The Ancient World

Prehistory - 476 C.E.

Great Lives from History

The Ancient World

Prehistory - 476 C.E.

Volume 2
Gaius Maecenas-Zoser
Indexes

Editor
Christina A. Salowey
Hollins University

Editor, First Edition
Frank N. Magill

SALEM PRESS
Pasadena, California   Hackensack, New Jersey

Editor in Chief: Dawn P. Dawson
Editorial Director: Christina J. Moose
Project Editor: Rowena Wildin
Copy Editor: Leslie Ellen Jones
Copy Editor: Elizabeth Ferry Slocum
Assistant Editor: Andrea E. Miller
Editorial Assistant: Dana Garey

Photograph Editor: Philip Bader
Acquisitions Editor: Mark Rehn
Research Supervisor: Jeffry Jensen
Research Assistant: Desiree Dreeuws
Production Editor: Joyce I. Buchea
Graphics and Design: James Hutson
Layout: Eddie Murillo

Cover photos: Library of Congress

Some of the essays in this work originally appeared in the following Salem Press sets: *Dictionary of World Biography* (1998-1999, edited by Frank N. Magill) and *Great Lives from History* (1987-1995, edited by Frank N. Magill).

Library of Congress Cataloging-in-Publication Data

Great lives from history. The ancient world, prehistory-476 C.E. / editor, Christina A. Salowey, editor, Frank N. Magill.— 1st ed.
    p. cm.
Includes bibliographical references and indexes.
    ISBN 1-58765-152-1 (set : alk. paper) — ISBN 1-58765-153-X (vol. 1 : alk. paper) — ISBN 1-58765-154-8 (vol. 2 : alk. paper)
    1. Biography—To 500. 2. History, Ancient. I. Title: Ancient world, prehistory-476 C.E. II. Salowey, Christina A. III. Magill, Frank Northen 1907-1997.
CT113.G745 2004
920.03—dc22

2004000705

First Printing

CONTENTS

Key to Pronunciation

Many of the names of personages covered in *Great Lives from History: The Ancient World, Prehistory-476 C.E.* may be unfamiliar to students and general readers. For these unfamiliar names, guides to pronunciation have been provided upon first mention of the names in the text. These guidelines do not purport to achieve the subtleties of the languages in question but will offer readers a rough equivalent of how English speakers may approximate the proper pronunciation.

Vowel Sounds

Symbol	Spelled (Pronounced)
a	answer (AN-suhr), laugh (laf), sample (SAM-puhl), that (that)
ah	father (FAH-thur), hospital (HAHS-pih-tuhl)
aw	awful (AW-fuhl), caught (kawt)
ay	blaze (blayz), fade (fayd), waiter (WAYT-ur), weigh (way)
eh	bed (behd), head (hehd), said (sehd)
ee	believe (bee-LEEV), cedar (SEE-dur), leader (LEED-ur), liter (LEE-tur)
ew	boot (bewt), lose (lewz)
i	buy (bi), height (hit), lie (li), surprise (sur-PRIZ)
ih	bitter (BIH-tur), pill (pihl)
o	cotton (KO-tuhn), hot (hot)
oh	below (bee-LOH), coat (koht), note (noht), wholesome (HOHL-suhm)
oo	good (good), look (look)
ow	couch (kowch), how (how)
oy	boy (boy), coin (koyn)
uh	about (uh-BOWT), butter (BUH-tuhr), enough (ee-NUHF), other (UH-thur)

Consonant Sounds

Symbol	Spelled (Pronounced)
ch	beach (beech), chimp (chihmp)
g	beg (behg), disguise (dihs-GIZ), get (geht)
j	digit (DIH-juht), edge (ehj), jet (jeht)
k	cat (kat), kitten (KIH-tuhn), hex (hehks)
s	cellar (SEHL-ur), save (sayv), scent (sehnt)
sh	champagne (sham-PAYN), issue (IH-shew), shop (shop)
ur	birth (burth), disturb (dihs-TURB), earth (urth), letter (LEH-tur)
y	useful (YEWS-fuhl), young (yuhng)
z	business (BIHZ-nehs), zest (zehst)
zh	vision (VIH-zhuhn)

COMPLETE LIST OF CONTENTS

VOLUME I

Volume 2

LIST OF MAPS AND TABLES

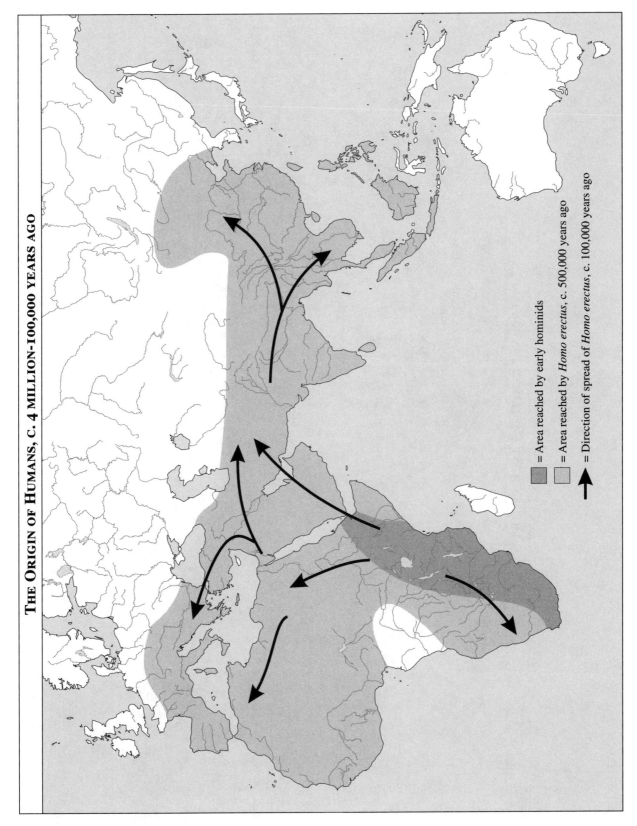

THE ORIGIN OF HUMANS, C. 4 MILLION-100,000 YEARS AGO

= Area reached by early hominids

= Area reached by *Homo erectus*, c. 500,000 years ago

= Direction of spread of *Homo erectus*, c. 100,000 years ago

THE ANCIENT WORLD, C. 200-500 C.E.

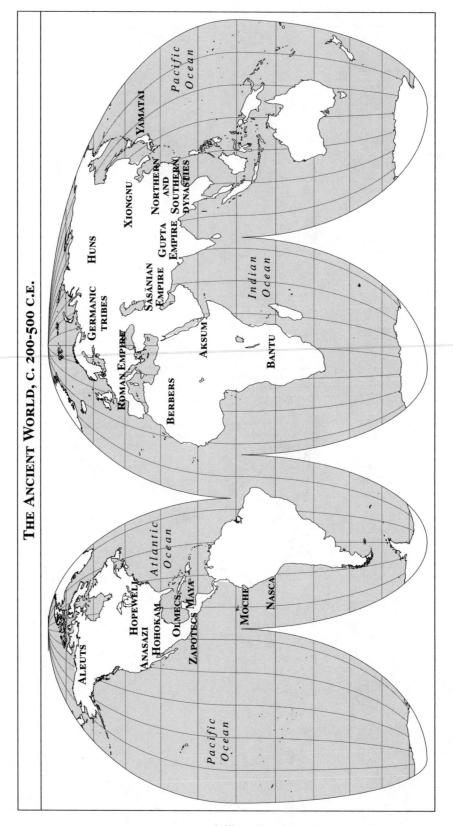

ALEUTS

ANASAZI
HOPEWELL
HOHOKAM
OLMECS
ZAPOTECS MAYA

MOCHE

NASCA

Pacific Ocean

Atlantic Ocean

Pacific Ocean

GERMANIC TRIBES
HUNS
XIONGNU

ROMAN EMPIRE
SASANIAN EMPIRE
GUPTA EMPIRE
NORTHERN AND SOUTHERN DYNASTIES
YAMATAI

BERBERS

AKSUM

BANTU

Indian Ocean

Pacific Ocean

ANCIENT NORTH AMERICA

Ipiutak

• Anangula

Norton • Onion
Portage

ALEUTS

PACIFIC

ARCTIC AND SUBARCTIC

Cape
Dorset

DORSET
Port
au Choix

PACIFIC COAST

CALIFORNIA

Head-Smashed-In

• Hoko River

*Pacific
Ocean*

Casper

**GREAT
PLAINS**

**GREAT
BASIN**
Danger Cave

ANASAZI
• Mesa Verde

MOGOLLON
Canyon de • Tularosa Cave
Chelly • Bat Cave (Cochise)
HOHOKAM

Blackwater Draw
(Clovis)

Marksville

OLD

COPPER
Osceola

Koster

Serpent
Mound

**RED
PAINT**
• Neville

Meadowcroft

EASTERN
• Adena
HOPEWELL

Indian Knoll

WOODLAND

*Atlantic
Ocean*

Poverty Point

• Porter

*Gulf
of
Mexico*

ZAPOTEC

OLMEC

MAYA

• = Sites
Cultures indicated by **BOLD SMALL CAPS**

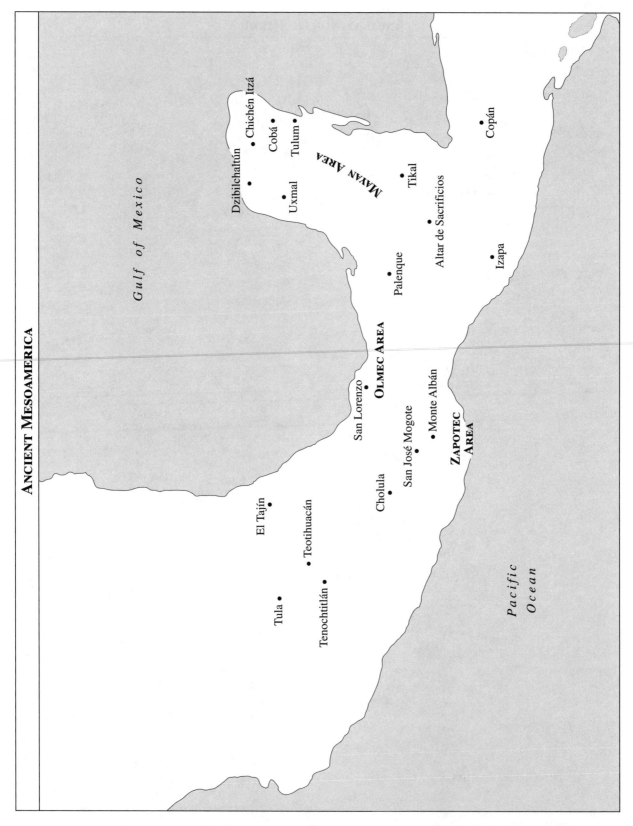

ANCIENT MESOAMERICA

Gulf of Mexico

Pacific Ocean

Tula
El Tajín
Teotihuacán
Tenochtitlán
Cholula
San José Mogote
San Lorenzo
Monte Albán
OLMEC AREA
ZAPOTEC AREA
Palenque
Altar de Sacrificios
Izapa
Dzibilchaltún
Uxmal
Cobá
Chichén Itzá
Tulum
MAYAN AREA
Tikal
Copán

ANCIENT SOUTH AMERICA

Valdivia

Moche
Chavín de Huántar
Recuay
Telarmachy Cave
El Paraíso
Pachacámac (Lima)
Paracas
Cahuachi (Nasca)
Lake Titicaca
Tiwanaku
Chinchorro

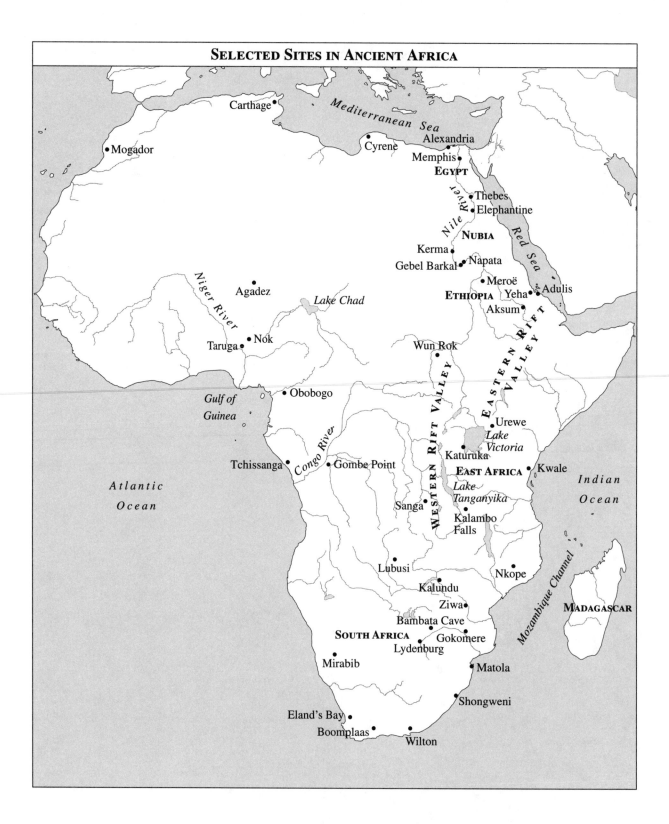

SELECTED SITES IN ANCIENT AFRICA

Mediterranean Sea

Carthage

Mogador

Cyrene

Alexandria

Memphis

EGYPT

Nile River

Thebes

Elephantine

Red Sea

NUBIA

Kerma

Gebel Barkal

Napata

Meroë

Adulis

ETHIOPIA

Yeha

Aksum

Niger River

Agadez

Lake Chad

Taruga

Nok

Wun Rok

Gulf of Guinea

Obobogo

EASTERN RIFT VALLEY

Urewe

Lake Victoria

Katuruka

Tchissanga

Congo River

Gombe Point

WESTERN RIFT VALLEY

EAST AFRICA

Kwale

Indian Ocean

Lake Tanganyika

Atlantic Ocean

Sanga

Kalambo Falls

Lubusi

Nkope

Kalundu

Ziwa

Mozambique Channel

MADAGASCAR

Bambata Cave

Gokomere

SOUTH AFRICA

Lydenburg

Mirabib

Matola

Shongweni

Eland's Bay

Boomplaas

Wilton

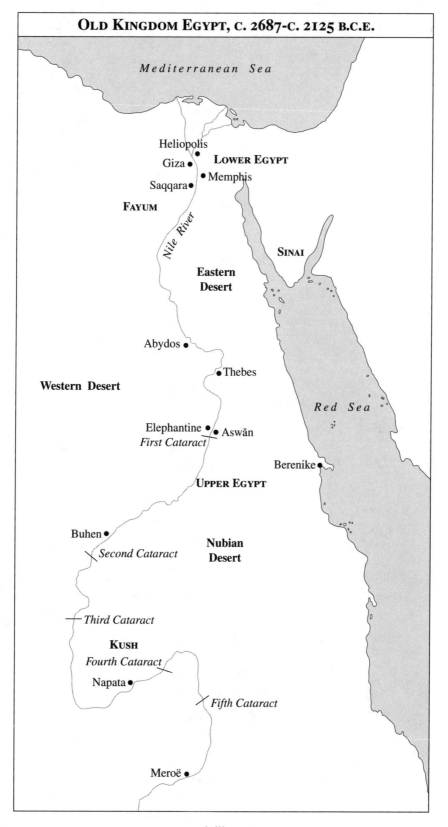

OLD KINGDOM EGYPT, C. 2687-C. 2125 B.C.E.

Mediterranean Sea

Heliopolis

Giza ●

LOWER EGYPT

Saqqara ● ● Memphis

FAYUM

Nile River

SINAI

Eastern Desert

Abydos ●

● Thebes

Western Desert

Red Sea

Elephantine ● ● Aswān
First Cataract

UPPER EGYPT

Berenike ●

Buhen ●

/ *Second Cataract*

Nubian Desert

— *Third Cataract*

KUSH
Fourth Cataract

Napata ●

Fifth Cataract

Meroë ●

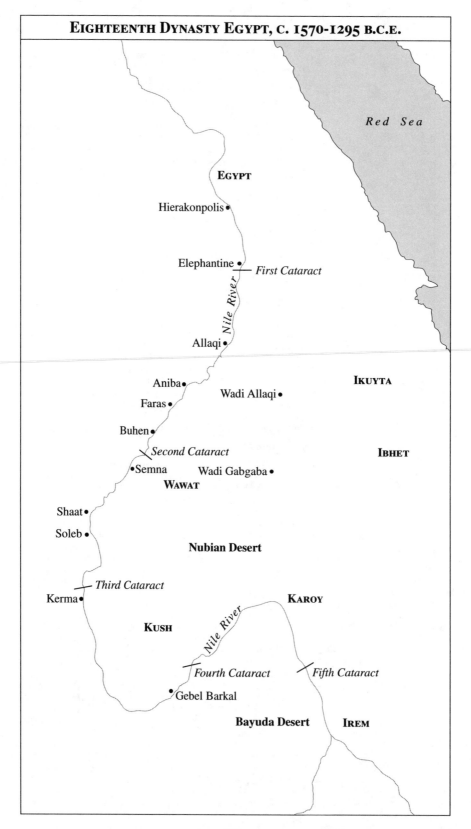

EIGHTEENTH DYNASTY EGYPT, C. 1570-1295 B.C.E.

Red Sea

EGYPT

Hierakonpolis •

Elephantine • — *First Cataract*

Nile River

Allaqi •

Aniba •

IKUYTA

Wadi Allaqi •

Faras •

Buhen •

Second Cataract

IBHET

• Semna   Wadi Gabgaba •

WAWAT

Shaat •

Soleb •

Nubian Desert

Third Cataract

Kerma •

KUSH

KAROY

Nile River

Fourth Cataract   *Fifth Cataract*

• Gebel Barkal

Bayuda Desert   IREM

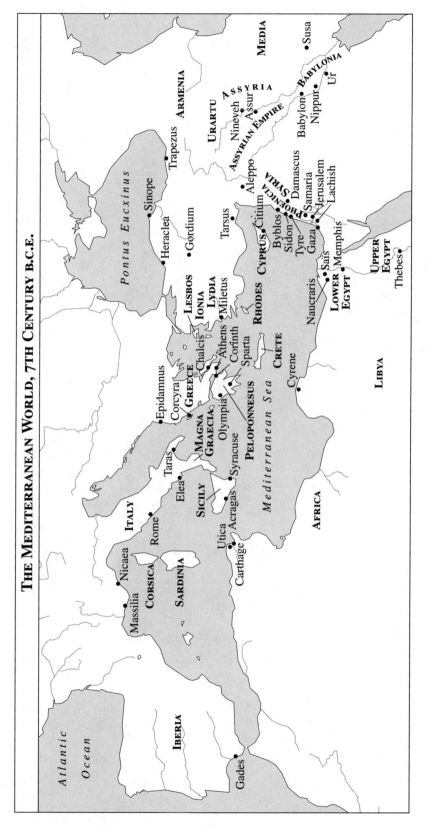

THE MEDITERRANEAN WORLD, 7TH CENTURY B.C.E.

Atlantic Ocean

Gades

IBERIA

Massilia

CORSICA

Nicaea

SARDINIA

Utica

Carthage

Rome

ITALY

Elea

Taras

SICILY

Acragas

Syracuse

MAGNA GRAECIA

Olympia

PELOPONNESUS

Epidamnus

Corcyra

GREECE

Chalcis

Athens

Corinth

Sparta

Mediterranean Sea

CRETE

Cyrene

AFRICA

LIBYA

Pontus Euxinus

Sinope

Heraclea

Trapezus

ARMENIA

Gordium

Tarsus

LESBOS

IONIA

LYDIA

Miletus

RHODES

CYPRUS

Citium

URARTU

ASSYRIA

Nineveh

Assur

ASSYRIAN EMPIRE

MEDIA

Susa

BABYLONIA

Babylon

Nippur

Ur

Aleppo

PHOENICIA

SYRIA

Damascus

Samaria

Jerusalem

Lachish

Byblos

Sidon

Tyre

Gaza

Saïs

Naucraris

Memphis

LOWER EGYPT

UPPER EGYPT

Thebes

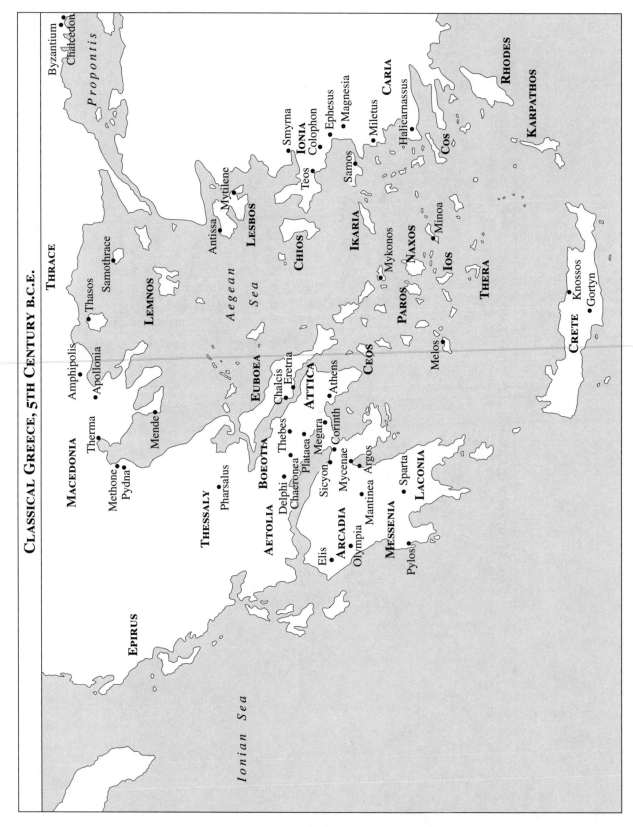

CLASSICAL GREECE, 5TH CENTURY B.C.E.

Byzantium
Chalcedon

Propontis

THRACE

RHODES

KARPATHOS

CARIA

Smyrna
IONIA
Colophon
Ephesus
Magnesia
Miletus
Halicarnassus
Cos

Teos
Samos
IKARIA

Mytilene

Antissa

LESBOS

Aegean Sea

Samothrace

Thasos

Amphipolis
Apollonia

THRACE

LEMNOS

CHIOS

Minoa
Mykonos
NAXOS
Ios

PAROS
THERA

MACEDONIA
Therma
Mende

Methone
Pydna

THESSALY
Pharsalus

EUBOEA
Chalcis
Eretria

ATTICA
Athens

CEOS

Melos

Knossos
Gortyn

CRETE

Delphi
Thebes
Chaeronea
Plataea

BOEOTIA

Megara
Corinth
Sicyon
Mycenae
Argos

AETOLIA

Elis
ARCADIA
Olympia
Mantinea

MESSENIA
Pylos

Sparta
LACONIA

EPIRUS

Ionian Sea

lxvi

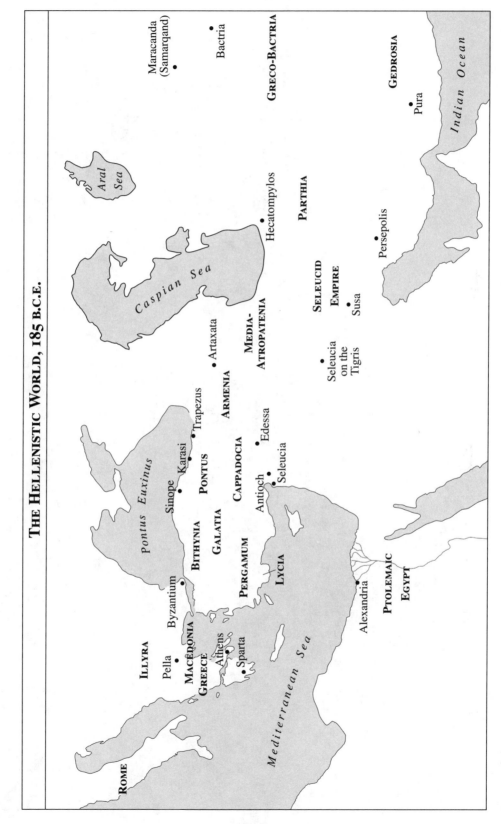

THE HELLENISTIC WORLD, 185 B.C.E.

Maracanda
(Samarqand)

Bactria

GRECO-BACTRIA

GEDROSIA

Indian Ocean

Pura

*Aral
Sea*

Hecatompylos

PARTHIA

Caspian Sea

Persepolis

SELEUCID
EMPIRE

Susa

MEDIA-
ATROPATENIA

Artaxata

Seleucia
on the
Tigris

ARMENIA

Trapezus

Pontus Euxinus

Karasi

PONTUS

Edessa

Sinope

CAPPADOCIA

BITHYNIA

GALATIA

Antioch

Seleucia

Byzantium

PERGAMUM

LYCIA

ILLYRA

Pella

MACEDONIA

GREECE

Athens

Sparta

Alexandria

PTOLEMAIC
EGYPT

Mediterranean Sea

ROME

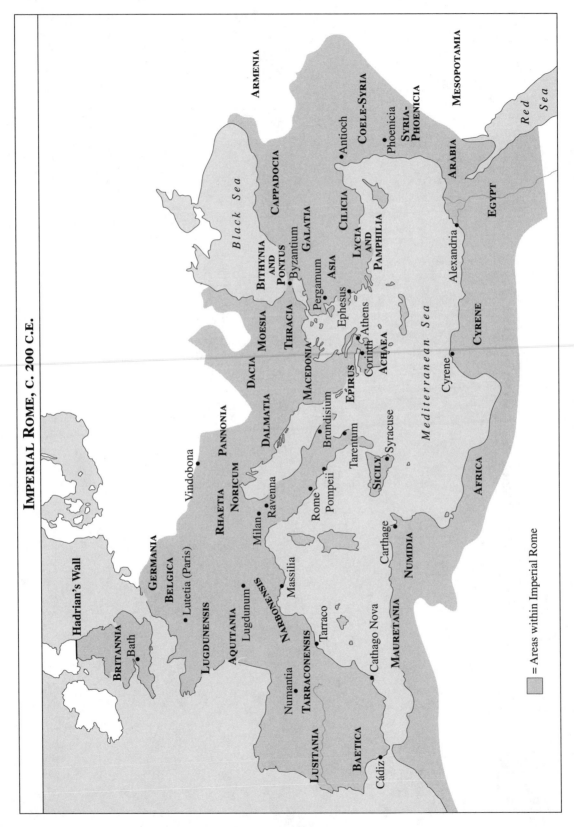

IMPERIAL ROME, C. 200 C.E.

Hadrian's Wall

BRITANNIA
Bath

Black Sea

GERMANIA

BELGICA
Lutetia (Paris)

LUGDUNENSIS

AQUITANIA
Lugdunum

NARBONENSIS
Massilia

RHAETIA
NORICUM
Milan
Ravenna

PANNONIA

Vindobona

DACIA

MOESIA

DALMATIA

MACEDONIA

THRACIA
Byzantium

BITHYNIA
AND
PONTUS

GALATIA
Pergamum

ASIA
Ephesus

CAPPADOCIA

ARMENIA

COELE-SYRIA
Antioch

SYRIA-
PHOENICIA
Phoenicia

MESOPOTAMIA

Red
Sea

CILICIA

LYCIA
AND
PAMPHILIA

ARABIA

EGYPT

Alexandria

Rome
Pompeii

EPIRUS

ACHAEA
Corinth
Athens

CYRENE
Cyrene

Tarraco

TARRACONENSIS

Numantia

LUSITANIA

BAETICA

Cádiz

Cathago Nova

MAURETANIA

MAURETANIA

Carthage

NUMIDIA

AFRICA

Brundisium

Tarentum

SICILY
Syracuse

Mediterranean Sea

= Areas within Imperial Rome

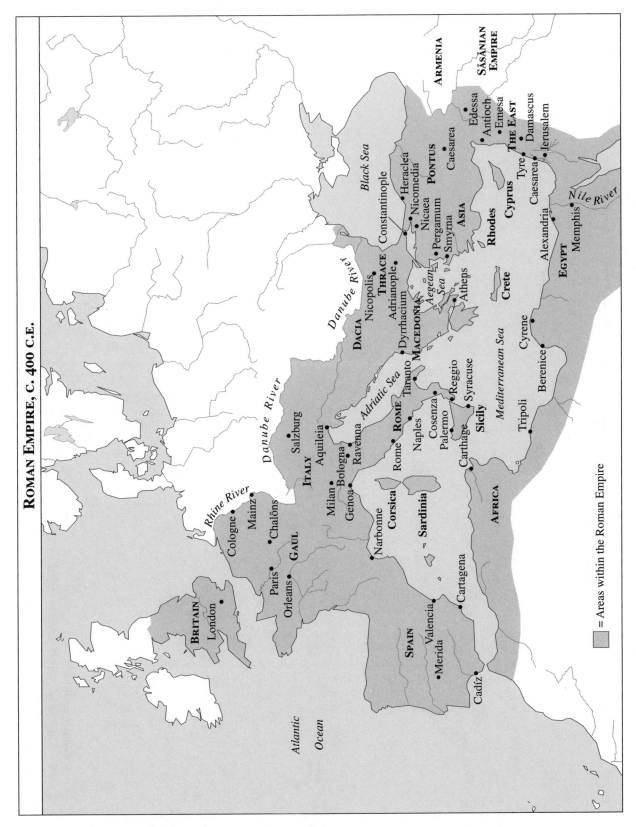

ROMAN EMPIRE, C. 400 C.E.

= Areas within the Roman Empire

BRITAIN
London

GAUL
Paris
Orleans
Chalôns
Cologne
Mainz
Narbonne

SPAIN
Merida
Valencia
Cartagena
Cadiz

ITALY
Salzburg
Aquileia
Milan
Bologna
Genoa
Ravenna
ROME
Rome
Naples
Cosenza
Palermo
Taranto
Reggio
Syracuse

Corsica
Sardinia
Sicily

AFRICA
Carthage
Tripoli

DACIA
Nicopolis
THRACE
Adrianople
Dyrrhacium
MACEDONIA
Atheps
Constantinople
Heraclea
Nicomedia
Nicaea
Pergamum
Smyrna
PONTUS
Caesarea
ASIA

Crete
Cyrene
Berenice

Rhodes
Cyprus
THE EAST
Edessa
Antioch
Emesa
Damascus
Jerusalem
Tyre
Caesarea
Alexandria

EGYPT
Memphis

ARMENIA
SĀSĀNIAN EMPIRE

Black Sea
Aegean Sea
Adriatic Sea
Mediterranean Sea
Atlantic Ocean
Nile River
Danube River
Rhine River

lxix

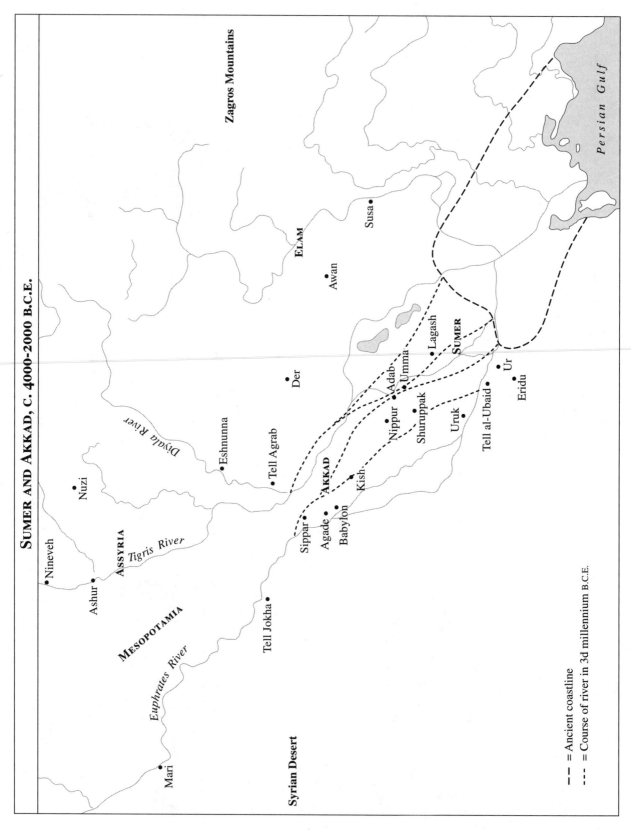

SUMER AND AKKAD, C. 4000–2000 B.C.E.

Persian Gulf

Zagros Mountains

ELAM

Susa

Awan

SUMER

Lagash

Umma

Adab

Ur

Der

Eridu

Nippur

Shuruppak

Uruk

Tell al-Ubaid

Diyala River

Eshnunna

Tell Agrab

AKKAD

Kish

Sippar

Agade

Babylon

Nuzi

ASSYRIA

Nineveh

Ashur

Tigris River

MESOPOTAMIA

Tell Jokha

Euphrates River

Syrian Desert

Mari

– – = Ancient coastline

– – – = Course of river in 3d millennium B.C.E.

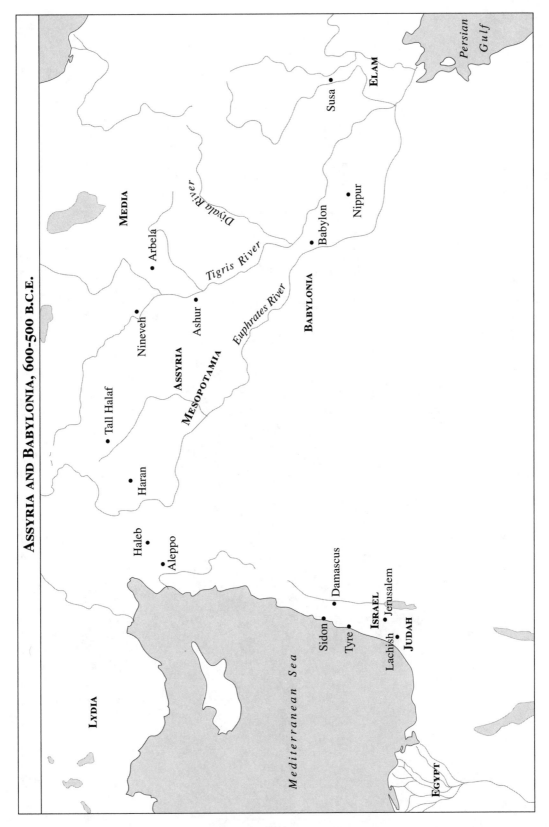

ASSYRIA AND BABYLONIA, 600-500 B.C.E.

Persian Gulf

ELAM

Susa

MEDIA

Nippur

Babylon

Arbela

Diyala River

Tigris River

BABYLONIA

Nineveh

Ashur

ASSYRIA

MESOPOTAMIA

Euphrates River

Tall Halaf

Haran

Haleb

Aleppo

Damascus

ISRAEL

Jerusalem

Sidon

Tyre

Lachish

JUDAH

Mediterranean Sea

LYDIA

EGYPT

lxxi

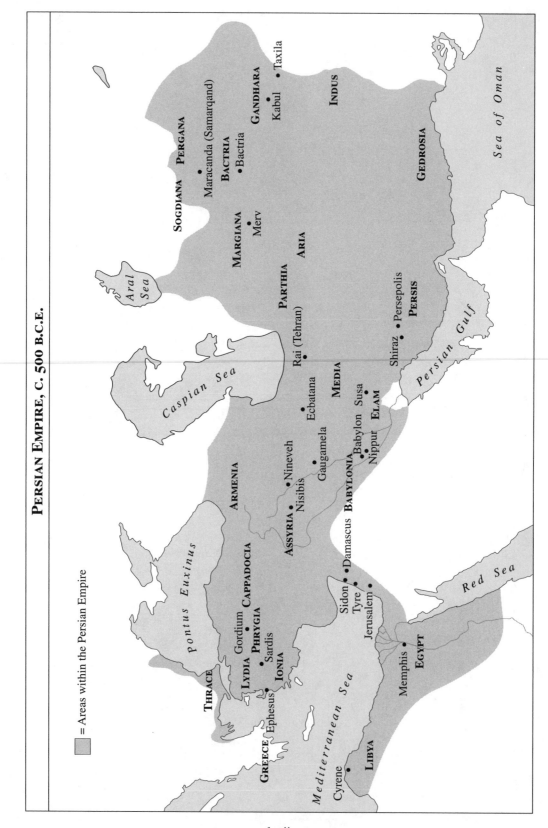

PERSIAN EMPIRE, C. 500 B.C.E.

= Areas within the Persian Empire

THRACE

GREECE
Ephesus
IONIA
Sardis
LYDIA PHRYGIA
Gordium CAPPADOCIA

Pontus Euxinus

ARMENIA

ASSYRIA Nineveh
Nisibis
Gaugamela

Ecbatana
MEDIA

Rai (Tehran)

PARTHIA

ARIA

MARGIANA
Merv

SOGDIANA
Maracanda (Samarqand)
BACTRIA PERGANA
Bactria

GANDHARA
Kabul Taxila

INDUS

Aral
Sea

Caspian Sea

Damascus
Sidon
Tyre
Jerusalem

BABYLONIA
Babylon Susa
Nippur ELAM

Shiraz Persepolis
PERSIS

Persian Gulf

GEDROSIA

Sea of Oman

Mediterranean Sea

Cyrene
LIBYA

Memphis
EGYPT

Red Sea

lxxii

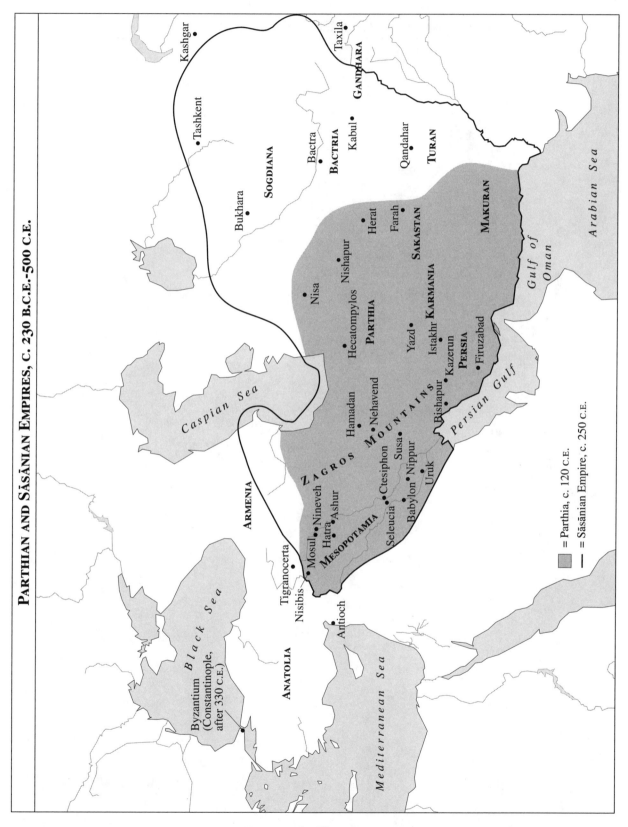

PARTHIAN AND SĀSĀNIAN EMPIRES, C. 230 B.C.E.-500 C.E.

Kashgar

Taxila

GANDHARA

Tashkent

Bactra
BACTRIA
Kabul

Qandahar

TURAN

SOGDIANA

Bukhara

MAKURAN

Herat

Farah
SAKASTAN

Nishapur

Nisa
PARTHIA
KARMANIA

Hecatompylos

Yazd
Istakhr
Kazerun
PERSIA
Firuzabad

Gulf of
Oman

Arabian Sea

Caspian Sea

Hamadan
Nehavend
Bishapur

Z A G R O S   M O U N T A I N S

Persian Gulf

Ctesiphon
Susa

Seleucia
Babylon   Nippur
Uruk

ARMENIA

Nineveh
Mosul   Ashur
Hatra
MESOPOTAMIA

Tigranocerta

Nisibis

Antioch

Black Sea

Byzantium
(Constantinople,
after 330 C.E.)

ANATOLIA

Mediterranean Sea

= Parthia, c. 120 C.E.

= Sāsānian Empire, c. 250 C.E.

lxxiii

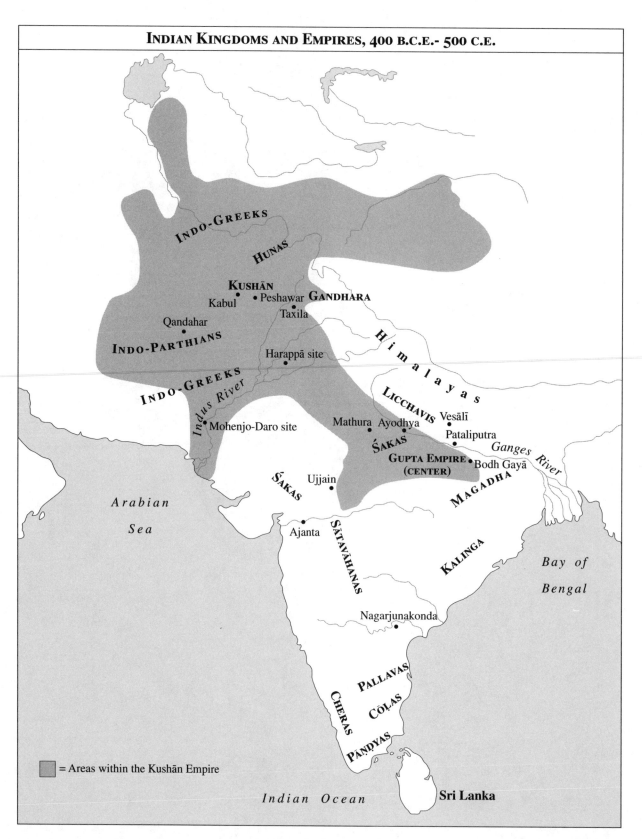

INDIAN KINGDOMS AND EMPIRES, 400 B.C.E.- 500 C.E.

INDO-GREEKS

HUNAS

KUSHĀN

Kabul • • Peshawar GANDHARA

• Taxila

Qandahar •

INDO-PARTHIANS

Harappā site •

Himalayas

INDO-GREEKS

Indus River

LICCHAVIS

Vesālī •

• Mohenjo-Daro site

Mathura • Ayodhya •

Pataliputra •

Ganges River

ŚAKAS

GUPTA EMPIRE • Bodh Gayā
(CENTER)

MAGADHA

ŚAKAS • Ujjain •

Arabian

Sea

Ajanta •

SĀTAVĀHANAS

KALINGA

Bay of

Bengal

Nagarjunakonda •

PALLAVAS

CHERAS CŌLAS

PĀNDYAS

█ = Areas within the Kushān Empire

Indian Ocean **Sri Lanka**

lxxiv

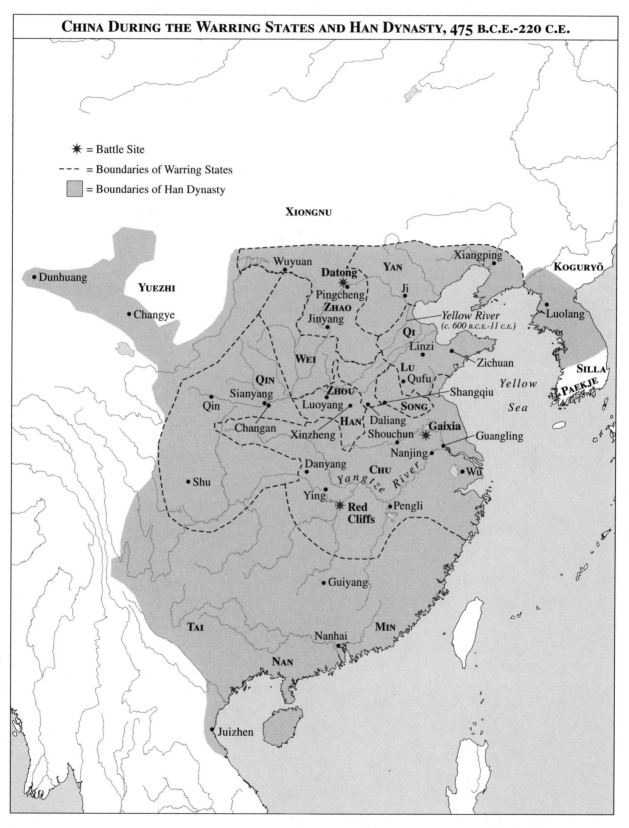

CHINA DURING THE WARRING STATES AND HAN DYNASTY, 475 B.C.E.–220 C.E.

✳ = Battle Site

--- = Boundaries of Warring States

■ = Boundaries of Han Dynasty

XIONGNU

Dunhuang

YUEZHI

Changye

Wuyuan

Datong

Yan

Xiangping

KOGURYŎ

Pingcheng

Zhao

Jinyang

Ji

Yellow River
(c. 600 B.C.E.–11 C.E.)

Luolang

Wei

Qi

Linzi

Zichuan

SILLA

PAEKJE

Qin

Sianyang

Lu

Qufu

Yellow
Sea

Qin

Zhou

Luoyang

Song

Shangqiu

Changan

Han

Xinzheng

Daliang

Shouchun

Gaixia

Guangling

Nanjing

Shu

Danyang

Chu

Yangtze River

Wu

Ying

**Red
Cliffs**

Pengli

Guiyang

Tai

Nanhai

Min

Nan

Juizhen

lxxv

The Ancient World

Prehistory - 476 C.E.

GAIUS MAECENAS
Roman statesman

Maecenas was one of the most powerful men in Rome of the first century B.C.E., often functioning as diplomatic arbiter and city administrator. His most significant role was as patron to a circle of writers who became known as the poets of the Golden Age of Latin literature.

BORN: c. 70 B.C.E.; Arretium (now Arezzo, Italy)
DIED: 8 B.C.E.; Rome (now in Italy)
ALSO KNOWN AS: Gaius Maecenas Cilnius (full name); Cilnius Maecenas
AREAS OF ACHIEVEMENT: Art and art patronage, government and politics

EARLY LIFE

Gaius Maecenas (mi-SEE-nuhs) was born in Arretium (modern Arezzo, Italy) to a wealthy equestrian family that traced its origins to Etruscan kings. Nothing is known of the first thirty years of his life, but he must have received an aristocratic education, for he knew Greek as well as Latin. He first emerges in the works of ancient writers as the intimate friend and financial and political supporter of Octavian (called Augustus after 27 B.C.E.), the heir of Gaius Julius Caesar, the junior member of the Second Triumvirate, and the future first emperor of Rome.

Maecenas greatly preferred the life of a private citizen, but he shocked Rome. He hosted extravagant parties, drank excessively, and wore his tunic unbelted (in opposition to proper Roman fashion). Two eunuchs frequently accompanied him through the streets. Although he became notorious as self-indulgent and effeminate, Maecenas appears to have been popular with the Roman people.

Octavian also liked, and trusted, Maecenas. In the years directly following 44 B.C.E., the year of Julius Caesar's assassination, the young heir found himself faced with the monumental task of avenging his adopted father's murder and making all Italy safe from disenfranchised Romans. Initially, Octavian struck an alliance with Marc Antony, then with Sextus Pompeius (Pompey the Younger), whose bands were raiding the southern coast of Italy. Repeated setbacks with these two, however, convinced Octavian to enlist the aid of friends. Marcus Vipsanius Agrippa became his general and Maecenas his diplomat and politician.

At Octavian's request, Maecenas arranged an engagement between Octavian and Scribonia, Pompey's sister-in-law, in the hope of allying Octavian with Pompey. When relations grew strained between Octavian and Antony, Maecenas helped arbitrate reconciliations at Brundisium, in 40, and at Tarentum, in 37 B.C.E. For unknown reasons, he was present at the Battle of Philippi (42 B.C.E.), where Octavian and Agrippa defeated the forces of Gaius Cassius Longinus and Marcus Junius Brutus, the major surviving assassins of Julius Caesar. Octavian again inexplicably summoned Maecenas to Actium (31 B.C.E.), where the troops of Antony and Cleopatra VII of Egypt were defeated. Maecenas may also have been present at the campaigns against Pompey.

When Maecenas's services were not required in the field, he was governing Rome and the rest of Italy. Octavian had entrusted Maecenas in his absence with temporary administration of the city, hoping to bolster popular support for himself and quash any resurgent popularity for his opponents. Maecenas now held all the powers of City Prefect but without the title. His power even extended to issuing official proclamations. He quelled a civil riot in 37 B.C.E., and in 30 B.C.E. he quietly crushed the assassination plot against Octavian that was led by the son of the recently deposed Triumvir, Marcus Aemilius Lepidus. Maecenas made the city streets safe after dark and may have helped rid Rome of magicians and astrologers. All these duties without benefit of public office endowed Maecenas with powers greater than those of any elected official.

LIFE'S WORK

Octavian's return to Rome in 29 B.C.E. ended Maecenas's role as public servant but not his influence in Rome. While he had been acting as diplomat and administrator, Maecenas had also begun befriending at Rome a number of writers whose talents he could use to the advantage of Octavian's new political order. With this growing group of friends he had assumed the position of literary patron, a role to which he now devoted all his energy. Literary patronage frequently included gifts of money or possessions. In addition, it usually included a larger audience for a poet's writings, circulation of his poems, and their publication. Maecenas entertained certain of his friends at his mansion to provide these benefits. Scholars disagree as to what extent Maecenas actually used his patronage to foster a state propaganda literature, but the works of his poets make it clear that they realized some expectation on the part of Augustus. In several of his

Odes written in 23 B.C.E. (English translation, 1621) the poet Horace answers with a polite refusal (*recusatio*) a request from his patron to write on a suggested topic. Sextus Propertius does the same when Maecenas suggests a change in theme from love to state matters. Because the literary refusal was standard in Alexandrian verse, it is uncertain how strongly Maecenas actually made his requests for propaganda poems. He may have done no more than give general guidance.

Maecenas's circle included many people who have become little more than names to posterity: Gaius Melissus, Lucius Varius Rufus, Domitius Marsus, and Plotius Tucca. His three most famous poets, however, whose works have survived to modern times have immortalized Maecenas. Vergil may have become Maecenas's protégé as early as 40 B.C.E. His three major works, the *Eclogues* (43-37 B.C.E., also known as *Bucolics*; English translation, 1575), the *Georgics* (c. 37-29 B.C.E.; English translation, 1589), written in honor of Maecenas, and the *Aeneid* (c. 29-19 B.C.E.; English translation, 1553), all glorify ideals that Octavian was trying to reinstate in society. In 38, Vergil and his friend Varius Rufus introduced Horace to Maecenas, who invited the young man to become one of his special "friends" eight months later when he returned from a diplomatic mission to the east on Octavian's behalf. Horace's lyric poetry, while not as universally patriotic as Vergil's, does reflect his respect for Octavian and the new regime. Propertius, who was already an established elegiac poet, became one of Maecenas's circle about 25 B.C.E. and dedicated the first poem of his second book to Maecenas, though his poetry is least indicative of Augustan ideals.

It is a paradox that the man who sought out and encouraged the most talented group of literary artists of his day was himself an author of the worst type. Enough fragments of his works survive to reveal that his compositions were oddly expressed and affected. Augustus disliked his style and parodied it unmercifully. From his semiretirement in 29 until about 20, Maecenas reigned as the predominant literary patron in Rome. This era saw the publication of Horace's *Odes* (books 1-3), Vergil's *Georgics*, and the second book of Propertius's *Elegies* (c. 24 B.C.E.). Thereafter, Augustus personally assumed the role of patron, and Maecenas returned completely to private life.

Ancients and moderns have speculated on this shift in literary power. Ancient historians supposed that Augustus never forgave Maecenas for telling his wife, Terentia, of the discovery of her brother's conspiracy against the emperor. Others say that Augustus's passion for his friend's wife led to the rift. Maecenas, for his part, may have wished, for personal or health reasons, to resume the life of a private citizen. Many modern scholars believe that Augustus was the real patron, Maecenas only his interim manager. Augustus, now secure in his position as princeps (first citizen) and at leisure to pursue more than war, no longer needed Maecenas as an intermediary between himself and the writers. As Maecenas always preferred the life of a private citizen, his retirement may have been mutually desirable.

Even in retirement, however, Maecenas retained influence with the emperor in public and private matters. Several times, Maecenas's sound judgment restored Augustus to an even temper. Moreover, it was supposedly on Maecenas's advice that Augustus married his daughter, Julia, to his general, Agrippa in 21 B.C.E.

The life of private citizen seems to have suited Maecenas's tastes well. Despite his years as Augustus's factotum, Maecenas chose to limit his involvement in politics, refusing all elective offices and remaining an equestrian all of his life. He erected a huge mansion on the Esquiline Hill, which he transformed from a plebeian cemetery into a magnificent residential area. The estate included a large house, a magnificent tower, lush gardens, and even a swimming pool. There he lived with his wife, Terentia, a beautiful but faithless woman whom he may eventually have divorced.

Despite his eccentricities, Maecenas retained his popularity with the Roman people and his intimacy with individual friends. After recovering from a serious illness, for example, Maecenas was greeted with resounding applause from the audience as he entered a theater. Whenever Augustus was ill, he slept at Maecenas's house. Vergil had a house on the Esquiline Hill very near Maecenas's. Horace, who became his personal as well as professional friend, was buried near the tomb of Maecenas on that same hill.

Maecenas's excesses, though tolerated by Augustus and the Roman people, seem to have caught up with him. He suffered from a chronic fever for the last three years of his life. When he died, he was mourned by his friends and especially by Augustus, to whom he had devoted so much of his life, talents, and energy.

SIGNIFICANCE

Maecenas, through his lifelong friendship with Augustus and his almost fifteen years' government service, helped Augustus establish a firm foundation for a smooth transition from the Roman Republic to the Roman Empire. It is his discovery, support, and nurturing of some of the greatest poets of Latin literature, however, that accounts for Maecenas's most lasting effect on the ancient world. He provided a buffer between the emperor and the poets, a role that had advantages for both factions. On the Imperial side, Augustus was protected by the figure of Maecenas from the embarrassment of being eulogized by any poet unworthy of his theme. On the other hand, poets who might have felt compelled to yield to a suggestion from Augustus as if it were a command still exercised their prerogative of saying no to Maecenas. In this way, the illusion of the Roman Republic that allowed freedom of choice was maintained. Maecenas's patronage supported Augustus's assertion that the Republic had been restored.

Maecenas believed in the idea of merit rather than wealth or social class. In the poets he selected he must have recognized their ability to form their own judgment and must have trusted that judgment to guide them in their writings. While he may have provided encouragement and general guidance to the poets, Maecenas shrewdly avoided demanding particular types of poems from his authors. This policy of nonintervention distinguished him from preceding centuries of literary patrons and set the standard for later generations of patrons in Europe. By fostering such poets as Vergil, Horace, and Propertius, Maecenas became identified with the Golden Age he helped Augustus establish. By giving the poets the freedom to express themselves as they saw fit, Maecenas became the model for future literary patrons. Immortalized by the Golden Age poets, Maecenas's name has become synonymous with the term literary patron.

—Joan E. Carr

FURTHER READING

DuQuesnay, I. M. Le M. "Horace and Maecenas: The Propaganda Value of *Sermones* I." In *Poetry and Politics in the Age of Augustus*, edited by Tony Woodman and David West. New York: Cambridge University Press, 1984. A convincing argument for the propagandist nature of the poems dedicated to Maecenas. Includes copious notes and bibliography.

Fraenkel, Eduard. *Horace.* Oxford, England: Clarendon Press, 1966. Focuses especially on Maecenas's relationship with Horace, with occasional references to the public Maecenas and fewer to the person. No bibliography, and the footnotes are in general useful only to readers of Latin.

Gold, Barbara K. *Literary Patronage in Greece and Rome.* Chapel Hill: University of North Carolina Press, 1987. Maecenas's role as patron is explored; carefully examines their dynamic relationship as seen through Horace's writings. Includes bibliography, index, and copious notes.

Griffin, J. "Augustus and the Poets: *Caesar Qui Cogere Posset.*" In *Caesar Augustus: Seven Aspects*, edited by Fergus Millar and Erich Segal. New York: Clarendon Press, 1984. Cites practical reasons for Maecenas, not Augustus, being the patron of the literary set. Endnotes provide little explanation but instead refer the reader to ancient works, most of which can be found in English translation.

Shackleton Bailey, D. R. *Profile of Horace.* Cambridge, Mass.: Harvard University Press, 1982. Maecenas is mentioned everywhere in this excellent literary criticism of Horace's *Epodes* and *Satires*. Gives more of a sense of who Maecenas was as a patron than actual data on his life. Latin passages are translated. Limited bibliography.

Syme, Ronald. *The Roman Revolution.* Reprint. New York: Oxford University Press, 2002. Maecenas is mentioned often as the close friend of Augustus, running personal and political errands for the leader and acting as a diplomat of invaluable skill. No straightforward biography. Minimal notes.

SEE ALSO: Marcus Vipsanius Agrippa; Augustus; Horace; Julia III; Sextus Propertius; Vergil.

RELATED ARTICLES in *Great Events from History: The Ancient World*: 43-42 B.C.E., Second Triumvirate Enacts Proscriptions; September 2, 31 B.C.E., Battle of Actium; 27-23 B.C.E., Completion of the Augustan Settlement; 19 B.C.E., Roman Poet Vergil Dies; November 27, 8 B.C.E., Roman Lyric Poet Horace Dies.

MARCUS AURELIUS
Roman emperor (r. 161-180 C.E.)

Although renowned as the last of Rome's "good emperors," Marcus Aurelius is also remembered for his simply written private notes that reflect the emperor's daily efforts to achieve the Platonic ideal of the philosopher-king and are the last great literary statement of Stoicism.

BORN: April 26, 121 C.E.; Rome (now in Italy)
DIED: March 17, 180 C.E.; Sirmium, Pannonia (now in Serbia) or Vindobona (now Vienna, Austria)
ALSO KNOWN AS: Marcus Aurelius Antoninus (full name); Marcus Annius Verus (given name)
AREAS OF ACHIEVEMENT: Government and politics, literature

EARLY LIFE

Marcus Aurelius (MAHR-kuhs oh-REHL-yuhs) Antoninus was born Marcus Annius Verus in Rome. His father was Annius Verus, a magistrate, and his mother was Domitia Calvilla, also known as Lucilla. The emperor Antoninus Pius was, by virtue of his marriage to Annia Galeria Faustina, the sister of Annius Verus, the boy's uncle. The emperor, who had himself been adopted and named successor by Hadrian, eventually adopted Marcus Annius Verus. The young man then took the name Marcus Aelius Aurelius Verus. The name Aelius came from Hadrian's family, and Aurelius was the name of Antoninus Pius. The young man took the title of Caesar in 139 and, on becoming emperor, replaced his original name of Verus with Antoninus. Hence, he is known to history as Marcus Aurelius Antoninus.

Marcus Aurelius was well brought up and well educated. Later, he would write of what a virtuous man and prudent ruler his uncle and adoptive father had been. To the fine example set by the emperor was added the dedicated teaching of excellent masters. Letters exist that attest the boy's industry and the great expectations engendered by his performance as a student. He studied eloquence and rhetoric, and he tried his hand at poetry. He was also trained in the law as a preparation for high office. Above all, Marcus Aurelius's interest was in philosophy. When only eleven years of age, he adopted the plain, coarse dress of the philosophers and undertook a spartan regimen of hard study and self-denial. In fact, he drove himself so relentlessly that for a time his health was affected. He was influenced by Stoicism, a sect founded by the Greek philosopher Zeno of Citium in the fourth century B.C.E.

LIFE'S WORK

Antoninus Pius became emperor on the death of Hadrian in July, 138. He adopted not only Marcus Aurelius but also Lucius Ceionius Commodus, who came to be called Lucius Aurelius Verus. The adoptive brothers could scarcely have been more different. Verus was destined to rule alongside Marcus Aurelius for a time, despite his manifest unworthiness. He was an indolent, pleasure-loving man, whereas Marcus Aurelius was proving himself worthy of more and more responsibility. The year 146 was a highly significant one, for it was at about that time that Antoninus Pius began to share with him the government of the Empire. Further, the emperor gave him Faustina, his daughter and the young man's cousin, in marriage. A daughter was born to Marcus Aurelius and Faustina in 147.

At the death of Antoninus Pius in March, 161, the senate asked Marcus Aurelius to assume sole governance of the Empire. However, he chose to rule jointly with Verus, the other adopted son. For the first time in its history, Rome had two emperors. Apparently, and fortunately for the Empire, Verus was not blind to his inadequacies. He deferred to Marcus Aurelius, who was in turn tolerant of him. Marcus Aurelius cemented their relationship by giving his daughter Lucilla to Verus as wife. That their joint rule lasted for eight years was really a credit to them both.

The first major problem to be faced by the joint rulers was the war with Parthia. Verus was sent to command the Roman forces but proved ineffectual. Fortunately, his generals were able, thus achieving victories in Armenia and along the Tigris and Euphrates Rivers. The war was concluded in 165, but as soon as Marcus Aurelius and Verus received their triumph—a huge public ceremony honoring the victors in war—Rome was struck by a virulent pestilence. As the plague spread throughout Italy and beyond, the loss of life was great.

At this time, barbarians from beyond the Alps were threatening to invade northern Italy. Although Marcus Aurelius was able to contain them, they would periodically renew their efforts. For the rest of the emperor's life, much of his time and effort was spent in holding these warlike people at bay.

Verus died suddenly in 169, and Marcus Aurelius became the sole emperor of Rome. His reign continued as it had begun, beset by difficulties on every front. He was almost constantly in the field, campaigning against one enemy or another. He was on the Danube River for three years, prosecuting the German wars, and by 174 he had gained a series of impressive victories.

In 175, Avidius Cassius, who commanded the Roman legions in Asia, led a revolt against the emperor. Up to that time, Cassius had been a fine general, but when he declared himself augustus, the emperor marched east to meet the threat. Before the emperor arrived, however, Cassius was assassinated by some of his officers. Marcus Aurelius's treatment of the family and followers of Cassius was magnanimous. His letter to the senate ask-

Marcus Aurelius. (Library of Congress)

ing mercy for them has survived. During this time, Marcus Aurelius suffered a severe personal tragedy. The empress, Faustina, who had accompanied her husband on the Asian march, abruptly died. Some historians have written that she was scandalously unfaithful and promiscuous, but their reports are contradicted by her husband's pronouncements. He was grief-stricken at her death, and his references to her are loving and laudatory.

It was during this decade of constant warfare, rebellion, and personal grief that Marcus Aurelius began to write the lofty, dignified contemplative notes that were originally known as *Tōn eis heauton* (c. 171-180 C.E.; *Meditations*, 1634). They were meant for no eyes but the emperor's, and their survival down through the centuries is a mystery (although scholars have no doubts as to their authenticity). They reflect his sense of duty, his high-mindedness, and his apparent inner peace. Two themes dominate the *Meditations:* that man, to the utmost of his ability to do so, should harmonize himself with nature and that it is not the circumstances of one's life that produce happiness but one's perception of those circumstances. According to the emperor, happiness always comes from within, never from without. The *Meditations* are also marked by their author's common sense. He observes that when one is seduced by fame and flattered by others, one should remember their want of judgment on other occasions and remain humble. A great emperor might be expected to be self-assured, perhaps even self-centered and self-satisfied; Marcus Aurelius strikes the reader as self-composed and self-contented.

Although the emperor's campaigns were generally successful (one victory, in which a fortuitous storm threw the enemy into a panic, was even viewed as a miracle), his reign was not unblemished. He was often forced to make concessions that allowed large numbers of barbarians to remain in Roman territory and that eventually resulted in a proliferation of barbarians within his own armies. (Some of his legions were already identifiably Christian in makeup.) He also seems to have been blind to the vices of Commodus, his son and successor. It is the persecution of the Christians, however, which brings his record into question.

The constant state of war, aggravated by widespread pestilence, caused the populace to demand a scapegoat. The Christians were a natural target, as their repudiation of the ancient gods was thought to have brought divine retribution on Rome. An ardent persecution was begun, especially in the provinces. At first, the persecutions seem to have progressed ad hoc. Eventually, however, a provincial governor appealed to the emperor for guidance. His directions were, by contemporary standards, severe. If the Christians would deny their faith, they should be released. Otherwise, they must be punished. Those unrepentant Christians who were Roman citizens were beheaded. The others were put to death in a variety of imaginative ways. Apologists for Marcus Aurelius have maintained that he had little to do with these persecutions, and they do seem out of character for the author of the *Meditations*. Still, in order to argue that Marcus Aurelius was in no way culpable, one must read history quite selectively. In 180, the emperor was conducting yet another successful, though somewhat inconclusive, campaign, this time along the upper Danube. He fell ill with the plague or some other contagious malady and died on March 17 of that year.

SIGNIFICANCE

The commemorative bust of Marcus Aurelius features a noble head indeed. Framed by a full head of curly hair and neat chin whiskers, the countenance is strong, honest, and handsome. Any idealization of the likeness is appropriate, for the emperor's demeanor as well as his words set one of the greatest examples in history. When his ashes were returned to Rome, he was honored with deification and, for long afterward, he was numbered by many Romans among their household gods. Commodus erected in his father's memory the Antonine column in Rome's Piazza Colonna. The emperor's statue was placed at the top of the column and remained there until Pope Sixtus V caused it to be replaced by a bronze statue of Saint Paul. The substitution is symbolic, as it was meant to be.

Throughout the Christian era, attempts have been made to associate the *Meditations* with Christian thought. Such efforts are understandable, for the emperor's self-admonitions to virtuous conduct for its own sake, steadfastness, magnanimity, and forbearance are congenial to the mind of the Christian apologist. The weight of evidence, however, indicates otherwise. Marcus Aurelius seems to have known little about the Christians, and what he knew he did not like. Even granting that he was not deeply involved in their persecution, he clearly regarded them as fanatical troublemakers. He should be viewed, then, not as an incipient Christian but as the voice of paganism's last great moral pronouncements.

The emperor was an able but not a great military figure. He was an intelligent but not a brilliant thinker. As a writer, he was a competent but not a formidable stylist. In short, Marcus Aurelius was great because he brought a human quality to his leadership and made optimal use of his limited talents.

—*Patrick Adcock*

FURTHER READING

Arnold, E. Vernon. *Roman Stoicism*. Reprint. Freeport, N.Y.: Books for Libraries Press, 1971. A series of lectures by a classical scholar, arranged in seventeen chapters. The thought of Marcus Aurelius receives ample treatment, as he is discussed in four chapters.

Aurelius Antoninus, Marcus. *The "Meditations" of the Emperor Marcus Aurelius Antoninus*. Translated by R. Graves. London: Robinson, 1792. Graves was a clergyman and an Oxford don. His assessment of Marcus Aurelius, written toward the end of the Enlightenment, is of historical interest. Accompanied by a biography and notes.

_____. *The Emperor's Handbook: A New Translation of the "Meditations."* Translated by C. Scot Hicks and David V. Hicks. New York: Scribner, 2002. A lucid translation. Includes index.

Birley, Anthony Richard. *Marcus Aurelius: A Biography*. New York: Routledge, 2000. An engagingly written yet scholarly review of the life and times.

Hadot, Pierre. *The Inner Citadel: The "Meditations" of Marcus Aurelius*. Translated by Michael Chase. Cambridge, Mass.: Harvard University Press, 2001. This analysis of the main themes in the *Meditations* also provides background to the work.

Morford, Mark P. O. *The Roman Philosophers: From the Time of Cato the Censor to the Death of Marcus Aurelius*. New York: Routledge, 2002. Places the philosopher in context.

Wenley, R. M. *Stoicism and Its Influence*. New York: Cooper Square, 1963. A defense of the importance of Stoicism against historians of philosophy who have tended to dismiss it lightly. Discussions of Marcus Aurelius are liberally sprinkled throughout the text.

SEE ALSO: Hadran.

RELATED ARTICLES in *Great Events from History: The Ancient World*: c. 300 B.C.E., Stoics Conceptualize Natural Law; 64-67 C.E., Nero Persecutes the Christians; October 28, 312 C.E., Conversion of Constantine to Christianity.

GAIUS MARIUS
Roman general

Marius was a successful Roman general whose military innovations created the professional army of the late Roman Republic and early Empire. Representing the Popular Party, he was elected consul seven times.

BORN: 157 B.C.E.; Cereatae, Arpinum, Latium (now Arpino, Italy)
DIED: January 13, 86 B.C.E.; Rome (now in Italy)
AREAS OF ACHIEVEMENT: War and conquest, government and politics

EARLY LIFE

Gaius Marius (MEHR-ee-uhs) was born on a farm near the village of Cereatae in the district of Arpinum, about sixty miles southeast of Rome. He was the son of a middle-class farmer. Marius received little formal education and grew to manhood with a certain roughness in speech and manner that characterized him throughout his life. He first saw military service in 134 B.C.E. in Spain under Scipio Aemilianus in the campaign against the Numantines. Marius readily adapted to military life and was decorated for valor. For the following ten years, he served as a junior officer in Spain and the Balearic Islands.

After returning to Rome, Marius began his political career. With the help of the powerful Metelli clan, he won the election for tribune of the people in 119 B.C.E. During his tribuneship, he showed his independence by carrying a bill for election reform despite opposition from the Metelli and the Senatorial Party. In the next year Marius stood for the office of aedile but was defeated. In 115 B.C.E. he was elected praetor but only with difficulty. In the following year he was appointed propraetor for Further Spain. About the year 111 B.C.E. Marius contracted a highly favorable marriage alliance with the ancient Julian clan. His marriage to Julia, a future aunt of Julius Caesar, gave him an important link to the aristocracy.

LIFE'S WORK

The Jugurthine War soon brought Marius to a position of prominence in Roman affairs. In 109 B.C.E. he was appointed staff officer to Quintus Caecilius Metellus, who, as consul, was given command of the army in the war against Jugurtha, the king of Numidia. Bringing his army to Africa, Metellus waged war against the wily Jugurtha for two years without success. Amid growing criticism of

the slowness of the campaign, Marius determined that he would seek the consulship for the year 107 B.C.E. If successful, he hoped to replace Metellus as commander and reap the glory of ending the war. Returning to Rome, he boldly attacked Metellus and the senate and promised to capture or kill Jugurtha if elected. He was supported by members of the business class, who desired stability in North Africa, and the plebeians, who used the war as an opportunity to criticize senatorial leadership. Marius won the consulship by a wide margin. Although the senate voted to extend the command of Metellus for an additional year, the tribal assembly passed a measure directing that the command be transferred to Marius.

In raising an army, Marius chose not to rely on conscription, which involved a small property qualification. Instead, he called for voluntary recruits from the proletariat, promising land at the end of military service. The innovation was made by Marius out of necessity, because conscription was viewed as a burden by the small farmers, whose numbers were diminishing and who were reluctant to leave their farms. Those who joined the army were often the poorest citizens. For them, the army offered hope for the future.

After arriving in North Africa, Marius began seizing and occupying the fortified strongholds of Jugurtha. By the end of 107, most of eastern Numidia was under Roman control. Jugurtha retreated westward, joining forces with his father-in-law, Bocchus, king of Mauretania. During the year 106, Marius marched across the western half of Numidia. He reached the river Muluccha, five hundred miles west of his base of operations, and seized the war treasure of Jugurtha in a remote mountain fortress. As the Roman army returned eastward, Bocchus and Jugurtha attacked but were repelled. Convinced now that he was on the losing side, Bocchus secretly offered to make peace. Marius sent his quaestor, Lucius Cornelius Sulla, to the Mauretanian camp. Sulla persuaded Bocchus to betray Jugurtha, who was kidnapped and turned over to the Romans. With the capture of Jugurtha, the war ended. Marius took credit for the victory, overlooking the critical role played by Sulla, who was to become his bitter rival. Marius returned to Rome in triumph with Jugurtha in chains; a few days later, Jugurtha was executed.

Marius had returned from Africa at a critical time, for two Germanic tribes, the Cimbri and the Teutons, had invaded the Roman province in southern France. In 105, the Cimbri had annihilated a Roman army at Arausio (Orange) in the lower Rhone Valley. Marius was elected consul for 104 even before he returned from Africa. With Italy threatened by invasion, the Romans disregarded the law requiring a ten-year interval between consulships. The need for Marius's military ability was so great that he was elected consul repeatedly between 104 and 101. Fortunately for Rome, the Cimbri migrated to Spain and the Teutons to northern France, giving Marius time to prepare for their return.

In raising an army, Marius again used voluntary recruits from the propertyless class. He increased the strength of the legion to six thousand men; each legion was divided into ten cohorts of six hundred men. Marius completed the process of making the cohort the standard tactical unit of the legion, replacing the smaller maniple. The cohort was subdivided into six centuries, led by veteran centurions who had risen through the ranks. Weapons were standardized to include the short sword and the hurling pilum. Each soldier was required to carry his own pack. Marius introduced the silver eagle as the standard for each legion; each developed its own traditions and *esprit de corps*.

In 102 the Cimbri and Teutons reappeared. The Teutons advanced toward Italy along the southern coast of France. Marius met them at Aquae Sextiae (now Aix). The battle took place in a narrow valley, with the Teutons advancing uphill against the Romans. At the height of the battle, the Teutons were attacked from the rear by a Roman force that had been concealed behind a hill. The Teutons panicked, and the battle became a rout. As many as 100,000 Teutons may have perished. The Cimbri invaded Italy through the Brenner Pass. The other consul, Quintus Lutatius Catulus, brought an army northward to intercept them but was driven back south of the Po River. In the spring of 101, Marius joined Catulus with additional troops. The decisive battle was fought on the Raudine Plain near Vercellae, located between Milan and Turin. The Cimbri, facing a burning sun, advanced against the Roman center. As soon as they were overextended, Marius attacked on the flanks. The Cimbri were dealt a severe defeat from which they could not recover. With the threat of the German invasion ended, Marius and Catulus returned to Rome to celebrate a joint triumph.

After these victories, Marius began a new phase of his career as a politician, but he failed miserably. He formed a coalition with two political opportunists, Lucius Appuleius Saturninus and Gaius Glaucia. In the elections for the year 100, Marius won the consulship for the sixth

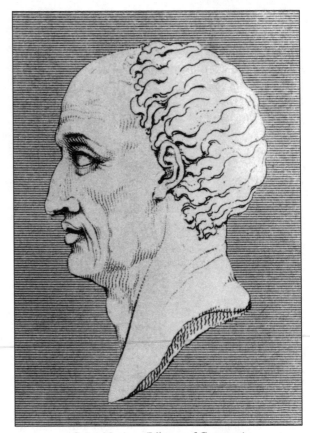

Gaius Marius. (Library of Congress)

time; Glaucia was elected praetor and Saturninus tribune. Soon afterward, Saturninus introduced bills to establish land grants for Marius's veterans in Transalpine Gaul and colonies in the east. Marius was to be given the right to bestow citizenship on a select number of the settlers. When the senate objected, Saturninus took the unprecedented step of requiring all senators to take an oath supporting the bills after passage or suffer exile. The urban proletariat also protested, for they judged the measures overly generous to the Italian allies, who made up a large part of the veterans. The bills were finally passed after Saturninus used Marius's veterans to drive off the opposition in the assembly.

In the elections for 99 B.C.E., Saturninus again won the tribuneship. Glaucia stood for consul but was defeated by Gaius Memmius. Seeking to intimidate their opponents, Saturninus and Glaucia ordered their henchmen to murder Memmius. The reaction to the slaying restored momentum to the senate, which passed a decree directing Marius to arrest Saturninus and Glaucia. After some hesitation, Marius ordered his veterans to seize his former friends, who were encamped on the Capitoline. He placed them in the senate building for protection, but the angry mob tore off the roof and pelted the prisoners to death with tiles. Marius completed his term as consul, but his influence and prestige disappeared. Under the pretext of fulfilling a vow to the goddess Cybele, he departed for the east.

After returning to Rome, Marius remained in relative obscurity until the outbreak of the Social War. When the allies gained early victories in the war, Marius was recalled to military service in the year 90 B.C.E. Although serving in a subordinate status, he was responsible for inflicting two defeats on the Marsi. Despite his success, he was given no assignment for the following year. The glory of concluding the war went to Sulla. In the year 88, when Mithradates VI Eupator, king of Pontus, led a revolt in the east, Marius sought to gain the command for the approaching war. The senate, however, ignored him and bestowed the command on Sulla, who was consul for 88. Marius gained the support of the tribune Publius Sulpicius Rufus, who initiated a tribal assembly measure transferring the command to him. Sulla, who was with his army in Campania, marched on Rome and ordered the executions of Marius and the leaders of the assembly. Sulpicius was captured and put to the sword; Marius fled to the coast, hiding in the marshes near Minturnae. At length he found refuge on the island of Cercina off the coast of Africa.

When Sulla departed for the east in 87, Marius returned to Italy and raised a new army. He joined forces with the democratic leader Lucius Cornelius Cinna, whom the senate had recently driven from Rome. With their combined armies, they advanced against Rome and forced its surrender. Marius now vented his anger after years of frustrations and disappointments by ordering wholesale executions of his enemies in the senate and among members of the nobility. Dispensing with the elections process, Marius and Cinna appointed themselves consuls for the year 86. Marius, now seventy-one years of age, entered his seventh consulship, but by this time he was gravely ill. He died of fever a few days after taking office in January, 86.

SIGNIFICANCE

One of the foremost generals of his age, Marius showed his resourcefulness and capability as a military commander in his successful campaigns in North Africa, Gaul, and Italy. His innovative recruitment of troops was of major significance for the future of Rome. By relying on volunteers from the proletariat class, Marius created an army of professional soldiers who were ready to serve for extended periods of time.

The new system was vastly superior to the short-term conscript militia of the past, but it also posed dangers. The soldiers of the professional army identified their interests with their general and expected to be rewarded with land following their service. They gave allegiance to their general rather than to the state. This system gave extraordinary power to any general who might desire to use the army for his own political ends. It led directly to the civil wars of the late Republic, when military strength became the key to political power.

Marius also introduced important reforms to improve the fighting ability of the army. His innovations in organization, weapons, and tactics produced a highly efficient fighting machine at a time when Rome was sorely pressed by its enemies. The new Marian army became the Roman army of the late Republic and early Empire.

Although Marius was a successful general, he failed as politician. His successive consulships are attributable not to political adroitness but to his skill as a general at a time when Rome was severely threatened. The year 100 marked a turning point in Marius's career. Elected consul for the sixth time and immensely popular after his recent victories, Marius devised no program for social reform beyond that of acquiring land for his veterans. Inept as a public speaker and vacillating in his political decisions, Marius allowed himself to be led by the demagogues Saturninus and Glaucia, whose radicalism and violence precipitated his fall. Driven by ambition, Marius spent the remaining years of his life trying to recover his former power and prestige. At his death, Rome had entered a new era of civil war and bloodshed that would last more than half a century.

—Norman Sobiesk

FURTHER READING

Carney, Thomas F. *A Biography of C. Marius*. Chicago: Argonaut, 1970. A concise, highly technical treatment of Marius's career. The notes present several directions in research. Includes numerous references and an appendix with tables listing all existing and nonextant contemporary sources.

Kildahl, P. A. *Caius Marius*. New York: Twayne, 1968. Highly readable, sympathetic account of the life of Marius. This book is intended for students and the general reader but will also be useful for scholars. Preface contains an analysis of contemporary sources. Chronology, map, useful notes, and select bibliography.

Last, Hugh. "The Wars of the Age of Marius." In *The Roman Republic*. Vol. 9 in *The Cambridge Ancient History*. 3d ed. New York: Cambridge University Press, 1998. Causes and historical background for both the Jugurthine War and the Cimbrian War are discussed. Detailed accounts of military campaigns, strategy, and battle tactics. Maps with physical features, mileage scales, and Roman place-names for areas of military operations. Description of military reforms under Marius. Includes notes and lengthy discussion of sources.

Parker, H. M. D. *The Roman Legions*. Chicago: Ares, 1980. A study of the composition of the Roman army through the periods of the Republic and the Empire. The chapter on the Marian army reforms offers technical explanations and details regarding Marius's innovations and contains valuable references to contemporary sources. The introduction provides a description of the pre-Marian army.

Scullard, H. H. *From the Gracchi to Nero*. New York: Routledge, 1988. An excellent account for the general background of the last century of the Roman Republic. Contains a detailed chapter on the career of Marius. Extensive notes include a discussion of sources for Marius, problems and conflicting interpretations arising from the sources, and numerous references for additional study.

SEE ALSO: Mithradates VI Eupator; Lucius Cornelius Sulla.

RELATED ARTICLES in *Great Events from History: The Ancient World*: 107-101 B.C.E., Marius Creates a Private Army; 90 B.C.E., Julian Law Expands Roman Citizenship.

MARTIAL

Roman poet

Martial perfected the epigram, the witty, sometimes salacious poem, typically of two to four lines, which points out the moral and social ills of the poet's day or lampoons prominent people.

BORN: March 1, 38-41 C.E.; Bilbilis, Hispania (now near Calatayud, Spain)
DIED: c. 103 C.E.; Hispania
ALSO KNOWN AS: Marcus Valerius Martialis (full name)
AREA OF ACHIEVEMENT: Literature

EARLY LIFE

Everything known about Martial (MAHR-shuhl) comes from his poems and from one letter of Pliny the Younger, written at the time of the poet's death. Martial alludes to his Spanish origins in an early poem, but by the age of fifty-seven he had already spent thirty-four years in Rome. His parents, of whom nothing more than their names is known, provided him with the standard rhetorical education designed to equip him to be a lawyer. In one of his poems, Martial depicts them as already in the underworld. Martial seems to have been in Rome by 64 C.E., perhaps under the patronage of the powerful Seneca family, also natives of Spain.

At some point he received the status of knight and an honorary military tribunate, but he does not mention which emperor bestowed on him those privileges. By contrast, it is clear that Titus gave Martial the privileges of a father of three children and that Domitian renewed the grant. His silence about the emperor who had provided the two earlier honors leads scholars to suspect that it was Nero, who fell into disgrace on his death in 68. It was important to Martial to have his honors known but impolitic to boast about who had given them to him.

Martial probably practiced law during Vespasian's reign (69-79), though it does not seem to have suited him. His comments about the profession are unkind, yet fairly late in his life he gibed someone who had failed to pay him for pleading his case in court.

Exactly when or why Martial turned to poetry cannot be determined. His first published effort was *Epigrammaton liber* (80 C.E.; *On the Spectacles*, 1980), a collection of short poems in honor of the dedication of the Flavian Amphitheater (the Colosseum) in 80. Between 86 and 98 he published his epigrams at the rate of roughly a volume a year. Publication order is not necessarily the order of writing. Epigrams 2.59 and 5.26, for example, refer to the same incident but were published several years apart. The twelfth and final volume appeared in 101, after he had returned to Spain. There are also two volumes of incidental poems that were meant to accompany gifts given at banquets. Probably written between 80 and 85, these are sometimes numbered books 13 and

14 of his collected works, but this classification does not seem to have been Martial's intention.

One of the great puzzles about Martial's early life is how he supported himself. Many of his poems complain about his poverty and the necessity of flattering the rich in the hope of a handout or a dinner invitation. He mentions his wretched third-floor apartment, and his ragged toga is a frequent subject of lament.

In other poems, however, Martial refers to his "Nomentan farm," a suburban villa not far from Rome, and to his private home in the city. He invites guests to dine with him and boasts about his kitchen and his cook, luxuries beyond the means of the urban poor who inhabited Rome's apartment houses. He asks permission from the emperor to tap into the city water supply and pipe the water directly into his house, a privilege reserved for the ruler's wealthy friends. The image that he tries to project of a poor poet scrounging handouts from stingy patrons may be nothing more than a literary pose.

LIFE'S WORK

This problem of the poetic persona complicates enormously the study of Martial's life and work. His poems are the only source of information about his life, but there is doubt that what he says about himself is to be taken seriously. For example, in one poem he complains about his wife having a lover, while in another he objects that she is too moralistic to engage in the deviant sexual behavior that he enjoys. Can these poems be talking about the same woman? As a result, some modern scholars contend that Martial was never married and that any reference to a wife is merely a literary convention. Another possibility is that he was married several times, something that was not at all uncommon in Rome in the late first century C.E.

If one cannot be certain whether, or how many times, Martial was married, it is difficult to ascertain anything else about his life. In one poem, he refers to a daughter but only once in passing. In another, he mourns deeply the death of the slave child Erotion, tending her grave for years and requiring the next owner of the property to observe the same rituals. It is conjectured that this was his daughter by a slave woman on his farm.

It is virtually impossible to know Martial from his poems, as the contradictions in his work are numerous. In some of the poems he pictures himself engaging in homosexual relations; in others he ridicules men who do the same. He praises the joys of simple country life, but he lived in Rome for thirty-five years. He claims that, although many of his poems are bawdy, his life is decent.

Every writer must please his readers, and Martial seems to have been slanting his material to the tastes of his audience. In one poem he claims that he "could write what is serious" but emphasizes entertainment value, for that is what makes people "read and hum my poems all over Rome." Most of his poetry was produced in the reign of Domitian, a cruel, self-indulgent emperor (according to the biographer Suetonius) who enjoyed brutal sex with prostitutes and initiated mixed nude bathing in Rome's public baths. After his death, the emperors Nerva and Trajan brought about a kind of Victorian reaction to the loose morality of Domitian's day. Martial found that his poetry no longer appealed to the general public, so he retired to Spain.

While he does not reveal himself to the reader, Martial does draw an intimate portrait of Roman society in the late first century. One commentator says that he "touched life closely at all levels." One of his poems describes a Roman's daily schedule, and several others focus on certain daily activities.

Martial's day would begin with a visit at daybreak to his patron, a wealthy man who would give him a small daily handout in exchange for Martial's accompanying him to public meetings and generally boosting his ego. Every Roman aristocrat had as many such clients as he could reasonably support. His status was measured by the size of the throng that surrounded him as he walked through the streets. Because Rome lacked a governmental welfare system, this informal arrangement redistributed some of the wealth that was concentrated in the hands of the aristocracy, a minute percentage of the population. In addition to the daily *sportula*, clients expected to receive gifts on their birthdays and at the festival of the Saturnalia in December. Martial's poems show that the clients would complain vociferously if the gift was not as large as they had expected.

One of the client's duties was to accompany his patron to court, an obligation that the litigious Romans faced frequently. Lawyers seem to have had difficulty collecting their fees, which was perhaps one reason that Martial abandoned the calling. The speeches in court were long and often irrelevant, but the client was expected to applaud his patron's case in the hope of influencing the jury.

By midday, everyone was ready for a rest, followed by exercise and a bath. Martial frequented the baths and pointed out the flaws—the stretch marks, the sagging breasts, the brand of the former slave—which other patrons tried to hide. From the numerous poems that discuss the baths, one can conclude that they served as Rome's social center. People went there to see and to be seen, to catch up on the latest gossip, and to wangle invitations to dinner. This last function was the most important to a client such as Martial. Failure to obtain an invitation meant that he had to provide his own meal, which marked him as a social outcast.

Dinner began in the late afternoon, as the Romans did not eat much, if anything, for breakfast or lunch. The city's social life revolved around these huge meals, at which the food was often intended to impress the guests as much as to nourish them. The seating arrangement indicated the guests' social standing, with the more prominent individuals reclined on couches closest to that of the host. Many aristocrats served two meals at once: elegant food for those eating immediately around them and cheaper fare for those in the farther reaches of the dining room. That this practice was common is evidenced by Pliny the Younger, who in a letter to a friend assured him that he did not engage in such habits.

Though these dinners did not often turn into orgies, the Romans had no compunctions about promiscuous sexual activity. Martial seems to have engaged in his share of such activity and was aware of what everyone else in his social circle was doing. His language is so explicit that no one dared to translate all of his poems into idiomatic English until 1968.

SIGNIFICANCE

Scattered through Martial's epigrams are the people of Rome, from the aristocracy to the prostitutes. He exposes their posturing and the vices they thought would remain secret. His picture of Roman society may be the most accurate available, for he does not adopt the bitterly satiric tone of Juvenal or the staid disdain of Pliny. Martial's poetry gained for him renown in his own lifetime, something that he openly pursued. What made him successful, he believed, was the shock value of his epigrams. Martial once wrote that it is the nature of the epigram, as he refined it, to jolt the reader while it amuses, just as vinegar and salt improve the flavor of food.

Martial's clearest statement of his purpose is found in epigram 6.60:

> Rome praises, adores, and sings my verses.
> Every pocket, every hand holds me.
> Look, that fellow blushes, turns pale, is stunned, yawns,
>   hates me.
> That's what I want. Now my poems please me.

Pliny's judgment on Martial's epigrams was that they were "remarkable for their combination of sincerity with pungency and wit.... His verses may not be immortal, but he wrote them with that intention." Later generations have agreed with Pliny's critique. Though the church fathers frowned on him in the Middle Ages, Martial's technique was much admired and palely imitated from the Renaissance until the eighteenth century. His Erotion poems directly influenced Ben Jonson's "On My First Daughter," and Robert Herrick's "Upon a Child That Died."

—*Albert A. Bell, Jr.*

FURTHER READING

Adamik, T. "Martial and the *Vita Beatior.*" *Annales Universitatis Budapestinensis* 3 (1975): 55-64. According to Adamik, Martial's personal philosophy of life seems to be closest to Epicureanism. He satirizes Cynics and Stoics especially.

Allen, Walter, Jr., et al. "Martial: Knight, Publisher, and Poet." *Classical Journal* 65 (May, 1970): 345-357. Discusses the problem of Martial's persona and concludes that he was not actually a poor, struggling poet but a reasonably successful writer and publisher.

Ascher, Leona. "Was Martial Really Unmarried?" *Classical World* 70 (April/May, 1977): 441-444. Surveys scholarly opinion on the question of Martial's marital status and finds the evidence inconclusive.

Bell, Albert A., Jr. "Martial's Daughter?" *Classical World* 78 (September/October, 1984): 21-24. Suggests that the girl Erotion, who is the subject of several of Martial's poems, was his daughter by a slave woman.

Carrington, A. G. *Aspects of Martial's Epigrams*. Eton, England: Shakespeare Head Press, 1960. A nonscholarly introduction to selected poems, especially those discussing Martial's life, Roman history, and the process of creating a book in antiquity.

Martial. *The Mortal City: One Hundred Epigrams of Martial*. Edited by William Matthews. Athens, Ohio: Ohio Review Books, 1995. Uses modern references and language to show the timelessness of Martial's epigrams.

Sullivan, J. P. "Martial's Sexual Attitudes." *Philologus* 123 (1979): 288-302. Though graphic by modern standards, Martial was merely expressing contemporary sexual values in his poetry. His explicit language is a convention of the epigram, as seen in Catullus and earlier poets.

SEE ALSO: Catullus; Juvenal; Nero.

RELATED ARTICLE in *Great Events from History: The Ancient World*: 100-127 C.E., Roman Juvenal Composes *Satires*.

MARY
Mother of Jesus

Though little is known about the historical Mary, the legendary virgin mother of Jesus Christ has been revered throughout the ages.

BORN: 22 B.C.E.; place unknown
DIED: Date unknown; probably Israel, perhaps Ephesus (now in Turkey)
ALSO KNOWN AS: Holy Virgin; Mother of God; Virgin Mary
AREA OF ACHIEVEMENT: Religion

EARLY LIFE

According to tradition, the parents of Mary (MEHR-ee) were Joachim and Anna, from the city of Nazareth in Galilee in present-day Israel. About five hundred years after their time, Saint Augustine declared that the sin of Adam and Eve infects all humanity and is passed down from generation to generation through biological conception. Mary was declared to have been exempt from this sin in preparation for her role as the mother of Jesus. This exemption became known and is still celebrated as the Immaculate Conception. The event is commemorated each year on December 8, nine months before her birthday, which is celebrated on September 8.

LIFE'S WORK

Almost nothing is known about the historical personage of the woman known as the Virgin Mary. She was the mother of the man Jesus, whom Christians worship as the Son of God. In the Christian Scriptures, only two of the four gospels, Matthew and Luke, feature Mary at the birth of Jesus. Matthew traces the ancestry of Jesus through Mary's husband, Joseph, and then immediately proceeds to create an image of Jesus as a new Moses. Like Pharaoh at Moses' birth, King Herod is threatened by portents at Jesus' birth and to avoid his fate, promises to kill all Hebrew baby boys. The Holy Family escapes into Egypt to await the death of the dreaded king. After Jesus' baptism, which takes place when Jesus is approximately thirty years old, he is followed by crowds up to the mountain, where Matthew depicts him, again like a new Moses, giving a new law to the people. Scholars agree that Matthew's narrative of Jesus' birth was written later than the rest of the gospels and that its purpose was not to relate a historical event but to convince his readers that Jesus was the Messiah for whom they were waiting.

In Luke's gospel, an angel appears to Mary and asks her to accept the privilege of being the mother of the savior. After questioning how this might happen, as she is not yet married, Mary is assured by the angel that the child will be born by the power of the Holy Spirit. It is thought that Mary was probably between the ages of twelve and fourteen at this time. Mary then immediately goes to the town of Ain Kerim to visit her cousin Elizabeth, who is pregnant with John the Baptist. Luke took excerpts from the song of Hannah, mother of Sampson, and put them into the mouth of Mary: "My heart extols the Lord. My spirit exults in God my savior." As soon as the child is born, an angel goes out to some shepherds and announces to them that a savior has been born. Luke recalls that Mary pondered all these things in her heart. Unlike Matthew's account, Luke's does not include a visit from the Magi or a flight into Egypt.

Outside of these infancy narratives, Mary is mentioned only a few more times in the Scriptures. Her next appearance is at a wedding in Cana, where the hosts run out of wine. Mary relates this fact to her son Jesus, who then changes water into wine. In Mark 3:20-35, Jesus' relatives are suspicious of him and think that he may be somewhat insane. They go to the place where he is preaching, and when they ask for him, the crowd yells out, "Your mother and brothers are outside asking for you." Jesus answers, "Who are my mother and my brothers? . . . Whoever does the will of God is my brother and sister and mother." At first, this answer seems to be a rebuke of his mother and his immediate family. However, Mark's purpose is to distinguish between Jesus' natural family and his followers. He is claiming that all people can be related to Jesus, not through blood ties but by doing the will of God.

In Luke 11:27-28, a similar incident takes place. A woman calls out from the crowd, "Blessed is the mother who bore you and nursed you!" Jesus answers, "You might better say, 'Blessed are those who hear God's message and observe it!'" Again, this seems to be a rebuke of his mother, but it can be interpreted to mean that kinship has no special claim on Jesus' friends.

John's gospel is the only one that puts Mary at the foot of the cross. Mary, her sister Mary (the wife of Clopas), Mary Magdalene, and John himself are present when Jesus looks down from the cross and says to his mother, "Woman, behold your son," and to the beloved disciple John, "Son, behold your mother," thus giving Mary into the care of John. According to later tradition, Jesus is taken from the cross and laid in the arms of his mother.

This scene has inspired many artistic sculptures and paintings, the most famous of which is the *Pietà* by Michelangelo, which now stands in the Vatican in Rome.

Whether Mary stayed in Jerusalem or went to Ephesus is not known. Ephesus boasts of a house in which Mary lived and died, but most scholars think she probably stayed in Jerusalem, where there is also a place honored as the site of her "falling asleep." There is a strong tradition in the Catholic Church that Mary did not die but only fell asleep and that she was assumed into heaven, body and soul. This "Assumption" was officially declared in 1950 and is celebrated each year on August 15. In 1954, Pope Pius XII officially proclaimed her "Queen of Heaven."

Before the fifth century C.E., references to Mary were rare. In about the year 100 C.E., Justin Martyr contrasted her with Eve, a theme later developed by Saint Irenaeus. Mary came into prominence until the 400's, when church councils debated whether Jesus was God. In 428, Nes-

torius, a Syrian, became bishop of Constantinople, the eastern capital of the Roman Empire. He preferred the term *christotokos* (mother of Christ) for Jesus' mother rather than the more popular *theotokos* (mother of God) because, he said, *theotokos* implies that Mary gave birth to God. Nestorius was quickly challenged by Cyril of Alexandria, and in 430 the bishops condemned Nestorius as a heretic. Since then, Mary has often been referred to as the "Mother of God." In popular piety, however, this title resulted in Mary's being referred to as a goddess; in 787, therefore, the Council of Nicaea clearly distinguished between worship of God alone and the lesser reverence due Mary and the saints.

The Middle Ages saw a proliferation of devotions and artistic works in honor of the Virgin and Mother Mary. She can be seen at the Annunciation, often reading a book of Scripture as the angel appears to her, a dove over her head representing the Holy Spirit. In one painting, the tiny baby can be seen flying through the window of the chapel to be implanted in her womb. Other favorite poses include the birth of Jesus in the stable, the Madonna and child, the crucifixion, and the pietà. At the time of the Reformation, Protestants deemphasized devotion to Mary. However, Martin Luther referred to her as the foremost example of God's grace and of proper humility.

In the nineteenth and twentieth centuries, Mary was reported to have appeared to various people: in Lourdes, France, in 1858; in Fatima, Portugal, in 1917; and since 1981 in Medjugorje, Bosnia. Some of the bishops at the Second Vatican Council in 1965 moved to declare her "corredemptrix" with Christ; that is, the co-redeemer of the world along with her son. The council did not approve of this, but it did include a chapter on Mary in the document *Lumen Gentium*. In his speech at the council, Pope Paul VI proclaimed Mary "Mother of the Church."

SIGNIFICANCE

After the Vatican Council, there was more activity in Roman Catholic Mariology. At first, women did not wish to venerate Mary, because she had always been idealized strictly for her biological function as the mother of Jesus. They saw her as weak, a woman who was always submissive to others, one who did not make her own decisions about her life. Feminist theologians, however, have begun to point out Mary's strengths. In the story of the annunciation, she questions the angel who wants her

Mary. (Library of Congress)

to be the mother of Jesus, and, after she understands what God wants, she decides on her own to go ahead, even though she realizes that she will be criticized by those who will not understand.

In her prayer, quoted from Hannah of the Hebrew Scriptures, Mary speaks of how she, along with others who had been considered humble and lowly, were lifted up by God: "He has satisfied the hungry with good things, and has sent the rich away empty-handed." Mary is seen here as a symbol for all women, who traditionally have been seen as insignificant but are now seen as equal to men and are highly regarded not only for their ability to reproduce but also for other strengths of intellect, will, and determination. Women throughout the ages have been able to relate to Mary in her difficult life, especially in the loss of her son.

—Winifred O. Whelan

FURTHER READING

Brown, Raymond, Karl P. Donfried, Joseph A. Fitzmyer, and John Reumann, eds. *Mary in the New Testament: A Collaborative Assessment by Protestant and Roman Catholic Scholars*. Philadelphia: Fortress Press, 1978. The role that Mary plays in salvation is one that has divided Protestants, Anglicans, and Roman Catholics over the centuries. This book is an effort to open the way for agreement.

Coll, Regina. "Mary, the Mother of Jesus." In *Christianity and Feminism in Conversation*. Mystic, Conn.: Twenty-Third, 1994. In this brief chapter, Coll speaks of how the Virgin Mary relates to the modern woman. Feminists now say that virginity is not simply a biological phenomenon but also connotes a person who is whole in herself, one whose being was not owned by a man.

Cunneen, Sally. *In Search of Mary: The Woman and the Symbol*. New York: Ballantine Books, 1996. This book reviews the New Testament references to Mary and then traces her cult through the ages into contemporary time. The author enters into the human aspects of Mary's life (her pregnancy, for example) and discusses how, very often, she did not understand what her son was doing. Cunneen quotes many different theologians, poets, and ordinary people to bring out the humanity of Mary as a person, a mother, and a model for the church.

Kung, Hans, and Jurgen Moltman, eds. *Mary in the Churches*. New York: Seabury Press, 1983. An ecumenical inquiry with contributions by Orthodox, Protestant, Jewish, and Catholic scholars. For the most part, Mariology has been anti- rather than pro-ecumenical and has been largely excluded from ecumenical dialogue. The authors wish to present Mary as an essential figure in the gospel of Christ.

Macquarrie, John. *Mary for All Christians*. Grand Rapids, Mich.: William B. Erdmans, 1990. John Macquarrie, a British theologian, takes up the questions of the Immaculate Conception, the Assumption, and Mary as corredemptrix. He states that Mary should not separate Christians from one another but should be seen in a wider context of Christian faith as a person who can point toward God.

Warner, Marina. *Alone of All Her Sex: The Myth and the Cult of the Virgin Mary*. New York: Vintage Books, 1976. This book relates the history of the titles of the Virgin Mary, such as the second Eve, queen, madonna, sorrowful mother, Immaculate Conception, and the Virgin among the moon and the stars. It also contains eight color and fifty-two black and white plates depicting scenes from the life of the Virgin.

SEE ALSO: Saint Augustine; Herod the Great; Jesus; John the Apostle; Saint John the Baptist.

RELATED ARTICLES in *Great Events from History: The Ancient World*: c. 6 B.C.E., Birth of Jesus Christ; c. 30 C.E., Condemnation and Crucifixion of Jesus Christ; c. 30 C.E., Preaching of the Pentecostal Gospel; c. 50-c. 150 C.E., Compilation of the New Testament.

MASINISSA
Numidian king (r. c. 201-148 B.C.E.)

*Through his alliance with the Roman Republic,
Masinissa helped to destroy the realm of Carthage,
opening the way to Roman suzerainty over the
Mediterranean region.*

BORN: c. 238 B.C.E.; Numidia, northern Africa (now in
Algeria)
DIED: 148 B.C.E.; Numidia, northern Africa
AREAS OF ACHIEVEMENT: Government and politics,
war and conquest

EARLY LIFE

Masinissa (MAHS-uh-NIHS-uh) was not born a king. He
was the son of a minor tribal chieftain of the Massylians, a
tribe of the North African group known to the Greeks and
Carthaginians as the Numidians. Numidia was roughly
equivalent to modern eastern Algeria (as far as present-
day Constantine) and western Tunisia. The Numidians
are generally considered the ancestors of the people later
known as the Berbers (the very word "nomad," according
to one etymology, derives from "Numidian"). For at least
three hundred years, the Numidians had been subjugated
by the Carthaginians, colonizers from Phoenicia. The
various Numidian tribes were used by Carthage as a
source of manpower, as they were usually more warlike
in nature than the commerce-minded Carthaginians.

Like many sons of Numidian nobility, young Masinissa was sent to Carthage to be educated, presumably
more in warfare and in science than in high culture. It is at
this point that a famous story begins, given credence by
ancient historians such as Livy and Appian but suspect to
more skeptical modern viewpoints. Masinissa, it is said,
met and fell in love with Sophonisba, an aristocratic Carthaginian girl of the family of Gisgo. Though Numidians
were subject peoples of Carthage, there were no particular racial or class differences between the two peoples,
and Sophonisba's father happily encouraged Masinissa's
interest in his daughter. The couple was betrothed around
216 B.C.E.

However, there was another suitor for Sophonisba, a
man named Syphax. Syphax was the leader of a larger
faction of Numidians, the Massaesylians, who coexisted
in an uneasy rivalry with Masinissa's group. While Masinissa was away in Spain serving in Carthage's war against
Rome under the command of Sophonisba's father, Syphax
exerted pressure on the Carthaginian leadership to prof-
fer Sophonisba to him. Because Syphax was on hand and
had a large military presence just outside Carthage, the

Carthaginian leadership consented to Syphax's marriage
to Sophonisba.

Masinissa was, understandably, infuriated; he also
felt personally endangered, as there were rumors that
Sophonisba's father was under orders from Carthage to
put him to death. Though he and his family had been
nothing but loyal to Carthage for several generations, he
felt so betrayed by the Carthaginians that he immediately
switched sides and offered his allegiance to Rome, which
was engaged in a life-and-death struggle with Carthage
for control of the Western Mediterranean region. Masinissa would continue as a Roman ally for the rest of his
long and productive life.

LIFE'S WORK

Masinissa joined the Roman side at about the time that
the tide was beginning to turn in the Second Punic War.
After Rome had been driven nearly to its knees after its
defeat at Cannae in 216 B.C.E., a new, young general,
Scipio, had taken command of Roman forces in Spain
and was reinvigorating the Roman war effort. In 204
B.C.E., Masinissa began an organized offensive against
Carthage in Africa. By now, Masinissa was in his early
thirties, and he impressed and motivated his men by his
physical energy, commanding appearance, and genius in
warfare.

The ascetic regimen that he mandated for his men
proved perfect for the desert locale of his attacks on
the Carthaginians. Lacking the heavy supply trains that
encumbered the Carthaginian troops, Masinissa's mobile and maneuverable army held off the Carthaginians
before Roman troops commanded by Scipio arrived in
force. Eventually, Masinissa's army engaged in direct
battle with that of Syphax, and the two rivals for Sophonisba's hand met each other in single combat. (It must
be stressed again that the entire Sophonisba story contains many legendary elements.) Masinissa prevailed
over Syphax at the Battle of the Great Plains, but there
was concern in the Roman camp that Sophonisba was potentially a Carthaginian agent who would turn Masinissa
against Rome. The Romans thus forced Masinissa to give
up the woman he loved.

Masinissa's most important service to Rome came in
202 B.C.E., when Hannibal, the great Carthaginian commander who had dealt Rome stunning blows earlier in
the war, returned to Africa to defend his homeland against
Scipio's invasion. Scipio linked up with Masinissa at

Zama, where the climactic battle occurred. Masinissa and his cavalry were stationed on Scipio's right flank. Masinissa's horsemen managed to circumvent Hannibal's front lines and, by wreaking havoc in the rear of his opponent's formation, contributed to Hannibal's defeat and that of Carthage overall.

As a reward for his participation in the victory, Rome made Masinissa king of Numidia, a position that had never before existed. Masinissa, of a formerly minor tribe, now exerted supreme authority over all the Numidians. His people's overall position in the region was also strengthened, as the peace Carthage was forced to conclude with Rome after the Battle of Zama left Carthage in a very weak position. Carthage was forced to cede to the Numidian kingdom any land that had ever belonged to Masinissa's ancestors in the past, a clause the Numidian leader was often to use as a pretext to harass Carthage over the next fifty years.

Even after Scipio's victory, Masinissa continued as an inveterate opponent of Carthage. This opposition was not ethnically or culturally motivated, as Masinissa, educated in Carthage, was an advocate of Punic (Carthaginian) culture and was far more part of the North African cultural world than the Roman. Masinissa's seemingly endless need for vengeance on Carthage perhaps caused ancient historians to attribute so much importance to the Sophonisba legend. More plausibly, Masinissa early on diagnosed the rising power of Rome and wanted to be on the winning side. Certainly, his kingdom benefited from Roman patronage over his career. Masinissa also made material improvements in his own realm, especially in the area of agriculture, as he convinced many Numidian herdsmen to settle down as farmers. He also established a new capital at Cirta that served as an appropriate focal point for his newly unified kingdom.

While his kingdom was developing internally, Masinissa continued to press against Carthage. In 174 B.C.E., he accused Carthage, which as part of its peace pact with Rome had to act as a Roman ally, of receiving ambassadors from Macedonia, with which Rome was fighting a fierce war. In fact, Carthage refused Macedonian overtures; Masinissa nevertheless continued to encroach on Carthaginian territory, plundering several Carthaginian coastal outposts.

Ironically, the Carthaginians came to despise Masinissa so much for these raids that even Rome, the city's true rival, had a far larger set of sympathizers among the Carthaginian people. For Carthage to surrender to Rome, a city of equivalent stature, was one thing, but for it potentially to surrender to Masinissa, king of a people who had once been Carthaginian subjects, was unthinkable. Carthage continually appealed to Rome to rein in their client king, but their pleas went unheeded until 151 B.C.E., when Rome suddenly restrained Masinissa from pursuing further gains. Some historians think that Rome had finally gotten suspicious of Masinissa and feared that the Numidian king was plotting to establish an empire that would encompass all of North Africa from Mauretania to Egypt, an aspiration that would eventually conflict with Rome's plans for expansion. Rome's restraint of Masinissa was probably a delaying tactic employed so that Rome's armies could be strong when the final push against Carthage came.

By now, Masinissa was in his late eighties. His sons, particularly Gulussa and Micipsa, began to take more of a role in commanding the Numidian armies. It was a Carthaginian attack on Gulussa that enabled Masinissa not only to besiege the city of Oroscopa but also to provoke Carthage into a full-scale battle that would enable Rome, which had been looking for an excuse to destroy Car-

Masinissa, top left, counsels Sophonisba to drink poison. (F. R. Niglutsch)

thage, to intervene. Through a brilliant set of military tactics, Masinissa appeared to pull back from Oroscopa, only to engage the Carthaginians in the open. He was victorious through a combination of combat and attrition, and a massacre led by Gulussa wiped out the Carthaginian army.

The Carthaginians now switched strategies and tried to make peace with Masinissa by appointing a grandson of his, Hasdrubal, to high command. This strategy did not seem to work, though Roman callousness in not consulting Masinissa as to strategy upset the old king and made him more distant toward Rome. He never, though, showed any sign of a break with Rome and an alliance with Carthage, and he thus left no obstacle to Carthage's final destruction. He did not, however, live to see the end of his old adversary, as he died in 148 B.C.E. at the age of ninety. He had forty-four children, of whom ten survived him. His sons Gulussa, Micipsa, and Mastanabal all served Rome loyally in the final assault on Carthage, which was destroyed in 146 B.C.E.

SIGNIFICANCE

Masinissa saw himself as a great Numidian leader. Rome saw him as a client king who could help the Romans gain control of Africa. Though they may have had different objectives, Rome and Masinissa worked hand in hand to subdue Carthage. Masinissa, indeed, was one of the most important and useful allies in all Roman history, and he gave major assistance to the process of Roman expansion. Although it might have seemed inevitable that the talented Masinissa would someday run afoul of his Roman patrons, there is no solid evidence of any important difference between Masinissa and Rome during the fifty years of their alliance.

Masinissa's long life, inveterate hatred of Carthage, and military skill make him a notable figure in ancient history. His enormous military achievements were complemented by his accomplishments in solidifying Numidia as a political and economic unity. By his death, Numidia was widely recognized as the preeminent realm in Mediterranean Africa. Masinissa can be seen as the first in a series of Berber leaders to offer resistance to colonizers seeking to occupy North Africa. He is also one of the most renowned indigenous Africans to make an impact on the Greco-Roman world.

—*Nicholas Birns*

FURTHER READING

Armstrong, Donald. *The Reluctant Warriors*. New York: Crowell, 1966. Probably the liveliest, most informative source on Masinissa, though the author's Cold War perspective skews the general argument somewhat.

Bagnall, Nigel. *The Punic Wars*. London: Hutchinson, 1990. A traditional military history that takes advantage of recent archaeological research. Useful for understanding the state of military practice in Masinissa's time.

Brett, Michael, and Elizabeth Fentress. *The Berbers*. Cambridge, Mass.: Blackwell, 1997. An anthropological and historical look at the people whom Masinissa helped launch onto the historical stage.

Fentress, Elizabeth. *Numidia and the Roman Army: Social, Military, and Economic Aspects of the Frontier Zone*. Oxford, England: British Archaeological Review, 1979. This look at Numidia after the Roman conquest is also relevant to Masinissa's era and takes account of his achievement in agriculture.

Lancel, Serge. *Carthage: A History*. Translated by Antonio Nevill. Cambridge, Mass.: Blackwell, 1995. This state-of-the-art history of the ancient region takes advantage of late twentieth century archaeological discoveries; also includes information on Punic culture.

Warmington, B. A. *Carthage*. New York: Praeger, 1969. A general history of Carthage that offers ten pages of detailed discussion of Masinissa's life and career. This book, frequently cited in subsequent scholarship, displays Masinissa in a North African context.

Wheeler, Sir Mortimer. *Roman Africa in Color*. New York: McGraw-Hill, 1966. This collection of photographs, with commentary by a famed archaeologist, gives a startlingly vivid picture of the physical and social environment in which Masinissa lived.

SEE ALSO: Hannibal; Scipio Africanus; Sophonisba of Numidia.

RELATED ARTICLES in *Great Events from History: The Ancient World*: c. 300-c. 100 B.C.E., Berber Kingdoms of Numidia and Mauretania Flourish; 218-201 B.C.E., Second Punic War; 202 B.C.E., Battle of Zama.

MAUSOLUS
Turkish satrap (r. 377-353 B.C.E.)

Mausolus established a multinational empire in southwest Turkey, but he became much more famous for his tomb at Halicarnassas, one of the Seven Wonders of the World.

BORN: Date unknown; Caria (now in Turkey)
DIED: 353 B.C.E.; Caria
ALSO KNOWN AS: Mausalous
AREAS OF ACHIEVEMENT: War and conquest, architecture

EARLY LIFE

Most information about Mausolus (maw-SOH-luhs) and his wife and sister Artemisia comes from various accounts dealing with the Seven Wonders of the World, a highly subjective compiling by Antipater of Sidon about 200 B.C.E. Artemisia built a huge and beautiful tomb for Mausolus in the capital city of the Carian Empire, Halicarnassus (now Bodrum, Turkey). This tomb, which survived for nearly eighteen hundred years, is the origin of the modern word "mausoleum."

Mausolus was a Carian, a group known for its many acts of piracy in the eastern Mediterranean region. King Minos of Crete forced the Carians into the mainland of Turkey, where they founded the cities of Mylasa and Halicarnassus. Mylasa was the official capital, but Halicarnassus had a more favorable geographic position, being located at the Gulf of Cos. The latter city would always have a mystic (and mysterious) reputation, with the Greeks claiming it had been founded by a descendant of the god of the seas, Poseidon. Herodotus, arguably the first historian, called Halicarnassus home. About a century after its defeat by the Greeks, Persia began expanding westward again, and by 387 B.C.E. had subjugated almost all of Asia Minor, including Caria.

The Persians were not as brutal as most conquerors, and they allowed the native Carian leader, King Hecatomnas, to remain in power as their chosen representative, or satrap. He obediently collected Persian taxes and enforced Persian law, and in exchange for these services, Caria was granted substantial autonomy.

Hecatomnus died in 377 and was succeeded by his son Mausolus and daughter Artemisia, who were married to each other. The Persians installed Mausolus as Caria's king and their agent, but, unlike his father, Mausolus was hugely dissatisfied by this arrangement. He wanted to free Caria of any Persian authority or influence, and through a campaign of intimidation, diplomacy, and war, he was able to do so.

LIFE'S WORK

King Mausolus, once fully sovereign, began to build a thoroughly cosmopolitan empire that combined Carian, Persian, and Hellenic culture. Although not Hellenic by birth, the king seemed to be particularly influenced by Greek architecture, as judged by the proliferation of temples, monuments, theaters, and marketplaces built during his reign. He expanded his realm by conquering nearby Lycia and Ionia, in addition to a number of islands in the eastern Mediterranean region. Carian power and influence would never again approach the heights established by Mausolus during his twenty-four year reign.

The Carian monarch soon grew tired with his inherited capital city of Mylasa and longed for a metropolis far grander and more Hellenic. He therefore decided to move the capital to Halicarnassus, a city that enjoyed the additional advantages of being farther west and more easily protected. Even Halicarnassus, however, did not meet his standards or fulfill his dream, so Mausolus decided extensive rebuilding was necessary. He built a new palace for himself in a place that provided a clear view of the harbor. He also extended the walls of the city, thus making available room for all of his anticipated projects. He then fortified the harbor to make it safe from attack and built a water passageway, which led directly to the new palace. Mausolus could thus keep up to one hundred ships near his residence, an armada entirely invisible to any potential conquerors from the sea. Wanting a capital to rival Athens, he decided a larger population was needed. Accordingly, parks, museums, and theaters were built, making Halicarnassus a major cultural attraction. When this failed to produce the desired population, he simply coerced the inhabitants of Mylasa and surrounding areas to move to the new capital.

All of these undertakings required enormous amounts of money, and Mausolus felt bound by neither law nor ethics in how he raised it. Early in his reign, he promised the people of Mylasa a new protective city wall, an improvement for which they dutifully paid. Then he took the revenues and spent them on building up Halicarnassus. When the people of Mylasa complained, he blithely informed them that the gods forbade the building of the promised fortification. He raised money from the Lycians by telling them that Persia had ordered all of them to shave their heads to provide hair for wigs for the Persian aristocracy. The only way to avoid this unfortunate circumstance was to offer up a huge cash payment, which Mausolus would pass on to Persia. Of course, there had been no such decree, and this money was also used on Halicarnassus.

He was as unscrupulous in foreign affairs as he was in appropriations. He joined a growing rebellion against Persia in 374. This rebellion, strongly supported by Egypt, was widely successful and helped lead to Carian independence. The very next year, however, he joined a punitive expedition led by Persia against Egypt. He waged war mercilessly, attacking without provocation Miletus and Ephesus and in the Social War (356 B.C.E.) he used duplicity to convince Rhodes and other islands to shift their allegiance from Athens to Caria.

A vain man, Mausolus routinely described himself as a superior physical specimen. Such an entity certainly deserved an eternal resting spot that would produce awe and homage for centuries, a tomb second to none on earth. He certainly wanted a larger and more intricate tomb than that of the Persian king Darius, his despised eastern rival. The Carian tyrant's goal was a burial place grander than any similar structure, more ornate than anything the Oriental world could offer and more stately than all Athenian structures.

Mausolus decided to place his tomb directly in the center of Halicarnassus, at the site where the capital's two main roads intersected. Interestingly, Alexander the Great, in choosing his own gravesite in Alexandria, Egypt, later in the same century, would also choose an intersection as his grave and memorial. Mausolus was nothing if not a builder, constructing two harbors, new city walls, a fortressed arsenal, a marketplace, and a luxurious palace. In this respect, perhaps he was more Roman than either Greek or Persian. A tremendously costly enterprise, the building of the tomb was to be financed as the earlier enterprises had been: forced homage, deceit, and crushing taxes.

It is likely that the mammoth structure was begun before the death of Mausolus in 353 B.C.E. Artemisia was to be the driving force behind the erection of the great monument. So consumed was she by grief on the death of her husband and brother, she reputedly had some of his remains mixed with wine, an eerie concoction she then drank. She meticulously planned his grandiose funeral activities, which included poetry readings, great orations, and the ritualistic slaughter of sacrificial animals (mostly chickens, oxen, sheep, and lambs). Artemisia was to outlive Mausolus by only two years, a period of

time dominated by the crushing of a rebellion in Rhodes, and primarily, the building of the tomb.

The most gifted of architects, the Greek Pythius, was commissioned for the final design, and the gifted artist Scopas was hired to lead a team of sculptors. Great progress was made on the tomb, but Artemisia's unexpected death in 351 B.C.E. threw the completion of the structure into great doubt. Without the queen's determination and adequate financing, it seemed the project might never be finished. The tomb, however, became a labor of love for the artisans constructing it, and they persevered. It was completed during the reign of Idreus, another son of Hecatomnus and Artemisia's successor. Respected sources such as Pliny of Rome and Philo of Byzantium vividly described its grandeur, and Alexander the Great, who conquered the area only twenty years later, was mesmerized by the tomb's beauty. Even thought he razed much of what Mausolus had built, he zealously protected the tomb.

The tomb measured 127 feet (39 meters) long and 108 feet (33 meters) in width. It was built on a leveled foundation with stone blocks held in place by metal clamps. A small hallway led to the burial chamber. On the foundation was a small series of steps leading to a rectangular basement area of stone and marble, which supported two contiguous friezes. A third frieze helped support a cella above it. The cella was surrounded by thirty-six Greek columns. Resting on the columns was a small pyramid, surmounted by a statue of life-sized horses pulling a chariot ridden by stone representations of Mausolus and Artemisia. The whole structure was adorned with stone carvings of gargoyles and real and mythical animals.

Amazingly, the tomb survived in good shape for more than eighteen centuries. At some point, an earthquake caused some of the artwork to collapse, including the statues of Mausolus and Artemisia. This wonder of the world, however, was tragically destroyed by human hands. A crusading Catholic order called the Knights of St. John of Jerusalem fled to Mecy, as Halicarnassus was then known, from eastern Turkey and the order's mortal enemy, the Ottoman Turks in 1402. The knights decided to build a protective fortress, and they used the stones and marble of the tomb to build it. The new structure, the fortress of St. Peter, incorporated into its outer walls some of the tomb's sculptured art. In 1542, the demolition was completed when the knights used what was left of the tomb to expand the fortress. All of this plundering was for naught, because the Ottomans soon captured the area anyway and again pushed the knights into exile. What the knights did not destroy was soon looted by thieves and pirates. The razing was so complete that only a century later few remembered exactly where the tomb had been.

SIGNIFICANCE

King Mausolus of Caria is not one of the more famous historical figures. He was, however, something of a prototype for many subsequent leaders. Alexander the Great admired the Carian's success on the battlefield, and city builders such as Roman emperor Constantine and Russia's Peter the Great apparently were influenced by Mausolus's great rebuilding of Halicarnassus.

The greatest contribution of Mausolus is, without doubt, his tomb. By the nineteenth century, many had come to believe it was entirely mythological. Charles Newton, an English diplomat and historian, believed the tomb to have been a reality and, accordingly, he began to excavate the Bodrum ruins in the 1850's. With a large and well-financed expedition and with the approval of the English and Turkish governments, his efforts were hugely successful. Much artwork, toppled by the ancient earthquake, was rediscovered and shipped to the British Museum. Stairways, a foundation wall, a casket, and decorative jars were also uncovered. Thanks to the efforts of ancient writers and modern anthropologists, the location, size, style, and general appearance of the tomb are today largely known, and its awe-inspiring and majestic aura continues to influence those who erect government buildings, arenas, and, of course, mausoleums.

—*Thomas W. Buchanan*

FURTHER READING

Banks, Edgar J. *The Seven Wonders of the Ancient World.* New York: G. P. Putnam's Sons, 1916. Dr. Banks was an archaeologist who taught at the University of Chicago, and his book reads more like a dissertation or ethnography than a modern research work, but it is nevertheless a thoroughly detailed and outstanding source.

Müller, Arthur. *The Seven Wonders of the World: Five Thousand Years of Culture and History in the Ancient World.* New York: McGraw-Hill, 1966. As a written source, this work does not contribute much new information. It does provide a thorough description of Artemisia's campaign against Rhodes after the death of Mausolus. The accompanying photographs of the tomb's relics and the surrounding Bodrum countryside make this work worthwhile.

Romer, John, and Elizabeth Romer. *The Seven Wonders of the World.* New York: Henry Holt, 1995. This is an excellent source, and it provides some background to the building of Halicarnassus and the Hellenic penchant for the ritualistic slaughtering of animals.

SEE ALSO: Alexander the Great; Imhotep.

RELATED ARTICLES in *Great Events from History: The Ancient World*: 336 B.C.E., Alexander the Great Begins Expansion of Macedonia; 327-325 B.C.E., Alexander the Great Invades the Indian Subcontinent.

MENANDER
Greek dramatist

Noted for his careful plotting, his accurate depiction of middle-class society, and his sympathetic treatment of character, Menander is considered the finest writer of Greek New Comedy.

BORN: c. 342 B.C.E.; Athens, Greece
DIED: c. 291 B.C.E.; Piraeus, Greece
AREA OF ACHIEVEMENT: Literature

EARLY LIFE

Although there is some disagreement about the exact date of his birth, Menander (muh-NAN-dehr) was probably born in 342 in Athens, Greece. His father was Diopeithes of Cephisia. Menander's family was evidently involved in both the social and the cultural life of Athens. His uncle Alexis was an important playwright in

the tradition of Middle Comedy; he had some two hundred plays to his credit. Menander attended the lectures of Theophrastus, who had succeeded Aristotle as head of the Peripatetic school and who was also a notable writer, now known chiefly for his *Charactēres ethikōi* (c. 319 B.C.E.; *Characters*, 1616), sketches of human types, which undoubtedly influenced Menander and the other dramatists of New Comedy.

Like all Athenian men, between the ages of eighteen and twenty Menander served a year in the military. It was at that time that he became a close friend of Epicurus, whose philosophy was influential in Menander's works. Another of Menander's early friends was important in his later life: Demetrius of Phalerum, a fellow student. When Menander was in his mid-twenties, Demetrius was appointed by the Macedonians as ruler of Athens. During the following decade, Demetrius constructed magnificent buildings in the city and drew the most brilliant and talented men of Athens to his court. Among them was Menander, who was already recognized as a playwright, having written his first work when he was nineteen or twenty.

The bust that has been identified as that of Menander suggests what an addition he would have been to the court of Demetrius. The classic features, well-defined profile, penetrating eyes, and strong jaw testify to strength of mind and character; the sensitive mouth and wavy hair soften the general impression. All in all, he was a strikingly handsome man.

When Demetrius fell, Menander is said to have been in some danger, and he was offered the protection of Ptolemy Soter if he would follow his friend Demetrius to Alexandria, Egypt. The playwright declined, however, as he also is said to have declined an invitation to Macedonia, and he spent the remainder of his life in Athens.

LIFE'S WORK

In somewhat more than thirty years, Menander wrote some one hundred comedies. Most of his work, however, has been lost. Until 1905, he was represented primarily by hundreds of lines quoted by other writers and by the four plays of Plautus and four others of Terence that were based on certain of his lost plays. Then, a fifth century C.E. papyrus book was discovered in Egypt; it contains one-third to one-half of three of Menander's plays, *Perikeiromenē* (314-310 B.C.E.; *The Girl Who Was Shorn*, 1909), *Epitrepontes* (after 304 B.C.E.; *The Arbitration*, 1909), and *Samia* (321-316 B.C.E.; *The Girl from Samos*, 1909). In 1958, another papyrus book was found in a private collection in Geneva; it holds not only a complete play, *Dyskolos* (317 B.C.E.; *The Bad-Tempered Man*, 1921, also known as *The Grouch*), but also half of *Aspis* (c. 314 B.C.E.; *The Shield*, 1921) and the almost complete text of *The Girl from Samos*.

Because so much of Menander's work is lost, and because the dating of those plays and fragments that have survived is very uncertain, it is difficult to analyze the playwright's development. It is known that his first work was written about 322 B.C.E. The only complete play that has survived, *The Bad-Tempered Man*, is an early one, performed in 317, which incidentally was the year that another of Menander's plays, now lost, won for him his first prize.

Greek comic playwright Menander. (Hulton|Archive by Getty Images)

In *The Bad-Tempered Man* one can see the careful plot construction and the realistic but sympathetic treatment of characters for which Menander was noted. The title character of the play is Cnemon, a misanthrope whose wife has left him because of his nasty temper and who lives alone with his daughter and a servant, while his virtuous stepson lives nearby. In the prologue to the play, the god Pan announces that he intends to punish Cnemon because he has offended against the principles Pan prizes, in particular good fellowship and love. It is not surprising, then, that this comedy, like Menander's other plays, must move toward suitable marriages, which symbolize reconciliation and which sometimes are accompanied by the reform of an older man who is angry, obstinate, or miserly. In this case, it must be admitted that the most interesting character, Cnemon, is not really reformed but instead is forced into participating in the final marriage feast. Other typical Menander characters in *The Bad-Tempered Man* include the parasite who profits from his attachment to a rich young friend, a fussy chef who does not realize how stupid he really is, and various comic servants.

The Girl from Samos is based on an even more complicated plot, involving the births of two illegitimate babies, one to a poor girl, the other to a woman from Samos. When the Samian woman's baby dies, it is decided that she will pretend that the other is hers. The result is a series of misunderstandings as to who is making love to whom, who are the parents of the baby, and who is related to whom. This plot enables Menander to analyze relationships between children and their fathers, who can move from love to anger to compassion as their perceptions of the truth alter. At the end of the play, the baby's parentage is revealed, the lovers marry, and parents and children are reconciled.

In *The Girl Who Was Shorn*, too, there is a problem of identity, in this case that of twins who were separated in infancy, while in *The Shield* the confusion arises from the supposed deaths of two men, who naturally must be resurrected in the final section of the play.

Because they see a greater depth in *The Arbitration*, critics believe it to be a later play. The basis of the play is a serious situation: Pamphila was raped by a drunken reveler, and the baby to whom she later gave birth was abandoned. When she married, she concealed the truth from her young husband, and when he learned from a servant about her past, he rejected her and threw himself into a dissolute life. At this point, the play begins. As single-minded as a tragic heroine, Pamphila remains faithful to her husband throughout the play, and though there are comic scenes, such as that in which a charcoal burner argues like a lawyer, and deliberate deception, masterminded by clever slaves, finally the husband is won by his wife's nobility. The baby reappears and is revealed to be the child of Pamphila and her husband, who did not remember raping her. At that point, presented with a grandchild, even Pamphila's father is happy.

Although *The Arbitration* has many of the elements of the other plays, such as the complex plot, the love intrigue, and the stock comic characters, the profound theme elevates it above the other surviving plays of Menander and suggests the basis of his high reputation. In *The Arbitration* can be seen not only the comic confusion that was the essence of New Comedy but also the compassionate treatment of human problems for which Menander was particularly admired.

In his early fifties, Menander drowned while swimming in the harbor of Piraeus, the seaport near Athens. According to Plutarch, Menander died at the height of his dramatic powers. It is unfortunate that his literary career lasted only slightly more than thirty years and that almost all of his plays have been lost. All that remains is a name, a reputation, and an influence.

SIGNIFICANCE

In his plot elements and stock characters Menander was probably similar to many of the other playwrights of New Comedy; his superior reputation rests on the fact that he rejected mere Dionysian horseplay for the presentation of a real moral drama. In this may be seen the influence of his friend Epicurus. In his penetration of character, he undoubtedly followed the tragedian Euripides.

Unfortunately, audiences of Menander's own time seem to have been less than enthusiastic about his kind of play, preferring the bawdy productions of his rivals. Of his one hundred plays, only eight won the coveted prize for comedy. After his death, however, his reputation rose rapidly. Among the Romans he was highly valued. Ovid admired him; Plutarch ranked him above Aristophanes, and others placed him just below Homer. During the period of the Empire, his philosophical maxims were frequently quoted and even collected.

Menander's greatest influence, however, came through the Roman playwrights Plautus and Terence, who adapted and imitated his works, devising their own complex plots, dramatizing Roman everyday life as Menander had the life of his own people, and working toward resolutions in which folly is exposed and lovers are united. Through Plautus and Terence, he survived to help establish the pattern of Renaissance drama. Menander's influence can be seen in the exaggeratedly humorous characters of Ben Jonson and the romantic lovers of William Shakespeare. Finally, his satire set in ordinary society provided the basis of the comedy of manners genre. Even though most of his work has been lost for centuries, Menander's comic vision persists in the plays of his successors.

—*Rosemary M. Canfield Reisman*

FURTHER READING

Allinson, Francis G. Introduction to *Menander: The Principal Fragments*. Translated by Francis G. Allinson. 1921. Reprint. Westport, Conn.: Greenwood Press, 1970. This brief but extremely scholarly essay includes a clear description of Menander's historical placement, concise comments about the playwright's use of prologue, plot, and character, and a statement about his Greek style.

Dover, K. J., ed. *Ancient Greek Literature*. New York: Oxford University Press, 1997. A concise and accurate treatment of the subject. For a full understanding of Menander's place in Greek literature, it would be helpful to read the entire book, although Menander is specifically treated in the chapter headed "Comedy."

Goldberg, Sander M. *The Making of Menander's Comedy.* Berkeley: University of California Press, 1980. An outstanding scholarly discussion of Menander's work. Explains clearly his relation to Old and Middle Comedy, delineates the problems of scholarship, and then proceeds to a lucid analysis of each of the surviving works.

Pickard-Cambridge, Arthur W. *The Dramatic Festivals of Athens.* Rev. ed. New York: Oxford University Press, 1988. The authoritative account of the production of Greek drama, ranging from the descriptions of the various festivals themselves to detailed explanations of acting style, costuming, and music, even including an analysis of the composition and character of the audience. Well illustrated.

Reinhold, Meyer. *Classical Drama: Greek and Roman.* Woodbury, N.Y.: Barron's Educational Series, 1965. In outline form, an excellent guide to its subject. Chapters 5 through 11—dealing with Euripides; Old,

Middle, and New Comedy; and Menander's Roman successors—are particularly recommended. Contains plot summaries, with hypothetical suggestions as to missing elements, of four of Menander's plays. Includes glossary and bibliography.

Sandbach, F. H. *The Comic Theatre of Greece and Rome.* New York: W. W. Norton, 1977. An excellent study of comedy from Aristophanes to Terence, with an illuminating discussion of Menander's themes, in the light of the newly discovered texts. Includes glossary and bibliography.

Walton, J. Michael, and Peter D. Arnott. *Menander and the Making of Comedy.* Westport, Conn.: Greenwood Press, 1996. This introduction to the comedy of Menander considers each of the plays as performance pieces. Includes bibliography and index.

SEE ALSO: Epicurus; Euripides; Plautus; Ptolemy Soter; Terence; Theophrastus.

RELATED ARTICLES in *Great Events from History: The Ancient World*: c. 385 B.C.E., Greek Playwright Aristophanes Dies; c. 320 B.C.E., Theophrastus Initiates the Study of Botany.

MENANDER
Greco-Bactrian king of India (r. c. 155-c. 135 B.C.E.)

Menander extended the Greco-Bactrian domains in India more than any other ruler. He became a legendary figure in a Pāli book as a great patron of Buddhism.

BORN: c. 210 B.C.E.; Kalasi near Alexandria, probably Alexandria-in-Caucaso (now Begram, Afghanistan)
DIED: c. 135 B.C.E.; Bactria (now in Afghanistan)
ALSO KNOWN AS: Milinda
AREAS OF ACHIEVEMENT: Government and politics, religion

EARLY LIFE

Menander (muh-NAN-duhr), not to be confused with the more famous Greek dramatist of the same name, was born somewhere in the fertile area to the south of the Paropamisadae or present Hindu Kush Mountains of Afghanistan. The only reference to this location is in the semilegendary Pāli *Milindapañha* (first or second century C.E.; *The Questions of King Milinda*, 1890-1894), a series of questions put to a Buddhist sage by King Milinda, along with their answers, which says that he

was born in a village called Kalasi near Alasanda, some two hundred *yojanas* (about eighteen miles) from the town of Sāgala (probably Sialkot in the Punjab). Alasanda refers to the Alexandria in Afghanistan and not to the one in Egypt. No evidence exists on the issue of whether Menander was an aristocrat, a commoner, or of royal lineage.

All surmises about the life of Menander are based on his coins, for information in Greek sources is very sparse. All that remains of a more extensive history of the east by Apollodorus of Artemita are two sentences in Strabo's *Geōgraphica* (c. 7 B.C.E.; *Geography*, 1917-1933) that the Bactrian Greeks, especially Menander, overthrew more peoples in India than did Alexander the Great. Strabo is dubious that Menander "really crossed the Hypanis River [Beas] toward the east and went as far as the Isamos [Imaus, or Jumna River?]." Plutarch in his *Ethika* (after c. 100 C.E.; *Moralia*, 1603) calls Menander a king of Bactria who ruled with equity and who died in camp, and after his death, memorials were raised over his ashes. If Menander became a convert to Buddhism, this could mean that Buddhist stupas, covering reliquaries, were built over his remains, which were divided among different sites. The final classical source that mentions Menander, the work of Pompeius Trogus, simply calls him a king of India together with Apollodorus.

The *Milindapañha* contains no historical data save those about Menander's birth, which may be legend, as well as moral precepts beloved to Buddhists. Another text of the period, the *Vāyū Purāna*, only mentions Menander as a Greek king in India. The last reference to Menander occurs in an inscription on a relic casket dedicated in the reign of Mahārāja Minedra (Menander), which is not informative. Modern students are left with the coins, the styles and legends of which have provided the basis of hypothetical reconstructions of the life of Menander. That he was married to a certain Queen Agathocleia, daughter of Demetrius, is suggested by historian W. W. Tarn on the basis of the coin style of Agathocleia, especially the figure of Pallas Athena, the favored deity of Menander's coins, on the reverse and the similarity in portraits between goddess and queen. The usual epithet on Menander's coins was the Greek word *soter* (savior), but what he saved, if anything, is unknown.

From the great number of extant coins of Menander and the widespread location of find spots, one may surmise that he had a fairly long rule over a kingdom extending from the Hindu Kush Mountains into the present-day United Provinces of north India. His rule over Mathura and especially Pataliputra on the borders of Bengal is uncertain and disputed, although the former is more likely than the latter. In any case, he obviously was that Greek king of India who made the greatest impression on the Indians, especially the Buddhists.

LIFE'S WORK

One of the two achievements that have earned for Menander a place in history books was the great extension of Greco-Bactrian rule in India, to the extent that his rule was probably the high point of Greek rule on the subcontinent. The second and equally significant factor in the life of Menander was his role in Buddhist legend. The *Milindapañha* was not popular only among Indians; a Chinese translation exists as well as the Pāli version. Although it is unproven whether Menander became a convert, and there is no tradition that he propagated Buddhism as Aśoka the Great and Kanishka are supposed to have done, he holds an eminent position as an enlightened Buddhist ruler in their tradition. Whether he was considered by his Indian subjects a Chakravartin, a su-

preme Buddhist ruler who conquered lands by persuasion and justice rather than by the sword, is unknown. If Plutarch's statement that memorials were raised over his ashes can be interpreted as meaning Buddhist stupas containing some part or ashes of him, then it is plausible that Menander was a Buddhist. The fact that legends did grow up about him at least indicates his importance in Buddhist circles.

The suggestion of Tarn that the Pāli book was modeled after a Greek original that might have had the title "Questions of Menander" is intriguing. It would imply that the Greek presence in India was neither simply a short-lived foreign military occupation nor a diluted, mixed Iranian-Indian culture with a thin Hellenistic veneer but that it did have a strong, purely Greek content. Furthermore, that content was responsible for the introduction in India of Greek genres of literature and philosophical and other ideas, as well as the canons of Greek art, which were to flower later under the sobriquet of Gandharan art.

SIGNIFICANCE

It may be argued not only that Menander was responsible for extending Greek arms on the Indian subcontinent to the fullest extent but also that he was much more than a conqueror. Because he has become a legend in Buddhist tradition and is praised by Plutarch as a just king, it may be further surmised that under his rule, Greek philosophy and culture met and influenced Indian civilization, which in the middle of the second century was dominated by Buddhism.

Whether a hypothetical Greek "Questions of Menander" influenced not only the Buddhists in India but also Hellenistic literature in Alexandria, Egypt, and elsewhere, as Tarn suggests, is even more speculative. The flowering of Gandharan art in the second century C.E., when Hellenistic origins are overwhelmingly indicated, probably owed as much to the legacy of Menander and his many successors as it did to the influence of Roman provincial art forms. Thus, Hellenism in India and Central Asia may owe much more than is now known to Menander and his legacy.

—Richard N. Frye

FURTHER READING

Bivar, A. D. H. "The Sequence of Menander's Drachmae." *Journal of the Royal Asiatic Society*, 1970: 128-129. A basic work on the coins of Menander's reign, with historical interpretations of their presence in certain locations.

Frye, Richard N. *The History of Ancient Iran*. Munich: Verlag C. H. Beck, 1984. A summary of the milieu and events in which the life and activities of Menander may be placed.

Majumdar, N. G. "The Bajaur Casket of the Reign of Menander." *Epigraphica Indica* 24 (1937): 1-8. An analysis of the only extant inscription of Menander's reign; includes translation and commentary.

Narain, A. K. *The Indo-Greeks*. Oxford, England: Clarendon Press, 1962. A response to Tarn's book (below), concentrating on translations of Chinese and Indian sources. Written from the Indian perspective.

Tarn, W. W. *The Greeks in Bactria and India*. 3d ed. Chicago: Ares, 1985. The basic study on Menander. Includes translations and analyses of classical sources. Highly speculative but fascinating reading.

SEE ALSO: Alexander the Great; Aśoka; Buddha; Kanishka.
RELATED ARTICLES in *Great Events from History: The Ancient World*: 6th or 5th century B.C.E., Birth of Buddhism; c. 155 B.C.E., Greco-Bactrian Kingdom Reaches Zenith Under Menander.

MENCIUS
Chinese philosopher

Through a lifetime of reflection, Mencius clarified and expanded the wisdom embodied in Confucius's works, rendering Confucian ideas more accessible. His own writings eclipsed other interpretations of Confucius and gained acceptance as the orthodox version of Confucian thought.

BORN: c. 372 B.C.E.; Zou, China
DIED: c. 289 B.C.E.; China
ALSO KNOWN AS: Mengzi (Pinyin), Meng-tzu (Wade-Giles); Mengke (Pinyin, given name), Mengk'o (Wade-Giles, given name)
AREA OF ACHIEVEMENT: Philosophy

EARLY LIFE

Mencius (MEHN-shee-uhs) was born probably about 372 B.C.E. in the small principality of Zou in northeastern China, not far from the birthplace of Confucius (551-479 B.C.E.), whose work Mencius spent his life interpreting. Knowledge of Mencius's early life is scarce. What evidence exists must be extracted from his own writing, most notably the *Menzi* (first transcribed in the early third century B.C.E.; English translation in *The Confucian Classics*, 1861; commonly known as *Mencius*), although many biographical observations are found in the great historian Sima Qian's *Shiji* (first century B.C.E.; *Records of the Grand Historian of China*, 1960).

Mencius was probably a member of the noble Meng family, whose home, like that of Confucius, was in the city-state of Lu, in what is now southwestern Shandong Province. Certainly Mencius's education was one that was common to the aristocracy, for he was thoroughly familiar with both the classical *Shijing* (traditionally fifth century B.C.E.; *The Book of Songs*, 1937) and the *Shujing* (compiled after first century B.C.E.; English translation in *The Chinese Classics*, Vol. 5, Parts 1 and 2, 1872; commonly known as *Classic of History*), which together provided the fundamentals of his classical training. Moreover, he had a masterly grasp of Confucius's work and quoted it frequently, leading to the assumption that he studied in a Confucian school, purportedly under the tutelage of Confucius's grandson, who was himself a man of ministerial rank in the central state of Wei.

Known as Menzi to his students, Mencius assumed the role of teacher early in his life and never abandoned it. Rejecting material well-being and position as ends in themselves, he, like many Confucians, nevertheless aspired to hold office inside one of the courts of the Chinese states. He did indeed become a councillor and later the minister of state in Wei. In such positions, he tutored students, not all of them noble, in classical works: the dynastic hymns and ballads anthologized in *The Book of Songs* and state papers from archives (from 1000 to 700 B.C.E.) that formed the *Classic of History*. These were works from which, by the end of the second century B.C.E., Confucian precepts developed. During these early years of observation and teaching, Mencius gained disciples, furthered his interpretations of Confucius, and enjoyed considerable renown in many parts of China.

LIFE'S WORK

Mencius was Mencius's principal work. It appeared late in his life. Had it incorporated less wisdom than his many years of diverse experiences and reflections allowed, or a less lengthy refinement of Confucius's thoughts, it would not be likely to rank as one of the greatest philosophical and literary works of the ancient world.

Mencius garnered experience through his wanderings and temporary lodgments in various Chinese courts and kingdoms. He was fortunate to live in an age when, despite continuous political turmoil, dynastic rivalries, and incessant warfare, high levels of civility prevailed in aristocratic circles. Teacher-scholars, as a consequence, were readily hosted—that is, effectively subsidized—by princely families eager to advance their children's education and to instruct and invigorate themselves through conversation with learned men.

Some of Mencius's temporary affiliations can be dated. Between 323 and 319 B.C.E., Mencius was installed at the court of King Hui of Liang, in what is now China's Szechwan Province. He moved eastward about 318 B.C.E. to join the ruler of the state of Qi (Ch'i), King Xun (Hsüan). Prior to his sojourn to Liang (although the dates are conjectural), Mencius visited and conversed with princes, rulers, ministers, and students in several states: Lu, Wei, Qi, and Song (Sung).

Mencius's journeys were not feckless. They related directly to his philosophical and historical perceptions. Like Confucius, Mencius believed that he lived in a time of troubles in which—amid rival feudatories and warring states, divided and misruled—China was in decline. Also like Confucius, Mencius looked back fondly on what he thought had been the halcyon days of Chinese government and civilization under the mythical kings (2700 B.C.E.-770 B.C.E.), when a unified China had been governed harmoniously.

Drawing on Chinese legends incorporated into literary sources familiar to him from the Xia (Hsia; c. 2100-1600 B.C.E.), Shang (1600-1066 B.C.E.), and Zhou (Chou; 1066 B.C.E.-256 C.E.) Dynasties, Mencius concluded that the ideal governments of these earlier days had been the work of hero kings—Yao, Shun, and Yu (Yü)—whose successors had organized themselves into dynasties. These were the sage kings, who, like kings Wen and Wu of the Zhou family, had been responsible for China's former greatness. Their dissolute successors, however, such as the "bad" kings of the Xia and the Shang Dynasties, were equally responsible for the subsequent debasement of the sage kings' remarkable achievements and erosion of their legacy.

For Mencius, a vital part of this legacy was the concept of the mandate of Heaven. It was an idea that he ascribed to the early Zhou kings, who justified their authority by it. These kings asserted that they had received the

Mencius, from an eighteenth century drawing. (Archivo Iconografico, S. A./Corbis)

mandate directly from the deity, who designated Zhou rulers sons of Heaven, viceroys of Heaven. Effectively, that charged them with the responsibilities of being the deity's fief holders. The Zhou kings, in turn, proceeded to impose lesser feudal obligations on their own fief holders and subjects. In Mencius's view, this arrangement was more than merely an arbitrary justification for Zhou authority; it was also a recognition of authority higher than man's. Because the mandate of Heaven was not allocated in perpetuity, it was essentially a lease that was operative during good behavior. When rulers lost virtue and thereby violated the mandate, the punishment of Heaven descended on them. Their subjects, their vassals, were constrained to replace them. It was on this basis, as Mencius knew, that the Zhou kings had successfully reigned for four centuries.

Equally important in this hierarchical scheme developed around the Zhou conception of the mandate of Heaven, of sage kings functioning in response to it, were the roles of sage ministers. It was these ministers whom Mencius credited with the rise and harmonious rule of the sage kings. In times when the mandate of Heaven had obviously been forgotten or ignored, Mencius wished not only that this ideal past would be restored but also that his presence at various courts would allow him to identify, assist, and guide potential sage kings, fulfilling the role of sage minister himself or through his disciples.

King Xun of Qi was one of the rulers at whose court he served and for whom he envisioned greatness as the ideal king. Xun, however, appeared lacking in will. King Hui of Liang also showed some promise, but Mencius despaired of Hui when he revealed his desire to rule the world by force. Briefly, Mencius saw potential in the king of Teng (T'eng), who ruled a small principality that, nevertheless, afforded a sufficient stage for a true king. That potential also went unrealized. To critics who charged that Mencius was simply unperceptive, his reply was that such rulers possessed ample ability but had not availed themselves of his services. After these encounters, despairing, he returned home to kindle his belief in the ideal king in the hearts of his disciples.

The basis for Mencius's initial optimism lay in his interpretation of China's history, for it reassured him that great kings had appeared in cycles of about five hundred years. Half a millennium lay between the reign of Tang (T'ang), founder of the Shang Dynasty, and Wuwang, first ruler of the great Zhou Dynasty. Consequently Heaven's dispatch of another sage king, according to Mencius, was overdue. In this interim and in expectation of the sage king's appearance, men such as himself—"Heavenly instruments"—had divine commissions to maintain the ideal.

There is no evidence that Mencius, any more than Confucius, was successful in the realization of such dreams. Although Mencius served briefly as a councillor, and although his knowledge was profound as well as wide-ranging, he revealed more disdain for than interest in (or understanding of) practical politics in his own highly politicized environment. Furthermore, areas of intellection such as religion, ethics, and philosophy were densely packed with rivals. A number of these, such as Micius (Mo-di; Wade-Giles, Mo-ti) the utilitarian or Yang Zhu (Yang Chu) the hedonist, enjoyed greater recognition and higher status than he did. Nor was Mencius ranked among the leading intellectuals or scholars of his day who were inducted into the membership of the famous Jixia (Chi-hsia) Academy.

Later generations would honor him, but in his own time Mencius was a relatively obscure, evangelizing teacher whose views were merely tolerated, a pedagogue who never penetrated beyond the fringes of power, a man without a substantial following. These conditions help explain his occasional haughtiness, manipulative argumentation, and assertive promulgation of Confucianism.

Nevertheless, not until two centuries after his death did Confucian principles gain significant influence.

Thus, Mencius's work can be examined for its intrinsic merit, outside the context of his own lifetime. He was, foremost, a devoted follower of Confucius. As such, he never wavered in the belief that it was not enough to be virtuous; men also had to model themselves after the sage kings. Antiquity represented the epitome of good conduct, good government, and general harmony. Consequently, the ways of old—or his interpretations of them—had to be accepted or rejected completely.

This position inevitably raised the issue of how the sages of yesteryear had become, both as men and as governors, such ideal models. Had such gifts been divinely bestowed? Mencius believed that they were like all men. This response led him therefore into an elaboration of the central tenets of his philosophy, into an embellishment of Confucius, and ultimately into formulating his major contribution to thought.

Whereas Confucius left only one equivocal observation on human nature, Mencius—probably because the contention of his time demanded it—placed the essence of human nature at the center of his work. Discussions of humanity (*ren*) and of justice (*yi*) accordingly became his preoccupations, and, subsequently, because of Mencius, became the focus of Chinese philosophy.

In defining humanity, he declared unequivocally that all men were born sharing the same human nature and that human nature is good. Mencius sought to demonstrate this belief through his maxims and parables: All men were endowed with sympathy for those whose lives were at risk or who had suffered great misfortune; all men felt best when they were instinctively being their best. Thus, all men who cultivated *ren* were capable of indefinite perfectibility; they were capable of becoming sages. Furthermore, men would find *ren* irresistible, for it nullified the menaces of brute physical force (*ba*). Writing with fewer logical inhibitions than had been displayed by Confucius, Mencius asserted that all things were complete within every man: Everyone, in microcosm, embodied the essences of everything: the macrocosm.

Consequently, men who knew their own nature also knew Heaven. In asserting this, wittingly or not, Mencius again went beyond Confucius, for knowing oneself first in order to know everything suggested meditative introspection, whereas Confucius had disparaged meditation and insisted on the superiority of observation and the use of the critical faculty. Mencius stressed the real incentives for the cultivation of one's humanity. Those who did so enjoyed wisdom, honor, and felicity. When such men became kings, the state was harmoniously governed and prospered. In turn, such kings won over the allegiance of the world, which to Mencius, as to all Chinese, meant China. *Ren* therefore also afforded men prestige and moral authority that constituted power (*de*) far greater than any physical force.

Mencius was all too aware of the extent to which his everyday world indicated just the opposite, that is, the appalling conditions men had created for themselves. He was also aware of misapplications of force, either as a result of these problems or as a result of attempts to resolve them. Yet to Mencius, the failure to cultivate one's humanity lay at the root of these difficulties. He was not naïve about some of the causes of inhumanity. Poverty and the misery of men's environments, he conceded, often left little chance for cultivating one's humanity, but that lent urgency to the search for a sage king who could mitigate or eradicate these conditions. He was also aware that men's appetites, as well as the conditions in which they lived, left little to differentiate them from other animals. Yet, the difference that did exist was a vital one: namely, their ability to think with their hearts.

Justice (*yi*) was a concomitant to Mencius's concept of humanity and was also central to his teaching. By justice, Mencius meant not only doing the right thing but also seeing that others received their rights. Clearly the "right things" consisted in part of rituals and formal codes of manners and of traditional civilities. They also embraced rights that were not necessarily embodied in law: the right of peasants to gather firewood in the forests, the right to subsistence in old age, and the right to expect civilities and to live according to traditional codes of behavior. If feeling distress for the suffering of others was, according to Mencius, the first sign of humanity, then feelings of shame and disgrace were the first signs of justice.

Mencius spent his lifetime forming his maxims and parables to illustrate what humanity and justice meant to him, or what he believed they should mean to all men. Appropriately for a teacher, he provoked more questions than he answered; he never arrived at his goal, nor did his disciples. He died about 289 B.C.E., probably near his place of birth on the Shandong Peninsula.

SIGNIFICANCE

A devoted Confucian, Mencius expanded and clarified Confucius's *Lun-yü* (later sixth-early fifth centuries B.C.E.; *The Analects*, 1861) and the principles of his master as they were being taught and debated a century after Confucius's death. Mencius, however, went beyond Confucius by placing human nature and his belief in its essential goodness at the center of philosophical discussion. Officially ranked a sage, he stands among the world's most respected literary and philosophical geniuses.

—*Clifton K. Yearley and Kerrie L. MacPherson*

FURTHER READING

Cao Raode and Cao Xiaomei. *The Story of Mencius.* Beijing: Foreign Language Press, 2001. A biography that uses Mencius's life and historical context to illuminate his thought.

Liu, Xiusheng, and Philip Ivanhoe, eds. *Essays on the Moral Philosophy of Mengzi.* Boston: Hackett, 2002. Eight essays, plus a very useful historical introduction, cover different aspects of Mencius's philosophy and place him in relation to traditional Chinese thought and modern Western philosophy.

Mencius. *Mencius.* Translated by D. C. Lau. New York: Penguin, 1970. Contains an interesting but dense introduction addressing the problems of dating events in Mencius's life. One of the best translations available. Five very informative appendices. With useful notes, glossary, and index.

Richards, I. A. *Mencius on the Mind: Experiments in Multiple Definition.* 1932. Reprint. New York: Routledge, 2001. Richards concentrates on Chinese modes of meaning as revealed in Mencius. The exploration is designed to see if beneath linguistic barriers there is material for comparative understanding. Thus, though ranking Mencius among the world's great thinkers, Richards deals critically with Mencius's methods of argument.

Shun, Kwong-loi. *Mencius and Early Chinese Thought.* Stanford, Calif.: Stanford University Press, 2000. An advanced discussion of Mencius's philosophy, relating his work to that of Confucius, Mozi, the Yangists, and others. After a philosophical and historical introduction, Shun examines key terms and concepts in Mencius's philosophy. Notes, index, character list, and concordance of Mencius's works.

SEE ALSO: Confucius; Hanfeizi; Laozi; Mozi; Xunzi.

RELATED ARTICLES in *Great Events from History: The Ancient World*: 479 B.C.E., Confucius's Death Leads to the Creation of *The Analects*; 475-221 B.C.E., China Enters Chaotic Warring States Period; Early 4th century B.C.E., Founding of Mohism; 104 B.C.E., Dong Zhongshu Systematizes Confucianism.

MENES
Egyptian pharaoh

Menes is described in classical Greek and Roman sources and late-period Egyptian king lists as the ruler who was responsible for the unification of Egypt, the building of the capital city of Memphis, and the founding of the First Dynasty of Egypt.

BORN: c. 3100 B.C.E.; Thinis, Egypt
DIED: c. 3000 B.C.E.; Memphis, Egypt
ALSO KNOWN AS: Menas; Min
AREA OF ACHIEVEMENT: Government and politics

EARLY LIFE

Virtually nothing is known about the early life of Menes (MEE-neez), since neither the extant classical sources nor the Pharaonic period Egyptian sources make any mention about his formative period.

LIFE'S WORK

The details of the life and work of Menes are few, scattered, and somewhat contradictory in some details. By classical times (c. 500 B.C.E.), Menes had been transformed into a culture hero whose life and accomplishments were embellished with semimythical anecdotes. He is thus at most a quasi-historical figure. According to the Egyptian historian Manetho (c. 300 B.C.E.), Menes, who came from the town of Thinis, about three hundred miles south of Cairo, was the first human ruler in Egypt after dynasties of demigods had ruled. He became the founder of the Egyptian state by uniting Upper and Lower Egypt; he was regarded as the first lawgiver and the leader who brought civilization to Egypt. The Greek historian Herodotus (c. 484-c. 425 B.C.E.) adds that Egyptian priests told him that Min (Menes) drained the plain of Memphis by damming up the Nile, laying the foundation for Egypt's first capital.

If Menes was indeed Egypt's first unifier, then Memphis was a prime location for a capital, as it was centered between Upper and Lower Egypt. According to Manetho, Menes ruled for about sixty years (although a variant text states a mere thirty years) and was the founder of the First Dynasty of Egypt, which lasted for more than 250 years. In addition, he "made a foreign expedition and won renown." The Greek historian Diodorus Siculus (fl. first century B.C.E.) adds the anecdotal statement that Menas (Menes) was pursued by his own dogs into the Lake of Moeris and was carried off by a crocodile that safely ferried him to the other riverbank. In gratitude, he founded the City of Crocodiles and demanded that the lo-

cals worship them as gods. Diodorus adds that Menes built his tomb there, a four-sided pyramid (although pyramids are not attested in Egypt until centuries later). Menes is also said by Diodorus to have built a labyrinth, although in another section, he attributes this to a king named Mendes. Manetho states that Menes was carried off by a hippopotamus and died.

Thus, the classical sources concerning Menes are in agreement concerning his position as the first king of Egypt and the founder of Memphis and the First Dynasty. The Pharaonic period Egyptian records, however, contradict the classical sources in many places. Menes is not listed as the first nondivine king and as the unifier of Egypt until king lists from the time of Thutmose III (late sixteenth century-1450 B.C.E.), fifth king of the Eighteenth Dynasty. The Karnak list of kings commences with Menes and lists all of Egypt's monarchs who ruled over the united kingdom (omitting any kings from the Intermediate periods) down to Thutmose III. Menes' preeminence is supported by the Turin Canon, or king list, and by a list of sixty-seven kings found inscribed on walls of a temple of Seti I (c. late fourteenth century-c. 1279 B.C.E.) at Abydos. Moreover, a palette from the Nineteenth Dynasty mentions the "Ptah of Menes," presumably a reference to a cult of the Egyptian god Ptah (the god of Menes). Interestingly, the Turin Canon has the name of Meni (Menes) twice, first with a human determinative before the name and again with a divine determinative. The purpose for this repetition is unknown. However, another king list inscribed in the tomb of a scribe at Saqqara (c. 1300 B.C.E.) omits mention of Menes and the first five kings of the First Dynasty.

It is not certain whether the New Kingdom lists reflect some documentary material that went back to an earlier time or whether they were constructed in conformity with ideas in vogue during their own period. For example, the fragmentary Palermo Stone, an annals text of the Fifth Dynasty (c. 2494-c. 2345 B.C.E.), does not list Menes. It does, however, list monarchs who ruled before the unification, although the text is severely fragmented for the earliest periods. In fact, it implies that there was a unification before the First Dynasty that broke down and thus had to be reinstated.

The issue becomes further complicated when one investigates the material remains from the First and Second Dynasties. An ivory plaque from the mastaba tomb of

Neithhotep at Naqada bears the name of Men (assumed to be Menes) and King Aha (likely the husband of Neithhotep). The relationship of these two is not immediately apparent. Was Menes the same person as Aha, or his father? Is one of the names a Horus name (the name a monarch took as the incarnation of the god Horus)? Some kings took as many as five different throne names. In fact, the royal tombs have different names than do the later king lists for monarchs of the first two dynasties, a fact attributed to the myriad names for the king. The name "Min," it has been argued, appears to be the Nebti name, the second name for the Egyptian king in his role as ruler over both parts of Egypt. A seal impression found at the Umm el-Qaʾab cemetery at Abydos in 1985 places Aha as the second king of the First Dynasty. The first king in this list is Narmer, presumably the father of Aha. He has also been associated with the Nebti name "Min" on jar sealings at Abydos. Thus, Min (Menes) is associated with both of these kings.

Narmer is well known from a mudstone ceremonial palette and a limestone macehead, both of which were excavated at Hierakonopolis in Upper Egypt. Both were found in poor archaeological contexts; the macehead seems to have been among a group of First Dynasty items buried beneath the floor of the Hierakonopolis temple complex dated to the Old Kingdom (c. c. 2687-c. 2125 B.C.E.), and the palette was found a few meters away. Both items have been dated stylistically to the period of the First Dynasty (c. 2925-c. 2775 B.C.E.). Though the macehead is severely fragmented and the palette in good condition, both are carved with reliefs that feature Narmer. On one side, he is shown with the white crown of Upper Egypt, striking a foreigner; on the other side, he is depicted with the red crown of Lower Egypt, taking his place in a procession that is moving toward a group of decapitated prisoners. The palette has been traditionally viewed as a memorial commemorating military successes over foreigners (usually identified as Libyans and Northern Egyptians). However, later studies have argued that the palette is an iconographic depiction of summaries of victories that occurred over the past year. If so, the palette was a votive object offered to the temple and may not express any particular historical reality.

The issue is still further complicated by the existence of a fragmentary limestone macehead containing an inscription of a king wearing the crown of Upper Egypt and identified as King Scorpion. Like the Narmer objects, it was found at Hierakonopolis in a poor archaeological context, although it also appears to date stylistically to the First or Second Dynasty. The king is shown excavating a ceremonial irrigation canal with the help of some subjects. More recently, a tomb at Umm el-Qaʾab at Abydos was excavated that contained many pieces of Predynastic Period (c. 3050-c. 2925 B.C.E.) pottery, many of which bore the scorpion hieroglyph. It is unclear whether these two items depict the same king, and his possible relationship to Menes is also uncertain.

SIGNIFICANCE

Menes is credited with being the unifier of Egypt, the builder of Memphis, and the founder of the First Dynasty of Egypt. However, it should be noted that it is impossible to identify Menes with any particular ruler from Egypt's First and Second Dynasties. Some scholars, however, have argued that Menes may later have become a name given to the unifier or unifiers of Egypt and thus may represent a composite of Narmer, Aha, and perhaps King Scorpion. Conversely, there are those who argue for identifying him either with Narmer or with Aha because of Menes' association with these monarchs in various inscriptions. No doubt the later classical tradition has become garbled because mistaken readings of the earliest cursive form of the Egyptian script were canonized by later dynasties.

Furthermore, the work of Manetho, the primary historian of ancient Egypt, is no longer extant and is known only from isolated statements in the writings of the Jewish historian Flavius Josephus (c. 37-c. 100 C.E.). An epitome of Manetho's work was made at an early date in the form of lists of dynasties and kingdoms, with short notes on kings and events. This was preserved in part primarily by the early Christian writers Sextus Julius Africanus (c. 180-c. 250 C.E.) and Eusebius of Caesarea (c. 260-339 C.E.). The original makeup of Manetho's *Aegyptica*, however, also appears to have included narratives. If ever recovered, the *Aegyptica* may hold the key to discovering the identity of Menes.

—*Mark W. Chavalas*

FURTHER READING

Assmann, Jan. *The Mind of Egypt: History and Meaning in the Time of the Pharaohs*. Reprint. Cambridge, Mass.: Harvard University Press, 2003. Although dense and best read by those with some background in the intricacies of Egyptian history, this book ably dissects the attitudes of Egyptians, from the most ancient times to the Alexandrian era, toward history and what it meant. Helps explain why the chronology of ancient Egypt is so tortuous.

Emery, W. B. *Archaic Egypt*. Harmondsworth, Middlesex, England: Penguin, 1961. Though dated, this work contains one of the most detailed discussions in English concerning the problem of the identification of Menes.

Redford, D. *Pharaonic King-Lists, Annals, and Day-Books: A Contribution to the Study of the Egyptian Sense of History*. Mississauga, Ont.: Benben Publications, 1986. A critical analysis of the historical value of Egyptian king lists, with a number of discussions of Menes and his identification.

Rice, Michael. *Egypt's Making: The Origins of Ancient Egypt, 5000-2000 B.C.* 2d ed. New York: Routledge, 1991. The introduction to ancient Egypt focuses on the psychology and culture of the people. The illustrations go beyond the standard images to give a broader understanding of Egypt's cultural inheritance.

Verbrugghe, Gerald P., and John M. Wickersham. *Berossos and Manetho, Introduced and Translated: Ancient Traditions in Ancient Mesopotamia and Egypt*. Ann Arbor: University of Michigan Press, 2001. The second half of this study provides an introductory chapter to what is known of Manetho, especially assessing his sources, reliability, and methods, and then provides the fragments of and references to his work that have been preserved in later authors. The final chapter provides a number of tables comparing Manetho's chronology and king lists with those from other sources.

SEE ALSO: Akhenaton; Amenhotep III; Flavius Josephus; Menkaure; Montuhotep II; Psamtik I; Ramses II; Sesostris II; Thutmose III; Tiy; Tutankhamen; Zoser.

RELATED ARTICLES in *Great Events from History: The Ancient World*: c. 6200-c. 3800 B.C.E., Ubaid Culture Thrives in Mesopotamia; c. 4000 B.C.E., Sumerian Civilization Begins in Mesopotamia; c. 3800 B.C.E., Cities and Civic Institutions Are Invented in Mesopotamia; c. 3500 B.C.E., Indus Valley Civilization Begins in South Asia; c. 3100 B.C.E., Sumerians Invent Writing; c. 3050 B.C.E., Unification of Lower and Upper Egypt.

MENKAURE
Egyptian pharaoh (r. 2532-c. 2503)

An important king of the Fourth Dynasty, Menkaure was the successor to the pharaohs Khafre and Khufu and builder of the third great pyramid.

FLOURISHED: 2532-c. 2503 B.C.E.; Egypt
ALSO KNOWN AS: Mykerinos (Greek); Mycerinus (Latin); Menkure; Menkara; Menkaura
AREAS OF ACHIEVEMENT: Architecture, art and art patronage

EARLY LIFE
Menkaure (mehn-KEW-ray) was the fourth (possibly fifth) Egyptian king of the Fourth Dynasty (c. 2613-c. 2494 B.C.E.), son of the pharaoh Khafre (r. 2558-2532) and nephew of the pharaoh Khufu (r. 2589-2566 B.C.E.). The exact duration of Menkaure's reign—eighteen or twenty-eight years—remains unclear. It has been noted that another short-lived monarch may have intervened between Khafre and Menkaure; this, however, remains speculation. The Greek historian Herodotus (c. 484-c. 425 B.C.E.) speaks of the Old Kingdom pharaoh as a man of refinement and beneficence, a pious, kind individual perhaps less forceful in character than his immediate predecessors. It must be noted, however, that Herodotus's rather damning descriptions of Khafre and Khufu as impious tyrants may be inaccurate. Their great pyramid-building projects may have functioned more as relief work to keep Egyptian farmers busy during their off-seasons rather than the forced slave-labor projects they were once thought to have been.

LIFE'S WORK
Menkaure's most lasting contributions, like those of his predecessors, were in the areas of art and architecture. Shortly after beginning his reign, Menkaure took the customary steps to ensure his continued existence in the afterlife by erecting a massive tomb in the form of a stone pyramid. Menkaure's pyramid still stands today, along with those of Khufu and Khafre, near the banks of the Nile River, the last surviving remnants of the Seven Wonders of the Ancient World. The pyramid of Menkaure is conspicuously smaller in volume (totaling 9 million cubic feet, or 4 million cubic meters) than the great pyramids of his more famous pharaonic predecessors, Khufu (78 million cubic feet; 34 million cubic meters) and Khafre (94 million cubic feet; 41 million cubic meters), that stand immediately to the northeast on the plateau at Giza.

Although less than half as tall as Khufu's Great Pyramid, Menkaure's has the distinction, along with one of its three smaller satellite pyramids, of having once been sheathed in costly rose-colored Ethiopian granite, of which, today, only the lowest courses remain; the rest is finished in common mud brick. As the pioneering Egyptologist James Henry Breasted (1865-1935) pointed out, the pyramids of Menkaure's two predecessors may have so depleted the resources of the state that he was unable to erect a more extravagant tomb. The financial strain that this type of labor-intensive construction exacted on the royal treasury was considerable enough to necessitate a reversion to simple sun-dried mud brick for the pharaoh's causeway and his unfinished mortuary temple, both of which were completed at the direction of Menkaure's son and successor. Even the casual observer is left with the impression of a monument hastened to completion during the eclipse of a dynastic era.

Menkaure's pyramid was opened and entered sometime during the seventh century B.C.E., probably by curious Egyptian antiquaries of the Twenty-sixth Dynasty who, finding the royal tomb already had been looted, replaced the scattered bones in a later style sarcophagus. In the mid-twentieth century, radiocarbon dating of these same human remains established that they were too recent to be those of Menkaure and may be, in all probability, those of an ill-fated looter who met his demise in the pharaoh's tomb. Unfortunately, the original basalt sarcophagus of Menkaure was lost off the coast of Spain in 1838 while being transported by sea to England.

Although the building projects of Menkaure appear comparatively modest by Old Kingdom standards, his sculptural artifacts are of very high quality and outnumber those produced under Khufu and Khafre. Surviving portraits from this era are predominantly either of the smaller freestanding sculptural type or larger semiengaged carvings in relief. *Ka* portraits, believed to provide a dwelling place for the pharaoh's shadow-self, are typical. In these representations, Menkaure is portrayed in an idealized manner, as was common practice in Old Kingdom statuary. Certain characteristic features, however, most notably his bulging eyes and snubbed-nose expression, are effectively conveyed as distinctive idiosyncratic traits. Notable representations of Menkaure include a sculptural dyadic portrait (now in the Boston Museum) of the royal couple, slightly under life size, showing Menkaure in the customary stiff-backed striding pose, accompanied by his sister-wife Khamerernebty II, who embraces the pharaoh with one arm while resting her left hand tenderly on his upper arm.

MAJOR KINGS OF THE FOURTH DYNASTY	
Ruler	*Reign (B.C.E.)*
Snefru	c. 2613-2589
Khufu	c. 2589-2566
Khafre	2558-2532
Menkaure	2532-c. 2503
Shepsekhaf	c. 2503-c. 2498

Note: Dynastic research is ongoing; data are approximate.

A much smaller triadic sculptural portrait in slate (now in the Cairo Museum) depicts Menkaure in company with Hathor, the Egyptian Venus, appearing in the guise of his favorite wife and accompanied, at his left, by one of the lesser female deities of the provinces (nomes). The evident regard that these female figures exhibit toward the central figure of the pharaoh, evidenced by their simultaneous embrace of him, conveys a sense of high esteem. Many similar sculptural portraits of Menkaure survive in fragmentary form and appear to have been abandoned as works-in-progress, perhaps lending credibility to the belief that the pharaoh's death came suddenly and without warning. Of all these similar works, of which there may have been as many as forty-two, only four have survived intact.

Herodotus tells that Menkaure suffered grievously over the death of a young daughter, then his only child. The pharaoh ordered built for her a wooden sarcophagus, covered in hammered gold, in the form of a heifer bearing the sun orb between its horns. Draped in scarlet cloth, this sacred effigy was said to have been brought forth into the sunlight one day each year in accordance with the daughter's dying wishes. Later authors, including the Roman Plutarch (c. 46-after 120 C.E.), have suggested that this story may actually allude to an annual agricultural ritual of rebirth and fertility associated with Osiris, green-skinned god of the Underworld, and his beautiful consort, Isis. Another ritual, which may actually allude to the sun's "return" in its yearly seasonal cycle, was said to have been inspired by an incident in the pharaoh's later life. An oracle decreed that Menkaure's beneficence had angered the ancient gods, who rather desired the people to be treated severely, and announced that the pharaoh had, as punishment, just six more years to live. The indignant pharaoh ordered all lamps to be lit unceasingly that he might live both by day as well as by night, thus doubling his effective remaining lifetime. In the end the prophecy proved false.

SIGNIFICANCE

Menkaure was the last of the three builders of the Great Pyramids. At his death, Menkaure was succeeded not by his oldest son (who may have predeceased him) but rather by Shepsekhaf (r. c. 2503-c. 2498 B.C.E.), a younger son by an unknown wife. Shepsekhaf's reign was only five years in duration and brought the Fourth Dynasty to a close. An indication that things began to go wrong at about this time is provided by Shepsekhaf's choice of Saqqara, rather than Giza, as his final resting place. Instead of erecting a pyramid as his forebears had done, he had built a tomb shaped like a plain sarcophagus with beveled sides whose simplicity echoed the prepyramid tomb style known as the mastaba (meaning "bench"). Ironically, this style of tomb was later copied at Giza in a monument, situated between the causeways of Khafre and Menkaure, that has come to be known as the fourth or "unfinished pyramid." This fourth pyramid is that of Menkaure's notable daughter, Khentkawes. Born of a second unknown 3wife, Khentkawes became a wife to the pharaoh Userkaf (r. 2494-c. 2487 B.C.E.), initiator of the Fifth Dynasty, and perhaps another, lesser pharaoh as well. A cult dedicated to Khentkawes flourished during the Fifth Dynasty, calling her the "mother of two kings, not only of one."

—Larry Smolucha

FURTHER READING

David, Rosalie. *The Pyramid Builders of Ancient Egypt: A Modern Investigation of Pharaoh's Workforce*. New York: Routledge, 1996. Using archaeological evidence from one of the first towns inhabited by pyramid laborers to be investigated, this book corrects many of the assumptions about the ways in which pyramids were built and the social conditions of their laborers.

Lepre, J. P. *The Egyptian Pyramids: A Comprehensive Reference*. Jefferson, N.C.: McFarland, 1990. A precise and detailed examination of ancient Egyptian pyramid construction from the predynastic era mastabas through the Twelfth and Thirteenth Dynasty revival. Well-illustrated with photos and architectural diagrams and containing appendices on hieroglyphics, principal explorers, and mathematical aspects of the various pyramid plans, etc.

Traunecker, Claude. *The Gods of Egypt*. Translated by David Lorton. Ithaca, N.Y.: Cornell University Press, 2001. A concise guide to Egyptian religion, including its significance in burial rituals and the mythology of death.

Verner, Miroslav. *The Pyramids: The Mystery, Culture, and Science of Egypt's Great Monuments*. Translated by Steven Rendall. New York: Grove, 2001. A very thorough review of the pyramids of Egypt, by a well-known Czech archaeologist, covering both cultural context and architectural properties. Bibliography, indexes, and appendices of the dimensions of the various pyramids, a list of Egyptologists and Egyptological scholars, a chronology of rulers and dynasties, and a glossary.

SEE ALSO: Imhotep; Ramses II; Tutankhamen; Zoser.
RELATED ARTICLES in *Great Events from History: The Ancient World*: c. 2687 B.C.E., Old Kingdom Period Begins in Egypt; c. 2575-c. 2566 B.C.E., Building of the Great Pyramid; From c. 1500 B.C.E., Dissemination of the Book of the Dead.

VALERIA MESSALLINA
Roman empress

Empress of Rome for more than seven years, Valeria Messallina was intimately involved in the highest level of Roman politics.

BORN: c. 20 C.E.; probably Rome (now in Italy)
DIED: 48 C.E.; Rome
ALSO KNOWN AS: Messallina
AREA OF ACHIEVEMENT: Government and politics

EARLY LIFE

Nothing is known of the childhood of Valeria Messallina (mehs-uh-LI-nuh). By the time she is first mentioned in historical sources, she had already married the Emperor Claudius I. Because their daughter, Octavia, was born in 40 C.E., the marriage is generally assigned to 39 C.E. The much older Claudius (born 10 B.C.E.) had three children by two earlier wives.

The Valerii Messallae (sometimes spelled with one *l*) were among the most illustrious families of Rome, one of the five *gentes maiores*—the inner circle of the patrician elite. Prominent through the early Republic, they faded into obscurity for more than a century after 164 B.C.E. An overview of the complicated family tree reveals the standing of the Valerii from the late Republic onward and goes far to explain Messallina's marriage to Claudius. Members of the high nobility often married for reasons of political advantage. This is true even of Claudius, who for fifty years was dismissed as an embarrassment to the Imperial house and kept largely out of public view.

LIFE'S WORK

Messallina presents major difficulties to students, as the ancient sources are uniformly extremely hostile. According to them, her only positive accomplishment was to produce two children for Claudius: Octavia and her brother, Britannicus, born in 42. According to the Roman writers, Messallina was addicted to sex and was utterly without principle, and she worked in tandem with the Imperial freedmen to manipulate her Imperial husband. Her scandalous life was known to everyone but Claudius. She had numerous lovers, participated in frequent orgies in the palace (on occasion compelling senators to watch their wives participate), destroyed several prominent politicians (some for refusing to have sex with her), and finally took reckless advantage of Claudius's absence to divorce him and marry her latest lover, Gaius Silius. Saved by the decisive action of the freedman Narcissus, Claudius ordered Messallina's death. She fled to her mother's gardens but lacked the courage to commit suicide and was executed by a soldier.

There are good reasons to disbelieve accounts that characterize Messallina as a world-class nymphomaniac. The writers all lived at least two generations later and doubtless used stories that had grown in frequent retelling. Further, these writers were all men, and the most important of them, Tacitus, was a senator. More important, they hated women who refused to conform to Roman expectations. Women were not allowed to participate in politics; no ancient state allowed women to hold office, command troops, or vote. Men were supposed to discipline their womenfolk. In his *Ab excessu divi Augusti* (c. 116 C.E., also known as *Annales*; *Annals*, 1598), Tacitus discredited individual emperors, the Imperial families, and the entire Imperial system; all had reduced the senate to subservience.

In this light, the accounts of Messallina are part of a larger drama involving the ferocious women of the ruling family: Augustus's wife Livia and her allies Urgulania and Munatia Plancina; Augustus's daughter Julia III; and Julia's daughters, Julia the Younger and Agrippina the Elder. The *Annals'* cast of infamous women culminates in Agrippina the Elder's daughter, Agrippina the Younger, who, though Claudius's niece, became his wife after Messallina's death and who reportedly murdered the emperor by poisoning his favorite snack, mushrooms.

The ancient writers also often omitted, minimized, or distorted the sound policies of the various reigns and hurried past them to put emphasis on scandals. Claudius is no exception, appearing as a bumbling fool, timid, addicted to wine, gambling, cruelty, sex, and—worst of all—unable to control either his wives or his freedmen. Messallina teamed with the powerful Narcissus to dominate the doddering man who became emperor almost by accident. The ancient historians give differing views of the era: Dio Cassius crams many good points into his opening survey of the reign (book 60); Suetonius categorizes events rather than proceeding chronologically; and Juvenal's *Saturae* (100-127 C.E.; *Satires*, 1693) are notoriously biased and bitter. The masterful Tacitus is the best source, but his account of the period from the accession of Caligula in March, 37, to midway through 47 C.E. is lost.

Recent scholarship sees Messallina as using whatever weapons were available to her, including sex, to secure political goals. Her aim was to keep Claudius alive and

Valeria Messallina. (Library of Congress)

at Ostia inspecting his new port facilities, Claudius's enraged return to Rome, her flight to her mother's house, and her death at the hands of the soldiers of the Praetorian Guard. Most would regard her as an adulteress to her lawful husband and as guilty of treason to the state. Tacitus speaks of her *furor*, or madness; he, too, was unable to make sense of the events.

SIGNIFICANCE

It is probably accurate to say that Messallina had relatively little significance in the long run. She was empress for a fairly short period, 41-48 C.E., and because women were excluded from office, she could not set government policies. Her influence over Claudius was limited to helping him eliminate their enemies, which she did ruthlessly. Her chief weapons were shrewd political sense and, evidently, sex. An inexplicable failure to control her political and sexual passions brought her to ruin in 48 C.E. Nero had her son, Britannicus, killed early in 55 C.E. and set aside her daughter, Octavia, a few years later, ending her bloodline. Tacitus's description of her has proved enduring. Moderns will find equally compelling the fictional account in Robert Graves's 1934 novels *I, Claudius* and *Claudius, the God and His Wife Messallina.* Also notable are the *Masterpiece Theater* productions of Graves's books, which introduced millions of television viewers to the intrigue and decadence of Imperial Rome.

—*Thomas H. Watkins*

FURTHER READING

Balsdon, J. P. V. D. *Roman Women: Their History and Habits.* 1962. Reprint. New York: Barnes & Noble, 1983. Valuable background, although many of Balsdon's views now seem quaintly dated.

Barrett, Anthony A. *Agrippina.* New Haven, Conn.: Yale University Press, 1996. Agrippina Major and Agrippina Minor were the dominant Roman women before and after Messallina. Agrippina Minor probably has the worst reputation of any Roman woman: empress for only five years as Claudius's wife but then powerful as the mother of Nero until he had her executed in 59. She may have learned much from close observation of Messallina.

_____. *Caligula: The Corruption of Power.* New Haven, Conn.: Yale University Press, 1990. Contains little on Messallina but much on Caligula's mother, Agrippina the Elder, and his sisters.

Bauman, Richard. *Women and Politics in Ancient Rome.* New York: Routledge, 1992. A detailed study of the period from about 330 B.C.E. to 68 C.E. Bauman ranks

on the throne until their son, Britannicus, was old enough to take control. Because Claudius had many opponents who thought they had better claims and better talents to be emperor and who were prepared to act ruthlessly to achieve their ends, Messallina responded in kind. Those whom she eliminated were all powerful politicians, actual or potential enemies, or their wives. One victim was Pompeius Magnus (Pompey the Great), married to Antonia, Claudius's daughter by an earlier wife; that combination of bloodlines was an obvious threat to Messallina's children. In several cases, she may have struck enemies only barely before they had their forces in place.

Messallina's orchestration of the downfall of D. Valerius Maximus in 47 C.E. was the beginning of the end. Her spectacular collapse remains an impenetrable mystery—her "marriage" to Gaius Silius while Claudius was

Messallina among the most powerful women of Rome, credits her with a sharp knowledge of criminal law, and dismisses some of the rumors about her sexual exploits as worthless.

Dudley, Donald R. *The World of Tacitus*. Boston: Little, Brown, 1968. A readable survey of the people who dominate Tacitus's historical works.

L'Hoir, Francesca Santoro. "Tacitus and Women's Usurpation of Power." *Classical World* 88 (1994): 5-25. A persuasive study of Tacitus's portrayal of women who "interfere" in politics and usurp men's place; according to Tacitus, any society that permits this "unnatural" occurrence is doomed.

Kokkinos, Nikkos. *Antonia Augusta: Portrait of a Great Roman Lady*. New York: Routledge, 1992. A sympathetic portrait of the mother of Claudius. She and her mother, Octavia, were perhaps the most dignified women of the Julio-Claudian Dynasty.

Levick, B. M. *Claudius*. New Haven, Conn.: Yale University Press, 1990. A good modern study of Claudius's reign; contains much useful information on Messallina.

Momigliano, Arnaldo. *Claudius: The Emperor and His Achievement*. Westport, Conn.: Greenwood Press, 1981. Though superseded by Levick's biography, this earlier study, originally published in 1934, remains valuable.

Syme, Sir Ronald. *The Augustan Aristocracy*. New York: Oxford University Press, 1989. An immensely detailed analysis of the Roman elite under the early Empire; much on the Agrippinas, Messallina, her mother, Domitia Lepida, and others. Family trees in the back are invaluable for sorting out the tangled aristocratic genealogies.

_____. *Tacitus*. 2 vols. Oxford, England: Clarendon Press, 1963. A magisterial study of the greatest Roman historian; however, like all of Syme's works, it is not for beginners.

Wiseman, T. P. "Calpurnius Siculus and the Claudian Civil War." *Journal of Roman Studies* 72 (1982): 57-67. Discusses a neglected poetic text that throws light on the opposition to Claudius at the beginning of his reign; the government crackdown reveals Messallina at work.

SEE ALSO: Agrippina the Younger; Arria the Elder; Arria the Younger; Arsinoe II Philadelphus; Claudius I; Clodia; Julia Domna; Julia Mamaea; Julia Soaemias; Julia III; Livia Drusilla; Lucretia; Nero; Poppaea Sabina; Zenobia.

RELATED ARTICLES in *Great Events from History: The Ancient World*: 8 C.E., Ovid's *Metamorphoses* Is Published; c. 50 C.E., Creation of the Roman Imperial Bureaucracy.

MILTIADES THE YOUNGER
Athenian general

Through innovative tactics and inspired battlefield leadership, Miltiades led Athens to victory over the Persians at the Battle of Marathon. He thus helped to secure Greek civilization from engulfment by Near Eastern influences and greatly enhanced Athenian prestige in the Greek world.

BORN: c. 554 B.C.E.; Attica, Greece
DIED: 489 B.C.E.; probably Athens, Greece
AREA OF ACHIEVEMENT: War and conquest

EARLY LIFE
Very little is known about the first thirty years of Miltiades (mihl-TI-uh-deez) the Younger. His family and clan relationships, however, would prove to be highly influential in the shaping of his career, as was commonly the case in ancient Athens. He was born into the very old and wealthy Philaidae clan, whose members had long played an active part in Athenian politics. This family's estates were located in rural Attica (the countryside that bordered Athens). As a member of a prominent, aristocratic family, Miltiades probably enjoyed the benefits of a fine education and certainly profited from extensive political connections.

Miltiades' father, Cimon, however, was notorious for his failure to advance in the Athenian political arena, a source of considerable shame for aristocrats in Greek society. Cimon was also widely known for intellectual torpidity, a trait that earned for him the nickname *koalemos*, meaning "the nincompoop." Nevertheless, his failure to earn a prominent place in public life was probably more a result of his opposition to the Pisistratidae clan, an aristocratic family and political faction that exercised an authoritarian rule over Athens from 560 to 510 B.C.E., with considerable popular support.

In order to secure his own place in politics, Miltiades was forced to disavow his father's opinions and seek allies elsewhere. He did not have to search outside his own clan, because his uncle, Miltiades the Elder, and his older brother, Stesagoras, had acquiesced to Pisistratidaen rule and had been dispatched to the Chersonese (modern Gallipoli Peninsula) to conquer, colonize, and rule the region for Athens. In roughly 524 or 523, Miltiades served as archon, a judicial-administrative post that he secured through his acceptance of the Pisistratidaen tyranny.

Sometime before 514, Miltiades married an Athenian woman, about whom nothing definite is known. Some historians believe that she was a relative of the Pisistratidae. The couple had at least one child. Around 516, the Pisistratidae sent Miltiades to the Chersonese to assume the duties formerly performed by Miltiades the Elder and Stesagoras, both of whom had recently died childless. Miltiades would utilize this opportunity to achieve renown in the Aegean world.

LIFE'S WORK

The Pisistratidae had entrusted Miltiades with an important assignment. By the latter half of the sixth century, Athens was importing unknown quantities of wheat from Black Sea regions through the Hellespontus strait to feed its burgeoning population. The Philaidae's mission was to preserve free access to the waterway by protecting the coastal regions from the depredations of pirates, Thracian tribes, and those Greek cities on the Asian side of the Hellespontus. Ancient sources tell little about the quality of Miltiades' service in the Chersonese, except that he continued the authoritarian rule over Athenian colonists and natives begun by his relations.

Miltiades' fame had its origins in the events surrounding the Scythian expedition, undertaken by Darius the Great, king of Persia. The Persians had extended their rule over the Greek cities of eastern Asia Minor (known as Ionia) in 545 and governed this region through Greek tyrants supported by their armies. From Ionia, around 513, Darius launched the first Persian invasion of Europe, using the Greek fleets for logistical support. Initially, he was successful, subduing Thrace and reducing Miltiades to vassalage. Darius's difficulties began when his army plunged into the lands of the Scythians, just north of the Danube River in modern Romania. The Persian army was doggedly harassed by the enemy and forced to retreat toward the Danubian boat-bridge maintained by the Ionians and their ships. At this crossing point, Miltiades urged the other Greeks to destroy the bridge and abandon Darius to his fate. Although his com-

patriots refused, Miltiades withdrew his forces to the Chersonese. His anti-Persian stand would serve him well politically in the future.

In the meantime, however, Darius's escape across the Danube left Miltiades in a precarious position. As the Persians retreated through the Chersonese into Asia, they were pursued by the Scythians. Miltiades and his family were expelled from their small kingdom. His whereabouts during the next eighteen years are not made known by the ancient sources, but it is likely that he spent time at the court of Olorus, king of Thrace.

There, sometime between 513 and 510, he married Olorus's daughter, Hegesipyle. The fate of his first wife is unknown. With his second wife he had four children: Cimon, destined to achieve greater fame than his father in the mid-fifth century as rival to Pericles and a founder of the Athenian Empire; Elpinice, a woman admired for her beauty and notorious for her free sexual behavior; and two other daughters whose names are unknown.

While Miltiades bided his time in exile, events in Ionia offered new political and military opportunities. In 499 the Ionian cities rose up in revolt against their Persian-imposed tyrants and thus began a six-year-long war in the eastern Aegean for Greek independence. Miltiades entered the fray in 495, when the inhabitants of the Chersonese invited him to return to rule over them. Installed once again in his kingdom, he used the Persians' preoccupation with the Ionian Revolt to seize the islands of Lemnos and Imbros, turning them over to the Athenians.

The Persian riposte was not long in coming. After suppressing Ionian resistance, their attentions focused on the Chersonese. When a Phoenician fleet in the service of the Persians closed in on Miltiades, he fled for the island of Imbros. In 493 he arrived in Athens, armed with vast political, and especially military, experience and widely admired for his consistently anti-Persian stance.

Politics in the Athens to which Miltiades returned had changed significantly since the days of his youth. Hippias, the last of the Pisistratidaen tyrants, had been expelled in 510. Around 508, Cleisthenes had introduced democratic reforms to the Athenian constitution, a political maneuver that greatly increased the strength of his clan, the Alcmaeonidae. Aristocrats seeking political power were thus forced to court the favor of the populace more strongly than ever before. It was a political culture alien to Miltiades' previous experience, but the looming Persian threat to Greek security—Athens had assisted the Ionian Revolt—made his military knowledge of the Persian Empire an important asset.

Miltiades the Younger. (F. R. Niglutsch)

Traditionally, historians have viewed Athenian politics during the 490's as a contest between political parties supporting well-defined ideologies. Some were appeasers of the Persians, while others were decidedly in favor of resistance to them. Some favored the new democratic constitution, and others longed for a return to an era of aristocratic predominance. Recently, most historians have rejected such theories, because they do not jibe with ancient sources, which describe political rivalries largely in personal and familial terms. Modern interpretations stress the general agreement of Athenian politicians on essential issues: strong opposition to the Persian threat and a generalized acceptance of—if not preference for—the democratic constitution. An exception to this rule was the Pisistratidae, still led by Hippias, who wanted to restore their tyranny with the backing of the Persians.

Miltiades' arrival on the political scene threatened to upset a delicate power balance. His appeal as a "Persian-fighter" instantly secured for him a power base, which promised to be troublesome to those clan factions that had grown used to the absence of the Philaidae. Although nearly all aristocratic politicians agreed with Miltiades' views, the essential issue in Athens in this era was not to what purposes power should be used but who should enjoy the benefits and prestige of power itself.

Shortly after Miltiades' arrival in Athens, he was brought to trial for exercising a tyranny over the Chersonese, possibly at the instigation of the Alcmaeonidae. During these proceedings, Miltiades probably strained to disassociate himself from his former affiliations to the Pisistratidae, giving rise to later legends of his youthful hostility to that clan. In any case, he was acquitted, thus foiling clever attempts to depict him as a reactionary aristocrat and to boost his enemies' popularity with the people.

In 490, with a Persian invasion imminent, Miltiades was elected to the ten-man board of generals from his tribe. Although this position was largely a command post—the Athenian army was organized tactically along tribal divisions—the board also functioned as an advisory council to the supreme commander, the polemarchos. Miltiades' expert advice was to play a crucial role in the impending campaign.

In July of 490, a Persian fleet, commanded by Datis and Artaphernes, sailed west from Ionia. King Darius's objectives were to punish Athens and another city-state, Eretria, for assisting the Ionian Revolt and to establish a base from which all mainland Greece could later be conquered. Ancient sources give grossly exaggerated numbers for this invasion force. Modern historians have variously estimated its military strength at fifteen thousand to thirty thousand infantry, including five hundred to one thousand cavalry. After subduing the Cyclades Islands and ravaging Eretria on Euboea Island, the Persians landed on the plain of Marathon, about twenty-file miles northeast of Athens. Most Athenian strategists favored a tough defense of the city's walls as the key to victory. Miltiades, however, who had personally observed skilled Persian siegecraft during the Ionian Revolt, argued for a pitched battle in the open field. He sponsored a decree to this effect in the Assembly. On its authority, the commander Callimachus led the ten-thousand-man hoplite force out to Marathon to meet the enemy.

For several August days, the Persians and Athenians observed each other across the plain. Both sides had compelling reasons for delay. The Persians were waiting for Hippias, who had accompanied them, to rally the Pisistratidaen faction to the invasion. The Athenians were anticipating the arrival of troops from Sparta, the most militarily powerful of the city-states in Greece.

Miltiades had different ideas about how this campaign should be fought. He persuaded Callimachus at a divided meeting of the board of generals to attack the Persians in the plain immediately. Ancient sources do not give explicit reasons for this precipitate decision to engage in battle, although modern historians have generally agreed that the Athenian commanders feared the collusion of the Pisistratidae—and possibly the Alcmaeonidae—in the invasion. An immediate victory would save Athens from the treachery of these opponents.

In the ensuing battle on August 12, Miltiades' innovative tactics capitalized on Persian weaknesses: a lack of heavy armor and reliable shock weapons and an overdependence on the missile power of their archers and cavalry. As the Greek hoplites advanced toward the Persian lines, their pace accelerated. Once within missile range, they rushed headlong into contact with the enemy. The vaunted Persian archery skills were thus rendered useless. The Persians were surprised by this tactic, as Greek armies normally walked into combat to preserve the solidity of their battle lines.

To avoid being outflanked, Miltiades had deliberately extended his weaker army to match the frontage of the Persians. This formation involved weakening the center of the phalanx. As the battle developed, this emaciated center gave way before the enemy onslaught. His stronger wings, however, were triumphant. Exercising firm control over his men, Miltiades diverted these flank hoplites from pursuit in order to turn them in against the Persian center. This section of the enemy army was almost annihilated. More than six thousand Persians fell in the battle. As the Persians sailed away in retreat, Miltiades and his men could congratulate themselves on a victory that had saved Greece from tyranny.

In the aftermath of this battle, known as the Battle of Marathon, Miltiades' popularity soared. His career, nevertheless, was already very close to an ignominious end. From the Assembly, he secured funds for a secret military mission that, he promised, would enrich Athens. His subsequent assault on the island of Paros ended in failure, while Miltiades received a critical leg wound. Back in Athens, he was brought to trial for deceiving the people, an accusation brought forth by Xanthippus, who had married into the Alcmaeonidae clan. Miltiades was convicted and assessed an enormous fine. Jealous political rivals had triumphed. He died shortly thereafter from gangrene.

SIGNIFICANCE

Miltiades' career provides a fine case study in the extremely competitive nature of Greek politics, a competition wherein clan and family loyalties, while very important, played a secondary role to the overpowering imperative to succeed. Aristocrats who won the political game were regarded as virtuous, while those who failed—such as Miltiades' father—were disgraced or shamed. Athenian political culture holds interesting clues to the reasons for the individual brilliance of the Greeks and their inability to achieve stable political organizations.

—Michael S. Fitzgerald

FURTHER READING

Burn, A. R. *Persia and the Greeks: The Defence of the West, c. 546-478 B.C.* Rev. ed. Stanford, Calif.: Stanford University Press, 1984. An excellent account of the titanic struggle between the Greeks and Persians. Interspersed with short sections on Miltiades' activities in this era, with references to the ancient sources on him. Includes a precise chronology of the Battle of Marathon.

Herodotus. *The Histories*. Translated by Robin Waterfield. New York: Oxford University Press, 1998. By far the most important ancient source on Miltiades and the Battle of Marathon—the place to start for those doing research. Aspiring scholars should use this volume only in conjunction with modern accounts because historians have discounted some of what Herodotus wrote.

Hignett, Charles. *Xerxes' Invasion of Greece.* Oxford, England: Clarendon Press, 1963. Despite its title, this book contains an excellent scholarly account of the Battle of Marathon. Provides references to nearly all the ancient sources and criticism of many of the modern attempts at reconstruction of the great event. Explains the modern tendency to regard Herodotus's writings as the most reliable of ancient sources on the Persian Wars.

Sealey, Raphael. *A History of the Greek City-States, 700-338 B.C.* Berkeley: University of California Press, 1976. Written by a prominent proponent of the prosopographical approach to Greek politics, that is, the concept that personal and familial relations overrode ideological issues in shaping events. Includes discussion of major aspects of Miltiades' life, with ancient sources referenced.

SEE ALSO: Cimon; Cleisthenes of Athens; Darius the Great.

RELATED ARTICLES in *Great Events from History: The Ancient World*: 520-518 B.C.E., Darius the Great Conquers the Indus Valley; 508-507 B.C.E., Reforms of Cleisthenes; 499-494 B.C.E., Ionian Revolt; September 17, 490 B.C.E., Battle of Marathon.

MITHRADATES VI EUPATOR
Pontic king (r. 120-63 B.C.E.)

Mithradates fought three wars with Rome in the first half of the first century B.C.E., resulting in the destruction and transformation into a Roman province of his own kingdom of Pontus.

BORN: c. 134 B.C.E.; probably Sinope, kingdom of Pontus (Sinop, Turkey)
DIED: 63 B.C.E.; Panticapaeum, Crimea (now Kerch, Ukraine)
ALSO KNOWN AS: Mithridates the Great
AREA OF ACHIEVEMENT: Government and politics

EARLY LIFE

Mithradates Eupator (mihth-ruh-DAYT-eez YEW-puh-tor), whose name means "good father," was probably born at Sinope, the capital of the kingdom of Pontus (in modern northern Turkey), in 134 B.C.E. He was the son of the Pontic king Mithradates V Euergetes (benefactor) and his wife, Laodice. When his father was assassinated in 120, Mithradates succeeded to the throne, possibly in conjunction with his brother Mithradates Chrestus (the good), under the regency of their mother. The details of his life at this time are shrouded in mystery. According to the Latin historian Pompeius Trogus, whose work in summary form is the only literary source to describe Mithradates' activity in these years, Mithradates went to live in the wild for the next seven years to avoid falling victim to various palace conspiracies. It is clear that this story is not strictly accurate, for a series of inscriptions in honor of Mithradates and other members of the Pontic court, dated to 116, found on the island of Delos in the Aegean Sea and an inscription discovered in southern Russia show that he was a presence in the palace during these years. The kingdom of Pontus was characterized by the difficult fusion of Greek and Iranian cultural traditions, as, indeed, was the court itself. It is therefore possible to interpret Trogus's story as a folkloric development stemming from the basic education of an Iranian noble in horsemanship and the hunt.

Whatever the case may be, it is clear from the course of his later life that Mithradates received a good education in Greek as well as in the traditional Iranian arts of war and the hunt. He was a man who truly represented the amalgam of these two powerful cultural traditions, and throughout his career there are many signs of these two sides in his upbringing. His coins suggest that he tried to model his appearance on that of Alexander the Great, for when he made war on Rome he presented himself to the cities of the Greek East as a champion against the Romans—the "common enemy"—and surrounded himself with officials of Greek descent. At the same time, he gave these officials titles such as satrap, which evoked the memory of the ancient Persian kingdom swept away by Alexander, and he offered massive sacrifices to the high god of the Persian pantheon, Ahura Mazda.

In general terms, he was a man of tremendous physical and intellectual gifts, preternatural brutality, and, evidently, severe paranoia. He could speak twenty-two (or, according to another tradition, twenty-five) languages and was a patron of the arts and a lover of music. He is said to have been able to control a chariot drawn by sixteen horses and in his late sixties could still ride a hundred miles in a day. He included prophylactics against poison in his meals, murdered three of his ten sons, and, in the course of his wars, perpetrated massacres that were to become legendary in antiquity.

LIFE'S WORK

In 115 or 114 B.C.E., Mithradates established himself as the sole ruler of Pontus, murdering his mother and then his brother in the process. At about the same time, he began a series of campaigns to extend his control in the Crimea, in southern Russia, and along the coast of what is now Bulgaria and Romania. He appears to have undertaken these operations for several reasons. One was to increase his prestige in the Greek world as a whole; as a result of these campaigns, he emerged as the protector of Greek cities against neighboring barbarian tribes. Another reason was to increase the overall power of Pontus, whose natural economic base was not sufficient to support a great nation. The territories that now came under his control were extremely wealthy; they had for centuries been an important source of grain and dried fish for the Aegean world and were to become an important source of revenue for Mithradates. In the next few years, he sent his armies to establish control over the eastern shore of the Black Sea as well. The success of these operations was vital for what seems to have been Mithradates' great ambition: the establishment of Pontus as a major power in Anatolia and the Aegean world, an ambition that he could achieve only if he could match the hitherto irresistible power of Rome.

In addition to strengthening his kingdom through acquisitions along the Black Sea coast, Mithradates worked to enhance the economic base of his ancestral territories, which extended along the northern coast of modern Turkey and just across the Caucasus Mountains into the Anatolian plateau. Many parts of this realm were at the time of his accession quite backward. The settled areas south of the mountains had retained their basic political structure from the time of the Persian Empire, or, indeed, of the Hittites, while the mountainous regions had always been the preserve of wild tribes whose primary occupations were the pasturing of flocks and brigandage. Mithradates sought to encourage urbanization, founding cities in the mountain valleys and bringing the tribesmen out of the hills. He was not altogether successful in this, but the effort is a good illustration of his comprehensive planning to build up the power of Pontus.

In the final decade of the second century, Mithradates began to turn his attention to the kingdoms that lay to his south and west: Bithynia, which bordered Pontus at its western extremity in Asia Minor; Paphlagonia, to the southwest; and Cappadocia on the central Anatolian plateau to the south. All these areas were essentially under the influence of Rome, which had established a presence in what is the central portion of modern western Turkey when in 132 it had accepted this area as a bequest from the last king of Pergamum (who had ruled these areas). This land had become the Roman province of Asia.

As a result of the potential might of Rome, Mithradates at first had to move against these areas through diplomacy and the promotion of domestic discord. On several occasions between 109 and 89, he sought to establish his relatives or supporters as the rulers in both Paphlagonia and Cappadocia. On each occasion, Roman embassies had ordered him to withdraw, and Mithradates, who did not believe that he could risk armed conflict, had done so.

The situation changed in 90, as a result of two events. First, a major civil war broke out in Italy between Rome and its Italian subjects, which initially went badly for Rome. Second, the incompetent Roman governor of Asia, Manius Aquillius, in conjunction with Cassius, the head of a Roman embassy that had recently ordered Mithradates out of Bithynia (from which he had expelled King Nicomedes), encouraged Nicomedes to attack the territory of Pontus. In 89, Mithradates struck with overwhelming force, thinking that he could no longer tolerate the intervention of Rome in his affairs and that Rome was now so weak that it would not be able to take effective action against him. His armies overwhelmed all resistance in Asia Minor, captured Aquillius (whom Mithradates executed by pouring molten gold down his throat) and Cassius, and began a wholesale massacre of Romans and their supporters throughout the region. In 88, at the height of

his power, his forces were established in Greece while he remained to administer his newly won territories.

In the same year, after the war against the Italians had turned decisively in Rome's favor, the Roman general Lucius Cornelius Sulla, after temporarily securing his personal domination by a military occupation of the city, set out to engage Mithradates. From 87 to 86 Sulla besieged Athens, the main base of the Pontic armies in Greece. In 86 he captured Athens, defeated in two battles the two main Pontic field armies, commanded by Mithradates' lieutenants, and prepared an invasion of Asia.

At the same time, a Roman army under the command of one of Sulla's rivals (Sulla's enemies had occupied Rome after heavy fighting in 87) moved directly against Mithradates. Although this army defeated him in several battles, it proved to be his salvation. When Sulla arrived in Asia Minor in 85, he was more interested in doing away with his rival and reestablishing his power in Italy than he was in destroying Pontus. Sulla struck a deal with Mithradates to restore the state of affairs before the outbreak of hostilities in return for a large indemnity, which Sulla could use to support the war that he then undertook in Italy. This deal, the Treaty of Dardanus, was signed in 85.

The treaty with Sulla saved Mithradates' kingdom and enabled him to rebuild his forces. He was able to do this rapidly enough to repulse an invasion by Murena, the officer whom Sulla had left in charge of Asia, in 82. This event is traditionally referred to as the Second Mithradatic War, even though it seems to have been no more than an unsuccessful plundering expedition. In the next several years, aided by Romans who had fled Sulla's bloody return to Italy and had continued the struggle abroad, Mithradates assembled a new army. At the same time, it is said, he offered encouragement to the pirates based in southern Asia Minor in their raids on Roman shipping.

Mithradates' third and final war with Rome began in 73 B.C.E. It was precipitated by the death of the king of Bithynia, who bequeathed his kingdom to the Romans. At first, Mithradates was completely successful. He defeated a Roman army, overran Bithynia, and again sent his troops into the province of Asia. However, his success was short-lived. At the end of the year, the Roman general Lucius Lucullus encountered Mithradates' main force as it was besieging the city of Cyzicus. At the beginning of 72, Lucullus destroyed this army and invaded Pontus itself. In 71 he drove Mithradates out of his kingdom.

Mithradates fled to Armenia, where he convinced his son-in-law, King Tigranes, to support him. Lucullus continued his invasion in 69 and defeated the combined forces of the two kings, leaving Mithradates roaming the hills with a small band of followers. Mithradates' career would have ended had it not been for a crisis of command on the Roman side. In 68, Lucullus's army mutinied, and he was forced to withdraw to Asia. Mithradates was then able to defeat the Roman army that had been left behind to occupy Pontus. This defeat led to the removal of Lucullus from command, though no effective officer relieved him until 66 when Pompey the Great arrived. Mithradates used this interval in an unsuccessful effort to consolidate the defenses of his old kingdom. At the end of 66, Pompey drove him from his kingdom and he was forced to withdraw, at the head of a small army, around the coast of the Black Sea to the Crimea. It was a difficult march, and its success is testimony to the enduring energy of the king.

In 63, while planning a new campaign against the Romans that is said to have involved the grandiose scheme of marching on Italy through the Balkans, Mithradates faced a serious palace revolt. His son, Pharnaces, launched a successful coup and took command of the army. Mithradates withdrew to his palace and, after killing his harem, tried to commit suicide. His efforts to poison himself failed, as a result of the drugs he had taken against poison throughout his life, and he had to call on one of his officers to stab him to death.

SIGNIFICANCE

Mithradates was a man of tremendous energy and ambition. It must also be conceded that this energy and ambition were fatally misdirected. No matter what steps he took, he would never have been able to match the power of Rome, and despite initial successes, he was never able to hold his own when Rome turned its superior military might against him. In fact, he was able to survive his first failure only because Sulla thought that he had more pressing business elsewhere.

Although Mithradates' determination, his refusal to admit defeat, and the broad vision he brought to the organization of his kingdom were impressive, his accomplishments were essentially negative. He initiated a series of wars that led to the expansion of Roman control in Anatolia and proved to be of great importance for Rome's subsequent organization of this area, precisely the end he sought to avoid. Furthermore, the process involved massive devastation by both Mithradates and his enemies. There can be no doubt that the course of Roman

expansion would have been very different if it had not been for Mithradates, but it can scarcely be argued that the course that Mithradates initiated was beneficial to those involved, as it resulted in the undoing of all that he had accomplished in the early part of his reign.

—David Potter

FURTHER READING

Appianus of Alexandria. "The Mithridatic Wars." In *Appian's Roman History*, translated by Horace White. Cambridge, Mass.: Harvard University Press, 1990-1999. Appian's account of the Mithradatic Wars, written in Greek during the first half of the second century C.E., is the basic source for information on Mithradates' reign.

Jones, Arnold H. M. *The Cities of the Eastern Roman Provinces*. Reprint. New York: Oxford University Press, 1998. This work contains a useful chapter on the history of Pontus.

Magie, David. *Roman Rule in Asia Minor to the End of the Third Century After Christ*. New York: Arno Press, 1975. Several chapters on Mithradates. Includes detailed analysis of the sources in extensive notes.

Plutarch. *Fall of the Roman Republic: Six Lives—Marius, Sulla, Crassus, Pompey, Caesar, Cicero*. Translated by Rex Warner. Rev. ed. Harmondsworth, Middlesex, England: Penguin, 1981. This volume contains Plutarch's biographies of Sulla and Pompey, both of which provide much information about the campaigns of Mithradates. Includes introduction and notes.

Sherk, Robert, ed. and trans. *Rome and the Greek East to the Death of Augustus*. New York: Cambridge University Press, 1984. Contains translations of a number of documents (inscriptions, papyruses, and classical texts for which other translations are not readily available) that are relevant to the career of Mithradates.

Sherwin-White, Adrian N. *Roman Foreign Policy in the East, 168 B.C. to A.D. 1*. Norman: University of Oklahoma Press, 1984. The central portion of the book deals with the history of Mithradates' reign, including valuable studies of the military aspects.

SEE ALSO: Alexander the Great; Pompey the Great; Lucius Cornelius Sulla.

RELATED ARTICLES in *Great Events from History: The Ancient World*: 133 B.C.E., Pergamum Is Transferred to Rome; 95-69 B.C.E., Armenian Empire Reaches Its Peak Under Tigranes the Great.

MONTUHOTEP II
Egyptian pharaoh (r. 2055-2004 B.C.E.)

Montuhotep II reunited Egypt after the First Intermediate Period and founded the Middle Kingdom Period.

FLOURISHED: 2055-2004 B.C.E.; Egypt
ALSO KNOWN AS: Mentuhotep II; Mentuhotpe II; Nebhepetra; Nebhepetre; Sankhibtawy (given name)
AREAS OF ACHIEVEMENT: Government and politics, war and conquest

EARLY LIFE

Not much is known about the early life of Montuhotep (MON-tew-hoh-tehp) II. He succeeded Intef III (r. 2063-2055 B.C.E.), whose son or heir he may have been. Montuhotep's family apparently was centered in Thebes; his name, Montuhotep ("Montu is content"), refers to Montu, the Theban god of war. Montuhotep's wives included Tem, his principal wife and the mother of his successor, Montuhotep III (Sankhkara).

LIFE'S WORK

On gaining the throne, Montuhotep II took as his first throne name "He who gives the Breath of Life into the Heart of the Two Lands" (that is, Upper and Lower Egypt), thus revealing his ambition to rule all of Egypt, though at this time he controlled only the area from the First Cataract up to the tenth nome (province) of Upper Egypt. Nonetheless, for about fourteen years an uneasy peace was maintained between Montuhotep II and the rulers of Lower Egypt. Although details are not clear, it is thought that the revolt of the Thinite nome in Lower Egypt against its ruler enabled Montuhotep to invade Lower Egypt. That his invasion was resisted strongly is evidenced by some sixty of his soldiers who are buried in a common tomb near Montuhotep's mortuary complex; it is thought that this location of honor may celebrate their heroism in his conquest of Lower Egypt.

The subsequent death of the ruler of Lower Egypt, Merykara, assisted Montuhotep's conquest of Lower Egypt. He celebrated his victory by taking a new title: Netjerihedjet ("The Wearer of the White Crown of Upper Egypt Is Divine"). References to fighting in the period after this reconquest indicate that pacification of Lower Egypt took some time. Gradually, however, peace and prosperity increased throughout the reunited land and in the thirty-ninth year of his long reign, Montuhotep took again a new title, Sematawy ("He Who Unites the Two Lands").

Once he had become ruler of all Egypt, Montuhotep made a number of administrative changes. Although Memphis was the traditional capital of the unified ancient Egypt, Montuhotep instead chose as his capital Thebes, the hometown of his dynasty. Montuhotep appointed mostly Theban men as his officials. To ensure the continued loyalty of the provincial governors (nomarchs) of Lower Egypt, Montuhotep created the office of "governor of Lower Egypt." Moreover, Montuhotep removed certain nomarchs, presumably for their support of the former king, Merykara. Montuhotep monitored the loyalty and effectiveness of his nomarchs by regularly traveling to the various nomes. The names and duties of some of Montuhotep's administrators are known. Meru, who held the position of chancellor, controlled the border territory of the eastern desert and its oases. Henenu, who held the position of steward ("overseer of horn, hoof, feather, and scale"), also traveled to Lebanon to acquire cedar for Montuhotep's building projects. Khety, who had been a steward of Intef III, was in charge of the patrols of the Sinai border.

During this time Montuhotep was active in asserting Egypt's power and prestige abroad. He led several invasions into Nubia, which had reverted to native rulers during the last years of the Old Kingdom. He was able to regain some mines and caravan trading routes by conquering Kurkur and ultimately occupied northern Nubia as far as the Second Cataract by establishing a garrison at Elephantine. To protect his western and eastern borders, Montuhotep led military campaigns against the Libyans and the nomads of the Sinai Peninsula.

Montuhotep reasserted the cult of the ruler as part of his strategy to enhance his reputation among his contemporaries and sustain his assumption of power. Two inscriptions describe him as the "son of the goddess Hathor," and he is depicted in some reliefs with the

KINGS OF THE ELEVENTH DYNASTY (ALL EGYPT)	
Ruler	*Reign (B.C.E.)*
Montuhotep II (Nebhepetra)	2055-2004
Montuhotep III (Sankhkara)	2004-1992
Montuhotep IV (Nebtawyra)	1992-1985

Note: Dynastic research is ongoing; data are approximate.

crowns of the gods Min and Amen. His Horus name, Netjerihedjet, and details of his funerary complex at Deir el-Bahri suggest that he presented himself as a god. Also, as part of this strategy, Montuhotep carried out extensive restorations or building projects in Upper Egypt at the sites of Deir el-Ballas, Dendera, Elkab, Gebelin, and Abydos. So far, no building site of Montuhotep in Lower Egypt has been identified.

Montuhotep selected as his burial site the valley basin called Deir el-Bahri, which is on the western bank of the Nile opposite Thebes. His well-preserved funerary complex at Deir el-Bahri is oriented east and west along the path of daily rebirth and death of the sun god Ra and was built in four stages. In the first stage, the entrances to the burial chambers for Montuhotep and his wives were out in the open air, but the second stage saw the construction of his burial chamber somewhat westward. In the third stage, a huge platform was constructed with a solid central core 86 feet (22 meters) square. Early modern reconstructions of the complex imagined that a pyramid surmounted this core.

Currently, it is thought that the top of the core was level and represented the primordial mound of creation in Egyptian mythology. Surrounding this core was an ambulatory of a triple row of octagonal sandstone columns that were, in turn, enclosed by a thick wall of limestone blocks. In the back of the ambulatory, cut into the cliffs, was the rear section of the complex. Extending westward (in the direction of the setting sun and hence symbolizing the afterlife) was an open courtyard, with pillared porticoes on all but the western side. Here, in the final stage of construction, was the entrance of the king's burial chamber in the form of a corridor running underground 490 feet (150 meters) into the cliff and terminating in a granite-lined chamber that held a shrine made of calcite. Above this chamber was a hall of ten rows of eight columns. A larger-than-life-size statue of the king stood in a niche in the middle of the western wall. During the fourth stage, the complex was made more impressive by additional colonnades and walls that protected the complex from rock and debris falling from the cliff. Statues of Montuhotep may have been placed along the inner sides of the inner walls. Other statues of the king, depicting him either standing or seated, were placed along the processional way of the forecourt between trees planted in deep beds. Those statues still extant show the king wrapped in the knee-length *sed*-festival cloak, holding the crook and flail of kingship in his hands crossed on his chest. Statues on the south side wore the white crown of Upper (southern) Egypt; those on the north side the red crown of Lower (northern) Egypt. On the front part of the temple's terrace were images of Montu and Amen, deities that Montuhotep identified with himself.

The design of this complex did not follow the mortuary temple plans of the Old Kingdom, but more probably drew on traditional Theban tombs, which also had large forecourts. The rock-cut tombs of Thebes also had pillared façades. Montuhotep did use, however, the traditional themes of the royal burials in the brightly painted reliefs that adorned the temple. These themes present, symbolically, the king as the restorer of order over chaos. Montuhotep spears hippos in the swamps, hunts desert animals, and defeats enemies in battle. He is also shown embraced by various deities and performing cult rituals. In another scene Montuhotep sits on his throne, which is adorned by the *sema-tawy* motif (the union of Upper and Lower Egypt), while the deities Seth and Nekhbet of Upper Egypt and Horus and Wadjit of Lower Egypt hand him the symbol of "millions of years." Montuhotep II reigned fifty-one years. He was succeeded by his second son, Montuhotep III.

SIGNIFICANCE

The unique plan of Montuhotep's mortuary temple was the inspiration for the basic plan of the mortuary complex of Hatshepsut (c. 1525-c. 1482 B.C.E.) that was built adjacent to it at Deir el-Bahri. His unification of Upper and Lower Egypt restored peace and prosperity and resulted in a resurgence of art, literature, and architecture of such high quality that the Middle Kingdom is generally considered the high point of Egyptian civilization.

—*Judith Lynn Sebesta*

FURTHER READING

Grimal, Nicolas. *A History of Ancient Egypt*. Boston: Blackwell Publishers, 1995. Discusses Montuhotep's reign within the overall political, cultural, and economic context of Egyptian history. Bibliography and index.

Habachi, Labib. "King Nebhetpetre Mentuhotpe: His Monuments, Place in History, Deification, and Unusual Representations in the Form of Gods." *Mitteilungen des Deutschen Archäologischen Instituts, Abteilung Kairo* 19 (1963): 16-52. Examines in detail his monuments and artifacts, titularies, inscriptions, and iconography as king and as deity.

Kemp, Barry J. *Ancient Egypt: Anatomy of a Civilization*. New York: Routledge, 1989. Examines city planning during the Middle Kingdom, including Thebes and Nubian forts, with detailed maps and plans. Bibliography and index.

Lichtheim, Miriam. *The Old and Middle Kingdoms.* Vol. 1 of *Ancient Egyptian Literature.* Berkeley: University of California Press, 1973. Lichtheim's translations are in clear English that give some idea of Egyptian style of phrasing. Each translation has a short preface describing the monument and aspects of the literary work and notes to the translation. The Middle Kingdom literature includes monumental inscriptions, coffin text, didactic literature, songs and hymns, and prose tales. Bibliography and indexes.

Parkinson, R. B., ed. and trans. *Voices from Ancient Egypt: An Anthology of Middle Kingdom Writings.* Norman: University of Oklahoma Press, 1991. Parkinson gives well-chosen selections from every kind of Middle Kingdom literature. His lucid translations include hymns, autobiographies, wisdom literature, etc., but also some "conversations" between workers in tomb wall-paintings (line-drawing of these paintings accompany these texts) as our best examples of "every-day" speech. His discussion of types of Egyptian writing systems and literary genres are clear even to the non-expert. Bibliography.

Robins, Gay. *The Art of Ancient Egypt.* Cambridge, Mass.: Harvard University Press, 1997. Extensively illustrated mostly with color photos, this volume surveys Egyptian art and architecture and covers the Middle Kingdom in two chapters. Bibliography and index.

Shaw, Ian, ed. *The Oxford History of Ancient Egypt.* New York: Oxford University Press, 2000. This well-illustrated volume provides detailed historical coverage of all of Egyptian history. The chapter on the Middle Kingdom (written by Gae Callender) examines in some detail the reign of Montuhotep II and includes information on Egyptian culture of the period.

Strudwick, Nigel, and Helen Strudwick. *Thebes in Egypt: A Guide to the Tombs and Temples of Ancient Luxor.* Ithaca, N.Y.: Cornell University Press, 1999. An in-depth survey of the monuments of Thebes, from prehistory through the post-dynastic period, with numerous photos (many in color), maps, and plans. The authors also include information on religious festivals and life in the city. Bibliography and index.

SEE ALSO: Akhenaton; Amenhotep III; Hatshepsut; Imhotep; Menes; Menkaure; Nefertiti; Psamtik I; Ramses II; Sesostris III; Thutmose III; Tiy; Tutankhamen; Zoser.

RELATED ARTICLES in *Great Events from History: The Ancient World*: c. 3050 B.C.E., Unification of Lower and Upper Egypt; c. 2687 B.C.E., Old Kingdom Period Begins in Egypt; c. 2575-c. 2566 B.C.E., Building of the Great Pyramid; c. 2160 B.C.E., First Intermediate Period Begins in Egypt; c. 2055 B.C.E., Middle Kingdom Period Begins in Egypt; c. 1650 B.C.E., Hyksos Create Second Intermediate Period.

MOSES
Hebrew religious leader

As the leader of tribal Israel who brought his people to the brink of nationhood in the thirteenth century B.C.E., Moses may be seen as the father of many governmental, social, and religious ideals that continue to influence the contemporary world. The codification of religious and ethical laws in the Pentateuch, the first five books of the Old Testament, is traditionally attributed to him.

BORN: c. 1300 B.C.E.; near Memphis, Egypt
DIED: c. 1200 B.C.E.; place unknown
AREAS OF ACHIEVEMENT: Religion, government and politics

EARLY LIFE

According to the biblical narrative, Moses (MOH-zuhz) was born to Jochebed, a Hebrew woman, during a period in which the children of Israel were under slavery to Egypt. The people of Israel had come to Egypt at the invitation of Joseph, one of Jacob's sons, who had become a prominent Egyptian leader in friendship with the pharaoh. Then, as the biblical text relates, "there arose a Pharaoh who knew not Joseph." As the Israelites grew in number and threatened the stability of Egyptian society, a more ruthless pharaoh began a policy of genocide toward newborn Hebrew boys (Ex. 1:22).

Immediately after Moses' birth, to spare him this fate his mother hid him in an arklike cradle and floated it down the Nile River, where it was discovered by an Egyptian princess who was bathing (Ex. 2:5-10). This princess found that Moses, whose name means "one drawn out of water," satisfied her longing for a son. Moses thus grew to manhood in the Egyptian palace, learning its language and culture, sheltered from his Hebrew heritage. Here he was exposed to the most sophisticated philosophies and science of the then known world, and he most likely learned how to write not only in the cuneiform and hieroglyphics of Egyptian textuality but also in the proto-Semitic alphabetic script known to have been used near Mount Sinai even before this historical period.

One day in his young adulthood, Moses was roused to justice on behalf of a Hebrew laborer who had been struck by an Egyptian (Ex. 2:11). In Moses' defense of this Hebrew, he killed the Egyptian; he was then forced into exile in Midian. There Moses began a new life with a wife, Zipporah, and family and tended the flock of his father-in-law, Jethro. It was evident that Moses' destiny lay in a higher calling, however, when the angel of the Lord appeared to him in a burning bush and then God spoke to Moses. He heard God's call to lead the Israelites out of Egyptian bondage (Ex. 3:1-17). In this divine commission, Moses was promised for his people a "land of milk and honey." It was during this encounter that God revealed his name to Moses as "Yahweh," or "I am that I am," the self-existing One who had chosen Israel to be his special people. Despite his initial hesitance, Moses accepted the call and was promised that his testimony would be corroborated with miracles.

Moses. (Library of Congress)

LIFE'S WORK

The first part of Moses' life had been exhilarating, as he grew from infancy to adulthood in a pharaoh's house. The remainder of his life, however, was spent in turmoil, verbal and physical warfare, and continuing challenges to his authority by his own people. On returning to Egypt, Moses called on his brother Aaron to accompany him and be his spokesman. In several bold and audacious audiences with the pharaoh, Moses demanded that the Egyptian leader free his people and allow them to worship Yahweh, who had called them to tabernacle at Mount Sinai. The pharaoh, amused by Moses' claim to authority and power, rejected his repeated pleas.

There ensued a series of ten plagues that brought Egyptian society to its knees, including the final plague—the death of the firstborn. That plague killed many Egyptian children while sparing the Hebrews, who had spread animal blood over their doorposts to avert the angel of death, who "passed over" them. This event came to be celebrated on the Hebrew holy day of Passover, which com-

memorates the preservation of the Hebrews and their deliverance from bondage in Egypt (Ex. 12-14).

When the pharaoh finally relented, Moses led his people in a mighty throng into the Red Sea, whose waters were miraculously parted for them and then closed on their Egyptian pursuers (Ex. 14-15). From their mountain encampment, Moses went to Mount Sinai for a momentous encounter with Yahweh, who revealed himself so spectacularly that Moses returned from the mountain with his countenance shining. The thunder and lightning that accompanied these events caused great fear among the people, and they asked Moses to be their intercessor lest they be consumed by Yahweh's omnipotence. Moses brought back to them the Covenant, a body of laws and relationships that was to bind Yahweh and the people of Israel together in a partnership (Ex. 19-20). Their task was to live in obedience to Yahweh's precepts—attributes of his holy character (justice, righteousness, peace, joy, and love)—for which he would continue to bless and protect them from their enemies. They were called on to acknowledge him as the only God and the surrounding civilizations as pagan and idolatrous.

Almost as soon as the people agreed to the covenant, they plunged into turmoil and rebellion. While Moses went to the mountain to receive further instruction from Yahweh, the people, impatient with Moses' absence, built a golden calf to worship, a reflection of their immaturity and naïveté and an action strictly forbidden by the covenant they had just ratified. Enraged at this apostasy, Moses returned from the mountain with vengeance, breaking the tablets on which the Ten Commandments had been written, destroying the idol, grinding it into powder, and forcing them to drink it. This lack of faith prefigured the continued disbelief and sin of the people, as the generation of Israelites who first left Egypt were destined to falter in their journey, never reaching the land promised them when Moses was called to God's service in Midian. During this time, however, Moses continued to meet with Yahweh and continued to build a record of Israel's experiences with this God who had brought them out of Egypt. Among the things that were presented to the people were the plans for building a tabernacle for worship, an elaborate ecclesiastical structure. Detailed specifications for its construction and use in the corporate life and worship of the Jewish people were supplied.

The other pivotal event in the history of this first generation who left Egypt is recounted in the Book of Numbers. Moses sent spies into the land of Canaan to determine when and how the Israelites might occupy the land promised to them by Yahweh. Of the twelve spies sent out, only two, Joshua and Caleb, brought a positive report. As a result, only Joshua and Caleb and their families were eventually permitted to enter Canaan. The other members of the first generation were refused entry by God as a result of their disbelief.

The Book of Deuteronomy records Moses' farewell speeches to the generation of Israel who would enter the Promised Land—a reiteration of the first covenant and an exhortation to obey the God who had called them out of bondage. In recounting the blessings and cursings that were to accrue to the Israelites, depending on their behavior, Moses advised, "I have set before thee this day, both death and life. Choose life" (Deut. 30:19).

Moses' egotism, briefly revealed in the biblical narrative, eventually prevented Aaron and Moses themselves from entering Canaan. During one trying episode, Moses became frustrated with the Israelites' continual bickering about the availability of food and water. At one point, Moses exclaimed, "Hear now, you rebels; shall we bring forth water for you out of this rock?" (Num. 20:10), thus presumptuously attributing to himself the power to provide for Israel's needs. This sin weighed heavily on Moses toward the end of his life. Psalm 90 in the Old Testament Book of Psalms is attributed to Moses; it contains this bittersweet comment on the brevity of life: "Thou dost sweep men away; they are like a dream, like grass which is renewed in the morning: in the morning it flourishes and is renewed; in the evening it fades and withers. For we are consumed by thy anger; by thy wrath we are overwhelmed."

Near the end of his days, Moses passed the mantle of leadership over to his aging comrade, Joshua, who would lead Israel into the land that had been promised. A heroic and dutiful life was then brought to rest with a series of blessings that Moses pronounced on the people of Israel. The concluding words of Deuteronomy offer this understated editorial judgment: "There has not arisen a prophet since in Israel like Moses, whom the Lord knew face to face" (Deut. 34:10).

SIGNIFICANCE

The law of Moses, his written legacy to subsequent generations, is matched only by Greek and Roman poetics and rhetoric in its impact on Western culture. Whatever editorial interventions there may have been over the centuries, it is clear that the five books of Moses—Genesis, Exodus, Leviticus, Numbers, and Deuteronomy—were intended to be histories of the Jewish people, beginning with the creation of the heavens and the earth. As a slave people fresh from redemption, this fledgling nation had few common experiences and little religious identity to bind them. Consequently, the Mosaic account of God's decision to choose the people of Israel as the blessed descendants of Abraham and to allow them to influence many civilizations can be seen as a primary attempt to solidify their nationhood during a precarious time. Moses' narrative gives the people of Israel a historical and moral vantage point from which to interpret their past and present experiences and, most important, to give praise to Yahweh, who called them out of Egypt to worship Him.

The religious foundation begun in the codification of legal and moral teaching became the scaffolding for Christianity, as Jesus Christ and his followers directly traced their heritage not only to Abraham but also to Moses. During his ministry, Jesus claimed to have come to fulfill the law of Moses and to inaugurate a new covenant of grace that would subsume and complete the covenants made with Abraham, Isaac, and Jacob. Islam, whose sacred text is the Qur'an, also owes much of its message to the framework established in the works attributed to Moses. Muhammad, the Prophet of Islam, claimed Abraham and Moses as his forerunners, proclaiming that he and his message stood in the same historical and intellectual genealogy as theirs.

It is not difficult to understand the nearly universal recognition of Moses as a pivotal leader in history. He was holy and devout, a man of action and contemplation, a diplomat and military strategist, and a shrewd political adviser. In witnessing the ongoing direct and indirect influences of Mosaic thought in contemporary Judaism, Christianity, and Islam as well as the continuing political significance of the lands that he helped secure and develop for his people, one must conclude that, indeed, Moses was a man of remarkable gifts.

—*Bruce L. Edwards*

FURTHER READING

Alexander, David, and Pat Alexander, eds. *Eerdmans' Handbook to the Bible*. Grand Rapids, Mich.: Wm. B. Eerdmans, 1987. A comprehensive handbook to biblical history and geography, with helpful interpretations that trace the history of Israel under Moses' leadership and rise to power in the ancient Middle East. Particularly useful are maps and word studies that illuminate Israel's relationships with Egypt and other Middle Eastern nations of 1400-1200 B.C.E.

Bright, John. *A History of Israel*. 4th ed. Louisville, Ky.: Westminster J. Knox Press, 2000. A thorough and compelling nontheological treatment of the history of Israel. Sections on the kingdoms and civilizations contemporary with Moses illuminate the story of his life and sustain the interest of both the common reader and the scholar.

Friedman, Richard Elliot. *Who Wrote the Bible?* San Francisco: HarperSanFrancisco, 1997. Friedman is representative of the majority of modern biblical scholars in rejecting Mosaic authorship of the Pentateuch. In this book, Friedman draws on a synthesis of scholarship to present his own, controversial answer to the question of authorship. Includes notes and a bibliography; lightly illustrated.

Harrison, R. K. *An Introduction to the Old Testament*. Grand Rapids, Mich.: Wm. B. Eerdmans, 1972. An overview of the origin, message, and impact of each book in the Old Testament. The volume addresses directly and comprehensively the issues of the chronology, authenticity, and influence of the life of Moses on the people of Israel in ancient times and in the present. A massive, comprehensive scholarly work with extensive documentation.

Kitchen, K. A. *The Bible in Its World*. Downers Grove, Ill.: Inter-Varsity Press, 1977. An insider's look at the world of archaeology and how it functions in validating ancient records and narratives. Particularly helpful in its extensive examination of antiquity's cultural artifacts and social conditions against the backdrop of the age of Moses and his people's sojourns in Egypt and wanderings in the wilderness.

Schultz, Samuel J. *The Old Testament Speaks*. San Francisco: Harper & Row, 1990. Written for the lay reader, this volume presents an objective historical analysis of the lives of the patriarchs. Includes a major section on Moses and the Pentateuch and their role in the evolution of ancient and modern Israel.

Thompson, J. A. *Handbook to Life in Bible Times*. Downers Grove, Ill.: Inter-Varsity Press, 1986. A colorful, lavishly illustrated reference tool with key sections on the domestic life, travel, family customs, and cultural preoccupations of the biblical world. The work illuminates the birth of Israel and its development under Moses' theological and political leadership.

Wenham, John. "Moses and the Pentateuch." In *New Bible Commentary: Revised*, edited by Donald Guthrie, Alec Moyer, Alan Stibbs, and Donald Wiseman. Grand Rapids, Mich.: Wm. B. Eerdmans, 1970. A concise and singularly wise assessment of the career of Moses, his personality and leadership qualities, and his continuing impact on both Jewish and Christian thought.

SEE ALSO: Aaron; Abraham; David; Jesus; Solomon.

RELATED ARTICLES in *Great Events from History: The Ancient World*: c. 1280 B.C.E., Israelite Exodus from Egypt; c. 1000 B.C.E., Establishment of the United Kingdom of Israel; c. 922 B.C.E., Establishment of the Kingdom of Israel.

MOZI

Chinese philosopher

Mozi founded the school of Mohism, which promoted beliefs in public ideals and meritocracy, contributing to the rise of the first empire in China (221 B.C.E.).

BORN: c. 470 B.C.E.; China
DIED: c. 391 B.C.E.; China
ALSO KNOWN AS: Mo-tzu (Wade-Giles); Mo Ti (Wade-Giles), Mo Di (Pinyin); Motze; Motse Meh Tzu; Mih Tzu; Micius (Latin)
AREAS OF ACHIEVEMENT: Philosophy, religion

EARLY LIFE

Virtually nothing is known of the life and background of Mozi (maw-dzih). Some scholars believe that he had been trained early in the Confucian school before he broke away to start his own line of thought. This claim, however, cannot be confirmed by the historical record; the earliest statement of the claim dates from three centuries after Mozi's life. On the basis of Mozi's known support for social mobility and the possible meanings for his name—"Mo" refers to ink—some scholars speculate that Mozi came from a lower-class background, possibly that of an artisan or craftsman, or even that of an erstwhile criminal (taking "mo" as a reference to the branding of criminals).

Such speculations seem to agree with the general tenor of Mozi's advocacy of ideas and institutions that hoped to eliminate contemporary practices of nepotism and the consolidation of power among a hereditary elite class. These speculations also make sense in light of the frequent references in Mohist writings to tools and the construction of objects as a metaphor for how to govern and act properly. However, since there is no explicit, reliable textual evidence concerning Mozi's personal background, it remains impossible to say with certainty that he stemmed from the lower class.

LIFE'S WORK

Mozi did not leave behind any writings of his own, and it is not known whether he even transmitted his ideas in written form. His thoughts are preserved today in the writings of his disciples and the many later followers and contemporaries of his school during the Warring States period (475-221 B.C.E.). These writings are collected in a text known as *Mozi* (fifth century B.C.E.; *The Ethical and Political Works of Motse*, 1929; also known as *Mo Tzu: Basic Writings*, 1963). Because of the impersonal, public style of the Mohist writings, there is very little in the corpus that reflects aspects of Mozi's life. Rather, accounts of his sayings recorded by his disciples convey a vivid sense of his religious, philosophical, and political orientations.

Much more can be said about Mohist schools of thought, which all claimed Mozi as their founder. The schools of Mohism rivaled the thought of the followers of Confucius (Kong Qiu; 551-479 B.C.E.) for centuries until the sudden disappearance of the school in the second century B.C.E. The disappearance of the school coincided with the rise of the Qin and Han Dynasties (221 B.C.E.-220 C.E.).

Mohists are mentioned sporadically in a few texts of the late Zhou (fourth-third centuries B.C.E.) and early Han (second century B.C.E.) periods, both in conjunction with Mozi and in connection with later groups, cultlike in organization, whose writings were much more specialized than those of their predecessors. Scholars refer to the "early Mohists" as those men who were responsible for leaving behind the earliest, core chapters of the Mohist text. These men were thought to be the direct disciples of the Master Mo himself, although the writings could possibly incorporate the words of one more generation of followers.

Early Mohists assembled together in groups according to a rigid hierarchy, all paying allegiance to their leader, known as the *juzi*. Since the structure of group was comparable to that of a military organization, Mohist groups fall more easily into the category of "schools" than any other early Chinese intellectual tradition. Mohist schools, both early and later, were spread out throughout many different states of the then multistate cultural and economic sphere. They functioned in society as cohesive military, religious, and intellectual units, renowned for acting out their values of loyalty and integrity to an extreme degree.

Early Mohists also became famous for their stance in opposition to certain Confucian practices of the day. The core chapters, which best represent the thought of the earlier schools, expound on ten basic precepts associated with the Mohist point of view. These precepts include such things as "universal caring," adherence to "heaven's will," "denying fatalism," "denouncing music," "elevating the achieved," "elevating conformity," and "negating the Confucians." The chapters against Confucian practices criticize elaborate burial practices and musical performances supported by Confucian ritual beliefs. Early Mohist criticism of music and burial practices is rooted in a belief that these practices demand the use of precious resources of the state and society that might otherwise be put to better use in maintaining social order and promoting the well-being of people. These chapters especially reveal Mozi's extreme tendencies toward frugality and political pragmatism, which permeate his philosophy.

Even the style of writing in the core chapters reflects a frugal aesthetic. Attributed to Mozi is the belief that flourishes and elements of literary style represent excessive additives that only detract from the truth. Whether consciously achieved or not, then, the core chapters themselves are notoriously terse, dry, and repetitive. At the same time, these chapters represent the first attempts known by early Chinese writers to establish a logical basis for utilizing and analyzing evidence that constitutes truth. Since these chapters express themselves in a fundamentally different way from the extant writings of the early Warring States, the prose style of the core chapters cannot be dismissed or neglected, despite its blunt style.

Another significant preoccupation of the early Mohists, continued by later proponents of their school, was with defensive warfare. Since the philosophy of Mozi condemns both the logic and practice of aggressive warfare, Mohists took up arms so as to dutifully aid those kingdoms under attack in their defense of regional aggressors. In such a manner, the Mohists found themselves embroiled in defensive warfare so as to act out their opposition to aggressive warfare. In addition to fighting for kingdoms under siege, later Mohists composed treatises on defensive warfare that provide fascinating details concerning the construction of defensive structures such as city walls.

Later Mohists, who lived and wrote from about 300 to 200 B.C.E., diverged quite radically from their predecessors. These groups occupied themselves primarily with specialized matters of defense and the linguistic and logical foundations of thought, knowledge, and speech. In the latter capacity, they became known for their achievements and prowess in dialectic, and they joined other thinkers, later known as Sophists, or members of the "School of Names," in actively engaging in formal, public debates held at court. Such debates came to represent a fairly standard means for intellectuals of the third century B.C.E. to engage in court politics and sway rulers and ministers to line up with their own ways of thinking. Writings on disputation and logic that stem from the later Mohists are represented in the Mohist "Canons" and "Explanations," along with smaller, isolated chapters transmitted as part of the Mohist corpus.

The last twenty chapters of the Mohist corpus constitute the literary works of the later Mohists on warfare.

These chapters focus heavily on engineering projects involving defensive structures. Inquiries into the more scientific and mathematical subjects of optics, geometry, mechanics, economics, and even traces of astronomy can be found throughout the "Canons." The epistemology of the Mohists appears to be grounded in a belief that objective truth exists and can be made intelligible through examination, study, and language. Hence, their detailed involvement in a wide array of practical topics in addition to disputation.

SIGNIFICANCE

Mozi is renowned for his sage wisdom and irreproachable behavior. He is also known as an ethicist and political philosopher who advocated a radical ideology of utilitarianism and universal human adherence to objective standards of Heavenly law. This ideology makes an explicit appeal to a meritocratic system of government appointment, which subsequently became associated more primarily with Legalist philosophies (writings on statecraft), and eventually became one of the benchmarks for empire in China at the beginning of the Three Kingdoms period (220-280 C.E.). Mohist ideology also makes an appeal to a new concept of "universal caring," which recommends that individuals extend their concern for people in their most private sphere to those stemming from a more impersonal and public realm.

Mozi's religious views are significant as well. While he upholds many traditional Zhou beliefs in the efficacy of ghosts and spirits as agents of heaven, Mozi also presents an extreme interpretation of heaven as an absolute moral force in the world. This latter vision is distinctive in the early Warring States period (475-221 B.C.E.) of the Zhou Dynasty because it supports a heavily monotheistic orientation that links individual human behavior directly with heavenly reward and punishment.The writings of the early Mohists reflect a singular interest in ethics and political philosophy. Early Mohist thought, which allegedly represents the teachings of Master Mo, is known for its advocacy of a type of utilitarianism centering around the concept of *li:* profit or benefit. This utilitarianism is grounded in a belief that heaven's system of justice translates into standards of behavior that can be measured through a calculus for bringing benefit to people. The early Mohist emphasis on the importance of having standards that can be defined and measured becomes apparent through such a claim.

Early Mohist ethical and political philosophy had a profound effect on politics and culture of the Warring States. Mencius (c. 372-c. 289 B.C.E.), a later Confucian lamented that the words of Mozi and of Yangzhu (known for his egoistic philosophy of the self) dominated the culture of his day. Mohist beliefs in meritocracy were absorbed so thoroughly in politics that they eventually became disassociated with the Mohist school and ascribed to general views on statecraft (Legalism). Indeed, some scholars speculate that the primary reason for the sudden demise of the Mohist school around 200 B.C.E. can be attributed to the fact that their beliefs enjoyed such popularity that they became absorbed into intellectual culture and mitigated against the necessity of having a Mohist school at all. None of this can be confirmed without more data on the particular contexts and circumstances surrounding their demise.

Mohism did not end with the demise of the school around 200 B.C.E. The writings of the Mohists were largely neglected for two millennia, until the influx of Western influences in China helped spark a renewed interest in the scientific foundations of China's past. Despite this neglect, it is undeniable that Mozi and his many schools played an integral part in the course of philosophical and political development during the critical period of empire-making. The influence of the Mohist concepts of meritocracy and objective law on the growth of empire cannot be overlooked, as it constitutes a lasting contribution to the shape of thought and institutions in imperial China and East Asia at large.

—Erica Brindley

FURTHER READING

Fung, Yu-lan. *A History of Chinese Philosophy.* Translated by Derk Bodde. 2 vols. Princeton, N.J.: Princeton University Press, 1967. Thorough overview of Chinese philosophy that includes a narrative of the Mohists and their place in the history of early thought.

Graham, A. C. *Disputers of the Tao: Philosophical Argument in Ancient China.* LaSalle, Ill.: Open Court, 1989. Provides one of the best discussions of the role of Mohist thought as a radical reaction to contemporary debates of the time.

_____. *Divisions in Early Mohism Reflected in the Core Chapters of Mo-tzu.* Singapore: Institute of East Asian Philosophies, 1985. Argues for the division of Mohist schools of thought on the basis of apparent differences in the Mohist corpus.

_____. *Later Mohist Logic, Ethics, and Science.* Hong Kong: Chinese University Press, 1978. A most thorough discussion of the later Mohist "Canon," its "Explanations," and other treatises that attest to the depth of later Mohist involvement in science and language, as well as more standard ethical pursuits.

Hu, Shih. *The Development of the Logical Method in Ancient China.* 2d ed. New York: Paragon, 1963. A twentieth century Chinese thinker's restatement of the value of China's own past. This view makes a claim for the indigenous roots of logic as reflected in Mohist writings of the classical period.

Schwartz, Benjamin. *The World of Thought in Ancient China.* Cambridge, Mass.: Harvard University Press, 1985. Provides a very good overview of early Chinese thought that includes Mohist concerns and pursuits.

Watson, Burton, trans. *Basic Writings of Mo Tzu, Hsün Tzu, and Han Fei Tzu.* New York: Columbia University Press, 1964. Selected translations of the core chapters of early Mohist ethical writings.

SEE ALSO: Confucius; Hanfeizi; Laozi; Mencius.

RELATED ARTICLES in *Great Events from History: The Ancient World*: 475-221 B.C.E., China Enters Chaotic Warring States Period; Early 4th century B.C.E., Founding of Mohism; c. 285-c. 255 B.C.E, Xunzi Develops Teachings That Lead to Legalism; 221-206 B.C.E., Legalist Movement in China; 221 B.C.E., Qin Dynasty Founded in China.

NABU-RIMANNI
Babylonian astronomer and mathematician

Nabu-rimanni copied and preserved astronomical tables for the computation of lunar, solar, and planetary phenomena. These accurate numerical parameters for the prediction of astronomical phenomena furthered the development and success of Greek spherical astronomy, developed to its fullest in the Ptolemaic system.

BORN: Early first century B.C.E.; probably Babylonia (now in Iraq)
DIED: Late first century B.C.E.; probably Babylonia
ALSO KNOWN AS: Nuburianos; Naburiannuos; Naburiannu; Naburimannu; Naburimani
AREA OF ACHIEVEMENT: Astronomy

EARLY LIFE

Because the nature of Babylonian sources is such that authors and authorship remain obscure, it is not possible to reconstruct for Nabu-rimanni (nah-BEW rih-MAHN-nee) a biography in the strict sense. The historical period with which he is associated, however, may be sketched. While Nabu-rimanni flourished in the mid-first century B.C.E., one may also define this period more broadly, that is, from roughly 300 B.C.E. to the beginning of the common era, as the Hellenistic period. As a result of the spread of Greek political influence across the Near Eastern territories once belonging to the empires of Persia, Babylonia, and Assyria, this era produced notable cultural and intellectual change from the cities of mainland Greece to Egypt in the south and Mesopotamia in the east. In particular, science flowered in Hellenistic intellectual centers such as Alexandria, and Greek astronomy, which had already begun in the fifth century, reached its height during the Hellenistic period, in part as a result of the transmission of astronomical knowledge from Mesopotamia.

LIFE'S WORK

The Hellenistic authors Strabo (64 or 63 B.C.E.-c. 25 C.E.) and Pliny the Elder (23-79 C.E.), who traveled and produced encyclopedic compendia of the knowledge and customs of the day, mention Babylonian astronomical "schools" and a few of the Babylonian astronomers by name. Thus, one finds in book 16 of Strabo's *Geōgraphia* (c. 7 B.C.E.; *Geography*, 1917-1933) the name Naburianos (Nabu-rimmani), and also Kidenas, Sudines, and Seleucus, all associated with Babylonian cities such as Babylon, Uruk, and possibly Borsippa. Nabu-rimanni's

particular or distinguishing role in the history of Babylonian astronomy, however, cannot be determined either from the Greek account or from Babylonian cuneiform sources.

Cuneiform texts yield information about the scribes only in the colophons at the ends of the inscriptions. These colophons, when complete, note the names of the owner of the document and the scribe who copied it as well as the date the tablet was written and who was king at the time. Nabu-rimanni's name is preserved on the colophon of an astronomical tablet from Babylon. The only fact, therefore, that can be established about him from Babylonian sources is that he was a scribe who copied, or possibly computed, a table of dates and positions in the sky of new and full moons for the year 49-48 B.C.E.

This particular colophon is the source for the claim that Nabu-rimanni was the inventor of the method of astronomical computation represented in his tablet. Far from showing this scribe as an innovator of Babylonian astronomy, however, Nabu-rimanni's tablet is one of the youngest of Babylonian lunar ephemerides; the oldest such tablets stem from the third century. Nabu-rimanni can therefore be credited only with preserving the tradition of Babylonian astronomy, not inventing it.

Because Nabu-rimanni is associated with a particular method of astronomical computation, but his individual contribution cannot be determined from the sources, the focus of any examination of his life's work must be Babylonian astronomy itself. Babylonian mathematical astronomy of the last three centuries B.C.E. is known from only two identifiable archives, one found in Babylon and the other in Uruk. The bulk of the texts are lunar or planetary ephemerides, which are supplemented by a smaller group of procedure texts outlining the steps necessary to generate ephemeris tables. The ephemeris tables contain parallel columns of numbers in specific sequences that represent occurrences of characteristic lunar and planetary phenomena. Each column represents a different periodic phenomenon—for example, new moons, eclipses, first visibilities, stationary points. The consecutive entries in each column correspond to dates, usually months. In the case of the ephemeris for the moon, the objective is to predict the evening of the first visibility of the lunar crescent. The appearance of the new moon defines the beginning of the month in a strictly lunar calendar. Indeed, the control of the calendar seems to have provided a major motivation for the development of mathematical methods for predicting astronomical phenomena.

For calculations, the Babylonians used a number system of base 60; that is, numbers are represented with special digits from 1 to 59, while 60, or any power of 60, is represented by 1. These "sexagesimal" numbers were written using a place-value notation system similar to decimal notation, so that for each place a digit is moved to the left, the value is multiplied by 60. The positional system was extended for fractions, which were expressed by moving digits to the right of the "ones" place, thereby dividing each time by 60. The Babylonian sexagesimal system is still preserved in the counting of time by hours, minutes (1 hour equals 60 minutes), and seconds (1 minute equals 60 seconds).

Babylonian lunar and planetary theory comprised two separate but coexistent systems, designated A and B, which are defined according to two different arithmetical methods of describing the distance covered each month by the sun. In this way, the velocity of the sun could be measured in terms of the progress of the sun in longitude, or degrees along its apparent path through the stars, the ecliptic. In system A, the progress of the sun along the ecliptic is described as being 30° per (mean synodic) month for one part of the zodiac (from Virgo 13° to Pisces 27°) and 28° 7′30″ for the other part (from Pisces 27° to Virgo 13°). A mathematical model is thereby created whereby the sun moves with two separate constant velocities on two arcs of the ecliptic. If the sun's velocity, reckoned in terms of progress in longitude (degrees along the ecliptic), is plotted against time, the resulting graph represents a "step function." System A also implies a certain length of the solar year, namely 1 year equals 12;22,8 months, expressed sexagesimally. (Sexagesimal numbers are represented in modern notation with a semicolon separating integers from fractions.) This method and its complementary system B were both used during the period from c. 250 B.C.E. to c. 50 B.C.E.

System B assumes the motion of the sun to increase and decrease its speed steadily from month to month. The variation in velocity is bounded by a minimum and a maximum value, and within this range of velocities, the monthly change is always by a constant amount. Plotting the progress of the sun by this model produces a graph representing a "linear zig-zag function." The name Kidenas, mentioned by Strabo, Pliny, and Vettius Valens (second century C.E.), may be associated with System B, as a scribe by the name of Ki-di-nu (Kidinnu) is known from colophons of system B-type ephemerides for the years 104-101 B.C.E. The Greeks credited him with derivation of the relation that 251 synodic months equals 269 anomalistic months. This numerical relation is in fact seen in system B computations.

Systems A and B constitute theoretical mathematical models of the motion of the sun that account for the varying lengths of the seasons of the year. By analogy with solar motion, the methods of systems A and B were applied to many celestial phenomena of a cyclic character. A Babylonian lunar table deals with the determination of conjunctions and oppositions of sun and moon, first and last visibilities, and eclipses, all of which are cyclic phenomena. Planetary tables for the planets Jupiter, Venus, Saturn, Mercury, and Mars predict the dates and positions in the zodiac of the cyclic appearances of planets, such as first visibilities, oppositions, stationary points, and last visibilities. The fact that each phenomenon had its own period enabled the Babylonians to compute them independently. No general theory of planetary and lunar motion was needed, as the strictly arithmetical methods of the two systems were sufficient to predict the individual appearances of the heavenly bodies.

The goal of Babylonian astronomy was, therefore, to predict when the moon or planets would be visible. In contrast, the Greeks' goal was to develop a single model that would serve to describe and account for the motion of celestial bodies in a general sense, and from which the individual appearances of celestial bodies would follow as a consequence. The achievement of this goal was found in geometrical methods and kinematic models (explaining motion), developed by Apollonius of Perga (third century B.C.E.) and perfected by Ptolemy in *Mathēmatikē suntaxis* (c. 150 C.E.; *Almagest*, 1948). Such geometrical concepts are not found in Babylonian astronomy.

The question of the identity of the Babylonian astronomers is not answered by the cuneiform astronomical texts. One scribe is hardly distinguished from another when the extent of one's information is the appearance of the scribe's name in a text colophon. Nevertheless, the question as to the significance of the scribes Nabu-rimanni and Kidinnu, whose names are remembered by later Greek and Roman authors, remains. The belief that they were the inventors of the systems A and B gains no support from the cuneiform texts. Indeed, the establishment of dates for the invention of systems A and B has proved difficult; thus, statements concerning the origins of Babylonian mathematical astronomy, in regard to both chronology and the role of individual scribes, must for the time being remain inconclusive.

SIGNIFICANCE

Babylonian lunar and planetary theory became the foundation for the development and further refinement of astronomy by the Greek astronomers Apollonius, Hipparchus, and Ptolemy. In very general terms, one can enumerate the various Babylonian contributions to Greek astronomy and thereby to the development of science in general as follows.

About 300 to 200 B.C.E., the Greek astronomers adopted the Babylonian sexagesimal number system for their computations and for measuring time and angles (360 degrees in a circle with degrees divisible by minutes and seconds). The use of arithmetical methods characteristic of Babylonian astronomical tables continued, particularly in the procedures used by Hellenistic astrologers. While Greek astronomical theory depended on geometrical and kinematic models, neither of which was used in Babylonian astronomy, the parameters used in constructing those models were Babylonian. Indeed, the success of Greek astronomical theory rests on the accuracy of the parameters established by Babylonian astronomers (such as the length of the solar year given above).

The concepts related to the parameters must also have been transmitted. Such concepts were, for example, the following components of lunar motion: longitude, latitude (angular distance of the moon from the ecliptic), anomaly (irregularity in motion), and the motion from east to west of the line of nodes (the two diametrically opposed points where the moon's orbital plane intersects the plane of the ecliptic) in a nineteen-year cycle.

Also of use for Greek planetary theory were the period relations essential to the determination of successive occurrences of a periodic phenomenon in Babylonian astronomy. Through the wide acceptance of the Ptolemaic tradition, as evidenced by Indian and Islamic astronomy, the direct influence of Babylonian astronomy on the Greek world had even greater impact as the ultimate impetus for the quantitative approach to celestial phenomena.

—*Francesca Rochberg-Halton*

FURTHER READING

Aaboe, Asger. "Observation and Theory in Babylonian Astronomy." *Centaurus* 24 (1980): 14-35. Suggests a reconstruction of the process by which the Babylonian systems of computing astronomical phenomena were developed.

_____. "Scientific Astronomy in Antiquity." In *The Place of Astronomy in the Ancient World*, edited by F. R. Hodson. London: Oxford University Press, 1974. Summary and explanation of the mathematical content of the Babylonian astronomical ephemerides and discussion of what constitutes a "scientific" astronomy.

Hunger, Hermann, and David Pingree. *Astral Sciences in Mesopotamia*. New York: Brill, 1999. This account of the beginnings of astronomy and astrology in the ancient Near East discusses the place a given tablet has in the development of astronomy both within Mesopotamian culture and outside it.

Neugebauer, Otto, ed. *Astronomical Cuneiform Texts*. New York: Springer Verlag, 1983. A transliteration and translation of the cuneiform astronomical texts, accompanied by an analysis.

_____. *The Exact Sciences in Antiquity*. 2d ed. New York: Dover, 1969. Concise history of mathematics and astronomy in Babylonia, Egypt, and Greece.

Van der Waerden, B. L. *The Birth of Astronomy*. Vol. 2 in *Science Awakening*. 4th ed. Princeton, N.J.: Scholar's Bookshelf, 1988. More accessible and less technical but also less reliable than Neugebauer. Gives an overall account of the phenomena of interest in Babylonian mathematical as well as pre-mathematical astronomy.

SEE ALSO: Anaximander; Apollonius of Perga; Hipparchus; Ptolemy (astronomer); Pythagoras; Sosigenes.

RELATED ARTICLES in *Great Events from History: The Ancient World*: c. 500-470 B.C.E., Hecataeus of Miletus Writes the First Geography Book; 325-323 B.C.E., Aristotle Isolates Science as a Discipline; c. 300 B.C.E., Euclid Compiles a Treatise on Geometry; c. 275 B.C.E., Greeks Advance Hellenistic Astronomy.

NEBUCHADNEZZAR II
Babylonian king (r. 605-562 B.C.E.)

One of the most ambitious and successful military leaders of ancient times, Nebuchadnezzar possessed excellent governing ability that made Chaldean Neo-Babylonia the most powerful and feared nation in the region.

BORN: c. 630 B.C.E.; place unknown
DIED: 562 B.C.E.; Babylon (now in Iraq)
ALSO KNOWN AS: Nabū-kudūrri-uṣur (Akkadian); Nabuchodonosor or Nabugodonosor (Greek); Nebuchadrezzar
AREAS OF ACHIEVEMENT: War and conquest, government and politics, religion

EARLY LIFE

Nebuchadnezzar (nehb-ew-kahd-NEHZ-ehr) II, the eldest son of Nabopolassar, king of the Chaldean Neo-Babylonians, who reigned from 625 to 605, entered the world's military arena in the early 600's. As crown prince, he led Chaldean forces against the remnants of the Assyrian army and a sizable Egyptian contingent in the decisive Battle of Carchemish, fought in what is modern Syria. For the remainder of his life, Nebuchadnezzar expanded on his father's conquests, until Babylonia was the richest, most prominent, and most renowned nation in the ancient world.

Nevertheless, his exploits, considerable though they were, would not have been so well known to later generations if he had not been the monarch who burned and looted Jerusalem, forcing its most able inhabitants into temporary exile in Babylonia. By so doing, Nebuchadnezzar unwittingly fulfilled the prophecies of Jeremiah, the most noted Jewish prophet of the time. Thus, the Bible has preserved the Babylonian ruler's most notable accomplishments.

After he succeeded his father as king in 605, Nebuchadnezzar gave the city of Babylon its most famous feature, the Hanging Gardens, as well as fiery furnaces used both for commercial enterprises and for the torture and destruction of Babylonia's foes; its grand celebrations of Marduk, Babylon's patron god, and the goddess Ishtar; and its huge brick outer walls, which dominated the desert for many miles. With these gifts, Nebuchadnezzar transformed Babylon from a dusty, shabby provincial city into an elegant world capital. With no remaining Assyrian enemy to engage and no significant Egyptian threat to counter, Nebuchadnezzar turned his attention not only to the rebuilding of Babylon but also to its terri-

torial expansion. He and his architects created enormous stepped ziggurats for the glory of Marduk and Ishtar, while he planned further forays against neighboring states.

Using the Code of Hammurabi as his basis, Nebuchadnezzar created a stable, generally lawful Babylonian society. Criminals faced severe penalties ranging from torture to death. The most notorious punishments, however, were reserved for enemy rulers and their retainers; on capture, these people were often flayed alive, partially dismembered, and cast alive into the furnaces, or were blinded and had gold clasps affixed to their tongues; with a leash attached to the clasp, the afflicted could be led around Babylon. By rigidly adhering to the Code of Hammurabi, Nebuchadnezzar reinforced his reputation for ferocity.

LIFE'S WORK

The battles that occurred after the flight of the Egyptian army brought many victories to the Chaldeans; each victory brought destruction and death to the vanquished tribe or nation. In 601 Nebuchadnezzar's forces were defeated by Necho II, the king of Egypt, an event that elevated the hopes of the kingdom of Judaea. Although Jehoiakim, appointed king of Judah by the pharaoh, had once submitted to Nebuchadnezzar, he had shortly thereafter covertly joined forces with the Egyptians in order to war against Babylonia. Jeremiah, one of the principal Old Testament prophets, warned his people that God intended to punish them for their worship of foreign gods and for their allegiance to Egypt.

Nebuchadnezzar fulfilled Jeremiah's prophecy by marching on Judah and its largest city in 597. King Jehoiakim had died before the city was captured, but Nebuchadnezzar took his son Jehoiachin into Babylonian exile. Later, in 586, after an eighteen-month siege, Jerusalem was burned and its leading citizens were sent into exile. As much as possible, Nebuchadnezzar attempted to erase all signs of Jewish civilization from the former kingdom. Zedekiah, the ruler of Judah-in-exile, paid for his dealings with Egypt by being blinded after witnessing the murder of his sons by Babylonian captors.

The enslavement of the Jews was nothing like the total servitude they had faced centuries before when Egyptian pharaohs forced them to make bricks for the pyramids and treated them like beasts of burden. Nebuchadnezzar, while never allowing them to return home, did allow them many freedoms, including the rights to work at trades and to mingle freely with the populace of Babylon. Still, the Jews were a miserable people who dreamed of one day going back to their ancestral towns and villages. In their midst was the prophet Ezekiel, Jeremiah's counterpart. Ezekiel prophesied that the Jews would be delivered from Babylonian captivity by a great king from the East, a vision that came true when Cyrus the Great of Persia invaded Babylon in the year 539.

After the destruction of Jerusalem and the capture and blinding of Zedekiah in 586, Nebuchadnezzar sent his armies against the Egyptians once again, finally capturing the important Phoenician city of Tyre in 571, thus adding considerably to the wealth, power, and authority of Babylonia. With Egyptian influence flagging, Babylonia became the unquestioned power of Asia Minor. Commerce with surrounding nations accompanied the empire's ascent as Babylon became the mercantile center of western Asia. With a storehouse of gold, silver, and precious

gems taken as tribute from vassal nations, Babylon could buy and trade virtually any commodity.

Nebuchadnezzar made certain that waterways and highways were constructed, making the city readily accessible to the heavy trade flowing into it. His earlier building program was intensified in the middle years of his reign so that Babylon would be an impregnable fortress as well as a center of commerce. The temples and ziggurats were made enormous, and the city walls rose higher, decorated with enameled figures of beasts. The Hanging Gardens were made even more elaborate so that the king and his harem could enjoy the delights of a large oasis in the middle of a desert city.

Little is known about the last years of Nebuchadnezzar. The final major event to occur before he faded from history was a battle with the Median leader Cyaxares, who had sacked Uratu and headed toward the kingdom of Lydia, which was close enough to Babylonian territory to make Nebuchadnezzar uneasy. Bitter fighting ended in May, 585, when darkness caused by a solar eclipse enveloped the Medes and the Neo-Babylonians; the event was interpreted as a sign from the gods to stop fighting. A truce was signed; nevertheless, the Medians remained a source of anxiety for Nebuchadnezzar.

There is much speculation about his final days. Some scholars believe that he gradually grew weary of the burdens of kingship and retired from active life, others that he may have suffered from senility or even mental illness. Perhaps the best-known source for the latter theory is the biblical account of Daniel, in which the king of Babylon is depicted as an insane old man, an eater of grass. In any event, his immediate successor, his son Evil-Merodach, the man he had hoped would continue his life's work in Babylonia, died in 559 (or, as some accounts have it, 560) after being overthrown. The short-lived Chaldean Dynasty founded by Nebuchadnezzar's father finally ended with the death of Nabonidus in 539, when Cyrus's army swept into Babylon and established Achaemenid rule.

SIGNIFICANCE

Nebuchadnezzar II's genius for conquering rival nations and tribes and then paralyzing them by taking their best-educated, most talented people into exile, as well as his great civic and military planning abilities, makes him one of

Nebuchadnezzar II, seated. (Library of Congress)

history's most influential leaders. He took chances in his military campaigns, but such risks were shrewdly calculated. By using the punishment of exile, he placed hostile governments directly under his own surveillance and, by so doing, nipped any potential revolution before it could grow into a threat. His cruelty toward certain unrepentant foes was unrivaled in the ancient world and established him as an enemy not to be resisted. Those who did resist brought on themselves death and destruction.

A lover of pomp, he made the city of Babylon into a magnificent fortress, its gardens, palaces, courtyards, and walls the marvels of their time. Almost single-handedly, the king magnified the power and prestige of his nation. Yet the end of Babylon was soon in coming, foretold by Ezekiel and those who shared his prophetic vision. Its magnificence was destroyed by enemies within and without, leaving it a warren of broken walls in the midst of a desert.

It is ironic that the Jews whom Nebuchadnezzar took into bitter exile were to portray him most memorably for later generations. To readers of the Old Testament, he is the cruel but brilliant monarch who fulfilled Jeremiah's predictions by destroying Jerusalem and creating the lengthy Diaspora as well as the man who threw Daniel into the den of lions and Shadrach, Meshach, and Abednego into a furnace. Like Daniel and his companions, the Jews survived Nebuchadnezzar's tortures, but Babylon itself, largely the creation of its king, left few traces after Cyrus made it into a wasteland. Like many empires, it had its golden age, followed by rapid decay. This golden age could not have occurred had it not been for the consummate genius of Nebuchadnezzar.

—*John D. Raymer*

FURTHER READING

Oates, Joan. *Babylon*. New York: Thames and Hudson, 1986. Considers many aspects of life in Babylon under various kings including Nebuchadnezzar. Discusses Babylonian law, religion, social customs, festivals, and military conquests and defeats and gives a fine overview of each king's contribution to Babylonia's rise and fall. An in-depth look at a sophisticated, complex society.

Oppenheim, A. Leo. *Ancient Mesopotamia: Portrait of a Dead Civilization*. Chicago: University of Chicago Press, 1977. Written by one of the foremost scholars dealing with the region, this work considers the development of the nation. Gives much insight into relationships between strong and weak nations.

_____. *Letters from Mesopotamia: Official, Business, and Private Letters on Clay Tablets from Two Millennia*. Chicago: University of Chicago Press, 1968. These letters shed light on the inner dynamics of the nations of the Near East in ancient times.

Saggs, H. W. F. *The Greatness That Was Babylon: A Survey of the Ancient Civilization of the Tigris-Euphrates Valley*. London: Sidgwick & Jackson, 1988. Written for both general and scholarly readers, this study covers the Babylonian monarchies. Invaluable for its lively depiction of the lives of both nobles and workers. Well-illustrated; includes extensive bibliography.

Way, Warren. *The Pride of Babylon: The Story of Nebuchadnezzar*. Philadelphia: Xlibris, 2001. Well-researched biography includes index and bibliographical references.

SEE ALSO: Cyrus the Great; Ezekiel; Hammurabi; Jeremiah.

RELATED ARTICLES in *Great Events from History: The Ancient World*: c. 607-562 B.C.E., Nebuchadnezzar Creates the First Neo-Babylonian State; 547 B.C.E., Cyrus the Great Founds the Persian Empire; October, 539 B.C.E., Fall of Babylon; c. 538-c. 450 B.C.E., Jews Return from the Babylonian Captivity.

NEFERTARI
Egyptian queen

Ramses II had at least eight wives, of whom Nefertari, his first and clearly his favorite, exercised significant political and religious influence on the pharaoh and on the society over which he reigned.

BORN: c. 1307 B.C.E.; Thebes, Egypt
DIED: c. 1265 B.C.E.; Nubia, or Pi-Ramses, Egypt
AREA OF ACHIEVEMENT: Government and politics

EARLY LIFE

Few facts have been unearthed regarding the early life of Nefertari (neh-fehr-TAH-ree), although she is thought to have been highborn, of noble, but not royal, birth. Because her name is often followed by a phrase indicating that she was beloved by Mut, a goddess associated with the area of Thebes, which is on the Nile River some hundred miles (160 kilometers) north of Aswān and fifty miles (80 kilometers) south of Abydos, it is generally thought that she was born in or around Thebes. The exact date of her birth is the subject of considerable conjecture.

It apparently was considered advantageous politically for Ramses to marry the daughter of a prominent nobleman from Thebes because his family was centered largely in Egypt's delta north of Cairo and did not share blood connections with Egyptian royalty. Ramses' forebears rose to power and prominence not through inheritance and blood ties but through their military service to the Eighteenth Dynasty pharaoh Horemheb, who, having no male heirs, chose as his successor Ramses' grandfather, Parameses, who changed his name to Ramses and, before his death in 1294 B.C.E., ruled for one year as Ramses I, first pharaoh of the Nineteenth Dynasty.

The name Nefertari was the name of the wife and sister of Pharaoh Ahmose I, founder of the Eighteenth Dynasty, and the mother of Amenhotep I. Ahmose-Nefertari dwelled in Thebes during its most exciting and successful period. Her husband fought off and banished Asian invaders, the Hyksos, around 1570 B.C.E. That Nefertari adopted Ahmose-Nefertari's headdress, a vulture between two plumes, suggests that she had ties to Thebes and likely was born there.

Nefertari married Ramses II before he became pharaoh. His father, Seti I, put his son under little direct pressure to marry, but, after he officially became prince regent, provided him with a harem and a goodly assortment of desirable women from whom to choose future mates. Nefertari, then in her early teens, was presumably one of the young ladies Seti selected as a prospective mate for the young Prince Ramses.

Polygamy was fully accepted among Egyptian royalty at that time and was also permitted among commoners, although more commoners were monogamous than polygamous. Among the primary functions of royalty was the production of heirs to feed leaders into the royal pipeline. Ramses and Nefertari made their initial contribution to this pipeline with the birth of their first son, Amenherwenemef, born shortly before Ramses ascended the throne around 1290 B.C.E.

During his lifetime, Ramses is thought to have fathered approximately one hundred children, some sixty of them sons. Ironically, none of the six children born to him by Nefertari outlived Ramses himself, who reigned for sixty-seven years and who died in his ninetieth year. On his death, Ramses was succeeded by Merenptah, then in his sixties and the eldest of Ramses' thirteen surviving sons.

Merenptah was Ramses' issue from Istnofret, Ramses' second wife, who, like Nefertari but unlike Ramses' other wives, was referred to by the epithet King's Great Wife. Nefertari alone bore the revered title Mistress of the Two Lands, meaning that she, like her husband, wielded power in both Upper and Lower Egypt. The designation Ruler of Two Lands was usually reserved for kings.

LIFE'S WORK

Aside from a few cuneiform tablets that provide researchers with some written record of Nefertari's life, most of what is known about her has been pieced together from such artifacts as statues, stelae, and wall paintings, many from her tomb in the Valley of the Tombs of the Queens at Abu Simbel, across the Nile River from Luxor. Although the meanings of these assorted artifacts have been subject to varied interpretations by cadres of archaeologists and Egyptologists, some quite reliable conclusions have been drawn from them.

Nefertari's marriage to Ramses II, usually referred to as Ramses the Great, was a genuine love match. Both were young, Nefertari in her early teens and Ramses only slightly older, at the time they married. Ramses adored Nefertari, who was among the most beautiful and accomplished women in his realm. His love for her was clearly greater than his love for any of his other wives, one of whom was his sister and two of whom were his daughters. Only Istnofret enjoyed anything resembling the sort of affection that Ramses lavished on Nefertari throughout their marriage.

After Ramses became pharaoh, Nefertari worked actively with him, traveling throughout his empire and, judging from various artifacts, sitting beside him during affairs of state. It is significant that two statues that depict her at the entry of her tomb are about 35 feet (11 meters) high, equal in size to the four statues of Ramses on the facade of the tomb. This indicates that she was considered of equal importance to him. Such statuary generally depicts women as smaller than the powerful men whom they married.

For the first few years of Ramses' reign, Nefertari played a significant role in the political and religious life of his realm. She traveled with the pharaoh from Pi-Ramses in the north up the Nile to Cairo and Gizeh, Abydos, Thebes, Gebel el-Silsila, Aswān, and Abu Simbel to the south, sometimes undertaking the 1,000-mile (1,600-kilometer) journey up the length of the Nile in the heat of summer. Her importance is documented by the titles she bore and by many images of her adorning monuments at the temples at Karnak and Luxor as well as at her tomb at Abu Simbel. Her impact on Nubia was especially strong.

The rock shrine at Gebel el-Silsila has statuary depicting the queen as appeasing the gods with offerings. This depiction was highly unusual because it is the king who, as chief priest of Egypt, generally made offerings to the gods. That Nefertari is depicted in a position normally reserved for pharaohs suggests the queen's special status and political power within Ramses' kingdom.

A few years into her marriage to Ramses, Nefertari more or less disappeared from public view for reasons that have not been adequately explained. Public record of her is found in the third year of Ramses' reign, when she is shown beside the king on the new pylon at the Luxor Temple. This was the last datable reference to Nefertari for nearly two decades. She was, it must be remembered, the mother of six children. Perhaps she opted to devote herself to raising them rather than delegate this responsibility to servants. Whatever accounted for this period of official silence, Nefertari did not emerge from it until the twenty-first year of her husband's reign.

It was in that year, 1268 B.C.E., that Hatti, the other major political power of that day, signed a peace treaty with Egypt. Apparently, this accord was something that Nefertari had longed for and probably had exerted her powers as the pharaoh's best-loved wife to help achieve.

When the treaty was signed, Padukhepa, queen of the Hatti, sent a letter to Nefertari expressing her delight that peace had been accomplished, marking the end of over twenty years of seething tensions between the two countries. Although Padukhepa's letter has not survived, Nefertari's cuneiform response has. She writes to the queen warmly, in a sisterly fashion, wishing her and her people good fortune and happiness. This letter demonstrates that Nefertari was, at this point, actively involved again in important affairs of state.

Ramses' love and high regard for Nefertari are attested to by his decision to have constructed to the north of his own elaborate tomb, dedicated to himself and to the official gods of Egypt, a corresponding tomb for her dedicated to Hathor, the patroness of motherhood and the goddess of love. This tomb, at Abu Simbel, is adorned with some 600 square feet (183 square meters) of elaborate and colorful wall paintings, which have been preserved and conserved through the efforts of the J. Paul Getty Conservation Institute and the Egyptian Antiquities Organization.

On the completion of the tombs of Ramses and of Nefertari, Ramses, his queen, and their daughter Meryetamen sailed a thousand miles up the Nile from Pi-Ramses for the pharaoh's official inauguration of the incredibly lavish structures. The viceroy of Nubia, Hekanakht, who was part of the extensive waterborne royal party, had a stele carved out of the nearby rock to commemorate the event. The stele depicts Ramses and Meryetamen engaged in the dedication rituals, while it shows Hekanakht attending Nefertari, who is seated, probably indicating that she is unwell. No later public images of Nefertari have appeared, suggesting that she died not long after her tomb was inaugurated.

SIGNIFICANCE

During the early years of her reign, Nefertari was a political and religious force, at times probably strongly influencing her husband's decisions. It was early assumed that her first-born, Amenhcrwenemef, would become Egypt's ruler on the death of Ramses, but Ramses outlived all of Nefertari's children, not dying until 1213 B.C.E.

Despite a period of seeming withdrawal from public life, Nefertari reemerged, probably as an indirect participant, in helping to bring about a peace treaty between Egypt and its longtime archrival Hatti. Nefertari was a highly independent person, as is suggested by several of the wall paintings in her tomb.

Ramses' name is absent from her tomb, indicating that she was considered to have the strength to negotiate alone the perilous and complicated ventures through the afterworld in which Egyptians strongly believed. This was traditionally a journey seldom taken by women without the guidance of men.

—*R. Baird Shuman*

FURTHER READING

Corso, Miguel Angel, ed. *Wall Paintings of the Tomb of Nefertari*. Santa Monica, Calif.: The Getty Conservation Institute, July, 1987. This initial report on the contents of Nefertari's tomb is essentially a catalog of what is in it.

Corso, Miguel Angel, and Mahasti Afishar, ed. *Art and Eternity: The Nefertari Wall Paintings Conservation Project, 1986-1992*. Santa Monica, Calif.: The J. Paul Getty Trust, 1993. Offers detail of how the Getty Conservation Project proceeded over a six-year period. The aim of the conservation project is conservation, not restoration. Salt deposits were removed and the wall paintings carefully washed. Missing parts were replaced with plaster. Richly illustrated.

The Editors of Time-Life Books. *Ramses II: Magnificence on the Nile*. Alexandria, Va.: Time-Life Books, 1993. Useful to those seeking information about Nefertari. Profusely illustrated, comprehensive index, extended bibliography. Chapter 3, "Of Queens, Consorts, and Commoners," is especially relevant.

The authors credit Ramses II with fathering more than ninety children, six of whom were born to Nefertari. Eight pages of color illustrations.

McDonald, John K. *House of Eternity: The Tomb of Nefertari*. Los Angeles: The Getty Conservation Institute, 1996. This is perhaps the most significant book about Nefertari to date. Its introductory sections and frequent sidebars offer useful biographical information, but it is the color reproductions of the wall paintings from Nefertari's tomb that distinguish the book. The story of how the tomb was discovered, how its contents have been cleaned and preserved, and how the various wall paintings have been interpreted is extremely valuable.

Menu, Bernardette. *Ramesses II: Greatest of the Pharaohs*. New York: Harry N. Abrams, 1999. A concise, well-balanced history of Ramses and his reign. Includes useful information such as lists of Ramses' known advisers, spouses, and children.

SEE ALSO: Cleopatra VII; Hatshepsut; Nefertiti; Ramses II; Tiy.

RELATED ARTICLES in *Great Events from History: The Ancient World*: c. 1570 B.C.E., New Kingdom Period Begins in Egypt; From c. 1500 B.C.E., Dissemination of the Book of the Dead; c. 1365 B.C.E., Failure of Akhenaton's Cultural Revival.

NEFERTITI
Egyptian queen

As queen of Egypt married to the iconoclastic pharaoh Akhenaton, Nefertiti helped in the temporary transformation of the culture's traditional religion into a monotheistic cult of sun worship. She also had an important role in ruling the empire and inspired standards of female beauty.

BORN: c. 1364 B.C.E.; Thebes, Egypt
DIED: c. 1334 B.C.E.; probably Egypt
ALSO KNOWN AS: Nefertiit; Nefretiri; Nofretete
AREAS OF ACHIEVEMENT: Government and politics, religion

EARLY LIFE

Nefertiti (NEH-fuhr-TEE-tee) was born in the royal city of Thebes on the Nile River in Upper Egypt; her name means "the beautiful one has come." Her origins and much about her life are unclear. Her supposed mother or

stepmother, Tiy, was also described as her nurse and governess. Her putative father was Ay, at first a scribe and keeper of the king's records. Eventually, Ay was to become grand vizier, or chief minister, as well as commander of the king's chariotry.

Perhaps her father's ascendancy made it possible for Nefertiti to secure an entrée to the court and to become friendly with the king's oldest son, the younger Amenhotep. Amenhotep happened to have her father, Ay, as tutor. Nefertiti had a younger sister, Mudnodjme, who some scholars posit became the chief wife of King Horemheb, a view contested by others.

Given her father's presumed ambitions and the young prince's affection for her, at age eleven Nefertiti already appeared to have been groomed to be queen. It is agreed that she spent much of her childhood in the royal palace at Thebes, a magnificent city beautified by Ay, this time in his capacity as chief architect to King Amenhotep III, the prince's father.

After the young King Amenhotep IV ascended the throne at about age fourteen on his father's death, he married Nefertiti, then fourteen. She thus became Queen Nefertiti, empress of the Two Egypts, Upper and Lower. During the Eighteenth Dynasty, royal couples were considered the intermediaries between the people and their gods; Amenhotep and Nefertiti, according to custom, were thus ascribed near-divine attributes.

The new king, however, broke rank with his predecessors. He evinced little interest in hunting, the affairs of state, or warfare. Rather, his focus was primarily theological. In fact, the sovereign became a religious reformer and was eventually considered a heretic. In contrast to his ancestors, Amenhotep IV replaced Amen-Ra, the supreme god of all Egyptian gods, with a new paramount, powerful, and eventually sole god, Aton, whose manifestation was the sun-disk, the physical embodi-

ment of the deity. Until then, Aton had been only a minor Theban god. Symbolically, in Year 5 of his reign, Amenhotep changed his name to Akhenaton. Because of mounting opposition to his iconoclasm and to his closure of the temples of the other gods, Akhenaton decided to build a new capital, Akhetaton (now Tell el-Amārna), on the Nile in Middle Egypt some 250 miles (400 kilometers) north of Thebes. The royal family and a good part of the court then moved there.

In the meantime, however, Meritaton and Mekitaton, two of the royal couple's six known daughters, had been born in Thebes. Four more girls—Ankhesenpaaton, Nefernefruaton the Younger, Nefernefrura, and Setepenra—were to follow. Some scholars suspect that the royal couple, or at least Akhenaton, may also have had a son, Smenkhare, who ruled briefly either with or following his father. Indeed, under a contemporary pharaonic tradition, the king may have sired other children either with his secondary wives such as his favorite, Kiya, or even with his own daughters, of whom he married three; incestuous couplings were favored to maintain the royal line. Various reliefs show the royal couple with their daughters, often in intimate, domestic surroundings that had never before been depicted.

LIFE'S WORK

The rise and fall of Egypt's new capital city, Akhetaton, with which Nefertiti became so closely associated, was little less than meteoric. In less than two decades, it was built with palaces, temples to the god Aton, monuments, residences, and burial places. A new style of art flourished during this brief Amarna period. In the fourteenth century B.C.E., Egypt was still the world's most important empire. Babylonia, Assyria, Syria, Palestine, Mitanni, and the region of Asia Minor where the Hittites lived all paid tribute in the form of slaves, animals, and princesses, who became royal spouses or concubines to reinforce political ties.

Because her husband's interests were primarily theological, Nefertiti helped to spread the new faith as Akhenaton's equal, participating enthusiastically in the new religious ceremonies. Unlike other chief wives, Nefertiti is shown taking part in daily worship, replicating the gestures of the king and making offerings similar to his. Yet since her husband was additionally focused on artistic innovations and poetry, not matters of state or war, Nefertiti necessarily found herself acting as a coregent, even though such a status was never formally announced. Indeed, stelae, monuments, tomb inscriptions, and other artifacts depict the

Nefertiti. (Library of Congress)

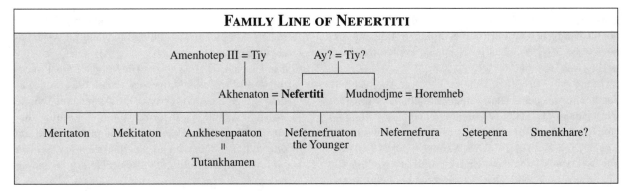

FAMILY LINE OF NEFERTITI

Amenhotep III = Tiy   Ay? = Tiy?

Akhenaton = **Nefertiti**   Mudnodjme = Horemheb

Meritaton   Mekitaton   Ankhesenpaaton   Nefernefruaton   Nefernefrura   Setepenra   Smenkhare?
                              ‖   the Younger
                         Tutankhamen

queen as assuming a major role at diplomatic receptions and in the ritual smiting of her country's foes. Even by the standards of Eighteenth Dynasty royal women, Nefertiti seems to have achieved unusual power and influence.

Whatever Nefertiti's role, and perhaps in part because of Akhenaton's orientation as a visionary rather than a warring pharaoh, the couple's reign was not a particularly good time for Egypt. There was restlessness in the empire, which in the fourteenth century B.C.E. stretched from Mesopotamia (roughly modern Iraq) to Nubia (approximately the modern Sudan), with some of these dependencies being at odds with one another in petty power struggles of their own as well. Akhenaton seems to have been unwilling to lead the traditional punitive expeditions to restore law and order.

Tragedy seems to have struck the royal family sometime after Year 11—probably in Year 14—of Akhenaton's sixteen-year reign. The couple's second daughter, Mekitaton, around age thirteen, died in childbirth. Her grief-stricken parents are shown in relief mourning over her lifeless body. This was the last known record of Nefertiti. There are several theories about her abrupt disappearance from public view.

One theory assumes that Nefertiti fell out of power and retired in disgrace in the northern palace as another wife—perhaps Kiya or even the royal couple's oldest daughter, Meritaton—came to monopolize the king's affection. Another view holds that Nefertiti came to disagree with Akhenaton on theological grounds; for example, he may have been shifting toward at least a partial restoration of the rival god Amen, while Nefertiti may have clung to Atonism. Still another theory has her committing suicide. Some theories stretch the imagination even further; one speculates that Smenkhare, Akhenaton's heir, was supposedly none other than Nefertiti, appearing from that point on as a male.

However, the view that the "great royal wife" died a natural death at about age thirty—a not-unusual lifespan even among royalty at the time—is endorsed by most modern scholars. Nefertiti's mummified remains have never been discovered, nor have her husband's been positively identified. This absence of evidence may be the result of the religious counterreformation that gathered momentum as the earlier principal god, Amen-Ra, was restored; references to Atonism and its sponsors were often obliterated and their records destroyed.

A few years after Akhenaton's death, moreover, the court returned to the earlier royal city of Thebes, and the late capital, Akhetaton, was laid to nearly complete ruin by enemies. Vandals and thieves may also have taken their toll. Yet it should be borne in mind that archaeologists discovered the famous limestone bust of Nefertiti—among other works in what had been the workshop of the master sculptor Thutmes in Amarna—only in 1912 C.E. This may logically suggest that the final chapter about Nefertiti has not yet been written.

SIGNIFICANCE

What is so striking about Nefertiti's life and work is that, even though her likeness—derived from Thutmes' bust of her, now located in the Egyptian Museum in Berlin, Germany—is one of the best-known and most frequently reproduced in the world, and while she lived at a time when Egypt was the most cultured and most powerful nation on earth, remarkably little is known about her. It is surmised that she must have been about 4.5 feet (1.4 meters) tall, the height of an average Egyptian woman of the time. It is known from her depictions that she often went about scantily dressed, as was customary in the warm climate. Otherwise, she appeared in the traditional garb of a clinging gown tied by a girdle with ends falling in front; at times, she is depicted coiffed with a short wig. She probably had a shaven head to improve the fit of her unusual tall blue crown. It is known that she identified with her husband's heresy and that, according to Akhenaton's poetry, he loved her dearly. It is also known that her beauty was legendary.

Many other details of her life, however, such as her personality and character, remain unfathomed. On the whole, then, "The Heiress, Great of Favor, Lady of Graciousness, Worthy of Love, Mistress of Upper and Lower Egypt, Great Wife of the King, Whom He Loves, Lady of the Two Lands"—as she is characterized in a contemporary inscription—though a historical figure of enormous importance, continues to be a riddle.

—Peter B. Heller

FURTHER READING

Aldred, Cyril. "The Amarna Queens." Chapter 19 in *Akhenaten: King of Egypt*. New York: Thames and Hudson, 1988. A foremost British Egyptologist tries to reconstruct the life and importance of Nefertiti and her controversial husband, carefully distinguishing between known facts, assumptions, and theories. Illustrated and annotated, with a select bibliography and index.

Dodson, Aidan. *Monarchs of the Nile*. London: Rubicon, 1995. While this work on the Egyptian pharaohs incorporates late research, the scanty information on Nefertiti suggests, by implication, the enigmas surrounding the queen's life and death. Illustrated, with a good annotated bibliography and index.

Freed, Rita E., et al., eds. *Pharaohs of the Sun: Akhenaten, Nefertiti, Tutankhamen*. Boston: Little, Brown, 1999. Originally the catalog accompanying an exhibition of remains from Amarna, this collection of essays focuses on Akhenaton, his wife, and his successor in overseeing the creation and destruction of a completely new city and a religious and cultural system to accompany it.

Redford, Donald B. *Akhenaten: The Heretic King*. Princeton, N.J.: Princeton University Press, 1984. A Canadian Egyptologist, director of the Akhenaton Temple Project excavations, theorizes about Nefertiti's "disappearance" but makes little attempt to profile the queen. Illustrated, with an excellent glossary, a select bibliography (including works on Nefertiti), and an index.

Samson, Julia. *Nefertiti and Cleopatra: Queen Monarchs of Ancient Egypt*. Rev. ed. London: Rubicon, 1990. A British Egyptologist tries to reconstruct, from the scanty artifacts, sites, monuments, and inscriptions contemporary with her, the life and importance of the queen. Illustrated and modestly annotated, with a short bibliography and index.

Tyldesley, Joyce. *Nefertiti: Egypt's Sun Queen*. New York: Viking, 1999. Another attempt at a biography of this largely unknowable subject. Provides much cultural and historical context, suggesting that the trend toward Aton worship was already beginning in the reign of Akehenaton's predecessor, Amenhotep III.

SEE ALSO: Akhenaton; Cleopatra VII; Hatshepsut; Nefertari; Tiy; Tutankhamen.

RELATED ARTICLES in *Great Events from History: The Ancient World*: c. 1570 B.C.E., New Kingdom Period Begins in Egypt; From c. 1500 B.C.E., Dissemination of the Book of the Dead; c. 1450 B.C.E., International Age of Major Kingdoms Begins in the Near East; c. 1365 B.C.E., Failure of Akhenaton's Cultural Revival; c. 1280 B.C.E., Israelite Exodus from Egypt.

NERO

Roman emperor (r. 54-68 C.E.)

As the fifth emperor of Rome, Nero continued the reign of terror of the Julio-Claudians while pursuing his own artistic career.

BORN: December 15, 37 C.E.; Antium, Latium (now Anzio, Italy)

DIED: June 9, 68 C.E.; Rome (now in Italy)

ALSO KNOWN AS: Lucius Domitius Ahenobarbus (given name); Nero Claudius Caesar Drusus Germanicus (full name)

AREAS OF ACHIEVEMENT: Government and politics, art and art patronage

EARLY LIFE

Born Lucius Domitius Ahenobarbus, Nero (NEER-oh) was a member of the Imperial Julio-Claudian family of Augustus through both parental lines. His formidable mother, Agrippina the Younger, was the granddaughter of Augustus's daughter Julia III. His dissolute father, Cnaeus Domitius Ahenobarbus, was the grandson of Augustus's sister Octavia and Marc Antony. When Nero was two years old, his mother was banished by her mad brother, the emperor Caligula, for treason. In the following year, Nero's father died, and his estate was seized by Caligula. The orphan was reared in the house of his paternal aunt Domitia Lepida until the accession of Claudius I in 41 C.E., when his mother was recalled from exile and his paternal inheritance was restored. The boy's early education was uncertain. He may have been cared for by a male dancer and a barber in his aunt's house. Later, he was given Greek tutors, including Anicetus and Beryllus, who remained advisers into his adulthood.

Nero's prospects improved significantly in 48 C.E., when the emperor Claudius married his niece Agrippina and her son came under the tutelage of the famous statesman and Stoic philosopher Lucius Annaeus Seneca (known as Seneca the Younger), who supervised the boy's education. Empress Agrippina schemed tenaciously to improve Nero's place in the line of succession. In 49 C.E. she persuaded her husband to betroth Nero to his daughter Octavia. On February 25, 50, Agrippina's son was legally adopted by the emperor and renamed Nero Claudius Caesar Drusus Germanicus even though Claudius had a natural son and heir, Britannicus. On March 5, 51, Nero took the *toga virilis* and was declared an adult, six months before he was legally entitled to do so; in the absence of the emperor, he served as prefect of the city of Rome. Two years later, Nero married Octavia and gave his first public speeches. On October 12, 54, the emperor Claudius died, perhaps poisoned by Agrippina, and the sixteen-year-old Nero was declared emperor the next day.

The physical description of Nero by his ancient biographer Suetonius is supplemented by images on contemporary coins. He was of average height, with blue eyes and light blond hair that he often set in curls and grew long in the back. He had a round, prominent chin, a squat neck, a protruding stomach, and spindly legs.

LIFE'S WORK

Nero's reign was marked by lavish public displays, a dissolute personal life, and the suspicious deaths of rivals. Nero endeared himself to the Roman populace by increasing the number of days on which public games were held. In 57 C.E. he built a new wooden amphitheater for gladiatorial contests and wild-beast shows. The emperor preferred extravagant and exotic artificial displays such as mock naval battles, controlled conflagrations during dramatic performances, and reenactments of mythological events. On such public occasions, the emperor often displayed great generosity to both the performers and the audience.

Nero enjoyed an uninhibited personal life. Rumors of an incestuous relationship with his mother cannot be proven. Nero certainly supplemented his marriage to Octavia with a long-term relationship with a Greek freedwoman named Acte. In 55 C.E. Britannicus became the emperor's first victim, poisoned at a banquet. About the same time, Agrippina fell into disfavor. By 59 this rift had developed to such an extent that Nero ordered a bizarre assassination attempt on a barge in the Bay of Naples. When this failed, a troop of Nero's henchmen killed Agrippina in her villa.

Throughout his reign, Nero relied heavily on others to govern the empire. At first, this dependence seemed the result of youthful inexperience; in later years, however, Nero spent much of his time composing poetry and songs that he performed publicly, much to the distaste of his subjects. While Agrippina's influence was short-lived, Nero benefited from the moderating counsel of Seneca and of Sextus Afranius Burrus, the commander of his Praetorian Guard until 62 C.E., when Seneca retired and Burrus died. Burrus was succeeded by Ofonius Tigellinus, whose heavyhanded tactics resulted in terror and bloodbaths.

The emperor had a cadre of epicurean friends on whom he could rely for help, especially in his debauchery. Marcus Salvius Otho, the future emperor, helped arrange Nero's rendezvous with Acte, and another friend, Petronius Arbiter, the author of the *Satyricon* (c. 60 C.E.; *The Satyricon*, 1694), is often called the emperor's "arbiter of elegance."

Several competent military commanders served Nero. Gnaeus Domitius Corbulo struggled with the difficult Armenian problem on the eastern border of the Empire. Gaius Suetonius Paulinus put down a dangerous revolt in the province of Britain in 60 C.E. Titus Flavius Vespasianus, the future emperor, suppressed the Jewish rebellion in Judaea in 67 C.E.

For the most part, Nero left the day-to-day management of the Empire to reliable freeborn Greeks such as Phaon, his finance minister, and Doryphorus, who managed the emperor's correspondence. Nero's reign was marked by few political initiatives. Rome's territory expanded modestly along the coast of the Black Sea. Some exploratory commercial expeditions were made to the Baltic and up the Nile River into the present Sudan. The Armenian problem was solved, at least temporarily, with the accession to the throne of the nominal Roman vassal Tiridates.

Agrippina's death was a turning point in Nero's reign. The emperor then pursued his artistic ambitions more openly. At the end of 59 C.E., the twenty-two-year-old emperor organized religious games called *Iuvenalia* to commemorate the first shaving of his beard. While such a celebration was an ancient Roman tradition, the emperor's competition as both singer and actor was a scandalous innovation. In the next year, Nero showed his fondness for Greek culture by founding the Neronian games, modeled on the Pythian games at Delphi, with competitions in the arts (music, poetry, and oratory), in athletics, and in chariot racing. While the emperor did not compete in these games, he was awarded the prize for oratory.

By 62 C.E. Nero had fallen into a passionate relationship with a woman named Poppaea Sabina, about whom little is known except that she was the former mistress of Otho. In order to marry the pregnant Poppaea, Nero had his childless wife Octavia summarily executed on a trumped-up charge of adultery. On January 21, 63 C.E., in Antium, the emperor's beloved birthplace, Poppaea gave birth to Nero's only child, a daughter named Claudia, who died the following May.

The events surrounding the Great Fire of Rome in 64 C.E. are among the most controversial of Nero's reign. When the fire broke out on July 19, the emperor was in Antium. He quickly returned to the capital, where he

Nero. (Hulton|Archive by Getty Images)

opened public buildings and his gardens on the Vatican hill to refugees and arranged for emergency food supplies. Despite these relief efforts, Nero was accused of starting the fire, partly because his agents cheaply bought up the large tracts of burned property, where his infamous Golden House was later built, and partly because of the rumor that Nero callously chose the backdrop of the burning city to perform his own composition about the fall of Troy. Nero's government responded to these rumors by charging the Christian population in Rome with arson. Saint Peter and Saint Paul are traditionally considered victims of the subsequent persecution.

It is unlikely that Nero's agents actually started the fire. It is uncertain whether he actually fiddled while Rome burned. However, Nero did take advantage of the fire to change the face of Rome. He rebuilt public buildings, such as the Temple of Vesta in the Roman Forum, and erected an opulent private residence spanning at least 125 acres (50 hectares) in the heart of Rome. This vast complex of buildings and gardens was filled with magnificent wall paintings, mechanical wonders such as a dining hall with a revolving ceiling, and great artwork, such as the Laocoon group now in the Vatican Museum. The Golden House became so closely associated with

Nero's extravagance that his successors, the Flavian emperors, used part of the site to build the Colosseum.

In 65 C.E. Nero faced a major conspiracy by Roman aristocrats, who planned to make Gaius Calpurnius Piso emperor. Among those implicated in the Pisonian conspiracy were Seneca, Seneca's poet nephew Lucan (Marcus Annaeus Lucanus), and Nero's old friend Petronius. In another conspiracy, led by Annius Vinicianus in 66, Nero's general Corbulo was forced to take his own life. These incidents left a permanent scar of Imperial suspicion and popular discontent on Nero's reign.

Shortly after the second celebration of the quincentennial Neronian games in 65 C.E., the empress Poppaea died. While acknowledging Nero's devotion to his wife, even the ancient historian Tacitus accepted the popular story that Nero had kicked the pregnant Poppaea after coming home late from the circus. Nero eventually married Statilia Messallina, who survived him but with whom he had no children.

In his final years, Nero turned increasingly to public display, and especially to personal performance, as a distraction from his political and personal troubles. Nero's reception for Tiridates, king of Armenia, in 66 C.E. was spectacular. Later in the same year, the emperor left for a tour of Greece, where he competed at a variety of festivals, including the Olympic Games. The emperor reportedly won 1,808 prizes, not only in artistic competitions but also in chariot racing. He also earned the enthusiastic gratitude of the Greeks by declaring the Greek province of Achaea free of Roman taxation. While in Greece, Nero also began work on an ambitious project to dig a canal across the isthmus of Corinth. Abandoned by Nero's successors, this canal was not finished until 1893.

Growing discontent led Nero to cut short his stay in the East and return to Rome in early 68 C.E., where he celebrated an extravagant triumph for his recent athletic victories. By March, Nero faced open revolt from Gaius Julius Vindex, one of his governors in Gaul (modern France). In April, Servius Sulpicius Galba, governor in Spain, followed Vindex in revolt. Although Vindex's army was defeated in May by troops loyal to the emperor at Vesontio (Besançon, France), Nero lost the support of his personal Praetorian Guard in Rome and prepared for escape to Egypt. Intercepted in headlong midnight flight from the city, he committed suicide with the help of an aide. His successor was Galba.

SIGNIFICANCE

In his final hours, according to Suetonius, Nero muttered, "What an artist perishes with me." While he cher-
ished his reputation as an artist, his work survives only in fragments. Instead, Nero's name became synonymous with incompetent government at best and despotic cruelty, debauchery, and wickedness at worst. His persecution of the Christians transformed his legend from that of a bad emperor to an antichrist whose second coming was anticipated with horror.

Nero's reign marked the end of the Julio-Claudian Dynasty founded by Augustus. While the Roman Empire slipped into temporary political chaos after Nero's death, the Empire was soon restabilized under new Imperial dynasties that preserved the Pax Romana, built on autocratic Julio-Claudian foundations, into the middle of the following century.

—*Thomas J. Sienkewicz*

FURTHER READING

Bishop, John. *Nero: The Man and the Legend.* New York: A. S. Barnes, 1964. This scholarly biography of Nero is mostly based on the ancient historian Tacitus but offers a controversial interpretation of the role of Christians in the burning of Rome in 64. Maps and illustrations.

Grant, Michael. *Nero.* New York: Dorset Press, 1989. A balanced and accessible biography with useful maps, illustrations, chronological lists, genealogical tables, notes, and bibliography.

Griffin, Miriam T. *Nero: The End of a Dynasty.* New York: Routledge, 2000. A scholarly examination of the reign of Nero is followed by a detailed explanation of the reasons for his fall. Includes illustrations, genealogical chart, maps, plans, and bibliography.

Henderson, Bernard W. *The Life and Principate of the Emperor Nero.* London: Methuen, 1903. Despite its publication date, Henderson's biography remains a major reference with extensive notes, maps, illustrations, genealogical table, and bibliography.

Weigall, Arthur. *Nero: The Singing Emperor of Rome.* Garden City, N.Y.: Garden City, 1930. This biography by a writer of popular history offers an uncritical retelling of the ancient sources. Includes notes and genealogical chart.

SEE ALSO: Agrippina the Younger; Augustus; Boudicca; Caligula; Claudius I; Julia III; Saint Paul; Saint Peter; Poppaea Sabina; Seneca the Younger.

RELATED ARTICLES in *Great Events from History: The Ancient World*: 43-130 C.E., Roman Conquest of Britain; 60 C.E., Boudicca Leads Revolt Against Roman Rule; 64-67 C.E., Nero Persecutes the Christians.

ŌJIN TENNŌ
Japanese emperor (traditionally r. 270-310 C.E.)

The first verifiable historical emperor of Japan, Ōjin Tennō consolidated imperial power, developed the empire, and supported cultural and political connections with Korea.

BORN: Late fourth century C.E.; Tsukushi, Kyūshū island, Japan
DIED: Early fifth century C.E.; Toyo-Akira, or Ohokuma Palace, Kinai region, Japan
ALSO KNOWN AS: Homuta; Homuda; Homutawake no Mikoto (personal name)
AREA OF ACHIEVEMENT: Government and politics

EARLY LIFE

According to Japanese tradition, the man who long after his death would be given the name Ōjin Tennō (oh-jeen tehn-noh), or Emperor Ōjin, was born in January, 201 C.E. Scholars now agree that this is much too early and place his birth in the late fourth century C.E. By 2003, most historians agreed that the parents ascribed to Ōjin in the earliest written Japanese histories are legendary figures, perhaps composite characters drawn around real people. The semimagic events around Ōjin's early life are similarly discounted as nonhistorical.

According to legend, about six months before his birth, Ōjin's father, the emperor Chūai, had died suddenly. This occurred after Chūai expressed his disbelief in a divine prophecy of the sun goddess Amaterasu, spoken through the mouth of his pregnant wife, the empress Jingū. Initially, the goddess had promised the emperor that he would conquer Korea. Now she angrily told him that it would be his son who would inherit the three Korean kingdoms then in existence.

When Ōjin's father died, Jingū kept this fact a secret. Dressed as a male warrior, she led an army, conquered Korea, and gave birth to her son the moment she returned to the Japanese island of Kyūshū. The baby was born with a flesh pad on his arm that looked like the protective leather shield worn by archers, and this was interpreted as a sign of his warrior nature.

After his birth, his mother outsmarted and defeated two hostile princes from the emperor's relations with his concubines. At age two, Ōjin was made the official heir to the throne. He exchanged his given name, Isasawake, with a god, and was thus called Homutawake no Mikoto, or Homuta (Homuda) for short. As was customary, later generations gave him the name of Ōjin the emperor, and it is by this name that Japanese history has referred to him

ever since. The boy grew up in the palace of his mother, Jingū, who gave banquets and held drinking games with her prime minister in his honor. Ōjin was quickly noted for his sharp intelligence and far-sightedness.

LIFE'S WORK

According to tradition, Ōjin's mother continued to rule for him until she died, and he did not become emperor until he was sixty-nine years old. Many historians believe that Ōjin was actually an outsider who took over the Yamato kingdom that formed the nucleus of the Japanese empire.

The oldest Japanese histories established the year of 270 as the start of Ōjin's reign. Comparing the early Japanese dating of events that are also described in other, primarily Korean histories, scholars have come to believe that the first Japanese historians deliberately predated their early national history. In the case of Ōjin's rule, scholars now believe that generally, two sixty-year cycles were subtracted from the true historical dates. Thus, his reign is most likely to have begun in 390 and to have ended in 430.

One year after he became emperor, Ōjin's wife Nakatsuhime was appointed empress. They had three children together. Their oldest son, Ohosazaki, became his father's favorite. Although he was not nominated to succeed Ōjin, Ohosazaki would become the next emperor and be given the name Nintoku. With his concubines, two of whom were the younger sisters of his wife, Ōjin had either twenty or twenty-six children. The Japanese sources of the eighth century spent considerable attention on his ample offspring, as many noble families of the seventh and eighth centuries later claimed these Imperial princes and princesses as the genuine founders of their clans. As some of these clan histories contained forgeries, not all of Ōjin's children mentioned may have been real people.

In the first years of his reign, Ōjin consolidated his power and dedicated himself to domestic politics. He used the workforce of tributary people to build roads and ponds, improving the Yamato region. He also organized the guilds, called *be* in Japanese, of the fishermen and gamekeepers, securing food supply for his domain. As such, Ōjin stands out, compared to most other historical emperors who performed fewer practical tasks and concerned themselves mostly with religious ceremonies.

Ōjin also got involved in foreign affairs in Korea. Here, the Japanese had an interest of their own and intervened in the affairs of the three Korean kingdoms of the period. Japanese and Korean sources vary considerably both about the nature of these struggles and their exact dates. Japanese tradition, for example, has it that Sinsã, the king of Paekche, disrespected Ōjin and was killed by his own people to atone for this transgression in 272. A Korean source states that Sinsã died in his traveling palace while hunting, in the year 392. While the Korean date is believed to be correct, the nature of the king's death is still subject to passionate debate between Japanese and Korean historians.

Ōjin continued his program of domestic improvements, often with foreign labor sent as tribute. He focused on shipbuilding and consolidation of his rule. There were also intrigues among the nobles. In 278 (traditional date), the man who had served as his father's and his mother's prime minister, Takechi no Sukune, was accused by his own younger brother of planning to usurp the throne. Sent to subdue a rebellion on the southwestern Japanese island of Kyūshū, Takechi secretly returned to the palace to defend himself. A judgment by ordeal involving boiling water was won by Takechi. However, Ōjin prevented the older brother from killing his younger brother afterward.

Ōjin's private life fascinated his contemporaries. Falling in love with the beautiful Kaminaga Hime in 282 (traditional date), Ōjin nevertheless yielded the young woman to his favorite son, Ohosazaki. He presented her to his son at a special banquet, and father and son expressed their desires in poems recorded for eternity. When Kaminaga responded to Ohosazaki favorably and slept with him without resistance, his status at court rose accordingly. Later, Ōjin allowed his beloved concubine Yehime, whom he had courted with romantic songs, to visit her parents. Thus, he showed humanity to his family and his subjects.

Ōjin's efforts at improving Yamato civilization also gained from his desire to have skilled professionals sent to Japan from Korea as tribute. The Korean seamstress Maketsu founded an important trade school, and the learned scribe Wani introduced writing to Japan. Historically, the Japanese acquired writing through Wani from the Chinese around 404, even though their legend uses the older, clearly wrong date of 284. Using Chinese characters to correspond phonetically to spoken Japanese, Japan finally became literary, a key event of Ōjin's reign.

Throughout his remaining years, Ōjin continued to intervene in Korea, occasionally sending Japanese troops to install his Korean protégés as kings there. Korean sources tell a different story and provide more historically accurate dates falling in the late fourth and early fifth centuries. Ōjin also demanded skilled immigrants to improve Japan's manufacture and infrastructure.

The exact historical nature of Ōjin's relationship with the three kingdoms of Korea is still a controversial issue

---

IMPORTANT CHILDREN OF EMPEROR ŌJIN

With his wife, Empress Nakatsuhime:
  Imperial Princess Arata
  Imperial Prince Ohosazaki, later Emperor Nintoku
  Imperial Prince Netori

*With his concubine Takaki Iribime
(younger sister of the empress):*
  Imperial Prince Nukada no Ohonakahiko
  Imperial Prince Ohoyamamori
  Imperial Prince Iza no Mawaka
  Imperial Princess Ohohara
  Imperial Princess Komida

*With his concubine Otohime
(younger sister of the empress):*
  Imperial Princess Ahe
  Imperial Princess Ahaji no Mihara
  Imperial Princess Ki no Uno

With his concubine Miyanushiyaka Hime:
  Imperial Prince Uji no Wakairatsuko, designated
    successor of Ōjin
  Imperial Princess Yata
  Imperial Princess Medori

With his concubine Oname Hime:
  Imperial Prince Uji no Wakairatsume

With his concubine Oto Hime:
  Imperial Prince Wakanoke Futamata

With his concubine Mago Hime:
  Imperial Prince Hayabusa Wake

With his concubine Naga Hime:
  Imperial Prince Ohohaye
  Imperial Prince Wohaye

in international scholarship. The traditional Japanese eighth century sources that Imperial Japan considered literal truth until 1945 are often contradicted by old Korean historical accounts. For 297, for example, Japanese history tells of a tribute to Ōjin by the North Korean state of Koguryo (or Kokuryo) that is accompanied by an insolent note. Even if the date is corrected by adding the usual 120 years, for 417, Korean historians have doubted that this kingdom would have sent tribute to Japan, with whom it was fiercely at war at that time.

Japanese legend has it that Ōjin lived well more than one hundred years, a life span that is not believed by most historians. According to Japanese tradition, when he was 107 years old, in 308 (traditional date), Ōjin received Shisetsu (Sin Chā To in Korean), the sister of the king of Paekche in Korea, as a fresh concubine.

Toward the end of his life, Ōjin gave clear preferences to his son Ohosazaki. Even as he appointed another son as heir apparent, he gave Ohosazaki a powerful position of his own, from which he would eventually become the emperor Nintoku. When Ōjin died, in 310 according to legend and most likely in the early fifth century in reality, he left behind an empire of considerable power.

SIGNIFICANCE

Ironically, later Japanese generations made Ōjin the god of war, called Yahata or Hachiman. However, his most enduring accomplishments lie in improving the domestic situation of his empire and the introduction of writing to Japan. His interventions in Korean politics brought Ōjin many skillful immigrants from this area. Traditionally, his reign also provided Japan's noble houses with many illustrious ancestors.

Indicative of the power, resources, and skills of the emperors of Yamato of Ōjin's time are the many impressive burial mounts of the period. One of the earliest and largest mausoleums, in Habikino in Ōsaka prefecture, is traditionally believed to be Ōjin's tomb. Like the others, it is built like a keyhole lying on the earth. It possesses three tiers, two moats, and two dikes. It is 1,362 feet (415 meters) long and rises over the plain landscape. Ōjin and his contemporaries' graves gave the period of his reign its name, *Kofun*, which is Japanese for keyhole.

With Ōjin, Japanese Imperial history leaves the realm of legend and enters that of history. Even though there are still shrines in Japan venerating this emperor as the god of war, it is clear that he was a real person. His emphasis on domestic development and the improvement of the

skills of his people advanced his nation, even though his office would become much more ceremonial in the decades and centuries to come, until the Meiji Restoration of 1868. Ōjin's kindness to his concubine Yehime is remembered as an important personal trait of this emperor, and his many children served Japanese nobility by legitimizing their position in society.

—R. C. Lutz

FURTHER READING

Aston, W. G., trans. *Nihongi: Chronicles of Japan*. 1896. Reprint. Rutland, Vt.: C. E. Tuttle, 1972. English translation of the *Nihon Shoki* (or *Shogi*) that contains one of the two original accounts of Ōjin's life.

Brown, Delmer M., ed. *Ancient Japan*. Vol. 1 in *The Cambridge History of Japan*. New York: Cambridge University Press, 1999. Chapter 2, "The Yamato Kingdom," contains an excellent historical account of the time of Ōjin's rule and places his reign in the context of early Japanese history.

Farris, William Wayne. *Sacred Texts and Buried Treasures*. Honolulu: University of Hawaii Press, 1998. Chapters 1 and 2 cover Japan's historical relationship with Korea in the time of Ōjin's rule. Excellent scholarly discussion of the textual and archaeological evidence for the events of his reign. Illustrated, with bibliography and index.

Philippi, Donald L., trans. *Kojiki*. Princeton, N.J.: Princeton University Press, 1969. Most generally available English translation of the first written Japanese account of Ōjin's life. However, Philippi's unique transcriptions of ancient Japanese names alter their English spelling and take getting used to.

Tarō, Sakamoto. *The Six National Histories of Japan*. Translated by John S. Brownlee. Vancouver: University of British Columbia Press, 1991. Chapter 2, on the *Nihon Shoki*, contains an excellent discussion on the source materials used by Japanese historiographers. Pages 63-64 deal directly with Ōjin. Includes appendix, bibliography, index.

OLYMPIAS
Molossian wife of Philip II of Macedonia and mother of Alexander the Great

During the reign of Alexander the Great, Olympias wielded political influence and authority in Macedonia and Greece. After Alexander's death, she died attempting to ensure the throne for his son.

BORN: c. 375 B.C.E.; Molossis, Epirus (now in Greece)
DIED: 316 B.C.E.; Macedonia (now in Greece)
ALSO KNOWN AS: Polyxena; Myrtale; Stratonice
AREA OF ACHIEVEMENT: Government and politics

EARLY LIFE

Most information about Olympias (oh-LIHM-pee-ahs) comes from narratives of the reigns of her husband, son, and grandson and from Plutarch's often hostile writings, but a few relevant inscriptions survive. All literary sources reflect southern Greek prejudice against political women as well as the propaganda wars of the period after the death of Alexander.

The daughter of Neoptolemus, king of the Molossians, Olympias belonged to a dynasty that claimed descent from Achilles. She had two siblings: a sister and a brother, Alexander, later ruler of the Molossians and husband of Olympias's daughter. Olympias may have been known by other names at various periods in her life.

Women in the Molossian-Epirote culture had more rights than elsewhere in the Hellenic world. The sources portray Olympias as fond of religion, particularly Dionysiac and other mystery cults. In this, she resembled women of the Hellenic and Hellenized world in general, much of the Macedonian and northern Greek population, and her own son. Indeed, Olympias and Philip II, king of the Macedonians, met at the mysteries of Samothrace. Their marriage, c. 357 B.C.E., was probably not a love match but the result of an alliance between Olympias's uncle Arybbas, who had succeeded her father as king, and Philip.

LIFE'S WORK

Olympias and Philip had two children: Alexander III (the Great), born in 356 B.C.E., and Cleopatra, born soon after. Philip fathered another son, Arrhidaeus, but he suffered from some mental disability that meant that he was unable to rule in his own right. By Alexander's early teens, Philip was treating him like an heir. Tradition says that Alexander and his mother were close and implies that he and his father were not. In the polygamous Macedonian court, mothers functioned as advocates for their sons' succession. Her son's status made Olympias the most

prominent of Philip's seven wives, but there is little evidence of the nature of her relationship with her husband and no proof that she exerted influence over him.

Philip's last marriage dramatically affected his public relationship with Olympias as well as Olympias's status. It occurred soon after the victory at Chaeronea in 338 B.C.E. that brought him domination of the Greek peninsula. Whatever Philip's motivation for this marriage, Alexander perceived a threat to his own status when the bride's guardian proposed a toast that brought into question Alexander's legitimacy as heir to the throne. Alexander, taking his mother with him, went into exile. When the public quarrel between father and son was settled, Alexander returned to court, possibly with Olympias.

Philip arranged a marriage between Olympias's daughter and Olympias's brother and turned the wedding into an international event. Some have seen this marriage as an indication that Olympias was being sidestepped, but others have seen it as part of the formal reconciliation between father and son, intended to reaffirm the status and importance of Alexander's Molossian heritage.

A Macedonian with a personal grievance assassinated Philip II at the wedding festivities in 336. Speculation in ancient (and modern) times assigned ultimate responsibility to Olympias or Alexander. Olympias and her son undeniably benefited by Philip's death. Others also benefited from his demise, however, some of whom ran less risk by participating in an assassination plot than did either Olympias or Alexander.

After the death of Philip, Alexander eliminated a number of his enemies, among them the guardian of Philip's last bride. At this time, though the evidence is poor, Olympias probably had Philip's last wife murdered, along with an infant she had born Philip. Olympias's motivation was similar to that behind Alexander's crimes: removal of dynastic rivals and revenge.

During her son's reign, Olympias played a more public role than she had in Philip's. Alexander's absence beginning in 334 meant that the only members of the dynasty not in Asia were women, and, of these, his mother remained the most prominent. In the cutthroat world of Macedonian power politics, mother and son had more reason to trust each other than any one else. Alexander and Olympias wrote frequently, and he sent booty home to her, from which she made splendid dedications to the gods.

Olympias also played a role in affairs of state, whether authorized by her son or opportunistic. She left Macedonia for her Molossian homeland and may have shared the regency of Molossia and Epirus with her now-widowed daughter, Cleopatra. Inscriptions suggest that, as early as 333-332, Olympias and her daughter functioned as heads of state. Contemporary literary evidence also indicates that Olympias had a position of some authority during her son's reign, although whether her power was based in Macedonia or Molossia or both is not certain.

Plutarch asserted that Olympias and Cleopatra formed a faction against Antipater, the general Alexander had left in military charge of Macedonian affairs, and that they shared Alexander's rule, Cleopatra taking Macedonia and Olympias Epirus. Olympias tried to influence her son's policy by means of epistolary attacks on Alexander's courtiers. She warned her son against those she considered dangerous to his interests. While most of these rivalries appear petty, typical of the competitive Macedonian court, her rivalry with Antipater had greater significance. Although Plutarch claimed Alexander was unaffected by her charges, her efforts against Antipater contributed to his demotion. Alexander ultimately came to interpret Antipater's actions, rightly or wrongly, as his mother did.

Although Olympias was remote from the fray precipitated by Alexander's death in 323 B.C.E., her life was now imperiled. She believed, probably wrongly, that Antipater and his sons were responsible for Alexander's death. Though her infant grandson Alexander IV and the limited Arrhidaeus were now nominally co-kings, in reality Alexander's generals (the Diadochi) struggled over his empire. Because her existence benefited none of the Diadochi and her demise might have pleased a number of them, for the first time she faced physical danger. Therefore, she sought support she had not previously deemed necessary. Probably at her bidding, Aeacides, Olympias's nephew, returned from exile and became ruler of the Molossians but consistently acted in her interests.

She also searched for a husband for her long-widowed daughter, Cleopatra. Ultimately, Olympias sent Cleopatra to Sardis (where most of the Macedonian army, Perdiccas the regent, and the kings were located) in the hope that she would marry Perdiccas, but this plan failed, and Cleopatra was effectively imprisoned in Sardis. Olympias, lacking control of either her daughter or grandson, was stymied, although still safe enough in Epirus.

Her opportunity for renewed power came with the death of Antipater in 319 and his replacement as regent by Polyperchon. Polyperchon asked Olympias to return to Macedonia, take over responsibility for her grandson, and accept some more general public role. Olympias refused his offer at least once, possibly twice: She distrusted her grandson's guardians, whom she believed wanted the rule for themselves. Nonetheless, Olympias changed her mind in the fall of 317 B.C.E. Arrhidaeus's wife (and Philip II's granddaughter) Adea Eurydice had formed an alliance with Antipater's son, Cassander, but the fundamental cause of Olympias's reversal was her conviction that the dual kingship created in 323—kings from different branches of the royal family that had been rivals for more than a generation—must be replaced by a return to unified monarchy.

Naturally, she hoped Alexander IV would become that single ruler, though, from the moment she heard of her son's death and the birth of Alexander IV, she must have known that the chances of her grandson surviving long enough to be more than a figurehead were slender and that if she became his advocate, she would lose what security her cousin's protection offered. Her caution in embracing the project indicates that she saw the dangers in becoming her grandson's supporter, yet she risked and lost her life in an attempt to ensure his sole rule.

Olympias returned to Macedonia with her grandson and mixed forces led by her nephew Aeacides and Polyperchon. Adea Eurydice and her husband met them on the Macedonian border, but their army immediately went over to Olympias, and Adea Eurydice and Philip Arrhidaeus were captured. Olympias executed them, killed one brother of Cassander, dishonored the tomb of another, and brought about the deaths of a hundred supporters of Cassander. Olympias's actions caused some Macedonians to dislike her, but they were not unique; many of the Diadochi were similarly brutal. The deaths of Adea Eurydice and Philip Arrhidaeus were considered a necessity. Left alive, Philip Arrhidaeus might become the tool of any faction. Adea Eurydice presented a threat because of her control of her husband but also because she had the potential to produce a child who was a descendant of Philip II as well as the son of one of Alexander's generals.

Olympias's slaughter of Cassander's supporters is more problematic. Though these deaths were probably intended as preemptive strikes, they alienated some public opinion and failed to eliminate opposition. Nonetheless, even if these murders constituted a partial political misjudgment, Olympias, her forces, and her allies, failed primarily because a series of military defeats eroded their support. Olympias either falsely believed that she herself had military skills sufficient to handle the situation or put her trust in men and in plans that made no sense.

When Olympias surrendered to Cassander on a (false) promise of personal safety, her fate was sealed. Had she succeeded in appearing at her own trial, as she wished, she might have survived. It proved difficult to find someone to kill Olympias (confirming that her failures were primarily military not political), but Cassander finally did so. She continued to scheme and plot to the end and faced death with resolve. With Olympias eliminated, Cassander took over rule of Macedonia and eventually murdered Alexander IV, but his dynasty failed to survive.

SIGNIFICANCE

In an era short on adult or competent royal males, Olympias used her skills as a succession advocate to make herself more powerful than any previous Macedonian royal woman, but, after the death of Alexander, she lacked the stable military base necessary to ensure the Macedonian throne for her descendants.

—*Elizabeth D. Carney*

FURTHER READING

Blackwell, Christopher W. *In the Absence of Alexander: Harpalus and the Failure of Macedonian Authority.* New York: Peter Lang, 1999. Examines Olympias's pivotal role in Greek events during Alexander's absence.

Borza, E. N. *In the Shadow of Olympus: The Emergence of Macedon.* Princeton, N.J.: Princeton University Press, 1990. Provides background on Macedonian monarchy and the cultural context of the Macedonian court.

Carney, Elizabeth D. *Women and Monarchy in Macedonia.* Norman: University of Oklahoma Press, 2000. Discusses the role of women in Macedonian monarchy and provides biographies.

Greenwalt, W. S. "Polygamy and Succession in Argead Macedonia." *Arethusa* 22 (1989): 19-45. Analyzes the dynamic between polygamy and succession in Macedonia.

SEE ALSO: Alexander the Great; Artemesia I; Arsinoe II Philadelphus; Atossa; Philip II of Macedonia; Ptolemy Philadelphus; Ptolemy Soter.

RELATED ARTICLES in *Great Events from History: The Ancient World*: 359-336 B.C.E., Philip II Expands and Empowers Macedonia; August 2, 338 B.C.E., Battle of Chaeronea; 336 B.C.E., Alexander the Great Begins Expansion of Macedonia; 332 B.C.E., Founding of Alexandria; 327-325 B.C.E., Alexander the Great Invades the Indian Subcontinent; c. 323-275 B.C.E., Diadochi Divide Alexander the Great's Empire.

ORIGEN

Alexandrian scholar and church father

Origen was the first to write extensive commentaries on most books of the Bible and also to study the main areas and problems within theology. What he wrote often determined the main lines of subsequent Christian thought.

BORN: c. 185 C.E.; Alexandria, Egypt
DIED: c. 254 C.E.; probably Tyre (now Sur, Lebanon)
AREAS OF ACHIEVEMENT: Religion, scholarship

EARLY LIFE

Origen (AHR-eh-jehn) was born at the end of the period that Edward Gibbon, the eighteenth century English historian, called the happiest and most prosperous the human race had known; he died during a time of civil war, plague, economic dislocation, and persecution of the Christian Church. Alexandria, the city of his birth, was one of the great cities of the world; it used Greek as its first language and was the home of the largest library in the Mediterranean basin. There many of the best scholars of the Greek world taught and studied.

Origen was the oldest of nine children. His father, whom tradition names Leonides, was prosperous enough to provide him with a Greek literary education and concerned enough about his Christian formation to teach him the Bible. From childhood, Origen was a serious Christian and a learned Greek. The Old Testament from which he studied, the Septuagint, was a Jewish translation of the Hebrew Bible into Greek. It contained, in addition to translations of those Scriptures originally written in Hebrew, books originally written in Greek. Although the canon, or list of books considered properly to be in the Bible, was not completely set in Origen's day, for most purposes his New Testament is that still used by Christians. While young, Origen memorized long passages of the Bible; thus as an adult he could associate passages from throughout the Bible on the basis of common words or themes. He, like other Christians of his day, also accepted as authoritative a body of teaching held to come from the Apostles.

Origen imbibed from his father and the Christian community the dramatic and heroic idea that he, as an individual Christian, was a participant in the drama by which the world was being redeemed. Like many other Christians, he was uneasy about wealth and marriage and tended to see Jesus calling the Christian to poverty and celibacy (that is, to a heroic mode of existence). Although martyrdom was still relatively infrequent, it was exalted in the Christian community, and in many ways Origen saw himself throughout his life as a living martyr doing battle for the spread of Christ's kingdom. At an unknown date, thoroughly instructed in the faith, he was baptized. Around 202, when Origen was seventeen, his father was martyred and the family property was confiscated by the state. It may be argued that for the rest of his life Origen saw himself continuing his martyred father's work.

LIFE'S WORK

In the following years, Origen added to his knowledge of grammar and Greek literature a familiarity with Gnosticism, a form of dualism very common in the Greek world of his day, which condemned all things material, especially the appetites and passions of the human body, and celebrated the spiritual, especially the human soul and spirit. Salvation was seen to lie in the separation of the soul from matter, and before Origen's day a form of Christian Gnosticism had developed. After his father's death, a Christian woman had taken Origen into her house so that he could continue his studies, and he subsequently began to teach grammar. In this woman's house Christian Gnosticism was practiced. Although Origen rejected much of what he heard there, he adopted the Gnostics' distinction between literal Christians, who understood only the literal sense of the Bible; psychic Christians, who went beyond this to consider the spiritual meaning of Scripture; and perfect Christians, who understood and followed the deepest meanings of the Bible. Origen also accepted a doctrine that was, after his death, to be condemned as heretical: He believed that ultimately all men, and even Satan himself, would be reconciled with God.

One of the second century Gnostic documents discovered at Nag Hammadi in Upper Egypt in 1945 contains many teachings similar to those found in Origen's writings and represents a form of Gnosticism more acceptable to the Christian tradition in which Origen had been formed. In this work, as in that of Origen, Christ was conceived of as very similar to God the Father, although subordinate to him in being. The work, and Origen, also conceived of human existence as a long process of education, in which evil and death prepare humans for union with God. Another writer, Marcion, whom Origen classified a Gnostic, provided a foil against which Origen developed the teaching that human suffering can be reconciled with God's power and goodness. Unlike Marcion, Origen held that difficult passages in the Scripture might be allegorized.

Sometime between 206 and 211, Origen added catechetical instruction (explanation of Christianity to those interested in conversion) to his duties as a grammar teacher. This period was again a time of persecution, and although he taught in secret, at one point Origen was discovered and almost killed; some of his students were martyred.

After the persecution, he gave up his work as a teacher of grammar, sold his books of Greek literature, became the chief Christian teacher in Alexandria, and gave himself totally to Bible study. He began to follow what became a lifelong practice of strictly imitating the most difficult sayings of Jesus, fasting regularly, sleeping very little (the Bible had said to "pray without ceasing"), and possessing only one cloak; he also castrated himself.

In the years between 211 and 215, Origen learned much of the Platonic tradition, and that had a deep influence on him, especially the Platonists' insistence on both Divine Providence and human freedom and—against the Gnostics—on the fundamental, if limited, good of the created order. Sometime before 217 Origen traveled briefly to Rome, where he was exposed to growing controversies over the definition of the relation of Jesus Christ to God the Father. Also sometime between 215 and 222, Origen met a Hebrew-speaking convert to Christianity who had been trained as a rabbi, with whom he began to study Hebrew and Jewish biblical interpretation. He also met an Alexandrian, Ambrose, who became his lifelong patron. The first problem facing Origen as a biblical scholar was the establishment of a reliable biblical text. His response was to write first *Tetrapla* (third century) and ultimately, after he had settled in Palestine, *Hexapla* (231-c. 245), each of which contained various Greek translations in parallel columns next to a transliterated Hebrew Old Testament. In this task he revealed lifelong characteristics—painstaking interests in textual criticism and historical problems. In his mind these were completely compatible with his interest in mystical interpretation of the Bible. Origen's growing reputation is evident from an incident that occurred about 222, when he was summoned to Arabia by the Roman governor for the discussion of an unknown subject.

Most of his early writings, from between 222 and 230, have been lost, but one of his most important, *Peri archōn* (220-230 C.E., also known as *De principiis*; *On First Principles*, 1936), survives. Heavily influenced by Platonism, it espoused the idea, later to be condemned, that the human soul before entering the body has existed eternally. Students were now flocking to Origen's lectures; of these he accepted only the most promising. Ambrose provided a staff of stenographers, who took down Origen's lectures in shorthand as he gave them, and of copyists, who then prepared a finished text.

Probably in 230, after unspecified conflict with Bishop Demetrius of Alexandria, Origen moved, at first briefly, to Caesarea, in Palestine. Having returned to Alexandria, he again left in 231, summoned by the dowager empress, Julia Mamaea, to Antioch to teach her more about Christianity. After a brief return to Alexandria, he left for Greece, traveling via Caesarea, where he was ordained a priest. In 233 a final break with Bishop Demetrius took place, and Origen moved to Caesarea. Finally, works that he had long been developing, such as a commentary on the Gospel of John and *Peri eykhēs* (c. 233; *On Prayer*, 1954), the first thorough Christian examination of prayer as contemplation of God, were finished.

Even more productive were the years from 238 to 244, when he regularly preached and was consulted in matters of doctrine. Again, although most of his work has been lost, some has survived, above all more than two hundred sermons. Following an estrangement from his bishop, Theoctistus, Origen departed for Athens, where he continued his writing. In 246 or 247, he returned to Caesarea, where he set to work on commentaries on the Gospels of Luke and Matthew and on *Contra Celsum* (c. 249; *Against Celsus*, 1954), a defense of Christianity. During roughly the last eight years of his life, he found himself in the midst of both theological controversy and serious persecution of the Christians by the emperor Decius. By 251, Origen, who had been imprisoned and tortured, was a broken man. The circumstances of his death are uncertain.

SIGNIFICANCE

Origen was more important than any other early Christian thinker in assimilating the Jewish and Greek traditions into Christianity. The former he accomplished

through his lifelong contact with rabbinic scholars and the latter through his lifelong devotion to the Platonic tradition. His conscious intent was always to be faithful to Christianity whenever there was a direct conflict between it and what he had inherited from the earlier traditions. Nevertheless, he also intended to be open to truth wherever it might be found. That Christians usually think of themselves as the heirs to both the Jewish and the Greek traditions is more his work than any other's. He was the first Christian to discuss at length central problems such as the nature of free will and of God's relation to the world; as the first to do so, Origen did not always arrive at conclusions deemed correct by later standards. Thus, in spite of his genius, he has often been the subject of some suspicion in later Christian tradition. Arguably, he had as much influence in setting the terms of later Christian theology as any writer, Saint Paul included.

Origen subjected himself to great ascetic discipline, usually surrounded by his community of scribes and students, and his mode of life may be justly described as protomonastic. Indeed, it was only about forty years after his death that the monastic movement began. Finally, with his great confidence in the ability of the disciplined intellect to rise above the world of sense to the vision of God, Origen stands near the source of the Christian contemplative tradition.

—*Glenn W. Olsen*

FURTHER READING

Caspary, Gerard E. *Politics and Exegesis: Origen and the Two Swords*. Berkeley: University of California Press, 1979. Centers on Origen's thought about the relation of Christianity to the political order but has much useful information about his biblical interpretation and political thought. A structuralist interpretation that mistakenly attributes pacifism to early Christians in general before the time of Constantine the Great.

Daniélou, Jean. *Gospel Message and Hellenistic Culture*. Vol. 2 in *A History of Early Christian Doctrine Before the Council of Nicaea*. Translated by John Austin Baker. London: Westminster Press, 1973. Contains fine sections on Origen's catechetical teaching, biblical interpretation, Christology, anthropology, demonology, and understanding of Christian Gnosticism. Daniélou is very precise on the meaning and practice of allegory for Origen.

_____. *Origen*. Translated by Walter Mitchell. New York: Sheed and Ward, 1955. Covers Origen's life and times but is especially strong on his theology, including his interpretation of the Bible, cosmology, angelology, Christology, and eschatology. This Roman Catholic reading of Origen gives a very fair account of scholarly disagreement over Origen's theology of the sacraments.

Origen. *Contra Celsum*. Translated by Henry Chadwick. Cambridge, England: Cambridge University Press, 1965. The introduction and notes of this translation of one of Origen's most important works are a mine of information. Well indexed.

Trigg, Joseph Wilson. *Origen: The Bible and Philosophy in the Third-Century Church*. Atlanta, Ga.: John Knox Press, 1983. The best general survey of Origen's life and thought in English. Daniélou's explanation (see entries above) of Origen's spiritual exegesis of the Bible is more perceptive than that of Trigg, but Trigg is consistently well-informed. A Protestant reading of Origen.

SEE ALSO: Saint Ambrose; Julia Mamaea.

RELATED ARTICLES in *Great Events from History: The Ancient World*: 200 C.E., Christian Apologists Develop Concept of Theology; 250 C.E., Outbreak of the Decian Persecution.

OVID
Roman poet

While his contemporaries Vergil and Horace were glorifying the Roman Empire or harking back to sober republican virtues, Ovid wittily celebrated the senses. He also preserved for later generations many of the classical myths, although he treated the gods with the same irreverence as he did his fellow mortals.

BORN: March 20, 43 B.C.E.; Sulmo, Roman Empire (now Sulmona, Italy)
DIED: 17 C.E.; Tomis on the Black Sea, Moesia (now Constanţa, Romania)
ALSO KNOWN AS: Publius Ovidius Naso
AREA OF ACHIEVEMENT: Literature

EARLY LIFE
Publius Ovidius Naso, or Ovid (AWV-ihd), was born in 43 B.C.E. in what is now central Italy. As his family was a locally prominent one, he enjoyed the advantages of an education and preparation for an official career. Ovid's youth was during a period of political chaos. Rome was still nominally a republic, but Julius Caesar had made himself dictator. When Caesar was murdered in the year before Ovid's birth, the Roman world was plunged into civil war. Peace was not truly restored until fourteen years later.

First, Octavian, great-nephew and adopted son of Julius Caesar, collaborated with Marc Antony and Marcus Aemilius Lepidus to defeat the chiefs of the Republican party, Marcus Junius Brutus and Cassius. Then Lepidus was shunted aside, and Octavian and Antony entered into a protracted struggle for power. In 30 B.C.E., the year after his disastrous naval defeat at Actium, Antony and his Egyptian ally, Cleopatra VII, committed suicide. Octavian was the complete military ruler of Rome. By 27, the senate had conferred on him the official title Imperator, or emperor, and the honorary title Caesar Augustus, or the august one. Henceforward he was known as Augustus.

The extent to which these wars affected Ovid's family is not known, but the eventual outcome proved beneficial for him. He had become a poet, and the Augustan Age was a favorable time for poets. Gaius Maecenas, a chief counselor to Augustus, was the protector and financier of poets. However, the fun-loving Ovid was destined to squander his advantages and fall afoul of his emperor.

LIFE'S WORK
Although Ovid was born one hundred miles east of Rome, he was early exposed to the atmosphere of the capital. As the scion of an established family, he was sent to Rome at the age of twelve to be trained in the law. His arrival at the capital roughly coincided with Augustus's final victory over Antony. The era of the Pax Romana had begun.

Ovid was twenty-two years younger than Horace and almost thirty years younger than Vergil. Because he had been a child during the civil war, his experience of those terrible times had been less immediate than that of the older poets. Vergil and Horace were conservative in temperament and viewed the emperor, despite his new title, as the embodiment of the traditional Roman virtues. Their approval of Augustus was apparently sincere as well as politically and financially expedient. Horace, who had fallen into poverty as a young man through his support of the ill-fated Brutus, received the gift of a farm from Maecenas in 33 B.C.E. Ovid, however, was not a member of Vergil and Horace's circle. His companions were young and less closely associated with the regime.

Ovid entered the Roman civil service but quickly abandoned the law for poetry. He was a born poet, who once wrote that whatever he tried to say came out in verse. For one element of patrician Roman society, the new era of peace and prosperity was a perfect time for pleasure seeking. Ovid was soon the darling of this brilliant society. He became a professional poet, and his social success equaled his literary success. His themes were often frivolous, but he treated them with great elegance and wit. Technically, his verse was dazzling. The tone of his work was skeptical and irreverent. He practically thumbed his nose at the official solemnity and high-mindedness of the Augustan establishment. *Gravitas* might be the prime Roman virtue, but it was not the poetic mode for Ovid.

Little is known of Ovid's appearance or personal behavior. A tradition grew up, totally unsubstantiated by evidence, that Ovid was a rake and a womanizer—a sort of ancient precursor to John Wilmot, Earl of Rochester, and George Gordon, Lord Byron. The legendary Ovid, the good-looking playboy, is largely the product of two of his poems. The first, the *Amores* (c. 20 B.C.E.; English translation, 1597), was also his first published work. The *Amores* unblushingly recounts the conquests of a Roman Don Juan. The second, the *Ars amatoria* (c. 2 B.C.E.; *Art of Love*, 1612), is a tongue-in-cheek seduction manual.

The *Art of Love* could hardly have endeared Ovid to Augustus. While the emperor's propagandists were portraying a Rome turning back to the virtuousness, dignity, and piety of its forefathers, the impudent Ovid portrayed an amoral and libertine Rome, where panting ladies were ripe for the plucking. (Both Romes probably existed simultaneously.) In addition to being wickedly amusing, the poem reveals many psychologically valid insights into the gamesmanship of love. Ovid recommends the theater, the arena, dinner parties, and large festivals as the most likely gathering places of pliant females. He artfully plays on the stereotypes, already centuries old in his day, of man as an unskilled dissembler and woman as a born actress. His advice to the would-be gallant is practical in nature: Never, even playfully, discuss any of your mistress's defects. Do not be so foolhardy as to demand her age; this information is not to be had. Last, if she is over thirty-five, do not be distressed; older women are more practiced, and therefore more desirable, lovers.

Ovid's passing reference to pederasty is made without apology and suggests that it was an all too common practice in his society. Perhaps the tone and theme of the poem are crystallized in one line: Ovid's assertion that, after dark, there are no ugly women. The poem contains self-mockery, too. Of the role poetry plays in wooing a woman, the poet says: Send her gold rather than verses, for, even if they are perfectly written and perfectly recited, she will consider them a trifling gift at best.

Over the next seven years, Ovid worked on his masterpiece, the *Metamorphoses* (c. 8 C.E.; English translation, 1567). The poem consists of fifteen books that retell the stories of classical mythology, beginning with the creation of the world. The title means "transformations," especially by supernatural means, but it is only loosely descriptive. Although many of the tales recount the transformation of human beings into animals or inanimate things, others do not. Fortunately for posterity, Ovid retold so many stories that his poem became a principal sourcebook of classical myths. One cannot read the great triumvirate of English literature—Geoffrey Chaucer, William Shakespeare, and John Milton—without noticing how often they allude to the *Metamorphoses* or choose Ovid's version of a familiar myth.

Ovid. (Library of Congress)

Some ancient writers later accused Ovid of lacking a proper respect for the gods. It is clear that the author of the *Metamorphoses* did not believe the stories he was telling or in the deities who populated them. It is equally clear that he had matured artistically since the composition of the *Art of Love*. The *Metamorphoses* is, like the *Art of Love*, witty, charming, and beautifully constructed; still, it is also more comic than frivolous, often seriocomic, occasionally even tragicomic. Ovid modernized the poem in a way that should have pleased the emperor. He portrays the ascension of the murdered Julius Caesar into the heavens, where he becomes a star, and hints that Augustus himself will one day be changed into a god.

By 8 C.E., however, Ovid was in deep trouble with his emperor. Although he was by that time Rome's leading poet, he was tried before Augustus on a charge that history has not recorded and was banished from Rome. Possibly the emperor's disapproval of the *Art of Love* had finally brought about the poet's downfall. That poem was completed about 1 B.C.E. and had been in published form since 1 C.E., though, so scholars suggest that the poet's offense may have been his involvement in a scandal, possibly one associated with the emperor's daughter Julia. For whatever reason, he was banished to Tomis (located in modern-day Romania), an outpost on the Black Sea. Tomis was a cultural and intellectual backwater—and menaced by hostile border tribesmen.

For the next nine years, Ovid pleaded, through a series of epistles in verse known as the *Tristia* (after 8 C.E.; *Sorrows*, 1859), for the lifting of his punishment. Augustus did not relent, nor did his stepson and successor, Tiberius. Given the excesses that were eventually to mark Tiberius's reign, one wonders how corrupting the poet's presence could have been in Rome. Nevertheless, Ovid died still in exile in 17 C.E.

SIGNIFICANCE

Aeneas, Vergil's self-sacrificing Trojan prince, and the manliness and common sense of Horace's odes express one aspect of the Augustan Age. It was probably the dominant aspect, stressing as it does the patriotism of the *Aeneid* (c. 29-19 B.C.E.; English translation, 1553) and the traditional religious, moral, and social values of Horace's *Odes* (23 B.C.E., 13 B.C.E.; English translation, 1621). Ovid, however, writing in the sensual tradition of Catullus, reflects another aspect of the age.

The Rome of Vergil and Horace gave to the Western world a legal system and a framework of political unity that only a serious and an industrious people could have

devised. However, there was also in the Roman nature a playfulness, a highly developed aesthetic sensibility, and a *joie de vivre*; these are the qualities found in Ovid's poetry. All people in every age are capable of excesses and base behavior, but the three great Augustan poets reflect the two faces of the Roman Empire at its best.

It is ironic that it was the skeptical Ovid who, in his *Metamorphoses*, breathed life back into the debilitated gods of Rome. Ovid lived at the dawn of the Christian era, and within a few centuries the Christians' monotheism would sweep aside the polytheism of Greece and Rome. Ovid preserved the gods as intriguing characters in dozens of charming stories told in elegant verse. His compendium of mythological tales has been so influential that few indeed are the great works of Western literature that contain no allusion to Ovid's *Metamorphoses*.

—*Patrick Adcock*

FURTHER READING

Brewer, Wilmon. *Ovid's "Metamorphoses" in European Culture*. Boston: Cornhill, 1933. A three-volume companion work to an English translation in blank verse. Begins with a long introductory survey that includes much biographical detail. Very valuable, because every story in the poem is discussed in the light of its cultural and literary antecedents, then of later works for which it served as antecedent.

Hardie, Philip, ed. *The Cambridge Companion to Ovid*. New York: Cambridge University Press, 2002. Chapters by well-known scholars discuss Ovid, his backgrounds and contexts, the individual works, and its influence on later literature and art. Includes bibliography and index.

Hoffman, Richard L. *Ovid and "The Canterbury Tales."* Philadelphia: University of Pennsylvania Press, 1966. Since John Dryden first compared Ovid and Chaucer in 1700, many Chaucerians have remarked that the great English poet studied, imitated, and relied on Ovid above all other authors. This study treats the *Metamorphoses* as a predecessor of *The Canterbury Tales*.

Rand, Edward Kennard. *Ovid and His Influence*. 1925. Reprint. New York: Cooper Square, 1963. A professor of Latin poses the question: What does our age owe to a professed roué, a writer so subtle and rhetorical as to strike some as thoroughly insincere? His 184 pages answer that question.

Syme, Ronald. *History in Ovid*. New York: Oxford University Press, 1978. Concentrating on Ovid's latest poems, the author develops a kind of manual designed to cover life and letters in the last decade of Caesar Augustus. Valuable because of the relative obscurity of that period.

Thibault, John C. *The Mystery of Ovid's Exile*. Berkeley: University of California Press, 1964. The author examines various hypotheses about Ovid's exile, describes their content, and evaluates the evidence and the cogency of the arguments.

SEE ALSO: Augustus; Horace; Gaius Maecenas; Vergil.

RELATED ARTICLES in *Great Events from History: The Ancient World*: 43-42 B.C.E., Second Triumvirate Enacts Proscriptions; September 2, 31 B.C.E., Battle of Actium; 27-23 B.C.E., Completion of the Augustan Settlement; 19 B.C.E., Roman Poet Vergil Dies; November 27, 8 B.C.E., Roman Lyric Poet Horace Dies; 8 C.E., Ovid's *Metamorphoses* Is Published.

PAPPUS
Alexandrian mathematician

Pappus provided a valuable compilation of the contributions of earlier mathematicians and inspired later work on algebraic solutions to geometric problems.

BORN: c. 300 C.E.; Alexandria, Egypt
DIED: c. 350 C.E.; place unknown
AREA OF ACHIEVEMENT: Mathematics

EARLY LIFE

Almost nothing is known about Pappus's life, including the dates of his birth and death. A note written in the margin of a text by a later Alexandrian geometer states that Pappus wrote during the time of Diocletian (284-305 C.E.). The earliest biographical source is a tenth century Byzantine encyclopedia compiled by Suidas. This work lists the writings of Pappus and describes him as a "philosopher," which suggests that he may have held some official position as a teacher of philosophy. Nevertheless, this reference to philosophy may be no more than an indication of his interest in natural science. The geometer had at least one child, a son, since he dedicated one of his books to him. In addition, Pappus mentions two of his contemporaries in his texts: a philosopher, Hierius, although the connection between the two is not clear; and Pandrosian, a woman who taught mathematics. Pappus addressed one of his works to her, not as a tribute, but because he found several of her students deficient in their mathematical education.

Pappus lived at a time when the main course of Greek mathematics had been in decline for more than five hundred years; although geometry continued to be studied and taught, there were few original contributions to the subject. To alleviate this lack, he attempted to compile all available sources of earlier geometry and made several significant contributions to the subject. As the first author in this new tradition, sometimes called the silver age of mathematics, Pappus provides a valuable resource for all of ancient Greek geometry.

LIFE'S WORK

Throughout his life, Pappus maintained a lively interest in a number of areas dealing with mathematics and natural science. The bulk of his surviving works can be found in the *Synagogē* (c. 340 C.E.; partial translation *The Collection*, 1986). Other works either are in fragmentary form or else are no longer extant, although mentioned by other writers. There exists part of a commentary on the mechanics of Archimedes which considers problems associated with mean proportions and constructions using straightedge and compass. There are two remaining books of a commentary on Ptolemy's *Mathēmatikē syntaxis* (c. 150 C.E.; *Almagest*, 1948) explaining some of the finer points of the text to the inexperienced reader. Pappus continued his interest in the popularization of difficult texts in a work, of which only a fragment survives, on Euclid's *Stoicheia* (c. 300 B.C.E.; *The Elements of Geometrie of the Most Auncient Philosopher Euclide of Megara*, 1570, commonly known as the *Elements*), in which Pappus explains the nature of irrational magnitudes to the casual reader. The lost works include a geography of the inhabited world, a description of rivers in Libya, an interpretation of dreams, several texts on spherical geometry and stereographic projection, an astrological almanac, and a text on alchemical oaths and formulas. Pappus was more than a geometer; he was a person who lived in a world where the search for new knowledge was rapidly declining and where political instability was the order of the day. Yet he expressed a continuing interest in the education of those less fortunate than himself and showed a lively interest in affairs outside his city.

Pappus's claim to historical and mathematical significance is found in a compendium of eight books on geometry. This collection covers the entire range of Greek geometry and has been described as a handbook or guide to the subject. In several of the books, when the classical texts are available, Pappus shows how the original proof is accomplished as well as alternative methods to prove the theorem. In other books, where the classical sources are not easily accessible, Pappus provides a history of the problems as well as different attempts at finding a solution. An overall assessment of these books shows few moments of great originality; rather, a capable and independent mind sifts through the entire scope of Greek geometry while demonstrating fine technique and a clear understanding of his field of study.

A summary of the contents of the eight books shows that some are of only historical interest, providing information on or elucidation of classical texts. Other books, particularly book 7, have been a source of inspiration for later mathematicians. All of book 1 and the first part of book 2 are lost. The remainder of book 2 deals with the problems of multiplying all the numbers between 1 and 800 together and expressing the product in words using the myriad (10,000) as base. Pappus refers to a lost work by Apollonius of Perga which seems to be part of the problem of expressing large numbers in words that began with Archimedes' *Psiammites* (c. 230 B.C.E.; *The Sand-Reckoner*, 1897). Book 3 deals with construction problems using straightedge and compass: finding a mean proportion between two given straight lines, finding basic means between two magnitudes (arithmetic, geometric, and harmonic), constructing a triangle within another triangle, and constructing solids within a sphere. Book 4 consists of a collection of theorems, including several famous problems in Greek mathematics: a generalization of Pythagoras's theorem, the squaring of the circle, and the trisection of an angle. Book 5 begins with an extensive introduction on the hexagonal cells of honeycombs and suggests that bees could acquire geometric knowledge from some divine source. This discussion leads to the question of the maximum volume that can be enclosed by a superficial area and to a sequence of theorems that prove that the circle has the greatest area of figures of equal parameter. His proof appears to follow those formulated by an earlier Hellenistic geometer named Zenodorus, whose work is lost. In a later section of this book, Pappus introduces a section on solids with a Neoplatonist statement that God chose to make the universe in a sphere because it is the noblest of figures. It has been asserted but not proved that the sphere has the greatest surface of all equal surface figures. Pappus then proceeds to examine the sphere and regular solids. Book 6 is sometimes called "Little Astronomy"; it deals with misunderstandings in mathematical technique and corrects common misrepresentations.

Book 7 is by far the most important, both because it had a direct influence on modern mathematics and because it gives an account of works in the so-called *Treasury of Analysis* or *Domain of Analysis*, of which a large number are lost. These are works by Euclid, Apollonius, and others that set up a branch of mathematics that provides equipment for the analysis of theorems and problems. Classical geometry uses the term "analysis" to mean a reversal of the normal procedure called "synthesis." Instead of taking a series of steps through valid statements about abstract objects, analysis reverses the procedure by assuming the validity of the theorem and working back to valid statements. Through the preservation of Pappus's account of these works it is possible to reconstruct most of them.

His most original contribution to modern mathematics comes in a section dealing with Apollonius's *Cōnica* (*Treatise on Conic Sections*, 1896; best known as *Conics*), where Pappus attempts to demonstrate that the product of three or four straight lines can be written as a series of compounded ratios and is equal to a constant. This came to be known as the "Pappus problem." Book 8 is the last of the surviving books of *Synagoge*, although there is internal evidence that four additional books existed. In this book, Pappus takes on the subject of mechanical problems, including weights on inclined planes, proportioning of gears, and the center of gravity.

There exist substantial references to various lost books of Pappus; among the lost works is a commentary on Euclid's *Elements*, although a two-part section does exist in Arabic. Several other works fit into this category, surviving only in commentary by later writers or in fragments of questionable authorship in Arabic. One of the more interesting Arabic manuscripts (discovered in 1860) shows that Pappus may have invented a volumeter similar to one invented by Joseph-Louis Gay-Lussac (1778-1850). Pappus was not merely a geometer; he was a conserver of classical tradition, a popularizer of Greek geometry, and an inventor as well.

SIGNIFICANCE

The works of Pappus have provided later generations with a storehouse of ancient Greek geometry, both as an independent check against the authenticity of other known sources and as a valuable source of lost texts. For modern mathematics, Pappus offers more than merely historical interest. In 1631, Jacob Golius pointed out to René Descartes the "Pappus problem," and six years later this became the centerpiece of Descartes's *Des matières de la géométrie*, which was a section of his *Discours de la méthode* (1637; *Discourse on Method*, 1649). Descartes realized that his new algebraic symbols could easily replace Pappus's more difficult geometric methods and that the product of the locus of straight lines generated from conic sections could generate equations of second, third, and higher orders.

In 1687 Sir Isaac Newton found a similar inspiration in the "Pappus problem" using purely geometric methods. Nevertheless, it was Descartes's algebraic methods that would be utilized in the future. Pappus also anticipated the well-known "Guldin's theorem," dealing with figures generated by the revolution of plane figures about an axis. It can be argued that Pappus was the only geometer who possessed the ability to work out such a theorem during the silver age of Greek mathematics.

—*Victor W. Chen*

FURTHER READING

Bulmer-Thomas, I. "Guldin's Theorem—or Pappus's?" *Isis* 75 (1984): 348-352. There exists some question whether the Pappus text is original or if the text was corrupted at a later date. A less significant issue here is the interpretation of the Pappus manuscript—a historical problem concerned with the extent to which Pappus anticipated Guldin.

Cuomo, Serafina. *Pappus of Alexandria and the Mathematics of Late Antiquity*. New York: Cambridge University Press, 2000. Sees Pappus's work as part of a wider context and relates it to other contemporary cultural practices, opening new avenues of research into the understanding of mathematics in antiquity.

Descartes, René. *The Geometry of René Descartes*. Translated by Davis E. Smith and Marcia L. Latham. Chicago: Open Court, 1952. It is possible to follow from Descartes's own text the relevant passages from Pappus's work, seeing how Descartes develops his new symbols and why this method would later become the preferred method.

Fried, Michael N. *Apollonius of Perga's "Conica": Text, Context, and Subtext*. Boston: E. J. Brill, 2001. An extensive discussion of this work, from which arose the "Pappus problem."

Heath, Sir Thomas. *From Aristarchus to Diophantus*. Vol. 2 in *A History of Greek Mathematics*. Reprint. New York: Dover Publications, 1981. This edition contains several long sections from the *Collection* as well as commentaries on the history and contents of these theorems.

Pappus. *Book 7 of the Collection*. Edited by Alexander Jones. 2 vols. New York: Springer-Verlag, 1986. These two volumes contain the most complete rendition of book 7; in addition, there are exhaustive commentaries and notes on every aspect of this text. Contains a detailed account of the history of various Pappus manuscripts and notes on the problems of translating ancient Greek text.

SEE ALSO: Apollonius of Perga; Archimedes; Diophantus; Euclid; Eudoxus of Cnidus; Hero of Alexandria; Hypatia; Pythagoras.

RELATED ARTICLES in *Great Events from History: The Ancient World*: 325-323 B.C.E., Aristotle Isolates Science as a Discipline; c. 320 B.C.E., Theophrastus Initiates the Study of Botany; c. 300 B.C.E., Euclid Compiles a Treatise on Geometry; c. 275 B.C.E., Greeks Advance Hellenistic Astronomy; c. 250 B.C.E., Discoveries of Archimedes; 415 C.E., Mathematician and Philosopher Hypatia Is Killed in Alexandria.

PARMENIDES
Greek philosopher

By exploring the logical implications of statements that use apparently simple terms such as "one" or "is," Parmenides established metaphysics as an area of philosophy.

BORN: c. 515 B.C.E.; Elea (now Velia, Italy)
DIED: Perhaps after 436 B.C.E.; possibly Elea
AREA OF ACHIEVEMENT: Philosophy

EARLY LIFE

In the mid-sixth century B.C.E., as the Persian Empire advanced through Asia Minor toward the Aegean Sea, some of the Greek city-states that were thus threatened accommodated themselves to the invaders. Others attempted to maintain their independence. In the case of one Ionian city, Phocaea, many of the inhabitants left Asia Minor entirely. They migrated to southern Italy, founding Elea around 540 B.C.E. Pyres, the father of Parmenides (pahr-MEHN-ih-deez), may have been one of the emigrants, or, like his son, he may have been born in Elea. At any rate, Parmenides' family background was in Ionia.

It is therefore entirely natural that Parmenides would eventually compose verse in the standard Ionic dialect that had earlier been used for Homeric epics. Philosophical influences on the young Parmenides must be more conjectural, but at least some interest in the Ionian philosophers of the sixth century, such as Thales of Miletus and Anaximander, seems entirely reasonable for someone growing up in a Phocaean settlement.

The ancient traditions about Parmenides, on the other hand, connect him with the poet and philosopher Xenophanes. Born c. 570 B.C.E., Xenophanes was from Colophon in Asia Minor, and like the Phocaeans, he fled before the Persians to the western Greek world. Some contact between him and Parmenides is therefore quite likely. It is not so clear, though, that one should regard Parmenides as being in any real sense Xenophanes' student. A better case can be made for a close association of Parmenides with the otherwise obscure Ameinias, to whom, after his death, Parmenides built a shrine, according to Diogenes Laertius (c. 200 C.E.). Ameinias was a

Pythagorean, and thus one should add the sixth century philosopher and mystic Pythagoras to the list of early influences on Parmenides.

The date that Diogenes Laertius gives for Parmenides' birth is around 540 B.C.E. Plato's dialogue *Parmenidēs* (399-390 B.C.E.; *Parmenides*, 1793), on the other hand, is inconsistent with this date. Most of the dialogue is clearly invented by Plato, as it includes details of argumentation that Plato himself developed in the fourth century. The conversation between Parmenides, Socrates, and others, therefore, can scarcely have taken place as described by Plato; still, the overall setting of the dialogue, which implies that the title character was born around 515 B.C.E., may be chronologically accurate. Possibly, the date given by Diogenes Laertius arose from a reference in one of his sources to the founding of Elea around 540 B.C.E. as a crucial event in Parmenides' background.

LIFE'S WORK

Pondering the implications of earlier philosophy, which saw a single unifying principle—such as water, the infinite, or number—behind the various phenomena of the world, Parmenides strove to uncover a paradox residing in any such analysis. He wrote one treatise, in poetic form, in which he set forth his views. This work is generally referred to as *Peri physeōs* (only fragments are translated into English), although it is not certain that Parmenides himself so entitled it. Of this poem, about 150 lines are preserved in Greek, along with another six lines in a Latin translation.

Parmenides' central concern, or at least that for which he is best known, lies in the implications of the Greek word *esti*, meaning "is." According to Parmenides, of the two predications "is" and "is not," only "is" makes sense. Merely to say "is not" gives some stamp of evidence to whatever one says "is not" and therefore involves self-contradiction. With "is not" thus rejected, all reality must somehow be single and unified, all-encompassing and unchanging. Such a view would seem to be essentially ineffable, but toward the middle of Parmenides' fragment 8, which gives the core of his argument, what "is" is compared to a well-rounded ball, perfectly poised in the middle, with nothing outside itself.

Despite this thoroughgoing monism, the opening of Parmenides' poem (fragment 1) refers to two paths of inquiry—one of *aletheia* (truth) and one of *doxa* (opinion). The argument about the primacy of "is" over "is not" follows the path of *aletheia*, while the latter part of fragment 8 follows the path of *doxa*. (These sections are generally

known as the *Aletheia* and the *Doxa*.) Ancient authors did not, on the whole, find the *Doxa* interesting. It was therefore not so much quoted in antiquity, and only about forty-five lines from it are preserved. As a result, many modern treatments of Parmenides concentrate on the better preserved *Aletheia*. Such an approach may also find a precedent in Plato's dialogue *Parmenides*. Other scholars, though, acknowledge *Doxa* as having been an integral part of the poem, and this approach is entirely supported by some of the ancient references to Parmenides. Aristotle (384-322 B.C.E.), for example, refers in *Metaphysica* (335-323 B.C.E.; *Metaphysics*, 1801) to Parmenides as having been constrained by phenomena to acknowledge change and multiplicity in the sensible world.

Aristotle's line of interpretation is probably correct. Despite the paucity of direct information about the *Doxa*, several crucial ideas in ancient science are consistently associated with Parmenides, either as originating with him or as being promulgated by him. For example, the simile that concludes the *Aletheia*—that what "is" resembles a well-rounded ball—may have a more prosaic but still-grander cosmic application to Earth as a sphere, poised in space. Fragment 14 refers to the moon's shining, not of its own accord but by reflected light. Aëtius (c. 100 C.E.) and Diogenes Laertius ascribe to Parmenides the observation that the evening and morning star are the same body (Venus) as it travels through space. Strabo (who flourished during the first century B.C.E.), quoting an earlier source, refers to Parmenides as having divided Earth into five zones. Such astronomical and geographic interests, along with various references to his treatment of biology, anatomy, and psychology, suggest that Parmenides had a mind more concerned with the investigation of physical phenomena than his austerely logical treatment of "is" and "is not" would suggest.

Nevertheless, Plato's contrary focus on Parmenides as primarily a metaphysician provides the earliest biographical and descriptive vignette of Parmenides. Plato's account places Parmenides in Athens in 450, at the time of a quadrennial festival to the goddess Athena. According to Plato, the Eleatic visitor to Athens was then about sixty-five years old, already white-haired but still of a forceful and commanding appearance and quite capable, as Plato reveals in the rest of the dialogue, of engaging in a complicated philosophical discussion.

Unfortunately, there is nothing very specific in Plato's physical description of Parmenides. One might hope that the picture would be filled out by the bust from the first century C.E. found during excavations at Elea in 1966.

The bust matches an inscription, "Parmenides the son of Pyres the natural philosopher," found in 1962; also, the inscription somehow connects Parmenides with Apollo as a patron of physicians. The existence of this statue obviously attests the regard in which Parmenides was held in Elea several centuries after his death. It is unlikely, however, that it actually portrays the visage of Parmenides, since it seems to be modeled on the bust of a later figure, the Epicurean Metrodorus (c. 300 B.C.E.), who was chosen to represent the typical philosopher.

In his account of Parmenides' visit to Athens, Plato includes the detail that Zeno of Elea, who accompanied Parmenides on that occasion, had once been his lover. Athenaeus (fl. c. 200 C.E.) objects to this point as a superfluous addition that contributes nothing to Plato's narrative. Whatever the case may be, Zeno and the slightly later Melissus (born c. 480 B.C.E.) are often grouped with Parmenides as the founders of an Eleatic school of philosophy. In particular, the intellectual connection between Parmenides and Zeno may be especially close. Both were from Elea (while Melissus was from the Aegean island Samos), and, according to Plato, Zeno's paradoxes, purporting to show the impossibility of motion, were designed to support Parmenides' doctrine concerning the unified nature of reality.

The determination of direct influences of Parmenides beyond the Eleatic school is more tenuous. Theophrastus (c. 372-287 B.C.E.), however, connects two other fifth century figures with him—the philosopher-poet Empedocles and Leucippus, the founder of atomism. Also, although he is from a later generation, it is generally agreed that Plato himself owed much to Parmenides.

Of Parmenides' life after his possible visit to Athens in 450, nothing definite is known. Theophrastus's implication that Leucippus studied with him at Elea should possibly be dated after 450. Also, Eusebius of Caesarea (c. 260-339 C.E.) implies that Parmenides was still living in 436 B.C.E.; this information leads scholars to believe Plato's chronology over that given by Diogenes Laertius. According to Plutarch, Parmenides was a lawgiver as well as a philosopher, and subsequent generations at Elea swore to abide by his laws.

SIGNIFICANCE

Some critics see fundamental flaws in Parmenides' reasoning. According to the modern scholar Jonathan Barnes, for example, it is perfectly acceptable to say that it is necessarily the case that what does not exist does not exist, but Parmenides erred in holding that what does not exist necessarily does not exist. Even if this objection

is valid, Parmenides' lasting influence on subsequent thought is undeniable. Often, his arguments are presented without quibble in modern treatments of the history of philosophy, as having uncovered difficulties with which any process of thinking must cope.

It is also important to keep in mind the poetic medium that Parmenides used. His sixth century predecessors, such as Anaximander and Anaximenes, had used prose for their philosophical treatises. Parmenides, however, chose verse, perhaps to give some sense of the majesty and dignity of the philosopher's quest. The ineffable quality that Parmenides claims for ultimate reality may also find an appropriate expression in poetry. Above all, the use of verse puts Parmenides in a rich verbal tradition, stretching back to the earliest extant Greek poetry, that of Homer and Hesiod, and to even earlier oral poetry. The most obvious parallels are with Homer's *Odyssey* (c. 725 B.C.E.; English translation, 1614). For example, the cattle of the Sun are described in the *Odyssey* as neither coming into being nor perishing, and this idea is also central to Parmenides' concept of what is. A close verbal parallel to Homer's description of the paths of night and day in the *Odyssey* is also found in Parmenides. More generally, one may note that Odysseus, after his manifold adventures in the outer reaches of the world, eventually returns home to Ithaca and to his wife, Penelope, exactly as Parmenides would both partake of and yet, somehow, eschew the realm of pure thought for the mundane world of *doxa*.

Parmenides thus emerges as a prime mediator between ancient Greek and later philosophy. While casting his thought in terms of the poetic imagery, metaphors, and formulas used by Homer and Hesiod, he still insisted emphatically on the paramount importance of reason that his contemporaries and successors, such as Zeno, Leucippus, and Plato, framed anew.

—*Edwin D. Floyd*

FURTHER READING

Barnes, Jonathan. *The Presocratic Philosophers*. New York: Routledge, 1996. Contains three chapters mainly on Parmenides, along with numerous other references. Barnes puts Parmenides' ideas into a modern philosophical framework, and although his use of technical jargon and symbols is sometimes a bit heavy, he nevertheless handles the ramifications of Parmenides' argument in magisterial fashion. Includes bibliography.

Burnet, John. *Early Greek Philosophy*. London: A. and C. Black, 1963. A classic work on pre-Socratic philosophy first published in 1892. Contains a clear, readable chapter on Parmenides and a chapter on Leucippus that suggests that Parmenides' reference to what "is" as a self-contained sphere may have given rise to atomism.

Finkelberg, Aryeh. "The Cosmology of Parmenides." *American Journal of Philology* 107 (1986): 303-317. Treating the *Doxa* as an important part of Parmenides' poem, this article deals principally with Aëtius's report of Parmenides as referring to various rings that compose Earth: a fiery region within it, airy rings that are associated with the heavenly bodies, and so on.

Lombardo, Stanley, ed. *Parmenides and Empedocles: The Fragments in Verse Translation*. San Francisco: Grey Fox Press, 1982. A spirited if somewhat free translation, but the best source for getting some sense in English of the fact that Parmenides wrote in verse and that this point is important for understanding the effect he wanted to achieve.

Mackenzie, Mary Margaret. "Parmenides' Dilemma." *Phronesis* 27 (1982): 1-12. Discusses the appearance of second-person verb forms in Parmenides' poem. The use of locutions such as "you think" must inevitably lead to an acknowledgment of plurality, and Parmenides' inclusion of the *Doxa* in his poem may be explained in these terms.

Mourelatos, Alexander P. D. *The Route of Parmenides*. New Haven, Conn.: Yale University Press, 1970. The main thrust of this work is Parmenides' philosophical program. There is also a good introductory chapter on Homeric prototypes for Parmenides' poetic technique. Contains Greek text of fragments of Parmenides but no translation.

Parmenides. *Parmenides of Elea, Fragments: A Text and Translation, with an Introduction*. Edited by David Gallop. Toronto: University of Toronto Press, 1984. This volume consists of Greek text and English translation of the fragments of Parmenides, with English translations of the contexts in which the fragments occur. Also contains brief biographies (one to three sentences) of the ancient authors who quote or refer to Parmenides. The most convenient source for getting a general view of the ancient sources concerning Parmenides. Includes a good bibliography.

Plato. *The "Parmenides" and Plato's Late Philosophy*. Translated by Robert G. Turnbull. Buffalo: University of Toronto Press, 1998. Primarily a translation of Plato's dialogue, with extensive commentary. Several pages deal specifically with Parmenides, however, and there are also other scattered references to his poem.

SEE ALSO: Anaximander; Empedocles; Homer; Plato; Pythagoras; Thales of Miletus; Xenophanes; Zeno of Elea.

RELATED ARTICLES in *Great Events from History: The Ancient World*: 600-500 B.C.E., Greek Philosophers Formulate Theories of the Cosmos; 547 B.C.E., Cyrus the Great Founds the Persian Empire; c. 530 B.C.E., Founding of the Pythagorean Brotherhood.

SAINT PAUL
Cilician religious leader

Paul spread the teachings of an obscure Jewish sect throughout the eastern Mediterranean region and eventually to Rome. As the educated apostle, he gave Christianity a measure of intellectual credibility and formulated much of what would later become doctrine.

BORN: c. 10 C.E.; Tarsus, Cilicia (now in Turkey)
DIED: c. 64 C.E.; Rome (now in Italy)
ALSO KNOWN AS: Paul the Apostle; Paul of Tarsus; Saul of Tarsus
AREA OF ACHIEVEMENT: Religion

EARLY LIFE
Saint Paul was born at Tarsus in Cilicia, a region in southeast Asia Minor, on the Mediterranean Sea. He was a Jew, known during his early years by the name of Saul. Little documentary evidence exists concerning these years, but certain things can be inferred from Paul's status at the time that he appeared on the historical scene.

Paul was trained as a rabbi in the Pharisaic tradition. His background as a Pharisee indicates a close adherence to both the written law and the oral, or traditional, law. This stance would have been a source of constant tension between Paul and the Apostles who arose out of the village culture of Palestine. In the Gospels, the term Pharisee takes on connotations of self-righteousness and sanctimoniousness. Further, Paul was a product of the city and of the Diaspora, the settlements of those Jews who had been dispersed throughout Asia Minor. Certain awkward phrases in his writings, when he is trying to be simpler, indicate that he was never comfortable with agricultural or bucolic topics. He was exposed early in life to Greek language, mythology, and culture. In the Hellenistic synagogues where he worshiped as a youth, he would have heard the Jewish scriptures read not in Hebrew but in Greek translation. Paul is identified in the Acts of the Apostles as a Roman citizen, so rare a status for a Jew that his family must have been influential and highly connected. Finally, he was for a time a leading persecutor of the new sect, seeing the followers of Jesus as a grave threat to the Jewish legal tradition.

For all the reasons cited above, it is little wonder that after his conversion many of his fellow Jewish Christians viewed him with suspicion and even with hostility. However, Paul's conversion was so total and the rejection of his past life so absolute that other writers have felt the need to dramatize it, even though Paul's own letters do not describe it at all.

LIFE'S WORK

Paul's great achievement was to take Christianity from Jerusalem throughout the eastern provinces of the Roman Empire and finally to the capital itself. He possessed the vision to see that the new faith had a message and an appeal that were not limited to the Jews.

During the years preceding the conversion of Saul of Tarsus, the future of Christianity was not promising. Rome had imposed a political order on the eastern Mediterranean and had inculcated its attitudes of tolerance (for the times) and materialism. The relative peace and prosperity of the period, however, apparently proved insufficient to meet the spiritual and psychological needs of the subject peoples. The major ancient religions had ossified and were the source of very little spiritual energy. Among the Greeks and Romans, religious practice had become almost purely conventional, and the Jews awaited the great supernatural event that would revitalize them.

In response to this state of affairs, philosophical and religious sects sprang up everywhere, including Greek syncretism, Mithraism, Zoroastrianism, and Christianity. The struggles of these and many other sects to win the minds and hearts of the people would continue for the next five hundred years (before Saint Augustine's conversion to Christianity in 386-387, he experimented with virtually all of its competitors). At the middle of the first century after the death of Jesus, Christianity—a provincial religion under the leadership of a small group of unsophisticated and unlettered men—seemed unlikely to

Saint Paul. (Library of Congress)

be the winner of this great competition. Thus, it is difficult to overstate the impact of the conversion of Saul of Tarsus.

He was a most unlikely Apostle of the crucified carpenter from Galilee. Far from being a man of the people, he was a member of the most learned Jewish party. He held Roman citizenship. He had not been personally associated with Jesus of Nazareth and viewed those who had been as a threat to the Jewish law, which he uncompromisingly supported. His nature was sometimes imperious, as his writings disclose. He did not leave a description of his conversion as Saint Augustine was later to do, but something in his thinking was leading him toward the profound change that would make him history's archetypal Christian convert. He developed a sense of the frailty and corruption of the world's institutions, a disgust for the secular materialism that surrounded him, and a conviction that humanity's only hope lay in dying to all worldly things. He gave up a comfortable, settled life for that of an itinerant preacher and religious organizer. He changed from a defender of the legal tradition of Judaism to the most zealous opponent of those Jewish Christians who sought to retain any part of it.

Saul first appears in the book of the Acts of the Apostles at Jerusalem, as a witness to the stoning of Stephen, the first Christian martyr. His complicity in the execution is strongly suggested, for he is reported to have consented to the death (as if he had some say in the matter), and the witnesses laid their clothes down at his feet. His age at the time is not known, but he is described as a young man. Succeeding chapters paint him as a fierce oppressor of the Christians. His persecutions culminate in a trip to Damascus, where, under authority from the high priests, he is to harry all the Christians he can find. It is on this journey that he has his famous conversion experience: He hears the voice of Jesus challenging him, and he is struck blind. After three days, his sight is restored. He is baptized and almost immediately begins to preach in the synagogues that Christ is the Son of God. Scholars who do not subscribe to a literal interpretation of the scriptural account suggest that it results from Paul's having left no account of his own. Presented with the sudden, total, and inexplicable change in Saul's behavior, perhaps his first biographer could not resist romanticizing it.

The remainder of his story in Acts is replete with adventure and conflict. Saul is so skilled in disputation that both his Jewish and Greek opponents plot to kill him; he makes narrow and dramatic escapes. Still the Christians in Jerusalem cannot fully trust him; they remember the old Saul, and send him back to Tarsus. By chapter 13 of Acts, Saul (whose name means "asked of God" in Hebrew) has become known as Paul (meaning "small" in Greek). He has also become the missionary to the Gentiles. He travels widely: preaching, healing, organizing Christian communities, and suffering periods of hardship and imprisonment. The Scriptures hint at but give no account of his eventual martyrdom in Rome; legend would later supply one.

Much of Paul's career as a missionary can only be the object of conjecture. Some of his work and the time of its accomplishment have been verified through seven of his letters whose genuineness is generally accepted—his epistles to the various fledgling Christian communities. The first letter to the church at Thessalonica, provincial capital of Macedonia, was written from Corinth, c. 51. At that time, Paul was in the company of Silvanus (known in Acts as Silas) and Timothy. About three years later, from Ephesus in western Asia Minor, he wrote a stinging letter to the Christians in Galatia. They had been entertaining rival missionaries, who apparently argued that pagan converts were subject to the Jewish law. In this letter, Paul defends his understanding of the Gospel and his teaching authority with occasionally bitter sarcasm.

The next year, near the end of his stay at Ephesus, he wrote the first of two extant letters to the church at Corinth, which he had founded c. 50. The church had developed several factions and incipient heresies (in the early church, it was largely Paul who delineated the orthodoxies and the heresies). In addition to responding to these matters, Paul offers sexual advice to husbands and wives, his famous pronouncement that the ideal Christian life is a celibate one, and his beautiful disquisition on love. A second letter to the Corinthians, written c. 56, asserts Paul's credentials and questions with heavy irony those of false prophets who have been wooing the flock. The letter addresses a number of other issues in such a curious chronology that it may well be a composite of several fragments, the work of some ancient editor. Paul's physical appearance is a mystery (early iconography seems based on little more than imagination), but in this letter he does allude to a "thorn in the flesh" from which three separate entreaties to the Lord have not relieved him. The nature of the illness is not known but has been the object of much speculation.

Around 57, during his last stay at Corinth, Paul wrote a long letter to Rome. It was both a letter of introduction and a theological treatise, written in anticipation of his preaching there. His letter to the church at Philippi was long held to have been written at Rome c. 62, during his two years of imprisonment there. Some scholars argue, however, that at least a part of it was written much earlier (c. 56) from a prison in Caesarea or Ephesus. Another letter from prison—a request that Philemon, a Colossian Christian, magnanimously take back a runaway slave whom Paul has converted—is also variously dated, depending on whether the missionary wrote from Rome or elsewhere. Other letters (such as Timothy and Titus) bear Paul's name, but their authenticity has been disputed.

The last of Paul's many arrests occurred in Jerusalem, where he was attempting to promote unity within the Christian community (ironically, he himself had been one of the divisive factors there). As a citizen, he appealed to Rome and was transported to the capital. His lengthy period of imprisonment there is described in some detail in Acts. It is presumed that around 64 he was executed—legend has it that he was beheaded—just preceding Nero's persecution of the Roman Christians.

SIGNIFICANCE

While Saint Peter and the other Palestinian Apostles were at first content to limit Christianity to converted Jews, Saint Paul determined to take it to the Gentiles. As the other Apostles moved back and forth among the villages of their native region, Paul spread the faith to the bustling cities of Asia Minor and southern Europe. He tirelessly plied the trade routes of the Eastern Roman Empire, setting up church after church in the major population centers. In his second letter to the Corinthians, he catalogs his sufferings: imprisonments, beatings, floggings, a stoning, shipwreck, assassination plots, hunger, thirst, and—above all else—anxiety for the welfare of his churches.

He believed, as did the other primitive Christians, that he lived at the end of history, that the second coming of his Lord was at hand. Even so, he threw himself into every aspect of church organization—doctrine, ritual, politics. He fought lethargy here, inappropriate enthusiasm there. He constantly sought to make peace between Jewish and non-Jewish Christians. His dictates on such subjects as Christian celibacy and the lesser role of women in the church continue to provoke controversy, thousands of years after they were written.

Paul has been called the man who delivered Christianity from Judaism. He has been called the man who furnished Christianity with its intellectual content. Because of his argument that the Crucifixion represents a covenant superseding the ancient law, he has been called the father of the Reformation, and it has been suggested that Protestantism derives from him as Catholicism derives from Saint Peter. He has been called a compulsive neurotic, whose works were instances of sublimation and whose thorn in the flesh was psychosomatic. Writer George Bernard Shaw characterized him as the fanatic who corrupted the teachings of Jesus. It would be extravagant to claim that Christianity would not have survived without Paul. It is safe to say that it would not have survived in its present form without him.

—*Patrick Adcock*

FURTHER READING

Bruce, F. F. *Paul: Apostle of the Heart Set Free*. Grand Rapids, Mich.: Wm. B. Eerdmans, 1983. This book, which is accessible to the general reader, focuses on Paul's life, though there is also discussion of his writings. Well illustrated, with indexes of names and places, subjects, and references.

Davies, William David. *Paul and Rabbinic Judaism: Some Rabbinic Elements in Pauline Theology*. Philadelphia: Fortress Press, 1980. Attempts to prove that Paul was in the mainstream of first century Judaism and that Hellenistic influences on him have been overestimated. The first of ten chapters assesses the degree of difference between Palestinian and Diaspora Judaism. Chapters 5 and 6 discuss Paul as preacher and teacher.

Meeks, Wayne A. *The First Urban Christians: The Social World of the Apostle Paul*. 2d ed. New Haven, Conn.: Yale University Press, 2003. This social history begins with the admission that great diversity existed within early Christianity. The author chooses to study Paul, his coworkers, and his congregations as the best-documented segment of the early Christian movement. The social level of Pauline Christians and the governance and rituals of their communities are discussed at length. Includes notes, indexes, and an extensive bibliography.

_____, ed. *The Writings of Saint Paul*. New York: W. W. Norton, 1972. A critical edition containing the Revised Standard Version of the undoubted letters of Paul and the works of the Pauline school, heavily annotated. Also contains more than two dozen essays and excerpts evaluating, from diverse points of view, Paul's thought, works, and influence on modern Christianity.

Schoeps, Hans J. *Paul: The Theology of the Apostle in the Light of Jewish History*. Translated by Harold Knight. Philadelphia: Westminster Press, 1979. The author begins by sketching the several approaches to interpretation (for example, the Hellenistic approach and the Palestinian-Judaic approach); then he treats Paul's position in the primitive church, his eschatology, his soteriology (theology of salvation), his views on the law, and his concept of history. Indexed to biblical passages and to modern authors. Heavily annotated.

Stendahl, Krister. *The Bible and the Role of Women: A Case Study in Hermeneutics*. Translated by Emilie T. Sander. Philadelphia: Fortress Press, 1976. This slim volume is composed of Stendahl's essay, a lengthy editor's introduction and author's preface, and a copious bibliography. The essay first appeared in 1958, growing out of a specific controversy over the proposed ordination of women as priests in the Church of Sweden (Lutheran). Part 2 of the essay, "The Biblical View of Male and Female," is devoted largely to an exegesis of Paul's pronouncements on the subject in his epistles.

SEE ALSO: Saint Augustine; Jesus; Saint Peter; Saint Stephen.

RELATED ARTICLES in *Great Events from History: The Ancient World*: c. 135 B.C.E., Rise of the Pharisees; c. 30 C.E., Condemnation and Crucifixion of Jesus Christ; c. 30 C.E., Preaching of the Pentecostal Gospel; January-March, 55 or 56 C.E., Paul Writes His Letter to the Romans; 64-67 C.E., Nero Persecutes the Christians.

PAUSANIAS OF SPARTA
Spartan military commander

Pausanias of Sparta led a coalition of allied Greeks to victory over the Persians at Plataea and helped liberate certain Greek cities from Persian control.

BORN: late sixth century B.C.E.; Sparta, Greece
DIED: c. 470 B.C.E.; Sparta, Greece
AREA OF ACHIEVEMENT: War and conquest

EARLY LIFE
Other than the fact that Pausanias (paws-AYN-ee-ahs) of Sparta was the son of Cleombrotus and a member of the oldest of Sparta's royal houses, the Agiads, virtually nothing is known about his early life.

LIFE'S WORK
In 480 B.C.E. the Spartan king Leonidas was killed while fighting against the Persians at the Battle of Thermopylae. Leonidas's son Pleistarchus was too young to assume the duties of king. Thus Pausanias, as member of a royal house and the young man's cousin, was appointed as his regent. After Leonidas's death, the Persians continued their advance south toward Athens. Persian forces under Mardonius had previously made their way to Athens, had destroyed the city, and had begun moving west toward Megara. The Spartans were summoned to assist their fellow Greeks, and in 479, Pausanias led the Spartan troops north to face the Persians.

The people of Argos, who had promised Mardonius they would oppose the Spartans, withdrew their resistance once they learned that Pausanias and his forces had set out from Sparta. The Persians, who had been advancing west from Athens, also retreated to the north into the region of Boeotia, as Thebes, the chief city of Boeotia, was friendly to their cause. Mardonius deployed his forces near Plataea north of the river Asopus, while Pausanias and the Spartans, bolstered by allies from other towns (including Athens and Tegea), encamped south of the Asopus. In the ensuing conflict, Pausanias would serve as the supreme commander of the Greek land forces.

Over the next several days, the Persian cavalry harassed the Greek forces, but neither army was prepared to make a decisive move. One of the leading Persians, Artabazus, advocated moving the Persian army within the walls of Thebes, where they would be well supplied and could conduct the campaign at their leisure. Mardonius, however, argued that the Greek ranks were increasing in numbers daily and that the Persians should attack while they still had an advantage in size. Certain oracles also led Mardonius to believe that the Persians would be victorious. In the end, Mardonius's view was adopted, and it was decided the Persians would attack at dawn the following day.

Fortunately for Pausanias and the Greeks, a Macedonian who had joined the Persian cavalry rode to the Greek camp in the middle of the night and informed the Greeks of Mardonius's intent. The historian Herodotus reports that when Pausanias heard this, he became frightened: The Spartan forces were posted directly opposite the Persian regular troops in the current battle formation. Accordingly, Pausanias proposed that because the Athenians had already battled the Persians successfully at Marathon, the Athenians and Spartans should trade places in the formation. The Athenians agreed, and the change was made. When the Persians noticed the change, they also changed positions, so that they themselves would have to face the Spartans. The Spartans again changed places, only to have the Persians move opposite them again.

Finally, the Persians began the battle by sending out their cavalry, who inflicted some damage to the Greek troops and cut off their water supply from the Gargaphian spring. The Greek forces managed to hold off the Persian cavalry for the rest of the day, and Pausanias planned to move the troops into a position where they could have access to the water of the Asopus River. When Mardonius learned that the Greeks had moved, he thought that they were fleeing and set out in pursuit. During the Greeks' maneuver, some of the various contingents took different paths. Thus, when Mardonius attacked, some of the Greek forces were so far out of position that they could not come to their army's aid. Accordingly, it happened that the Spartans and the Tegeans bore the brunt of the Persian attack. Eventually, Pausanias and his heavily armed troops gained the advantage over the Persians, who wore no armor. When Mardonius was killed in the battle, the Persian forces fell apart, and those who retreated to their camp were cut down. After the battle, the Athenian commander Aristides urged that both Pausanias and the Spartans receive prizes for their valor in the battle. Eleven days after the battle at Plataea, Pausanias marched on and besieged the town of Thebes, which had allied itself with the Persians. Pausanias demanded that those responsible for the alliance with Persia be handed over. When the responsible Thebans turned themselves over to Pausanias, he had them executed.

KINGS DURING THE LIFE OF PAUSANIAS	
King	*Reign (B.C.E.)*
Darius the Great of Persia	c. 522-486
Cleomenes I of Sparta	c. 519-c. 490
Leonidas of Sparta	490-480
Xerxes I of Persia	486-465

In 478 B.C.E. the Spartans turned their sights toward liberating Greek cities that remained under Persian control. Pausanias, with help from Aristides, assembled a fleet of some eighty ships, sailed out, and liberated both Cyprus and Byzantium. Some of the leading Persians in Byzantium, however, were turned over by Pausanias to an Eretrian named Gongylus. Supposedly, Pausanias had given these Persians to Gongylus for punishment, but in fact they were to be taken to the Persian king Xerxes, with whom Pausanias had made a secret alliance and whose daughter was engaged to Pausanias. Furthermore, the Persian general Artabazus, who served as go-between for Xerxes and Pausanias, had been giving Pausanias large amounts of money to win over various Greeks to the Persian cause.

Pausanias's betrayal of the Greeks was soon discovered, though, as he began using his Persian riches to finance a luxurious lifestyle. While in Byzantium, he began to dress and dine in the Persian fashion as well as surround himself with bodyguards, including Persians and Egyptians. Additionally, Pausanias had begun to treat the Spartans who served under him in a tyrannical manner, which engendered their hatred of him. Eventually, some of Pausanias's allies returned to Greece and began complaining to the Spartans about him.

Pausanias had also made himself unpopular because of an inscription he had placed on an offering to Apollo to commemorate the victories at Plataea and Salamis. This inscription implied that Pausanias himself was primarily responsible for the victories. Accordingly, in 477 the Spartans recalled Pausanias and put him on trial for various offenses, the most serious of which was treasonous behavior in collusion with the Persians. He was convicted of some of the lesser accusations but acquitted on the charge involving the Persians.

Following this trial, Pausanias, without authorization from the Spartan government, sailed to Byzantium and took up residence there. Ancient sources say that he intended to continue his relationship with the Persians and had aims of ruling the whole of Greece. After some time,

though, Pausanias became a source of trouble in Byzantium. In his *Life of Cimon*, contained in *Bioi paralleloi* (c. 105-115; *Parallel Lives*, 1579), Plutarch relates how Pausanias accidentally killed a maiden named Cleonice, with whom he intended to have sexual relations, and then was haunted by her ghost.

Around 475 B.C.E., after being driven from Byzantium by the Athenian Cimon, Pausanias sailed to Colonae (in the Troad) and lived there. In Colonae, he continued his treacherous relationship with the Persians. When Pausanias's behavior gained the attention of the Spartans, they again recalled him in the late 470's. Wishing to avoid suspicion, Pausanias obligingly returned to Sparta and was there imprisoned. After he offered to stand trial for any crimes of which he might be accused, he was released. The Spartans, however, had no irrefutable proof of any wrongdoing on Pausanias's part and so decided legal prosecution might be futile. The Spartans also heard a rumor that Pausanias had promised the helots (the Spartans' slaves) freedom and citizenship if they would help him in a revolt against the Spartans. Even this rumor was not credible enough to prompt the Spartans to take legal action against Pausanias.

Finally, a trusted servant of Pausanias, who was supposed to take a letter from his master to Artabazus, noticed that none of Pausanias's other messengers had ever returned from their missions. The servant opened the letter. On seeing that the letter's contents included, among its treasonous material addressed to the Persians, a request from Pausanias to have the servant executed, the servant showed the letter to the Ephors (five Spartan magistrates who were annually elected).

Even with this information, the Ephors wanted to hear Pausanias for themselves. Accordingly, they arranged for the servant to go as a suppliant to Taenarus, a town south of Sparta, and construct a hut that was divided by a partition. Apparently Pausanias was summoned to the hut to meet with his servant, while some of the Ephors hid on the other side of the partition. When Pausanias met with the servant, the servant accused Pausanias of planning to have him killed and discussed the other details of the letter with him. During their conversation, Pausanias spoke of his dealings with the Persian king. Pausanias promised the servant that no harm would come to him and urged him to deliver the letter as previously instructed.

After the meeting between Pausanias and his servant, the Ephors decided to arrest Pausanias back at Sparta. This plan, however, was thwarted. As Pausanias was walking down a certain street, he saw the Ephors approaching. One of the Ephors, who was still on friendly terms with Pausanias, signaled him that he was about to be arrested. Perceiving the threat, Pausanias ran to the nearby temple of Athena of the Brazen House. He entered a small, sheltered room that adjoined the temple and took asylum there. The Ephors followed, barricaded Pausanias within this room, guarded the area, and then began to starve him.

Just before Pausanias died, the Ephors removed him from the temple. They buried Pausanias nearby, but, according to the scholiast on Euripides (in *Alcestis* 1128), his ghost began harassing those who tried to enter the temple. To discover a remedy for this curse, the Spartans consulted the Delphic oracle, who directed them to move Pausanias's tomb to the place where he died and to give Athena two bodies instead of one. Accordingly, the Spartans moved Pausanias's place of burial and dedicated two bronze statues to the goddess.

SIGNIFICANCE

Pausanias's leadership at the Battle of Plataea and in the liberation of various Greek cities from Persia helped allow the Greek civilization to develop on its own. What Pausanias did at Plataea, however, may not be as significant as what he was prevented from doing after his military successes: plotting with the Persians to gain mastery over his fellow Greeks. Had Pausanias of Sparta been successful in his ambitions, the course of Western civilization might have been altered as the Athenians failed to flourish without interference from the outside world.

—*John E. Thorburn, Jr.*

FURTHER READING

Diodorus Siculus. *Bibliotheca historica*. Cambridge, Mass.: Harvard University Press, 1962-1983. Diodorus, writing from 60 to 30 B.C.E., composed a history of the world up to his own times in which are included accounts of the Battle of Plataea, Pausanias's activities in Byzantium, and Pausanias's death.

Herodotus. *The Histories*. Translated by Robin Waterfield. New York: Oxford University Press, 1998. Herodotus, writing in the fifth century B.C.E., provides an extensive early account of Pausanias's activities at Plataea.

Lazenby, J. F. *The Defence of Greece, 490-479 B.C.* Warminster, England: Aris & Phillips, 1993. Lazenby provides military history of the first two Persian invasions of Greece, which the author considers within the context of the fifth century B.C.E. Attention is also given to Herodotus's insight and skill as a military historian.

_____. "Pausanias, Son of Kleombrotos." *Hermes* 103 (1975): 235-251. Lazenby argues that it is wrong to consider Pausanias as only a traitor. Despite evidence of Pausanias's personal ambition in Byzantium, he could have had Sparta's interests in mind.

Loomis, W. T. "Pausanias, Byzantium, and the Formation of the Delian League." *Historia* 39 (1990): 487-492. Loomis argues that because Byzantium was not captured until spring of 477 B.C.E., Pausanias could not have been recalled to Sparta before that time.

Lord, Louis E. *Literary Criticism of Euripides in the Earlier Scholia and the Relation of This Criticism to Aristotle's "Poetics" and the Aristophanes*. Göttingen, Germany: W. F. Kaestner, 1908. Includes a discussion of the scholia of Euripides.

Plutarch. *Cimon*. London: Institute of Classical Studies, University of London, 1989. Writing in the latter half of the first century C.E. and the first quarter of the second century C.E., Plutarch, in his biography of Cimon, provides scattered details about Pausanias, especially his time in Byzantium.

Simonides. "Anthologia Palatina." In *Simonides: Selected Epigrams*. Translated by Timothy Sean Quinn. Edgewood, Ky.: Robert L Barth, 1996. Composed by Pausanias's contemporary, this two-line poem records Pausanias's dedication of a bronze tripod to Apollo at Delphi after his victory at Plataea.

Thucydides. *The Peloponnesian Wars*. Translated by Benjamin Jowett. New York: Washington Square Press, 1963. Writing in the latter half of the fifth century B.C.E., Thucydides provides a detailed account of the attempted arrest and death of Pausanias.

SEE ALSO: Cimon; Cleomenes; Darius the Great; Leonidas; Xerxes I.

RELATED ARTICLES in *Great Events from History: The Ancient World*: c. 550 B.C.E., Construction of Trireme Changes Naval Warfare; 547 B.C.E., Cyrus the Great Founds the Persian Empire; 520-518 B.C.E., Darius the Great Conquers the Indus Valley.

PAUSANIAS THE TRAVELER
Greek travel writer

Pausanias the Traveler spent many years traveling and wrote a travel guide to Greece, covering all cities and sanctuaries, with historical, artistic, and religious information on each.

BORN: c. 110-115 C.E.; Lydia, Magnesia, Asia Minor
(now in Turkey)
DIED: c. 180 C.E.; Greece
AREAS OF ACHIEVEMENT: Geography, literature

EARLY LIFE

Nearly all the information about the life of Pausanias (paws-AYN-ee-ahs) comes from his only surviving work, the *Periegesis Hellados* (between 143 and 161 C.E.; *Description of Greece*, 1794). In fact, the author's name is only known as Pausanias, thanks to a late Byzantine lexicographer called Stephanus. The ten-book travel guide to Greece that survives under Pausanias's name is the only work of its kind to have survived from antiquity, and it has been translated into many languages. Pausanias appears to have traveled widely in the territories of the Roman Empire and probably spent ten to twenty years in Greece, gathering material for his guide.

Pausanias does not supply a preface or an epilogue and generally keeps a low profile in his writing. He hardly ever says anything about himself or the circumstances of his travels, but some details of his life can be pieced together from the few references he does make. He was born around 110 or 115 C.E., most probably in a town in Lydia, in the province of Asia Minor, now Turkey, called Magnesia. This was located near Mount Sipylus, not far from Pergamum, one of the major cities of the eastern part of the Roman Empire, renowned for its cultural activity. Pausanias mentions the area around Mount Sipylus so frequently in his work that it is widely believed that he came from there. Although not born in Greece proper, he would have identified himself as Greek in every sense of the word: socially, culturally, and even politically. He was the rough contemporary of such famous writers as the astronomer Ptolemy, the satirist Lucian, and the physician Galen, as well as of many Greek Sophists, who traded on their rhetorical, rather than their intellectual, skills.

In view of the education he received and his ability to travel so widely—which in his day involved considerable expense—one can assume that Pausanias came from a wealthy family. He would have received a traditional Greek education in rhetoric and literature. He quotes from a long list of classical writers, ranging from historians such as Herodotus and Thucydides to poets such as Homer and Apollonius of Rhodes and clearly possessed an excellent memory. His family were probably members of the provincial aristocracy and were most likely Greeks who held Roman citizenship. Some have suggested that Pausanias was a medical doctor, but the evidence for this is highly questionable. It is more likely that he was a wealthy, well-educated man who undertook extensive travels and decided to write a guide for others who wished to follow in his footsteps.

At what age he began these travels, it is impossible to say, but one may conjecture that he started while quite young: His journeys included tours of western and central Asia Minor, Ionia, Caria, Galatia, Syria, and Palestine. He says he never visited Babylon but did go to Egypt, where he saw, among other sites, the pyramids. He visited several islands in the Aegean, including Rhodes and Delos, and may also have gone to Sardinia and Sicily. In Italy, he traveled to Rome and through the Greek towns of the south, including Capua and Metapontum. In all these places, he undertook a careful survey of sites and objects of historical, artistic, and religious interest. While staying in the large metropolitan centers of Pergamum, Athens, Alexandria, and Rome, he would have encountered Imperial administrators, local dignitaries, famous scholars, writers, artists, and athletes. He mentions several senators in his book.

Pausanias appears to have written his *Description of Greece* between 143 and 161 C.E. This means that he wrote it when he had reached mature adulthood. While he may have produced other works before this, it is clear that the *Description of Greece* was his life's work.

LIFE'S WORK

The genre of travel literature in which Pausanias is to be placed began in the Hellenistic era, in the third century B.C.E., when the Greek world expanded dramatically beyond the boundaries of mainland Greece. The ultimate origin lies in the early books of Herodotus's *Historiai Herodotou* (c. 424 B.C.E.; *The History*, 1709) with their descriptions of Persia, Egypt, and Scythia—all regions largely unfamiliar to Greeks—and in the tradition of the *periploi* (circumnavigations), descriptions of seas and coastlines written to guide sailors. Most of the travelwriters before Pausanias restricted themselves to describing a single city or a particular monument within a city. What makes Pausanias's *Description of Greece* unique and uniquely impressive is that he took as his subject virtually the whole of mainland Greece.

Pausanias seems to have placed the activity of travel writing on a completely new intellectual and scientific level. His method was not to rely on what previous writers had said and simply patch together a group of sources but to travel to places, so that he could see them for himself and write from personal observation. He wrote book 1, on Athens and Attica, first, for it shows signs of experimentation and the search for a cohesive methodology. Book 2 dealt with Corinth and Argos and books 3 through 8 the rest of the Peloponnese, including Sparta and Messenia. There are two books (5 and 6) devoted to Elis because that is where the Olympic festival was held, and Pausanias treats the site of Olympia, which was filled with cultural and artistic significance, at great length. In book 9, he moves out of the Peloponnese into central Greece and describes Boeotia, continuing in book 10 with an account of Phocis, paying particular attention to the renowned sanctuary of Apollo at Delphi. The guide is most likely complete or very nearly complete. Some scholars have thought that Pausanias wrote one or more books beyond the ten that survive, citing the absence of an epilogue, but the evidence is inconclusive. There may have been an eleventh book devoted to Euboea, but more than that cannot be said.

Pausanias arranged his guide geographically, treating first one region, then moving on to the next. From Athens, he does a circle of the Peloponnese, ending up in central Greece. Each book is arranged topographically, with the exception of the first, in which the method is more haphazard. The pattern in the remaining nine books is clear: When Pausanias crosses the border into a region, he makes his way directly to the capital, from which he provides an account of the significant sites and objects to be seen there. Then he follows another road out to the border, describing everything that he finds worth mentioning. He returns to the capital and takes another road out to the border, doing the same thing until all the major locations in the region have been visited, at which point he crosses the frontier into the next region.

Most books open with a general introduction in which the history and myths relating to the region are summarized. Pausanias clearly considered this an important element of his work, and elsewhere on occasion he interrupts his descriptions of sites to provide the reader with some historical or cultural background. This suggests that he saw his guide as more than a catalog of interesting sights and perhaps rather as a grand work of cultural

transmission. The guide is a literary work as well as a practical handbook: He wanted to make it both useful for travelers and entertaining for readers. The selection of what to describe, from what was certainly an overwhelming mass of available material, and the careful arrangement of these selections into a coherent structure, are indicative of a highly systematic and sophisticated mind. Judicious selectivity was especially vital with regard to the "big" sites of Olympia and Delphi, and the city of Athens, whose cultural richness was unique in Greece.

Pausanias had his preferences in matters of architecture and art, and they come through quite clearly. He prefers religious buildings like temples and shrines to public or administrative constructions, and he elevates artwork from the archaic and classical periods above all subsequent forms. One can see these preferences at work most often by omission: He simply chooses not to comment on what he does not admire. His tone is more emotional when he describes sacred images or old statues.

It is reasonable to wonder, then, for what kind of audience Pausanias saw himself composing his *Description of Greece*. Without any doubt, the guide is intended for Greek speakers, but that would have included not just Greeks living in the homeland, but also Greeks spread more widely afield across the empire, like his own family. The guide would also have been accessible to Greek-speaking Romans and might have appealed particularly to philhellene circles in the aristocratic and Imperial elite. It is striking that Pausanias avoids almost all mention of matters Roman: Like many educated Greeks of his day, he probably felt a degree of cultural hostility, a hostility that perforce remained unexpressed. Some have viewed his *Description of Greece* as a document of cultural warfare, a work glorifying the treasures and traditions of Greece through its sheer weight of detail.

The date of Pausanias's death is not known, but is assumed to have occurred around the year 180 C.E. By this time, the "golden age" of the second century was coming to a close and it would not be long before travel of the kind undertaken by Pausanias became more difficult. The fate of the *Description of Greece* is unknown: it slips into obscurity and we do not know whether it was widely read or not, whether it made Pausanias's name or not. It is only in recent times that its value for tourists has been realized.

SIGNIFICANCE

Pausanias's *Description of Greece* provides detailed information on what a traveler could expect to find of cultural, religious, and artistic significance in just about every town in mainland Greece. It continues to be an important source for archaeologists and historians, as well as the basis of many modern travel guides. It stands out from the ancient tradition of such travel-writing by virtue of its scope, organization, and reliance on personal observation. Scholarly investigation has tended to confirm Pausanias's accuracy in reporting what he saw during his extensive travels throughout Greece. The guide is revealing on several levels about the intellectual position of Greeks living under Roman rule, for it turns the landscape of Greece into a discourse, in which places and objects come to embody what it means to be Greek. Although the author remains something of a mystery, in the sense that little is known about him, his work continues to be read with fascination by travelers and nontravelers alike.

—*David H. J. Larmour*

FURTHER READING

Alcock, Susan. *Pausanias: Travel and Memory in Roman Greece*. New York: Oxford University Press, 2001. Volume of essays discussing Pausanias and his work, including the sources he used, his guides, his artistic interpretations, and the impact of Pausanias's work on later travel writers and on the genre. Includes bibliography and index.

Arafat, K. W. *Pausanias's Greece: Ancient Artists and Roman Rulers*. New York: Cambridge University Press, 1996. Covers what Pausanias has to say about the Greek past, the Roman rulers of Greece, and phil-hellenic benefactors like Herodes Atticus. Includes bibliography and index.

Frazer, James G., and A. Van Buren. *Graecia Antiqua: Maps and Plans to Illustrate Pausanias's "Description of Greece."* London: Macmillan, 1930. A volume of maps and other topographical information produced to supplement Frazer's 6-volume translation of the guide.

Habicht, Christian. *Pausanias's Guide to Ancient Greece*. Berkeley: University of California Press, 1998. Groundbreaking reevaluation that argues for Pausanias's essential accuracy and reliability and seeks to place his guide in its historical and social context.

Pausanias. *Pausanias's "Description of Greece."* 6 vols. Translated by J. G. Frazer. 1898. Reprint. New York: Biblo and Tannen, 1965. Includes substantial commentary on Pausanias's work, with detailed investigation of what he has to say about the artistic, historical, and religious material at each site visited. A comprehensive edition. Includes index.

SEE ALSO: Galen; Lucian; Ptolemy (astronomer).

RELATED ARTICLES in *Great Events from History: The Ancient World*: c. 440 B.C.E., Sophists Train the Greeks in Rhetoric and Politics; 159 B.C.E., Roman Playwright Terence Dies; c. 157-201 C.E., Galen Synthesizes Ancient Medical Knowledge.

PERICLES
Athenian statesman

The Age of Pericles was a crucial period in the history of Athens. Pericles' transformation of the Delian League into the Athenian Empire provided the financial basis for the flowering of Athenian democracy.

BORN: c. 495 B.C.E.; Athens, Greece
DIED: 429 B.C.E.; Athens, Greece
AREA OF ACHIEVEMENT: Government and politics

EARLY LIFE

Pericles (PEHR-ih-kleez) was born in Athens around 495 B.C.E., the son of Xanthippus and Agariste (the niece of Cleisthenes of Athens). As the son of a wealthy aristocratic family in Athens and possessed of an above-average intelligence, Pericles received an excellent education from private tutors. The two men who had the greatest influence on Pericles' life were the musician Damon and the philosopher Anaxagoras. Damon taught Pericles the moral and political influence of music, and Anaxagoras taught him political style, effective speech making, and analytical rationalism.

Although Pericles had prepared himself for a political life, he did not openly side with any of the factions in Athens until 463, when he joined in the prosecution of the Athenenian statesman and general Cimon. During this period, various political factions frequently brought charges against their opponents, with the goal of diminishing the prestige of the accused. Cimon, having recently returned from a two-year military campaign against the island of Thasos, which had rebelled against the Delian League, was brought to trial by the democratic faction on charges of bribery. In this instance, Cimon was acquitted.

In 462 Sparta requested military aid from Athens because of a revolt among the helots (serfs). Sparta, a city-state unfamiliar with siege warfare, needed help in trying to dislodge the helots who had fled to and fortified Mount Ithome in Messenia. Cimon urged the Athenians to cooperate with the Spartans, while the democratic faction, led by Ephialtes and Pericles, opposed any form of cooperation. On this occasion, Cimon won popular support and led an Athenian force to Mount Ithome. The Spartans, however, having reconsidered their request, dismissed Cimon and his men when they arrived. Because of this humiliation, Cimon's influence with the people declined rapidly.

With Cimon in disgrace, the democratic faction now focused its attention on the Areopagus, the council of former archons (magistrates). In 461 Ephialtes and Pericles led the people in stripping the Areopagus of any real power. Cimon, unable to rally the conservative opposition, was ostracized in the same year. Not long after, a member of the conservatives assassinated Ephialtes, and Pericles became the new leader of the democratic faction.

LIFE'S WORK

Pericles' main achievement as the leader of Athens was the conversion of the Delian League into an Athenian Empire. The Delian League was originally formed in 476 B.C.E. as an offensive and defensive alliance against Persia. Although it was composed predominantly of Ionian maritime city-states individually bound by treaty to Athens, with all member states considered equal, only Athenians were league officials. The league collected annual tribute from its members to maintain a fleet. For all practical purposes, it was an Athenian fleet, built and manned by Athenians but paid for by the allies. Because the allies had been paying tribute every year since 476, the income of the league far exceeded its expenditures. When the league treasury was transferred from Delos to Athens in 454, it contained a vast sum of money that was essentially at the disposal of the Athenians.

Pericles, believing that the Athenians had every right to enjoy the benefits of empire, introduced numerous measures that provided pay to Athenians for their services as soldiers, magistrates, and jurors. An estimated twenty thousand Athenians were on the government payroll. In addition, so that no Athenian would be deprived of the opportunity to attend the plays of the Dionysiac Festival, even the price of admission to the theater was given to the poor.

The city of Athens itself was not to be neglected in Pericles' plans for the Delian League treasury. Pericles

Pericles. (Library of Congress)

was building commissioner for the Parthenon and many other important building projects in Athens. The Parthenon, Propylaea, Odeum, and Erectheum are merely a few of the many temples and public buildings that were built or planned under the direction of Pericles but financed with league funds.

To increase the power of Athens, Pericles attempted to enlarge the Delian League. When the island of Aegina, located in the Saronic Gulf near Athens, declared war on Athens in 459, Pericles saw an opportunity to expand the league by creating an Athenian land empire that would complement the sea empire already embodied in the league. After the Athenians captured Aegina and forced it to become a member of the Delian League, the Peloponnesian coastal area of Troezen, facing Aegina, joined the league in self-defense. When Sparta tried to counter Athens by helping Thebes to dominate the Boeotian League in 457, Athens sent troops to fight the Spartans in the Battle of Tanagra. Although Athens lost the battle, Sparta soon withdrew its forces, and Athenian troops returned to rally the Boeotian League against Thebes. With the Boeotian League joined to the Delian League, the neighboring areas of Phocis and Locris joined the league, along with Achaea. By 456, the Periclean strategy of creating an Athenian land empire was a success, and the empire had reached its greatest territorial extent.

The Athenian land empire, however, disintegrated almost as quickly as it had been created. In 447 B.C.E., the Boeotian League revolted against Athens. As a result, Athens lost not only control of Boeotia but also the support of Phocis and Locris. When the five-year truce with Sparta expired in 446, Sparta invaded Attica with a Peloponnesian army and encouraged the Athenian allied island of Euboea to revolt. Pericles quickly dealt with the two problems by bribing the Spartan commander of the Peloponnesians to leave Attica and by personally leading the Athenian reconquest of Euboea. While the Athenians were temporarily distracted, Megara broke its alliance with Athens and joined the Peloponnesian League, along with Troezen and Achaea. All that remained now of the Athenian land empire was Aegina, Naupactus, and Plataea. Because Athens was in no position to reverse the situation, Athens and Sparta agreed in 445 to the Thirty Years' Peace.

Pericles successfully led the democratic faction in its control of Athenian politics from 461 until his death. He was a political genius in that he was able to provide leadership to the Athenian people without being led by them. The only surviving contemporary evidence of the opposition to Pericles is from Attic comedy. In general, the opponents of Pericles resented his oratorical skill, his family's wealth, and his political successes. Pericles was a very reserved and private individual, and his enemies interpreted these personality traits as signs of haughtiness and arrogance. Having earned the confidence of the people, however, Pericles was frequently elected *strategos* (general) in the 450's. When his chief political opponent, Thucydides, son of Melesias, was ostracized in 443, Pericles led the people virtually unopposed and was elected *strategos* every year until his death in 429 B.C.E.

The Peloponnesian War broke out in 431, when Athens and Sparta found that they could no longer observe the Thirty Years' Peace. Pericles believed that Athens and the Delian League had strategic advantages over Sparta and the Peloponnesian League. While the Peloponnesians had access to greater numbers of troops than the Athenians and had more agricultural land on which to produce food to support those troops, the Peloponnesians lacked a large fleet and so were more or less restricted to conducting a land war. The plan of Pericles was for the Athenians to abandon their property and

homes in Attica and withdraw into the city of Athens. With its long walls assuring access to the port of Piraeus, Athens could withstand a siege of any length. In addition, Athens controlled the Delian League treasury and possessed a large fleet that could be used for hit-and-run raids on the Peloponnesians. As a safety precaution, however, Pericles set aside one thousand talents from the league treasury and reserved one hundred ships to be used only in the extreme emergency of defending Athens itself.

As Pericles predicted, the Peloponnesians invaded Attica in 431 and ravaged the countryside, trying to lure the Athenians from their walled city to fight a pitched battle. The Athenians, however, held firm. Instead of fighting in Attica, the Athenians, under Pericles' direction, mounted an attack on the Peloponnese. After they ravaged the territory of Epidaurus and Troezen, the Athenians sailed to Laconia to bring the war directly to the Spartans. After the Peloponnesians had withdrawn their troops from Attica, Athens prepared to bury its dead. It was the custom of the Athenians to choose their best speaker to give the funeral oration for the first men who had fallen in a war. As expected, Pericles was chosen for this honor. Pericles' funeral oration was more a speech extolling the virtues of Athens than a speech of mourning. He clearly wanted to impress on the living Athenians the greatness of their city and the enlightened life they were privileged to lead.

In the second year of the war, the Athenians continued to follow the Periclean strategy. The people withdrew from Attica into Athens when the Peloponnesians returned to ravage the land. Athenian morale, however, was devastated by a plague that broke out in the city, killing many people. In their anger and frustration, the people blamed Pericles for their suffering and drove him from office. Though he was tried for embezzlement, convicted, and fined, he was soon elected *strategos* once again. Within six months, however, Pericles contracted the plague; he died in 429. The Athenians would have to endure the rest of the Peloponnesian War without the guidance of their greatest leader.

SIGNIFICANCE

Pericles was the dominant political figure during the most important period in Athenian history. Rather than being a demagogue who flattered the people and pandered to their base instincts, Pericles won the people over to his policies by his forceful and energetic oratory. While some politicians sought to win a following by agreeing with whatever was currently popular, Pericles used his oratorical skill to lead the people to decisions that he thought were correct. Possessing an incorruptible character, Pericles gained the confidence of the people and knew how to keep it. By respecting their liberties and by offering the Athenians a consistent policy, Pericles prevented the people from making what he considered grave errors in judgment. What Pericles failed to understand, however, was that personal government was, in the long run, harmful to the state because it limited the ability of the people to govern themselves. In addition, while Athens enjoyed its democracy, the Athenians refused to recognize that it was based on the political, military, and financial oppression of others in the empire.

Although Athens and Sparta did go to war in 431, Pericles had worked for peace twenty years before. In 451, Sparta and Athens agreed to a five-year truce; in 449, Persia and Athens reached an understanding in the Peace of Callias. With Athens assured of peace, Pericles called for a meeting of all Greek city-states to consider the issue of peace throughout the Greek world. According to Pericles, representatives at the proposed meeting were to discuss the rebuilding of all temples destroyed during the Persian Wars, the elimination of piracy, and the promotion of trade and commerce between and among all Greek city-states. Although because of Spartan opposition such a meeting was never held, Pericles' proposal showed that the Athenians were content with the territories they had and that they wanted peace.

—*Peter L. Viscusi*

FURTHER READING

Andrewes, A. "The Opposition to Pericles." *Journal of Hellenic Studies* 98 (1978): 1-8. While Plutarch is the main source of information on the struggle between Pericles and Thucydides, son of Melesias, Andrewes shows that he is unreliable because of his anti-imperialist bias. Although there were opponents to Pericles' building program, the argument that it was wrong to use league funds would not have been made, for Athenians viewed the empire as theirs to be enjoyed.

Bloedow, Edmund F. "Pericles' Powers in the Counter-Strategy of 431." *Historia* 36 (1987): 9-27. Bloedow tries to discover the constitutional basis for the power of Pericles through a close study of Thucydides. Although Pericles was only one of ten generals (*strategoi*) who led the state, he wielded authority that went far beyond that of a general.

Cawkwell, George. "Thucydides' Judgment of Periclean Strategy." *Yale Classical Studies* 24 (1975): 53-70. Cawkwell examines Thucydides' belief that the Athenians brought ruin on themselves when they strayed from Periclean strategy after the death of Pericles.

Ehrenberg, Victor. *Sophocles and Pericles*. Oxford: Blackwell, 1954. More than a third of this work directly concerns Pericles and his leadership role in Athens. The author provides an excellent analysis of all the dramatic and comedic references to Pericles and the politics of his time. The comments of the author on Plutarch's use of sources are invaluable.

Hignett, C. *A History of the Athenian Constitution to the End of the Fifth Century B.C.* Oxford, England: Clarendon Press, 1975. Contains three chapters that cover the Athenian democracy from the revolution of 462 to the fall of the Athenian Empire. The author covers all Periclean laws and their impact on the Athenian constitution. Although a very specialized study, this work is seminal.

Kagan, Donald. *The Outbreak of the Peloponnesian War.* Ithaca, N.Y.: Cornell University Press, 1989. The author discusses the position taken by Thucydides that the Peloponnesian War was inevitable. Kagan reexamines the foreign and domestic decisions made by Pericles and the Athenians and concludes that the war was not inevitable, but was the result of poor judgment and bad decisions.

_____. *Pericles of Athens and the Birth of Democracy.* New York: Free Press, 1998. Biography chronicles the years leading into the great war between the Athenians and Spartans. Kagan argues that Pericles was a visionary political leader whose great mistake was to expect everyone to think and behave as rationally as he did.

Meiggs, Russell. *The Athenian Empire*. New York: Oxford University Press, 1979. This is an attempt to bring together all the available evidence for the Athenian Empire and to evaluate it in the light of archaeological and epigraphic evidence. The coverage is comprehensive. Seventeen appendices cover controversial points of interpretation.

Plutarch. *The Rise and Fall of Athens*. Translated by Ian Scott-Kilvert. Baltimore: Penguin Books, 1975. Contains a chapter on Pericles, together with other chapters on some of his political rivals. Plutarch preserves much material regarding Pericles' time; the interpretations, however, are often biased. Still, the work is useful in showing the opinion of the opposition.

Ste. Croix, G. E. M. de. *The Origins of the Peloponnesian War.* Ithaca, N.Y.: Cornell University Press, 1972. An in-depth study of the reasons for the Peloponnesian

War, based on a detailed reexamination and reevaluation of the primary sources. Includes forty-seven appendices and an extensive bibliography.

Thucydides. *History of the Peloponnesian War.* Translated by Charles Forster Smith. 4 vols. Cambridge, Mass.: Harvard University Press, 1977. Books 1 and 2 of the first volume of Thucydides constitute the primary source on Pericles' background, his political career, and his strategy for the transformation of the Delian League into the Athenian Empire. While his-

torians may interpret and reinterpret Thucydides, he remains the indispensable beginning point for any study of Pericles.

SEE ALSO: Aspasia of Miletus; Cimon; Cleisthenes of Athens; Phidias.

RELATED ARTICLES in *Great Events from History: The Ancient World*: 478-448 B.C.E., Athenian Empire Is Created; 447-438 B.C.E., Building of the Parthenon; May, 431-September, 404 B.C.E., Peloponnesian War.

SAINT PETER
Christian religious leader

During Jesus' life, Peter was the most faithful and outspoken of the disciples. After Jesus' death he gave leadership to the early Church at Jerusalem and was active in missionary work. In Catholic tradition, he is the founder of the Christian Church and of the Papacy.

BORN: Date unknown; Bethsaida, Galilee (now in Israel)
DIED: c. 67 C.E.; Rome (now in Italy)
ALSO KNOWN AS: Simon (given game); Simeon; Petrus (Latin); Simon Peter; Cephas
AREA OF ACHIEVEMENT: Religion

EARLY LIFE
Peter (PEE-tuhr) was born Simon (or Simeon), son of Jonah in Bethsaida; the date is uncertain, but it is believed that he was born in the first few years of the Christian era. The name Peter was given to him later by Jesus; the Greek word *petros* means "rock" and translates into the Aramaic Cepha or Cephas. Nothing is known of Peter's life before his call to discipleship. At the time of the call, he was working as a fisherman in partnership with his brother Andrew. According to the Gospel of Luke, he was also partners with James and John, thus beginning an intimacy with John that continued until both left Palestine.

Peter was a married man; it is recorded that Jesus cured Peter's mother-in-law of a fever. That his wife later accompanied him on missionary journeys is suggested by Paul in 1 Corinthians 9: "Have we not power to lead about a sister, a wife, as well as other apostles, and as the brethren of the Lord, and Cephas?" According to another tradition, Peter's wife was martyred at the same time as Peter.

Concerning Peter's call, there are two accounts. The Synoptics (Matthew, Mark, and Luke) make Peter and

Andrew the first to be called as they were fishing (or washing their nets); henceforth, they were to be "fishers of men." According to the Gospel of John, Andrew was the first to follow Jesus and afterward recruited Simon, whom Jesus immediately christened Peter.

LIFE'S WORK
In the accounts given of Jesus' ministry in the four Gospels, Peter plays a more prominent part than any of the other disciples, even John. When the Twelve are listed, Peter is always listed first and is even identified as "the first." He is noted as first, too, of an inner circle that includes James and John. These three were present (with Andrew) at the healing of Peter's mother-in-law and also at the healing of Jairus's daughter. Together they were present at the Transfiguration, where Peter proposed building tabernacles ("shelters" in the New English Bible) for Jesus, Moses, and Elijah (Matt. 17).

Of all the Apostles, Peter was the most talkative—or the most often quoted. It was Peter who asked how often he should forgive his brother, who asked for the interpretation of a parable, who commented on the withered fig tree, and who protested that the Apostles had left all to follow Jesus. He also attempted to imitate his master by walking on the water and then lost his faith and had to be rescued. It was Peter who first realized that Jesus was indeed the Christ, "the son of the living God" (Matt. 16). It was Peter who refused to believe that Jesus had to "be killed, and the third day be raised up" (Matt. 16) and earned the rebuke "Get thee behind me, Satan."

Peter was also prominent in the events of the Passion. According to Luke 22, Jesus sent Peter and John ahead to prepare the Passover. When Jesus washed the disciples' feet, Peter alone resisted, and when Jesus insisted, Peter asked that "not my feet only, but also my hands and my head" be washed (John 13). When Jesus foretold that "one of you shall betray me," Peter prompted "the disciple whom Jesus loved" (presumably John) to ask Jesus who it was. When Peter protested that he was ready "to go both to prison and to death," Jesus answered, "Peter, the cock shall not crow this day, before that thou shalt thrice deny that thou knowest me" (Luke 22).

In the Garden of Gethsemane, when Jesus went aside to pray for the last time, he took Peter, James, and John with him. Three times he found them sleeping; according to Matthew and Mark, it was to Peter that he directed his reproach: "What, would you not watch with me one hour?" (Mark 14). According to John, when the officers came to arrest Jesus, again Peter alone resisted and cut off the ear of the high priest's servant. He followed Jesus to Caiaphas's house and sat in the court with the officers, warming himself by a fire; it was there that, being questioned by the servants, he denied Jesus thrice.

Though in the First Epistle of Peter, Peter calls himself a witness of Christ's sufferings (implying that he was present at the Crucifixion), he next appears in the Gospels in the aftermath of the Resurrection. According to Luke and John, Mary Magdalene, perhaps with some other women, found the tomb empty and reported the fact to Peter (and "the beloved disciple," according to John); Peter went to the tomb and found only the linen cloths in which Jesus' body had been wrapped. Luke speaks also of an appearance of the Lord "to Simon." Otherwise, aside from the appearance to Mary and to the two on the road to Emmaus, Jesus first appeared to the Eleven (or the Eleven without Thomas); neither here nor in most of the subsequent appearances was Peter particularly distinguished. An exception is John's report of an appearance by the Sea of Galilee. Peter had gone fishing with his old partners, James and John, and some others, when they became aware of a figure on the shore, whom the "beloved disciple" recognized as the Lord. It was then that Jesus gave Peter a pointed commandment, "Feed my sheep," and prophesied "by what manner of death he should glorify God."

In the period following the Resurrection appearances, one sees the Apostles gradually, and perhaps at first not intentionally, forming themselves into a church at Jerusalem, of which Peter was the natural, if not the official, leader. (Paul speaks of Peter and John and James, the Lord's brother, as "reputed pillars" of the Church.) Peter took the initiative in urging the appointment of a twelfth Apostle to replace Judas. When the Holy Spirit descended on the Apostles at Pentecost and they spoke in tongues, Peter spoke boldly to the astonished multitude, defending the speaking as the fulfillment of prophecy and proclaiming Jesus as the Messiah; thus he added thousands to the Church.

When, in company with John, Peter healed a crippled man, he and John were for the first time arrested and

Saint Peter. (Library of Congress)

625

brought before the high priest and the Sanhedrin, but they were released after being warned to desist from preaching in the name of Jesus. When further miracles followed, the whole body of Apostles was arrested, and although (it is said) the Apostles miraculously escaped from prison, they appeared before the high priest the next day and might have been executed except for the cautiousness of Gamaliel, a teacher of the law.

After the martyrdom of Saint Stephen, the infant church was dispersed, and adherents carried the Gospel into the country districts. Philip preached in Samaria with such success that Peter and John were sent down to support him. This was apparently the beginning of Peter's missionary work outside Jerusalem. Tours of Lydda and Joppa, which followed, were important to the history of the Church. Peter had performed two miracles; soon afterward, he had a vision that seemed to abolish the Jewish distinction between clean and unclean food. The next day, he received a message from one Cornelius, a Roman centurion and convert to Judaism, who had had a vision urging him to send for Peter. The result was that the Holy Spirit was poured out on Gentiles, and they were baptized. Peter understood that he could no longer reject food as unclean or refuse to eat with the uncircumcised. For the time being, the disciples in Jerusalem seemed to accept Peter's position. It was about this time that Herod Agrippa I executed John's brother James. (He would have done the same with Peter if Peter had not miraculously escaped from prison.)

Meanwhile, Paul had undergone his conversion, and his missionary activity raised again the problem of the status of gentile converts. In Paul's letter to the Galatians, Paul asserts that three years after his conversion he went to Jerusalem and spent two weeks with Peter, without seeing any of the other Apostles except James, the Lord's brother. Fourteen years later, Paul went again to Jerusalem with Barnabas to discuss the problem raised by those Jewish Christians who would have imposed on gentile converts the burden of observing the Jewish ceremonial law. According to Paul, the meeting concluded amicably, with James, Peter, and John agreeing that they would minister to the Jews and Paul would minister to the Gentiles. The account in Acts of the Apostles (assuming that the same meeting is meant) adds that Peter spoke up on behalf of the Gentiles and was supported by James, who, however, made the condition that the Gentiles should abstain "from pollutions of idols, fornication, and from things strangled, and from blood" (Acts 15). The fragmentary evidence would suggest that by this time Peter, though apparently still the most outspoken of the

FIRST FIVE ROMAN CATHOLIC POPES (BISHOPS OF ROME)	
Popes	*Dates (C.E.)*
Peter	c. 33-c. 67
Linus	67-76
Anacletus	76-88
Clement I	88-97
Evaristus	97-105

group at Jerusalem, had yielded some of his influence to James. The compromise did not prevent further misunderstandings: Later, at Antioch, Peter, under pressure from James, refused any longer to eat with gentile converts and was rebuked by Paul (Gal. 2).

This, except for what can be conjectured from the Epistles of Peter, is the last that Scripture tells of Peter. The episode does not do credit to him, and yet the whole business of the controversy about the gentile converts fits with what is already known about Peter. The Gospels uniformly depict him as loyal, enthusiastic, courageous, and open to change, but he is also depicted as possessing that quality of irresolution that appeared most spectacularly in the episode of the denial.

SIGNIFICANCE

Even though Scripture breaks off with the quarrel at Antioch, this does not mean that Peter ceased to serve the Church. Indeed, tradition has much to say about his further career, though some of the statements have proved highly controversial. It seems obvious from Scripture that Peter held a special place among the disciples. Matthew 16 elaborates on this:

> Thou art Peter, and upon this rock I will build my church; and the gates of Hades shall not prevail against it. I will give unto thee the keys of the Kingdom of Heaven: and whatsoever thou shalt bind on earth shall be bound in Heaven: and whatsoever thou shalt loose on earth shall be loosed in Heaven.

This passage has been used to support the claims of the Roman Catholic Church regarding the authority and infallibility of the papacy. Connected with this is the question of Peter's residence and martyrdom in Rome. According to tradition, Peter was martyred in Rome by Nero between 64 and 67 C.E., after having lived in Rome for about twenty-five years, serving as bishop. Tradition also asserts that Peter was in contact with Mark in Rome and furnished material for his Gospel. It is natural for Protestants to deny not only that Peter was in effect the first pope but also that he was ever in Rome at all. The controversy has of late become less intense. It seems to be agreed that Peter was in Rome, though hardly for twenty-five years, and that he was crucified there, in the vicinity of the Vatican Hill; the question of his burial is still uncertain.

Peter showed himself a leader of the Apostles even during the lifetime of Jesus, and he was also a leader of the early Church, though sharing his authority at first with John and later with James and Paul. He almost certainly was martyred in Rome. Whether he had any authority in the Roman church and whether he could transmit that authority to others are questions on which even believers are likely to remain divided.

—John C. Sherwood

FURTHER READING

Alter, Robert, and Frank Kermode, eds. *The Literary Guide to the Bible*. Cambridge, Mass.: Harvard University Press, 1987. Especially relevant on the subject of Acts, which contributor James M. Robinson treats less as history than as "dramatized theology." The section "English Translations of the Bible," written by Gerald Hammond, explains the preference for the King James Version, used in this article.

Cullmann, Oscar. *Peter—Disciple, Apostle, Martyr: A Historical and Theological Study*. Translated by Floyd V. Wilson. 2d ed. Philadelphia: Westminster Press, 1962. Although thorough and scholarly, this volume is less a biography than a Protestant criticism of Catholic claims.

O'Connor, Daniel William. *Peter in Rome: The Literary, Liturgical, and Archaeological Evidence*. New York: Columbia University Press, 1969. An exhaustive survey of the evidence for Peter's presence in Rome. The account of the archaeological investigations (heavily illustrated) is particularly interesting.

Ray, Stephen K. *Upon This Rock: St. Peter and the Primacy of Rome in Scripture and the Early Church*. San Francisco: Ignatius Press, 1999. Tackling the issue of authority that divides Catholics and Protestants, Ray asserts that the early Christians had a clear understanding of the primacy of Peter in the See of Rome. Contains a complete compilation of Scriptural and Patristic quotations on the primacy of Peter and the Papal office of any book currently available.

Reicke, Bo. Introduction and notes to *The Epistles of James, Peter, and Jude*. New York: Doubleday, 1973. Accepts that the First Epistle was written by Peter, probably with assistance from Silvanus. The First Epistle was written from "Babylon," by which Rome is almost certainly meant; there is a reference to Mark, presumably the author of the Gospel of Mark.

Smith, Terence V. *Petrine Controversies in Early Christianity: Attitudes Toward Peter in Christian Writings of the First Two Centuries*. Tübingen, West Germany: J. C. B. Mohr, 1985. In his opening statement, Smith confesses, "To talk of the Apostle Peter is to enter into a world of disaccord, polemic, and controversy." Contains an extensive bibliography.

SEE ALSO: Jesus; John the Apostle; Saint Paul; Saint Stephen.

RELATED ARTICLES in *Great Events from History: The Ancient World*: c. 30 C.E., Condemnation and Crucifixion of Jesus Christ; c. 30 C.E., Preaching of the Pentecostal Gospel; c. 50-c. 150 C.E., Compilation of the New Testament; January-March, 55 or 56 C.E., Paul Writes His Letter to the Romans; 64-67 C.E., Nero Persecutes the Christians.

PHAEDRUS
Greek fabulist

As a prolific writer of fables and reputed translator of Aesop, Phaedrus elevated the fable from a rhetorical device, used incidentally in writing and speaking, to a completely independent genre with a recognizable place in literature.

BORN: c. 15 B.C.E.; Pieria, Thessaly, Macedonia (now in Greece)
DIED: c. 55 C.E.; place unknown
ALSO KNOWN AS: Gaius Iulius Phaeder; Phaidros
AREA OF ACHIEVEMENT: Literature

EARLY LIFE

The little that is known about Roman fabulist Phaedrus (FEE-druhs) is derived either directly or by deduction from his own writings. He was born Gaius Iulius Phaeder in Pieria, Thessaly, which was at the time part of a Roman province. He was presumably the son of a schoolteacher and was instructed by a highly educated poet and teacher of Greek. He spent part of his early youth in Italy, where he received the customary education in Latin and Greek. He studied, among others, Vergil, Euripides, Simonides, and particularly Quintus Ennius, who, together with Lucilius and Horace, had previously employed the fable in Roman literature.

During some portion of his youth, Phaedrus was attached to the retinue of Lucius Calpurnius Piso Frugi, who spent about three years settling disturbances in Thrace. After Piso's return to Rome, Phaedrus was brought, as a personal servant and tutor, to the house of Augustus, where he taught Greek to the emperor's grandson and heir, Lucius, while he himself attended the school of the famous scholar and philologist Marcus Verrius Flaccus. Years later, Phaedrus was granted his freedom by the emperor; however, his manumission did not confer upon him complete civil rights. As a freedman under Augustus, Phaedrus continued to live under the repressive tutelage and influence of the Imperial rules.

Phaedrus's writing was strongly influenced by folklore, especially the fables collected in the writings of Aesop (c. 600 B.C.E.). The fable, which originally came from the "wisdom literature" of numerous civilizations, migrated, in oral or written form, to Europe. There, Aesop, considered to be one of the wisest men of Greece, developed it and came to be known as the father of the fable. Aesop had also been a freed slave and, through his fables, he became, in scholar H. J. Blackham's words,

"idealized as spokesman of the wisdom of the common man." Aesop himself explained that, in giving the use of speech to animals (actually the poet Hesiod's invention), he "laid the plan of teaching the most beautiful and useful maxims of philosophy under the veil of fables."

Aesop's influence on Phaedrus cannot be underestimated. "Where Aesop made a footpath, I have built a highway," wrote Phaedrus. He not only adopted the fable as a form of writing that he would later elevate to an independent genre but also, as a slave and later a freedman under Augustus and Tiberius, became increasingly preoccupied with the fortunes (or misfortunes) of the common people and used the fable to give a voice to those who were not allowed to speak openly. In the prologue to book 3 of his fables, he wrote:

> The slave, being liable to punishment for any offence, since he dared not say outright what he wished to say, projected his personal sentiments into fables and eluded censure under the guise of jesting with made-up stories.

On more than one occasion, his allusions to the atmosphere of unfairness and injustice in which he lived got him into trouble. His audacity even brought him to the point of persecution at the hands of Sejanus, the most powerful minister of Tiberius's reign. However, it is not known which poem or poems in books 1 and 2 offended Sejanus or what form of punishment Phaedrus received.

LIFE'S WORK

Much of Phaedrus's work is lost. His only surviving work, *Phaedri augusti Liberti Fabularum Aesopiarum* (*The Fables of Phaedrus*, 1646), is a collection based on Aesop's fables that had been gathered in prose by Demetrius of Phalerum in about 300 B.C.E. Using Demetrius as his only source, Phaedrus translated Aesop's fables into Latin, cast them into verse form, and compiled them in the first collection of fables ever published as poetry and thus as literature. The five-book collection contains a total of ninety-three fables, but it is thought to be incomplete, because the length of each volume varies considerably. In particular, volumes 2 and 5 are thought to have originally contained much greater numbers of fables. Later editions include some thirty additional fables compiled by Niccolò Perotti (Archbishop of Manfredonia, 1430-1480 C.E.) in the *Appendix Perottina* (1470;

Perotti's Appendix, 1826). Except for *Perotti's Appendix*, each volume begins with a prologue in which Phaedrus stresses his independence from his source and defends his poetry from the attack of what he calls "malign critics."

The fables were written during a span of twenty years. Books 1 and 2 were published during the last years of Tiberius's reign and contain some of Phaedrus's most famous animal fables, such as "The Wolf and the Lamb," "The Wolf and the Crane," and "The Frogs Complain Against the Sun." Book 3 appeared under the reign of Caligula somewhere between 37 and 41 C.E. Book 4 differs from the previous volumes in that it includes a large number of fables composed by Phaedrus himself. This volume marked Phaedrus's return to writing after he had determined to put an end to his work. Book 5 was written without much enthusiasm under the reign of Claudius I (41-54 C.E.) or during that of Nero (54-68 C.E.), when Phaedrus was at a very advanced age and probably close to death.

Phaedrus's collection of fables is far from being a mere compilation of Aesop's work. Phaedrus went beyond his source, refining and rewriting the fables in iambic senarii (a simple meter composed of lines of six iambic feet with variations that provide varying rhythms), the standard meter used by Greek and Roman dramatists. He also included some of his own fables using "the old form but with modern content." As a result, the collection includes a variety of stories, proverbs, sayings, and jests of varied length. Not all of them are animal fables. In fact, volumes 3, 4, and 5 include progressively fewer animal characters and more poets, priests, farmers, and shepherds, in conversation among themselves and sometimes even with Aesop himself (as in "The Poet," "The Thief and His Lamp," "Aesop and the Farmer," and "Aesop and the Saucy Fellow").

This difference in the form, however, does not affect their main purpose, which, following the example set by Aesop, was to convey a moral or useful truth beneath the shadow of an allegory. Thus, "The Sheep, the Dog, and the Wolf" teaches the reader that liars are liable to lose in the end, while "Aesop and the Imprudent Fellow" instructs the reader that success dooms people to their downfalls. To stress the didactic purpose of the fables, Phaedrus usually inserted a separate moral, either at the beginning (*promythion*) or at the end (*epimythion*) of each fable. It is believed that he may have derived this feature from Demetrius; it was definitely not from Aesop, who rejected such trite and wearisome additions that left little to the imagination.

Phaedrus wrote the fables in the language that characterized the early Augustan period: lucid, simple, and free from ornaments. At times, he uses a colloquial and coarse language, but it is always in agreement with his characterizations. His style, often satirical but at times serious, is defined by an extreme brevity that other fabulists both admired and envied but that most critics judged on account of the rather obscure effect some of his extremely brief sentences yielded. Only occasionally, such as in "The Poet, on Believing and Not Believing," and "The King, the Flute Player," is the language less concise, yielding a rather tedious effect. His tone has been defined sometimes as charming and humorous, other times as querulous and cantankerous, and, in one critic's opinion, embittered, particularly when commenting on the "law of the stronger."

Throughout his lifetime, Phaedrus suffered much stern criticism. Not only were his fables condemned by Sejanus, but he was also constantly ridiculed by jealous and hostile critics who underrated his writing and condemned it to a level below that of poetry. In books 3 and 4, he asked Eutychus and Particulo, two of his patrons, to vindicate him in the eyes of the public. Their defense must not have made much of an impact, for he was rarely mentioned in classical literature. Neither Seneca the Younger nor Quintilian, both of whom wrote in the first century C.E., mentioned him in their writings, and even Flavius Avianus, himself a fabulist writing in the fourth century C.E., claims to have been influenced by Babrius (who wrote in the second half of the first century C.E.) rather than Phaedrus.

If, however, Phaedrus's contemporaries failed to recognize his literary merit, he regained the respect he had always sought after the fifteenth century, when his fables were rediscovered and were read by the public, paraphrased among respected fabulists, and even used for teaching Latin in school.

SIGNIFICANCE

Phaedrus admitted that his ambition was to carry on, in Latin, the literary tradition of Greece, which he had inherited. He chose the fable because it combined the two traditional functions of poetry: entertainment and instruction. Some scholars suggest, however, that his main motive in adopting the fable as a literary form and Aesop as his subject was to fight against moral degradation during the reigns of Augustus and Tiberius. Because slaves were not allowed to speak outright, he chose a genre in which he was able to elude censure and thus remain immune. This may well have been true. Behind the speech of his animals and his inanimate objects such as trees, there is the constant reminder of some of his prevalent themes: the advantage of the stronger over the weak ("The Wolf and the Lamb"), the futility of protest ("The Frogs Ask for a King"), the safety found in poverty ("The Dog Carrying a Piece of Meat Across the River"), the pervasiveness of power ("The Eagle and the Crow"), and the praise of freedom ("The Wolf and the Sleek Dog"). Phaedrus was not a highly inventive fabulist nor a poet of great achievement. However, no other fabulist did for the fable what Phaedrus did: By adapting the Greek genre of the fable to Latin, he made it a subject of poetic composition and gave it a recognizable voice in literature.

—*Silvia P. Baeza*

FURTHER READING

Blackham, H. J. *The Fable as Literature*. Dover, N.H.: Athlone Press, 1985. Chapter 1 gives a detailed account of the fable as early popular narrative, including its Indian and Aesopic origins. Phaedrus is mentioned tangentially throughout the discussion.

Conte, Gian Biagio. *Latin Literature: A History*. Translated by Joseph B. Solodow. Baltimore: The Johns Hopkins University Press, 1994. The section "Phaedrus: The Fable Tradition" includes a discussion of Phaedrus's merit as a man of letters and a social commentator of his time.

Duff, J. Wight. *A Literary History of Rome in the Silver Age: From Tiberius to Hadrian*. Westport, Conn.: Greenwood Press, 1979. Chapter 5, "Phaedrus and Fable: Poetry of the Time," is a long discussion on Phaedrus's life and work within the Roman context.

Perry, Ben Edwin. *Babrius and Phaedrus*. Cambridge, Mass.: Harvard University Press, 1990. The lengthy introduction covers the Aesopic fable in antiquity, its origin, and the roles of Aesop, Babrius, and Phaedrus in its development.

Phaedrus. *The Fables of Phaedrus*. Translated by P. F. Widdows. Austin: University of Texas Press, 1992. Translation includes a lengthy introduction discussing Phaedrus's life and work, his fables, his reputation, his use of meter, and Christopher Smart's 1764 translation of his work.

SEE ALSO: Aesop; Augustus; Quintus Ennius; Euripides; Horace; Simonides; Tiberius; Vergil.

RELATED ARTICLES in *Great Events from History: The Ancient World*: 19 B.C.E., Roman Poet Vergil Dies; November 27, 8 B.C.E., Roman Lyric Poet Horace Dies.

PHEIDIPPIDES
Athenian courier

Pheidippides delivered a message, on foot and over a long distance, concerning the Battle of Marathon fought between Persia and Athens in 490 B.C.E. Despite problems with the ancient tradition, Pheidippides' feat of running is still popularly associated with the announcement of the Athenian victory and also with the introduction of the so-called marathon race in modern times.

BORN: Probably c. 515 B.C.E.; Athens, Greece
DIED: Perhaps 490 B.C.E.; perhaps Athens, Greece
ALSO KNOWN AS: Philippides
AREA OF ACHIEVEMENT: War and conquest

EARLY LIFE

No information is available about the early life of Pheidippides (fi-DIHP-ih-deez) prior to his famous run, which occurred in 490 B.C.E., either shortly before or shortly after the Battle of Marathon, a pivotal conflict of the Greco-Persian Wars. At Marathon, located in Athe-

nian territory to the northeast of the city of Athens, a smaller army of Athenians courageously faced and dramatically defeated a larger Persian army, and Pheidippides' run has become famous as a symbol of that victory.

The Battle of Marathon showed the effectiveness of the Greek infantry, and it greatly enhanced the self-confidence of the Greeks, especially the Athenians, in their military and cultural prowess. Along with the "birth of democracy" at Athens a few years earlier, the victory at Marathon marked the transition from the early Archaic Age of Greece (c. 750-500 B.C.E.), a time of independent development for the Greek city-states. After Marathon, acting more in concert than ever before, Athens, Sparta, and other Greek states went on to repel an even greater Persian attack on Greece in 480 to 479 B.C.E., and in the classical age of Greek glory in the fifth century B.C.E., the Greeks made phenomenal achievements in the areas of politics, literature, philosophy, and the arts.

The best source on Pheidippides is Herodotus, the "father of history," the fifth century B.C.E. author of *Historiai Herodotou* (c. 424 B.C.E.; *The History*, 1709), a work on the Persian Wars. Herodotus says that Pheidippides was an Athenian and a trained *hemerodromos*, a "day-runner," which means that he delivered messages by running long distances on foot. Clearly, he was well trained and in excellent physical shape, and he had run long distances before. Probably, but not necessarily, he was a fairly young man in 490.

LIFE'S WORK

Pheidippides' achievement was a physically impressive feat of long-distance running performed in the context of one of history's most famous battles, but details of his actions were confused and at least semilegendary, even in antiquity. Even his name is a matter of debate. Some ancient manuscripts of Herodotus and some other ancient sources name the runner Philippides, a more common name in ancient Athens. Nevertheless, the name Pheidippides is still popularly associated with the "messenger of Marathon," the heroic soldier who supposedly fought at the Battle of Marathon and then ran approximately twenty-five miles to Athens, delivered the message, "Rejoice! We have won," and dropped dead.

Recent studies have reexamined the ancient sources and shown that this inspirational event perhaps never happened at all and certainly did not happen as is traditionally assumed. According to Herodotus, in 490 B.C.E. a Persian force landed in Athenian territory and occupied the plain of Marathon. One of the Athenian generals, Miltiades the Younger, convinced the Athenians to send out a force of heavily armed infantry soldiers (called hoplites) to meet the Persians. Before the army departed for Marathon, the Athenian generals decided to send a herald to appeal to Sparta, the leading military power in Greece, for help against Persia.

The Athenian Pheidippides, a courier trained at delivering messages over long distances by running, carried the appeal from Athens to Sparta, a distance of about 140 miles (225 kilometers). Later, on his return, Pheidippides told the Athenians that while he was running over Mount Parthenion in Arcadia (a region of Greece along the route to Sparta) the god Pan (a Greek god, part human and part goat in form, associated with flocks, shepherds, and fertility) called him by name. Pan, Pheidippides claimed, told him to ask the Athenians why they had failed to worship the god with a state cult when he had been friendly to them, he had helped them in the past, and he was willing to do so in the future. Herodotus adds that, after the return

to peace and prosperity, the Athenians built a shrine to Pan and established annual sacrifices and a torch race to honor the god.

According to Herodotus, on the second day after leaving Athens, the messenger arrived in Sparta. He addressed the Spartan leaders and begged them to help save Athens from slavery at the hands of the Persians. The Spartans said they wanted to help but that they were busy with an important festival, the Carnea, in honor of Apollo, and so their religion obliged them to stay at Sparta until the arrival of the full moon later in the month. As Herodotus recounts, a force of about ten thousand Greeks (mostly Athenians, with a few soldiers from Plataea, a state allied with Athens) were heavily outnumbered, perhaps by two to one, by the Persian forces. Nevertheless, the Greeks charged and defeated the Persians in an infantry battle that, Herodotus claims, cost the lives of 6,400 Persians but only 192 Athenians.

Herodotus notes that immediately after the battle, the Athenian troops hurried back to the city to defend it against a possible Persian attack by sea. Troops from Sparta did arrive at Marathon but only after the battle was over. Significantly, Herodotus makes no mention of a post-battle run by Pheidippides. Herodotus loved stories of heroic feats and wonders, so his silence about a "Marathon run" seriously undermines the credibility of the later traditions about the runner.

The popular version of the story comes from later authors. Writing around 100 C.E., Plutarch, a Greek biographer of famous ancient leaders, stated that Herakleides of Pontus, a Greek philosopher of the fourth century B.C.E., had said that the messenger who brought the news from Marathon was one Thersippus of Erchia. This suggests that some story of a messenger announcing the victory at Marathon at Athens was known in the mid-fourth century B.C.E. but that the messenger's name was not Pheidippides. Furthermore, Plutarch says most (probably later) sources say that the messenger was a certain Eukles and that he ran directly from the battle, still in full armor, to Athens, said "Rejoice! We have won," and then died. Elsewhere, Plutarch tells a suspiciously similar story about a man named Euchidas: that in 479 B.C.E., after another Greek land victory against Persia, he ran from Plataea to Delphi and back to Plataea, covering the distance of about 125 miles (202 kilometers) in one day, carrying a torch burning with sacred fire, that he greeted his fellow citizens, handed them the torch, and died.

The latest ancient source on the tradition is Lucian, a prolific literary figure who, around 170 C.E., wrote that the name of the messenger from Marathon was Philippides and that, with his dying words, he announced the victory to the Athenian officials. Lucian thus is the only ancient author to combine all the now-popular details—a messenger named Philippides or Pheidippides who ran from Marathon to Athens and announced the victory with his last words before dying. In sum, because the best source, Herodotus, omits the story, and the "Marathon run" turns up only in later, less reliable sources, the popular story perhaps was a romantic invention of the type that commonly grow up around famous battles and famous figures.

Adding to the tradition and the confusion, Robert Browning's 1879 poem "Pheidippides" mixed ancient accounts with poetic creativity to produce a full-blown modern version of the tale. Browning's poem has Pheidippides run to Sparta to request help, then run back to fight at Marathon, and then run to Athens, arriving, with his heart bursting with joy, to announce the victory and die. This amounts to a truly impressive but much less credible historical accomplishment. Nevertheless, Browning's expanded, romantic version of the story inspired (or was used to suggest an ancient precedent for) the introduction of the modern marathon race in the Olympic Games held in Athens in 1896.

Despite modern misperceptions, Pheidippides' run to Sparta should not be associated with any sporting contest but rather with the abilities of ancient messengers. There simply was no marathon or ultra-long-distance running in ancient Greek athletics. At ancient Greek athletic meets, the longest footrace, the *dolichos*, was run over a distance of at most 3 miles (5 kilometers). However, other ancient examples, modern studies, and the feats of modern long-distance athletes have shown that even such a lengthy run as 140 miles (225 kilometers) could have been accomplished by a well-trained runner in two days. Moreover, the story that the runner saw Pan provides a convincing detail, for long-distance runners sometimes do experience altered states of consciousness as part of the so-called runner's high.

SIGNIFICANCE

Ironically, Pheidippides has not been immortalized for his historically credible and physically very impressive (though ultimately militarily futile) run from Athens to Sparta but rather for a much shorter and historically much less credible run from Marathon to Athens, a run associated with a great military victory and his own dramatic death. Indeed, there probably was a fifth century B.C.E. Pheidippides (or Philippides) who carried a mes-

sage from Athens to Sparta, quite conceivably covering the distance in two days. However, the popular version of the story, that a soldier running miles from the victory at Marathon to Athens and then dropping dead as he delivered the news, is surely a product of a tradition begun by later, less reliable ancient authors, amplified by Browning's 1879 poem and memorialized by the introduction of the marathon race at the Olympics in 1896.

Although the story remains a cherished part of the folklore of ancient Greece and of modern sport, the "Marathon run" should not be associated with Pheidippides; moreover, marathon running as a sport rather than as a form of messenger service is of historically recent origin. Not actually derived from ancient sport but rather invented for the Athens Olympic Games of 1896, the marathon race has nevertheless become both a symbol of the Olympic Games and an internationally popular athletic event.

—*Donald G. Kyle*

FURTHER READING

Burn, A. R. *Persia and the Greeks: The Defence of the West, 546-478 B.C.* 2d ed. Stanford, Calif.: Stanford University Press, 1984. A readable, traditional, but still useful military history of the conflicts between Greece and Persia.

Frost, Frank J. "The Dubious Origins of the Marathon." *American Journal of Ancient History* 4 (1979): 159-163. An important article challenging the value of sources after Herodotus on the runner, whom Frost argues was actually named "Philippides."

Herodotus. *The Histories*. Translated by Robin Waterfield. New York: Oxford University Press, 1998. A convenient translation of the classic ancient history of the background to and course of the Persian Wars.

Lazenby, J. F. *The Defence of Greece, 490-479 B.C.* Warminster, England: Aris & Phillips, 1993. An excellent account of the failure of the Persian invasions of Greece.

Lee, Hugh M. "Modern Ultra-Long-Distance Running and Philippides' Run from Athens to Sparta." *Ancient World* 9 (1984): 107-113. Offers modern comparisons to show that a run from Athens to Sparta in two days was possible for a trained runner.

Matthews, V. J. "The *Hemerodromoi:* Ultra-Long-Distance Running in Antiquity." *Classical World* 68 (1974): 161-167. The author, a classicist and marathon runner, thoroughly examines several ancient accounts of long-distance running.

Sweet, Waldo E. *Sport and Recreation in Ancient Greece.* New York: Oxford University Press, 1987. A sourcebook of ancient texts on sport. Includes sources on Pheidippides in a chapter on running in ancient Greece.

SEE ALSO: Cyrus the Great; Darius the Great; Miltiades the Younger; Xerxes I.
RELATED ARTICLES in *Great Events from History: The Ancient World*: September 17, 490 B.C.E., Battle of Marathon; 480-479 B.C.E., Persian Invasion of Greece.

PHIDIAS
Greek sculptor

Phidias's work embodied the high classical ideal in sculpture; his renditions of the gods became standards to which later artists aspired. He was best known for his cult images of Athena in Athens and of Zeus in Olympia.

BORN: c. 490 B.C.E.; Athens, Greece
DIED: c. 430 B.C.E.; Elis, Greece
AREA OF ACHIEVEMENT: Art and art patronage

EARLY LIFE

Phidias (FIHD-ih-ahs), the son of Charmides, was born just before the wars that pitted his fellow Athenians against the invading Persians in 490 and 480 B.C.E. This fact is of great importance in understanding his development and that of his country, for these wars proved to the Athenians that with their own resources and the gods' favor, the fledgling democracy could succeed against overwhelming odds. Phidias's sculptures came to reflect confidence in men and the gods' grace.

After the wars, Athens became the preeminent Greek state and led a confederation that continued to fight the Persians. Athenian leadership led to Athenian domination, and any city that tried to leave the Delian League was disciplined. Pericles led the state during Phidias's adult lifetime and created a strong Athens by pursuing an expansionist policy. Phidias grew up knowing that he lived in one of the most powerful and influential of the Greek states.

Little is known of Phidias's early training beyond the fact that—like other Athenian children—he would have received his education in the gymnasium, learning athletics, music, mathematics, and poetry, including the Homeric epics. The works of Homer in particular were to have a profound impact on Phidias's vision of the gods, which expressed itself in his sculpture. Along with the sculptors Myron and Polyclitus, he received artistic training from Ageladas (also called Hageladas) of Argos, who worked mainly in bronze and is known for a great statue of Zeus that he made for the Messenians.

Phidias attended the dramatic festivals of Dionysus, where he saw performances of Aeschylus's tragedies, including *Persai* (472 B.C.E.; *The Persians*, 1777), a triumphant paean to Athenian success and divine favor, and the *Oresteia* trilogy (458 B.C.E.), which extols the gods Zeus and Athena and ends with an encomium to justice as practiced in Athens. Phidias grew up to be proud of his land's traditions and the accomplishments of its citizens. The tragic vision revealed in Athenian drama, with the grace of the immortals contrasting with human limitations, was to have a profound effect on the sculptor's works.

Another formative influence on the sculptor was the humanistic teachings of Sophists such as Protagoras, who held that "man is the measure of all things," and Anaxagoras, who insisted on the divine supremacy of reason. With their notions of subjectivity and emphasis on the potential for human progress, these new thinkers saw people as responsible for their own advancement. Thus, they represented an anthropocentric view of life that encouraged the development of the arts, because to them civilization was advanced by *technē* (artistic skill). Phidias's work was a physical manifestation of this confidence in human accomplishment. At the same time, his statues reflected the measured relationships that Anaxagoras saw as the reflections of the divine world-reason.

Phidias was a product of his age, which was characterized by confidence in human rationality, the tragic notion of human limitation in the face of divine power, and the idea of civilization's triumph over barbarism. His sculptures both reflected his age and recalled epic notions of Homeric gods and heroes.

LIFE'S WORK

During Phidias's early years, the temples and sanctuaries that the Persians had destroyed remained untouched because the Greeks, in the Oath of Plataea, had agreed to leave the ruins as memorials to barbarian sacrilege. Consequently, Phidias's earlier sculptures were monuments to the Athenian victory over the Persians at Marathon. In fact, two of them were built with spoils from that battle. One, a colossal bronze statue of armed *Athena Promachos* (c. 470-460 B.C.E.; Athena, first in battle), stood prominently on the Acropolis at Athens; approximately 50 feet (15 meters) high, its shining spear tip and helmet crest could be seen from far out at sea. The other, a bronze group containing Athena, Apollo, the legendary heroes of Athens, and the victorious Athenian general Miltiades, was dedicated at the panhellenic sanctuary at Delphi (c. 465 B.C.E.).

Phidias's *Athena Lemnia* was commissioned and dedicated by Athenian colonists settling on Lemnos around 450. This bronze stood on the Athenian Acropolis and had a reputation for extraordinary beauty. Later copies and ancient descriptions indicate that it showed the goddess contemplating her helmet in her right hand.

Pericles respected the Oath of Plataea as long as a state of belligerence with Persia—fostered by the Athenian general Cimon—kept the issue alive. When Cimon died in 449 and a peace treaty was arranged with the Persians, Pericles no longer felt the need to maintain the Athenian temples in ruins. The stage was set for a rebuilding of the sanctuaries on the Acropolis, and the next year, construction of the Parthenon began. Pericles named Phidias general supervisor for the project.

The Parthenon—the temple of Athena the Maiden—was a major synthesis of architecture and sculpture. Phidias coordinated the sculptural program, which consisted of ninety-two metopes with battle scenes (Greeks/Trojans, Greeks/Amazons, lapiths/centaurs, and gods/giants; in place by 443), a 525-foot (160-meter) sculptured frieze the Panathenaic Procession (complete by 438), the cult statue of *Athena Parthenos* (complete by 438), and pediments (the birth of Athena and the contest of Athena and Poseidon; complete by 432). The sculpted decoration of the Parthenon was unique: No other temple had both sculpted metopes and a continuous frieze, so Phidias's genius had the maximum opportunity to show itself.

Phidias himself was completely responsible for the chryselephantine (gold and ivory) statue of Athena inside, which stood more than 40 feet (12 meters) high. No original pieces of this statue have survived, but later copies and descriptions give an idea of its appearance. Athena stood with a statue of Nike (victory) in her right hand, which rested lightly on a Corinthian column. She was dressed in her aegis, a magical breastplate surrounded by snakes, and wore a three-crested helmet and a belt of snakes. A spear and shield stood at her left side, the latter decorated with relief figures of gods battling giants (inside) and Greeks fighting Amazons (outside). These motifs reflected those of the Parthenon's other sculptures: the forces of order battling those of barbarity—another sign of Athenian pride in the Persian defeat. Beneath the shield rose the form of a great snake, representing the local god Erichthonius. The statue stood on a rectangular base showing Pandora being adorned by all the gods.

After the cult image was dedicated in 438, Phidias was accused by Pericles' enemies of hav-

Statue of Minerva by Phidias, in the Parthenon. (F. R. Niglutsch)

ing stolen some of the gold from the statue. This charge was proved false when it was revealed that the gold on the statue, weighing more than 454 pounds (1,000 kilograms), had been designed to be easily removed. When it was weighed, no gold was found missing. On his acquittal on that charge, Phidias was accused of sacrilege, for it was commonly believed that he had represented himself and Pericles on the shield of Athena. This charge provides the circumstances for the description of Phidias: He was shown as a bald old man lifting up a stone with both hands. On his conviction, Phidias had to leave Athens, probably around 437 B.C.E.

Fortunately for Phidias, the Elians at this time invited him to come to Olympia to make a chryselephantine cult image of Zeus for the recently completed temple of Zeus. Phidias set up a workshop behind the temple, where he worked for five years, helped by his nephew Panaenus. Pieces of the molds for the golden drapery have been found there, in addition to a cup with the inscription "I belong to Phidias."

Phidias's Zeus at Olympia represented a new conception in Greek art. Until that time, Zeus had been usually depicted striding forward with a thunderbolt in his hand. Phidias portrayed him seated on a throne in Olympian calm, seven or eight times life size—more than 40 feet (12 meters)—his head almost touching the roof. The throne was four-fifths of the height of the whole and was decorated with ebony, gold, and ivory. The golden cloak was decorated with lilies and glass inlay. The majesty of the statue impressed all who saw it. Quintilian asserted that it enhanced traditional religion, Dio Cocceianus (Chrysostomos) that the sight of it banished all sorrow. According to one anecdote, Phidias said that he had been inspired by the image of Zeus in Homer's *Iliad* (c. 750 B.C.E.; English translation, 1611), in which the god on his throne nodded and caused all Olympus to shake. Pausanias related that Phidias carved his signature beneath the god's feet and that when the statue was complete, the god sent a flash of lightning to show that he approved of the work. The men in charge of cleaning the great statue were said to be the descendants of Phidias himself.

Phidias died shortly after having completed the Olympian Zeus, probably in Elis around 430. Many other works have been attributed to him, including a bronze Apollo near the Parthenon, a marble Aphrodite in the Athenian Agora, a chryselephantine Aphrodite in Elis, and a famous Amazon in Ephesus. In addition, literary sources indicate that he was skilled in paintings, engraving, and metal embossing. None of these works survives.

SIGNIFICANCE

Phidias's life spanned three important periods in the development of Greek art. He was born toward the end of the Archaic period, when sculpture was quite formal, orderly, and stylized, with a quality of aloofness. Phidias lived as a young man in the Early Classical period, a time of artistic transition, when statues were more representational and heavily charged with specific emotions. When he matured, Phidias worked in a style that avoided the extremes of both: the High Classical, whose statues had expressions that were neither overly remote nor involved, but simultaneously detached and aware. This attitude of idealism, congenial to Phidias's strong Homeric tendencies, colored his work and gave it its distinctive quality.

The sculpture on the Parthenon came to embody what later generations considered "classical," and Phidias's style influenced all cult images subsequent to his Athena and Zeus, setting a standard for later sculptors to follow. For example, his pupil Alcamenes was responsible for the cult images in the Hephaesteum and the temples of Dionysus Eleuthereus and Ares in Athens as well as the Aphrodite of the Gardens. Agoracritus, another pupil, created the cult statue and base for the temple of Nemesis at Rhamnus.

The chief characteristics of Phidias's style were sublimity, precision, and an "Olympian" rendering, showing the gods as detached from the human realm yet still concerned for men. Their expressions were calm and dignified. They were so pure in their conception that stories arose that Phidias had seen the gods themselves. His works brought the divine down to earth and made heavenly forms manifest for mortals; the gods of Homer came alive under his touch.

Since so few of Phidias's works survive—the Parthenon sculptures are most likely his design but not of his hand—scholars try to re-create his sculptures on the basis of later copies, mostly of Roman date. The *Athena Lemnia*, for example, has been reconstructed from ancient references, combined with a marble head now in Bologna and a torso in Dresden; the *Athena Parthenos* from later copies, including the *Varvakeion Athena* of Roman date; the Olympian Zeus from coins and gems depicting it in Roman times. Identifications of copies of Phidian originals cannot be proved for the most part, but the quest continues to exercise the ingenuity of scholars. For example, some assign to Phidias the bronze warrior statues found in 1972 in the sea off Riace in southern Italy, while others oppose the attribution.

—Daniel B. Levine

FURTHER READING

Boardman, John. *Greek Art*. Rev. ed. New York: Thames and Hudson, 1996. Regarded as a standard work in the field of classical art, this book provides an overview of the masterpieces of ancient Greece as well as commentary on discoveries and controversies of interpretation surrounding the world's best-known works of art and architecture.

Boardman, John, and David Finn. *The Parthenon and Its Sculptures*. Austin: University of Texas Press, 1985. Contains hundreds of large, clear photographs and illustrations. Excellent discussion of the history of the building, the role of Phidias, the nature of the sources, historical context, interpretation of the sculpture, and relation to religious festivals. Includes bibliography and index.

Harrison, Evelyn B. "The Composition of the Amazonomachy on the Shield of *Athena Parthenos*." *Hesperia* 35 (1966): 107-133. Exhaustive study of literary sources that describe the battle scene said to include a representation of Phidias himself, with an analysis of the ancient copies. Discussion of composition and iconography, including illustrations with discussion of each figure. Includes extensive bibliography, catalog of figures, and detailed reconstruction.

Leipen, Neda. *"Athena Parthenos": A Reconstruction*. Toronto: Royal Ontario Museum, 1971. Devoted to the problem of reconstructing Phidias's Parthenon cult statue, this is a photographic documentation of all relevant artifacts, with a discussion of literary descriptions, the Royal Ontario Museum's own construction of a model of the statue, and a detailed description of each part of the figure, including accessories. Includes notes and bibliography.

Palagia, Olga. "In Defense of Furtwangler's *Athena Lemnia*." *American Journal of Archaeology* 91 (1987): 81-84. Discussion of a reconstruction of Phidias's most beautiful statue. Contains an illustration of the most accepted reconstruction and of other sculptures that support that interpretation. A good example of scholarly methodology used to re-create a Phidian original. Includes bibliography.

Pollitt, J. J. *Art and Experience in Classical Greece*. Cambridge, England: Cambridge University Press, 1999. Describes the intellectual influences on Phidias, his influence on other media, his style and spirit, and the problems with writing his biography. Includes illustrations and bibliography.

Richter, Gisela M. "The Pheidian Zeus at Olympia." *Hesperia* 35 (1966): 166-170. Excellent summary of what is known about the statue that was considered one of the seven wonders of the world. Includes descriptions of the statue as rendered in literature and on gems and coins. Generously illustrated and footnoted.

_____. *The Sculpture and Sculptors of the Greeks*. New Haven, Conn.: Yale University Press, 1970. Definitive work on the lives and works of Greek sculptors. Treats anatomy, technique, composition, copies. Long and detailed section on Phidias, discussing all of his works, with extensive bibliography of ancient and modern sources. Two indexes, numerous photographs, chronological table of Greek sculptors and their works.

SEE ALSO: Anaxagoras; Homer; Pericles; Polyclitus; Praxiteles; Protagoras.

RELATED ARTICLES in *Great Events from History: The Ancient World*: September 17, 490 B.C.E., Battle of Marathon; 480-479 B.C.E., Persian Invasion of Greece; 447-438 B.C.E., Building of the Parthenon; c. 440 B.C.E., Sophists Train the Greeks in Rhetoric and Politics.

PHILIP II OF MACEDONIA
Macedonian king (r. 359-336 B.C.E.)

Philip inherited a backward kingdom on the verge of collapse and made it a powerful state. His military innovations revolutionized warfare and created the army that would conquer the Persian Empire.

BORN: 382 B.C.E.; Macedonia (now in Greece)
DIED: 336 B.C.E.; Aegae, Macedonia
ALSO KNOWN AS: Philip II
AREAS OF ACHIEVEMENT: Government and politics, war and conquest

EARLY LIFE

Situated on the northern frontier of the Greek world, Macedonia had long remained a kingdom without real unity. From their capitals of Aegae and Pella near the Aegean coast, the ancestors of Philip (FIHL-ihp) had ruled the eastern area of lower Macedonia since the seventh century B.C.E. They exercised only a tenuous rule inland over upper Macedonia, however, and suffered repeated invasions and interference from their neighbors, barbarian and Greek alike. Philip's direct experience of these problems during the reigns of his father and two older brothers helps explain his determination as king to reverse Macedonia's precarious position.

In 393, Philip's father, Amyntas, suffered his first expulsion at the hands of the Illyrians, his neighbors to the west. Amyntas soon regained his throne, but he secured peace with the Illyrians only by paying tribute. As part of the settlement, he also married an Illyrian princess, Eurydice—the future mother of Philip. Ten years later a second Illyrian invasion forced Amyntas to entrust a portion of this kingdom to the Chalcidian Greeks, who refused to relinquish it. By 382, the year of Philip's birth, they had extended their control westward to include Amyntas's capital, Pella. An intervention by Sparta, then the most powerful of the Greek states, restored Amyntas to his capital in 379, but the Spartans demanded Macedonia's subservience to Sparta.

When Philip's older brother Alexander II assumed the throne in 370, the now-adolescent Philip went as a hostage to the Illyrians, who also demanded tribute as the price of peace. The boy returned home to find Alexander in a civil war that invited intervention by Thebes, the ascendant Greek city-state since the defeat of Sparta in 371. In 368, after the Thebans resolved the conflict in favor of Alexander, Philip and thirty other sons of Macedonian nobles were sent to Thebes as a guarantee of Macedonian obedience to Theban wishes.

For three years Philip observed Thebes at the peak of its diplomatic and military power. Later accounts of the military lessons of this visit are probably exaggerated, but this experience must have influenced Philip. At the very least it allowed him to understand how the Greeks conducted their affairs, and it may explain his later severe treatment of Thebes. Following the assassination of Alexander, a second Theban intervention saved the throne for Philip's other brother, Perdiccas III, and brought more hostages to Thebes.

Back in Macedonia after 365, Philip received a district of his own and witnessed seizures of Macedonian coastal territory by the Athenians. In 359 he may have taken part in the disastrous Illyrian expedition that resulted in the death of Perdiccas and four thousand Macedonian soldiers. After the death of his brother, Philip—at age twenty-three—became the eighteenth king of Macedonia.

LIFE'S WORK

Philip inherited a kingdom on the verge of disintegration. Rival heirs challenged his right to the throne, the army threatened to collapse, and enemies menaced on all sides. Fortunately, the Illyrians did not choose to follow their victory with an invasion. To the north, however, the Paeonians began to raid Macedonian territory, while

Philip II of Macedonia. (Library of Congress)

a Thracian king supported a pretender who claimed the kingship. Diplomacy and bribery forestalled these threats, while Philip dealt with a more immediate danger: Another pretender, backed by the Athenians, marched on the ancestral capital, Aegae, with three thousand mercenaries. After ensuring the loyalty of the capital, the young king trapped and disposed of his rival. Wisely, he then made conciliatory gestures to the Athenians in order to neutralize them while he returned his attention to the barbarians.

The opportune death of the Paeonian king allowed Philip to force an alliance on his weaker successor, and by 358 Philip felt secure enough to lead a revitalized Macedonian army west against his most dangerous foes, the Illyrians. The details of his first major battle remain unclear, but Philip won a decisive victory and inflicted unusually severe casualties on his defeated enemy—three-quarters of the Illyrian army reportedly died. Followed by his marriage to an Illyrian princess, this victory secured his western frontier and allowed him to consolidate his position in Macedonia. As part of that consolidation, Philip began the transformation of Macedonia from a largely pastoral society to a more agriculturally based and urbanized state. Less visible than his military activities, these internal changes were equally important to the rise of Macedonia.

His dramatic victory over the Illyrians indicates that Philip had already begun the reorganization of the Macedonian army that would revolutionize warfare and make Macedonia the supreme military power in the Mediterranean region. One year after his unfortunate brother had lost four thousand men to the Illyrians, Philip fielded a force of ten thousand foot soldiers and six hundred horsemen. (By the time of Philip's death, the Macedonian army would comprise at least twenty-four thousand infantry and four thousand cavalry, with numerous supporting troops.) As important as the increase in manpower was Philip's use of heavy cavalry as a primary instrument of attack against infantry, a tactic that explains the remarkably high rate of casualties among his foes. Equally significant was his redesign of the traditional Greek phalanx infantry formation, which he used in expert combination with his horsemen. Superbly trained to fight as a unit, Philip's phalangites used a novel fifteen-foot pike, the *sarissa*, and wore minimal defensive armor. Their success depended on careful coordination with cavalry and lighter armed infantry. Philip's army also included specialists in siege techniques, who introduced the torsion catapult and tall siege towers. The evolution of this fighting force is obscure, but Philip

MACEDONIAN KINGS OF THE LATER ARGEAD AND EARLY HELLENISTIC PERIODS	
King	*Reign (B.C.E.)*
Philip II	359-336
Alexander the Great	336-323
Philip III Arrhidaeus	323-317
Alexander IV	323-311
Cassander	315-297

clearly began his military reform early—he suffered only one defeat in his entire career.

With his kingdom more or less secure from barbarian threats, Philip abandoned his conciliatory posture toward the Athenians and moved to eliminate their presence on his eastern frontier. In 357 he seized the strategic city of Amphipolis, founded by the Athenians eighty years previously. This move gave Philip access to the rich gold and silver mines of neighboring Mount Pangaeus, which eventually rendered him an annual revenue of one thousand talents. Philip next took Pydna, one of two Athenian-controlled cities on the lower Macedonian coast. In 354 his successful siege of Methone eliminated the last Athenian base in Macedonia but at a considerable cost to Philip: During the assault on the city an arrow destroyed his right eye.

Once he had placed Athens on the defensive, Philip moved against two nearby Greek districts that had threatened Macedonia during his youth: Thessaly to the south, Chalcidice to the east. His venture into Thessaly in 353 produced the only serious defeat of his career, but Philip came back the next year to win the Battle of the Crocus Plain, in which six thousand enemy soldiers died. This victory, followed by his election as president of the Thessalian League and his marriage to a Thessalian princess, brought Thessaly, with its renowned supply of horses, securely under Macedonian control. In 349 Philip began his move against the thirty-odd cities of the Chalcidian League, which he subdued one by one. Olynthus, the most important city of the league and the last holdout, fell after a two-month siege in 348. Philip razed the city and enslaved its inhabitants. Having eliminated most threats in the north, Philip now turned his attention to the city-states of central and southern Greece. The former victim of Greek interventions had become the intervener.

In 346, after obtaining a peace with Athens recognizing his right to Amphipolis, Philip in a surprise move came south and forced an end to the so-called Sacred War, which had been waged for nearly a decade. By intervening against the Phocians, whose sacrilegious seizure of the international sanctuary at Delphi had brought them almost universal condemnation, he cleverly played to Greek public opinion. Moreover, his refusal to punish the Athenians, despite their aid to the Phocians, suggests that already Philip had decided to attack Persia and hoped to use the Athenian navy in that effort. Philip withdrew from Greece late in 346 to continue his work of consolidation in Macedonia.

A shattered shinbone in 345 kept Philip out of military action for a few years, but in 342 he began a systematic attack on Thrace and in 340 laid siege to the strategic cities of Perinthus and Byzantium, which overlooked the sea lane through the Bosporus. This move threatened the grain supply of the Athenians, who responded with aid to Byzantium. When the sieges of these well-fortified cities proved more difficult than expected, Philip abandoned them, declared war on Athens, and in 339 invaded Greece. At Chaeronea in August of 338 Philip faced a Greek army headed by Athens and Thebes. The battle was long, and Philip appears to have won through a controlled retreat of his right wing that created a break in the Greek line. Philip's son Alexander, who would be known later as Alexander the Great, struck through this gap with the cavalry against the Theban contingent, while Philip with his infantry crushed the Athenian wing. The elite Sacred Band of Thebes was completely destroyed, and half the Athenian participants were killed or captured. Greece lay at Philip's mercy, and many city-states anxiously expected the worst.

Philip sought their compliance, however, not their destruction, and with the exception of Thebes and Sparta he treated them leniently. He summoned representatives from all the Greek states to a congress at Corinth, where they swore to a common peace and formed what modern historians call the League of Corinth. Its members accepted Philip as their leader and agreed to provide troops for a common armed force. Early in 337, at Philip's request, the council of the league declared war on Persia and named Philip the supreme commander for the anticipated conflict.

Returning home in triumph, Philip began final preparations for the attack on Persia and took as his seventh wife a young Macedonian noblewoman named Cleopatra. His previous marriages had all shown political shrewdness, but this one was most impolitic and alienated Philip's primary wife-queen, Olympias, and her son, the crown prince Alexander. After a drunken encounter

in which Philip drew his sword against Alexander, both mother and prince fled Macedonia.

With advance units of the Persian expedition already in Asia, military and political necessities forced him to arrange a reconciliation of sorts with Alexander, but Philip did not live to lead the invasion. In the summer of 336, as he attended the wedding festival of his daughter, one of his bodyguards, Pausanias, stabbed him to death. Although the murderer was almost certainly driven by a private grievance, the rift within the royal family brought suspicion on Alexander and Olympias, who were the primary beneficiaries of Philip's untimely death. Whatever the truth of this matter, Alexander succeeded Philip as king of Macedonia at a most opportune moment. Using Philip's army, he would make himself the most famous conqueror in history.

SIGNIFICANCE

Philip II of Macedonia inherited a backward, largely pastoral kingdom on the verge of disintegration and in his twenty-three-year reign transformed it into a major power. Less visible than his military endeavors, his domestic reforms were no less important. By bringing new areas under cultivation, founding new towns, and resettling upland populations, he made Macedonia a more advanced and cohesive kingdom. His military innovations revolutionized warfare and produced the best army the world had yet seen. With it he won three major pitched battles, suffered only one significant defeat, and successfully besieged nine cities. A general of great bravery and energy, Philip also possessed good strategic sense and never lost sight of his objectives. He saw war as an instrument of policy, not an end in itself, and used it along with diplomacy to achieve realistic ends.

Unfortunately for Greece, Philip's success meant the end of Greek independence, and his victory at Chaeronea effectively ended the era of the autonomous city-state. Philip created the army that Alexander would employ to destroy the Persian Empire. Had he lived, it is likely that Philip would have used it in a more restrained and constructive fashion than did his brilliant son.

—James T. Chambers

FURTHER READING

Adcock, Frank E. *The Greek and Macedonian Art of War.* Berkeley: University of California Press, 1957. This small volume provides an excellent brief introduction to Greek warfare, with appropriate references to Philip's innovations.

Bradford, Alfred S. *Philip II of Macedon: A Life from the Ancient Sources.* New York: Praeger, 1992. Compiled from fragments of ancient writings, epitomies, and passages from the orators, this volume integrates all the significant classical writings about Philip. Includes maps and illustrations based on ancient artifacts.

Bury, J. B., S. A. Cook, and Frank E. Adcock, eds. *The Cambridge Ancient History*. 12 vols. New York: Cambridge University Press, 1989. Chapters 8 and 9 in volume 6 describe Philip's rise to power with emphasis on his relations with the Greeks, especially the Athenians.

Cawkwell, George. *Philip of Macedon*. London: Faber and Faber, 1978. An excellent—though brief—biography, with outstanding maps. References to secondary works are minimal, but the notes contain a full record of the primary sources. The discussion of Greek military practices and Philip's part in their evolution is especially good.

Diodorus Siculus. *Diodorus of Sicily*. Translated by C. H. Oldfather et al. 12 vols. Cambridge, Mass.: Harvard University Press, 1962-1983. Book 16 in volumes 7 and 8 provides the only surviving ancient narrative of Philip's reign, interspersed with descriptions of activities in other parts of the Greek world. Diodorus must be used with care, because his account is sometimes inconsistent and chronologically confused.

Hammond, N. G. L., and G. T. Griffith. *A History of Macedonia*. 3 vols. New York: Oxford University Press, 1972-1988. Volume 2, chapter 4 (by Hammond) provides a fine picture of Macedonia's weak condition in the forty years before Philip's accession. Chapters 5 through 20 (by Griffith) form the fullest, most authoritative biography of Philip available, with complete discussion of sources and chronological problems.

Hatzopoulos, Miltiades B., and Louisa D. Loukopoulos, eds. *Philip of Macedon*. London: Heinemann, 1981. A collection of thirteen essays by leading scholars of Macedonian history. Included are chapters on Philip's personality, his generalship, his coinage, his foreign policy, his achievement in Macedonia, his death, and the royal tombs at Vergina. This volume is beautifully illustrated and includes excellent maps, a chronological table, and a bibliography.

SEE ALSO: Alexander the Great; Olympias.

RELATED ARTICLES in *Great Events from History: The Ancient World*: c. 700-330 B.C.E., Phalanx Is Developed as a Military Unit; 359-336 B.C.E., Philip II Expands and Empowers Macedonia; August 2, 338 B.C.E., Battle of Chaeronea; 336 B.C.E., Alexander the Great Begins Expansion of Macedonia.

PHILO OF ALEXANDRIA
Alexandrian philosopher

Philo harmonized Old Testament theology with Greek philosophy, especially Platonism and Stoicism; his thought contributed much to that of Plotinus, originator of Neoplatonism, and to the ideas of the early church fathers.

BORN: c. 20 B.C.E.; Alexandria, Egypt
DIED: c. 45 C.E.; possibly outside Alexandria, Egypt
ALSO KNOWN AS: Philo Judaeus
AREA OF ACHIEVEMENT: Philosophy

EARLY LIFE

Philo (FI-loh) came from one of the richest and most prominent Jewish families of Alexandria. The city had a large Jewish community, with privileges granted by its founder, Alexander the Great, and confirmed by his successors, the Ptolemies. The intellectual climate was Greek, and the resident Jews read their Scriptures in the Greek Septuagint version. According to ancient sources, the Greek population of Alexandria showed great hostility toward Jews.

Philo's brother Alexander held the Roman post of alabarch and collected taxes from Arab communities. He also managed the financial affairs of Antonia, mother of Emperor Claudius, and supplied a loan to Herod Agrippa, Caligula's choice as Jewish king.

In 39 C.E., anti-Semitism flared in the city, touched off by the visit of Herod Agrippa. The ensuing pogrom, permitted by the Roman governor Aulus Avilius Flaccus, resulted in a mission of opposing delegations to Caligula in Rome. The delegations consisted of three Greeks, led by the famous anti-Semite Apion, and five Jews, of whom Philo was eldest and spokesman. Caligula rudely dismissed the Jews and ordered his statue placed in their temples. In 41, under Claudius, Jewish rights were restored.

LIFE'S WORK

At least sixty-four treatises attributed to Philo are known. Only four or five are spurious; a few others, whose names have survived, no longer exist. The dates of the treatises, and even the order of their composition, are not known, except when a treatise refers to a previous one or to a dated event, such as the delegation to Rome. All the treatises have been translated into English (1854-1855), but some retain their original titles.

Foremost among Philo's writings are the exegetical works on the Pentateuch. These were arranged by Philo himself. Of the cosmogonic works, *De opificis mundi* (*On the Creation*, 1854), an allegorical explanation of Genesis, is most important. The historical works, allegorical commentaries on various topics in Genesis, are known as *Quod Deus sit immutabilis* (*On the Unchangeableness of God*, 1854), *De Abrahamo* (*On Abraham*, 1854), *De Josepho* (*On Joseph*, 1854), *De vita Moysis* (*On the Life of Moses*, 1854), and *De allegoriis legum* (*Allegorical Interpretation*, 1854). Philo also wrote legislative works, commentaries on Mosaic legislation, such as *De Decalogo* (*On the Decalogue*, 1854) and *De praemiis et poenis* (*On Rewards and Punishments*, 1854). Philosophical writings, such as *De vita contemplativa* (*On the Contemplative Life*, 1854), and political writings, such as *In Flaccum* (*Against Flaccus*, 1854) and *De legatione ad Gaium* (*On the Embassy to Gaius*, 1854), are attributed to Philo as well.

As a devout Jew, Philo's intent was to reconcile the prevalent Alexandrian philosophical thought of Platonism and Stoicism with the sacred law of Israel (the Old Testament). He wanted to show the identity of the truths of philosophy and of revelation—and the priority of the latter. He thus suggests not only that Moses had been a consummate philosopher but also that the "holy assembly" of Greek philosophers (Philo includes Plato, Xenophanes, Parmenides, and Empedocles—and the Stoics Zeno and Cleanthes) had access to Holy Scripture.

Beyond the notion of the unity of God, on which the Bible, Stoicism, and Plato's *Timaeos* (365-361 B.C.E.; *Timaeus*, 1793) clearly agree, the Old Testament bears little relation to Greek philosophy. Philo thus adopted for the Old Testament the Stoic technique of reading the Greek myths as allegories illustrating philosophical truths. Even as a Jew he was not original in this, for the Jewish philosopher Aristobulus (fl. mid-second century B.C.E.) and others had employed this method. Jews, however, could not gratuitously disregard the literal sense of the Old Testament stories. Philo resolved the problem by asserting that Scripture has at least two levels of meaning: the literal, for the edification of simple folk, and a deeper spiritual meaning, of which the literal account was merely an allegory. This higher meaning was avail-

Philo of Alexandria. (Library of Congress)

able to subtler minds capable of comprehending it. Indeed, the allegorical method seems imperative when the literal sense presents something unworthy of God or an apparent contradiction and when the text defines itself as allegorical.

Philo rejects the anthropomorphism of God in the Old Testament as a concession to weaker minds. His teaching is that Yahweh, God, is perfect existence (*to ontos on*) and absolutely transcendent, that is, outside creation, beyond comprehension, and inexpressible. One can know of his existence but nothing of his essence; one cannot predicate anything of him, for he is unchangeable. In this Philo went beyond Plato and the Stoics. Having described God in such terms, Philo was compelled to harmonize this with the scriptural concept of Yahweh as a personal God, immanent in the world and intimate with his people.

In order to bridge the gulf between this transcendent God and the created cosmos, Philo adopted the Stoic doctrine of divine emanations, or intermediaries, as the means of God's extension to the physical world. The first emanation and—according to Philo's various terminology—God's firstborn, His mediator, administrator, instrument, or bond of unity, is the divine Logos. The

Logos is, in Stoic symbolism, the nearest circle of light (fire) proceeding from God, defined as pure light shedding His beams all around. In the Old Testament, the angel of God is an allegory for the Logos. The Logos is also identified with Plato's Demiurge.

Philo varied his conception of the intermediary beings of creation, including the Logos. Sometimes they are forces, ideas, or spiritual qualities of God; sometimes they are spiritual personal beings, which Philo identifies with the biblical "powers" (*dynameis*, an order of angels). They derive from the Logos as Logos derives directly from God. God created first an invisible, spiritual world as a pattern (*paradeigma*) for the visible world. This is identified as the Logos *endiathekos* (organizer). Thus Logos is the location of Plato's Ideas. From this pattern, Logos *prophorikos* (forward-carrying) created the material world. Like the Greeks, who believed that nothing could be produced out of nothing, Philo assumed primeval lifeless and formless matter (*hyle*) as the substratum of the material world. At the same time, this matter became, for Philo, the source of the world's imperfection and evil.

God made the first preexistent, ideal man through Logos. This was man untainted by sin and truly in the divine image. His higher soul (*nous*, or *pneuma*) was an emanation of the purely spiritual Logos; it permeated man as his true, essential nature. Man's body and lower nature, or soul, with its earthly reason, were fashioned by lower angelic powers, or Demiurges. In a flight of Platonic dualism of body and soul, Philo saw the body as the tomb of the *pneuma*. The soul's unfolding was retarded by the body's sensuous nature, which it must overcome in order to gain salvation.

Philo's ethical doctrine employs the Logos in yet another, Stoic guise: operating as man's conscience and as teacher of the virtues. Men should strive for Stoic *apatheia*, apathy—the eradication of all passions. They should cultivate the four cardinal virtues of the Stoics (justice, temperance, courage, and wisdom). As this is an interior task, public life was discouraged by Philo; man, however, will never succeed by himself in getting free of the passions. God, through his Logos, can help man build virtue in the soul. It follows that man must place himself in correct relationship to God.

For this last and most important task, the sciences—grammar, rhetoric, dialectics, mathematics, music, and astronomy—are helpful. Yet they have never been sufficient to produce the Stoic ideal man of virtue. Contemplation of God alone is true wisdom and virtue. Thus Philo forges a link between Greek philosophy and the world of the mystery religions. He advocates going beyond ordinary conceptual knowledge, which recognizes God in his works, to an immediate intuition of the ineffable Godhead. In this ecstasy, the soul sees God face-to-face. Having passed beyond the original Ideas within the Logos, already beautiful beyond words, the soul is seized by a sort of "sober intoxication." As it approaches the highest peak of the knowable (*ton noeton*), pure rays of divine light come forth with increasing brilliance, until the soul is lost to itself and understands all.

Philo says that he himself had frequently been so filled with divine inspiration but that the ecstasy was indeed available to all the "initiated." These statements lend credence to the possibility that he ended his life as a member of the sect of the Therapeutae, an Essene-like community near Alexandria that he described affectionately in *On the Contemplative Life*. Eusebius of Caesarea, quoting Philo, wrote that such communities in Egypt were founded by Mark the Evangelist and that their lives epitomized Christian practice in the seminal days of the new faith.

SIGNIFICANCE

Though Photius's remark that Philo of Alexandria was a Christian cannot be accepted, his philosophy exerted a profound influence on early Christian theology. The Logos of John's Gospel certainly seems identical with one or more senses of the Logos in Philo. Ultimately, however, the Christian Logos, meaning the incarnate Word of God, can never be traced to Philo, for whom Logos was always incorporeal. Common to both Philo and many church fathers was the belief that philosophy was a special gift from God to the Greeks, just as revelation was His gift to the Jews. The fathers also used the allegorical method in interpreting Scripture beyond its literal meaning.

Philo's importance in Christian thought is underscored by the extensive commentary on and frequent reference to him by early Christian writers. Eusebius, Saint Jerome, and Photius all provide lists of his tractates. Philo's philosophical language regarding God's transcendence influenced Christian apologists such as Justin, Athenagoras, Clement of Alexandria, and Origen.

Philo's greatest influence extended to Plotinus, founder of Neoplatonism. Though Plotinus may have pursued philosophy in India, many of his principles echo those of Philo: that the body is the prison of the soul, that politics is trivial and distracting, that God (the One) is utterly transcendent yet the source of all truth and goodness, that Creation was effected by emanations from the One, and that pure souls may hope to return to the One, though in this life it is possible to encounter the One in a mystical experience. Thus, Philo had an impact on the two major theological systems of the Roman Empire.

—*Daniel C. Scavone*

FURTHER READING

Colson, F. H., and G. H. Whitaker. *Philo.* 12 vols. Cambridge, Mass.: Harvard University Press, 1966-1981. These volumes provide the original Greek with English translation on facing pages. They supply ample introductory sections, copious footnotes, and a complete bibliography addressing all problems of Philo scholarship.

Copleston, Frederick. "Greece and Rome." In *A History of Greek Philosophy*, edited by W. K. C. Guthrie. London: Cambridge University Press, 1986. Contains a short but encyclopedic survey of Philo's chief doctrines. Greek terms and references in Philo's writings are given for each specific teaching of Philo.

Philo of Alexandria. *The Works of Philo: Complete and Unabridged.* Translated by C. D. Yonge. Peabody, Mass.: Hendrickson, 1993. Includes an introduction, bibliographical references, and an index. Philo is not easy reading.

Wolfson, Harry A. "Greek Philosophy in Philo and the Church Fathers." In *The Crucible of Christianity*, edited by Arnold Toynbee. New York: World, 1969. Wolfson isolates the primary similarities and oppositions in the thought of the earliest Christian fathers and Philo. The chapter is fully documented for further research.

_____. *Philo: Foundations of Religious Philosophy in Judaism, Christianity, and Islam.* Cambridge, Mass.: Harvard University Press, 1982. This is the most thorough, complete, useful, and current treatment of Philo available in English.

Zeller, Eduard. *Outlines of the History of Greek Philosophy.* Translated by Wilhelm Nestle. New York: Meridian Books, 1955. Includes an overview of Philo's key ideas. Zeller defines major differences between Philo and Greek thought.

SEE ALSO: Empedocles; Eusebius of Caesarea; Moses; Parmenides; Plato; Plotinus; Xenophanes.

RELATED ARTICLES in *Great Events from History: The Ancient World*: c. 380 B.C.E., Plato Develops His Theory of Ideas; c. 300 B.C.E., Stoics Conceptualize Natural Law; 51-30 B.C.E., Cleopatra VII, Last of Ptolemies, Reigns.

PONTIUS PILATE
Roman governor

A provincial Roman official, Pontius Pilate became infamous as the magistrate who presided over the trial of Jesus Christ.

BORN: Date and place of birth unknown
DIED: After 36 C.E.; place unknown
AREAS OF ACHIEVEMENT: Government and politics, religion

EARLY LIFE

Nothing is known of the life of Pontius Pilate (PI-laht) before he was appointed prefect of Judaea and Samaria; even subsequent references to him, except in the New Testament and religious writings, are cursory. He belonged to none of the great Roman families and apparently left no descendants. Even his first or given name is unknown. The name Pontius, representing his *gens*, or tribe, would indicate that he was not Roman in ancestry but Samnite. The Samnites were an Italian people conquered by the Romans in 295 B.C.E. His family name, Pi-

late, means "cap," "helmet," or "spear," a fact that is of little help in tracing his lineage.

Pilate was of the equestrian class, a rank roughly equivalent to the knighthood of later European history. Because of this social rank and the fact that his patron Lucius Aelius Sejanus was commander of the Praetorian Guard, the elite troops who protected the emperor and served as the local police force, it is almost certain that Pilate gained recognition through military service, most likely in the Praetorian Guard itself.

The military background and apparent lack of any administrative or political experience would explain Pilate's mistakes in governance. One of the reasons for the success of the Roman Empire was that it respected, or at least permitted, the exercise of the religions, customs, and laws of subject peoples as long as these did not interfere with Roman control. While they could be ruthless, the Romans did not impose a totalitarian regime on conquered peoples, who had their own local officials and were generally free of Roman control in their day-to-day lives. The function of a Roman governor was to maintain order and to see that taxes were collected and sent to Rome. Pilate, however, would needlessly provoke the local Jewish population; a more experienced or more competent official would probably have had a better understanding of his subjects, their religion, and their sensibilities.

LIFE'S WORK

Pilate was appointed the fifth prefect of Judaea and Samaria in 26 C.E., during the reign of the emperor Tiberius. Pilate succeeded Valerius Gratus, who had a relatively quiet term of office and managed to avoid conflict between the Roman troops and the turbulent Jewish revolutionaries, or zealots. Gratus resided in Caesarea; his primary concern was the acquisition of wealth, which he managed to secure through his control of appointments, especially to the office of high priest. During his tenure, he made four appointments to the office.

On assuming his duties, however, Pilate took a more hands-on—and more confrontational—approach toward the Jewish people. On his arrival in Palestine, the new governor, in accordance with plans made beforehand with Sejanus, moved the headquarters of the Roman garrison from Caesarea to Jerusalem. Pilate himself also was to take up winter residence there.

The Roman army entered Jerusalem with their standards under cover of darkness. The standard consisted of the figure of an eagle with outspread wings and a thunderbolt in the claws mounted on the end of a spear. A banner or bust with the likeness of the emperor was attached. When the city awoke to find the Roman eagles before the Herodian palace, which was to be Pilate's residence, the populace was furious. To bring the standards with their graven images almost within the precincts of Holy Temple was, to the Jews, an abomination of abominations, a gross violation of God's commandment.

Because Pilate had not yet taken up residence in Jerusalem but was still in Caesarea, a good part of the crowd, together with Jews from other areas, hurried to Caesarea. There, they surrounded Pilate's house, demanding that the standards be removed. After five days of demonstrations, Pilate lost patience. The demonstrators were asked to move to an open area where Pilate would speak to them and respond to their grievances. This was part of a plan by Pilate to get the demonstrators in an area where they could be surrounded by his troops, who had weapons concealed under their mantles. When his troops were in position, Pilate told the crowd that unless they dispersed and left him in peace, he would order the soldiers to cut them down. To Pilate's chagrin, they reportedly answered that they would rather die than permit idolatry and disobedience to a commandment of their God; they then lay down and bared their necks, ready to die as martyrs. At this point, Pilate relented and ordered the standards removed from Jerusalem.

Another disturbance arose when Pilate ordered temple funds to be used for the construction of an aqueduct to

Pontius Pilate, seated, foreground, interviews Jesus Christ. (Library of Congress)

bring water into Jerusalem. This time Pilate did not relent and ordered his troops to use force to disperse a crowd of protesters. The Roman soldiers showed no mercy, killing many Jews with blows with their cudgels; many others were killed in the stampede that followed. Other massacres are mentioned by Flavius Josephus, a Jewish historian of the period. Still others are set forth in the Talmud and in the Gospel of St. Luke (13.1), which refers to the massacre of Galilean pilgrims who were in the act of sacrificing. Galilean zealots frequently took a leading part in the insurrections. As Galilee was not under Pilate's jurisdiction but ruled by Herod Antipas, a puppet king, the inability of Herod to control his subjects was a source of friction with Pilate.

Pilate would be little more than a footnote in history except for his role in the trial and execution of Jesus. Pilate's role and actions during the trial are set forth in the Gospel accounts of the four evangelists in the New Testament. There are no other historical accounts in existence.

Following the crucifixion of Jesus, it is almost certain that Pilate made a written report to Emperor Tiberius. Such correspondence between Roman officials and the emperor was routine. Justin Martyr, defending himself and his fellow Christians before Antonius Pius around 140 C.E., refers to reports from Pilate that were at that time in the Roman archives. This was confirmed forty years later by Tertullian, a Christian writer.

In the year 311, Emperor Maximian was engaged in persecuting the Christians. To discredit them, he caused to be circulated throughout the Empire a forgery called the "Acts of Pilate." If the genuine reports and correspondence from Pilate were still in existence, they would likely have been destroyed by the emperor, as they might have been used to debunk the forgery.

In 36 C.E., Pilate was deposed by his immediate superior, Vitellius, the legate of Syria. The reason for Vitellius's action was Pilate's gross mishandling of an incident involving the Samaritans, a people who were loyal and submissive to Rome. The incident arose out of a visionary's claim that Moses had hidden certain golden vessels on Mount Gerizim, on which the Samaritans worshiped. This caused a large group of armed Samaritans to begin a search for the golden vessels. Pilate dispatched his troops, who surrounded the treasure seekers and killed many of them. Pilate then had several of the organizers of the treasure search beheaded.

A Samaritan delegation went to Vitellius to complain about the atrocities. After hearing the complaint, Vitellius sent one of his subordinates to relieve Pilate of his duties and ordered Pilate to return to Rome to answer the charges. By the time Pilate arrived in Rome after removal from his office, Tiberius had died and had been succeeded by Caligula. Pilate was held in prison and was ultimately banished from Rome, reportedly to Vienne in Gaul. Eusebius of Caesarea, a historian of the early Christian church, says that Pilate ended his life by suicide; other sources allege that he converted to Christianity. The Coptic church even honors him as a saint.

SIGNIFICANCE

Pilate made his mark in history by presiding over the trial of Jesus Christ. The biblical account has Jesus condemned to death against Pilate's better judgment. Pilate at first sought to save Jesus by having him scourged, thinking that this would satisfy the mob. He then, according to custom, gave the mob the choice of releasing either Jesus or Barrabas, a notorious murderer; the crowd chose Barrabas. Pilate's wife then intervened and cautioned him to have no part of the blood of this innocent man. Pilate, failing in all attempts, then washed his hands and said that he was free of Christ's blood. He agreed to the Crucifixion only when his loyalty to Caesar was questioned. Pilate is portrayed as a weakling unable to withstand the clamor of the crowd.

Critics of the biblical account, who became especially vocal in the 1990's, dismissed it as Christian propaganda. These critics contended that Jesus was a fanatic who posed a threat to Roman rule and that Pilate had no scruples about having such people executed. At the time the Gospels were being written, Christianity was spreading throughout the Roman Empire. According to the critics, the Gospels were slanted in favor of Pilate because the Christian cause would not have been furthered by blaming Rome for Jesus' execution.

There is, however, nothing other than the biblical accounts to relate what happened at the trial. There are passing references to the event by Josephus, Eusebius, and other writers, but these are of little help. Everything written about the matter since is based on interpretation and conjecture.

—Gilbert T. Cave

FURTHER READING

Brown, Raymond E. *The Death of the Messiah: From Gethsemane to the Grave.* New York: Doubleday, 1994. A comprehensive and definitive two-volume work on the arrest, trial, and execution of Jesus.

Crossan, John Dominic. *Who Killed Jesus? Exposing the Roots of Anti-Semitism in the Gospel Story of the*

Death of Jesus. San Franciso: HarperSanFrancisco, 1995. Crossan argues that it was the Roman government that tried and executed Jesus as a social agitator and views the Gospel accounts of the trial of Jesus as anti-Semitic and nonhistorical.

Latimer, Elizabeth Wormeley. *Judaea from Cyrus to Titus: 537 B.C. to 70 A.D.* Chicago: A. C. McClurg, 1900. Covers six centuries of Jewish history. Chapter 18 is devoted exclusively to Pontius Pilate. Written in a flowery and hortatory nineteenth century style.

Maier, Paul L., ed. and trans. *Josephus: The Essential Writings*. Grand Rapids, Mich.: Kregel, 1988. Covers Jewish history from its beginning to the fall of the Masada fortress in the first century. Easy reading; highly recommended for anyone who enjoys history. Contains only a few references to Pilate but is important because it is one of the few primary sources.

Philo of Alexandria. *The Works of Philo*. Translated by C. D. Yonge. Peabody, Mass.: Hendrickson, 1993. The Jewish scholar Philo makes several references to Pilate in a writing titled "On the Embassy to Gaius." Philo is not easy reading.

Sanders, E. P. *The Historical Figure of Jesus*. London: Penguin Group, 1993. A comprehensive account of the life of Jesus. Sanders contends that Pilate ordered the execution of Jesus because his fanaticism posed a threat to law and order. He argues that the biblical accounts of Pilate's reluctance and weakness of will are best explained as Christian propaganda meant to lessen conflict between the Christian movement and Roman authority.

Watson, Alan. *The Trial of Jesus*. Athens: University of Georgia Press, 1995. Argues that the Sanhedrin, or supreme Jewish court, had the authority to put Jesus to death but could not convict him because of stringent trial procedures. He was therefore handed over to Pilate, who had no scruples about ordering an execution.

SEE ALSO: Caligula; Herod the Great; Jesus; Tiberius.

RELATED ARTICLES in *Great Events from History: The Ancient World*: c. 30 C.E., Condemnation and Crucifixion of Jesus Christ; c. 30 C.E., Preaching of the Pentecostal Gospel; c. 50-c. 150 C.E., Compilation of the New Testament.

PINDAR
Greek lyric poet

As the greatest lyrical poet of classical times, Pindar influenced literature, music, and culture for centuries.

BORN: c. 518 B.C.E.; Cynoscephalae, near Thebes, Boeotia, Greece
DIED: c. 438 B.C.E.; Argos, Greece
ALSO KNOWN AS: Pindaros (Greek); Pindarus (Latin)
AREAS OF ACHIEVEMENT: Literature, music

EARLY LIFE

Pindar (PIHN-dehr), the greatest of ancient Greek lyric poets, was born in Cynoscephalae, near Thebes, around 518 B.C.E. A city rich in history and legend, Thebes was located in the region known as Boeotia, north of the Gulf of Corinth. Pindar came from a noble Dorian family whose lineage went back to ancient times and included heroes whom he celebrated in his poems. His uncle was a famous flute player; Pindar, who excelled at that instrument, may have acquired his skills from him. Lyric poems were written primarily for solo or choral singing, with instrumental accompaniment, and Pindar learned his craft in writing poetry from two important lyric poets, Lasus of Hermione and Corinna of Tanagra. It is said (but

disputed by some) that Corinna defeated Pindar five times in lyric competition.

In the framing of his poetry, Pindar drew from the vast store of myths—many of them associated with Thebes—that he had learned in his youth. To him, the Olympians and other figures from ancient stories were not mythical but real. He accepted reverently, for example, the stories of the oracle of Delphi, and he devoutly worshiped Zeus (even composing a famous hymn to him) and other gods and goddesses all his life. He was also the heir to several priestly offices, which buttressed his natural inclination toward religion. In addition to being educated near Thebes, he is said to have received instruction in Athens, which was a great academic and cultural center. Studying in Athens would account for his having known the Alcmaeonids, a politically active family in Athens for which he wrote laudatory poems—probably, as was customary, under commission.

Pindar was schooled in history, philosophy, religion, music, and literature. His poetry is filled with allusions to those fields as well as to his homeland and relatives. He secured his reputation as a young man, and fabulous leg-

Pindar performs a lyric poem. (Library of Congress)

ends grew up around him. For example, one story explaining his talent claimed that as he slept out in the fields one day, bees had deposited honey on his lips.

Pindar received a constant flow of engagements to write poems for important figures, including the victors of athletic contests, the odes for which are the only surviving works of the poet. Usually these victory odes, the *Epinikia* (498-446 B.C.E.; *Odes*, 1656) were performed in processionals welcoming the heroes home. Pindar's odes are named for the particular games at which they were performed—the *Olympian Odes, Pythian Odes, Nemean Odes*, and *Isthmian Odes*. This celebratory tradition was at one with the Greek belief that great deeds—including the greatest of all, the creation of the world—should be artistically remembered so as not to pass into oblivion. For a time, Hieron, tyrant of Syracuse, was a patron of Pindar and of other poets, such as Simonides, Bacchylides, and the great tragedian Aeschylus. This activity helped Syracuse to rival Athens and Thebes as an intellectual center and helped perpetuate Pindar's already considerable fame.

LIFE'S WORK

In the Alexandrian list of the nine best lyric poets, Pindar's name came first. In his own time and in later centuries he was remembered as "soaring Pindar." The fact of music is inseparable from the fact of lyric poetry in Pindar, for it is clear that his poems were written to be sung. What is not known is how to reproduce for modern performance the melody and the meter of his lyrics, all of which were written in celebration of an individual or an event, often an athletic victory. This is to speak only of the four books that have survived, for there are fragments of his other works (or allusions to them) that prove that his genius was not limited to the choral lyric. He produced thirteen books in genres other than the *epinikia*, including hymns, processionals, and dirges.

Another obstacle to the comprehension of Pindar's poetry is its allusiveness. Those people hearing the performance of a victory ode had an immediate awareness of Pindar's allusions, whether to the Olympians, the heroes of myth, the rulers of the times, the athletes or families being honored, or even autobiographical refer-

647

ences. Only one who has read widely in Greek history, philosophy, literature, and legend can begin to understand these allusions or the stirring effect they would have had on Pindar's audience.

The poems are, then, locked into a time frame in their references and in their constructions. The themes, however, are accessible. A central theme in Pindar is the emulation of divinity. Humans are of the same race with gods but lack their powers; thus they are ever striving toward perfection, in an effort to be as much like the gods as possible. This view required the poet to overlook or disbelieve scandalous stories in mythology (which, to Pindar, was religion) that belied the perfection of the gods. Remembrance of the greatness of Zeus—Zeus unsullied by rumors about his lust, his violence, his unreasonableness—gave humanity a standard by which to live. Life is the thing of a day—another theme in Pindar—and to live it with constant reverence for the lessons taught by gods and heroes was to give reverence to oneself and to give a degree of permanence to life.

Virtue, bravery, manliness, and competitive physical activities were far more important to Pindar than was (as with Homer) intelligence, and he expressed scorn toward those who displaced these attributes with intellectual measures. The intelligent, resourceful Odysseus, for example, he found less praiseworthy than a man of physical prowess. Physical things—bodily strength and athletic skills and other things of the earth—were the things of heaven. Acquired learning paled beside innate talent, inborn greatness of soul and body.

Pindar always wrote his odes as if those they celebrated were joined with the immortals. Poets were said to have Zeus speaking through them; subjects celebrated by odes were, similarly, raised above the ordinary lot of humankind. There was a mystical link between the human being and divinity, a link that could not, to Pindar's way of thinking, be achieved by education. A basic belief of the aristocracy that Pindar represented was that qualities of goodness—humanistic ideals—could not be taught; universal edification being impossible, therefore, society depended on an aristocracy that was morally and spiritually enlightened. Pindar's place as a poet was to praise heroes in order to raise humankind.

Rooted in tradition as he was, Pindar was conservative; still, he was an innovator and a searcher. He was always seeking profound meanings from human events, ideals and nobility from everyday realities. He supported the rule of Eunomia (law, or good constitution) as a way for a moderate aristocracy to succeed tyranny. Such an aristocracy would be made up not only of those from the traditional aristocracy but also of those from the wealthy class. Those with leisure to contemplate new possibilities for humanity would most likely be those who would bring about new achievements for the betterment of humanity; the wealthy, the aristocratic, had freer minds. Large audiences listened to Pindar, audiences accustomed to hearing Homeric epics recited and therefore prepared for the exceptionally long, whirling passages of Pindar sung by an enthusiastic chorus.

Pindar's fame was even greater after his death than in his own time. His writings proved not to be locked in time; rather, they were one more link of many links in Greek literature going back to a time even before Homer, and extending through Aeschylus to Plato, which, while glorifying aristocratic tradition, pointed the way to the political principle that came to be known as democracy. The highest virtue that elitism had, in other words, was the knowledge that what was available at first to only the privileged few was ultimately accessible to all. Pindar's poetry was one of the main avenues making accessible this Greek ideal: that the commonest individuals have within them resources of divine inspiration, divine identity, divine glory.

SIGNIFICANCE

Pindar's complex style as preserved in the *epinikia* challenged later generations of poets to compose "Pindaric odes," in which colorful images shifted rapidly and imaginatively, like rushing water. Although the content of Pindar's surviving works is obscure for the modern reader, his inspired style remains a model of purely beautiful language.

—David Powell

FURTHER READING

Carne-Ross, D. S. *Pindar*. New Haven, Conn.: Yale University Press, 1985. A brief work addressed to the general reader, with a short but useful bibliography.

Crotty, Kevin. *Song and Action: The Victory Odes of Pindar*. Baltimore: The Johns Hopkins University Press, 1982. Devoted to individual examinations of the performances of the odes for which Pindar is most remembered. Includes notes, bibliography, and index.

Finley, Moses I. *The Ancient Greeks*. New York: Penguin, 1991. Gives brief but interesting and useful information on Simonides, Bacchylides, and Pindar.

Grant, Mary A. *Folktale and Hero-Tale Motifs in the Odes of Pindar*. Lawrence: University of Kansas Press, 1967. Straightforward account of the subject, with an index of motifs and an index of mythological characters.

Hamilton, Edith. *The Greek Way.* New York: W. W. Norton, 1993. An excellent short book on the Greek way of life; devotes a chapter to Pindar. Bridges scholarship and general readership. Includes seven pages of references, especially to works of ancient Greek writers.

Highet, Gilbert. *The Classical Tradition: Greek and Roman Influences on Western Literature.* New York: Oxford University Press, 1985. The best work available on the Greco-Roman influences on Western literature. Lengthy discussion—perhaps the most accessible anywhere for general readers—on Pindar's poetical forms and on his direct influences on poetry. Extensive notes in lieu of a comprehensive bibliography.

Pindar. *Pindar.* Edited and translated by William H. Race. Cambridge, Mass.: Harvard University Press, 1997. Translation of all the surviving odes. Contains a preface on Pindar and his poetry.

Race, William H. *Pindar.* Boston: Twayne, 1986. Comprehensive in biography, criticism, and bibliography. For both scholarly and general audiences.

SEE ALSO: Aeschylus; Homer; Plato; Simonides.

RELATED ARTICLES in *Great Events from History: The Ancient World*: 478-448 B.C.E., Athenian Empire Is Created; c. 456/455 B.C.E., Greek Tragedian Aeschylus Dies; c. 438 B.C.E., Greek Lyric Poet Pindar Dies.

PISISTRATUS
Athenian ruler (r. 540-527 B.C.E.)

As benevolent tyrant of Athens, Pisistratus prepared the way for the birth of Athenian democracy by introducing social, religious, and political reforms that raised popular expectations and possibilities.

BORN: c. 612 B.C.E.; near Athens, Greece
DIED: 527 B.C.E.; Athens, Greece
ALSO KNOWN AS: Peisistratus
AREAS OF ACHIEVEMENT: Government and politics, art and art patronage

EARLY LIFE
The family of Pisistratus (pi-SIHS-tra-tuhs) reputedly came from Pylos on the Peloponnese peninsula. His father, Hippocrates, claimed a family tie to Nestor, Homeric king of Pylos, and named Pisistratus for Nestor's son. The family estates of Pisistratus were at Brauron, near Marathon, in the hill country outside Athens. Pisistratus's mother was cousin to Solon, a connection that much elevated Pisistratus's social status. During Pisistratus's youth, Solon was the genius who guided Athens to economic and political leadership among the Greek states. Pisistratus was attractive, intelligent, and a good speaker. Solon once remarked that, except for his ambition, no one would make a more virtuous man and a better citizen.

In about 570 B.C.E., Solon won a great victory over Megara by which Athens recovered the island of Salamis. Pisistratus reportedly served Solon as commander in the capture of Nisaea, Megara's eastern port. One of Solon's reforms was the *seisachtheia*, which "shook off" the debts of Athenian farmers. These farmers, or *hektemoroi* (referring to the 16 percent interest they owed), had pledged their labor as a means of repayment and had become virtual slaves to their creditors. Solon had decreed that ceding their lands to their creditors would absolve them from debt. Free but landless, they now made up the Party of the Hill (the *hyperakrioi*), and Pisistratus became their champion. The party included downtrodden miners from Laurium and people from his hometown of Brauron, to whom were added the poorest urban Athenians (the *thetes*).

In 561, Pisistratus deliberately wounded himself and blamed his political enemies. Pisistratus was given a bodyguard of fifty men. With these, he seized the Acropolis and entered his first period of tyranny. Solon, who reportedly opposed the tyranny by speeches, died the same year. By 556, Pisistratus was driven out by a new coalition of the other parties. These parties, entrenched in their authority, were the Coast (*Paraloi*), led by the Alcmaeonids under Megacles, and the Plain (*Pediakoi*), under Lycurgus and later Miltiades. Megacles, though, fell out with the Plainsmen and befriended Pisistratus as a needed ally. Their families were united by Pisistratus's marriage to Megacles' daughter. In about 550, a clever plan was devised to trick the Athenians into accepting their tyrant. A tall and beautiful woman named Phya lived in the town of Paeonia. They dressed her as Athena and drove a chariot into Athens with Pisistratus at her side. The plan was completely successful.

Megacles later regretted his daughter's marriage to Pisistratus and realigned himself with the Plain. Pisistratus was again driven into exile by the coalition. Operating from Eretria in Euboea, he raised money and troops and made important friends, especially Lygdamis of Naxos, Amyntas of Macedonia, and the leaders in Thessaly, Thebes, and even Sparta.

His control of the silver mines and gold deposits of Mount Pangaeus in Thrace enabled his third ascendancy. In 540, after a ten-year exile, his army landed at Marathon. His partisans flocked to him, and his enemies were easily defeated. Pisistratus entered the city unopposed and ruled Athens for twelve years until his death in 527 B.C.E.

LIFE'S WORK

To secure his position in Athens, Pisistratus maintained a private army. While he did not alter Solon's laws or the government, his adherents and relations usually held the highest offices, while Pisistratus presumably ruled in the background. He took hostages from the leading families and sent them to Lygdamis on Naxos. The Alcmaeonids and his other Athenian opponents fled or were exiled, leaving their estates in the tyrant's control.

Pisistratus's expenses were now met from the Mount Laurium silver mines of Attica as well as the Pangaean

mines. It is not known how he came to control the Thracian mines; perhaps it was through King Amyntas of neighboring Macedonia, who later gave a town to Pisistratus's son Hippias.

With this monetary base, Pisistratus arranged state support of citizens disabled in war. He strengthened Athenian tetradrachm coinage, guaranteeing its purity and metallic content, and thereby improved the commerce of the city. He gave land from confiscated estates to sons of *hektemoroi* for them to farm. A moderate tax was levied on all citizens to permit him to advance seed and cattle money to the new proprietors and also to refurbish the city's defenses. By colonizing the Thracian Chersonese and recovering Sigeum, he established control of the grain routes from Pontus and secured the city's grain supply.

It must be partially owing to Pisistratus that Attic pottery was traded all over the Mediterranean world, both east and west. Pisistratus thus oversaw the blossoming of the first great styles of Attic vase painting, black figure and red figure.

Pisistratus is carried through the streets by Athenians celebrating his return. (F. R. Niglutsch)

Pisistratus employed the urban poor in building projects. These included roads and the construction of the *enneakrounos*, or Nine-Conduit Fountain, which improved Athens's water supply. Among his public buildings were a temple of Pythian Apollo; a magnificent temple to Olympian Zeus, left unfinished (to be completed in the Corinthian style by Roman emperor Hadrian in the second century C.E.); the stately buildings of the Lyceum garden; possibly a new and larger shrine at Eleusis for the local mystery cult; and, not least, the first temple to Athena, the Hecatompedon. Its pediment held the vigorous terra-cotta statue of striding Athena, part of a gigantomachy group. Traces of once-brilliant colors can still be seen on her skin and clothing. The Hecatompedon, predecessor of the famous Parthenon, was destroyed by the Persians in 480 B.C.E.

In connection with the worship of Athena, Pisistratus either instituted the Greater Panathenaea or enhanced a festival newly established about 566. Every fourth year, a new *peplos* ("shawl") was sewn by Athenian women and was borne by them as a gift to be placed on the statue of Athena. The ceremony included a long procession of all the citizens from the agora (marketplace) to the temple, which stood close to where the present Parthenon stands on the Acropolis.

Pisistratus also initiated the Panathenaeic competitions in Homeric recitation. Each contestant memorized the texts of Homer and recited from precisely where the previous contestant had left off. Thus they were called "rhapsodists," or "stitchers of song." Pisistratus is thus credited as the first to have the texts of Homer's epics written down and preserved essentially as they exist today. He also encouraged literature and literacy by collecting a library and allowing public access to it.

He created the city festival in honor of Dionysus. This cult was essentially a religion of the small farmer, and it harmonized with the popular stance of the tyrant. It was in association with this Dionysiac cult festival that Greek tragedy was first performed. The religious highlight of the festival was a hymn to Dionysus (the *dithyramb*) sung by a chorus of citizens. According to the Marmor Parium, a marble tablet from Paros containing a chronology of important events down to 264 B.C.E., it was in 534, not long after the inception of the festival, that the *choregos* ("poet" or "producer") Thespis of Icaria introduced a soloist as interlocutor with the chorus. This new "dialogue" opened the way for the creation of individual characters and for the evolution of classical Greek tragedy as best seen in the plays of Aeschylus, Sophocles, and Euripides.

Pisistratus endeared himself and his city to Apollo of Delos by carrying out the purification of that island sanctuary: This was achieved by removing all tombs visible from the vicinity of the god's temple. This is but one example of the wise and moderate foreign policy that has already been suggested by Pisistratus's cordial and peaceful relations with neighbors.

On Pisistratus's death in 527, his sons Hippias and Hipparchus, the *Pisistratidae*, succeeded him in the tyranny. The brothers seem to have ruled jointly and admirably. Some scholars even believe that it was Hipparchus who actually arranged the manner in which the rhapsodists recited the Homeric poems at the Panathenaea. Several poets resided in Athens at the court of the *Pisistratidae*: Simonides of Ceos, Anacreon of Teos, Lasus of Hermione, and Onomacritus, who, with the support of the brothers, introduced a new Orphic religious influence in the city, as can be seen in many parts of Greece in the sixth century.

Hippias and Hipparchus, however, brought the tyranny into disrepute. After Hipparchus's assassination, his older brother became morose, suspicious, and arbitrary in his rule. Citizens were executed, taxes were increased. The Pisistratid family was finally expelled by a force led by the rival Alcmaeonids with Spartan assistance, which was gained by trickery. The Alcmaeonids bribed the Delphic oracle to urge Sparta to free Athens from the tyranny. A Spartan army under Cleomenes drove Hippias into perpetual banishment. A monument recording the offenses of the tyrants was set up on the Acropolis.

Soon after, however, the Spartans learned of the trick and learned that the oracle had actually foretold the Athenians' enmity against them. They therefore invited Hippias to Sparta and held a congress of their allies to form an army to reinstate him in Athens, but the idea was voted down. Hippias next went to the court of King Darius the Great of Persia, applying for his aid. It was Hippias who led the Persians to Marathon, where the story was told that, as he was now quite old, Hippias's tooth fell out and was buried in the sand when he sneezed. This seemed to augur the failure of the Persian expedition. The Persians were defeated, and Hippias met his death on the field of Marathon. Afterward, members of Hippias's family were back at the court of Persia under Darius's son Xerxes I. There the known line of Pisistratus becomes lost in the sources.

SIGNIFICANCE

Herodotus, a reliable historian and a major source for information on Pisistratus's life, regarded him highly. Herodotus considered tyranny to be the negation of law and order and the arbitrary rule of an individual. Pisistratus, however, gave to that title a temporary respectability that was ruined by the behavior of most other Greek tyrants. Herodotus said, "He was no revolutionary, but governed excellently without disturbing the laws or the political offices."

As if in anticipation of the Magna Carta, Pisistratus observed the laws and submitted himself before the Areopagus court. He foreshadowed Augustus, Rome's first emperor, in founding a principate (a monarchy under the guise of a republic). For the common people, Pisistratus's rule was a golden age.

—Daniel C. Scavone

FURTHER READING

Aristotle. *Athenian Constitution*. Translated by H. Rackham. 5th ed. Cambridge, Mass.: Harvard University Press, 1981.

_____. *Politics*. Translated by H. Rackham. 4th ed. Loeb Classical Library. Cambridge, Mass.: Harvard University Press, 1932. Both works of Aristotle give details of Pisistratus's career but draw heavily from Herodotus and Thucydides. Aristotle saw tyranny as the derogatory side of monarchical rule.

Day, James, and Mortimer Chambers. *Aristotle's History of Athenian Democracy*. Berkeley: University of California Press, 1962. An excellent commentary on Aristotle's treatment of Pisistratus.

Herodotus. *The Histories*. Translated by Robin Waterfield. Cambridge, Mass.: Harvard University Press, 1998. The primary source for Pisistratus's political career.

How, W. W., and J. Wells. *A Commentary on Herodotus*. 2 vols. New York: Oxford University Press, 1989-1990. The authors argue that too few Athenian freemen worked in the mines to serve as a power base for Pisistratus; the main struggle was between the old landed aristocracy and the rising merchant class.

Lesky, Albin. *A History of Greek Literature*. Indianapolis: Hackett, 1996. Discussion of the literary contributions of the *Pisistratidae*.

Thucydides. *The Landmark Thucydides: A Comprehensive Guide to the Peloponnesian War*. Edited by Robert B. Strassler. New York: Simon & Schuster, 1998. Among the primary sources for Pisistratus. Includes introduction, maps, bibliography, and index.

SEE ALSO: Augustus; Cleomenes; Homer; Miltiades the Younger; Solon.

RELATED ARTICLES in *Great Events from History: The Ancient World*: c. 594-580 B.C.E., Legislation of Solon; September 17, 490 B.C.E., Battle of Marathon; 483 B.C.E., Naval Law of Themistocles Is Instituted; 480-479 B.C.E., Persian Invasion of Greece.

PITTACUS OF MYTILENE
Mytilenian ruler (r. 590-580 B.C.E.)

Elected tyrant by the people of Mytilene, Pittacus brought an end to his state's bitter aristocratic party struggles and established a government that remained stable for years after he had relinquished power. Though he was vilified by his political opponent Alcaeus, later Greeks considered Pittacus one of the "Seven Sages."

BORN: c. 645 B.C.E.; Mytilene, Lesbos, Greece
DIED: c. 570 B.C.E.; Mytilene, Lesbos, Greece
AREA OF ACHIEVEMENT: Government and politics

EARLY LIFE

Pittacus (PIHT-ah-kuhs), the son of Hyrras (or Hyrrhadius), was raised in Mytilene on the island of Lesbos, famous for its wine and the richest and most powerful of the Aeolian Greek settlements in the eastern Aegean Sea.

Mytilene had colonized territories on the mainland (notably Sestos, c. 670), had dealings with the nearby Lydian kingdom, and maintained commercial connections throughout the northeastern Aegean. The citizens of Mytilene were enterprising and bold in their projects and vigorous in defense of their mainland interests. Furthermore, Mytilene's citizens fought in the service of Asiatic rulers, and the city was the only one of its Aeolian neighbors to take part in the Greek trading colony at Naucratis in Egypt. In short, Pittacus was reared in a cosmopolitan city, familiar with merchants, soldiers, and colonists.

In addition to being a progressive and dynamic state, the Mytilene of Pittacus's childhood was steeped in its old Aeolian traditions. Lesbos was within sight of the territory of Troy, and heroic poetry dealing with the Trojan saga was prominent in its early literature. Pittacus's younger contemporary Alcaeus wrote a poem describing with pride a collection of armor that harked back to the heroic age.

In addition, a rich tradition of popular song on the island gave rise to the lyric monodies of Sappho and Alcaeus, performed at *symposia* (drinking parties). The Aeolians valued their descent from the house of Agamemnon, the victor of the Trojan War, and young Pittacus respected the traditions of his ancestors and the hereditary rights of his family. Although Pittacus's father's name was Thracian, there is every indication that the family was a member of the nobility.

The civic strife in the aristocracy at Mytilene was the single most important factor in Pittacus's early life. At that time, his city was involved in bitter quarrels among the nobles vying for control of the state. During his childhood, the Penthilid clan ruled at Mytilene, claiming descent from Agamemnon's son Orestes, whose own son Penthilus was said to have colonized Aeolis. The Penthilids gained a reputation for cruelty and were said to have clubbed their aristocratic rivals. Pittacus witnessed an uprising against that family, led by Megacles, followed by Smerdis's murder of Penthilus and the establishment of a tyranny by Melanchrus.

During Pittacus's youth, the aristocratic government of Mytilene functioned through a council that submitted its deliberations to an assembly for discussion and approval. As a young man, Pittacus attended the meetings of the assembly and probably became familiar with the council through his father's connections.

LIFE'S WORK

There are two main sources for Pittacus's life and work: the poetry of his political enemy Alcaeus, which is hostile, and the writings of other writers, which extol his wisdom and place him among the so-called Seven Sages of the Greeks. From the praise and blame of the two traditions a somewhat coherent picture of his life emerges.

During the forty-second Olympiad (612-608 B.C.E.), Pittacus and the older brothers of Alcaeus deposed Melanchrus, an aristocrat of Mytilene who had made himself tyrant and become odious to the other noble families of the city. Pittacus's role in the action is unclear, but he must have established a reputation for leadership and daring, for soon afterward the people of Mytilene put him in charge of their army in a military encounter against the Athenians in a territorial dispute over Sigeum, near Troy. One early story records that in the course of this struggle he fought and won a duel with the Athenian general and

Olympic victor Phrynon (c. 607 B.C.E.), killing him with a trident and knife, having first caught him in a net (perhaps a reference to a popular song describing Pittacus as a fisherman hunting his prey).

In the power struggle that ensued after the fall of Melanchrus, Pittacus allied himself with the political coterie of Alcaeus against Myrsilus, another aristocratic claimant to power. After an indeterminate period of maneuvering, Pittacus forsook the coalition that he had pledged to help and gave his support to Myrsilus's party. Alcaeus and his supporters went into exile on Lesbos, where they railed against Pittacus's defection. Pittacus married into the Penthilid family, probably during Myrsilus's rule, thereby gaining a larger political base. His wife, a sister of a man named Draco, was said to be the daughter of one Penthilus. Pittacus's son Tyrraeus was murdered in nearby Cyme while sitting in a barbershop. Pittacus was said to have forgiven his murderer.

Myrsilus ruled as tyrant until he died in 590. Alcaeus was overjoyed at his death and wrote a poem calling for everyone to get drunk in celebration. The poet's hopes of repatriation, however, were disappointed, for the people of Mytilene immediately chose Pittacus to succeed Myrsilus. The new tyrant maintained a policy of subduing party strife by forcing Alcaeus and his supporters to leave Lesbos altogether. Although poems of Alcaeus call for his overthrow and mention Lydian support for the rebels, there is no indication that Pittacus's rule was ever seriously threatened from without or within. One anecdote tells of Alcaeus falling into Pittacus's hands during this period. Instead of punishing his enemy for his savage attacks, the tyrant is reported to have freed him and uttered the maxim "Pardon is better than revenge." Pittacus held supreme power in Mytilene until 580, when he voluntarily gave up his post and returned to private life.

Pittacus's rule at Mytilene was benevolent and was probably the source of his excellent reputation in later years. He did not overthrow the traditional constitution but respected its institutions while adding new laws to those already in existence. His respect for the law produced his description of the best rule as one of "the painted wood" (that is, of laws written on wooden tablets). His most famous statute, aimed at curbing alcohol abuse, provided a double penalty for anyone committing a crime while drunk. This law calls to mind both the reputation of Lesbian wine and the poems of Alcaeus extolling its use.

The only physical descriptions of Pittacus come from Alcaeus's abusive poems and therefore can probably be dismissed as rhetorical excess. Alcaeus calls Pittacus flat-footed, dirty, and pot-bellied. Yet everything known about Pittacus from other sources makes doubtful the validity of these libels. Indeed, Alcaeus also calls Pittacus "base-born," a charge that can also be explained as simply part of the vocabulary of invective.

Several sayings of Pittacus are preserved, including "Even the gods do not fight against Necessity" and "Office reveals the man." Because of the fighting he had witnessed all of his life, Pittacus is credited with a rather un-Greek notion when he urged people to seek "victories without blood." His statement that "It is a difficult thing to be good" was the basis of a poem by Simonides and a long discussion in Plato's *Prōtagoras* (399-390 B.C.E.; *Protagoras*, 1804) Numerous other quotations of his are preserved, mostly commonplace sentiments.

A number of stories tell that Pittacus had dealings with the Lydian king Croesus, and although chronology of their lives makes it unlikely that they ever met while both were in power, Croesus was the governor of the Lydian province close to Lesbos before he became king, and therefore it is possible that he could have met Pittacus at that time. It is most likely that stories relating the two are the result of an ancient attempt to create stories analogous to those that connected the Athenian sage and lawgiver Solon with the Lydian king. Pittacus's name has been identified on an inscription of his contemporary Nebuchadnezzar II, king of Babylonia, providing evidence that Mytilene did have important relations with the great powers to the east.

Pittacus died in 570 B.C.E., having lived more than seventy years. He left behind a stable and prosperous city as well as an enviable reputation—despite the protests of Alcaeus's poetry. Few ancient biographies have such happy endings. His traditional epitaph is:

> With her own tears, Holy Lesbos who bore him
> Bewails Pittacus who has died.

SIGNIFICANCE

Pittacus of Mytilene must have been very successful in quelling the party strife that had troubled the state for so long. He felt comfortable enough with the political situation to retire after only ten years, and there is no evidence of further civil disturbances thereafter. Indeed, Pittacus entered the ranks of the traditional Greek Seven Sages for his work. The Seven Sages were contemporaries of Pittacus who held similar positions as lawgivers and tyrants and included Periander of Corinth and Solon of Athens. More is known of them than of Pittacus, although Pittacus is admired as much as the others by later tradition.

Diodorus of Sicily said that Pittacus not only was outstanding for his wisdom but also was a citizen whose like Lesbos had never before produced—nor would produce, until such time as when it would make more and sweeter wine (that is, never). Diodorus called Pittacus an excellent lawgiver and a kindly man who was well-disposed toward his fellow citizens. He released his homeland from the three greatest misfortunes: tyranny, civil strife, and war. In addition, he was serious, gentle, and humble, perfect in respect to every virtue. His legislation was just, public-spirited, and thoughtful, and he himself was courageous and outstandingly free from greed.

Encomiums such as this made up the bulk of the later tradition dealing with Pittacus and form a strong contrast with the poetry of his contemporary Alcaeus. Diogenes Laertius wrote a "Life of Pittacus" in his *Peri biōn dogmatōn kai apophthegmatōn tōn en philosophia eudokimēsantōn* (early third century C.E.; *Lives and Opinions of Eminent Philosophers*, 1688), which includes numerous anecdotes illustrating his wisdom and justice. In his "Life of Thales," Diogenes Laertius gives various ancient lists of the Seven Sages, and Pittacus appears in each one. Plutarch provided a similar portrait of Pittacus in his work "Banquet of the Seven Sages," in *Ethika* (after c. 100; *Moralia*, 1603). Strabo's *Geōgraphica* (c. 7 B.C.E.; *Geography*, 1917-1933) twice mentions Pittacus, each time emphasizing that he was one of "The Seven Wise Men," and notes that Pittacus used his monarchic powers to rid the state of dynastic struggles and to establish the city's autonomy. Aristotle wrote that Pittacus's position of elective tyrant was a distinct form of rule called *aesymneteia*, but he gives no other examples of it, and no others are known.

The impression made by Pittacus on his countrymen is revealed in the fact that the rich Lesbian folk song tradition preserves his memory:

> Grind, mill, grind.
> For even Pittacus grinds,
> As he rules great Mytilene.

Historians have few details to illustrate these ancient generalizations about Pittacus's exceptional character and achievements. Further discoveries of ancient evidence about archaic Lesbos and its most admired citizen would help fill in the gaps about Pittacus's life.

—Daniel B. Levine

FURTHER READING

Andrewes, Antony. *The Greek Tyrants*. Reprint. New York: Harper and Row, 1963. Solid and balanced discussion of the tyrannies at Mytilene, of Alcaeus, and of Pittacus in the chapter "Aristocratic Disorder at Mytilene." Best comparative material with other archaic tyrannies, and general discussion of the phenomenon. Puts Pittacus in perspective. Notes, index, bibliography.

Campbell, David A., ed. *Greek Lyric Poetry*. Bristol, Gloucestershire, England: Bristol Classical Press, 1982. Contains all fragments of Sappho and Alcaeus, translations, and brief notes to each poem. Includes an introduction with good discussion of how to date events in the life of Pittacus. Lists ancient evidence for lives of Alcaeus and Pittacus. With an index.

Lefkowitz, Mary R. *The Lives of the Greek Poets*. London: Duckworth, 1981. Includes important perspective on ancient biography, claiming that most material in the lives is fiction—based on the poems, not history. Relevant to Alcaeus's information used for his life and that of Pittacus. With a chapter on ancient lyric poets and an index and bibliography.

Murray, Oswyn. *Early Greece*. Cambridge, Mass.: Harvard University Press, 1993. Good general background on ancient Greece, with a short section on Alcaeus and Pittacus and examples of Alcaeus's poems. Points out the unique political position held by Pittacus. With maps, illustrations, useful chronological chart, and annotated list of primary sources.

Podlecki, Anthony J. *The Early Greek Poets and Their Times*. Vancouver: University of British Columbia Press, 1984. A substantial chapter on Alcaeus and Sappho offers chronological analysis of Pittacus and his contemporaries on Lesbos, with analysis of the use of Alcaeus's poems in creating the picture of Pittacus. A thoughtful and readable treatment, with good use of all available sources. Includes an index and bibliography.

Romer, F. E. "The *Aisymneteia:* A Problem in Aristotle's Historic Method." *American Journal of Philology* 103 (1982): 25-46. Discusses sources for the rule of Pittacus and Aristotle's definition of the *aisymneteia*, or elective tyranny. Proves that this definition originated in his own philosophical ideas about civil strife and political harmony. Well documented, with many notes and a list for further reading.

SEE ALSO: Croesus; Nebuchadnezzar II; Solon.

RELATED ARTICLES in *Great Events from History: The Ancient World*: c. 645-546 B.C.E., Lydia Rises to Power Under the Mermnad Family; c. 607-562 B.C.E., Nebuchadnezzar Creates the First Neo-Babylonian State; c. 594-580 B.C.E., Legislation of Solon; 547 B.C.E., Cyrus the Great Founds the Persian Empire.

PIYE
Kushite king and Egyptian pharaoh (r. 742-716 B.C.E.)

A dynamic and forceful king of Kush, Piye invaded a divided Egypt, conquered it, and initiated an almost century-long Kushite rule over the entire Nile Valley.

BORN: c. 769 B.C.E.; place unknown
DIED: 716 B.C.E.; place unknown
ALSO KNOWN AS: Piankhi; Piankhy
AREAS OF ACHIEVEMENT: War and conquest, government and politics

EARLY LIFE

Nothing is known of the early life of Piye (Pi). He was the son of Kashta (r. c. 783-747/746 B.C.E.), the Kushite chieftain who controlled northern Nubia, the land immediately south of Egypt. Relatively early in its history, the kingdom of Egypt was attracted to this neighboring territory up the Nile; gold, incense, and slaves, among other things, were obtained there. Nubia also was the corridor for Egyptian trade with the lands farther south in inner Africa, Nubian middlemen being essential in this commerce. Beginning in the Old Kingdom (c. 2687-c. 2125 B.C.E.), Egypt's rulers thought it necessary to control northern Nubia and therefore established permanent bases there. Gradually, as the Egyptian hold weakened through the centuries, local leadership produced a state known as the Kingdom of Kush. The nature of its relationship with the greater power to the north depended on the latter's internal stability and the successive pharaohs' ability periodically to reassert firm imperial control over this outlying territory.

By the seventeenth century B.C.E., Kush's rulers had their capital at Kerma, just south of the Third Cataract on the Nile River. While they looked to Egypt's impressive culture for inspiration and imported luxury goods, these presumably black kings of Kush enjoyed political independence for long periods. Inevitably, however, the Egyptians took back northern areas near the Egyptian border and sometimes absorbed all of Kush. During the Second Intermediate Period (c. 1650-1570 B.C.E.), Egypt itself was invaded for the first time, and much of its territory was conquered by a chariot army of the Hyksos, a people from western Asia. They ruled the country for more than one hundred years and recognized Kush, independent once again, as an equally great power whose rule extended as far north as Elephantine (opposite Aswān).

Kush clearly was under heavy Egyptian cultural influence from early times, borrowing religious beliefs, architectural styles, and writing from the long-established northern civilization. Not only Egyptian soldiers and merchants worked there; many craftsmen, builders, and priests are also believed to have ventured up the Nile for employment under rich Kushite kings.

LIFE'S WORK

By the time Piye ascended the throne in 742 B.C.E., Kush's royal capital was Napata, just north of the Fourth Cataract on the Nile. He inherited a strong kingship, one that had replaced an Egyptian viceroyalty lasting about four hundred years that had been imposed on Kush by pharaohs of the Eighteenth and Nineteenth Dynasties (c. 1570-1186). The Kushites, partly emulating Egypt's institution of divine monarchy, believed their king was the adopted son of several deities. A council composed of high priests, the queen mother, clan chiefs, and military commanders determined the royal succession, usually selecting one of the dead king's brothers. Piye is an obvious exception, since he followed his father to the throne.

More than a political capital, Napata also was an important religious center. The seat of Egyptian royal power long had been the city of Thebes in Upper Egypt, which in addition was the principal center for the worship of the sun god, Amen. In the Twenty-second Dynasty, Egyptian kings moved their capital downstream to the delta region and emphasized dedication to the god Ptah rather than Amen. This alienated Amen's priests, who consequently shifted their religious headquarters to Napata, already the site of major temples erected by the Egyptians to honor Amen. The extensively Egyptianized Kushite population—or at least its leaders—thus became even more zealous devotees of Amen. It is likely that these newly moved religious authorities, in need of strong sup-

port in their new base, established an alliance with local chieftains who in time became the new Kushite monarchs from whom Piye descended. It cannot be determined, however, if this new dynasty could trace its bloodline back to the original royal lineage of Kerma.

As Kush became an increasingly centralized state under native rulers by the eighth century B.C.E., Egypt, in contrast, was experiencing political division. Indeed, ever since the tenth century, Egypt had been torn by dissension. By the eighth century that country was a confusing scene of about eleven major political entities, each under its own local potentate and more or less independent of the central authority of the weak Twenty-second Dynasty (945-715). The next dynasty returned the capital to Thebes, but evidently this did not help it overcome the political turmoil that prevailed with so many regional seats of power contending with one another. Such confusion and disunity eventually would draw Kush into Egyptian politics in a very dramatic way.

A major figure aspiring to leadership in Egypt during the mid-eighth century was Tefnakht (r. 730-720 B.C.E.), lord of Saïs, a principality in the western delta. He managed to extend his rule over a large part of Lower Egypt. In addition, this aggressive prince brought all the eastern- and middle-delta rulers into an alliance system dominated by him. Tefnakht was the major power in all Lower Egypt and even a part of Middle Egypt. The man who would resist his efforts to reunify Egypt under a delta monarchy was Piye, who now reigned at Napata. This situation was not only one of political rivalry; Piye considered the northern Egyptians religiously and culturally inferior and thus unfit to govern Egypt.

When Tefnakht sent his army south to besiege Heracleopolis, a center in Middle Egypt that had held out successfully against him earlier, the king of Kush recognized that this expanding force might be a potential threat to his own position. Still, he did not yet move against Tefnakht. Ultimately, however, other Egyptian princes, seeing fellow rulers forced to submit to Tefnakht's control, appealed to Piye to interfere. Piye dispatched one of his armies, already in Egypt, to liberate the city of Hermopolis. Another force was sent to assist in that task but, having passed slightly north of Thebes, it encountered Tefnakht's river fleet carrying many troops. The Kushites won a furious battle, inflicting heavy casualties on the enemy and taking many prisoners.

When Piye's two contingents joined farther northward, they fell on Tefnakht's forces besieging Heracleopolis. Again the men from the south were successful, and the losers were driven out of the area. The victori-

RULERS OF THE TWENTY-FIFTH (KUSHITE) DYNASTY

Ruler	Reign (B.C.E.)
Piye	742-716
Shabaka	716-702/698
Shebitku	698-690
Taharqa	690-664
Tanutamuni	664-656

Note: Dynastic research is ongoing; data are approximate.

ous Kushites then pushed on to Hermopolis, where they began their own siege of that city. When informed of his army's triumphs, King Piye, still in Napata, naturally was pleased. Satisfaction turned to rage, however, when he heard that his antagonist's surviving forces had been allowed to escape toward the delta. Deciding to take personal command of the campaign, Piye left for Egypt.

The Kushite ruler was slow to overtake his army. When he arrived in Thebes he spent some time engaged in elaborate ceremonials dedicated to Amen in the great temple complex of Karnak. This monarch was nothing if not a pious servant of his favorite god. It has been suggested that such ostentatious worship also was intended to convince Egyptians that this foreign leader enjoyed divine sanction for his impending conquest of the country. In any case, on the completion of his devotions, Piye reached his army and soon ended the siege of Hermopolis by agreeing to spare its ruler's life if he surrendered. As Piye led his army to the north, his military strength as well as his reputation for clemency toward his enemies encouraged towns in his path to capitulate.

Tefnakht, now concerned about the approaching Kushites, established his base at Memphis, the ancient city just south of the delta region. It was strongly defended, but Piye devised a shrewd plan of attack. Since the eastern side of the city was under water, its defenders thought it unnecessary to worry about an assault from that direction. Grasping the opportunity this presented, the royal commander ordered his men to seize all the enemy's boats in the harbor, which, along with the Kushite's own flotilla, were then utilized quickly to ferry his fighting men to the city walls. These were mounted easily before the opposition could react effectively. When the city fell, Piye characteristically gave credit to Amen.

This spectacular victory led to the submission of the surrounding country. In keeping with his religious habits, Piye celebrated each of his military successes by publicly worshiping in local sanctuaries, including, especially, those of Memphis. Ptah, the artificer god, was the major deity of that city and believed to be the creator of Amen. The bold conqueror from the distant south could now announce that Ptah had recognized him as the legitimate King of Egypt. All the princes of the delta eventually submitted to Piye's authority, demonstrating their homage by delivering their substantial treasures to him. It is interesting that Piye, the religious puritan, refused to meet some of these leaders personally, as he considered such "fisheaters" to be unclean.

The Kushite's principal target, however, eluded him. Even though Tefnakht's army was destroyed, that ambitious and determined leader defied his adversary, ultimately taking refuge on an island in the northern delta. Piye settled for Tefnakht's pledge of allegiance rather than continuing pursuit in the difficult, unfamiliar swampland. Thus, when the few other notable rulers of outlying territories swore obedience to him, Piye, the prince of a longtime colony of Egypt, was now the lord of that great imperial nation by the Nile.

Having achieved such success, the man from Napata packed his accumulated prize wealth aboard his riverboats and made his way up the river to his own desert land. Although it was short-lived, political unity had been restored to Egypt by a foreign conqueror. Nevertheless, Tefnakht soon resumed his efforts to acquire control of Egypt himself and enjoyed considerable success in the north. Kushite dominance in Upper Egypt was secure, however, during the remainder of Piye's reign. That king evidently was content to have imposed his nominal authority over the entire Nile Valley without troubling to remain in Egypt in order to enforce his sovereignty over the long term. As long as Upper Egypt, particularly the holy city of Thebes, was not threatened by the "unclean" northerners, he rested easily.

Piye's last known accomplishment, which seems fitting for a king so obsessed with pleasing the gods, was his reconstruction of and addition to the great temple of Amen at Napata. It remained for his brother and successor, Shabaka (r. 716-c. 702/698 B.C.E.), to return to Egypt and firmly establish his dynasty's rule by residing there as pharaoh.

SIGNIFICANCE

Piye's extended military effort in Egypt was the foundation for Kushite control of that country for almost a century. His control of Egypt from Kush paved the way for Shabaka's foundation of the Twenty-fifth (Kushite) Dynasty, which reigned from c. 742 to c. 656 B.C.E. His achievement, consequently, established Kush as a major power in the ancient world. If the other important states of the time had not noticed inner Africa before, they did after Piye's conquest.

The Kushites' appearance in force in Egypt undoubtedly was feared by the proud Egyptians as the coming of barbarian hordes, but it was not the calamity they expected. Piye and his men represented a culture that was heavily Egyptianized. Admittedly, Kush was an African kingdom and never completely lost its unique identity under the Egyptian façade. Yet the influence of Egypt's long-established and admired civilization had brought Kush within the northern cultural orbit to a considerable extent. These were not savage barbarians but fellow residents of the Nile Valley whose leaders were literate worshipers of Egyptian gods and who expressed themselves in cultivated Egyptian terms.

Piye, in the twenty-first year of his reign, erected a stela in Napata that recounts his Egyptian expedition. It is acknowledged as one of the most interesting and revealing documents in Egyptian and Kushite history, vividly describing the military exploits of the king and his army as well as clearly communicating details about the fiery temperament, religious piety, and generosity of Piye. Now exhibited in the Cairo Museum, it is a fitting memorial to one of the great figures in African history.

—*Lysle E. Meyer*

FURTHER READING

Adams, William Y. *Nubia: Corridor to Africa.* 1977. Reprint. Princeton, N.J.: Princeton University Press, 1988. Comprehensive account of the region from prehistoric times to the nineteenth century. Provides excellent coverage of the "heroic age" of the Nabatan kings and their rule in Egypt. Extensive end notes and chapter bibliographies are included.

Breasted, James Henry. *The Twentieth to the Twenty-sixth Dynasties.* Vol. 4 in *Ancient Records of Egypt.* 1906-1907. Reprint. Urbana: University of Illinois Press, 2001. Contains a translation of the Piye stela as well as the editor's excellent scholarly summary of it. An essential source.

Miyasliwiec, Karol. *The Twilight of Ancient Egypt: The First Millennium B.C.E.* Translated by David Lorton. Ithaca, N.Y.: Cornell University Press, 2000. Contains substantial coverage of Piye's reign and of his successors. Illustrations, maps, bibliography, and index.

O'Connor, David. *Ancient Nubia: Egypt's Rival in Africa.* Philadelphia: University of Pennsylvania Press, 1994. Compiled as a catalog for an archaeology exhibit, this volume has numerous illustrations. The text covers Nubia's politics, religious beliefs, society, culture, and history from the Bronze Age to the Napatan-Meroitic period.

Torok, Lazlo. *The Kingdom of Kush: Handbook of the Napatan-Meroitic Civilization.* New York: Brill Academic Publishers, 1998. A guide to Kushite history and culture. Bibliograpy.

PLATO
Greek philosopher

Plato used the dialogue structure in order to pose fundamental questions about knowledge, reality, society, and human nature—questions that are still alive today. He developed his own positive philosophy, Platonism, in answer to these questions, a philosophy that has been one of the most influential thought-systems in the Western tradition.

BORN: c. 427 B.C.E.; Athens, Greece
DIED: 347 B.C.E.; Athens, Greece
ALSO KNOWN AS: Aristocles; Platon; Son of Ariston
AREA OF ACHIEVEMENT: Philosophy

EARLY LIFE

Plato (PLAY-toh) was originally named Aristocles but may have acquired the nickname Plato ("broad" or "wide" in Greek) on account of his broad shoulders. Both of Plato's parents were from distinguished aristocratic families. Plato himself, because of family connections and expectations as well as personal interest, looked forward to a life of political leadership.

Besides being born into an illustrious family, Plato was born into an illustrious city. He was born in the wake of Athens's Golden Age, the period that had witnessed Athens's emergence as the strongest Greek power (particularly through its leadership in repelling the invasions of Greece by the Persians), the birth of classical Athenian architecture, drama, and arts, and a florescence of Athenian cultural, intellectual, and political life. By the time of Plato's youth, however, the military and cultural flowers that had bloomed in Athens had already begun to fade. A few years before Plato's birth, Athens and Sparta—its rival for Greek supremacy—had engaged their forces and those of their allies in the Peloponnesian War.

This long, painful, and costly war of Greek against Greek lasted until Plato was twenty-three. Thus, he grew up witnessing the decline of Athens as the Greek military and cultural center. During these formative years, he observed numerous instances of cruelty, betrayal, and deceit as some unscrupulous Greeks attempted to make the best of things for themselves at the expense of other people (supposedly their friends) and in clear violation of values that Plato thought sacred.

It was also at an early age, probably in adolescence, that Plato began to hear Socrates, who engaged a variety of people in Athens in philosophical discussion of important questions. It could fairly be said that Plato fell under the spell (or at least the influence) of Socrates.

When, as a consequence of losing the Peloponnesian War to Sparta, an oligarchy was set up in Athens in place of the former democracy, Plato had the opportunity to join those in power, but he refused. Those in power, who later became known as the "Thirty Tyrants," soon proved to be ruthless rulers; they even attempted to implicate Socrates in their treachery, although Socrates would have no part in it.

A democratic government was soon restored, but it was under this democracy that Socrates was brought to trial, condemned to death, and executed. This was the last straw for Plato. He never lost his belief in the great importance of political action, but he had become convinced that such action must be informed by a philosophical vision of the highest truth. He continued to hold back from political life, devoting himself instead to developing the kind of training and instruction that every wise person—and political people especially, because they act on a great social stage—must pursue. Plato maintained that people would not be able to eliminate evil and social injustice from their communities until rulers became philosophers (lovers of wisdom)—or until philosophers became rulers.

LIFE'S WORK

In his twenties and thirties, Plato traveled widely, becoming aware of intellectual traditions and social and political conditions in various areas of the Mediterranean region. During these years, he also began work on his earliest, and most "Socratic," dialogues.

When he was about forty years old, Plato founded the Academy, a complex of higher education and a center of communal living located approximately one mile from Athens proper. Plato's Academy was highly successful. One famous pupil who studied directly under the master was Aristotle, who remained a student at the Academy for twenty years before going on to his own independent philosophical position. The Academy continued to exist for more than nine hundred years, until it was finally forced to close in 529 C.E. by the Roman emperor Justinian I on the grounds that it was pagan and thus offensive to the Christianity he wished to promote.

In 367 B.C.E., Plato went to Sicily, where he had been invited to serve as tutor to Dionysius II of Syracuse. The project offered Plato the opportunity to groom a philosopher-king such as he envisioned in *Politeia* (388-368

B.C.E.; *Republic*, 1701) but this ambition soon proved to be unrealizable.

One of the main tasks Plato set for himself was to keep alive the memory of Socrates by recording and perpetuating the kind of impact that Socrates had had on those with whom he conversed. Virtually all Plato's written work takes the form of dialogues in which Socrates is a major character. Reading these dialogues, readers can observe the effects that Socrates has on various interlocutors and, perhaps more important, are themselves brought into the inquiry and discussion. One of the explicit aims of a Platonic dialogue is to involve readers in philosophical questioning concerning the points and ideas under discussion. In reading essays and treatises, readers too often assume the passive role of listening to the voice of the author; dialogues encourage readers to become active participants (at least in their own minds, which, as Plato would probably agree, is precisely where active participation is required).

The written dialogue is an effective mode of writing for a philosophy with the aims of Plato, but it sometimes leaves one uncertain as to Plato's own views. It is generally agreed among scholars that the earlier works—such as *Apologia Sōcratis* (*Apology*, 1675), *Euthyphrōn* (*Euthyphro*, 1804), and *Gorgias* (English translation, 1804), written between 399 and 390 B.C.E.—express primarily the thought and spirit of Socrates, while middle and later dialogues—such as *Menōn* (*Meno*, 1769), *Symposion* (*Symposium*, 1701) *Politeia, Theaetētos* (*Theaetetus*, 1804; all 388-366 B.C.E.), *Philēbos* (*Philebus*, 1779), and *Nomoi* (*Laws*, 1804; both 360-347 B.C.E.)—gradually give way to the views of Plato himself.

The dialogues of Plato are among the finest literary productions by any philosopher who has ever lived, yet there is evidence that Plato himself, maintaining the superiority of the spoken word over the written word, and of person-to-person instruction over "book learning," regarded the written dialogues as far less important than the lectures and discussions that took place in the Academy. There is, however, very little known about those spoken discussions, and the best evidence available for Plato's views is in his many dialogues.

The fundamental thesis of Plato's work is the claim that there are "forms" or "ideas" that exist outside the material realm, that are the objects of knowledge (or intellectual cognition), and that, unlike material objects, do not come into existence, change, or pass out of existence. These forms, rather than material things, actually constitute reality. This is Plato's well-known theory of forms (or theory of ideas).

The theory attempts to take two points of view into consideration and to define their proper relationship. The two points of view give the questioner access to a changing world (of sensible or material things) and an unchanging world (of intellectual objects). From the first perspective, human beings know that they live in a changing world in which things come into existence, change, and pass out of existence. If one tries to pin something down in this world and determine whether various predicates apply to it (whether it is big, or red, or hot, or good, for example), one finds that the object can be viewed from a variety of standpoints, according to some of which the predicate applies and according to some of which it does not apply. Socrates, for example, is big compared to an insect but not big compared to a building. This train of thought leads one, however, to the other point of view. An insect, Socrates (that is, his body), and a building belong to the changing physical world in which the application of predicates is problematic or changing.

In the nonphysical, or intellectual, world, however, there must be some fixed points of reference that make possible the application of predicates at all. These latter

Plato. (Library of Congress)

660

fixed points do not change. Whether one compares Socrates with the insect or with the building, when one judges which is bigger one is always looking for the same thing. Bigness or largeness itself, Plato thought, must always exist, unchanging, and it must itself be big. It is this abstract or intellectual element with which a person must be familiar if the person is to be in a position to decide whether various objects in this changing material world are big.

The forms, or objects of intellect, are quite different from (and superior to) physical objects, or objects of sense. Plato thought of knowledge as occurring only between the intellect (or reason) and its objects, the forms. The bodily senses give human beings only belief, he said, not true knowledge.

Plato considered human beings to be composed of a rational aspect and an irrational aspect. The intellect or reason, that which communes with the forms, is rational. The body, which communes with the physical world, is irrational. Plato looked down on the body, considering it merely the seat of physical appetites. Additionally, there is a third, intermediate aspect of people: passions, which may follow intellect (and thus be rational) or follow the bodily appetites (and thus be irrational).

In each person, one aspect will dominate. Reason is best, but not everyone can achieve the state in which his or her life is under the direction of reason. Thus, communities should be organized in such a way that those who are rational (and not led by physical appetites) will be in command. The philosopher-king is one who both attains philosophical insight into the world of the forms and holds power in the day-to-day changing world.

SIGNIFICANCE

Plato defended the role of reason in human life, in opposition to many ancient Greek teachers who were called Sophists. The Sophists traveled from city to city and claimed to be able to teach young men how to be successful in life. They offered such services for a fee. Although the Sophists were never a unified school and did not profess a common creed, certain beliefs are characteristic of them as a group and are almost diametrically opposed to the views of Plato. The Sophists mainly taught the art of speaking, so that a person could speak well in public assemblies, in a court of law, and as a public leader. Plato thought, however, that such speakers were probably more likely to appeal to feelings and emotion than to reason. Such speakers may hold forth and sound impressive, but they tend not to be acquainted with the objects of the intellect, the ground of true knowledge.

Plato argued that such speakers may, for example, be persuasive in getting a man who is ill to take his medicine, but it is only a real doctor who can prescribe the right remedy. Plato also compared the Sophist to a makeup artist, who makes only superficial changes in people's looks. The true philosopher, on the other hand, is compared to a gymnastic trainer, who is genuinely able to bring health and soundness to people's bodies.

In Plato's view, however, the stakes are really much higher, for both Sophists and philosophers actually affect people's souls or inner selves, not their bodies, and Plato followed Socrates in thinking of the cultivation of the soul as much more important than the cultivation of the body. Moreover, Plato went beyond the views of other Greek philosophers and beyond the cultural norms of ancient Athens by affirming that women and men had the same potential for philosophical wisdom and community leadership. Many writers in the twentieth century have referred to Plato as the first feminist, although it is also true that the vast majority of ancient, medieval, and modern philosophical Platonists did not follow him in this particular. The Sophists, in any case, were false teachers and false leaders, in Plato's view. True leaders must have wisdom, and the acquisition of such wisdom, he believed, could only come about in a cooperative community of inquirers who were free to follow argument, not carried away by speech making.

Throughout the history of more than two millennia of Western philosophy, Plato has been one of the most influential thinkers. One twentieth century philosopher, Alfred North Whitehead, has said that philosophy since Plato's time has consisted mainly of a series of footnotes to Plato. There have been numerous revivals of Plato's thought in Western philosophy. Platonists, Neoplatonists, and others have made their appearances, but Plato's influence is probably better gauged in terms of the importance of the questions he has raised and the problem areas he has defined, rather than in terms of the numbers of his adherents or disciples. From both dramatic and philosophical points of view, Plato's dialogues are so well constructed that even today they serve well as a student's first encounter with the philosophical practice of inquiry and argument.

—*Stephen Satris*

FURTHER READING

Cropsey, Joseph. *Plato's World: Man's Place in the Cosmos*. Chicago: University of Chicago Press, 1995. Discusses Plato's views on human nature, with attention to his political theories.

Gonzalez, Francisco, ed. *The Third Way: New Directions in Platonic Studies.* Lanham, Md.: Rowman and Littlefield, 1995. A helpful sampling of late twentieth century research on Plato, his continuing significance, and trends of interpretation in Platonic studies.

Irwin, Terrence. *Plato's Ethics.* New York: Oxford University Press, 1995. A thorough study of Plato's moral philosophy, including its political implications.

Kahn, Charles H. *Plato and the Socratic Dialogue: The Philosophical Use of a Literary Form.* New York: Cambridge University Press, 1996. A study of Plato's use of the dialogue form as a means for exploring and developing key philosophical positions and dispositions.

Kraut, Richard, ed. *The Cambridge Companion to Plato.* Cambridge, England: Cambridge University Press, 1992. Eminent Plato scholars analyze and assess key Platonic dialogues and issues in Plato's thought.

Moravcsik, J. M. E. *Plato and Platonism: Plato's Conception of Appearance and Reality in Ontology, Epistemology, and Ethics and Its Modern Echoes.* Cambridge, Mass.: Blackwell, 1992. A scholarly study of Plato's key distinction between appearance and reality and the continuing impact of that distinction.

Pappas, Nikolas, ed. *Routledge Philosophy Guidebook to Plato and the "Republic."* New York: Routledge, 1995. Helpful articles that clarify key Platonic concepts and theories.

Rutherford, R. B. *The Art of Plato: Ten Essays in Platonic Interpretation.* Cambridge, Mass.: Harvard University Press, 1995. Well-informed essays on key elements of Plato's theories.

Sayers, Sean. *Plato's "Republic": An Introduction.* Edinburgh: Edinburgh University Press, 2000. An accessible commentary on the works of the philosopher.

Tarrant, Harold. *Plato's First Interpreters.* Ithaca, N.Y.: Cornell University Press, 2000. An examination of the earliest debates about Plato's ideas.

Tuana, Nancy, ed. *Feminist Interpretations of Plato.* University Park: Pennsylvania State University, 1994. Scholarly essays evaluate Plato's understanding of gender issues and appraise his philosophy from the perspectives of feminist theory.

Williams, Bernard A. O. *Plato.* New York: Routledge, 1999. An excellent biographical introduction to the thoughts of the philosopher, clearly presented. Includes bibliography.

SEE ALSO: Aristotle; Socrates.

RELATED ARTICLES in *Great Events from History: The Ancient World*: c. 440 B.C.E., Sophists Train the Greeks in Rhetoric and Politics; May, 431-September, 404 B.C.E., Peloponnesian War; September, 404-May, 403 B.C.E., Thirty Tyrants Rule Athens for Eight Months; 399 B.C.E., Death of Socrates; c. 380 B.C.E., Plato Develops His Theory of Ideas.

PLAUTUS
Roman playwright

Plautus's action-packed, middle-class comedies, built from a contrived structure of disguises, mistaken identities, and the obligatory revelatory scene, were sensationally popular in his time and influenced future comedic dramatists William Shakespeare, Richard Brinsley Sheridan, Molière, and Jean Giraudoux.

BORN: c. 254 B.C.E.; Sarsina, Umbria (now in Italy)
DIED: 184 B.C.E.; Rome (now in Italy)
ALSO KNOWN AS: Titus Maccius Plautus (full name)
AREA OF ACHIEVEMENT: Literature

EARLY LIFE

The sparse biographical details on Titus Maccius Plautus (PLAW-tuhs) are drawn from historians and writers such as Livy and Cicero. From his birthplace, Sarsina, a mountainous rural region of Italy, where the native tongue was Umbrian, Plautus escaped, joining a traveling group of players (probably as an actor). He learned the technical intricacies of the profession, acquired a mastery of Latin—and perhaps some Greek—and became the unequaled practitioner of his comedic craft.

In Rome, Plautus worked in the theater, lost money in trade, and eventually became a mill worker, writing in his leisure moments. No record remains of his life except the plays that he wrote, and even some of these claim authenticity only on the basis of ascription. Plautus became so popular that dramas by other writers were attributed to him in order to gain production and popular reception. In his time, it was enough merely that a play bore his name; a generation later, it was enough that the prologue to the play *Menaechmi* (*The Twin Menaechmi*, 1595) contain the words "I bring you Plautus"—words that remain in that prologue forever as guarantors of laughter.

LIFE'S WORK

Although he may have written more than fifty plays, only twenty-one manuscripts of works attributable to Plautus survive, the oldest of these dating to the fourth or fifth century C.E. Only twenty of these are complete plays. In an age when records were shoddily kept, or not kept at all, and when aspiring contemporary playwrights did not hesitate to attach Plautus's name to their plays, a large number of comedies were attributed to him.

In an attempt to clear up the chaos of authorship, Marcus Terentius Varro, a contemporary of Cicero, compiled three lists of plays: those given universal recognition as being written by Plautus, those identified by Varro as plays by Plautus, and those recognized as Plautus's work by others but not by Varro. The first list, labeled by scholars the "Varronianae fabulae," contains the twenty-one plays that succeeding generations of scholars have agreed on as belonging to Plautus. Other plays remain outside the canon.

The dates of Plautus's plays are as speculative as are the details of his life. Only two of them—*Pseudolus* (191 B.C.E.; English translation, 1774) and *Stichus* (200 B.C.E.; English translation, 1774)—are attached to specific dates. About half the remainder are unidentified chronologically, and the rest are qualified with terms such as "probably early" or "late." Like William Shakespeare nearly fifteen hundred years later, Plautus borrowed his plots and reworked Greek originals; some sources have been identified, but others remain unknown.

Among the most famous stock situations and character types associated with Plautine comedy are the vain soldier-braggart (*miles gloriosus*), which finds its most complex realization in Shakespeare's Falstaff; the farcical chaos caused by mistaken identity, a chaos to which order is eventually restored; the servant who, wiser than his superiors, extricates them from a web of near-impossible entanglements, sometimes of the master's making; and finally, a happy ending. The plays, whether serious—such as *Amphitruo* (*Amphitryon*, 1694)—or farcical—such as *The Twin Menaechmi*—are always comic in the Aristotelian definition of comedy as a play that begins in an unfortunate situation and ends fortunately.

Like the commercial playwright of modern times, Plautus wrote for a broad audience, basing his appeal on laughter and a good story, love and money forming an integral part of the story. Preceding his plays, as was the custom, with a prologue devoted to a summary of the borrowed story, he then developed his plot by highly improbable complications, witty native dialogue, slapstick scenes, and an infinite variety of jests, all kept within the limits of popular recognition. That recognition is embodied in the characters, the most famous of which in his time and, perhaps, in any time is the *miles gloriosus* figure, the Greek *alazon* or "overstater" (commonly translated as the soldier-braggart), whose vanity and consequent exposure have never failed to entertain. In Plautus's time, the Punic Wars created an audience receptive to fast-paced action and to the adventures of the returning soldier.

On a broader social scale, the element of recognition is drawn from the merchant-class milieu of his time, in which servants, wiser than their masters, extricate their superiors from entrapments of one sort or another, thereby resolving problems and bringing the play to its happy conclusion. Molière's middle-class comic heroes and villains stem from this Plautine tradition. The stories borrowed from Greek comedies became merely the scaffolding for the native Roman ribaldry, schemes, and jests that characterize the famous Plautine humor, and the upper-class characters are frequently a part of that scaffolding. In the course of the play, they give way to the servants or peasants. Thus, in the tradition of the New Comedy of Menander (as opposed to the old Aristophanic satire, which was topical), Plautus opened the comic stage to the common man. What social satire is present is a part of the more broadly based humor, concerned with the outwitting of the upper classes by their inferiors. Like death, humor becomes the great leveler.

Of the twenty-one surviving plays, the two that remain the most famous are *The Twin Menaechmi*—frequently translated as *The Two Menaechmi*—and *Miles gloriosus* (*The Braggart Warrior*, 1767), the date and source of the former unknown, the latter dated about 205 B.C.E. Both are placed by scholars in the early or early middle of the agreed-on chronology of Plautus's writing. Respectively, they are the direct source of Shakespeare's play *The Comedy of Errors* (c. 1592-1594) and of his most famous and complex comic figure, Falstaff. Indirectly, they have influenced both literary style and popular humor in most succeeding comedies. Both plays exude the festive spirit to which C. L. Barber attributes Shakespeare's comedies and which distinguishes Plautine humor, heavily dependent on robust and fast-moving physical actions, from that of traditional satire, invective, or other modes of comedy in which ideas are prominent.

The Twin Menaechmi, more directly imitated perhaps than any other play, builds its comedy on a set of separated twins, whose lives develop complications that, once begun, take on a life of their own in a seemingly endless web of mistaken identities and consequent misunderstandings. Only the most skillful plotting of events by the author can extricate the twins from that web created by disguises and accidental meetings.

The title figure of *The Braggart Warrior* (variously titled *The Soldier-Braggart*), the soldier Pyrgopolynices, is considered by scholars to be Plautus's most brilliant creation. Convinced of his bravery and appeal to women and recently returned from the wars, Pyrgopolynices (who is characterized by lechery and stupidity as well as vanity) falls victim to the elaborate deceptions of a slave whose master is in love with a woman whom the braggart soldier has brought to Ephesus against her will. The slave concocts a pattern of disguises and misunderstandings that befuddle the vain soldier, and the lovers are reunited. Again, disguises, misunderstandings, and deceptions create a farcically intricate plot, delightful in its escalating complications and ingenious in its resolution.

SIGNIFICANCE

In addition to being "the dean of Roman drama," Plautus has directly provided the plots for at least three illustrious successors: Shakespeare's *The Comedy of Errors*, based on *The Twin Menaechmi*; Molière's *L'Avare* (1668; *The Miser*, 1672), based on *Aulularia* (*The Pot of Gold*); and Jean Giraudoux's *Amphitryon 38* (1929; English translation, 1938), based on *Amphitryon*. Edmond Rostand's *Cyrano de Bergerac* (1897; English translation, 1898), Nicholas Udall's *Ralph Roister Doister* (1552), Ben Jonson's *Every Man in His Humour* (1598, 1605), and the contemporary American musicals *The Boys from Syracuse* (1938) and *A Funny Thing Happened on the Way to the Forum* (1962) are among the popular descendants of Plautus's work.

Erich Segal, writing about Plautine humor, quotes the psychiatrist Ernst Kris, who describes comedy as a "holiday for the superego." A "safety valve for repressed sentiments which otherwise might have broken their bonds more violently," Plautine comedy provides release from the conventions of a socially prescribed life. It produces a resolution of the tension between dreams and actuality, order and chaos, and finally between the vital and repressive forces in life, as it acts out that resolution for the audience. In the end, a kind of ironic equilibrium is achieved, an equilibrium that reconciles dream with reality, providing the release necessary to avoid the violence inherent in the tragic mode.

—*Susan Rusinko*

FURTHER READING

McCarthy, Kathleen. *Slaves, Masters, and the Art of Authority in Plautine Comedy*. Princeton, N.J.: Princeton University Press, 2000. A look at the relation of slaves to their masters, with emphasis on the work of Plautus. Bibliography and index.

Moore, Timothy. *The Theater of Plautus: Playing to the Audience*. Austin: University of Texas Press, 1998. A study of Plautus that focuses on his endeavors to adapt works to suit his audience's taste and culture. Bibliography and indexes.

Riehle, Wolfgang. *Shakespeare, Plautus, and the Humanist Tradition*. Rochester, N.Y.: D. S. Brewer, 1990. A comparison of William Shakespeare and Plautus, examining Plautus's influence on Shakespeare. Bibliography and index.

Segal, Erich. *Roman Laughter: The Comedy of Plautus*. New York: Oxford University Press, 1987. A sprightly treatment of the social milieu that spawned Plautus's comedies, with extensive notes, an index of passages quoted, and a general index.

_____, ed. *Oxford Readings in Menander, Plautus, and Terence*. New York: Oxford University Press, 2002. A collection of papers tracing the development of the "New Comedy." Segal's introduction draws connections between these Latin plays and modern comedy.

Slater, Niall W. *Plautus in Performance: The Theater of the Mind*. Amsterdam: Harwood Academic, 2000. This study focuses on the production of the plays of Plautus. Bibliography and index.

Sutton, Dana Ferrin. *Ancient Comedy: The War of the Generations*. New York: Twayne, 1993. An examination of early comedy that looks at Plautus, Aristophanes, Menander, and Terence.

SEE ALSO: Aristophanes; Menander (dramatist); Marcus Terentius Varro.

RELATED ARTICLES in *Great Events from History: The Ancient World*: c. 385 B.C.E., Greek Playwright Aristophanes Dies; 264-225 B.C.E., First Punic War; 159 B.C.E., Roman Playwright Terence Dies.

PLINY THE ELDER
Roman science writer

Pliny's history of natural science preserved for later times priceless information on the ancients' beliefs in countless areas. His work had great influence on later antiquity, the Middle Ages, and the early Renaissance, and he remains a major figure in the history of science.

BORN: Probably 23 C.E.; probably Novum Comum (now Como, Italy)

DIED: August 25, 79 C.E.; Stabiae, near Mount Vesuvius (now Castellammare di Stabia, Italy)

ALSO KNOWN AS: Gaius Plinius Secundus (given name)

AREAS OF ACHIEVEMENT: Science, natural history

EARLY LIFE

Gaius Plinius Secundus, or Pliny (PLIHN-ee) the Elder, was in his fifty-sixth year when he died during the famous eruption of Mount Vesuvius in August of 79 C.E. He therefore was probably born in late 23 C.E. His family was prominent in Novum Comum and most scholars believe that he was born there, although some prefer to use the evidence that points to Verona. Clues to his career are found in his own writing, in a life by Suetonius, and in the letters of his nephew and adopted ward Gaius Plinius Caecilius Secundus, better known as Pliny the Younger.

It can be inferred from certain remarks in his work that Pliny came to Rome at an early age to study, as befitted his status as the son of a prominent northern Italian family. He obtained the normal education of the time and thus would have been thoroughly trained in rhetoric, a discipline to which he would later return, as well as several of the fields that he would cultivate for the next thirty years until he wrote *Naturalis historia* (77 C.E.; *The Historie of the World*, 1601; better known as *Natural History*). The next natural step for a young man in his position was one of military service and therefore, at about the age of twenty-three, he went to Germany as a military officer and, in addition to holding other posts, was put in command of a cavalry troop. Later comments in the *Natural History* lead scholars to believe that he traveled throughout the area and took copious notes on what he saw during his stay there.

Although all Pliny's writings except the *Natural History* are lost, his nephew published a chronological, annotated bibliography of his uncle's works, and the titles from this early period are instructive. His first work was a single-volume book titled *De iaculatione equestri* (on throwing the javelin from horseback), and his next was a two-volume biography of his patron Lucius Pomponius Secundus. His third book was a twenty-volume history of all the wars Rome had ever waged against Germany. Pliny claimed that he was instructed to begin this work at the behest of the ghost of Drusus Germanicus (the brother of Tiberius and the father of Claudius I), who was concerned that the memory of his deeds would be lost. Scholars also suspect a certain amount of Imperial flattery in this story. It was probably also during this German campaign that Pliny became close to the future emperor Titus, to whom he dedicated the *Natural History*. A belief that he served under Titus later during the campaign in Judaea is somewhat suspect.

After a fairly lengthy stay in Germany, Pliny returned to Rome and began the second phase of his career as a writer and public servant.

LIFE'S WORK

During this time, generally thought to begin during the reign of Claudius I, Pliny turned to the life of a professional pleader, a natural choice for one of his station and education. There is no record of any great successes in this regard, and none of his speeches survives, but his next book, *Studiosi* (the scholar, sometimes translated as the student), reflects again his tendency to write about matters with which he was concerned. In it, Pliny traced the training of a rhetorician from the cradle onward. The work encompassed three books in six volumes and very likely occupied Pliny during the early years of Nero's reign. It was consulted by Quintilian and earned some cautious praise from that author. The later, more turbulent, years of Nero's reign were occupied with an eight-volume study of grammar. Pliny, who later would call Nero an enemy of humankind, was clearly keeping out of the maelstrom of Neronian politics by retreating to his study. It is therefore not surprising that near the end of Nero's reign Pliny accepted a posting as procurator of Spain, perhaps to remove himself completely from the city during troubled times.

It may have been during this period that Pliny also found time to write a thirty-one-book history that continued the work of Aufidius Bassus. Bassus's history seems to have ended with the events of Claudius's reign, and Pliny began there and ended perhaps with the events of 69. It is likely that this work was published posthumously. It was also at this time that Pliny's brother-in-law died and entrusted the care of his son, Pliny's nephew, to

Pliny the Elder. (Library of Congress)

this now-distinguished Roman figure. Pliny could not care for the lad from Spain but chose a guardian for him until he adopted him on his return to Rome. He held his post in Spain until Vespasian emerged victorious from the turmoil that followed Nero's death in 69, a year of civil war commonly referred to as the Year of the Four Emperors.

Vespasian brought stability to a war-weary city, and for Pliny he represented political patronage as the father of Pliny's army friend Titus. After Pliny's return to Rome, he held several high-ranking posts abroad, and it can be surmised from his first-person reports in the *Natural History* that one of these trips may have taken him to Africa, where he made copious notes on what he saw. At this time, he was also made an official "friend of the court" and thus became an Imperial adviser, regularly called to Vespasian's court for meetings at daybreak.

The demands of Pliny's renewed public life were thus intense, and yet he was also finishing the *Natural History* at the same time he held these offices. Pliny had been amassing information for this work for years. His nephew writes that his uncle never read without taking notes and that one of his mottoes was that no book was so bad that he could not find something of use in it. He always read or was read to whenever possible—even while bathing, eating, or sunbathing (one of his favorite pastimes). He read or dictated while riding in a sedan chair, and he once chastised his nephew for walking, because it

was impossible to read while one did so. He even devised a sort of glove to ensure that his slave could take notes on such trips in cold weather. To find more time for his studies, Pliny retired early and rose even earlier, reading and writing by lamplight in the early morning darkness. So diligent was he that on his death he left his nephew 160 books of notes written in a tiny hand.

The *Natural History* became the great showcase for these notes. Its thirty-seven books cover virtually every aspect of nature's works and several of those of humankind. After an entertaining preface, book 1 offers a full table of contents and a list of authorities cited—a rare and welcome practice in antiquity. The remaining books range far and wide across the realms of zoology, entomology, botany, mineralogy, astronomy, geography, pharmacology, anthropology, physiology, folklore, and metallurgy. There are countless long digressions on such subjects as the history of art, the manufacture of papyrus, the growing of crops, religious practices, aphrodisiacs, and magic spells. In his preface, Pliny claims to have studied about two thousand volumes, to have emerged with twenty thousand noteworthy facts, and to have cited one hundred principal authors. In reality, the total number of authors cited by name is almost five hundred. Although it is surmised that the work was published in 77, there are certain signs that it is unfinished; Pliny may well have been revising the work when he met his death.

On August 24, 79, Pliny was on duty at Misenum as prefect of the fleet in the Bay of Naples. On seeing the volcanic cloud from Vesuvius, he sailed across the bay both to investigate further and to help in possible evacuation plans. Once at his destination, he sought to calm his hosts by a casual attitude and even fell asleep amid the danger, a fact attested by those who overheard his characteristic loud snoring. The volcanic eruption intensified, and by the next morning Pliny and his hosts had to flee to the shore with pillows tied over their heads for protection.

The sea was too rough to set sail, and Pliny was exhausted from his labors, being rather obese and prone to heavy and labored breathing. He lay down for a while on a sail and requested cold water, but on rising fell suddenly dead, the victim either of the foul air or of a heart attack. His body was found the next day, looking, according to his nephew, more like one asleep than one who had died.

SIGNIFICANCE

It is fashionable to criticize Pliny the Elder as an uncritical encyclopedist, an assiduous notetaker with little or no discrimination. It is charged that his work is devoid of literary style and is almost completely lacking in organization. It is clear that most of his information came from late-night note-taking and not from fieldwork, a point in which he suffers by comparison to Aristotle.

However, in Pliny's time he was much consulted. One can see traces of his rhetorical and grammatical works in the works of Quintilian and Priscian and of his histories in the works of Tacitus, Plutarch, and Dio Cassius. The popularity of the *Natural History* is shown in the number of authors who used it as a treasure trove of facts, in its imitators such as Solinus, Martianus Capella, and Isidore of Seville, and by the great number of manuscript versions of the text, in whole or in part, which survived into the Middle Ages.

The work was much used by medieval scholars, who mined it for whatever information they needed. Several produced topical condensations, and in the early 1100's a nine-volume "reader's edition" was prepared. Its traces are frequently to be seen, often cited by name, in such authors as Thomas of Cantimpre, Bartholomaeus Anglicus, Vincent of Beauvais, and Saint Albertus Magnus. Not surprisingly, it was printed as early as 1469 and was so popular that by 1499 six more corrected editions had been printed. It was translated into Italian in 1476 and 1489.

Such popularity merits consideration and should cause the work to be judged on its own terms. In the first place, posterity owes Pliny much for preserving so many intriguing facts and the names of authors that would otherwise be lost. Clearly, it is not meant to be read as literature. It is a volume of antiquity, wherein a reader can wander, fascinated, at leisure. It is a book for browsers and, as such, offers the rewards of hours of pleasurable discovery to those people who, like Pliny, believed that knowledge was inherently good.

—*Kenneth F. Kitchell, Jr.*

FURTHER READING

Beagon, Mary. *Roman Nature: The Thought of Pliny the Elder.* Oxford, England: Clarendon Press, 1992. Examines Pliny's portrayal of the relationship between nature and humankind. Also places both the author and his work in their wider literary and historical contexts.

Chibnall, Marjorie. "Pliny's *Natural History* and the Middle Ages." In *Empire and Aftermath: Silver Latin II*, edited by T. A. Dorey. Boston: Routledge and Kegan Paul, 1975. Careful and clear study of the influence of the *Natural History* from late antiquity through the Middle Ages.

French, Roger, and Frank Greenway, eds. *Science in the Early Roman Empire: Pliny the Elder, His Sources and Influence.* Totowa, N.J.: Barnes and Noble Books, 1986. Twelve essays occasioned by a Pliny symposium, with a brief life and studies centering on such subjects as medicine, pharmacy, botany, zoology, metallurgy, and astronomy.

Healy, John F. *Pliny the Elder on Science and Technology.* New York: Oxford University Press, 2000. Reexamines Pliny's work in the light of modern experiments, simulating Pliny's techniques.

Pliny the Younger. *Letters and Panegyricus.* Translated by Betty Radice. Cambridge, Mass.: Harvard University Press, 1972-1975. Letters 3.5, 6.16, and 6.20 are vivid, firsthand accounts of the elder Pliny, his writings, lifestyle, and death.

SEE ALSO: Dio Cassius; Pliny the Younger; Plutarch; Tacitus.

RELATED ARTICLES in *Great Events from History: The Ancient World*: 64-67 C.E., Nero Persecutes the Christians; 68-69 C.E., Year of the Four Emperors.

PLOTINUS

Egyptian philosopher

As the founder of Neoplatonism, Plotinus has exerted a profound influence on Western philosophical and religious thought, from his own day to the present.

BORN: 205 C.E.; possibly Lycopolis, Upper Egypt
DIED: 270 C.E.; Campania (now in Italy)
AREA OF ACHIEVEMENT: Philosophy

EARLY LIFE

Plotinus (ploh-TI-nuhs) was born in 205 C.E., but there is almost no information about his origins or his early life. His nationality, race, and family are unknown, and information about his birthplace comes from a fourth century source that may not be reliable. Plotinus told his disciples little about himself; he would not even divulge the date of his birth. Only one thing can certainly be said: Plotinus's education and intellectual background were entirely Greek. This fact can be deduced from his writings; Plotinus shows little knowledge of Egyptian religion and misinterprets Egyptian hieroglyphic symbolism. Porphyry (c. 234-c. 305 C.E.), Plotinus's pupil and biographer, reports that Plotinus had a complete knowledge of geometry, arithmetic, mechanics, optics, and music, and he must have acquired some of this knowledge during the early years of his education.

Porphyry reports that in 232 C.E., when Plotinus was twenty-seven, he felt a strong desire to study philosophy. He consulted the best teachers in Alexandria, but they all disappointed him. Then a friend recommended a teacher named Ammonius Saccas (c. 175-242 C.E.). Plotinus went to hear him and immediately declared, "This is the man I was looking for." Little is known, however, of Ammonius's philosophy; he was self-taught, wrote nothing, and made his followers promise not to divulge his teachings.

Beginning in late 232 or early 233 C.E., Plotinus studied with Ammonius for eleven years (Plotinus's long stay in Alexandria may be the only reason for the common belief that he was originally from Egypt). Following that, Plotinus wanted to learn more of the philosophy of the Persians and the Indians, and he joined the army of Emperor Gordianus III, which was marching against the Persians.

It is not known in what capacity Plotinus served; he may have been a scientific adviser, or he may have occupied a more lowly position. The expedition, however, did not achieve its objective. Gordianus was assassinated in Mesopotamia, and Plotinus escaped with difficulty to Antioch. He made no attempt to return to Ammonius (nor did he ever return to the East). Instead, in 245 C.E., at the age of forty, he traveled to Rome, where he was to remain for twenty-five years, until shortly before his death. The stage was set for him to emerge as the last great pagan philosopher.

LIFE'S WORK

For the next ten years, Plotinus established himself in Rome. He accepted private students and based his teaching on that of Ammonius. During this time he wrote nothing, but by the time Porphyry joined him in 264 C.E., Plotinus no longer considered himself bound by the restrictions on publication that Ammonius had imposed; other pupils of Ammonius, such as Origen (c. 185-c. 254 C.E.) and Erennius, had already published. Plotinus had therefore written twenty-one treatises by 264 C.E., although none of them had circulated widely. Porphyry urged him to write more, and twenty-four treatises followed during the six years that Porphyry was his pupil.

Only one story survives about Plotinus's life in Rome before Porphyry's arrival. A philosopher named Olympias, from Alexandria, who was also a former pupil of Ammonius, attempted to "bring a star-stroke upon him [Plotinus] by magic." Plotinus, who apparently believed in the power of magic, felt the effects of this attack, but Olympias found his attempt recoiling on himself. He ceased his attack and confessed that "the soul of Plotinus had such great power as to be able to throw back attacks on him on to those who were seeking to do him harm."

During the time that Porphyry was his pupil, Plotinus lived comfortably in what must have been a large house, owned by a wealthy widow named Gemina. He earned a reputation for kindness and gentleness and was always generous in offering help to others. Many people entrusted their sons and daughters to his care, "considering that he would be a holy and godlike guardian." Although Plotinus was an otherworldly philosopher, he also believed in the importance of the social virtues, that the practice of them contributed to the soul's ultimate liberation. He was therefore practical, wise, and diplomatic in daily affairs, taking good care of the worldly interests of the young people in his charge. For example, they would be encouraged to give up property only if they decided to become philosophers, and even this was a decision that they would have to make for themselves. The same was true of Plotinus's attitude toward the physical body and its desires. Although he believed in self-discipline, he acknowledged that legitimate physical needs must be looked after, and he never advocated the kind of asceticism that was found in some other ancient philosophical schools.

Plotinus often acted as arbitrator in disputes, without ever incurring an enemy. The only opposition he appears ever to have aroused (apart from that of Olympias) was when some Greek philosophers accused him of stealing some of his philosophy from fellow Neoplatonist Numenius, a charge that modern scholars have not accepted. Plotinus was also a good judge of character, and his advice was sound. When Porphyry, for example, confessed that he was contemplating suicide, Plotinus told him that the desire was caused by physiological reasons, not by rational thought, and advised him to take a vacation. Porphyry accepted his advice.

Plotinus had a number of aristocratic friends, and members of the senate attended his lectures. One of them, Rogatianus, relinquished his property and became an ascetic after being exposed to Plotinus's teaching. Emperor Gallienus, sole emperor from 260 to 268 C.E., and his wife Salonia venerated Plotinus. Plotinus once asked them to found a "city of philosophers" in Campania, to be called Platonopolis, which would serve as a monastic retreat for him and his followers. The scheme failed, however, as a result of opposition in the Roman senate. Gallienus's assassination in 268 C.E. must have been a blow to Plotinus, since Gallienus's successors showed no interest in Greek philosophy.

Plotinus's lectures were more like conversations; discussion was always encouraged. One of his pupils once complained that he would prefer to hear Plotinus expound a set treatise and was exhausted by Porphyry's continuous questions. Plotinus replied, "But if when Porphyry asks questions we do not solve his difficulties we shall not be able to say anything at all to put into the treatise." Plotinus was a thoroughly engaging teacher; when he was speaking, "his intellect visibly lit up his face: there was always a charm about his appearance . . . kindliness shone out from him."

Plotinus would never revise his written work; he complained that writing gave him eyestrain. He was careless in the formation of the letters, and he showed no interest in spelling. Porphyry comments that Plotinus would compose everything in his mind. When he came to write, the thoughts were already fully formed, and he wrote "as continuously as if he was copying from a book." Even if someone engaged him in conversation, he would con-

tinue writing and not lose his train of thought. This ability to focus on the inner life enabled him to achieve a high level of mystical experience. He attained complete mystic union four times during Porphyry's stay with him, and in a treatise written before Porphyry's arrival, Plotinus says that he had experienced it often.

In his final years he suffered from a painful illness that may have been leprosy. Although he stopped teaching and withdrew from his friends and pupils, who feared contagion, he continued to write. Nine treatises appeared in his last two years (268-270 C.E.)—bringing the total to fifty-four—which were collected and edited by Porphyry, at Plotinus's request. Finally, Plotinus went away to the estate of his late friend Zethus in Campania, where he died alone, except for the presence of his doctor, Eustochius. His last words, according to Eustochius, were "Try to bring back the god in you to the divine in the All!"

SIGNIFICANCE

As the last great philosopher of antiquity, and the only one to rank with Plato and Aristotle, Plotinus's philosophy has exerted an enormous influence both on the thought of his own period and on that of later times. Although he probably thought of himself as no more than an interpreter of Plato, Plotinus became the founder of Neoplatonism. His thought lived on in his pupils Porphyry and Amelius, and all later Neoplatonic philosophers regarded him as a respected, although not a supreme, authority.

Plotinus's system was a comprehensive and original one. He brought to the best of Greek philosophy a dimension of mystical thought, which in its force, immediacy, and beauty has rarely, if ever, been equaled in the West. The *Enneads* (c. 256-270 C.E.; English translation, 1918) are not merely an ethical or metaphysical system; they are a guide to the soul's liberation, culminating in the experience and contemplation of the One. This experience is seen as the goal of the philosopher's quest, and that of all humankind.

Plotinus, and Neoplatonism in general, were also major influences on the development of Christian theology. Saint Augustine (354-430 C.E.) knew all the six *Enneads* and quotes Plotinus by name five times. The fourth century Cappadocian Fathers, especially Gregory of Nyssa (c. 335-c. 394 C.E.), also came under his spell. His thought emerged again in the Renaissance in the work of Marsilio Ficino (1433-1499), who translated Plotinus into Latin, and Giovanni Pico della Mirandola (1463-1494). In modern thought, Plotinus's influence can be traced in the work of German Idealist philosopher Friedrich Schelling (1775-1854), French philosopher Henri Bergson (1859-1941), and poets such as William Blake (1757-1827) and William Butler Yeats (1865-1939), whose interest in Plotinus was prompted by the translations made by the English Platonist Thomas Taylor in the late eighteenth and early nineteenth centuries.

—*Bryan Aubrey*

FURTHER READING

Dodds, E. R. *Pagan and Christian in an Age of Anxiety*. 1965. Reprint. New York: Cambridge University Press, 1991. This brief but wide-ranging book by a renowned classical scholar discusses the historical and social background of Neoplatonism, the conflict between Neoplatonism and Christianity, and the many types of religious and psychological experience that flourished during the period. The section on Plotinus's mysticism is particularly valuable. Well written and scholarly, but accessible to the general reader.

Dufour, Richard. *Plotinus: A Bibliography, 1950-2000*. Boston: E. J. Brill, 2002. A very useful guide for further research.

Edwards, M. J., ed. *Neoplatonic Saints: The Lives of Plotinus and Proclus by Their Students*. Philadelphia: University of Pennsylvania Press, 2001. A translation of Porphyry's work on his teacher.

Gerson, Lloyd P., ed. *The Cambridge Companion to Plotinus*. New York: Cambridge University Press, 1996. Fifteen essays explore the facets of Plotinus's philosophy and its legacy. Requires some familiarity with Neoplatonic philosophy.

Mayhall, C. Wayne, Steve Wainwright, and Worth Hawes. *On Plotinus*. Belmont, Calif.: Wadsworth, 2002. A concise introduction to Plotinus's thought and legacy. Intended for students first encountering his philosophy.

Miles, Margaret Ruth. *Plotinus on Body and Beauty: Society, Philosophy, and Religion in Third Century Rome*. Boston: Blackwell, 1999. This introduction to Plotinus's philosophy explores his thought by relating his Neoplatonism to modern concerns. Bibliography and index.

O'Meara, Dominic J. *Plotinus: An Introduction to the Enneads*. New York: Oxford University Press, 1995. An introduction devoting separate chapters to important themes in Plotinus's philosophy.

Plotinus. *The Enneads*. Translated by Stephen MacKenna. Burdett, N.Y.: Larson, 1994. A well-respected translation of Plotinus's work.

SEE ALSO: Aristotle; Plato; Porphyry; Proclus; Pythagoras; Socrates.

RELATED ARTICLES in *Great Events from History: The Ancient World*: 600-500 B.C.E., Greek Philosophers Formulate Theories of the Cosmos; 399 B.C.E., Death of Socrates; c. 380 B.C.E., Plato Develops His Theory of Ideas; 332 B.C.E., Founding of Alexandria.

PLUTARCH
Greek biographer

Plutarch was the greatest biographer of antiquity. He taught his successors how to combine depth of psychological and moral insight with a strong narrative that evokes the greatness and excitement of subjects' lives.

BORN: c. 46 C.E.; Chaeronea, Boeotia, Greece
DIED: After 120 C.E.; Chaeronea, Boeotia, Greece
AREA OF ACHIEVEMENT: Literature

EARLY LIFE

Plutarch (PLEW-tahrk) did not accomplish most of his writing until his late middle age. He was born in a Roman province to an old and wealthy Greek family. He received a comprehensive education in Athens, where he studied rhetoric, physics, mathematics, medicine, the natural sciences, philosophy, and Greek and Latin writing. His worldview was strongly influenced by Plato, and he took considerable interest in theology, serving as the head priest at Delphi in the last twenty years of his life. By the time he was twenty, he had rounded out his education by traveling throughout Greece, Asia Minor, and Egypt. Before his writing career began, Plutarch worked in Chaeronea as a teacher and was its official representative to the Roman governor. Later, he undertook diplomatic trips to Rome, where he befriended several important public servants.

The prestige of Greek learning stood very high in the Roman Empire, and Plutarch eventually was invited to lecture in various parts of Italy on moral and philosophical subjects. Sometime in his late thirties, he began to organize his notes into essays. There is evidence to suggest that by the time he was forty, Plutarch enjoyed a highly receptive audience for his lectures. This was a time in which the Roman emperors were particularly favorable to Greek influences.

Although Plutarch could easily have made a career of his Roman lecture tours, he returned to his home in Chaeronea at about the age of fifty. There, he served in many administrative posts with the evident intention of reviving Greek culture and religion. His principal great work, *Bioi paralleloi* (c. 105-115 C.E.; *Parallel Lives*, 1579), was written in these years when his sense of civic responsibility and leadership had matured and when he was able to draw on his considerable experience of political power.

LIFE'S WORK

In *Parallel Lives*, better known simply as *Lives*, Plutarch chose to write about historical figures. The lives were parallel in the sense that he paired his subjects, so that Alexander the Great and Julius Caesar, Demosthenes and Cicero, could be discussed in terms of each other. It was important to have a basis of comparison, to show how equally famous men had arrived at their achievements in similar and different circumstances, with personalities that could be contrasted and balanced against each other. Plutarch's aim was not merely to describe lives but to judge them, to weigh their ethical value and to measure their political effectiveness. Clearly, he believed that human beings learned by example. Thus, he would present exemplary lives, complete with his subjects' strengths and weaknesses, in order to provide a comprehensive view of the costs and the benefits of human accomplishment.

Plutarch has often been attacked for being a poor historian. What this means is that sometimes he gets his facts wrong. On occasion he is so interested in making a moral point, in teaching a lesson, that he ruins the particularity and complexity of an individual life. He has also been guilty of relying on suspect sources and of taking reports at face value because they fit a preconceived notion of his subject.

While these faults must be acknowledged and compensated for, they should not be allowed to obscure the enormous value of Plutarch's biographies. In the first place, he realized that he was not writing histories but lives and that some of his sources were questionable. Unlike the historian, he was not primarily interested in the events of the past. On the contrary, it was the personalities of his subjects that had enduring value for him. To

Plutarch. (Library of Congress)

Plutarch, there was a kind of knowledge of human beings that could not be found in the close study of events or in the narration of historical epochs. As he puts it, "a slight thing like a phrase or a jest often makes a greater revelation of character than battles where thousands fall, or the greatest armaments, or sieges of cities." Plutarch found his evidence in the seemingly trifling anecdotes about great personages. He was of the conviction that an intense scrutiny of the individual's private as well as public behavior would yield truths about human beings not commonly found in histories.

Plutarch thought of himself as an artist. He was building portraits of his subjects:

> Just as painters get the likenesses in their portraits from the face and the expression of the eyes, wherein the character shows itself, but make very little account of the other parts of the body, so I must be permitted to devote myself rather to the signs of the soul in men, and by means of these to portray the life of each, leaving to others the description of their great contests.

As the founder of modern biography, Plutarch was pursuing psychological insight. Individuals were the expressions of a society, the eyes and face of the community, so to speak. He would leave to historians the description of society, "the other parts of the body."

What makes Plutarch convincing to this day is his keen perception. No biographer has surpassed him in summing up the essence of a life—perhaps because no modern biographer has believed as intensely as Plutarch did in "the soul in men." Each line in Plutarch's best biographical essays carries the weight and significance of a whole life. It is his ability to make his readers believe that he is imagining, for example, Caesar's life from the inside, from Caesar's point of view, that makes the biographer such an attractive source that William Shakespeare and many other great authors borrowed from him.

It has often been said that no biographer can truly penetrate his or her subject's mind. Plutarch perfected a way of reading external events, of shaping them into a convincing pattern, until—like a great painting—his prose seems to emit the personality of his subject. Here, for example, is his account of Caesar's ambition:

> Caesar's successes . . . did not divert his natural spirit of enterprise and ambition to the enjoyment of what he had laboriously achieved, but served as fuel and incentive for future achievements, and begat in him plans for greater deeds and a passion for fresh glory, as though he had used up what he already had. What he felt was therefore nothing else than emulation of himself, as if he had been another man, and a sort of rivalry between what he had done and what he purposed to do.

These two long sentences, with their complex clauses, are imitative of Caesar's life itself, for they demonstrate how ambition drove him on—not satisfying him but actually stimulating more exploits. Here was a great man who had set such a high example for himself that his life had turned into a competition with itself. Plutarch manages the uncanny feat of having Caesar looking at himself and thereby gives his readers the sensation of occupying Caesar's mind.

Plutarch was by no means interested only in men of great political and military accomplishment. His pairing of Demosthenes and Cicero, for example, is his way of paying respect to mental agility and the power of the word. Both men prepared for their public careers as orators through long, careful training, but their personalities were quite different. Cicero was given to extraordinary boasting about himself, whereas Demosthenes rarely spoke in his own favor. If Cicero was sometimes undone by his penchant for joking, there was nevertheless a pleasantness in him almost entirely lacking in Demos-

thenes. That two such different men should have parallel careers is surely part of Plutarch's point. There is no single pathway in life to success or failure, and personal faults—far from being extraneous—may determine the fate of a career. Shakespeare realized as much when he based much of his *Coriolanus* (c. 1607-1608) on Plutarch's interpretation of the Roman leader's choleric character.

SIGNIFICANCE

Most of the *Lives* and its companion volume, *Ethika* (after c. 100; *Moralia*, 1603), seem to have been written in the last twenty years of Plutarch's life—precisely at that point when he was most seriously occupied as a religious official, statesman, and diplomat. It is likely that his *Moralia*, or moral reflections on life, helped to give him the worldly perspective, tolerance, and acute judgment that are so evident in his masterpiece, the *Lives*. His studies of philosophy and religion surely gave him the confidence to assess the lives from which he would have his readers learn. He died an old man in peaceful repose, recognized for his good services by his fellow Boeotians, who dedicated an inscription to him at Delphi.

It has been suggested that Plutarch was most concerned with the education of his heroes, whose stories proceeded from their family background, education, entrance into the larger world, climax of achievement, and their fame and fortune (good and bad). He exerted a profound influence on the Roman world of his time, on the Middle Ages, and on a group of important writers—chiefly Michel Eyquem de Montaigne, Shakespeare, John Dryden, and Jean-Jacques Rousseau. If his impact is less obvious in modern times, it is probably because there is less confidence in the moral patterns Plutarch so boldly delineated. What modern biographer can speak, as Plutarch did, to the whole educated world, knowing that he had behind him the prestige and the grandeur of Greek literature and religion?

—*Carl Rollyson and Lisa Paddock*

FURTHER READING

Barrow, Reginald Hayes. *Plutarch and His Times*. Bloomington: Indiana University Press, 1967. Emphasizes Plutarch's Greek background, with chapters on his role as a teacher and his relationship to the Roman Empire. The bibliography is divided between English and foreign titles. Includes map of central Greece.

Duff, Tim. *Plutarch's "Lives": Exploring Virtue and Vice*. New York: Oxford University Press, 2002. Explains how Plutarch's *Parallel Lives* offers insight into issues of psychology, education, morality, and cultural identity in ancient Greece and Rome.

Gianakaris, C. J. *Plutarch*. New York: Twayne, 1970. An excellent short introduction to Plutarch. Includes detailed chronology, discussions of all Plutarch's important works, an annotated bibliography, and a useful index. Gianakaris writes with a firm grasp of the scholarship on Plutarch, corrects errors of earlier writers, and conveys great enthusiasm for his subject.

Russell, Donald Andrew. *Plutarch*. London: Duckworth, 1973. Draws on the best English and French scholarship. Slightly more difficult than Gianakaris as an introduction. Includes chapters on language, style, and form, on the philosopher and his religion, and on Plutarch and William Shakespeare. Contains several ap-

pendices, including one on editions and translations, and a general bibliography and index.

Scardigli, Barbara, ed. *Essays on Plutarch's "Lives."* New York: Oxford University Press, 1995. Collection includes essays on Plutarch's life, his methodology; choice of subjects and sources, compositional techniques, and more.

SEE ALSO: Alexander the Great; Julius Caesar; Cicero; Demosthenes; Polybius; Tacitus.

RELATED ARTICLES in *Great Events from History: The Ancient World*: c. 594-580 B.C.E., Legislation of Solon; 483 B.C.E., Naval Law of Themistocles Is Instituted; 58-51 B.C.E., Caesar Conquers Gaul; 51 B.C.E., Cicero Writes *De republica*.

POLYBIUS
Greek historian

Through the advancement of sound historiographic methods, Polybius contributed to the development of history as a significant area of inquiry having primarily a didactic rationale.

BORN: c. 200 B.C.E.; Megalopolis, Arcadia, Greece
DIED: c. 118 B.C.E.; Greece
AREA OF ACHIEVEMENT: Historiography

EARLY LIFE

Polybius (puh-LIHB-ee-uhs) was born about 200 B.C.E. in Megalopolis, Arcadia, in Greece. He was the son of Lycortas, a prominent Achaean diplomat and political leader; nothing is known of Polybius's mother. His family's wealth was based on extensive and productive land holdings. During his youth Polybius developed an interest in biography, history, and military topics. He wrote a biography of Philopoenen, a legendary leader in Arcadia, and a military treatise, *Tactics*, which has not survived. As a young nobleman, Polybius complied with the expectation that he be trained as a warrior in order to support the policies of the Achaean League.

At the age of twenty, Polybius was named a hipparch, a commander of cavalry, in the army of the league, and he remained in that position for a decade. Shortly after 170, the fragile tranquillity of the Greek world was disrupted by the Roman war against Perseus of Macedonia. Amid this crisis, which saw a heightened Roman distrust of the various Greek states, Polybius declared his support for the Romans and offered his cavalry to assist the Roman

forces, which were under the leadership of Quintus Marcius Philippus. Not only did the Romans not accept Polybius's offer of support, which was a result of their lack of trust, but they also seized him and about a thousand other Achaeans and transported them to Italy. This episode marked a transformation in the life and work of Polybius.

LIFE'S WORK

On arriving in Rome, Polybius came under the protection of Scipio Aemilianus, a prominent Roman general who had befriended the exiled Achaean. Polybius traveled with Scipio to Spain, Africa, and southern France; they witnessed the destruction of Carthage in 146 at the close of the Third Punic War. In the same year, Polybius was in Corinth, which had been destroyed by the Romans. He exhibited effective diplomatic skills as he arranged an end to hostilities and a reasonable settlement for the Achaeans.

Throughout his travels and contacts with the Romans, Polybius developed his interest in history and formulated a plan to write a history of the emergence of Rome to a position of hegemony in the Mediterranean world. At first, he intended to conclude his work in 168 with the victory of the Romans over Perseus in the Battle of Pydna. He later decided, however, to continue the history through to the fall of Carthage and Corinth in 146. It appears that his history was published in forty books; although only the first five books have survived intact, fragments and collaborative evidence provide considerable information on the remaining thirty-five books.

In his work *The Histories* (English translation, 1889), Polybius clarified and expanded the role of the historian and the importance of the study of history. He maintained that historians must be familiar with the geography of the regions they cover, knowledgeable about the practice of politics, and informed of the appropriate documentary sources relating to their topics. Polybius viewed history as an analysis of political developments that would better equip leaders to increase political wisdom.

He advanced a philosophy of history that was based on the frequency of constitutional changes or revolutions in societies and cultures. Polybius argued that in the earliest years of a society's history, people banded together and designated a leader whose primary purpose was to provide protection for the group; the consequence of this action was the appearance of despotism. As the society expanded and the concept of law emerged, the despotism was transformed into monarchy, which eventually led to tyranny and an aristocratic reaction. The aristocratic regime yielded to oligarchy, which was then replaced by democracy. The democracy survived for a few generations until the memory of the oligarchy passed and democracy was corrupted to mob rule, during which the conditions that first resulted in the emergence of despotism were re-created. A despot would again seize power, and the politically oriented and driven process would resume. Polybius argued that Rome would be exempt from the processes of decay because of the fluid nature of the constitution of the Roman Republic.

In collecting his sources, Polybius exercised a thoroughness and discrimination that were revolutionary in the study of history. He relied heavily on the use of oral testimony; indeed, he structured the chronological limits of his study so that he could emphasize the material that he gathered from oral sources. These sources could be used as collaborative evidence and were capable of being verified. In addition to oral history, Polybius had access to and made use of a wide range of written sources. From Achaean and Roman official records to earlier histories, Polybius effectively used all the available sources.

The Histories constitute an apologia, an explanation for the emergence of Rome as the leader of the Mediterranean world. Polybius contended that Rome deserved its preeminent position because the Roman leaders and people had developed a progressive political system. The other Mediterranean peoples, Polybius believed, did not possess the realistic political worldview of the Romans and, as a consequence, lost their independence. In the development of this notion as well as others, Polybius demonstrated his concern with causation. On several occasions he discussed the concept of cause and effect and noted contrasts between the larger causes of a development and the immediate activities that resulted in it. It should be noted, however, that Polybius also ascribed to Tyche (the Greek goddess of chance) developments that were inexplicable. Throughout his writings Polybius repeated that history should be instructive,

> for it is by applying analogies to our own circumstances that we get the means and basis for calculating the future; and for learning from the past when to act with caution, and when with greater boldness, in the present.

Polybius repudiated partisan histories, such as the writings of Timaeus, the Greek antiquarian, and warned against the worthlessness of deliberately biased works. He was interested in determining the truth and, once it was determined, learning from it.

Both in his own time and in subsequent generations, critics noted the shortcomings of Polybius's style, which in many ways appears to have been as tedious as modern bureaucratic English. Polybius was repetitious, exercised a penchant for ambiguity, and developed his arguments in such an indirect fashion that his principal points were frequently submerged. Nevertheless, Polybius, along with Herodotus and Thucydides, raised the study and writing of history to a new level of serious inquiry. Polybius's emphasis on proper methodology, his vision of a universal political historical process, and his advocacy of history as a didactic art resulted in the enhancement of the Greco-Roman historical tradition. Polybius allegedly died at about the age of eighty-two in approximately 118 in Greece, as a result of injuries suffered when he was thrown from a horse.

SIGNIFICANCE

While Polybius was a leading Achaean during his lifetime and used his abilities and connections to develop an accommodation with Rome for his native Arcadia, his more significant legacy consisted of his contributions to the development of the study and writing of history. In the tradition of the earlier Greek historians Herodotus and Thucydides, Polybius considered the multitude of issues relating to historical methodology and developed an expanded notion of historical evidence. His use of oral history and his approach to collaborative evidence were significant contributions to his craft. Polybius's methodology and his concept of history influenced Roman historians such as Livy and Tacitus.

While much of *The Histories* of Polybius has been lost, the first five books provide the reader with more than a glimpse of Roman history at a time when the Mediterranean world was in a state of crisis. In this context, Polybius's contributions to the study of constitutions and political cycles should be emphasized. His thesis on the progression from despotism to monarchy to tyranny to aristocracy and then on to democracy and the return to despotism via mob rule not only advanced a historical analysis but also provided a framework for the discussion of constitutionalism.

—*William T. Walker*

FURTHER READING

Breisach, Ernst. *Historiography: Ancient, Medieval, and Modern*. Chicago: University of Chicago Press, 1994. Breisach discusses Polybius's work in the context of early Roman historiography, emphasizing his concept of political history. The author also provides a schema for Polybius's cycle of constitutional revolutions. This work constitutes one of the best single-volume reviews of historiography available. Includes an excellent bibliography.

Magie, D. *Roman Rule in Asia Minor*. New York: Arno Press, 1975. An excellent introduction to the expansion of Rome in the eastern Mediterranean, this volume provides a valuable insight into the world and writing of Polybius.

Scullard, H. H. *Scipio Africanus in the Second Punic War*. Cambridge, England: Cambridge University Press, 1930. A classic study of the Second Punic War and the emergence of Rome as the major power in the Mediterranean region. This book provides an excellent examination of Roman policy at the end of the third century.

Walbank, Frank A. *A Historical Commentary on Polybius*. 3 vols. Oxford, England: Clarendon Press, 1967-1979. This is the preeminent scholarly study of Polybius by one of the major classical scholars of the twentieth century. The work includes extensive details on Polybius, textual commentary, and criticism on *The Histories*.

_____. *Polybius, Rome, and the Hellenistic World: Essays and Reflections*. New York: Cambridge University Press, 2002. Walbank's volume, which treats the life of Polybius and his work stands as a significant contribution to biography and historiography as well as to the study of this particular historian. The work is well documented and includes a useful bibliography.

SEE ALSO: Herodotus; Livy; Scipio Aemilianus; Tacitus; Thucydides.

RELATED ARTICLES in *Great Events from History: The Ancient World*: 218-201 B.C.E., Second Punic War; 149-146 B.C.E., Third Punic War; 146 B.C.E., Sack of Corinth.

POLYCLITUS
Greek sculptor

Polyclitus was a highly accomplished sculptor, famous for his idealized depictions of the male body and for his masterpiece, a sculpture of a spear bearer, which defined the classical ideal in European art for centuries.

BORN: c. 460 B.C.E.; Argos or Sicyon, Greece
DIED: c. 410 B.C.E.; Greece
ALSO KNOWN AS: Polykleitos; Polycleitus
AREA OF ACHIEVEMENT: Art and art patronage

EARLY LIFE

Not much is known about the early life of Polyclitus (paw-lee-KLI-tuhs). Ancient sources reveal next to nothing about his family background. According to the Roman historian Pliny the Elder, Polyclitus was born at Argos, an ancient city in Southeast Greece on the gulf of Argolis in the eastern Peloponnese. Polyclitus's artistic career probably began by the late 450's B.C.E.

As a young man, Polyclitus became a student of another highly accomplished Greek sculptor, Hageladas, who also taught Phidias, the architect and sculptor of the Parthenon in Athens. From Hageladas, Polyclitus learned the intricate skills of design and how to work in marble, bronze, stone, chryselephantine (works overlaid with gold and ivory), and other media. He also studied under Pythagoras of Rhegion, another sculptor who worked in bronze. Although no work of Pythagoras of Rhegion can be identified today, historians remember him for his artistic innovations; Pythagoras is thought to have been the first sculptor to represent veins and muscle sinews in his statues, a noticeable feature of Polyclitus's masterpiece, the *Doryphorus*, or spear bearer. Pythagoras also had a deep interest in sculptural theory and was the first Greek sculptor to aim for mathematical precision, rhythm, and symmetry. A skilled craftsman like Polyclitus probably earned a good income as the Greek Mediterranean trade economy developed; some sculptors became wealthy from the demand for their art for use in commemorations and religious shrines.

LIFE'S WORK

Polyclitus became famous for working almost exclusively in bronze. All of his famous sculptures of heroes, gods and goddesses, athletes, politicians, and statesmen were made of metal except for the magnificent *Hera of Argos* (c. 423 B.C.E.), which was chryselephantine. Polyclitus excelled so highly at the art of depicting the human form that his works were considered unsurpassed by anyone in ancient Greece.

Probably around 440 B.C.E., Polyclitus set up a workshop at the shrine of Zeus and Hera at Olympia, where he produced bronze representations of victorious young athletes seen in competition. When Polyclitus first became known in the ancient world, he was making heavy and idealized statues of young, muscular gods and heroes. Just before he traveled to Ephesus to work on a new sculpture of an Amazon warrior for a temple competition, he changed his sculptural style by lengthening the limbs of his stocky figures. He started to make their appearance softer, more lifelike, and evenly proportioned. Polyclitus's statue the *Diadumenos*, or fillet binder, shows these new artistic inclinations as it depicts an athletically robust form that expresses grace, lightness, and ease. It shows the symbolic gesture of tying up the victor's hair with a ribbon after successful competition in wrestling or track and field.

At the bustling seaport of Ephesus on the southeast Ionian coast c. 435 B.C.E., Polyclitus created a statue of an Amazon warrior that was included in the Ionic Temple of Artemis (goddess of the hunt), regarded as one of the Seven Wonders of the World. This female sculpture accentuates the idea of grace combined with athleticism and power. The warrior raises her right arm upward as she gently touches the back of her head in repose, and her robe bunches up between her exposed breasts.

Legend says that five accomplished sculptors in a competition at Ephesus were asked to vote for their first and second choices for the best Amazon statue. Each of the five chose his own creation as the best, and three chose Polyclitus's Amazon for second place, so he was judged to have won. After this work, the sculpture of Polyclitus becomes lighter, less muscular, and more youthful, focusing almost entirely on adolescent male athletes. Polyclitus's experience at Ephesus must have sharpened his artistic eye for detail and softened the edge of his chisel. From the more slender and graceful sculpture of the years after 435 B.C.E. emerged much of the humanistic element in Greek art of the fourth century B.C.E. Greek sculpture before Polyclitus had been stylized and less realistic, but after *Doryphorus*, Greek sculptors such as Praxiteles carried forth the Polyclitean ideal of youthful, appropriately muscular athletes. This approach to the human figure has been the central idea of European art ever since.

Besides his work in the sculpture studio, Polyclitus also wrote a book called the *Canon* (fifth century B.C.E.) that elucidates the guiding ideals behind his art; most of the discussion of dimensions and proportions is based on his sculpture *Doryphorus*. Polyclitus's *Canon* was the most famous ancient theoretical work on art and possibly the first professional treatise on sculpture in the world. Although no complete copy survives, enough information in fragmentary quotes and allusions exists in the work of other writers to create a reasonable understanding of its content and scope. In the *Canon*, Polyclitus writes that perfection is attained little by little, through many numbers. He describes a mathematical hierarchy of human proportions in which every part of the body, from the fingers and toes through the head, neck, torso, and legs, is related to every other part using numbers. The body as a whole thus contains many mathematical relationships. Galen, a physician and medical writer states:

> Beauty does not reside in the overall ratios of the body, but in the commensurability of their individual parts, as for instance of finger to finger and of all the fingers to the metacarpus and carpus, and of these to the forearm, and of the forearm to the entire limb, precisely as is written in the "Canon" of Polykleitos, who supported his theory by producing a statue consonant with its prescriptions.

The purpose of Polyclitus's *Canon* was not only to explain the technique of an artist but also to describe "the beautiful" and "the good" in the sculpture, which was a mastery of symmetry and commensurability of each individual part to the whole. The *Canon* attempts to find an underlying pattern in a visual phenomenon, demonstrating a fascination with numbers associated with the belief that in mathematics lies the founding principles of beauty and even abstract ideas like love and justice. Ancient Greeks such as Pythagoras of Rhegion and Polyclitus explored musical harmony and remarked how the intonation needed for harmony on a stringed instrument could be translated into numbers such as 2:1, 3:4, and so forth. This caused Polyclitus to look for these patterns in nature in visual events such as the movement of the stars and planets. He thought that underlying harmonic patterns could be found throughout nature.

SIGNIFICANCE

Polyclitus was a sculptor. He was also a theoretical and practicing artist whose views were studied five hundred years later by Roman artists and historians. Polyclitus's reputation today rests largely on a single sculpture, the *Doryphorus*, which appears in almost every museum book on ancient Greek sculpture and on history of art of the ancient world. The *Doryphorus* is the pivotal statue in the development of Greek sculpture and in the evolution of Polyclitus's career. Polyclitus made Argive sculpture synonymous with dignified, minutely detailed, muscular portrayal of the strong and graceful male athlete in monumental bronze or marble. The *Doryphorus* is only preserved through Roman copies of the Greek original, and the severe, exaggerated lines of the Roman copy do not convey the subtle beauty of the original. No ancient writer describes it in detail, but fragments identify it as a nude, virile boy holding a spear, ready for athletics or warfare.

Polyclitus's masterpiece can be understood from the perspective of the harmony of opposing forces and the balance of opposites. The *Doryphorus* rests on his right leg, with his left leg slightly bent and relaxed. His right arm hangs at his side, while his left is curved upward, with fingers bent around a spear handle. This structural design brings together disparate elements by setting up cross-relationships between rigid and relaxed limbs. Known as the Greek letter *chi*, or X, the design became the standard for both Greek and Roman sculptors. The *chiastic* principle throws light on the composition of *Doryphorus*. Two lines crossing form the Greek letter chi, but the line descending right to left is straight, while the other is curved like an inversed *S*. If the letter X is imposed on *Doryphorus*, the two sides of the sculpture are opposed, with the left side as the straight side and the right side as curved. These oppositions are then balanced with the contrasts between active and passive parts of the body. The right leg is engaged and active, while the left leg is passive, relaxed, and somewhat withdrawn. The

same is true of the arms, although turned around. The same is true of the balancing of the torso, because the chest is turned toward the left, while the *Doryphorus*'s head turns toward the right. The left shoulder is lowered and balanced by the lowered right hip.

When the *Doryphorus* is compared with earlier Greek sculpture such as the *Kritios Boy*, the *contrapposto* (off-balance position with one of the opposing legs extended slightly forward) has now become more natural and emotive. The *Doryphorus* shows much more distinct differentiation between the right and left halves of the body, with every crease of skin and layer of muscle uniquely pronounced. The *Doryphorus*'s slight turn of the head and precise anatomical detail, combined with the harmonious proportions of the figure, made it renowned as the standard embodiment of the classical ideal of the human body. The *Doryphorus* became so famous to antiquity that it was simply known as the *Canon*.

The Roman historian Pliny the Elder wrote of Polyclitus's accomplishments in his *Naturalis historia* (77 C.E.; *The Historie of the World*, 1601; better known as *Natural History*):

> Polykleitos . . . made an athlete binding the diadem about his head, which was famous for the sum of one hundred talents which it realized. This . . . had been described as "a man, yet a boy"; the spear-bearer as "a boy, yet a man." He also made the statue which sculptors call the "canon," referring to it as a standard from which they can learn the first rules of their art. He is the only man who is held to have embodied the principles of his art in a single work.

—Jonathan L. Thorndike

FURTHER READING

Boardman, John. *Greek Art*. Rev. ed. New York: Thames and Hudson, 1996. Regarded as a standard work in the field of classical art, this book provides an overview of the masterpieces of ancient Greece as well as commentary on recent discoveries and controversies of interpretation surrounding the world's best-known works of art and architecture.

Carpenter, Rhys. *Greek Sculpture: A Critical Review*. Chicago: University of Chicago Press, 1960. An exploration of the evolution of sculptural style in ancient Greece, with special attention paid to the technical procedures, craftsmanship, and changing styles of the artist's craft as he seeks to emulate the human form.

Moon, Warren G. *Polykleitos, the "Doryphoros," and Tradition*. Madison: University of Wisconsin Press,

1995. Scholarly essays by eighteen experts in classical sculpture and art history, from a symposium devoted to assessing the career of fifth century Greece's most renowned sculptor, Polyclitus of Argos.

Vermeule, Cornelius. *Greek Sculpture and Roman Taste.* Ann Arbor: University of Michigan Press, 1977. Lectures on the installation of sculpture in Greek and Roman times, creative commercialism for architectural display, and literary and archaeological evidence for understanding how the Greeks and Romans displayed sculpture.

_____. *Polykleitos.* Boston: Museum of Fine Arts, 1969. A brief but highly informative introduction to the career of Polyclitus with an assessment of his accomplishment and the influence he had on Greek, Hellenistic, and Roman sculptors.

SEE ALSO: Galen; Phidias; Praxiteles; Scopas.
RELATED ARTICLES in *Great Events from History: The Ancient World*: 447-438 B.C.E., Building of the Parthenon; c. 157-201 C.E., Galen Synthesizes Ancient Medical Knowledge.

POLYGNOTUS
Greek painter

Polygnotus was the first great Greek painter. His murals at Delphi and in Athens established his reputation as the preeminent painter of the fifth century B.C.E. and probably the most famous in antiquity.

BORN: c. 500 B.C.E.; Thasos, Thrace, Greece
DIED: c. 440 B.C.E.?; Thasos or Athens, Greece
AREA OF ACHIEVEMENT: Art and art patronage

EARLY LIFE

Little is known about the early life of Polygnotus (pahl-ihg-NOH-tuhs). He was born on the Greek island of Thasos, near Thrace, and was the son and pupil of the prominent painter Aglaophon. His brother Aristophon was also an artist; a later painter named Aglaophon may have been his son or nephew. Polygnotus's family appears to have been politically active, and he may have been related to the famous seventh century poet Archilochus, whose family had colonized Thasos.

Polygnotus was already being employed as a painter, and probably also as a sculptor, for major projects on the Greek mainland during the first quarter of the fifth century. He eventually made his way to Athens, where he spent much of his life, and became the first known artistic adviser to an Athenian politician—Cimon, whom he recognized as his patron. Cimon was the dominant political figure in Athens from the late 470's to 461, and it was undoubtedly through his influence that Polygnotus became an Athenian citizen, a rare honor. Cimon's free-spirited sister, Elpinice, was Polygnotus's lover and model.

Polygnotus may have been persuaded to enter Cimon's service when the latter conquered Thasos, which had revolted from Athens and the Delian League in 465, but it is more likely that the association had begun in the previ-

ous decade. There is plausible evidence to suggest that Polygnotus helped decorate the Theseum in Athens, the shrine for the bones of the hero Theseus, which Cimon had discovered and returned to the city in the mid-470's. The relationship could have begun as early as 479, when Polygnotus was painting in a shrine commemorating the Battle of Marathon, in which Cimon's father, Miltiades the Younger, had been the hero.

LIFE'S WORK

The destruction of Athens in 479 during the Second Persian War left the city in ruins; the necessity of rebuilding and beautifying the city provided an opportunity for artists such as Polygnotus. Polygnotus's friend Cimon was responsible for an extensive building program, and the artist was actively employed in decorating Cimon's structures. The most significant of these was the Stoa Poecile (painted stoa), which was funded by Cimon's brother-in-law and probably completed by 460. Polygnotus (who may have been the artistic director for the building) and other prominent artists created a "Cimonian" picture gallery in the Stoa Poecile, choosing mythological and historical themes that could call attention to Cimon's family and his accomplishments. Like many ancient murals, these paintings were executed not directly on the walls but on wooden panels that were pinned to the walls with iron pegs.

Polygnotus was responsible for the *Iliupersis*, a mural depicting Troy fallen. The theme evoked memories of Cimon's great victory at the Eurymedon River in Asia Minor in 469, where the Athenian general had inflicted so crushing a defeat on the Persians that, at the time, it seemed as final as the legendary Greek triumph over the

Trojans. Polygnotus also used the opportunity to paint the face of Elpinice on Laodice, the most prominent Trojan woman in the mural, further indication that the mural honored Cimon.

Among other works in Athens attributed to Polygnotus was a depiction of the marriage of Castor and Pollux to the daughters of Leucippus, a painting that appeared in the sanctuary of the Dioscuri, another building associated with Cimon. In the Propylaea on the Acropolis, his murals of Achilles among the virgins on Scyros and Odysseus's encounter with Nausicaa were displayed. What he painted in the Theseum cannot be determined.

Polygnotus's greatest works were not in Athens but at Delphi, in the Cnidian Lesche (clubhouse), which had been dedicated to the god Apollo by the people of Cnidus, a Greek city in Asia Minor, soon after the Battle of the Eurymedon. In that structure, the artist painted what would become the most famous murals of antiquity—the *Iliupersis* (*Troy Fallen*), a much larger and earlier version of the painting with the same name in Athens, and the *Nekyia*, or *Odysseus's Visit to the Underworld*.

The paintings were gigantic by contemporary standards and covered the interior walls of the clubhouse, which measured 55 feet (17 meters) long and 25 feet (7.5 meters) wide. Their dozens of mythological figures, which were arranged on at least three different levels on a surface perhaps 15 feet (4.5 meters) tall, were almost life-sized, and the themes of the murals, like the themes of most of Polygnotus's paintings in Athens, related directly to Cimon—in this case, his victory at the Eurymedon. The Cnidians, devotees of Apollo, had themselves participated in the battle. They had been among the forces led by Cimon, whose fleet had departed for the final engagement from their harbors and whose triumph at Eurymedon guaranteed their freedom from further Persian domination. Nothing would have been more appropriate for them than to celebrate the victory by making an offering of thanks to Apollo at Delphi and commissioning paintings whose symbolism would reflect favorably on the god's agent at the battle—Cimon.

The fact that Polygnotus, Cimon's close friend and client, was chosen to execute the paintings in the Cnidians' clubhouse is further evidence of the political intent of the paintings—although, politics aside, the artistic merits of the two great murals were so impressive that the artist was voted free food and lodging for life by the Amphictionic Council (the "common council" of Greece). As Athens was a member of that council, the patriotic tradition that Polygnotus painted in the city without fee becomes understandable. He had no reason to charge, because Athens was already contributing to his upkeep, and, certainly, Cimon saw to it that his material needs were met.

Polygnotus's later life is largely a subject of conjecture. When Cimon was ostracized from Athens in 461, there is no reason to believe that the artist was adversely affected or forced to leave. He was, after all, an Athenian citizen. He may have continued to work on the Stoa Poecile; it is known that other artists who had worked on Cimonian projects or were close to Cimon were able to remain in Athens. One was the great sculptor Phidias, who became the intimate friend of Pericles, the man who had helped engineer Cimon's exile and became the single dominant politician in Athens after him. The Polygnotean paintings displayed in the Propylaea, built by Pericles in the 430's, may be indication that the artist stayed, though it is not known whether these murals were actually painted while Pericles was in power or were earlier works collected from other places and deposited there. When and where Polygnotus died is uncertain. He held political office on Thasos sometime after 450, as did his brother Polydorus, but whether he remained there for the rest of his life cannot be determined.

SIGNIFICANCE

Polygnotus was the first great Greek painter. A friend and client of the powerful Athenian politician Cimon, he painted murals in Athens that reflected favorably on his patron. His *Iliupersis* and *Nekyia* at Delphi were the two most famous paintings of antiquity, and their mythological themes celebrated Cimon's crushing victory over the Persians at the Eurymedon River in 469.

Polygnotus represented a break from the conventions of earlier times, freeing painting from its archaic stiffness. He did not confine his figures to a single ground line but arranged them on several levels, scattering them about at various points in space and adding landscape elements such as rocks and trees to give an additional feeling of depth.

Among other innovations attributed to him were painting women in transparent drapery, representing their heads in multicolored headdresses, depicting the mouth open and teeth showing, and more natural treatment of the face. There was an emotional quality to his work, with figures or groups of figures reacting to events. Aristotle, at least, came close to assigning Polygnotus a didactic intent, saying that he represented men as better or more virtuous than they were and was concerned with portraying good character. Later critics maintained his greatness but considered him almost a primitive, citing his simplicity of color and lack of shading. The assertion by Cicero that Polygnotus painted in only four colors is probably erroneous. He is said to have been among the first to paint with yellow ochre.

During the early years of the Roman Empire, Quintilian averred that any serious survey of art must begin with Polygnotus, and his work was considered meritorious enough over the centuries to justify frequent restorations. Pausanias the Traveler, who provides the most complete account of Polygnotus's paintings, was still impressed by them in the second century C.E., about six hundred years after they were painted. Some of Pausanius's descriptions are corroborated in the surviving work of ancient potters, who borrowed Polygnotus's themes, figure groupings, and figure poses and applied them to their own work.

—*Robert B. Kebric*

FURTHER READING

Barron, J. P. "New Light on Old Walls: The Murals of the Theseion." *Journal of Roman Studies* 92 (1972): 20-45. A detailed discussion of the murals in the Theseum in Athens, attempting to reconstruct their content and identify who painted them. A full discussion of Polygnotus's role in the decoration of this building.

Boardman, John. *Greek Art*. Rev. ed. New York: Thames and Hudson, 1996. Regarded as a standard work in the field of classical art, this book provides an overview of the masterpieces of ancient Greece as well as commentary on recent discoveries and controversies of interpretation surrounding the world's best-known works of art and architecture.

Jeffery, L. H. "The *Battle of Oinoe* in the Stoa Poikile: A Problem in Greek Art and History." *Annual of the British School at Athens* 60 (1965): 41-57. A discussion of the paintings in the Stoa Poecile, including Polygnotus's *Iliupersis*.

Kebric, Robert B. *The Paintings in the Cnidian Lesche at Delphi and Their Historical Context*. Leiden, Netherlands: E. J. Brill, 1983. This study is a complete analysis of the political content of Polygnotus's major paintings and his relationship with Cimon. The major historical and chronological questions surrounding the paintings at Delphi, in particular, are discussed fully. Includes extensive bibliography.

Meiggs, R. *The Athenian Empire*. New York: Oxford University Press, 1979. Thorough study of the Athenian Empire provides a detailed analysis of the period of Polygnotus's activity and of Cimonian Athens. Polygnotus himself is given a three-page treatment.

Pollitt, J. J. *The Art of Greece, 1400 B.C.E.-31 B.C.E.* New York: Cambridge University Press, 1990. An accessible sourcebook that contains relevant passages from ancient writers about Polygnotus and his work.

Pomeroy, Sarah B., Stanley M. Burstein, Walter Donlan, and Jennifer Tolbert Roberts. *Ancient Greece: A Political, Social, and Cultural History*. New York: Oxford University Press, 1999. This volume, beginning with early Greece and the Bronze Age, provides good background in Greek culture; the section on the growth of Athens discusses Polygnotus's style.

Robertson, Martin. *A History of Greek Art*. 2 vols. London: Cambridge University Press, 1976. This survey of ancient Greek art contains an excellent introduction to Polygnotus's art and paintings.

SEE ALSO: Cimon; Miltiades the Younger; Pericles; Phidias.

RELATED ARTICLE in *Great Events from History: The Ancient World*: 480-479 B.C.E., Persian Invasion of Greece.

POMPEY THE GREAT
Roman statesman and military leader

As a military leader and Imperial proconsul, Pompey greatly extended the bounds of the Roman Republic and, with Julius Caesar and Marcus Crassus, was one of the three leading figures whose careers and ambitions coincided with the final downfall of the Republic.

BORN: September 29, 106 B.C.E.; probably near Rome (now in Italy)
DIED: September 28, 48 B.C.E.; Pelusium, Egypt
ALSO KNOWN AS: Gnaeus Pompeius Magnus (full name)
AREAS OF ACHIEVEMENT: Government and politics, war and conquest

EARLY LIFE

Little is known of the early years of Pompey the Great, or Gnaeus Pompeius Magnus. His family rose to prominence in Rome only during the second century B.C.E. and thus was not among the ancient patrician nobility. Pompey's father, Pompeius Strabo, was an ambitious and successful general during the Social War (91-87 B.C.E.). As a result of his military success, Strabo extended his political influence, gaining many supporters, or *clientela*, whom he then used in advancing his own career.

The centuries-old Roman Republic was dominated by a number of ancient aristocratic families who ruled the state through the senate, with individuals from the plebeian class who had achieved wealth. This government had been under tension for some time, however, as it proved to be less and less suitable as Rome gained in territory. In the resulting political instability, victorious generals and their armies often played a prominent role. Strabo, like his contemporaries Gaius Marius and Lucius Cornelius Sulla, hoped to parlay his military conquests into ruling strength. Many were relieved when he died suddenly of a plague.

Pompey had served under his father during the Social War, but after the unpopular Strabo's death, he had to forge new connections in order to advance his political career. When Sulla, victorious in the east, returned to Italy at the head of his army in 83 B.C.E., Pompey raised an army from his own clients and took Sulla's part. After Sulla was elected dictator, Pompey divorced his first wife, Antistia, and married Sulla's stepdaughter, Aemilia. Through Sulla's influence, Pompey was given a military command to pursue opponents of the new regime. He did so, bloodily and efficiently, in Africa and Sicily.

After his victories, his troops hailed him *imperator* and *magnus*, but when Sulla attempted to retire Pompey, he resisted disbanding his army. He returned to Rome and demanded a triumph, a recognition of his military exploits. Sulla reluctantly granted his request, and by 80 Pompey had become one of the most significant figures in the unstable landscape of republican Rome.

Because of his handsome looks, his youth, and his military accomplishments, Pompey was compared by his contemporaries to Alexander the Great, the Macedonian king who had conquered Persia and much of the known world. However, Pompey's wars and his political machinations were directed toward placing himself among the first citizens of the Roman Republic. He was obsessively concerned with his own dignity and honor but not with absolute power for its own sake, and although he was a military hero, he often resorted to charm and tact rather than the threat of force.

LIFE'S WORK

From 80 B.C.E., when he was in his mid-twenties, until the end of his life, Pompey remained among the leading figures in the Republic. After Sulla resigned his dictatorship, there was another period of civil war, directed against Sulla's system of reformed oligarchy. Pompey supported the government against attack in Italy, and then he was awarded an important military command in Spain. From 76 to 72, he pursued Quintus Sertorius, who had fled Rome during the events that had brought Sulla to power and had subsequently established control over much of Spain. Pompey succeeded militarily and also added to his influence by increasing the number of his personal supporters, or clients, in Spain.

Pompey returned to find Italy in the throes of a slave uprising led by a Thracian gladiator, Spartacus. The Third Servile War (73-71 B.C.E.) led to several defeats of the Roman armies until Crassus took charge. Although the war was almost over when he arrived, Pompey claimed to have attained the final victory, much to the disgust of Crassus. The two rivals were elected consuls in 70 despite Pompey's youth and political inexperience; the exception was made because of his previous heroic accomplishments.

After Pompey's year as consul, he stepped down, but he remained a major figure, one of the *principes civitatis*. Then, in 67, he was granted the authority to eliminate the threat posed by pirates to Mediterranean shipping, particularly to the grain supply necessary to Roman peace and survival. Although there was considerable senate opposition to giving such power to one individual, the price of bread dropped in Rome in anticipation of Pompey's success. Beginning in the west, Pompey swept the pirates east, successfully ending the campaign in three months.

Using his still-increasing popularity and political influence, Pompey next obtained a military command against the continuing threat from Mithradates the Great, ruler of the eastern kingdom of Pontus. Again, his selection was controversial, partially because it would add to Pompey's stature and power. Turning down a peace initiative by Mithradates, Pompey pursued him ruthlessly, forcing Mithradates to retreat into the Crimea region of the Black Sea. Pompey then successfully brought the kingdom of Armenia into the Roman orbit. With the threat from Pontus and Armenia ended, Pompey turned south, into Syria, ending the Seleucid kingdom, which had been founded in the aftermath of the conquests of Alexander. He conquered Jerusalem and created a client kingdom in Judaea, as he did elsewhere in the Middle East. By the time he returned to Rome in 62, Pompey had successfully extended the boundaries of the Roman Empire almost to the Euphrates River. He had emulated Alexander and had justly earned the title of Pompeius Magnus, Pompey the Great.

In Rome, Pompey was awarded another triumph, during which he wore a cloak once worn by Alexander. By then, he was probably the richest individual in the Republic. His conquests in the east and his wealth, however, did not easily translate into political power. The senate, led by Cato the Censor, denied his demands for rewards for his soldiers and himself. To avoid even the appearance of wishing to assume dictatorial power, Pompey disbanded his armies on reaching Italy. He divorced his wife, Mucia, on grounds of adultery, and planned to marry Cato's niece, but Cato refused to accept an alliance with someone he believed was a threat to the Republic. Pompey expected honors and respect, but his return was anticlimactic.

His failure to gain senate ratification of his proposals coincided with a demand by some of Crassus's supporters for changes in the tax collection laws in the east. Pompey and Crassus had been rivals, but the senate's opposition forced the two together. Caesar, returning from campaigning in Spain, desired both a triumph in Rome and to be elected consul; his ambitions were also blocked. To gain the support of Pompey and Crassus, Caesar promised both what they had failed to receive

from the senate. By the end of 60, the somewhat misleadingly named First Triumvirate had come into being; formed for practical short-term goals, it was not intended to subvert the government of the Republic.

With Caesar as consul and with the public support of Pompey and Crassus, the desired legislation was passed. As a further reward, Caesar received a military command in Gaul. However, Pompey's popularity declined. He had returned from Asia, expecting to be accepted as Rome's principal citizen, but in order to achieve his other goals, he had been forced into an alliance with Caesar and Crassus, which cast doubt on Pompey's republican patriotism. The alliance soon began to experience difficulties in Rome because of the ambitions of others, such as Clodius Pulcher. Although Pompey had to maintain the coalition for fear that his long-desired legislation might be reversed, Caesar, concerned about the possibility of Pompey's abdication, forged a new bond between them; Caesar's daughter, Julia, was married to Pompey.

Clodius soon became Pompey's chief threat. Through his own clients and his ability to manipulate the city mobs, Clodius neutralized Pompey's authority by threatening violence. Pompey's successful solution to a grain shortage—perhaps the single greatest political issue in

Pompey the Great. (Library of Congress)

the lives of most Romans—restored much of his lost popularity by 57. When it appeared that the triumvirate might end, Pompey and Caesar met and renewed the alliance, with Pompey and Crassus becoming joint consuls for the second time in 55. They, in turn, ensured that Caesar's command in Gaul would be extended for another five years. Only with bribery and violence, however, were Pompey and Crassus able to defeat their opponents in the senate.

As a reward, Crassus gained a military command in Syria in anticipation of a war against Parthia, which would add to his fame. In Rome, Pompey sponsored a large building program, culminating in the Theatrum Pompeii, Rome's first stone-built theater. The traditionalists objected to still another departure from the republican past; again, it was rumored that Pompey wished to become dictator, and again he denied it.

By 53, the triumvirate had collapsed. Julia died in childbirth, removing one bond between Pompey and Caesar, and Crassus met death in his armies' defeat by the Parthians at Carrhae. When Pompey married again, to Cornelia, daughter of Metellus Scipio, it was an alliance not with Caesar but with another ancient family. Renewed violence in Rome bolstered Pompey's position as the only person with the necessary authority who might save the state, and even Cato, defender of the Republic, proposed that Pompey become sole consul in order to deal with the emergency.

In Gaul, Caesar desired a second consulship for himself, but he was unwilling to give up the military *imperium* to return to Rome in order to seek election. Pompey was not opposed to having Caesar stand for consul while still keeping his command in Gaul, but he supported legislation that might reduce the period Caesar could keep control of his province. Pompey stated that it was not directed against Caesar, but Pompey was still committed to maintaining his position as the first citizen. He had positioned himself so that Caesar depended on him for protection from the senate, and the senate depended on Pompey for protection from Caesar.

Pompey's position between Caesar and the senate was inherently unstable. In the summer of 50, Pompey suffered a serious illness, and public prayers and declarations of sympathy and gratitude at his recovery indicated to Pompey that his support was both wide and deep. When in December it was rumored that Caesar had already invaded Italy, Pompey was given the command to mobilize the necessary legions and defend the Republic. He hoped that a show of strength would cause Caesar to back down, ensuring Pompey's own position of superiority. Pompey became convinced that Caesar was a threat to Rome itself, but even then Pompey hoped to avoid war. Only pressure sufficient to stop Caesar, but not destroy him, would maintain Pompey's own position.

Pompey proved to be wrong on two counts: Caesar reacted more quickly than was anticipated, invading Italy in early January, 49, and Pompey's support was less than expected. In reaction to Caesar's invasion, Pompey abandoned Rome. He had not been given supreme power and continued to face the possibility of senate opposition. Both Caesar and Pompey probably wished to avoid war, but the senate, particularly Cato and his faction, opposed any compromise. In March, 49, Pompey left Italy for the east, and public opinion began to turn against him. Caesar wisely pursued a policy of clemency, and some began to claim that Pompey had intended all along to establish a dictatorship on the model of Sulla.

Pompey and a majority of the senate retreated to Greece. When Caesar later arrived in Greece, Pompey had three options: He could return to Italy ahead of Caesar, he could retreat and allow Caesar to exhaust his resources, or he could fight a pitched battle. Pompey's supporters demanded a confrontation, and on August 9, 48, both sides met at Pharsalus, where Caesar was victorious. Pompey fled to Egypt, but on the day he landed, September 28, 48, the day before his fifty-eighth birthday, he was stabbed to death. His head was presented to Caesar, and his ashes were returned to Italy.

SIGNIFICANCE

Two sons of Pompey the Great continued the struggle against Caesar. After Pompey's murder, they retreated first to Africa and then to Spain, where they had much success in an area of their father's earlier conquests. The elder, Gnaeus, however, met defeat at the hands of Caesar in 45 and was executed. The younger, Sextus, continued the family's battles and survived Caesar's assassination in 44. During the conflicts of the next decade, Sextus took sides against Caesar's heir, Augustus, and was eventually executed in 36.

The verdict on Pompey's career is divided between claims that both Caesar and Pompey sought the same thing—supreme power—and arguments that Pompey was the last of the republicans, a man who gave his life for the ideals of ancient Rome. Perhaps the best estimate is that Pompey was a man of his own time, reflecting the ambiguous politics of the late Republic, when the institutions of the past no longer proved entirely adequate. Following the example of his father and others, he used his military conquests to influence politics. He wished to be honored as the premier citizen of Rome, but it is doubtful that he ever intended to replace the senate as the governing body of the Republic. Still, Pompey's personality, his ambitions, his conquests, and his ultimate position in Roman society undoubtedly played a part in the fall of the Republic.

—*Eugene S. Larson*

FURTHER READING

Greenhalgh, Peter. *Pompey: The Roman Alexander.* Columbia: University of Missouri Press, 1981. This work carries the subject's biography to the formation of the triple alliance among Pompey, Caesar, and Crassus. The story is presented in a theatrical style, as the author is writing for the general reader.

_____. *Pompey: The Republican Prince.* Columbia: University of Missouri Press, 1982. The second and concluding volume of the author's study of Pompey. Like its predecessor, it is written in dramatic form and is especially strong on Pompey's military conquests as well as on the pageant and spectacle of Rome.

Gruen, Erich S. *The Last Generation of the Roman Republic.* Berkeley: University of California Press, 1995. An important revisionist study. The author's thesis is that there was nothing inevitable about the end of the Roman Republic and that there was no predestined decline that led to the triumph of Caesar. Instead, Gruen focuses on the continuity and the traditions of the earlier Republic, which were still viable during Pompey's era.

Leach, John. *Pompey the Great.* Dover, N.H.: Croom Helm, 1986. This brief biography praises Pompey's military abilities and accomplishments. The author also admires Pompey's political talents. Leach supposes that if Pompey had defeated Caesar, he would have more likely pursued the later path of Augustus, as *princeps*, instead of Caesar's more dangerous road to the dictatorship.

Scullard, H. H. *From the Gracchi to Nero.* Reprint. New York: Routledge, 1988. One of the standard works on the late Republic and the principate through Nero, this volume is scholarly but well written and includes considerable information on Pompey and his peers. The author's judgment of Pompey is that he excelled on the battlefield but lacked forcefulness in the political arena, always preferring glory to power.

Seager, Robin. *Pompey: A Political Biography.* Malden, Mass.: Blackwell, 2002. One of many biographies of Pompey, it is both brief and scholarly and concentrates primarily on the political and constitutional issues of the late Republic rather than on Pompey's activities and conquests in Spain and in the east.

Syme, Ronald. *The Roman Revolution.* Reprint. New York: Oxford University Press, 2002. The author of this classic work on Roman history places the actions and activities of Pompey, Caesar, and Augustus in the wider context of Roman politics, including family, clan, and faction.

SEE ALSO: Julius Caesar; Cato the Censor; Gaius Marius; Mithradates the Great; Spartacus; Strabo; Lucius Cornelius Sulla.

RELATED ARTICLES in *Great Events from History: The Ancient World*: 107-101 B.C.E., Marius Creates a Private Army; 73-71 B.C.E., Spartacus Leads Slave Revolt; 58-51 B.C.E., Caesar Conquers Gaul.

POPPAEA SABINA
Roman noblewoman

Poppaea Sabina established herself as a pivotal figure in the popular support for the regime of the Roman emperor Nero.

BORN: 31 C.E.; Pompeii, Campania (now in Italy)
DIED: 65 C.E.; place unknown
ALSO KNOWN AS: Augusta; Sabina Poppaea
AREA OF ACHIEVEMENT: Government and politics

EARLY LIFE

Poppaea Sabina (paw-PEE-ah sa-BI-nah), a woman of noble birth and financial resources, was an immensely influential figure in Nero's Imperial court. As she became an increasingly public figure, many of her decisions seem to have been driven by a desire to legitimize her position in the Imperial household. Indeed, the position and influence of Poppaea Sabina were, on more than one occasion, matters of such considerable interest to the populace at Rome that on them rested the support of the Imperial regime.

Poppaea Sabina was the daughter of Titus Ollius and the granddaughter of Poppaeus Sabinus (from whom her name was derived). Poppaeus Sabinus, as a confidant of both Augustus and Tiberius, had held the consulship and was awarded a military triumph. Her mother (also Poppaea Sabina), known for her beauty, was accused of adultery by Valeria Messallina during the reign of Claudius I and driven to suicide in prison. It is reasonable to conjecture that the examples of both her mother and Messallina early awakened the younger Poppaea Sabina to the possibilities and hazards for beautiful and powerful women in the house of the emperor.

Beyond this, almost nothing is known of the early life of Poppaea Sabina. She married Rufius Crispinus, a distinguished man of the equestrian order who had served as Praetorian Prefect under Claudius. With Rufius, Poppaea had a son, also named Rufius Crispinus, whom Nero had drowned on a fishing expedition sometime after the death of his mother. Poppaea is said to have cultivated art and learning and to have been an excellent conversationalist. Further, she was known as a beauty with a taste for the finer things. In her tours of elite Roman society, Poppaea made the acquaintance of Marcus Salvius Otho (later to be heralded as the Emperor Otho by the Praetorians in 69 C.E.), who at the time served as a close adviser to Nero. After she had a brief, clandestine affair with him, the two were legitimately married. Rufius Crispinus, for his part, continued to live in Rome and serve in the government until he was banished by Nero in 64; the allegations in the case of Crispinus's banishment are unknown, but his crime in Nero's eyes was surely his past marriage to Poppaea.

LIFE'S WORK

Nero took notice of Poppaea. Otho, having previously been most trusted by Nero, was now increasingly excluded from the emperor's inner circle. The historian Tacitus reports that Nero appointed Otho as governor of Lusitania in order to remove him as a rival for Poppaea's affections, but it is not possible to say with certainty that Nero's true goal in making Otho a provincial governor was to remove him from Rome. Otho served well in his administrative post until the death of Nero in 68. Poppaea remained at Rome after her husband's departure. An alternate story, told in Tacitus's *Ab excessu divi Augusti* (c. 116 C.E., also known as *Annales*; *Annals*, 1598) and Suetonius's "Life of Otho" (in *De vita Caesarum*, c. 120 C.E.; *History of the Twelve Caesars*, 1606), is that Nero himself may have orchestrated Otho's marriage to Poppaea Sabina in order to keep her available in the Imperial court until he was able to divorce his own wife, Octavia. Whatever the circumstances of their original introduction, Otho's affection for Poppaea was genuine; after his accession as emperor, he had statues of her restored throughout the city of Rome at public expense, despite her general lack of popularity.

Poppaea's initial effect on Nero's actions can be traced to her desire to secure her position as the legitimate wife of the emperor. At the time he fell in love with Poppaea, Nero was legally married to Octavia, daughter of Agrippina. Poppaea knew that popular support for Nero had flagged under the weight of his notorious relationship with a freedwoman named Acte and the widespread rumors that he had engaged in an incestuous relationship with his mother. She further knew that, regardless of whether the rumors of the relationship were true, Agrippina exercised a powerful control over Nero's actions.

Sensing that she would never be able to marry Nero without removing Agrippina's influence, she encouraged the emperor in a plot to murder his mother. This plot came to fruition in southern Italy when Nero invited Agrippina to join him at Baiae. Although the notorious attempt to drown her at sea in a staged shipwreck ultimately failed, she was eventually dispatched by Anicertus, commander of the fleet at Miseunum, who volunteered for this task. The story of what actually happened circulated widely among the people despite the official Imperial position that Agrippina had died after being discovered in a conspiracy to assassinate the emperor.

After returning to Rome, Nero sought to regain popular support for his regime though the introduction of entertainments and the destruction of his increasingly popular subordinates, Sulla and Plautus. After the assassinations of these two (Sulla at Massilia, or Marseilles in Gallia Narbonesnis and Plautus in Asia), the emperor felt sufficiently recovered from the scandal of Agrippina's murder and the treachery of his seditious operatives to go forward with his original intention of divorcing Octavia to marry Poppaea.

Nero at first removed Octavia from his household on the grounds that she was unable to provide him with a son, but Poppaea then suborned one of Octivia's domestics to declare that her mistress had engaged in a sexual relationship with a slave named Eucaeus. Although subsequent investigation failed to evince any more evidence than the highly suspect testimony of slaves from Octavia's house (some of whom corroborated the original accusation under torture by Nero's minister Tigellinus), the emperor nonetheless obtained an ordinary divorce under the provisions of which Octavia was to be allowed to depart with considerable property. However, the further step of banishing her to Campania under military guard was taken as an executive action by Nero and seems to have been instigated by the exhortations of Poppaea, desirous to be publicly married and to remove any possible influence from Octavia. The banishment of Octavia so offended the populace and resulted in such widespread expressions of displeasure that Nero was forced once again to recognize Octavia as his wife.

As soon as Nero's reversal of the divorce was made public, demonstrations of disdain for Poppaea Sabina erupted throughout the city of Rome. Her images were desecrated, while those of Octavia were decorated. In an excess of thanks and celebration, one mob ascended the Palatine and approached the Imperial residence to salute and thank the emperor. They were greeted by an armed guard that turned them back; it now became clear that Poppaea's influence with Nero was far from extinguished and that further outbursts of this sort would not be tolerated in the city. Octavia was not recalled from Campania, and Nero considered his options.

Driven by her own need for legitimacy and conscious of Nero's paranoia, Poppaea Sabina began to take action to establish a greater control over the emperor. She attempted to convince him that the popular uprising they had just witnessed was a precursor to a revolution that would come to fruition should Octavia ever return to Rome; the common people had begun to see in Octavia a heroine of the opposition who could lead a revolution against Nero. Persuaded by these arguments, Nero decided to bolster the claim that Octavia had engaged in an extramarital affair with a slave by manufacturing yet more compelling evidence. He enticed Anicetus, the same lieutenant who had been involved in the assassination of Agrippina, to declare that he had himself intrigued with her against the emperor. Compelled to this service, Anicetus was rewarded with a lifetime in exile on Sardinia without loss of his property. There, he would die a natural death. The crime of Octavia now sufficiently established, Nero had her banished to the island of Pandateria, where, after a short time, she was cruelly executed by Imperial decree. Only days later, Nero married Poppaea. They had a daughter they named Claudia Augusta, but she died in infancy.

Poppaea is said to have died at the emperor's hands in 65 C.E., perhaps after he kicked her in a fit of rage. Suetonius testifies that Poppaea, pregnant with a second child and also ill, had enraged Nero by complaining because he had returned home late from the races. Poppaea was given a lavish state funeral at which her corpse was burnt with a legendary amount of incense. Nero also decreed Poppaea deified, and she was thus incorporated into the state cult at Rome.

However, the people of Rome were quietly pleased when they heard of the death of Poppaea Sabina, and the reception of her demise is surely testimony to the degree of importance that she had taken on in the popular imagination. She had come to symbolize the capricious cruelty that was to be the mark of the last few years of Nero's reign. The noted senator Thrasea Paetus is said to have been conspicuously absent from Poppaea's funeral and refused to recognize her divinity. Many stories, some probably apocryphal, circulated about her lust and indulgence. The younger Pliny claims that it was well known that Poppaea kept she-goats with her at all times because she liked to bathe in their milk to enhance her beauty. Not long after Nero's death, the *Octavia* was composed. A Latin tragedy in the style of Seneca, the *Octavia* tells the story of Nero's cruelty toward his first wife following his affair with Poppaea. The image of Poppaea Sabina as femme fatale lived on in the classical tradition, again surfacing in Claudio Monteverdi's 1642 opera *L'incoronazione di Poppaea*.

SIGNIFICANCE

Poppaea Sabina caught the popular imagination in ancient Rome as the quintessence of women who stood against the traditional values of the ruling classes. For many, she came to represent the woman who is more concerned with her own needs than the affairs of the state. At the same time, she shrewdly manipulated power and influenced several of Nero's policies. The historical tradition does not treat Poppaea Sabina well, but this may, in part, reflect a growing resentment of the power wielded by women in the household of the Julio-Claudian emperors.

—*Wells S. Hansen*

FURTHER READING

Suetonius. *The Histories of the Twelve Caesars*. Translated by Robert Graves. New York: Welcome Rain, 2001. By referring to Suetonius's chapter on Nero, the reader will find much valuable information in this primary source document, which is one of history's best guides to the Julio-Claudian emperors.

Syme, R. *Tacitus*. Oxford, England: Clarendon Press, 1963. The reader should consult the index for references to Poppaea Sabina in Syme's text. Syme not only discusses the evidence from Tacitus; he also brings to bear expert knowledge of a broad variety of sources in an interesting and readable way.

Tacitus. *The Annals of Imperial Rome*. Translated by Michael Grant. New York: Penguin Books, 1996.

_____. *The Histories*. Translated by W. H. Fyfe. New York: Oxford University Press, 1999. Tacitus described the reign of Nero and role of Poppaea Sabina in two sections of his work: The first starts at *The Annals* 13.45 and the other at *The Histories* 1.13. Tacitus's prose is readable, and the comparison of his testimonies with those of Suetonius provide the reader with a good sense for some of the problems of interpretation that attend understanding the details of history in this period.

Wiedemann, T. E. J. "Tiberius to Nero." *The Cambridge Ancient History*. 2d ed. New York: Cambridge University Press, 1996. Wiedemann provides a clear examination of the political significance of Nero's relationship with Poppaea Sabina during the various stages of their involvement.

SEE ALSO: Agrippina the Younger; Arsinoe II Philadelphus; Cleopatra VII; Nero; Olympias.

RELATED ARTICLE in *Great Events from History: The Ancient World*: 64-67 C.E., Nero Persecutes the Christians.

PORPHYRY
Greek scholar and philosopher

As the devoted disciple of Plotinus, who is credited as the founder of Neoplatonic thought, Porphyry undertook to compile and edit his master's philosophical works. He also wrote extensive commentaries on Greek philosophers and on the allegorical interpretation, or exegesis, of the Homeric myths.

BORN: c. 234 C.E.; Tyre, Phoenicia (now in Lebanon)
DIED: c. 305 C.E.; probably Rome (now in Italy)
ALSO KNOWN AS: Malchus (given name); Malchos; Basileus; Porphyry of Tyre
AREAS OF ACHIEVEMENT: Philosophy, scholarship

EARLY LIFE

Porphyry (POHR-feh-ree) was born of well-to-do Syrian parents in the Phoenician city of Tyre, where he spent most of his early years. His original name was Malchus, which in the Syro-Phoenician language signifies a king. He first Hellenized his name to Basileus, the Greek word for king. Later, at the suggestion of one of his teachers, Cassius Longinus, he changed it to Porphyry, which alludes to the royal purple color of the regal garments.

Sometime in his teens, Porphyry went to Athens to continue his education. There, he attended the lectures of the erudite critic and philosopher Cassius Longinus. From Longinus, he first learned of and was influenced by the Platonism of the time. At the age of thirty, he went to Rome to become the pupil of Plotinus. He remained with Plotinus for six years, during which time he gained his confidence and respect, enjoying prolonged private discussions with him. He was entrusted by Plotinus with the arrangement and editing of his writings, the *Enneads* (c. 256-270; *The Enneads*, 1918). At the end of his six years with Plotinus, Porphyry suffered an acute depression and was contemplating suicide. Plotinus persuaded him to leave Rome. He traveled to Sicily and remained there for several years. He was in Sicily when Plotinus died in 270.

LIFE'S WORK

During his stay in Sicily, Porphyry wrote some of his most important philosophical works. He wrote commentaries on the Platonic and Aristotelian systems of philosophy, none of which survives. One of his works, the *Isagoge* (*The Introduction of Porphyry*, 1938), a commentary on Aristotle's *Categoriae* (fourth century B.C.E.; *Categories*, 1812), served as an introduction to the elementary concepts of Aristotelian logic. The *Isagoge* was translated into Latin and interpreted by the medieval philosopher and theologian Boethius. The work's views on the ontological status of universals, stated in the beginning, exercised great influence on the early medieval controversy between realism and nominalism, as well as being the subject of many commentaries. In Sicily, Porphyry also composed, in fifteen books, the polemic *Kata Christanōn* (c. 270 C.E.; *Against the Christians*, 1830). It was not a particularly philosophical work but a defensive reaction against the growing popularity of Christianity. This work was often imitated in later years, but it also provoked a number of Christian replies and brought on Porphyry much slander and verbal abuse.

Very little is known of the remainder of Porphyry's life. He returned to Rome several years after the death of Plotinus, supposedly to take over Plotinus's school. It was in Rome that he edited the works of Plotinus, wrote his biography, and gained a reputation as teacher and public speaker by his expositions of Plotinus's thought. At the advanced age of seventy, c. 304, he married Marcella, the widow of a friend with seven children. As he states in *Pros Markellan* (*Porphyry, the Philosopher, to His Wife, Marcella*, 1896; better known as *Ad Marcellam*), the letter he sent to his wife while on a trip away from home, they married so that he could help to raise and educate her children.

Porphyry was very successful in popularizing the thought of Plotinus and in expounding it in a clear, concise, comprehensible manner. It was the Porphyrian version of Neoplatonism that influenced Western thought, both pagan and Christian, until the ninth century. His views are basically those of his master Plotinus. History does not credit Porphyry with any original views. Still, Porphyry did not follow Plotinus slavishly. The main emphasis of his thought was on the salvation, or ascent, of the individual soul, and he wanted to find a universal way

of salvation that could be practiced by all individuals. Thus, he placed a greater emphasis on the moral and ascetic aspects of Neoplatonism, was much more interested in the popular religious practices than his master, and introduced the idea of theurgy into Neoplatonism. Porphyry's views on the ascent of the soul are found in the following works: *Aphormai pros ta noēta* (*Auxiliaries to the Perception of Intelligible Natures*, 1823; better known as *Sententiae*), a disjointed collection of ideas; *Peri apochēs empsychōn* (*On Abstinence from Animal Food*, 1823; better known as *De abstinentia*), a treatise defending vegetarianism; and the *Ad Marcellam*, which deals with the practice of virtue and self-control.

Like Plotinus, Porphyry believed that the soul of an individual is of divine origin and has fallen into matter—the body. While in the body, the soul must purify itself by turning its attention from the bodily and material things to contemplation of the absolute supreme deity—the One, or God. Contemplation, or love of God, cannot be combined with concern for or love of the body. Thus, the soul must purify itself by liberating itself from the bonds of the body. This liberation is not attained by death only but by freeing the soul from its bodily concerns. The soul's purification is achieved through the practice of the virtues. Systematizing Plotinus's treatise on the virtues, Porphyry classifies them into four main types: the political (or civic), the purifying, the contemplative, and the paradigmatic. The political/civic and purifying virtues are acquired on the conscious level, while the soul is still aware of and concerned with matters of the material world, and are preparatory to the other virtues, which are acquired purely through the intellect, when the soul has entered the realm of true being or intellect.

The first and lowest class of virtues, the political/civic, produce moderation and free the soul from excessive bodily concern and indulgences, tempering the individual's behavior toward his fellow humans. Mastery of that leads to the purifying virtues. These virtues completely free the body from all bodily and material attachments and lead the soul toward contemplation of true being. Porphyry believed that the soul's purification and ascent were facilitated by the practice of asceticism. In *De abstinentia*, he stressed the abstinence from animal food, as well as from all external pleasures and desires, and the practice of celibacy. At the third stage of the ascent, the soul is directed toward the world of the intellect, is filled by it and guided by it; the soul has realized its true self, its divinity. Finally, in the fourth and last stage, the soul completely discards all the qualities of a mortal or material nature and its affection for them and becomes pure intellect, living by reason alone and becoming one with the supreme being: God.

Porphyry believed that philosophy was the best means by which the soul could achieve salvation. However, he realized that the discipline of philosophy as a means of salvation was not possible for all. His interest in and search for a universal way of salvation common to all nations and levels of humankind led him to accept external aids that would lead an individual to that end. He acknowledged the religious practices, rites, and superstitions of the popular polytheism of the time and accepted their gods as symbols, giving their myths an esoteric interpretation. Unlike his master, Plotinus, he upheld the worship of the national gods, claiming that it is important to show respect for the ancient religious practice of a nation.

The early centuries of the Christian era were times of increasing insecurity and anxiety that led individuals to long for salvation, a release from the misery and failure of human life. People turned to the practice of magic and the utterances of the oracles or inspired prophets for answers to their everyday concerns and solutions to their spiritual needs. Astrology and the mystery cults with their purification rites, their enthusiasm and ecstasy, and their rewards of immortality through deification enjoyed immense popularity. The Chaldaean Oracles in particular, composed about 200 C.E. in hexameter verse, were purported to be a divine revelation containing both a theology and a way of salvation communicated by the gods through an entranced medium or prophet. They presented a sure method of salvation through ritual magic, by means of which a divine force could be incarnated in a human being, resulting in a state of prophetic trance.

This approach to salvation and union with the divine was known as theurgy. Porphyry acknowledged theurgy as an alternative approach to salvation. Theurgy became one of the major influences in the development of later Neoplatonism from the time of Porphyry to the eleventh century. Porphyry believed that theurgy had some validity and in some way connected the individual with the gods—but only on the lower, or conscious, level. Remaining basically loyal to the philosophy of Plotinus, Porphyry maintained that it is only philosophy that can lead the soul to final union with God.

SIGNIFICANCE

Although Porphyry has been considered an unoriginal and uncritical thinker, his contributions to learning are far from insignificant. He had an insatiable intellectual curiosity and thirst for knowledge that led him to delve into and become well-versed in many subjects. In addi-

tion to the preservation and intelligible interpretation of Neoplatonism, his main contribution, Porphyry wrote on numerous and varied subjects: rhetoric, grammar, numbers, geometry, music, philology, and philosophy. History credits him with seventy-seven titles. Unfortunately, many of his works are either no longer extant or available only in scanty fragments. Being a detailed scholar, he quotes his authorities by name in his works and thus has preserved numerous fragments of scholarship that otherwise would not have been maintained.

His *Isagoge* became a standard medieval textbook of logic. Of his non-philosophical works, *Homērika zētēmata* (*The Homeric Questions*, 1993) is considered a milestone in the history of Homeric scholarship concerning the meaning and exegesis of the Homeric works and reveals his vast knowledge of the epics. The essay on the Homeric cave of the nymphs in the *Odyssey* (c. 725 B.C.E.; English translation, 1614) is an excellent example of the type of mystical allegorizing of the Homeric epics that was prevalent at the time and is the oldest surviving interpretive critical essay.

In the field of religion, his polemic against the Christians is a study in biblical criticism that was not equaled until modern times, and he anticipated modern scholars in discovering the late date of the biblical Book of Daniel through sound historical scholarship. Although the text was condemned by the Christian church in 448, sufficient fragments remain to show Porphyry's expert knowledge of Hebrew and his wide and accurate knowledge of both Hebrew and Christian Scriptures. Applying the standards of historical criticism to the Scriptures, he denied the authenticity and prophetic character of the Book of Daniel, disputed the authorship of the Pentateuch, and pointed out the discrepancies within the different Gospel narratives and the Epistles of Saint Paul. He is believed to have been the first individual to apply the rules of historical criticism to the Scriptures.

Porphyry stands at the end of the creative phase of Greek philosophical thought. After him, Neoplatonism became more a religion than a philosophy. In an attempt to rescue pagan religion and culture from the overwhelming strength of Christianity, Neoplatonism sacrificed Greek rationalism for occult magico-religious practices that were meant to secure the salvation of the soul.

—*Antonia Tripolitis*

FURTHER READING

Lamberton, Robert. *Homer the Theologian*. Berkeley: University of California Press, 1986. Contains an ex-

cellent study of Porphyry's work on the Homeric ep-
ics. It analyzes in detail the surviving fragments of
Homērika zētēmata and presents an in-depth study of
Porphyry's essay on the cave of the nymphs.

Porphyry. *Neoplatonic Saints: The Lives of Plotinus and
Proclus by Their Students*. Translated by Mark Edwards. Liverpool: Liverpool University Press, 2000.
A major source of information for the life of Porphyry, this work is primarily a biography of Plotinus.
However, it contains many facts of Porphyry's early
life and discusses his association with Plotinus and
with Cassius Longinus. It also presents an interesting
profile of Porphyry's personality.

_____. *On the Cave of the Nymphs*. Translated by
Thomas Taylor. Grand Rapids, Mich.: Phanes Press,
1991. An example of Porphyry's method of allegorically interpreting the poetic mythology current at that
time. The work is a mystical interpretation of the cave
of the nymphs in Homer's *Odyssey*.

_____. *Porphyry, the Philosopher, to His Wife, Mar-
cella*. Translated by Alice Zimmern. London: George
Redway, 1896. An old work, but invaluable. It is the
only translation of Porphyry's *Ad Marcellam* in English. The lengthy introduction, comprising more
than half of the book, includes a summary of the development of Neoplatonism, a review of Porphyry's
emphases, and a discussion of the letter to Marcella,
showing its religious character and its emphasis on
the practice of virtue.

Smith, Andrew. *Porphyry's Place in the Neoplatonic
Tradition*. The Hague, Netherlands: Martinus Nijhoff,
1974. A study in post-Plotinian Neoplatonism. It
presents an analysis of Porphyry's views of the soul
and its means of salvation and compares them with
those of Plotinus and Iamblichus, Plotinus's pupil and
successor. Includes an extensive bibliography of ancient and modern sources and an appendix listing the
works of Porphyry relevant to the doctrine of the soul.

SEE ALSO: Homer; Saint Paul; Plato; Plotinus.
RELATED ARTICLES in *Great Events from History: The
Ancient World*: c. 750 B.C.E., Homer Composes the *Iliad*; c. 380 B.C.E., Plato Develops His Theory of Ideas;
c. 335-323 B.C.E., Aristotle Writes the *Politics*; 325-
323 B.C.E., Aristotle Isolates Science as a Discipline;
c. 300 B.C.E., Stoics Conceptualize Natural Law.

POSIDONIUS
Greek philosopher

*Though virtually none of his writings survives, it is
clear that Posidonius was one of the most influential
thinkers of the ancient world. He made important
contributions in the fields of philosophy, history,
astronomy, mathematics, natural history, and
geography.*

BORN: c. 135 B.C.E.; Apamea ad Orontem, Syria
DIED: c. 51 B.C.E.; place unknown, possibly Rhodes
   (now in Greece)
AREA OF ACHIEVEMENT: Philosophy

EARLY LIFE

Posidonius (pohs-ih-DOH-nih-uhs) was born in Syria
around 135 B.C.E. Some ancient writers refer to him as
"The Apamean," from his birthplace in Syria, which, at
that time, was part of the Roman Republic. This vast
nation had greatly facilitated the international exchange
of knowledge. The dominant philosophy that emerged
was Stoicism, named for the Stoa Poecile (the "painted
porch") of the building in Athens where the originators
of the doctrine taught. The earliest expression of Stoic
philosophy comes from Zeno of Citium (c. 335-261) in
Cyprus and Cleanthes of Assos (c. 331-c. 232) in Asia
Minor; they were of the Early Stoa, the first period of this
doctrine, which lasted from 300 B.C.E. to the beginning of
the second century B.C.E. The thinkers of the Middle Stoa
introduced this philosophy to Roman culture during the
second and first centuries B.C.E. Panaetius of Rhodes
(185-109) and his prize student, Posidonius, were the
most important figures of the Middle Stoa. Though Stoicism was to remain the dominant philosophy until the
second century C.E., Posidonius was the last of the Greek
Stoic philosophers.

Posidonius left his home country early in his life and
traveled to Athens, where he studied philosophy under
Panaetius. After his teacher died in 109, Posidonius traveled for several years throughout North Africa and the
western Mediterranean region, including Spain, Italy,
and Sicily. During these travels he conducted extensive
scientific research. He returned to Greece and settled in
Rhodes, the largest island in the Dodecanese group, off
the southwest coast of Asia Minor. In Rhodes, he was ap-

pointed head of the academy that he would later make the center of Stoic philosophy. Posidonius also became involved in local politics and influenced the course of legislation on more than one occasion. In 87 the Rhodians sent him as an envoy to Rome with the charge of appeasing Gaius Marius. The result of this visit was that Posidonius developed an extreme dislike for Marius and later heavily criticized him in his historical writings.

The Stoic philosophy that Posidonius studied at Athens and taught at Rhodes consisted of three domains of concern: logic, physics, and ethics. Stoic logic included the study of grammar but emphasized the formal nature of reasoning, that is, relations between words, not between words and what they stand for. The relations in rational discourse (as studied by logic) were regarded as reflecting the processes of the cosmos (as studied by physics).

The dominant theme of Stoic physical theory was that the universe is an intelligent living being. The physical theory of the Stoics was equivalent to their theology, for the rational totality was equated with God, Zeus, the logos, or the ordering principles of the universe (all these terms being synonymous within their philosophy). In the physical theory of the Stoics, matter is inert or passive and is acted on by God, the rational active cause. All gradations of being in the universe were regarded as having been formed by this action. According to this philosophy, the action of the rational cause on the matter is cyclical. Throughout the aeons, each cycle begins with the pure active cause organizing the four fundamental elements and ends with a universal conflagration in which all created matter is consumed and the totality reverts to its purified state. Stoic ethical doctrines were perhaps the most famous element of their philosophy and were connected to their cosmological conceptions.

The basic precept of the Stoic ethical system was to live according to the order of the universe. The ultimate goal of ethical action was to achieve self-sufficiency, the only guarantee of happiness. Happiness was regarded as possible only through that which was entirely within the individual's control, and this state was to be achieved through the practice of the virtues. The most important of the virtues were wisdom, courage, justice, and self-control. The Stoics emphasized two ways of acquiring the virtues: the imitation of exemplary lives and the study of ethics and physics.

It was in the context of these broad doctrines that Posidonius developed his conceptions of humankind and the universe. Though only a few fragments of Posidonius's writings have survived, he is mentioned by more

Posidonius. (Library of Congress)

than sixty ancient writers, and it is through their comments that scholars have been able to reconstruct his philosophy. He is mentioned primarily in the works of Cicero, Strabo, Seneca, and Galen.

Posidonius differed from the Stoic tradition in which he was educated in his concern with empirically oriented scientific investigations. He did, however, adhere to the Stoic division of philosophy into the branches of logic (or dialectics), ethics, and physics. His teacher, Panaetius, admired Plato, and it was with the development of Posidonius's philosophy that the influence of Plato on Stoicism truly began. Posidonius also emphasized his agreement with the doctrines of Pythagoras, and, in general, he argued for the reconciliation of all opposing philosophies.

LIFE'S WORK

While developing his own version of Stoic philosophy at his academy in Rhodes, Posidonius became quite famous. In 78, the famous Roman orator Cicero attended his school. In fact, Cicero requested of Posidonius that he edit his account (in Greek) of the conspiracy of Catiline. Posidonius declined the request.

Posidonius's most famous visitor was the Roman general Pompey the Great, who visited Posidonius's school on two different occasions in order to attend lectures: in 72, when Pompey returned from the eastern part of the Empire after action in the Mithradatic War, and again five years later, after a victorious campaign against pirates in the Mediterranean Sea. As a gesture of respect for the great philosopher, Pompey ordered his officers to lower their fasces (bundles of rods with axes in them, which were used as scepters by Roman leaders) at the door of Posidonius's school. Posidonius greatly admired Pompey and added an appendix to his *Histories* (now lost), which was devoted exclusively to Pompey's campaigns in the East.

Posidonius's history of the world began with the year 146 B.C.E. (the point at which the famous history of Polybius ended) and continued up to the dictatorship of Lucius Cornelius Sulla around 88 B.C.E. Virtually none of this work has survived, but its influence was tremendous, both at the theoretical level (that is, in the conception of history) and in terms of the sheer mass of factual information that the work contained. All the following historians were influenced by it: Sallust, Julius Caesar, Tacitus, Plutarch, Timagenes, Pompeius Trogus, and Diodorus Siculus.

Posidonius's *Histories* was noteworthy for including the histories of the Eastern and Western peoples with whom the Romans had come into contact, such as the Germans and the Gauls. His study of primitive cultures led him to hypothesize that these cultures represented the original state of the more advanced cultures. The work was written from a standpoint that favored the nobility and opposed the Gracchi and the equestrian party. It was also opposed to the independent Greeks, who were supported by Mithradates. In short, the work was strongly pro-Roman, and in it Posidonius attempted to show that Roman imperialism embodied the commonwealth of all humankind and ultimately reflected the commonwealth of God. To this latter commonwealth only those statesmen and philosophers who had lived worthy lives were to be admitted after their stay on earth. In addition, Posidonius argued that lesser civilizations should accept and even welcome Roman domination for the sake of their own self-betterment. This theory had a tremendous influence on Cicero and provided the foundations for the eventual development of the doctrine of natural law.

Posidonius's conception of the history of the human race was intimately linked to his conceptions of ethics. Politics and ethics were fused within his system, as political virtue consisted in attempting to bring back the natural condition of humanity. In this condition, the philosopher-statesman apprehends the world of God (from which morality is derived) and conveys this vision to the rest of humanity living solely in the material world. Morality and religion were fused in Posidonius's view, as any moral or political duty was also a religious duty. In a work titled *On Duty*, Posidonius argued that by adhering to duty, the philosopher-statesman gained knowledge of the spiritual world and freedom and was prepared for the superior forms of existence after death. The highest state to be achieved by a person in this life was regarded by Posidonius as contemplation of the truth and order of the universe (without distraction by the promptings of the irrational part of the soul). Posidonius parted with Stoic orthodoxy on the connection between virtue and happiness, however, and argued that the former was not a sufficient condition for the latter and that external bodily goods were also needed to achieve happiness.

Posidonius also made modifications of Stoic psychological doctrines. The most significant of these was his reaffirmation, in *On the Soul*, of the division of the soul into rational and irrational parts (the latter being the source of the emotions and appetites). Stoic tradition held to the essential unity of the soul. Posidonius claimed, in *On Emotion*, that the emotions of the irrational part of the soul have two distinct origins: the body, and judgments of good and evil. He took as evidence for this view the fact that animals, which are irrational creatures, experience emotion. This doctrine also parted from the standard Stoic conception of emotion as based solely on false judgments about good and evil. In this theory, Posidonius drew a connection between the union of the soul and the body and the external influences on that union. He argued that some conditions of the human being are predominantly bodily, whereas others are predominantly spiritual or mental. Some influences pass from the body to the soul, and others pass from the soul to the body. He based a system of character on the idea that permanent modifications of character can be caused by certain bodily organizations.

More fundamental aspects of Posidonius's psychology are contained in his metaphysical system, in which he followed the standard Stoic conception of two fundamental principles governing the universe: the passive principle (matter) and the active principle (God). God, for Posidonius, did not create the human soul, though the soul was believed to be composed of the same stuff out of which the heavenly bodies are composed. As a result, on the death of the body the soul "escapes" and returns to the heavens. In addition, for Posidonius, God was not the creator of matter, and matter was endowed with its own form and quality. The divine principle merely shaped and modeled this matter (that is, God does not endow matter with form). As part of this cosmology, Posidonius posited, in *On Heroes and Daemones*, the existence of beings that were intermediary between God and human. These beings were regarded as immortal and were revealed to mortals in visions, divinations, and oracles. Posidonius also regarded the gap between reason and matter as bridged by mathematical forms. Of all the Stoics, only Posidonius was a realist with regard to mathematical entities. In *On the Void*, he argued that the vacuum beyond the universe was not infinite (a standard Stoic conception) but only large enough to allow for the periodic dissolution of the universe. He also argued that the end of the universe would occur not by fire but by this dissolution.

Among the scientific achievements of Posidonius that were related to his metaphysics was his construction of a model of the celestial system. This planetarium allowed the apparent motions of the sun, moon, and planets around the earth to be exhibited. An important inference he made concerning astronomy, in a work titled *On the Sun*, was that the sun is larger than the earth because the shadow cast by the earth is conical. He rejected the heliocentric conception of the solar system in favor of a geocentric conception. He also succeeded in calculating the distance between the earth and the sun at 502 million stadia (one stadium equals approximately 600 feet, or 183 meters). The diameter of the sun he calculated at 4 million stadia, and the circumference of the earth at 180,000 stadia, figures that were generally accepted by thinkers in his day. Posidonius also considered the moon to be larger than the earth and to be composed of matter that is transparent. Because of the moon's size, light does not pass through it during eclipses. In another work on astronomy, *On Astronomical Phenomena*, Posidonius argued that the Milky Way is composed of igneous material and is intended to warm those parts of the universe that the sun cannot warm. This view was also widely accepted by other thinkers. He had collected considerable geographical data on his various travels, and in *On the Ocean* he charted the currents of the ocean and pointed out the connection between the tides and the moon. In about 51 B.C.E., Posidonius left Rhodes on another trip to Rome,

where he died soon after his arrival. On his death, the school in Rhodes was taken over by his grandson Jason.

SIGNIFICANCE

Posidonius had an extremely influential personality—he was reported to have a good sense of humor and was known as a man of dignity. He also developed a reputation as the most learned man in the world and was especially known for his dialectical skills, shrewd powers of observation, and love of poetry. Though he was extremely influential in his own time and for two centuries afterward, his writings disappeared at some point, and he is not mentioned after the second century C.E. Virtually all the important Roman philosophers and historians were influenced by Posidonius. His disciples and students included Phanias, Asclepiodotus, C. Velleins, C. Cotta, Q. Lucilius Balbus, and perhaps Marcus Junius Brutus. His influence on thought in the ancient world has been compared to that of Aristotle. He was the last compiler of the Greco-Roman heritage, furthered the development of Greek rationalism, and was influential in the development of Neoplatonism. Nevertheless, from the Renaissance through the nineteenth century, Posidonius was considered to be only a minor figure in the history of Stoicism. It was not until the beginning of the twentieth century that his influence was attested and classicists began to discover references to Posidonius in many of the writings of his time.

—Mark Pestana

FURTHER READING

Dobson, J. F. "The Posidonius Myth." *Classical Quarterly* 12 (1918): 179-191. Attacks the source criticism method of assessing Posidonius's influence, suggesting that Posidonius's achievements have been exaggerated.

Edelstein, Ludwig. "The Philosophical System of Posidonius." *American Journal of Philology* 57 (1936): 286-325. Reconstructs the philosophical system of Posidonius from the existing fragments. Written by the foremost authority on Posidonius of the twentieth century.

Kidd, I. G. "Posidonius on Emotions." In *Problems in Stoicism*, edited by A. A. Long. London: Athlone Press, 1971. Contains a detailed analysis of Posidonius's modification of the standard Stoic conception of the emotions.

Mattingly, John Robert. "Cosmogony and Stereometry in Posidonian Physics." *Osiris* 3 (1937): 558-583. Contains an extensive explication of the cosmological system developed by Posidonius.

Posidonius. *Fragments, Volume 1*. Translated by I. G. Kidd. 1972. Rev. ed. New York: Cambridge University Press, 1989. This edition contains sixty new readings, nearly eighty alterations to the apparatus criticus, corrections of errors, and cross-references to recently published works.

_____. *Fragments, Volume 2: Commentary*. Translated by I. G. Kidd. New York: Cambridge University Press, 1992.

_____. *Translation of the Fragments, Volume 3*. Translated by I. G. Kidd. New York: Cambridge University Press, 1999. The translations are accompanied by contextual introductions and explanatory notes, and a general introduction assesses the importance of Posidonius and his contribution. The order of fragments follows exactly that of the ancient texts collected and edited by L. Edelstein and I. G. Kidd in Posidonius Vol. 1 and completes (with Vol. 2, Commentary) what has become the definitive modern edition.

Rist, John Michael. *Stoic Philosophy*. Cambridge, England: Cambridge University Press, 1977. Contains a chapter devoted to the ethical system of Posidonius.

Solmsen, Friedrich. *Cleanthes or Posidonius? The Basis of Stoic Physics*. Amsterdam, Netherlands: Noord-Hollandsche Uitg. Mij., 1961. The best available discussion of the relative influence of Cleanthes and Posidonius on developments in Stoic thought concerning science and the relation between science and the cosmos.

SEE ALSO: Cicero; Gaius Marius; Plato; Polybius; Pompey the Great; Pythagoras.

RELATED ARTICLES in *Great Events from History: The Ancient World*: c. 300 B.C.E., Stoics Conceptualize Natural Law; 107-101 B.C.E., Marius Creates a Private Army; Late 63-January 62 B.C.E., Catiline Conspiracy; 51 B.C.E., Cicero Writes *De republica*.

PRAXITELES
Greek sculptor

The subtle expression of personal emotions, such as tenderness and laziness, through marble statuary is the trademark of Praxiteles. His most famous work, a rendering of the Aphrodite of Knidos, established Western civilization's standard of perfection in the female figure.

BORN: c. 370 B.C.E.; Athens, Greece
DIED: c. 330 B.C.E.; place unknown
AREA OF ACHIEVEMENT: Art and art patronage

EARLY LIFE

Although very little is known of his early life, Praxiteles (prak-SIHT-uhl-eez) came from a long line of Greek sculptors. His grandfather and father were both sculptors, as were his two sons and perhaps a nephew. At least seven of the line were also named Praxiteles.

Praxiteles' father was the Athenian sculptor Kephisodotos (sometimes spelled Cephisodotus), whose most famous sculpture is titled *Peace and Wealth*. The original statue, which was probably erected soon after Athens's victory over Sparta in 375 B.C.E., depicts a mother, the goddess Peace, fondly holding her infant son, Wealth. The tenderness of the mother and the playfulness of the child display a marked departure from earlier Greek statues, which expressed such public virtues as courage and

honor. Also, the subject, a family scene, is very different from the usual subjects of Olympian gods and heroic humans. Praxiteles carried on and far surpassed the subtler, intimate tradition established by his father.

In addition to *Peace and Wealth*, Kephisodotos carved another statue, *Hermes Carrying the Infant Dionysus*, which had a more direct effect on the son. Kephisodotos's *Hermes* and Praxiteles' *Hermes* share both subject matter and arrangement. Although the original is lost, the fact that there are several Roman copies attests the popularity of Kephisodotos's statue. On the other hand, most historians agree that the *Hermes* found in the Olympia excavations is indeed the original work of the son. Fortunately, the condition of the statue is quite good, as it is missing only the right forearm and the two legs below the knee. Because the *Hermes* is the most muscular of Praxiteles' known statues, it is probably an early work. The smooth, sensuous young men appear to belong to a later period, during which Praxiteles was sculpting his famous female figures.

No statues of Praxiteles can be dated with absolute certainty, but his major works were carved between about 370 and 330. Early, dated works include portions of the *Altar of Artemis* at Ephesus, which was begun around 356, and the *Artemis at Brauron*, around 346.

LIFE'S WORK

Although ancient writers mention almost sixty works by Praxiteles, the surviving originals include only three heads and the major portion of one statue, the aforementioned *Hermes*. The *Hermes* was found on May 8, 1877, at the temple of Hera at Olympia. In Greek legend, Hermes, the messenger of the gods, is charged with taking young Dionysus back to the nymphs of Crete. Dionysus is a great embarrassment to Zeus, as the baby is the result of Zeus's indiscretion with a human woman. In banishing Dionysus to Crete, Zeus hopes to escape the jealousy of his wife, Hera. In Praxiteles' conception, the statue is a masterpiece of psychological complexity. Hermes, gazing tenderly at the young god, is clearly in no hurry to leave Olympus. Leaning lightly against a tree, he has placed the babe in his left arm and amuses himself by dangling in his right hand something, probably a bunch of grapes, for Dionysus. The fact that the infant Dionysus, who is eagerly grabbing at the grapes, will grow up to be the god of wine and intoxication is evidence of Praxiteles' urbane sense of humor.

Another statue that illustrates the Praxitelean sense of humor is the *Apollo Sauroctonos*, or *Lizard Slayer*. Here Praxiteles makes fun of the Greek legend in which the fierce young sun god Apollo slays Pythus, a fire-breathing dragon, in order to win control of Delphi. Leaning dreamily against a tree trunk and holding an arrow in his right hand, Praxiteles' Apollo seems to have barely enough energy to swat an everyday lizard that is climbing up the trunk. While the original bronze statue is lost, reproductions occur on the coins of several city-states and in several Roman replicas, notably a marble statue in the Louvre and one in the Vatican.

Related to the *Lizard Slayer* in stance is the *Satyr*. Both statues bear Praxiteles' personal stamp. In fifth century statuary, satyrs were savage half-goat, half-man beasts with large tails and devilish eyes. Praxiteles' satyr is instead a strong and active youth with pointed ears and a small stub of a tail. There is in his face, however, a strong sensual expression that suggests that some of the old animal instinct still lingers.

The original *Satyr* of Praxiteles, which stood in a temple of Dionysus at Athens, was a favorite collector's piece among the Romans, as more than seventy copies still exist. One of the best is the copy in the Capitol Museum in Rome. It is this statue that Nathaniel Hawthorne saw in 1858 and that inspired him to write his novel *The Marble Faun* (1860). Hawthorne, intrigued by the possibility of a real man who actually embodied all the characteristics he saw in the faun, or satyr, created a character whose combination of total innocence and animalistic instincts made him unprepared to exist in the real world. The Louvre has a fragmentary version of the *Satyr*, but the execution of that statue is generally considered to be quite good. A few writers have theorized that it might be the original. Although the *Satyr* in the Capitol is complete, it is clearly a Roman copy.

Evidence that the *Satyr* was one of Praxiteles' personal favorites is related by the ancient historian Pausanias. According to the story, Phryne, Praxiteles' mistress, asked for the most beautiful of the sculptor's works.

Praxiteles' Hermes with Infant Dionysus. (Archivo Iconografico, S.A./Corbis)

Praxiteles agreed, but he refused to say which one of his works he thought the most beautiful. Phryne secretly arranged for one of her slaves to run in and declare that Praxiteles' studio was on fire. On hearing the news, Praxiteles ran for the door, claiming that all of his labor was lost if the flames had taken the *Satyr* and *Eros*.

Phryne chose the *Eros*, god of love, and gave it to her native town of Thespiae in Boeotia. This statue made Thespiae famous. Unfortunately, the very popularity of the statue may have led to its destruction. Pausanias explains that the Roman emperor Caligula took it, but when Claudius I assumed power, he restored the sacred statue to Thespiae. Then Emperor Nero took it away a second time. Pausanias believes that the *Eros* eventually perished by fire in Rome. On the other hand, some art historians theorize that the *Eros* of Thespiae may survive in a headless statue that was excavated from the Palatine in Rome and is now held in the Louvre. Others have speculated that a torso in the Museum of Parma may, in fact, be the original.

What is certain is that the *Eros* once more illustrates Praxiteles' distinctive style. As Greek legend developed over the centuries, the character of Eros grew younger. In his poem *Theogonia* (c. 700 B.C.E.; *Theogony*, 1728), Hesiod describes Eros as one of the oldest gods. In that version, Eros comes into existence before Aphrodite and even accompanies her at her birth from the sea to Mount Olympus. After Praxiteles, third century artists would conceive of Eros as the child of, rather than the companion to, Aphrodite. Eventually, the child becomes a mischievous, winged baby, the Cupid on a Valentine's Day card. In the Praxitelean conception, Eros stands between those surface interpretations. He is a delicate, dreamy youth, symbolizing the power of love to capture the soul, a fitting gift from the artist to his mistress.

All the works thus far discussed have been statues depicting male figures. However, it is Praxiteles' conception of the female form for which he is best known and most admired. His most celebrated work was the *Aphrodite of Knidos*, for which Phryne was the model. About 360, the city of Kos commissioned the sculptor to carve an Aphrodite, but the citizens were scandalized when they found that their statue of Aphrodite was nude. Praxiteles then made a clothed goddess of love, but the city of Knidos (sometimes spelled Knidus or Cnidus) was delighted to buy the nude *Aphrodite*. It was an enormously popular statue. Tourists came from all over the Mediterranean region to see the work of Parian marble, and Pliny the Elder pronounced it the finest statue yet made in Greece. King Nicomedes of Bithynia offered to buy the statue and in return excuse the city's huge public debt, but the Knidians refused. A number of ancient poets composed verses honoring the statue; the legend has it that men were crazed with desire on viewing it.

The statue, which is thought to have been the first freestanding female nude, was put in an open shrine so that the goddess could be seen and admired from all sides. *Aphrodite* stands in a graceful pose, one hand held in front of her, the other grasping her drapery, which falls on a water jar. The goddess is represented at the moment that she steps into her bath. Her gaze is turned to the left, supposedly to see an intruder. Only her right hand makes any effort to cover up, and the slight smile displays a hint of welcome.

Reproductions of the *Aphrodite* are found on Roman coins of Knidos as well as in small, practically complete statuettes. The best replicas of the head are those in the Louvre and in Toulouse. Full-sized Roman copies exist in the Vatican, Brussels, and Munich museums, the most-often photographed and reprinted one being the Vatican version.

As a result of the *Aphrodite of Knidos* and other sculptures of Aphrodite by Praxiteles, the nude female figure became one of the most common forms of statuary, but the goddess was increasingly portrayed as a mortal. One example is the statue titled *Venus of Medici*, which may have been carved by Kephisodotos and Timarchos, the sons of Praxiteles. Here the magnificent Praxitelean ideal woman has been transformed into a mere coquette.

SIGNIFICANCE

Coming from a long line of sculptors, Praxiteles stands at the climax of a family of distinguished artists. Inspired by his father's softer, subtler treatment of subjects that the fifth century artists had treated with monumental but impersonal dignity, Praxiteles imbued statues with psychological complexities that give his work its universal appeal. The fleet-footed Hermes pauses for a moment of tenderness, the infant Dionysus turns greedy, the mature Eros becomes a sensual young man, and the heroic Apollo loses his fighting spirit so that he seems to lack the energy even to engage in lizard slaying, a popular Mediterranean boy's sport.

The crowning achievement of Praxiteles' work is his series of Aphrodites, especially the famous nude that he sold to the Knidians. The fifth century sculptors tended to carve nude males and clothed females. For example, the *Peace* by Kephisodotos is weighted down with heavy drapery. Praxiteles' female nude created a sensation and a whole new style of artistic expression. The intricately worked hair, the finely chiseled facial features with their play of emotions, and the perfectly proportioned body of the *Aphrodite of Knidos* set the standard for female beauty. Although Praxiteles did not invent the concept of a statue's standing free in order to be seen in a three-dimensional space, the success of the *Aphrodite*'s backside (her dimpled buttocks were especially admired) inspired other artists to carve freestanding nude females also.

Another Praxitelean innovation, although certainly not an invention, was the expanded employment of the S-curve, or *contrapposto*, for the body outline, which allows for a more natural, animated stance. The S-curve allows the *Apollo Sauroktonos* to lean casually against his tree trunk and the *Hermes* to hold the babe in one arm while he raises the other arm over his head.

Also, the surface of Praxitelean statues was technically outstanding. Ancient writers who saw the original, painted statues remarked that the body surfaces were smoothly polished and that the modeling of the hair was particularly realistic. Unfortunately, the *Hermes* is the only fairly complete work that can be taken to be an original, and many historians and archaeologists dispute even that attribution. It is so far superior to any of the Roman copies of other works by Praxiteles that the more admired original statues must have been exquisite indeed.

The many facets of Praxiteles' work meant that his work was difficult to copy accurately. While many contemporaries and the sculptors of the third and second centuries were able to capture the outward forms of the statues, they were unable to evoke the complex human emotions. The effect of the Praxitelean style in the hands of inferior artists seems to be merely mannered and elegant.

—Sandra Hanby Harris

FURTHER READING

Boardman, John. *Greek Art*. Rev. ed. New York: Thames and Hudson, 1996. Regarded as a standard work in the field of classical art, this book provides an overview of the masterpieces of ancient Greece as well as commentary on recent discoveries and controversies of interpretation surrounding the world's best-known works of art and architecture.

Furtwängler, Adolf. *Masterpieces of Greek Sculpture*. Edited by A. L. N. Oikonomides. Chicago: Argonaut, 1964. Takes a close look at the original monuments in order to reevaluate generally held theories of attribution and dating.

Kjellberg, Ernst, and Gösta Säflund. *Greek and Roman Art: 3000 B.C. to A.D. 550*. Translated by Peter Fraser. New York: Thomas Y. Crowell, 1970. Catalogs all the major examples of the Greek and Roman art forms. Dates, sizes, and describes included works.

Paris, Pierre. *Manual of Ancient Sculpture*. Edited by Jane E. Harrison. New Rochelle, N.Y.: Aristide D. Caratzas, 1984. A chapter on Scopas and Praxiteles discusses the works of both sculptors at length. Of particular interest is a reproduction of the *Aphrodite of Knidos* seen on a Knidian coin.

Pollitt, J. J. *Art and Experience in Classical Greece*. New York: Cambridge University Press, 1999. Focuses on the period between c. 480 and 323 B.C.E. and seeks to integrate art styles with historical experience. Particularly useful in describing the emotional states depicted in various statues by Praxiteles.

Richter, Gisela. *A Handbook of Greek Art*. Oxford, England: Phaidon, 1987. For many years curator of Greek and Roman art in the Metropolitan Museum in New York, Richter presents one of the most authoritative accounts of Greek architecture and sculpture. Traces the historical evolution of Greek sculpture and adds biographical information wherever possible. Includes extensive bibliography and lucid chronology.

_____. *The Sculpture and Sculptors of the Greeks*. Rev. ed. New Haven, Conn.: Yale University Press, 1970. Contains a consecutive, chronological study of the human figure, drapery, and composition. Includes extensive footnotes and bibliography.

Waldenstein, Charles. "Praxiteles and the Hermes with the Infant Dionysus." In *The Art of Pheidias*. Washington, D.C.: McGrath, 1973. Originally published only seven years after the discovery of the *Hermes*, this article contains an in-depth study of the state of the statue when it was first excavated, its importance to the Greeks for whom it was carved, and its relation to other sculptors' versions of the messenger god.

SEE ALSO: Phidias; Polyclitus; Scopas.
RELATED ARTICLES in *Great Events from History: The Ancient World*: c. 350 B.C.E., Diogenes Popularizes Cynicism; c. 335-323 B.C.E., Aristotle Writes the *Politics*.

PRISCILLIAN
Spanish bishop

Priscillian provides an example not only of the popularity of ascetic practices in the Christian church but also of what can happen when such activities are carried to extremes and challenge established Church beliefs and lines of authority.

BORN: c. 340 C.E.; Spain
DIED: 385 C.E.; Trier (now in Germany)
AREA OF ACHIEVEMENT: Religion

EARLY LIFE

The latter half of the fourth century was a great age of Christian ascetics. These individuals withdrew from the secular world and practiced a life of fasting, deprivation, nightly vigils, and spiritual contemplation. Churchmen such as Saint Antony of Egypt, Saint Martin of Tours in Gaul, Saint Jerome in Italy and Palestine, and many others popularized this style of asceticism. In theory, these practices were merely part of the ideal Christian life. Groups of ascetics could become very influential; their members often were chosen as bishops. Extreme forms of asceticism, however, especially those that rejected established church practices and teachings, were looked on with less favor.

Priscillian (prihs-SIHL-yahn) was a well-educated Spanish nobleman said to have been versed in secular and Christian literature as well as in astrology and the occult. He was possessed of a keen intellect and was an eloquent speaker. After his conversion to Christianity, he, like many others of his day, adopted an ascetic life. He also claimed to have prophetic powers. He became a wandering lay preacher and assumed the title "doctor." During the 370's, he began to teach his own peculiar brand of Christianity.

LIFE'S WORK

Insight into just what Priscillian's teachings were can be gained not only from his contemporary detractors but also from eleven treatises that were first published in 1889. Although only a few of them may have been written by Priscillian himself, or by his supporter Instantius, they do reflect Priscillian's teachings. The Priscillianists were very ascetic, recommending vegetarianism and abstinence from wine. On Sundays, they fasted. They generally walked barefoot. They also were opposed to marriage and to other aspects of the organized Church. They preferred, for example, to meet in secret, either in their own country villas or in mountain retreats. They held Communion outside the established Church. At some times of the year, such as during Lent and in the days before Epiphany, which was then recognized as the day of Christ's birth, they seemed simply to disappear from sight.

As to their theological beliefs, the Priscillianists had a marked preference for the New Testament and for some of the apocryphal writings, such as the lives of the Apostles Peter, John, Andrew, and Thomas. They also believed in direct, divine inspiration. Aspects of Priscillian's works to reflect a Manichaean dualism: He distinguished, for example, between darkness and light and saw Satan not as a fallen angel but as having an independent existence. His denial of the preexistence of Christ could have been tinged with Arianism. As a result, great controversy soon arose over Priscillian's teachings and practices. The contemporary Gallic writer Sulpicius Severus, in his chronicle, noted, "there followed portentious and dangerous times of our age, in which the churches were defiled and everything was disturbed by an unaccustomed evil."

Priscillian soon gained a large following in Galicia and Lusitania (the northern and western parts of Spain). A large number of women were attracted to him; they held meetings of their own apart from the regular church services. He also was joined by two western Spanish bishops, Instantius and Salvianus. He initially was opposed, however, by more worldly bishops such as Hyginus of Cordova and, in particular, Hydatius of Emerita. Some of his detractors accused him of Manichaeanism. It also was rumored that two of his followers, the noblewoman Agape and the rhetorician Helpidius, had infected him with the Gnostic teachings of Mark of Memphis, an Egyptian who had moved to Spain. The Priscillianists soon were joined by another bishop, Symphosius of Astorga in Lusitania (modern Portugal). Hyginus of Cordova also changed his mind and withdrew his initial objections.

In 380, a council was assembled at Saragossa to consider Priscillian's case. Ten Spanish bishops attended as well as two Gallic bishops, Delphinus of Bordeaux and Phoebadius of Agen, the latter presiding over the meeting. Priscillian himself, however, did not attend, although he did submit a written reply. The council declined to condemn him by name, although it did denounce some Priscillianist practices, such as the speaking and teaching of women in religious "conventicles" (gatherings), the activities of lay preachers, and the absence from church during Lent. Perhaps in response to the second of these, Priscillian was consecrated shortly thereafter as bishop of Avila in Lusitania by Salvianus and Instantius. The Priscillianists then made scandalous accusations of their own against Hydatius. In 381 Priscillian's opponents, who had been joined by Bishop Ithacius of Ossonoba, appealed to the Emperor Gratian with the help of Bishop Ambrose of Milan. Gratian then issued a decree condemning "false bishops and Manichees."

Priscillian himself realized the efficacy of such a tactic, noting, "with our names disguised [Hydatius] sought a rescript against pseudobishops and Manichees, and of course obtained it, because there is no one who does not feel hatred when he hears about pseudobishops and Manichees." The Italian writer on heresies Philastrius of Brescia made similar connections, referring to the "so-to-speak ascetics in Gaul, Spain, and Aquitania, who likewise follow the most pernicious belief of the Gnostics and Manichees," despite Priscillian's own explicit anathematization of Manichaeanism.

It was a popular tactic in ecclesiastical debates of this time, however, to attempt to associate one's opponents with some other universally detested heresy. Priscillianism was related to Origenism, for example, by the Spanish writer Paulus Orosius in his *Commonitorium de errore Priscillianistarum et Origenistarum* (c. 414; reminder about the error of the Priscillianists and Origenists). Other heresies by which the Priscillianists also were accused of being influenced included Gnosticism, Montanism, Novatianism, Ophitism, Patripassianism, Photinianism, and Sabellianism.

Priscillian, Instantius, and Salvianus, though the Imperial edict had not specifically named them, left Spain seeking additional support. At Eauze in southwestern Gaul, they made many converts. After being expelled from Bordeaux by Bishop Delphinus, they were received by the noblewoman Euchrotia and Procula, the widow and daughter of the professor Attius Tiro Delphidius. They then continued on to Italy. At Rome, where Salvianus died, they were rebuffed by Pope Damasus. Thereafter, they received a similar response from Ambrose of Milan. They were successful, however, in gaining the help of Ambrose's enemies at the Imperial court, and they obtained an Imperial rescript of their own, authorizing them to reclaim their sees, which they then did. Ithacius even was forced to go into exile in Trier.

Soon thereafter, however in 383, Gratian was murdered by the usurper Magnus Maximus, who subsequently was baptized as an orthodox Christian. Ithacius

proceeded to place his case before the new emperor, with whom the Priscillianists had no influence. Maximus, desiring to conciliate the established Gallic and Spanish clergy, ordered a council to be convened in 384 or 385 at Bordeaux under the presidency of Priscillian's enemy Delphinus. Instantius, whose case was heard first, was declared deposed, but before Priscillian could be tried, he appealed to Maximus himself.

A hearing was therefore convened before the praetorian prefect of Gaul at Trier. Priscillian's principal accuser, Ithacius, took the lead in the prosecution. Priscillian was accused, according to Sulpicius Severus, "of witchcraft, of studying obscene teachings, of organizing nocturnal gatherings of shameful women, and of praying in the nude." Some of these crimes were capital offenses. Two other influential bishops who coincidentally happened to be in the city at the time, Martin of Tours and Ambrose of Milan, refused to take part and argued that a bishop should be tried before his fellow bishops. Other bishops, however, supported the proceedings.

In the end, Priscillian and six of his followers, including Euchrotia and the Spanish nobleman Latronianus, were condemned to death and executed. Others, such as Instantius, were sent into exile. Martin was able to prevent the sending of an Imperial commission to root out the Spanish Priscillianists, but purges did take place. The aged Hyginus, for example, was sent into exile, and ascetics in general continued to be harassed.

The role of Maximus is seen especially in his letter to Bishop Siricius of Rome informing him of the affair: "Our arrival found certain matters so contaminated and polluted by the sins of the wicked that, unless foresight and attention had quickly brought aid, great disturbance and ruin immediately would have arisen, . . . but it was then disclosed how great a crime the Manichees recently had committed, not by doubtful or uncertain rhetoric or suspicions, but by their own confession." According to the emperor, the Priscillianists were Manichees: In fact, he never referred to Priscillian or Priscillianists by name at all. He may have seen no need to try to define a new heresy when Manichaeanism, a perfectly good, universally detested one, was available. An accusation of Manichaeanism would have allowed Priscillian to be tried under the statutes that made it a capital crime.

This heavy-handed secular interference in church activities led to a split in the Gallic church. Bishops such as Felix of Trier, who associated themselves with Priscillian's accusers, were seen as responsible for his execution by others, such as Martin, who had declined to participate. Thus arose the so-called Felician controversy, in which bishops of the two sides excommunicated each other.

The anti-Felicians, who had opposed the executions, came back into Imperial favor in 388, when Maximus was defeated and Valentinian II, Gratian's younger brother, was restored to the throne. Both Ithacius and Hydatius were exiled and imprisoned at Naples. The remains of Priscillian and his followers were returned to Spain and buried with great ceremony. Priscillian was venerated as a martyr and saint, and his teachings continued to have many followers. Subsequently, a number of Priscillianists were chosen as bishops in Galicia, with Symphosius as one of their leaders.

The Council of Toledo in 400 was able to reconcile some of the Priscillianists, such as Symphosius, but Priscillianism continued to have many adherents. Outbreaks are attested in the 440's, in the mid-530's, and as late as the Councils of Braga in 561 and 572, when seventeen supposed Priscillianist teachings were condemned. Some Priscillianist practices were reflected even later in those of the medieval Albigensians (c. 1200), southern French ascetic, anticlerical dualists, and Adamites, who practiced nudity. The Priscillianist preference for clerical continence, moreover, did eventually become standard Catholic practice.

SIGNIFICANCE

The Priscillianist controversy did not concern ecclesiastical dogma as much as it did church authority. Even in the modern day, scholars have a difficult time finding obvious heresy in Priscillian's writings. Nevertheless, his advocacy of uncontrolled scriptural interpretation, lay ministry, the participation of women, and the carrying out of the sacraments outside the established structure excited much opposition from the existing church hierarchy. His and his followers' acquisition of episcopal office, and their attempts to take over the church hierarchy themselves, only served to arouse more opposition against them. The result was a power struggle in which both sides sought assistance from the secular government. Priscillian was the loser and paid with his life. In the future, the state would become more and more intimately involved in church activities and controversies.

—Ralph W. Mathisen

FURTHER READING

Birley, A. R. "Magnus Maximus and the Persecution of Heresy." *Bulletin of the John Rylands Library* 66 (1983): 13-43. A detailed discussion of the part played by the emperor Magnus Maximus in the Priscillianist controversy. This incident illustrates the increasing interference of the Imperial government in the operation of the Church. Includes references to recent scholarship on Priscillian and notes.

Burrus, Virginia. *The Making of a Heretic: Gender, Authority, and the Priscillianist Controversy.* Berkeley: University of California Press, 1995. Explores the concept of heresy from the point of view of the followers of Priscillian. Reevaluates the reliability of the historical record. Burrus's analysis includes the concepts of gender, authority, and public and private space that informed established religion's response to this early Christian movement.

Chadwick, Henry. *Priscillian of Avila: The Occult and the Charismatic in the Early Church.* Oxford, England: Clarendon Press, 1976. The standard English-language biography of Priscillian. Concentrates on the religious and theological aspects of Priscillian's teaching. Includes thorough documentation and bibliography, with references to many other sources, especially in foreign languages.

De Clercq, V. C. "Ossius of Cordova and the Origins of Priscillianism." *Studia patristica* 1 (1957): 601-606. A brief discussion of the background of the Priscillianist controversy; De Clercq seeks to identify possible forerunners of Priscillian's beliefs and theology in earlier Christian teachings, especially those of Ossius of Cordova.

SEE ALSO: Saint Ambrose; Saint Anthony of Egypt; Saint Jerome; Origen.

RELATED ARTICLES in *Great Events from History: The Ancient World*: c. 286 C.E., Saint Anthony of Egypt Begins Ascetic Life; October 28, 312 C.E., Conversion of Constantine to Christianity; 313-395 C.E., Inception of Church-State Problem; 380-392 C.E., Theodosius's Edicts Promote Christian Orthodoxy; c. 382-c. 405 C.E., Saint Jerome Creates the Vulgate; October 8-25, 451 C.E., Council of Chalcedon.

PROCLUS
Greek philosopher

Proclus is known for his detailed systematization of the various theological and philosophical doctrines that he inherited from his predecessors and for his immense commentaries on the works of Plato, which consumed most of his activity.

BORN: c. 410 C.E.; Constantinople, Byzantine Empire (now Istanbul, Turkey)
DIED: 485 C.E.; Athens, Greece
AREA OF ACHIEVEMENT: Philosophy

EARLY LIFE
Proclus (PROH-kluhs) was born of patrician Lycian parents from the city of Xanthus. They wanted him to be educated in their city; thus, he was sent to Xanthus at a very early age. Later, he went to Alexandria to study rhetoric and Roman law in order to follow his father's profession, law. He soon became interested in philosophy and abandoned the study of law, choosing instead to attend lectures on mathematics and the philosophy of Aristotle. About the age of twenty, he went to Athens and studied under the Athenian Plutarch and his successor, Syrianus, at the Academy, the Athenian school that traced its ancestry to Plato's Academy. There, he continued his study of Aristotle and was introduced to Plato's philosophy and to mystical theology, to which he became a devotee. Proclus was such an intense, diligent student, with extraordinary powers of comprehension and memory, that by the age of twenty he had read the whole of Aristotle's *De anima* (348-336 B.C.E.; *On the Soul*, 1812) and Plato's *Phaedros* (399-390 B.C.E.; *Phaedrus*, 1792), and by twenty-eight he had written several treatises as well as his commentary on Plato's *Timaeos* (360-347 B.C.E.; *Timaeus*, 1793).

Although a devoted disciple of Platonic thought, which he considered his main influence and inspiration, Proclus was a great enthusiast of all sorts of religious practices, beliefs, and superstitions and a champion of pagan worship against Christian Imperial policy. He practiced all the Orphic and Chaldean rites of purification religiously, was a celibate, pursued a strict vegetarian diet, observed the fasts and vigils for the sacred days (more than was customary), devoutly revered the sun and moon, faithfully observed all the Egyptian holy days, and spent part of each night in prayer and in performing sacrifices. He believed that he was in complete possession of the theurgic knowledge, that he was divinely inspired, and that he was a reincarnation of the neo-Pythagorean

Nichomachus. Through the practice of theurgy, a type of ritual magic, it is claimed that he caused rainfall in a time of drought, prevented an earthquake, and was able to persuade the god Asclepius to cure the daughter of his friend Archiadas. Proclus had a vast and comprehensive knowledge of philosophy, mythology, religious practices, and cults, and he attempted to harmonize all these elements into a comprehensive system.

Marinus, his biographer, who was also his pupil and successor, describes Proclus as having lived the perfect life of a philosopher, a model of all the virtues, both social and intellectual, the life of a divine man. His only shortcomings were a quick temper and a fiercely competitive nature. On the death of Syrianus, Proclus succeeded him as the head of the Academy. Because of his position as the head of the Academy and his devotion to Platonic thought, he has often been called "diadoches," or successor of Plato.

LIFE'S WORK
Proclus believed that his philosophy was a further and necessary development of Plato's thought. In reality, his views are a systematization of those found in other Neoplatonists' interpretations of Plotinian thought, and most can be traced to the teachings of Iamblichus, a follower of Plotinus. Of the many works that Proclus wrote, the most important and the one that best displays his schematization of Neoplatonic thought is *Stoikheiōsis theologikē* (*The Elements of Theology*, 1933). This work is basically a doctrine of categories. It consists of a series of 211 propositions with deductive proofs. Each succeeding proposition follows on the basis of the preceding one, following the Euclidean procedure in geometry.

At the head of Proclus's system is the One, the ultimate First Principle existing beyond being and knowledge, ineffable and incomprehensible. Proclus often identifies God with the First Principle or One. From the One emanates or radiates innumerable lesser independent realities, reflecting the multiplicity of the world order, which strive to return to union with it. Unlike Plotinus, who held that the process of emanation was continuous and equal in degree, Proclus believed that all things emanate by triads and return to the One by triads. Every emanation is less than that from which it evolves but has a similarity or partial identity to its cause. In its emergence from its cause, the derived is also different. However, because of its relation to and dependence on its cause, it attempts to imitate its cause on a lower plane and return to and unite itself with it. It is only through the intermediate existences in triadic aspects that an existence can return to the highest reality, the One.

Although not original with him, Proclus was the first to emphasize and apply throughout his system the principle of universal sympathy, the view that everything is in everything else, each according to its proper nature. According to this, every reality in the universe is mirrored in everything else, but appropriately, in accordance with its nature. Eternal things exist in temporal existences temporally, and temporal things exist in eternal things eternally. This principle unifies and interweaves every part of the universe with every other part, from the One to the last stage of being or matter. In his attempt to unify the totality of the universe, Proclus also effected a total synthesis of religion with philosophy. His system is a chain of many carefully constructed links that include the traditional pagan gods, heroes, and other supernatural beings of late pagan syncretistic mythology and cult, as well as the divine principles of Greek philosophy.

Similar to his Neoplatonic predecessors, Proclus believed that the ultimate goal of the individual soul was to lose its identity and return to union with the One, or God. Although he accepted the Neoplatonic view that philosophy was important in the attainment of this goal, he added that theurgy provided an even better avenue. Philosophy is intellectual activity, is discursive, and, as such, is divided. Thus, it is impossible to achieve union with the undivided One through philosophy alone. Philosophy serves only as a preparation. Union with God is best achieved through the method of theurgy, or, as Proclus calls it, the sacred art, a collection of magical practices based on the principle of universal sympathy, a common sympathy existing between all earthly and divine things. According to this, there can exist in herbs, stones, and other material substances a magical or divine property. On a higher level, divinity could also be found in the names of gods, certain symbols, and even numbers. A skilled theurgist, by placing together the materials that possess divine properties and effacing others, could set forth a chain reaction of sympathies proceeding upward through a whole series of things to a divine being. The result would be a divine illumination, by means of which an individual could come into external communion with a god. Thus, theurgy was considered by Proclus superior to philosophy, for, unlike philosophy, theurgy can lead an individual to the gods themselves.

Proclus posited two types of theurgy, a lower and a higher. The lower uses the unities found in specific material things to stimulate the soul toward self-knowledge, an understanding of its unity and divinity. Union with God, Himself, however, is attained only through a higher theurgy, the power of faith. Faith, according to Proclus, is when the individual goes beyond words, ritual actions, and conceptual thought and arrives at a state of simplicity, or self-unity. That leads to an unexplainable and incomprehensible belief in and love of God. When that occurs, the soul finds itself in a mystical silence before the incomprehensible and ineffable Supreme Being, and to the degree that a soul can, it becomes God.

In its later years, Neoplatonism came to be more a religion than a philosophy in order to compete with Christianity, which was becoming increasingly popular. Neoplatonism's followers were concerned with matters similar to those of their Christian counterparts: constructing a theology and interpreting and reconciling sacred texts. They also adopted some of the tenets fundamental to Christianity and other religions. Because faith is indispensable for salvation in any religion, it became for the later Neoplatonists a basic requirement for salvation or union with God. Proclus understood the problem of combating Christianity and attempted to construct a system that would bring into harmony elements of religion and Greek thought.

SIGNIFICANCE

Proclus is considered the last of the major pagan Greek philosophers. His works represent the culminating point of Neoplatonic philosophers and the final form of Neoplatonism's doctrines. It is in the Proclian form that Neoplatonic doctrines had considerable influence on Byzantine, Arabic, and early medieval Latin Christian thought. Proclus exerted the greatest influence, indirectly, on Latin Christendom through the writings of Dionysius, or Pseudo-Dionysius, as he is now called. It is not known who Dionysius was or when he lived. All that is known is that sometime in the late fifth or early sixth century a Christian follower of Proclus adopted his philosophy in toto, disguised it as apostolic teaching, and claimed it to be that of Dionysius the Areopagite, Saint Paul's first Athenian convert and disciple. Despite the fact that they were fraudulent, the works of Dionysius were highly regarded in the West, and beginning in the early sixth century to the eighth, elaborate commentaries were written defending both their orthodoxy and their genuineness. They soon acquired authority second only to those of Saint Augustine. Through the Dionysian corpus, Proclus's Neoplatonism influenced the thought of Western theologians for many centuries.

In the Byzantine world, the Dionysian theology had influence on the eighth century Eastern theologian Saint John of Damascus, but in general the works of Proclus were not as widely accepted as in the West, although they were well-known and often refuted. The main reason for their nonacceptance was that the Christian East considered Proclus's views on the eternity of the world heretical. It was not until the eleventh century, with the revival of Platonism, that Proclus's philosophy became widely known, studied, quoted, and commented on in the East. The Muslim world was also influenced by Proclus. His works were translated into Arabic and influenced the thought of Arabic thinkers, especially those mystically inclined, such as al-Ghazzali and the Sufis, and Ibn Gabirol and the Cabalists.

Proclus's influence on both the East and the West continued down to the eighteenth century and was especially prominent during the Middle Ages and the Renaissance, when he was considered the great pagan master. His works were translated into many languages, and his influence can be found in the philosophies of John Scotus Erigena (c. 810-c. 877), Saint Thomas Aquinas (1225-1274), Meister Johannes Eckhart (c. 1260-1327), Nicholas of Cusa (1401-1464), René Descartes (1596-1650), Gottfried Wilhelm von Leibniz (1646-1716), and others. Traces of Proclus's philosophy can also be found in many modern works, literary and philosophical.

—*Antonia Tripolitis*

FURTHER READING

Lowry, J. M. P. *The Logical Principles of Proclus's "Elements of Theology" as Systematic Ground of the Cosmos.* Amsterdam: Rodopi, 1980. A study of the development of a logical structure of the cosmos as set forth in the logical systematic construction of the 211 propositions in Proclus's *The Elements of Theology.* It contains a good introductory chapter that includes a synopsis of Greek philosophy, Proclus's place in the history of philosophy, his relation to Iamblichus and Plotinus, and his influence on medieval and Renaissance thought.

Proclus. *The Elements of Theology.* Translated by E. R. Dodds. Rev. ed. Oxford, England: Clarendon Press, 1977. Greek text and English translation, with an excellent introduction and commentary on *The Elements of Theology.* The introduction includes a general description of the work, its place in the philosophical works of Proclus, a summary of Proclus's place among his Neoplatonic predecessors, and his influence during the Middle Ages.

Rosán, Laurence Jay. *The Philosophy of Proclus: The Final Phase of Ancient Thought.* New York: Cosmos, 1949. A compendium of Proclus's writings, with a detailed discussion and annotated bibliography.

Wallis, R. T. *Neoplatonism.* Indianapolis: Hackett, 1995. The study is intended as an updated account of Neoplatonism. It is a summary of Neoplatonic thought from Plotinus to the end of the Athenian Academy, but it also includes two brief chapters on the aims and sources of Neoplatonism and a lengthier chapter on the influence of Neoplatonism through the years. Includes bibliography.

Whittaker, Thomas. *The Neo-Platonists.* New York: Olms-Verlag, 1987. A study in the history of Hellenism, with emphasis on Neoplatonic philosophy, from Plotinus to Proclus, and its influence. Chapter 9 contains a study of Proclus's life and a descriptive account of many of the propositions found in *The Elements of Theology.* At the end of the book, there is a supplementary section of summaries on Proclus's extant commentaries.

SEE ALSO: Aristotle; Plato; Plotinus; Porphyry.

RELATED ARTICLES in *Great Events from History: The Ancient World*: 600-500 B.C.E., Greek Philosophers Formulate Theories of the Cosmos; c. 380 B.C.E., Plato Develops His Theory of Ideas.

SEXTUS PROPERTIUS
Roman poet

Sextus Propertius expanded the scope and power of the Roman love poem in the passionate poems to and about Cynthia.

BORN: c. 57-48 B.C.E.; Asisium (now Assisi, Umbria, Italy)
DIED: c. 16 B.C.E.-2 C.E.; Rome (now in Italy)
AREA OF ACHIEVEMENT: Literature

EARLY LIFE

Sextus Propertius (proh-PUR-shuhs) was born between 57 and 48 B.C.E. in Umbria, in the small town of Assisi. He was the son of a knight who was a well-off landowner. Propertius's father died while Propertius was still a child, and his world was further dislocated by the appropriation of land in Umbria to settle the soldiers of Marc Antony and Octavian (later known as Augustus).

Propertius grew up under the shadow of the continuing civil wars among Antony, Octavian, and Pompey the Younger—and the early consolidation of power by Augustus. His first book of poems was published about 30 B.C.E., and it attracted the attention of Gaius Maecenas, the patron of Vergil and Horace. This support improved Propertius's financial situation, but he continued to refuse to write poems in celebration of Augustus.

LIFE'S WORK

Propertius's poetry came at the end of the great period of the Roman love poem. His work does not have the passion of Catullus or the polish of Horace, but it does have a complexity and an intensity not found in the poetry of his predecessors. Some critics have complained about Propertius's heavy use of myth, but the allusions in his poetry are well employed—especially the contrasting of the distant gods to the immediate relationship with a woman he called Cynthia.

Propertius's poetry survives in four books. At the heart of the poems are those on Cynthia, and while commentators have been unsuccessful in discovering an autobiographical sequence, the poems do give one of the fullest portrayals of an intense relationship in all literature. The first poem (book 1, elegy 1) immediately evokes this intensity: "She was the one to enslave me, and she did it with her eyes;/ till then I'd never felt love's poison arrows."

For Propertius, love is not a pleasant or a sentimental state but a terrible visitation and a loss of control. He contrasts his subject state to mythic figures and urges the powers of love to visit his mistress with the same poison. The poem shifts at the end, as Propertius becomes adviser rather than victim and warns his friends to avoid this sorry state of unrequited love by sticking "to your own love."

In the poems that follow, Propertius frequently complains about Cynthia's mistreatment, yet in book 1, elegy 7, the poet defends his choice of the love poem over the more traditional and valued epic. Propertius's poems are his "life's work" and come from bitter and joyful experience, while the epic of one Ponticus—according to Propertius—is straight out of books. Propertius writes that when Ponticus falls in love, in vain he will try to turn his hand to love poems, while Propertius will be celebrated as "the greatest poet of them all."

In book 1, elegies 21 and 22, Propertius addresses war, not love. The speaker in elegy 21 is a dead man who advises a fleeing soldier. The dead man urges the soldier not to be brave but to "Save yourself/ and bring your parents joy." He also asks the soldier to bring a message of "tears" to his sister. The poem ends ironically, for the dead man was also a soldier and had escaped "the swords of Caesar," only to fall to robbers. It is a personal and a political poem; it evokes the sorrow of the dead soldier and points unmistakably to its cause, the wars of Antony and Octavian.

Elegy 22 is also a political poem. It begins with a question from a man named Tullus about Propertius's origins. The answer is that he comes from "the graveyard of our fatherland/ when civil war set Roman against Roman. . . ." Once more he evokes a landscape littered with "my kinsman's bones" but ends with an opposite image, life and birth: "where the fertile plain touches the foothills/ Umbria gave me birth."

The first poem in book 2 is addressed not to Cynthia but to Propertius's patron, Maecenas. Once more, he contrasts the supposedly trivial love poem to the great epic, but because Cynthia is his inspiration "each trivial incident begets/ a mighty saga." Even if he had the power to write an epic, he would avoid the usual subjects, because they are all clichés. If he had the power he would write about "your Caesar's wars" (another example of the distancing of the poet from the emperor). Yet he has no such power or ability; he can only write "of the battles I fight in bed." The poem ends in an amusing fashion, as Propertius asks Maecenas to visit his obscure tomb, drop a tear, observe the burial rites, and say, "Here lies one for whom destiny/ Was a Cruel mistress." As the poems show, Propertius's destiny was a cruel mistress, Cynthia.

Most of the poems in book 2 complain about Cynthia's ways or lack of faithfulness. Elegy 5 is the most interesting of these. It begins with a series of accusations as Cynthia is called a "whore" and the poet looks forward to following her example and acquiring a new love. The focus of the poem shifts, however, as Propertius looks not to the future but to past moments they shared like "tender sacraments." He then lists all the brutal things he will not do to her; he will, instead, "mark" her with his poetic curse that will last to her dying day.

Book 2, elegy 7, speaks of a more tender relationship between the poet and Cynthia as well as of the complex relationship he has with Augustus. It begins with relief that some "law" was not put into operation by Augustus that would separate the poet and his beloved. The relief is tinged with defiance, as the poet declares that "mighty Caesar cannot conquer love." Nor is the poet a fit candidate to be a husband or a breeder of sons for Rome; the only war he will fight is in the name of his mistress. The last lines of the poem are an affirmation of the poet's love, "which is greater to me than the name of father."

In book 2, elegy 10, Propertius seems to have reversed his earlier position and now wishes to sing of "war and war's alarms," because "Cynthia's song is sung." By the end of the poem, however, he sees poems about war as beyond his reach, like a statue that "towers too high." He will, instead, write of and from the lower strain of love. Propertius is very clever in praising Augustus, but, finally, he relocates his art in a private rather than a public arena.

Elegy 34, the last poem in book 2, brings together many of the themes of the earlier poems. It is addressed to another poet, Lynceus, who has attempted to steal the poet's beloved. Lynceus is identified as a student of the "Socratic books," but they will be of no help to a man in love—nor will the usual epic themes. Lynceus must make himself into a love poet in the manner of Propertius if he wishes to succeed. The second section contrasts Propertius's poems with the political and nationalistic ones of Vergil and the pastoral ones of Lynceus. In the end, however, the epic and pastoral poets are left behind, as Propertius places himself in the line of Catullus and Calvus. If he is allowed to join that company, both he and Cynthia will live forever. So the poem is both a disguised love poem that praises Cynthia and a defense of lyric poetry against the epic and the pastoral.

Book 3 continues the themes of Cynthia and the championing of the love poem over the epic. Elegy 4, however, seems to be a surrender to the claims of Rome. The poem praises the new victories of Augustus against the Parthians. Propertius even prays to see "the wheels of Caesar heaped with the spoils of war." However, where will the poet be while this triumph is celebrated? He will be lying in his "sweetheart's arms watching the sights" rather than taking an active role or even writing about war. The last two lines define the difference between the two areas: "Let those who earned it bear the spoil away,/ and leave me to stand and cheer on the Sacred Way." The role of the poet is to sing and cheer, not to take part in public life.

Elegy 11 deals with the power that women have over men. It begins with Propertius speaking of his bondage to Cynthia and asserting that it should be no "surprise." He cites Medea and others as examples of this same situation, but the main comparison is to Cleopatra VII. She has "brought into disrepute" the "walls of Rome" and made senators slaves. According to Propertius, however, Augustus was not awed by this woman and has recently defeated and destroyed her; the poet sings out "your triumph, Rome" over these forces. The subjection to women that seemed to be universal at the beginning is now broken, and the poet tells the reader to "remember Caesar."

Elegy 22 also discusses Rome but from a more personal perspective. It is addressed to Tullus, who has been roaming among the various wonders of the world. After listing those exotic sights, however, the poet reminds Tullus that "all the wonders of the world/ are not a patch on Rome." Not only is Rome victorious, it is also free from the crimes and vices common in other places. So Tullus is welcomed back to a Rome that is "worthy of your eloquence," where children and "a wife to match your love" await. It is clearly a Rome in which there is no mention of Cynthia and her destructive passion.

Book 4 also begins with a celebration of Rome, in the first elegy. A "stranger" is invited to look around at "the grandeur of Rome." He is reminded of Roman history and myth from Romulus and Remus through the founding of Rome by the Trojans, as the poet offers up his song "to the service of my country." He imagines his homeland, Umbria, now proud as the birthplace of "Rome's Callimachus." In the second part of the poem, however, Horus, a god of time and an astrologer, appears and criticizes Propertius's new project. He tells him that he should be fashioning love poems to "provide a model for the scribbling mob," since Apollo "banned you from thundering in the frantic forum." Propertius's fate is Cynthia and the creation of poems about her: "It's she who tells you whether it's day or night;/ your teardrops fall at her command."

In book 4, elegy 6, however, Propertius returns to the subject of Augustus's wars. After listing the triumphs of his emperor, the poet focuses on the victory over Cleopatra that has made Augustus into a god. There is one more poem on Cynthia in book 4. It speaks of her as a ghost who is "very much alive," snapping her fingers at the poet and ordering him around. She accuses him of not attending her funeral and of sleeping soon after her death. She has come, however, not to accuse but to bring information about the underworld and to instruct the poet. She tells him, first, to burn all the poems he has written about her and to place "this poem" on her tombstone: "Here in the fields of Tivoli/ Lies golden Cynthia/ Adding a new glory/ To the banks of the Anio." She then leaves him to other women until they can be reunited in the afterlife. It is a fitting end to the sequence.

SIGNIFICANCE

The poems of Sextus Propertius portray the growth, flowering, decay, and death of an intense love relationship with the elusive Cynthia. From the very first, it is seen as an unconquerable obsession. There are moments of union between the two, but, for the most part, he complains about her neglect and unfaithfulness. The Cynthia sequence can be compared to the one dealing with Lesbia in the poems of Catullus. Catullus goes through a similar wrenching experience of hate and love that defines his existence.

There is, however, another side to the poetry of Propertius. He accepted the patronage of Maecenas, but he did not become an official spokesman for Augustus, as Vergil and Horace did. Instead, he defended his right to a private life and a private art, the love poem. The tension created by the struggle to remain free without insulting the emperor gives another dimension to the passionate love poems and adds subtlety to their structure.

—*James Sullivan*

FURTHER READING

Highet, Gilbert. *Poets in a Landscape.* Westport, Conn.: Greenwood Press, 1979. Contains an evocative discussion of Propertius and other Roman poets that concentrates on the poets' biographies and societies. Well written, providing background information but no interpretation.

Janan, Micaela Wakil. *The Politics of Desire: Propertius IV.* Berkeley: University of California Press, 2000. Reassesses Propertius's last elegies using psychoanalytic theory. Includes bibliography and index.

Luck, G. *The Latin Love Elegy.* Hamden, Conn.: Archon Books, 1981. A useful study of some of the techniques and concerns of the Roman love poem. It is quite good on the literary tradition but not much of a guide to individual poems.

Propertius, Sextus. *The Poems of Propertius.* Edited by Ronald Musker. London: J. W. Dent, 1972. A brief and adequate introduction to the poetry of Propertius, with an excellent translation. Good introduction to Propertius for readers without knowledge of Latin.

Stahl, Hans-Peter. *Propertius: Love and War, Individual and State Under Augustus.* Berkeley: University of California Press, 1985. A superb study of Propertius's ambiguous relationship with Augustus and the themes of love and war. It is written primarily for an academic audience, but other readers will find it clear and informative.

Williams, Gordon. *Tradition and Originality in Roman Poetry.* New York: Oxford University Press, 1983. A scholarly treatment of many aspects of Propertius's thought and interests. The book is very good on the background and tradition of the poems but assumes knowledge of Latin.

SEE ALSO: Augustus; Catullus; Clodia; Horace; Gaius Maecenas; Vergil.

RELATED ARTICLES in *Great Events from History: The Ancient World*: 54 B.C.E., Roman Poet Catullus Dies; September 2, 31 B.C.E., Battle of Actium; 19 B.C.E., Roman Poet Vergil Dies; November 27, 8 B.C.E., Roman Lyric Poet Horace Dies.

PROTAGORAS
Greek philosopher

Protagoras was among the first of the Greek Sophists, itinerant teachers who professed to be able to teach virtue for a fee. His ideas on learning, morality, and the history of human society have influenced the system of education since the fifth century B.C.E.

BORN: c. 485 B.C.E.; Abdera, Greece
DIED: c. 410 B.C.E.; place unknown
AREA OF ACHIEVEMENT: Philosophy

EARLY LIFE
Most of what is known of Protagoras (proh-TAG-oh-ruhs) comes from select writings of Plato, Aristotle, Aristophanes, and certain later authors. Protagoras was born about 485 B.C.E. in Abdera, a coastal town of Thrace to the east of Macedonia. The town was remarkable for producing several famous philosophers, including Democritus, and as the third richest city in the Delian League, a fifth century alliance established to expel the Persians from Greece.

Protagoras's father, Maeandrius (or by some accounts, Artemon), was said to have been one of the most affluent citizens of Abdera and was thus able to obtain a good education for his son. When Xerxes I, king of the Persians, stopped in the town with his army prior to invading Greece, Maeandrius supposedly gained permission for his son to be educated by the magi who were part of Xerxes' retinue. The magi were supposed to have been the source of Protagoras's well-known agnosticism. No trace of their influence, however, can be seen in his work, so the story is largely discounted.

A story arose that Protagoras invented the shoulder pad that porters used, because he himself had been a porter in his youth. A longer version of the tale claims that his fellow citizen, the philosopher Democritus, saw him working at a menial task and was so impressed by his methodical arrangement of firewood that he first made the boy his secretary, then trained him in philosophy and rhetoric. Because Democritus was actually younger than Protagoras, this story must also be rejected. However, he may have been a "hearer" of Democritus, as some accounts claim.

The numerous stories from ancient times that have largely been discounted by later generations prove that nothing certain can be said about Protagoras's early life. It is stated authoritatively, however, that at the age of thirty Protagoras began his career as a Sophist, traveling up and down the peninsula of Greece and into Sicily and southern Italy, giving lessons to wealthy young men for a fee.

LIFE'S WORK
Prior to the mid-400's B.C.E. no schools or professional teachers existed, yet the city-states experienced an increasing need for well-educated, informed leaders. The older Sophists, Protagoras, Prodicus, Hippias, and Gorgias, filled this need by teaching upper-class young men how to acquire political and personal success. They held similar views on education and had similar aversions to the objective scientific doctrines of their day. They claimed superiority in wisdom, the ability to teach that wisdom, and the right to charge a fee for their lessons. In this atmosphere Protagoras gained fame by lecturing and by writing books.

Many disapproved of the Sophists' methods, especially Socrates and Plato. Socrates argued that wisdom was a quality that could not be taught. Plato, who disparaged the rhetorical tricks used specifically by Protagoras, brought ill repute to all the Sophists. A generation later, Aristotle branded their teaching as the furthering of the appearance of wisdom without the reality, and the Sophists as men who made money on this pretense.

Still, Protagoras was clearly more than a specious philosopher. Plato consistently portrayed him as witty, intellectual, moral, and sincere in his praise of Socrates—and thought Protagoras's ideas important enough to refute in several dialogues. Aristotle's extensive refutation of Protagoras's beliefs attests the fact that he, too, took Protagoras seriously.

Protagoras's instruction was practical. He emphasized skill in persuasive speaking and effective debating. He taught his students the importance of words by the study of grammar, diction, and poetic analysis. He may have been the first to emphasize the importance of proper timing. Armed with these skills, Protagoras believed, his students would excel as civic leaders and political advisers. The Athenian orator Isocrates and Protagoras's fellow Sophist Prodicus were two of his most famous students. He also influenced Aristophanes and Euripides.

On his journeys, Protagoras no doubt stayed with influential families and read his speeches to select audiences. His most famous visits were to Athens, which he first saw in 444 B.C.E., when the Athenian ruler Pericles asked him to write the constitution for the new Panhellenic colony of Thurii in southern Italy. This assignment probably required him to live in Italy for some years. He spent enough time in Sicily to have won fame as a teacher. He returned to Athens about 432, when he engaged in the debate with Socrates described in Plato's dialogue *Prōtagoras* (399-390 B.C.E.; *Protagoras*, 1804). He may have visited the city once more in 422 or 421.

Protagoras's high fee of one hundred minae was notorious; according to Plato, Protagoras earned more money in his forty years of teaching than did the famous sculptor Phidias and ten other sculptors combined. Protagoras claimed that a student was not compelled to pay the fee if he did not think the instruction worth the price.

Protagoras was known to have written at least two books, though many more titles have survived. *Aletheia* (*The Truth*) was an early, and his most important, composition. He wrote another titled *Antilogion* (*Contrary Arguments*) and may also have written a third called *Peri theon* (*On the Gods*). Only two substantial fragments of his writing remain. In conjunction with numerous shorter fragments, they reflect the two main philosophies of Protagoras's life and portray him as a person interested in philosophy, rhetoric, grammar and syntax, and literary criticism. The statement for which he is most famous introduces *The Truth*: "Man is the measure of all things, of the things that are, that they are, of the things that are not, that they are not." The saying, perhaps a reply to the mathematicians, has been interpreted since Plato to mean that what a man perceives to be true for him is true for him. A new fragment discovered in 1968 expounds further on the remark.

Protagoras's subjectivism, as it was called, was not well received by philosophers. Aristotle declared the statement absurd. Plato argued that a pig or a baboon was equally capable of being the measure. The flaw in Protagoras's argument was that if others believed the maxim to be false, then by that very maxim their perceptions must be true for them and his maxim was false for them. Despite these objections, the dictum represented an original contribution to fifth century philosophy.

On the Gods is said to have opened with the following statement:

> With regard to the gods, I cannot know whether they exist or do not exist, nor what they are like in form; for the factors preventing knowledge are many: the obscurity of the subject, and the shortness of human life.

Such agnosticism shocked Protagoras's contemporaries. The Athenians reportedly expelled him from the city for impiety. Nearly seven hundred years later, Sextus Empiricus labeled Protagoras an atheist for this remark, as did Diogenes Laertius.

In *Contrary Arguments*, Protagoras stated that two contradictory propositions existed for every issue. Aristotle rejected the saying as contradicting Protagoras's own belief that all views were equally true, and Aristophanes lampooned the idea in his comedy *Nephelai* (423 B.C.E.; *The Clouds*, 1708). Modern views of sophistry stem from the comic playwright's portrayal of these rhetorical tricks.

Minor fragments reveal Protagoras's interest in speech, grammar, and education in general. He wrote on existence, he refuted mathematics, and he discussed such varied topics as wrestling, ambition, virtues, laws, human error, and the underworld. Protagoras's influence on his contemporaries is apparent from later authorities. Porphyry claims that Plato plagiarized substantial passages from the *Contrary Arguments* for his work, the *Politeia* (388-366 B.C.E.; *Republic*, 1701). Protagoras's personal friend Pericles may have chosen him to draft laws for Thurii, partly because he respected the Sophist and partly because Protagoras was already familiar to Western Greeks. The drafting of the laws may have brought him into contact with the historian Herodotus, who was also involved in founding Thurii. Protagorean influence has been noted in part of Herodotus's *Historiai Herodotou* (c. 424 B.C.E.; *The History*, 1709).

The circumstances of Protagoras's death remain shrouded in mystery. By one account, he died in a shipwreck. Diogenes believed he died fleeing Athens when he was banished for impiety. Probably closest to fact is Plato's statement that he died after forty years of teaching, that is, about 410 B.C.E.

SIGNIFICANCE

Protagoras's importance in the realm of Greek philosophy has been largely underrated because of the refutations of Plato and Aristotle and the lampoons of Aristophanes. He and his fellow Sophists initiated the practice of instructing students. Before this time, young men had had to rely on the dramatists and their plays for lessons in how to be good citizens. After the Persian War, this brand of instruction was inadequate for the demands of the city-states, especially Athens. The Sophists provided a necessary service by establishing a definite curriculum.

The system was not without flaws. The aim from the beginning was to educate only the leaders of society, not the general populace. Protagoras's claim to teach virtue was too weak an assertion to support, as Plato, Aristotle, and others clearly saw. Still, it is interesting that after the death of Socrates, who vehemently protested that he taught nothing and never charged a fee, his student Plato founded the Academy, where he lectured to paying students in the area of philosophy. In this respect, Plato much more closely resembled Protagoras than Socrates.

Protagoras's influence has spanned generations. He was known in the Middle Ages and early Renaissance through the writings of Cicero, Seneca, and Aulus Gellius—and in the Latin translations of Aristotle. Some scholars have seen evidence for sophistic origins of Renaissance Humanism. Greek Sophists founded the type of intellectual movement with which the Italian Humanists are identified. There seems to have been a Humanist character to the Sophists, a character that arguably makes the Sophists, through Cicero and his knowledge of them, the progenitors of the thoughts and ideas expressed in Italian Humanism of the 1400's. Protagoras's myth on the origin of human society corresponds to the Humanists' concepts of their own moral and educational role in society.

As historian W. K. C. Guthrie so aptly claims:

> Protagoras's innovation was to achieve a reputation as a political and moral thinker without supporting any political party, attempting political reform, or seeking power for himself, but simply by lecturing and speaking and offering himself as a professional adviser and educator.

Protagoras made people think about their lives in relation to society and sparked some very strong objections from philosophers regarding the direction of learning. In this way, he helped advance education.

—Joan E. Carr

FURTHER READING

Balaban, Oded. *Plato and Protagoras: Truth and Relativism in Ancient Greek Philosophy*. Lanham, Md.: Lexington Books, 1999. The conclusion of this analysis is that Plato and Protagoras do not exemplify characteristic moralism or relativism. Includes index and bibliography.

Barnes, Jonathan. *Empedocles to Democritus*. Vol. 2 in *The Presocratic Philosophers*. New York: Routledge, 1996. The author's special contribution is interpreting Protagoras's sayings according to ancient commentators. Includes extensive bibliography, endnotes, and index.

Freeman, Kathleen. *The Presocratic Philosophers*. Cambridge, Mass.: Harvard University Press, 1971. Still an excellent discussion in English of all the fragments of Protagoras, fact and fiction. Freeman puts him in historical perspective with his predecessors, contemporaries, and successors.

Guthrie, W. K. C. *The Fifth-Century Enlightenment*. Vol. 3 in *A History of Greek Philosophy*. New York: Cambridge University Press, 1986. Compiles ancient evidence on Protagoras and presents it in a clear, straightforward manner. Also provides a good historical background to the Sophists and a discussion of their importance.

Jaeger, Werner. *Archaic Greece: The Mind of Athens*. Vol. 1 in *Paideia: The Ideals of Greek Culture*. Translated by Gilbert Highet. 1945. Reprint. New York: Oxford University Press, 1979. Jaeger's evaluation of the role and importance of the Sophists and of Protagoras's role is one of the best critical accounts. Includes extensive endnotes.

Plato. *Plato's "Protagoras": A Socratic Commentary*. Edited by B. A. F. Hubbard and E. S. Karnofsky. Chicago: University of Chicago Press, 1984. This translation of Plato's dialogue provides a clear portrayal of Protagoras as Sophist and as intellectual. In the commentary, the translators refer to sections of the dialogue that reveal bits of Protagoras's life, and a succinct biography appears in one of the indexes. Includes bibliography.

SEE ALSO: Aristotle; Democritus; Isocrates; Pericles; Plato.

RELATED ARTICLES in *Great Events from History: The Ancient World*: 480-479 B.C.E., Persian Invasion of Greece; 447-438 B.C.E., Building of the Parthenon; c. 440 B.C.E., Sophists Train the Greeks in Rhetoric and Politics; c. 380 B.C.E., Plato Develops His Theory of Ideas.

PSAMTIK I
Egyptian pharaoh (r. c. 664-610 B.C.E.)

Psamtik carved out political independence for Egypt after almost a century of foreign rule, inaugurating a renewal of its society and culture.

BORN: c. 684 B.C.E.; place unknown
DIED: 610 B.C.E.; place unknown
ALSO KNOWN AS: Psammetichus I
AREA OF ACHIEVEMENT: Government and politics

EARLY LIFE

Little is known about the early life of Psamtik I (SAHM-tihk); even the date of his birth is based on conjecture. He was the son of Necho I, a local Egyptian ruler in the western Delta region. For nearly a century, after the kingdom of Egypt had fragmented into several small principalities, Kushite invaders had held the Nile Valley, calling themselves the Twenty-fifth (Kushite) Dynasty (c. 742-c. 656). Assyria was beginning to expand westward; under Esarhaddon and Ashurbanipal (c. 685-627 B.C.E.), it vied for control of the valley, which led to confrontations with the Kushites.

Psamtik's ancestors, especially his great-grandfather Tefnakht, had unsuccessfully tried to reunite the land. Necho, his father, pursued a precarious course between the Assyrians and Kushites, trying to carve out a maximum of independence for himself and the principality of Saïs, which he controlled. This political game would prove fatal: He later died on the battlefield in 664 B.C.E.

LIFE'S WORK

A year earlier, Psamtik had participated in a mission to Nineveh together with his father; at that time, Ashurbanipal appointed the two his vassals in Egypt. Necho became king of Memphis and Saïs, while Psamtik (in the Assyrian records called Nabu-shezibanni) was to rule Athribis in the central Delta. On the death of his father, Psamtik became ruler of Memphis and Saïs. An invasion of the Delta by the Kushites forced him to flee to the Assyrians.

He returned in 664 B.C.E. when Ashurbanipal conducted a campaign against Tanutamuni (r. 664-656), a Kushite ruler, which led to the expulsion of the latter and the sacking of Thebes by the Assyrians. Psamtik was reinstated and had to pay tribute to his Assyrian overlord. With both great powers removed, Psamtik craftily worked to consolidate his position and to expand his rule. A major step toward this goal was the reorganization of his army; with the help of Gyges of Lydia (c. 705-c. 645

B.C.E.), he hired Carian and Ionian mercenaries—the "bronze men who would make their appearance from the sea" in the romantic account of the Greek historian Herodotus (c. 484-c. 425 B.C.E.). For these soldiers, the first coins were struck in Egypt.

By 657 B.C.E., Psamtik had gained full control over the various principalities of the Delta and Middle Egypt. How he accomplished this is not known in detail. Herodotus relates a fictitious tradition: An oracle had foretold that the one who would perform the divine libation from a bronze helmet would become king of all Egypt. At a ceremony in the temple of Ptah-Hepaistos—so the story goes—the golden cups for the ritual libation were one short and Psamtik quickly took his helmet to perform for the god.

The final unification of Egypt under Psamtik was completed in 656 B.C.E., when Thebes peacefully accepted him. This development was negotiated for Thebes by a local dignitary named Mentuemhat and was formalized by the appointment of Psamtik's daughter Nitocris as "Wife of Amen," the priestess who controlled the eco-

Psamtik I. (Library of Congress)

nomic resources of the temple of the Theban god Amen at this time. With great pomp and lavish gifts, the young Nitocris, probably in her teens at the time, sailed to Thebes. Since Psamtik refrained from any interference in prevailing political situations, he did not stir up any opposition; Thebes remained an integral part of Egypt for the next 130 years.

Following the expansion into Thebes, Psamtik was faced with an attack from Libya; some of the invaders were former Delta princes who had fled there. In 655 B.C.E. he repelled this last challenge to his rule. To prevent any recurrence of outside attacks, he set up garrisons at Egypt's borders, such as Elephantine in the south and Daphne in the northeast. The troops stationed there were foreign mercenaries, including Greeks, Hebrews, and Carians.

By 655 B.C.E. Psamtik not only had consolidated his rule over Egypt but also was able to shed his dependence on an Assyria exhausted from years of incessant warfare and growing internal tensions. A period of peace and economic renewal was inaugurated for Egypt. Memories of Egypt's former greatness were carefully cultivated, leading to a conscious antiquarianism that found its most visible expression in the arts, where the style of the Old Kingdom, the Pyramid Age, served as model. This interest in the past also had its impact on the administration of the country, as indicated by the reappearance of official titles after an absence of fifteen hundred years. The motive seems to have been a desire to emulate the achievements of the past, an illusion sustained by the prosperity following half a millennium of internal strife, political insignificance, and economic stagnation. Despite the antiquarian mold, there were numerous intellectual impulses. The traditional way of writing became increasingly replaced by a smoother, more cursive script called demotic. Medicine flourished, especially in Saïs. There was religious fervor, and the cults of Isis and Amen, among others, profited.

The long reign of Psamtik coincided with major shifts in the balance of power in the eastern Mediterranean basin. Assyria, which at the beginning of his reign had been the dominant nation, was losing its importance. Following years of external and internal strife, it was no longer able to exercise influence in Syria and Palestine. In return for military assistance to Assyria, Psamtik was able to expand Egypt's political might northward, filling the vacuum that developed in the Levant as a result of Assyria's withdrawal. By 612 B.C.E. Egypt's control over parts of Lebanon and Palestine was reestablished, while Psamtik joined the Assyrians in their fight against the

RULERS OF THE TWENTY-SIXTH (SAITE) DYNASTY	
Ruler	*Reign (B.C.E.)*
Psamtik I	664-610
Necho II	610-595
Psamtik II	595-589
Apries	589-570
Ahmose II	570-526
Psamtik III	526-525

Note: Dynastic research is ongoing; data are approximate.

Babylonians under Nabopalassar (r. c. 626-605) in 616 and 610 B.C.E. Ashdod was seized by Psamtik, but the Egyptian did not concern himself with the affairs of Judah, which under Josiah (c. 648-609 B.C.E.) was concentrating on religious reforms. Being landlocked at the time, Judah did not fall into the overall political plan Psamtik followed at this time in the Levant.

Unlike any of his predecessors on the throne, Psamtik was interested in making Egypt into a naval power on the Mediterranean and later also on the Red Sea. It is not clear from where the technical expertise came, but some Greek participation is feasible. These naval plans coincided with the political expansion into Palestine. Psamtik prepared the basis for Egypt's subsequent role as a truly international power, not only in its traditional land-based form but also as a naval force, culminating in the construction of a canal linking the Mediterranean—via the Nile system—to the Red Sea and the first known circumnavigation of Africa, which took place under his son and successor Necho II (r. 610-595 B.C.E.).

SIGNIFICANCE

When Psamtik I died in 610, he left an entirely different Egypt from the one with which he began his reign fifty-four years earlier. Caught between the Kushites and the Assyrians, the political ambitions of the local ruler of Memphis and Saïs faced considerable odds, which were overcome. Since the unification of Egypt was achieved peacefully, however, it did not generate new tensions; instead, it marked the beginning of a period of political, cultural, and economic flowering, known as the Saite Renaissance, which lasted until the Persian invasion in 525 B.C.E. Marked by a reawakened national spirit, which took the glorious past, especially the Pyramid Age, as its model, Egypt's last fully indigenous period was a time when the land of the pharaohs exerted considerable cultural influence, on the Greeks especially. Egypt developed its Hellenic contacts, in the process entering the Mediterranean theater. A void in the international political structure not only gave Egypt the opportunity to consolidate its newly attained national identity but also offered the country the chance to become once more a major power, bringing the coastal regions of part of Syria and Palestine under Egyptian authority.

—*Hans Goedicke*

FURTHER READING

Assmann, Jan. *The Mind of Egypt*. Translated by Andrew Jenkins. New York: Henry Holt, 2002. This rather dense book discusses the antiquarianism of the late period dynasties in looking backward to and modeling themselves on the Old Kingdom.

Clayton, Peter A. *Chronicle of the Pharaohs*. New York: Thames and Hudson, 1994. This brief overview of Egyptian chronology provides a reign-by-reign account of all known pharaohs of Egypt. Psamtik is covered in the section on the Late Period. Includes a very useful section on the five royal names of the pharaohs, helping to clarify one of the more confusing aspects of Egyptian history.

Gardiner, Alan. *Egypt of the Pharaohs*. 3d ed. New York: Oxford University Press, 1966. This volume is a fine general account of the history of ancient Egypt. Includes a short bibliography, some illustrations, and an index.

Kitchen, K. A. *The Third Intermediate Period in Egypt, 1100-650 B.C.* Warminster, Pa.: Aris and Phillips, 1973. A well-documented, authoritative study; discusses the Twenty-sixth Dynasty, beginning with Psamtik, extensively. General bibliography.

Spanlinger, Anthony. "Psammetichus, King of Egypt: I." *Journal of the American Research Center in Egypt* 13 (1976): 133-147. The only scholarly treatment of Psamtik written in English. Includes citations.

SEE ALSO: Akhenaton; Amenhotep III; Hatshepsut; Imhotep; Menes; Menkaure; Montuhotep II; Nefertiti; Ramses II; Sesostris III; Thutmose III; Tiy; Tutankhamen; Zoser.

RELATED ARTICLES in *Great Events from History: The Ancient World*: 1069 B.C.E., Third Intermediate Period Begins in Egypt; 745 B.C.E., Tiglath-pileser III Rules Assyria.

PTOLEMY (ASTRONOMER)
Alexandrian scientist

Ptolemy's scientific work in astronomy, mathematics, geography, and optics influenced other practitioners for almost fifteen hundred years.

BORN: c. 100 C.E.; possibly Ptolemais Hermii, Egypt
DIED: c. 178 C.E.; place unknown, possibly Egypt
ALSO KNOWN AS: Claudius Ptolemaeus
AREAS OF ACHIEVEMENT: Astronomy, mathematics, geography

EARLY LIFE

Very little is known about the life of Ptolemy (TOL-uh-mee). He was born in Egypt at the end of the first century C.E., but his birth date and birth place and his life thereafter are subjects of speculation. It is thought that he might have been born in the Grecian city of Ptolemais Hermii in Upper Egypt and that he might have lived to the age of seventy-eight. It has been suggested that he studied and made astronomical observations, staying for more than half of his life among the elevated terraces at the temple of Serapis in Canopus near Alexandria, where pillars

were erected with the results of his astronomical discoveries engraved on them. He was probably the descendant of Greek or Hellenized ancestors and obtained Roman citizenship as a legacy from them.

Much more is known about the age in which Ptolemy lived. It was a century during which Rome ruled the Mediterranean world and during which four successive Roman emperors, Trajan, Hadrian, Antoninus Pius, and Marcus Aurelius, built roads and bridges, opened libraries and colleges, and maintained Rome's power and peace. It was a time when educated men spoke Greek as well as Latin, when Athens was still honored for its cultural traditions, when Marcus Aurelius wrote his *Tōn eis heauton* (c. 171-180; *Meditations*, 1634) in Greek, and Greek was still the language of science and the arts.

Ptolemy, who probably used the libraries at Alexandria, was strongly influenced by a Greek scientist, Hipparchus (fl. 146-127 B.C.E.), who propounded the geocentric theory of the universe. As far back as the fourth century B.C.E., the leading view of the nature of the universe had the sun, moon, and planets revolving around the fixed Earth in concentric spheres. The competing theory was first advocated by Aristarchus of Samos (fl. c. 270 B.C.E.). Aristarchus discovered that the sun was much larger than Earth, and this discovery was the basis for his argument that Earth and all other planets revolved around a fixed sun and stars in circles. Yet the heliocentric theory could not be demonstrated by observable phenomena as long as it was thought that the sun was the center of a circle rather than of an ellipse. Hipparchus rejected the contention of Aristarchus, insisting on "saving the phenomena," that is, adhering to the observations. His further scientific speculations founded on the geocentric theory were the legacy to Ptolemy some two centuries later.

LIFE'S WORK

Some historians maintain that Ptolemy merely plagiarized from Hipparchus; others have said that Ptolemy superseded Hipparchus and made the work of the earlier scientist superfluous. In fact, it could be said that Ptolemy immortalized Hipparchus by acknowledging the debt he owed to his distant predecessor and by frequently quoting from him.

Whatever historical assessment is more correct, there is no doubt that Ptolemy's work in astronomy alone lasted for more than fourteen hundred years, until the great scientific achievements of Nicolaus Copernicus (1473-1543) and Johannes Kepler (1571-1630). Ptolemy used new instruments or improved on old ones to make his observations. In the *Mathēmatikē syntaxis* (c. 150 C.E.; *Almagest*, 1948), one of his most significant books, he utilized the mathematical methods of trigonometry to prove that Earth was a sphere and went on to postulate that the heavens were also spheres and moved around an immobile Earth in the center of the solar system. He dealt with the length of the months and the year and the motion of the sun; he covered the theory of the moon; and he figured out the distance of the sun, and the order and distances of the planets, from Earth. Much of this was not new, not original; the *Almagest* was essentially a restatement of astronomical knowledge available three hundred years earlier. Yet Ptolemy was able to synthesize that scientific information into a system and to expound it in a clear and understandable manner. He was a teacher, and he taught well.

Ptolemy's contribution to mathematics was even more significant. Hipparchus had invented spherical and plane trigonometry for the use of astronomers. Ptolemy then perfected this branch of mathematics so that, unlike

his astronomical system, which was finally discredited, the theorems that he and Hipparchus devised form the permanent basis of trigonometry.

The *Almagest*, in which trigonometry was utilized to measure the positions of the sun, Earth, moon, and planets, was later translated into Arabic and then Latin, and so also was Ptolemy's *Geōgraphikē hyphēgēsis* (second century C.E.; *The Geography of Ptolemy*, 1732). Ptolemy attempted with considerable success to place the study of geography on a scientific foundation. His book, written after the *Almagest*, was modeled after the work of Marinus of Tyre (fl. second century C.E.), but Ptolemy added a unique dimension by placing his predecessor's information into a scientific structure. He assumed that Earth was round, that its surface was divided into five parallel zones, and that there were other circles from the equator to the poles. He was the first geographer to write of "parallels of latitude" and "meridians of longitude." Ptolemy, however, did make one crucial mistake. Along with other ancient geographers, he underestimated the circumference of Earth, and as a consequence few latitudes were established correctly (and, since the means were not available, no longitudes were established).

What most attracted the interest and attention of earlier geographers and of Ptolemy was the size of the inhabited world: in the north, Thule (the present Shetland Islands); in the west, the Fortunate Islands (the Canary Islands and Madeira); and in the south and east, the vast continents of Africa and Asia. Although they overestimated the size of both the eastern and southern continents, Ptolemy's findings, and Marinus's before him, were based on new knowledge derived from travelers' accounts of the silk trade with China and from sea voyages in the Indian Ocean. Ptolemy revised some of Marinus's estimates of the length and breadth of Asia and Africa, extending Asia eastward and Europe westward. More than a thousand years later, Christopher Columbus (1451-1506), who relied on Ptolemy's *Geography*, was led to believe that it was possible to reach Asia by a direct route across the Atlantic Ocean.

Ptolemy's *Geography* is restricted to mathematical calculations; he did not write about the physical attributes of the countries he charted or the people who inhabited them. His tables, stating the location of places in terms of latitude and longitude, gave a false impression of precision; he made frequent errors because of his basic misestimate of the size of Earth. Still, Ptolemy's objective to draw a world map was noteworthy. His educated guess as to the location of the sources of the Nile River

Ptolemy the astronomer. (Library of Congress)

was remarkable, and his use of the terms "latitude" and "longitude" was a distinct contribution to the advancement of geographical knowledge.

While Ptolemy is well-known among historians of science for his volumes on astronomy and geography, it is also necessary to consider his writings on astrology, which in the ancient world was the "science" of religions. His volume *Apotelesmatika* (second century C.E.; *Ptolemy's Quadripartite: Or, Four Books Concerning the Influences of the Stars*, 1701; commonly called *Tetrabiblos*, "four books") is important partly because it was more famous than the *Almagest* and partly because it reflects the popular thinking of his age. The *Tetrabiblos* is a summary of Egyptian, Chaldean, and Greek ideas. It attributes human characteristics to the planets, such as masculine and feminine, beneficent and malevolent. It predicts the future of races, of countries and cities, and speaks of catastrophes, natural and human: wars, famine, plagues, earthquakes, and floods. It also expounds on such subjects as marriage, children, the periods of life, and the quality of death. Translated into Arabic, Latin,

Spanish, and English, it influenced generations of Europeans (and, later, Americans) and formed the basis of modern astrological beliefs.

There are many historians of science who deplore the superstitions that pervade the *Tetrabiblos* and dismiss it as an unfortunate effort. The great historian George Sarton wrote, however, that "we should be indulgent to Ptolemy, who had innocently accepted the prejudices endemic in his age and could not foresee their evil consequences. . . ."

SIGNIFICANCE

It would be unreasonable to expect great scientific breakthroughs during the second century C.E., and they did not happen. What did occur was the gradual advancement of knowledge to which Ptolemy contributed. Not only did Ptolemy write the *Almagest* and the *Geography*, adding new and significant materials to those of his predecessors, but he also attempted to illuminate the science of optics and the art of music. In the first case, although little was known about the anatomical and physiological structure of the eye, he devised a table of refraction, and his book reveals that he understood that a ray of light deviates when it passes from one medium into another of a different density. He addressed the role of light and color in vision, with various kinds of optical illusions and with reflection. Ptolemy's volume on music theory, known as the *Harmonika* (second century C.E.; *Harmonics*, 2000), covers the mathematical intervals between notes and their classification. He propounded a theory that steered a middle ground between mathematical calculations and the evidence of the ear. Observation was again a guiding principle of his art as well as his science.

Other work on mechanics, dimensions, and the elements was done but has not survived. What did survive had great influence on the Arabic science of astronomy, led to the rise of European astronomy, and influenced the work of Copernicus himself in the fifteenth century. The *Geography*, also translated into Arabic in the ninth century, was amended to describe more accurately the territories under Islamic rule; in the West, where the work became known in the fifteenth century, it was a catalyst of cartography and to the work of the Flemish cartographer Gerardus Mercator (1512-1594). Ptolemy's work on optics inspired the great improvements made by the Arabic scientist Ibn al-Haytham (d. 1039), and his work became the foundation of the *Perspectiva* of Witelo (c. 1274), the standard optical treatise of the late Middle Ages.

Just as there is no exact knowledge of Ptolemy's birth date, there is no reliable information about when and where he died and under what circumstances. Yet those biographical facts are not that important; what is significant is the scientific legacy that was transmitted through the centuries. Ptolemy was not, as one expert has argued, an "original genius"; his forte was to take existing knowledge and to shape it into clear and careful prose.

—*David L. Sterling*

FURTHER READING

Barker, Andrew. *Scientific Method in Ptolemy's "Harmonics."* New York: Cambridge University Press, 2001. This study illuminates not only the *Harmonics* but also Ptolemy's observational methods in general.

Grasshoff, Gerd. *The History of Ptolemy's Star Catalog.* New York: Springer-Verlag, 1989. A careful study of the relationship between Ptolemy's work and that of Hipparchus, showing that charges of plagiarism are anachronistic and based in a misunderstanding of Ptolemy's scientific objectives.

Irby-Massie, Georgia L., and Paul T. Keyser. *Greek Science of the Hellenistic Era: A Sourcebook.* New York: Routledge, 2001. Chapters cover the main scientific disciplines in the Hellenistic era, providing a historical and scientific context for Ptolemy's work in many fields.

Ptolemy. *Harmonics: Translation and Commentary.* Translated by Jon Solomon. New York: Brill Academic Publishers, 2000.

_____. *Ptolemy's "Almagest."* Translated by G. J. Toomer. 1984. Reprint. Princeton, N.J.: Princeton University Press, 1998.

_____. *Ptolemy's "Geography."* Translated by Alexander Jones and J. Lennart Berggren. Princeton, N.J.: Princeton University Press, 2000.

_____. *Tetrabiblos.* Translated by F. R. Robbins. Loeb Library. Cambridge, Mass.: Harvard University Press, 1980. For students and readers who may want to sample the scientific works of Ptolemy. All have useful introductions and annotations.

SEE ALSO: Anaximander; Apollonius of Perga; Hipparchus; Nabu-rimanni; Pythagoras; Sosigenes.

RELATED ARTICLES in *Great Events from History: The Ancient World*: c. 3100-c. 1550 B.C.E., Building of Stonehenge; 600-500 B.C.E., Greek Philosophers Formulate Theories of the Cosmos; c. 500-470 B.C.E., Hecataeus of Miletus Writes the First Geography Book; 332 B.C.E., Founding of Alexandria; 325-323 B.C.E., Aristotle Isolates Science as a Discipline; c. 320 B.C.E., Theophrastus Initiates the Study of Botany; c. 300 B.C.E., Euclid Compiles a Treatise on Geometry; c. 275 B.C.E., Greeks Advance Hellenistic Astronomy; c. 250 B.C.E., Discoveries of Archimedes.

PTOLEMY PHILADELPHUS
Hellenistic pharaoh (r. 288-246 B.C.E.)

Under Ptolemy, the domestic institutions and the foreign policy characteristic of Hellenistic Egypt matured. His patronage of the arts and sciences established Alexandria as the most important cultural center of the Greek world.

BORN: February, 308 B.C.E.; Island of Cos, Greece
DIED: 246 B.C.E.; Alexandria, Egypt
ALSO KNOWN AS: Ptolemy II
AREA OF ACHIEVEMENT: Government and politics

EARLY LIFE

In 308 B.C.E., Ptolemy Soter (367/366-283/282 B.C.E.), fighting to secure his place among the Macedonian dynasts eager to claim their share of the legacy of Alexander the Great (356-323 B.C.E.), personally led an expedition into the Aegean in order to anchor his influence in the region through alliances and a series of naval bases. Along with Ptolemy Soter went his third wife, Berenice, who gave birth to Ptolemy Philadelphus (TOL-uh-mee fihl-uh-DEHL-fuhs) on the island of Cos. Berenice was the least well connected of the polygamous Ptolemy's three wives. She had come to Egypt in the retinue of Eurydice, when that daughter of Antipater came as Ptolemy's bride. Despite her political insignificance, Berenice was Ptolemy's favorite spouse, and her son Ptolemy Philadelphus became heir to Egypt over the claims of an older son of Eurydice, Ptolemy Ceraunus ("thunderbolt").

Ptolemy Philadelphus was not to be the man of action his father had been. Reared at an urbane court in the greatest city of the Greek world, he was a devotee of a softer, more culturally inclined life. He had the best of educations under the likes of the Aristotelian Strato of

Lampsacus (d. c. 270 B.C.E.) and became a king who preferred to rule from his capital, rather than personally oversee his varied foreign interests.

In order to facilitate the transfer of authority to his chosen son, Ptolemy Soter elevated Ptolemy Philadelphus to the throne in 288 B.C.E., and they ruled jointly until Ptolemy Soter died about three years later. On the accession of his half brother, Ptolemy Ceraunus fled Egypt to the court of Lysimachus (c. 360-281 B.C.E.) in Thrace. There his sister, Lysandra, was married to Lysimachus's son Agathocles (361-289 B.C.E.). Lysimachus, furthermore, was married to Arsinoe II Philadelphus (c. 316-270 B.C.E.), the sister of Ptolemy Philadelphus. Probably to foster the inheritance of her own young sons, Arsinoe II convinced her husband that Agathocles was engaged in treason. Lysimachus had Agathocles executed, and, as a result, both Lysandra and Ceraunus fled to the Asian court of Seleucus I Nicator (358/354-281 B.C.E.). When Seleucus defeated and killed Lysimachus in 281, Ceraunus fought on the winning side.

The true nature of Ceraunus's loyalty, however, revealed itself when he soon after assassinated Seleucus and seized Thrace. Arsinoe II fled to Macedonia on the death of Lysimachus, to secure it for her children. Not satisfied with the murder of Seleucus, Ceraunus also aspired to add Macedonia to his realm, which he accomplished by marrying Arsinoe II, his half sister. For reasons that are not entirely clear, Ceraunus eventually butchered two of Arsinoe's three sons. Perhaps Ceraunus limited his wife's freedom, but she remained in Macedonia until he was killed fighting Gauls in 279 B.C.E. With Macedonia overrun by barbarians, Arsinoe II and her surviving son, Ptolemy, again fled, this time home to Egypt.

Ptolemy Philadelphus's queen was another woman named Arsinoe (a daughter of Lysimachus), by whom he already had three children. Nevertheless, not long after Arsinoe II came to his court, Ptolemy exiled his first wife, and sometime before 274 B.C.E. he married his sister. It was this union that later earned for Ptolemy the name "Philadelphus" ("brother-loving"; Arsinoe II alone bore the title in life.) The marriage scandalized many of Ptolemy's Greco-Macedonian subjects, but royal brother-sister unions were known in Egypt, and its consummation had the effect of drawing the Europeans in Egypt closer to native tradition.

LIFE'S WORK

Ptolemy ruled Egypt at the height of its Hellenistic power, but before the return of Arsinoe II to Egypt, little is known of Ptolemy's foreign ambitions. In the early 270's B.C.E. he was interested in fostering a regular spice trade with Arabia and as a result recut a neglected ancient canal from the Nile's delta to the Gulf of Suez. Ptolemy subsequently patronized the exploration of the Red Sea (complete with colonies along the African coast) and voyages to India. His desire to tap the exotic luxuries of the East found a counterpart in his interests in sub-Saharan Africa. In fact, the only known foreign expedition personally led by Ptolemy went to Ethiopia in order to strengthen trade to the south. Perhaps Ptolemy's most interesting foreign policy initiative came in 273 B.C.E., when he sent an embassy to Rome and became the first Hellenistic monarch to establish friendly relations with the Republic, which had only recently unified peninsular Italy.

Arsinoe II's holdings in the Aegean (a legacy from her days as Macedonian queen) expanded the interests of Egypt in that region and eventually pitted Ptolemy against Antigonus II Gonatas (c. 320-239 B.C.E.), whose victories over the Gauls won for him Macedonia. Perhaps prompted by his wife's more assertive personality, in the 270's Ptolemy initiated an aggressive foreign policy that challenged not only Antigonus II, but the Seleucids as well.

His first conflict of note, the First Syrian War (c. 276-271 B.C.E.), was fought against the Seleucid Antiochus I (324-260/261 B.C.E.) over the Phoenician coast. This land not only lay astride the best approach to Egypt but also was an important terminus for trade that stretched eastward along several routes. In this war, Antiochus secured Damascus and successfully incited Magas (Ptolemy's half brother and governor of Cyrene) to rebellion, but Ptolemy's superior fleet was a scourge to Seleucid coastal settlements and eventually won the war for him. By its end, Ptolemy had regained Cyrene and extended his control of the coast northward into Syria. Arsinoe II was probably instrumental in planning the war, since soon after its conclusion, Ptolemy approved worship of her under the auspices of a state-cult, the first attested worship of a living human being since Alexander the Great. Indeed, Arsinoe's political clout must have been enormous, since her portrait appeared with that of Ptolemy on Egyptian coins—an honor exclusively reserved for Hellenistic monarchs. Arsinoe died in July, 269 B.C.E.

In the Balkans, Ptolemy was a party to the Chremonidean War (266-261 B.C.E.) in which Athens, expecting strong Egyptian backing, led a Greek coalition against Macedonia. Accounts of this war are extremely fragmentary, making a reconstruction of its significance difficult. The reason Ptolemy did not order his forces in the Aegean to exploit the war more effectively is not known, but by and large they remained on the fringes while Antigonus II Gonatas defeated his opponents. Perhaps there is more than a grain of truth in the hypothesis that Ptolemy was an indecisive strategist when not influenced by the forceful Arsinoe II.

Whether the Egyptian success in the First Syrian War was because of Arsinoe, the Second Syrian War (c. 260-253 B.C.E.) saw Ptolemaic losses. Not long after his accession, the Seleucid Antiochus II (c. 287- 246 B.C.E.) attacked Ptolemaic possessions along the coast of Asia Minor. A complicated and elusive struggle followed, until Ptolemy conceded much of the Syrian coast under his garrison. The resulting peace was fixed by the marriage that joined Ptolemy's daughter by Arsinoe I, Berenice, to Antiochus II.

At home, Ptolemy II faced a brief challenge to his authority in the 270's from a brother, Argaeus, and was forced to recognize the semiautonomy of King Magas in Cyrene. Ptolemy was very successful, however, in establishing a variety of institutions that anchored the legitimacy of his dynasty in Egypt. For example, for the Macedonians who still remembered their native land and its traditions, at the beginning of his reign, Ptolemy established a royal cemetery in Alexandria around the remains of Alexander the Great and Ptolemy Soter. This foundation re-created in Egypt an institution from the homeland and provided a focus for the loyalties of the Macedonians in Egypt. It also acted as a bridge between the legitimacy of the extinct house of Alexander and the new authority of Ptolemy's dynasty. Its political purpose is manifest: Ptolemy laid first claim to the authority of Alexander.

It was under Ptolemy that the apparatus that ruled Hellenistic Egypt matured. The native pharaonic system was too efficient a revenue producer to be abandoned, but the Ptolemies could not afford to trust their security to the loyalty of native Egyptians. As a result, the Ptolemies grafted an immigrant Greco-Macedonian ruling class onto the stock of Egyptian society and tried as much as possible to maintain the distinctiveness of the two social orders (for example, by severely limiting native Egyptian access to the city of Alexandria). Such a policy was doomed, at least in the Egyptian countryside, but in the time of Ptolemy it worked. Egypt was the sole possession of the Ptolemaic kings. Except for those estates alienated by the Ptolemies to attract European settlement, it remained their private property. The geographical isolation of Egypt made it possible to sever all but officially sanctioned foreign trade, and its economy was monopolized in the interests of the dynasty. Native Egyptians were compelled to render to Ptolemy at a fixed rate a percentage of their grain, which he thereafter sold abroad at a huge profit, while the immigrants paid significant taxes for the use of their land. In turn, these profits paid not only for such things as cultural patronage and the construction of a city that was home to about one million people but also for the domestic and foreign security ensured by Ptolemy's sizable Greco-Macedonian military establishment.

Like his father before him, Ptolemy elevated his heir, Ptolemy III Euergetes (r. 246-221 B.C.E.), a son of Arsinoe I, to royal authority before his own demise. Ptolemy Philadelphus, having no sons by Arsinoe II, seems originally to have selected as his heir Arsinoe II's only surviving son, but this Ptolemy apparently died in 258 B.C.E. Ptolemy Philadelphus died shortly after passing on the burdens of his office to his son.

SIGNIFICANCE

The domestic and foreign policies that made Ptolemy Philadelphus's Egypt the most stable Hellenistic power of his day were very expensive and pushed Egypt to its financial limit. Although an adequate defense of Egypt proper was maintained, the rivalries with Antigonid Macedonia and Seleucid Asia drained the treasury greatly. Arsinoe II may have been responsible for unleashing an aggressive foreign policy, but without her decisiveness to carry the stratagem through, Ptolemy's remote interests languished, taking second place to Alexandrian pleasures.

Evidence suggests that Ptolemy was both intellectually curious and self-indulgent. He was a renowned cultural patron, attracting outstanding poets such as Theocritus (c. 310-c. 250 B.C.E.) and Callimachus (c. 305-c. 240 B.C.E.) to his court. Although Ptolemy patronized the greatest Hellenistic poets, perhaps his most important cultural legacy resulted from his support of scientific and technological investigation. Ptolemy encouraged such investigation through the great museum and library in Alexandria, which were to be the cultural mainstays of the Hellenistic tradition for the rest of antiquity. The concentration of talent attracted to Alexandria by royal patronage brought the city a luster that drew intellectuals who did not directly enjoy Ptolemy's largess. Jews in large numbers took advantage of the city's resources and there produced a Greek version of their sacred texts, which was to begin the process whereby the Jewish and

Hellenistic traditions would intermingle. Ptolemy personally enjoyed the artistic fruits of his patronage, but he also benefited in practical ways: Figures such as the poet Apollonius of Rhodes gave him political advice, and his engineers constantly improved the technological efficiency of the Ptolemaic navy, thus enabling the fleet to remain competitive while Ptolemy was occupied elsewhere.

It is unfair to describe Ptolemy as lazy or hedonistic, for he was very much concerned with the administration of his kingdom at a time when his dynasty's hold on Egypt was anything but traditionally anchored. Nevertheless, his talents were hardly those of his Macedonian predecessors. He did not feel comfortable leading troops into battle as had Philip II (382-336 B.C.E.), Alexander the Great, Ptolemy Soter, or even men such as his own contemporary, Pyrrhus (319-272 B.C.E.). His style of kingship—surrounding himself with elaborate layers of court officials and a well-oiled administration—tempered the martial spirit that underscored the foundation of Alexander's Macedonian Empire and its division. A new age had dawned, an age that based its legitimacy on conquest but aspired to more peaceful pursuits.

—*William S. Greenwalt*

FURTHER READING

Burstein, Stanley. "Arsinoe II Philadelphos: A Revisionist View." In *Philip II, Alexander the Great, and the Macedonian Heritage*. Washington, D.C.: University Press of America, 1982. Argues that Arsinoe II should not be credited with single-handedly devising Ptolemy's foreign policy.

Fraser, Peter Marshall. *Ptolemaic Alexandria*. 3 vols. Oxford, England: Clarendon Press, 1972. The authoritative study of the Ptolemaic capital and virtually every institution associated with the Ptolemaic Dynasty.

An essential work for anyone interested in the development of Ptolemaic society.

Holbl, Gunther. *A History of the Ptolemaic Empire*. Translated by Tine Saavedra. New York: Routledge, 2000. Ptolemy Philadelphus is covered in part 1 of this study. Includes bibliography, index, and maps.

Macurdy, Grace Harriet. *Hellenistic Queens*. 1932. Reprint. Chicago: Ares, 1985. Includes excellent reviews of what is known of the careers of Arsinoe I and Arsinoe II and, in connection with the latter, a standard summary of her influence over her brother and husband, Ptolemy.

Shipley, Graham. *The Greek World After Alexander, 323-30 B.C.* New York: Routledge, 2000. This overview of the Hellenistic world provides insight into the complicated interrelationships between Alexander's heirs. Includes some useful dynastic tables and genealogical charts, as well as index and bibliography.

Turner, E. G. "Ptolemaic Egypt." *The Hellenistic World*. Vol. 7 in *The Cambridge Ancient History*. 2d ed. New York: Cambridge University Press, 1984. A review of the Ptolemaic system in Egypt. Includes a good discussion of the social structures harnessed and exploited by Ptolemy.

SEE ALSO: Alexander the Great; Arsinoe II Philadelphus; Callimachus; Philip II of Macedonia; Ptolemy Soter; Seleucus I Nicator.

RELATED ARTICLES in *Great Events from History: The Ancient World*: 359-336 B.C.E., Philip II Expands and Empowers Macedonia; 336 B.C.E., Alexander the Great Begins Expansion of Macedonia; 332 B.C.E., Founding of Alexandria; 323 B.C.E., Founding of the Ptolemaic Dynasty and Seleucid Kingdom; c. 323-275 B.C.E., Diadochi Divide Alexander the Great's Empire.

PTOLEMY SOTER
Hellenistic general and ruler (r. 305-285 B.C.E.)

A companion of Alexander the Great during the conquest of the Persian Empire, Ptolemy came to rule Egypt shortly after Alexander died—first as a satrap under Philip III and Alexander IV, and after the extinction of the Argead royal family as a king in his own right. Ptolemy thereby founded the dynasty that ruled Egypt until the death of Cleopatra VII in 30 B.C.E.

BORN: 367 or 366 B.C.E.; the canton of Eordaea, Macedonia (now in Greece)
DIED: 283 or 282 B.C.E.; Alexandria, Egypt
ALSO KNOWN AS: Ptolemy I
AREAS OF ACHIEVEMENT: Government and politics, war and conquest

EARLY LIFE

The origins of Ptolemy Soter (TOL-uh-mee SOH-tuhr) are obscure—and were so even in his lifetime, when jokes were made about his grandfather's lack of distinction. Ptolemy's father was named Lagus, although in order to enhance his legitimacy among the Macedonians he later ruled in Egypt, rumor maintained that he was an illegitimate son of Philip II of Macedonia (382-336 B.C.E.) and thus that he was the half brother of Alexander the Great (356-323 B.C.E.). Ptolemy's mother was named Arsinoe, and she may have been distantly related to the Argead house, the royal line of Macedonian kings of which Philip was a member. Ptolemy was born in Eordaea, a region in western Macedonia that was firmly brought within the political orbit of the Argead royal house only during the reign of Philip II.

Ptolemy probably came to live at the Argead court in the 350's B.C.E. (after Philip's victory over an Illyrian coalition that threatened Macedonia from the northwest), as Eordaea then fell under direct Argead rule. In order to control the newly incorporated cantons of Upper Macedonia, Philip invited the sons of aristocratic western families to his court at Pella. These youths served as royal pages, responsible for (among other things) the protection of the king's person. The honor associated with becoming a member of the pages was augmented by the military, political, and cultural educational opportunities available at court. The selection of royal pages, however, served not only to redirect the loyalty of young aristocrats but also to provide the king with hostages in order to secure the good behavior of their families.

Ptolemy is first mentioned in ancient sources with respect to the so-called Pixodarus affair. In 337 B.C.E., as Philip was searching for political connections in Asia as a prelude to his proposed attack on the Persian Empire, he made diplomatic contact with the satrap of Caria, Pixodarus, to whose daughter he betrothed his handicapped son, Philip III Arrhidaeus. At the time of this initiative, Alexander the Great was temporarily alienated from his father as a result of Philip's last marriage and was in self-imposed exile.

When Alexander learned of Philip's move, he was afraid that Philip had jeopardized his own status as heir to the throne. As a result, Alexander rashly interfered with Philip's plans by offering himself to Pixodarus in lieu of Arrhidaeus. The Carian was delighted with the proposed substitution, but Philip was not. On learning of Alexander's obstruction, Philip both broke off diplomatic contact with Pixodarus and severely chastised his son. In the wake of Philip's anger, several of Alexander's associates, including Ptolemy, were exiled from Macedonia.

Many have seen Ptolemy's exile as a result of his longstanding intimacy with Alexander, but such a close friendship between the two is doubtful since Ptolemy was eleven years older than Philip's heir—almost as close in age to Philip as he was to Alexander. By the 330's B.C.E. Philip seemed to have appointed Ptolemy as a counselor to Alexander, with a responsibility to advise the son according to the interests of the father. When Alexander embarrassed Philip in the Pixodarus affair, the king drove out of Macedonia those who had failed him. Fortunately for Ptolemy, Philip was assassinated in 336 B.C.E., and when Alexander became king, he brought home those who had suffered exile.

LIFE'S WORK

Although Ptolemy accompanied Alexander into Asia, he did so initially in a minor capacity—proving that Ptolemy had not been an intimate of Alexander. Ptolemy's first command came in 330 B.C.E., when he led one of several units at the battle that gave the Macedonians access to Persia proper. Ptolemy became a figure of the first rank shortly afterward, when he replaced a certain Demetrius as one of Alexander's seven eminent bodyguards, whose duty it was to wait closely on the king in matters of consequence. Ptolemy further distinguished himself in 329, when he personally brought to Alexander Bessus, Alexander's last rival for the Persian throne.

Having attained Alexander's confidence, Ptolemy alternated his service at the side of the king with indepen-

RULERS OF THE PTOLEMAIC DYNASTY

Ruler	Reign (B.C.E.)
Philip III Arrhidaeus	323-317
Alexander IV	323-311
Ptolemy Soter	305-285
Ptolemy II Philadelphus	288-246
Ptolemy III Euergetes	246-221
Ptolemy IV Philopator	221-205
Ptolemy V Epiphanes	205-180
Ptolemy VI Philometor	180-145
Ptolemy VII Neos Philopator	145
Ptolemy VIII Euergetes II	170-116
Ptolemy IX Soter II	116-107
Ptolemy X Alexander I	107-88
Ptolemy IX Soter II (restored)	88-80
Ptolemy XI Alexander II	80
Ptolemy XII Neos Dionysos	80-51
Cleopatra VII	51-30
Ptolemy XIII	51-47
Ptolemy XIV	47-44
Ptolemy XV Caesarion	44-30

dent assignments. In 328 he commanded one of five columns as Alexander drove into Sogdiana, in 327 he was instrumental in the capture of the fortress of Chorienes, and, while the Macedonians campaigned along the Indus River (327-325 B.C.E.), Ptolemy often led both Macedonian and mercenary troops. Alexander's return to Susa in 324 brought Ptolemy military honors, his first wife (the Persian Artacama), and additional commands in coordination with Alexander.

The death of Alexander at Babylon in 323 precipitated a constitutional crisis, since the only male Argead living was the mentally deficient Arrhidaeus. Alexander's son by Roxana, Alexander IV (r. 323-311 B.C.E.), would be born several months after his father's passing. Perdiccas (365-321 B.C.E.), the officer to whom the dying Alexander had given his signet ring in a gesture of unknown significance, dominated the discussions concerning succession and advised the Macedonians to accept an interregnum until it could be determined whether Roxana would give birth to a son. Along with others, Ptolemy objected to the unprecedented leadership role Perdiccas had delegated himself. Dissension infected the Macedonian army until a compromise averting civil war was adopted. It was agreed that the throne should go to Arrhidaeus (who was given the throne name of Philip III, r. 323-317 B.C.E.), until such time as Roxana gave birth to

a son. When that eventuality occurred, a dual monarchy was established. Since neither king was competent, both were put under the protection of Perdiccas. There followed a general distribution of satrapies in which Ptolemy received Egypt.

Once in Egypt, Ptolemy asserted control over the satrapy and extended his authority to incorporate the region around Cyrene. He then used his considerable resources to challenge the authority of Perdiccas. His first open act of defiance concerned the body of Alexander the Great. Whether the Macedonians originally meant to bury Alexander in Macedonia or at the oracular shrine of Amen located at the oasis of Siwah in the Egyptian desert, when Alexander's funeral procession reached Syria, Ptolemy diverted the remains to Memphis, where they were enshrined until the late 280's B.C.E., when they were transferred to a complex in Alexandria. Perdiccas saw the appropriation of Alexander's corpse as a rejection of his own authority and in 321 B.C.E. led an expedition to Egypt against Ptolemy.

By this time, others had begun to question the ambitions of Perdiccas, and a coalition including especially Ptolemy, Antipater (397-319 B.C.E.), and Antigonus (382-301 B.C.E.) formed to strip Perdiccas of his office. In the resulting war, Perdiccas failed miserably in an attempt to force his way into Egypt and was assassinated by his own men for his failure. Ptolemy thereafter successfully appealed to the Macedonians of Perdiccas's army and persuaded many of them to settle in Egypt. Ptolemy refused the option of replacing Perdiccas as the guardian of the kings, preferring to retain his Egyptian base.

Although Perdiccas was dead, Eumenes (362-316 B.C.E.), his most important ally, remained free in Asia. In response to this new situation, a redistribution of satrapies occurred at Triparadisus. Ptolemy again received Egypt, while Antipater returned to Macedonia with the kings and Antigonus waged war against Eumenes. Ptolemy anchored an expanded influence by taking Antipater's daughter, Eurydice, as a second wife. (A third, Berenice I, was culled from Eurydice's retinue. Ptolemy's polygamy had a precedent in the Argead house.)

The death of Antipater in 319 B.C.E. initiated a new era. The royal family split behind the claims of the two kings, and a civil war erupted. Eventually, both kings were murdered: Philip III by Olympias in 317, and Alexander IV by Antipater's son Cassander (c. 358-297 B.C.E.) in 311. Through inscriptions and coins, however, it is known that Ptolemy remained loyal to the kings of the Argead house until they were no more. Despite his professed Argead loyalties, Ptolemy continued to secure

Egypt at the expense of rivals. In particular, he seized the coast of Palestine in order to safeguard the only viable access to Egypt by land.

In addition to these problems, Antigonus's success and ultimate victory over Eumenes in 316 destabilized the balance of power that had been established among the Macedonian officers at Triparadisus. High-handed actions, such as Antigonus's expulsion of Seleucus I Nicator (358/354-281 B.C.E.) from his Babylonian satrapy, created a fear of a second Perdiccas. An alliance consisting of Ptolemy, Cassander, Lysimachus (c. 360-281 B.C.E.), and Seleucus demanded that Antigonus surrender his authority. When Antigonus refused, war erupted anew. This conflict continued intermittently until Antigonus was killed at a battle near Ipsus in 301. Ptolemy saw action in Palestine, where he defeated Demetrius (336-283 B.C.E.), the son of Antigonus, at a battle near Gaza in 312, and amid the confusion built the beginnings of a maritime empire in the eastern Mediterranean.

Although this period saw the expansion of Ptolemy's influence, most of his early gains beyond Egypt were tenuously held and setbacks occurred. For example, in 306, Demetrius defeated the Ptolemaic navy off the island of Cyprus in an action so decisive that both he and his father subsequently claimed the title of "king." Once Antigonus and Demetrius claimed the royal mantle from the defunct Argead house, others followed suit, including Ptolemy in 305.

After Ipsus, Ptolemy reestablished influence abroad, retaking Cyprus and actively engaging in Aegean affairs. His occupation of Palestine after 301, however, precipitated a series of wars with the Seleucids in the third century. These civil wars established a rough balance among the emerging powers of Macedonia, Egypt, and Seleucid Asia. This balance was constantly under strain and ever shifting in its precise makeup, composed as it was of infant dynasties seeking legitimacy and leverage.

Egypt also claimed Ptolemy's attention. He inherited an efficient bureaucratic apparatus of great antiquity, capable of funneling great wealth to his coffers. Nevertheless, Ptolemy could not afford to rely on the loyalty of native Egyptians. Rather, he grafted a new Greco-Macedonian aristocracy onto the existing political structure. Recruitment was a major concern, and Ptolemy made every effort to attract Greek mercenaries, military colonists, and professionals accomplished in administration. The wealth of Egypt made possible these initiatives, and each recruit was guaranteed a respectable status as long as Ptolemy remained secure.

In part to unify these enlistees of varied background,

Ptolemy combined elements of the Egyptian worship of Osiris and Apis to manufacture the cult of a new deity: Serapis. Traditionally, religion helped to define the parameters of Greek political communities, and the invented Serapis successfully drew Ptolemy's immigrants together. In addition, in an age of emerging ruler cults, Ptolemy posthumously was worshiped as a god (indeed, to the Egyptians, who worshiped him as pharaoh, he was naturally considered divine), receiving the epithet "Soter" (savior) from the Rhodians for his naval protection.

Under Ptolemy, Alexandria became the foremost city of the Hellenistic world. Planned on a grand scale, it held architectural wonders and became the greatest literary and intellectual center of the age, with its focus being the great museum and library complex. In 288, after decades of molding Egypt to his liking, Ptolemy shared royal authority with a son by Berenice, Ptolemy II, better known as Ptolemy Philadelphus. Ptolemy Soter died in 283 or 282 B.C.E. at the age of eighty-four.

SIGNIFICANCE

Ptolemy Soter was the one great link between Greece's classical age—characterized by its narrow geographical orientation and exclusive appreciation of the Greek cultural heritage—and the Hellenistic age, with its expanded horizons. He took advantage of the opportunities presented by the moment to rise as far as hard work could take him and was instrumental in combining Hellenistic traditions with those of the Orient—a mixture that was a hallmark of the Hellenistic period. Not the most talented of Alexander's successors in military affairs, Ptolemy nevertheless understood, even better than Alexander himself, how long-term stability depended on the careful selection of a defendable base coupled with a steady consolidation of resources. His success can be appreciated best once it is realized that he alone of the officers who received assignments in Babylon in 323 B.C.E. passed his legacy on to his descendants. He did more than politically anchor Egypt in a time of unprecedented change: Because of his patronage, which brought so many fertile minds to Alexandria, he was also able to shape the cultural experience that would dominate the civilized Western world for hundreds of years.

The range of Ptolemy's talents is not fully appreciated until it is realized that he was not only an active ruler and a cultural patron but also a historian of note. Late in life, he wrote an account of Alexander's conquests based not only on his own observations but also on important written sources (including a journal that detailed the king's activities on a daily basis, at least for the end of Alexander's reign). Although Ptolemy's account was slanted in his own favor, no other eyewitness account of the Macedonian conquest can claim greater objectivity. No longer extant, Ptolemy's work was one of the principal sources used in the second century C.E. by Arrian, whose history is the best extant account of Alexander's life. Without Ptolemy's attention to detail, present knowledge about Alexander would be considerably less accurate.

—*William S. Greenwalt*

FURTHER READING

Bowman, Alan K. *Egypt After the Pharaohs*. 1986. Reprint. Berkeley: University of California Press, 1996. This work is a broad introduction to Egypt between the conquests of Alexander and the Arabs. As such, it covers the Ptolemaic period, especially insofar as its political and social institutions evolved.

Ellis, Walter M. *Ptolemy of Egypt*. New York: Routledge, 1995. A thorough, detailed biography of Ptolemy and his role in the formation of Hellenistic society.

Fraser, Peter Marshall. *Ptolemaic Alexandria*. 3 vols. New York: Oxford University Press, 1972. The authoritative study of the Ptolemaic capital and virtually every institution associated with the Macedonian presence in Egypt. An essential work for anyone interested in how Ptolemy developed the infrastructure of his realm.

Holbl, Gunther. *A History of the Ptolemaic Empire*. Translated by Tine Saavedra. New York: Routledge, 2000. Ptolemy Soter is covered in part 1 of this study. Includes bibliography, index, and maps.

Shipley, Graham. *The Greek World After Alexander, 323-30 B.C.* New York: Routledge, 2000. This overview of the Hellenistic world provides insight into the complicated interrelationships between Alexander's heirs. Includes some extremely useful dynastic tables and genealogical charts, as well as index and bibliography.

Turner, E. G. "Ptolemaic Egypt." *The Hellenistic World*. Vol. 7 in *The Cambridge Ancient History*. 2d ed. Cambridge, England: Cambridge University Press, 1984. A review of Ptolemy's accomplishment in Egypt, with special attention devoted to the domestic difficulties associated with stabilization of Macedonian authority.

Walbank, R. W. *The Hellenistic World*. Rev. ed. Cambridge, Mass.: Harvard University Press, 1993. One of the best introductions to the period in English, especially insofar as it traces the emergence of Hellenistic kingdoms.

SEE ALSO: Alexander the Great; Arsinoe II Philadelphus; Callimachus; Philip II of Macedonia; Ptolemy Philadelphus; Seleucus I Nicator.

RELATED ARTICLES in *Great Events from History: The Ancient World*: 359-336 B.C.E., Philip II Expands and Empowers Macedonia; 336 B.C.E., Alexander the Great Begins Expansion of Macedonia; 332 B.C.E., Founding of Alexandria; October 1, 331 B.C.E., Battle of Gaugamela; 323 B.C.E., Founding of the Ptolemaic Dynasty and Seleucid Kingdom; c. 323-275 B.C.E., Diadochi Divide Alexander the Great's Empire.

PYRRHON OF ELIS
Greek philosopher

The founder of skepticism, Pyrrhon, a companion of Alexander the Great, taught that the nature of things is inapprehensible; his attitude greatly influenced science and philosophy throughout antiquity.

BORN: c. 360 B.C.E.; Elis, Greece
DIED: c. 272 B.C.E.; buried in village of Petra, near Elis, Greece
ALSO KNOWN AS: Pyrrho
AREA OF ACHIEVEMENT: Philosophy

EARLY LIFE

Few details about the life of Pyrrhon (PIHR-ohn) have been preserved. Born in Elis, Pyrrhon was the son of Pleistarchus or, by other accounts, Pleitocrates. Apparently of humble background, Pyrrhon first studied painting, no doubt influenced by the master Apelles in nearby Sikyon, then briefly turned his hand to poetry.

Pyrrhon's early philosophical training must have begun soon thereafter; he studied under Bryson and Anaxarchus (a pupil of Democritus and adviser to Alexander the Great), whom he joined in the Macedonian invasion of Persia and India in 331 B.C.E. During that invasion, Pyrrhon gained a reputation for high moral conduct among the quarrelsome Macedonians. After returning to his native Elis, he was awarded a high priesthood and was exempted from taxes; he also received honorary Athenian citizenship and knew Aristotle, Epicurus, the Academic Arcesilaus, and Zeno of Citium. A tradition that

Alexander had provided Pyrrhon with a comfortable endowment may help to account for the philosopher's high social standing. Although probably a man of some means, he was renowned for his modest and withdrawn life.

Pyrrhon's Greece witnessed a major revolution in philosophical thinking as the old political order of independent city-states yielded to the Hellenistic empires. Pyrrhonistic philosophy joined the Epicurean and the Stoic in seeking ways to achieve *ataraxia*—a personal state of freedom from worldly cares. Pyrrhon differed both from his contemporaries and from the previous skeptical trends of Xenophanes, Heraclitus, Democritus, and the Sophists, in that he held no dogmatic position concerning the nature of truth. According to Pyrrhon and his followers, the phenomena of sense experience are neither true nor false, and there is no access to any proof of reality beyond the empirical world. The wise and happy man takes an agnostic stance on the nature of reality.

Pyrrhon did not establish a formal school, as did Epicurus and Zeno, though he was the mentor of Philo of Athens, Nausiphanes of Teios, and Timon of Phlius, his only true successor. In his third century C.E. *Peri biōn dogmatōn kai apophthegmatōn tōn en philosophia eudokimēsantōn* (*Lives and Opinions of Eminent Philosophers*, 1688), Diogenes Laertius quotes extensively from the writings of Timon and from the life of Pyrrhon written by Antigonus of Carystus shortly after the philosopher's death. Diogenes Laertius's account, together with Cicero's somewhat problematic references, provides an important check on the portrait presented by later skeptical thinkers, including the major work of second century C.E. skeptic Sextus Empiricus.

LIFE'S WORK

The second century C.E. Peripatetic philosopher Aristocles of Messana quotes Timon, saying that the happy man must examine three questions: What is the nature of things, what attitude should one adopt with respect to them, and what will be the result for those who adopt this attitude?

Pyrrhon held that things by nature are inapprehensible (*akatalypsias*) and indeterminate (*adiaphora*). Making use of the established distinction between appearances and reality, Pyrrhon elaborated, stating that sense experiences and beliefs are neither true nor false because the true nature of things, if one exists, cannot be known.

Pyrrhonistic skepticism is summed up in the following formula: The nature of things no more is than is not, than both is and is not, than neither is nor is not. Shortened to the phrase "no more," the indeterminability of nature leads the wise man to withhold judgment (*aprosthetein*). According to Pyrrhon, "That honey is sweet I do not grant; that it seems so, I agree." The objective world cannot be perceived, and no ultimate truth can be assigned to subjective observations.

Pyrrhon did not urge the cessation of inquiry into the natural world. On the contrary, he held that the skeptic should continue to seek truth; this position influenced the development of medicine and science in Cos and in Alexandria. A suspension of judgment for Pyrrhon was a system (*agoge*) that leads to the desired goal of mental imperturbability, *ataraxia*.

While the essential origins of Pyrrhonism clearly are to be found in a purely Greek philosophical dialogue, it is possible that Pyrrhon's epistemology had been influenced by Buddhist thought. Contemporary accounts of Alexander show that the Greeks did have access to interpretations of Indian gymnosophists (literally, "naked wise men"). Alexander and his men, presumably including the youthful Pyrrhon, watched a certain Sphines (called Calanus in Greek) voluntarily mount his own funeral pyre, declaring that it was better for him to die than to live. The extent to which Pyrrhon was aware of Buddhist agnosticism or the dictum that happiness was freedom from worldly desires cannot be determined. Pyrrhon's penchant for wandering in deserted places searching for knowledge and his attempt to achieve that state of mind he called "silence" (*aphasia*) may well have had their roots in the asceticism of India.

Given the dominance of ethical questions in Greek thought after Plato, it is not surprising that Pyrrhon also addressed the problem of virtue. The testimony of Timon and Cicero shows that Pyrrhon was a stern moralist who led an exemplary life. Rejecting all definitions of virtue, Pyrrhon declared that without any true guide to moral conduct, one must observe traditional laws and customs. Withdrawn from active life though he may have been, Pyrrhon nevertheless was a good citizen.

It is unfortunate that testimony on Pyrrhon reveals little else about his positions. It may be surmised that the debate between Stoics and later skeptics over possible criteria of right conduct had its origin in Pyrrhon's thought. A poem by Timon mentions a right standard (*orthon canona*) by which he can question those who hold that the nature of the divine and the good makes men live most equably. In this poem, Timon inserts the qualification "as it seems to me to be," perhaps to indicate that the Pyrrhonic standard is the incommensurability of appearance and reality.

Pyrrhon was not original in doubting the ultimate truth of sensory experiences. His true contribution to Greek philosophy lay in his denial of the possibility that true knowledge can be gained by pure reason: If the only access to the world is through phenomena, there is no way to judge these phenomena against any objective model. Pyrrhon thus turned away from the monumental intellectual systems of Plato and Aristotle and helped to usher in an age of empiricism.

SIGNIFICANCE

Pyrrhon's empirical skepticism did not outlive his pupil Timon. Skeptical thought did persist, however, in the new Academy of the Aeolian Arcesilaus (315-240 B.C.E.) and of Carneades (214-129 B.C.E.). This Academic skepticism was more a second version of skepticism than a direct continuation of Pyrrhonism. The Academics used the Platonic dialectic as their basis for a suspension of judgment on the true nature of things. This Academic skepticism was a direct attack on the Stoic position, which held that some sense impressions were true. Unlike the Pyrrhonists, however, the Academic skeptic did maintain that sense impressions can be representative of an objective, external world.

After Carneades, the next important skeptical thinker was the enigmatic Aenesidemus, who lived sometime between the first century B.C.E. and the second century C.E. in Alexandria. Aenesidemus reorganized skeptical sayings into ten "tropes," a not-too-original attack on the possibility of deriving true knowledge from perceptual experiences.

The last major figure in the history of ancient skepticism was Sextus Empiricus, a Greek physician who lived sometime between 150 and 250 C.E. The large corpus of Sextus's writing that has been preserved provides the most complete statement of ancient skepticism. A true disciple of Pyrrhon, Sextus used the Pyrrhonistic suspension of judgment in his attacks on the dogmatic positions of contemporary philosophers and physicians. Through

Sextus Empiricus, the original philosophy of Pyrrhon of Elis has been saved from oblivion.

—*Murray C. McClellan*

FURTHER READING

Bett, Richard. *Pyrrho, His Antecedents, and His Legacy.* New York: Oxford University Press, 2000. Bett investigates the origins of Pyrrhon's ideas; in particular, Plato is singled out as an important inspiration.

Burnyeat, Miles F, ed. *Original Sceptics: A Controversy.* Indianapolis: Hackett, 1997. Five essays on the nature and scope of ancient skepticism.

Long, A. A. *Hellenistic Philosophy: Stoics, Epicureans, Sceptics.* Berkeley: University of California Press, 1986. A general work on the three main philosophical schools of the Hellenistic age. Includes a chapter on Pyrrhon and the later skeptics.

Schofield, Malcolm, Myles Burnyeat, and Jonathan Barnes, eds. *Doubt and Dogmatism: Studies in Hellenistic Epistemology.* New York: Oxford University Press, 1980. This work is a collection of ten essays from a 1978 Oxford conference. Presents detailed studies on Hellenistic theories of knowledge.

Tarrant, Harold. *Scepticism or Platonism? The Philosophy of the Fourth Academy.* New York: Cambridge University Press, 1985. An original investigation of the first century B.C.E. philosophies of Philo and Charmadas. Discusses the influence of early Pyrrhonists.

Zeller, Eduard. *The Stoics, Epicureans, and Sceptics.* Translated by Oswald Reichel. New York: Russell and Russell, 1962. Part of Zeller's massive nineteenth century history of Greek philosophy, this work contains a useful chapter on Pyrrhon. Includes bibliographical footnotes.

SEE ALSO: Alexander the Great; Aristotle; Epicurus; Zeno of Citium.

RELATED ARTICLES in *Great Events from History: The Ancient World*: 336 B.C.E., Alexander the Great Begins Expansion of Macedonia; 325-323 B.C.E., Aristotle Isolates Science as a Discipline; c. 300 B.C.E., Stoics Conceptualize Natural Law.

PYTHAGORAS
Greek philosopher and mathematician

Pythagoras set an inspiring example with his energetic search for knowledge of universal order. His specific discoveries and accomplishments in philosophy, mathematics, astronomy, and music theory make him an important figure in Western intellectual history.

BORN: c. 580 B.C.E.; Samos, Ionia, Greece
DIED: c. 500 B.C.E.; Metapontum, Lucania (now in Italy)
AREAS OF ACHIEVEMENT: Philosophy, mathematics, astronomy, music

EARLY LIFE
Pythagoras (pih-THAG-oh-ruhs), son of Mnesarchus, probably was born about 580 B.C.E. (various sources offer dates ranging from 597 to 560). His birthplace was the Greek island of Samos in the Mediterranean Sea. Aside from these details, information about his early life—most of it from the third and fourth centuries B.C.E., up to one hundred years after he died—is extremely sketchy. On the other hand, sources roughly contemporary with him tend to contradict one another, possibly because those who had been his students developed in many different directions after his death.

Aristotle's *Metaphysica* (335-323 B.C.E.; *Metaphysics*, 1801), one source of information about Pythagorean philosophy, never refers to Pythagoras himself but always to "the Pythagoreans." Furthermore, it is known that many ideas attributed to Pythagoras have been filtered through Platonism. Nevertheless, certain doctrines and biographical events can be traced with reasonable certainty to Pythagoras himself. His teachers in Greece are said to have included Creophilus and Pherecydes of Syros; the latter (who is identified as history's first prose writer) probably encouraged Pythagoras's belief in the transmigration of souls, which became a major tenet of Pythagorean philosophy. A less certain but more detailed tradition has him also studying under Thales of Miletus, who built a philosophy on rational, positive integers. In fact, these integers were to prove a stumbling block to Pythagoras but would lead to his discovery of irrational numbers such as the square root of two.

Following his studies in Greece, Pythagoras traveled extensively in Egypt, Babylonia, and other Mediterranean lands, learning the rules of thumb that, collectively, passed for geometry at that time. He was to raise geometry to the level of a true science through his pioneering work on geometric proofs and the axioms, or postulates, from which these are derived.

A bust now housed at Rome's Capitoline Museum (the sculptor is not known) portrays the philosopher as having close-cropped, wavy Greek hair and beard, his features expressing the relentlessly inquiring Ionian mind—a mind that insisted on knowing for metaphysical reasons the *exact* ratio of the side of a square to its diagonal. Pythagoras's eyes suggest an inward focus even as they gaze intently at the viewer. The furrowed forehead conveys solemnity and powerful concentration, yet deeply etched lines around the mouth and the hint of a crinkle about the eyes reveal that this great man was fully capable of laughter.

LIFE'S WORK
When Pythagoras returned to Samos from his studies abroad, he found his native land in the grip of the tyrant Polycrates, who had come to power about 538 B.C.E. In the meantime, the Greek mainland had been partially overrun by the Persians. Probably because of these developments, in 529 Pythagoras migrated to Croton, a Dorian colony in southern Italy, and entered into what became the historically important period of his life.

At Croton he founded a school of philosophy that in some ways resembled a monastic order. Its members were pledged to a pure and devout life, close friendship, and political harmony. In the immediately preceding years, southern Italy had been nearly destroyed by the strife of political factions. Modern historians speculate that Pythagoras thought that political power would give his organization an opportunity to lead others to salvation through the disciplines of nonviolence, vegetarianism, personal alignment with the mathematical laws that govern the universe, and the practice of ethics in order to earn a superior reincarnation. (Pythagoras believed in metempsychosis, the transmigration of souls from one body to another, possibly from humans to animals. Indeed, Pythagoras claimed that he could remember four previous human lifetimes in detail.)

His adherents he divided into two hierarchical groups. The first was the *akousmatikoi*, or listeners, who were enjoined to remain silent, listen to and absorb Pythagoras's spoken precepts, and practice the special way of life taught by him. The second group was the *mathematikoi* (students of theoretical subjects, or simply "those who know"), who pursued the subjects of arithmetic, the theory of music, astronomy, and cosmology. (Though *mathematikoi* later came to mean "scientists" or "mathematicians," originally it meant those who had attained advanced knowledge in a broader sense.) The *mathematikoi*, after a long period of training, could ask questions and express opinions of their own.

Despite the later divergences among his students—fostered perhaps by his having divided them into two classes—Pythagoras himself drew a close connection between his metaphysical and scientific teachings. In his time, hardly anyone conceived of a split between science and religion or metaphysics. Nevertheless, some modern historians deny any real relation between the scientific doctrines of the Pythagorean society and its spiritualism and personal disciplines. In the twentieth century, Pythagoras's findings in astronomy, mathematics, and music theory are much more widely appreciated than the metaphysical philosophy that, to him, was the logical outcome of those findings.

Pythagoras developed a philosophy of number to account for the essence of all things. This concept rested on three basic observations: the mathematical relationships of musical harmonies, the fact that any triangle whose sides are in a ratio of 3:4:5 is always a right triangle, and the fixed numerical relations among the movement of stars and planets. It was the consistency of ratios among musical harmonies and geometrical shapes in different sizes and materials that impressed Pythagoras.

His first perception (which some historians consider his greatest) was that musical intervals depend on arithmetical ratios among lengths of string on the lyre (the most widely played instrument of Pythagoras's time), provided that these strings are at the same tension. For example, a ratio of 2:1 produces an octave; that is, a string twice as long as another string, at the same tension, produces the same note an octave below the shorter string. Similarly, 3:2 produces a fifth and 4:3 produces a fourth. Using these ratios, one could assign numbers to the four fixed strings of the lyre: 6, 8, 9, and 12. Moreover, if these ratios are transferred to another instrument—such as the flute, also highly popular in that era—the same harmonies will result. Hippasus of Metapontum, a *mathematikos* living a generation after Pythagoras, extended this music theory through experiments to produce the same harmonies with empty and partly filled glass containers and metal disks of varying thicknesses.

Pythagoras determined that the most important musical intervals can be expressed in ratios among the numbers 1, 2, 3, and 4, and he concluded that the number 10—the sum of these first four integers—comprehends the

Pythagoras. (Library of Congress)

entire nature of number. Tradition has it that the later Pythagoreans, rather than swear by the gods as most other people did, swore by the "Tetrachtys of the Decad" (the sum of 1, 2, 3, and 4). The Pythagoreans also sought the special character of each number. The tetrachtys was called a "triangular number" because its components can readily be arranged as a triangle.

By extension, the number 1 is reason because it never changes; 2 is opinion; 4 is justice (a concept surviving in the term "a square deal"). Odd numbers are masculine and even numbers are feminine; therefore, 5, the first number representing the sum of an odd and an even number (1, "unity," not being considered for this purpose), symbolizes marriage. Seven is *parthenos*, or virgin, because among the first ten integers it has neither factors nor products. Other surviving Pythagorean concepts include unlucky 13 and "the seventh son of a seventh son."

To some people in the twentieth century, these number concepts seem merely superstitious. Nevertheless, Pythagoras and his followers did important work in several branches of mathematics and exerted a lasting influence on the field. The best-known example is the Pythagorean theorem, the statement that the square of the hypotenuse of a right triangle is equal to the sum of the squares of the other two sides. Special applications of the theorem were known in Mesopotamia as early as the eighteenth century B.C.E., but Pythagoras sought to generalize it for a characteristically Greek reason: This theorem measures the ratio of the side of a square to its diagonal, and he was determined to know the *precise* ratio. It cannot be expressed as a whole number, however, so Pythagoras found a common denominator by showing a relationship among the *squares* of the sides of a right triangle. The Pythagorean theorem is set forth in book 1 of Euclid's *Stoicheia* (*Elements*), Euclid being one of several later Greek thinkers whom Pythagoras strongly influenced and who transmitted his ideas in much-modified form to posterity.

Pythagoras also is said to have discovered the theory of proportion and the arithmetic, geometric, and harmonic means. The terms of certain arithmetic and harmonic means yield the three musical intervals. In addition, the ancient historian Proclus credited Pythagoras with discovering the construction of the five regular geometrical solids, though modern scholars think it more likely that he discovered three—the pyramid, the tetrahedron, and the dodecahedron—and that Theaetetus (after whom a Platonic dialogue is named) later discovered the construction of the remaining two, the octahedron and the icosahedron.

The field of astronomy, too, is indebted to Pythagoras. He was among the first to contend that the earth and the universe are spherical. He understood that the sun, the moon, and the planets rotate on their own axes and also orbit a central point outside themselves, though he believed that this central point was the earth. Later Pythagoreans deposed the earth as the center of the universe and substituted a "central fire," which, however, they did not identify as the sun—this they saw as another planet. Nearest the central fire was the "counter-earth," which always accompanied the earth in its orbit. The Pythagoreans assumed that the earth's rotation and its revolution around the central fire took the same amount of time—twenty-four hours. According to Aristotle, the idea of a counter-earth—besides bringing the number of revolving bodies up to the mystical number of ten—helped to explain lunar eclipses, which were thought to be caused by the counter-earth's interposition between sun and moon. Two thousand years later, Nicolaus Copernicus saw the Pythagorean system as anticipating his own; he had in mind both the Pythagoreans' concept of the day-and-night cycle and their explanation of eclipses.

Like Copernicus in his time, Pythagoras and his followers in their time were highly controversial. For many years, the Pythagoreans did exert a strong political and philosophical influence throughout southern Italy. The closing years of the sixth century B.C.E., however, saw the rise of democratic sentiments, and a reaction set in against the Pythagoreans, whom the democrats regarded as elitist.

Indeed, this political reaction led either to Pythagoras's exile or to his death—there are two traditions surrounding it. One is that a democrat named Cylon led a revolt against the power of the Pythagorean brotherhood and forced Pythagoras to retire to Metapontum, where he died peacefully about the end of the sixth century B.C.E. According to the other tradition, Pythagoras perished when his adversaries set fire to his school in Croton in 504 B.C.E. The story is that of his vast library of scrolls, only one was brought out of the fire; it contained his most esoteric secrets, which were passed on to succeeding generations of Pythagoreans.

Whichever account is true, Pythagoras's followers continued to be powerful throughout Magna Graecia until at least the middle of the fifth century B.C.E., when another reaction set in against them, and their meeting-houses were sacked and burned. The survivors scattered in exile and did not return to Italy until the end of the fifth century. During the ensuing decades, the leading Pythagorean was Philolaus, who wrote the first systematic exposition of Pythagorean philosophy. Philolaus's influence can be traced to Plato through their mutual friend Archytas, who ruled Taras (Tarentum) in Italy for many years. The Platonic dialogue *Timaeus* (360-347 B.C.E.), named for its main character, a young Pythagorean astronomer, describes Pythagorean ideas in detail.

SIGNIFICANCE

"Of all men," said Heraclitus, "Pythagoras, the son of Mnesarchus, was the most assiduous inquirer." Pythagoras is said to have been the first person to call himself a philosopher, or lover of wisdom. He believed that the universe is a logical, symmetrical whole, which can be understood in simple terms. For Pythagoras and his students, there was no gap between the scientific or mathematical ideal and the aesthetic. The beauty of his concepts and of the universe they described lies in their simplicity and consistency.

Quite aside from any of Pythagoras's specific intellectual accomplishments, his belief in universal order, and the energy he displayed in seeking it out, provided a galvanizing example for others. Sketchy as are the details of his personal life, his ideals left their mark on later poets, artists, scientists, and philosophers from Plato and Aristotle through the Renaissance and down to the twentieth century. Indirectly, through Pythagoras's disciple Philolaus, his ideas were transmitted to Plato and Aristotle, and, through these better-known thinkers, to the entire Western world.

Among Pythagoras's specific accomplishments, his systematic exposition of mathematical principles alone would have been enough to make him an important figure in Western intellectual history, but the spiritual beliefs he espoused make him also one of the great religious teachers of ancient Greek times. Even those ideas of his that are seen as intellectually disreputable have inspired generations of poets and artists. For example, the Pythagorean concept of the harmony of the spheres, suggested by the analogy between musical ratios and those of planetary orbits, became a central metaphor of Renaissance literature.

—*Thomas Rankin*

FURTHER READING

Guthrie, Kenneth Sylvan, ed. *The Pythagorean Sourcebook and Library: An Anthology of Ancient Writings Which Relate to Pythagoras and Pythagorean Philosophy*. Grand Rapids, Mich.: Phanes Press, 1988. This anthology of Pythagorean writings contains the four ancient biographies of Pythagoras as well as later Pythagorean and Neopythagorean writings.

Kahn, Charles H. *Pythagoras and the Pythagoreans*. Indianapolis: Hackett, 2001. Surveys Pythagorean tradition from Pythagoras's time to early modern times, including his influence on early modern math, music, and astronomy. Indexed by ancient and early modern name and by modern name.

Kirk, Geoffrey S., and John E. Raven. *The Presocratic Philosophers*. New York: Cambridge University Press, 1983. Provides a good account of Pythagoras and his followers, in their historical context, from a philosopher's point of view.

Muir, Jane. *Of Men and Numbers*. New York: Dover, 1996. Written for lay readers. Contains a chapter on Pythagoras's mathematical work and its influence on later scientists, especially Euclid.

Philip, J. A. *Pythagoras and Early Pythagoreanism*. Toronto: University of Toronto Press, 1968. Attempts to separate the valid information from the legends surrounding Pythagoras and his teachings. Includes notes and a selected bibliography.

Strohmeier, John, and Peter Westbrook. *Divine Harmony: The Life and Teachings of Pythagoras*. Berkeley, Calif.: Berkeley Hills Books, 2003. Describes Pythagoras's travels in Egypt, Phoenicia, Babylonia, and Greece and examines Pythagorean ideas as taught at his scholarly community in southern Italy. Includes illustrations, map, introduction, and bibliography.

SEE ALSO: Euclid; Thales of Miletus.
RELATED ARTICLES in *Great Events from History: The Ancient World*: 547 B.C.E., Cyrus the Great Founds the Persian Empire; c. 530 B.C.E., Founding of the Pythagorean Brotherhood; c. 300 B.C.E., Euclid Compiles a Treatise on Geometry.

PYTHEAS
Gallic explorer

Pytheas undertook the first lengthy voyage to the North Atlantic and may have circumnavigated England. This knowledge of the West, together with his astronomical observations, provided the basis for centuries of study.

BORN: c. 350-325 B.C.E.; Massalia, Gaul (now Marseilles, France)
DIED: After 300 B.C.E.; perhaps Massalia, Gaul
ALSO KNOWN AS: Pytheas of Massalia
AREAS OF ACHIEVEMENT: Science, geography

EARLY LIFE

It is a special characteristic of the study of antiquity that the fewer facts scholars know about a figure, the more they seem to write about him or her. So it is that an enormous bibliography about Pytheas (PIHTH-ee-uhs) of Massalia, the first known man to explore the far reaches of the North Atlantic, has evolved.

The time period of Pytheas's voyage has been determined with some certainty. He seems to have used a reference work that dates to 347 B.C.E., but because he is not mentioned by Aristotle, perhaps the voyage had not occurred before Aristotle's death in 322 B.C.E. Also, according to Strabo, Pytheas is quoted by Dicaearchus, who died c. 285 B.C.E. Thus, the voyage most definitely occurred between 347 and 285. At this time Carthage was the leading city of the western Mediterranean and controlled all traffic in and out of the Pillars of Hercules (Gibraltar). It is, therefore, sometimes claimed that Pytheas could have escaped this blockade only while Carthage was distracted in the war with Syracuse. If these assumptions are correct, the voyage took place between 310 and 306. Further, because Pytheas was surely a mature adult when he undertook the journey, scholars place his birth roughly between 350 and 325.

The date for the voyage is important, for it is believed that Pytheas opened the world of the West to Greek exploration at the same time that the wonders of the Far East were trickling back to the Mediterranean region as a result of the conquests of Alexander the Great. The cosmopolitan Hellenistic age was being born, and a quest for knowledge of far-off lands and their marvels was to play a large role in it. Apart from this tenuous but probable date, only two firm facts about Pytheas's life—his financial condition and his place of origin—are known. Polybius, also quoted by Strabo, sneers at Pytheas's voyage, asking if it was likely that a private citizen, and a poor one at that, ever undertook such a venture. Although Polybius was far from impartial, this comment may indicate that the voyage was state-sponsored.

His place of origin, Massalia, was founded c. 600 B.C.E. by Phocaea in Asia Minor. One of the most ambitious seafaring Greek towns, it soon controlled the coast, from its fine harbor down to modern Ampurias, seventy-five miles northeast of Barcelona. A Massaliote named Euthymenes was said to have sailed south along Africa until he saw a river filled with crocodiles (possibly the Senegal), and Massalia had early trading connections with metal-rich Tartessus in Spain. Friction with Carthage was inevitable, as the two powers sought control of these rich trade routes. Into this tradition of Massaliote adventurism Pytheas was born, poor but ambitious.

LIFE'S WORK

Not a word of Pytheas's works remains. It has been suggested that Pytheas's own works were not available to such authors as Diodorus Siculus (who wrote under Julius Caesar and Augustus), Strabo (who wrote under Augustus), and Pliny the Elder, who preserved for posterity meager fragments of Pytheas's research by quoting from or citing his works.

Nevertheless, it is clear that Pytheas was remembered fondly as an astronomical scientist. Using only a sundial, he calculated the latitude of Massalia with remarkable accuracy. He noted first that the pole star was not really at the pole and was also the first to notice a relationship between the moon and the tides. Much of the information on latitudes and geography that he brought back from his voyages was deemed sufficiently accurate to be used by such famous ancient scholars as Timaeus, Hipparchus, and Ptolemy.

Pytheas the explorer, however, had another reputation entirely, neatly summed up by Strabo's calling him "the greatest liar among mortals." The nature and name of the work that reaped such abuse are unknown. The work may have been called "On the Ocean," "The Periplus" (meaning "voyage"), or "Travels Around the World." Modern scholars generally believe that it was a single work and that it recounted Pytheas's voyage. There is much to be said, however, for the theory that it was a general work of geography in which he reported his own firsthand observations, along with the rumors and reports he heard from others. If this is so, the scorn of later antiquity, relying on a spurious text, is more understandable. One can imagine the same comments being directed at Herodotus if only the more marvelous passages of his work had survived in this fashion.

With all that as warning, it is still customary to take the scattered references to Pytheas's voyage and reconstruct his route. If this approach is valid, his travels are impressive indeed. He left the Pillars of Hercules and cruised around Spain and the coast of France to the coast of Brittany and Ushant Island. Instead of continuing his coastal route, as was customary for ancient mariners, he apparently struck out across the channel to Land's End, at the southwest tip of Britain at Cornwall. Here he described local tin mining. It is often asserted that Pytheas then circumnavigated the entire island of Britain. This belief is based on the fact that he describes the shape of the island correctly, describes its relationship to the coast better than did his critic Strabo, and, although doubling their true lengths, still correctly determines the proportion of the three sides. He probably made frequent observations of native behavior, and he may have conducted investigations inland. Diodorus, probably relying on Pytheas, reported correctly that the natives' huts were primitive, that they were basically peaceful but knew the chariot used for warfare, that they threshed their grain indoors because of the wet climate, and that they brewed and consumed mead.

Pytheas undoubtedly passed by Ireland, although no specific mention of this is found. It is often claimed, however, that his observations on the island enabled subsequent ancient geographers to locate it accurately on their maps. He apparently moved on to the northern tip of Britain, where he blandly described incredible tides 80 cubits (120 feet) high. Modern scholars see in this the gale-enhanced tides of the Pentland Firth.

It is the next stop on Pytheas's voyage that generates the most discussion. Pytheas claims that the island of Thule lay six days to the north of Britain and only one day from the frozen sea, sometimes called the Cronian Sea. Here, he states, days have up to twenty hours of sunlight in summer and twenty hours of darkness in winter. As if that information were not sufficiently incredible, he claims that the island lay in semicongealed waters in an area where earth, sea, and air are all mixed, suspended in a mixture resembling "sea lung" (perhaps a sort of jellyfish).

Where, if anywhere, is this Thule? Pytheas only claims that he saw the sea lung, getting the rest secondhand. Some parts of his tale ring true, such as long northerly days of light or darkness and a mixture of fog, mist, and slush so thick that one cannot tell where sea ends and sky begins. Scholars variously identify Thule as Iceland,

Norway, the Shetland Islands, or the Orkney Islands, but no one solution is entirely satisfactory.

Pytheas soon turned south and completed his circumnavigation until he recrossed the channel. Here, again, there are problems, for he claims to have visited amber-rich lands as far as the Tanais River, acknowledged as the boundary between Europe and Asia. Scholars claim either that Pytheas reached the Vistula River and thus, remarkably, the heart of the Baltic Sea or that he stopped at the Elbe River. In either case, it is generally assumed that from there he retraced his steps along the European coast and returned home. Even by the most conservative estimates, he had traveled a minimum of seventy-five hundred miles in ships designed for the Mediterranean and manned by sailors unfamiliar with the rigors of the northern seas.

SIGNIFICANCE

How can one assess a man and voyage so beset with problems of historicity? Did Pytheas in fact make a voyage at all? Was it a single voyage or were there two—one to Britain and one to the land of amber? In either case, how far did he go, and how much information is from his own experience and how much is from what he learned through inquiry?

Barring the remarkable discovery of a long-lost Pytheas manuscript, these questions will never be answered. A coin from Cyrene, found on the northern coast of Brittany and dating to this time, has been cautiously set forth as evidence of Greek intrusion at this date, but the caution is well deserved.

Despite the poor evidence and the hostility of the ancient authors, scholars can gauge Pytheas's importance from the impact he had on those who came after him. Pytheas opened Greek eyes to the wonders of the West, and it was his reports, for better or worse, which formed the basis for all writers on this area of the world for two centuries to come. In the same way, his scientific observations were respected and used by the best geographical minds of antiquity.

Still, it is highly likely that Pytheas did undertake a voyage himself and that he pushed fairly far to the north. Several thorny problems are solved if one believes that many of his wilder statements were not based on firsthand information but on tales he heard along the way. Much of the difficulty regarding Thule, for example, disappears when one views Pytheas's "discoveries" in this light.

The purpose of this voyage is also unclear. Some have hailed it as the first purely scientific voyage known to humankind. However, if Pytheas was, in fact, a poor man and thus had public funds behind him, it is highly unlikely that the elders of Massalia would have found reports of sea lung proper repayment for their investment. It is wiser to see the voyage as primarily commercial, aimed at rivaling Carthaginian trade routes to lands rich in tin and amber, although Pytheas clearly lost no opportunity to engage in scientific enquiry along the way. (To be sure, his entire trip north of Cornwall seems guided more by a sense of adventure than of mercantilism.)

The world soon forgot about Pytheas's contribution to Massaliote trade routes. In fact, there is no evidence that an increase in trade followed his maiden voyage. Less ephemeral were Pytheas's tales of gigantic tides, sea lung, or Thule. His appeal extends into modern times, as the term "ultima Thule" remains a synonym for "the ends of the earth."

—*Kenneth F. Kitchell, Jr.*

FURTHER READING

Bunbury, E. H. *A History of Ancient Geography Among the Greeks and Romans from the Earliest Ages till the Fall of the Roman Empire.* Amsterdam: J. C. Gieben, 1979. A very sensible and cautious reconstruction of the probable circumstances surrounding Pytheas's voyage.

Carpenter, Rhys. *Beyond the Pillars of Heracles.* New York: Delacorte Press, 1966. A very lengthy section devoted to Pytheas treats several issues in great detail. The discussion of Thule is very well done.

Cary, Max, and E. H. Warmington. *The Ancient Explorers.* 1929. Reprint. Baltimore: Penguin Books, 1963. A somewhat uncritical re-creation of the voyage, with a tendency to gloss over several of the thornier issues.

Cunliffe, Barry. *Extraordinary Voyage of Pytheas the Greek.* Baltimore: Penguin, 2003. Chronicles the journey of Pytheas; demonstrates just how much of a pioneer he was, even if some of his accounts of his voyage were based merely on hearsay.

Whitaker, Ian. "The Problem of Pytheas's Thule." *Classical Journal* 77 (1982): 148-164. A fine, careful study not only of Thule but also of most of the crucial problems surrounding Pytheas. Contains excellent documentation and bibliography, with translations of crucial passages from ancient authorities.

SEE ALSO: Hamilcar Barca; Pausanias the Traveler; Pliny the Elder; Ptolemy (astronomer).

RELATED ARTICLES in *Great Events from History: The Ancient World*: 336 B.C.E., Alexander the Great Begins Expansion of Macedonia; 325-323 B.C.E., Aristotle Isolates Science as a Discipline; c. 250 B.C.E., Discoveries of Archimedes.

QU YUAN
Chinese statesman and poet

A skilled statesman who always tried to speak the truth no matter what the cost, Qu Yuan exemplified the Confucian ideal of the virtuous official; his country's first widely known poet, he became one of the founding fathers of Chinese literature.

BORN: c. 343 B.C.E.; Chu, central China
DIED: 278 B.C.E.; in the Miluo River, China
ALSO KNOWN AS: Ch'ü Yüan (Wade-Giles); Qu Ping (Pinyin), Ch'ü P'ing (Wade-Giles)
AREAS OF ACHIEVEMENT: Government and politics, literature

EARLY LIFE
Qu Yuan (chew ywahn) was born about 343 B.C.E. in the southern Chinese state of Chu (Ch'u), which was centered in what is the modern province of Hubei. The Warring States period (475-221 B.C.E.) was characterized by China's fragmentation into a multitude of rival kingdoms, of which Chu was one of the major powers. Although little is known of Qu Yuan's childhood, tradition holds that his father's name was Boyong (Po-yung) and that he was related to Chu's royal family. Qu Yuan is also reputed to have achieved great distinction as a student and to have been marked for high government service from an early age.

In his late twenties, Qu Yuan was appointed to the important post of *zuodu*, or "left counselor," in his country's bureaucracy. He became the most influential confidant of the reigning King Huai Wang, and his advice was sought on all significant matters of both foreign and domestic policy. As a young man who believed in the ethical ideals inculcated by Confucianism, Qu Yuan tried to convince the king that he should look for these qualities in his new officials and cease the automatic preferment of the nobly born that had been the traditional way of doing things.

The king's son, Ze Lan (Tse Lan), successfully argued that to do so was obviously not in the interest of the aristocracy; Qu Yuan fell out of favor, his counsels were disregarded, and eventually, he was banished to a remote area in Chu's northern hinterlands. In the years to come, Qu Yuan's star would rise and fall several times as his country changed rulers and policies, but he never again would wield the kind of influence he had with Huai Wang. It was the disappointment of these youthful hopes for thorough reform that turned Qu Yuan toward literature, in which he was destined for far greater fame than he could ever have achieved in his homeland's civil service.

LIFE'S WORK
Qu Yuan's political aspirations had received a crushing blow, but his profoundly idealistic nature was not much affected by his being sent away from court. His poem "In Praise of the Orange Tree," which was written about this time, articulated his confidence in what the future would have to say about his unwillingness to play partisan politics with his country's future:

> Oh, your young resolution has something different from the rest.
> Alone and unmoving you stand. How can one not admire you!
> Deep-rooted, hard to shift: truly you have no peer!

The rural region north of the Han River to which Qu Yuan was banished proved to be a rich source of myths and folktales, many of them related to the shamanistic cults that still flourished in the area. A set of poems known as *Jiu ge* (third century B.C.E.; *The Nine Songs*, 1955), thought to be among his earliest literary works, includes many references to such deities as the River God and the Mountain Spirit, and it is possible that the songs were originally sacred hymns that Qu Yuan used as a basis for poetic composition.

Whatever their origin, *The Nine Songs* combined religious and romantic impulses in a manner completely new to Chinese poetry. Just as the Greek poet Homer (ninth century B.C.E.) described a world in which gods and men were akin in terms of psychology if not in their respective powers, so Qu Yuan envisaged crossing the barriers that divided humanity from the deities it worshiped. This excerpt from "The Princess of the Xiang" depicts a god waiting for his human lover:

> I look for my queen, but she comes not yet:
> Of Whom do I think as I play my reed-pipes?
> North I go, drawn by flying dragons . . .
> And over the great River waft my spirit:
> Waft, but my spirit does not reach her;
> And the maiden many a sigh heaves for me.

The Nine Songs immediately established Qu Yuan as the foremost literary figure of his time.

During the first of what would prove to be several periods of banishment for Qu Yuan, Huai Wang was murdered in 297 B.C.E. while participating in a supposed peace conference—which Qu Yuan had warned him against attending—in the neighboring state of Qin (Ch'in). This shocking event sparked one of Qu Yuan's most fervently emotional poems, "Great Summons"; the refrain "O soul, come back!" expresses both general fear of death and specific anxiety as to what would now become of the poet. For the moment, however, his fortunes took a turn for the better: The new king of Chu, Jing Xiang (Ching Hsiang), remembering that Qu Yuan had argued against the visit to Qin, recalled him to the court and at first followed his adviser's policy of breaking off relations with those who had executed his father. For the next two or three years, Qu Yuan was once again his country's most respected political adviser.

Despite this esteem, Jing Xiang's younger brother Ze Lan, who had engineered Qu Yuan's first downfall, worked unremittingly to bring about his second. The crisis came when Qin attacked and subdued one of Chu's neighbors in 293 B.C.E. and threatened to invade Chu unless normal relations were restored. Qu Yuan counseled against this, but Ze Lan's opposing faction won the day: Jing Xiang married a Qin princess, Chu and Qin reestablished diplomatic contact, and Qu Yuan was once more banished, this time to another remote province south of the Yangtze River.

In the remaining fifteen years of his life, Qu Yuan was several times recalled to court when Qin aggression seemed imminent, but his refusal to compromise with Ze Lan's pro-Qin faction led to his swift dismissal each time. After one of these disappointments, he considered emigrating to some other country but finally decided that it was his destiny to set an example for those who would come after him. He now wrote the autobiographical poem that is considered his finest achievement: *Li Sao* (c. 293-278 B.C.E.; *The Li Sao*, 1895), literally "encountering sorrow," offers a moving account of the agonies and ecstasies of his turbulent career as poet and politician.

The Li Sao opens with the birth of Qu Yuan, who is given the names "True Exemplar" and "Divine Balance" by his father. His youthful enthusiasm is soon quenched by a sobering dash of political reality: He learns that "All others press forward in greed and gluttony" while he alone seems to care about leaving behind "an enduring name." His greatest disappointment comes when he learns that even the king is subject to an all-too-human inconstancy of mind, but Qu Yuan is nevertheless determined to continue campaigning for what he believes is right: "But I would rather quickly die and meet dissolution/ Before I ever would consent to ape their behaviour."

Qu Yuan presents his love of beauty and poetry as a kind of contrapuntal relief from his political misfortunes, and it is these passages that make *The Li Sao* such a landmark in Chinese verse. Just as he had combined religion and romanticism in his early poetry, so this later work merges the conduct of contemporary affairs with the more permanent consolations offered by aesthetic accomplishment and appreciation. In a world where most people are too busy seeking power to care about either art or morality, Qu Yuan argues that a sensitive soul must protect its natural heritage of grace and good conduct against the constant temptation to conform.

The implications of the conclusion of *The Li Sao*, which announces that the author intends to "go and join P'eng Hsien [Peng Xian] in the place where he abides," are still a matter of some disagreement among students of Chinese literature. The statement has been interpreted as a decision to become a hermit as well as a desire to commit suicide; since nothing is known about Peng Xian, it seems unlikely that the issue will ever be resolved. This ongoing debate demonstrates how timelessly relevant *The Li Sao* is to questions of individual and social morality and of the artist's role in the world, and it helps to explain why Qu Yuan is so important a figure in Chinese literature.

After years of gradual encroachment, the Qin armies sacked Chu's capital in 278 B.C.E. and threw the country into turmoil. This final disaster was too much for Qu Yuan to bear: He drowned himself in the Miluo River, a tributary of the Yangtze, shortly thereafter. Nevertheless, his name lived on as a symbol of selfless dedication to both the highest standards of morality and the good of his country; in addition, he was commemorated by a national holiday. On the day of the annual Dragon Boat Festival, small boats are raced as an expression of the desire to rescue him from drowning, while specially prepared rice balls are thrown into the water so that his spirit will not go hungry.

SIGNIFICANCE

Very few people have been accorded the degree of respect given to Qu Yuan in traditional Chinese culture. He exemplified the ideal Confucian official, so loyal to the state that he would not compromise his opinions even when aware that they would be negatively received; his development of his literary talents exemplified the Renaissance-man wholeness that Confucius had advocated but which was often neglected by bureaucrats who found it easier to conform to tradition than attempt to expand it.

Even the People's Republic of China, which has discouraged the respect paid to many traditional historical figures on the grounds that they were reactionary influences, considers Qu Yuan's exemplary loyalty to the state a model of correct social behavior. This esteem has had the important incidental effect of maintaining his status as one of the founding fathers of Chinese literature, and his work has thus been preserved as an important element of his country's cultural heritage. Many poets of subsequent generations, among them Song Yu (Sung Yü; 298-265 B.C.E.), Tao Qian (T'ao Ch'ien; 365-427 C.E.), and Li Bo (Li Po; 701-762 C.E.), were deeply affected by Qu Yuan's energetic defense of the highest ethical and aesthetic standards. Even today he is often acknowledged as an influence by writers striving for a balance between imaginative idealism and moral realism. Wherever Chinese is spoken, his name remains synonymous with personal integrity above and beyond worldly success.

—Paul Stuewe

FURTHER READING

Hawkes, David, trans. *Ch'u tz'u: The Songs of the South, an Ancient Chinese Anthology*. 1959. Reprint. New York: Penguin, 1995. Hawkes's versions of the poems, which are accompanied by excellent notes, are somewhat different from those of earlier translators and are generally considered more accurate by his fellow scholars.

_____. "The Quest of the Goddess." In *Studies in Chinese Literary Genres*, edited by Cyril Birch. Berkeley: University of California Press, 1974. This essay places Qu Yuan's work in its cultural perspective, compares it with that of his predecessors and successors, and argues that he represents the victory of a written, secular approach to literature over earlier oral and religious modes of expression. A seminal discussion by Qu Yuan's foremost modern interpreter.

Qu Yuan. *Li Sao: And Other Poems of Qu Yuan*. Translated by Yang Xianyi and Gladys Yang. Honolulu, Hawaii: University Press of the Pacific, 2001. A translation of the complete corpus of Qu Yuan's poems.

Schneider, Laurence A. *A Madman of Ch'u: The Chinese Myth of Loyalty and Dissent*. Berkeley: University of California Press, 1980. A well-researched account of the development of Qu Yuan's reputation into a synonym for political rectitude. The treatment is basically historical and culminates in a convincing demonstration of how he became the patron saint of modern Chinese intellectuals. The poetry is used merely as thematic evidence, but even those more interested in Qu Yuan as a poet will find the book a useful source for social and cultural insights.

Waley, Arthur. *The Nine Songs: A Study of Shamanism in Ancient China*. 2d ed. San Francisco: City Lights Books, 1973. Waley stresses the religious origins of Qu Yuan's verse, suggesting that its depth of feeling may be an indication of the author's madness. Although his grasp of the historical context is second to none and makes the book still worth consulting, Waley was not a very sophisticated literary critic; his diagnosis has been disregarded by most subsequent commentators.

Watson, Burton. *Early Chinese Literature*. New York: Columbia University Press, 1962. Includes a detailed discussion of Qu Yuan's work in its historical and textual aspects. A descriptive rather than interpretive approach that occasionally ventures opinions regarding symbolic or thematic significances; a good introduction for the general reader.

_____, trans. *Records of the Grand Historians of China: Translated from the Shih Chi of Ssu-ma Ch'ien*. 2 vols. 3d ed. New York: Columbia University Press, 1995. Includes the original historical evidence on which all subsequent research about Qu Yuan is based. Its biographies of his era's political contemporaries provide a vivid sense of what life was like during the Warring States period.

SEE ALSO: Sima Xiangru; Tao Qian.

RELATED ARTICLES in *Great Events from History: The Ancient World*: 479 B.C.E., Confucius's Death Leads to the Creation of *The Analects*; 475-221 B.C.E., China Enters Chaotic Warring States Period; 221 B.C.E., Qin Dynasty Founded in China; c. 220 C.E., Cai Yan Composes Poetry About Her Capture by Nomads; c. 405 C.E., Statesman Tao Qian Becomes Farmer and Daoist Poet.

RAMSES II
Egyptian pharaoh (r. 1279-1213 B.C.E.)

Renowned for his statesmanship, military leadership, administrative abilities, and building activity, Ramses set a standard by which subsequent rulers of Egypt measured themselves.

BORN: c. 1300 B.C.E.; probably the Eastern Delta of Egypt
DIED: 1213 B.C.E.; probably Pi-Ramesse (Qantir), Egypt
ALSO KNOWN AS: Rameses II
AREAS OF ACHIEVEMENT: Government and politics, war and conquest, architecture

EARLY LIFE

Born of Egypt's great god Amen (personified by King Seti I) and Queen Tuya, Ramses (RAM-zeez) was designated "while yet in the egg" as Egypt's future king: Such is Ramses II's account of his own birth. The period into which he was born, that of the New Kingdom, was a time when Egypt was attempting to maintain control of an extensive empire that ranged from the Fourth Cataract of the Nile in the Sudan to the provinces of North Syria.

Some fifty years prior to his birth, during the Eighteenth Dynasty, Egypt had undergone a period of turmoil. Akhenaton (Amenhotep IV, r. 1377-1360 B.C.E.), reacting against the ever-growing power of the Amen priesthood, had abandoned the traditional religion and proclaimed the sun god, represented as the sun disk Aton, as sole god of the country. He worshiped the Aton at the virgin site of Amarna. He died without heirs; after his demise, a series of relatively ineffectual kings, including Tutankhamen (r. 1361-1352 B.C.E.), ruled for brief periods as the Amen priesthood set about reestablishing religious domination and refurbishing Amen's temples.

Meanwhile, using this period of uncertainty in Egypt to best advantage, vassal states in Syria held back their tribute and fomented revolt. When Tutankhamen died without living heirs, a military man of nonroyal birth, Ay, assumed the throne. He was followed only four years later by another, the general Horemheb, who also ruled only a short period before his death, but not before designating another man with a military background, his vizier Pa-Ramessu, as his heir. Pa-Ramessu (Ramses I, first king of the Nineteenth Dynasty) had what rulers since Akhenaton had lacked: viable male descendants. Thus, when Ramses I died after only a two-year rule, his son, Seti I (r. 1294-1279 B.C.E.), assumed the throne. Immediately, Seti began an active program of military campaigns in Canaan, Syria, and Libya. During many of these excursions, his son, the young Ramses II, was at his side, learning the art of warfare.

Seti I instructed his son in civil and religious affairs as well, and Prince Ramses accompanied his father or acted as his deputy on state occasions and at religious festivals. As prince-regent, Ramses received the rights of Egyptian kingship, including his titulary (five royal names attributing to him divine power and linking him with Egypt's divine past) and a harem.

When his father died, after a rule of between fifteen and twenty years, Ramses II oversaw Seti's burial in the Valley of the Kings and assumed the throne. At that time, he was probably in his mid-twenties. He was about 5 feet, 6 inches (1.7 meters) tall and had auburn hair. Many children had already been born to him and his numerous wives.

LIFE'S WORK

With great ceremony, on the twenty-seventh day of the third month of summer, 1279 B.C.E., Ramses II acceded to the throne of Egypt. Following an age-old tradition, the great gods of Egypt, in the persons of their high priests, placed the crowns of Upper and Lower Egypt (Nile Valley and Delta) on his head and presented him with other symbols of rulership: the divine cobra (uraeus) to protect him and smite his enemies, and the crook and flail. At the sacred city of Heliopolis, his name was inscribed on the leaves of the sacred *ished* tree, and birds flew in all directions to proclaim his names to all Egypt. With this ceremony concluded, the divine order (or balance) in the universe, a concept known as *Ma'at*, was once again in place. It would be Ramses' duty, as it had been of every

KINGS OF THE NINETEENTH DYNASTY	
Ruler	*Reign (B.C.E.)*
Ramses I	1295-1294
Seti I	1294-1279
Ramses II	1279-1213
Merenptah	c. 1213-1203
Amenmessu	1203-1200?
Seti II	1200-1194
Saptah	1194-1188
Queen Tausret	1188-1186

Note: Dynastic research is ongoing; data are approximate.

king before him, to maintain *Ma'at*, thereby guaranteeing peace and prosperity for all.

Ramses II set out with determination to ensure the preservation of *Ma'at*. He was a shrewd politician from the start; one of his first acts as king was to journey south to Thebes to act as high priest in the city's most important religious event, the Opet Festival. Amid great and joyous celebration, Amen's cult image was carried from his home at Karnak to the Luxor temple. There, through a reenactment of his divine conception and birth, the ceremonies of Opet Festival assured the divinity of Ramses' kingship and promoted his association with the god Amen, whose cult image was recharged with divine energy during its stay at Luxor.

Afterward, Ramses II headed north to Abydos, restored that city's holy sites, and promoted a member of the Abydos priesthood to the position of high priest of Amen at Thebes, the highest and most powerful religious office in the land. In this way, he kept Amen's priesthood under his control and averted the power struggles that had beset earlier kings.

From Abydos, Ramses continued his northerly journey to the eastern Nile Delta. There, in his ancestral homeland near Avaris, he established a new capital, naming it Pi-Ramesse (the house of Ramses). Scribes extolled its magnificence, likening the brilliant blue glaze of its tile-covered walls to turquoise and lapis lazuli.

Not only at Pi-Ramesse but also at Memphis, Egypt's administrative capital, at Thebes, her religious capital, and at numerous other sites throughout Egypt and Nubia, Ramses II built extensively and lavishly. Indeed, few ancient Egyptian cities were untouched by his architects and artisans. Monuments that Ramses II did not build he often claimed for his own by substituting his name for those of his predecessors. Colossal statues of the king erected outside temples were considered to function as intermediaries between the villagers and the great gods inside. They also reminded every passerby of Ramses' power.

The territorial problems and general unrest that had compelled Seti I to travel to the Levant continued during Ramses II's rule. When the growing Hittite empire annexed the strategically important city of Kadesh in northern Syria, an area formerly under Egyptian sovereignty, Ramses rose to the challenge.

In April of the fifth year of Ramses' reign, he led an army of about twenty thousand men to meet about twice as many enemy soldiers. As the Egyptian army neared Kadesh, two Hittites posing as spies allowed themselves to be captured. The main Hittite army, they assured the Egyptians, was still far to the north. Thinking that he had nothing yet to fear, Ramses marched ahead, accompanied by only his personal guard. Two more captured Hittites, this time true spies, revealed, on vigorous beating, that the Hittites were encamped just on the other side of Kadesh, a few miles away. Suddenly, the enemy attacked the Egyptian line, sending surprised soldiers fleeing in confusion and fright.

With valor and courage, Ramses succeeded virtually single-handedly in holding the Hittite attackers at bay. Relief came at a critical moment in the form of the king's advance guard arriving from the north. Gradually, the rest of Ramses' army regrouped and joined battle. The day ended with no clear victor. The second day also ended in a stalemate, and both sides disengaged.

Ramses II. (Library of Congress)

Ramses headed home in triumph, having, after all, saved his army (and himself) from great disaster. Although during the next fifteen years Ramses returned frequently to the Levantine battlefield, no battle made as great an impact as the Battle of Kadesh. For decades following, on temple walls throughout the land, the king's artists told the story of this battle in prose, poetry, and illustration, with each telling more elaborate than the one before. What the chroniclers neglected to mention each time was the battle's outcome: The disputed city, Kadesh, remained a Hittite possession.

Sixteen years after the Battle of Kadesh had made Ramses a great military leader, at least in his own eyes, it cast him into the role of statesman as well. A new generation of leadership in the Hittite Empire, the lack of military resolution with Egypt, and the rising power of Assyria made the prospect of continued warfare with Egypt unattractive to the Hittites. Accordingly, a peace treaty was proposed (by the Hittites according to Ramses and by Ramses according to the Hittites). Its terms are as timely today as they were in 1258 B.C.E.: mutual non-aggression, mutual defense, mutual extradition of fugitives, and rightful succession of heirs. A thousand gods of Egypt and a thousand gods of Hatti were said to have witnessed this treaty, which survives today in both the Egyptian and Hittite versions.

Former enemies became fast friends following the treaty's execution, as king wrote to king and queen to queen. In Year 34, the Hittite king even sent his daughter to Ramses. Chronicles of Ramses' reign indicate his pleasure on his first sight of her, accompanied by her dowry of gold, silver, copper, slaves, horses, cattle, goats, and sheep.

Matnefrure, as Ramses II named his Hittite bride, joined a harem that was already quite large. In the course of his long rule, the king had at least eight great royal wives and numerous lesser wives. To Nefertari (c. 1307-c. 1265 B.C.E.), who must have been his favorite wife, he dedicated a temple at Abu Simbel, and on her untimely death he buried her in a tomb whose wall paintings are the finest in the Valley of the Tombs of the Queens. Ramses II fathered at least ninety children (some fifty sons and forty daughters), who were often represented in birth-order procession on temple walls or sculpted knee-height beside images of their father.

In 1213 B.C.E., nearly ninety years old and after more than sixty-six years of rule over the most powerful country in the world, King Ramses II died. His carefully mummified body was laid to rest in a splendidly carved tomb in the Valley of the Kings, and he was succeeded on the throne of Egypt by his thirteenth son, Merenptah (r. c. 1213-1203 B.C.E.).

SIGNIFICANCE

Military leader, statesman, builder, family man, and possibly pharaoh of the biblical Exodus, Ramses II left a legacy that history never forgot. He distinguished himself in battle in the early years of his reign, and during the remainder of his lengthy rule—the second longest in Egyptian history—he maintained an interlude of peace in an increasingly tumultuous world. Egypt under his leadership was a cosmopolitan empire. Foreigners were free to come to Egypt to trade or settle; others were taken as prisoners of war and joined Egypt's labor force. It was an era of religious permissiveness, and foreign gods were worshiped beside traditional Egyptian deities. The cultural climate of Ramses' Egypt is similar to the one described in the Bible just prior to the Exodus (an event for which no archaeological record has been found).

The monuments Ramses II built to Egypt's gods (and to himself) are larger and more numerous than those of any other Egyptian king. Nine kings named themselves after him and patterned their lives after his. During his own lifetime, he promoted himself as a god, and he was worshiped as such for the next thousand years.

Greek and Roman tourists marveled at his monuments and immortalized them in their writings, just as the poet Percy Bysshe Shelley did hundreds of years later in his 1818 poem "Ozymandias." (The name Ozymandias is the Greek rendering of *User-Ma'at-Ra*, throne name of Ramses II.) When the greatest of all Ramses' monuments, Abu Simbel, was threatened by the rising waters of the Aswān High Dam in the 1960's, ninety countries around the world contributed funds and expertise to save it. In this way, they too paid homage to Ramses, as do millions of tourists who travel thousands of miles to visit his monuments.

Although his tomb was plundered and his body desecrated, Ramses II has gained the immortality he sought. His monuments and his actions bear testimony to his importance and justify the appellation Ramses the Great.

—*Rita E. Freed*

FURTHER READING

Bierbrier, Morris. *The Tomb Builders of the Pharaohs.* New York: Charles Scribner's Sons, 1984. A delightfully written description of the community of workmen who built the tombs of the New Kingdom kings, including that of Ramses II. An intimate picture of their day-to-day lives. Includes a description of how they built the tombs.

Healy, Mark. *The Warrior Pharaoh: Ramses II and the Battle of Qadesh*. Mechanicsburg, Penn.: Stackpole, 2000. A military history detailing the battle, its causes, and its consequences. Discusses Ramses' military tactics and the equipment used by the armies; describes the location of the battle and other matters of interest to military historians.

James, T. G. H. *Ramses II*. New York: Sterling, 2002. A lavishly illustrated biography that accompanies a major traveling exhibit from the British Museum.

Menu, Bernardette. *Ramesses II: Greatest of the Pharaohs*. New York: Harry N. Abrams, 1999. A concise, well-balanced history of Ramses and his reign. Includes useful information such as lists of Ramses' known advisors, spouses, and children.

Murnane, William. *The Road to Kadesh*. 2d ed. Chicago: University of Chicago Oriental Institute, 1990. Background for the understanding of Egypt's far-flung empire. Consideration of Egypt's relations with Syria and the Hittites through the reign of Ramses' father, Seti I, and detailed analyses of Seti's military campaigns.

Tyldesley, Joyce A. *Ramesses: Egypt's Greatest Pharaoh*. New York: Penguin, 2001. An approachable, well-written biography of Ramses and his time.

Weeks, Kent. *The Lost Tomb*. New York: William Morrow, 1998. In 1995, an expedition led by Weeks discovered the enormous tomb complex of Ramses II's fifty sons, possibly the most important find in modern Egyptology. This book is more of an archaeological memoir than a site study, but it offers an inside look at the archaeological site and provides Weeks an opportunity to explain why this tomb is so important.

_____, ed. *The Valley of the Kings*. New York: Sterling, 2001. Essays by experts interpret the archaeological evidence from the Valley of the Kings and the Valley of the Queens for the nonspecialist reader. Includes many illustrations, as well as plans, diagrams, and bibliography.

SEE ALSO: Akhenaton; Nefertari; Tutankhamen.

REGULUS
Roman statesman

Through legendary embellishments of his actual exploits, Regulus has served as an example, variously, of moral courage and devotion to duty, of arrogance in the face of victory, and of the reversals of fortune that history records.

BORN: c. 300 B.C.E.; probably Rome (now in Italy)
DIED: c. 249 B.C.E.; probably Carthage (now in Tunisia)
ALSO KNOWN AS: Marcus Atilius Regulus
AREA OF ACHIEVEMENT: War and conquest

EARLY LIFE
Marcus Atilius Regulus (REHG-ew-luhs) was a Roman, born, in all probability, into a noble but not wealthy family when Rome was consolidating its takeover of Italy. Consul in 267 B.C.E., Regulus participated in the conquest of southern Italy by capturing Brundisium (modern Brindisi), the most important seaport on Italy's eastern coast, and subduing the people around it. The reputation he earned in the engagement was no doubt instrumental in his selection to replace Q. Caedicus as consul in 257, when Caedicus died at a crucial moment in the First Punic War.

LIFE'S WORK
It was as replacement consul (*consul suffectus*) that Regulus entered the stage of history. The long cold war between Rome and Carthage, competitors for dominance in the Mediterranean world, had finally exploded into hot war in 264. In 258, the year before Regulus assumed the consulship, Rome had laid siege to fortress-towns throughout Sicily, then a Carthaginian possession. Successful in conquering many of the towns, Rome was disabused of its enemy's invincibility and grew confident of its own military ability. Rome planned to use its navy in a daring attack on Carthage itself. The Carthaginians, trusting their superiority in naval resources, resolved to meet the Roman navy at sea, defeat it, and so protect the

African mainland, which was not well fortified for defense.

In 256, with Regulus and the other consul, L. Manlius Vulso Longus, in command, a Roman fleet of 330 battleships and 140,000 infantry met the more numerous (350 ships and 150,000 infantry) Carthaginians at Ecnomus. The advantage seemed to belong to the Carthaginians; their ships were more maneuverable, as the Roman ships were weighed down with land weapons. After a long battle the Romans won the day, destroying or capturing many Carthaginian ships.

The Carthaginian navy under Hanno withdrew to Africa to protect the sea lanes to Carthage, while Hamilcar Barca stayed with the land army in Sicily. A few months later, the Roman consuls led their invasion forces to Africa. It is said that en route, the tribune Nautius stirred up the fears of the already nervous Roman soldiers and that Regulus, learning of Nautius's cowardly speeches, threatened him with an ax. Thus Regulus used fear to inspire his soldiers with courage.

The Romans landed at Cape Hermaeum (modern Cape Bon) and proceeded to Clupea, a town they captured and established as their base of operations. The consuls sent to the senate at Rome for further orders; when the reply came, Manlius returned to Rome with the fleet, while Regulus remained in Africa with forty ships and the land army of fifteen thousand men. With the army, Regulus subdued three hundred fortresses and towns throughout Libya. Stories survive that Regulus had to fight "huge monster-serpents" that harassed his camp. Perhaps in this period Regulus can be faulted for his insistence on conquest and plunder. If he had enlisted the aid of the Libyans and Numidians, who hated Carthage and might have made willing allies, he could have acquired a cavalry, the lack of which would prove fatal to his plans.

Up to this point, the Carthaginians had not comprehended the scale of the Roman invasion. They now sent for Hamilcar, who was in Sicily with their land army. Immediately on his return with five thousand men, he persuaded Carthage to engage Regulus in battle. While both sides possessed roughly the same number of infantry, the Carthaginians held an advantage in cavalry and elephants, animals unfamiliar to the Romans. Hamilcar was wary of confronting the Romans on a plain, though it was a terrain favorable to his cavalry and elephants, and occupied the high ground. Regulus seized the initiative and attacked the Carthaginian camp from two sides, causing a

Regulus. (Hulton|Archive by Getty Images)

panic in the enemy and putting them to flight to Carthage. Regulus then advanced to nearby Tunis to set up winter quarters.

The Carthaginians were aware that they had been defeated at Ecnomus despite their superior navy. Their land army had been defeated in Africa. The Roman army was just outside their gates and plundering their territories with impunity. Even their Numidian subjects were raiding and plundering. Morale was at a low point. Now Regulus sent an overture suggesting willingness to settle on easy terms. Regulus's motives are not known, but Roman terms of office were one year; when his term as consul ended, he would lack the authority to carry on the struggle. If, however, he worked out a treaty with Carthage, he would leave to posterity a reputation as the man who ended the First Punic War. Perhaps thinking of glory, then, Regulus entered into negotiations with a delegation headed by Hamilcar's son Hanno.

It is not known with certainty what Regulus's terms of settlement were, though ancient historians agree that they were excessively severe. Perhaps Regulus wanted the Carthaginians to give up Sardinia, Sicily, and their entire fleet except for one symbolic ship, and to pay an indemnity as well. By these terms, Carthage would have become virtually a subject state to Rome, and the wealthy merchants who ruled Carthage chose to prolong the war rather than agree to Regulus's demands.

The desperation of Carthage was a source of courage to the Carthaginians, and they were preparing a fight to the death when there arrived in Carthage some Greek mercenaries, among them the Spartan Xanthippos, a man trained in the military tradition of Sparta. He examined the Carthaginian military and criticized it as inadequate. The Carthaginians were impressed and gave him the command. Confident that they had in Xanthippos a man who knew what he was doing, the Carthaginians took the field against Regulus in late spring. While the advantage perhaps lay with the Romans in infantry, the Carthaginians were again superior in cavalry and elephants. Under Xanthippos, at Tunis the Carthaginians were not reluctant to fight on a plain. Regulus, anticipating that he would defeat this nation of shopkeepers as easily as he had before, took to the field. Now, however, the outcome was quite different. The Carthaginian cavalry chased the smaller Roman cavalry from the field. Elephants trampled large numbers of Roman infantry . It is said, too, that Regulus's men were worn out from the heat and thirst and the heaviness of their weapons. Of Regulus's army, only a few escaped to Clupea. The rest were killed or captured, including Regulus.

It is not known what actually happened to Regulus after his capture. It may be that he simply died in captivity; it may be that some form of the tales the historians and poets tell is true. However, no account of Regulus would be complete without these tales. While he was held captive in Carthage, the fortunes of war shifted back and forth for the next few years between Carthage and Rome. In 251, the Punic commander Hasdrubal advanced on Panormus in Sicily but met a devastating defeat. He was recalled to Carthage and impaled. Then, probably in 250, according to traditional accounts, Regulus was ordered by his Carthaginian captors to return to Rome and to negotiate either an exchange of prisoners (by some accounts) or a peace on lenient terms (by other accounts). He was on his oath to persuade the Roman senate or, failing to do so, to return to Carthage to meet torture and death.

When he arrived in Rome, accompanied by Carthaginian ambassadors, he entered the senate clad as a prisoner in Punic clothes. When the ambassadors had left, Regulus is said to have disclosed the full crisis of Car-

thage's desperation and to have advised peace on much harder terms than the Carthaginians wished—or, if Carthage did not accept such terms, a renewed aggressive war. Then, although he could have remained in Rome with his loving family, he kept his oath to Carthage and returned there, knowing that he would be punished for his failure to obtain a generous peace. There are varying accounts of his torture at Carthage. According to Cicero, he was kept awake until he died. According to the more common and more detailed account, he was confined in a wooden box designed so that he was forced to remain standing. Through the planks of the box were placed iron spikes to prevent his lying down or resting; abused in this way, he eventually died. According to some writers, the stories of his oath and torture are inventions to cover up an atrocity by Regulus's widow. According to this version, when Regulus died in captivity, his widow was so distressed that she tortured two Punic boys held captive by her family.

SIGNIFICANCE

The story of Regulus has achieved prominence because of the moral lessons it instills. For some writers, the tale of Regulus is a lesson in the fickleness of fortune. Victorious in his battles and unyielding in his demands to Carthage, he was then defeated and forced to sue for his life. Thus, he illustrates the law that fortune most likes to afflict those who enjoy extreme prosperity. For other moralists, Regulus's arrogance was his undoing. If he had not pressed excessively harsh terms on Carthage, he would have won glory for himself and peace for Rome. It was his contumelious belief in his powers and luck that struck him down.

To traditional patriotic Romans, Regulus became a symbol of Roman probity, the man who kept his oath, even unto death. The great orator and statesman Cicero held him as a model. For Cicero, Regulus was a glorious example of a man who rejected what seemed to be his private advantage—his life and a comfortable existence at Rome as a former consul—for what was honorable and noble.

—James A. Arieti

FURTHER READING

Caven, Brian. *The Punic Wars*. New York: St. Martin's Press, 1980. Covers all the Punic Wars in annalistic form. Includes plates and maps that help the reader to follow the strategic plans of both sides.

Goldsworthy, Adrian. *The Punic Wars*. London: Cassell, 2000. Each of the wars is described in detail, including an account of the long stalemate over Sicily in the

First Punic War. Provides background to the conflict as a whole and its context in military history.

Lancel, Serge. *Carthage: A History.* Translated by Antonia Nevill. Cambridge, Mass.: Blackwell, 1997. Detailed study of Carthage from its founding and rise in the early centuries of the first millennium to its defeat and Roman absorption by the end of the period.

Livy. *The Rise of Rome.* Translated by T. J. Luce. New York: Oxford University Press, 1998. Includes introduction, notes, bibliography, and index.

_____. *The War with Hannibal.* Translated by Aubrey de Sélincourt. Baltimore: Penguin Books, 1965. Along with Polybius's work, it is the best source of information on the Punic Wars. Useful for the more knowledgeable reader.

Polybius. *The Rise of the Roman Empire.* Translated by F. W. Walbank. New York: Penguin, 1979. By one of the great historians of the ancient world. Drawing from a great many earlier histories that have been lost, Polybius is the main source for the early story of Regulus.

Walbank, F. W. *A Historical Commentary on Polybius.* 3 vols. Oxford, England: Clarendon Press, 1967-1979. An annotated commentary on the Greek text of the influential ancient historian. Carefully assesses Polybius's sources and weighs the evidence in the conflicting accounts of the story of Regulus.

SEE ALSO: Fabius; Hamilcar Barca; Hannibal; Hanno; Scipio Africanus.

RELATED ARTICLES in *Great Events from History: The Ancient World*: 264-225 B.C.E., First Punic War; 218-201 B.C.E., Second Punic War; 149-146 B.C.E., Third Punic War; 146 B.C.E., Sack of Corinth.

SALLUST
Roman historian

Sallust's most important accomplishments were influential works of history composed after his retirement from a checkered political career. The tone, style, and subject matter of his writings reflect the perils and disenchantments of his earlier career.

BORN: 86 B.C.E.; Amiternum, Samnium (now San Vittorino, Italy)
DIED: 35 B.C.E.; Rome (now in Italy)
ALSO KNOWN AS: Gaius Sallustius Crispus (full name)
AREA OF ACHIEVEMENT: Historiography

EARLY LIFE

Gaius Sallustius Crispus, or Sallust (SAL-uhst), was born in 86 B.C.E. in the town of Amiternum in the Sabine uplands, some fifty-five miles northeast of Rome in the central Italian peninsula. Though likely a member of a locally eminent family, Sallust was in Roman terms nonaristocratic, that is, a plebeian. As a politician, he was thus a *nouus homo* (new man). Although by the first century B.C.E. plebeians regularly attained political office and senatorial rank, the highest offices—the praetorship and especially the consulship—remained almost exclusively the preserve of a few wealthy, aristocratic families and such men as they chose to support. To fulfill his political ambitions, the new man needed skill, sagacity, tact, perseverance, luck, and, most particularly, powerful friends. This helps to explain both Sallust's general dislike of the entrenched conservative aristocracy and his affiliation with Julius Caesar.

Sallust was elected quaestor (a junior official with financial responsibilities) around 55 and tribune of the people in 52. In the latter position, he was involved on the side of the prosecution in the murder trial of a notorious right-wing politician (defended by Cicero) who habitually used intimidation and mob violence. This involvement, along with various other anticonservative actions, gained for Sallust numerous political enemies, who retaliated by having him expelled from the senate in 50 on apparently trumped-up charges of sexual immorality.

Hoping for a restoration of status, Sallust sided with Julius Caesar against Pompey the Great in the civil war that broke out in the year 49. He was rewarded with a second quaestorship (c. 49), a praetorship (47), and various military commands. His service in these posts was undistinguished and occasionally incompetent. He failed to quell a troop mutiny, for example, and was not entrusted with a battle command during Caesar's African cam-

paign. Caesar did, however, see fit to appoint Sallust as the first governor of the province of Africa Nova in 46, a fact that implies at least minimal faith in his administrative abilities. After his governorship, Sallust was charged with abuse of power—extortion and embezzlement—but saved himself from conviction by sharing his spoils with Caesar, who was by then dictator. Still, the scandal severely limited Sallust's political prospects and forced him into an early retirement, from which the assassination of Caesar in 44 made it impossible to return.

LIFE'S WORK

Sallust's inglorious political career was marred by factional strife, sensational scandals, sporadic ineptitude, and outright misconduct. Whatever he may have lost in public esteem, however, Sallust handsomely recouped in property and possessions. The wealth he amassed in office ensured an opulent style of retirement. Sallust purchased a palatial villa at Tivoli, said to have been owned at one time by Caesar himself. At Rome, he began construction of the famed Horti Sallustiani (gardens of Sallust), in which an elegantly landscaped complex of parklands surrounded a fine mansion. The loveliness of this estate in the capital city later attracted the attention of Roman emperors, whose property it eventually became.

Sallust did not, however, simply settle into a genteel life of disillusioned and indolent leisure. He used his knowledge of the dynamics of Roman government as a lens through which to examine the gradual disintegration of the political system in the late republican period.

The personalities and events in Sallust's historical works are typical of a period of decline and fall. His first work, the *Bellum Catilinae* (c. 42 B.C.E.; *The Conspiracy of Catiline*, 1608), is a historical monograph devoted to the failed conspiracy of Catiline, a disgruntled, impoverished aristocrat who intended to make good his electoral and financial losses by resorting to armed insurrection. The planned *coup d'état* was quashed by the actions of Cicero during his consulship in 63. The story of the exposure of the plot and of the measures taken by consul and senate to eliminate the threat—ultimately in battle—is familiar from Cicero's four Catilinarian orations.

Sallust's telling of the Catiline story differs from Cicero's in several respects. He sees the conspiracy in the context of a general moral deterioration within the governing class in Rome. Many in the senatorial nobility placed their own advancement ahead of concern for the commonweal. Catiline found supporters not only among disaffected political have-nots but also among members of the ruling elite who—at least for a time—saw in his machinations opportunities for furthering their own selfish interests. This was not surprising in an era that had seen the bloodshed and confiscation of property that marked the dictatorship of Lucius Cornelius Sulla Felix. In *The Conspiracy of Catiline*, two men of strong moral character—Marcus Porcius Cato (Cato the Younger) and Julius Caesar—stand out in contrast to the surrounding moral decay. Though representing very different political persuasions, both men are portrayed as admirable for their integrity. Sallust is sometimes accused of being an apologist for his erstwhile patron, Julius Caesar, but his favorable portrait of Cato argues a more nonpartisan outlook. Cicero, too, though not the triumphant savior paraded in his own writings, is given his due by Sallust.

Sallust's second work, the *Bellum Iugurthinum* (c. 40 B.C.E.; *The War of Jugurtha*, 1608), recounts the war between Rome and an upstart king of Numidia (now eastern Algeria) between 111 and 105. This was an apt subject, in part because of Sallust's familiarity with North Africa and because of the many hard-fought battles, but especially because it afforded another case of mismanagement and corruption among the Roman ruling elite. In *The War of Jugurtha*, the handling of the conflict by the senate and its representatives is portrayed as ineffective, again largely because of divisions among the aristocrats who had allowed their own lust for power or money to displace their obligation to govern well. Some in the government were willing to accept bribes in return for their support of Jugurtha over other claimants to the Numidian throne. The phrase "everything at Rome has its price" rings like a death knell in the monograph. It was finally a new man—Gaius Marius— who succeeded in gaining victory for Rome. Marius, too, in Sallust's account, had flaws of character: He is depicted as a demagogue who connived to damage the reputation of his predecessor in command. Furthermore, though he would have other spectacular military successes (against invading Germanic tribes on Italy's northern frontier), Marius's long career ended in civil war against Sulla.

Sallust's other major work, his *Historiae* (begun c. 39 B.C.E.; English translation of fragments, *Histories*, 1789), survives only in fragments. It was more extensive in scope than the monographs, covering in annalistic fashion the years from 78 apparently to the early 60's; a continuation to perhaps 50 may have been envisaged, but Sallust's death in 35 prevented it.

Sallust does not meet the standards of modern historical scholarship. His chronology is sometimes awry; he neglected or suppressed relevant information, while including long digressions. He sometimes perpetuated patently distorted reports of personalities and events and, in general, did not assess available sources with sufficient care. Still, no ancient Greek or Roman historian is entirely free from such shortcomings, and Sallust's works are historically valuable despite them, particularly as a check against the record furnished by Cicero, who has so colored the modern picture of the late Republic.

Sallust is most compelling and influential as a stylist and moralist. His language is deliberately patterned on the ruggedly direct and archaic syntax of the stern Cato the Censor and, among Greek precedents, on the brevity and abnormal grammatical effects of the greatest Greek historian, Thucydides. His terse sentence structure contributes to a forceful and dramatic progression of thought. This style is well suited to the moral outlook of a historian of decline and fall. Like Thucydides, Sallust wrote from the vantage point of a man of wide experience forced out of an active political life into that of an analyst of the causes of deterioration of character and commitment in the ruling elite of a great imperial power. This analysis is achieved by remarkably concise and trenchant sketches of, and judgments on, persons and motives. The historical figures who are Sallust's subjects act out of clearly defined and exhibited passions—sometimes noble, mostly base, never lukewarm.

SIGNIFICANCE

Sallust's qualities as stylist and moralist have always won for him readers, admirers, and imitators. In classical antiquity, he was recognized as the first great Roman historian; the eminent teacher and critic Quintilian even put him on a par with Thucydides. This judgment is a literary one. The most brilliant classical Roman historian, Cornelius Tacitus, was profoundly influenced by the Sallustian style of composition. The poet Martial concurred with Quintilian's high estimation of Sallust, and Saint Augustine's favorable opinion helped to ensure the historian's popularity in the Middle Ages. German and French translations of his work appeared by the fourteenth century, the first printed edition in the fifteenth, and the first English versions early in the sixteenth. The great Renaissance Humanist, Desiderius Erasmus, preferred Sallust to Livy and Tacitus for use in school curricula. In modern times, Sallust has appealed to many, including Marxist readers who find in him an indictment of decadence in a corrupted aristocracy.

Sallust produced the first true masterpieces of historical writing in Latin. His political career served as preparation, in the school of hard experience, for his work as a writer. In modern times, some have charged him with hypocrisy, noting the glaring inconsistency between his own quite dismal record as a public servant and the lofty moral tone he adopts in his histories. Moreover, doubts tend to arise regarding the presentation and interpretation of facts in the writings of a retired politician. Nevertheless, these considerations do not detract from the worth of Sallust's writings in and of themselves. His works are valuable inquiries into and reflections on sociopolitical developments in an exciting and critically significant period in Roman history.

—*James P. Holoka*

FURTHER READING

Earl, D. C. *The Political Thought of Sallust.* Cambridge, England: Cambridge University Press, 1961. Earl discusses Sallust's views of the political environment of the late Republic, in particular his attitude toward moral degeneracy (declining *virtus*) as a fatal element. Explicates the individual works as reflective of this political perspective.

Gruen, Erich. *The Last Generation of the Roman Republic.* Berkeley: University of California Press, 1995. Account of the last years of the Roman Republic provides a context for understanding the career and motivations of politicians of the day.

Kraus, Christina Shuttleworth, and A. J. Woodman. *Latin Historians.* New York: Oxford University Press, 1997. Describes and assesses the works of Sallust.

Laistner, M. L. W. *The Greater Roman Historians.* Berkeley: University of California Press, 1966. Contains a chapter on Sallust giving a harsh assessment of his worth as a historian.

Syme, Ronald. *The Roman Revolution.* Reprint. New York: Oxford University Press, 2002. An important and influential scholarly work on "the transformation of state and society at Rome between 60 B.C.E. and A.D. 14."

_____. *Sallust.* Reprint. Berkeley: University of California Press, 2002. An authoritative work on the life, times, and writings of its subject.

SEE ALSO: Julius Caesar; Catiline; Cato the Younger; Cicero; Gaius Marius; Lucius Cornelius Sulla; Thucydides.

RELATED ARTICLES in *Great Events from History: The Ancient World*: Late 63-January 62 B.C.E., Catiline Conspiracy; 58-51 B.C.E., Caesar Conquers Gaul; 51 B.C.E., Cicero Writes *De republica*; 46 B.C.E., Establishment of the Julian Calendar; 43-130 C.E., Roman Conquest of Britain.

SAMMU-RAMAT
Assyrian queen (r. c. 823-807 B.C.E.)

Sammu-ramat was a legendary queen of Assyria who enjoyed extraordinary prominence in the Assyrian court in life and whose fame grew to mythological proportions after death.

BORN: c. 840 B.C.E.; place unknown
DIED: After 807 B.C.E.; place unknown
ALSO KNOWN AS: Semiramis (Greek name); Sammuramat
AREA OF ACHIEVEMENT: Government and politics

EARLY LIFE

Nothing is known of the early life of Sammu-ramat (SAW-mew RAW-maht) except for that which is provided in the fanciful stories of her life originally collected by the Greek author Ctesias of Cnidus, who referred to her as Semiramis. He incorporated the legends regarding this remarkable woman in his *Persika* (*The Fragments of the Persika of Ktesias*, 1888) while he also served as a physician in the court of the Persian king Artaxerxes in the fifth century B.C.E. While his work no longer survives, his account of the beautiful, adventurous, and cruel Assyrian queen was subsequently included in the writings of Diodorus Siculus, who wrote a universal history in the first century B.C.E.

According to Ctesias, Sammu-ramat was the daughter of the Syrian goddess Derketo and a handsome Syrian youth for whom she developed a great passion. However, after giving birth to a daughter, the goddess was consumed with shame. She killed the father of her child, left the infant to die in the fields, and threw herself into a lake, where she was transformed into a fish. Abandoned, the beautiful baby girl was cared for by doves until she was discovered by shepherds who gave her to Simmas, the chief shepherd, to raise until she was of a marriageable age. When an officer of the Assyrian court by the name of Onnes was sent to inspect the royal flocks, he was so entranced by Sammu-ramat's beauty that he married her and took her back to Nineveh, the Assyrian capital, where she eventually gave birth to two sons, Hyapates and Hydaspes. Once there, however, her beauty, intelligence, and courage brought her to the attention of Ninus, the king and founder of Nineveh.

Ninus was engaged in the conquest of Bactria, and Onnes had accompanied him on the campaign. As the campaign wore on, Onnes began to miss his wife and sent for her to join him. When she arrived at the siege of the city of Bactria, she noticed a weakness in the defense of the city's acropolis. She then led an attacking force that captured the acropolis; as a result, the defense of the city collapsed, and the conquest of Bactria was complete. Ninus, now aware of Sammu-ramat's cunning and bravery as well as her beauty, prevailed on Onnes to relinquish any claims he had on his wife so that he, Ninus, could marry her. Because of the threats of the king and his sorrow at the prospect of losing his wife, Onnes hanged himself. Sammu-ramat was now free to marry the Assyrian king. Ninus fathered a son, Ninyas, with Sammu-ramat but then died before Ninyas was old enough to rule. This allowed Sammu-ramat to engage in the series of exploits on which her fame rests.

In addition to the account above, Diodorus Siculus preserved an alternate account of Sammu-ramat's rise to power given by Athenaeus and other unnamed historians. They contended that Sammu-ramat had been a courtesan in her early life. Captivated by her beauty, the king of Assyria married her and then elevated her to a position of power in his court. According to this account, she repaid her husband for his love by contriving to imprison him so that she could rule in his stead, which she did into her old age.

LIFE'S WORK

Historically, Sammu-ramat was, as a boundary stone (annotated in 1990 by Veysel Donbaz) proclaimed, the "palace woman of Shamshi-Adad (king of Assyria from 824-811 B.C.E.), mother of Adad-nirari III (king of Assyria from 811-782 B.C.E.), and daughter-in-law of Shalmaneser (king of Assyria from 858-824 B.C.E.)." While it is tempting to believe the legendary stories of her reign as a sovereign, it should be noted that Assyria did not typically have queens who ruled in the modern sense. Nevertheless, the prominent inclusion of her name in

this boundary stone, along with references to her in two other inscriptions, indicates that she was an important figure within the Assyrian court. As such, it is believed that, following the death of her husband, she served as regent for her son, Adad-nirari, for at least four years until he was old enough to take the reins of power himself.

The legend of Sammu-ramat outstripped these historical references to her reign, increasing her fame as numerous fanciful activities and exploits were attributed to her. The fifth century historian Herodotus briefly mentioned that she ruled over the city of Babylon for five generations, during which time she was credited with building a series of levies to control the flooding of the Euphrates River. Ctesias, by contrast, credited her with the founding of Babylon itself. These claims may be a confused memory of the work of Naqi'a-Zakutu, wife of Sennacherib of Assyria (r. 704-681 B.C.E.), who supervised the reconstruction of Babylon after her husband had destroyed it c. 689 B.C.E. Nevertheless, one may suppose that the woman who revealed her unbridled pride by inscribing her triple relationship with Assyrian royalty (Shamshi-Adad, Adad-nirari, and Shalmaneser) on border stones must have been a formidable woman in her own right.

According to the legend recorded by Ctesias, Sammu-ramat first determined to construct her own fame after her husband, Ninus, died by engaging in a number of building projects. She erected a large mound over the tomb of her husband that could be seen at a great distance from Nineveh. Then she began the construction of the city of Babylon, with its imposing walls and towers and numerous temples and palaces. Ctesias presented a detailed account of how she divided the work of construction among large cadres of workers and gathered the greatest artisans to outfit the city with remarkable embellishments. Ctesias also included a lengthy catalog of wonders that she included in her construction of the city. He credited her with the construction of protective walls so thick that two chariots could be driven abreast of each other around the entire circuit of the city.

Reportedly, she spanned the Euphrates, which flowed through the city, with a massive bridge and ordered the construction of a tunnel that went under the river to connect the palaces she built on both sides of the river. She also erected an exceedingly high temple, from which astronomical observations were made, and then placed enormous statues of Zeus, Rhea, and Hera fashioned of beaten gold on its top. After completing the construction of Babylon, she turned her attention to other places in

Mesopotamia and surrounding lands to build several other cities, parks, and palaces.

Ctesias also claimed that Sammu-ramat led numerous military expeditions, which allowed her to subjugate Egypt and Libya and to attempt the conquest of India. In this latter venture, he said that she crossed the Indus River on a bridge that she commanded to be built in order to engage Strabrobates, the king of the Indians, in combat. To counter the superiority of his forces—which included elephants—she commissioned the manufacture of several dummy elephants to inspire dread in the enemy. Despite her preparations and bravery in battle, however, the Indian forces of Strabrobates bested Sammu-ramat and her army in battle, forcing her to retreat beyond the Indus. While retreating, the daring queen received both an arrow wound in her arm and a javelin wound in her back. Nevertheless, she preserved the remnants of her army by bravely enduring pain while she cut the moorings of the bridge that she had constructed over the Indus, thus thwarting Strabrobates' pursuit.

In addition to her building projects and military exploits, Sammu-ramat was famous for her sensuality coupled with extreme cruelty. In addition to the account that reported an early career as a courtesan, she allegedly engaged in numerous affairs after becoming queen. Freed from the constraints of marriage following Ninus's death and intending to retain her freedom to rule alone, Sammu-ramat refused to marry again, according to Ctesias. Instead, she selected lovers from among the most handsome of her soldiers and, after consorting with them, had them executed.

The legend asserts that, after her several exploits, Sammu-ramat abandoned her throne in favor of her son Ninyas. According to Ctesias, she did this to fulfill a prophesy that she had received from the priests of Amen while sojourning in Egypt. The oracle stated that "she would disappear from among men and receive undying honor among some of the peoples of Asia, and that this would take place when her son Ninyas should conspire against her." According to Ctesias, when Sammu-ramat discovered a conspiracy against her in which Ninyas was involved, she relinquished the throne in favor of her son, rather than punish the conspirators. After commanding the governors of her realm to obey Ninyas as they had obeyed her, Sammu-ramat turned into a dove and flew away.

The legendary stories regarding Sammu-ramat that found their way into the writings of the Greek authors did not fare well with Berosus, a Babylonian priest (fl. c. 290

B.C.E.) who compiled lists of kings who had ruled in Mesopotamia as part of his *Babylfnḷaka* (c. 290 B.C.E.; *The Babyloniaka of Berossus*, 1978). While the full scope of his refutation of Herodotus and Ctesias is not known, it is certain that he contradicted their identification of Sammu-ramat as a queen of Babylon. Diodorus Siculus was also rightfully skeptical of the legendary exploits and fate of Sammu-ramat as recorded by Ctesias; nevertheless, Ctesias was correct when recounting these stories in stating that Sammu-ramat was among "the most renowned of all women of whom we have any record."

SIGNIFICANCE

Historically, Sammu-ramat joined the small but important sorority of powerful women who enjoyed unusual prominence in the male-dominated ancient world. Whatever the true details of her life might have been beyond the few inscriptional references that have survived, her legend as Sammu-ramat became part of the recollection of Assyria's fabled power long after its cities had been reduced to rubble.

—*Carlis C. White*

FURTHER READING

Donbaz, Veysel. "Two Neo-Assyrian Stelae in the Antakya and Kahramanmaras Museums." *Annual Review of the Royal Inscriptions of Mesopotamias Project* 8 (1990): 9. Describes the commemorative stelae found at the site of ancient Assyria, one of which mentions Sammu-ramat.

Luckenbill, D. D., trans. *Ancient Records of Assyria and Babylonia.* London: Histories & Mysteries of Man, 1989. A collection of inscriptions found in Mesopotamia from the period of Sammu-ramat.

Oldfather, C. H., trans. *Diodorus of Sicily.* Cambridge, Mass.: Harvard University Press, 1962-1983. A translation of Diodorus's work, which includes Ctesias of Cnidus's account of the legends regarding Sammu-ramat.

Roux, Georges. *Ancient Iraq.* New York: Penguin Books, 1992. A treatment of the full sweep of history in ancient Mesopotamia, which places Sammu-ramat in the full historical context of the region.

Verbrugghe, Gerald P., and John M. Wickersham, trans. *Berossos and Manetho, Introduced and Translated: Native Traditions in Ancient Mesopotamia and Egypt.* Ann Arbor: University of Michigan Press, 1996. This history contains an introduction, bibliography, and index.

SAMUEL
Israeli religious leader

Though famed as a priest and prophet, Samuel is chiefly remembered as the instrument by which the monarchy was established in Israel.

BORN: c. 1090 B.C.E.; Ramathaim-Zophim (or Ramah), Israel
DIED: c. 1020 B.C.E.; Ramah, Israel
ALSO KNOWN AS: Shmu'el (Hebrew name)
AREAS OF ACHIEVEMENT: Religion, government and politics

EARLY LIFE
When Samuel (SAM-yew-ehl) was born, the twelve tribes of Israel had conquered and settled the greater part of the Promised Land but had as yet no unified government. The tribes occasionally united against a common enemy and submitted their disputes to judges, but leaders such as Gideon and Jephthah achieved victory in battle without establishing any office or administration.

Samuel's birth followed a pattern common in the Old Testament. He was the son of Elkanah, who had two wives. One, Hannah, was barren; though she had the love of her husband, she was mocked for her barrenness by his other wife. When the family went to sacrifice at Shiloh, Hannah vowed that if the Lord gave her a boy child, she would dedicate the child to divine service for "all the days of his life." Thus, her son, Samuel, after he had been weaned, became servant to Eli, the priest at Shiloh.

One night Samuel thought that he heard Eli calling; after the third time, Eli realized that the Lord was calling to the boy. Samuel learned that God's favor was withdrawn from the house of Eli because of the misconduct of Eli's sons. Shortly thereafter, these sons were killed in battle against the Philistines, and Eli died. The ark of the covenant was captured, but it was soon restored when it occasioned plagues among the Philistines. Samuel was now the priest and was also recognized as a prophet who received direct revelations from God, as Eli had not.

LIFE'S WORK
Twenty years later, Samuel decided that aggressive action was needed against the Philistines, a people from overseas who had settled on the coast of Palestine. The Philistines were a constant threat to Israel because they were technologically more advanced, especially in the use of iron. In order to regain divine favor, Samuel persuaded the Israelites to abandon their worship of "strange gods" (the Baalim and Ashtoreth, Canaanite fertility gods). When the Israelites gathered at Mizpeh, and the Philistines attacked them, Samuel sacrificed, and

> as Samuel was offering up the burnt offering, the Philistines drew near to battle against Israel: but the Lord thundered with a great thunder that day on the Philistines, and discomfited them; and they were smitten before Israel.

Several cities were recovered from the Philistines, and Samuel returned to his priestly and judicial duties, traveling "from year to year in circuit to Bethel, and Gilgal, and Mizpeh, and judged Israel in all those places; and his return was to Ramah; for there was his house" (1 Sam. 7).

In the Book of Judges, there are several examples of leaders, such as Gideon, who might have established a monarchy, but they either refused or behaved so badly that the Israelites repudiated them. Samuel seems almost to have been thought of as a king, but he could not have been accepted as one because his sons, like Eli's, were unworthy: They "turned aside after lucre, and took bribes, and perverted judgment." At this point, Samuel became less a judge or military leader and more a kingmaker, one who as prophet communicated the Lord's intentions to make or unmake a particular monarch. (The narrative of 1 Samuel shows certain inconsistencies that are thought to be the result of combining two accounts, one friendly and one hostile to the idea of a monarchy. Note that the idea of monarchy implies not only authority in war and peace but also succession, the orderly passing of rule from father to son.)

"When Samuel was old," the elders of Israel asked him to give them a king "to judge us like all the nations," to "go out before us, and fight our battles." Samuel con-

Samuel. (Hulton|Archive by Getty Images)

drawing of lots, again chose Saul king. Saul did not begin his reign but went home to Gibeah; he could not even collect taxes, for the sons of Belial "despised him and brought him no presents."

The crisis came when the Ammonites besieged Jabesh-gilead. Saul behaved like a king at last: "And he took a yoke of oxen, and hewed them in pieces, and sent them throughout all the coasts of Israel by messengers, saying, Whosoever cometh not forth after Saul and after Samuel, so shall it be done to his oxen" (1 Sam. 11:7).

According to the phrase "after Saul and after Samuel," Samuel was still a power in Israel when Saul "slew the Ammonites until the heat of the day." Samuel's response to this victory was twofold. First, he conducted a formal coronation ceremony for Saul. Second, Samuel gave a formal abdication speech, stressing his function as judge: "Whom have I defrauded? whom have I oppressed? or of whose hand have I received any bribe?" Samuel further reminded the people of all that the Lord had done for them since He delivered them from Egypt. Emphasizing his point by calling down thunder and rain in the midst of harvest, he concluded grimly, "But if ye shall still do wickedly, ye shall be consumed, both ye and your king."

Saul's reign started auspiciously; he and his son Jonathan were victorious in their campaigns against the Philistines and other enemies of Israel. However, there were two occasions when Saul acted in ways that caused him to forfeit divine favor. Saul had mobilized the people to meet a Philistine invasion and expected Samuel to meet him and offer sacrifices. When, after seven days, Samuel had not appeared, Saul, seeing his army melting away, offered the sacrifice himself. Immediately thereafter, Samuel arrived and told Saul that because of his disobedience to the Lord, his kingdom, which otherwise would have been established forever, would not continue but would be given to another, a man after the Lord's own heart. Nevertheless, afterward, Samuel ordered Saul, in the name of the Lord, to attack the Amalekites, who had interfered with the Israelites during the Exodus, and massacre them, "both man and woman, infant and suckling, ox and sheep, camel and ass." Saul defeated the Amalekites, but he spared their king, Agag, and kept the best of the sheep and oxen for later sacrifice. This, to Samuel, was another sin of disobedience; the Lord, he said, re-

sulted the Lord, who answered, "They have not rejected thee, but they have rejected me, that I should not reign over them." Nevertheless, he directed Samuel, after listing all the forms of oppression that a king might inflict, to give them a king.

Thus Samuel became involved in the tragic career of Saul. The younger son of a Benjaminite named Kish and a "choice young man and a goodly," Saul had been sent with a servant to find some lost asses. They were ready to abandon the search when the servant suggested that they consult a man of God, a seer in the city of Zulph, who might advise them about the asses for a present of one-fourth of a shekel of silver. They went to the seer, who was Samuel. Having been forewarned by the Lord, Samuel entertained Saul cordially and anointed him. This anointing did not imply that Saul would immediately become king. Instead, he was sent home. On the way, he met a company of ecstatic prophets and prophesied with them (perhaps an alternative account is again being presented). Samuel called the people to Mizpeh and, by a pented having made Saul king. "And Samuel came no more to see Saul until the day of his death: nevertheless Samuel mourned for Saul."

The Lord had one more duty for Samuel to perform before his death; he was to go to Bethlehem and anoint David as Saul's successor. Saul, meanwhile, was troubled by an evil spirit sent from the Lord; the modern reader may recognize symptoms of paranoia and depression. The remainder of 1 Samuel has little to do with Samuel; it primarily concerns David's rise and Saul's decline. It is recorded simply that Samuel died; "all the Israelites were gathered together, and lamented him, and buried him in his house at Ramah."

SIGNIFICANCE

Whether Samuel is considered a prophet or a judge, the Bible portrays him playing a variety of roles in Israel. He was, first, a priest, presiding over a shrine and offering sacrifices there; on special occasions, such as war, he may have offered sacrifices elsewhere. His powers as a prophet varied greatly; he was apparently not insulted at the idea of finding lost cattle for a small sum in silver. He also claimed, however, to receive divine communications regarding the public welfare: In this he resembled the classic prophets, such as Jeremiah and Isaiah. Samuel enforced the lesson that national prosperity meant obedience not merely to general moral principles but also to direct instruction from the Lord, as communicated through His prophets. One form of prophecy Samuel seems not to have practiced: He was not one of the ecstatic prophets who performed in bands and in whose performances Saul twice joined. Samuel also occasionally performed secular functions. At least once, he commanded the armies of Israel, and his function as a judge should not be forgotten.

Samuel's influence did not end with his death. The modern reader does not automatically side with Samuel but asks whether Saul's premature sacrifice was such a fatal piece of disobedience and whether it was necessary to carry out such a ruthless sacrifice of the Amalekites. In part, the Bible answers these doubts: After Samuel's death, Saul's depression deepened, and his jealousy and persecution of David must have weakened him politically. When the Philistines gathered their army once more, Saul "was afraid, and his heart greatly trembled." Unable to gain divine guidance, Saul, who had driven the witches and wizards from the land, in his desperation sought out a woman who had a familiar spirit and asked her to call up Samuel. Samuel appeared, an old man covered with a mantle, and pronounced a grim sentence: "The Lord will also deliver Israel with thee into the hand of the Philistines: and to morrow shalt thou and thy sons be with me." Thus it happened, but the author or last editor of 1 Samuel must have had compassion for Saul; he recorded that the men of Jabesh-gilead recovered Saul's body from the Philistines and gave it honorable burial.

—*John C. Sherwood*

FURTHER READING

Alter, Robert, and Frank Kermode, eds. *The Literary Guide to the Bible*. Cambridge, Mass.: Harvard University Press, 1987. Contains an essay on 1 and 2 Samuel by Joseph Rosenberg that emphasizes Samuel's role in the establishment of the monarchy. See also Gerald Hammond's "English Translations of the Bible," which justifies the continued use of the King James Version.

Blenkinsopp, Joseph. *A History of Prophecy in Israel*. Louisville, Ky.: Westminster John Knox Press, 1996. Places Samuel in the context of Old Testament prophecy and in the context of other Near Eastern cultures.

Bright, John. *A History of Israel*. 4th ed. Louisville, Ky.: Westminster John Knox Press, 2000. A thorough, nontheological treatment of the history of Israel. Includes anecdotal commentary on life in ancient times.

Bruce, F. F. *Israel and the Nations: The History of Israel from the Exodus to the Fall of the Second Temple*. Carlisle, Cumbria, England: Paternoster Press, 1997. A comprehensive historical analysis of the kings of Israel, beginning with Saul and David and continuing through the Davidic line.

Kuntz, J. Kenneth. *The People of Ancient Israel: An Introduction to Old Testament Literature, History, and Thought*. New York: Harper and Row, 1974. Useful for the historical context and for chronology. Includes extensive bibliographies.

Sternberg, Meir. *The Poetics of Biblical Narrative: Ideological Literature and the Drama of Reading*. Macon, Ga.: Mercer, 1989. The final chapter contains an interesting study of the literary strategies used to handle the downfall of Saul.

SEE ALSO: David; Ezekiel; Ezra; Jeremiah; Moses; Solomon.

RELATED ARTICLES in *Great Events from History: The Ancient World*: c. 1280 B.C.E., Israelite Exodus from Egypt; c. 1100 B.C.E., Arameans Emerge in Syria and Mesopotamia; c. 1000 B.C.E., Establishment of the United Kingdom of Israel; 587-423 B.C.E., Birth of Judaism.

SAPPHO
Greek lyric poet

Regarded by ancient commentators as the equal of Homer, the lyric poet Sappho expressed the human emotions with honesty, courage, and skill.

BORN: c. 630 B.C.E.; Eresus, Lesbos, Asia Minor (now in Greece)
DIED: c. 580 B.C.E.; Mytilene, Lesbos, Asia Minor (now in Greece)
ALSO KNOWN AS: Psappho
AREA OF ACHIEVEMENT: Literature

EARLY LIFE
Sappho (SAF-oh) was born about 630 in Eresus on the island of Lesbos, just off the western coast of Turkey. Her father was probably a rich wine merchant named Scamandronymus, and her mother was called Cleis, as was Sappho's daughter. The poet had three brothers: Charaxus and Larichus, who served in aristocratic positions in Mytilene, and Eurygyius, of whom no information is available. Charaxus, the oldest brother, reportedly fell in love with and ransomed the courtesan Doricha, which displeased Sappho. Conversely, she often praised her other brother, Larichus, whose name, passed down in Mytilenian families, was the same as that of the father of a friend of Alexander the Great.

About 600, when the commoner Pittacus of Mytilene gained political power in Lesbos, Sappho reportedly went into exile in Sicily for a short time. She was already well-known. She married Cercylas, a wealthy man from Andros, with whom she had her daughter, Cleis.

Although much of the information available regarding the Aeolian culture of seventh century Lesbos derives only from the poetry of Sappho and her contemporary Alcaeus, scholars have described the society as more sensual and free than those of the neighboring Dorians, Ionians, Spartans, and Athenians. Political unrest, freedom for women, and enjoyment of the senses appear to have characterized the aristocratic circle with which Sappho mingled.

LIFE'S WORK
Sappho's poetry, her principal life's work, consisted of nine books, which the grammarians of Alexandria arranged according to meter. The earliest surviving texts date from the third century B.C.E. Because the first book contained 1,320 lines, it can be surmised that Sappho left approximately twelve thousand lines, seven hundred of which have survived, pieced together from several sources. Only one complete poem remains, quoted by Dionysius of Halicarnassus, the rest ranging in completeness from several full lines to one word. Many of the lines lack beginning, middle, or end because they have survived on mummy wrapping in Egyptian tombs, the papyrus having been ripped crosswise of the roll, lengthwise of the poem. The long rolls of papyrus, made from the stalks of a water plant, also survived in battered condition in the dry Egyptian climate in garbage dumps and as stuffing in the mouths of mummified crocodiles.

Other lines remain because ancient grammarians used them to illustrate a point of grammar or comment on a text; literary critics quoted them to praise Sappho's style or talk about her metrics; and historians, orators, and philosophers used brief quotes from her work to illustrate their points. One fragment was recorded on a piece of broken pottery dating from the third century B.C.E. Important discoveries of eighth century manuscripts near Crocodilopolis were made in 1879, and two Englishmen made comparable finds in 1897 in an ancient Egyptian

Sappho. (Library of Congress)

garbage dump. One nineteenth century German scholar who rescued Sappho's poetry from its battered condition lost his eyesight, and one of the English scholars temporarily lost his sanity during the arduous process of transcription.

The surviving poetry consists primarily of passionate, simple, love poems addressed in the vernacular to young women. "Ode to Aphrodite," the only remaining complete poem, pleads with the goddess to make the object of the poet's passion return her love with equal intensity, which Aphrodite promises to do. Sappho's equally famous poem, "Seizure," is usually interpreted as an objective description of the poet's extreme jealousy when she sees her beloved conversing with a man. She writes that her heart beats rapidly and "a thin flame runs under/ [her] skin"; she cannot speak or see anything and hears only her "own ears/ drumming"; she sweats, trembles, and turns "paler than/ dry grass." Her jealousy can also burst into anger, as when she warns herself

> Sappho, when some fool
> Explodes rage
> in your breast
> hold back that
> yapping tongue!

Or she can restrain her emotions, stating quietly, "Pain penetrates/ Me drop/ by drop." The intensity of Sappho's passion becomes clear in the brief metaphor "As a whirlwind/ swoops on an oak/ Love shakes my heart." In a quieter mood, she can reveal another facet of her feelings:

> Really, Gorgo,
> My disposition
> is not at all
> spiteful: I have
> a childlike heart.

Sappho's subject matter helps explain the low survival rate of her poetry. Her reputation reached such greatness during the Golden Age of Greece that Solon of Athens reputedly remarked that he wished only to learn a certain poem by Sappho before he died, and Plato referred to her as the "Tenth Muse." The writers of the urbane and sophisticated Middle and New Comedy of Greece in the fourth and third centuries B.C.E., however, six of whom wrote plays they titled "Sappho," ridiculed Sappho's simplicity and openness, depicting her as an immoral, licentious courtesan. Although the Romans Theocritus, Horace, and Catullus praised and imitated her, Ovid referred to her both as a licentious woman lust-

ing after a young man and as one who taught her audience how to love girls, characteristics that the Christian church did not value.

Consequently, in 180 C.E. the ascetic Tatian attacked her as being whorish and love-crazy. Gregory of Nazianzus, bishop of Constantinople, in about 380, ordered that Sappho's writings be burned, and eleven years later Christian fanatics partially destroyed the classical library in Alexandria, which would certainly have contained her work. In 1073, Pope Gregory VII ordered another public burning of her writings in Rome and Constantinople. The Venetian knights who pillaged Constantinople in April, 1204, further vanquished her extant poetry. Thus, no single collection of her work survived the Middle Ages.

During the Renaissance, however, when Italian scholars recovered *Peri hypsous* (first century C.E.; *On the Sublime*, 1652), attributed to Cassius Longinus, and Dionysius of Halicarnassus's treatise on style, they found "Hymn to Aphrodite" and "Seizure." At this point, scholars began to collect all the remaining words, lines, and stanzas by Sappho.

During the nineteenth century, English and German scholars began to idealize Sappho and her work. Many of them viewed her as a moral, chaste woman, either a priestess of a special society of girls who devoted themselves to worship of Aphrodite and the Muses, or as the principal of a type of girls' finishing school. Although they sometimes acknowledged the intensity of her passion for her "pupils," they denied that it resulted in physical expression, a sentiment that persisted in the work of Maurice Bowra in 1936 and that Denys L. Page began to challenge in 1955. Succeeding critical works have increasingly accepted and explored the existence of Sappho's physical love for her young female companions. Although Sappho's expressed lesbian feelings or practice have little bearing on her skill as a poet, the stance almost doomed her work to extinction in a predominantly Christian society, in which sexual values differed significantly from those accepted in the ancient world, especially in seventh century Lesbos.

SIGNIFICANCE

The poetry of Sappho provides its reader with a direct experience of intense, stark emotions. Its unadorned honesty allows readers from various cultures and time periods a glimpse of the culture in which she lived, but, more important, into the human heart at its most vulnerable. Sappho loves and hates, feels jealousy and anger, and is able to transmit her emotions so immediately that the reader must respond to her stimuli.

Sappho defends the private sphere and shows the power of love within the individual heart. She has caused succeeding cultures to express their values in relation to her openness. To examine the history of Western civilization in reaction to Sappho's work is to stand back and observe as succeeding generations gaze into the mirror that she provides. Many have smashed the mirror, unable to confront the naked human heart. Some have seen themselves as they would like to be, and a few have learned more fully what it means to be feeling, passionate human beings.

—*Shelley A. Thrasher*

FURTHER READING

Bowra, C. Maurice. *Greek Lyric Poetry: From Alcman to Simonides*. 2d ed. Oxford, England: Clarendon Press, 1961. A classic review of seven Greek lyric poets stressing their historical development and critiquing important works. Offers groundbreaking theories of the poets as a group and as individual writers. Views Sappho as the leader of a society of girls that excluded men and worshipped the Muses and Aphrodite.

Burnett, Anne Pippin. *Three Archaic Poets: Archilochus, Alcaeus, Sappho*. Cambridge, Mass.: Harvard University Press, 1983. Rejects theories of ancient Greek lyrics as either passionate outpourings or occasional verse. Describes Sappho's aristocratic circle and critiques six major poems.

Jenkyns, Richard. *Three Classical Poets: Sappho, Catullus, and Juvenal*. Cambridge, Mass.: Harvard University Press, 1982. Stresses the relativistic view that no one theory can elucidate ancient poetry. Detailed analysis of Sappho's principal poems and fragments, concluding that she is a major poet.

Rayer, Diane, trans. *Sappho's Lyre: Archaeic Lyric and Women Poets of Ancient Greece*. Berkeley: University of California Press, 1991. The introduction and notes to this analogy of works of Sappho and her contemporaries provide historical and literary contexts for the ancient poetry. Written for the reader who does not know Greek.

Reynolds, Margaret, ed. *The Sappho Companion*. New York: Palgrave, 2001. Analogy contains narratives of the way societies in different times have accepted or rejected Sappho's works. Includes an introduction as well as translations of the fragments of the poems, a bibliography, and an index.

Sappho. *If Not, Winter: Fragments of Sappho*. Translated by Anne Carson. New York: Knopf, 2002. Presents all of Sappho's fragments in English accompanied by the Greek text.

SEE ALSO: Catullus; Enheduanna; Homer; Horace; Hypatia; Ovid; Pittacus of Mytilene; Sulpicia.

RELATED ARTICLES in *Great Events from History: The Ancient World*: c. 750 B.C.E., Homer Composes the *Iliad*; c. 594-580 B.C.E., Legislation of Solon; c. 580 B.C.E., Greek Poet Sappho Dies; c. 1st century B.C.E., Indian Buddhist Nuns Compile the *Therigatha*.

SARGON II
Neo-Assyrian king (r. 721-705 B.C.E.)

Through incessant, successful warfare and widespread resettlement of conquered populations, Sargon II brought an embattled Assyria to a late zenith of power and reshaped the structure of its empire; the dynasty he founded would last until the fall of Assyria.

BORN: Second half of eighth century B.C.E.; Assyria (now in Iraq)
DIED: 705 B.C.E.; north of Assyrian Empire
ALSO KNOWN AS: Sharru-kin
AREAS OF ACHIEVEMENT: War and conquest, government and politics

EARLY LIFE

There exists no known record of his life before Sargon (SAHR-gawn) II assumed the title of king of Assyria from his predecessor, Shalmaneser V, in December, 722, or January, 721. He never followed the royal custom of mentioning his father and grandfather by name in his annals but simply referred to his ancestors as "the kings his fathers." For this reason historians believe Sargon to have usurped the throne, although some insist that he was a son of the successful king Tukulti-apal-esharra (Tiglath-pileser III). In any case, he must have been born to a noble family of some renown; after surviving infancy—no small achievement in a society plagued by high infant mortality—the young warrior most likely pursued the customary education for his class: archery, horseback riding, and chariot driving and perhaps reading and writing.

From the ninth century B.C.E. on, Sargon's royal predecessors had worked to reverse the decline of Assyrian power that had begun with the death of the powerful king Tukulti-Ninurta I in 1208. Their expansionist policy had given birth to the Neo-Assyrian Empire, a state that found a most able leader in Tiglath-pileser III from 744 to 727.

During his reign, Egypt in the southwest and Urartu in the northeast were defeated, and Palestine, Syria, and Babylonia were conquered and subjected to political reorganization. Indeed, Tiglath-pileser bequeathed to Assyria a legacy that defined the direction of that country's interest and armed struggle for more than a century.

During a prolonged punitive mission in Samaria, when the absence of the king paralyzed official life and the work of justice at home, Tiglath-pileser's successor, Shalmaneser V, lost his throne to Sargon. The name that the young king took for himself at his accession shows some clever political maneuvering and suggests the need to legitimize this succession, or at least to stress its rightfulness. In its original Semitic form, Sharru-kin, Sargon's name, means "established" or "true and rightful king." In addition to this literal claim, there is the implicit reference to the Mesopotamian king Sargon of Akkad, who had reigned more than a thousand years before and whose fame had given rise to popular myths.

LIFE'S WORK

Sargon's kingship placed him at the helm of an embattled empire to whose expansion he would dedicate his life. Immediately after his succession, Sargon reaped unearned fame abroad when the city of Samaria fell and 27,290 Israelites were captured and resettled eastward in Mesopotamia and Media; this event is well-known because it is mentioned in the biblical book of Isaiah. At home, the new king secured his position by supporting the priesthood and the merchant class. His immediate reestablishment of tax-exempt status for Assyria's temples was the first demonstration of Sargon's lifelong policy of supporting the national religion.

During the first year of his reign, Sargon had to face opposition in the recently conquered territories. Sargon's annals, written in cuneiform on plates at his palace, record how he first marched south against Marduk-apal-iddina II or "Merodachbaladan, the foe, the perverse, who, contrary to the will of the great gods, exercised sovereign power at Babylon," a city that this local potentate had seized the moment Sargon became king. In league with Ummannish, king of the Elamites to the east of Babylon, the rebel proved able to prevent Sargon's advance through a battle in which both sides claimed victory.

Merodachbaladan remained ruler over the contested city for the next twelve years.

Turning west toward Syria and Palestine, Sargon's army defeated the usurper Ilu-bi'di, who had led an anti-Assyrian uprising, in the city of Karkar. Sargon's revenge was rather drastic; he burned the city and flayed Ilu-bi'di before marching against an Egyptian army at Raphia. There, Sargon decisively defeated the Egyptians and reestablished Assyrian might in Palestine. For the next ten years, neither Egypt nor local rebels would contest Assyrian power in the southwestern provinces, and Sargon began to look north toward another battlefield. There, at the northeastern boundary of the Assyrian Empire around the Armenian lakes, King Ursa (Rusas I) of Urartu and King Mita of Mushki (the Midas of Greek legend) habitually supported Sargon's enemies and destabilized the Assyrian border. For five years, between 719 and 714, Sargon battled various opponents in mountainous territory and waged a war of devastation and destruction on hostile kingdoms and their cities. Once they had overcome their enemies, the Assyrians plundered and burned their cities, led away the indigenous population, hacked down all trees, and destroyed dikes, canals, and other public works. In neighboring territories that Sargon intended to hold, a new population of Assyrians would follow the wave of destruction and deportation and settle in the land, and a new city with an Assyrian name would be founded at the site of the ruined old one.

In 714, Sargon finally defeated King Rusas and, on its ready surrender, plundered the city of Musasir, the riches of which were immense. A year later, a minor campaign against his son-in-law Ambaridi, a northern chieftain, showed the extent of resistance that Assyrian officers and nobles encountered in dealing with their neighbors and the populations of their provinces. The Assyrian response was swift and successful, and after Ambaridi's defeat and the leading away of his family and supporters, a large number of Assyrians settled in the pacified country, as was the usual pattern by then.

The next year saw a new campaign in the west, where pro-Assyrian rulers had been murdered or replaced with anti-Assyrians, who sometimes commanded considerable local support. In all cases, Sargon proved successful. The siege of Ashdod, where an Egyptian contingent was captured as well, is the second of Sargon's exploits mentioned in the Bible.

After his successful conquests and campaigns of pacification in the north and the southwest, Sargon prepared himself for a new showdown with his old enemy

Merodachbaladan. Marching southward, the Assyrian king wedged the two halves of his army between Babylon and the Elamites; his strategy proved successful when Merodachbaladan left his capital for Elam. In 710-709, Sargon triumphantly entered the open city and became the de facto king of Babylon, where he "took the hand of Bel," the city's deity, at the new year's celebration. Again, Sargon showed himself profoundly sympathetic to the cause of the priesthood and made large donations to the Babylonian temples; in turn, priests and influential citizens celebrated his arrival. Merodachbaladan, in contrast, failed in his attempt at persuading the Elamites to fight Sargon and retreated south to Yakin, close to the Persian Gulf. In April, 709, Sargon defeated him in battle there but let him go in return for a large payment of tribute.

After the fall of Yakin, Sargon ruled over an empire that stretched from the Mediterranean to the mountains of Armenia and encompassed Mesopotamia up to the Persian Gulf in the east. He left the remaining military missions to his generals, made his son and heir apparent, Sennacherib, commanding general in the north, and dedicated his energy to the building of his palatial city at what is now Khorsabad in Iraq. There, besides commissioning his annals to be written on stone plates, Sargon had his artists create impressive reliefs of the Assyrian king. These reliefs show a strong, muscular man taking part in various royal ceremonies and functions, among which is the blinding of prisoners of war. Sargon's head is adorned with an elaborately dressed turban and bejeweled headband. As was the fashion among the Assyrians, he wears a golden earring and a long, waved beard that is curled at the end. On his upper arms he wears golden bands, and his wrists sport bracelets. His multilayered garment bears some resemblance to a modern sari; the cloth has a rich pattern of rosettes and ends in tassels that touch the king's sandals at his ankles.

In 705, Sargon died under circumstances that are as mysterious as is his rise to kingship. Some historians believe that he died in an ambush during a campaign in the north when he led a small reconnaissance unit, as he was wont to do. According to others, he died at the hands of an assassin in his newly built capital, Dur-Sharrukin, a city that was abandoned after his death.

SIGNIFICANCE

For all of his aggression against neighboring states, which was the accepted mode of national survival in his times, Sargon showed statesmanship when it came to domestic politics and the treatment of the vast populace of his empire. He was a fair ruler who showed care for the material and spiritual well-being of his subjects. His annals make proud mention of how he paid fair market price for confiscated private land and strove "to fill the store houses of the broad land of Asshur with food and provisions . . . [and] not to let oil, that gives life to man and heals sores, become dear in my land, and regulate the price of sesame as well as of wheat." Sargon was also well aware of the fact that his nation, in which resettlement of conquered people and colonization by Assyrians eradicated older national structures, possessed no real racial or religious unity. To achieve a sense of national homogeneity and coherence, he employed the Assyrian language. Dur-Sharrukin, his new capital, was the best example of Sargonian domestic policy. His annals record how he populated the new metropolis:

> People from the four quarters of the world, of foreign speech, of manifold tongues, who had dwelt in mountains and valleys . . . whom I, in the name of Asshur my lord, by the might of my arms had carried away into captivity, I commanded to speak one language [Assyrian] and settled them therein. Sons of Asshur, of wise insight in all things, I placed over them, to watch over them; learned men and scribes to teach them the fear of God and the King.

Thus, Sargon's successful wars and domestic policy firmly established the power of the Neo-Assyrian Empire and left behind a great nation that would last for a century and help fight the northeastern barbarians who were beginning to threaten the ancient civilizations of the Middle East.

—*R. C. Lutz*

FURTHER READING

Kristensen, Anne. K. G. *Who Were the Cimmerians, and Where Did They Come From? Sargon II, the Cimmerians, and Rusa I.* Translated by Jorgen Laessoe. Copenhagen: Munksgaard, 1988. Slim volume on the history of western Asia includes bibliography.

Luckenbill, D. D., trans. *Ancient Records of Assyria and Babylonia.* London: Histories & Mysteries of Man, 1989. This work contains a fine translation of Sargon's letter to the god Ashur, in which the king reports on his northern campaign against Urartu. Sargon's text, far from dry, reveals a remarkable poetic bent.

Olmstead, Albert T. E. *History of Assyria.* Reprint. Chicago: University of Chicago Press, 1975. Chapters 17 to 23 deal with Sargon in a detailed discussion that closely follows original sources and points out where Sargon's reign connects with biblical events. Richly illustrated with maps and photographs of Assyrian artifacts, ruins, and the present look of the country.

_____. *Western Asia in the Days of Sargon of Assyria*. New York: Holt, 1908. Historically accurate and highly readable book on Sargon and his times that brings alive the Assyrians and their king. Illustrated and with helpful maps.

Roux, Georges. *Ancient Iraq*. New York: Penguin Books, 1992. A treatment of the full sweep of history in ancient Mesopotamia, which places Sargon within the full historical context of the region.

Saggs, H. W. F. *The Might That Was Assyria*. London: Sidgwick and Jackson, 1984. Pages 92-97 deal directly with Sargon. An account of Assyrian history and culture by an author who enjoys his subject. Relatively short on Sargon, but invaluable for its modern insights into Assyrian life. Has maps and interesting

illustrations, including representations of both kings and everyday objects. Very readable.

Sargon II. *The Correspondence of Sargon II*. Edited by Simo Parpola. Helsinki, Finland: Helsinki University Press, 2001. From the State Archives of Assyria project. Includes map and indexes.

_____. *Letters from Assyria and the West*. Edited by Simo Parpola. Helsinki, Finland: University of Helsinki Press, 1987. In English and Akkadian.

_____. *Letters from the Northern and Northeastern Provinces*. Edited by Giovanni B. Lanfrachi and Simo Parpola. Helsinki, Finland: Helsinki University Press, 1990. Includes bibliography and index.

SEE ALSO: Sennacherib; Tilgath-pileser III.

RELATED ARTICLES in *Great Events from History: The Ancient World*: 745 B.C.E., Tiglath-pileser III Rules Assyria; 701 B.C.E., Sennacherib Invades Syro-Palestine.

SCIPIO AEMILIANUS
Roman general

Combining a genius for military conquest with an appreciation for literature and the arts, Scipio Aemilianus embodied—perhaps better than any other figure of his day—the paradoxical forces that swept through Rome during the central years of the Republic.

BORN: 185/184 B.C.E.; probably Rome (now in Italy)
DIED: 129 B.C.E.; Rome
ALSO KNOWN AS: Publius Cornelius Scipio Aemilianus Africanus Numantinus (full name); Scipio the Younger
AREAS OF ACHIEVEMENT: War and conquest, government and politics, literature

EARLY LIFE
Scipio Aemilianus (SIHP-ee-oh ee-mihl-ih-AY-nuhs), also known as Scipio the Younger, was born into Roman society in 185/184, about the time that Cato the Elder was beginning his famous censorship. Scipio's earliest years were thus spent during one of the most interesting periods of the Roman Republic. From his vantage point as a member of the distinguished Aemilian *gens* (family), the young Scipio was in a perfect position to witness events that would shape the course of Roman history. In addition to this, because of his father, Lucius Aemilius Paulus, and his interest in Greek culture, Scipio was sur-

rounded almost from birth by Greek tutors, orators, and artists. Together, these two factors—the political distinction of his family and his father's philhellenism—were to inspire in Scipio his interest in a military career and his lifelong enthusiasm for Greek civilization.

Scipio's mother, Papiria, was a member of one of Rome's leading families: Her father had been a victorious general, the first general, in fact, to hold a triumphal procession on the Alban Mount because he had been denied an official triumph back in Rome. Scipio's father had also served as a general and had already been elected to the curule aedileship and the Spanish praetorship. At the time of Scipio's birth, Paullus was only a few years away from the consulship, the highest political office in Rome.

Ironically, at about the same time that Paullus's tenure as consul began, his marriage ended. He divorced Papiria, remarried, and soon had two other sons with his second wife. Perhaps as a result of conflicts between these two families, Paullus decided to allow Scipio and his brother to be adopted into other households. Scipio, as his name implies, was adopted by Publius Cornelius Scipio, the son of Scipio Africanus, who had won his greatest fame as victor over the Carthaginians at Zama during the Second Punic War. His elder brother was adopted into the household of Quintus Fabius Maximus Cunctator, perhaps by a son or grandson of the famous general himself. Both Scipio and his brother, now known as Quintus Fabius Maximus Aemilianus, remained close to their birth father. Indeed, they both accompanied Paullus on an important expedition against Macedon in 168, during Paullus's second consulship.

The climactic battle of this expedition, at Pydna in 168, was both the crowning glory of Paullus's career and, possibly, Scipio's first battle. The Macedonians, led by King Perseus, were defeated, and Paullus, in accordance with his literary tastes, chose only one prize for himself out of the spoils: Perseus's library. This mixture of military and literary interests was also apparent in Scipio himself at this time. It was during his stay in Greece that Scipio met the future historian Polybius, an author who would come to be his lifelong friend.

LIFE'S WORK

In 151, nearly a decade after the death of his father, Scipio was finally given a chance to develop a military reputation of his own. He was offered the position of military tribune under the consul Lucius Licinius Lucullus, who was about to assume command of the Roman forces in northern Spain. Though the campaign against the Celtiberian tribesmen would nearly be over before Lucullus finally arrived, Scipio did manage to win the *corona muralis* (an honor awarded to the first soldier who scaled the wall of an enemy), and, on a mission to obtain reinforcements in Africa, he witnessed a major battle between the Numidians and the Carthaginians. Thus, in this single campaign, Scipio journeyed to both of the regions that would one day see his greatest victories: Spain and Africa. Later, in 149 and 148, during the Third Punic War, Scipio served again as military tribune. The high honors that he won during the early campaigns of this war prompted his election to the consulship of 147, though neither in age nor in magistracies already held did he meet the requirements for the office.

The task assigned to Scipio during the final campaigns of the Third Punic War was to besiege the city of Carthage itself. Despite fierce opposition from the local inhabitants, Scipio managed to breach the fortifications of the city; six days of bitter fighting from house to house ensued. The Carthaginians resisted the Romans with unexpected vigor, though they had only makeshift weapons with which to defend themselves. While the battle raged in the streets below, the Roman soldiers were surprised to discover that they were being pelted with rocks and roofing tiles cast down from the houses above. However, in

the end, Carthage was set ablaze, and the Romans proceeded to demolish all remaining structures. As these orders were being carried out, many Carthaginians were trapped and buried alive in their own homes.

Some days later, as the final task of razing Carthage was completed, Polybius noticed tears in Scipio's eyes. When asked the reason for these tears, Scipio replied that he was afraid lest someday the same order might be given for his own city. He then quoted a famous passage of Homer's *Iliad* (c. 750 B.C.E.; English translation, 1611): "There will come a day when sacred Ilium shall perish/ and Priam and the people of Priam of the fine ash-spear." Scipio's sentiments notwithstanding, the site of Carthage was declared accursed, and its fifty thousand survivors were sold into slavery.

The years following the destruction of Carthage brought Rome once again into conflict with an old enemy: the Celtiberian tribesmen of Spain. For nearly ten years, from 143 until 134, a succession of Roman commanders had tried unsuccessfully to capture a Celtiberian fortress located on the hill settlement of Numantia. In the end, the Romans elected Scipio to be consul for a second time with the hope that he might bring this prolonged campaign to a successful conclusion. Scipio collected a force of nearly sixty thousand men, far outnumbering the four thousand Celtiberians who remained at Numantia. He then adopted the plan of surrounding the fortress with a ring of seven camps. The ploy was successful, although once again at an appalling cost of human life. The inhabitants were starved out, and some of them had even been reduced to cannibalism before their surrender. In any case, when Numantia finally capitulated to the Romans in 133, Scipio ordered the fortress to be destroyed and its survivors sold into slavery. Once again, this general who had been steeped in Greek culture since childhood felt compelled to resort to extreme measures in his efforts to subdue a Roman enemy. In order to understand this event, however, it is necessary to realize how formidable an opponent Numantia must have seemed at the time: Nearly a century after the fall of the city, Cicero could still refer, without fear of contradiction, to Carthage and Numantia as having been "the two most powerful enemies of Rome."

While these military conquests were still under way, however, Scipio's reputation was also on the rise because of his support for a group of artists and intellectuals who would come to make up the most famous "salon" in Roman history. The group was later to be known as the Scipionic Circle, though it is doubtful that this title was ever used in Scipio's lifetime. The discussions of the

Scipionic Circle covered a wide range of issues, and one of these discussions was later dramatized by Cicero in his dialogue titled *De republica* (51 B.C.E.; *On the State*, 1817). Though the membership in the Scipionic Circle varied from year to year, it eventually came to include such figures as Scipio, Polybius, the comic playwright Terence, the Roman legate Gaius Laelius, and the philosopher Panaetius. Membership in the group seems to have been based not only on these individuals' talents but also on Scipio's genuine affection for those with whom he discussed the issues of the day. Indeed, Scipio's friendship with Laelius became so renowned in later generations that Cicero based his philosophical dialogue *Laelius de amicitia* (44 B.C.E.; *On Friendship*, 1481) on Laelius's supposed recollections of Scipio shortly after his death.

In 129, Scipio, on the verge of being given an important new position in the Roman government, was found dead in his bed. He had been in perfect health, it was said, only the night before. As a result, no one knew whether he had been murdered or had died of an illness. Indeed, the question was so vexing that it was still being debated even in the time of Cicero. At first, suspicions fell on Gaius Papirius Carbo, a keen supporter of the reformer Tiberius Gracchus and a politician known for his oratorical ability. Carbo had been tribune in 131 and had proposed that tribunes be eligible for reelection year after year. Scipio had opposed this measure and led the fight against it. It is possible, therefore, that this political struggle eventually cost Scipio his life.

SIGNIFICANCE

While his contemporaries probably believed that Scipio Aemilianus would best be remembered for his military conquests and the political reputation of his family, scholars of later ages have come to view Scipio in a different light, as the center of the Scipionic Circle more than as a conquering general. Though Scipio destroyed Carthage, it was his adoptive grandfather, the defeater of Hannibal, whose name became tied to that city. Though Scipio consolidated Roman rule in Spain, it was Cato the Elder—who had tried and failed to accomplish the same task—whose military vision for Rome has remained clearer throughout the succeeding generations.

The Scipio who is recalled today is thus the Scipio of Cicero's dialogues: the student of Greek civilization, the friend of Polybius and Laelius, the magnet for Roman intellectuals of his time. While this is not an inaccurate picture, it is a picture that is largely incomplete. It is important, therefore, that Scipio Aemilianus be remembered not only as the man who wept and quoted Homer at the fall of Carthage but also as the victorious strategist who brought about the city's destruction.

—Jeffrey L. Buller

FURTHER READING

Astin, A. E. *Scipio Aemilianus*. Reprint. Oakville, Conn.: Oxbow Books, 2002. An accurate study of Scipio Aemilianus. Contains complete biographical data on Scipio, including references to all ancient sources. Family trees of the Aemilii Paulli and the Scipiones are provided. Includes extensive and well-chosen bibliography.

Brown, Ruth Martin. *A Study of the Scipionic Circle*. Scottdale, Pa.: Mennonite Press, 1934. Still the most complete and readable analysis of the Scipionic Circle. Includes information on the history and nature of the Scipionic Circle, its members during various periods in its development, and its influence in Roman society. Brown's book is helpful in tracking down many primary sources; two appendices listing the members of the Scipionic Circle in tabular and chronological form are still useful.

Cicero. *Cicero's "Republic."* Edited by J. G. F. Powell. London: Institute of Classical Studies, University of London, 2001. English translation includes index and bibliography.

_____. *"On Friendship" and the "Dream of Scipio."* Edited by J. G. F. Powell. Oakville, Conn.: David Brown Book Company, 1991. The Scipio of Cicero's dialogues is shown to be a student of Greek civilization, the friend of Polybius and Laelius, and the magnet for Roman intellectuals of his time.

Earl, D. C. "Terence and Roman Politics." *Historia* 11 (1962): 469-485. Earl demonstrates that the political views—or lack thereof—of Terence can be traced directly to his participation in the Scipionic Circle and the Hellenic influence on that body.

Scullard, H. H. "Roman Politics." *Journal of Roman Studies* 50 (1960): 59-74. Scullard examines the policies of Scipio and those in his immediate circle. The article is valuable for those interested in tracing the rise of the Roman reform movement before the time of Tiberius Gracchus.

SEE ALSO: Cato the Elder; Cicero; Hannibal; Hanno; Polybius; Terence.

RELATED ARTICLES in *Great Events from History: The Ancient World*: 202 B.C.E., Battle of Zama; 149-146 B.C.E., Third Punic War; 146 B.C.E., Sack of Corinth.

SCIPIO AFRICANUS
Roman general

Scipio's military victory over Carthaginian forces in Spain and North Africa, brought about by his genius as strategist and innovator of tactics, ended the Second Punic War and established Roman hegemony in the Western Mediterranean region.

BORN: 236 B.C.E.; Rome (now in Italy)
DIED: 184 or 183 B.C.E.; Liternum, Campania (now Patria, Italy)
ALSO KNOWN AS: Publius Cornelius Scipio (full name); Scipio the Elder
AREAS OF ACHIEVEMENT: War and conquest, government and politics

EARLY LIFE
Publius Cornelius Scipio, known as Scipio Africanus (SIHP-ee-oh ahf-rih-KAY-nuhs) or Scipio the Elder, was born to one of the most illustrious families of the Roman Republic; his father, who gave the boy his name, and his mother, Pomponia, were respected citizens of the patrician dynasty of the gens Cornelii. At Scipio's birth, Rome had begun to show its power beyond the boundaries of Italy, and the young nation was starting to strive for hegemony west and east of the known world. Coinciding with expansion outward was Rome's still-stable inner structure; nevertheless, the influence of the Greek culture had begun a softening, or rounding, of the Roman character.

Scipio's early life clearly reflects this transition. His lifelong sympathy with Greek culture made him somewhat suspect in the eyes of his conservative opponents, who accused him of weakening the Roman spirit. On the other hand, as a patrician youth, he must have received early military training, for Scipio entered history (and legend) at the age of seventeen or eighteen, when he saved his father from an attack by hostile cavalry during a skirmish with the invading forces of Hannibal in Italy in 218.

His military career further advanced when Scipio prevented a mutiny among the few survivors of the disastrous Battle of Cannae in 216. As a military tribune, the equivalent of a modern staff colonel, he personally intervened with the deserters, placed their ringleaders under arrest, and put the defeated army under the command of the surviving consul.

In 211, another serious defeat for Rome brought Scipio an unprecedented opportunity. In Spain, two armies under the command of his father and an uncle had been defeated, and the commanders were killed. Although he was still rather young—twenty-seven according to the ancient historian Polybius—and had not served in public office with the exception of the entry-level position of *curulic aedile* (a chief of domestic police), Scipio ran unopposed in the ensuing election and became proconsul and supreme commander of the reinforcements and the Roman army in Spain.

His election attests the extraordinary popularity that he enjoyed with the people of Rome and later with his men. So great was his reputation, which also rested partly on his unbounded self-confidence and (according to Polybius) a streak of rational calculation, that people talked about his enjoying a special contact with the gods. A religious man who belonged to a college of priests of Mars, Scipio may himself have reinforced these adulatory rumors. Whether his charisma and popularity were further aided by particularly "noble" looks, however, is not known. Indeed, all the extant representations of him, no matter how idealized, do not fail to show his large nose and ears, personal features that do not detract from the overall image of dignity but serve to humanize the great general.

His marriage to Aemilia, the daughter of the head of a friendly patrician family, gave Scipio at least two sons and one daughter, who would later be mother to the social reformers Gaius and Tiberius Gracchus.

LIFE'S WORK
Arriving in Spain, Scipio followed the strategic plan of continuing the offensive warfare of his father and uncle and thus trying to tear Spain, their European base, away from the Carthaginians. After he had reorganized his army, Scipio struck an unexpected blow by capturing New Carthage, the enemy's foremost port, in 209. A year later he launched an attack on one-third of the Carthaginian forces at Baecula, in south central Spain. While his light troops engaged the enemy, Scipio led the main body of Roman infantry to attack both flanks of the Carthaginians and thus win the battle. Hasdrubal Barca, the Carthaginian leader, however, managed to disengage his troops and escape to Gaul, where Scipio could not follow him, and ultimately arrived in Italy.

The decisive move followed in 206, when Scipio attacked the united armies of Hasdrubal, the son of Gisco, and Mago at Ilipa (near modern Seville). Meanwhile, his generous treatment of the Spanish tribes had given him native support. Scipio placed these still-unreliable allies in the center of his army, to hold the enemy, while Roman infantry and cavalry advanced on both sides, wheeled around, and attacked the Carthaginian war elephants and soldiers in a double enveloping maneuver that wrought total havoc.

Scipio's immediate pursuit of the fleeing enemy succeeded so completely in destroying their forces that Carthage's hold on Spain came to a de facto end. After a punitive mission against three insurgent Spanish cities and the relatively bloodless putting down of a mutiny by some Roman troops, Scipio received the surrender of Gades (Cádiz), the last Carthaginian stronghold in Spain.

When Scipio returned to Rome, the senate did not grant him a triumph. He was elected consul for the year 205, but only his threat to proceed alone, with popular support, forced the senate to allow him to take the war to Carthage in North Africa rather than fight an embattled and ill-supported Hannibal in Italy. In his province of Sicily, Scipio began with the training of a core army of volunteers; uncharacteristically for Roman thought, but brilliantly innovative in terms of strategy, he emphasized the formation of a strong cavalry.

Scipio Africanus. (Library of Congress)

In 204, Scipio landed in North Africa near the modern coast of Tunisia with roughly thirty-five thousand men and more than six hundred cavalry. He immediately joined forces with the small but well-trained cavalry detachment of the exiled King Masinissa and drew first blood in a successful encounter with Carthaginian cavalry under General Hanno.

Failing to capture the key port of Utica, Scipio built winter quarters on a peninsula east of the stubborn city. One night early the next spring, he led his army against the Carthaginian relief forces under Hasdrubal and King Syphax, who had broken an earlier treaty with Scipio. The raid was successful, and the camps of the enemy were burned. Now Scipio followed the reorganized adversaries and defeated them decisively at the Great Plains. The fall of Tunis came soon after.

Beaten, Carthage sought an armistice of forty-five days, which was granted by Scipio and broken when Hannibal arrived in North Africa. Hostilities resumed and culminated in the Battle of Zama. Here, the attack of the Carthaginian war elephants failed, because Scipio had anticipated them and opened his ranks to let the animals uselessly thunder through. Now the two armies engaged in fierce battle, and, after the defeat of the Carthaginian auxiliary troops and mercenaries, Scipio attempted an out-flanking maneuver that failed against the masterful Hannibal. In a pitched battle, the decisive moment came when the Roman cavalry and that of Masinissa broke off their pursuit of the beaten Carthaginian horsemen and fell on the rear of Hannibal's army. The enemy was crushed.

After the victory of Zama, Scipio granted Carthage a relatively mild peace and persuaded the Roman senate to ratify the treaty. When he returned to Rome, he was granted a triumph in which to show his rich booty, the prisoners of war (including Syphax), and his victorious troops, whom he treated generously. It was around this time that Scipio obtained his honorific name "Africanus."

There followed a period of rest for Scipio. In 199 he took the position of censor, an office traditionally reserved for elder statesmen, and in 194 he held his second consulship. An embassy to Masinissa brought Scipio back to Africa in 193, and in 190 he went to Greece as a legate, or general staff officer, to his brother Lucius. In Greece, the Romans had repulsed the Syrian king Antiochus the Great and prepared the invasion of Asia Minor. Because of an illness, Scipio did not see the Roman victory there.

At home, their political opponents, grouped around archconservative Cato the Censor, attacked Scipio and his brother in a series of unfounded lawsuits, known as "the processes of the Scipios," concerning alleged fiscal mismanagement and corruption in the Eastern war. Embittered, Scipio defended his brother in 187 and himself in 184, after which he left Rome, returning only when the opposition threatened to throw Lucius in jail. Going back to his small farm in Liternum in the Campania, Scipio lived a modest life as a virtual exile until his death in the same year or in 183. His great bitterness is demonstrated by his wish to be buried there instead of in the family tomb near the capital.

SIGNIFICANCE

The military victories of Scipio Africanus brought Rome a firm grip on Spain, victory over Carthage, and dominion over the Western Mediterranean. Scipio's success rested on his great qualities as a farsighted strategist and innovative tactician who was bold enough to end the archaic Roman reliance on the brute force of its infantry; he learned the lesson of Hannibal's victory at Cannae. His newly formed cavalry and a highly mobile and more maneuverable infantry secured the success of his sweeps to envelop the enemy.

On the level of statesmanship, Scipio's gift for moderation and his ability to stabilize and pacify Spain secured power for Rome without constant bloodletting. His peace with Carthage would have enabled this city to live peacefully under the shadow of Rome and could have prevented the Third Punic War, had the senate later acted differently.

Finally, Scipio never abused his popularity to make himself autocratic ruler of Rome, although temptations to do so abounded. At the height of his influence in Spain, several tribes offered him the title of king; he firmly refused. After his triumph, the exuberant masses bestowed many titles on the victor of Zama, but he did not grasp for ultimate power. Unlike Julius Caesar, Scipio Africanus served the Roman state; he did not master it. He is perhaps the only military leader of great stature who achieved fame as a true public servant.

—*R. C. Lutz*

FURTHER READING

Eckstein, Arthur M. *Senate and General*. Berkeley: University of California Press, 1987. Generally scrutinizes who had the power to make political decisions. Chapter 8 illuminates various aspects of Scipio's struggle with the senate. Includes a good, up-to-date bibliography.

Goldsworthy, Adrian. *The Punic Wars*. London: Cassell, 2000. Each of the wars is described in detail; provides background to the conflict as a whole and its context in military history.

Hart, B. H. *Scipio Africanus: Greater than Napoleon*. 1926. Reprint. New York: Da Capo Press, 1994. Readable, well-balanced biography emphasizes the subject's military achievements. Scipio is judged sympathetically and praised for tactical innovations and rejection of "honest bludgeon work." Contains many helpful maps.

Haywood, Richard M. *Studies on Scipio Africanus*. 1933. Reprint. Westport, Conn.: Greenwood Press, 1973. Revises the account by Polybius, who rejected old superstitions about Scipio but made him more calculating and scheming than Haywood believes is justified. The bibliography is still useful.

Lancel, Serge. *Carthage: A History*. Translated by Antonia Nevill. Cambridge, Mass.: Blackwell, 1997. Detailed study of Carthage from its founding and rise in the early centuries of the first millennium to its defeat and Roman absorption by the end of the period.

Scullard, Howard H. *Roman Politics 220-150 B.C.* 2d ed. Reprint. Westport, Conn.: Greenwood Press, 1981. Chapters 4 and 5 deal with Scipio's influence on Roman politics and place his career in the context of political and dynastic struggle for control in the Roman Republic. Shows where Scipio came from politically and traces his legacy. Contains appendix with diagrams of the leading Roman families.

_____. *Scipio Africanus in the Second Punic War*. Cambridge, England: Cambridge University Press, 1930. An in-depth study of Scipio's campaigns and military achievements, highly technical but readable and with good maps. Brings alive Scipio while dealing exhaustively with its subject.

_____. *Scipio Africanus: Soldier and Politician*. Ithaca, N.Y.: Cornell University Press, 1970. General study and excellent, comprehensive biography. Carefully balanced and well-researched work. Written with a feeling for its subject, which makes it interesting to read. Contains useful maps.

SEE ALSO: Cato the Censor; Fabius; Gracchi; Hannibal; Hanno; Masinissa; Scipio Aemilianus.

RELATED ARTICLES in *Great Events from History: The Ancient World*: 218-201 B.C.E., Second Punic War; 202 B.C.E., Battle of Zama; 149-146 B.C.E., Third Punic War; 146 B.C.E., Sack of Corinth.

SCOPAS
Greek sculptor

Scopas created works of relaxed gracefulness on one hand and of strong emotion, stress, and turbulence on the other. With Praxiteles of Athens and Lysippus of Sicyon, his work dominated the art of the fourth century B.C.E.

BORN: Possibly as early as 420 B.C.E.; Paros, Greece
DIED: Late fourth century B.C.E.; place unknown
ALSO KNOWN AS: Scopas of Paros
AREA OF ACHIEVEMENT: Art and art patronage

EARLY LIFE

No biographical information on Scopas (SKOH-pahs) survives. He may have been the son of the Parian sculptor Aristander, who was working in 405 B.C.E.

LIFE'S WORK

Scopas worked as an architect and sculptor. His most celebrated works are sculptures designed to fit into a specific architectural setting. Ancient sources report that he worked on three important monuments of the early and mid-fourth century B.C.E.: the temple of Athena Alea at Tegea, the temple of Artemis at Ephesus, and the Mausoleum of Halicarnassus. It is indicative of his prominence that the last two of these three projects became famous as two of the Seven Wonders of the World.

Modern students of Scopas consider the temple of Athena Alea at Tegea the most important of his achievements because its fragments are the basis of whatever judgments can be made about his style. Pausanias the Traveler (b. c. 110-115 C.E.; d. c. 180 C.E.) says that he was the architect of the building as a whole; judging from the consistent style of the surviving pieces, it is likely that the temple sculptures were executed by a team of artisans working under Scopas's supervision. The original temple, in southern Arcadia, had been destroyed by a fire in 394 B.C.E. The rebuilding took place about a generation later, on a scale of size and magnificence designed to overshadow all other temples in the Peloponnese. The central image of the temple, an ivory carving of Athena Alea, had been saved from the earlier temple. Everything else was for Scopas to create, and it is likely that he conceived of the temple itself as a vehicle for the display of the ornamental sculptures he designed. Pausanias, who saw the building intact, reports that the sculptures of the front pediment represented the Calydonian boar hunt referred to in the ninth book of Homer's *Iliad* (c. 750 B.C.E.; English translation, 1611). The figure of Meleager on

this pediment, though lost, is believed to survive in copies, of which the best two are in the Vatican and in Berlin. The rear pediment showed the duel between Telephus (the local Arcadian hero) and Achilles, which took place just before the Trojan War. Of these sculptures, only fragments of the heads and various body parts survive. Scopas also created the freestanding statues of the healer Asklepios and the health goddess Hygieia, which flanked the ivory figure of Athena that stood in the interior. A marble head of a woman that may be that of Hygieia was found by French excavators of the site in the early 1920's.

Scopas's role in the creation of the Artemisium at Ephesus is more problematical. There is only the authority of Pliny the Elder that he executed one of the thirty-six ornamented columns that were commissioned for this colossal structure, one of the Seven Wonders of the World. The sixth century B.C.E. temple of Artemis had burned in 356 B.C.E., reportedly on the night of Alexander the Great's birth, and construction began immediately on what would be (like Athena's temple at Tegea) considerably grander than its predecessor. The remains of this larger second temple are now in the British Museum. Of the three surviving ornamented column bases, one is dubiously attributed to Scopas. It shows Hermes leading the soul of Alcestis, who had offered to die in place of her husband, Admetus, toward a winged figure representing Thanatos, or death.

Scopas's third major work in architectural ornamentation was the Mausoleum of Halicarnassus, ordered by Queen Artemisia as a monumental tomb for her husband Mausalaus, satrap of Caria, who died in 353. This building, constructed entirely of white marble, stood until the fifteenth century, when it was brought down by an earthquake. It was excavated by the British in 1857, and many of its best pieces were taken to the British Museum. Though not its chief architect, Scopas was one of four famous artists brought in to decorate the four sides of the building with relief sculpture. His colleagues in this project, according to Pliny the Elder and Vitruvius, were Bryaxis, Timotheus, and Leochares. The best preserved of the three friezes found near the site by the British team represents an Amazonomachy, any of a number of legendary battles between Greeks and Amazons. Seventeen slabs, more or less defaced, represent this scene. Numerous attempts to attribute sections of the frieze to Scopas have been made, but they are problematical as a result of the lack of a single distinctive style that can serve as a signature of the master's work. Four slabs found near the northeast corner are commonly attributed to Scopas, but the touchstone of Scopadic style remains the fragments from Tegea.

Other works by Scopas are known through descriptions in ancient sources, which have led to the attribution of copies that seem to fit the ancient descriptions. A poem by Callistratus describes a Bacchante in ecstasy, carrying a kid she has killed. This image has been identified with a Maenad in the Dresden Sculpture Museum whose head is thrown up and back over her left shoulder. Her light dress, fastened over her right shoulder and held in place by a cord knotted above her waist, is blown by the wind, laying bare her left side, and her back is arched sharply backward as she strides, right leg forward. *The Dresden Maenad*, commonly attributed to Scopas, is representative of the late Classical and Hellenistic fondness for figures in action, gripped by powerful emotion. One of his most popular sculptures was a statue of Pothos (Longing), a young male nude leaning on a pillar, or thyrsus, with a cloak over his left arm and a goose at his feet. He stands with his weight on one foot, his left leg relaxed and crossing in front of his right. He looks upward in an abstracted way, as if thinking of an absent lover.

Although the original of this masterpiece no longer survives, there are many Roman copies (and gemstone engravings) that testify to its popularity. This work represents the late classical departure from the powerfully built, erect, and concentrated figures of the earlier severe style. The body lines are gentle, the geometry of the figure is sloping rather than erect, and the effect is of grace rather than power. Pausanias mentions a bronze Aphrodite Pandemos in a precinct of Aphrodite at Elis; the image has survived on Roman coins. Other works believed to show Scopas's influence are Roman reproductions of his statue of Meleager and the *Lansdowne Heracles* at the Getty Museum in Malibu, California, thought to be modeled on an original made for the gymnasium at Sikyon. Nearly all these derivative pieces are statues of gods and goddesses: Asklepios and Hygieia, Aphrodite, Apollo, Dionysus, Hestia, and Hermes.

SIGNIFICANCE

Scopas must remain an enigmatic figure because no existing work of sculpture can safely be attributed to him; indeed, not much is known about the man or his work. Nevertheless, the testimony of ancient writers such as Pausanias, Pliny the Elder, and Vitruvius affirms that he was famed in the ancient world as both sculp-

tor and architect, that his work was in great demand, and that he was widely imitated. The consensus of ancient opinion represents him as the preeminent sculptor of passion.

Modern students of ancient art are also unanimous in attributing to Scopas an individuality of manner that they perceive in works closely associated with his name. While the best authorities are reluctant to make dogmatic attributions of specific works, they agree in attributing to his style an impetuous force in the rendering of figures, delicate workmanship, and the rhythmical composition of a master sculptor.

Scopas's technical virtuosity is perhaps less important than the human content of his work, which reveals an emotional fervor and a sensitivity to the sadness of life. This interpretation was one of his great contributions to Hellenistic culture. Another aspect of his contribution is the representation of the human form under stress, where the body's tension symbolizes a turbulent emotional state. Hellenistic mannerism grows naturally out of this style. Scopas's unique achievement in recording the deeper recesses of human experience has been appropriately compared to that of Michelangelo in the Renaissance.

—*Daniel H. Garrison*

FURTHER READING

Ashmole, Bernard. "Skopas." In *Encyclopedia of World Art*. New York: McGraw-Hill, 1959-1983. An excellent summary in English supplemented by an extensive bibliography of books and articles in English, French, German, and Italian.

Barron, John. *An Introduction to Greek Sculpture*. New York: Schocken Books, 1984. This volume is brief but well illustrated.

Bentley, Diana, and Sarah Warburton. *The Seven Wonders of the Ancient World*. New York: Oxford University Press, 2002. Describes the architectural achievements of the ancient world known as the Seven Wonders of the World, including the Temple of Artemis at Ephesus and the Mausoleum of Halicarnassus.

Bieber, Margarete. *The Sculpture of the Hellenistic Age*. New York: Hacker Art Books, 1981. A detailed account of the major works still surviving, those described by ancient sources, and existing sculptures in Scopas's style. Finely illustrated; includes a bibliography and references to museum catalogs.

Jeppeson, Kristian. *Maussolleion at Halikarnassos, Reports of the Danish Archaeological Expedition to Bodrum*. Copenhagen: Jutland Historical Society,

2000. Describes the mausoleum's structure, art and adornments, and the sacrificial deposit.

Lawrence, A. W. *Greek and Roman Sculpture*. London: Cape, 1972. This work concentrates on the Tegea figures, with notices of several pieces attributed to Scopas. Limited bibliography.

Richter, G. M. A. *The Sculpture and Sculptors of the Greeks*. New Haven, Conn.: Yale University Press, 1970. Attentive to the ancient sources, which are quoted freely, and most sensitive to the problems of identification. Well documented with references to ancient and modern sources.

Stewart, Andrew F. *Skopas of Paros*. Park Ridge, N.Y.: Noyes Press, 1977. Detailed attention to features of style, based chiefly on the Tegea fragments. Richly illustrated, with a full set of ancient testimonia and detailed references to modern scholarship. Likely to remain the standard authority for some time.

SEE ALSO: Artemisia I; Lysippus; Mausolus; Praxiteles.

RELATED ARTICLES in *Great Events from History: The Ancient World*: c. 750 B.C.E., Homer Composes the *Iliad*; 447-438 B.C.E., Building of the Parthenon.

SELEUCUS I NICATOR
Seleucid king (r. 305-281 B.C.E.)

By his courage and practical common sense, Seleucus created the Seleucid Empire, maintaining the loyalty of a heterogeneous population by fair government.

BORN: 358 or 354 B.C.E.; Europus, Macedonia (now in Greece)

DIED: August/September, 281 B.C.E.; near Lysimachia, Thrace (now in Greece)

AREAS OF ACHIEVEMENT: Government and politics, war and conquest

EARLY LIFE

Seleucus (seh-LEW-kuhs) was born in 358 or 354 B.C.E. in Europus, Macedonia. Although ancient sources do not agree on when he was born, no one disputes that he was the son of a man named Antiochus and his wife, Laodice. Nothing is known of Seleucus's early life, but both Diodorus Siculus and Appian indicate that he was with the army of Alexander the Great that marched against the Persians in 334. He must have distinguished himself in the following years, for by 326 he had assumed command of the royal hypaspists (elite infantry) in the Indian campaign and had gained a position on the king's staff. When Alexander crossed the Hydaspes River, he took with him in the same boat Ptolemy (later Ptolemy Soter), Perdiccas, Lysimachus, and Seleucus.

One of Alexander's final acts was to preside over the festival at Susa during which his generals married Persian brides. His two fiercest opponents had been Oxyartes and Spitamenes. Alexander had already married Oxyartes' daughter Roxane; he gave Apama, daughter of Spitamenes, to Seleucus. This marriage provided Seleucus with his son and successor, Antiochus. According to Appian, he named three cities after Apama.

When Alexander died in 323, Perdiccas took over as regent for Alexander's retarded half brother and his unborn child. The empire was divided among the generals, who were to serve as satraps (governors). Seleucus was named chiliarch (commander of the Companion cavalry), a position of extreme military importance but with no grant of land. For this reason, he played a relatively unimportant role for the next ten years, although he led the cavalry rebellion that resulted in the death of Perdiccas in 321. When a new appointment of satraps was made shortly after this, Seleucus gave up his position as chiliarch to become governor of Babylonia.

Babylonia, in the center of what had been Alexander's empire, was the perfect position from which to dominate the entire empire, but its security was threatened by the arrogant satraps of Media (Pithon) and Persia (Peucestas). Pithon seized Parthia to the east, was driven out by Peucestas, and subsequently sought an alliance with Seleucus. Meanwhile, Eumenes, the outlawed former satrap of Cappadocia, appeared in Babylonia with an elite Macedonian force far superior to Seleucus's army. Seleucus was forced to call on Antigonus I, the most powerful of the satraps, for help. Although Antigonus, Seleucus, and Pithon started the campaign together in 317, once they had taken Susiana, Seleucus was left behind to besiege the citadel of Susa while the other two pursued Eumenes. In rapid succession, Antigonus defeated and killed Eumenes, ordered the execution of Pithon, and masterminded the "disappearance" of Peucestas. When he returned to Babylonia, Seleucus tried to appease Antigonus with the treasure from Susa, but it was only a short time later, in 316, that he wisely fled Babylon and sought refuge with Ptolemy in Egypt.

LIFE'S WORK

Seleucus would seem to have lost everything at this point, but this was actually the beginning of his climb to even greater power. Antigonus was now the dominant figure among Alexander's successors, but he wanted the whole empire. The three other powerful leaders—Ptolemy in Egypt, Lysimachus in Thrace, and Cassander in Macedonia—formed a coalition against him. In the first phase of the resulting war, Seleucus served as commander in Ptolemy's navy, seeing action in both the Aegean Sea and the eastern Mediterranean around Cyprus. In the beginning of the second phase, he took part in the attack on Gaza by the Ptolemaic army. Antigonus had sent his son Demetrius to hold this strategically important fortress, and his defeat was a severe blow to Antigonus's plans. According to Diodorus (c. 40 B.C.E.), Ptolemy showed his gratitude to Seleucus by giving him a small army, which he then led into Babylonia.

The troops at first were fearful of their mission, but Seleucus convinced them that an oracle of Didymean Apollo had proclaimed him king. The Seleucids would eventually claim Apollo as an ancestor. Better than the oracle, however, was the fact that during his previous governorship Seleucus had ruled wisely and well. Reinforcements flocked to him as he marched into the territory, and he took the city of Babylon with little trouble. This feat launched the Seleucid Empire.

Seleucus regained Babylonia but not without antagonizing Nicanor, the satrap of Media, who proceeded to march on Babylon. Seleucus, however, swiftly leading an army out to meet him, surprised and routed Nicanor, whose troops deserted to the victor.

The East was now open to Seleucus. He rapidly took Susiana and Persia before turning to Media, where, according to Appian, Nicanor was killed in battle. Between 311 and 302, Seleucus gained control of all Iran and the lands extending to the Indus River. At the Indus, he reestablished contact with the Indian chieftains of the region and returned home finally with 480 elephants.

Meanwhile, in the West, Alexander's family had been exterminated. In 306, Antigonus proclaimed himself king, and the other four satraps, Ptolemy, Lysimachus, Cassander, and Seleucus, followed suit. Antigonus still had designs on all of Alexander's empire, and by 302, the other kings considered his power so threatening to their own security that they formed a coalition against him.

The armies met at Ipsus in 301, where Seleucus's elephants played a major role in the defeat of Antigonus, who died in battle. In the redivision of land that followed, Seleucus gained Syria, and Lysimachus was awarded Asia Minor. A new war could have started between Seleucus and Ptolemy, as the king of Egypt had previously occupied Coele-Syria (Palestine) and now refused to give it up. Seleucus, however, remembered that Ptolemy had stood by him in a difficult time and decided to ignore the issue, although he did not give up his claim to the land.

Seleucus now held more land than any of the other kings, and that made them uneasy. In order to balance the power, Ptolemy and Lysimachus joined in marriage alliances; this, in turn, disturbed Seleucus. Although his marriage to Apama was still firm, Seleucus sent word to Demetrius to ask for his daughter Stratonice in marriage. (Macedonian kings practiced polygamy.) Demetrius agreed, and the marriage took place. Seleucus and Stratonice had a daughter, whom Seleucus eventually gave in marriage to his eldest son, Antiochus. He sent them to Babylon to reign as king and queen in the East. Seleucus ruled in the West from his new capital city of Antioch, named for his father.

Seleucus spent most of the twenty years following the Battle of Ipsus consolidating his empire. One of his major policies was the division of the empire into East and West, with the heir to the throne ruling from Babylon; this would become a standard policy of the Seleucids. His major problem throughout most of this period was Demetrius, who had become king of Macedonia but would not be satisfied until he had regained his father's lost kingdom. Demetrius invaded Asia Minor in 287, but two years later, Seleucus held him captive. At first, Demetrius believed that he would soon be set free, but as that hope faded, so did his self-control. By 283, he had drunk himself to death.

There might have been a peaceful old age for Seleucus if it had not been for Ptolemy's disinherited eldest son, Ptolemy Keraunos. After causing the death of Lysimachus's son in Thrace, Keraunos fled to Seleucus, thus precipitating war between the two former allies. The two met at Corypedium in Asia Minor in the spring of 281. Lysimachus was killed in the battle. Seleucus, who was now in his seventies, suddenly saw himself as Alexander reuniting his empire. He pressed on to Thrace, only to meet death treacherously at the hand of Ptolemy Keraunos outside the capital city of Lysimachia in the following summer. His common sense had deserted him in the end, but he left behind an heir who was experienced in ruling and a well-established empire based on sound government.

SIGNIFICANCE

Seleucus I Nicator ruled an empire made up of many diverse ethnic groups. He had inherited the Persian system of administration and was wise enough to realize its value. He continued the Persian policy of respecting the cultures and religions of the people he ruled at the same time that he proceeded to establish a governmental system entirely made up of Greeks. Unlike most of Alexander's generals, Seleucus retained and respected his Persian wife, but there were few, if any, non-Greeks in his administration. His son and successor, who was half Persian, married a Macedonian woman. Seleucus spread Hellenism throughout the major parts of his empire by the typical Greek method of founding colonies. Antioch, his capital in the West, became one of the great cities of the ancient world.

The first of the Seleucids was a man of honor. He gained his position in Alexander's army through hard work and his empire in the same way. He was able to reclaim Babylonia because he had ruled well throughout his first governorship, and he refused to fight Ptolemy over Coele-Syria out of gratitude for past favors. Later, when he held Demetrius prisoner, Seleucus declined to turn him over to Lysimachus, who had offered a large sum of money in exchange. Demetrius was treated honorably during his imprisonment, but Seleucus realized that he was too troublesome ever to be released. Seleucus was loyal to his friends and treated his enemies fairly. Unfortunately, Ptolemy Keraunos had none of these attributes, and Seleucus died as the result of a cowardly attack by a man who had first called on him for help and then killed him to gain a kingdom he was not wise enough to keep.

—*Linda J. Piper*

FURTHER READING

Bar-Kochva, B. *The Seleucid Army: Organization and Tactics in the Great Campaigns.* Cambridge, England: Cambridge University Press, 1976. This study addresses only military affairs, but Bar-Kochva points out Seleucus's courage and tactical ability. Part 1 concentrates on manpower and organization.

Bevan, Edwyn Robert. *The House of Seleucus.* 1902. Reprint. New York: Ares, 1985. Analytical account of Seleucus's rise to power based on the ancient sources.

Cohen, Getzel M. *The Seleucid Colonies: Studies in Founding, Administration, and Organization.* Weisbaden, West Germany: Steiner, 1978. Contains information on the founding, administration, and organization of new colonies. Attempts to answer questions on the nature of the poorly documented Seleucid colonization program. The answers are tentative but thought-provoking.

Cook, S. A., F. E. Adcock, and M. P. Charlesworth, eds. *The Hellenistic Monarchies and the Rise of Rome.* Vol. 7 in *The Cambridge Ancient History.* New York: Cambridge University Press, 1984-2000. Contains a systematic account of the organization of both the central and satrapy governments in the Seleucid Empire.

Grainger, John D. *Seleukos Nikator: Constructing a Hellenistic Kingdom.* New York: Routledge, 1990. Biography traces the stages of Seleucus's rise as he added province to province and kingdom to kingdom. Includes maps, index, and bibliography.

Seyrig, H. "Seleucus I and the Foundation of Hellenistic Syria." In *The Role of the Phoenicians in the Interaction of Mediterranean Civilizations.* Beirut, Lebanon: American University Press, 1968. Part of a series of articles edited by W. A. Ward. (Phoenicia was a part of the satrapy of Syria claimed by Seleucus in 301 B.C.E.)

SEE ALSO: Alexander the Great; Antiochus the Great; Ptolemy Soter.

SENECA THE YOUNGER
Roman philosopher and statesman

An influential intellectual, Seneca also showed great abilities as coadministrator of the Roman Empire during the first years of Nero. In literature, Seneca's essays and tragedies were influential from the Middle Ages to the Renaissance, when English playwrights took his dramas as models.

BORN: c. 4 B.C.E.; Corduba (now Córdoba, Spain)
DIED: April, 65 C.E.; Rome (now in Italy)
ALSO KNOWN AS: Lucius Annaeus Seneca (full name)
AREAS OF ACHIEVEMENT: Government and politics, philosophy, literature

EARLY LIFE
Although Seneca (SEHN-ih-kuh) the Younger was born in Corduba, his father, known as Seneca the Elder, was a conservative Roman knight who had achieved fame as an orator and teacher of rhetoric in Rome. His mother, Helvia, was an extraordinarily intelligent, gifted, and morally upright person whose love for philosophy had been checked only by her husband's rejection of the idea of education for women.

The familial conflict was handed down to the next generation: The oldest of the three brothers, Gallio, pursued a splendid political career, but the youngest, Mela, spent his life making money and educating himself (the poet Lucan was his son). Lucius Annaeus Seneca, the second child and bearer of his father's name, was torn between public life in the service of a corrupted state and life as philosopher and private man.

Going to Rome at a very early age, Seneca received an education in rhetoric, which was the first step toward becoming an orator with an eye to public offices. The youth also saw teachers of Stoic philosophy who taught a life of asceticism, equanimity in the face of adversity, and an evaluation of the daily work of the self, which laid the foundations of Seneca's eclectic philosophical beliefs.

In Rome, Seneca lived with an aunt; she guarded the precarious health of the thin, feeble boy. His physical deficiencies and what were perhaps lifelong bouts with pneumonia almost led the young man to suicide; only the thought of how much this act would hurt his aging father stopped him. As intense studies distracted his mind from his sufferings, Seneca would later state that he owed his life to philosophy. In the light of his physical afflictions and his own description of himself as small, plain, and skinny, scholars doubt the veracity of the only extant antique copy of a bust of Seneca, which shows the philoso-

pher and statesman as a corpulent old man with sharp but full features and receding hair.

Seneca's ill health apparently caused him to spend a considerable portion of his youth and early manhood in the healthier climate of Egypt. It was not before 31 C.E. that he permanently left the East for Rome.

LIFE'S WORK
As a result of the lobbying of his aunt, Seneca successfully entered public service as quaestor (roughly, secretary of finances), in 33. Although it is no longer known which positions he held during this period, it is most likely that he continued in ever more prestigious offices.

Besides serving the state under two difficult emperors, Tiberius and Caligula, Seneca began to achieve wealth and fame as a lawyer. From the later works that have survived, one can see how his witty, poignant, almost epigrammatical language fascinated Seneca's listeners and how his pithy sentences, which reflected his enormous vocabulary, must have won for him cases in court. Further, Seneca's consciously anti-Ciceronian style, which avoided long sentences and ornamental language, established his fame as an orator. Early works (now lost) made him a celebrated writer as well. Seneca's first marriage, dating from around this time, cannot have been a very happy one; he fails to mention the name of his wife, despite the fact that they had at least two sons together, both of whom he wrote about in the most affectionate terms.

Under the reign of Caligula (37-41 C.E.), Seneca's ill health proved advantageous. His oratorical success had aroused the envy of the emperor, who derogatorily likened Seneca's style to "sand without lime" (meaning that it was worthless for building), and Caligula sought to execute Seneca. Seneca was spared only because one of the Imperial mistresses commented on the futility of shortening the life of a terminally ill man. Later, Seneca commented, tongue in cheek, "Disease has postponed many a man's death and proximity to death has resulted in salvation."

In 41, the first year of the reign of Claudius I, a struggle for power between Empress Valeria Messallina and Caligula's sisters Agrippina and Julia Livilla brought Seneca into court on a trumped-up charge of adultery with Princess Julia. Found guilty, Seneca escaped death only because Claudius transformed the sentence into one of banishment to the barren island of Corsica. There, for the next eight years, Seneca dedicated his life to philosophy, the writing of letters, and natural philosophy; he also began to draft his first tragedies. The most powerful nonfiction works of this era are his letter of advice to his mother *Ad Helviam matrem de consolatione* (c. 41-42 C.E.; *To My Mother Helvia, on Consolation*, 1614) and the philosophical treatise *De ira libri tres* (c. 41-49 C.E.; *Three Essays on Anger*, 1614). Both works are deeply influenced by Stoic philosophy and argue that to deal with misfortune is to bear the adversities of life with dignified tranquillity, courage, and spiritual strength; further, violent passions must be controlled by the man who is truly wise.

The execution of Messallina for treason in 48 and the ensuing marriage of Claudius to Agrippina the Younger brought the latter into a position of power from which she could recall Seneca. Intent on using the famous orator and writer, Agrippina made Seneca the tutor of her son by a previous marriage, a young boy whom Claudius adopted under the name of Nero. Rather than being allowed to retire to Athens as a private man, Seneca was also made a member of the Roman senate and became praetor, the second highest of the Roman offices, in 50.

Seneca the Younger. (Library of Congress)

Further, his new marriage to the wealthy and intelligent Pompeia Paulina drew Seneca into a circle of powerful friends—including the new prefect of the Praetorian Guard, Sextus Afranius Burrus.

The death of Claudius in 54 brought highest power to Seneca and Burrus. Their successful working relationship began when Burrus's guard proclaimed Nero emperor, and Seneca wrote the speech of accession for the seventeen-year-old youth. For five years, from 54 to 59, the statesmen shared supreme authority and successfully governed the Roman Empire in harmony, while Nero amused himself with games and women and let them check his excesses and cruelty. Internally, the unacknowledged regency of Seneca and Burrus brought a rare period of civil justice, harmony, and political security. Seneca's Stoicism led him to fight the cruelty of gladiatorial combat and to favor laws intended to limit the absolute power of the master over his slaves. At the frontiers of the empire, the generals of Burrus and Seneca fought victoriously against the Parthians in the East and crushed a rebellion in Britain, after which a more reformist regime brought lasting peace to this remote island.

Seneca's fall was a direct result of Nero's awakening thirst for power. Increasingly, Seneca and Burrus lost their influence over him and in turn became involved in his morally despicable actions. In 59, Nero ordered the murder of his mother, Agrippina, and Seneca drafted the son's address to the senate, a speech that cleverly covered up the facts of the assassination.

Burrus's death and replacement by an intimate of Nero in 62 led to Seneca's request for retirement, which Nero refused; he kept Seneca in Rome, although removed from the court. Seneca's best philosophical work was written during this time; in his remaining three years, he finished *De providentia* (c. 63-64; *On Providence*, 1614) and wrote *Quaestiones naturales* (c. 62-64; *Natural Questions*, 1614) and his influential *Epistulae morales ad Lucilium* (c. 62-65 C.E.; *Letters to Lucilius*, 1917-1925), in which he treats a variety of moral questions and establishes the form of the essay.

Early in 65, a probably false accusation implicated Seneca in a conspiracy to assassinate Nero, who ordered him to commit suicide. With Stoic tranquillity and, loosely, in the tradition of Socrates and Cato the Younger, Seneca opened his arteries and slowly bled to death. Fully composed, and with honor, the Roman noble ended a life in the course of which he had wielded immense political power and enjoyed great status as statesman and writer.

SIGNIFICANCE

Consideration of the life and work of Seneca the Younger remains controversial. On a professional level, critics have attacked his philosophical work as eclectic and un-original, but it is through Seneca that more ancient ideas were handed down before the originals became known. For example, Seneca's tragedies are easily dismissed as static, bombastic, lurid, and peopled by characters who rant and rave; still, English Renaissance works such as John Webster's *The Duchess of Malfi* (1613-1614) could not have been created without their authors' knowledge of Seneca.

The reputation of Seneca the man has suffered from his political alliance with Nero, one of the most monstrous creatures of popular history. The ancient historian Tacitus is among the first to censure Seneca for his complicity in the cover-up of Agrippina's murder: "It was not only Nero, whose inhuman cruelty was beyond understanding, but also Seneca who fell into discredit."

A final evaluation of Seneca cannot overlook the fact that his public service ended in moral chaos after a period of doing much good for the commonwealth. It is interesting to note, however, that Seneca's most mature writing came after his de facto resignation from political power and responsibility. It is for his brilliantly written letters to Gaius Lucilius that Seneca achieves the status of philosopher, and these words have been with Western civilization ever since.

—*R. C. Lutz*

FURTHER READING

Griffin, Miriam Tamara. *Seneca: A Philosopher in Politics*. Oxford, England: Clarendon Press, 1992. Definitive study of Seneca; dramatizes the problem of public service for a corrupted state. Clearly written. Contains a good bibliography.

Harrison, George, ed. *Seneca in Performance*. London: Duckworth with The Classical Press of Wales, 2000. Twelve papers discuss characterization, staging, and Seneca's place in the history of Roman art and literature.

Henry, Denis, and Elisabeth Henry. *The Mask of Power: Seneca's Tragedies and Imperial Power*. Chicago: Bolchazy-Carducci, 1985. An interpretative study of Seneca's tragedies, placing them in their cultural context. Includes a good bibliography.

Holland, Francis. *Seneca*. 1920. Reprint. Freeport, N.Y.: Books for Libraries Press, 1969. For a long time, this work was the only biography on Seneca available in English. Still useful and readable, Holland's study is thorough and aware of the problematic status of its subject.

Motto, Anna Lydia, ed. *Essays on Seneca*. New York: P. Lang, 1993. Collection of critical articles on Seneca's life and work, written with a focus on his philosophical and dramatic work.

_____. *Further Essays on Seneca*. New York: P. Lang, 2001. This volume continues the criticism and interpretation begun in *Essays on Seneca*.

Roller, Matthew B. *Constructing Autocracy: Aristocrats and Emperors in Julio-Claudian Rome*. Princeton, N.J.: Princeton University Press, 2001. This book takes as its subject Rome's transition from a republican system of government to an Imperial regime and how the Roman aristocracy reacted to this change. According to Roller, writers and philosophers negotiated and contested the nature and scope of the emperor's authority; among these were Lucan and Seneca the Younger, on whom the text focuses.

Sorensen, Villy. *Seneca: The Humanist at the Court of Nero*. Translated by W. G. Jones. Chicago: University of Chicago Press, 1984. A well-written, scholarly work that is understandable to a general audience. Brings alive the man, his time, and his political and philosophical achievements. Includes interesting illustrations.

Sutton, Dana Ferrin. *Seneca on the Stage*. Leiden, Netherlands: E. J. Brill, 1986. This volume argues against tradition that Seneca's tragedies were not merely written to be read but crafted to be performed. Supports its claim with its discovery of stage directions that are "clues" hidden in the text of the dramas.

SEE ALSO: Agrippina the Younger; Caligula; Claudius I; Valeria Messallina; Nero; Tiberius.

SENNACHERIB

Neo-Assyrian king (r. 704-681 B.C.E.)

Sennacherib's military campaign into Judah in 701 B.C.E. was a significant event in biblical history, the historical record of which has proven helpful to modern historians and archaeologists.

BORN: c. 735 B.C.E.; place unknown
DIED: January, 681 B.C.E.; Nineveh, Assyria (now in Iraq)
ALSO KNOWN AS: Senherib; Sinakhkheeriba; Sin-ahhe-eriba; Sin-akhkheeriba ("the god Sin has compensated the death of the brothers")
AREA OF ACHIEVEMENT: Government and politics

EARLY LIFE

Little is known concerning the early life of Sennacherib (seh-NA-kur-ihb). His father, Sargon II (r. 721-705 B.C.E.), greatly expanded the Neo-Assyrian Empire in all directions, forcing tribute from Midas, king of Phrygia; the pharaoh of Egypt; Uperi, the king of Dilmun; and several kings from Cyprus. During the final years of Sargon's life, Sennacherib functioned as a military leader and governor in the troubled regions of the north, where he gained experience both as a soldier and as an administrator. Sennacherib inherited the Assyrian Empire when his father was killed in battle against the Cimmerians in 705 B.C.E.

LIFE'S WORK

On his father's untimely death, Sennacherib moved the capital from the newly established city of Khorsabad (Dur-Sharrukin) to the ancient city of Nineveh, home to the chief temple of the goddess Ishtar. Here Sennacherib spent the first two years of his reign reconstructing and enlarging the city. Previously the city had a circumference of about 8 miles (5 kilometers). Sennacherib enlarged it to include some 1,850 acres (750 hectares), surrounded by a wall whose circuit was about 20 miles (12 kilometers). On the largest hill in the city, Tel Kuyunjik, he constructed a magnificent palace for himself, the so-called Palace Without Rival. This palace comprised more than seventy rooms. Its decorations featured colossal human-headed bulls standing guard at entryways, and the walls of each room were lined with stone reliefs depicting Sennacherib's early military campaigns in Babylonia, the Zagros mountains, and Palestine.

Sennacherib protected the city with a moat and a double wall. The outer wall was composed of a mud-brick core with a limestone facing, and incorporated a crenellated parapet and regularly spaced towers. The taller, inner wall was built completely of mud brick. More than a dozen gates pierced this massive double wall. Water was furnished to the city through a complex irrigation system that was large enough to supply water for fields and orchards in addition to the needs of the city itself. This was accomplished through an ingenious system of dams, canals, and aqueducts that brought water from multiple sources as far as 73 miles (45 kilometers) away.

Throughout his reign, Sennacherib was troubled by enemies on his southern border. This opposition centered mainly around the city of Babylon. The policy of Sargon II had been to support an independent but friendly Babylon. Sennacherib continued this policy, but it did not turn out well for him. The first challenger he had to face was Merodachbaladan, a Chaldaean prince whom Sargon II had expelled from Babylon in 721. Merodachbaladan renewed his claim to kingship in Babylon in 703. In an attempt to raise opposition to Sennacherib from several sides at once, Merodachbaladan sent envoys to Hezekiah, king of Judah (2 Kings 20:12-19; Isaiah 39), and undoubtedly to other kings, including to the king of Egypt. Sennacherib responded quickly, routing Merodachbaladan and his allies, first at Cuthah and then at Kish in 703. The following year was also spent suppressing the rebellion. A native Babylonian, Bel-ibni, was then placed on the throne in Babylon. He proved to be an incompetent ruler, unable to control the regions under his rule.

In 701 Sennacherib launched a campaign south into Syria and Palestine. This campaign was in response to the threat posed by Merodachbaladan's allies. The Phoenician coast was Sennacherib's first target, and his quick reduction of Sidon induced many of the lesser rulers in that area to renew their allegiance to the Assyrians through the payment of tribute. Sennacherib then moved down the coast, capturing Joppa, Ekron, and Gath.

Sennacherib's palace reliefs in Nineveh recount his capture of the next city, Lachish. The reliefs occupied the central room in the building, indicating the importance Sennacherib attached to his conquest of this city. Lachish was better fortified than the cities Sennacherib had encountered previously, and it put up a fierce resistance. Sennacherib's army built a large siege ramp at the southwestern corner of the city, which was protected by a double wall. The defenders built a counter-ramp inside the city wall. As indicated on the palace reliefs, the defenders attempted to burn the siege machines with torches thrown from the city walls. The excavations at Lachish produced a length of chain that may have been used in an attempt to grapple the head of the battering ram from above. Despite the strong resistance, the Assyrian battering rams eventually prevailed. Sennacherib's palace art depicts the aftermath of the siege quite graphically—prisoners were decapitated, impaled, or flayed. Excavators at Lachish uncovered a cave on the site that contained the remains of some fifteen hundred inhabitants of the city, including men, women, and children. The remaining population of Lachish was deported to Assyria. Sennacherib's army then met and defeated a weak Egyptian force, led by Taharqa, near Eltekeh on the Mediterranean coast.

One island of resistance remained. Jerusalem was the capital of Judah. It was located in the hills east of Lachish and was ruled by King Hezekiah. Hezekiah had not been idle in the preceding months. Archaeological evidence indicates he made preparations for Sennacherib in a variety of ways. He provisioned Jerusalem and other key cities with emergency rations. Especially prominent were four-handled wine jars, each specially marked with the royal stamp *lamelek* (Hebrew "belonging to the king"). These wine jars have been found in numerous locations throughout Judah, including in the destruction level at Lachish that resulted from Sennacherib's attack. Hezekiah also made preparations at Jerusalem for a secure water supply. His workmen cut a tunnel some 1,777 feet (542 meters) long through the hill beneath Jerusalem, the ancient Jebusite city known as the City of David (1 Kings 20:20). This tunnel diverted water from the Gihon spring on the east to the Siloam pool, located within the city wall on the west. This served the dual purpose of securing the water supply for the city and denying water to those besieging it. Also, recent excavations have revealed an additional city wall built by Hezekiah that ran further down the eastern slope of the City of David than the former wall. This provided both a secondary defensive wall for the city and additional, walled space for an influx of Judaean refugees. It is also likely that the city wall was extended and strengthened on the western side of the city in preparation for Sennacherib's imminent attack. In the end, however, these defenses proved unnecessary. According to the Bible, the angel of the Lord struck down a large contingent of his army (2 Kings 19:35-36). Sennacherib himself simply recorded that, having exacted tribute from Hezekiah and "shut him up in his capital Jerusalem like a bird in a cage," he decided to return home.

The remainder of Sennacherib's reign was given over to three additional campaigns in the south, once again concentrated mainly around Babylon. The first of these campaigns came in 700. It was a fairly limited action in response to a revolt by Chaldean tribes. Sennacherib then placed the crown prince of Assyria, Ashur-nadin-shumi, on the throne of Babylonia. This worked well, and there were about six years of peace. In 694 Sennacherib launched another attack against Elam, presumably to root out rebels who had fled there after the campaign in 700. Ashur-nadin-shumi was captured by the Elamites in the early phase of the ensuing campaign, which lasted more than a year. A Chaldean, Mushezib-Marduk, replaced him on the throne at Babylon in 693. In 691 Sennacherib returned again. After several battles and a protracted siege, Babylon was captured in 689. This time the city was looted and sacked, and Sennacherib took for himself the title "King of Sumer and Akkad," indicating a change in policy. He no longer attempted to support the city as an independent kingdom but became its king himself. The city was then an Assyrian vassal with an Assyrian ruler, and the succeeding years were quiet.

Sennacherib's death came at the hands of his sons on the 20th of Tebet (January), 681 B.C.E. According to the biblical account (2 Kings 19:37), he was slain as he worshiped in the house of his god in Nineveh. The annals of Ashurbanipal implicate Babylonians, which may be taken to indicate that an elder son attempted to take the throne that had already been promised to the younger son Esarhaddon.

SIGNIFICANCE

Sennacherib's reign can be characterized as a time of relative stability for the Assyrian Empire. He did not gain new territory beyond what had been conquered by his father, but he was able to retain most of the territory his father had acquired. He wisely restrained himself from taking more territory than he would have been able to hold, even when he had been victorious in battle. Sennacherib was cautious in both his soldiering and his policies.

Sennacherib's greatest significance is related to his campaign into Palestine in 701 B.C.E. The destruction he left at the forty-six fortified cities he conquered, and especially at Lachish, has provided valuable chronological evidence for the archaeology of the area. This event is one of the rare instances in which archaeological, biblical, and Assyrian records converge. This convergence has provided a chronological benchmark that is helpful for archaeology by pinpointing the precise date of a destruction layer in many cities. The convergence is also helpful for constructing an accurate chronology of Judah, as the biblical account records that Sennacherib's campaign took place in Hezekiah's fourteenth year (2 Kings 18:13). Finally, the detailed reliefs that decorated Sennacherib's Palace Without Rival, which centered on the conquest of Lachish, are a rich source of information on Assyrian culture, warfare, and life.

—Kriston J. Udd

FURTHER READING

Bates, Robert D. "Assyria and Rebellion in the Annals of Sennacherib: An Analysis of Sennacherib's Treatment of Hezekiah." *Near East Archaeological Society Bulletin* 44 (1999): 39-61. Argues that accounts of Sennacherib's treatment of Hezekiah, recorded in both the Assyrian annals and the Bible, are consistent with his treatment of other rebellious cities.

Kuhrt, Amelie. *The Ancient Near East c. 3000-330 B.C.* Vol. 2. New York: Routledge, 1995. A detailed account of Mesopotamian history with an emphasis on primary texts, especially court documents and royal inscriptions. Includes bibliography and index.

Levine, Louis D. "Sennacherib's Southern Front: 704-689 B.C." *Journal of Cuneiform Studies* 34, no. 1/2 (1982): 28-55. Provides a detailed account of Sennacherib's campaigns to the south against the Babylonians, Chaldeans, and Elamites.

Roaf, Michael. *Cultural Atlas of Mesopotamia and the Ancient Near East.* 1966. Reprint. New York: Facts on File, 2000. Provides a short overview of Sennacherib's accomplishments in the greater context of Assyrian history. Contains a diagram of the capital city of Nineveh. Includes bibliography, glossary, and index.

Russell, John. "Nineveh." In *Royal Cities of the Biblical World*, edited by Joan Westenholz. Jerusalem: Bible Lands Museum, 1996. Traces the history of Nineveh, Sennacherib's capital city, from prehistoric times to its fall in 612 B.C.E.

Ussishkin, David. *The Conquest of Lachish by Sennacherib.* Tel Aviv: The Institute of Archaeology, 1982. An oversized book that focuses on the excavation of the city conquered by Sennacherib. Contains a lengthy section on the Lachish reliefs from Sennacherib's palace. Includes maps, illustrations, and bibliography.

SEE ALSO: Ashurbanipal; David; Ezekiel; Ezra; Sargon II; Solomon.

RELATED ARTICLES in *Great Events from History: The Ancient World*: 701 B.C.E., Sennacherib Invades Syro-Palestine; c. 320 B.C.E., Theophrastus Initiates the Study of Botany.

SESOSTRIS III
Egyptian pharaoh (r. 1878-1843 B.C.E.)

Sesostris's egocentric nature inspired him to be the first king of ancient Egypt to pursue a truly imperialistic policy, conducting war in the Levant and extending Egypt's southern border. His lasting impact was on Egypt's social structure, where he eliminated the vestiges of the indigenous nobility.

BORN: Date unknown; place unknown
DIED: 1843 B.C.E.; place unknown
ALSO KNOWN AS: Senwosret; Senusert
AREAS OF ACHIEVEMENT: Government and politics, war and conquest

EARLY LIFE

Sesostris (sih-SOH-strihs) III is commonly considered the son of Sesostris II, who ruled from 1897 to 1878 B.C.E., and Queen Nefertiti II, but his origins are not certain. The same uncertainty concerns a possible coregency with the latter, for which there is no indisputable evidence. It is assumed that he became king of Egypt in 1878 B.C.E. and ruled until 1843 B.C.E., a thirty-five year span, although year 19 is the latest attested year of his reign. Sesostris adopted the official name Netjerikheperu.

LIFE'S WORK

Nothing is known about Sesostris's life prior to his ascent, or about events during the early years of his reign. The earliest preserved inscription dates from his fifth year of rule. It was found in Ezbet el-Saghira, in Egypt's northeastern delta. This find is not isolated; other material relating to Sesostris has been discovered in the same region. A seated statue of the king was found at Tell Nebesheh, in addition to material at Qantir, Bubastis, and Tanis. These finds may indicate the concern of Sesostris with Egypt's northeastern border.

Yet Sesostris's interests did not end at this border. There is a report about a military campaign by a follower of Sesostris named Khu-Sobek, leading to the capture of a region called Sekemem. This region has been identified with Shekhem (biblical Sichem), but because a deep military penetration into Palestine lacks substantiation, this identification has been disputed.

That there was a concerted political interest in the Levant during the reign of Sesostris is suggested by the considerable number of Egyptian objects found in the Levant, namely at Megiddo and Gezer, which date to Sesostris's reign. These objects probably reflect diplomatic rather than military activity. Such an evaluation is supported by a group of Egyptian texts commonly labeled Execration Texts. These texts consist of magical incantations pronounced to influence the chiefs in a wide range of city-states in Palestine and Syria. Although their political effectiveness could be questioned, they display a detailed familiarity with the political situation in the Levant at the time. The claim in a hymn to Sesostris that "his words control the Asiatics" also points to the influence of Sesostris on the affairs of Syria and Palestine by diplomatic means rather than by military interference.

Sesostris III. (Gianni Dagli Orti/Corbis)

Egypt's interests in the exploration of the mineral resources of the Sinai Peninsula seem to have been a major force in the political contacts to the East. During the reign of Sesostris, mining in Serabit el-khadim on Sinai's western side was limited. Further, no addition to the local sanctuary of the goddess Hathor was constructed during his reign. During the ensuing reign of Amenemhet III, the Sinai mines were extensively explored. This exploration was probably a result of Sesostris's influence on the Levant scene.

The chief military activity of Sesostris was directed southward against Nubia and was specifically intended to gain control over the area of the Nile's Second Cataract. Four campaigns by the king are attested by inscriptions, namely in the eighth, tenth, sixteenth, and nineteenth years of his reign. There is no indication that this military activity was in response to any prior aggression or danger. Instead, it seems that Sesostris embarked on the campaigning for imperialistic goals and personal vainglory. At that time, Egyptian authority extended as far south as the northern end of the Second Cataract, where the fortress of Buhen (opposite modern Wadi Halfa) guarded the border. The very inhospitable terrain of the cataract region appears to have been scarcely populated, but south of it was an important Nubian state with Kerma as its center. Apparently, Sesostris aspired to subdue it and to incorporate it into his realm, goals that he ultimately failed to achieve.

Major preparations preceded the first campaign in the eighth year of his reign. In order to move troops and equipment southward, a canal more than 200 feet (61 meters) long, 75 feet (23 meters) wide, and 22 feet (6.7 meters) deep was cut through the rocks forming the First Cataract. Sesostris met with fierce resistance, and the advance proved much more difficult than anticipated. Although the king directed the campaign in person, the proclaimed goal "to overthrow the wretched Kush" turned out to be a more difficult task than the repelling of nomadic tribesmen. At least three more campaigns followed. As a result of these military efforts, Egypt's southern frontier was pushed some 40 miles (65 kilometers) southward, but it did not advance into the fertile stretch beyond. At strategically dominating places, Sesostris had fortresses built on either side of the Nile River, specifically at Semna (Heh) and Kumna,

KINGS OF THE TWELFTH DYNASTY

Ruler	Reign (B.C.E.)
Amenemhet I	c. 1985-1956
Sesostris I	c. 1971-1926
Amenemhet II	1926-1897
Sesostris II	1897-1878
Sesostris III	1878-1843
Amenemhet III	1843-1798
Amenemhet IV	1802-1785
Sebeknefru	1785-1782

Note: Dynastic research is ongoing; data are approximate.

to shield the dearly won frontier. An inscription there states the king's political principles:

> Southern boundary made in the Year 8 under the majesty of the King of Upper and Lower Egypt Sesostris, may he be given life forever, in order to prevent any Nubian from crossing it by water or by land, with a ship or any herd, except a Nubian who shall come to do trading at Yken or with a commission. Every good thing shall be done to them, but without allowing a ship of Nubians to pass by Heh going north—forever.

The conquest itself held hardly any advantages, except as a potential bridgehead for later operations. The resistance it encountered prevented those plans from succeeding, an indication that a state of considerable military power opposed Sesostris's expansionist efforts.

By his sixteenth year in power, Sesostris apparently realized the futility of his aspirations and decided to make the frontier permanent at Semna and Kumna. Despite his limited success, he announced it as a great personal achievement:

> Every successor of mine shall maintain this boundary which my majesty has made—he is my son born to my majesty. He who shall abandon it and shall not fight for it—he is not my son, he is not born to me.
>
> My majesty had a statue of my majesty set up at this boundary which my majesty made in order that one might stay with it and in order that one fight for it.

The egocentric attitude of Sesostris is clearly apparent in these lines. Indeed, Sesostris was the first king of ancient Egypt to receive worship as a god during his lifetime; this divinization, however, was limited to Nubia. Three hundred years later, Thutmose III (r. 1504-1450 B.C.E.) erected a temple for him at Semna as the "god of Nubia." Sesostris's personality left its lasting mark on Egypt proper. Few monuments of him, however, are preserved; they are especially scarce in Middle Egypt. Sesostris favored the temple of Osiris at Abydos and was also active at Thebes.

During Sesostris's reign, all traces of the indigenous nobility of Egypt disappeared. There are no texts expounding a specific policy, but from the results there can be no question that Sesostris intended to be the sole Egyptian leader, eliminating any potential competition. His methods remain obscure, but the possibility of forced exile is likely. While Sesostris streamlined the social structure by enforcing one single center, the disappearance of the hereditary nobility had its dangers. As long as a strong personality occupied the throne, the affairs of Egypt prospered. When such a ruler was lacking, however, there was nobody in the society to provide the leadership necessary to keep the ship of state on course. It is fitting that fifty-seven years after Sesostris's death the political structures disintegrated rapidly.

Sesostris had a large mud-brick pyramid built at Dahshûr. Attached to it are the burial places for the members of the royal family. From these tombs come some stunning jewelry, a part of which is housed in the Metropolitan Museum of Art. Later traditions adopted Sesostris as a legendary hero, and stories about him were related by the Greek historians Herodotus (c. 484-c. 425 B.C.E.) and Diodorus Siculus (fl. first century B.C.E.). The stories conflate some of his exploits with those of other kings, especially Ramses II (1279-1213 B.C.E.), to create a romantic quasihistory.

SIGNIFICANCE

While Sesostris III was unquestionably an exceptionally strong personality on the throne of Egypt, his excessive ego brought not only blessings but also potential dangers. He demonstrated military determination unparalleled by any earlier king and opened the conquest of Upper Nubia. By concentrating the social structure exclusively on himself and eliminating the indigenous nobility, he initiated the transformation of Egypt from a conservative, traditional society into a politically motivated populace.

—Hans Goedicke

FURTHER READING

Adams, William Yewdale. *Nubia: Corridor to Africa.* Princeton, N.J.: Princeton University Press, 1977. Primarily concerns Egypt's advance into Nubia. Contains twelve pages of illustrations, bibliographic references, and an index.

Hayes, William C. "The Middle Kingdom in Egypt." *Early History of the Middle East*. Vol. 1 in *The Cambridge Ancient History*, edited by I. E. Edwards, C. J. Gadd, and N. G. L. Hammond. 3d ed. Cambridge, England: Cambridge University Press, 1971. A thorough discussion not only of one reign but also of the political tendencies of the time.

Parkinson, R. B., ed. *Voices from Ancient Egypt: An Anthology of Middle Kingdom Writings*. Norman: University of Oklahoma Press, 1991. This collection of translated texts includes the inscription on a stela of Sesostris III and also a hymn to him.

Ziegler, Christiane, ed. *The Pharaohs*. New York: Thames and Hudson, 2002. This collection of essays includes one on the history of the Middle Kingdom, as well as two that cover the political role of the pharaoh and his place in religious ritual, as both worshiper and deity.

SEE ALSO: Akhenaton; Amenhotep III; Cleopatra VII; Hatshepsut; Imhotep; Menes; Menkaure; Montuhotep II; Psamtik I; Ramses II; Thutmose III; Tutankhamen; Zoser.

RELATED ARTICLES in *Great Events from History: The Ancient World*: c. 2300-c. 2000 B.C.E., First Great Expansion of Berber Peoples Across North Africa; c. 2160 B.C.E., First Intermediate Period Begins in Egypt; c. 2055 B.C.E., Middle Kingdom Period Begins in Egypt; c. 1900-1527? B.C.E., Kerma Kingdom Rules Nubia; c. 1650 B.C.E., Hyksos Create Second Intermediate Period; 8th century B.C.E., Kushite King Piye Conquers Upper Egypt; c. 783-c. 591 B.C.E., Napata Kingdom Flourishes in Kush; c. 712-698 B.C.E., Shabaka Reunites the Nile Valley; c. 6th century B.C.E.-c. 350 C.E., Meroitic Empire Rules from Southern Egypt to the Blue Nile.

SHĀPŪR II

Sāsānian shah (r. 309-379 C.E.)

Shāpūr was one of the greatest rulers of the Sāsānian Empire in pre-Islamic Iran. Succeeding to the throne after a period of internal confusion, he restored the fortunes of the empire and extended its frontiers in all directions.

BORN: 309 C.E.; place unknown
DIED: 379 C.E.; place unknown
ALSO KNOWN AS: Sapor II; Shāpūr II the Great
AREAS OF ACHIEVEMENT: Government and politics, war and conquest

EARLY LIFE

Shāpūr (sha-POOR) II was the eighth in the long line of rulers of the Sāsānian Empire, which dominated much of the Middle East between 224 and 651. The first two Sāsānian shahs (kings), Ardashīr I and Shāpūr I, descendants of hereditary priests of the Zoroastrian fire temple at Istakhr in the southwestern Iranian province of Fars, replaced the disintegrating rule of the Parthians with an aggressive military monarchy based on domination of the Plateau of Iran and expansion outward in all directions. In the east, the Sāsānians advanced deep into Afghanistan as far as the land near the upper Indus River. To the northeast, they crossed the Amu Darya River and the Hisar range. In the northwest, they claimed overlordship in Armenia, Iberia, and Albania (areas corresponding to modern Armenia, Republic of Georgia, and Azerbaijan).

In the west, they disputed hegemony with the Romans over upper Mesopotamia, between the Tigris and Euphrates Rivers (the conjunction of modern Turkey, Iraq, and Syria). Shāpūr I enjoyed spectacular successes over three Roman emperors, celebrated in his bas-reliefs at Naqsh-e Rustam and Bishapur: Gordianus III, who was murdered by his troops in 244 while campaigning against the Sāsānians; Philip the Arabian, who was compelled to negotiate a humiliating peace; and Valerian, who was taken prisoner by Shāpūr after a battle near Edessa in 260 and who died in captivity.

Ardashīr and Shāpūr I ruled over an empire of diverse races, religions, and languages; from their Parthian predecessors they inherited a situation of regional fragmentation, a society Iranologists refer to as "feudal." The first two Sāsānian shahs recognized the pluralistic composition of their empire, but they were determined to crush the independence of the feudal nobility. They wanted to establish a highly centralized autocracy in which the Shahanshah (King of Kings) shone with a refulgence derived from his being endowed with the unique qualities of *farr* (the divine favor reserved for monarchs) and *hvarna* (the charisma of kingship).

Following Shāpūr I's death in 272, his immediate successors failed to maintain the momentum: A series of short-lived, unimpressive rulers allowed the army to deteriorate, and the Romans counterattacked with vigor.

In 283, Emperor Carus advanced to within sight of the walls of Ctesiphon, the Sāsānian metropolis near modern Baghdad. His successor, Diocletian (c. 245-316), then determined to stabilize Rome's eastern frontiers by constructing limes (a defensive line of forts and earthworks) from the great bend of the Euphrates northward into Armenia, the traditional bone of contention between Romans and Iranians. As a result, war broke out, and in the ensuing campaigns the Iranians fared badly. On one occasion, the family of Narses, the shah, fell into Roman hands, together with a large booty. By the Peace of Nisibis of 298, Narses was forced to relinquish not only upper Mesopotamia between the Tigris and Euphrates but also territory on the east bank of the Tigris. All trade between the two empires was to go through Nisibis, and Armenia passed definitively into the Roman sphere of influence, to which it tended to be drawn anyway, as a consequence of the Armenian king's adoption of Christianity around 303.

With the death of Hormizd II, a grandson of Shāpūr I, in 309 the imperial line appeared to have ended, but a ray of hope lay with a pregnant wife or concubine of the late ruler. Tradition has it that the future Shāpūr II was designated shah while still in his mother's womb by the crown being placed on her belly. In another version of the story, the high priest sat the woman on the throne, a diadem was held over her head, and gold coins were poured into the crown.

The events of Shāpūr's long reign are fairly well documented in Latin, Syriac, and Arabic sources, although there is a dearth of source material in Middle Persian. Moreover, later Arabic and Persian accounts, although quite detailed, have a tendency to confuse happenings in the reign of Shāpūr II with those in the reign of Shāpūr I.

Of Shāpūr II's early years nothing is known. The first third of his reign was probably spent learning the business of government, consolidating the royal authority, and taming the habitually turbulent nobility. Such campaigning as there was occurred on the exposed Arabian marches of the empire, where Bedouin raiders penetrated the prosperous agricultural settlements of lower Mesopotamia and perhaps even threatened Ctesiphon. One solution to the problem was to construct defensive lines similar to the Roman limes, with which the Iranians were already acquainted in upper Mesopotamia, but Shāpūr also resorted to a "forward policy" of punitive expeditions. There may be more than a grain of truth in late accounts of the shah leading his handpicked warriors, mounted on racing dromedaries, into the fastnesses of the Arabian Desert, but it is probable that he campaigned

MAJOR RULERS OF THE LATER SĀSĀNIAN EMPIRE	
Ruler	*Reign (C.E.)*
Shāpūr II	309-379
Kavadh I	488-531
Khosrow I	531-579
Khosrow II	590-628
Yazdgard III	633-651

against the Ghassanid Arab clients of the Romans in the direction of Syria rather than, as much later traditions assert, crossing the central plateau to attack Yathrib (modern Medina) or to invade Yemen. More plausible are references to Arab piratical raids on the coastline of Fars that prompted Shāpūr to send out a naval expedition to raid the island of Bahrain and the mainland behind it.

LIFE'S WORK

During the first thirty years of Shāpūr's life, roughly coinciding with the long reign of Constantine the Great (306-337), Rome was the dominant power on the frontier, but in 337 the accession of Constantius II, who controlled only the eastern provinces and whose future seemed uncertain, signified a change. At the same time, in Armenia, a party among the Armenian nobles opposed to the recent Christianization of the kingdom expelled their ruler and turned to Iran for assistance. Shāpūr took the field and, crossing the Tigris, besieged Nisibis in 338 (but without success), while the Romans forcibly reinstated the Armenian king. For the next decade or more, an undeclared peace settled on the western frontier, broken by sporadic border forays, while the shah campaigned in the East.

Since the time of Ardashīr, the former Kushan territories of Bactria (north of the Hindu Kush Mountains, in Afghanistan), Sogdiana (beyond the Amu Darya River), and Gandhara (in eastern Afghanistan and the upper Indus country) had been ruled by Sāsānian governors, probably a cadet line of the royal house, who used the title of Kushanshah (King of the Kushans). During the 340's, this arrangement seems to have broken down, perhaps as a result of a steady flow of nomads into these regions from the steppes to the north.

This nomadic influx diverted Shāpūr's attention from the West, and it may have been partly the fear of an attack from that quarter while he was preoccupied in the East that prompted him to order the systematic persecution of his Christian subjects, a campaign that had begun in 337 at the time of his first confrontation with Rome. The reason for this policy lay in Constantine's adoption of Christianity for the Roman Empire, some two decades after the Christianization of Armenia. Thus Shāpūr viewed the Christian communities in the Sāsānian Empire as a fifth column that would rise up in support of their coreligionists in the event of the Romans' breaking into the Iranian homeland. He may also have undertaken this policy with the idea of endearing himself to the intolerant Zoroastrian priesthood. Certainly, the persecution, ferocious in the extreme, ended the notion that the Sāsānian Empire was a kind of religious melting pot, for at this time, Manichaeans and Jews were also exposed to harassment (although less severe than that experienced by Christians). In the course of the persecutions, the ancient city of Susa in southwestern Iran, which sheltered a Christian see and a large Christian population, revolted. It was, therefore, razed, and several hundred war elephants were brought in to help with the demolition.

In 350, Shāpūr returned to the offensive in the West. Constantius was embroiled in civil wars, while in Armenia, Tigranes V had been pursuing a crooked policy of playing off Rome against Iran. Shāpūr, exasperated by his double-dealing, now had him seized and executed, replacing him with Tigranes' son, Arshak II. Meanwhile, the shah planned to besiege Nisibis. Once more, the prize eluded him. This time, a looming crisis in the East demanded his immediate presence there. The former penetration of the eastern provinces by nomadic bands had given way to the threat of all-out invasion by a people who appear in the sources as "Chionites." This nomadic confederacy probably consisted of a majority of people of Iranian stock led by a ruling elite of Huns, who now made their appearance in Iranian history for the first time. Several years of hard campaigning against the Chionites resulted in their defeat in 356 and, in the following year, their submission as tributaries of the empire.

With the East now pacified, Shāpūr turned to the West again and in 359 undertook the siege of the great fortress of Amida (modern Diyarbakir, in Turkey) on the upper Tigris. The fighting went on for seventy-three days before the final successful assault. The Roman historian Ammianus Marcellinus watched from the battlements as "the king himself, mounted on a charger and overtopping the others, rode before the whole army, wearing in place of a diadem a golden image of a ram's head set with precious stones. . . ." A leading scholar has hypothesized that Ammianus Marcellinus was mistaken, because Shāpūr wore a different headdress, and that the wearer of the

ram's head was another Kushanshah, who was serving as an auxiliary to his overlord. Early in the course of the siege, the son of Grumbates, the Chionite ruler, was killed, and after his body had been burned in accordance with Hunnish custom, his father demanded vengeance. The city was then closely besieged. The Iranian contingents were deployed on every side. Of the allies, the Chionites were on the east, the Gelani (tribesmen from Gilan and Mazandaran in northern Iran) were on the south, the Albanians (from modern Azerbaijan) were on the north, and the Sakas (from Seistan in eastern Iran) were on the west. Ammianus Marcellinus wrote: "With them, making a lofty show, slowly marched the lines of elephants, frightful with their wrinkled bodies and loaded with armed men, a hideous spectacle, dreadful beyond every form of horror. . . ."

Eventually, Amida fell after heavy casualties on both sides. It was to be Shāpūr's supreme triumph. In the following year, more cities in upper Mesopotamia were taken by the Iranians, but thereafter the fighting seems to have entered a desultory phase that continued until Emperor Julian (r. 361-363) resolved to restore Rome's fortunes in the East. Julian moved swiftly. He traversed Mesopotamia virtually unopposed to within sight of the walls of Ctesiphon, the Iranians preferring not to give battle and adopting a "scorched earth" strategy. Julian was killed in a skirmish, and his successor, Jovian (r. 363-364), was eager to extract his forces at minimal cost. Shāpūr obtained possession of Nisibis at last, together with all upper Mesopotamia, and Rome abandoned its protectorate over Armenia. Arshak II, who had initially demonstrated commitment to the Iranian connection, had long since proved himself duplicitous, openly aligning himself with the Romans at the time of Julian's campaign. Now he was abandoned to the wrath of his erstwhile overlord, who had him seized and held captive until his death (c. 367).

By then, however, Shāpūr had systematically ravaged Armenia, deporting thousands of captives, who were redistributed throughout the empire during the course of a campaign that also took him into Iberia (that is, modern Georgia), where he expelled a Roman client ruler and installed his own candidate (c. 365). The emperor Valens reacted to this humiliation by sending troops into both Armenia and Iberia to restore the status quo. In Iberia, the country was now divided between two kings, both bearing the same name—one was a puppet of Rome, the other a puppet of Iran.

In Armenia, the Romans installed Pap, the son of Arshak II, as king. As with other Armenian kings, however, Pap could not resist the temptation of seeking to play one power off against the other. At various times between 370 and 374, he seems to have entered into negotiations with Shāpūr that probably included some kind of submission. Getting wind of Pap's treachery, Valens summoned him to Tarsus to answer charges of treason, but he escaped and made his way back to Armenia, where he was subsequently assassinated at a banquet given by local Roman commanders.

Pap was replaced by a kinsman, Varazdat, whom a considerable section of the Armenian nobility was unwilling to acknowledge, while Shāpūr refused to recognize his accession and sent troops to oust him. With the Goths in the Balkans threatening Adrianople, Valens needed a speedy settlement of the eastern frontier. Thus some kind of arrangement was negotiated between the two great powers around 377, although the sources do not specify the existence of a peace treaty at that time. Armenia was de facto, if not de jure, partitioned, the greater part of the country passing under Iranian control. Thus, Shāpūr had attained a major objective of Sāsānian rulers: Armenia and Iberia were partitioned into spheres of influence, and with Albania tributary, Iran dominated almost the entire region between the Caspian Sea and the Black Sea. After Shāpūr's death, a formal treaty between Iran and Rome during the reign of Shāpūr III (383-388) regularized the previous partition arrangements regarding Armenia. Then, when the king of Iranian Armenia died in 392, Bahram IV installed his own brother, Vramshapuh, on the throne, while Roman Armenia was formally integrated into the Roman provincial administration.

Little is known regarding the internal conditions of Iran during the time of Shāpūr II, but the evidence suggests that he vigorously pursued his predecessors' goals of curbing the power of the nobility. The favors that he lavished on the Zoroastrian priesthood (to which may be added his relentless persecution of the Christians) were probably intended to secure the support of this influential class. In the course of helping to create an official Zoroastrian state church, well endowed, privileged, and powerful, he also ensured that it was firmly under the control of the Shahanshah.

Like his namesake, Shāpūr I, Shāpūr II played an active role in promoting new urban centers and in restoring older foundations that had been languishing. Thus, he enlarged the city of Gundeshapur in Khuzestan (southwestern Iran), originally built by Shāpūr I's Roman prisoners, where he founded the university, observatory, and medical school that were to become so famous in the early Is-

lamic period. Having carried out the destruction of Susa around 350, he ordered an entirely new city to be constructed nearby, known as Iran-khwarra Shāpūr (Shāpūr's fortune of Iran), while another city, Iranshahr-Shapur, often referred to by its Aramaic name of Karkha de Ledan, was founded upstream from Susa. He also rebuilt Nishapur (or Niv-Shapur, meaning "the good deed of Shāpūr").

SIGNIFICANCE

The reign of Shāpūr II marks one of the climactic phases of Sāsānian rule. With the frontiers of his empire stretching from Diyarbakir in the west to Kabul in the east and from the Caucasus Mountains to the southern shores of the Persian Gulf, with his effective—if brutal—subjugation of all internal elements that seemed to challenge his autocratic exercise of power, and with his tight grip on the Zoroastrian church, Shāpūr II must be rated as one of the most successful of all Sāsānian monarchs. At his death, he was succeeded by Ardashīr II, whose relationship to him is a matter of dispute but who was probably his son.

In the light of Shāpūr II's long reign, it is surprising that so few major monuments have survived from this period. One of the six bas-reliefs carved in the gorge at Bishapur in Fars known as "Bishapur VI" has been widely attributed to him, although some scholars have identified it with Shāpūr I. Those who believe that it dates from Shāpūr II's reign have variously interpreted it as commemorating a victory over Kushan, Roman, or even internal Iranian foes, while a recent study claims that it represents the submission of Pap.

The surviving sources do not allow for much speculation about the personality of Shāpūr II, although the known facts point to a ruler of great energy, ambition, and pride. Like those of most Sāsānian rulers, his profile can be readily identified on coins, seals, and metal objects by virtue of a distinctive crown. Shāpūr's crown consists of the characteristic *korymbos* (a balloon-shaped bun of hair wrapped in a fine cloth and perhaps symbolizing the terrestrial or celestial globe) above a tiara of stepped crenellations with long ribbons billowing out behind. Several formal representations of him survive in the royal hunting scenes that decorate ceremonial silver dishes. One of the finest of these shows the shah in profile, mounted, turning about in his saddle to shoot a springing lion, while a second lion is being trampled beneath his horse's hooves. He wears a tunic and the baggy pantaloons favored by other Iranian peoples, his long, straight sword hangs loosely from his belt, and he draws the typical compound bow of the steppe peoples, the weapon so feared by the Romans and other adversaries of the Iranians. As with all Sāsānian art, including a remarkable silver-overlay head attributed to Shāpūr II in the Metropolitan Museum of Art in New York, the expression is highly stylized but proclaims calm concentration, fearlessness, and regal dignity, attributes that fit well with what is known of Shāpūr II.

—Gavin R. G. Hambly

FURTHER READING

Ammianus Marcellinus. *Res gestae.* Translated by John C. Rolfe. 3 vols. Cambridge, Mass.: Harvard University Press, 1935-1939. Sometimes described as the last classical historian of the Roman Empire, Ammianus Marcellinus served in the Iranian campaigns of Constantius and Julian and was an eyewitness at the siege of Amida. His history includes a topographical description of the Sāsānian Empire as well as an account of contemporary Iranian manners and customs.

Azarpay, Guitty. "Bishapur VI: An Artistic Record of an Armeno-Persian Alliance in the Fourth Century." *Artibus Asiae* 43 (1981-1982): 171-189. An absorbing discussion of the Bishapur bas-relief attributed to Shāpūr II, identifying the scene as representing the submission of Pap to the Sāsānian shah.

Bivar, Adrian David Hugh. *Catalogue of the Western Asiatic Seals in the British Museum.* London: British Museum Publications, 1986. For the student of the Sāsānian period, this book is essential for understanding Sāsānian iconography.

_____. "The History of Eastern Iran." In *The Cambridge History of Iran*, edited by Ehsan Yarshater, vol. 3. Cambridge, England: Cambridge University Press, 1983. This chapter, by one of the leading authorities on the eastern Iranian lands in pre-Islamic times, is essential for elucidating the still-obscure relations of the Sāsānian shahs with their Kushan, Chionite, and Ephthalite neighbors.

Frye, Richard N. "The Political History of Iran Under the Sasanians." In *The Cambridge History of Iran*, edited by Ehsan Yarshater, vol. 3. Cambridge, England: Cambridge University Press, 1983. Recommended as the best account in English of the reign of Shāpūr II within the overall setting of Sāsānian rule, by one of the leading scholars in the field. For an alternative, see the same author's *The History of Ancient Iran* (1984).

Göbl, Robert. "Sasanian Coins." In *The Cambridge History of Iran*, edited by Ehsan Yarshater, vol. 3. Cambridge, England: Cambridge University Press, 1983. In Göbl's own words, "this coinage is an invaluable source of information about the history, culture, and economic life of the Sasanian state." Easily the best introduction to the subject.

Herrmann, Georgina. *The Making of the Past: The Iranian Revival.* Oxford, England: Elsevier-Phaidon, 1977. Beyond any doubt, the best general introduction to the Sāsānian period, accompanied by fine illustrations. Written by an acknowledged authority on Sāsānian bas-reliefs.

Neusner, Jason. *A History of the Jews in Babylonia: From Shapur I to Shapur II.* 5 vols. Leiden, Netherlands: Brill, 1997. The volumes present a glimpse at a long period in the history of Judaism in Mesopotamia (c. 227 B.C.E.-700 C.E.), which was, almost entirely, under the control of two successive Iranian dynasties, the Arsacid and Sasanid. Traces and discusses the Persian/Iranian influence on Judaism and its history.

Whitehouse, David, and Andrew Williamson. "Sasanian Maritime Trade." *Iran: Journal of the British Institute of Persian Studies* 11 (1973): 29-49. An interesting discussion of a little known aspect of Sāsānian history, prefaced by an account of Shāpūr II's activities in the Persian Gulf.

SEE ALSO: Constantine the Great.

RELATED ARTICLES in *Great Events from History: The Ancient World*: 284 C.E., Inauguration of the Dominate in Rome; 309-379 C.E., Shāpūr II Reigns over Sāsānian Empire; October 28, 312 C.E., Conversion of Constantine to Christianity.

SHI HUANGDI
Chinese emperor (r. 221-210 B.C.E.)

Shi Huangdi established the first unified empire that ruled China. His short-lived Qin Dynasty was marked by uniform laws, harsh justice, massive public works, and the ruler's elevation into an almost divine figure. Shi Huangdi redefined the Chinese notion of the state, and his conduct established a model that all later Chinese emperors attempted to emulate, modify, or avoid.

BORN: 259 B.C.E.; Qin, China
DIED: 210 B.C.E.; China
ALSO KNOWN AS: Shih Huang-ti (Wade-Giles); Qin Shi Huangdi (Pinyin), Ch'in Shih Huang-ti (Wade-Giles); Zheng (Pinyin), Cheng (Wade-Giles)
AREA OF ACHIEVEMENT: Government and politics

EARLY LIFE

The future Shi Huangdi (shur hwahng-dee) was born into the family of a secondary prince of the state of Qin (Chin) in 259 B.C.E. China was divided into a number of feudal states, and Qin was a formidable power with a strong army, an efficient administration, and an excellent geographical location in the Wei River valley, west of the center of Chinese civilization on the North China plain. The future First Emperor's father, Prince Zichu (Tzuch'u), lived as a hostage in the state of Zhao (Chao). He was a living pledge that Qin would uphold its agreements with the ruler of Zhao.

Prince Zichu had no male heirs, but he acquired a concubine from his confidant, the merchant Lu Buwei (Lu Pu-wei), and she bore him the son who was to become Shi Huangdi. After his son's birth, Zichu made the child's mother his legitimate first wife.

Both Prince Zichu and his son grew up in an era known as the Warring States Period (475-221 B.C.E.), which was marked by almost continuous warfare that eliminated small feudal territories, leaving seven large states ruled by kings. In spite of the lack of peace, ideas and technology flourished. The state of Qin's importance grew in the fourth and third centuries B.C.E. because of its association with a school of thinkers called Legalists, who emphasized simple administration, harsh justice, and mobilization of the state's subjects to enhance the kingdom's power. This Legalist approach contrasted with Confucianism, which stressed that the ruler and his officials must be good men of high moral character who sought peace, prosperity, and justice for the common people. The Legalist style, so named for an emphasis on rules rather than good men, appeared more than a century before Shi Huangdi's birth but reached its height during his rule. It has thus been associated with him ever since.

Prince Zichu's chief supporter, Lu Buwei, returned to Qin, where he spent his wealth freely to gain advantage for the prince and himself. Lu Buwei managed to have Zichu placed in direct line of succession for the Qin throne. In 251 B.C.E., Zichu's grandfather died, and the throne passed to his adoptive father (actually his paternal uncle), who ruled for less than a year. Zichu then ascended to the kingship, but ruled for only four years (250-246 B.C.E.). On his death, Lu Buwei ensured that the future Shi Huangdi, then a boy of thirteen, would be crowned King Zheng (Cheng) of Qin.

For nine years, Lu Buwei continued as King Zheng's chief minister, but in 237 B.C.E. a scandal linked him to a plot to overthrow his young charge. The historian Sima Qian (c. 145-86 B.C.E.) produced an account of these events that has shaped the contemporary view of Shi Huangdi as a morally bad man. Sima Qian, an advocate of Confucianism and an opponent of Legalism, wrote that Lu Buwei was Shi Huangdi's biological father because, when he had given the concubine to Prince Zichu, she was already pregnant. Sima Qian further tarred the First Emperor's parentage by claiming that his mother, after the death of her spouse Zichu, resumed sexual relations with Lu Buwei. Unable to satisfy her, he provided a highly virile but uncouth partner named Lao Ai, who fathered children with her. She is said to have plotted with Lao Ai to remove her illegitimately conceived son from the throne and substitute one of their children as king of Qin.

These lurid tales paint Shi Huangdi as the bastard son of a déclassé merchant and loose woman who was so base that she could join a plot to kill her own first-born son. Such behavior violated the prevailing moral standards of the time, which stressed the importance of proper blood descent for rulers, the strong ties between parents and children, and the propriety of female chastity, especially for widows. Sima Qian, as the official historian of the succeeding Han Dynasty (206 B.C.E.-220 C.E.), surely meant to defame Shi Huangdi with this account.

LIFE'S WORK

Whatever the truth of these stories, the events of 237 B.C.E. mark the beginning of King Zheng's active rulership. First, he ordered the deaths of Lao Ai and his family, required his mother to return to live in the Qin court under supervision, and banished Lu Buwei, who, fearing further punishment, committed suicide. For the next sixteen years, King Zheng of Qin focused on defeating his rivals. He relied on civilian ministers to run his kingdom and on generals to fight his wars, while living in grand style. His most important adviser was a former protégé of Lu Buwei, Li Si (Li Ssu), whom many historians have seen as a Legalist genius for his role in creating the empire. Li Si became chief minister after the Qin Dynasty was established in 221 B.C.E. and served in that post until 208 B.C.E., two years after the First Emperor's death.

Beginning in 230 B.C.E., Qin conquered all six of its rival states. These states, realizing the ambitions of Qin, had attempted alliances, but these always failed. Qin won a reputation of being as ferocious as a wolf or tiger. In 221 B.C.E., the last of these states, Qi (Ch'i), located in China's present-day eastern coastal Shandong Province, fell, and King Zheng declared himself a new kind of ruler, an emperor, with the title "Shi Huangdi."

Over the next eleven years, Shi Huangdi fashioned a remarkable new political order by applying the Legalist approach to governing, which had worked in Qin, to the whole of China. He divided the empire into a hierarchy of territorial administrative units: thirty-six commandaries and one thousand counties. Appointed officials, serving at the emperor's pleasure, administered the law, meted out justice, and collected revenue. In Legalist fashion, the Qin worked through simple but oppressive statutes applied to common people with uniform harshness.

During the Warring States era, different practices had grown up in the feudal states, but, under Shi Huangdi, the Qin ways became the standard through the empire. He established one set of weights and measures, one coinage, one standard way of writing Chinese characters, and one standard width for cart axles.

The First Emperor required the wealthy and powerful families from the East—meaning the survivors in the six defeated rival states—to reside in his capital of Xianyang (Hsien-yang; near the modern city of Xi'an in Shaanxi province). He let them live privileged lives but forestalled their participation in plots of rebellion in their old homelands. He confiscated weapons from around the empire and brought them to Xianyang, where they were melted down into twelve great statues. He also ordered the burning of the archives in the former rival states, thereby destroying many philosophical works of ancient China and acquiring a reputation as an anti-intellectual tyrant.

At Xianyang, as a reflection of his own megalomania, he began work on an enormous palace and a huge tomb of unprecedented size and magnificence. It is said that 700,000 workers were employed at the tomb site alone. The First Emperor seemed to care nothing for the cost and the sacrifices his subjects made for these extravagances.

Among his most remarkable achievements were a series of great public works undertaken by huge armies of corvée laborers and tens of thousands of families uprooted and relocated as colonists at the First Emperor's whim. Impressive roads connected Xianyang with the territory of the empire that extended east, north, and south of the original state of Qin. Newly dug canals moved grain to the capital, where it was used to feed its large population or dispatched to armies and workers. In the Warring States period, the rival states had raised walls and earthen dikes for defensive purposes. Shi Huangdi had some of these removed but ordered the walls along the northern border of the empire, meant to protect against the Turkic people called Xiongnu (Hsiung-nu), linked together into the Great Wall, which remains one of the best-known features of ancient China.

Shi Huangdi thought himself omniscient and ruled in a highly autocratic manner. Following a challenge from a Confucian in 212 B.C.E., he ordered four hundred Confucian scholars killed. It was this, along with the burning of Confucian texts on the advice of Li Si, that earned him the undying enmity of Confucianists for the next two thousand years.

Shi Huangdi undertook imperial tours to the far reaches of his newly won empire. These trips served to unify his control and acquaint him with the various parts of his great state. On these journeys, he visited mountain temples associated with local gods for whom he conducted proper ceremonies, thus fulfilling a key responsibility of the rulers he had defeated and replaced.

Shi Huangdi had great personal interest in the Daoist theories of nature. These notions embodied both proto-scientific ideas and superstitious occult beliefs centered around yin-yang dualism, which saw the world in terms of an unceasing alteration of forces operating through five elements or powers (*wuxing*). Shi Huangdi delighted in the elaborate systems of correspondence developed by devotees of this approach and, during his imperial tours, sought out those claiming to be able to prolong life or to unlock the secret of immortality.

Returning from one of these trips in 210 B.C.E., Shi Huangdi became ill and died at Shachu (Sha-ch'iu), on the North China plain, some distance from his capital at

Xianyang. Shi Huangdi intended for his eldest son to succeed him, but his chief traveling companions—a favorite younger son named Hu Hao, the chief minister Li Si, and a court eunuch named Zhao Gao (Chao Kao)—attempted to hide the First Emperor's death until they could return to Xianyang and put Hu Hao on the throne. By the crude but effective ruse of loading the imperial entourage with dead fish to cover the odor of the putrefying First Emperor's corpse, the plotters managed to make the court think the First Emperor was still alive and that he had declared Hu Hao to be his successor before his own death.

The First Emperor was buried in his vast and splendid tomb along with many palace women, who were to accompany him in the afterlife, and the chief builders of the tomb, who died so they could not reveal its secrets. In the 1970's, Chinese farmers digging a well accidentally revealed portions of a huge army of terracotta soldiers ranged in front of the tomb. The main tomb mound itself remained unexcavated, but the newly opened sections yielded a major attraction for Chinese and foreign tourists alike at Xi'an.

As Er Huangdi (Second Emperor), Hu Hao aped the style of his father and murdered several of his brothers on the recommendation of the eunuch Zhao Gao, who thus won a place in history as the first of a long series of notorious eunuchs who have harmed various Chinese ruling houses. Revolts broke out around the empire, the most important led by commoners drafted for corvée service. At the Qin court, Zhao Gao became chief minister and engineered an attack on the Second Emperor, who committed suicide. One of Shi Huangdi's surviving sons succeeded to the Qin throne, but with the title of king (*wang*), not emperor. This ruler quickly surrendered to Liu Bang (Liu Pang) in late 207 B.C.E. Liu Bang went on to consolidate his power and established the Han Dynasty, which endured for four centuries.

SIGNIFICANCE

Shi Huangdi is the most famous and best-known of all China's emperors. Some features of his rule became generally accepted by Confucianist rulers and scholars, including appointed officials administering territorial units organized in a hierarchical fashion, uniform laws throughout the society, canals for grain transportation, wall construction to mark China's northern boundary, extravagant magnificence at court, and grand imperial tours around the empire. Still, later Confucians always added condemnation of his ruthlessness, his anti-intellectualism, and his lack of concern over the common

people's suffering. Nevertheless, many dynamic rulers in China, Korea, Japan, and Vietnam emulated the style and substance of the First Emperor in their own careers. Shi Huangdi's influence lasted into the twentieth century when, in the 1970's, Mao Zedong (Mao Tse-tung) accepted comparisons of his own attempts to revolutionize China with those of the First Emperor.

—David D. Buck

FURTHER READING

Bodde, Derk. "The State and Empire of Ch'in." In *The Ch'in and Han Empires 221 B.C.-A.D. 220.* Vol. 1 of *The Cambridge History of China*, edited by Denis Twitchett and Michael Loewe. New York: Cambridge University Press, 1986. The best summary of Shi Huangdi's life in English.

Cottrell, Arthur. *The First Emperor of China.* New York: Holt, Rinehart, and Winston, 1981. A well-illustrated volume emphasizing early excavations at the First Emperor's tomb. Contains a long section summarizing the Qin conquest and Shi Huangdi's life.

Guisso, R. W. L., Catherine Pagani, and David Miller. *The First Emperor of China.* New York: Birch Lane, 1989. A book to accompany the National Film Board of Canada's docudrama film *The First Emperor of China.* Lavishly illustrated, but the text is somewhat disjointed.

Li Yu-ning, ed. *The First Emperor of China: The Politics of Historiography.* White Plains, N.Y.: International Arts and Sciences, 1975. Emphasizes Chinese fascination with Shi Huangdi during the Maoist era in China (1949-1976 C.E.). Contains a translation of Hong Shidi's popular biography of Shi Huangdi, which was first published in Chinese in 1972.

Sima Qian. *Records of the Grand Historian: The Qin Dynasty.* Translated by Burton Watson. 3d ed. New York: Columbia University Press, 1995. Contains translation of thirteen sections of Sima Qian's famous first century B.C.E. work *Shiji*, which include his accounts relating to Qin Shi Huangdi. Extracts from the *Records of the Grand Historian of China* dealing with Qin Shi Huangdi are frequently included in various anthologies concerning Chinese history and literature, but this is the best.

SEE ALSO: Sima Qian.

RELATED ARTICLES in *Great Events from History: The Ancient World*: c. 1066, Western Zhou Dynasty Begins in China; 770 B.C.E., Eastern Zhou Dynasty Begins in China; 475-221 B.C.E., China Enters Chaotic Warring States Period; c. 420 B.C.E.-c. 100 C.E.,

B.C.E., Liu Bang Captures Qin Capital, Founds Han Dynasty; 140-87 B.C.E., Wudi Rules Han Dynasty China; 1st century B.C.E., Sima Qian Writes Chinese History; 220 C.E., Three Kingdoms Period Begins in China.

Yuezhi Culture Links Persia and China; c. 285-c. 255 B.C.E, Xunzi Develops Teachings That Lead to Legalism; 221 B.C.E., Qin Dynasty Founded in China; c. 221 to 211 B.C.E., Building the Great Wall of China; c. 212-202? B.C.E., Construction of the Qin Tomb; 206

SIMA QIAN
Chinese historian

Sima Qian wrote the first major history of China, 130 chapters covering the major events and people in China from the reign of the legendary Yellow Emperor to the late first century B.C.E.

BORN: 145 B.C.E.; Longmen, Hancheng county, Shaanxi Province, China
DIED: 86 B.C.E.; China
ALSO KNOWN AS: Ssu-ma Ch'ien (Wade-Giles)
AREA OF ACHIEVEMENT: Historiography

EARLY LIFE

Nearly all information concerning the life of Sima Qian (soo-mah chee-yen) comes from his lifework, the *Shiji* (first century B.C.E.; *Records of the Grand Historian of China*, 1960). This comprehensive history of China from antiquity to Sima Qian's lifetime has been partially translated in a number of editions but is commonly referred to by its original title. In this work, as was customary, Sima Qian traced his genealogy to legendary figures of high station and high repute. In the mid-ninth century B.C.E., the family suffered a loss of position and became known by the name Sima. In about 140 B.C.E., his father, Sima Tan (Ssu-ma T'an), had been appointed the Grand Historian of the court of Emperor Wudi (Wu Ti; r. 141-87 B.C.E.). Since before his son's birth, Sima Tan had been collecting materials to write a major historical work. On his deathbed, he charged his son with completion of the history.

Little is known of Sima Qian's specific training for this task. His father served as court astrologer and historian, and his family apparently earned a living farming and keeping livestock in the hills south of the Huang River. Sima Qian's early education purportedly consisted of village schooling, which was continued after his father had been appointed to serve in the court. By his tenth year, Sima Qian reportedly was reading old texts.

Between his boyhood and his twentieth year, Sima Qian traveled extensively. He reported going south to the Yangtze and the Huai Rivers. He climbed Huiji, where the mythical emperor Yu, a great cultural hero who had

saved humankind and Earth from flooding, supposedly had died, and searched for a fabled cave atop the mountain. He saw the famed Nine Peaks, where the legendary emperor Shun, whose reign had brought humankind unmatchable happiness, was interred, and then sailed down the Yuan and Xiang Rivers. Farther north, he crossed the Wen and the Si Rivers. He traveled onward to study in Lu, the home state of the philosopher Confucius, and in Qi (Ch'i), the home state of Confucian philosopher Mencius. He also participated in an archery contest at a famed mountain near Confucius's home and encountered local toughs in Xue and Pengcheng. After passing through Liang and Chu (Ch'u), he returned home to Longmen probably around 122 B.C.E.

There, his father's influence, careful training, and good grades brought him into government service as a *langzhong*, a traveling court attendant. In this capacity, he wrote of having participated in imperial expeditions as well as many other journeys, which made him one of the most widely traveled men of his era.

The event critical to his career occurred in 110 B.C.E., as Emperor Wudi prepared for the sacred Feng sacrifice, symbolic of the divine election of the Han Dynasty (206 B.C.E.-220 C.E.). Having already reported to the authorities in Chang-an (now Xi'an) on his recent mission, Sima Qian traveled eastward to join the emperor at Luoyang. On his way, he saw his dying father, who asked him to succeed him as Grand Historian. Sima Qian had a family, although nothing is known of his wife, and only brief mention is made of a daughter.

LIFE'S WORK

What had begun as the private initiative of Sima Tan became in the hands of his son and successor one of the acknowledged masterworks of historical writing. Creation of most of the 130-chapter *Shiji* absorbed Sima Qian for twenty years, almost until his death. In carrying out the spirit of his father's injunction, however, he produced a history that was not only monumental but also unique in the implementation of its creative perceptions. Previous "histories" had consisted essentially of genealogical records, bland chronicles of a single regime, mere cautionary tales, essays propagandizing current political morality, or work dedicated to individual or institutional glorification.

Contrary to these precedents, Sima Qian sought to depict, as far as his sources allowed, the entire past of the Chinese people—basically a universal history, but one that fortunately illuminated the presence of many non-Chinese of whom no written record would otherwise have existed. His purpose was to record what had happened with judicious objectivity. Although the assumption of objectivity was not novel in Sima Qian's day (objectivity had been the goal of previous chroniclers, his father included), the degree of objectivity with which Sima Qian wrote, together with the chronological span and geopolitical range of his study, was unparalleled.

The *Shiji* is organized into five extensive sections. The "Basic Annals" are composed of a dozen chapters relating the histories of early dynastic families—back to the mythic Yellow Emperor, whose reign is said to have begun in 2697 B.C.E.—and the lives of individual Han emperors. Ten "Chronological Tables," graphing and dating important events of the past, follow. Subjects such as astronomy, rites, pitch pipes, music, the calendar, religion, and political economy subsequently are discussed in eight "Treatises." In turn, there follow thirty chapters on "Hereditary Houses," which cover political and diplomatic events before the Qin Dynasty (Ch'in; 221-206 B.C.E.). The next seventy chapters relate the "Accounts," or biographies, of famous men—including invaluable information on kings, ministers, sages, rebels, Confucian scholars—as well as reports on foreign governments and "barbarian" peoples with whom the Chinese had contact. Internally, the organization of sections and chapters is chronological, although some mixing of events and biographies leads to repetition of the narrative and a dispersal of information. Such confusions notwithstanding, the singularity of the organization is undoubtedly a result of Sima Qian's research, imagination, and sheer capacity for work.

Because of losses sustained in uprisings, wars, and the Hans' wanton destruction of documents relating to the Qin, their predecessors, sources for early dynasties were scarce and Sima Qian's narrative was parsed out by legends. The historian, however, disliked superstitions and wrote fairly accurate, three-dimensional portrayals when he had access to more abundant and more easily substantiated sources, such as those for events and personalities of the Han Dynasty, including those of his own lifetime.

He rarely obtruded his own personality directly, although almost the entire work (some sections may be later emendations) bears his imprimatur. Similarly, as was the case with most Chinese historians, he avoided forthright insertion of his own opinions. He was also inclined to present the most favorable aspects of his subjects first while introducing harsher facts later.

For dramatic effect, like the historians of ancient Greece and Rome, Sima Qian composed speeches for his principal characters, though not, as was the case in the West, so that they could be declaimed publicly. He wrote of the past as a sequence of dramas; therefore, the narrative portions of the *Shiji* are actually speeches by the principal figures instead of the author's descriptions of the action. In fact, very little pure description exists in the text. The Chinese preferred the directness of speech, as did readers of Greek and Roman historians such as Thucydides, Herodotus, or Cornelius Tacitus. The terseness of the classical Chinese language, however, lends a fluidity to the *Shiji* that is not present in analogous Western writings.

Scholars have sought to discover the personality and beliefs of Sima Qian beneath his literary devices. Although the historian may have been objective in many respects, his purpose was often didactic. Concentration on heroes, important figures, and grand events, insofar as his sources allowed, was subtly designed to convey moral judgments. He doubtless believed that goodness triumphs over evil. In this respect, he was at one with Confucius, whom he admired. He was the philosopher's first full-length biographer in the *Shiji*'s section titled "Hereditary House of Confucius." It seems unlikely, however, that Sima Qian extended his admiration for Confucius to all Confucianists or to Daoists.

Whether Sima Qian as a historian believed in an evolutionary process, in the inevitability of decline, in cycles, or in continuous flux is uncertain. His selection of emperors, sages, ministers, bandits, rebels, and even nonentities (as well as his structuring of events) is too complex to suggest a firm conclusion. If, as he explained, his motive in writing was to glorify Wudi, then the universal history that he produced was unnecessary. This obeisance to his emperor aside, it appears that he intended to create a new form of history.

Sima Qian was engaged in his private historical enterprise while officially attending to observance of rites and other courtly duties. Among these was his reformation of the Chinese calendar, which remains in use today. He suffered as a result of a dispute with Wudi over the actions of the historian's friend, a general named Li Ling.

Li Ling had fought brilliantly on the western frontier but, failing to receive the support essential to saving his army, went over to the enemy. For his efforts to explain Li Ling's behavior, Sima Qian was imprisoned and sentenced to be castrated in 99 B.C.E. Reportedly, rather than take the "honorable" choice of suicide, he chose castration in order to complete his history, which he finished around 90 B.C.E. Still a minor and largely unrecognized court official, he died shortly afterward, in 86 B.C.E. The *Shiji* remained unknown until the marquess of Pingtong, Yang Yun (mid-first century B.C.E.), Sima Qian's grandson, succeeded in having it widely circulated.

SIGNIFICANCE

Sima Qian's *Shiji* provides the principal written source of knowledge about ancient Chinese history and culture. It continues to be an invaluable resource for understanding and interpreting a substantial portion of China's past. Although it embodies many dramatic elements and important writings already familiar to his predecessors, it remains unique for its scope, substantive richness, and literary distinction. It must also be regarded as a fresh form of historical writing. Unlike previous historians, who had been content with the production of dynastic or personal eulogies and cautionary or moralizing tales in which a recounting of the past was merely a convenient vehicle for their views, Sima Qian sought to offer an objective perspective on the whole experience of the Chinese people. Scholarly difficulties in ascertaining precisely what his final estimates of many personalities and events were and in determining what his philosophy of history might have been tend to reaffirm his objectivity. This objective cast to the *Shiji* has lent it a timeless quality, despite Sima Qian's obvious inventions and despite later and inferior emendations. In subsequent generations, the *Shiji* continued to be admired for its organization, execution, and objectives.

—*Clifton K. Yearley and Kerrie L. MacPherson*

FURTHER READING

Dawson, Raymond. Introduction to *Historical Records* by Sima Qian. Translated by Raymond Dawson. New York: Oxford University Press, 1994. Classical Chinese scholar Dawson looks at Sima Qian's role as a historian and provides background material on the

Qin Dynasty, which is the focus of this translation of the *Shiji*. Index.

Durrant, Stephen W. *The Cloudy Mirror: Tension and Conflict in the Writings of Sima Qian*. Albany: State University of New York Press, 1995. Durrant examines both the man, Sima Qian, and the work, *Shiji*, tracing the relationship between the historian's narrative of the past and his narrative of his own life through an analysis of the chapters in which the historian describes himself and of the chapters that form his history of China. Bibliography and index.

Hardy, Grant. *Worlds of Bronze and Bamboo: Sima Qian's Conquest of History*. New York: Columbia University Press, 1999. Hardy provides biographical information on Sima Qian as he compares his work with that of the early Greek historians. He focuses on the Chinese historian's objectives in creating the *Shiji*, arguing that his intent was not what Westerners would regard as an accurate and objective representation of the past. Bibliography and index.

Watson, Burton. Introduction to *Records of the Grand Historian of China* by Sima Qian. Translated by Burton Watson. 3d ed. 3 vols. New York: Columbia University Press, 1995. Discusses the life and times of the historian and provides background to the translation that follows. This translation, the most extensive in English, focuses on the Qin and Han Dynasties. Index.

_____. *Ssu-ma Ch'ien: Grand Historian of China*. 1958. Reprint. New York: Columbia University Press, 1963. The only full-length, English-language biography of Sima Qian. Watson places the subject in the context of his times and examines the beginnings of Chinese historiography, the structure of his work, and the subject's thought. Includes two appendices, notes, a brief bibliography, glossary, and index.

SEE ALSO: Ban Gu; Ban Zhao; Dio Cassius; Herodotus; Livy; Polybius; Sallust; Tacitus; Thucydides; Wudi.
RELATED ARTICLES in *Great Events from History: The Ancient World*: c. 450-c. 425 B.C.E., History Develops as a Scholarly Discipline; 1st century B.C.E., Sima Qian Writes Chinese History; c. 99-105 C.E., Ban Zhao Writes Behavior Guide for Young Women.

SIMA XIANGRU
Chinese poet, scholar-official, and musician

China's greatest composer of a type of rhapsodic poem in a complex and highly stylized language, Sima Xiangru also was one of Imperial China's most revered players of the seven-string zither prized by the literati for its evocative expression. The marriage of Sima Xiangru and his young wife Zhuo Wenjun is a classic love story in traditional Chinese culture.

BORN: 179 B.C.E.; Chengdu, China
DIED: 117 B.C.E.; Maoling, Nan Yue, China
ALSO KNOWN AS: Ssu-ma Hsiang-ju (Wade-Giles); Sseu-ma Siang-jou (French transliteration); Sima Zhangqing (Pinyin), Ssu-ma Chang-ch'ing (Wade-Giles)
AREAS OF ACHIEVEMENT: Government and politics, literature, music, scholarship

EARLY LIFE

Sima Xiangru (sur-mah shyang-rew) lived during the Western, or Former, Han Dynasty (206 B.C.E.-23 C.E.). Information about his life, including versions of his most important writings, comes primarily from biographies—largely similar to each other—in the early histories the *Shiji* (first century B.C.E.; *Records of the Grand Historian of China*, 1960, rev. ed. 1993) of Sima Qian (Ssu-ma Ch'ien, 145-86 B.C.E.) and the *Han Shu* (also known as *Qian Han Shu*, completed first century C.E.; *The History of the Former Han Dynasty*, 1938-1955) of Ban Gu (Pan Ku; 32-92 C.E.).

Sima Xiangru was from a well-to-do family in Chengdu (Ch'eng-tu), the principal city of the prosperous southwestern region of Shu (modern-day Sichuan Province). He was provided with an excellent education in literature, history, and philosophy and is said to also have studied swordsmanship in his youth. Sometime around age twenty-five he was able to use his family wealth to purchase an appointment at the imperial court. Finding this posting not to his liking due to the emperor's lack of interest in literary composition, he resigned on the pretext of illness in 151 or 150 B.C.E. and joined the literary coterie gathered under the patronage of the emperor's younger brother Liu Wu (r. 168-143 B.C.E.), then king of the state of Liang (in modern-day Henan Province). Sima Xiangru had been impressed by Liu Wu and his entourage during their recent stay in the imperial capital; the group included such literary luminaries as Zou Yang (Tsou Yang; c. 206-129 B.C.E.), Mei Sheng (Mei Cheng; d. 141 B.C.E.), and Zhuang Ji (Chuang Chi, also known as Yan Ji; c. 188-105 B.C.E.). It is during the period when Sima Xiangru was associated with the Liang court circle that he produced the first of the poetic compositions that would gain him recognition and praise both in his time and throughout history.

LIFE'S WORK

Sima Xiangru composed the *Zixu fu* (second century B.C.E.; *Sir Fantasy*, 1971) a few years after joining the group of highly talented literati at Liu Wu's court. It was an imagistic tour-de-force description of the royal hunting preserve in the old state of Chu (located in Hubei and Hunan Provinces), framed as a dialogue between two characters who boast of the relative merits of their states. Sir Fantasy, on a visit to the state of Qi (located in Shandong Province), is taken on a hunt in the royal park. When asked about his experience, he launches into a description of the vast Yunmeng Park in his native state of Chu, detailing the park's natural attributes and the fantastic progress of the royal hunt. His rhapsodic outburst overwhelms his interlocutor and he is accused of poor manners and inappropriate, overt boasting. An example of the descriptive vocabulary and complex prosody Sima Xiangru used throughout the composition is seen in David Knechtges's translation (1987, vol. 2, pp. 55-57):

> The mountains:
> Twisting and twining, tortuously turning,
> Arch aloft, precipitously piled.
> Peaked and pointed, jaggedly jutting,
> They leave the sun and moon covered and eclipsed.
> Multifariously merging, complexly conjoined,
> Upward they invade the blue clouds.
> Slanting and sloping, sloping and slanting,
> Below they join the Jiang and He.
> In their soil:
> Cinnabar, azurite, ochre, white clay,
> Orpiment, milky quartz,
> Tin, prase, gold, and silver,
> In manifold hues glisten and glitter,
> Shining and sparkling like dragon scales.

Another example (Knechtges, p. 63) recounts the carnage of hunting:

> Swift and sudden, fleet and fast,
> They move like thunder, arrive like a gale,
> Course like stars, strike like lightning.
> Their bows are not fired in vain;

Hitting the mark they are certain to split an eye,
Impale a breast, pierce a foreleg,
Or snap the heart cords.
The catch, as if it had rained beasts,
Overspreads the grass, covers the ground.

When Liu Wu died in 144 B.C.E., Sima Xiangru returned, impoverished, to his home in Shu. However, he soon found the support of an old acquaintance, now a local official in Linqiong, a smaller town to the southwest of Chengdu, where he soon attracted the attention of some of the richest men in the area. One of these, an iron merchant and manufacturer named Zhuo Wangsun, whose household included eight hundred indentured servants, paid a visit to Sima Xiangru and was immediately won over, all the more so after Sima Xiangru performed a few songs for him on the *qin* (seven-string zither). As it happened, Zhuo Wangsun had a recently widowed seventeen-year-old daughter who had a passion for music, and thus began one of the most renowned love stories of early China.

Sima Xiangru was invited to the Zhuo estate, where he arrived fully intent on winning the rich man's daughter. While Sima Xiangru was ostensibly entertaining Zhuo Wangsun by playing the *qin* during the drinking festivities, his music and song really were directed toward seducing the daughter, Zhuo Wenjun (Cho Wen-chü), who spied on him through a crack in the doorway and lost her heart. Sima Xiangru bribed the young lady's servants, and the two eloped to Chengdu. Disinherited by her father and with no other means of support, Zhuo Wenjun soon convinced her new husband that they should move back to Linqiong, where they could borrow from her brother. They sold their property and set up a small wine shop, where she minded the bar and he washed the pots. Zhuo Wangsun was mortified, but after a time he was persuaded to reconcile with his daughter. He sent his daughter servants, cash, and all of the property she had accumulated in her first marriage, and the couple returned to live in wealth on an estate in Chengdu.

Sima Xiangru is portrayed as a confident man with great flair, although with a weak physical constitution and some tendency toward aloofness. The song that he is supposed to have played to woo Zhuo Wenjun, with unambiguously pathetic and provocative lyrics, is about finding one's ideal mate. The highly attractive characters, complex web of circumstances, and evocative, romantic nature of the tale have contributed to its perennial popularity. It also is one of the few romantic stories in which a marriage for love finds success, rather than ending prematurely and tragically.

After a period of easy living, around the year 137 B.C.E., a townsman from Shu gave a copy of the *Zixu fu* to the recently installed emperor Wudi (Wu-ti; r. 140-87 B.C.E.). The sixteen-year-old emperor was greatly impressed and exclaimed that he regretted that the author of the piece was of a different time. Surprised to learn that the author was alive, the emperor had Sima Xiangru brought to the capital. The poet suggested that, as his previous compositions merely concerned the affairs of vassal lords, he wished now to compose a *fu* (rhapsody or long descriptive literary work in a complex and highly stylized language) on the excursions and hunts of the Son of Heaven for the emperor's delectation. This lengthy two-part composition pairs the *Zixu fu* with a new, longer, and more embellished sequel, *Shanglin fu* (second century B.C.E.; imperial park).

This *fu* continues the fictional discourse of three interlocutors: Sir Fantasy (Zixu; "hollow, empty words"), who delineates the grandness of the hunting preserve in Chu; Master Improbable (Wuyou xiansheng; "how could something like this exist?") of the state of Qi, who upbraids him for his churlishness; and Lord Nosuch (Wushigong; "someone who does not exist"), who humbles them both with his exhaustive exposition on the majesty of the Shanglin hunting park of the Former Han emperors, located to the west of the capital city Chang-an (modern-day Xian, Shaanxi Province), adding a final didactic section on the moral correctness of curbing excess. As the satiric names of its characters suggest, the *fu* is full of hyperbole, exhibiting a descriptive power and imagistic vocabulary that surpasses anything found in Chinese literature. It is indisputably the greatest of all *fu* and one of the monuments of world literature.

The *Shanglin fu* continues the imagistic descriptive mode of the *Zixu fu*, cataloging the attributes of the locale and the progress of the hunt. Replete with exaggerated exuberance and a confluence of the real and the imaginary, it weaves together sections about the park's topography and geophysical qualities, the diversity of its flora and fauna, the terrible efficacy and carnage of the hunt, the architectural intricacies of the hunting lodges, and the emperor's elegant entourage. Finally, the *fu* shows the emperor becoming aware of the implications of such extravagance and setting his attention to reform, implementing economic and land-use policies favorable to the people and adopting proper administrative and ritual conduct for the correct governance of the empire.

The *fu* is a euphonic and rhythmic prosodic form comprising both rhymed and unrhymed sections; early *fu* were meant for oral recitation, even while being highly valued and influential as written texts. The ornate language of Sima Xiangu's *fu* is quite unrivaled and often entirely original, and had a tremendous influence on Chinese descriptive vocabulary. Sonorous and euphemistic disyllabic expressions and binomial descriptives that characteristically are amalgams of alliteration and/or rhyme bring a palpable sensuality and a rhythmic sense of flow to the description. Whole lines often consist of paired disyllabic words that impart an affective image or impression rather than a static or unambiguous likeness. For example, in Knechtges's superb English rendition (1987, p. 77), which captures much of the force of the original (although in translation its musicality can only be imagined), the movement of dashing rivers is described as:

> Soaring and leaping, surging and swelling,
> Spurting and spouting, rushing and racing,
> Pressing and pushing, clashing and colliding,
> Flowing uncontrolled, bending back,
> Wheeling and rearing, beating and battering,
> Swelling and surging, troublous and turbulent,
> Loftily arching, billowing like clouds,
> Sinuously snaking, twirling and whirling,
> Outracing their own waves, they rush to the chasms,
> Lap, lap, they descend to the shoals.

Elsewhere (Knechtges, 1987, p. 109), palace women are described as:

> Beguiling and bewitching, elegant and refined,
> Faces powdered and painted, hair sculpted and trimmed,
> Lithe and lissome, decorous and demure,
> Soft and supple, gracile and graceful,
> Winning and winsome, slender and slight.

Sima Xiangru's *fu* ostensibly was a depiction of the imperial hunting preserve, but the fantastic portrayal might better be seen as a symbolic re-imagining of the park as a microcosmic representation of the realm and its full panoply of plants and animals, where all is under the control of the enlightened and just emperor. Emperor Wudi was suitably impressed, swayed by the rhetorical flourishes of Sima Xiangru's literary extravaganza. His lavish description gained Sima Xiangru the emperor's favor, and he again took up a position at court.

Sima Xiangru was twice sent as imperial envoy to his native Shu. Around 133 B.C.E. his mission was to allevi-

ate tensions that had arisen due to an imperial general's oppressive treatment of the local population in an attempt to assert Han rule over the area. For this, Sima Xiangru composed a proclamation to the local governors on the part of the emperor assuring them of the emperor's good will. One year later, Sima Xiangru was sent to bring more of the area under Han control; to allay criticism from some of the emperor's economic advisors, Sima Xiangru composed a dialogue between the elders of Shu and an imperial envoy arguing for the benefits of benevolent Han interests. Sima Xiangru was successful in opening up new roads and extending imperial authority over the various ethnic populations; while in Shu, he was honored by his wealthy and influential father-in-law.

Sima Xiangru was a particularly talented and persuasive writer; he is said to have stuttered, yet nevertheless he was especially renowned for his *fu*, a form generally intended for oral performance. Following his success with his *Shanglin fu*, around 120 B.C.E. he composed for the emperor *Da ren fu* (c. second century B.C.E.; *The Great Man*, 1996), which both praises the grandness of his sovereign and also, through indirection, admonishes him for his excesses. The Great Man is characterized as a transcendent being in control of mystical arts who goes on a distant journey through the cosmos, freed of the constraints of the material world; the emperor again was greatly pleased, as if he himself had roamed about heaven and earth. While some of Sima Xiangru's writings would seem, at face value, to be laudatory or occasional compositions written after excursions with the emperor, most of his writings also carried a clear didactic lesson or a political commentary. His *fu* lamenting the second Qin emperor, written after a visit to the tomb of the last ruler of the previous dynasty, clearly addressed the consequences of inattention to correct rulership.

Sima Xiangru retired to Maoling (just west of modern Xianyang, Shaanxi) around the year 119 B.C.E., where he passed away in 117 B.C.E. Shortly before his death, hearing of the poet's poor state of health, the emperor personally sent a messenger to collect his writings to ensure that they were not lost to posterity. However, the functionary arrived after he had died; he was told that Sima Xiangru never kept copies of his writings, but that he had left behind one composition in anticipation of the man's arrival. This was a memorial to the throne, which Sima Xiangru had composed at the end of his life, recommending that the emperor perform for the first time the important sacrificial rites of legitimation at Mount Tai (in Shandong); this resulted in the institution of a state cult five years later, and an imperial progress to each of three mountains for the official sacrifices.

Sima Xiangru is said to have composed twenty-nine rhapsodies in all, but only five still are extant. All of his writings display highly crafted rhetorical flourishes. He also is credited with having compiled a dictionary—which would seem appropriate for such a wordsmith—and a few other writings, including the two songs that won the love of Zhuo Wenjun; these songs and their instrumental music still are part of the *qin* repertory.

Sima Xiangru is described sometimes as a dashing fellow, sometimes as a quiet, frail sort who disdained high company. Due to both his literary excellence and his personality, he shows up as a character in later writings, for instance in the *fu* by Xie Huilian (Hsieh Hui-lien; 379-433) on snow. The romantic love story of Sima Xiangru and Zhuo Wenjun has been the subject of operas and other dramatic productions; one example is *Qin xin ji* (sixteenth century C.E.; record of the heart of the zither). Several places in China have landmarks commemorating places where Sima Xiangru is said to have played the *qin*, enticed his lover, or had his wine shop.

SIGNIFICANCE

Sima Xiangru is one of the most famous literary personalities of traditional China. His writings had a tremendous influence on Chinese descriptive language and literature, and his life story has struck a romantic chord throughout the millennia. During the Han Dynasty, he perfected the highly embellished literary form and style known as *fu*, or rhapsody, perhaps the most exuberant and complex of Chinese forms of descriptive literature. His long, imaginative compositions wove together fantastic images in an outpouring of alliterative and rhyming descriptive expressions that gave sensual impressions of movement, sound, and color, a mode of expression whose evocative nature has often been copied. The story of Sima Xiangru's musical seduction of Zhuo Wenjun and the story of their free and independent life underlies many later romances. It is a very rare example of a successful marriage on the basis of love, perhaps the first in literary history, and it is all the more cherished because of its happy ending.

—*Alan Berkowitz*

FURTHER READING

Gong, Kechang. *Studies on the Han Fu*. Translated and edited by David R. Knechtges, et al. New Haven, Conn.: American Oriental Society, 1997. Includes an excellent chapter on Sima Xiangru's literary writings.

Idema, W. L. "The Story of Ssu-ma Hsiang-ju and Cho Wen-chü in Vernacular Literature of the Yüan and Early Ming Dynasties." *T'ung Pao* 70, nos. 1-3 (1984): 60-109. Full treatment of the love story and its influence.

Knechtges, David R. "Problems of Translating Descriptive Binomes in the *Fu*." *Tamkang Review* 15, nos.1-4 (1985): 329-347. Good introduction to aspects of the distinctive language used by Sima Xiangru and others.

Sage, Steven F. *Ancient Sichuan and the Unification of China*. Albany: State University of New York Press, 1992. Chapter 6 discusses Sima Xiangru's diplomatic missions.

Xiao, Tong. *Rhapsodies on Sacrifices, Hunting, Travel, Sightseeing, Palaces and Halls, Rivers and Seas*. Vol. 2 of *Wen xuan*. Translated by David R. Knechtges. Princeton, N.J.: Princeton University Press, 1987. Elegant and true translations of Sima Xiangru's most important writings with copious annotation. The introduction also discusses his use of language.

SEE ALSO: Ban Gu; Catullus; Horace; Pindar; Qu Yuan; Sappho; Sima Qian; Tao Chien; Wudi; Xie Lingyun.
RELATED ARTICLES in *Great Events from History: The Ancient World*: c. 580 B.C.E., Greek Poet Sappho Dies; c. 438 B.C.E., Greek Lyric Poet Pindar Dies; 206 B.C.E., Liu Bang Captures Qin Capital, Founds Han Dynasty; 140-87 B.C.E., Wudi Rules Han Dynasty China; 54 B.C.E., Roman Poet Catullus Dies; November 27, 8 B.C.E., Roman Lyric Poet Horace Dies; c. 405 C.E., Statesman Tao Qian Becomes Farmer and Daoist Poet.

SAINT SIMEON STYLITES
Syrian monk

An ascetic who spent the greater part of his career perched in prayer atop a sixty-foot pillar, Simeon was one of the most controversial figures of the fifth century. Although he left behind no works of enduring value, he was the conscience and spiritual example for Syrian Christians in the patristic period.

BORN: c. 390 C.E.; Sisan, Cilicia (now in Syria)
DIED: 459 C.E.; Telanissos (now Deir Samaan, Syria)
ALSO KNOWN AS: Simeon the Elder; Stylites ("pillar dweller")
AREA OF ACHIEVEMENT: Religion

EARLY LIFE

Simeon Stylites (sti-LI-teez) was born of Christian parents in the town of Sisan, Cilicia (now in northern Syria), around 390. He was baptized in his youth by his very pious parents, who provided a home life in which religious matters were a frequent topic of conversation. Until he was about thirteen years old, Simeon spent his time shepherding his father's flocks in the neighborhood of Sis; this was a task that, according to the Syriac biography of Simeon, he discharged with great diligence and sometimes to the point of exhaustion.

The occupation of shepherd improved Simeon's strength, gentleness, speed, and endurance but had little effect on his slight build. A dreamy boy, he would often meditate while watching the campfire flame and burn storax as a tribute to the ubiquitous God of his parents. Because of his kindly disposition, he was a favorite with the other shepherds, and to show his generosity he would often forgo food until his friends had eaten.

The turning point in Simeon's life occurred shortly after his thirteenth birthday. One Sunday, while attending church, he was deeply moved by the Gospel reading for that day, which included the Beatitudes "Blessed are they that mourn" and "Blessed are the pure of heart." Simeon asked the congregation the meaning of these words and how one might attain the blessedness referred to in the Gospels. An old man who was present suggested that the monastic life was the surest but steepest path to holiness because it was characterized by prayer, fasting, and austerities designed to mortify the flesh and purify the soul.

On hearing this reply, it is said, Simeon withdrew to the pasture lands with his flocks to burn storax and meditate on what the old man had said. One day, in the course of his meditations, Simeon had the first of the many visions described in his biographies. In it, Jesus Christ appeared to him under the disquieting visage of the apocalyptic Son of Man and commanded him to build a sound foundation on which it would be possible to erect the superstructure of an edifice unparalleled in all human history.

Simeon took this vision to mean that it was his life that was to be the foundation of a great work that Christ would complete. The marvelous nature of this work, however, demanded a foundation of extraordinary strength and endurance. In Simeon's reckoning, that meant that special sacrifices would be required, and these would best be accomplished within the confines of a monastic community.

LIFE'S WORK

The various biographies differ about how Simeon spent his monastic period. Less reliable biographies mention an initial two-year sojourn, near Sis, at the monastery of the abbot Timothy, where Simeon is said to have learned the psalter by heart. Theodoret's biography and the Syriac biography, on the other hand, indicate that Simeon first took the tonsure at the monastery of Eusebona at Tell 'Ada, between Antioch and Aleppo. Whichever is the accurate narrative, the sources agree that Simeon's stay at Eusebona was charged with many extraordinary occurrences.

To mortify his flesh, Simeon engaged in fasts lasting many days, exposed himself to extremes of inclement weather, and humbly but steadfastly endured the jeering of envious monastics and the onslaught of demonic forces (whether real or imagined). One peculiar austerity, which Theodoret identifies as the principal cause of Simeon's eviction from Eusebona, serves as an example of this ascetic's willpower (and fanaticism). Finding a well rope made of tightly twisted, razor-sharp palm leaves, Simeon wrapped it snugly around his midriff. So tight was the wrapping that the flesh swelled on either side of the coils as they cut progressively deeper into his flesh. Finally, after Simeon had begun to show some signs of discomfort, the abbot of Eusebona had the bindings forcibly removed, despite Simeon's protestations. So deep had the rope cut into Simeon's body that the bloody wound had matted the bindings and robes together. For three days, the monks had to apply liquids to soften Simeon's clothes in order to remove them, the result being that when the rope was finally uncoiled it brought with it pieces of Simeon's flesh and a torrent of blood.

From this last austerity, Simeon's recovery was slow, nearly leaving him an invalid. Tired of the bickering and petty jealousies that Simeon's practices had aroused among his monastic brothers—and probably not a little horrified at Simeon's fanatical zeal—the abbot of Eusebona discharged Simeon, giving him his blessing and forty dinars for food and clothing.

Simeon's expulsion from the monastery at Eusebona was significant because it was typical of the response of abbots to ascetic practices that went beyond the bounds of good sense. Simeon's own desire to perform acts of supererogation, even at the expense of disobedience to his superior, may seem to suggest that he deserves to be classed among the Sarabaitic monks—those who were described by Saint Jerome and John Cassian as thwarting all authority. The various biographies, however, are unanimous in proclaiming Simeon's freedom from the grasping, care-ridden personality of a Sarabaite.

After leaving the monastery, Simeon's life more closely resembled the lives of the anchorites, described by Cassian as hermits who were the most fruitful of the monastics and achieved greater heights of contemplation because they withdrew to the desert to face the assaults of demons directly. According to Cassian, John the Baptist was the forerunner of the anchorites. It is this group that most probably can claim Simeon as its own.

After his dismissal from the monastery at Eusebona, Simeon wandered to the foot of Mount Telneshae in northern Syria. Intent on beginning a special set of austerities for the Lenten season, he approached an almost deserted hermitage and asked its keeper to provide a cell in which he might seclude himself. There, Simeon fasted for forty days. Not satisfied with this feat of extraordinary endurance, he determined to undertake a three-year fast. Frightened by the duration and severity of the proposed fast, the keeper of the hermitage, Bassus, convinced Simeon that such a work was imprudent and that he ought to divide the period in half, lest he kill himself. Simeon agreed.

It was the completion of the year-and-a-half fast that established a name for Simeon. News of his endurance and holiness was carried abroad. Everywhere people began to talk about the Syrian phenomenon: The backwater of Telneshae had been graced by God; a saint had come to dwell there. People began to flock to the hermitage to seek the wisdom of this holy man and his curative powers. When they returned home, they brought with them stories of his marvelous abilities, abilities that were the fruit of his extreme asceticism.

Saint Simeon Stylites sitting on a column, from a sixteenth century Russian icon. (Bettmann/Corbis)

For about ten years, Simeon practiced his asceticism in an open cell on Mount Telneshae, each year repeating the particulars of his original Lenten fast. One day, sometime around the year 422, Simeon had a vision that was to distinguish him forever as an ascetic of a special kind. Twenty-one days into his Lenten fast, Simeon beheld an apparition. He saw a man, noble in stature, dressed in a military girdle, face radiant as the sun, praying aloud. After finishing his prayer, the stranger climbed up on the pillar-shaped stone, three cubits (about four and a half feet) high, which stood near Simeon's cell and served as a makeshift altar. Standing on the stone, the stranger folded his hands behind his back, bowed toward Simeon, and looked heavenward with his hands outstretched. For three days and three nights the stranger thus prayed before vanishing.

Simeon regarded this experience as a decisive revelation. From that point onward, he was to practice his fasts standing on a column of stone, exposed to the extremes of weather. He had been called to be a stylite (from the Greek *stulos*, meaning "pillar").

At first Simeon's new practice aroused the ire of the Christian leaders in the region. It may have been the novelty of Simeon's practice that angered them or it may have been that Simeon's peculiar form of worship seemed a retrogression, a return to the adoration practiced in Syria in pre-Christian times—particularly in Hierapolis. Lucian of Antioch wrote that in Hierapolis, twice a year, a priest would ascend a tall column to commune with the goddess Attar'athae and the rest of the Syrian pantheon. It may have seemed to the local religious leaders that Simeon was reviving the form, if not the content, of this pagan worship.

Whatever the cause of the displeasure of the Christian leaders, its expression diminished as quickly as the public adulation of Simeon increased. One can imagine what a powerful sight the stylite must have been, a sight that awakened deep and elemental associations in the pilgrims (particularly the Syrians). He must have been a spectacle: an emaciated figure, arms raised in unceasing prayer, perched atop a narrow column whose diameter provided barely enough room for the saint to recline. Simeon's figure could be seen on his spindle 365 days a year, regardless of the weather, at all times of day. He could be seen silhouetted against the rising and setting sun, shining in the midday azure sky, and brilliantly illuminated against Stygian thunderclouds by stroboscopic flashes of lightning. Finally, add to the image a constant procession of pilgrims winding their way up Mount Telneshae (some nearly exhausted from the great distances traveled but still hopeful that they might be healed, find advice, or discover a holy truth) and one has some idea of the deep impression that Simeon Stylites made on his age.

For thirty-seven years, Simeon stood atop pillars of various sizes under all conditions. Many pagans were converted by his miracles and example, and even those barbarians who remained unconverted held the saint in the highest esteem. If the biographers are to be trusted, three emperors (Theodosius, Leo I, and Marcian) sought his advice about difficult state matters. Also, two surviving, but possibly spurious, letters attributed to Simeon indicate that he intervened on the side of the Christians when Emperor Theodosius issued an edict to restore Jewish property unlawfully seized by Christians and that he wrote to Emperor Leo I to approve the opening of the Council of Chalcedon in 451.

Concerning the exact time of Simeon's death, his biographers give different accounts. They mark the date as Friday, July 24, Wednesday, September 2, or Friday, September 25, in the year 459. Whatever the precise date, the accounts agree that Simeon died in prayer, surrounded by his disciples.

For four days the corpse of the saint was paraded throughout the region, and on the fifth day it was carried through the streets of the great city of Antioch to the accompaniment of chanting, the burning of incense and candles, a constant sprinkling of fine perfumes, and many miraculous cures and signs. The body of the blessed Simeon was laid to rest in the great cathedral of Constantine, an honor that had never before been awarded either saint or statesman. There it remained for a while, despite even the attempts of Emperor Leo to have it transported to his own court as a talisman against evil. Eventually, the cult of Simeon grew so significantly that a pilgrimage church, in the style of Constantine's cathedral, was built at Qual'at Saman to house Simeon's remains.

SIGNIFICANCE

Unlike great philosophers, theologians, and statesmen, Simeon Stylites left no great works of intellect or polity behind. Of the surviving letters attributed to him, it is difficult to say which are spurious and which are original because of their contradictory doctrinal positions and obvious redactions. What, then, can be made of Simeon's life? What was its impact on the world of the fifth century?

It is possible to describe the impact of Simeon as twofold. First, he contributed a peculiar ascetic technique that was imitated and extended by other stylites, such as Daniel, Simeon Stylites the Younger, Alypius, Luke, and Lazarus. As an ascetic practice, Simeon's method was one of the most severe. Yet, if practiced in a pure spirit, it held great promise: It could transform its adherent into a channel of supernatural grace.

Second, Simeon contributed something symbolic to the world of the fifth century. Regardless of which accounts of his wisdom and his importance to the social and theological controversies are accurate, all of his biographers asserted that Simeon's chief significance was as a religious symbol. His was a life whose worth must be measured in terms of the possibilities of the human spirit, not in terms of practical results or durable goods. His actions—like the actions of many other saints in the various world religions—were a testimony to the existence of values that transcend those of the visible world. Because he demonstrated the power of these values through a concrete form of supererogatory practice, people could grasp them easily. That is the reason he was so respected: He enacted his belief.

—Thomas Ryba

FURTHER READING

Brown, Peter. *The Cult of the Saints: Its Rise in Latin Christianity.* Chicago: University of Chicago Press, 1981. Useful for its general analysis of the phenomena associated with saint devotion. Although Brown's work is about the cult of the saints in the patristic Latin West, some of his arguments can be extended by analogy to Eastern Christianity. Particularly pertinent are his discussions of saintly patronage, the gift of perseverance, and the power associated with saintly presence. The cult of devotion that developed after Simeon's death manifests these features as clearly as any Western cult.

Doran, Robert, trans. *The Lives of Simeon Stylites.* Kalamazoo, Mich.: Cistercian, 1992. Includes English translations of two Greek biographies of Saint Simeon, by Theodoret of Cyrrhus and Antonius. Also includes translation of an anonymus Syriac version, which is more episodic and contains more details that are historically questionable yet is useful for capturing the spirit of the man. Contains map, bibliography, and index.

Downey, Glanville. *Ancient Antioch.* Princeton, N.J.: Princeton University Press, 1963. An accessible book on the history of ancient Antioch from its origins to the decline of the Roman Empire, it is a condensation of another work by Downey, cited below. As Simeon was at the center of many political and theological controversies of his day, this book helps situate his involvement within the social, cultural, and religious history of Syria's most important city. Contains some maps and illustrations.

_____. *A History of Antioch in Syria: From Seleucus to the Arab Conquest.* Princeton, N.J.: Princeton University Press, 1961. One of the most ambitious histories of Antioch from the time of the Seleucids until the Arab conquest, this work contains a wealth of historical information on ancient Christian and pre-Christian Antioch. Contains maps and illustrations.

Voobus, Arthur. *History of Asceticism in the Syrian Orient: A Contribution to the History of Culture in the Near East.* 3 vols. Stockholm: Louvain, 1958-1988. The seminal work on Syrian asceticism and spirituality. Contains much material on the life of Simeon as well as his successors. The most useful work for anyone interested in studying the phenomenon of asceticism and the forms it assumed in the Syrian environment.

SEE ALSO: Saint Anthony of Egypt; Diogenes; Saint John the Baptist; Theodoret of Cyrrhus; Theodosius the Great.

RELATED ARTICLES in *Great Events from History: The Ancient World*: c. 286 C.E., Saint Anthony of Egypt Begins Ascetic Life; c. 382-c. 405 C.E., Saint Jerome Creates the Vulgate; 428-431 C.E., Nestorian Controversy; October 8-25, 451 C.E., Council of Chalcedon.

SIMONIDES
Greek lyric poet

Having advanced the quality of Greek lyric poetry through his elegies and epigrams, Simonides brought the dithyramb and Epinician ode to a level of perfection comparable only to that of Pindar.

BORN: c. 556 B.C.E.; Iulis, Island of Ceos (now Kéa), Greece

DIED: c. 467 B.C.E.; Syracuse, Sicily (now in Italy)

AREA OF ACHIEVEMENT: Literature

EARLY LIFE

One of the epigrams of Simonides (si-MON-ih-deez), number 203, reveals both its author's place and year of birth; it is in this poem that he celebrates a victory prize he won at the age of eighty in the archonship of Adeimantus. Other ancient sources confirm these dates, and one can be certain that Simonides lived to the age of eighty-nine or ninety or even longer, if one believes the testimony of Lucian.

Unlike many of the Greek lyric poets, a surprisingly complete genealogy remains extant for Simonides. His father's name was Leoprepes, and his maternal grandfather's name was Hyllichus. His paternal grandfather, also named Simonides, and a grandson known as Simonides Genealogus were poets as well. In addition, the dithyrambic poet Bacchylides was his nephew. It is clear that literary inclinations ran deeply in Simonides' family.

According to traditional accounts, the family of Simonides held some form of hereditary post in connection with Dionysus, and this would account for Simonides' early access to music and poetry festivals held in that god's honor. Supposedly, while still a boy, Simonides instructed the choruses and celebrated the worship of Apollo at Carthaea. Pindar, who became Simonides' bitter rival, criticized both Simonides and Bacchylides for these early involvements, castigating them both as *tous mathontas* ("the teachers"), with the implication that they were pedants.

Sometime after 528 B.C.E., the tyrant Hipparchus invited Simonides to his court at Athens, and it was here that the poet acquired his first major celebrity. The poets Anacreon and Lasus, the teacher of Pindar, were present at Hipparchus's court at this time. Simonides appears to have had only minimal contact with Anacreon. The relationship between Simonides and Lasus appears, however, to have been contentious from the outset. They engaged in a number of poetry contests filled with personal invective, and Lasus's student Pindar would carry on this enmity to the final years of Simonides' life.

Based on encomia attributed to him, Simonides appears to have weathered the political storms that resulted from the murder of Hipparchus and the expulsion of his successor Hippias. With consummate irony, an inscription attributed to Simonides praises the tyrannicide committed by Harmodius and Aristogiton and calls the death of his patron "a great light rising upon the Athenians." This inscription probably appeared at the base of a publicly displayed statue of Harmodius and Aristogiton. The point at which one might consider the career of Simonides to be established, approximately 510 B.C.E., thus coincides with the death or expulsion of those who had helped him achieve recognition.

LIFE'S WORK

The unstable situation in Athens following the overthrow of the Pisistratids probably led Simonides to seek the patronage of the Aleuads and the Scopads in Thessaly. If the assessment of the poet Theocritus is correct, the names of these ruling families escaped oblivion only through the encomia that Simonides wrote in their honor to celebrate the victories of their horses at the sacred games. Most noteworthy among the extant works of Simonides is the substantial fragment of the Epinician ode on the victory of the four-horse chariot of Scopas. Plato preserves and comments on this poem (number 13) in his *Prōtagoras* (399-390 B.C.E.; *Protagoras*, 1804). "Fragments on the Fall of the Scopads" (number 46) and "Antiochus the Aleuad" (number 48) are among Simonides' most familiar works. It is even possible that a threnody on Danae is a poem originally written for one of the Scopads.

Despite this considerable involvement with the tyrants of Thessaly, it seems that Simonides' relationship with them was never an easy one. The region was rugged, and the arts, praised as they might have been in the abstract, always took second place when it came to the granting of subventions. Cicero, in *De oratore* (56 B.C.E.; *The Orations*, 1741-1743), cites the poet Callimachus as his authority for the story that Scopas, having heard Simonides' Castor and Pollux ode, gave the poet only one-half the agreed payment, telling Simonides that he should request the other half from the Tyndarids, because they had received half the praise in Simonides' poem. The tale assumes a somewhat fantastic character at this point. Having received a message that two young men wished to speak to him, Simonides, just humiliated by Scopas's behavior, left the hall to see the two young men supposedly waiting for him at the entrance to the banquet hall. When he left the hall, however, he could find no one, but he heard a sudden crash, and the entire hall fell on Scopas, killing him and the other revelers who had ridiculed Simonides.

It is, of course, hardly likely that this event occurred as Cicero relates it. The tale concludes with the implication that the two young men were the Dioscuri themselves, Castor and Pollux. They made their half of the payment due Simonides, and the larger moral lesson of the tale is that those who treat artists with unkindness incur the wrath of the gods. Presumably, the legend also implies that tyrants such as Scopas fall from power because of their own hubris. Evidently, this was a popular narrative in the ancient world, as variations of it appear in a diverse number of ancient writings, including those of Callimachus, Quintilian, Valerius Maximus, Aristeides, and Phaedrus. Ironically, assuming that the part about Scopas's refusal of full payment is true, only the part of the poem that refers to his family line survives; that which refers to the Dioscuri is no longer extant. Fantastic though the story is on the literal level, it nevertheless reflects the high esteem that cultured people of the day felt for Simonides even as it records the sudden historical demise of odious rulers such as Scopas. In this, it follows the same structure as the myth of Arion, who was saved by a dolphin, or of lbycus, who was avenged by cranes.

In any event, the period of this tale approximates the time of the Persian invasion, and it is at this juncture that Simonides must have returned to Athens, for his poems from this time celebrate Athenian bravery in the Persian Wars.

At this stage in his career, Simonides began to associate himself with the military leaders of Athens, his career again reflecting the prevailing political winds. It was Miltiades who, in 490 B.C.E., commissioned an epigram (number 188) for a statue of Pan, dedicated to commemorate the Battle of Marathon (490 B.C.E.). One measure of the incredible success Simonides had achieved since his first departure from Athens is the fact that, in the following year, he defeated no less a poet than Aeschylus in the contest to produce an elegy that would honor those who had fallen at Marathon (fragment 58).

Simonides' works written during this period include the epigrams inscribed on the tombs of those Spartans who fell at Thermopylae as well as an accompanying encomium (epigrams 150-155, fragment 9). His circle of

acquaintance remained among the powerful, including the statesman Themistocles. An apocryphal story that parallels the Scopas narrative surrounds their acquaintance. In this story, cited by Plutarch in "Themistocles" (in *Bioi paralleloi*, c. 105-115; *Parallel Lives*, 1579), the statesman criticizes the poet for making extraordinary demands on public resources when commissioned to write commemorative verse for public occasions.

The extant works of Simonides reveal that many such commissions must have been forthcoming in the wake of the Persian Wars. The Battle of Plataea (479 B.C.E.) provided the occasion for an elegy (fragment 59) as well as the famous epigram (198) inscribed on the tripod fabricated from Persian spoils and dedicated collectively at Delphi by the victorious Greek cities. Thucydides reported that, because this inscription too completely attributed the Greek victory to the general Pausanias, the Spartans erased Pausanias's name and substituted, as though for an epic catalog, the names of all the Greek states that had taken part in the war. In any event, the zenith of Simonides' career was clearly his victory in the dithyrambic chorus competition held in 477 B.C.E. during the archonship of Adeimantus. Simonides would have been eighty years of age at this time, and this would have been, by his own reporting (epigrams 203-204), his fifty-sixth victory prize.

The final stage in Simonides' career began about 476 B.C.E. with his decision to accept the invitation of the tyrant Hiero to establish himself at Syracuse. Tales of his diplomatic prowess at Hiero's court describe his mediation of a peace between Hiero and Theron of Agrigentum, and the historian Xenophon records a dialogue between Simonides and Hiero on the positive and negative arguments for government by tyranny. Cicero, in *De natura deorum* (44 B.C.E.; *On the Nature of the Gods*, 1683), describes Simonides' evasive answer to Hiero on the nature of divinity.

SIGNIFICANCE

It seems that Simonides' continuing dependence on tyrants arose from practical necessity, but it also seems that he was able consistently to assemble a circle of personal friends who could support his aesthetic needs. The wife of Hiero, for example, protected his interests to some degree by interceding with her husband when necessary; she also became Simonides' interlocutor in philosophic conversations. At one time or another Pindar, Bacchylides, and Aeschylus were in residence at Hiero's court so that Simonides had little want of stimulating conversation, even when opinions differed. In all, Simonides had few wants at any time in his life. Indeed, despite his often uneasy relationship with the Syracusan tyrant and stories of Hiero's reluctance to pay for commissioned works, Simonides received such a generous allowance of daily supplies from the royal household that he often sold what he did not need and thereby provided himself with additional income.

Perhaps Simonides' distaste for opulence also led him to sell his excess supplies. His poems reveal that he held the conservative philosophic view traditional with the Greeks, in which *sophrosyne* ("genuine wisdom"), temperance, and order arose from moderation. Moreover, he reverenced traditional religion, and this appears in his treatment of the ancient myths. The polemical character of his political poems indicates that he considered one function of poetry to be educational and that those most in need of such education were often his patrons. In some sense, his works imply a kind of philosophic stoicism. One should enjoy, as much as possible, the calm reflection that literature offers despite the storms and stresses of the moment.

There is, of course, the other side of the argument. Simonides did live amid and depend on the very excesses his philosophic outlook condemned. If inclined to view these facts cynically, one could accuse him of hypocrisy, but perhaps it is better to consider him a realist. He believed in the power of the arts to change human behavior, and if he used support from unsavory sources in order to achieve the results he desired, he was simply making use of the instruments available to him.

In any event, his reputation among the popular audience never suffered, and his patriotic poems always won immediate general acclaim. These, primarily because they reflected a Panhellenic view rather than the local perspective prevailing at the various locations in which he resided, encouraged a spirit of Greek identity not present in actuality until the Hellenistic period.

—*Robert J. Forman*

FURTHER READING

Bowra, C. M. *Greek Lyric Poetry: From Alcman to Simonides*. New York: Oxford University Press, 2001. Volume of criticism and interpretation includes bibliography and index.

Bowra C. M., and T. F. Higham, eds. *Oxford Book of Greek Verse in Translation*. Rev. ed. Oxford, England: Oxford University Press, 1972. Contains the largest selection of Greek verse in a single source; more than seven hundred items with good notes that cite parallels and explain content.

Hutchinson, G. O. *Greek Lyric Poetry, a Commentary on Selected Larger Pieces: Alcman, Stesichorus, Sappho, Alcaeus, Ibycus, Anacreon, Simonides, Bacchylides, Pindar*. New York: Oxford University Press, 2003. Provides excellent translations and a good selection of poems as well as easy accessibility.

Molyneux, John H. *Simonides: A Historical Study*. Chicago: Bolzchazy Carducci, 1992. Thoroughly examines the documentary evidence available with respect to Simonides and the dating of events and poetry in the various stages of his career.

Skelton, Robin. *Two Hundred Poems from the Greek Anthology*. London: Methuen, 1971. Generally good translations of a variety of poems. The introduction is particularly suitable for general readers new to Greek verse, though there are no notes to the individual poems.

SEE ALSO: Aeschylus; Hipparchus; Lucian; Miltiades; Pindar; Themistocles.

RELATED ARTICLES in *Great Events from History: The Ancient World*: 520-518 B.C.E., Darius the Great Conquers the Indus Valley; September 17, 490 B.C.E., Battle of Marathon; 480-479 B.C.E., Persian Invasion of Greece; 478-448 B.C.E., Athenian Empire Is Created; c. 456/455 B.C.E., Greek Tragedian Aeschylus Dies.

SAINT SIRICIUS
Roman bishop

Siricius was the first pope to exercise his authority throughout the Roman Empire. In the process, he set precedents that were to be used to great effect by his successors.

BORN: c. 335 or 340 C.E.; probably in or near Rome (now in Italy)
DIED: November 26, 399 C.E.; Rome
AREA OF ACHIEVEMENT: Religion

EARLY LIFE

Siricius (sih-RIHSH-ee-uhs), who was born c. 335 or 340, was Roman by birth. Little of his early life is known. He was ordained by Pope Liberius as a lector and later as a deacon. Siricius received the standard Roman clerical education, and he may well have been classically educated also. His entire career was spent in the church of Rome.

On December 11, 384, Liberius's successor, Damasus I, died. By this time, the papacy had become increasingly politicized, and there followed intense campaigning for his office. The candidates included Siricius; Ursinus, who had also been a candidate and was responsible for rioting in the election of 366; and Jerome, who seems to have been Damasus's favorite. Later that month, or perhaps early in January of 385, Siricius was elected and consecrated the next pope; a congratulatory letter from the emperor still survives. Ursinus and his partisans were then officially expelled from Rome. Jerome, perhaps believing that he was no longer welcome, also departed, settling in Palestine with several of his protégés.

LIFE'S WORK

Siricius's activities during his pontificate are known primarily from the letters he sent or received and from the account given in the sixth or seventh century *Liber Pontificalis* (*The Book of the Popes*, 1916), compiled by many writers and written over many years.

Siricius became pope at a time when the bishops of Rome were just beginning to exercise their claimed large-scale ecclesiastical authority. Several of his letters, for example, contain the first of the papal decrees later collected as canon law.

Some of Siricius's letters document his desire to formalize ecclesiastical discipline and practices. He was concerned, for example, that the proper procedures be followed in the choice of bishops and in appointments to other ranks of the clergy. On February 10, 385, he replied to a letter that Bishop Himerius of Tarragona in Spain had written to Damasus. He discussed the proper way to deal with converted Arians and Novatians (they were not to be rebaptized); the proper times for baptism (Easter and Pentecost but not Christmas); and various classes of individuals, such as penitents, incontinent monks and nuns, and married priests. This epistle is the first of the papal decretals. Elsewhere, Siricius decreed that new bishops must have more than one consecrator, that bishops should not ordain clerics for another's church or receive those deposed by another bishop, and that a secular official, even if baptized, could not hold a clerical office.

Decrees such as these exemplify the papal role of overseer of ecclesiastical procedures throughout the Roman Empire. Siricius and his successors portrayed themselves as the inheritors of the authority of Peter. Siricius even claimed to have something of Peter within himself: "We bear the burdens of all who are weighed down, or rather the blessed apostle Peter, who is within us, bears them for us. . . ." Siricius also claimed that the bishop of Rome was the head of the college of all the bishops and that bishops who did not obey him should be excommunicated. He asserted that his decisions, the *statuta sedis apostolicae* (the statutes of the apostolic see), should have the same authority as church councils. Like other bishops, Siricius also appropriated some of the trappings and authority of the secular government. For example, he referred to his decrees with the technical word *rescripta*, the same word used by the emperors for their responses to official queries.

At this time, however, it appeared that the authority of the Roman see was on the wane. In the east, the Council of Constantinople in 381 had assigned the bishop of Constantinople, the capital of the eastern part of the Empire, the same honorary status as the bishop of Rome. Siricius was not even the most influential bishop in Italy: He was overshadowed by Ambrose in Milan. Ambrose not only was a man of greater abilities but also was the bishop of an Imperial capital. Milan, not Rome, was where emperors tended to reside at that time. As a result, Ambrose had the ear of the emperors. Despite his claims, Siricius was able to impose his direct authority only on some of the local, rural bishops, whose elections he oversaw. He is said to have ordained thirty-two bishops "in diverse locations" as well as thirty-one priests and sixty deacons for the city of Rome.

In spite of the limitations on him, Siricius energetically tried to assert the authority of his see. In the east, he attempted to assume some administrative responsibility in Illyria by instructing Archbishop Anysius of Thessalonica to see to it that episcopal ordinations were carried out properly. The pope wished to restrict the influence not only of the see of Constantinople, which also claimed authority over Thessalonica, but also of Ambrose in Milan. Ambrose, however, had anticipated Siricius and already exercised a supervisory role in Illyria. In 381, at the emperor's request, he had assembled a council at Aquileia to investigate irregularities in the Illyrian church. As a result, Siricius made little progress there.

Siricius also belatedly became involved in a schism that had occurred at Antioch, where there were rival claimants to the bishopric. Ambrose in 391 had been instrumental in the summoning of a church council in southern Italy, at Capua, to consider the matter, and the results were forwarded to the East. Although Siricius must have been involved, the extent of his participation is uncertain. Subsequently, according to the writer Severus

Saint Siricius. (Library of Congress)

of Antioch, Siricius wrote to the Antiochenes on his own initiative. He recommended that there should be only one bishop, whose election conformed with the canons of the Council of Nicaea. Shortly thereafter, the Council of Caesarea did in fact recognize the claimant who met Siricius's criteria.

In the north, Siricius became involved in other ecclesiastical controversies. In 386, he wrote to the emperor Magnus Maximus, then resident in Trier, about a priest named Agroecius, whom Siricius accused of having been wrongfully ordained. Maximus's reply survives. Noting that the matter should be dealt with by the Gallic bishops themselves, the emperor answered:

> But as regards Agroecius, whom you claim had wrongly risen to the rank of presbyter, what can I decree more reverently on behalf of our catholic religion than that catholic bishops judge on this very matter? I shall summon a council of those who dwell either in Gaul or in the Five Provinces, so it may judge with them sitting and considering the matter.

Maximus also forwarded to Siricius the results of his investigations into the Priscillianists, whom he referred to as "Manichees." Priscillian and his followers already had appealed to Ambrose and to Siricius's predecessor Damasus and had been rebuffed by both. In 386 they were condemned at a synod at Trier, and Priscillian and several of his supporters were executed; others were sent into exile. This heavy-handed secular interference in ecclesiastical affairs was considered a bad precedent, and Siricius, like Ambrose and Martin of Tours, seems to have denied Communion to those bishops, such as Felix of Trier, who had supported the executions. The resultant "Felician schism" lasted until c. 400. This incident may be behind the curious account in *The Book of the Popes* of Siricius's discovery of Manichaeans in Rome and his exiling of them.

Like many of his successors, Siricius attempted to impose his authority through church councils held in Rome, attended at this time primarily by local bishops. A synod assembled on January 6, 386, dealt with matters of ecclesiastical discipline. A council of 385-386 issued nine canons concerning ecclesiastical discipline, which were sent to the African church on January 6, 386. This council met in Saint Peter's Basilica and is the first known to have met at the Vatican.

Another local concern of Siricius was a problem caused by a certain Jovinian, who, after abandoning his life as a monk, began to teach that ascetic practices such as celibacy and fasting served no useful purpose.

Jovinian even went so far as to claim that Mary, by having children, had ceased to be a virgin. He also asserted that those who had been properly baptized were incapable of sin. Jovinian was denounced to Siricius, who in 390 or 392 assembled a local synod that excommunicated the former monk and eight of his followers. This news was carried to Milan, where Jovinian had fled, but Ambrose assembled another synod and excommunicated him again.

Siricius's papacy also saw the final decline of pagan worship. The emperor Theodosius I, in a series of decrees, formalized Christianity as the only legal religion in the Empire. As a result, this period saw the construction and expansion of the churches and sacred buildings at Rome, often at the expense of pagan temples. The Basilica of Saint Paul on the Via Ostiensis (Ostian Way) was rebuilt during Siricius's papacy in the same general shape it now has and was dedicated in 390. Siricius also rebuilt the Church of Saint Pudentiana. On November 26, 399, Siricius died, and he was buried in the cemetery of Priscilla, at the Basilica of Sylvester, on the Via Salaria. By the seventh century, his tomb was venerated by pilgrims coming to Rome.

SIGNIFICANCE

A man of only middling talents, Siricius was more of an administrator than an innovator. In the realm of ecclesiastical politics, he had to compete with others, such as the bishops of Milan and Constantinople, who were situated in Imperial capitals and who had Imperial support. Nevertheless, Siricius, who had a strong view of the rights and responsibilities of the bishop of Rome, did what he could to strengthen the position of his see. During his tenure, the pope ceased to be merely another bishop and truly began to assume an empire-wide presence.

Siricius established a secure foundation for papal authority on which several of his fifth century successors were to build. His Italian rival Ambrose had died in 397, and with the withdrawal of the Imperial administration to Ravenna, Milanese authority rapidly declined. In the fifth century, Innocent I and Leo I were successful in establishing a papal vicariate in Illyria. Leo, later called "the Great," also was able to gain the support of the Imperial government in his attempts to assert his ecclesiastical hegemony at least in the western part of the Empire.

The last years of the fourth century were a very critical period of Church history. Not only was the Roman Empire beginning to split into eastern and western halves, but also the "barbarian invasions" already had begun in the East, even though they had yet to affect the West. As the influence of the state weakened, the Church assumed greater authority. Even though Siricius could not foresee the fall of the Western Empire later in the fifth century, his attempts to establish the authority of the see of Rome set many precedents for the great power the popes soon were to exercise.

—Ralph W. Mathisen

FURTHER READING

Duchesne, Louis. *Early History of the Christian Church from Its Foundation to the End of the Fifth Century.* Reprint. London: John Murray, 1957-1960. Still one of the best histories of the early Church, placing Siricius's activities in their broader historical context. Based primarily on the original sources.

Duffy, Eamon. *Saints and Sinners: A History of the Popes.* New Haven, Conn.: Yale University Press, 2001. Examines the history of the Roman papacy, from its beginnings nearly two thousand years ago to the reign of Pope John Paul II.

Loomis, Louise Ropes, trans. *The Book of the Popes.* Vol. 3. New York: Octagon, 1965. This volume contains a translation of the biography of Siricius found in *Liber pontificalis,* a compilation that dates back to the sixth or seventh century. It is a mixture of tradition, myth, and solid historical fact.

McBrien, Richard P. *Lives of the Popes: The Pontiffs from Saint Peter to John Paul II.* San Francisco: HarperSanFrancisco, 1999. Profiles all 262 Roman popes to date and includes essays on the papal election process as well as timelines of papal, ecclesiastical, and secular persons and events. Also rates all the popes, from the best to the worst.

MacDonald, J. "Who Instituted the Papal Vicariate of Thessalonica?" *Studia Patristica* 4 (1961): 478-482. A discussion of Siricius's role in the ecclesiastical politics of Illyria in the late fourth century, with references to other, similar studies.

SEE ALSO: Saint Ambrose; Saint Jerome; Saint Peter; Priscillian.

RELATED ARTICLES in *Great Events from History: The Ancient World*: October 28, 312 C.E., Conversion of Constantine to Christianity; 313-395 C.E., Inception of Church-State Problem; 325 C.E., Adoption of the Nicene Creed; November 24, 326-May 11, 330 C.E., Constantinople Is Founded; 380-392 C.E., Theodosius's Edicts Promote Christian Orthodoxy; c. 382-c. 405 C.E., Saint Jerome Creates the Vulgate; 445-453 C.E., Invasions of Attila the Hun.

SOCRATES
Greek philosopher

Socrates was a leader in the intellectual advancement that drew attention to human and social questions (in addition to physical questions) and developed the Socratic method of learning by question and answers.

BORN: c. 470 B.C.E.; Athens, Greece
DIED: 399 B.C.E.; Athens, Greece
AREA OF ACHIEVEMENT: Philosophy

EARLY LIFE

The lives of many philosophers are quite undramatic, yet Socrates (SOK-rah-teez) is a striking exception. First, he wrote no philosophy at all. He walked through the public places of Athens and engaged people of all types in philosophical discussions. In this way, he came to have many followers, especially among the young. Second, he acquired strong enemies, and eventually his enemies had him condemned to death.

Socrates—who was said to have had a broad, flat nose, bulging eyes, and a paunch—was a powerful and eccentric individual. His philosophy is intensely personal. More than any other philosopher, he successfully united his personal character with his professional career. For Socrates, there was ultimately no difference between his private life and his public career.

Socrates was the son of a stonemason (or sculptor) and a midwife. He does not appear to have spent much time in his father's line of work, although it was traditional for sons to do what their fathers did, and Socrates was probably trained in stoneworking. He later claimed that he was following in his mother's footsteps, that he was an intellectual midwife. That is, he said, he assisted other people with the birth of the ideas they carried, while he himself had none. Clearly, he had ideas too; such a statement can be understood as an expression of typical Socratic irony.

Socrates was born, lived, and died in Athens. The only significant amount of time he spent outside the city was during his military service, when he earned a reputation for bravery, steadfastness in battle, and a general toughness of character. While on military campaigns in the northern parts of Greece, he reportedly went barefoot over ice and snow. In Athens, he became known for his unkempt appearance, his moral integrity, his probing questions, his self-control, his ability to outdrink anyone, and his use of questions and dialogue in the pursuit of wisdom.

A friend of Socrates once asked the Delphic oracle—which was believed by the Greeks to speak with the divine authority of Apollo—whether anyone was wiser than Socrates. The answer was that no one was wiser. When Socrates heard this, he was confused. The oracle often spoke in riddles, and Socrates wondered what this saying could mean. He believed that he knew nothing and was not wise at all. He went to those who had a reputation for wisdom—to political leaders, authors, and skilled craftsmen—and questioned them. He found, to his surprise, that they really were not wise, although they thought that they were. He reasoned that because they were no wiser than he (as the oracle had said) but he knew nothing except that he was not wise, then they must know even less. Socrates' conclusion was that while others mistakenly believed that they were wise, his own wisdom consisted in knowing that he was not wise.

LIFE'S WORK

Socrates was a central figure in the revolution in fifth century B.C.E. Greek thought that turned attention away from the physical world (of stars and eclipses) and toward the human world (of the self, the community, the law). It has been said that Socrates brought philosophy down to earth.

Because Socrates wrote nothing himself, the evidence for his views must be somewhat indirect. Even if other sources are useful, scholars generally agree that the early, or Socratic, dialogues of Plato are the most important sources of information about Socrates' philosophy. Himself one of the foremost philosophers in the Western tradition, Plato was a student of Socrates. Moreover, although all the early dialogues were written after the death of Socrates, they were written while many of those who knew him were still alive, and Plato presumably would not paint a false picture of Socrates before the eyes of those who knew him.

The inquiries of Socrates, as represented dramatically in the dialogues of Plato, generally revolve around a particular concept, usually a moral concept. In the dialogue called the *Lachēs* (399-390 B.C.E.; *Laches*, 1804), for example, Socrates inquires into the definition of courage; in the *Euthyphrōn* (399-390 B.C.E.; *Euthyphro*, 1804), he asks what piety is; and in the *Theaetētos* (388-366 B.C.E.; *Theaetetus*, 1804), he examines the nature of knowledge. Often, the dialogues follow a pattern. At first, Socrates' partners in conversation are confident of their knowledge of the subject at hand. Socrates claims to seek enlightenment and asks them seemingly simple questions, such as

"What is courage?" The speaker gives an example to which the concept applies, but Socrates replies that if the item given is only an example, then the speaker should know the larger concept that it represents. He says that it is precisely this relationship between the example and the concept that should be explained. The speaker then considers one definition after another, but Socrates, by a skillful use of questioning, is able to show the speaker that the definitions are unsatisfactory. The speaker often complains that Socrates has robbed him of the confidence he once had. Socrates, although he had been claiming that he only wanted to learn from the speaker, has all the while been orchestrating this very result by means of his questions. The speaker is led to see for himself that he really does not know what he thought he knew. The speaker, thus divested of false notions, is in a position to become a partner of Socrates in the quest for positive knowledge and wisdom. The ancient Greek term for this sort of question-and-answer testing of ideas is *elenchus*.

It is sometimes noted that in the dialogues Socrates refuses to suggest any positive ideas but only questions others and destroys their views (and sometimes their composure). Indeed, that is often the case. However, there are some positive views that Socrates is willing to defend. For example, he defends the thesis that virtue is knowledge and thus that all wrongdoing stems from ignorance, and he claims that it is far more important to care for one's soul than for one's body. These statements require some explanation, however, especially in their English and other non-Greek versions.

Socrates and other Greeks asked, "What is virtue?" The Greek word that is generally translated as "virtue" is *aretē*. Another translation for this term is "excellence." (Virtue is a poor translation if it suggests ideas such as Christian charity, humility, and the like, because Socrates lived prior to Christianity, and the Greeks did not greatly admire charity and humility.) It was Socrates' belief, then, that human excellence consists in knowledge. If a person knew what was the best thing to do, for example, then the person would do it. Some critics have objected that this idea might be true for Socrates, who had great self-control, but that other, more ordinary people might see one course of action as superior to another and yet choose to do that which was not superior. The other side of the coin, according to Socrates, is that if a person has done something wrong, then it must be concluded that the person did not have the knowledge that what was being done was wrong. All wrongdoing, Socrates holds, is really the result of ignorance.

Socrates continually compares questions about hu-

Socrates. (Library of Congress)

man nature, the purpose of life, and the nature of virtue (or excellence) to considerably more down-to-earth and sometimes humble questions. He discusses carpenters, shoemakers, horse trainers, and others. One could say that Socrates' discussions are dominated by a craft analogy. For example, the shoemaker's function is to make shoes, and he fulfills his function well when he makes good shoes. The shoemaker must know what he is doing; otherwise, he would probably produce poor shoes. Similarly, a person must know what his business in life is. "Know thyself," a Greek saying inscribed on the temple walls of Delphi, was a prominent theme of Socrates. He is also credited with saying that for a human being "the unexamined life is not worth living." A person will be an excellent human being only if that person subjects his life to examination and attains self-knowledge. Like excellence in shoemaking, excellence in human life is indeed an achievement, and it follows on training from others and self-discipline from within.

Finally, Socrates believed that the disposition of the soul is more important than the body or any material thing. The word translated as "soul" here is the Greek *psychē*. Other translations might be "inner self" or "mind." It is the inner self that Socrates sees as inhabiting the body, just as a body can be thought of as inhabiting clothes. This *psychē*, or inner self—and not the appetites or passions or demands of the physical body—is what should give direction to one's life.

In 399 Socrates was tried in Athens on two charges: for not worshiping the Athenian gods (and introducing new divinities) and for corrupting the young. The first charge was unfair. It was a standard charge used to persecute threatening individuals, but Socrates had, in fact, been rather faithful in his observance of local religious customs. The only grain of truth in the charge was that he did claim to hear a voice within him—a daimon, or supernatural voice, that warned him not to do certain things. (The voice never encouraged actions but sometimes stopped Socrates when he considered doing or saying something.) Socrates and his fellow Greeks believed in many such divine signs and had little trouble accepting oracles and dreams as bearers of supernatural messages. The inner voice of Socrates did not replace the traditional gods; rather, it was supposed to be an additional source of divine messages.

The second charge was quite serious and, in some respects, plausible. As youths, Alcibiades, Critias, and Charmides had heard Socrates. As men, Alcibiades became a ruthless traitor and opportunist, and Critias and Charmides overthrew Athenian democracy (for a time) with a violent revolution, instituting a bloodthirsty regime. Moreover, Socrates himself had been a vocal critic of democracy.

It could be that this last charge was only a case of guilt by association. Socrates was not responsible for the fact that a few of his students proved troublesome. He certainly did not encourage violent revolution and bloodthirstiness; he stressed argument and discussion. In fact, his criticism of Athenian democracy reflects this very point. He criticized the way Athenian democracy awarded some positions by lot (as potential jurors are selected today) and some by vote. The random lottery method is unreasonable precisely because it is not responsive to argument. In general, Socrates believed that those who know, those who are wise, should rule. Why, he reasoned, should a community leave important social and political decisions in the hands of voters—who may well be ignorant and are likely to be swayed by their own self-interest or by smooth-talking politicians—rather than in the hands of those who have wisdom and knowledge.

At his trial, Socrates was not contrite. He asserted that he would never stop asking his questions, the questions that some Athenians found so bothersome, and refused to accept the idea that he be banished to another place. He would stay in Athens and would remain who and what he was. The jury condemned him to death by drinking hemlock.

While Socrates was being held in prison, but before he was to drink the hemlock, he was visited by a friend who proposed to get him out of prison—bribing the guards if necessary—and to arrange for him to live at some distance beyond the reach of Athenian law. Socrates investigated this option with his usual methods and concluded that there were better arguments in favor of conforming to the legal judgment and drinking the hemlock—which, when the time came, he did.

SIGNIFICANCE

To the philosophers who came after him, Socrates not only left the example of his life but also a new sort of inquiry (that is, social inquiry) and a new way of pursuing that inquiry, namely through the use of the Socratic method of question and answer.

Several schools of philosophers claiming to follow Socrates arose after his death. One of the best known, Cynicism, took up the view that virtue is an inner knowledge that has nothing to do with externals, such as material things or even other people. Diogenes, the most prominent Cynic, rejected conventional values and is said to have lived in a tub. He claimed that the life of the dog ("Cynic" comes from a Greek word that means "like a dog"), free and unfettered by human conventions, was a good model for the natural life. The Cynics invented the concept of the cosmopolitan (citizen of the cosmos or universe) when they claimed allegiance only to the universe at large and not to particular humanly instituted and local political units—such as Athens.

The Cyrenaics, also claiming to follow Socrates, held that inner, subjective experiences were far more important for life than the existence and nature of external objects. From this view, they derived the conclusion that the best life was one that was directed by subjective feelings of pleasure and pain. This school practiced a form of hedonism that was in many respects at odds with Cynicism. The Megarics, another minor Socratic school, practiced the art of refutation, which they modeled after Socrates' destructive criticism of the views of others. In this way, several schools of thought emerged, at variance with one another but all claiming to follow Socrates. One could say that each school followed some strands of thought in Socrates but that no school was able to capture him completely.

That is one reason that Socrates remains a giant in philosophy. It is possible to go back to the stories of his life and practice many times and each time discover some new aspect or line of thought. Moreover, the Socratic method of inquiry can be used by those less wise than the giant himself. Each new generation is enabled by this method to question received opinion, alleged wisdom, and even its own values.

Socrates said that he was a gadfly who stimulated his fellows to think more clearly. This applies both to his fellow citizens in Athens and to his fellow philosophers, or seekers after wisdom. With respect to his fellow citizens, it might be said that Socrates failed, because in the end they turned on him and had him condemned to death. With respect to philosophers who have come after Socrates, however, it could well be said that his mission has proved successful, for he has had a permanent effect on the direction of philosophy, an effect that can never be undone.

—*Stephen Satris*

FURTHER READING

Colaiaco, James A. *Socrates Against Athens: Philosophy on Trial*. New York: Routledge, 2001. Intended to be used alongside Plato's *Apology* and *Crito*. Provides historical and cultural context to the trial.

Guthrie, W. K. C. *Socrates*. Part 2 in *The Fifth-Century Enlightenment*. Vol. 1 in *A History of Greek Philosophy*. New York: Cambridge University Press, 1972. Part of the author's monumental, thorough, and scholarly treatment of Greek life, character, and philosophy.

May, Hope. *On Socrates*. Belmont, Calif.: Wadsworth, 2000. Aims to assist students in understanding Socrates' philosophy and thinking so that they can more fully engage in useful, intelligent class dialogue and improve their understanding of the dialogues.

Plato. *The Last Days of Socrates*. Translated by Hugh Tredennick. New York: Penguin Books, 1993. The translator provides an introduction and notes, but this work is mainly a rendering into English of four of Plato's Socratic dialogues, including Socrates' speech at his trial, his conversation in prison, and his last conversations and death.

Santas, Gerasimos X. *Socrates: Philosophy in Plato's Early Dialogues*. Boston: Routledge and Kegan Paul, 1982. A contribution to the Arguments of the Philosophers series, this volume emphasizes the logical reconstruction of the arguments of Socrates and sometimes uses formal logical symbolism. The book focuses on the Socratic method and Socrates' views on ethics.

Stone, I. F. *The Trial of Socrates*. New York: Anchor Books, 1989. Stone attempts to get behind the scenes at the trial of Socrates. He aims to show that political motivations, largely stemming from Socrates' negative attitude toward democracy and his friendships with those who supported a contrary regime, were powerfully at work in the trial, even though they were not openly acknowledged.

Strathern, Paul. *Socrates in Ninety Minutes*. Chicago: I. R. Dee, 1999. A concise account of Socrates' life and ideas, including selections from his observations, a list of suggested readings, and chronologies that place Socrates within his own age and in the broader history of philosophy.

Vlastos, Gregory, ed. *The Philosophy of Socrates: A Collection of Critical Essays*. Notre Dame, Ind.: University of Notre Dame Press, 1980. A wide-ranging collection of articles by scholars in Socrates' philosophy. Consideration is given to the problem of the reliability of the various ancient sources for Socrates' views, the thesis that virtue is knowledge, and problems associated with the Socratic denial that one can do wrong willingly and knowingly.

SEE ALSO: Alcibiades of Athens; Aristotle; Diogenes; Plato; Xanthippe; Xenophon.

RELATED ARTICLES in *Great Events from History: The Ancient World*: 600-500 B.C.E., Greek Philosophers Formulate Theories of the Cosmos; c. 530 B.C.E., Founding of the Pythagorean Brotherhood; 478-448 B.C.E., Athenian Empire Is Created; 399 B.C.E., Death of Socrates; c. 380 B.C.E., Plato Develops His Theory of Ideas.

SOLOMON
Israeli king (r. c. 961-930 B.C.E.)

Through the application of his famous wisdom and the construction of the Temple, Solomon not only made a major contribution to the Judeo-Christian tradition but also forged the twelve tribes of Israel into a true nation, giving them an identity that would survive succeeding dispersions and persecutions.

BORN: c. 991 B.C.E.; Jerusalem, Israel
DIED: 930 B.C.E.; Jerusalem, Israel
AREAS OF ACHIEVEMENT: Government and politics, religion

EARLY LIFE

Solomon (SAHL-oh-muhn) was the second child born to King David and Bathsheba and the fifth of David's sons. Although the sources are silent about Solomon's childhood, it is known that the prophet Nathan, who had enormous court influence, was his tutor. Accordingly, Solomon would have received a very thorough grounding in Jewish civil and religious teachings. His position at the court was enhanced by his mother, a remarkably intelligent figure with influence over the king.

Although David had promised the throne to Solomon, David's eldest surviving son, Adonijah, harbored the ambition to be king, an ambition that to him seemed perfectly justifiable. His older brothers, Amnon, Absalom, and Chileab, had died, so should not the throne naturally devolve to the next oldest son? In order for him to secure the throne for himself, however, Adonijah needed allies. Through intrigue, he gained the support of his other brothers; of Joab, the commander of the army; and of Abiathar, the high priest in Jerusalem. These were powerful people, but Solomon had an even more potent group backing his claim. These included Zadok, the high priest at Gilbeah, Benaiah, commander of David's mercenaries (David's "Mighty Men," who had fought with him since the king's early days and had never lost a campaign), Nathan, and Bathsheba.

To have any hope of success, Adonijah, then, had to act boldly before Solomon was consecrated king. As David lay on his sickbed, Adonijah, with an escort of fifty men and his supporters, had himself anointed king in the royal gardens at Enrogel. Nathan quickly learned of this and, alarmed, informed Bathsheba. It was vital that David reaffirm his oath concerning Solomon and have him anointed king immediately, or Solomon and his supporters would be killed. Confronted by Nathan and Bathsheba with Adonijah's acts, David ordered Benaiah and the royal troops to escort Solomon on the king's donkey and to have him anointed king by Zadok. When Adonijah and his followers realized that this had occurred, their coup attempt collapsed. His guests scattered, and Adonijah fled to the sanctuary altar and would not leave until Solomon promised not to harm him.

Solomon was now king. Shortly before David died, he advised Solomon on how to deal with his enemies, counseling him to stay true to the Lord's commandments. It was useful advice, for Adonijah quickly tried another tactic. Through Bathsheba, he asked Solomon's permission to marry Abishag, who was a member of David's harem. If this marriage were permitted, it would establish Adonijah's rightful claim to the throne. Solomon reacted swiftly. Adonijah was immediately executed, as was Joab. Abiathar was removed from his priestly office and exiled to Anathoth, fulfilling the prophecy regarding Eli's descendants (1 Sam. 2:27-37). Three years later, Shimei, an opponent whom Solomon had confined to Jerusalem, violated the terms of his punishment and was executed.

LIFE'S WORK

With his throne now secure, Solomon could concentrate on consolidating his kingdom, in order to secure the empire that his father had created. To achieve this end, Solomon initiated a sophisticated program based on three policies: There would be no further territorial conquests for the Israelite empire, he would take advantage of the economic opportunities presented by Israel's strategic location, and he would build the Temple in Jerusalem to provide a unifying political and spiritual focal point for his people.

Although there were no significant foreign threats during his reign, Solomon realized that to attain his goals he needed to secure his borders through a combination of peaceful dealings with his neighbors and a modernized army at home. Accordingly, he launched a bold foreign policy initiative: an alliance with Egypt. After some difficult negotiations, the alliance was confirmed by Solomon's marriage to Pharaoh Siamon's daughter—a clear indication of the importance Egypt gave to the alliance, for Egyptian princesses were rarely given in marriage to foreign potentates. Solomon received the fortified city of Gezer as a dowry after the pharaoh had plundered it. The land route for the transport of goods from Phoenicia to Egypt thus secured was mutually beneficial for Egypt and Israel. The main advantage with which this alliance provided Solomon, however, was that it gave him access to Egypt's building expertise and military technology: chariots, horses, and technical advisers to train the Israelites in their proper use.

Solomon could now proceed to modernize his army. This involved creating a large chariot force of fourteen hundred chariots and twelve thousand horsemen and constructing forts with stables at strategic points around the kingdom. For example, excavations at the thirteen-acre site at Megiddo, which controlled the vital highway running through the Plain of Esdraelon between Egypt and Syria, show that this fortress could house 450 horses and 150 chariots. Similar fortresses were apparently built at Beth-horon, Baalath, Hamath-zobah, and Tadmor.

Solomon also cemented relations with Hiram of Tyre. Tyre was a vital maritime city with colonies in Cyprus, Sicily, Sardinia, and southern Spain. Hemmed in by the Lebanon Mountains, Tyre had to depend on commerce for survival. Solomon needed cedar lumber as well as skilled artisans and architects from Tyre for his building projects; in return, Hiram received food and protection for his city.

Solomon's political program required not only safe borders backed by a military force capable of protecting important trade routes but also a firm revenue base. To meet this need, Solomon divided the nation into twelve districts. The official in charge of each district had to provide the supplies for the central government for one month of the year. The rest of the time, he collected and stored the necessary provisions. The required items for a single day's supply for the king and his court are enumerated in 1 Kings 4:22-23; though the list appears excessive, it is similar to the daily victual lists for other kingdoms in Mesopotamia.

Central to Solomon's overall policy was his building program. He built not only forts and cities but also ports, mines, highways, and shipyards. Solomon is most famous, however, for two major projects completed by the middle of his reign: the construction of the royal palace and of the Temple. These two undertakings played a major role in his plan of consolidation. The palace, which in addition to the king's personal residence included the complex of buildings housing the various governmental offices, took thirteen years to complete. Cedar, gold, ivory, and silver were liberally used; the resulting grandeur was a source of national pride. The building that was the cornerstone of Solomon's political program, however, was the Temple.

The erection of the Temple was the most important event in the Israelites' religious history since they had left the Sinai; accordingly, Solomon must have overseen every detail of construction. With a work force of 150,000 men, the project took seven years. The Bible gives a very detailed description of the finished Temple. Though it was once thought that it was a unique structure in the ancient

Solomon, shown kneeling. (Library of Congress)

world, recent archaeological finds have revealed that the Temple was quite similar to other temples in Mesopotamia.

It is difficult to overstate the deep significance of the Temple for Israel. Moses had prophesied that a kingdom would be created; with the construction of the Temple, divine confirmation of the Davidic throne was established. Thus, Solomon, by the act of building the Temple, firmly cemented his mandate to rule. Further, by placing the ark in the Temple, he focused the religious fervor of his people on the Temple, making Jerusalem their holy city and their national center. Solomon also was able to control the Temple and therefore gained a reputation for piety.

While the Bible says much about the Temple, it gives little space to discussion of the commercial ventures of Solomon. These played a significant part, however, in financing his other programs, and archaeological evidence indicates that they were extensive. Solomon was the middleman in the region's lucrative horse and chariot market. His involvement in and control of the major caravan routes passing through the Negev have been well documented. Excavations at Ezion-geber have shown that Solomon was also very involved in shipping and shipbuilding. His ships carried copper and iron ore (and their related products) dug from his mines throughout the Wadi al-'Araba (biblical Arabah) as far as Yemen and Ethiopia, returning with gold, silver, ivory, and monkeys.

His shrewd commercial activities made Solomon incredibly wealthy. Eager to meet this legendary and successful king, other rulers came to Jerusalem bearing gifts and riches to establish relations with Solomon. The Queen of Sheba may have come to learn his wisdom, but she also wanted to create trade relations with Israel.

Solomon's power and grandeur were believed to have arisen from his exceptional wisdom. The Bible states that immediately after Solomon assumed the throne, the Lord, appearing to him in a dream, granted his request for wisdom and added that he would also receive riches, honor, and long life, as long as he obeyed the Lord's commandments. Eventually, Solomon became world renowned for his sagacity. His decision regarding the two women fighting over the custody of one living child is an example of his judicial wisdom. Because Solomon's reign was a time of peace, literature and scholarship flourished. Much of Israel's history, up to that point preserved orally, was set down in writing during this period. Solomon is credited with the authorship of the Song of Songs, the Book of Proverbs, and Ecclesiastes. While there is some question regarding Solomon's authorship

THE KINGS OF ISRAEL	
Ruler	*Reign* (B.C.E.)
Saul	c. 1020-1000
David	c. 1000-c. 962
Solomon	c. 961-930

of the Song of Songs, there is little doubt that he did write most of Proverbs, and the weight of evidence leans toward him as the author of Ecclesiastes. These works of genius, stamped with the character of Solomon, reveal a deep spiritual insight and have formed a vital part of the Judeo-Christian tradition.

SIGNIFICANCE

The final years of Solomon's reign present an interesting historical problem. Chapter 11 of 1 Kings makes it clear that Solomon, king of Israel, recipient of godly wisdom, vast wealth, and international recognition, ended his reign amid predictions of failure. Indeed, immediately after his death, the kingdom was split into the kingdoms of Israel and Judah. Some of the causes that have been advanced to explain the stresses that finally fractured Solomon's empire include the increasing bureaucratization of government, the excessive taxes needed to support Solomon's programs, the use of Israelites for forced labor, the unequal distribution of wealth, and the Israelites' inability to identify fully with their king's vision of a united Israelite state. According to the biblical interpretation, however, these problems were only symptoms of the disease. The root cause was Solomon's religious apostasy.

Early in his reign Solomon had followed the Lord's commandments, but eventually he fell into disobedience in two important areas. First, he violated the command not to take foreign wives (Deut. 17:17). At the height of his power he reputedly had seven hundred wives and three hundred concubines. The wives were usually taken for diplomatic or political reasons, but concubines were given as sexual gifts that Solomon could have refused but did not. These wives and concubines were his downfall, for in his efforts to please them, Solomon fell into idolatry.

Solomon not only tolerated idolatry but indeed officially recognized it. He gave official sanction for the worship of the fertility goddess Ashtoreth (Astarte) and constructed altars near Jerusalem for the worship of Moloch and Chemosh. During his reign, a valley just outside Jerusalem became known as the site of child sacrifices to

Moloch; its name, Gê Hinnom, in later years was rendered Gehenna, which became a synonym for the word "hell."

Such religious apostasy, then, clearly moved Solomon away from the sound principles of rule that had governed the first half of his reign and induced him to adopt methods that in the eyes of his people undermined the legitimacy of his vision of a permanent, unified state. As a result, Solomon suffered rebellion at home by Jeroboam, son of Nebat, and the loss of various parts of his realm, and the welfare and prosperity of the kingdom would be endangered.

Despite his failings, however, Solomon was a great king. Without his efforts, one of the great achievements of history would have been impossible: that despite unprecedented persecutions, invasions, and sufferings, the Jews would retain their distinct national identity. Furthermore, Solomon's contributions to the Old Testament have proved to be a valuable legacy to countless generations and must be counted as one of the pillars of Western civilization.

—Ronald F. Smith

FURTHER READING

Barker, Kenneth, ed. *The Full Life Study Bible*. Grand Rapids, Mich.: Zondervan, 1990. In this edition, each book is preceded by a detailed introduction, and there are verse-by-verse explanations on each page. There are also indexes, essays, notes, time lines, maps, and charts. For an excellent archaeological supplement, see the *Thompson Chain-Reference Bible*, also published by Zondervan.

Beers, V. Gilbert. *The Nation Divides*. Vol. 12 in *The Book of Life*. Grand Rapids, Mich.: Zondervan, 1980. Beers combines the accounts of 1 Kings and 2 Chronicles to provide a cogent picture of Solomon and his times. Includes excellent photographs and illustrations. The text brings the period and people alive for the reader.

Maly, Eugene H. *The World of David and Solomon*. Englewood Cliffs, N.J.: Prentice-Hall, 1966. Consistently cited by later works, this book makes excellent use of twentieth century archaeological findings and interpretations. The chapter on Solomon provides valuable insights into his political program and commercial activities. Includes bibliographies at the end of each chapter and an index.

Schultz, Samuel J. *The Old Testament Speaks: Old Testament History and Literature*. San Francisco: Harper & Row, 1990. This is an outstanding book in which to begin one's research on Solomon. Makes use of other scholarly works and archaeological revelations to fill in the biblical gaps.

Shah, Tahir. *In Search of King Solomon's Mines*. London: John Murray, 2002. This book takes up the search for King Solomon's astonishing wealth, using as leads the Septuagint, the earliest form of the Bible, as well as geological, geographical, and folkloric sources.

Thieberger, Frederick. *King Solomon*. Oxford: East and West Library, 1947. Remains one of the few books in English that focus exclusively on Solomon. The author did not have the benefit of later archaeological discoveries, but he does depend greatly on the extensive textual research into the Old Testament that was done in Germany in the nineteenth and twentieth centuries. For that alone the book is worthwhile. Includes extensive notes and index.

Torijano, Pablo A. *Solomon the Esoteric King: From King to Magnus, Development of a Tradition*. Boston: Brill, 2002. Examines the esoteric characterization of King Solomon that became popular in some currents of Judaism and Christianity in Late Antiquity.

SEE ALSO: Bathsheba; David; Moses.
RELATED ARTICLES in *Great Events from History: The Ancient World*: c. 10th century B.C.E., Queen of Sheba Legends Arise; c. 1000 B.C.E., Establishment of the United Kingdom of Israel; c. 966 B.C.E., Building of the Temple of Jerusalem; c. 950 B.C.E., Composition of the Book of Genesis; c. 922 B.C.E., Establishment of the Kingdom of Israel.

SOLON
Greek statesman

Through his law code, Solon averted a civil war at Athens and established the political and social foundations for the development of Athenian democracy.

BORN: c. 630 B.C.E.; probably Athens, Greece
DIED: c. 560 B.C.E.; probably Athens, Greece
AREAS OF ACHIEVEMENT: Government and politics, law, literature

EARLY LIFE
The ancient sources include many details about the life of Solon (SOH-luhn) before 594 B.C.E., but most of these are probably romantic inventions about what the life of a great man ought to have been like. The fragments of Solon's poems tell little about his early life. Plutarch, in his biography of Solon (in *Bioi paralleloi*, c. 105-115; *Parallel Lives*, 1579), writes that Solon's mother was the cousin of the mother of Pisistratus, the tyrant of Athens who ruled between 561 and 527 B.C.E. This is one of many probably spurious attempts to link Solon's and Pisistratus's families. There is a stronger argument that Solon's father was Execestides, a member of one of Athens's noblest families. Execestides could trace his ancestry back to Codrus, a semilegendary king of Athens, and even to Poseidon, a wholly legendary god. Plutarch maintains that Execestides exhausted his wealth through lavish gift giving and that Solon traveled widely as a trader to recoup his fortunes, even though there were many Athenians who would have repaid his father's gifts. Another possibility mentioned by Plutarch is that Solon traveled solely to visit foreign lands.

Solon won a reputation as a poet, and several of his works are quoted at length by Plutarch and in the *Athenaiōn politeia* (335-323 B.C.E.; *The Athenian Constitution*, 1812), attributed to Aristotle. Many early Greek statesmen were poets; poetry had an important role in politics, and Plutarch writes that Solon used his verse to catapult himself into political prominence, probably around 610. Plutarch further relates that Solon used a ruse to be put in charge of a war against Megara to win back the island of Salamis. The Athenians were so humiliated by their defeat some years before that they passed a law forbidding anyone even to mention their claim to Salamis. Solon circumvented this restriction by feigning insanity and then publicly reciting poems urging revenge. The Athenians were inspired by this act and soon won the island back. Like many other incidents in Solon's early life, however, this story may be attributing to Solon events that really happened later in the sixth century.

According to a second story, around 600 Solon had the Alcmaeonid family put on trial for the massacre of the followers of Cylon, who staged an unsuccessful coup in Athens in the 630's. The murders had ritually polluted Athens, and Solon supposedly brought in the semilegendary seer Epimenides of Crete to help purify the state. It is quite likely that this event was made up to provide a Solonian precedent for the expulsion of the Alcmaeonids during political strife around 500. A third account links Solon to the possibly fictitious First Sacred War in the 590's, fought for control of the oracle at Delphi.

LIFE'S WORK
Whatever the truth of these stories about political crises, one thing is certain: Around 600, Athens was torn by social unrest. In the words of Aristotle:

> For a long time there was strife between the rich and the poor. For the state was oligarchic in all ways, and the poor, along with their wives and children, were enslaved to the rich. And they were called "clients" and "sixth-parters," for it was at this rate that they worked the fields of the rich. All the land belonged to a few people; and if the poor did not render these dues, they and their children could be sold overseas. And before Solon, all loans were made on the security of the person; but he became the first champion of the people.

Fearing civil war, the Athenian nobles elected Solon chief magistrate (archon) in 594, to draw up new laws to avert the crisis.

Other than Solon's poems, which are often obscure, the earliest source for his laws is Herodotus's *Historiai Herodotou* (c. 424 B.C.E.; *The History*, 1709), which simply mentions that "at the request of his countrymen he had made a code of laws for Athens." Solon's laws were publicly displayed on wooden boards, and it is believed that these boards survived for later writers such as Aristotle to consult. The laws fall into three main groups: economic reforms, political reforms, and other laws.

In an economic reform known as the "shaking off of burdens" (*seisachtheia*), Solon cancelled all debts and forbade enslavement for debt. He said he would try to bring back to Athens all those who had been sold as slaves overseas. He also addressed land tenure, removing from the soil certain markers called *horoi*, which probably stood on mortgaged fields. The meaning of the *horoi* is unclear, but by this act Solon claimed, "I have made free the dark earth, which was enslaved." These reforms led to the disappearance of the serflike statuses of "clients" and "sixth-parters." Solon is also credited with a reform of weights, measures, and coinage, but that is probably a later fabrication (coinage only appeared at Athens c. 550 B.C.E.).

Solon also instituted political reforms. He divided the adult male population into four groups, based on the annual agricultural production of their land. The top class, the "five hundred bushel men" (*pentakosiomedimnoi*), monopolized the highest political offices. The next class was called the *hippeis*, or "knights," who could produce three hundred to five hundred bushels, and the third class was the *zeugitai* ("infantrymen," or perhaps "yoke men"), who could produce two hundred to three hundred bushels. These two groups could hold lesser political offices. Below them were the *thetes* (usually translated as "laborers," although most of these men probably owned some land), who could vote in the assembly and sit in the law courts but not hold office.

It is difficult to uncover the details of other political reforms because of later fabrications. In 403 the Athenians were forced by the Spartans to abandon their democracy and to return to an undefined "ancestral constitution." In the years that followed, various Athenians tried to project their own political programs back onto past statesmen, claiming that their own ideology was taken from the ancestral constitution. Solon was commonly said to have founded the democracy. According to Aristotle, Solon established the Council of Four Hundred to prepare measures to be voted on by the assembly of all citizens and set up the law courts as the central democratic organ. These institutions are uncannily like those of the fourth century B.C.E. and were possibly falsely attributed to Solon by propagandists at that time.

Solon is said to have legislated on all aspects of life, from mourning at funerals to the placing of trees near field boundaries and the digging of wells. While some of the laws attributed to him can be proved to have originated centuries later, the scope of his code reflects the general tendency of early Greek lawgivers to assume responsibility for every dimension of life.

According to his own notes, Solon had enough support to set himself up as a tyrant over Athens, but because of his moderation, he chose not to do so. This moderation made his position difficult after 594: The poor demanded a complete redistribution of land, which he resisted, while the rich believed that he had already relinquished too much power. It is said that he left Athens for ten years

of travel, making the Athenians agree not to tamper with his laws while he was away. Similar stories are attributed to other early Greek lawgivers, however, and this story may be no more than a literary flourish.

SIGNIFICANCE

Solon's moderation probably saved Athens from a self-destructive civil war. The greatness of his achievement was recognized in his status as one of the so-called Seven Sages of early Greece. He did not resolve all Athens' social, economic, and political troubles (unrest continued during the sixth century), but he did lay the foundations on which Athenian greatness was built. By freeing the poor from their serflike status and from the threat of bondage resulting from debt, he provided the basis of a relatively unified citizen body. His time also marked the beginning of one of the great paradoxes of Athenian society: the interdependence of democracy and slavery. Legally unable to reduce fellow Athenians to bondsmen after 594, wealthy men were forced to look elsewhere for labor to work their fields, workshops, and mines and began to import increasing numbers of non-Greeks, mainly from the Black Sea area, as chattel slaves. By the fifth century B.C.E., as much as one quarter of the resident population of Athens may have been slaves completely lacking civil rights.

Solon is one of the most important figures in Greek history, but also one of the most obscure, hidden beneath layers of later fabrications. Almost no detail in his biography is beyond question, but his overall contribution—averting civil war and setting Athens on the path to democratic rule—was a decisive one.

—Ian Morris

FURTHER READING

Aristotle. *Aristotle: "The Athenian Constitution."* Translated by P. J. Rhodes. Harmondsworth, Middlesex, England: Penguin Books, 1984. Fine translation, with excellent introduction and notes, of one of the main sources for Solon's reforms.

Edmonds, John Maywell. *Greek Elegy and Iambus.* Cambridge, Mass.: Harvard University Press, 1993. Parallel edition of the original Greek texts with a fairly literal translation of all the surviving fragments of several early Greek poets' works, including Solon.

Finley, Moses I. *Ancient Slavery and Modern Ideology.* Reprint. Princeton, N.J.: Marcus Wiener, 1998. Brilliant discussion of modern attitudes toward ancient slavery and the logic of slave economies, including an analysis of the relationships between Solon's reforms and the rise of both slavery and the ideology of citizen equality in ancient Athens.

_____. *The Use and Abuse of History*. New York: Penguin, 1987. Contains Finley's lecture "The Ancestral Constitution," which looks at the reinterpretation and invention of Solonian laws in Athens around 400 B.C.E. and compares this practice to similar distortions of past politics in seventeenth century England and early twentieth century United States.

Forrest, William George Grieve. *The Emergence of Greek Democracy: 800-400 B.C.* New York: McGraw-Hill, 1966. Classic, beautifully written, and well-illustrated overview of the rise of democratic institutions in Athens, setting the Solonian agrarian crisis in the context of similar problems in a number of other states in seventh century Greece.

Gallant, T. W. "Agricultural Systems, Land Tenure, and the Reforms of Solon." *Annual of the British School of Archaeology at Athens* 77 (1982): 111-124. A sophisticated discussion of the archaeological data relating to Solon's economic reforms, drawing on comparative anthropological evidence from modern societies facing similar problems of agrarian debt. Includes bibliography.

Hignett, Carl A. *A History of the Athenian Constitution*. New York: Oxford University Press, 1975. A detailed study of constitutional developments. Hignett works within the very critical tradition of nineteenth century German scholarship and offers penetrating discussions of the sources. He is best known for his attempt to date Solon's reforms to the 570's.

Murray, Oswyn. *Early Greece*. Cambridge, Mass.: Harvard University Press, 1993. Highly readable account of Greek history from 800 to 480 B.C.E., combining the literary and archaeological evidence with judicious use of comparative material. Recommended as an introductory text.

Plutarch. *Plutarch: "The Rise and Fall of Athens."* Translated by Ian Scott-Kilvert. Baltimore: Penguin, 1967. Translations of nine of Plutarch's lives, including that of Solon, along with a brief introduction. Solon was of interest to Plutarch mainly as a moral example. His writing includes many clearly fictional elements but has remained popular through the ages for its lively style and content.

SEE ALSO: Cleisthenes of Athens; Draco; Hammurabi; Pisistratus.

RELATED ARTICLES in *Great Events from History: The Ancient World*: 621 or 620 B.C.E., Draco's Code Is Instituted; c. 594-580 B.C.E., Legislation of Solon; 478-448 B.C.E., Athenian Empire Is Created; September, 404-May, 403 B.C.E., Thirty Tyrants Rule Athens for Eight Months; 325-323 B.C.E., Aristotle Isolates Science as a Discipline.

SOPHOCLES
Greek playwright

One of the most important ancient Greek tragedians, Sophocles was an innovative and skilled master of character development and dramatic irony.

BORN: c. 496 B.C.E.; Colonus, near Athens, Greece
DIED: 406 B.C.E.; Athens, Greece
AREA OF ACHIEVEMENT: Literature

EARLY LIFE
The life of Sophocles (SAHF-uh-kleez) is known from a variety of ancient sources but especially from an Alexandrian biography included in the manuscript tradition of his plays. The playwright was born about 496 B.C.E. in Colonus, a suburb of Athens, which Sophocles commemorated in his last play, *Oidipous epi Kolōnōi* (401 B.C.E.; *Oedipus at Colonus*, 1729). His father, Sophilus, was a wealthy industrialist who owned many slaves and operated a prosperous weapons factory. The young Sophocles was given a good education. He won several prizes in school for music and wrestling, and his music teacher, Lamprus, was famous for a sobriety and restraint in composition that would later be noted in the style of his student.

The childhood of Sophocles parallels his city's long conflict with Persia, which began shortly after his birth with Darius the Great's invasion, continued with Darius's defeat at the Battle of Marathon in 490, and climaxed in 480 with Xerxes' capture of Athens and defeat in the sea battle of Salamis. Sophocles was probably too young to have seen action at Salamis, but his family status—as well as his own personal talent and beauty—may account for his selection as a chorus leader in the public celebration that followed Athens's unexpected defeat of the Persian fleet.

Record of Sophocles' dramatic career begins in 468,

when he entered an annual competition at Athens with a group of plays. It is not known if the young Sophocles was competing for the first time in this year, but his victory over the established playwright Aeschylus at this festival must have raised a sensation among the Athenians, especially if, as is recorded, the officiating public servant requested Cimon and nine other generals to replace the judges usually chosen by lot. Sophocles did not compete in the following year, but a papyrus fragment discovered in the twentieth century suggests that in 463 Sophocles was defeated by Aeschylus, who produced his Danaid trilogy.

Sophocles performed in many of his earlier plays, none of which survives. His appearance as the ball-playing heroine in one play and his lyre playing in another are recorded in his ancient biography. Later in his career, Sophocles abandoned such performances, perhaps because his voice was weakening or because the roles of actor and playwright became increasingly specialized in the second half of the fifth century.

LIFE'S WORK

The second half of Sophocles' life was dedicated to public service, both in the theater and in government. In general, the several civic offices held by the mature Sophocles are better documented than are the dates of Sophocles' extant tragedies. The most difficult extant plays to put in a chronology are probably *Aias* (early 440's B.C.E.; *Ajax*, 1729) and *Trachinai* (435-429 B.C.E.; *The Women of Trachis*, 1729), usually placed somewhere between 435 and 429.

In 443 or 442, Sophocles served as a *Hellenotamias*, one of the financial officials in the Delian League of the Athenian Empire. This appointment may have been the result of the great wealth of Sophocles' family. It may also be attributable to the well-known patriotism of Sophocles, who did not follow the example of many contemporary artists, including Aeschylus and Euripides, in leaving Athens for the court of a foreign patron.

In 441 or 440, Sophocles was elected to serve as general along with the great Athenian leader Pericles during the rebellion of Athens's ally Samos. As the ancient *hypothesis*, or introduction, to *Antigonē* (441 B.C.E.; *Antigone*, 1729) says that his election was encouraged by the success of this play, Sophocles' military service is often considered to have been more honorary than practical, but it is almost certain that the playwright traveled with the fleet on the campaign.

In 438, Sophocles was back in Athens, where he defeated Euripides' entry, including *Alkēstis* (438 B.C.E.;

Alcestis, 1781), with an unrecorded group of plays. Sometime in this decade Sophocles may also have produced a group of plays, now lost, although it is doubtful that these plays were connected thematically in the same way that the plays of Aeschylus's *Oresteia* (458 B.C.E.; English translation, 1777) were linked. When Euripides' *Mēdeia* (*Medea*, 1781) was defeated in a competition of 431 by Euphorion, the son of Aeschylus, Sophocles received second place with unknown plays.

Shortly after the beginning of Athens's long conflict with Sparta known as the Peloponnesian War and following the Athenian plague recorded in the histories of Thucydides, Sophocles produced his most famous play, *Oidipous tyrannos* (c. 429 B.C.E.; *Oedipus Tyrannus* 1715) and was voted second place to Philocles, the nephew of Aeschylus. In the following year Sophocles made no production, and around 427 he was probably elected general again, this time with Nicias.

A combination of patriotism and piety may have again motivated Sophocles in 420 to help introduce to Athens the worship of Asclepius, the deified physician and son of Apollo. Sophocles is also known to have composed for Asclepius a paean, or hymn of praise, which survives in fragments. The playwright was also a priest of Halon, a

Sophocles. (Library of Congress)

hero connected ritually with Asclepius, and was honored after his death with Halon's epithet, *dexion*, or "receiver."

Based on comparison with Euripides' *Ēlektra* (413 B.C.E.; *Electra*, 1782), Sophocles' extant play of the same name is variously dated by scholars between 418 and 410, except for 415, when Sophocles made no entry in the dramatic competitions. In the same decade, the octogenarian Sophocles was once again called to public office. In 413 he was one of the ten *probouloi* elected to deal with the crisis caused by the disastrous defeat of the Athenian fleet in Sicily.

In the last years of his life, Sophocles continued to produce plays. The extant *Philoktētēs* (*Philoctetes*, 1729) is known to have won first prize in 409. Three years later, Sophocles apparently again entered the competition, where he displayed a chorus in mourning for the dead Euripides. Sophocles himself died within a few months. He was certainly dead by early 405, when Aristophanes produced *Batrachoi* (*The Frogs*, 1780), in which Sophocles' death is mentioned.

The ancient biographers were not content to accept Sophocles' advanced age as sufficient cause of death. They recorded several more colorful versions, including choking on a grape, overexertion while reciting *Antigone*, and overexcitement after a dramatic victory. At the time of the dramatist's death, Spartan garrisons were in control of the road to Decelea, where the family burial plot was located, and the family had to seek special permission from the Spartan general Lysander to complete the funeral.

Like many of his contemporaries, Sophocles appears to have had two families. He had one son, Iophon, by a lawful wife, Nicostrata, and another son, Ariston, by a Sicyonian *hetaira*, or mistress, named Theoris. Iophon followed his father into the theater, where he even competed with Sophocles at least once. In *The Frogs*, Aristophanes suggests that Iophon was often helped in his career by his more famous father, but that may be an example of comic exaggeration. Of Ariston, all that is known is that he produced a son named Sophocles, who was favored by his grandfather; Ariston produced his grandfather's last play, *Oedipus at Colonus*, in 401 and won first prize.

Iophon brought a suit of senility against his elderly father, perhaps because of the attentions shown to a cherished, but illegitimate, grandson. At the trial, Sophocles is said to have told the jury, "If I am Sophocles, I am not insane; if I am insane, I am not Sophocles" and to have proven his sanity to the jury by reciting lines from his current work, perhaps *Oedipus at Colonus*.

In his long life Sophocles was associated with many of the great men of fifth century B.C.E. Athens. His political sentiments are difficult to verify because of strong links with both the pro-Spartan and aristocratic Cimon, who may have assured Sophocles his first dramatic victory in 468, and with the democratic champion Pericles, with whom Sophocles served as general in the early 440's. Other members of Sophocles' circle of friends included Polygnotus, an outstanding painter who produced a famous portrait of the dramatist holding a lyre; Archelaus of Miletus, the philosopher and teacher of Socrates; the dramatist Ion of Chios, whose home Sophocles is said to have visited during the Samian Revolt; and the historian Herodotus of Halicarnassus. With some of these men, Sophocles may have formed the *thiasos*, or religious guild in honor of the Muses, which is mentioned in his ancient biography.

SIGNIFICANCE

To the ancients, Sophocles' career as civil servant, as priest of Asclepius, and, especially, as dramatist at the festival in honor of the god Dionysus, proved he was a man of great patriotism and piety, although some modern scholars have tried to find a different, more questioning Sophocles in the extant plays. Certainly this man called by his ancient biographer *philathenaiotatos*, or "a very great lover of Athens," exhibited throughout his life a high level of personal involvement in his beloved city.

During his career, Sophocles is known to have written more than 120 plays, always produced in groups of three tragedies plus one satyr play. Sophocles, therefore, competed dramatically at least thirty times, perhaps every other year during the course of his career. If his ancient biography is correct that he won first prize twenty times, second prize many times, and third prize never, then Sophocles may have won first prize in two-thirds of the competitions he entered—a great testimony to his contemporary popularity.

There is some evidence that Sophocles was interested in literary theory. Besides his book, now known as "On the Chorus," which does not survive, Sophocles' analysis of his own dramatic style is recorded in Plutarch's *Bioi paralleloi* (c. 105-115 C.E.; *Parallel Lives*, 1579). Here Sophocles suggests that there were three stages in his work. The first was influenced by "the majesty and pomp of Aeschylus." The second displayed an originality in the creation of painful effects. In the third he had characters speak in languages appropriate to their personalities. Because the date of this statement is unknown and because so few of Sophocles' plays survive, it is not possible to follow these stages in Sophocles' seven extant plays.

Traditionally, in addition to abandoning the practice of a playwright acting in his own plays, Sophocles may have introduced several important innovations to the theater. He is said to have increased the size of the tragic chorus from twelve to fifteen members and to have added a third actor, scenery, and other dramatic paraphernalia. Sophocles received particularly high commendation in Aristotle's *De poetica* (c. 334-323 B.C.E.; *Poetics*, 1705), in which *Oedipus Tyrannus* was praised for displaying the Aristotelian ideal of tragic plot and character. In the modern world Sophocles has become known for his masterful and dramatic development of character and irony.

—*Thomas J. Sienkewicz*

FURTHER READING

Edinger, Edwin F., and Sheila Dickman Zarrow, eds. *The Psyche on Stage: Individuation Motifs in Shakespeare and Sophocles*. Toronto: Inner City Books, 2001. The third and final section is titled "*Oedipus Rex:* Mythology and the Tragic Hero." Includes bibliography and index.

Knox, Bernard MacGregor Walker. *Oedipus at Thebes: Sophocles' Greatest Hero and His Time*. New Haven, Conn.: Yale University Press, 1998. Looks at Sophocles' *Oedipus Tyrannus* in the context of Athens in the fifth century B.C.E. Includes preface and a list of suggested readings.

Lefkowitz, Mary. *The Lives of the Greek Poets*. Baltimore: The Johns Hopkins University Press, 1981. A translation and discussion of the Alexandrian biography of Sophocles are included in this book, which also includes a bibliography.

Lesky, Albin. *Greek Tragedy*. New York: Barnes and Noble Books, 1965. A scholarly introduction to Aeschylus's dramaturgy, with a brief summary of his life. A bibliography is included.

_____. *A History of Greek Literature*. Indianapolis: Hackett, 1996. Sophocles' place in the literature of ancient Greece can be traced in this standard history, which includes biographical evidence and a bibliography.

Scodel, Ruth. *Sophocles*. Boston: Twayne Publishers, 1984. A good introduction written for the general reader, this book includes a chronological chart and a select annotated bibliography.

Webster, T. B. L. *An Introduction to Sophocles*. London: Methuen, 1969. An excellent and carefully documented life of Sophocles can be found in the first chapter of this standard study.

SEE ALSO: Aeschylus; Aristotle; Cimon; Euripides; Herodotus; Polygnotus.

RELATED ARTICLES in *Great Events from History: The Ancient World*: 520-518 B.C.E., Darius the Great Conquers the Indus Valley; September 17, 490 B.C.E., Battle of Marathon; 480-479 B.C.E., Persian Invasion of Greece; May, 431-September, 404 B.C.E., Peloponnesian War.

SOPHONISBA OF NUMIDIA
Numidian queen and Carthaginian patriot

Through her marriage to the Numidian king Syphax, Sophonisba secured an important alliance between Numidia and Carthage against the Romans in the years 205-203 B.C.E.

BORN: Date unknown; Carthage, North Africa (now in Tunisia)

DIED: c. 203 B.C.E.; near Campi Magni (now Souk el Kremis, Tunisia) or Cirta (now Constantine, Algeria)

ALSO KNOWN AS: Sophoniba; Çafonbaal (Punic, "She whom Baal has protected"); Saphanba‘al

AREA OF ACHIEVEMENT: Government and politics

EARLY LIFE

The story of Sophonisba (saw-fon-IHZ-bah) is inextricably entwined with the story of the great conflict between Rome and Carthage known as the Second Punic War (218-202 B.C.E.). In tracing her life one must also trace a part of the history of this war as well as variations in the details of her life given in the primary sources, the works of Polybius, Diodorus Siculus, Livy, Appian, and Dio Cassius. In 218 the Carthaginian general Hannibal led an invasion force from Spain into Italy, where he inflicted a series of devastating military defeats on the Romans. Meanwhile, Roman forces contested Carthaginian dominance in Spain. One of the Carthaginian commanders in Spain (214-206 B.C.E.) was Hasdrubal (d. 202), son of Gisco and the father of Sophonisba. The sources are unanimous in describing Sophonisba as young, beautiful, educated in literature and music, and exceptionally charming. Her desirability coupled with her deep devotion to Carthage made her an important foreign relations asset.

The Berber tribes who occupied the region of north Africa west of Carthage called Numidia (northeast Algeria) were of strategic importance in the deadly struggle between the two Imperial powers, able to offer a huge supply of manpower, especially cavalry, to whichever side could gain their alliance. The preeminent Numidian king at this time was Syphax (d. 201), who ruled a confederacy of tribes known as the Masaesylii. In 213 Syphax made war on the Carthaginians and entered into relations with the Roman commanders in Spain. The Carthaginians made an alliance with Gala, the leader of a second important confederacy of Numidian tribes. Gala's son Masinissa (c. 238-148 B.C.E.) won a large-scale battle against Syphax in Africa and then went to Spain as an ally of Hasdrubal (212-206 B.C.E.). Masinissa was young, handsome, noble, educated in Carthage, and an outstanding military asset. Accordingly, Hasdrubal attempted to seal their alliance by offering him Sophonisba's hand in marriage.

LIFE'S WORK

In 206 when Scipio Africanus (d. 184) dealt a crushing blow to Hasdrubal's forces, effectively ending the war in Spain, Masinissa secretly went over to the Romans and returned to Africa. Apparently, his betrothal to Sophonisba was not sufficient to secure his loyalty in the absence of military success. Now Gala died and Masinissa was defeated by Syphax and forced to go into hiding with a small guerrilla force. Thus, when Scipio's advance force landed in Africa in 205, Syphax was the man the Carthaginians had to talk to in order to ensure that the resources of Numidia would be on their side in the coming war in Africa. To this end, Hasdrubal now offered Sophonisba to the elderly Syphax. Sophonisba must have been of marrying age by now, for she was immediately summoned from Carthage, and the ceremony was performed. Along with the marriage came a treaty with Carthage, and the king was even persuaded to send messengers to Scipio in Sicily warning him not to make the crossing to Africa. Thus, when the Romans crossed in force to Africa in 204 they were joined only by Masinissa and his small rebel force, while, thanks to Sophonisba, the Carthaginians enjoyed the support of Syphax and his large Numidian army.

Finding no success at first, Scipio spent the winter of 204-203 in negotiations with the opposing armies, which were all camped in the vicinity of Utica (Utique). Specifically, he hoped that Syphax's love for Sophonisba would weaken over time and with it his loyalty to Carthage. However, the king remained as rigid in his commitment to Carthage as he was, reportedly, in his passion for his bride. Nevertheless, the prolonged peace negotiations gave the inventive Roman commander the opportunity to gather intelligence that he exploited in a successful scheme to set the enemy camps on fire and inflict massive casualties in the ensuing confusion. Following this costly defeat, the Carthaginian assembly considered suing for peace but, under the influence of Hasdrubal and the Hannibalic faction, decided to gather new forces and continue fighting. Syphax wavered but, according to a fragment of Polybius's work, was persuaded to keep fighting by two things: the arrival of a force of Spanish mercenaries and the now-desperate imprecations of the "young girl," Sophonisba.

Within a few days Hasdrubal and Syphax had joined forces but were again defeated by Scipio and forced to flee. Masinissa soon arrived in Numidia along with a Roman force under Gaius Laelius, where the Maesylians made Masinissa their king. Syphax, defiant to the end, gathered a huge army of inexperienced recruits that was routed by Masinissa and Laelius. Syphax himself was captured alive while recklessly riding out in front of his troops in an effort to shame them into fighting. Masinissa, with his cavalry, pressed on ahead to take Syphax's capital, Cirta, while Laelius followed behind with the infantry. The people of Cirta refused to capitulate until they were presented with the spectacle of their king in chains.

When Masinissa entered the palace at Cirta he met Sophonisba. Most sources write of the meeting as a reunion, since they had met before, presumably when Masinissa was being educated in Carthage, and Sophonisba had originally been betrothed to him. Livy, however, records that the two had never met, a variation that allows him to emphasize Sophonisba's almost supernatural powers of persuasion as well as the irrational and passionate nature of the Numidians. Masinissa barred the exits to the city to prevent anyone from escaping and was entering the forecourt of the palace when he was accosted by Sophonisba. She clutched his knees and begged that he punish her in any way he saw fit, so long as he not give her to the Romans as a prize of war. She preferred to suffer punishment at the hands of a fellow African rather than foreigners. Clutching his hand, her tone changed from pleading to alluring, and Masinissa, "a victor caught by love of his captive," gave her his word that he would honor her wish. All accounts agree that he married her that very day. However, it would not prove so easy to deprive the Romans of their spoils.

The sources agree that Syphax was dragged in chains before Scipio and required to account for his violation of the treaty. The fallen monarch gave an answer that both ameliorated his own guilt and struck a blow against his rival in love and politics. He claimed that it was Sophonisba's irresistible ability to beguile men, combined with her diehard patriotism, that had caused him to break faith with the Romans and had brought about his downfall. His only consolation, he claimed, was that she would likewise bring destruction on his enemy Masinissa, because she would never be loyal to Rome. This made a profound impression on Scipio, and when Laelius and Masinissa returned from Numidia he demanded that the king give up the woman on the grounds that she belonged to the Romans by right of conquest. From this point the ancient accounts again diverge.

Appian has it that Sophonisba was still in Cirta. Riding on ahead of the Roman party sent with him to fetch her, Masinissa brought the girl poison, giving her the option to drink or be taken captive. After he had ridden away, Sophonisba chose a glorious death by drinking the poison. Dio, Livy, and Diodorus presume that Sophonisba was present in Scipio's camp. Dio has Masinissa take the poison to his wife, who drinks willingly and dies content in her freedom from Rome. Livy's account is the most vivid version: In it, Masinissa retreats to his tent, from which groans and sighs emanate as he deliberates. Finally, he sends a slave to his new bride's tent bearing the poison and a message claiming that this is the only way he can keep his promise to her. Sophonisba accepts the poison as a wedding gift and sends a message back to her husband: "I would have died better, if my wedding had not been at my funeral."

It has been noticed that in all of these narratives, Sophonisba's death appears to have been influenced by accounts of the death of Cleopatra VII, who also chose a noble death over capture by the Romans in 30 B.C.E. Both figures used their charms to undermine the loyalty of those whose duty was to serve Rome, both committed suicide to avoid the humiliation of being paraded in a Roman triumph, and both revealed their strength by accepting death willingly. Diodorus alone preserves a separate and certainly earlier tradition: Masinissa himself went to Sophonisba's tent and *forced* her to drink the poison. This account, which is to be preferred, reveals Sophonisba's deep loyalty to Carthage. Masinissa knew that the intractable Sophonisba's death was necessary if he was to remain secure and prosperous in his position as sole monarch of Numidia under Rome's Imperial patronage. In the end, the historical Sophonisba emerges as a noble, beautiful, and persuasive young woman whose loyalty to her people was stronger than her love of life.

SIGNIFICANCE

As politically important as Sophonisba may have been in the final years of the Second Punic War, her lasting significance has been as a literary character. In book 5 of Petrarch's unfinished Latin epic *Africa* (1396; English translation, 1977), she appears as a dangerous seductress who suffers defeat but robs Rome of joy in victory.

Later Giovanni Boccaccio emphasized the greatness of her death in his Latin *De mulieribus claris* (c. 1361-1375; *Concerning Famous Women*, 1943). Petrarch's depiction also influenced the first neoclassical tragedy, G. G. Trissino's *Sofonisba* (1515, performed in 1556), which in turn influenced sixteenth and seventeenth century tragedies in French, German, and English. Among these is the *Sophonisba* of Nathaniel Lee (first performed in 1675 and incorporating theater music by Henry Purcell in 1695), which presents Sophonisba and Masinissa as lovers doomed by the tyrannical oppression of Rome. John Marston's *The Wonder of Women: Or, The Tragedie of Sophonisba* (1606) diverged from this tradition, Sophonisba appearing as a model of stoic virtues in a world of chaotic passion and self-interest.

In the eighteenth century, the story was used to elucidate political ideas in works by James Thomson and parodied by Henry Fielding in his *Tom Thumb: A Tragedy* (1730). Voltaire's *Sophonisbe* was published in 1770. The theme also provided material for numerous operas, including works by C. W. Gluck (1744), B. Galuppi (1753), and T. Traetta (1762). In the nineteenth century Sophonisba took off in Germany, with no less than eleven tragedies bearing the heroine's name in the period 1808-1868.

From at least the sixteenth century Sophonisba has also been a popular subject in the pictorial arts, inspiring, for instance, major frescoes by the Veronese school painters G. A. Fasolo and G. B. Zelotti and the Venetian master G. B. Tiepolo, as well as important paintings by G. F. Caroto, M. Preti, and G. Pittoni.

—*James M. Quillin*

FURTHER READING

Dorey, T. A. "Masinissa, Syphax, and Sophoniba." *Proceedings of the African Classical Associations* 4, nos. 1/2 (1961). Brief but pithy historical comparison of the evidence on Sophonisba and the conflict between Syphax and Masinissa.

Haley, S. P. "Livy's Sophonisba." *Classica et Mediaevalia* 40 (1989): 171-181. A useful article highlighting the story's literary function in Livy as part of the moralizing agenda of his work. Also demonstrates the influence of accounts of Cleopatra's death on the accounts of Livy, Appian, and Cassius Dio.

Trissino, Giovanni G., and Pietro Aretino. *Trissino's "Sophonisba" and Aretino's "Horatia."* Edited by Michael Lettieri and Michael Ukas. Lewiston, N.Y.: Edwin Mellen Press, 1997. Translations of the two Italian Renaissance tragedies.

SEE ALSO: Cleopatra VII; Hannibal; Masinissa; Scipio Africanus.

RELATED ARTICLES in *Great Events from History: The Ancient World*: c. 300-c. 100 B.C.E., Berber Kingdoms of Numidia and Mauretania Flourish; 264-225 B.C.E., First Punic War; 218-201 B.C.E., Second Punic War; 202 B.C.E., Battle of Zama.

SOSIGENES
Egyptian or Greek astronomer

Sosigenes advised Julius Caesar on the development of the Julian calendar, which, with only slight modification, is still in use today.

BORN: c. 90 B.C.E.; place unknown
DIED: First century B.C.E.; place unknown
ALSO KNOWN AS: Sosigenes of Alexandria
AREAS OF ACHIEVEMENT: Astronomy, mathematics

EARLY LIFE

Virtually nothing is known about the life of Sosigenes (soh-SIHJ-eh-neez), an Alexandrian astronomer and mathematician who flourished in the first century B.C.E. Even the place of his birth is disputed. Some sources maintain that he was born in the Roman-controlled Egyptian city of Alexandria; others say that he came to Alexandria from Greece.

Since the ancient days of the pharaohs, Egypt had been besieged by foreign powers. Its people had been conquered by the Assyrians, then the Persians, and finally, in the fourth century B.C.E., by Alexander the Great, for whom the city of Alexandria is named. In the years just before Sosigenes' life, the Ptolemies, who ruled following the collapse of Alexander's realm, had made Alexandria into a world center for commerce and cultural development. Trading vessels arrived from lands as diverse as Britain and China. Science and art flourished. The city had several parks, a university, and a library with 750,000 volumes. It became a mecca for philosophers and scientists, producing such great scholars as Hipparchus, Ptolemy, Euclid, and Hero of Alexandria. It is no wonder, then, that Sosigenes ended up in Alexandria.

Interest in Alexandria was not limited, however, to intellectuals. Foreign leaders continued to see Egypt as a prize. During the century before the birth of Sosigenes, the ruler of Macedon, Philip V, conspired with the king of Syria to conquer and divide Egypt. This move attracted the attention of the great and expanding Roman Empire. Though the Romans were embroiled in the Second Punic War with Carthage, they managed to send an army east to punish the two rulers. After both countries had been conquered, the Romans set up a protectorate in Egypt. Thus, the Alexandria of Sosigenes' time was under profound Roman influence. The Romans did not, however, interfere with the growth and development of the city, which now held more than half a million inhabitants—more than Rome itself.

After ending a bloody civil war in 48 B.C.E., Julius Caesar rested a year in Egypt before returning to Rome to become dictator. Perhaps it was during this visit that he became acquainted with Sosigenes, who by that time had come to be considered an authority on astronomy. One of Caesar's goals, as ruler of the Roman Empire, was to make radical reforms to the calendar in use at that time. The Roman republican calendar was so out of synchronization with the natural year that the vernal equinox, the springtime event when the sun's path crosses the celestial equator, had occurred months later, in early summer. Caesar called on Sosigenes to advise him on this matter and to develop a new calendar to replace the problem-ridden one of old.

LIFE'S WORK

The earliest calendars were lunar in that they followed the phases of the moon. Each month was designed to chart a complete cycle of lunar phases, from new moon to full moon and then on to the next new moon. Lunar calendars were easy to use, especially because they were tied to readily observable astronomical events. Their main problem was that they were independent of important phenomena on Earth. Most notably, they did not follow the seasons. The progression of seasons follows the solar year, the time it takes Earth to complete a revolution around the sun, roughly 365 days. The phases of the moon, however, follow the synodic period (the time between successive new moons) of about thirty days. A lunar year might consist of twelve such cycles (twelve months), or 360 days. The five-day discrepancy meant that seasonal events (monsoons, river flooding, snowfall, and the like) would drift five days forward each lunar year. Thus, by the time a calendar had been in use for two decades, the cold-weather days of winter would occur three months later, in the "spring" months.

Agricultural concerns dictated a need for a calendar that would closely follow the seasons. Farmers would then know when to plant and when to harvest. Such seasonal, or solar, calendars would be based on the observed motion of the sun through the constellations of the sky (ancient astronomers did not realize that this drifting of the sun through the constellations was actually caused by the revolution of Earth). The difficulty with solar calendars was that they did not follow the phases of the moon—which were important for setting the dates of religious feasts and events.

It seemed impossible to reconcile these two demands. Egypt, at the time of Sosigenes, had no fewer than three calendars in use. The oldest calendar was actually a very good one, by modern standards. It was a lunar calendar but was corrected each year by the rising of the star Sirius (the day on which a given star rises at the moment the sun sets is a seasonal year constant). Thus, this calendar—lunar, but regulated by the solar year—accurately predicted seasonal events such as the flooding of the Nile River, an important consideration for farmers.

Governmental and administrative personnel, however, wanted something more: a calendar that would not vary from year to year, so that they could set predictable dates for treaties and business contracts. Therefore, a true seasonal calendar was developed. It consisted of twelve months, each of which contained exactly thirty numbered days. As this worked out to 360 days, the Egyptians then intercalated five extra days at the end of each year. At first, this calendar worked as well as the lunar calendar. As the decades passed, however, the seasonal calendar grew out of synchronization with the seasons. Farmers went back to the Sirius-regulated lunar calendar. Astronomers tried to determine the reasons for the failure of the seasonal calendar. They developed a new lunar calendar. This one, instead of being corrected by Sirius, was tied to the civil year (the seasonal calendar). This helped the religious leaders set their events but was of no use to the farmers, who continued to use the old calendar.

Sosigenes realized that the reason for the problems that developed in the civil calendar was that the solar year did not consist of exactly 365 days. His calculations revealed that the year actually consisted of 365.25 days, so that any calendar based on a 365-day year would lose a whole day every four years. He decided that the way to solve the problem would be to intercalate an extra day every fourth year. Though the Egyptian government did not listen to his proposals, his work attracted the attention of Julius Caesar, who sought his advice on amending the Roman calendar.

This task proved quite a challenge, for the calendar of the Roman Republic was in a shambles. It consisted of twelve months, each having either twenty-nine or thirty-one days except for February, which had twenty-eight. The year ended up having 355 days, far too few to be in step with the seasons. A Roman administrative office known as the Pontifices was assigned to intercalate whole months when necessary to reconcile the calendar with the seasons. Sosigenes must have seen this solution as a rather messy one—and it was not made any better by the actual practice of the Pontifices. It seems that these officials chose to add extra months not as needed by the solar year but instead to increase the time in office of their favorite politicians. As a result, when Sosigenes took the job, the Roman calendar was several months off the solar year.

Sosigenes' task was twofold. First, he had to correct the current year, 46 B.C.E., so that it would align itself with the seasons. Second, he was to develop a new calendar that would keep synchronization with the solar year. A fixed system of intercalation would also be helpful, to prevent the Pontifices from changing the calendar according to their whims. Sosigenes accomplished the first task by intercalating a full ninety days into the year 46, making that year have 445 days. Then he designed a new calendar, which was to start on the first of January in 45 B.C.E. For this calendar, which came to be called the Julian calendar after Caesar, Sosigenes used his knowledge of the problems with the Egyptian calendars. He made each standard year consist of 365 days, with each of the twelve Roman months having either thirty or thirty-one days, except for February, which he left at twenty-eight days. In order to keep the calendar in precise synchronization with the solar year, he required that every fourth year an extra day should be intercalated in February.

This calendar, with its extremely simple and fixed method for intercalation, should have finally ended all the confusion and discrepancies caused by the old calendar and the meddling Pontifices. Sosigenes and Caesar seemed to have considered everything in their new calendar. They even prescribed that the intercalary day, the *punctum temporis*, should be inserted between the twenty-third and the twenty-fourth of February (Roman custom for adding days in the past) and that persons born on the intercalary day would, for legal purposes, be considered to have been born on the twenty-fourth.

Unfortunately, both men completely overestimated the capabilities of an ignorant bureaucracy. The Pontifices managed to misinterpret the command to add the extra day every fourth year. They counted the year in which they added the day as the first year of the cycle and thus managed to insert the extra day every three years. Julius Caesar was assassinated in 44 B.C.E., and Sosigenes had no authority over the Pontifices. It was not until 8 B.C.E. that Augustus remedied the problem and enforced the correct observance of the Julian calendar. It is probable, however, that Sosigenes did not live to see this accomplished.

SIGNIFICANCE

The Julian calendar that Sosigenes developed has survived to the present time. The names of a few months have been changed, and the extra day is now inserted at the end of February rather than after the twenty-third. Still, the basic structure of the calendar has changed little through the centuries. In fact, the only significant difference between the modern calendar and the Julian one has to do with how often the extra day is intercalated. For the most part, the four-year rule is still followed; the years of 366 days are referred to as leap years. After several centuries of using the Julian calendar, however, it was noticed that the seasonal events were again out of synchronization with the dates. This problem was traced to Sosigenes' figure of 365.25 for the length of the year. Advances in astronomy were able to determine the number more precisely, finding it to be 365.24219 days. Sosigenes was only off by eleven minutes per year, but over the centuries this error propagated into several days. It was finally corrected in 1582 by Pope Gregory XIII, who omitted ten days from the calendar that year to bring the dates back into alignment with the vernal equinox. Then he instituted the policy of making centurial years (1600, 1700, 1800, and so on) common years instead of leap years, unless they were evenly divisible by four hundred. Thus, 1900 was not a leap year, but 2000 was.

Besides his achievement with the Julian calendar, little is known of Sosigenes. The few bits of available information are intriguing. It is known that he wrote three treatises on astronomy. One of them, on "revolving spheres," was likely a primary source for Pliny the Elder's chapters on the sky in the second book of his massive *Naturalis historia* (77 C.E.; *The Historie of the World*, 1601; better known as *Natural History*). Unfortunately, none of Sosigenes' texts is extant. All that has survived are a few isolated fragments. One of these fragments indicates that Sosigenes believed that the planet Mercury revolved about the sun—a truly remarkable insight. Hipparchus, the great Alexandrian astronomer who lived before Sosigenes, maintained that all celestial objects revolve about Earth, and Ptolemy, the great Alexandrian astronomer who lived after Sosigenes, developed a model of the solar system based on Hipparchus's data and ideas. Sosigenes' view was ignored. It would be some fourteen centuries before anyone would advance such a notion again.

—*Greg Tomko-Pavia*

FURTHER READING

Duncan, David Ewing. *Calendar: Humanity's Epic Struggle to Determine a True and Accurate Year*. New York: Avon Books, 1999. A sweeping history of calendars, including Caesar's scrapping of the Roman system in favor of one based on Alexandrian science. More Eurocentric than Richards's book.

Michels, Agnes Kirsopp. *The Calendar of the Roman Republic*. Princeton, N.J.: Princeton University Press, 1967. The best work available on the pre-Julian calendar. It includes a discussion of the peculiarities of the Roman enumeration of dates, which continued into the Julian calendar of Sosigenes.

Mommsen, Theodor. *The History of Rome*. Translated by William P. Dickson. 4 vols. New York: Charles Scribner's Sons, 1887. This work gives the political background for the calendar reform of Julius Caesar and Sosigenes.

Packer, George. *Our Calendar*. Williamsport, Pa.: Fred R. Miller Blank Book Co., 1892. This work describes the Julian calendar and Pope Gregory's reform. Though out of date, the book is useful for anyone who seeks a mathematical examination of the calendar.

Philip, Alexander. *The Calendar: Its History, Structure, and Improvement*. Cambridge, England: Cambridge University Press, 1921. The best overarching discussion of Sosigenes' work with the Julian calendar. It explains, in accessible terms, both the astronomical and the anthropological concerns that influenced the development of the modern calendar.

Pliny the Elder. *Natural History*. Translated by John Bostock. London: Henry G. Bohn, 1855. Has extensive annotations; one of the most useful translations of Pliny's great work. In the second book, Pliny writes of Sosigenes' work on the planet Mercury. He discusses the calendar reform in his eighteenth book.

Richards, E. G. *Mapping Time: The Calendar and Its History*. New York: Oxford University Press, 2000. A history of the development of calendars worldwide, more global in perspective than Duncan's book.

Steel, Duncan. *Marking Time: The Epic Quest to Invent the Perfect Calendar*. New York: John Wiley, 2000.

From the Sumerians to the present day, astronomer Steel traces the history of the calendar as it paralleled the growth of civilization.

SEE ALSO: Augustus; Julius Caesar; Hipparchus; Pliny the Elder; Ptolemy.

RELATED ARTICLES in *Great Events from History: The Ancient World*: c. 275 B.C.E., Greeks Advance Hellenistic Astronomy; 46 B.C.E., Establishment of the Julian Calendar.

SPARTACUS
Roman rebellion leader

A gladiator of great courage and capacity for leadership, Spartacus was the main leader of the largest and most violent slave insurrection in the history of Roman civilization.

BORN: Late second century B.C.E.; Thrace (now in Bulgaria)
DIED: 71 B.C.E.; Lucania (now in Italy)
AREA OF ACHIEVEMENT: War and conquest

EARLY LIFE

There is little reliable information about the early life of Spartacus (SPAHR-tah-kuhs). He grew up in Thrace, then an independent region in which various ethnic tribes were struggling against the imperialistic ambitions of the Roman Republic. For a short period, Spartacus served as a Roman soldier, but he deserted and apparently joined a group of brigands. Captured by the Romans, he was condemned to a life of slavery, a common fate of criminals, prisoners of war, and any rebels who opposed Roman hegemony. A skillful and experienced fighter, Spartacus was purchased by Lentulus Batiates, the owner of a large school of gladiators in the city of Capua, about 130 miles south of Rome on the Appian Way.

In training to become a gladiator (from the Latin word *gladius*, which means "sword"), Spartacus was entering a profession in which he would be required to fight to the death in either public arenas or private homes. These violent exhibitions had originated at Roman funerals, because many Romans believed that those who died in combat would serve as armed attendants in the afterlife. By the time of Spartacus, gladiatorial shows had long been a popular form of entertainment, and many of the larger contests would feature approximately three hundred pairs of combatants. Only a small minority of Ro-

mans expressed any concerns about the way that crowds of thousands enjoyed the savage combats. Even Cicero, a sensitive moral philosopher, believed that the shows were socially useful as long as only convicted criminals killed one another.

Although a few men voluntarily chose to become gladiators for financial reasons, the vast majority, like Spartacus, were forced into the deadly work as a form of punishment. Not surprisingly, the gladiatorial schools had to maintain constant vigilance to prevent rebellion or escape. Plutarch's *Bioi paralleloi* (c. 105-115 C.E.; *Parallel Lives*, 1579) reports that Batiates' school in Capua had an especially bad reputation for its cruelty. Before Spartacus, there had been sporadic cases of gladiatorial uprisings in southern Italy, and the island of Sicily had experienced two large slave revolts in 136-132 B.C.E. and 104-100 B.C.E.

LIFE'S WORK

In 73 B.C.E. Spartacus, along with two hundred other gladiators, mostly of Thracian and Celtic background, attempted an escape from Batiates' school, and seventy-eight, including Spartacus, succeeded. Contrary to several historical novels and a popular film, there is no documentary evidence that Spartacus ever had any idealistic vision of abolishing the institutions of slavery or gladiatorial contests. Rather, it appears that his first goal was to regain freedom for himself and his associates and to return to his home in Thrace. The historical sources also suggest that Spartacus had not entirely given up the ways of the brigand and that he wanted to steal as much wealth as he could from the Romans. Although the Romans considered Spartacus as nothing more than a ruthless criminal, Plutarch later described him as "a man not only of high spirit and valiant, but in understanding, also, and in gentleness superior to his condition."

At first, the fugitives were armed with only kitchen knives, but they had the good fortune of capturing wagons that transported gladiatorial arms. After leaving Capua, the escapees selected Spartacus as their main leader, and they also chose two Gauls, Crixus and Oenomaus, as lieutenant commanders. In desperation, the group sought refuge on Mount Vesuvius, but Roman officials soon learned of their location. One of the praetors, Clodius Glaber, pursued them with a small contingent of well-armed soldiers, and the soldiers soon blockaded the accessible parts of the mountain. The rebels, however, managed to descend a steep cliff by holding onto wild vines, and they were then able to rout the Romans with a surprise attack from the rear. Shortly thereafter, the rebels also defeated small detachments of soldiers commanded by two other praetors, L. Cossinius and Publius Varinius, and Spartacus captured Varinius's horse. With each victory, the rebels captured valuable weapons that could be used in future confrontations.

As word of the initial successes of the rebellion spread, the rebels were soon joined by numerous slaves and landless laborers from the *latifundia* (large estates) located in the countryside of southern Italy. Eventually, the rebellion grew into a large army that included between 70,000 and 120,000 men, many accompanied by their wives and children. Plutarch, who is not always reliable in such details, wrote that Spartacus acquired a wife, but Appian, a more critical Roman historian of the second century C.E., did not provide this information.

The rebels bitterly disagreed about the best course of action. Spartacus reportedly recognized that the Romans would soon muster a large army against them and that their wisest decision would be to march north out of Italy and return to their various homelands. Crixus and several others, however, pointed out the financial advantages of plundering the estates of southern Italy, and the majority of the rebels agreed with this second option. During the winter of 73-72, therefore, there was widespread devastation throughout the south.

The Roman senate, faced with insurgents in Itruria and Spain, was slow to realize the seriousness of the slave rebellion, but it finally commissioned the two Roman consuls of that year, Publius Cornelius Lentulus and L. Gellius Publicola, to pursue Spartacus with four legions (about sixteen thousand soldiers). In late 73, the Roman army managed to defeat Crixus's forces near Mount Garganus. Following the death of Crixus, Spartacus decided to head north according to his original plan; he got as far as Cisalpine Gaul, where he encountered an army led by the proconsul and governor of the region, Cassius Onginus. After Spartacus defeated Cassius's troops in the Battle of Mutina, he and his horde could have escaped north by way of the Alps but instead decided to head south, probably because the rebels preferred to continue seeking the spoils of plunder. Spartacus defeated the forces of the two consuls in Picenum, and the rebels then faced little opposition as they pillaged the southwestern provinces of Lucania and Bruttium. Spartacus entered into negotiations with some Cilician pirates for transportation to Sicily, a province known for

Spartacus. (Library of Congress)

its large numbers of discontented slaves and landless laborers.

In Rome, the senate relieved the two disgraced consuls of their military command, and it conferred Marcus Licinius Crassus with the special command of proconsular imperium. Crassus, who had served as one of Lucius Cornelius Sulla's commanders, was an extremely wealthy landowner with unbridled ambition. When one of his legates, Mummius, disobeyed orders, Crassus restored order by reviving the punishment of decimation (the execution of every tenth man). Crassus then led ten well-armed legions into Bruttium. Meanwhile, the pirates failed to keep their promise to provide Spartacus with transportation to Sicily. During the winter of 72-71, Crassus was able to construct a fortified blockade around the bulk of Spartacus's forces in the toe of Italy between the towns of Scyllaeum and Rhegium.

Spartacus's forces managed to escape the blockade in their third attempt, and the rebels went on to win two battles against relatively small Roman units in Lucania. In resources and training, however, Spartacus's rebels were no match for the ten legions that Crassus commanded, and they were decisively defeated when they directly encountered these legions in a battle that was probably near the head of the Silarus River. Spartacus was killed in this battle, and his body was never identified. Crassus pursued the surviving rebels as they fled northward, and he ordered the crucifixion of six thousand rebels along the Appian Way from Capua to Rome. The rotting bodies were left hanging for months as a warning to anyone who might contemplate rebellion. Returning to the city of Rome, Crassus was allowed to wear a crown of laurel and received enthusiastic ovations.

During the six months that Crassus was pursuing Spartacus, the senate had decided (probably without Crassus's knowledge) that it was necessary to recall Pompey the Great's large army from Spain. Pompey arrived in northern Italy about the time that Crassus was concluding his successful campaign, and Pompey's army encountered and annihilated about five thousand fugitives who were trying to escape to their homes. Based on this minor engagement, Pompey sent the senate a message claiming that it was he who had finally put the slave rebellion to an end. The competing claims of Pompey and Crassus intensified the animosity that the two men had for one another.

SIGNIFICANCE

Spartacus fought courageously to end the grievous oppression he and his colleagues experienced, but the historical sources do not suggest that the Thracian gladiator wished to end slavery or reform the nature of Roman society. He and his followers did manage, nevertheless, to keep the Roman army at bay for almost two years, a great achievement for that period. Despite claims to the contrary, there is no evidence that Spartacus's rebellion had any humanitarian influence on the ways that the Romans treated their slaves and gladiators. From the Roman perspective, the rebellion demonstrated the need for harsh punishment as an example to dissidents, and the Romans apparently responded to the rebellion by increasing security over both slaves and gladiators. Although it would be five hundred years before the Western Roman Empire would come to an end, the Romans would never again have to contend with a major slave insurrection.

Spartacus has often served as a mythical symbol of a courageous revolutionary, fighting for social justice and the abolition of slavery. For example, during World War I, socialist militants in Germany took the name "the Spartacist League." At the time of the American Civil Rights movement, in contrast, there was a tendency to portray Spartacus as an enlightened reformer who opposed violence and oppression. Ironically, the limited nature of the ancient sources describing the persona of Spartacus has added to the protean character of the legend.

—*Thomas Tandy Lewis*

FURTHER READING

Bradley, Keith. *Slavery and Rebellion in the Roman World*. Bloomington: Indiana University Press, 1998. An interesting and scholarly account of the three large slave rebellions during the late Republic, with chapter 5 devoted to Spartacus. The detailed notes provide the most extensive documentation available. The best single account.

Fast, Howard. *Spartacus*. New York: Dell, 1979. Although much of the material is fictional, this is probably the most readable and interesting of the novels devoted to Spartacus.

Grant, Michael. *Gladiators*. New York: Delacorte Press, 1995. A concise, fascinating, and scholarly treatment of the Roman gladiators, including a short analysis of the Spartacus insurrection. Highly recommended.

Gruen, Erich. *The Last Generation of the Roman Republic*. Berkeley: University of California Press, 1995. A fascinating account of the politics and leaders of the time, with pages 20-22 giving a good summary of Spartacus's revolt.

Harris, W. V. "Spartacus." In *Past Imperfect: History According to the Movies*, edited by Mark Carnes. New York: Henry Holt, 1995. A most interesting analysis of both the historical and fictional aspects of Stanley Kubrick's popular 1960 film.

Yavetz, Zvi. *Slaves and Slavery in Ancient Rome.* New Brunswick, N.J.: Transaction Books, 1988. In addition to general information about Roman slavery,

pages 83-112 contain translations of almost all the ancient sources dealing with Spartacus, including the writings of Cicero, Appian, Plutarch, and Florus.

SEE ALSO: Cicero; Pompey the Great.

RELATED ARTICLES in *Great Events from History: The Ancient World*: 73-71 B.C.E., Spartacus Leads Slave Revolt; 51 B.C.E., Cicero Writes *De republica*.

SAINT STEPHEN
Samarian theologian

By means of his innovative theology, his courage, and his martyrdom, Stephen helped to universalize the early Christian Church by encouraging its expansion beyond the doctrinal confines of Judaism and the political confines of Jerusalem.

BORN: c. 5 C.E.; Samaria (now in Palestine)
DIED: c. 36 C.E.; Jerusalem (now in Israel)
ALSO KNOWN AS: Stephanos
AREA OF ACHIEVEMENT: Religion

EARLY LIFE

All that is known of the life and thought of Saint Stephen (STEE-vehn) is derived from chapters 6 and 7 of Saint Luke's Acts of the Apostles. The former chapter tells of Stephen's rise to prominence in the early Christian Church, his election to the protodiaconate (the earliest board of deacons), his theological disputations with the Jews, and his arrest on trumped-up charges of heresy. The latter chapter relates his impassioned and provocative defense before the Sanhedrin, a group of Jewish leaders who became so enraged at his ideas that they stopped his defense short and dragged him away for execution. His death at their hands made Stephen the first in a long line of Christian martyrs.

From his Greek name and the ecclesiastical task to which he was elected, on one hand, and from his idiosyncratic theological beliefs, on the other, scholars believe that Stephen was both a Hellenist and a Samaritan prior to his conversion to Christianity. A Hellenist was not only a Greek-speaking Jew but also one who was influenced by Greek (Hellenic) culture and open to Greek ideas. That is, Hellenists had a broader outlook and a more liberal education than did those Jews whose persuasion and practice were more separatistic. That Stephen was a Hellenist is deduced from the fact that his parents gave him a Greek name (Stephanos—the other

deacons also had Greek names) and that the segment of Christian people he was elected to serve were Hellenists themselves.

The Samaritans, those who came from Samaria (in central Palestine, between Judaea and Galilee), were known for their unorthodox religious beliefs: Though they were Jews, they deplored the temple worship conducted at Jerusalem. They opted instead for worshiping at Mount Gerizim in Samaria. Besides an intense messianism, they also had their own version of the five books of Moses, a version known as the Samaritan Pentateuch, which, though it is largely the same as the standard Pentateuch, differs in a few significant ways. Stephen's recorded defense not only contains a Samaritan-like attack on the Temple and a presentation of Jesus as Messiah; it also contains allusions to numbers and events found only in the Samaritan Pentateuch. This remarkable fact underscores not only his Samaritanism but also the historical reliability of Saint Luke's account, which in all other places employs a different version of the Old Testament Scriptures. Thus, Stephen appears to have been a Hellenist and a Samaritan.

Because no record of Stephen's conversion to Christianity has been preserved, scholars are unable to date it precisely or to identify its causes. A late and unreliable ecclesiastical tradition, however, numbers Stephen among the seventy evangelists sent out by Jesus.

LIFE'S WORK

According to the second chapter of Acts, the early Church experienced periods of remarkable growth. On the day of Pentecost alone, for example, approximately three thousand people were converted to the faith. As time passed, the Church's numbers continued to swell. While desirable, this growth brought with it some knotty organizational problems, among them the problem of how the

Saint Stephen. (Library of Congress)

small band of twelve Apostles could oversee the distribution of the Church's extensive program of charitable outreach while still devoting sufficient time and energy to teaching and preaching the Christian message, a task they considered their supreme assignment.

Especially needy among the early converts were the Hellenistic widows. Financially, they were in a precarious position. With no husbands as breadwinners and faced with a language barrier that seems to have prevented them from making their needs known to the Church, they faced severe difficulties. In an effort, therefore, to free the Apostles for teaching and preaching, and in order to relieve the Hellenistic widows' distress, the Church appointed "seven men of honest report, full of the Holy Spirit and wisdom," among whom Stephen, as the subse-

quent biblical narrative shows, was most prominent.

From Luke's account, it is clear that Stephen did not restrict himself to the duties attached to the care of the poor. Stephen was an impressive theological debater, one who carried his Christian message into the Hellenistic synagogues in and around Jerusalem, one whom his opponents found difficult to gainsay.

Added to his Hellenism and his Samaritanism, his Christianity aroused the ire of the established Jewish leaders. His theological adversaries, bested in argument and distressed at what they deemed his unconscionable heresies, resorted to arousing opposition to him by distorting his teachings. They raised charges against him that they not only exaggerated but also corroborated with what Luke calls "false witnesses." By prearrangement, these false witnesses testified before the Sanhedrin to Stephen's "heresies." He was accused (like Jesus before him) of advocating the destruction of the Temple and of the overthrow of the Jewish law. The former idea they extrapolated from his Samaritanism and the latter from his Christianity. That is, like the Samaritans, he opposed worship in the Jerusalem Temple, and like Saint Paul after him (who now, as Saul, was in charge of the proceedings against Stephen), he was opposed to trying to achieve salvation through observance of the Jewish ceremonial laws.

Stephen's defense before the Sanhedrin was not so much a defense of himself as a defense of the early Christian message and a counterattack against his accusers and judges. He spoke against the Temple and the system of sacrifices followed there by maintaining that, because God was not confined to buildings made by human hands, the true worship of God was not a temple-based function. Furthermore, by condemning Jesus to death, Stephen asserted, the Jews of his day had merely acted in accord with the spiritual failures of their ancestors, who had also resisted the revelation of God. In his view, the will of God had been made known by means of the prophets, and the prophets had been killed by their own people. The fate of the Messiah, whose coming the prophets had predicted, was no different: He, too, suffered at the hands of his own people. Thus, Stephen's defense chastised the Jews for what he believed to be their spiritual intransigence and wickedness. They did not grow closer to God or obey him, even though they had the spiritual light to do so.

Quite predictably, such a speech served only to enrage his judges. In the midst of the ensuing turmoil, the council bypassed the normal procedures for passing a sentence. As they began to converge on him, Stephen offended his opponents even more by declaring that he saw, at that very moment, the heavens opened up and Christ, as if to welcome Stephen or to assist him, standing at the right of his Father. To Stephen's accusers, this was rank blasphemy. He was dragged unceremoniously out of the chambers to a place now known as Stephen's Gate, where he was stoned to death. Remarkably, in the midst of this torture, he knelt to pray aloud for his executioners. This startling sight, many believe, was the catalyst behind the conversion of Saul, soon to be the Apostle Paul, perhaps the greatest theologian and missionary of the apostolic era. As Saint Augustine later wrote, "If Stephen had not prayed, the Church would not have had Paul."

As is the case with many other notable ancient Christians, pious but unhistorical legends grew up around Saint Stephen's memory. The apocryphal apocalypse known as "The Revelation of St. Stephen" is unquestionably false and bears no genuine connection to the first Christian martyr, either by its content or by its authorship. This book purports to be a narrative of Saint Stephen's reappearance after his death; it was popular among Manichaean heretics and survives only in garbled segments. The discovery of Stephen's alleged relics occurred early in the fifth century.

SIGNIFICANCE

Saint Stephen's not inconsiderable influence can be summarized under four important headings. First, he was the Paul before Paul. His personal conviction and courage in the face of death and his unique combination of Samaritanism and Hellenism in a dynamic system of Christian belief undoubtedly influenced the zealous Pharisee Saul of Tarsus in his pilgrimage toward a new identity as Saint Paul the Apostle. Second, Stephen's death was the immediate impetus behind the Church's leaving its nest in Jerusalem and spreading itself and its message, as Luke writes, from Jerusalem, to Judaea, to Samaria, and to "the uttermost parts of the earth." Third, Stephen's defense was the basis of an effective strategy of theological defense, one that seems to have been employed in various segments of the early Church. Fourth, Saint Stephen has served as a stimulus to piety. Christians in all ages have been strengthened by his courage and spirituality. The Roman Catholic Church celebrates the feast of Saint Stephen on December 26.

—Michael E. Bauman

FURTHER READING

Barnard, L. W. *Studies in the Apostolic Fathers and Their Background.* New York: Schocken Books, 1966. Chapter 6, "St. Stephen and Early Alexandrian Christianity," is a technical examination of Stephen's theology and his influence on one segment of the early Church. The extensive bibliography is of use primarily for biblical and theological specialists.

Bruce, F. F. *Peter, Stephen, James, and John: Studies in Non-Pauline Christianity.* Grand Rapids, Mich.: Wm. B. Eerdmans, 1980. Chapter 2, "Stephen and the Other Hellenists," is a well-balanced and well-documented account of the theology of Saint Stephen, especially as it is seen in the context of Jewish Hellenism. Apart from the biblical account itself, this chapter is perhaps the best and most easily accessible introduction to the man, his life, his beliefs, and his theological tradition.

Bunson, Matthew, Margaret Bunson, Stephen Bunson, and Timothy M. Dolan. *Our Sunday Visitor's Encyclopedia of Saints.* Rev. ed. Huntington, Ind.: Our Sunday Visitor, 2003. Encyclopedia is arranged alphabetically by saint's name. Most entries contain biographical information and feast day. Includes twelve appendices, glossary, calendar of feast days, and index. Illustrated.

Kilgallen, John. *The Stephen Speech: A Literary and Redactional Study of Acts 7, 2-53.* Rome: Biblical Institute Press, 1976. An extensive treatment of Stephen's defense before the Sanhedrin, this book is both thorough and demanding. Though specialists will benefit from its detailed analysis (and will be able to detect its weaknesses), the beginning student will quickly be overwhelmed. Includes unannotated bibliography.

Munck, Johannes. *The Acts of the Apostles.* Garden City, N.Y.: Doubleday and Co., 1967. Appendix 5, "Stephen's Samaritan Background," notes thirteen reasons scholars identify him as a Samaritan. It also explains how the presence of these Samaritanisms in the Stephen account underscores Luke's historical reliability and clarifies Luke's use of sources.

Rufus, Anneli. *Magnificent Corpses: Searching Through Europe for St. Peter's Heart, St. Stephen's Hand, and Other Saints' Relics.* New York: Marlowe, 1999. A charmingly grotesque guide to the saintly relics of Europe. Saint Stephen's alleged hand was discovered in the fifth century.

Schmithals, Walter. *Paul and James.* Translated by Dorothea M. Barton. Naperville, Ill.: Alec R. Allenson, 1965. Chapter 1, "Stephen," is an idiosyncratic examination, from a theologically radical point of view, of the beliefs and practices of the Jewish Hellenists. Schmithals's bibliographical citations are quite numerous and technical, and almost all reflect a theologically liberal stance.

Watson, Alan. *The Trial of Stephen: The First Christian Martyr.* Macon: University of Georgia Press, 1996. This volume discusses both Jewish law and Roman law. Includes bibliography and index.

SEE ALSO: Jesus; Saint Paul.
RELATED ARTICLES in *Great Events from History: The Ancient World*: c. 966 B.C.E., Building of the Temple of Jerusalem; c. 6 B.C.E., Birth of Jesus Christ; c. 30 C.E., Condemnation and Crucifixion of Jesus Christ; c. 30 C.E., Preaching of the Pentecostal Gospel; January-March, 55 or 56 C.E., Paul Writes His Letter to the Romans.

FLAVIUS STILICHO
Roman general

For a period of some fifteen years, Stilicho acted as the generalissimo of the Western Roman Empire (and as much of the Eastern as he was allowed), repeatedly staving off barbarian assaults on Rome and on Constantinople.

BORN: c. 365 C.E.; location unknown
DIED: August 22, 408 C.E.; Ravenna (now in Italy)
AREA OF ACHIEVEMENT: War and conquest

EARLY LIFE
The father of Flavius Stilicho (FLAY-vee-uhs STIHL-ih-koh) was a Vandal cavalry officer, his mother a Roman. The Vandals at that time did not have the reputation for ferocity and destruction that they were later to acquire. Nevertheless, it was never forgotten that Stilicho was a "half barbarian." He was never fully trusted by all of his Greek or Roman civilian masters and colleagues. He began his career as a protector, a member of the personal bodyguard of Theodosius the Great (c. 347-395). Following the normal course of events, he was presumably made a tribune, attached to the Roman Imperial general staff, and sent on a diplomatic mission to Persia in 383 or 384.

Shortly after this, an unexpected event took place that catapulted Stilicho firmly into prominence: He married Serena, niece and adopted daughter of Theodosius. It has been suggested that this was a love match instigated by Serena, and though historians have been reluctant to accept this sentimental theory, no more plausible one exists. Stilicho was at that time quite undistinguished, had no important relatives, and was not a likely candidate for a diplomatic marriage. The poet Claudian (c. 370-c. 404), who is admittedly biased in favor of Stilicho, wrote that his hero surpassed the demigods of antiquity in strength and size; wherever he walked, the crowds

moved out of his way. These observations must have some basis in fact and could explain how the young officer attracted the attention of the emperor's niece.

Naturally, after the marriage promotion was rapid. Stilicho was made "count of the stable," then chief of the Imperial Guard. He seems to have held independent command in a campaign in Thrace in 392, and from 393 onward he was called *magister utriusque militiae*, meaning "master of both arms," that is, of the infantry and the cavalry. While still firmly under the wing of Theodosius, he had become the approximate equivalent of field marshal, a position from which many earlier and later generals aimed at seizing Imperial power. In 394, he marched with Theodosius from the eastern half of the Empire toward Italy, to put down the revolt and usurpation of the general Arbogast and his puppet emperor Eugenius, installed in 388. In early September, 394, the armies of the Eastern and Western Roman Empires clashed at the Battle of the Frigidus River, and after initial failure the easterners won a decisive victory. Both enemy leaders were killed. Theodosius marched toward Rome but died soon after, on January 17, 395. He left Stilicho in charge of both the eastern army and the pardoned survivors of the western army. Remote from the control of Constantinople and related by marriage to the Imperial house, Stilicho was in a position of unusual power.

LIFE'S WORK
One certainty about Stilicho's life is that he did not use his power to the full. He never made himself emperor, though no one was in any position to stop him. For the rest of his life he claimed that Theodosius had appointed him guardian of both his sons, Arcadius (c. 377-408), the eastern emperor, and Flavius Honorius (384-423), declared emperor of the West by his father in 393. It seems

that no one else was present at Theodosius's deathbed, so naturally people have been skeptical about Stilicho's mandate. The fact remains that Stilicho always obeyed Imperial orders, even foolish ones, and made no move against his former master's children (although Honorius, at least, was widely disliked).

Stilicho was left, however, with at least two problems. One was the division now accepted between the two halves of the Empire. This was dangerous and unproductive, as neither side was willing to help the other very much, and there was always danger of civil war—for example, over the border province of Illyricum, the modern Balkans. However, neither half of the Empire could afford civil war, for both were hard-pressed by constant waves of barbarian invasion. In the immediate background of all events of Stilicho's life was the disaster of Adrianople, August 9, 378, when the Goths, driven on by fear of the Huns and fury at Imperial treachery, had totally destroyed the main Imperial army and killed Emperor Valens (c. 328-378). The barbarians then knew that the Romans were not invincible.

Stilicho had a difficult hand to play. In 395 he led his joint army out of Italy toward Constantinople, again threatened by the Goths under Alaric (c. 370-410). No decisive battle was fought, but the Goths withdrew, and Stilicho—with apparently characteristic selflessness—released the eastern army from his control, returning it to Arcadius. The following year, he led an expedition into the west, along the Rhine River, possibly as a demonstration of force and to "show the flag." In 397 Alaric once again moved into Greece, and Stilicho launched an amphibious expedition against him. Alaric was beaten, but in some unexplained way—there were accusations of treachery—he managed to make an orderly withdrawal. Stilicho then returned to Italy, only to find that North Africa had broken its allegiance to Rome and cut off the corn supply on which Rome depended—and had done so under the pretense of authorization from the eastern emperor, whom Stilicho had just rescued. Stilicho dispatched a naval force against North Africa, which rapidly brought the province back under control.

In late 401, Alaric invaded Italy; it was the start of a series of barbarian invasions that led to the sack of Rome in 410. Alaric and Stilicho fought a bloody battle at Pollenza in 402, which both sides claimed as a victory. Alaric withdrew, however, and was decisively beaten at Verona in the summer of the same year. Once again Alaric escaped; Claudian ascribes this to the poor discipline of Stilicho's auxiliaries. In early 406, a later invasion under one Radagaisus, with a mixed force of barbarians, was defeated outside Florence, with very few Roman casualties (Claudian claims that there were none at all).

Matters soon worsened: The Rhine froze, Gaul was invaded by hordes of German barbarians (Vandals, Burgundians, Swabians, and Alans), the army of Britain elected the usurper Constantine as emperor and launched a cross-Channel invasion, Alaric reinvaded, and, in 408, Arcadius died, leaving the eastern Empire insecure and leaderless. Stilicho could hardly have known which way to turn. What he did, in fact, was to leave Gaul to itself; he persuaded the bitterly resentful Roman senate to buy off Alaric with four thousand pounds of gold and dispatch him against Constantine. Stilicho then prepared to leave for Constantinople to take charge of Arcadius's seven-year-old heir, Theodosius II (401-450). These measures were too pragmatic for the Roman people to accept; thus, Stilicho was accused of treachery. Honorius launched a massacre of his supporters: His Hunnish bodyguard was murdered, and Stilicho was arrested at Ravenna. It is clear that even then Stilicho could have fought and probably cracked Honorius's stronghold on power. Instead, he obeyed orders and surrendered to execution.

SIGNIFICANCE

Flavius Stilicho has long proved a puzzle to historians. It is very tempting to see him as the noble upholder of an impractical and decadent Imperial ruling class that rewarded his support and obedience only by murder. There is a kind of justice, in this view, in the sack of Rome by Alaric's Goths two years later. The Roman senate and emperor did not realize how much they had relied on Stilicho until they had killed him. In favor of this view is the unswerving loyalty that Stilicho displayed, almost to the point of quixotism.

There are odd features in Stilicho's career. He hardly ever won a major battle, except against the unimportant Radagaisus. Alaric always seemed to slip away from him. Did Stilicho, in fact, retain a kind of alliance with the Gothic king, who had been his ally at the Frigidus River in 394? Or should Stilicho be seen as essentially a warlord, whose trade was war and whose capital was soldiers? Could it be that Stilicho would not risk casualties and did not particularly want a major victory, which would only bring peace? It has also been noted that rivals of Stilicho—such as the commander of the North African expedition in 408 or Arcadius's main adviser in 395—were inclined to meet with strange accidents or be openly murdered. Stilicho was also very quick to marry his daughters to Honorius and seems to have planned to marry his son into the Imperial family also. As a "half barbarian," he could not be emperor, but his design may have been to have a grandson as ruler over a reunited empire. In this way, he was quite capable of ruthlessness.

The questions are insoluble, but Stilicho may not have had as much choice as modern historians tend to suppose. Accusations of military ineptitude rest on the assumption that Roman armies were competent and reliable. After Adrianople, this may not have been the case. Stilicho had continuous trouble in recruiting good Roman troops, and the barbarians he used instead were often badly disciplined and unreliable. He may, in fact, have done as well as anyone could expect. Possibly his underlying weakness was something as elementary as a desperate shortage of real Roman drill sergeants.

—*T. A. Shippey*

FURTHER READING

Bury, John B. *A History of the Later Roman Empire.* London: Macmillan, 1889. Rev. ed. *A History of the Later Roman Empire from the Death of Theodosius I to the Death of Justinian (A.D. 395 to A.D. 565).* London: Macmillan, 1923. This volume may be considered the nineteenth century alternative to Gibbon, cited below. It is strong on dates and events and determinedly personal in interpretation. Lacks the twentieth century awareness of social forces demonstrated, for example, by Jones, below.

Cameron, Alan D. E. *Claudian: Poetry and Propaganda at the Court of Honorius.* Oxford, England: Clarendon Press, 1970. This work attempts to distinguish truth from flattery in the work of Stilicho's greatest propagandist. Perhaps by inevitable reaction from its subject, this book takes a severely negative view of Stilicho.

Claudian. *Claudian.* Translated by Maurice Platnauer. Cambridge, Mass.: Harvard University Press, 1972-1976. This edition of Claudian's poems makes it possible for students to see both what data can be extracted from the poems on Stilicho and how carefully data are at times concealed. The information Claudian does not mean to give is more revealing than his surface intention.

Gibbon, Edward. *The Decline and Fall of the Roman Empire.* 6 vols. Reprint. New York: Modern Library, 1995. This set of volumes is only one of innumerable reprints of Gibbon's classic work, first published from 1776 to 1788. In spite of their age, chapters 29 and 30 are well worth reading for their style and recondite learning. Gibbon succeeded at an early stage in catching the ambiguous quality of Stilicho's achievement.

Isbell, Harold, trans. *The Last Poets of Imperial Rome.* Harmondsworth, Middlesex, England: Penguin Books, 1971. Among other poems, this volume offers Claudian's *Raptus Proserpiae* (c. 397 C.E.) and the *Epithalamium* (398 C.E.) for the marriage of Honorius and Stilicho's daughter Maria. The former poem is valuable as a reminder that there was still an important pagan faction among the Roman aristocracy.

Jones, A. H. M. *The Later Roman Empire, 284-602: A Social, Economic, and Administrative Survey.* 3 vols. Baltimore: The Johns Hopkins University Press, 1986. These volumes provide essential data for considering the complicated social, administrative, and military structures within which Stilicho functioned.

O'Flynn, John M. *Generalissimos of the Western Roman Empire.* Edmonton: University of Alberta Press, 1983. The three chapters of this work devoted to Stilicho give an able summary of what is known and attempt to answer some of the riddles of his career in terms of the power structures of the time. There is some interest in the comparison with Stilicho's successors, who appear to have shed some of his inhibitions and solved some of his problems.

Randers-Pehrson, Justine D. *Barbarians and Romans.* Norman: University of Oklahoma Press, 1983. This work is organized geographically; the chapters on Milan, Rome, and Ravenna all have relevance to Stilicho's career. Includes good illustrations: for example, a photograph of the monument celebrating the victory at Pollenza, with Stilicho's name carefully removed.

SEE ALSO: Attila; Theodosius the Great.

RELATED ARTICLES in *Great Events from History: The Ancient World*: August 9, 378 C.E., Battle of Adrianople; 380-392 C.E., Theodosius's Edicts Promote Christian Orthodoxy; August 24-26, 410 C.E., Gothic Armies Sack Rome.

STRABO
Greek geographer

Strabo wrote a description of the known inhabited world, valuable for its philosophy of geography, its historical digressions, and the current scientific notions it contains. His work stands out for its diverse subjects, encyclopedic scope, and contemporary view of the ancient world at the dawn of the Christian era.

BORN: 64 or 63 B.C.E.; Amasia, Pontus, Asia Minor (now Amasya, Turkey)
DIED: After 23 C.E.; probably Amasia, Pontus, Asia Minor or Rome (now in Italy)
AREAS OF ACHIEVEMENT: Geography, historiography

EARLY LIFE
Strabo (STRAY-boh) was born at Amasia in Pontus, about 55 miles (90 kilometers) inland from the southeastern shore of the Black Sea. Formerly a royal capital of Pontus, Amasia was located in a deep valley on the Iris River. It was a well-fortified place, with striking mountains towering above the town. Located there were the tombs of the kings of Pontus. Amasia controlled the surrounding river valleys and villages, which doubtless contributed to its wealth. It is inferred that Strabo belonged to a rich family who could afford to give their son a good education. Although his lineage was a mixture of Asiatic and Greek, Strabo's training and language were purely Greek.

The area had been conquered by the Romans immediately before Strabo's birth. In the generation before, Mithradates the Great of Pontus had extended the kingdom's borders through Asia Minor, the islands of the Aegean Sea, and the southern and eastern shores of the Black Sea. He fought the Romans Lucius Cornelius Sulla, Lucius Licinius Murena, and Lucullus before succumbing to Pompey the Great. A most formidable foe of Rome, he died about the time Strabo was born.

Strabo thus grew up appreciating both the power of Rome and the legacy of Pontus. His mother's ancestors had been on close terms with the royal house, and one of them, the general Dorylaus Tacticus, had been a friend of King Mithradates V Euergetes. Mithradates the Great patronized Strabo's great-grandfather Lagetas and granduncle Moaphernes, appointing the latter to a governorship. The king also made Dorylaus's nephew the priest of Ma at Comana, a position that gave him power second only to Mithradates himself.

Strabo's education in grammar and rhetoric included lessons from Aristodemus, who was also the tutor of Pompey's sons. When he was nineteen or twenty years old, Strabo went to Rome and was instructed by Tyrannio, a tutor of Cicero's sons and an expert on geography. It is likely that Strabo got his passion for the subject from this master. Also in Rome, Strabo learned from Xenarchus, who, like Tyrannio, was an Aristotelian. Nevertheless, references throughout the *Geōgraphica* (c. 7 B.C.E.; *Geography*, 1917-1933) indicate that Strabo became a follower of the Stoics, perhaps under the influence of Augustus's teacher and friend Athenodorus. In addition to his early educational trips, Strabo made other visits to Rome, most likely in 35 and 29.

As a youth, Strabo read widely and became especially enamored of Homer, as shown by his later passionate defense of the epics' historical and geographical accuracy. He also read Herodotus's *Historiai Herodotou* (c. 424 B.C.E.; *The History*, 1709), which he did not value, and the work of Polybius, which he considered useful and accurate. He became familiar with the historical, scientific, and geographical works of Posidonius, Eratosthenes of Cyrene, Hipparchus, Artemidorus, and Ephorus. In addition, Strabo read the works of the historians of Alexander the Great, especially concerning Alexander's eastern travels.

By adulthood, Strabo had visited a good portion of Asia Minor and made several trips to Rome. He had met influential Romans and Greeks and had been introduced to the best in literature and history—all of which were to influence his later writings.

LIFE'S WORK
Probably between 25 and 19, Strabo resided in Alexandria, Egypt. At the beginning of his sojourn there, he accompanied his friend Aelius Gallus, the Roman prefect of Egypt, on a trip up the Nile River, reaching the border of Ethiopia. His time in Egypt gave him opportunity to observe the country—and perhaps to use the library at Alexandria. Afterward, he returned to Rome for an undetermined amount of time.

Strabo's travels continued through his life and reached as far west as Etruria and as far east as the border of Armenia, south to the northern edge of Ethiopia, and north to the Black Sea. Around 26, Strabo wrote a historical work, now known as *Historical Memoirs*, none of which has survived, although Plutarch and Flavius Josephus refer to it. It comprised forty-three books, covering the period from the destruction of Corinth and Carthage in

146 B.C.E. to (perhaps) the Battle of Actium in 31 B.C.E., thus forming a continuation of Polybius's history.

Strabo's magnum opus was the *Geography*, a work in seventeen books describing the inhabited world of the three continents Europe, Asia, and Africa. Its scope included mathematical, physical, political, and historical aspects of geography. His was a general treatise on the subject: the first ancient attempt to synthesize all known geographical knowledge.

The first two books of the *Geography* deal with the history of the discipline, including attacks on the ideas of Eratosthenes and others, whom Strabo considered to have made mistakes in their published works on geography. He discourses at length on Homer, naming him the first geographer. Strabo was often at pains to "prove Homer right" and saw the ship catalog in the second book of the *Iliad* (c. 750 B.C.E.; English translation, 1611) as preserving historical locales and the voyages of Odysseus and Jason's quest for the Golden Fleece as actual events. Strabo also suggests that as the inhabited world that he knows only makes up one-third of the temperate zone, it is likely that other continents exist.

Apparently not relying on Roman writers, Strabo addresses Spain in book 3, drawing mainly on Greek sources in his description of the natural resources and physical traits of the country. This book also makes mention of the mythical island home of Geryon and the Tin Islands, which Strabo does not recognize as connected with Britain in any way.

Relying heavily on the *Comentarii de bello Gallico* (52-51 B.C.E.) and the *Comentarii de bello cinli* (45 B.C.E.; both translated into English as *Commentaries*, 1609) of Julius Caesar, Strabo wrote the fourth book about Britain, France, and the Alps. Although he used Caesar's description of the Gallic tribes, for some reason Strabo ignored his descriptions of the dimensions of Britain, thereby making the island much broader and shorter than it actually is. Strabo believed that Ireland lay to the north of Britain. His description of the Alps is somewhat accurate, including discussions of trade, alpine passes, and avalanches.

Because maps of Italy and the surrounding islands were common in his day, Strabo probably had one before him while writing about this area in his fifth and sixth books. In addition, Strabo was personally familiar with Italy and aware of several Greek and Roman writers on the subject. Impressive in this section is his description of Mount Vesuvius, which he describes as having every appearance of a volcano, although it had not erupted in living memory. His words were oddly appropriate, for Vesuvius erupted in 79 C.E. Strabo never visited Sicily, so his description is not as accurate as that of Italy proper, but his descriptions of the volcanic activity of Mount Etna and the Aeolian Islands are well done.

Northern Europe forms the bulk of the seventh book, and the lack of information handicapping Strabo is very evident in this section. It is strange that Strabo ignores things that the Romans knew about these regions: the amber trade and the testimony of Herodotus about the region. When he describes the area north of the Black Sea, however, his accuracy increases, probably because of Mithradates' recent conquests in the area.

The next three books deal with Greece and its islands and is surprisingly lacking in geographical information; Strabo probably assumed that his readers were familiar with the area, and Strabo knew little of it at first hand. In addition, his preoccupation with identifying sites mentioned in the Homeric catalog of ships skewed Strabo's account here. Finally, Greece's diminished status in the period left little outstanding to describe. Many cities lay in ruin, while others were reduced to the status of sleepy villages in Strabo's lifetime. His interest in volcanoes does not flag in this section, which describes the volcanic activity of mountains at Thera and near Methone.

Strabo. (Library of Congress)

Books 11 through 16 deal with Asia. Strabo's accounts of Asia Minor—especially the northern sections—are rather accurate, for he had seen much of it, his home being in Pontus. The section includes a discussion of the site of Homeric Troy. Strabo believed that the Caspian Sea connected to the northern ocean and even describes what a sailor would see while sailing southward into this arm of the surrounding sea. Strabo admits that he knows nothing about the extreme north of Asia, and, although he knows the name of silk producers, he does not mention the silk trade at all, although it had already become quite important. He provides an interesting account of India, derived from the lost works of those who accompanied Alexander the Great to that land. Strabo concentrates on the customs of the inhabitants there—at the expense of the actual geography of the territory. Africa, the subject of the seventeenth book, is well described along the Nile because of Strabo's acquaintance with the territory. He describes the antiquities of the land and gives an account of the Ethiopians. The rest of Africa is not as well delineated; in fact, Strabo reduced its size by more than two-thirds, having no idea how far to the south it actually extended. In fact, Strabo seems to have ignored or not to have known of the works of his younger contemporary Juba II, king of Mauretania, who had written extensively on North African geography and history.

Strabo died some time after completing the *Geography*, possibly in his homeland. His acquaintance with eminent Romans of his time and the admiration for the Roman Empire, which he consistently shows in his writing, could not ensure instant success at Rome for his work, which came to be appreciated only by later generations.

SIGNIFICANCE

Strabo said that his work would be useful to administrators and generals, calling geography a practical and philosophical science. He thus avoids tedious listings of the insignificant in favor of major points relating to places under discussion. His work is encyclopedic and comprehensive—a storehouse of information about his world.

The date and place of composition are uncertain. The latest date in it is 23 C.E., but few believe that he began his work in his eighties. It has been argued that he composed it while in his fifties, around 7 B.C.E., and later revised, for it lacks references to events between 3 B.C.E. and 19 C.E. Rome seems a likely place for its publication, but some have argued that Strabo returned to Amasia to write it, because Pliny the Elder and Ptolemy ignore the work. Had it been published in Rome, one would expect that it

would have gained some attention. In fact, however, there are only a few minor references to the *Geography* before Stephanus of Byzantium made frequent use of it at the end of the fifth century C.E. Other possibilities for Strabo's residence at the end of his life include the eastern Mediterranean region or Naples.

Although Strabo boasts of his wide travels, he evidently did not make detailed studies of all the places he visited. He probably saw Cyrene in Libya only as he sailed by and probably did not even visit Athens. In Italy, he kept to the main roads leading to and from Rome.

Strabo assumed a spherical Earth at the center of the universe. An island surrounded by ocean, it was admissible of being divided into five zones, uninhabitable at the extreme north because of the cold and at the extreme south because of the heat. Aside from assuming a geocentric universe, Strabo made a number of mistakes, mainly resulting from the lack of accurate observations and reliable sources of information. Where data were available, they were often misleading. As a result, he distorted the shape of the whole of the Mediterranean and Europe. Other mistakes include the assumption that the northern coast of Africa was practically a straight line, and that a line from the Pillars of Hercules to the Strait of Messina was equidistant from Europe and Africa. Also in error are his statements that the Pyrenees form a line from north to south, that Cape St. Vincent is the most westerly point of Europe, and that eastern Crete does not extend much to the east of Sunium Promontorium (when in fact four-fifths of the entire island lies east of it). Describing Palestine, he asserted that the Jordan River flowed into the Mediterranean Sea, being navigable for ships sailing east from the sea.

In spite of its inaccuracies, Strabo's *Geography* is the most important geographical treatise from the ancient world. Its great value lies not only in his own observations that, when firsthand, are accurate and lucid—but also in the preservation of so many previous authors whose work it summarizes, especially Eratosthenes and Posidonius.

—Daniel B. Levine

FURTHER READING

Bunbury, E. H. *A History of Ancient Geography Among the Greeks and Romans from the Earliest Ages till the Fall of the Roman Empire.* 1879. Reprint. Amsterdam: J. C. Gieben, 1979. The standard handbook on the subject of ancient geography. Putting Strabo in historical perspective, it has four long sections on the *Geography*, with detailed discussions of each book, commenting on Strabo's sources, errors, and value. With maps, notes, and an index.

Dilke, O. A. W. *Greek and Roman Maps*. Baltimore: The Johns Hopkins University Press, 1998. Evidence for cartography in the ancient world, from the work in Mesopotamia to the Renaissance. Chapters on ancient Greece and geographical writers, the latter containing a section on Strabo: his cartographic terms, construction of a globe, contribution to mapmaking, use of myth, and lack of scientific accuracy. Contains maps, charts, photographs, notes, appendices, and bibliography, and an index.

Dueck, Daniela. *Strabo of Amasia: A Greek Man of Letters in Augustan Rome*. New York: Routledge, 2000. A biography that covers the life and works of the ancient geographer. Bibliography and index.

Kish, George. *A Source Book in Geography*. Cambridge, Mass.: Harvard University Press, 1978. Selections from Strabo and other ancient geographers, putting the *Geography* in context. Casts light on the geographical theory. Includes selections from Plato, Aristotle, Greek travelers' reports, Greek heliocentric theory, and selections from Strabo on geography in general, the inhabited world, changes in the earth, volcanoes, and Asian lands.

Magie, David. *Roman Rule in Asia Minor to the End of the Third Century After Christ*. 2 vols. New York: Arno Press, 1975. Exhaustive historical discussion of Strabo's homeland. Essential for understanding the geographer's background. A chapter on "The Rise of the Power of Pontus," chapters on Mithradates, Pompey, and the years of Strabo's youth. Told from the Roman perspective, it is dependent on Strabo's *Geography* as the copious notes show.

Strabo. *The "Geography" of Strabo with an English Translation*. Translated by Horace Leonard Jones. 8 vols. Cambridge, Mass.: Harvard University Press, 1982-1989. Contains the complete Greek text and English translation, with notes and bibliography. Includes diagrams illustrating complex mathematical discussions, maps, and index. Useful introduction discusses Strabo's life and works. Identifies the sources of Strabo's many quotations, contains useful cross-references, and points out textual variations.

Thomson, J. Oliver. *History of Ancient Geography*. New York: Biblo and Tannen, 1965. Numerous useful maps and pertinent chapters on geography in the Roman Republic, theory in the same period, and the great days of the Roman Empire. With a brief section on Strabo. Contains an index and addenda.

SEE ALSO: Eratosthenes of Cyrene; Homer; Pausanias the Traveler; Polybius.

RELATED ARTICLES in *Great Events from History: The Ancient World*: c. 300 B.C.E., Stoics Conceptualize Natural Law; 146 B.C.E., Sack of Corinth; September 2, 31 B.C.E., Battle of Actium; August 24, 79 C.E., Destruction of Pompeii.

LUCIUS CORNELIUS SULLA
Roman general and statesman

Sulla played an extremely important role in the transformation of the Roman Republic into the Roman Empire. While attempting to prevent others from using force to influence Roman politics, Sulla became the first Roman to use the military to gain a political end.

BORN: 138 B.C.E.; Rome (now in Italy)
DIED: 78 B.C.E.; Puteoli (now Pozzuoli, Italy)
ALSO KNOWN AS: Lucius Cornelius Sulla Felix (full name)
AREAS OF ACHIEVEMENT: Government and politics, war and conquest

EARLY LIFE

Lucius Cornelius Sulla (LEW-shee-uhs kawr-NEEL-yuhs SUHL-uh) was born into an old Roman patrician family in 138 B.C.E. Although not much is known of his youth, Sulla did receive an excellent education in the Greek and Roman classics. He grew to be a handsome man with golden red hair and sharp, piercing blue eyes. Sulla had a very pale complexion, and a severe skin condition badly scarred his face. Because his family had little wealth and his father left him nothing when he died, Sulla had to live on the income from a relatively small investment. As a consequence of his modest means, he lived in a small apartment in one of the less desirable neighborhoods of Rome, a circumstance he found demeaning. To an ambitious patrician, wealth was a necessary prerequisite to participation in politics.

Sulla's life changed, however, when he inherited the

estates of both his stepmother and his mistress, allowing him to pursue his dream of public service.

Although Rome had been at war with Jugurtha in North Africa since 111, the Roman army had not made much progress toward victory. In 108, Gaius Marius was elected consul for the following year, and the people voted to transfer the command of the war from Quintus Caecilius Metellus to Marius. In the same election, they elected Sulla quaestor and chose him to serve under Marius.

During his years of military service in Africa, Sulla proved himself an able and courageous soldier, popular with common soldiers as well as officers. Although Marius was more successful against Jugurtha than Metellus had been, he was unable to capture the elusive enemy leader. Sulla was entrusted with the task of convincing Bocchus (king of Mauretania and father-in-law of Jugurtha) to betray Jugurtha to the Romans. Through skillful diplomacy, Sulla was able to win the friendship of Bocchus, capture Jugurtha, and end the war.

After the war, Marius returned to Rome in triumph on January 1, 104. Although Sulla captured Jugurtha, Marius claimed the triumph as his. Sulla, as a military subordinate, was in no position to dispute Marius's claim. Immediately after their victory in Africa, the Romans faced a new war against two German tribes, the Cimbri and the Teutons. Because of his recent triumph, the Romans now elected Marius consul to defend Italy. Sulla served as a legate of Marius and once again used his diplomatic skills to detach the Marsi from the German alliance.

After his latest tour of duty, Sulla returned to Rome in 99 to stand for the praetorship. Despite his military successes, Sulla failed to win office. The next year, however, the people elected Sulla urban praetor. The senate assigned Sulla to Cilicia for his propraetorial governorship. On reaching his province, Sulla received a senatorial order to restore Ariobarzanes to the throne of Cappadocia. After his success in Cappadocia, Sulla had the opportunity to negotiate Rome's first diplomatic relations with the Parthians.

LIFE'S WORK

Sulla now returned to Rome to seek the consulship. When his political enemies prosecuted him in an unsuccessful campaign to discredit him, Sulla had to postpone his canvassing for office. With the failed campaign for the consulship came public notice of Sulla's feud with Marius. Many of the Roman aristocracy viewed Marius as an upstart (*novus homo*) who did not know his proper

Lucius Cornelius Sulla. (Library of Congress)

place. Sulla's capture of Jugurtha, his military successes, and his patrician background made him the perfect man to challenge Marius. When Sulla received sufficient backing, he gained the consulship for 88.

Because of the territorial expansion of Mithradates the Great, king of Pontus, the senate decided to give Sulla the command of the war against Mithradates. The tribune Publius Sulpicius Rufus, however, introduced a bill in the Tribal Assembly to transfer the command to Marius. Because no public business could be conducted during a public holiday, Sulla and a consular colleague declared a public holiday to prevent the vote from taking place. Sulpicius claimed that this was illegal and incited the people to riot. To save himself from the mob, Sulla rescinded the holiday decree and pretended to accept the transfer of his command. Sulla then went to address his troops gathered in Campania for the war against Mithradates. After he explained the political developments in Rome, the troops urged Sulla to lead them to

Rome to reclaim his rightful command. With the backing of his soldiers, Sulla marched on Rome and took the city by force.

Although these events marked the first time in history a Roman army had violated the *pomerium* (the sacred boundary of Rome), Sulla believed that he was defending legally constituted authority and that he was saving Rome from tyrannical demagogues. Once in control of Rome, Sulla had the senate declare Marius and Sulpicius public enemies, subject to immediate execution. Although Marius managed to escape from Rome, Sulpicius was captured and killed. After having the senate annul the laws of Sulpicius, Sulla sent his army away and allowed the election of the consuls for the next year. Gnaeus Octavius (a supporter of Sulla) and Lucius Cornelius Cinna (an enemy of Sulla) were elected consuls for the year 87. Sulla, eager to fight the war with Mithradates, left for Greece.

With Sulla out of Italy, Cinna declared Sulla a public enemy but did nothing to hinder him in the East. After pushing the forces of Mithradates out of Greece and defeating them in Asia Minor, Sulla made peace with Mithradates. On hearing that Cinna had been murdered by his own troops, Sulla invaded Italy in the spring of 83. Within a year, Sulla defeated all the forces ranged against him. He massacred the Italians who sided with Cinna and who were still in rebellion and confiscated some of their lands.

Having Rome firmly in his control, Sulla ordered the execution of all magistrates and high military officers who had served Cinna's government. To limit the executions to those guilty, Sulla published proscription lists of those subject to the death penalty. Sulla confiscated the properties of those proscribed and auctioned them to his supporters. Motivated by greed, some Sullan supporters arranged for the proscription of certain wealthy individuals in order to acquire their money and lands. The death toll among the upper classes included seventy senators and sixteen hundred equestrians. The sons and grandsons of those proscribed were barred from holding public office in the future.

From Sulla's point of view, he meted out various punishments under his authority as proconsul. The drawback to being a proconsul, however, was that Sulla could not enter Rome. When the death of Gnaeus Papirius Carbo, Cinna's former consular colleague, became known, Sulla suggested that the dictatorship be revived after a lapse of 120 years. Although the usual term of office for a dictator in Rome was six months or less, Sulla wanted no time limit placed on him. Accordingly, the people elected

Sulla dictator and granted him complete immunity. Sulla's having the title of "Dictator for the making of laws and the settling of the Constitution" allowed his every decree to become law immediately.

As dictator in 81 Sulla instituted a constitutional reform that placed the senate in total control of the state. Sulla increased senate membership from the traditional number of three hundred to six hundred by including pro-Sullan equestrians and by automatically making all former quaestors members of the senate. The number of praetors was increased to eight and the number of quaestors to twenty. To create an orderly career ladder, Sulla established a strict *cursus honorum* in which politicians had to hold the quaestorship and praetorship before holding the consulship (the minimum age for holding this office was to be forty-two). Because tribunes had caused so much political turmoil in the past, men holding the tribuneship were now limited in the use of the veto and were barred from holding any higher office. In addition, prior senatorial approval was required before bills from a tribune could be introduced into an assembly.

At the height of his power, Sulla stepped down from the dictatorship and restored constitutional government. He was elected consul for 80, after which he retired to one of his villas in Puteoli (in Campania) to write and to relax by hunting and fishing. In his extensive memoirs, Sulla minimized the humble circumstances of his early years and emphasized his career from the time of war with Jugurtha. Sulla wanted to create the image of having possessed *felicitas* (good luck) from childhood. After a lifetime spent in active service to Rome, Sulla died of liver failure in 78. His body was taken to the Forum in Rome, where it lay in state. After thousands of Sullan veterans and ordinary people passed the funeral bier to pay their respects, the body was cremated. So great was Sulla's following that the matrons of Rome mourned Sulla for a full year, just as they would have done for their own fathers.

SIGNIFICANCE

Although Lucius Cornelius Sulla was not a talented orator, he had the ability to establish an immediate personal rapport with people. Whether commanding troops, leading the state, or managing delicate diplomatic negotiations, Sulla was always able to earn the respect of the people with whom he dealt. Sulla's contemporaries of all classes were most impressed by his personal charm and by this highly developed sense of humor. In addition, Sulla believed that he possessed a special divine gift, *felicitas*. With his natural abilities and his good luck backing him, Sulla was always confident.

Unknowingly, Sulla played an important historical role in Rome's transition from a Republic to an Empire. Despite his passionate belief in Rome's republican form of government, Sulla felt compelled to defend the state by being the first to use military force against it. As Roman politics became more polarized, adversaries used violence as the means to a political end. Although angered at the prospect of losing his command against Mithradates, Sulla looked on Marius, Cinna, Carbo, and Sulpicius as men intent on violating the Roman constitution. Sulla, therefore, saw his actions in a broader context than a mere factional dispute. As a patriotic Roman, Sulla could not stand by and watch the subversion of the Republic.

When Marius allowed the Roman legions to recruit from among the urban proletariat, he made possible the rise of a man such as Sulla. Generals now recruited armies whose only loyalties were to their commanders. When Sulla's men believed their general to have been wronged, they rose to his defense, not to that of the state. Although Sulla exercised absolute power over Rome, he did not use his power to establish a Hellenistic-style monarchy. Sulla viewed the senate as representing traditional republican government: He attempted to restore it to its former central role. In short, Sulla tried to repair the Roman constitution after self-serving politicians had damaged it.

Using as many historical precedents as possible, Sulla tried to resolve Rome's problems in a constitutional manner. In reviving the dictatorship with no time limit, he was harking back to 387 B.C.E., when Marcus Furius Camillus required more than six months to save Rome from the Gauls. Just as the Romans thought Camillus the savior of Rome, Sulla hoped for the same recognition. When the Romans needed a thorough revision of their laws in 451, they turned to the *decemviri* for leadership. In Sulla's view, the Romans needed a new constitutional reform.

Despite his great talents and his extreme patriotism, Sulla ultimately failed to accomplish what he had set out to do. The Sullan reforms were not permanent, and they did not stop the Roman constitution from changing. By 70, Sulla's own supporters, Marcus Licinius Crassus and Pompey the Great, annulled or changed much of Sulla's work. Although his efforts to preserve the Republic were well-meaning, they demonstrated that he did not understand Rome's deep-seated problems. The very situation he sought to prevent, the use of force in politics, became the established norm as a result of Sulla's march on Rome and his use of proscription lists. Rome did not achieve political stability until Augustus established the Roman Empire in 27 B.C.E.

—Peter L. Viscusi

FURTHER READING

Appianus of Alexandria. *Appian's "Roman History."* Translated by Horace White. 4 vols. Cambridge, Mass.: Harvard University Press, 1990-1999. Appian's "The Civil Wars," "The Mithridatic Wars," and "Numidian Affairs" cover the time periods for Sulla's participation in these events. Although Appian lived during the late first and early second centuries C.E., he preserved some very valuable information from an unknown early Imperial annalist.

Badian, E. "Waiting for Sulla." *Journal of Roman Studies* 52 (1962): 47-61. The author attempts to bring modern critical historiographical analysis to the study of the period of Sulla. Through a reexamination of the sources, Badian maintains that Sulla's ambition drove him into rebellion against lawful authority. Sulla's contemporaries did not, according to Badian, believe that Sulla was a champion of the Roman nobility.

Baker, G. P. *Sulla the Fortunate.* 1927. Reprint. Lanham, Md.: Rowan and Littlefield, 2001. Baker's classic biography of Sulla as the bloody, fearless forerunner of Julius Caesar. Index.

Keaveney, Arthur. *Sulla: The Last Republican.* London: Croom Helm, 1982. The first full-scale biography of Sulla to appear in English. The author gathered and analyzed all the available evidence on the life of Sulla and presents it in a most convincing manner. A very favorable interpretation of Sulla.

Lovano, Michael. *The Age of Cinna: Crucible of Late Republican Rome.* Stuttgart: Franz Steiner, 2002. Chronological treatment of the period from the consulship of Cinna (87 B.C.E.) to Sulla's seizure of Italy (82 B.C.E.). Attempts to view these events from the perspective of Sulla's opponents, who are not treated well in the ancient sources.

Plutarch. *Fall of the Roman Republic, Six Lives: Marius, Sulla, Crassus, Pompey, Caesar, Ciero.* Translated by Rex Warner. Harmondsworth, Middlesex, England: Penguin Books, 1981. This volume contains a chapter on Sulla together with other chapters on some of his political rivals. Because Plutarch used many sources unavailable today, he preserved much anecdotal material that may be contemporaneous with Sulla. Although Plutarch's work lacks historical perspective and is very moralistic, it portrays Sulla vividly.

Sallust. *"The Jugurthine War" and "The Conspiracy of Catiline."* Translated by S. A. Handford. Baltimore: Penguin Books, 1967. A useful and interesting but brief account of Marius and Sulla in the war against Jugurtha. Despite his prejudice against the Roman nobility and his inaccuracies in chronology and geography, Sallust is an important source of information. It is highly probable that Sallust used Sulla's memoirs as one of his sources.

Scullard, H. H. *From the Gracchi to Nero: A History of Rome from 133 B.C. to A.D. 68.* New York: Rout-

ledge, 1988. This book contains two chapters, "The Rise and Fall of Marius" and "The Rise and Fall of Sulla," which give an exceptionally clear account of this most crucial period in Roman history. Points of interpretative discussion with secondary source citations are included in the notes at the back of the book.

SEE ALSO: Catiline; Gaius Marius; Pompey the Great.

RELATED ARTICLES in *Great Events from History: The Ancient World*: 107-101 B.C.E., Marius Creates a Private Army; Late 63-January 62 B.C.E., Catiline Conspiracy; 51 B.C.E., Cicero Writes *De republica*; 46 B.C.E., Establishment of the Julian Calendar.

SULPICIA
Roman poet

Sulpicia wrote at least six brief but well-crafted elegies, the only substantial body of poetry written by a Roman woman that has survived.

FLOURISHED: Late first century B.C.E.; place unknown
AREA OF ACHIEVEMENT: Literature

EARLY LIFE

Sulpicia (suhl-PIH-shuh) was a descendant of the most aristocratic of Roman families. In one of her poems, she proudly identifies her father as Servius (Servius Sulpicius Rufus), who, critics now agree, was the son of the distinguished jurist of the same name. Sulpicia's grandfather was a close friend of Cicero, the Roman statesman, orator, and philosopher. In 50 B.C.E., Cicero approached the elder Servius Sulpicius, praising his friend's son for his good character and his intellectual gifts and proposing that the son become the third husband of Cicero's daughter Valeria. It is assumed that Sulpicia was born of that union.

Sulpicia's father was a highly educated man, a polished orator, and a poet. Evidently he died young, and his wife chose not to remarry. Valeria's brother, Marcus Valerius Messalla Corvinus, who, like his father, was a prominent statesman and orator, may well have been named his niece's guardian. At any rate, Sulpicia's uncle Messalla obviously played an important role in her life during her early years, and the second of her elegies shows that their close relationship continued after she became an adult.

As an upper-class girl growing up in the first century B.C.E., Sulpicia would probably have been educated by

private tutors. Although her sex would have precluded her being trained in oratory, her education would not otherwise have been much different from that of a boy, in that it was liberal in nature, stressing fluency in both Greek and Latin as well as knowledge of the literatures in both languages. Sulpicia would have been free to make use of the family library. Moreover, because both her father and her uncle Messalla wrote poetry, she may have learned from her association with them.

LIFE'S WORK

There is no way to know at what age Sulpicia began writing poetry, but it is obvious from her surviving elegies that at the time they were written she was a young woman and almost certainly unmarried. The fact that her poems survived is due to her belonging to a literary coterie, a group of friends who reviewed one another's works before they were "published" (meaning circulated from hand to hand, made available for sale in bookshops, and placed in public libraries).

Sulpicia is the only Roman woman who is known to have been a member of such a coterie. She owed this distinction to Messalla, who was one of Rome's most important literary patrons. Recognizing Sulpicia's poetic talent, he undoubtedly encouraged her to write, made suggestions about her work, and helped her to publish, just as he did for other young poets in his coterie, including Ovid and Tibullus, who became one of the most famous poets of his time but who, ironically, is now remembered primarily because of his connection with Sulpicia. It is in the collection bearing his name, the *Cor-*

pus Tibullianum, which contains works not only by Tibullus but also by several other poets, that Sulpicia's poems appear.

In keeping with the long-standing notion that modest women keep their feelings to themselves, for centuries it was assumed that Sulpicia's poems were meant merely to be read by the persons addressed and that she would never have permitted them to be published during her lifetime. However, as scholar Matthew Santirocco and others point out, if the poem now usually printed first is read as an introduction to the elegies, one must note that in it Sulpicia rejects the idea of secrecy. In fact, she explicitly states her intention of making her feelings about her lover known to the world. Moreover, in this poem she credits the Muses for persuading Venus to send her a worthy lover. This makes it clear that Sulpicia did not merely dabble in poetry. She was a devotee of the Muses, a conscious artist, whose seemingly simple poems are in reality as carefully crafted as those of her contemporary, the poet Catullus, to whom Sulpicia is often compared.

The six poems whose authorship is not in question relate a brief history of a love affair. In the introductory poem, Sulpicia emphasizes her joy that at last she has found a man worthy of her love. Not until the second poem does she give his name, and even then she uses the pseudonym "Cerinthus." This is significant, for by admitting her identity while shielding that of the lover, Sulpicia is reversing the traditional pattern of love poetry. In this case, it is the woman who glories in the relationship, while the object of her love is not identified. The implication is that his role in the relationship is more passive than that of Sulpicia.

Sulpicia's conscious artistry is again evident in the fact that she presents the second and third poems in the series as a pair, a device often used in Roman elegies. Initially she writes a poem addressed to her uncle Messalla, who had planned to celebrate her birthday with a trip to the country. In it, she urges Messalla to reconsider, pointing out that her birthday would hardly be a happy one if she had to spend it away from her lover. In the poem that follows, Sulpicia announces happily that the trip has been called off; one may speculate that perhaps her uncle took heed of her pleas. Sulpicia is delighted that she will be able to celebrate her birthday in Rome, presumably in the company of her lover.

In the fourth poem, true love encounters a more serious obstacle. In lines dripping with sarcasm, Sulpicia pretends to be pleased that her lover has taken steps to keep her from falling more deeply in love with him. What he has done, it becomes evident, is to become involved with a low-class woman, thus seeming to value her more than the daughter of an aristocrat. The poem ends with a veiled threat: Sulpicia asserts that people are worrying about her. However, she does not make it clear whether they are concerned about her feelings, worried that she will break off with her lover, or hopeful of taking his place. Again, Sulpicia's artistry is evident, for example, in her use of the hissing, snakelike "s" sound that dominates the lines in the Latin original.

The fifth poem begins with a gentler rebuke. Sulpicia is ill with a fever, and she is uncertain whether Cerinthus is concerned about her. Sulpicia's use of the ambiguous Latin word "calor," which means both bodily temperature and sexual passion, suggests that she may be troubled as much by passion as by real illness. After these two poems questioning the sincerity of Cerinthus, in her final poem Sulpicia admits that she has precipitated a crisis in the relationship. She should not have left her lover alone the previous night, she admits; her only excuse is that she wanted to conceal her passion from him. By thus seeming to reject the honest expression of emotion, Sulpicia appears to be retreating from her earlier posture. However, the fact that this sixth poem was written and distributed like the other five suggests that Sulpicia's comments either reflected a mood or were a calculated ploy. Perhaps it was just that in the final analysis, her devotion to her art always triumphed over her womanly modesty.

It is not known what happened to Sulpicia in later life. She may have continued to write poetry; she may have been the author of other elegies in the *Corpus Tibullianum* collection, where there are five poems listed as being written by a mysterious *amicus Sulpiciae*, that is, a friend of Sulpicia. In any case, after centuries in which her works were sometimes attributed to Tibullus, sometimes dismissed as no more than one would expect from a mere female, and more often just ignored, Sulpicia has finally been recognized as the artist she was.

SIGNIFICANCE

Sulpicia adheres to the tradition of the short, autobiographical love poem in elegiac form as practiced by her Greek predecessors and by her contemporary Catullus. However, by taking an active part in the love affair she described and by making it clear that her primary allegiance was not to any man but to her muse, Sulpicia brought a voice to Roman poetry that had not previously been heard: that of a strong, independent woman. Her membership in Messalla's coterie proves that she was highly respected during her lifetime. However, there is no way to ascertain how much she may have influenced other poets, either women or men.

—*Rosemary M. Canfield Reisman*

FURTHER READING

Flaschenriem, Barbara L. "Sulpicia and the Rhetoric of Disclosure." *Classical Philology* 94 (January, 1999): 36-54. The author uses detailed textual analysis to support her belief that Sulpicia was a woman in conflict with herself. Though the poet expresses her thoughts and feelings honestly, she makes herself somewhat less vulnerable through the skillful use of conventional literary techniques. A thoughtful study.

Hallett, Judith P., and Marilyn B. Skinner, eds. *Roman Sexualities*. Princeton, N.J.: Princeton University Press, 1997. A collection of essays in which feminist critical tools are used to explore the hierarchy of power in ancient Rome. It is pointed out that women writers like Sulpicia, who inverted the traditional gender roles of males as the pursuers and females as the pursued, were viewed as posing a threat to traditional power structures.

Heath-Stubbs, John. Preface to *The Poems of Sulpicia*, translated by John Heath-Stubbs. London: Hearing Eye, 2000. This volume contains a translation of Sulpicia's poems by a highly respected English scholar. In his prefatory comments, Heath-Stubbs points out how much more favorably scholars now look on Sulpicia than they did in the past. He also deals with the issue of the two poems tentatively attributed to her and with the question of the Sulpicia mentioned by Martial.

Hemelrijk, Emily A. *Matrona Docta: Educated Women in the Roman Élite from Cornelia to Julia Domna*. New York: Routledge, 1999. Two chapters in this invaluable volume describe the education of upper-class women, thus providing a sound basis for conjectures about Sulpicia's early life and education. Other especially useful sections of the book explore the attitudes of Sulpicia's society toward women's sexual behavior and their artistic endeavors. The chapter titled "Women and Writing: Poetry" contains a lengthy discussion of Sulpicia's life and her work. Includes notes, bibliography, and indexes.

Parker, Holt N. "Sulpicia, the Auctor de Sulpicia, and the Authorship of 3.9 and 3.11 of the Corpus Tibullianum." *Helios* 21 (1994): 39-62. Argues that two additional poems in Tibellius's collection, traditionally included in a group by an unnamed writer, were in fact written by Sulpicia. Though controversial, this theory deserves consideration, for the poems have significant biographical content.

Santirocco, Matthew. "Sulpicia Reconsidered." *Classical Journal* 74 (1979): 229-239. The author refutes the long-standing assessment of Sulpicia as merely an emotional amateur, thus setting the stage for serious study of her poetry as the work of a conscious artist.

Skoie, Mathilde. *Reading Sulpicia: Commentaries 1475-1990*. New York: Oxford University Press, 2002. Selections show how the attitudes toward Sulpicia and her works have altered over time. An appendix includes her six poems in Latin and in translation. Two bibliographies, one organized chronologically and the other alphabetically. Includes index.

Snyder, Jane McIntosh. *The Woman and the Lyre: Women Writers in Classical Greece and Rome*. Carbondale: Southern Illinois University Press, 1989. Explains the biographical references in Sulpicia's poems and notes how her work fits into the established elegaic tradition. Includes map, bibliographies, and index.

SEE ALSO: Catullus; Cicero; Enheduanna; Ovid; Sappho.

RELATED ARTICLES in *Great Events from History: The Ancient World*: 54 B.C.E., Roman Poet Catullus Dies; 51 B.C.E., Cicero Writes *De republica*; 19 B.C.E., Roman Poet Vergil Dies; November 27, 8 B.C.E., Roman Lyric Poet Horace Dies; 8 C.E., Ovid's *Metamorphoses* Is Published.

TACITUS
Roman historian

Combining a successful career in the Roman civil service with a lifelong interest in his nation's past, Tacitus devoted his mature years to exploring the many facets of history. His portraits of the famous and the infamous, especially during the early years of the Roman Empire, are among the most vivid and influential descriptions in all Roman literature.

BORN: c. 56 C.E.; place unknown
DIED: c. 120 C.E.; probably Rome (now in Italy)
ALSO KNOWN AS: Cornelius Tacitus (full name)
AREAS OF ACHIEVEMENT: Government and politics, historiography

EARLY LIFE

Cornelius Tacitus (TAS-ih-tuhs), considered by many scholars to be Rome's greatest historian, is an enigma. Neither the exact date of his birth nor that of his death is known. His *praenomen*, that name that distinguished each Roman from his relatives, is a mystery, as is his birthplace. Tacitus never mentioned his parents or any siblings in any of his writings. He imparts to his readers much information about his contemporaries and a number of historical personages, but he never reveals a single solid fact about himself.

Almost everything that is known about Tacitus has been gleaned from the writings of his close friend Pliny the Younger, an author in his own right and the nephew of the great scientist and historian Pliny the Elder. The friendship seems to have been of long duration, a fact that has led authorities to speculate that Tacitus was actually the son of one Cornelius Tacitus, who served as a financial agent of the government in Gallia Belgica and was a friend of Pliny the Elder. The public career of Tacitus is a matter of record, and by carefully noting the dates of his terms of office in each position it is possible to place his birth early in the reign of Nero, probably the year 56.

Clearly, Tacitus received an excellent education with special emphasis on rhetoric, because he was recognized in later life as a fine public speaker and an outstanding lawyer. He may have studied with the great Quintilian, who taught Pliny the Younger, but Tacitus never mentions his teachers or his fellow students. The elegance of his prose and his reputation denote one of good birth who received all the advantages belonging to his class, but the actual details must remain speculative. From natural modesty, Tacitus may have thought it unnecessary to repeat facts well known to his readers, or he may have done

so out of caution. Most of his youth was spent during troubled times when the slightest notoriety might mean death.

In his late teens Tacitus probably had the opportunity to hold his first public offices. Usually, young men were assigned minor posts in one of the four minor magistracies. During these brief terms of service it was possible to judge their preparation as well as their potential for success in government service. Having tested his mettle as a civilian, a young man then entered the military for a brief time to experience the rigor and discipline of the Roman army. This tour of duty was usually performed under a relative or close friend of the family. If a career in the military were not his choice, a young Roman of good birth reentered civilian life by selecting a wife and offering himself for a place in the civil service. Because a candidate with a wife was given priority, marriage at an early age was not unusual. In 77 Tacitus, his military service completed, was betrothed to the daughter of the noted general Gnaeus Julius Agricola.

LIFE'S WORK

Tacitus took the first step in the *cursus honorem*, or the Roman civil service, in 82, when he was chosen a quaestor. He was one of twenty young men who for a year had the opportunity to prove their potential for a political career by fulfilling the duties of the lowest regular position in the civil service. If the quaestor's command of the law earned for him the commendation of the consul under whom he served, he might be offered another year under a proconsul in one of the Imperial provinces.

For Tacitus, the next rung in the ladder of preferment was probably the position of aedile. These magistrates might perform any number of duties in Rome. Some of them saw to the care of the city and supervised the repair of public buildings. Others were responsible for regulating traffic within the capital. The organization of public games or the supervision of the morals of the populace might prove more difficult than the checking of weights and measures, but all these duties could fall to an aedile during his term of office, and each was a test of his ability. Tacitus obviously succeeded, because he was elected a praetor in 88.

By the time of the Roman Empire, the office of praetor, originally a military title, had essentially become a legal position. The experience gleaned during his term as an aedile would prepare the praetor for dealing with offenses from oppression and forgery to murder and treason. During his term as praetor, Tacitus was elected to the priesthood of one of the sacerdotal colleges, quite an honor for one so young. This election may have indicated not only his aristocratic birth but also the patronage of the influential and the powerful, including the emperor. The following year Tacitus left for a tour of duty somewhere in the provinces.

He probably spent the next three years serving in the army, and he may have commanded a legion. During his last year abroad, Tacitus may have served as a proconsul in one of the lesser provinces of the Empire. In 93, the year that he returned to Rome, his father-in-law, Agricola, died. Requesting permission to write a biography of Agricola, Tacitus was rebuffed by Domitian, who had already begun the judicial murder of anyone who he believed threatened his position or his life. While many of his friends and colleagues were slaughtered, Tacitus buried himself in his research and the subsequent writing of the forbidden biography, which he finished in 96, the year in which Domitian was assassinated.

De vita Julii Agricolae (c. 98; *The Life of Agricola*, 1591) was more than a simple biography. While recounting the various stages in the career of Agricola and imparting to the reader varied details about the Britons, their history, and their country, Tacitus began to examine a theme on which he would comment for the next twenty years: the conflict between liberty and the power of the state. He also had the opportunity to serve the state in the aftermath of the reign of terror of Domitian. In 97 he was elected consul during the first year of the reign of Nerva, a distinguished and respected senator.

In 99 Tacitus's public career reached its zenith when he and Pliny the Younger successfully prosecuted the case of Marius Priscus, who had used his government position to abuse the provincials of Africa. Both men received a special vote of thanks from the senate for their preparation of the case for the state. Tacitus also received much attention for his second book, *De origine et situ Germanorum* (c. 98, also known as *Germania*; *The Description of Germanie*, 1598). Based on his observation and research while serving with the army, it was an immediate success. While Tacitus saw the Germans as a potential threat to the security of the Empire, he was impressed with their love of freedom and the simplicity of their lives when contrasted to the servility and decadence of his fellow Romans. With few flaws, *Germania* is an impressive and persuasive work of scholarship.

Having embarked on the study of the past, Tacitus devoted his next work, *Dialogus de oratoribus* (c. 98-102;

Tacitus. (Library of Congress)

A Dialogue Concerning Oratory, 1754), to the apparent decay of the art of oratory. Quintilian had addressed the problem a generation earlier, and while he may have had a strong influence on Tacitus's thoughts on the subject, it was to Cicero whom Tacitus turned for stylistic inspiration. The culprit appeared to be the decline of education, but as Tacitus developed his theme using the time-honored device of the dialogue, it became apparent that the age of the Antonines was not suited to great oratory because it lacked the tension and turmoil that inspires great public speakers. The consolation for the decline of this discipline was the universal peace that had replaced the chaos of the reign of Domitian.

In 115, after serving as proconsul of the province of Asia, Tacitus finished his narration of the events between 69, when Servius Sulpicius Galba assumed the *imperium*, and the death of Domitian in 96. *Historiae* (c. 109; *Histories*, 1731) was followed the next year by *Ab excessu divi Augusti* (c. 116, also known as *Annales*; *Annals*, 1598), which concentrated on the period from the beginning of the reign of Tiberius in 14 through the death of Nero in 68. As examples of historical scholarship, these works are flawed, punctuated with misinformation that might have been easily corrected had Tacitus troubled to do so. Tacitus was a student of human nature, not of politics, a moralist who sometimes reshaped history to suit his narrative. Having chosen the most turbulent period in Rome's history for his subject, Tacitus filled both works with his own prejudices, but his delineation of his characters is at times brilliant and redeems the *Histories* and the *Annals* from being mere gossip. Unfortunately, neither work exists intact. Tacitus died several years after completing the *Annals*, around 120, probably in Rome.

SIGNIFICANCE

Raised in the tradition of sacrifice and service to Rome that had characterized the Republic, Tacitus dedicated himself to the best interests of the state, and he distinguished himself as a man of great promise from the beginning. At the age of forty, he witnessed the beginning of a three-year-long nightmare in which many of his friends and colleagues were murdered on the orders of Domitian because they espoused and publicly proclaimed many of those same principles that Tacitus held dear. For the rest of his life, Tacitus was haunted by the events of those years, and their memory runs like a dark thread through everything he wrote.

Either consciously or unconsciously, Tacitus sought to ease his fears, his guilt, and his confusion through the study and writing of history. The past held the key to Rome's gradual decay as well as the source of her possible salvation, and to reveal both was a duty Tacitus could not avoid. In his first book, *The Life of Agricola*, Tacitus not only celebrated the deeds of his father-in-law but also explored for the first time the conflict between liberty and the power of the state. The theme of freedom is also a strong element in his second book, *Germania*. Much of what is known about the early Britons and Germans is found in these two works, and while there may be some doubt about the accuracy of some facts, it would be hard to question the admiration of Tacitus for those who prized liberty above life.

His third work, *A Dialogue Concerning Oratory*, seems a pleasant interlude between his earlier works and his histories of contemporary Rome, the *Histories* and the *Annals*. Tacitus was able to unleash a flood of criticism of the Imperial system and question the character of a number of his fellow countrymen, because the Antonine emperors under whom he served, Nerva, Trajan, and Hadrian, tolerated free inquiry. Thus, his vivid portraits have colored the opinions of countless generations of writers and historians. They are boldly drawn to serve not only as records of past deeds but also as warnings to the future leaders of the Roman state. Tacitus accepted the Imperial system as inevitable, but he believed that it could be revitalized by a return to the noble virtues that had made the Republic unique. It is as a moralist more than as a historian that Tacitus has had his most positive and enduring effect.

In the years following his death, the scholars and writers who succeeded Tacitus as the guardians of the traditions of the Roman state created a vogue for everything pre-Imperial, and the Republic, despite its violent history, was idealized as a golden age. The emperor Marcus Claudius Tacitus, who reigned briefly at the end of the third century, sought to claim descent from the great historian. As an act of filial piety, he ordered statues of his supposed ancestor to be erected in every public library and ten copies of his works to be produced every year. The latter edict certainly was a fitting memorial to Rome's great historian.

—Clifton W. Potter, Jr.

FURTHER READING

Chilver, G. E. F. *A Historical Commentary on Tacitus's Histories I and II*. New York: Oxford University Press, 1985. Containing a wealth of information, this work will prove very helpful to students of the period, because the author takes great care to trace each source and reference used by Tacitus.

Luce, T. J., and A. J. Woodman. *Tacitus and the Tacitean Tradition*. Princeton, N.J.: Princeton University Press, 1993. A collection of essays from a symposium on Tacitus, addressing both his major and his minor works as they may originally have been composed and as they survive.

Mellor, Ronald. *Tacitus*. New York: Routledge, 1993. Argues for reclaiming an ironic genius whose cynicism is suited to an analysis of the brutality of the current age.

O'Gorman, Ellen. *Irony and Misreading in the Annals of Tacitus*. New York: Cambridge University Press, 2000. Literary analysis and close reading of the language and style of the *Annals*, in the political context of first and second century Rome. Includes a full translation of the Latin.

Sinclair, Patrick. *Tacitus the Sententious Historian: A Sociology of Rhetoric in Annales*. University Park: Pennsylvania State University Press, 1995. Examines Greek and Latin rhetorical and historical culture, centering on Tacitus's use of aphorisms and maxims (*sententiae*).

Syme, Ronald. *Tacitus*. 2 vols. Oxford, England: Clarendon Press, 1963. This superb biography is a remarkable work of scholarship that examines the life and work of Tacitus against the background of Rome in the first century. Its bibliography is an excellent resource for the student.

Tacitus, Cornelius. *Agricola*. Translated by Anthony R. Birley. New York: Oxford University Press, 1999. With the original Latin as well as line-by-line English translations. Enriched with excellent notes and scholarly essays.

_____. *The Annals of Imperial Rome*. Translated by Michael Grant. Rev. ed. New York: Penguin Books, 1996. Contained in these volumes are books 4 through 6 and books 11 through 14 of the *Annals*. Also included is an index to the other volumes in the Loeb Classical Library containing parts of the *Histories* and the *Annals*. With excellent maps.

_____. *Histories*. Translated by W. H. Fyfe. New York: Oxford University Press, 1999. This bilingual text contains an excellent introductory essay to the life and works of Tacitus.

Woodman, A. J. *Tacitus Reviewed*. New York: Oxford University Press, 1998. Collects the great Tacitus scholar's thoughts on the historian over twenty-five years, with emphasis on the *Annals*.

SEE ALSO: Gnaeus Julius Agricola; Boudicca; Cicero; Nero.

RELATED ARTICLES in *Great Events from History: The Ancient World*: 180 B.C.E., Establishment of the *Cursus honorum*; 51 B.C.E., Cicero Writes *De republica*.

TANAQUIL
Etruscan aristocrat; wife of King Tarquin the First of Rome

Tanaquil, an Etruscan aristocrat, participated in the making of two Roman kings.

FLOURISHED: Mid- to late seventh century B.C.E;
   Tarquinii, Etruria (now Tarquinia, Italy) and Rome
ALSO KNOWN AS: Thanchvil (Etruscan)
AREA OF ACHIEVEMENT: Government and politics

EARLY LIFE
Virtually nothing is known of Tanaquil (TAN-ah-kwihl) before she married Lucumo, a half-Etruscan and half-Greek man from Corinth, renamed Lucius Tarquinius Priscus and known in history as Tarquin the First, the first Etruscan king of the Romans. The accounts of her in literature, however, allow one to suppose that she had an aristocratic upbringing and education that, coupled with her own characteristics, apparently shaped a decisive but generous woman with quick intelligence and ambition.

The main ancient source for Tanaquil's life and exploits is the Roman historian Livy's account of the early history of Rome, *Ab urbe condita libri* (c. 26 B.C.E.-15 C.E.; *The History of Rome*, 1600), and he credits Tanaquil with influence in six distinct events: her and her husband's abandonment of her native town Tarquinia for Rome; the interpretation of an omen on their arrival at Rome; the interpretation of an omen concerning their boy slave, Servius Tullius; action taken regarding the mother of Servius; in placing Servius Tullius, now her son-in-law, on the throne at the death of Tarquin; and the actions of her granddaughter, the younger Tullia, who was determined to emulate Tanaquil's successes.

LIFE'S WORK
Tanaquil enters Livy's narrative in his discussion of Lucumo. Livy reports that Lucumo was perceived by his fellow Tarquinians as an alien (his father was Corinthian) and therefore despised. He realized that despite his inherited wealth he would never be able to rise to a high position in Tarquinia. His wealth added to his pride, as did his marriage to Tanaquil, a young woman who Livy says "was not of a sort to put up with humbler circumstances in her married life than those she had been previously accustomed to." He says she also could not tolerate the indignity of her husband's position, as she wanted him to be highly regarded and, having suppressed her affection for her native town, decided that they should go to Rome, where opportunities for advancement—even for foreigners—abounded. Lucumo readily agreed, and they left for Rome.

On their arrival, while they were sitting in their carriage, an eagle descended gently on them and snatched Lucumo's hat. The eagle rose with great commotion and then swooped down again and replaced the hat before disappearing into the blue. Tanaquil, Livy reports, joyfully hugged her husband and interpreted the omen to mean that "no fortune was too high to hope for," because the bird had come as a messenger from the gods, gone to Lucumo's "highest part," taken the hat (or crown, as she

TRADITIONAL DATES OF THE EARLY KINGS OF ROME AND THEIR WIVES

King and Wife	Reign (B.C.E.)
Romulus (Alba Longa) + Hersilia (Sabine)	753-715
Numa Pompilius (Sabine) + unnamed poet	715-673
Tullus Hostilius (Latin)	673-642
Ancus Marcus (Latin) + unnamed mother of two sons	642-617
Lucius Tarquinius Priscus (Etruscan) + Tanaquil	616-579
Servius Tullius (Etruscan) + daughter of Tanaquil	579-535
Lucius Tarquinius Superbus (Etruscan) + Tullia	534-510

Note: Ethnicity appears in parentheses.

now declared) to heaven, and restored it with divine approval. Livy remarks that Tanaquil, like most Etruscans, was well skilled in reading celestial signs.

Throughout Livy's description of Lucumo—now Lucius Tarquinius Priscus—and his martial and civic successes in Rome, Tanaquil remained in the background until a strange event happened in the palace. As a young boy, named Servius Tullius, who was being raised in the royal palace as a slave, slept, his head burst into flames. The commotion brought both Tanaquil and Tarquin to the scene, but Tanaquil took charge of the situation. She forbade anyone from putting the flames out and instead insisted that the boy not be disturbed until he woke naturally. When he awoke a few minutes later, the flame went out. In secret, she discussed the matter with Tarquin, claiming that the flame portended that "he will one day prove a light in our darkness, a prop to our house in the day of its affliction." She therefore took him under her wing, providing him with a prince's education and treating him as a prince as well. His nature proved to be royal, and Tarquin betrothed him to his daughter. Livy suggests that Servius and his mother were never slaves but instead had been captured and brought to Rome, where Tanaquil, "as a tribute to her rank," did not enslave them but allowed them to live freely in the palace and became close friends with the mother and loved the boy.

When Tarquin was murdered by an ax wound to the head, Tanaquil immediately took precautions to ensure her safety and reputation, fearing again that she would become a "creature of contempt in the eyes of those who hated her." She ordered the palace gates to be closed, prepared salves for the wound to make people believe the king still lived, and called for Servius. She bid him to rise to his destiny and then went to an upper room of the palace. From the window, she urged the crowd below to be calm and patient, as the king had suffered only a surface wound and would soon recover. In the meantime, she bade them to give their loyalty to Servius. From this beginning, he gradually secured his place on the throne.

Tarquin had two sons (or grandsons), Lucius Tarquinius and Aruns. They had married Servius's two daughters, both called Tullia. The younger Tullia was unhappily married to the mild-mannered Aruns; he lacked ambition and fire. Tullia instead burned for Lucius Tarquinius and approached him with a murderous scheme. Soon thereafter they were both widowed and, without King Servius's approval, married each other. Tullia, tortured by the thought of Tanaquil's success with kingmaking, determined to emulate her, reasoning that if Tanaquil, a foreigner, had had enough influence to twice confer the crown, then she, of royal blood, must also be of some influence in the making of kings. She spurred her husband to action, causing her father's death and seeing her husband take the throne as Lucius Tarquinius Superbus, or Tarquin the Proud, the last of the kings of Rome.

SIGNIFICANCE

Much of what is known about the Etruscans comes from material remains and written accounts of them in non-Etruscan literature; no Etruscan literature survives. The classical writers Aristotle, Theopompus (a fourth century B.C.E. historian from Chios), and Livy report events inaccurately or with their own biases. To the Greeks and the Romans, the Etruscans were an unusual people who lived in luxury and enjoyed a prosperity that made them wanton and self-indulgent. Etruscan women, according to classical writers, participated in the decadence of their society, and their prerogatives and habits piqued the curiosity of non-Etruscan writers. Much of the material remains tends to corroborate the written evidence that presents the upper-class Etruscan women of the Archaic period (seventh to fifth century B.C.E.) as having a freedom and autonomy that was atypical in the ancient Greek and Roman world.

Wall paintings from tombs in Tarquinia and Cerveteri and other Etruscan cities depict scenes of luxurious feasts at which husbands and wives share equally in the festivities. Sarcophagi depict affectionate couples reclining together for eternity. Unlike Greek and Roman women, Etruscan women, as evidenced from funerary inscriptions and literature, had their own names, independent of their fathers' or mothers'. Evidence for female literacy exists in the numerous inscribed mirrors. From what can be gathered from these ancient sources, Tanaquil was not unusual in her predilection to take an active role in the lives of those around her.

This apparent high status and visibility of Etruscan women helped lead J. J. Bachofen in the 1860's to postulate his theory of matriarchy, a theory now well disproven, though still influential in Etruscology, and scholarly debate continues on the political role of Etruscan women. One side, best represented by the writings of L. Bonfante, concludes that Etruscan women did indeed enjoy a freedom and power unfamiliar to the rest of the ancient world and that the classical writers discuss the Etruscans in terms of "otherness" precisely to portray negative role models for contemporary Roman matrons. The other side, represented most eloquently by Iain McDougall, argues that social freedom does not necessarily imply political clout and looks instead to understand the historical account of Livy in its context. Focusing on the tendency of Livy to present ancient history in modern garb, these scholars conclude that Livy's account reflects contemporary phenomena rather than those of an ancient, and nearly completely assimilated, society. Examples include the similarity of the behavior of Tanaquil at Tarquin's death to that of Livia, wife of Augustus, at his death, or the similarity of the omens of Tarquin's hat and Augustus's bread as told by Suetonius, who records that when Augustus was having a picnic by the Appian Way, an eagle removed a piece of bread from his hands, soared in the air, and replaced it between his fingers.

For the story of Tanaquil in particular, it is also imperative to uncover the biases of Livy. D. S. Gochberg organizes these biases into five categories: Roman history for Livy is diagnostic, therapeutic, culturally imperialistic, militaristic, and—above all—moralistic. In his account of Tanaquil it is not explicit whether Livy considers her actions the result of ambition or of normal aristocratic sensibilities or whether he admires or finds fault with her (though he clearly finds fault with Tullia's behavior, and one might conclude that because she bases her behavior on Tanaquil's, Livy finds fault with both). The moralistic impetus that drives Livy's work is that simplicity and modesty are preferable to greed and ambition and that the study of ancient history provides examples or situations to reject or repeat.

Because Livy is writing in an age of political unrest, his history is both escapist and self-protective. By writing history, he can either ignore or confront modern troubles while avoiding the possibility of offending politicians like the young Augustus. It remains a question of scholarly debate whether Tanaquil appears in Livy's histories to provide a foil for Roman matrons like Lucretia or whether he uses Tanaquil in lieu of contemporary Roman women, who may be, in fact, his target.

The Tanaquil whom Livy presents clearly exhibits general traits of aristocracy: solidarity with other aristocrats, awareness of aristocratic privilege and the envy it may arouse in less fortunate people, and ambition that overrides natal family or national connections. At the same time, Livy highlights her Etruscan characteristics: her name, her independence, and her facility in interpreting omens.

—*Elise P. Garrison*

FURTHER READING

Bachofen, J. J. *Das Mutterrect*. 1861. Reprint. Basel, Switzerland: B. Schwabe, 1984. Bachofen proposed a theory of matriarchy and supported it for the Etruscans from the narrative of Livy. The theory of matriarchy has been disproven.

Bonfante, L. "Etruscan Couples and Their Aristocratic Society." In *Reflections of Women in Antiquity*, edited by H. Foley. New York: Gordon and Breach Science, 1981. Discusses the differences between Etruscan and Roman women. Bonfante argues that the archaeological evidence for the independence and power of Etruscan women is supported by the accounts of the classical writers.

_____, ed. *Etruscan Life and Afterlife. A Handbook of Etruscan Studies*. Detroit: Wayne State University Press, 1986. This is a collection of essays that discuss Etruscan history, politics, trade, art, architecture, coinage, language, daily life, and afterlife.

Heurgon, Jacques. *Daily Life of the Etruscans*. London: Phoenix, 2002. Heurgon is a proponent of the view that Etruscan woman played a role in civic life to which Roman matrons could never aspire.

Livy. *The Early History of Rome*. Translated by Aubrey de Sélincourt. New York: Penguin Books, 2002. Livy is the primary source for information on Tanaquil. Quotations in this article are taken from this translation.

McDougall, Iain. "Livy and Etruscan Women." *The Ancient History Bulletin* 4, no. 2 (1990): 24-30. McDougall argues that the literary evidence for Tanaquil provided by Livy does not support the notion of the political power of Etruscan women.

Nulle, Stebelton H., ed. *Classics of Western Thought: The Ancient World.* 4th ed. New York: Harcourt Brace Jovanovich, 1988. Organizes Livy's biases into five categories. To Gochberg, Roman history for Livy is diagnostic, therapeutic, culturally imperialistic, militaristic, and moralistic.

Ogilvie, R. M. *A Commentary on Livy Books 1-5.* Oxford, England: Clarendon Press, 1965. Notes the tendency of Livy to present ancient history within the context of his own time.

Richardson, Emeline Hill. *The Etruscans: Their Art and Civilization.* Chicago: University of Chicago Press, 1976. Richardson presents a comprehensive and accessible general overview of the Etruscan people and their customs, art, architecture, and religious beliefs.

SEE ALSO: Agrippina the Younger; Antonia Minor; Arria the Elder; Arria the Younger; Julia Domna; Julia Mamaea; Julia Soaemias; Julia III; Livia Drusilla; Lucretia; Valeria Messallina; Poppaea Sabina; Tarquins.

RELATED ARTICLES in *Great Events from History: The Ancient World*: 625-509 B.C.E., Rise of Etruscan Civilization in Rome; 509 B.C.E., Rape of Lucretia; c. 509 B.C.E., Roman Republic Replaces Monarchy.

TAO QIAN
Chinese poet

Tao Qian's insistence on directness and simplicity in both form and content, although largely unappreciated during his lifetime, was in subsequent generations recognized as a major contribution to the development of Chinese poetry.

BORN: 365 C.E.; Xinyang (now in Henan), China
DIED: 427 C.E.; Xinyang, China
ALSO KNOWN AS: T'ao Ch'ien (Wade-Giles); Tao Yuanming (Pinyin), T'ao Yüan-ming (Wade-Giles)
AREA OF ACHIEVEMENT: Literature

EARLY LIFE

Tao Qian (dow chyehn) was born on his parents' farm near the city of Xinyang (Hsin-yang) in what is now the province of Henan. His family had once been prominent among the local gentry, but by Tao Qian's time their property had shrunk to a few acres. In an autobiographical sketch written for his sons, he described himself as a bookish youth, fond of quiet and never happier than when observing the changing of the seasons. He received a conventional education in the Confucian classics and, on completing his studies, was awarded a minor position in the civil service.

It did not take him long, however, to become bored with this post, and he resigned to return to the life of a small farmer. He married and soon found himself with several young children to support; the unremitting toil of farming soon took its toll on his health. In 395 C.E., when he was thirty, his first wife died, and for a short time he was employed as a general's secretary. Once again, he found that he could not abide the life of an official, and he was soon back tilling his meager farm.

After remarrying and having more children, thus putting additional pressure on his already straitened circumstances, Tao Qian made one final attempt at occupying the sort of position for which his education had prepared him. In 405 C.E., an uncle with influence at court arranged for him to be appointed magistrate at Pengze (P'eng-tse), not far from his home. Before long, however, he had to resign, because "my instinct is all for freedom and will not brook discipline or restraint." For the remainder of his life, he would eke out a subsistence living on his farm and refuse all further offers of government employment, while exercising the poetic gifts that would not be widely acknowledged until well after his death.

LIFE'S WORK

China was racked by dynastic warfare during much of Tao Qian's life, and some commentators have suggested that his reluctance to assume official positions was caused by an awareness of the punishments that awaited those who supported the losing side. It is far more probable, however, that it was his profound dislike of being at a superior's beck and call that made it impossible for him to take on the kinds of responsibilities society expected of him. His independent attitude was incomprehensible to most of his peers, and as a result it was commonly assumed that Tao Qian must be some sort of hermit or recluse.

This he was not, although it is true that he studiously avoided anything that carried with it formal duties or organizational affiliations. He was at one point on the verge of accepting an invitation to join the Lotus Society, an exclusive group of Buddhist intellectuals and literary men, but at the last moment he declined when he realized that no matter how convivial its members might be, it was still an organization with rules and regulations. Tao Qian was not antisocial—he was reputed to have been well liked by his neighbors, and he knew quite a few of his fellow poets—but he definitely was an advocate of the simple life, which for him meant staying close to home and nature and ignoring almost everything else.

It is this fundamental love of simplicity that distinguishes Tao Qian's verses from the works of court poets of his time, who utilized obscure allusions and complicated stylistic devices to fashion verses that appealed only to the highly educated. Tao Qian, by way of contrast, seldom made any literary allusions whatsoever, and he wrote for the widest possible audience. As a consequence, he was slighted by his era's critics and fully appreciated only by later generations of readers. It was more than a century after his death before a complete edition of his works appeared. The first writers to champion his reputation seriously were the Tang Dynasty (T'ang; 618-907 C.E.) poets Meng Haoran (Meng Hao-jan; 689-740 C.E.) and Wang Wei (701-761 C.E.), who ensured that his name would not be forgotten by honoring him as a spiritual predecessor of what would become one of the most brilliant periods in Chinese literary history.

The charms of Tao Qian's poetry are subtle. The fifth poem in his series of poems on drinking wine is perhaps as good an example as any of how simple words and thoughts can yield complex emotions:

> I built my cottage among the habitations of men,
> And yet there is no clamor of carriages and horses.
> You ask: "Sir, how can this be done?"
> "A heart that is distant creates its own solitude."
> I pluck chrysanthemums under the eastern hedge,
> Then gaze afar towards the southern hills.
> The mountain air is fresh at the dusk of day;
> The flying birds in flocks return.
> In these things there lies a deep meaning;
> I want to tell it, but have forgotten the words.

The irony resides in the concluding line's apparent confession of failure, which is superficially true—the poem's meaning has not been formally defined in words—but in a more profound sense false, since meaning has been suggestively expressed in the cumulative interaction of these direct and vivid images. Such images might strike self-consciously sophisticated readers, which was how many of the court officials of Tao Qian's time viewed themselves, as nothing more than bucolic snapshots. For those who approach them without patronizing preconceptions, however, their evident simplicity is resonant with intimations of elemental natural forces.

In order to appreciate the full impact of Tao Qian's decision to concentrate on realistic description of his humble surroundings, the reader needs to compare his approach with that of the dominant aristocratic and scholarly poets of the period. Their ideal was the mannered evocation of court life in lyrics that were rigidly controlled by parallel structures and recurring tonal patterns. A literal translation of one of the poems by Shen Yue (Shen Yüeh; 441-513 C.E.) reads:

> slackening reins, dismounts carved carriage,
> changing clothes, attends jade bed.
>
> slanting hairpin, reflects autumn waters,
> opening mirror, compares spring dresses.

Each line contains exactly two parallel images, the Chinese ideograms follow a set sequence of tones, and the content is characteristically taken from upper-class life.

Compare the above to the third section of Tao Qian's "Returning to the Farm to Dwell":

> I planted beans below the southern hill
> The grasses flourished, but bean sprouts were few.
> I got up at dawn to clear away the weeds
> And come back now with the moon, hoe on shoulder.
> Tall bushes crowd the narrow path
> And evening dew soaks my clothes.
> Wet clothes are no cause for complaint
> If things will only go as hoped.

Here the conversational tone of the narrative, the way that content is restricted to the mundanities of farm life, and the *in medias res* beginning all work together to convey an impression of natural reality that is the polar opposite of Shen Yue's sort of poetry.

Tao Qian was not, however, averse to enlivening his rural existence with an overindulgence in the pleasures of wine. He was renowned for his drinking, which in the social context of his period was an acceptable way of temporarily escaping worldly preoccupations rather than a sign of moral weakness. Tao Qian's name is thus often linked with those of two other poets who were also serious imbibers: Chu Yuan (Ch'u Yüan; c. 343 B.C.E.-c. 277 B.C.E.) and Li Bo (Li Po; 701-762 C.E.). Some of his best poems were written while enjoying this favorite pastime.

Tao Qian's life ended in the same pastoral setting in which it had begun, with no dramatic anecdote to set the day of his death apart from the days that had preceded and would follow it. During his final twenty-two years, he had become both a material and a spiritual part of his natural environment. In a prose sketch written just before he died, Tao Qian described how, as was the custom, his old friends gave him a farewell banquet in honor of what he had meant to their lives. With typical unhurried deliberation, he enumerated the foods and wines that were served as he prepared "to depart from this lodging house to return for all time to his own home," where he would become one of the immortal figures of Chinese literature.

SIGNIFICANCE

It is the high value Tao Qian set on immediacy and immanence that has led many literary historians to see his work as pivotal in the development of Chinese poetry. Although there were advocates of simplicity who came before him and apostles of aestheticism still to come after him, it was his lyrics, more than any others, that served as a continuous source of inspiration for succeeding ages and would be rediscovered whenever poetry seemed in danger of becoming too mannered and removed from common experience.

In addition to his importance as a literary model, Tao Qian is admired for his decision to remain true to himself rather than subordinate his feelings to the demands of conventional lifestyles. The writers and intellectuals of his day were, broadly speaking, split into the opposing camps of conformist Confucians and antiauthoritarian Daoists, and when Tao Qian rejected the former it would have been normal for him to have gravitated to the vagabond life of the latter. He chose, however, to pilot his own idiosyncratic course between these polar opposites, and he suffered much personal hardship in so doing.

Even more important than his position in literary history or his personal qualities, however, is the candid beauty of his poetry. The freshness of his images, his homespun but Heaven-aspiring morality, and his steadfast love of rural life shine through the deceptively humble words in which they are expressed, and as a consequence he has long been regarded one of China's most accomplished and accessible poets.

—*Paul Stuewe*

FURTHER READING

Cotterell, Yong Yap, and Arthur Cotterell. *The Early Civilization of China*. London: Weidenfeld and Nicolson, 1975. Chapter 6, "The Age of Disunity: The So-Called Six Dynasties," gives a good general account of historical developments during Tao Qian's time. This chapter also includes useful sections on the religion and art of the period.

Davis, A. R. *T'ao Yüan-ming: His Works and Their Meaning*. 2 vols. New York: Cambridge University Press, 1983. This thorough study consists of a volume of translation and commentary, and a second volume of commentary, notes, and a biography of the poet.

Kwong, Charles Yim-tze. *Tao Qian and the Chinese Poetic Tradition: The Quest for Cultural Identity*. Ann Arbor, Mich.: The Center for Chinese Studies, 1995. One of the few English-language literary studies of Tao Qian's work. Discusses the poet in his cultural and literary contexts, comparing his work to that of both Chinese and Western poets.

Tao Qian. *The Poems of T'ao Ch'ien*. Translated by Lily Pao-hu Chang and Marjorie Sinclair. Honolulu: University of Hawaii Press, 1953. This beautifully produced volume includes original brush drawings reminiscent of a deluxe Chinese-language edition. Chang and Sinclair opt for inclusiveness in translating all the poems attributed to Tao Qian, several of which are the objects of scholarly debate. The translations themselves are reliable if not always idiomatic. A brief biography of the poet is included in an appendix.

_____. *The Poetry of T'ao Ch'ien*. Translated and edited by James Robert Hightower. Oxford, England: Clarendon Press, 1970. The standard edition in English. The translations themselves are not noticeably superior to those of his predecessors, but Hightower's notes make the book an essential reference for anyone doing serious work on Tao Qian. It is by far the best guide to its subject's use of traditional elements of the Chinese literary tradition.

SEE ALSO: Sima Xiangru.

RELATED ARTICLES in *Great Events from History: The Ancient World*: c. 405 C.E., Statesman Tao Qian Becomes Farmer and Daoist Poet; 420 C.E., Southern Dynasties Period Begins in China.

TARQUINS
Roman royal family of Etruscan origin

The Tarquins were an influential and aristocratic Etruscan-Roman royal family clan whose members include the last three kings of Rome and the founders of the Roman Republic.

Lucius Tarquinius Priscus (Lucumo; Tarquin the First), traditionally r. 616-579 B.C.E.

BORN: Seventh century B.C.E.; Tarquinii, Etruria (now Tarquinia, Italy)
DIED: 579 B.C.E.; Rome (now in Italy)

Lucius Tarquinius Superbus (Tarquin the Proud), traditionally r. 534-510 B.C.E.

BORN: Sixth century B.C.E.; Rome (now in Italy)
DIED: After 510 B.C.E.; Cumae (now Cuma, Italy)
ALSO KNOWN AS: Tarquinii (Latin); Tarchna (Etruscan)
AREAS OF ACHIEVEMENT: Architecture, government and politics, religion, war and conquest

EARLY LIVES

The Tarquins (TAR-kwihns) play a colorful part in the Roman traditions recorded by the historians Livy and Dionysius and, by all accounts, they were the most influential family in Rome's transition from monarchy to republic in the late sixth century B.C.E. Tradition brings their founder, Demaratus, to Tarquinii as a fugitive from the Corinthian tyrant Cypselus in the sixth century B.C.E. Once settled, Demaratus married his sons, Lucumo and Aruns, into the Etruscan nobility. Lucumo emigrated to Rome with his wife, Tanaquil, as Lucius Tarquinius Priscus (LOO-shus tar-KWIHN-ee-us PRIS-cus). (Whether Lucumo is actually an Etruscan title like "sir" or an Etruscan name equivalent to Lucius is debated.) There, through diligent work and strategic planning, the ambitious couple became influential with the king, Ancus Marcius. Appointed guardian of the king's sons, Priscus sent the princes out of town on their father's death and contrived to have himself elected king. Despite his success, some years later, he was assassinated by the disgruntled followers of Ancus's displaced sons, during an attempt to reclaim the throne.

Nevertheless, rule passed to Priscus's popular son-in-law, the Latin Servius Tullius, husband of the king's daughter Tarquinia. Servius's throne became the object of two ambitious royals: Priscus's grandson (or possibly son) Lucius and Servius's daughter Tullia, the wife of Lucius's brother Aruns. Lucius and Tullia found common cause and, after their respective spouses met convenient ends, married. They then set about undermining Servius's popularity. During a riotous confrontation in the senate, Lucius threw the aged Servius out into the streets, where he was dispatched by assassins. Tullia, who had rushed into town to be the first to proclaim Lucius king, drove her carriage over her father's body as she returned home. Lucius, who had already taken care to eliminate other potential family rivals to the throne, seized power with the backing of the army and ruled as Lucius Tarquinius Superbus (soo-PER-bus; "the Proud"). He and his immediate family were ultimately driven out by the aristocratic revolution that established the Roman Republic.

According to tradition, Superbus was both a successful and cunning military leader and a murderous despot. Rome chafed under his rule until his son Sextus Tarquinius raped Lucretia, the wife of his kinsman Lucius Tarquinius Collatinus. While Collatinus's pedigree is uncertain, it looks as though he was a descendant of Lucumo's brother Aruns. Lucretia committed suicide after exposing the rape to her husband and father. Sextus's cousin Lucius Junius Brutus, Superbus's nephew, then led Collatinus and others in an outraged revolt that drove Superbus's family from Rome. Rome became a republic under the executive power of two Tarquin consuls: Lucius Junius Brutus and Lucius Tarquinius Collatinus. The family of Superbus made several attempts to retake power, aided in part by the military support of the Etruscan warlord Lars Porsenna of Clusium and Brutus's own sons (whom he executed), but the Republic endured.

LIVES' WORKS

Roman tradition treats Servius as strictly Latin in origin and temperament (and therefore to be excused from his royal connections) and separates the republican heroes Brutus and Collatinus from the monarchy. This entry therefore primarily engages the work of Tarquinius Priscus and Tarquinius Superbus. However, the fact that these other characters were intimately connected with the royal line should not be missed. Lucius Junius Brutus, for example, was an heir to the throne who escaped suspicion by playing a simpleton (hence his cognomen "Brutus," or "Blockhead") and who executed his own sons for conspiring to bring back the expelled Tarquin monarchy (to which they were also heirs).

There is also some debate as to whether Priscus and Superbus are two versions of the same historical person (a "doublet"), for many of Priscus's achievements seem to be echoes of Superbus's better evidenced accomplishments. Nevertheless, scholarship generally inclines toward tradition in making Priscus a genuine historical figure. Of Superbus, however, Roman tradition, contemporary sources, archaeological evidence, and scholarship all agree: He was Rome's last king. His primary legacy (whether legitimately earned or promoted by those who deposed him) was to give Rome a distaste for monarchy—and even for the word "rex" (king)—that endured throughout the nearly five hundred years of the Roman Republic. Nevertheless, the Tarquins, especially if the reign of Servius Tullius reflects any measure of continuity in Tarquin policy, must receive a considerable share of credit for Rome's accomplishments during the sixth century B.C.E.

Both Priscus and Superbus are credited with beginning and completing major civic projects that made a unified city out of Rome's mixture of ethnic villages and that brought prestige, wealth, and influence to Rome. Principal among these projects were the Cloaca Maxima ("Great Sewer"), which drained the area for Rome's central forum (creating a common civic and judicial center of the city), and the foundation of an impressive temple of Jupiter Optimus Maximus (Jupiter the Best and Greatest) on the Capitoline hill overlooking the forum. It was to this temple that victorious Roman generals proceeded in triumph to offer their spoils as thanks for victory. Superbus is also credited with the erection of wooden stands at the Circus Maximus for citizens to view games and events. Rome's early defensive wall (the so-called Servian Wall), ascribed to Servius Tullius, was probably a later addition to the city's defenses.

The last three Roman kings worked to unify and organize their city's growing population with civil and military reforms and with the foundation of temples to gods revered by Rome's mixture of Latin, Etruscan, Sabine, and other ethnicities. They made provisions for both the increasing number of clans (and clan leaders) and independent poor who arrived to become part of the city. Under Priscus, clan leaders were added to the senate's num-

Sextus Tarquinius, third from left, meets Lucretia. (F. R. Niglutsch)

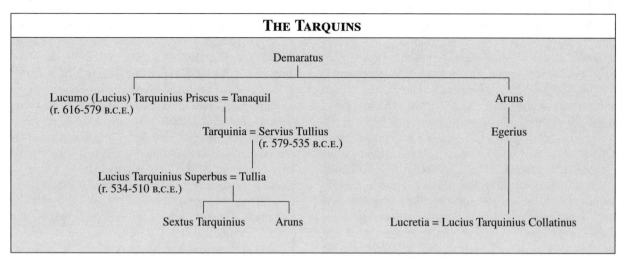

THE TARQUINS

Demaratus

Lucumo (Lucius) Tarquinius Priscus = Tanaquil
(r. 616-579 B.C.E.)

Aruns

Tarquinia = Servius Tullius
(r. 579-535 B.C.E.)

Egerius

Lucius Tarquinius Superbus = Tullia
(r. 534-510 B.C.E.)

Sextus Tarquinius   Aruns   Lucretia = Lucius Tarquinius Collatinus

---

bers, and tradition assigns to Servius Tullius the most important reforms of the military and civic structure (such as the Comitia Centuriata, an elective assembly of citizen males organized by classes according to wealth and ability to furnish weapons). The so-called Servian Constitution, associated with these reforms, probably reflects the Romans' desire to anchor all positive elements of their "traditional" constitution firmly to a Latin king. However, the Servian reforms can likely be seen as falling within a greater Tarquin program, at least until the reign of Superbus went awry. In any event, the foundational organization of the Roman army and state were laid down in this regal period.

From these developments, the Tarquins engaged in successful conquests and treaties that expanded Rome's sphere of influence. Priscus is said to have conquered a number of surrounding Latin and Sabine towns and to have put his sons in charge of them. Servius is (probably correctly) credited with the completion of a favorable treaty with the Latin League. Superbus (whom even Livy concedes was a successful military leader) continued an aggressive policy of expansion, conquest, and inclusion in a protective ring around Rome's growing domain. A treaty with the city of Gabii, which was inscribed on a hide shield and legible until the late first century B.C.E., names a Tarquin of Rome (probably Superbus) and seems indicative of this policy. In any case, the last three kings increased Rome's territorial control from a few miles to nearly 350 miles (565 kilometers) around the city, backed by an effective and disciplined citizen army and a growing number of interrelated constituencies.

Given their broad engagement in and around Rome, the Tarquins' influence outlasted both the fall of the mon-

archy and the struggles of the young Republic. In fact, a fourth century B.C.E. Etruscan tomb painting (the "François" tomb) by a Marcus Camitlnas at the Etruscan city of Vulci depicts the rescue of a Caelius Vibenna by Mastarna and Aulus Vibenna and the killing of Gnaeus Tarquinius of Rome, who had captured Caelius. While the exact identification of these characters and the story to which the painting refers are a matter of dispute, this and other historical evidence show that the Tarquin family exercised a continuing influence on the entire area's early development and imagination.

Even against this background, the story of Priscus's surprise arrival in Rome, Superbus's tyrannical behavior, Brutus's clever masquerade, Sextus's unbridled lust, Lucretia's noble suicide, and the ensuing revolt of liberation reads much more like political melodrama than history. Indeed, Roman historians modeled much of the story of the Roman tyrants' fall on the fall of Greek tyrants recorded by Herodotus. After all, besides oral tradition, the Romans had only a scant few relics and records of events until the history of Fabius Pictor, nearly three hundred years after the events. Subsequent evidence by and large corroborates the traditional history in broad outline, and although Roman historians wrote in the personalities, many of the events and accomplishments ascribed to the historical characters seem to cling stubbornly, in a most Roman way, to credibility.

SIGNIFICANCE

The Tarquins, as a clan, oversaw enduring civic, military, political, architectural, religious, and cultural developments that marked Rome's rise from a relatively minor Latin city of mixed peoples to a major player in Latium, the region inhabited by the Latins, now Lazio and Etruria (modern Tuscany and portions of Umbria). Moreover, instead of a history of sharply demarcated ethnic communities (as it is sometimes portrayed), the overall record of the Tarquins' regime shows a fusion of elements—particularly Etruscan and Latin—that set the stage for Rome's eventual supremacy in Italy.

—*Eric D. Nelson and Susan K. Allard-Nelson*

FURTHER READING

Dionysius. *The Roman Antiquities of Dionysius of Halicarnassus*. Translated by Ernest Cary. Cambridge, Mass.: Harvard University Press, 1971-1990. Dionysius was a Greek who lived in Rome from 30 to 8 B.C.E., and wrote a history of Rome to 246 B.C.E. Contains notes and index.

Gantz, T. N. "The Tarquin Dynasty." *Historia* 24 (1975): 539-554. Gantz presents a view of the Tarquins that is sympathetic to the original sources' contention that there was, in fact, a Tarquin Dynasty. Includes a full family tree and argues for the interesting speculation that the Gnaeus Tarquinius pictured in the François Tomb may be the father of Superbus.

Holloway, R. R. *The Archaeology of Early Rome and Latium*. New York: Routledge, 2000. A fine presentation of archaeological findings and their significance for an understanding of the development of early Rome and the surrounding area. Holloway also gives the reader a strong understanding of the different controversies involved with interpreting the evidence. Includes notes and index.

Livy. *The Early History of Rome*. Translated by Aubrey de Sélincourt. New York: Penguin Books, 2002. Books 1-5 of Titius Livius's (late first century B.C.E.) comprehensive history of Rome to the time of Augustus. Contains the traditional and vivid account of the Tarquins and their exploits. Offers a useful introduction as well as the translation. Includes maps, bibliography, and index.

Ogilvie, R. M. *Early Rome and the Etruscans*. Atlantic Highlands, N.J.: Humanities Press, 1976. Ogilvie presents a substantial overview of the evidence for the Etruscan influence on Rome. Includes a date chart, description of primary sources, notes for further reading by chapter, and index.

SEE ALSO: Lucretia; Tanaquil.

RELATED ARTICLES in *Great Events from History: The Ancient World*: 625-509 B.C.E., Rise of Etruscan Civilization in Rome; 509 B.C.E., Rape of Lucretia.

TERENCE
Roman playwright

As a Roman comic playwright whose adaptations of Greek dramas depicted in graceful Latin the social realities operating in his ancient world, Terence strongly influenced the development of sophisticated theater in the West.

BORN: c. 190 B.C.E.; Carthage
DIED: 159 B.C.E.; en route to Greece
ALSO KNOWN AS: Publius Terentius Afer
AREA OF ACHIEVEMENT: Literature

EARLY LIFE

Ancient materials reporting on the life of Terence (TEHR-uhns) frequently present contradictory information. Certain facts, however, fall into the realm of probability: Publius Terentius Afer (Terence) was born at Carthage and came to Rome as the slave of Terentius Lucanus, a senator who educated him and set him free. Because Terence's life fell between the Second and Third Punic Wars, he could not have been a slave captured in combat; thus, he may have been owned and sold by a Carthaginian trader.

Terence was of average height, medium build, and dark complexion. His cognomen "Afer" is thought to indicate his African birth; however, one cannot be completely certain that Terence was actually ever a slave. Roman biographers, who often wove a web of fiction around their subjects, commonly recorded playwrights as having sprung from slavery, and "Afer" need not positively establish African birth. Nevertheless, many commentators have marveled at the significant achievement of the onetime slave who learned Latin as a second language and who came to use it with such outstanding artistry and precision.

In Rome, the young man's intelligence and talent soon gained for him entry into the Scipionic circle of study, a group of patrician literati behind a philhellenic movement. So close was the involvement of Terence and particular associates in this group—including Scipio

Africanus and Gaius Laelius—that rumors circulated suggesting that Terence was simply a front for these august patrons of the arts who had really authored the plays. Terence, in fact, inadvertently helped the malicious gossip along by never definitively attempting to refute the charges. Indeed, in the prologues to his plays he concentrated on stating his theories of dramatic art, trying to deflect the scurrilous accusations. Unfortunately, Terence's short life came to be plagued by constant innuendo.

When Terence offered his first drama to the aediles, the officials at the public games where the performances were held, he was ordered to show his work to Caecilius Statius, a revered comic playwright of an earlier era whose successes had been, in part, a result of the abilities of noted actor Lucius Ambivius Turpio. Legend describes the youthful Terence, poorly dressed, arriving at the dramatist's home during the dinner hour, sitting down on a bench near the old man's couch, and beginning to read from his first effort. It took only a few minutes for Caecilius to recognize the genius of his young visitor, and Terence was invited to take a seat at the table. Not only did his career as dramatist begin at that moment but also the actor Turpio, now in old age, performed in Terence's plays, giving them the same public notice and authoritative support he had given to Caecilius. Thus promoted, Terence appeared an assured success from the beginning.

LIFE'S WORK

Terence looked to the New Comedy of Greece for his major literary resource and composed, therefore, in the tradition of *palliatae*, plays derived from Greek models, and acted in Greek dress, or *pallium*. Of the twenty-six complete plays surviving from the second century B.C.E. Roman stage, six are the work of Terence, whose chief model was Menander, an artist with a reputation in the ancient world superseded only by Homer and Vergil. While the Old Comedy had dealt with affairs of state, the New Comedy exemplified by Menander focused on domestic issues, particularly on wealthy youths and the tangled dilemmas of their often complicated love lives. Filial duty, which on occasion ran counter to the young men's casual self-indulgence, and the devious machinations of crafty slaves helped generate comic situations at times to farcical extremes.

Terence found his métier in these intricate plots and, by artfully adapting the Greek models, brought with his distinctive translations a conscious artistry to the Roman stage. He developed prologues that articulated literary principles and that did not simply explain the action to follow. He developed a "doubling technique" to balance Menander's character creations. Alongside these innovations, Terence sensitively rendered the impact of behavioral fashion on the ethical values of his time. While Terence realized that in his models the characters were standard, the action was predictable, and the themes were formulaic; under his original touch the plays not only embody a vivid realism but also detail a sociological compendium of the age.

The complete works of Terence, produced over a six-year period, include the following extant plays: *Andria* (166 B.C.E.; English translation, 1598), *Hecyra* (165 B.C.E.; *The Mother-in-Law*, 1598), *Heautontimorumenos* (163 B.C.E.; *The Self-Tormentor*, 1598), *Eunuchus* (161 B.C.E.; *The Eunuch*, 1598), *Phormio* (161 B.C.E.; English translation, 1598), and *Adelphoe* (160 B.C.E.; *The Brothers*, 1598). While the dramas—all based on the work of either Menander or Apollodorus of Carystus—reveal the extent of Terence's achievement, of greater significance to his biography are the *didascaliae* (production notes attached to the dramas) and the prologues, for these writings candidly reveal information that chronicles the way Terence's creative life was progressing. These statements sometimes indicate his strategy for dealing with

Terence. (Library of Congress)

the hurtful charges of plagiarism and the jealous accusations of *contaminatio*, that is, adulterating his literary sources.

Even before the presentation of his first play, Terence was forced to defend his unorthodox, innovative literary practices. Luscius Lanuvinus, a jealous competitor who had either seen *Andria* in rehearsal or read it in manuscript, began a vendetta of slander by accusing Terence of contaminating the plays he had used in his adaptation. During the next few years, these accusations were repeated and, apparently, escalated into charges of plagiarism. Terence went about defending the legitimacy of his literary methods as well as the originality of his artistry, going so far as to point out the Roman historical precedent for adapting work from the Greek stage. On one occasion, Terence flatly charged that his accuser was simply trying to force him into early retirement, to drive a young competitor from the theater by wounding him with invective. Insisting that he would prefer to exchange compliment for compliment rather than engage in verbal skirmishes, Terence urged his audiences to enjoy his plays, to be fair in their assessments, and to disregard the gossip of an evil-tempered old man, especially one whose talent was weak.

Another difficulty in his career Terence accepted with benign amusement: the problem with presenting *The Mother-in-Law*, a drama that suffered two failures before its eventual success. The first time Terence offered the play (165 B.C.E.), his audience rushed out of the performance to view a prizefight and a tightrope walker. Trying again five years later, Terence watched as the audience hurriedly left to watch some gladiators. A few months later, the play was successfully performed, with Terence in his prologue requesting courteous support for his efforts and urging his audience to abstain from irreverent behavior that might expose him to more unfair criticism by his enemies.

In his plays, Terence used the stock themes—boastful soldiers, crafty slaves, kindly prostitutes, professional parasites, and confused sons, all involved in innocent mistakes and switched identities—and held the mirror up for the examination of moral and ethical principles, touching such concerns as the limits of filial duty, the question of a slave's loyalty, the role of women in Roman society, and the proprieties of legal deportment. While comedy did not readily lend itself to didacticism, Terence's plays, nevertheless, were epitomes of both entertainment and instruction, especially in portraying the emotional and psychological complexities involved in all human relationships.

SIGNIFICANCE

As Terence's brief life was filled with controversy and speculation, so were the events surrounding his death. The playwright left Rome for Greece and never returned. He had undertaken the journey possibly to study at first hand the culture from which his plays were derived or to scrutinize the work of Menander—maybe even to discover other works modeled after Menander's or to escape for a time the Roman atmosphere of jealousy and acrimony that had spawned the petulant attacks of his rivals as they jockeyed for favor among patrons of the arts and theater audiences. Terence died in 159 B.C.E., either of an illness in Greece or in a shipwreck that also may have destroyed more than one hundred adaptations from Menander that he was bringing home.

Terence's reputation as a master dramatist has clearly withstood the passage of centuries; his accomplishments in the development and advancement of world theater are clear. His painstaking artistry in portraying psychological motivation and social reality set benchmarks for dramatists to follow in establishing the seriousness of comedy. In eliminating the prologue as simply a means to explain plot, Terence ensured that the drama had to depend on characterization and dialogue. When sophisticated theatrical tastes came to govern the stage, Terence became a major literary source. During the Restoration in England, when the comedy of manners reigned supreme, Terence's work influenced such masters as William Congreve and Thomas Otway. In France, Molière looked to Terence for inspiration. In addition, the expository prologue as a means for critical expression and advancement of dramatic theory came to be a mark of identity for George Bernard Shaw.

The facts of Terence's life will be forever clouded by rumor and hearsay, for speculation and gossip were often freely intermingled with fact among ancient biographers. On Terence's death, records Suetonius, he left a twenty-acre estate on the Appian Way; Licinus Porcius, however, asserts that at the end of his life Terence possessed not even a rented house where his slave might announce his master's death.

—*Abe C. Ravitz*

FURTHER READING

Beare, W. *The Roman Stage: A Short History of Latin Drama in the Time of the Republic.* New York: Barnes & Noble, 1965. An authoritative study of the Roman stage, particularly useful regarding the stage practices, customs, and techniques of the time. Includes a detailed examination of the charge of contamination leveled against Terence. With extensive notes, bibliography, and appendices.

Copley, Frank O. *The Comedies of Terence.* Indianapolis: Bobbs-Merrill, 1967. Translations of each play with a useful introductory note on each drama. A fourteen-page essay surveys the problems encountered in attempting to reconstruct Terence's life and in trying to analyze his art.

Duckworth, George E. *The Nature of Roman Comedy: A Study in Popular Entertainment.* Norman: University of Oklahoma Press, 1994. A vital source on the ancient stage and its conventions as well as on the contributions of Terence. This work is a detailed study of themes, treatments, methods, and influences of Terence, including the critical problems in studying his texts and the biographical problems in studying his life. With an extensive index and bibliography.

_____, ed. *The Complete Roman Drama.* 2 vols. New York: Random House, 1942. This work includes Terence's production notes, which date the performances, describe some of the staging techniques, identify some of the actors, and help both in setting the Terentian ambience and in establishing the plays' chronologies. A general introduction provides a sound overview of the era and gives important information on ancient stage discipline.

Forehand, Walter E. *Terence.* Boston: Twayne, 1985. A sound, basic work that outlines the major controversies surrounding Terence's life and productions. Contains a full account of Terence's literary career, surveying the plays and illuminating the theater background of the times. Includes bibliography.

Goldberg, Sander M. *The Making of Menander's Comedy.* Berkeley: University of California Press, 1980.

This study of Menander's art sheds light on Terence, whose adaptations came mainly from this Greek model. Terence's work in relation to Menander is discussed in detailed, analytical fashion throughout.

_____. *Understanding Terence.* Princeton, N.J.: Princeton University Press, 1986. A perceptive, analytical study focusing on Terence and the Latin tradition of New Comedy rather than on Terence as an adapter of Menander; this work analyzes the prologues and the plays for their language and themes. The critical problems in dealing with Terence are studied. Contains a bibliography for the individual plays as well as for further study of ancient Greece.

Harsh, Philip Whaley. *A Handbook of Classical Drama.* Stanford, Calif.: Stanford University Press, 1976. Contains an informative survey of Terence's life and work set within the context of the total range of classical drama. Extensive notes as well as bibliographies for Terence and his peers are included.

Konstan, David. *Roman Comedy.* Ithaca, N.Y.: Cornell University Press, 1983. An examination of the New Comedy genre within contexts of the ideology and the institutions of the Roman state. With a reading of Roman plays—including those of Terence—from the social and philosophical perspective to determine how the plays reveal the ethical standards and moral imperatives of the age. Includes bibliography.

SEE ALSO: Juvenal; Martial; Menander; Phaedrus; Plautus; Plutarch; Scipio Africanus; Seneca the Younger.

RELATED ARTICLES in *Great Events from History: The Ancient World*: c. 385 B.C.E., Greek Playwright Aristophanes Dies; 159 B.C.E., Roman Playwright Terence Dies.

TERTULLIAN
Roman theologian

Tertullian was the most outstanding spokesman for Christianity in the Latin West before Saint Augustine; his polemical treatises set the direction for much of Western theology.

BORN: c. 155-160 C.E.; at or near Carthage (now in Tunisia)
DIED: After 217 C.E.; probably near Carthage
ALSO KNOWN AS: Quintus Septimius Florens Tertullianus (full name)
AREAS OF ACHIEVEMENT: Religion, literature

EARLY LIFE

Quintus Septimius Florens Tertullianus, known as Tertullian (tur-TUHL-yuhn), left a strong mark on the history of Latin literature and exercised more influence than anyone but Saint Augustine on the development of theology in the Western church. However, he left but few scraps of biographical information. A short paragraph in Saint Jerome's *De viris illustribus* (392-393; *On Illustrious Men*, 1999) yields few assertions, and only deductions can be drawn from the writings of Tertullian, which are remarkable for their lack of self-revelation. Each item has been closely examined by scholars, and while virtually nothing can be said with certainty about the man, the following picture emerges from a cautious balancing of ancient tradition and modern skepticism.

Tertullian was certainly born and raised in Roman North Africa, in or near the proconsular capital of Carthage, to a prosperous pagan family. His father was probably a career military officer attached to the staff of the proconsul, and several relatives were active in the literary life of the city. Any birth date assigned to Tertullian (usually 155-160 C.E.) is reached by subtracting from 197 C.E., the secure date of one of his earliest works, the *Apologeticus* (*Apology*, 1642), enough years—roughly forty—to account for its character as a mature masterpiece of style, argumentation, and Christian apologetics.

Tertullian received the standard education of a well-to-do Roman, culminating in extensive rhetorical training, in which he must have excelled, judging from his subsequent literary career. It is difficult to avoid identifying Tertullian of Carthage with Tertullian the jurist, whose writings are quoted in later Roman law codes. The men were contemporaries; the jurist wrote on questions of military law, and the Carthaginian had a penchant for legalistic language and argument and was declared by Eusebius of Caesarea to have been eminent at the Roman bar. If they were indeed the same person, Tertullian of Carthage traveled to Rome, became a pupil of the great jurist Pomponius, and established among legal scholars of the Empire a reputation that was later vindicated by his apologetic works.

It was probably in early middle age, not long before 197, that Tertullian converted to Christianity. He never discusses his conversion, though he expresses repeatedly an admiration for the constancy of Christian martyrs, their steadfastness in persecution, and their stubborn defiance of Roman authority in the face of death. It was he who coined the saying "The blood of Christians is seed." He may have been ordained a priest, as Jerome claims, for some of Tertullian's works are clearly sermons. While Tertullian uses two or three turns of phrase that place him among the laity, these may be rhetorical poses—devices that he uses more frequently than any other Latin writer. He was certainly married, but though he addressed several treatises to his wife, they reveal nothing of her personality or of their relationship. This opacity is characteristic of Tertullian's writings: He turned consistently outward toward problems and enemies but seldom inward to reflect on himself or friends.

LIFE'S WORK

In the first three or four years of his career as a Christian, Tertullian devoted his rhetorical talents to apologetics—for example, in *Ad nationes* (197 C.E.; *To the Nations*, 1869) and the *Apology*—defending Christianity against pagan hostility with the aim of ending official persecution. These writings provide an invaluable window on primitive Christian belief and practice, but they are so self-righteous and vehement that they must have increased the pagans' animosity rather than diminishing it. Tertullian's strategy is often to argue that pagan Romans do not live up to their own beliefs, values, laws, and civic traditions as well as Christians do. This pose claims for the writer a privileged ability to interpret the texts and traditions of others. He denies repeatedly the right of Roman magistrates to judge Christians, on the ground that God's law is higher than humankind's, and he makes the claim, remarkable for a lawyer, that no law has binding force unless it is accepted by the individual's conscience. Such claims to unfettered autonomy of belief and action recur throughout Tertullian's works.

Tertullian's theological vision centered initially on the Church, seeing it as the community mediating between God and humans and thus the authoritative interpreter of Scripture and channel of God's grace. He argued against certain rigorists that postbaptismal sins could be forgiven by the Church, but his lawyer's training led him to think of sin chiefly in terms of Roman law, the categories of which he introduced into Christian theological vocabulary. He uses the term *delictum* (crime) much more often than *peccatum* (sin) and demands confession before a judge, and the imposition of a penalty, to complete the process of expiating wrongdoing. Correspondingly, penances or good deeds "hold God a debtor" and oblige him to grant the doer forgiveness, favor, and eventually salvation.

Tertullian's logical prowess and penchant for fine distinctions served him well in dogmatic theology. He was the first to use the term "trinity" to describe the relation of Father, Son, and Spirit, and he pioneered the description of Jesus as one person with a divine and a human nature. These positions antedate the Nicene Creed by more than a century and have become standard in all the main branches of Christianity.

Not long after the year 200, Tertullian's energies turned to polemical treatises against Gnostics and other heretics, especially the ascetic Marcionites. In these contentious and angry pieces he seems to take on many of the characteristics of his opponents, sinking deep into moral rigorism and antisocial attitudes. He was forced consequently to make ever more contorted and idiosyncratic interpretations of Scripture to score points against them. By around 210, he had drifted away from the mainstream of orthodox Christianity into Montanism, a sect that claimed that its private revelations superseded those of the New Testament and that opposed a pure, invisible, "spiritual" Church to the corrupt, visible church of the bishops and clergy. Thereafter, Tertullian increasingly stressed the role of private illuminations from the Spirit and the ability of each Christian to interpret Scripture for himself, outside, or even against, the tradition of the Church.

Though he is famous for comparing classical philosophy unfavorably with Christian theology—"What . . . has Athens to do with Jerusalem?"—he does not reject the formulations and arguments of philosophy but only their claim to compel assent—so strong was his determination to be utterly unfettered in his choice of belief. In fact, he formulates his own positions much more often in philosophical than in biblical terms, quoting Scriptures more for slogans and proof texts than to develop any genuine biblical theology. His major treatise *De anima* (210-213; *On the Soul*, 1870), for example, is based on Stoic theory,

affirming that the substance of the cosmos is all one, with no distinction of matter and spirit. Tertullian drew the explicit conclusion that soul-substance, as well as body-substance, is passed on from parents to children and laid thereby the foundation for the doctrine of Original Sin, unknown previously.

Having always tended toward absolutism, Tertullian became more extreme and rigorous in his Montanist phase. He reversed his earlier position that sins could be forgiven, claimed that anything that is not explicitly commanded by Scripture is forbidden, and became so confident of his own interpretations as to revoke divine commands from the Old Testament and apostolic counsels in the New. In his last writings his tone is bitterly antisocial and misanthropic; here he pictures himself as living in a world bound for damnation and gloats over the impending deaths of his enemies. Apparently he broke with Montanism in his last years to found his own sect, the Tertullianists, which survived some two centuries until the time of Augustine. His last datable writing was done in 217; according to Jerome, however, he lived to an advanced age.

SIGNIFICANCE

Tertullian's Latin prose style is the most vehement, tortuous, and pyrotechnic ever produced, the ultimate flower of the genre of controversy, lush with innovative vocabulary and quotable phrasing. This power, however, was in the hands of a tortured spirit, a man who was hostile, suspicious, and self-righteous, alienated from the world, from others, and, ultimately, from himself. His writings exhibit many of the traits associated with the authoritarian personality. Rejecting first pagan religion, then the Roman Empire, then orthodox Christianity, and finally the Montanist heresy, he ended his days in an idiosyncratic splinter group defined solely by himself.

Though Tertullian's writings were condemned by the Church in the sixth century, his genius blazed theological paths that are followed to this day: the doctrine of Original Sin, the Trinity of Persons in God, and the dual natures of Jesus. His legalism and penchant for quid pro quo justice set the tone for Western Christianity's outlook on sin, forgiveness, grace, and salvation for fourteen centuries, until Martin Luther supplied a corrective. His insistence on the validity of philosophical concepts led to the Roman Catholic tradition of reasoning from natural law, as his rejection of the binding force of philosophical conclusions on his absolute God led to the primacy of scriptural authority in Protestantism. His early argument that Scripture belongs to the Church and can only be interpreted rightly by the Church in accord with its traditions is still a mainstay of Catholic and Eastern Orthodox thinking. His later emphasis on private interpretation of scriptural texts provided a strong impetus to the Protestant Reformation. Combined with his moral rigorism and rejection of a visible Church in favor of a "spiritual" or personally defined one, it has exerted continuing influence on Fundamentalism.

—John D. Madden

FURTHER READING

Barnes, T. D. *Tertullian: A Historical and Literary Study.* New York: Oxford University Press, 1985. This specialized work presents all the evidence ever likely to be available concerning Tertullian's life and the dates of his writings. Barnes subjects the material to an extremely narrow and skeptical criticism, ignoring or dismissing ancient testimony. His conclusions must be taken into account, but their radical denials should be balanced by the recognition that ancient authorities had available to them more and better sources than do modern scholars.

Bray, Gerald L. *Holiness and the Will of God: Perspectives on the Theology of Tertullian.* Atlanta: John Knox Press, 1979. An excellent overview of Tertullian's thought. It is particularly helpful in synthesizing his positions, which often appear fragmentarily in scattered works and which changed drastically during his writing career.

Morgan, James. *The Importance of Tertullian in the Development of Christian Dogma.* London: K. Paul, Trench, Trübner, 1928. Classic work surveying Tertullian's contributions in various areas, and thus somewhat superficial in each. Bray's work (see above) supplies more up-to-date interpretations.

Osborn, Eric. *Tertullian, First Theologian of the West.* New York: Cambridge University Press, 2003. A major reappraisal of Tertullian's theology and its influence on the West and Christianity.

Roberts, A., and J. Donaldson, eds. *The Ante-Nicene Fathers.* Vols. 3 and 4. Reprint. Peabody, Mass.: Hendrickson, 1994. This is a reprint of the 1925 American edition of the nineteenth century British *Ante-Nicene Christian Library.* The translation is somewhat archaic, and it is sparsely annotated, but these volumes offer the only English versions of many of Tertullian's works, including *Ad Scapulam.*

Tertullian and Minucius Felix. *Apology, De spectaculis, Octavius.* Translated by T. R. Glover and G. H. Rendall. Cambridge, Mass.: Harvard University Press, 1998. A translation of Tertullian's best-known work, with Latin text. The text of Minucius Felix is interesting as he is the only known Christian Latin writer before Tertullian. "Minucius" may in fact be a pseudonym used by Tertullian for his first Christian work.

Warfield, B. B. *Studies in Tertullian and Augustine.* Reprint. Westport, Conn.: Greenwood Press, 1970. This essay on Tertullian gives the best treatment of his power and originality as a theologian, using his Trinitarian doctrine as focus for the study.

SEE ALSO: Saint Augustine; Saint Jerome.

THALES OF MILETUS
Greek philosopher

Through his various theories, Thales countered supernatural and mythical explanations of nature, attempting to replace them with empirically derived answers. He became a transitional figure between the worlds of philosophy and science.

BORN: c. 624 B.C.E.; Miletus, Ionia, Asia Minor (now in Turkey)
DIED: c. 548 B.C.E.; Miletus, Ionia, Asia Minor
AREAS OF ACHIEVEMENT: Philosophy, science

EARLY LIFE

Few details are known about the life of the man many call "the father of philosophy." Ancient tradition often fixed a person's birth date by a major event. According to Apollodorus, an Athenian historian of the second century B.C.E., the major event in the life of Thales (THAY-leez) was the solar eclipse of 585-584 B.C.E., when he was forty years old. If this is correct, Thales was born c. 624. He was a member of a distinguished family from the port city of Miletus, Ionia, on the west coast of Asia Minor. Thales' upper-class background meant that he had the luxury of spending his life engaged in intellectual pursuits.

Although probably from Phoenicia originally, Thales' family most likely lived in Miletus for several generations. Besides his social standing, his place of birth is also significant. Miletus was the major trading center of the Aegean Sea in the sixth century B.C.E. The coastal city entertained merchants from Egypt, Greece, and the Persian Empire. It possessed both a frontier spirit and a cosmopolitan, intellectual environment. A thriving economic center with a rich mixture of Near Eastern and Greek cultures, Miletus had no traditional, government-imposed beliefs that it sanctioned; life in Miletus was unconventional.

The body of knowledge familiar to the young Thales came principally from two sources: the earliest Greek writers and the scholars of Egypt and Babylon. Their ideas played a significant role in the philosophy of Thales, not because of their influence on him but rather because of his departure from them. Among the first ideas Thales encountered were those from the writings of Homer and Hesiod. Both these Greek writers speculated on the origins of the world and certain natural phenomena. Their answers, however, were always found within the realm of the Olympian gods. Homer and Hesiod did gather some factual data that they incorporated into their writings, but scientific advancement was impossible as long as nature was interpreted as the supernatural caprices of the gods. Greek thinkers before Thales had some knowledge of natural occurrences but never moved toward a more rational analysis. Theirs was an anthropomorphic world. Mythology served as both science and history prior to the revolution in thought that occurred in Miletus during the mid-sixth century.

The other information common to scholars such as Thales came from the Near East. The ancients of Egypt and Babylon had long experimented with their own forms of science and mathematics. The wonders of the Egyptian pyramids and other structures interested the Ionians, and the Babylonians claimed the attention of scholars for their study of the stars. While the achievements of these Near Eastern civilizations were remarkable, they were also limited in their scope. The Egyptians never converted their practical knowledge of mathematics and engineering into theories and principles. The Babylonians compiled volumes of notes on the heavens and developed astrology, a discipline hardly resembling astronomy. This was the intellectual climate, complete with preconceptions and misconceptions about natural "science," into which Thales was born.

LIFE'S WORK

The philosophy Thales espoused must be gleaned from the excerpts and comments of other authors. Herodotus, Aristotle, and Diogenes are the most notable ancient writers who included Thales in their works, and Thales' contributions are represented consistently in all three accounts. Thales bridged the gap between superstition and reason. Aristotle credited Thales with being the first recorded Milesian in a line of pre-Socratic philosophers who attempted to define nature in terms of nature itself. The questions Thales asked and the assumptions he proposed changed philosophy and science and laid a rational foundation on which others could build.

Thales searched for the "stuff," as the ancients referred to it, which composed all existing matter. He assumed that among the infinite variety of things on Earth there must be one underlying source of their existence. Though the stuff might change its form, it essentially retained its properties. Through observation, Thales concluded that the first principle of the world must be water. It was the prime substance of all things, and Earth floated on a cushion of it.

The matter of Thales' theory also possessed the quality of fluidity. It was to some degree alive and caused the change perceived in the visible world. Thales compared the inner power of water to a magnet that moves a piece of iron. This animism was typical of sixth century philosophy. It compelled Thales to conclude that all things are "full of gods." Although he used religious language, Thales did not adhere to a prevalent religious system—nor did he attempt to deify water in the traditional sense of ancient custom. To Thales, that which gave continual life must, in the vernacular of the time, be to some extent divine. Water was that life-giving substance that, in one form or another, composed everything and thus merited the term "god," not an anthropomorphic Olympian god but a new secular and rational god of Thales' making.

There is no extant record of the reason Thales chose water as the stuff of the world. Certainly the importance of water was not lost on ancient people. Water was central in the mythology of Greece, Egypt, and Babylon as well as in the Hebrew creation account. Some historians suggest that these myths exerted the greatest influence on Thales. In the epics of the Near East, Earth rises out of primeval water. The principal focus of these myths, however, was the origin of the world, not a common substance underlying all things in the world. Thus, Thales probably did not draw from them. Further, none of the ancient commentators on Thales mentions any influence

Thales of Miletus. (Library of Congress)

of Near Eastern thought on Ionian philosophy developing in the sixth century B.C.E.

Many modern scholars have asserted that there is a rational explanation for Thales' choice of water. Because Thales' theory was founded on observation only, not experimentation, the three phases of water would have been readily apparent to him. Water, appearing in such numerous forms, fits the description of the stuff that changes but is fundamentally constant. From the sources on Thales, however, it is never established that he even understood the three states of water.

Aristotle postulated another reason that led Thales to his conclusion. It is a variation of the rational explanation fashioned by modern scholars. Given the proximity of Aristotle to Thales, this may be the closest to the latter's own thinking. As Aristotle suggested, there existed a close link in the ancient mind between water and life. There were the rivers and seas without which humans could not nourish themselves. Trees contained sap, and plants had liquid within their stems. Growth, and therefore change, was inextricably tied to water—and nowhere was this clearer than in the ancient world. Even the human body testified to the importance of moisture. From conception to death, water was an integral part of human existence. As Aristotle observed, when the body died two things occurred: It became cold, and it dried up. Even that which was hot and dry required water. A popular fifth century B.C.E. idea held that the sun drew water to itself for nourishment and then rained it back to Earth to complete the cycle. Whether myth or logic influenced Thales, his attempt to look outside the divine process for answers to the puzzles of nature was monumental. By so doing, he attributed an orderliness to the cosmos that had heretofore been regarded as the disorderly and mystical playground of the gods.

Contemporaries hailed Thales as a politician, diplomat, civil engineer, mathematician, and astronomer, but his achievements in those roles are uncertain. Among the more important feats attributed to Thales was his prediction of a solar eclipse in 585-584 B.C.E. During a significant battle between the Medes and Lydians, Thales is said to have forecast a solar eclipse that, when it occurred, caused such trepidation among the combatants that they ceased fighting and called a truce. The ancients certainly believed the tale, but modern scholars doubt that Thales could predict an eclipse (such a prediction requires sophisticated astronomical calculations). A more likely astronomical achievement attributed to Thales is his idea of steering ships by the constellation Ursa Minor.

Tradition also credits Thales with introducing Egyptian principles of geometry to Greece. In Egypt, Thales is said to have taken the practical knowledge of Egyptian scholars and devised a method for accurately measuring the pyramids by their shadows. Altogether, five theorems are attributed to Thales. It is impossible to know the exact contribution of Thales to mathematics; it is likely, however, that he made some fundamental discoveries that enabled later mathematicians to build a framework for a variety of theorems.

In the minds of his contemporaries, Thales was not only a philosopher but also a sage. The Greeks named him one of the Seven Sages, because he urged the Ionian states to unite lest they fall easy prey to the Persian Empire. Thales was so respected by his countrymen that it is difficult to determine to what extent the legends that surround him are apocryphal. In antiquity, attributing great discoveries or achievements to men with reputations for wisdom was a common practice. The ancient authors themselves often recorded conflicting accounts of the accomplishments of Thales. It seems that they chose whatever Thalesian story would substantiate the point they were trying to make. Whatever the veracity of the stories enveloping Thales, it seems logical that his reputation for rational thinking would spread from his cosmological interests to such fields as mathematics, astronomy, and politics.

SIGNIFICANCE

Were all the legends surrounding Thales false, his speculations on the principal substance of the world would be enough to accord him special recognition. It is not the theory itself that is so significant but the revolution in thinking that it produced. Thales placed the study of nature on a new plane: He lifted it from the realm of the mythical to the level of empirical study. Scholars began to evaluate and analyze theories on the basis of the factual data available. Thales was the first of what has been called the Milesian group of the Ionian school of philosophy. Anaximander and Anaximenes, who followed him, produced more sophisticated philosophical systems, but they regarded Thales as the master.

To the modern scholar, the limitations of Thales' thinking are apparent. There remained elements of anthropomorphism and mythology in the work of Thales and the other pre-Socratic philosophers. While Thales rejected a universe controlled by the gods with his assertion "all things are water," he did not anticipate an atomic theory, as Democritus did. Thales attributed to nature an animism that prevented him from seeing it as a neutral agent in the world. In this sense, his ideas are less abstract than the ideas of those who came after him. Thales does not properly belong to the world of modern science, and yet he is equally misplaced when his ideas are classified with the cosmologies of Homer and Hesiod. Thales transcended, through rational analysis, the established supernatural explanations of nature, laying the foundation for major advances in philosophy and science in the following centuries.

—Linda Perry Abrams

FURTHER READING

Anglin, W. S. *The Heritage of Thales*. New York: Springer-Verlag, 1995. A textbook on the history, philosophy, and foundations of mathematics intended for undergraduate students.

Brumbaugh, Robert S. *The Philosophers of Greece*. New York: State University of New York Press, 1981. Evaluation of Greek philosophy from Thales to Aristotle. Takes a "romantic" approach to the subject that depicts Thales as a Renaissance man. Includes bibliography.

Burnet, John. *Early Greek Philosophy*. 1892. Reprint. London: A. and C. Black, 1963. Still considered one of the first major pieces on the subject. Emphasizes the Greeks as the earliest scientists and philosophers. Includes elaborate notes on source material.

Guthrie, William Keith Chambers. *The Earlier Presocratics and Pythagoreans*. Vol. 1 in *A History of Greek Philosophy*. New York: Cambridge University Press, 1978-1990. A standard general account of the subject, beginning with Thales and continuing through to the works of Heraclitus. Concentrates on how early Greek writers of myths and theogonies influenced the early ideas of the pre-Socratic philosophers and adheres to the traditional claim of Thales as the first European philosopher. Includes bibliography.

Hussey, Edward. *The Presocratics*. Indianapolis: Hackett, 1995. An introduction to early Greek thought, designed for the reader with no background in Greek. Deals with philosophy and science within the political and cultural setting of the ancient world and stresses the importance of political development on the emergence of the ideas of Thales. Includes maps and bibliography.

Nahm, Milton C., ed. *Selections from Early Greek Philosophy*. Englewood Cliffs, N.J.: Prentice-Hall, 1968. Short translated excerpts from the works of ancient authors in early Greek philosophy. Book spans the period from the Milesians through the atomists. Includes commentaries on Thales by Diogenes, Aristotle, and Plutarch.

Wightman, William P. D. *The Growth of Scientific Ideas*. Westport, Conn.: Greenwood Press, 1974. Critically explores the advance of science from the Ionians through Charles Darwin. Somewhat critical of Thales' theories, even within the context of the ancient world. Contains a limited annotated bibliography of general works, but a more specific list of sources concludes each chapter. Includes several illustrations and a chronology of scientific discoveries and innovations.

SEE ALSO: Anaximander; Anaximenes of Miletus; Aristotle; Hesiod; Homer.

RELATED ARTICLES in *Great Events from History: The Ancient World*: c. 750 B.C.E., Homer Composes the *Iliad*; c. 700 B.C.E., Hesiod Composes *Theogony* and *Works and Days*; 600-500 B.C.E., Greek Philosophers Formulate Theories of the Cosmos; 499-494 B.C.E., Ionian Revolt.

THEMISTOCLES
Athenian statesman and admiral

Themistocles engineered the naval defeat of the Persians at Salamis and thus made possible the subsequent Golden Age of Athens.

BORN: c. 524 B.C.E.; Athens, Greece
DIED: c. 460 B.C.E.; Magnesia, Asia Minor (now in Turkey)
AREAS OF ACHIEVEMENT: Government and politics, war and conquest

EARLY LIFE

Themistocles (thee-MIHS-toh-kleez) was born about 524 B.C.E. to an Athenian father, Neocles, and a non-Athenian mother. His father's family, the Lycomidai, was respected, but his father achieved no great prominence. Six centuries later Plutarch related a number of anecdotes showing Themistocles to be clever, resourceful, and interested in politics from the start. In one of these stories, Themistocles was walking home from school when he saw coming toward him the tyrant Pisistratus. When the boy's tutor cautioned him to step aside, Themistocles answered, "Isn't the road wide enough for him?"

The political and military events of the final decades of the sixth century B.C.E. shaped the course of Themistocles' life. Even before he was born, the rapidly expanding Persian Empire had entrenched itself in Lydia, directly east from Athens across the Aegean Sea, with its countless islands available as stepping-stones to the Greek mainland. In his teenage years, Themistocles would have heard older Athenians discussing the ominous Persian advance across the Bosporus into Thrace and Macedonia to the north as well as into the easternmost Greek islands.

He was growing up in an increasingly commercial culture fostered by Pisistratus and maintained by his successors until Sparta, the strongest Greek state, expelled Hippias in 510 and enrolled Athens in its Peloponnesian League. Athens found itself the focus of a struggle between the militant Spartans and the advancing Persians. It might have occurred to Themistocles early in his manhood that a strong naval force might become the key to Athenian defense.

The career of Hippias must have seemed particularly instructive. Having fled to Persia after his deposition, Hippias was first offered reinstatement as the price Athens must pay for Persian neutrality. Sparta later brought Hippias back and offered to restore him in Athens to block any increase in Persian influence. Given these political situations, freedom was precarious, and Themistocles certainly would have learned how participation in such maneuvers could impair the credibility of a leader. Despite achievements much more brilliant than those of Hippias, he would eventually face both exile and suspicion himself.

LIFE'S WORK

By 493, Themistocles had attained sufficient stature to be chosen an archon in Athens, then a post of considerable authority. Nothing is known of his role in the famous Battle of Marathon in 490, which resulted in victory for the Athenian general Miltiades the Younger, and because the whereabouts of Themistocles are unknown until 483, some historians doubt the earlier archonship. In the latter year, however, he manifested his leadership by persuading the Athenians to use the proceeds of a newly discovered silver mine to modernize the navy and expand its fighting strength to two hundred vessels. Accepted as the unquestioned leader of Athens, Themistocles directed the campaign against the great Persian commander Xerxes I. Ordering a series of strategic retreats as the Persians, fresh from their victory at Thermopylae, swept down on Athens from the north, Themistocles at length committed the newly enlarged fleet to battle at Salamis, off the Attic coast, in 480. He used deception—at which he excelled—to lull the Persian fleet into overconfidence, and he used eloquence to bolster Athenian morale. Along with its Greek allies, the Athenian navy maneuvered the larger Persian fleet into a narrow strait and decisively defeated the invaders, who fled back across the Aegean.

Themistocles resented the Athenian failure to honor him sufficiently and went to Sparta, where he was given an olive crown and a chariot described by the historian Herodotus as the most beautiful in Sparta. After a shower of praise, Themistocles enjoyed an escort of three hundred Spartan soldiers, who accompanied him to the border. Back in Athens, which had borne the brunt of the Persian offensive, only remnants of the city wall stood, and a massive rebuilding project loomed. A Spartan delegation tried to persuade the Athenian leaders not to reconstruct the wall, ostensibly so that no foreign invader could capture the city and hold it as the Persians had before Salamis. In reality, as Themistocles saw it, Sparta and its other allies to the south feared that with its new naval eminence, a fortified Athens represented too strong a potential foe. Regarding the rebuilding as essential, Themistocles persuaded his fellow Athenians to send him back to Sparta to negotiate the matter and meanwhile to put all men, women, and children to work at the reconstruction. In Sparta, Themistocles used all of his wiles to postpone the talks. He explained that he could not proceed without his colleagues, who had been unaccountably delayed. When reports came back that the wall was already rising, he labored to convince the Spartans of their falsity. Eventually he suggested that a trustworthy inspection team be sent, while at the same time he secretly sent instructions to delay the visitors in every possible way.

With the wall in place, Themistocles admitted the deception but defended it stoutly. The Athenians, he pointed out, had abandoned their city in the first place on their own; furthermore, they had devised the strategy that had lured the invaders to their defeat. Whenever they had consulted with their allies, the Athenians had displayed good judgment. Now it was the Athenian judgment that without walls Athens could not contribute equally with

Themistocles. (Library of Congress)

other walled cities of the alliance. Sparta had no doubt expected such arguments from Themistocles, though not after the fact. Nevertheless, he extricated himself from Sparta without drawing any overt hostility. Through his deception, he had obtained improvements that he never could have negotiated, for the workers had substantially increased both the thickness of the walls and the area they enclosed. Following Themistocles' advice, they had also fortified the "lower city," Piraeus, in accordance with his theory that as long as Athens maintained naval superiority, safety lay in the lower city, with its natural harbors on both sides of the peninsula that it straddled.

Within five years of the victory at Salamis, a reaction set in against Themistocles. He probably contributed to this reaction through boasting and heavy-handed attempts to exact payments toward the cost of his military campaign from Athenian allies. He appears to have had little to do with the ascendancy of Athens in the Delian League, formed in 477 to combat future Persian aggression. It is difficult to determine whether Themistocles' absence from leadership in this important defensive alliance springs from distrust on the part of his colleagues or his own perception that Sparta, not Persia, represented the most likely future enemy. While the new leaders, Cimon and Aristides, supported Sparta and the alliance,

Themistocles opposed any extension of Spartan influence. In this respect, he showed more foresight than the men who had replaced him in power.

Themistocles had obvious faults. Herodotus depicts him as constantly seeking personal gain; even if his assiduous fund-raising went largely for the common good, suspicions to the contrary were bound to arise. He appears to have been vain and egotistical. Even his wiliness, so valuable against enemies, posed a threat. Like Homer's Odysseus, Themistocles had built his reputation not so much on valor as on duplicity. In the Athens of the 470's, it would not have been difficult to see this devious man with his unpopular anti-Spartan bias as dangerous to Athenian security.

For whatever reason, around the year 472, he was ostracized. Many prominent citizens were exiled without specific accusations or formal trials in that era, and ostracism was only temporary, but Themistocles never returned to Attic soil. He first chose anti-Spartan Argos as his refuge, but in his absence he was condemned as a traitor. He found it necessary to flee to the island of Corcyra in the Ionian Sea, but he found no welcome there and continued to Epirus in northwestern Greece. His odyssey continued in the land of the Molossians to the east and then to Pydna on the Aegean coast. Thucydides reports him to have sailed on a merchant ship to Ionia, but a storm carried the ship to Naxos, an island then under Athenian siege. Bribing the captain, Themistocles persuaded him to sail to the coast of Asia Minor, and there he applied to his old enemies the Persians for refuge. He was granted not only refuge but also honors, in fact the governorship of Magnesia, in what is now west-central Turkey, probably after the death of his old adversary Xerxes in 465. Magnesian coins bearing his imprint have survived.

One story of Themistocles' death has him committing suicide by drinking bull's blood to avoid the necessity of leading a military expedition against the Greeks, but it is much more likely that he died a natural death around 460.

SIGNIFICANCE

An Odyssean leader, Themistocles excelled at outwitting his military and political opponents. He demonstrated the true leader's capacity to resist the popular mood and to redirect popular energy toward prudent ends. His decision to devote windfall profits from silver mines, which others wanted to divide up among the populace, to naval defense, saved Athens from almost sure defeat at the hands of the Persians and preserved Athenian autonomy in the face of Spartan ambition. Although Themistocles did nothing personally to promote Athenian democracy, its later flowering surely depended on his actions in defense of a strong and independent city-state.

Not always a good man, Themistocles was an indisputably great leader. Despite the fact that at various times he opposed all of them, the three major states of his region—Athens, Sparta, and Persia—all heaped honors on him. Thucydides reports that the Magnesians, whom Themistocles led in his last years, erected a monument to him in the marketplace. They saw him not as a former enemy but as a man whose talent for governance, frustrated in his own land, needed scope and opportunity. His brilliance and energy in public projects outweighed the devious means by which he achieved them and his penchant for boasting of them afterward. Thucydides regarded him as an intuitive genius who could operate successfully in matters for which neither his training nor his experience had prepared him. Adversity brought out the best in him and inspired him to bring out the best in the troops and citizens whom he led.

—*Robert P. Ellis*

FURTHER READING

Gomme, A. W. *A Historical Commentary on Thucydides*. Ann Arbor: University of Michigan Press, 1997. One section of Gomme's learned commentary on the work of the most respected ancient Greek historian deals with Themistocles. Gomme is particularly interested in the gap between his archonship and ship-building activity a decade later. Skeptical of the theories advanced to explain the gap in Themistocles' career, Gomme is inclined to doubt the archonship and places his rise to power in the 480's rather than the 490's.

Herodotus. *The Histories*. Translated by Robin Wakefield. New York: Oxford University Press, 1998. Of the two great ancient Greek historians who write of Themistocles, Herodotus is more likely than Thucydides to accept fanciful sources of information and shows less understanding of military affairs, but his subject encompasses the years of Themistocles' most notable exploits. Herodotus lived and wrote at a time when many witnesses of the Persian Wars were still living.

Keaveney, Arthur Peter. *Life and Journey of Athenian Statesman Themistocles, 524-460 B.C. as a Refugee in Persia*. Lewiston, N.Y.: Edwin Mellen Press, 2003. This volume seeks to illuminate the years in Themistocles' career between his finally leaving Athens for exile and his death some years later as a refugee in the Persian Empire.

Lenardon, Robert J. *The Saga of Themistocles*. London: Thames and Hudson, 1978. This is the only true biography of book-length form for English-speaking readers. Lenardon's method is to place before the reader the full variety of evidence, with many substantial quotations from ancient sources, and encourage readers to draw their own conclusions in cases of dubious or conflicting evidence. His cautious approach can be maddening to anyone looking for an authoritative assessment of his subject, but his presentation of the facts could not be more scrupulous.

Plutarch. *Life of Themistocles*. Edited by J. L. Marr. Warminster, England: Aris & Phillips, 1998. Plutarch is the ancient biographer most skillful at conveying a sense of his subjects' personalities. There can be little doubt that many of his anecdotes are inventions, but

others may have a basis in fact. His semi-fictionalized life of the Athenian leader makes absorbing reading.

Thucydides. *The Landmark Thucydides: A Comprehensive Giude to the Peloponnesian War*. Edited by Robert B. Strassler. New York: Simon & Schuster, 1998. This early historian's general reliability and his relative closeness to Themistocles in time (his birth came close to Themistocles' death) make his account preferable wherever, as often happens, early authorities disagree.

SEE ALSO: Cimon; Pisistratus; Xerxes I.

RELATED ARTICLES in *Great Events from History: The Ancient World*: 520-518 B.C.E., Darius the Great Conquers the Indus Valley; September 17, 490 B.C.E., Battle of Marathon; 483 B.C.E., Naval Law of Themistocles Is Instituted; 480-479 B.C.E., Persian Invasion of Greece; 478-448 B.C.E., Athenian Empire Is Created.

THEODORE OF MOPSUESTIA
Greek theologian

The most important representative of the Antiochene school of biblical exegesis and theology, Theodore served as bishop of Mopsuestia from 392 until his death in 428. Primarily because of alleged similarities with Pelagianism and Nestorianism, Theodore's theological views were condemned by Emperor Justinian and by the Fifth Council of Constantinople in 553.

BORN: c. 350 C.E.; Antioch (now Antakya, Turkey)
DIED: 428 C.E.; Mopsuestia, Cilicia (now Yakapinar, Turkey)
AREA OF ACHIEVEMENT: Religion

EARLY LIFE

Theodore, generally known by the name of his bishopric as "of Mopsuestia" (mahp-soo-EHS-chee-uh) was born at Antioch about 350. Little is known about his parents or family, except that his father held an official position at Antioch and the family was reportedly wealthy. Theodore's brother, Polychronius, eventually became bishop of Apamea on the Orontes; a cousin, Paeanius, held an important civil post at Constantinople.

Theodore belonged to the nobility in Antioch, thus his early education was under the most renowned professor of rhetoric of his day, the Sophist Libanius. Theodore was an early companion, fellow student, and friend of

John Chrysostom, who was also born in Antioch, although a few years before Theodore. John, usually known simply as Chrysostom, became famous for his eloquent preaching and eventually became Patriarch of Constantinople.

Theodore and Chrysostom enjoyed an excellent philosophical education along with another friend and fellow student, Maximus, who later became bishop of Isaurian Seleucia. It seems that the three friends came to enjoy the luxurious life of polite Antioch. Chrysostom was the first to turn back from the pleasures of that world, and he then succeeded in winning back his fellow students, Theodore and Maximus. The three friends shortly thereafter sought a retreat in the Asketerion, a famous monastic school of Diodore (later bishop of Tarsus) and Carterius, near Antioch.

According to Chrysostom, Theodore's conversion was sincere and fervent, and he threw himself into the monastic discipline with characteristic zeal. He may have been baptized at this time as well. His days were spent in study, his nights in prayer. He practiced almost every conceivable form of ascetic self-discipline, including lengthy fasts and sleeping on the bare ground. He is reported to have found inexpressible joy in the service of Christ as a Christian celibate until "the world" beckoned to him again.

Theodore had become fascinated by the charms of a beautiful young girl named Hermione, and he was seriously contemplating marriage and a return to the secular life. This proposal became a matter of great concern to his fellow ascetics in the monastery, with many prayers offered and various efforts made for his "recovery" from his "fall." Such efforts included the earliest known literary compositions of Chrysostom—two letters appealing to Theodore to abandon his infatuation and remain true to his monastic vows. Theodore was not yet twenty years of age, but the appeal of his friends prevailed. He remained true to his vow of celibacy throughout his life.

From 369 to 378, Theodore remained under the spiritual leadership of Diodore, who was at that time elevated to the See of Tarsus. Theodore probably became closely acquainted with both Scripture and church doctrine during these years. He may also have developed his principles of interpretation of the Bible and his views of the person of Christ, which eventually led him into theological controversy. He subsequently came under the influence of Flavian, bishop of Antioch, who ordained him as a priest in 383, three years before his friend Chrysostom was ordained. Chrysostom almost immediately rose to the full height of his oratorical powers in the pulpit of Antioch. Theodore may have felt himself eclipsed by his friend's greater power as a preacher, or a visit from his old master Diodore to Antioch may have caused him to move to Tarsus, where he stayed until 392, at which time he was elevated to the See of Mopsuestia, in Cilicia, where he remained for the final thirty-six years of his life.

LIFE'S WORK

Nothing is known about the physical appearance or general health of Theodore. He died in 428, at the age of seventy-eight, reportedly exhausted from more than fifty years of literary and pastoral work. Most of his later years were marked by theological controversy, but he died peacefully with a great reputation from his many books and other writings. His long episcopate was marked by no outstanding incidents, and his many friends and disciples left few personal recollections. He impressed Emperor Theodosius I, however, who heard him preach once, and Theodosius is said to have declared that he had "never met with such a teacher." (Theodosius had also heard Saint Ambrose and Saint Gregory of Nazianzus.) A letter from Chrysostom when he was an exile also reveals that the two friends always retained a high regard for each other. Chrysostom declared that he could "never forget the love of Theodore, so genuine and warm, so sincere and guileless, a love maintained from early years,

and manifested but now." He assured Theodore that, "exile as he is, he reaps no ordinary consolation from having such a treasure, such a mine of wealth within his heart as the love of so vigilant and noble a soul."

Theodore wrote widely on a great variety of topics. Active in the theological controversies of his time, he is said to have written at least fifteen books on the Incarnation of Christ before he began his serious exegetical work in 402. Unfortunately, many of Theodore's writings have not survived, and those that have do not give a true indication of the scope of his work. He began with a commentary on the Psalms and eventually wrote commentaries on practically every book of the Bible. In addition, he wrote at least thirty-seven other works on a variety of theological, ecclesiastical, and practical problems: the Incarnation, the sacraments, the Holy Spirit, exegetical method, monasticism, and other topics.

Theodore is doubtless best known today as a theologian, and in particular for his views on Christology and anthropology. Although his theological ideas were condemned by the Fifth Council of Constantinople more than a century after his death, during his lifetime he enjoyed the reputation of an orthodox teacher. It is ironic that this untiring foe of theological heresies was later condemned as a heretic himself. In his opposition to heresy, Theodore's attention was particularly directed toward the Christological views of Apollinaris of Laodicea. His fifteen-volume *On the Incarnation* was primarily directed against Apollinaris, and Theodore's extreme views on the "two natures" of Christ were largely by way of response to Apollinaris's teachings concerning the subordination of the human nature of Christ.

Theodore insisted on the complete manhood of Christ and roundly condemned the theory of Apollinaris that the divine Logos had taken the place of Christ's rational soul. Theodore reasoned that if the Godhead had replaced human reason, Jesus would not have experienced fear or any other human emotion. He would not have wrestled in prayer or needed the Holy Spirit's assistance; the story of the temptations of Christ, for example, would have been meaningless. Christ would have had nothing in common with humanity, which would render the Incarnation itself devoid of meaning.

Theodore also insisted that the two natures of Christ, human and divine, were perfect and always remained two. He refused to contemplate the spiritual and material as confused in any manner. His emphasis on this theological point may have been derived from a careful analysis of human personality. Since only elements of the same substance can become unified, Theodore could not conceive of any sort of union between the two natures of Christ. This view, later held in somewhat modified form by Nestorius, was condemned by the Third Ecumenical Council at Ephesus in 431.

SIGNIFICANCE

By his insistence on maintaining the human nature of Christ along with the divine, Theodore of Mopsuestia held his own against the ontological speculations of the Alexandrian school, which were, in fact, derived primarily from philosophical abstractions. In principle, his position was vindicated by the great Council of Chalcedon in 451, which recognized in Christ two natures "without confusion, change, division, or separation in one person and subsistence." Through his emphasis on the human nature of Christ and his keen awareness of the biblical evidence, Theodore may have saved Christendom from falling into endless theological speculation.

As the greatest exegete and spiritual leader of the Antiochene school, Theodore became the acknowledged leader of numerous ecclesiastical figures of the fourth and fifth centuries. In his theological writings he also stressed the importance of free will and the human contribution to salvation. Human achievements were ascribed to free will; thus, Theodore opposed the doctrines of predestination and original sin. Because of such views, Theodore was regarded by some as a forerunner to Pelagius, whose views were also condemned by the council at Ephesus in 431.

Theodore's theological views, considered orthodox during his lifetime, became controversial after his death, particularly when Nestorians and Pelagians appealed to his writings. In the end, the Alexandrian school succeeded in bringing Theodore and his writings under ecclesiastical anathema. Indeed, the primary reason so few of his writings survive today is that many of them were intentionally destroyed by church authorities. Rabboula, orthodox Syriac bishop of Edessa from 411 to 436, vehemently attacked Theodore and his teachings and ordered all existing copies of his works confiscated and burned. It may have been Monophysite reaction to the Council of Chalcedon that first brought Theodore's theological views into question. He was condemned as a heretic by Emperor Justinian in 544. Under Imperial pressure Pope Vergilius condemned sixty propositions from Theodore's writings as heretical, and the Fifth Council of Constantinople in 553 placed his writings under anathema.

As an interpreter of Scripture, Theodore stood out among the scholars of his day. His scholarship is said to have astounded his contemporaries. In thoroughness, accuracy, and consistency of thought he had no peer, not even Chrysostom. His followers called him simply "the interpreter." He became the most remarkable and original representative of the Antiochene school of exegesis, noted for its insistence on the plain, literal meaning of Scripture and its opposition to the fanciful, allegorical interpretations so typical of Origen and the Alexandrian school.

Theodore was also a pioneer in the use of critical methods of Bible study unheard of in his day. He made careful use of scientific, critical, philological, and historical methods, thereby anticipating by more than a millennium the rise of modern historical-critical methods of Bible study. He consistently tried to take into account the historical circumstances under which biblical books were written; subsequently, he rejected several books as uncanonical, including Job, Chronicles, the Song of Songs, Ezra, Revelation, and the Catholic Epistles (except 1 Peter and 1 John). The few of his writings that survive demonstrate something of the power and authority of his work. The only commentary that survives in the original Greek is *On the Twelve Prophets*, but many of his writings were translated into Syriac very early and have been preserved, at least in part, primarily by Nestorians. His commentary on John had long been known, but later discoveries included commentaries on the Lord's Prayer, the Nicene Creed, and the sacraments. His massive work on the Incarnation was discovered early in the twentieth century in a codex in Seert, Turkey, but unfortunately seems to have been destroyed during World War I.

—*C. Fitzhugh Spragins*

FURTHER READING

Bellitto, Christopher M. *The General Councils: A History of the Twenty-one General Councils from Nicaea to Vatican II*. New York: Paulist Press, 2002. Noted Church historian Bellitto traces the history of twenty-one general councils. Written for the nonspecialist, the first section, "Councils of the Early Church," is of particular note. Bellitto addresses not only the historical context, goals, successes and failures of the councils but also the impact on their times.

Dewart, Joanne McWilliam. *The Theology of Grace of Theodore of Mopsuestia*. Washington, D.C.: Catholic University of America Press, 1971. An important study of Theodore's teachings about the grace of God. Emphasizes Theodore's scriptural understanding of grace as divine benevolence, best understood against the background of the Pelagian controversy. Demonstrates Theodore's insistence on the cooperation of divine grace and the human will.

Greer, Rowan A. *Theodore of Mopsuestia: Exegete and Theologian*. London: Faith Press, 1961. A sympathetic assessment of the theology of Theodore from the point of view of biblical criticism. Greer uses Theodore's *Commentary of St. John* as representative of his critical and exegetical work and as a vantage point from which to illustrate the basic differences between the Antiochene and Alexandrian schools. He concludes that Theodore was a biblical critic first of all; his theology sprang from his study of the Bible.

Norris, Richard A. *Manhood and Christ: A Study in the Christology of Theodore of Mopsuestia*. Oxford, England: Clarendon Press, 1963. A thorough survey of Theodore's anthropological presuppositions and their impact on his Christological thought. This highly recommended theological analysis contains valuable appendices on fifth and sixth century discussion of Theodore as well as more recent treatment of his thought.

Patterson, Leonard. *Theodore of Mopsuestia and Modern Thought*. London: Society for Promoting Christian Knowledge, 1926. Although dated, this is an important study of Theodore's life and thought. Particularly interesting is Patterson's discussion of Theodore's relation to modern thought (for example, evolutionary theory and the mind-body relationship).

Sullivan, Francis S. J. *The Christology of Theodore of Mopsuestia*. Rome: Apud Aedes Universitatis Gregorianae, 1956. A careful study of Theodore's thought concerning the unity of Christ. Sullivan treats some of the problems involved in making use of existing fragments of Theodore's works, mostly in Syriac translation. He concludes that Theodore was indeed, despite his orthodox intentions, the "father of Nestorianism."

Swete, Henry B. "Theodore of Mopsuestia." In *A Dictionary of Christian Biography, Literature, Sects and Doctrines During the First Eight Centuries*, edited by William Smith and Henry Wace, vol. 4. London: John Murray, 1887. Dated but extremely valuable and sympathetic study of Theodore's life and work. Excellent use made of primary sources, despite the fact that many of Theodore's writings had not yet been discovered when Swete prepared this article.

SEE ALSO: Saint John Chrysostom; Theodoret of Cyrrhus.

RELATED ARTICLE in *Great Events from History: The Ancient World*: October 8-25, 451 C.E., Council of Chalcedon.

THEODORET OF CYRRHUS
Greek theologian

Theodoret served as the bishop of Cyrrhus for forty-one years. Aside from carrying out an effective and sensitive bishopric, he authored works on practically every aspect of Christian thought and practice. He is perhaps best remembered for his contribution to the Christological debates that led to the Council of Chalcedon.

BORN: c. 393 C.E.; Antioch, Roman Syria (now Antakya, Turkey)
DIED: c. 458 C.E.; Cyrrhus, Roman Syria (now in Syria)
ALSO KNOWN AS: Theodoretus; Theodoret of Cyrus
AREA OF ACHIEVEMENT: Religion

EARLY LIFE
Theodoret (thee-AHD-uh-ruht) was born in Antioch in the Roman province of northern Syria c. 393 C.E. to moderately wealthy Christian parents. He spent the first twenty-three years of his life in the city of Antioch, leaving in 416-417 for the monastery at Nicerte. While Theodoret wrote sparingly of these formative years in Antioch, his remarks as well as what can be deduced from his later writings reveal that he drew deeply from both the rich Greco-Roman culture of the city and the monks who lived on the fringes of Antioch. His writings reflect the education typical of the privileged population of large Greco-Roman cities in late antiquity. Such an education would have entailed training in Greek grammar, speech, and the classics of Greek literature and philosophy from Homer to Demosthenes.

From his parents, Theodoret inherited a fondness for the monks who lived in the caves and wilderness surrounding Antioch. Theodoret's mother had sought out these monks to cure an eye ailment, and his father had sought help when after thirteen years of marriage no child had been conceived. In both cases, the monks were given credit for solving the problem; from childhood, Theodoret was taken on weekly visits to them. Theodoret fondly recalled his visits to the monks Peter of Galatia and Macedonius and noted that Peter had given him a piece of linen girdle that was treasured by the family when it proved a remedy for a variety of physical afflictions.

On the death of his parents, Theodoret left Antioch to become a monk himself. He joined the monastic community at Nicerte near Apamea and there enjoyed some seven years of quiet seclusion. It was during his tenure at Nicerte that Theodoret composed his celebrated apology for the Christian religion, *Therapeutica* (c. 424; *A Treatise of Laws*, 1776). This apology displays the breadth of his knowledge of Greek philosophy and religion as he juxtaposes the claims of Christianity to those associated with a host of Greek philosophical schools and religious cults.

LIFE'S WORK

After seven years in the monastery at Nicerte, Theodoret was called to assume the duties of bishop of the diocese of Cyrrhus. Theodoret says he "unwillingly assumed" the office, as it meant leaving behind the beloved tranquillity of the monastery and taking on the demands of an exceptionally large and unruly diocese on the eastern edges of the Roman Empire. Theodoret's reluctance did not prevent him from fulfilling his appointed task: He served as bishop there from the year 424 until his death in 458.

The boundaries of the diocese were the same as those of Cyrrhestica, a territory of the province of Euphatensis in eastern Syria. The diocese was subject to the Metropolitan at Hierapolis and covered 1,600 square miles (2,580 square kilometers). Theodoret described the diocese as mountainous and bare. This bleak landscape had not, however, discouraged the establishment and spread of Christianity; Theodoret also refers to the existence of eight hundred parishes, each with its own church. The area also contained a significant population of monks, with whom Theodoret maintained a cordial relationship.

The town of Cyrrhus, where Theodoret was to reside, was located approximately sixty-five kilometers northeast of Antioch at the confluence of the Aphreen and Saboun Souyou rivers. Cyrrhus had been an important Roman military outpost, but, like many other Roman frontier towns, it was in a state of decline by the fifth century. Theodoret called it "a solitary and ugly village." During his residence, he spent much time and energy in rebuilding and improving Cyrrhus. Using funds collected from the diocese, he constructed two bridges and public galleries, rebuilt a major aqueduct, and improved the public baths. The bishop also paid to have skilled physicians move to the town and secured the service of educators and engineers.

Theodoret's responsibilities were numerous. He describes such tasks as visiting and encouraging the monks living in the diocese, driving out heretics, playing ecclesiastical politics, and writing a number of tracts on practically every aspect of Christian life and thought. Aside from the apology mentioned earlier and the treatises on Christology to be discussed below, the extant works from Theodoret's vast corpus include historical studies, biblical commentaries, a series of sermons on Providence, and a collection of letters.

While Theodoret's interests and contributions were wide-ranging, his place in the history of Christianity has consistently been recorded in terms of his role in the Christological controversies that began with the Council of Ephesus in 431 and culminated with the Council of Chalcedon in 451. In 431, Theodoret was called on to represent the Antiochene interpretation of Christ (the two-nature Christology) against the Alexandrian interpretation as it was put forth by Cyril of Alexandria. Theodoret's response took the form of a tract entitled *Reprehensio duodecim capitum seu anathema anathematismorum Cyrilli* (431), in which he stressed the biblical foundation for the fullness of the two natures of Christ and argued that Cyril's formula implicated the divine Christ in the passion and suffering of the Crucifixion. The Council of Ephesus was called to resolve the differences between Cyril and Theodoret; it decided in favor of Cyril.

In the years between the First Council of Ephesus and the Council of Chalcedon, Theodoret continued to be involved in the debates over the proper interpretation of the nature of Christ. In 447, he composed a work entitled *Eranistes seu Polymorphus* (*Dialogues*, 1892) as an attack on the position held by the monk Eutyches, who had succeeded Cyril as the leader of the Alexandrian one-nature school of interpretation. This work and the ensuing debate led to the Second Council of Ephesus in 449; Theodoret again lost and was deposed from his bishopric in Cyrrhus. He was apparently restored soon thereafter, and the Council of Chalcedon in 451 closed the chapter on Theodoret's involvement in the Christological debates. In fact, from the end of the Council of Chalcedon till his death in 458, Theodoret must have lived a comparatively quiet and uninvolved life as bishop, as there is no record of any further writing or involvement in ecclesiastical politics.

SIGNIFICANCE

Theodoret of Cyrrhus was one of the most prolific writers and influential voices for Christianity in the East during late antiquity. He wrote against a rich and complex background that was at once deeply indebted to the language, ideas, and ideals of the long-established Greco-Roman culture and that at the same time increasingly felt the influence of Christianity and its otherworldly monks and theological squabbles. Theodoret labored as a bishop in the eastern provinces of the later Roman Empire to improve the life and resources for his congregation, to establish the proper interpretation of the Bible, to chronicle the history of the Church and its monks, and to clarify what the Church taught about the person and work of Christ. While in the end, Theodoret found himself on the losing side of the Christological debates, his contributions to those debates have been judged the clearest and most profound statements on the two-nature view of Christ.

—*C. Thomas McCullough*

FURTHER READING

Ashby, Godfrey, and William Ernest Candler. *Theodoret of Cyrrhus as Exegete of the Old Testament*. Grahamstown, South Africa: Rhodes University Press, 1972. Provides, in largely summary fashion, a guide to Theodoret's exegesis of the Old Testament. While the author provides few critical insights, the work nevertheless proves valuable as it offers an entry into an enormous collection of biblical commentary, most of which is available only in Greek or Latin.

Bellitto, Christopher M. *The General Councils: A History of the Twenty-one General Councils from Nicaea to Vatican II*. New York: Paulist Press, 2002. Noted Church historian Bellitto traces the history of twenty-one general councils. Written for the nonspecialist, the first section on the "Councils of the Early Church" is of particular note. Bellitto addresses not only the historical context, goals, successes and failure of the councils but also the impact on their times.

Chesnut, Glenn F. *The First Christian Histories*. Paris: Éditions Beauchesne, 1977. A well-researched work that compares the ecclesiastical histories of Eusebius, Socrates, Sozomen, and Theodoret. The author demonstrates how each brought to his historical studies a distinct theological and philosophical bias and shows the extent to which these early Christian historians were dependent on classical Greco-Roman models of history writing.

Grillmeier, Alois. *From the Apostolic Age to Chalcedon*. Vol. 1 in *Christ in Christian Tradition*. Translated by John Bowden. Rev. ed. Atlanta: John Knox Press, 1975. This book provides a thorough treatment of the development of Christology in the early Church and includes a long and helpful discussion of Theodoret's contribution. The book has an extensive bibliography of works in English and European languages.

Jones, A. H. M. *The Later Roman Empire*. 2 vols. 1964. Reprint. Norman: University of Oklahoma Press, 1975. The standard work on this period, it provides not only an account of the major events and persons but also useful insights into the contemporary social world.

Theodoret of Cyrrhus. *"The Ecclesiastical History," "Dialogues," and "Letters" of Theodoret*. Translated by B. Jackson. Grand Rapids, Mich.: Wm. B. Eerdmans, 1975. This English translation of the letters and two of Theodoret's works was originally published in 1892. In the case of *Ekklēsiastikē historia* (c. 449; *The Ecclesiastical History*, 1612) and *Dialogues*, newer editions of the Greek text have been published. The translations are competent and since they are the only modern English translations of these works of Theodoret, they are invaluable for those wishing to read his words who are limited to reading publications in English. A brief historical and theological introduction has been appended to the collection.

_____. *A History of the Monks of Syria*. Translated by R. M. Price. Kalamazoo, Mich.: Cistercian Publications, 1985. One of the rare English translations of a work by Theodoret. The text and translation are based on the French edition of Pierre Canivet. The history itself offers a rare glimpse into the provocative world of Syrian monasticism. The translation is clear, and the introduction and notes do a splendid job of situating the work historically and literally.

Urbainczyk, Theresa. *Theodoret of Cyrrhus: The Bishop and the Holy Man*. Ann Arbor: University of Michigan Press, 2002. Urbainczyk discusses Theodoret's writings and arguments in relationship to his life and political circumstances. Includes bibliographical references and indexes.

Young, Frances M. *From Nicaea to Chalcedon: A Guide to the Literature and Its Background*. Philadelphia: Fortress Press, 1983. This is a clearly written handbook intended as an introduction to the major figures and writings of Christianity from the period between the Council of Nicaea and the Council of Chalcedon. Many of Theodoret's works are discussed, with special attention paid to *The Ecclesiastical History* and his Christological treatises. There is a substantial bibliography.

SEE ALSO: Theodore of Mopsuestia.

RELATED ARTICLE in *Great Events from History: The Ancient World*: October 8-25, 451 C.E., Council of Chalcedon.

THEODOSIUS THE GREAT
Byzantine emperor (r. 379-395 C.E.)

Theodosius restored peace to the Eastern Roman Empire after the Roman defeat at Adrianople and established a dynasty that held the throne for more than seventy years. His settlement of Visigoths inside the Empire may have contributed to the fall of the western part of the Empire, and his religious policies were a major step in the development of a theocratic state in the East.

BORN: January 11, 346 or 347 C.E.; Cauca, Gallaecia (now in Spain)

DIED: January 17, 395 C.E.; Mediolanum (now Milan, Italy)

ALSO KNOWN AS: Flavius Theodosius (full name)

AREAS OF ACHIEVEMENT: Government and politics, war and conquest

EARLY LIFE

Flavius Theodosius (FLAY-vee-uhs thee-oh-DOH-see-uhs), known as Theodosius the Great, was the son of Count Flavius Theodosius, a Hispano-Roman nobleman whose family estates were located at Cauca in northwestern Spain. Theodosius's father distinguished himself in commands in Britain and North Africa. The younger Theodosius probably served under his father in Britain. He became military commander on the Danube River, in what is now Yugoslavia, and made a name for himself by winning victories over the Sarmatians, non-Germanic peoples who had been filtering into the Danube area from southern Russia since the first century C.E.

Theodosius's military career ended suddenly in 376 C.E., when his father, who had just suppressed a revolt in North Africa, was accused on some charge and executed at Carthage. The whole incident seems to have occurred just after the death of the emperor Valentinian I (321-375 C.E.), and it is assumed that Valentinian's young son Gratian (359-383 C.E.), the new emperor, was persuaded to authorize the execution by a newly powerful faction at court that included enemies of Count Theodosius. The younger Theodosius may have been in danger himself; at any rate, he retired to the family estates in Spain, his official career apparently over. He married Aelia Flavia Flacilla and had a son, Arcadius, during the two years spent in Spain.

A crisis in the Eastern Roman Empire brought Theodosius from retirement to the highest responsibility. The Germanic Visigoths had been defeated by the Huns as the latter advanced westward. The Visigoths asked for and received from the Romans permission to cross the Danube River and find refuge inside the Empire. When Roman officials sent to supervise their reception abused the Goths, they revolted and in August, 378, defeated and killed the emperor Valens in a great battle at Adrianople in Thrace. The Goths were then free to pillage the Balkans and Thrace.

Gratian, who had broken off wars with Germanic tribes in eastern Gaul to assist Valens, only to find that Valens had gone into battle without waiting for his aid, now had to find someone to restore Roman control in Thrace. The men who had accused Theodosius's father were now out of favor; a new faction made up of friends and connections of the Theodosian family had the emperor's ear. They suggested the younger Theodosius as a good candidate for emperor of the East. Gratian summoned Theodosius from Spain and apparently first gave him a military command, in which he again won victories against the Sarmatians, and then named him emperor. Theodosius officially took power on January 19, 379.

LIFE'S WORK

Theodosius's next few years were spent in campaigns against the Goths, first from headquarters at Thessalonica in northeastern Greece and then, after November, 380, from Constantinople. Very little is known about these wars, but Theodosius was unable to destroy the Goths or even to drive them out of the Empire, in part, perhaps, because of a manpower shortage caused by the losses at Adrianople. As part of an attempt to conciliate at least some of the Goths and perhaps disunite them, the emperor welcomed the Gothic chieftain Athanaric to Constantinople on January 11, 381, and, when the Gothic leader died two weeks later, gave him an elaborate state funeral. Such treatment impressed the Goths and may have disposed them to negotiate.

In October, 382, Theodosius, apparently having concluded that victory was not attainable, ordered one of his generals to make a treaty with the Goths. By its terms, they were allowed to settle in Thrace as *federati*. They owed military service to the Empire, but unlike earlier settlements of barbarians inside the Empire, the Goths were allowed to retain their arms as well as their own rulers and laws. In effect, they were a separate nation inside the Imperial borders. Many contemporaries criticized this arrangement; some modern scholars have even suggested that it was a factor in the fall of the Western Roman Empire.

On the other hand, Theodosius reorganized the eastern armies in a way that greatly contributed to the internal security of the Eastern Roman Empire. He set up five separate armies, each with its own commander who reported directly to the emperor. No single commander could concentrate power in his own hands as was still possible in the West.

In the same years in which he was engaged in campaigns against the Goths, Theodosius involved himself in religious affairs. He was baptized in the autumn of 380, when he was believed to be near death from illness. Many people in this period preferred to delay baptism until their deathbed, since the ritual absolved sins committed before the sacrament. There is no way of knowing whether baptism on threat of death caused Theodosius to have some sort of conversion experience or whether it only intensified an already strong adherence to the Church. Certainly he took vigorous steps shortly after his recovery to demonstrate his support of the Nicene Creed (which maintained that Father and Son were of the same substance). The Arians, who were especially powerful in

Theodosius the Great. (Hulton|Archive by Getty Images)

the Eastern Roman Empire, believed that the Son was not divine, but only a creature, and thus subordinate to the Father.

Within two days after entering Constantinople on November 24, 380, Theodosius expelled the Arian bishop Demophilus and established his own candidate, the orthodox Catholic Gregory of Nazianzus (329 or 330-389 or 390 C.E.), as bishop. On February 28, 380, he had issued an edict requiring everyone to accept the Trinity. Yet the new decree was enforced mainly against bishops and priests, who lost their churches if they refused to accept it. It did not, apparently, represent an attempt to force all laymen to adhere to the Nicene Creed.

Toward paganism, Theodosius adopted a more conciliatory approach, at least in the early years of his reign, even reopening a pagan temple on the Euphrates River in 382 as long as no sacrifices took place there. In January, 381, he issued another edict ordering that all churches be turned over to the Nicene Catholics, and in May through July he held the Council of Constantinople, at which about 150 eastern bishops reaffirmed the divinity of Son and Holy Spirit.

Soon Theodosius was faced with a situation in which his loyalty to the Church conflicted with the duty he owed to the man who had made him emperor. In 383, Magnus Clemens Maximus (d. 388 C.E.) in Britain proclaimed himself emperor of the West and invaded Gaul, where Gratian's army went over to the usurper and Gratian himself was killed, perhaps by his own men. Magnus Maximus controlled Britain, Spain, Gaul, and North Africa. In Italy and the middle Danube provinces Valentinian II (371-392 C.E.), Gratian's younger brother, ruled under the tutelage of his mother, Justina, an Arian. Theodosius was placed in something of a dilemma. Loyalty to Gratian would have demanded that he avenge his patron's death and restore all the western provinces to Valentinian. Religion complicated the picture, however, since Magnus Maximus was presenting himself as a champion of orthodox Catholicism. How could the defender of orthodoxy in the East put down a Catholic ruler in the West in order to put an Arian in his place?

There may also have been personal ties between Theodosius and Magnus Maximus; Maximus came from Spain, was apparently some sort of dependent of the Theodosian family, and may have served in Britain alongside Theodosius under Count Theodosius. His concern for his eastern frontier could have increased the emperor's reluctance to divert his armies to a campaign in the West. When the envoys of Magnus Maximus arrived in Constantinople to ask for official recognition, the King

ROMAN EMPERORS FROM THEODOSIUS THE GREAT TO LEO I	
Ruler	*Reign (C.E.)*
Theodosius the Great (all)	379-395
Maximus (West, usurper)	383-388
Eugenius (West, usurper)	392-394
Honorius (West)	393-423
Arcadius (East)	395-408
Theodosius II (East)	408-450
Constantius III (East)	421
Valentian III (West)	425-455
Marcian (East)	450-457
Petronius Maximus (West)	455
Avitus (West)	455-456
Majoran (West)	457-461
Leo I (East)	457-474

of Persia, Ardashīr II, had just died, and it was not known whether his successor planned to attack the Romans. A revolt of tribes on the Arabian frontier, in modern Jordan, complicated the situation. Religion, personal ties, and military concerns apparently decided the issue. Theodosius not only made no attempt to get rid of Magnus Maximus but also gave him official recognition as ruler of Britain, Spain, and Gaul.

Many of the difficulties that had held Theodosius back in 383 were resolved in the next few years. In 384, the new ruler of Persia sent envoys to Constantinople with lavish gifts for the emperor, presumably to signal friendly intentions. The tribes in revolt on the eastern frontier had submitted in 385, and in 387 a treaty was signed with Persia. In an agreement similar to those made by Rome and Parthia in earlier centuries, Theodosius allowed the Persians to name a ruler for most of Armenia, a mountainous area in eastern Asia Minor that controlled the roads between Roman Asia Minor and Persia. This Persian treaty and the earlier one with the Goths gave the Eastern Roman Empire a long period of peace in which to rebuild its forces.

Although repeated incursions by bands of Huns and other tribes kept the frontier forces on the alert, the only major wars Theodosius fought in the remainder of his reign were against usurpers in the West, the first not until about ten years after Adrianople. In those ten years, he had succeeded in rebuilding his armies to a point where they could win victories over other Roman armies. Whether Theodosius's decision to make peace with foreign enemies but to fight internal rivals was best for the whole empire in the long run is a question fundamental to any assessment of his accomplishments as ruler.

In the same year in which the Persian treaty was signed, Maximus invaded Italy, causing Valentinian II, his mother, and his sister Galla to flee to Theodosius for help. Theodosius was now militarily in a much better position to confront Maximus, and by marrying Galla he could claim that family loyalties outweighed the claims of religion. In June, 388, he led an army from the East, defeated Maximus twice in Pannonia, at Siscia and Poetovio, and forced him to retreat to Aquileia, at the head of the Adriatic Sea. There, Maximus surrendered and was killed by Theodosius's soldiers, who feared that the emperor might pardon him. Indeed, Theodosius punished very few of Maximus's supporters and issued a general pardon for the rest. He installed Valentinian as emperor in the West under the supervision of Arbogast (d. 394 C.E.), an army commander of mixed Germanic and Roman parentage. Valentinian converted from Arianism to Catholicism at Theodosius's urging and established his court at Vienne in southern Gaul.

Theodosius spent considerable time in Italy between 388 and 391. On June 13, 389, he made a formal entry into Rome with his younger son Flavius Honorius. By generous gifts, reforms in the laws, and deference to powerful individuals, he cultivated the support of the senate. While in Italy, Theodosius himself came under the influence of Bishop Ambrose of Milan (c. 339-397 C.E.), one of the Fathers of the Church. If Theodosius had given orders to church officials in the East, he now found himself submitting to the demands of a western bishop. In 390, after the people of Thessalonica murdered one of the emperor's German officers, soldiers were allowed to massacre thousands of spectators in the city's stadium. Ambrose demanded that Theodosius do penance for the massacre, and after long negotiations the emperor conceded. Stripping himself of the diadem and purple cloak that symbolized his power, he knelt before the bishop in the cathedral in Milan to ask for a pardon. It was a vivid demonstration of the western Church's power in relation to the government.

Having returned to Constantinople in 391, Theodosius found himself facing another western usurper in the following year. As Valentinian II grew into his late teens, the young man realized that Arbogast meant to keep real power in his own hands. In frustration, he apparently committed suicide, although many at the time and later accused Arbogast of murdering the young emperor. Arbogast named a teacher of rhetoric, Eugenius, as the emperor of the West.

Arbogast, a pagan himself, seems to have hoped for the support of the surviving pagan aristocracy, and a number of distinguished pagan nobles did rally to Eugenius's cause. Pagan support for Eugenius allowed Theodosius to present himself as the defender of Christianity. In 394, Theodosius again led his armies westward; on September 6, 394, at the Battle of the Frigidus, a river in Yugoslavia, he defeated Arbogast and Eugenius. On the first day of the battle, ten thousand Visigoths in Theodosius's army died in a frontal assault, and the emperor's officers advised retreat. Theodosius refused to give up and on the next day won a decisive victory with the aid of a sudden windstorm. Eugenius was captured and executed; Arbogast escaped but killed himself two days later. Many consider this final defeat of the forces of paganism in the Roman Empire to have been Theodosius's greatest achievement.

The emperor, however, had only a few months to enjoy the victory; he died in Milan in January, 395. He left the Empire to his sons Arcadius and Honorius—Arcadius to rule in the East and Honorius in the West. It has been argued that this division led to the fall of the Western Roman Empire because the wealthier East not only did not send aid when barbarians attacked the West but also diverted invaders westward to save itself, in some cases.

SIGNIFICANCE

Theodosius the Great brought peace to the Eastern Roman Empire through diplomacy, rebuilt the eastern armies, and used them to win victories against western Roman armies. He ruled the East for fifteen years in which no one successfully disputed his authority, and he founded a dynasty that held power in the East until 450 and in the West until 455. In his zeal for Catholic orthodoxy, he issued orders to lay people and bishops on matters of doctrine, conciliated the senate with high offices, and won the people's favor. He made sure that Constantinople had a secure supply of grain, extended the walls, and embellished the city with a forum and a column depicting his victories. He even managed to lower taxes.

By most of the standards applied to earlier emperors, Theodosius was successful; the Church thought he deserved the title "Great." One could argue that the Eastern Roman Empire benefited substantially from his rule, in both the short and the long terms. Whether his settlement of the Goths and his division of the Empire between his sons did not in the long run prove disastrous to the West is a question still disputed.

—*Carolyn Nelson*

FURTHER READING

Ferrill, Arthur. *The Fall of the Roman Empire: The Military Explanation*. New York: Thames and Hudson, 1986. Chapter 4 on Theodosius is a careful evaluation of his military accomplishments, with a description of the Roman armies in 395. With table of emperors, bibliography, and illustrations, including a sculptural portrait of Theodosius and a map of the Battle of the Frigidus.

Holum, Kenneth G. *Theodosian Empresses: Women and Imperial Dominion in Late Antiquity*. 1982. Reprint. Berkeley: University of California Press, 1990. Part of chapter 2, "Theodosius the Great and His Women," provides a useful summary of some of the main issues of Theodosius's reign as well as a description of Theodosian Constantinople, a discussion of the position of the emperor's first wife, and an account of the implications of his second marriage for the war against Maximus. With detailed footnotes, a plan of Constantinople under Theodosius, a genealogical table of the Theodosian family, illustrations with an emphasis on coins, extensive bibliography, and an index.

Jones, A. H. M. *The Later Roman Empire, 284-602: A Social, Economic, and Administrative Survey*. 2 vols. 1964. Reprint. Baltimore, Md.: The Johns Hopkins University Press, 1986. Detailed, authoritative treatment of the period includes material on Theodosius's reign, his religious policy, and his laws. Third volume contains notes, three appendices, lists of collections and periodicals cited, and an exhaustive list of sources with abbreviations. With seven maps in a folder.

Matthews, John. *Western Aristocracies and Imperial Court: A.D. 364-425*. 1975. Reprint. New York: Oxford University Press, 1990. Chapters 4 through 9 deal with Theodosius's reign in considerable detail, intermingled with extensive and occasionally digressive treatment of the social and cultural background of the aristocracies under his rule.

Williams, Stephen, and Gerard Friell. *The Rome That Did Not Fall: The Survival of the East in the Fifth Century*. New York: Routledge, 2000. A well-illustrated analysis of the breakup of the Roman Empire and its division into the Eastern and Western Empires. A good presentation of the results of Theodosius's reign and the consequences of his political decisions.

_____. *Theodosius: The Empire at Bay*. New Haven, Conn.: Yale University Press, 1998. This biography analyzes Theodosius's military, political, and religious impact on Western history, using archaeological, literary, and numismatic evidence.

THEOPHRASTUS
Greek scientist and philosopher

Successor of Aristotle as head of his school, the Lyceum, Theophrastus became father of the sciences of botany, ecology, and mineralogy. He also wrote literary sketches of human psychological types.

BORN: c. 372 B.C.E.; Eresus, Lesbos, Greece
DIED: c. 287 B.C.E.; Athens?, Greece
ALSO KNOWN AS: Tyrtamus
AREAS OF ACHIEVEMENT: Science, philosophy, literature

EARLY LIFE

Theophrastus (thee-uh-FRAS-tuhs), originally named Tyrtamus, was born in Eresus, a small city-state on the Greek island of Lesbos, near the coast of Asia Minor. His father was Melantas, a cloth-fuller. He studied under the philosopher Alcippus in Eresus, later traveling to Athens to broaden his intellectual horizons. It is not known when he became Aristotle's student. It was Aristotle who called him Theophrastus, "he of godlike speech," a compliment to his polished Greek style. According to tradition, both men studied under Plato, but in Theophrastus's case this study must have been brief.

Theophrastus was in his mid-twenties when Plato died. Since Plato had not made Aristotle head of his school, the Academy, Aristotle moved to Assos at the invitation of its ruler, Hermias, and stayed three years. Theophrastus followed him there. When the Persians threatened Hermias, Theophrastus took Aristotle to the relative safety of his native island, Lesbos. The men were only twelve years apart in age, and the relationship between them was as much that of friends and colleagues as that of master and disciple. Soon Philip II, King of Macedonia, invited Aristotle to come there as tutor of his son, the future Alexander the Great. He accepted, and Theophrastus went with him, remaining until after Philip's death seven years later.

LIFE'S WORK

In 335, Aristotle returned to Athens and founded a school at the Lyceum, a cult center with a colonnade and park, where the Peripatetic philosophy flourished under his leadership for thirteen years. Theophrastus lived there, discussing, lecturing, and writing. It was a creative period. Alexander was conquering the East as far as India, and philosophers who went with him, at first including Aristotle's nephew, Callisthenes, sent back scientific specimens never seen before in Greece. Not least among these were seeds and living plants that were tended in the garden of the Lyceum and studied by Theophrastus. His books on botany thus contain descriptions of the plants of India. He traveled through Greece collecting plants and making observations of natural phenomena.

Around the time of Alexander's death in 323, Aristotle retired to Chalcis, and a few months later he also died. His choice of Theophrastus as his successor at the Lyceum proved to be a wise one. At this time Theophrastus was about fifty years old, and statues give some idea of his appearance. He was a vigorous, healthy man, but lines around his eyes and the hollows of his cheeks suggest the heavy responsibilities of leadership and the hard work of empirical research. He remained at the Lyceum as *scholarch* (senior professor) until his death in about 287. His will provided for the maintenance of the Lyceum garden, where he asked to have his body buried. He designated Strato of Lampsacus, known as "the physicist," his heir as head of the school.

Theophrastus taught some two thousand students, among them Demetrius of Phalerum, who became ruler of Athens and presented Theophrastus with the land on which the Lyceum and its garden were located. Thus the school came to possess its own real estate, instead of leasing its grounds from the city. This step was important, because many Athenians regarded Aristotle and his followers as pro-Macedonian; Theophrastus had even been charged with sacrilege in 319. He had managed to stay in the city, and the reestablishment of Macedonian power in Athens two years later had made Demetrius governor. Demetrius was not popular, and when his rule ended in 307 a law was passed forbidding the operation of philosophical schools without special permission. Theophrastus then had to leave Athens, but the law was repealed within a year, and he was able to return.

Theophrastus produced his most important writings during his years at the Lyceum. He continued to revise them until the end of his life. The titles of 227 works by Theophrastus have been recorded, but only a small fraction have survived. They fall into three major categories: scientific, philosophical, and literary.

It is in science that Theophrastus made his most significant contributions. Here he continued the work of Aristotle, achieving important insights of his own. He pointedly repeated Aristotle's statement that "nature does nothing in vain" and added his own comment, "Anything which is contrary to nature is dangerous." In describing natural objects, Theophrastus established sets of opposing characteristics, such as cold and hot, wet and dry, male and female, wild and domestic. This method is typical of the Peripatetic school and is derived from Aristotle. In some respects, however, such as his emphasis on the autonomous purposes of living things and his avoidance of the ideas of final causation and the prime mover, he rejected Aristotle's authority and marked out an independent line of investigation.

His longest extant writings are the nine books of *Peri phytikōn historiōn* (translated in *Enquiry into Plants and Minor Works on Odours and Weather Signs*, 1916; often designated by the Latin title, *De historia plantarum*) and the six books of *Peri phytikōn aitiōn* (translation in *De causis plantarum*, 1976-1990). Aristotle had written on animals; Theophrastus's works are the first careful treatment of botanical subjects. *Enquiry into Plants* describes the parts of plants and the characteristics of more than five hundred species, arranged in four groups: trees, shrubs, sub-shrubs, and herbs. *Peri phytikōn aitiōn* discusses generation, propagation, cultivation, and diseases of plants, as well as their tastes and odors. Theophrastus originated many terms in the botanical vocabulary and distinguished some of the main divisions of the vegetable kingdom. These works are also notable for their ecological viewpoint. Theophrastus always discusses a plant in the context of its relationships to the environment: sunshine, soil, climate, water, cultivation, and other plants and animals. His conclusions are sometimes wrong—for example, he believed in spontaneous generation—but even in such cases he showed caution and skepticism.

The works of Theophrastus dealing with other sciences are extant only in fragmentary form. Only excerpts remain of his *Peri physikōn* (on physics) and *Peri pyros*

(*De Igne: A Post-Aristotelian View of the Nature of Fire*, 1971). Geology is represented by *Peri lithōn* (translated in *Theophrastus's History of Stones*, 1746; also as *On Stones*), a long fragment that investigates the properties of metals, minerals, gems, and substances whose animal origin he recognized, such as pearls, coral, and ivory.

Theophrastus. (Library of Congress)

873

Fossils are handled in *Peri ichthyōn en xera katastasei* (on fishes in dry condition). Then there are fragments on meteorology such as *Peri semeiōn hydatōn kai pneumatōn kai cheimonōn kai eudiōn* and *Peri anemōn* (translated together in *On Winds and On Weather Signs*, 1894); the treatise on winds accurately describes many of the Mediterranean winds and goes beyond Aristotle in affirming that winds are moving air. Human physiology is discussed by Theophrastus in other treatises on sense perception, odors, weariness, fainting, paralysis, and perspiration. One called *Peri hypnou kai enypniōn* (on sleep and dreams) has disappeared.

The surviving philosophical work of Theophrastus is an important section of the *Tōn meta ta physika* (*Metaphysics*, 1929), which criticizes Aristotle's doctrine that all things have a final cause, or *telos*. Aristotle said that the final cause of all living things is the service of the higher rational nature, that is, of human beings. Rejecting his teacher's excessive teleology, Theophrastus remarked,

> We must try to find a certain limit . . . both to final causation and to the impulse to the better. For this is the beginning of the inquiry about the universe, that is, of the effort to determine the conditions on which real things depend and the relations in which they stand to one another.

So he maintained that, by nature, each living thing always aims at assimilating its intake to its own goal, and the goal of a plant is not to feed humans or to give them wood but to produce fruit containing seed for the perpetuation of its species—in other words, to produce offspring similar to itself. Aristotle would not have denied species perpetuation as a goal but would have made it a subsidiary cause in his hierarchical organization of nature. For Theophrastus, it is the whole point.

Other authors often quoted from his now-lost reference works, *Physikon doxai* (doctrines of natural philosophers), a history of philosophical opinions about major problems, and the *Nomoi* (laws), a compilation of the statutes and traditions of Greek cities. *Charactēres ethikōi* (c. 319; *The Moral Characters of Theophrastus*, 1616, best known as *Characters*) is Theophrastus's only surviving literary work and his most famous writing. In it he sketches thirty aberrant human personality types, giving as much care to their description as he did to plant species in his botanical works. These are not objective treatises, but satirical, dryly humorous jabs at disagreeable people such as the flatterer, the faultfinder, and the miser. This genre established by Theophrastus was much imitated, particularly in Great Britain and France in the seventeenth and eighteenth centuries.

SIGNIFICANCE

Theophrastus was, as Diogenes Laertius wrote, "a man of remarkable intelligence and industry." His fame has suffered because he has remained in the shadow of Aristotle. In the areas where he differed from his teacher, he was more scientific, more dependent on observation, and less ready to make universal statements of principle that could not be supported by perceptible facts. Aristotle had moved away from Plato in that direction; Theophrastus went even further.

In doing so, Theophrastus anticipated some of the methods of modern science. More than Plato's or Aristotle's, his philosophical stance was congenial with scientific discovery, emphasizing as it did efficient causes, not final causes. He has been recognized as the founder of the science of botany, having made many observations about plants for the first time and having established the basic terminology in that field. In modern times, he is also recognized as the first ecologist, for he viewed species not as isolated phenomena but in interaction with their physical environment and other species. He was distinguished as a perceptive investigator of lithology and mineralogy. Many of his ideas have been corrected in the light of later work; many others have so far withstood the test of time. It is hard to criticize him too severely, since he was among the first to set out on the journey of scientific inquiry. All told, he is impressive for his rationality and good sense and for his wish to depend on observations and to criticize the reports that he received. His practical attitude may be discerned in his rejoinder to those who advised him to plant and fell trees by the moon and signs of the zodiac: "One should not in fact be governed by the celestial conditions and revolution rather than by the trees and slips and seeds."

Among those who followed him were the researchers of the Museum and Library of Alexandria in Egypt in the second and first centuries B.C.E. The Latin natural historian Pliny the Elder quoted him extensively, and his influence can be traced in other ancient writers on sciences such as botany and medical pharmacology. Arabic commentators studied, preserved, and translated his writings during the medieval period. When interest in the sciences was reawakened in early modern Europe, the botanical works of Theophrastus were revived and printed. A Latin translation appeared in 1483, and the Greek text was published in Venice between 1495 and 1498. An English translation of the *Peri phytikōn historiōn* was published in 1916 and of the first two books of the *Peri phytikōn aitiōn* in 1976.

—*J. Donald Hughes*

FURTHER READING

Baltussen, H. *Theophrastus Against the Presocratics and Plato: Peripatetic Dialectic in the "De sensibus."* Boston: Brill Academic, 2000. Interprets and offers insights into Theophrastus's *De sensibus* and criticizes the methods of the Presocratics and Plato. Includes bibliographical references and indexes.

Diogenes Laertius. "Theophrastus." In *Lives of Eminent Philosophers*, edited by R. D. Hicks. Vol. 1. Cambridge, Mass.: Harvard University Press, 1925. Because Diogenes wrote his set of biographies about five hundred years after the death of Theophrastus, his work is not entirely reliable, but it does preserve many ancient traditions about him.

Fortenbaugh, William W., et al., eds. and trans. *Theophrastus of Eresus: Sources for His Life, Writings, Thought, and Influence.* New York: Brill Academic, 1992. An ambitious series of volumes dedicated to the translation of and commentary on Theophrastus's works. See in particular the volumes of commentary.

Fortenbaugh, William W., Pamela M. Huby, and Anthony A. Long, eds. *Theophrastus of Eresus: On His Life and Work.* New Brunswick, N.J.: Transaction Books, 1985. Contains numerous scholarly essays on the major issues in literary, philosophical, scientific, and historical research on Theophrastus. Three of these deal with the Arabic tradition.

Fortenbaugh, William W., and Robert W. Sharples, eds. *Theophrastus as Natural Scientist and Other Papers.* New Brunswick, N.J.: Transaction Books, 1987. Volume 3 in the Rutgers Studies in Classical Humanities series and a companion to *Theophrastus of Eresus*, this is another collection of articles on Theophrastus's shorter scientific works, and others on botany and ecology, metaphysics, ethics, religion, and politics.

Theophrastus. *The Character Sketches.* Translated with an introduction and notes by Warren Anderson. Kent, Ohio: Kent State University Press, 1970. A translation of the *Characters*, with useful explanatory notes and an introductory essay on the development of the "character" as a literary genre.

_____. *De causis plantarum.* Translated with an introduction by Benedict Einarson and George K. K. Link. Cambridge, Mass.: Harvard University Press, 1976-1990. This translation of the *Peri phytikōn aitōn* has the Greek and English texts on facing pages and includes a fine introduction on the author and the work, Theophrastus's predecessors, his calendar, and more.

_____. *Enquiry into Plants and Minor Works on Odours and Weather Signs.* Translated with an introduction by Sir Arthur Hort. 2 vols. Cambridge, Mass.: Harvard University Press, 1916. This has the Greek text and English translation on facing pages; it includes a short but useful introduction. The difficult Greek of Theophrastus is rendered accurately, but in an eccentric English style.

SEE ALSO: Aristotle; Philip II of Macedonia; Plato.

RELATED ARTICLES in *Great Events from History: The Ancient World*: 336 B.C.E., Alexander the Great Begins Expansion of Macedonia; 325-323 B.C.E., Aristotle Isolates Science as a Discipline; c. 320 B.C.E., Theophrastus Initiates the Study of Botany

THESPIS
Greek actor and playwright

Though perhaps more legendary than historical, as none of his plays has survived, Thespis is credited with introducing the first actor into the Dionysian festival of song and dance. Thus, he is the traditional originator of Greek drama.

BORN: Before 535 B.C.E.; probably Icarios (Icaria) or Athens, Greece
DIED: After 501 B.C.E.; probably Athens, Greece
AREA OF ACHIEVEMENT: Literature

EARLY LIFE

In the sixth century B.C.E. or earlier, the Greeks established an annual festival to honor the god Dionysus. This "god of many names," as the great dramatist Sophocles would later call him, was also known as Bacchus and Iacchos. He was associated with wine and other bounty and fecundity. His festival, the City Dionysia, was celebrated in March and featured a chorus of fifty singers and dancers whose performance was a part of the religious rites. Eventually, the cosmopolitan City Dionysia was succeeded by a second, domestic festival called the Lenaea ("wine press") and held in January.

A performance of song and dance is not a drama, and it was Thespis (THES-puhs), an Athenian of whom little is known historically, who is said to have converted the former into the latter. According to one tradition, Thespis's home was Icarios, or Icaria, in northern Attica, near Marathon. Yet an extant ancient source refers to him simply as "Athenian." If "Thespis" is the name of a real person, he may have been born to a father who was an epic singer or honored with a nickname later in life, for the name comes from a word that means "divinely speaking" or from a similar word that means "divinely singing."

The first evolution of the chorus produced a leader who, presumably, would take occasional solo turns during the performance. Until a performer existed apart from the chorus to ask its members questions, to be questioned by them, and perhaps to challenge assertions made in their lyrics, however, no absolute dramatic form was possible. Thespis is not known to history until he makes an appearance to introduce such a performer, the first actor.

Scholars do not agree on the date of Thespis's achievement. The traditional date for the appearance of tragedy as a part of the City Dionysia, or Great Dionysia, is 534 B.C.E., but late in the twentieth century some scholars argued for a later date, 501 B.C.E. Whatever the correct date, tragedies appear to have been acted as a part of the festival every year thereafter. No comedy is mentioned as having been performed at the City Dionysia until 486 B.C.E. The dramas at the Lenaea were solely comic in 442 B.C.E., and although tragedy was added in 432 B.C.E., comedy continued to dominate. None of these developments would have been possible without Thespis's innovation.

LIFE'S WORK

Thespis's career as actor-playwright is inextricably connected with the awarding of dramatic prizes at the Dionysian festivals. Some classical scholars have speculated that the prize originally was a goat, a not insignificant award in ancient Greece. Eventually, the winning dramatist received a monetary prize that was donated by a prominent Athenian. Each donor was chosen by the city government before the competition began.

According to tradition, the first official presentation of drama at Athens occurred in 534 B.C.E. The prize was won by Thespis. It is believed that at least as late as the time of Aeschylus, the next great Athenian playwright, who died in 456 B.C.E., the dramatist combined in his own person the roles of writer, director, composer, choreographer, and lead actor. Thus, when Thespis invented the first actor, it may be assumed that he played the role himself. His revolutionary contribution was the creation of a character who established a dialogue with the chorus. The character did not merely inquire of the chorus what happened next. Thespis impersonated someone interacting with the chorus, contributing to the unfolding plot. He was both the first dramatist and the first actor. Thus, it is appropriate that actors are still called "thespians" in his honor.

The little that is known of Thespis is filtered through the accounts of others, accounts that may themselves be apocryphal. For example, Solon, the famed Athenian lawgiver, supposedly reproached Thespis after witnessing his first play. He felt that it was inappropriate for the playwright to tell the assembly lies. His belief that these lies might actually be believed by the audience is a testament to the seriousness and the persuasiveness of the artifice. Thespis responded that it was appropriate in a play to persuade people that imaginary things are true. Solon, according to the story, was troubled by the idea that such deception might spread into the practice of politics. The problem with this amusing anecdote is that a commonly accepted date of death for Solon is c. 559 B.C.E., fully a quarter of a century before one of the proposed dates for Thespis's first play. If the story is true, Thespis must have exhibited in Athens before 560 B.C.E., as other sources suggest.

Despite the absence of historical evidence, certain features of Thespis's dramaturgy may be inferred. The identities of several of Thespis's immediate successors are known, foremost among them Phrynichus. By 499 B.C.E. the great Aeschylus was competing at the Festival of Dionysus. He was so popular and so critically esteemed that seven of his plays have survived. In the earliest of these, *Hiketides* (463 B.C.E.?; *The Suppliants*, 1777), the chorus numbers fifty members. In Aeschylus's later plays, he reduces the chorus to twelve members, and Sophocles, his younger contemporary, finally fixes the number at fifteen. Reasoning backward thus supports the inference that all of Thespis's plays employed the original fifty-member chorus, since documentary evidence attests that its reduced number was a much later innovation.

One scholarly school of thought rejects Thespis as a historical personage, viewing him instead as an effort to explain an interesting development in a mythic pattern very ancient and widespread throughout the Near East. Dionysus, through his association with spring and nature's bounty, is linked to the primitive god who dies over and over only to be reborn over and over, saving humankind by means of his resurrection. This powerful myth, incorporating the deepest mysteries of life and death, has produced countless stories in cultures ranging from Egypt to India. It also accounts, according to this theory, for the emergence of drama as a central element in the worship of Dionysus.

The Greek dramatists came to play a role in their culture very similar to the role played by the prophets in Hebrew culture. The God of the Hebrews was all-wise, all-good, the very source of order in the universe. The gods of the Greeks were willful, inconstant in their sympathies, frequently the source of disorder and strife. For the Hebrews, God was the ultimate moral arbiter. Such was not the case with the Greeks, but as a highly rational and civilized people, they realized their religious practice must address the thorny moral issues of life. To the playwrights fell the lot of supplying this moral dimension to the worship of Dionysus. It can thus be argued that the innovation of Thespis—or whoever or whatever that legendary figure represents—made possible in the next century the works of the great Aeschylus and Sophocles, dramatizing the deepest and subtlest conflicts of humankind.

For virtually every theory about Thespis and his work, there exists a countertheory. Some scholars argue that his plays grew out of the dithyramb, a wildly emotional choric tribute to Dionysus. Others insist that his first performances were given in his native region at country festivals and later brought to Athens by him and his players and that these were rather crude representations of the doings of satyrs, lustful, mischievous goat-men. Support for this theory comes from the fact that the etymology of "tragedy" can be traced to a word meaning "song of goats." Some sources indicate that Thespis gave only the most general direction to his reveling masquers and that a later poet, Pratinas, was the first person to write words for the players to learn by heart. This assertion, however, cannot be correct if, as Aristotle reportedly wrote, "Thespis invented a prologue and a (set) speech" for the chorus. Thespis is not discussed in the extant part of *De poetica*, c. 334-323 B.C.E. (*Poetics*, 1705), Aristotle's treatise on the drama, but other ancient authors quote from the lost portion.

The Roman poet Horace says that Thespis and his actors toured the Attic countryside in a wagon. By some accounts, Thespis, as the only one of his players to impersonate individual characters, would play one part after another in the same story. Since this activity necessitated frequent changes of mask and disguise, Thespis had a *skene*, a temporary booth, set up for the purpose. Thus, Thespis would also have invented the first traveling stock company and the first dressing room.

Still, whether the most minimal or the most extravagant view of Thespis's accomplishments prevails, his essential contribution to the drama was enormous. Without his brilliant conception of a character separate from the original chorus, the great comedies and tragedies produced during the next one hundred years would never have come to be.

SIGNIFICANCE

Thespis is a fascinating figure, in large part because of his historical elusiveness. Scarcely two classical scholars agree in every respect about his life and work. An example noted above is the belief of some experts that Thespis was producing what were essentially plays as early as 560 B.C.E. Others are equally convinced that a true tragedy was not acted in Athens until thirty or even fifty years later. Were Thespis's first plays crude, bucolic representations of the antics of the half-man, half-goat satyrs? Or, were they another solemn evolutionary step in the worship of the archetypal god who dies and is reborn yearly? Perhaps these jousting theories will never be reconciled.

It is clear, however, that Thespis, no matter what the precise details of his accomplishment, can be favorably judged—and honored—by the fruits of his labor.

Before Thespis, there was no drama. By c. 534 B.C.E., a competition among tragic dramatists had become a part of the City Dionysia (with Thespis himself identified as the earliest victor). The competitions began with tragedy and were expanded to include comedy. The festival's third, fourth, and fifth days were given over to tragic and comic contests. During the period of the Peloponnesian War, 431-404 B.C.E., tragedies were performed in the mornings, comedies in the afternoons.

At the Lenaea, the number of comedies was reduced to three for the duration of the Peloponnesian War. Before and after the war, however, five comic poets and two tragic poets regularly competed. This explosion of dramatic activity in the sixth and fifth centuries B.C.E. was lit by the spark of Thespis's innovation.

—Patrick Adcock

FURTHER READING

Else, Gerald F. *The Origin and Early Form of Greek Tragedy.* 1967. Reprint. New York: W. W. Norton, 1972. References to Thespis are sprinkled throughout the 102 pages of text, and chapter 3, pages 51-77, is titled "Thespis: The Creation of *Tragôidia*." Especially interesting is a discussion on pages 51-52 of the origin and meaning of the dramatist's name.

Gaster, Theodor H. *Thespis: Ritual, Myth, and Drama in the Ancient Near East.* 1961. Reprint. New York: Harper & Row, 1966. Here Thespis is used as a metaphor for the beginnings of European literature. Gaster argues that drama everywhere derived from a religious ritual designed to ensure the rebirth of the dead world. Traces the myth through Canaanite, Hittite, and Egyptian sources, concluding with biblical and classical poetry.

Gould, John. *Myth, Ritual, Memory, and Exchange: Essays in Greek Literature and Culture.* New York: Oxford University Press, 2001. An examination of early Greek drama and literature that looks at the role of ritual and myth. Bibliography and index.

McLeish, Kenneth. *A Guide to Greek Theatre and Drama.* London: Methuen, 2003. A study of Greek theater, including its development.

Sommerstein, Alan H. *Greek Drama and Dramatists.* New York: Routledge, 2002. An examination of the world of Greek drama.

Thomson, George. *Aeschylus and Athens: A Study in the Social Origins of Drama.* New York: Haskell House, 1972. Thomson infers elements of Thespian dramaturgy by reasoning backward from what is known of the plays of Aeschylus.

SEE ALSO: Aeschylus; Sophocles.

RELATED ARTICLES in *Great Events from History: The Ancient World*: c. 456/455 B.C.E., Greek Tragedian Aeschylus Dies; 406 B.C.E., Greek Dramatist Euripides Dies; c. 385 B.C.E., Greek Playwright Aristophanes Dies; 159 B.C.E., Roman Playwright Terence Dies.

SAINT THOMAS
Christian Apostle

As one of the handpicked followers of Jesus, Thomas played a role in the epoch-making spread of the Christian message in the first century. He continues to be venerated in Christendom.

BORN: c. early first century C.E.; Galilee, Palestine (now in Israel)
DIED: Second half of the first century; possibly Mylapore, India
ALSO KNOWN AS: Didymus
AREA OF ACHIEVEMENT: Religion

EARLY LIFE

Little specific information is available, but the general conditions of the early life of Thomas are reasonably certain. The signs point to his birth around or slightly after the traditional date of Jesus' nativity (c. 6 B.C.E.). Also like Jesus, he hailed from the area of Galilee, a district some sixty miles north of Jerusalem. His Jewish heritage furnished him with knowledge of the history of his race, respect for the religious customs of his forefathers, and familiarity with the Hebrew scriptures, perhaps in Aramaic or even Greek form.

A Galilean Jew such as Thomas (also called Didymus in the New Testament, a Greek word meaning "twin") likely differed somewhat from his countrymen in Jerusalem to the south. There are several reasons for this circumstance. First, Galilee had long been extensively affected by foreign cultural influences and had a large non-

Jewish population. Foreign merchants and settlers were encountered everywhere. Second, the Galileans' dialect was different from that spoken by Jews in Jerusalem (Matt. 26:73). Third, Jews of Galilee were regarded with some disdain by their southern neighbors for their less strict observance of the oral religious tradition, which formed the basis for faith and practice among the Pharisees, the most respected and influential Palestinian Jewish sect of the day. Finally, Galileans would most likely have been bilingual, both Aramaic and Greek being widely used throughout the district. A Jewish male would probably have had some command of Hebrew, the language of most of the Old Testament, as well.

Thomas's early years, then, would have been marked not only by thorough grounding in Judaism but also by considerable exposure to non-Jewish language and culture. The radical separation of Jew from Gentile practiced by some in Jerusalem would have been most difficult in Galilee. This cultural background helps account for, though it does not totally explain, his apparent willingness to become a disciple of Jesus of Nazareth (a village in south-central Galilee), whose views met forceful opposition from certain more strictly traditional Jewish authorities based in Jerusalem.

Thomas's early years would also have instilled in him, along with the vast majority of all Jews of his locale and time, a profound distaste for the presence of Roman military and political power, for Galilee was part of the Roman Empire throughout the first century. This loathing, which eventually erupted in the First Jewish Revolt (66-70 C.E.), was coupled in many persons with a distinct religiopolitical expectation, even longing. That is, the Jews hoped that the promises of the Hebrew Scriptures (understood quite literally as God's very words to his chosen people) were soon to come true in a new and dramatic fashion. God would send his designated deliverer, the Messiah (in Greek, *Christos*), to liberate the land from foreign domination and mightily bless his ancient covenant people, the Jews. The kingdom of God would one day soon arrive in tangible form.

Thomas was most likely an heir of such a theological and political outlook. His life's work as a disciple of Jesus was a response to what he understood as God's fulfillment, as promised in the Scriptures, of his and his nation's heartfelt longing.

LIFE'S WORK

The scanty available evidence points to Thomas's achievement in two settings: Galilee and surrounding districts during and after the life of Jesus of Nazareth, and

Saint Thomas. (Library of Congress)

areas to the east of the Roman Empire in the second half of the first century.

In his native Galilee, Thomas came into contact with Jesus, whose influence in the mid- to late 20's was felt from Roman Syria southward through Galilee and on to Jerusalem. Galilean Jews would have been aware of John the Baptist's prophetic proclamation; Jesus rode on John's coattails into the public arena, attracting followers such as Thomas.

Thomas was, according to available evidence, one of only twelve persons selected by Jesus from a much larger group of followers to receive special instruction and responsibilities (Matt. 10:3, Mark 3:18, Luke 6:15). For a period of some three years, Thomas observed and participated in a religious movement (not without political implications, however) led by Jesus and bent on intensifying, if not ushering in, the earthly reign of Israel's covenant God, Yahweh ("the kingdom of God"). Thomas was among the twelve sent out to call his countrymen to repentance (Mark 6:7-13), a recognition of personal and corporate need for moral reform in the light of impending divine judgment. In this way, he and his colleagues saw their mission, like that of John the Baptist and Jesus himself, as preparation for a decisive act of God in the near future (Luke 19:11, Acts 1:6).

Thomas was as disillusioned as his comrades were when Jesus' activity culminated in his arrest and execution by local and Imperial authorities in Jerusalem. Like the other disciples, he fled the scene (Matt. 26:56), presumably to avoid being incriminated himself because of association with an alleged criminal. Were this the last hint of Thomas's activity, his name would long ago have been forgotten. Ancient sources, however, afford three specific glimpses into his life and thought that have for centuries enshrined him in the memories of those whose own personal religious experience resonates with that of Thomas. These traditions, all in the Gospel of John, merit specific mention as a result of their continuing religious relevance as well as their probable historical significance.

At the crucial point in Jesus' life, when his sense of destiny beckoned him from Perea (where he was fairly safe from arrest) to Jerusalem (where he was not), it was Thomas who rallied his comrades with the declaration, "Let us go with him so that we may die with him." Scholars debate whether this evinces a fatalistic or a courageous spirit. In either case, Thomas helped to galvanize the other disciples into accompanying Jesus, against their own better judgment (Mark 10:32), to the eventual site of his death. He models a stoic, or perhaps selfless, response to perceived duty.

Some days later, according to John's gospel, Jesus sought to console his disciples on the eve of his imminent betrayal. Again Thomas focused the collective spirit of his fellows. This time, however, his words betrayed not courage but curiosity, if not incredulity. Jesus spoke enigmatically of departing in order to make ready a place for his followers: Thomas observed: "We do not know where you are going; how can we know how to get there?" Thomas demonstrates here a searching if not critical temperament that articulates the heartfelt inquisitiveness, or even frustration, of many religious persons in the first century, and others since that time.

Thomas is most remembered, however, for the independent yet ultimately pliant spirit he exhibited during the days when, according to sources preserved in the New Testament, Jesus appeared to his disciples alive following his death by crucifixion (John 20:24-31). Thomas refused to give credence to hearsay evidence, saying that unless and until he had personal, tangible proof that Jesus had indeed somehow risen from the dead—which, one surmises, Thomas doubted he would receive—he refused to set any store by his friends' astonishing claims.

One week later, Thomas's skepticism was forced to contend with the corporeal presence of the person whose existence he had so roundly questioned: Jesus. Thomas was invited to satisfy his doubt and then draw the appropriate conclusions. In John's account, Thomas becomes the first person to affirm, in the wake of Jesus' resurrection, unqualified recognition of Jesus as master and deity.

Apart from his activity in Galilee, Thomas is also connected in ancient sources with missionary activity east of the Roman Empire. *The Acts of Thomas*, dating from about the third century, speaks of Thomas's presence in India. (The second century *Gospel of Thomas* gives little if any information on Thomas and was in any case not written by him.) Much of the material in this apocryphal book may be safely regarded as fiction. There seems, however, to be a historical core that supports the view, held by several communities of Indian Christians to this day, that the Gospel was first brought to their ancestors by Thomas in the first century. According to traditions preserved in these communities, Thomas was fatally stabbed on July 3, 72, for refusing to worship Kali, a Hindu goddess.

Other ancient sources speak somewhat vaguely of Thomas's labors in Parthia, an ancient nation southeast of the Caspian Sea. Scholars theorize that these reports reflect not an actual visit by Thomas to Parthia but written communication between Thomas and Christians in the Parthian city of Edessa. In any case, the Parthian tradition corroborates the assertion that in the early years of Christianity's expansion Thomas was instrumental in bearing the Gospel message to lands far to the east of his native Galilee.

SIGNIFICANCE

Saint Thomas was hardly a pivotal figure in the history of early Christianity. It cannot even be said that he occupies a prominent place in the Gospel records where he receives direct mention. During Jesus' life, he was overshadowed by Peter, James, and John, while his activity in the first decades of early church expansion is now nearly hidden.

However, there is good evidence that he played a more integral role in the spread of Christianity to India—where thousands have revered his memory for centuries—and perhaps even farther eastward than Western Christendom and historians generally acknowledge.

Thomas in his milieu may perhaps be compared to someone such as Martin Bucer in the Reformation: Both men played significant roles, but in historical perspective both are eclipsed by more dominant personages and events in which they had only tangential involvement. Still, the careful student of ancient Christianity will be as loath to overlook Thomas's place as will the student of the Reformation to overlook Bucer.

Wherever the New Testament has been read through the centuries, which is virtually everywhere in the West, Thomas has served as an example, both good and bad, for Christian faith. Commentators such as John Calvin, stressing his incredulity, have criticized his obduracy and contributed to a view of him epitomized in the expression "doubting Thomas." Augustine sees in Jesus' words to Thomas ("Blessed are they who have not seen, and yet believe," John 20:28) a commendation of those who in coming centuries and God's predestinating plan place personal trust in God through Jesus. Origen refutes the claims of Augustine's adversary Aulus Cornelius Celsus by adducing Thomas's testimony as proof of the corporeality of Jesus' resurrected body.

In these and many other cases, Thomas takes his place as a continuing witness to both the objective reality and the subjective impact of the person of Jesus in the experience of one who examines his claims. Thomas himself would perhaps affirm an assessment of his contribution to religion, and even history, which would stress not his own achievement but the merit of the one whose reality convinced his questioning mind and, as a result, his heart.

—Robert W. Yarbrough

FURTHER READING

Barclay, William. *The Master's Men.* New York: Abingdon Press, 1959. Popular level but learned discussion. A renowned New Testament scholar devotes a chapter to an insightful, if slightly overimaginative, character sketch that attempts to assess all significant historical references to Thomas. Also discusses Thomas traditions in works by ancient historians as well as in *The Acts of Thomas.*

Barker, Kenneth, ed. *The New International Study Bible.* Rev. ed. Grand Rapids, Mich.: Zondervan Bible Publishers, 2002. Makes available, in modern English translation, all extant first century references to Thomas (indexed in a concordance). Includes explanatory comments on Thomas's remarks in the Gospel of John and other Gospel references to him. Maps aid in picturing the geographical dimensions of the world in which Thomas lived.

Bonney, William. *Caused to Believe: The Doubting Thomas Story as the Climax of John's Christological Narrative.* Boston: Brill Academic Publishers, 2002. A literary study of John's gospel and the doubting Thomas story. Shows how the story reveals Jesus' nature in relationship to God and humanity.

Bremmer, Jan N., ed. *The Apocryphal Acts of Thomas.* Leuven, Belgium: Peeters, 2001. Based on a conference held at the Rijksuniversiteit Groningen in 1998 and part of the Studies on Early Christian Apocrypha series. Provides criticism and interpretation and includes bibliographical references.

Finegan, J. *Hidden Records of the Life of Jesus.* Philadelphia: Pilgrim Press, 1969. The extended subtitle reads "An Introduction to the New Testament Apocrypha and to Some of the Areas Through Which They Were Transmitted, Namely, Jewish, Egyptian, and Gnostic Christianity, Together with the Earlier Gospel-Type Records in the Apocrypha, in Greek and Latin Texts—Translations and Explanations." Contains a valuable discussion of the Gospel of Thomas with extensive bibliography. Cites portions in the original languages, then gives translation and analysis. Concludes with the verdict that alleged sayings of Jesus in the Gospel of Thomas generally have little chance of being authentic. Implies that Jesus' disciple Thomas is not the author.

Freyne, Seán. *Galilee from Alexander the Great to Hadrian, 323 B.C.E. to 135 C.E.: A Study of Second Temple Judaism.* Wilmington, Del.: Michael Glazier, 1980. The standard history of Galilee in the days of Thomas. Useful for general background on living conditions and social environment. Discusses the languages spoken in Galilee, the religious views of Galileans, and the political currents of the time. Useful maps and full bibliography.

The Gospel According to John. 2 vols. Introduction, translation, and notes by Raymond Brown. Garden City, N.Y.: Doubleday and Co., 1966-1970. The most significant primary source for information on Thomas is the New Testament, especially John's gospel. This critically acclaimed entry in the Anchor Bible series is among the most competent and thorough investigations of John, and therefore of the Thomas traditions as they occur in the New Testament.

Medlycott, A. E. *India and the Apostle Thomas: An Inquiry, with a Critical Analysis of the "Acta Thomae."* London: David Nutt, 1905. The seminal study in English of the ancient extra-New Testament Thomas traditions in the light of modern historical and archaeological findings. Medlycott is among the first to furnish, and at times deny, solid historical footing for certain ancient ecclesiastical traditions concerning Thomas. His observations and arguments are foundational to subsequent discussion.

Mundadan, A. M. *From the Beginning up to the Middle of the Sixteenth Century (up to 1542)*. Vol. 1 in *History of Christianity in India*. Bangalore, India: Theological Publications in India, 1982. Chapter 1 of this critical history focuses primarily on the traditions that link Thomas to India. Mundadan's evaluation of both primary and secondary evidence in some respects supersedes all previous discussion in its breadth and depth of treatment. He concludes that the Indian community's ancient traditions of Saint Thomas are rooted in the historical fact of Thomas's first-century labors there. Exhaustive bibliography.

Perumalil, A. C. *The Apostles in India*. 2d enl. ed. Patna, India: Xavier Teachers' Training Institute, 1971. Elaborates on ancient traditions concerning both Thomas and Bartholomew. Not always sufficiently analytical and critical in dealing with historical evidence, but this is more than compensated for by the complete listing of all references to India in both Greek and Latin sources from the second to the thirteenth century.

SEE ALSO: Jesus; John the Apostle; Saint John the Baptist; Saint Paul; Saint Peter.

RELATED ARTICLES in *Great Events from History: The Ancient World*: c. 200 B.C.E.-c. 100 C.E., Composition of the Intertestamental Jewish Apocrypha; c. 30 C.E., Condemnation and Crucifixion of Jesus Christ; c. 30 C.E., Preaching of the Pentecostal Gospel; c. 50-c. 150 C.E., Compilation of the New Testament.

THUCYDIDES

Greek historian

For the methods he employed in his account of the Peloponnesian War, Thucydides is considered one of the founders of the discipline of history.

BORN: c. 459 B.C.E.; probably Athens, Greece
DIED: c. 402 B.C.E.; place unknown
AREA OF ACHIEVEMENT: Historiography

EARLY LIFE

Thucydides (thew-SIHD-uh-deez) was born around 459 into a wealthy and conservative Athenian family. He grew up in Periclean Athens, an exciting place for a young, intelligent aristocrat. He followed the traditional course of education founded on the study of Homer, but leavened it with the rational skepticism of the Sophists. Thucydides could listen to the teachings of Protagoras, Socrates, Herodotus, and other major intellectual and creative figures who lived in or visited Athens.

Little is known about Thucydides' personal life. His family was politically active and opposed the democratic forces led by Pericles, but Thucydides evidently did not involve himself in political intrigues. It is known that he inherited gold mines in Thrace and had an estate there. He married a Thracian woman and had a daughter. He seems to have been a slightly detached but observant young man, studying the social and political turbulence around him. He did not break openly with his family, nor did he enter actively into Athenian politics. Though he

criticized the people when they acted as a "mob," he did not approve of oligarchy. He respected the wisdom and moderation of Athenian leaders such as Nicias but was stirred by the boldness of Pericles, Themistocles, and Alcibiades.

When the Peloponnesian War began in 431, Thucydides perhaps first intended to record for posterity the events and the deeds of men in a dramatic conflict. He soon saw that the war provided instruction in something basic about human nature and the fortunes of nations. He started collecting material for his *Historia tou Peloponnesiacou polemou* (431-404 B.C.E.; *History of the Peloponnesian War*, 1550), at the outbreak of the twenty-seven-year conflict.

LIFE'S WORK

A generation before Thucydides was born, the victory of the Greeks over the Persians at Plataea in 479 B.C.E. ushered in the golden age of Athenian history. The city's economy flourished, its government became more democratic than in the past, its art, literature, and freedom of expression attracted creative people from throughout the Greek world, and its navy established it as a power over the Aegean Islands and many coastal cities. Though Athens and Sparta had cooperated against the Persians, they soon went separate ways. The slow-moving, conservative Spartans watched Athens build an empire and, under

Thucydides. (Library of Congress)

masterful clinical description of the plague that hit Athens and chronicled the degeneration of morale and morals as disease swept the hot, overcrowded city. People gave themselves up to lawlessness and dissipation: "No fear of god or law of man had a restraining influence. As for the gods, it seemed to be the same thing whether one worshipped them or not, when one saw the good and the bad dying indiscriminately." With the gods silent in the face of human tragedy and no one expecting to live long enough to be punished for violating society's laws, people took what pleasure they could.

Revolution also spread through the city-states, with war between democratic and oligarchic forces. Brutality within cities equaled that between them. Thucydides wrote that in times of peace and prosperity most people acted decently: "But war is a stern teacher; in depriving them of the power of easily satisfying their daily wants, it brings most people's minds down to the level of their actual circumstances." His observations have rung true throughout the centuries to the present time; take for example his words about fanaticism:

> What used to be described as a thoughtless act of aggression was now regarded as the courage one would expect to find in a party member; to think of the future and wait was merely another way of saying one was a coward; any idea of moderation was just an attempt to disguise one's unmanly character; ability to understand a question from all sides meant that one was totally unfitted for action.

With both sides battered by war and revolution, leaders of Athens and Sparta negotiated a shaky truce in 421, but resolved none of the larger issues. The first war had revealed something basic about human affairs, Thucydides believed. The Athenians had told the Spartans before the war opened that always the weak had been subject to the strong. When the Spartans raised questions of right and wrong, the Athenians answered: "Considerations of this kind have never yet turned people aside from the opportunities of aggrandizement offered by superior strength."

War started again. The Athenians mounted a disastrous expedition to Sicily. Soon, Thucydides wrote, the Athenians, intending to enslave, were totally defeated and themselves enslaved. Athens was in turmoil, and oligarchic leaders overthrew its democracy. Vicious bloodletting occurred as the two sides fought for control. Disaster followed disaster, and the Athenians surrendered in 404. The Spartans forced them to renounce their empire, destroy their navy, and tear down the Long Walls.

Pericles' leadership, reach for more power and wealth. "What made war inevitable," Thucydides wrote, "was the growth of Athenian power and the fear which this caused in Sparta."

War began in 431. It opened with ten years of fighting, followed by some years of shaky truce, before fighting continued for another ten years. After Sparta established its power on land, the Athenians retreated into the city, which was joined by the Long Walls to the port of Peiraeus. The Athenians supplied themselves by sea and harassed the Spartans and their allies. The war was brutal. Besieged cities turned to cannibalism, and conquerors sometimes put defeated males to death and enslaved their women and children.

Despite Thucydides' renowned objectivity—he was acclaimed at one time as "the father of scientific history"—later military historians have seldom matched the emotional intensity and striking visual images conveyed by his calm prose. He described trapped Plataeans counting bricks in the besieging wall to determine how high to build scaling ladders. They began a desperate dash for freedom through a dark, rainy night, each man wearing only one shoe for better traction in the mud. He gave a

Thucydides was himself caught up in the war. In 424, Athens elected him a general but then exiled him for twenty years when he failed to prevent the brilliant Spartan general Brasidas from taking the strategically important city of Amphipolis. Exile meant withdrawing a short distance from Amphipolis to his Thracian estate, where he had time to think, write, and talk to Brasidas and other opponents and to central figures in Athenian politics, such as Alcibiades.

Unlike his older contemporary, the great historian Herodotus, Thucydides did not leave much room for the divine in human affairs; he believed that human activities could be understood in human terms. Like Herodotus, Thucydides displayed breadth of sympathy for all sides in the conflict. He weighed his oral evidence carefully, seeking accuracy and precision. He stated his purpose eloquently:

> It will be enough for me . . . if these words of mine are judged useful by those who want to understand clearly the events which happened in the past and which (human nature being what it is) will, at some time or other and in much the same ways, be repeated in the future. My work is not a piece of writing designed to meet the taste of an immediate public, but was done to last forever.

Thucydides found meaning in history, evidence of a pattern or cycle. Unless human nature changed, states would continue to overreach themselves, create defensive resistance, and then decline and fall. Even the second part of the Peloponnesian War repeated the first, with new actors making much the same mistakes for the same reasons. People could, however, use their intelligence and reason. They might not escape the cycle, but some few could at least come to understand what was happening and perhaps moderate the cycle. Thucydides did not believe that cycles were endlessly repeating series of events that allowed historians to predict the future, but he thought that people could use history to interpret their times.

It is unclear when Thucydides wrote his history. Most scholars believe that changes in style and conflicting statements about events suggest that it was written in stages; Thucydides died before putting it in final form. He probably died around 402.

SIGNIFICANCE

Thucydides and Herodotus, the first historians, retain their rank among the very greatest. Few historians who followed would equal Herodotus's breadth of sympathy for the diversity of human culture, and seldom would

they match Thucydides' clarity and precision and his emotional and intellectual power.

Thucydides found a scholarly audience more easily than did Herodotus. Thucydides' objective tone, rational skepticism, and focus on the military and on politics fit the modern temper. His writing on war and revolution seemed directed at the modern age. His message seemed clear, especially after World War II, when in the Cold War atmosphere it was easy for Americans to identify themselves with the free Athenians, confronting dour, warlike Spartans in the form of the totalitarian Soviets. Thucydides, viewed by some scholars as the father of realpolitik, seemed to give a clear warning: Democracies must be strong and alert in a dangerous world.

When the Vietnam War changed historians' understanding of the Cold War, Thucydides did not drop from favor among scholars, but his message came to seem different. To some scholars, he seemed to be the first revisionist, revealing Athens for what it was: an arrogant and aggressive state aimed at dominating and exploiting the weak and inciting fear of the Spartans to help keep Athenian allies in line. Today Thucydides' observations continue to resonate in the post-Soviet era as political and religious ideologies clash.

Changing times will continue to shed light on Thucydides' thoughts and work. Like every genius, he speaks to some members of each generation, who find in him insights into human affairs that clarify their understanding of their own time.

—*William E. Pemberton*

FURTHER READING

Connor, W. Robert. *Thucydides*. Princeton, N.J.: Princeton University Press, 1984. A meditation on Thucydides and an analysis of the text, especially to determine the source of Thucydides' emotional impact on his readers.

Edmunds, Lowell. *Chance and Intelligence in Thucydides*. Cambridge, Mass.: Harvard University Press, 1975. A study of Thucydides' theory of reason and chance in human affairs and of the interplay of pessimism and optimism in his work.

Gomme, Arnold W. *A Historical Commentary on Thucydides*. 5 vols. Oxford, England: Clarendon Press, 1945-1981. Gomme's monumental work is a classic of Thucydides scholarship.

Gustafson, Lowell S., ed. *Thucydides' Theory of International Relations: A Lasting Possession*. Baton Rouge: Louisiana State University Press, 2000. Essays by nine political scientists consider Thucydides as a theorist of international relations, including his concepts of how history informs modern events, realism vs. pluralism, the impact of internal events on international politics, and culture as it operates in world affairs.

Hornblower, Simon. *Thucydides.* London: Duckworth, 1994. Places Thucydides in the intellectual atmosphere of Periclean Athens and carefully distinguishes the various influences on his thought.

Luginbill, Robert D. *Thuycidides on War and National Character.* Boulder, Colo.: Westview Press, 1999. Examines Thucydides' analysis of human character and its tendency toward war, behaviors of individuals and states in times of stress, and what lessons can be drawn by modern audiences.

Pouncey, Peter R. *The Necessities of War: A Study of Thucydides' Pessimism.* New York: Columbia University Press, 1980. A study of Thucydides' theory of human nature and its influence on history; Pouncey finds an "essential pessimism" that holds that human nature carries within it drives that destroy human achievements.

Price, Jonathan J. *Thucydides and Internal War.* New York: Cambridge University Press, 2001. Argues from internal evidence that Thucydides viewed the Peloponnesian War as an internal war, or stasis. Readable and accessible to nonscholars.

Rawlings, Hunter R., III. *The Structure of Thucydides' History.* Princeton, N.J.: Princeton University Press, 1981. Provides insights into Thucydides based on an analysis of the structure of his work.

Thucydides. *The Peloponnesian War.* New York: Penguin Books, 1954. This translation by Rex Warner, with an introduction by M. I. Finley, is highly regarded and easily accessible.

SEE ALSO: Alcibiades; Herodotus; Pericles; Themistocles.

RELATED ARTICLES in *Great Events from History: The Ancient World*: 480-479 B.C.E., Persian Invasion of Greece; 478-448 B.C.E., Athenian Empire Is Created; c. 450-c. 425 B.C.E., History Develops as a Scholarly Discipline; May, 431-September, 404 B.C.E., Peloponnesian War; June, 415-September, 413 B.C.E., Athenian Invasion of Sicily; 406 B.C.E., Greek Dramatist Euripides Dies.

THUTMOSE III
Egyptian pharaoh (r. 1504-1450 B.C.E.)

During a reign of nearly fifty-four years, Thutmose III consolidated Egypt's position as primary power in the ancient Near East and North Africa. He laid the groundwork for some two hundred years of relative peace and prosperity in the region.

BORN: Late sixteenth century B.C.E.; probably near Thebes, Egypt

DIED: 1450 B.C.E.; probably near Thebes, Egypt

ALSO KNOWN AS: Menkheperre' Thutmose (full name)

AREAS OF ACHIEVEMENT: Government and politics, war and conquest

EARLY LIFE

Thutmose (THUHT-mohz) III, son of Thutmose II and a minor wife named Isis, became the fifth king of Egypt's Eighteenth Dynasty (c. 1570-1295 B.C.E.) while still a child. It is very likely that Thutmose III was not the obvious heir to Egypt's throne. According to an inscription at Karnak carved late in his reign, the young Thutmose spent his early life as an acolyte in the Temple of Amen. Thutmose III asserted that the god Amen personally chose him as successor to his father: During a ritual procession of Amen's statue through the temple, the god sought out Thutmose; an oracle revealed that he was the god's choice to be the next king. Thutmose thus became his father's legitimate heir.

The historical value of this account has been doubted. It was recorded late in Thutmose III's reign. Furthermore, it closely parallels an earlier text describing the accession of Thutmose I. Whatever the historical value of this account for determining the legitimacy of Thutmose III's claim to succeed his father, he did ascend to the Egyptian throne on the death of Thutmose II. Contemporary inscriptions make clear, however, that during the first twenty-one years of the reign, real power was held by Hatshepsut (c. 1503-1482 B.C.E.), the chief queen or Great King's Wife of his father.

The relationship between Thutmose III and Hatshepsut in these early years has been the subject of scholarly controversy. By year 2 of Thutmose III's reign, Hatshepsut had assumed all the regalia of a reigning king. Yet it is not at all certain that she thrust Thutmose III into the background in order to usurp his royal prerogative, as early twentieth century commentators have claimed. Hatshepsut probably crowned herself coregent to obtain the authority to administrate the country while Thutmose III was still a minor. Hatshepsut's year dates are often recorded alongside dates of Thutmose III. There is also evidence that his approval was necessary for significant decisions such as installing a vizier, establishing offering endowments for gods, and authorizing expeditions to Sinai.

In any case, there is no question that Thutmose's early years were spent in preparation for his eventual assumption of sole authority. His education included study of hieroglyphic writing. Contemporaries comment on his ability to read and write like Seshat, the goddess of writing. His military training must also have occurred during this time.

When Hatshepsut died in the twenty-second year of Thutmose III's reign, he assumed sole control of the country. Whether it was at this point that an attempt was made by Thutmose III to obliterate the memory of Hatshepsut is open to doubt. It is clear that Thutmose III emphasized his descent from Thutmose II as part of the basis for his legitimate right to rule Egypt.

The mummy of Thutmose III reveals a man of medium build, almost 5 feet (1.5 meters) in height—for his time, he was relatively tall. He appears to have enjoyed good health throughout most of his life, avoiding the serious dental problems common to other Egyptian kings.

LIFE'S WORK

The ancient Egyptians expected their pharaoh's career to follow a preconceived pattern that was ordained by their gods. This pattern was always followed in the historical texts that the Egyptians wrote describing the accomplishments of their kings. There is good reason to believe that Thutmose III became the prototype for a successful king. His achievements were emulated by his successors throughout most of the New Kingdom (c. 1570-c. 1069 B.C.E.). The pattern included conquests abroad, feats of athletic prowess, and building projects at home.

Between the twenty-third and thirty-ninth years of his reign, Thutmose III undertook fourteen military campaigns. These campaigns are documented in a long historical text carved on the walls at the Temple of Karnak, called the Annals. Various stelae (inscriptions on upright slabs of stone) found in other Egyptian temples also provide information on his career. The most significant campaigns occurred in year 23 and in year 33 of his reign.

The campaign of year 23 was fought against a confederation of Syro-Palestinian states led by Kadesh, a Syrian city-state on the Orontes River. The forces allied with Kadesh had gathered at a city called Megiddo on the Plain of Esdraelan in modern Israel. The Egyptian description of the battle that took place in Megiddo follows a pattern known from other inscriptions yet contains many details that attest its basic historical value.

Thutmose III set out for Syria-Palestine with a large army. On reaching the town of Yehem, near Megiddo, Thutmose III consulted with his general staff on tactics and strategy. The general staff urged caution on the king, suggesting that the main road to Megiddo was too narrow and dangerous for the Egyptian army to pass safely on it. They argued for an alternative route to Megiddo that would be longer, yet safer. Thutmose III rejected his staff's advice, judging that the bolder course was more likely to succeed. The staff acceded to the king's superior wisdom; the Egyptian army proceeded along the narrow direct path, surprised the enemy, and encircled Megiddo. The enemy emerged from the city only to be routed

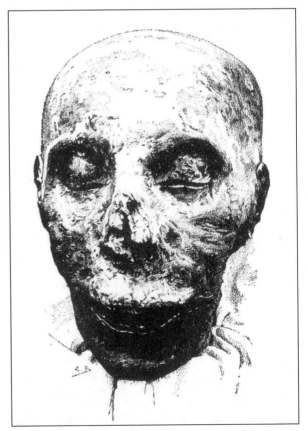

Head of the mummy of Thutmose III. (Library of Congress)

through Thutmose's personal valor. As the enemy retreated, however, the Egyptian forces broke ranks and fell on the weapons that the enemy had abandoned. This unfortunate break in discipline allowed the leaders of the Kadesh confederation to escape back into the city of Megiddo. Thutmose was forced to besiege the city. The siege ended successfully for the Egyptians after seven months, when the defeated chieftains of the alliance approached Thutmose with gifts in token of their submission.

This total defeat of the enemy became synonymous in later times with utter disaster. The name of the Battle of Megiddo—*Har Megiddo* (Mount Megiddo) in Hebrew—entered English as Armageddon, a word that designates a final cataclysmic battle.

Thutmose was equally wise in his handling of the defeated chieftains as he had been in war. The chieftains were reinstalled on their thrones, now as allies of Egypt. Their eldest sons were taken back to Egypt as hostages to guarantee the chieftains' cooperation with Egyptian policy. As the various Syro-Palestinian rulers died, their sons would be sent home to rule as Egyptian vassals. These sons, by that time thoroughly trained in Egyptian customs and culture, proved to be generally friendly to Egypt.

Thutmose's ambitions for Egyptian imperialism extended beyond Syria-Palestine. In the thirty-third year of his reign, he campaigned against the Mitanni, who occupied northern Mesopotamia (modern Iraq), the land the Egyptians called Nahrain. This battle also demonstrated Thutmose's mastery of strategy. He realized that his major problem in attacking the Mitanni would be in crossing the Euphrates River. To that end, he built boats of cedar in Lebanon and transported them overland 250 miles (403 kilometers) on carts. Once again, the element of surprise worked in Thutmose's favor. He was easily able to cross the river, attack the enemy, and defeat them.

Thutmose demonstrated his athletic prowess on the return trip from Nahrain. He stopped in the land of Niy, in modern Syria, to hunt elephants as had his royal ancestors. His brave deeds included the single-handed slaughter of a herd of 120 elephants.

Thutmose was responsible for initiating a large number of building projects within Egypt and in its Nubian holdings. The chronology of these projects is not understood in detail, but it is clear that he either built or remodeled eight temples in Nubia and seven temples in Upper Egypt. In the Egyptian capital of Thebes, he built mortuary temples for his father and grandfather as well as for himself. He added important buildings to the complex of temples at Karnak. These projects included the site of the Annals and a temple decorated with relief sculptures showing the unusual plant life Thutmose had observed during his campaigns to Syria-Palestine and Mesopotamia. Though it is difficult to identify the plants that interested Thutmose and his artists, this unusual form of decoration for a temple illustrates the king's interest in scholarly pursuits.

Thutmose's foresight included planning for his own successor. In the fifty-second year of his reign, his son Amenhotep II was designated coregent. The custom of naming and training an heir to the throne while the father still lived had been known since at least the Middle Kingdom (c. 2055-c. 1650 B.C.E.). Thutmose showed wisdom in choosing as his successor Amenhotep, a son who would largely follow his father's policies.

The last twelve years of Thutmose III's reign passed relatively peacefully. The Annals for this period record only the yearly delivery of goods for the king's and the god's use.

Little is known of Thutmose III's personal life. Scholars are in disagreement as to whether he ever married Neferure, the daughter of Hatshepsut. His earliest wife was probably Sit-iakh; she was the mother of Amenemhet, a son who probably died young. A second wife, Meryetre-Hatshepsut II, was the mother of Amenhotep II. Nothing is known of a third royal wife, Nebtu, aside from her name. Four other royal children are known.

During the fifty-fourth year of a reign largely dedicated to war, Thutmose III died peacefully. He was buried by his son Amenhotep II in the tomb that had been prepared in the Valley of the Kings.

SIGNIFICANCE

Despite the clichés and preconceived patterns that characterize the sources available for reconstructing the life of Thutmose III, he emerges as a truly remarkable man. His conquests in Syria-Palestine and Mesopotamia laid the groundwork for at least two hundred years of peace and prosperity in the ancient Near East. Vast quantities of goods flowed into Egypt's coffers from colonial holdings during this time. The royal family, the noblemen, and the temples of the gods came to possess previously unimagined wealth. The threat of foreign domination that had haunted Thutmose's immediate ancestors was finally dissipated. Egypt looked confidently toward a future of virtually unquestioned dominance over its neighbors.

Thutmose III himself was long remembered by Egyptians as the founder of their country's prosperity and security. Succeeding kings of the Eighteenth and Nineteenth Dynasties modeled their reigns on the historic memory of the founder of the Egyptian empire.

—Edward Bleiberg

FURTHER READING

Goedicke, Hans. *The Battle of Megiddo*. Baltimore, Md.: Halgo, 2001. An in-depth analysis of the battle, including the events leading up to it and its place in Thutmose's personal mythology.

Redford, Donald B. *The Wars in Syria and Palestine of Thutmose III*. New York: Brill, 2003. Discusses the political and military aspects of Thutmose's reign.

Tulhof, Angelika. *Thutmosis III, 1490-1436 B.C.E.: First Conqueror of the Middle East, Artist, and Multiculturalist*. London: Karnak House, 2003. A popular biography portraying Thutmose's accomplishments in modern terms.

Tyldesley, Joyce A. *Hatshepsut: The Female Pharaoh*. New York: Viking, 1996. This well-researched, scholarly biography of Hatshepsut of necessity also covers the early years of Thutmose's life as well.

SEE ALSO: Akhenaton; Amenhotep III; Cleopatra VII; Hatshepsut; Imhotep; Menes; Menkaure; Montuhotep II; Piye; Psamtik I; Ramses II; Sesostris III; Tutankhamen; Zoser.

RELATED ARTICLES in *Great Events from History: The Ancient World*: c. 1600-c. 1300 B.C.E., Mitanni Kingdom Flourishes in Upper Mesopotamia; c. 1570 B.C.E., New Kingdom Period Begins in Egypt; From c. 1500 B.C.E., Dissemination of the Book of the Dead; c. 1450 B.C.E., International Age of Major Kingdoms Begins in the Near East; c. 1365 B.C.E., Failure of Akhenaton's Cultural Revival; c. 1280 B.C.E., Israelite Exodus from Egypt.

TIBERIUS
Roman emperor (r. 14-37 C.E.)

As the second emperor of Rome, Tiberius solidified and firmly established the new system of power—but not without devastating impact on his personal life and the Roman upper classes.

BORN: November 16, 42 B.C.E.; Rome (now in Italy)
DIED: March 16, 37 C.E.; Misenum (now in Italy)
ALSO KNOWN AS: Tiberius Claudius Nero Caesar Augustus (full name)
AREA OF ACHIEVEMENT: Government and politics

EARLY LIFE

Tiberius (ti-BIHR-ee-uhs) Claudius Nero, the second emperor of Rome, came from a very ancient family of Sabine origin, the Claudians, who had moved to Rome shortly after the foundation of the city. Among the most patrician of Rome's residents, the Claudians expressed an aristocratic disdain for the other, less ancient, less noble inhabitants of Rome.

Tiberius's father, also named Tiberius Claudius Nero, was an associate of Julius Caesar and served as a quaestor (a sort of deputy) under him. The elder Tiberius fought with Caesar during the campaign in Egypt, which ended the civil war between Caesar and Pompey the Great, but after the murder of Julius Caesar in 44 B.C.E. he went over to the side of the republicans.

This decision made the Claudian family enemies of Octavian (later Augustus), Marc Antony, and Marcus Aemilius Lepidus, the three men who formed the socalled Second Triumvirate which succeeded Caesar in power. The triumvirs were anxious to eliminate any traces of republican sentiment, and Tiberius the elder, his wife Livia, and his young son were forced into flight, often coming close to capture and death.

When Tiberius was only four years old, even stranger events happened. Augustus imposed a divorce between Livia and her husband, and soon married Livia—although she was pregnant at the time. Despite the adverse early influences, Tiberius was reared to be a loyal and dutiful servant of Augustus, ready to serve him in civil, military, and personal capacities. For twenty-two years Tiberius was an associate of Augustus; Tiberius was to be emperor himself for an equal period of time.

He began his service early. In 26 B.C.E., while only a teenager, he was sent to Spain on military service. Two years later, he was made quaestor in charge of the grain supply in Rome. Later, he served primarily in military positions, commanding armies in the east and in Europe. During several hard-fought campaigns, Tiberius subdued Illyricum and Pannonia (modern Yugoslavia and Hungary) and helped secure the Empire's northern border with the dangerous German tribes. For these efforts, he was awarded a triumph, the highest honor bestowed on a victorious general.

His personal life was less triumphant. He was forced by Augustus to divorce his beloved wife, Agrippina, and marry Julia, the daughter of Augustus. The match was arranged to strengthen the chance of succession of a descendant of Augustus to power; it failed, for Tiberius and Julia were incompatible and soon lived apart. For this reason, because Augustus was advancing his grandsons, and perhaps because of simple fatigue with his exhausting duties, Tiberius retired to the island of Rhodes in 6 B.C.E. He remained there for eight years, until the premature deaths of Augustus's grandsons forced his return, and he was adopted by the emperor as his son and heir.

There followed more campaigns in the north, interspersed with time at Rome. During the latter years of Augustus's reign, Tiberius seems to have been virtual co-emperor, and in 14 C.E., when Augustus died, Tiberius assumed sole power of the whole Roman world.

Tiberius was a large, strong man, well above average height. He had a fair complexion, which was sometimes marred by outbreaks of skin disease. According to the ancient historian Suetonius, he wore his hair long in back, an old-fashioned style perhaps adopted in memory of his distinguished ancestry.

For most of his life, Tiberius enjoyed excellent health, although he was reported to have indulged in excessive drinking and an astounding number and variety of sexual pleasures. He was stiff and formal in manner and seemed ill at ease in the senate chambers. He was quite well educated in Latin and Greek literature and was devoted to astrology.

LIFE'S WORK

Tiberius came to the throne at the age of fifty-six. He had served Augustus all of his adult life, helping to establish the political system of the Roman Empire, also known as the principate (after one of Augustus's titles, *princeps*, or first citizen). The new system was a delicate and highly personal one, in which Augustus balanced traditional Roman republican forms with the new reality of one-man rule; the creation and maintenance of this balance required considerable skill and tact.

Because of his nature, Tiberius found it impossible to adopt his predecessor's role completely. Although he assumed actual power, he seemed to do so unwillingly and refused most of the titles that the senate offered him. Many, including the eminent Roman historian Cornelius Tacitus, have seen this as hypocrisy; others believe that Tiberius was genuinely reluctant to become an autocrat.

Tiberius. (Library of Congress)

During the early years of his rule, he made a great show of consulting the senate on all matters, great and small. After years of Augustus's rule, however, the old methods were simply inadequate to govern a worldwide empire, and increasingly Tiberius was forced to assume and exercise absolute powers.

At first, these powers were used for the common good. In matters of religion and morals, Tiberius took firm steps against foreign beliefs, which he believed threatened traditional Roman virtues: He expelled adherents of the Egyptian and Jewish religions from Rome and banished astrologers on pain of death—although he firmly believed in the practice himself. Perhaps he was protecting himself against possible conspiracies inspired by favorable horoscopes; such things were taken very seriously in ancient Rome.

Tiberius was also firm in his suppression of riots and

other civil disturbances, which often afflicted Rome and the other large cities of the Empire. Many of these problems were caused by an excessively large unemployed population, which was fed by the public dole and amused by public games; with little to lose, this group was easily incited to violence. As one measure against this violence, Tiberius established a central camp for the Praetorian Guard in Rome, so this elite military unit could be called out to quell civil violence. At the same time, this concentration of troops gave enormous potential power to its commander, and soon that man, Lucius Aelius Sejanus, made a bold play for power.

Sejanus came from the equestrian order, the group below the senate in social standing and generally ineligible to hold the higher offices of the state. From about 23 C.E., however, Sejanus worked on the psychological and political insecurities of Tiberius, increasing his own hold over the emperor. It seems possible that Sejanus may even have aimed at the Imperial power for himself—or, at least, as regent over Tiberius's successor. Sejanus aspired to marry Livia Julia, Tiberius's daughter, and worked to increase the emperor's fear and distrust of other members of his family. At the instigation of Sejanus, many senators (and others) were accused and condemned on charges of treason.

During this time, Tiberius left Rome, never to return. He settled on the island of Capri, off the coast of Naples. It was a spot well chosen for a man grown increasingly paranoid: No boat could approach it without being seen, and there were only two landing places, both easy to defend. By 31 C.E., Sejanus was named to a shared consulship with Tiberius and was at the height of his powers.

That same year saw the abrupt fall of Sejanus. Tiberius had become convinced that the Praetorian commander was aiming to become ruler of the state, and in a carefully worded letter to the senate, read while the unsuspecting Sejanus sat in the chamber, Tiberius bitterly denounced him. Sejanus's former lieutenants and others privy to the plot quickly acted, and Sejanus and his family were brutally executed, and his aspirations ended.

After this incident, Tiberius continued to rule Rome and the Empire from the isolation of Capri. Important appointments were left unmade or, if made, were not allowed to be filled: Provincial governors sometimes spent their entire terms in Rome, having been denied permission to leave for their posts. Governing by letters, Tiberius often confused and mystified the senate, which was often unable to decipher his enigmatic messages.

His fears were clear enough, however, and resulted in an endless series of treason trials. During the latter years,

a virtual reign of terror descended on the Roman upper classes, as they were accused of the vague but heinous crime of *maiestas* (roughly, treason). Executions of prominent Romans became commonplace, and many of those accused by professional informers chose not to wait for the show of a trial, committing suicide instead.

Meanwhile in Capri, Tiberius is reported by Suetonius to have engaged in a series of gaudy vices and perversions. His character, weakened first by years of hard work and worry and then the intense pressures of solitary rule, gave way to tyranny, debauchery, and paranoid suspicion. Having outlived his own sons, he settled the succession on his nephew Gaius (later the emperor Caligula). Tiberius died on March 16, 37 C.E.; there was widespread rejoicing instead of mourning in Rome, and it was not until April 3 that his body was cremated and his remains interred in the Imperial city he had vacated so many years earlier.

SIGNIFICANCE

When Augustus adopted Tiberius as his son and heir, he took a formal oath that he did so only for the good of the Roman state and people. Historians have puzzled over this statement ever since. Some have argued that Augustus meant it as a sincere compliment, underscoring Tiberius's high qualifications for rule and indicating Augustus's confidence in his abilities. Others, however, have perceived a darker meaning in the words: that the action was one Augustus would have preferred not to take but was forced to by the lack of other, more preferable candidates.

Assessments of Tiberius as emperor similarly take two differing views. There are those who believe that, on the whole, he was a fairly good emperor, maintaining peace at home and security along the borders. While there is little doubt that after the fall of Sejanus Tiberius turned increasingly suspicious and vengeful, these dark elements cloud only the latter part of his rule, and the so-called reign of terror affected only a handful of the Empire's inhabitants. It was only the senatorial and equestrian orders in Rome itself that felt the weight of the treason trials, and their hostility to Tiberius and the Imperial system was to a large extent responsible for these events.

On the other hand, there are those who believe that from the first Tiberius was a cruel and tyrannical ruler, one who delighted in the suffering of his victims and whose life was given over to vice and debauchery. Foremost of these critics is the celebrated Roman historian Tacitus, whose brilliant writings paint a vivid portrait of Tiberius as a completely evil despot, a ruler who used his unlimited powers to destroy his supposed enemies. So great is Tacitus's genius that his version of history and his view of Tiberius seem almost irrefutable. Yet it must be remembered that Tacitus was a firm believer in the virtues of the vanished Republic and hated the Empire that replaced it. In a sense, he used Tiberius as a symbol of an entire system that he believed to be evil and unjust.

Those with a more balanced view maintain that Tiberius was a man of considerable abilities, both military and political. While serving under Augustus, Tiberius used these abilities to the benefit of Rome and, following his own succession to power, continued for many years to provide effective, proper rule for the Empire. A series of causes—plots against him, the hostility of the upper classes, mental and physical exhaustion caused by overwork—wrought profound and disastrous changes in his personality. In the end, the task of ruling the Roman Empire proved too great a burden for one man to bear alone.

—*Michael Witkoski*

FURTHER READING

Grant, Michael. *The Roman Emperors: A Biographical Guide to the Rulers of Imperial Rome, 31 B.C.-A.D. 476.* New York: Charles Scribner's Sons, 1985. Reprint. London: Weidenfeld & Nicolson, 1996. For a fast-paced yet comprehensive introduction to Tiberius and his reign, the relevant section in this volume is unsurpassed. Grant, an outstanding historian of Rome, combines information and explanation in a narrative that provides as much pleasure as knowledge.

_____. *The Twelve Caesars.* New York: Charles Scribner's Sons, 1975. Working from the base of Suetonius's historical scholarship, Grant approaches Tiberius from the perspectives of psychology, power politics, and common sense. He asks intriguing questions about what it must have been like to be the sole ruler of the vast Roman Empire, and his answers are thought-provoking. An excellent place to start a study of this enigmatic emperor.

Levick, Barbara. *Tiberius the Politician.* Rev. ed. New York: Routledge, 1999. An exhaustive and scholarly account of Tierius's life, from his ancestry to the impact of his reign after his death. Includes bibliographical references and an index.

Marsh, Frank Burr. *The Reign of Tiberius.* 1931. New York: Barnes and Noble, 1959. Still the definitive modern biography of Tiberius, this volume brings together an impressive amount of scholarship in a generally readable and often entertaining fashion. Especially good in its knowledge of the detail and connections of ancient Roman political life.

Seager, Robin. *Tiberius.* Berkeley: University of California Press, 1972. A balanced and scholarly (but not pedantic) biography that shows how, under the early Roman Empire, the personality of the ruler had a profound impact on the state. Seager is careful to place Tiberius within the context of his times and his position, both of which were unique and difficult.

Smith, Charles Edward. *Tiberius and the Roman Empire.* Baton Rouge: Louisiana State University Press, 1942. Reprint. Port Washington, N.Y.: Kennikat Press, 1972. A work more concerned with Tiberius the ruler than Tiberius the man or tyrant, this book is strong on events and happenings outside the arena of Rome itself and is thus useful to counteract the popular image of that time created by Tacitus, that of unrelieved terror.

Suetonius. *Lives of the Twelve Caesars.* Edited, notes, and introduction by Joseph Gavorse. New York: Modern Library, 1959. This is one of the enduring classics of the ancient world, and it combines shrewd personal insight, revealing anecdotes, and a contemporary point of view. The section on Tiberius also has a longfamous description of his alleged sexual escapades on the isle of Capri; readers unfamiliar with Latin should be careful to choose an unexpurgated version, such as this one.

Tacitus, Cornelius. *The Complete Works.* Edited and introduction by Moses Hadas, translated by Alfred Church and William Brodribb. New York: Modern Library, 1942. The *Annals* of Tacitus covers the period of Tiberius's reign, and this work is perhaps the most impressive production of classical history. Tacitus has fashioned a Tiberius who is a monster of deceit, hypocrisy, tyranny, and cruelty. This view may be distorted, but its impact has profoundly influenced history and historians ever since its conception.

SEE ALSO: Augustus; Caligula; Livia Drusilla; Tacitus.
RELATED ARTICLES in *Great Events from History: The Ancient World*: 15 B.C.E.-15 C.E., Rhine-Danube Frontier Is Established; c. 50 C.E., Creation of the Roman Imperial Bureaucracy.

TIGLATH-PILESER III
Neo-Assyrian emperor (r. 745-727 B.C.E.)

Tiglath-pileser III was the founder of the Neo-Assyrian Empire. His achievements as both a warrior and an administrator reversed a forty-year decline experienced by Assyria and established that nation's control over a region spanning from beyond Babylonia to the border of Egypt.

BORN: Early eighth century B.C.E.; Kahlu?, Assyria (now Nimrud, Iraq)

DIED: 727 B.C.E.; Babylonia (now in Iraq)

ALSO KNOWN AS: Tiglath-pilneser; Tukulti-Apil-Esharra (full name); Pulu; Pul

AREAS OF ACHIEVEMENT: War and conquest, government and politics

EARLY LIFE

Nothing is known of the early life of Tiglath-pileser III (TIHG-lath-pihl-ay-sehr). Certainly, he benefited from a revolt that erupted in 745 B.C.E. in the Assyrian royal residential city of Kahlu (now Nimrud). The revolt was doubtless stimulated by popular dissatisfaction with the previous regime and the failure of its kings to reassert Assyrian hegemony over those western territories that had lately fallen under the control of the kingdom of Urartu. The Assyrian problem with Urartu had grown increasingly dire: Except for a brief resurgence of Assyrian power under Adad-nirari III (809-783 B.C.E.)—who was not able to hold the West—the fortunes of the empire had waned through the successive reigns of that monarch's three sons. By 745, the year of the revolt that brought Tiglath-pileser to power, Assyrian influence had so eroded that the nation verged on losing its autonomy to Sarduri III, king of Urartu. Where Tiglath-pileser's predecessors had failed, however, he was soon to succeed.

Although the new king seems likely to have been a usurper, his lineage remains mysterious. On one hand, the Assyrian king list implies he was not royal, because the list stops with the reign of Adad-nirari III's third ruling son, Ashur-nirari V (755-745 B.C.E.), even though the document itself dates from 738 B.C.E., long after Tiglath-pileser III began to rule. On the other hand, the possibility that Tiglath-pileser came from royal blood is suggested by a later copy of that same document that names Tiglath-pileser as the son of his predecessor. Whatever his paternity, after 745 Tiglath-pileser held power over the troubled kingdom of Assyria. Indeed, and contrary to Assyrian royal tradition, he claimed his predecessor's last regnal year as the first year of his own regime.

The Assyrian spelling of the name Tiglath-pileser was Tulkulti-Apil-Esharra, but the biblical writers knew the Assyrian monarch as Tiglath-pileser (Hebrew *tiglat pil'eser*; 2 Kings 15:29; 16:7, 10) or as Tiglath-pilneser (Hebrew *tiglat pilne'eser*; 1 Chronicles 5:6, 26; 2 Chronicles 28:20), Hebraized versions of the Assyrian name. Tiglath-pileser III is also remembered in the Hebrew scriptures as Pul (2 Kings 15:19; 1 Chronicles 5:26) which, in turn, reflects his Babylonian throne name, *Pulu*. The latter may be an abbreviation for the element *apil* in his name, or it may simply be his nickname. In any case, the name Pul serves as an appropriate referent for the relentless empire-builder, for Pul (Assyrian *pulu/pilu*) means "limestone block."

LIFE'S WORK

On seizing the throne, Tiglath-pileser III marched the Assyrian army southeast as far as the Karkheh River in order to relieve the beleaguered Babylonian king Nabu-nasir (best known as Nabonassar). His purpose, evidently, was to support this vassal king and thus secure his own eastern borders. In so doing, however, he campaigned extensively in territories nominally controlled by Babylonia, even implying suzerainty over Babylonia by assuming the ancient titles of King of Sumer and King of Arad. Nevertheless, Tiglath-pileser did not interfere with the governance of Babylonia until after the death of Nabu-nasir in 734 and the subsequent murder of that monarch's son and heir.

His eastern front secure, Tiglath-pileser turned his attention to the west. In 743 he attacked Mati'-ilu, who was, simultaneously, the king of Arpad, the leader of a league of Neo-Hittite and Aramaean princes, and a vassal of the king of Urartu. The latter monarch, Sarduri III, came to assist Mati'-ilu against the Assyrians but was crushingly defeated and forced to flee the vicinity by night on the back of a mare. Nevertheless, the fortified city of Arpad managed to resist siege for three years before finally falling in 741. Arpad immediately became the capital of a newly created Assyrian province.

The details of the next several years are difficult to reconstruct owing to the fragmentary and sometimes contradictory nature of the inscriptions. Evidently, while the siege of Arpad was still under way, Tiglath-pileser pushed farther west and accepted the surrender of a number of smaller kingdoms, thus bringing northwestern Syria and probably Phoenicia under Assyrian hegemony. Several petty monarchs of the region brought Tiglath-pileser tribute in 740, including Ethbaal of Tyre, Rasunu (Rezin) of Damascus, and Menahem of Samaria (2 Kings 15:19-20).

In 739 Tiglath-pileser directed the Assyrian army against Ullubu, located on the upper Tigris River. That campaign was followed by the 738 defeat of the neo-Hittite state of Unqi. The resulting new Assyrian province Kullana (biblical Calneh) took its name from the fallen Unqi capital city.

In 738 Tiglath-pileser was still in the west, combating a coalition of smaller kingdoms led by one Azriyau, king of Yaudi. The identity of Azriyau and his nation remain controverted. The early suggestion that Azriyau was the king of Samal gave way to an identification of Azriyau with Uzziah, king of Judah. Others regard the circumstances whereby the aged Judaean king could have been involved in an affair in central Syria at this time as improbable, averring instead that Azriyau was an otherwise unattested king of either Hamath or Hadrach. Whatever the solution to this puzzle may be, it is certain that Azriyau was not successful in withstanding Assyrian might, and the western kings once again offered tribute to the Assyrian emperor.

Turning his attention toward the east once more in 737 and 736, Tiglath-pileser brought most of the region of the central Zagros mountains into Assyrian control and even launched an expedition that penetrated Mede territory as far south as Mount Bikni (best known as Mount Demavend) and to the so-called salt desert located southwest of Teheran. It was probably in 735 that he attacked Urartu's capital, Tushpa, apparently without success.

The order of the campaigns of 734-732 remains difficult to determine. Apparently, in 734 Tiglath-pileser returned his armies to the Mediterranean coast, where he found Tyre and Sidon rankled under Assyrian-imposed restrictions on timber exports while the Philistine rulers of Gaza and Ashkelon led a growing anti-Assyrian coalition. Resistance by these rebellious states proved futile. Tiglath-pileser had no difficulty in killing the prince of Ashkelon while "the man of Gaza" escaped to Egypt. Continuing his southern push, Tiglath-pileser stopped only on reaching the Wadi al-'Arīsh, which formed the Egyptian border, where he erected a monument. During this same campaign, most of the western kingdoms surrendered to Assyria. Kings of Amen, Edom, Moab, and Judah, as well as Shamshi, queen of the Arabs, signaled their subjugation through tribute and gifts.

The fidelity of the western vassal states was short-lived. Soon after the Assyrians returned to their homeland in 734, a new anti-Assyrian coalition emerged. This alliance included Rezin of Aram, Pekah of Israel, Hanun of Gaza, Hiram of Tyre, and Shamshi, queen of the Arabs. Rezin and Pekah attacked Ahaz and Jerusalem (the so-called Syro-Ephramitic War), probably because Ahaz would not cooperate with the coalition's resistance to Assyria. Ahaz, in turn, sent gift-laden emissaries to Tiglath-pileser, asking for assistance and protection (2 Kings 16:5-9).

The Assyrian's response was robust and devastating. The army of Assyria marched again in 733-732. Early in this latest campaign, portions of Aram were taken, and Rezin was besieged in Damascus, while Shamshi's Arabs and a number of nomadic tribes surrendered. Israelite possessions in the Transjordan were conquered, and the residents of Reuben, Gad, and Manasseh were deported (2 Kings 15:29; 1 Chronicles 5:6, 22, 25-26). By 732, Tiglath-pileser had completed the conquest of Aram and Israel. Damascus fell, Rezin was executed, and Tiglath-pileser divided Aram into four provinces (2 Kings 16:9). As punishment for Israel's part in the resistance, Tiglath-pileser conquered Galilee and emptied the region of its citizens (2 Kings 15:29). He doubtless also conquered all major Israelite cities except Samaria, leaving the latter as the capital of a rump state, now headed by the pro-Assyrian Hoshea (2 Kings 15:30), whom Tiglath-pileser claimed he put on the throne.

KINGS OF THE NEO-ASSYRIAN EMPIRE

King	Reign (B.C.E.)
Tiglath-pileser III	745-727
Shalmaneser V	726-722
Sargon II	721-705
Sennacherib	704-681
Esarhaddon	680-669
Ashurbanipal	669-627
Ashur-etil-ilāni, Sin-shum-lishir, and Sīn-shar-ishkun	627-612
Ashur-uballit II	612-609

Meanwhile, affairs in Babylon drew Tiglath-pileser's attention to the east. Nabu-nasir had died in 734, and his son was soon thereafter killed in the first of a series of *coups d'état*. In 731 an Aramaean chieftain Ukin-zer claimed the Babylonian throne. When diplomatic efforts by Tiglath-pileser's ambassadors failed to remove Ukin-zer, the emperor resolved the matter militarily. Ukin-zer and his son were executed and, in 729 (and again in 728) Tiglath-pileser ritually "took the hands of [the statue of] Bel" (the god Marduk) and was thereby proclaimed king of Babylon under the name of Pulu. Not all Babylonians were happy with the dual monarchy. The Chaldean sheikh Merodachbaladan led a resistance that plagued Tiglath-pileser for what little time remained of his life. The Assyrian monarch died the following year.

SIGNIFICANCE

Tiglath-pileser established Assyrian dominance over a territory that extended from the Persian Gulf to the border of Egypt. For well more than a century Assyrian monarchs were able to maintain control of this vast empire, in large measure because of Tiglath-pileser's administrative innovations. Royal authority was strengthened by circumscribing the authority of vassal kings and governors through a deliberate reduction in the size and a corresponding increase in the number of districts in Assyria. Likewise, countries annexed to Assyria were constrained to heed royal control: Vassal kings who submitted to Assyrian authority, as did Ahaz of Judah, were allowed to remain on their thrones. Those who resisted were conquered and their territories routinely converted to Assyrian provinces, administered by a district lord or governor responsible to the king.

Tiglath-pileser's practice of deportations also discouraged rebellion. He did not invent the tactic, but the monarch did distinguish himself in terms of the size and character of deportations under his reign. Following the conquest of Galilee, for example, the Assyrian's *Annals* report a deportation of 13,520 prisoners out of a population recently estimated to have numbered only 18,000. Another year, 154,000 were displaced in southern Mesopotamia. Although the deportees were typically well treated and "counted among the people of Assyria" (as citizens and not slaves), they were transferred to a distant part of the empire. Thus, deportation effectively discouraged any rebellion based on devotion to native territories, traditions, or deities, even as it made the displaced population dependent on the central government. Moreover, the practice served to populate remote districts and to provide Assyria with laborers, craftsmen, and soldiers. Tiglath-pileser's success in this quarter would later inspire Babylonian policy.

Tiglath-pileser served the vast administrative demands of the expanding empire through the development of a new and efficient system of communication. Ordinary messengers, special runners, or personal representatives of the monarch relayed messages between the king and his governors.

Finally, in contrast to his predecessors, Tiglath-pileser established a standing army. Previously, Assyrian armies had consisted of crown dependents doing military service in exchange for land grants and peasants and slaves supplied by those landlords. This conscripted force was now supplemented by a standing army, mainly composed of soldiers levied in peripheral provinces. Some of these served in cavalry units—another innovation of Tiglath-pileser. The presence of an aggressive standing army, headed by this able warrior king, established the Neo-Assyrian Empire as the dominant power of the Middle East until the accession of the Babylonians at the end of the following century.

—*Walter C. Bouzard, Jr.*

FURTHER READING

Cogan, Mordechai, and Hayim Tadmor. *II Kings: A New Translation, with Introduction and Commentary.* New York: Doubleday, 1988. This biblical commentary includes a description of Assyria under Tiglath-pileser III and of his role in the biblical drama. Useful appendices feature chronology charts.

Galil, Gershom. "A New Look at the Inscriptions of Tiglath-pileser III." *Biblica* 81, no. 4 (2000): 511-520. The author's interpretation of inscriptions leads to a cogent reconstruction of the relationship between Assyria and the western states in the days of Tiglath-pileser III.

Roux, Georges. *Ancient Iraq.* 3d ed. New York: Penguin Books, 1992. This excellent survey of ancient Mesopotamian civilizations includes significant discussion of Tiglath-pileser III and other emperors of the Neo-Assyrian period.

Tadmor, Hayim. *The Inscriptions of Tiglath-pileser III, King of Assyria. Critical Edition, with Introductions, Translations, and Commentary.* Jerusalem: Israel Academy of Sciences and Humanities, 1994. Although this singularly important publication of the inscriptions associated with Tiglath-pileser III is aimed at the specialist, the commentary and especially the supplementary studies provide important and accessible insight about the life of the Assyrian monarch.

Younger, K. Lawson, Jr. "The Deportations of the Israelites." *Journal of Biblical Literature* 117, no. 2 (1998): 201-227. The essay includes a description of the devastating effects of Tiglath-pileser III's deportation policies on ancient Israel.

SEE ALSO: Cyrus the Great; Sammu-ramat; Sennacherib.

RELATED ARTICLES in *Great Events from History: The Ancient World*: c. 883-c. 824 B.C.E., Second Assyrian Empire Displays Military Prowess; 745 B.C.E., Tiglath-pileser III Rules Assyria; 701 B.C.E., Sennacherib Invades Syro-Palestine.

TIGRANES THE GREAT
Armenian king (r. 95-55 B.C.E.)

As king of Armenia between 95 and 55 B.C.E., Tigranes the Great defied the growing power of Rome and carved out a vast but short-lived empire that stretched from upper Mesopotamia to the Mediterranean Sea.

BORN: c. 140 B.C.E.; Armenia
DIED: c. 55 B.C.E.; Armenia
ALSO KNOWN AS: Tigran; Dikran; Tigranes II
AREA OF ACHIEVEMENT: Government and politics

EARLY LIFE

The Armenia of Tigranes (ti-GRAY-neez) the Great consisted of the uplands that run from the Black Sea to the Caspian Sea and from the Caucasus Mountains south to the upper Tigris and Euphrates Rivers. Armenia had long been politically and culturally related, on one hand, to the great civilizations of Mesopotamia and the Iranian Plateau and, on the other, to those of Asia Minor and the eastern Mediterranean. Centered on the fertile plain of the Araxes River between the alkaline Lake Van and Lake Sevan, Armenia had maintained a large measure of autonomy despite its status as a satrapy of the Persian Empire and, following the Macedonian conquest of Persia, a nominal part of the Seleucid Empire. After the Roman victory over Antiochus the Great at Magnesia in 190 B.C.E., the Seleucid Empire was stripped of its possessions north of the Taurus Mountains. In the resulting political vacuum, independent kingdoms were established in Lesser Armenia (known in antiquity as Sophene) and in Greater Armenia by the former governors of these regions, Zariadris and Artaxias, the ancestor of Tigranes the Great.

Practically nothing is known about the early life of Tigranes. Second century Greek writer Appian stated that Tigranes' father was also named Tigranes (Tigranes I) and other scholarship has supported this claim; however, different opinions hold that Tigranes was the son of Artavasdes. Tigranes' birth date of c. 140 B.C.E. is deduced from the tradition that he was eighty-five years

old at the time of his death in 55 B.C.E. It is known that, at some point in his early years, Tigranes was taken hostage by Mithradates II (the Great) of Parthia when that king besieged Armenia. In 95 B.C.E. Mithradates placed Tigranes on the Armenian throne, having made Tigranes cede to Parthia seventy fertile valleys of eastern Armenia.

Tigranes came to power at a time that was ripe for the expansion of the Armenian kingdom. The apparently inexorable growth of Roman power in the east had been severely hampered by Rome's internal social problems and by the transformation of the Black Sea kingdom of Pontus into a significant military threat under the leadership of Mithradates VI Eupator. The Seleucid Empire had continued to disintegrate and was on the verge of total collapse.

LIFE'S WORK

On his accession to the throne of Greater Armenia in 95 B.C.E., Tigranes began immediately to enlarge his dominion. His first act as king was to invade Sophene and depose its ruler, thus uniting all Armenia under his rule. That same year, Tigranes made an extremely important political alliance by marrying Cleopatra, a daughter of Mithradates VI Eupator. For the next thirty years, the political and military fortunes of Tigranes and Mithradates were to be closely linked in their joint struggle against Rome.

The first conflict between Rome and the alliance of Tigranes and Mithradates was precipitated by Mithradates' struggle with Nicomedes III of Bithynia for the control of Cappadocia. To forestall a Roman attempt to intervene and appoint a pro-Roman king over Cappadocia, Tigranes overran the country with his Armenian army and secured it for his father-in-law. In 92 B.C.E., the Roman senate dispatched an army under the command of Lucius Cornelius Sulla, who cleared Cappadocia and installed the Roman candidate, Ariobarzanes I, as king. As soon as Sulla withdrew from Asia, however, Mithradates deposed both Ariobarzanes and the new Bithynian king, Nicomedes IV, from their thrones. In 89 B.C.E., with the

Tigranes the Great. (Library of Congress)

support of another Roman army, both kings were reinstated, and Nicomedes, urged on by the Roman legates, provoked a full-scale war by invading Mithradates' Pontic homeland.

Mithradates responded to the provocation of Nicomedes IV and, taking advantage of the disruption of the Roman Social War, launched a major attack on the Roman province of Asia. After more than eighty thousand Roman officials and citizens were massacred in the Greek cities of Asia Minor, Mithradates invaded the Aegean. In 87 B.C.E., Sulla once again responded to this threat and swept Mithradates out of Roman territory. As a result of political troubles back in Rome, Sulla was unable to capitalize on his victory, and in 86 B.C.E. a peace between Mithradates and Rome was arranged.

In 88 B.C.E., Mithradates II died, and Tigranes used the opportunity to recover the Armenian territory he had ceded to the Parthians in 95 B.C.E. Tigranes followed this success by invading northern Parthia, taking the important regions of Gordyene and Adiabene and the city of Nisibis. Tigranes then turned his attention to the east and annexed a large tract of Media Atropatene into his growing Armenian Empire. Tigranes now called himself by the archaic title of "King of Kings" and had vassal kings wait on him in his court.

With Mithradates VI Eupator in temporary retirement from active campaigning and with Asia Minor temporarily quiet, Tigranes moved against the tottering Seleucid Dynasty. In 83 B.C.E., the Armenian army defeated the last Seleucid king, Antiochus Eusebius, and the entire eastern Mediterranean coast from Cilicia to the borders of Egypt became a part of Tigranes' empire. Tigranes was now at the height of his power. He divided his empire into 120 satrapies, following the old Persian model, and set an Armenian feudal lord as governor over each. As the evidence of his silver coinage shows, Tigranes now added the traditional Seleucid title "Divine" to the eastern "King of Kings."

With his kingdom stretching from the Caspian to the Mediterranean, the old Armenian capital of Artaxas on the Araxes River was far removed from the center of Tigranes' empire. Thus, Tigranes set about building a new capital in the west, near the head of the Tigris River, and named it Tigranocerta, for himself. Tigranes populated his city by forcibly displacing Greeks and natives from Syria (and later from Cappadocia), in addition to encouraging Jewish and Arab merchants to settle there.

For the next decade, Tigranes apparently was able to govern his massive empire without major incident. When trouble arose, it was once again caused by Mithradates, who dragged Tigranes into his struggle against Rome. In 74 B.C.E., Nicomedes IV died and willed his Bithynian kingdom to Rome. Mithradates responded by invading Bithynia, and Tigranes again invaded Cappadocia. Rome then sent out Lucius Licinius Lucullus, who, in a series of engagements from 74 to 72 B.C.E., was able to drive Mithradates out of Pontus.

When Mithradates fled to the safety of Armenia, Lucullus sent his brother-in-law, Appius Claudius, to Tigranes to ask him to turn over Mithradates. Initially, Tigranes employed a delaying tactic by refusing to give an audience to either Appius Claudius or his father-in-law, who was kept under virtual house arrest in an Armenian castle. When the Roman envoy finally did speak to Tigranes, Appius's haughty and peremptory tone so infuriated the king that he refused the Roman request. In 69 B.C.E., Lucullus invaded Armenia, with a force that Tigranes is said to have described as "too large for an embassy, too small for an army." Nevertheless, Lucullus was able to besiege Tigranocerta and, after Tigranes had fled into the Armenian hills and joined forces with Mithradates, inflict a serious defeat on the combined Armenian and Pontic armies. Lucullus's army was unwilling, however, to fight further, and when the Roman garrison that had been left in Pontus revolted, Lucullus was forced to retire. Both Tigranes and Mithradates were able to recover much of the territory that had been seized, though Tigranes had lost Syria forever.

The final blow to Tigranes' imperial rule was soon to follow. In 67 B.C.E. Pompey the Great cleared the Mediterranean of pirates by destroying their bases in Cilicia; in the following year, he was awarded the command against Mithradates VI. When Pompey quickly moved against Pontus, Mithradates once again tried to seek refuge in Armenia. In the meantime, however, Tigranes was facing a new enemy. His third son, also named Tigranes, had married into the family of Phraates III, King of Parthia, and, urged on by his father-in-law, raised a revolt against his father.

As Pompey marched into Armenia, the elder Tigranes banished Mithradates from his kingdom and made overtures of submission to the Roman general. Perceiving that a weakened Tigranes would serve Roman interests, Pompey switched his support from Phraates to Tigranes, though he did set Tigranes' son on the throne of Lesser Armenia. The younger Tigranes soon intrigued again against his father, and Pompey thereupon took him prisoner and brought him back to Rome, where he perished. The next two years witnessed intermittent hostilities between Tigranes and Phraates until Pompey finally negotiated a peace between Armenia and Parthia. Tigranes the Great continued to rule as King of Armenia, albeit a king completely subservient to Rome, until his death.

SIGNIFICANCE

The ancient Armenians themselves left no historical records, and the earliest extant Armenian history, written sometime between the fifth and eighth centuries C.E. by Moses of Khorene, presents only a very unreliable legendary account of the reign of Tigranes. Except for a single reference to Tigranes in a Parthian document and the evidence of Tigranes' coinage, all that is known about this king is what is preserved in the writings of a handful of Greek and Latin authors, who wrote from a Roman perspective.

The main sources for the life of Tigranes are Strabo, Plutarch, Dio Cassius, Appian of Alexandria, and Justin. It is hardly surprising, therefore, that the Tigranes portrayed by these authors is an arrogant tyrant who through his own stupidity and hubris was unable to maintain his empire. In large part, this negative picture of Tigranes simply reflects a general Greco-Roman hostility toward absolute monarchs. In spite of his sincere philhellenism, which was shared by most of the eastern aristocracy of the Hellenistic age, Tigranes was above all an Oriental ruler.

After the death of Tigranes the Great, his descendants continued to rule as client-kings of Rome until 1 B.C.E., when Augustus attempted to put his own grandson, Gaius, on the throne. When Gaius was killed during an Armenian uprising in 4 C.E., the kingship was reinstated, and the Armenian throne continued to be a matter of contention between Rome and Parthia for another century. Finally, by 114 C.E., the usefulness of Armenia as a buffer state had ended, and Trajan annexed it as a Roman province.

—*Murray C. McClellan*

FURTHER READING

Foss, Clive. "The Coinage of Tigranes the Great: Problems, Suggestions, and a New Find." *Numismatic Chronicle* 146 (1986): 19-66. A major reclassification of the silver and bronze coinage of Tigranes based on metrology, iconography, and style. Identifies mints and reassigns one type to Tigranes the Younger.

Lang, David M. *Armenia: Cradle of Civilization.* 3d ed. Boston: Unwin Hyman, 1980. Presents a general overview of Armenia from the Neolithic to the present. In general, the chapters on early Armenia are marred by historical errors and a strong pro-Armenian bias.

McGing, B. C. "The Date of the Outbreak of the Third Mithridatic War." *Phoenix* 38 (1984): 12-18. Suggests that the beginning of the war should be downdated from 74 B.C.E. to 73 B.C.E.

Musti, D. "Syria and the East." In *The Hellenistic World,* edited by F. W. Walbank, A. E. Astin, M. W. Frederiksen, and R. M. Ogilvie. Vol. 7 in *The Cambridge Ancient History.* 3d ed. Cambridge, England: Cambridge University Press, 1984. The best general account available on the relations between the Seleucids and the Eastern kingdoms.

Ormerod, H. A., and M. Cary. "Rome and the East." In *The Roman Republic, 133-44 B.C.,* edited by S. A. Cook, F. E. Adcock, and M. P. Charlesworth. Vol. 9 in *The Cambridge Ancient History.* 2d ed. Cambridge, England: Cambridge University Press, 1966. Still the best narrative on the Third Mithradatic War and Tigranes' battles against Lucullus.

Peters, F. E. *The Harvest of Hellenism: A History of the Near East from Alexander the Great to the Triumph of Christianity.* 2d ed. New York: Barnes and Noble, 1996. In this massive history of the Hellenistic East, chapter 8, "The Romans in the Near East," presents a solid general account of the conflicts between Rome and the Eastern kingdoms from Cynoscephalae to Carrhae.

SEE ALSO: Mithradates VI Eupator; Pompey the Great; Lucius Cornelius Sulla.

RELATED ARTICLE in *Great Events from History: The Ancient World*: 95-69 B.C.E., Armenian Empire Reaches Its Peak Under Tigranes the Great.

DĒVĀNAṂPIYA TISSA
Sri Lankan king (r. 247-207 B.C.E.)

Dēvānaṃpiya Tissa was the first Buddhist king of Tambapanni, now called Sri Lanka. A great patron of the faith, he was the country's first convert and was responsible for creating Tambapanni's first Buddhist establishments.

BORN: Date unknown; Anuradhapura, Tambapanni (now Sri Lanka)

DIED: 207 B.C.E.; Anuradhapura, Tambapanni

AREAS OF ACHIEVEMENT: Religion, government and politics

EARLY LIFE

Little is known of the early years of Dēvānaṃpiya Tissa (deh-vah-nawm-pee-yah tee-sah), and the exact year of his birth is uncertain. The earliest record tells that he was anointed king and took the throne after the demise of his father, Mutasiva, in 247. In pre-Buddhist Sri Lanka there were neither proper kings nor a central government. His father probably was a provincial chieftain ruling over a large part of central Tambapanni; the capital was located at Anuradhapura. The Anuradhapura domain was important enough, however, to establish diplomatic connections with Madhura in South India and Pataliputra, the Mauryan capital in North India. A popular tale relates that, when Tissa ascended the throne, jewels immediately sprang up from the earth because of his meritorious past lives.

The Sri Lankan chronicle, the *Mahāvamsa* (fifth or sixth century C.E.; *The Mahāvamsa: Or, The Great Chronicle of Ceylon*, 1912), states that, after he took office, Dēvānaṃpiya Tissa sent various valuable gifts, including some of the gems rising from the earth, to his neighbor the mighty Mauryan king Aśoka as a token of his friendship. On learning from the Sinhalese ambassador that King Tissa had only a modest ceremony of investiture of kingship, Aśoka decided to send all the requisite implements for a full royal coronation, including a fan, a diadem, a sword, a parasol, shoes, a turban, ear ornaments, a pitcher, sandalwood, sumptuous garments, red-colored earth, water from Anotatta Lake and the Ganges River, one hundred wagonloads of mountain rice, golden platters, and a fine litter.

Once the gifts were delivered, Dēvānaṃpiya Tissa was installed a second time with the elaborate coronation ceremony prescribed by Aśoka. It may be that the honorific term Dēvānaṃpiya, or "Beloved of the Gods," was an imperial title conferred by Aśoka on the neighboring king. The second coronation, with all its new stately regalia, connotes the friendly and intimate connections between India and Tambapanni. It also crystallized the authority of the king in a way that ensured his political dominance on the island.

LIFE'S WORK

In response to the growing friendship with Dēvānaṃpiya Tissa, Aśoka sent his own son Mahinda Thera, a Theravāda monk, as a Buddhist missionary to the southern island. Before the advent of Buddhism, Tambapanni had no systematically organized state religion. Only the cults of Yakshas and Yakshis (male and female nature deities often associated with the spirits of the dead) and a form of tree worship seem to have been prevalent and popular forms of worship. The missionary Mahinda, on the other hand, offered a wholly new, organized, and profoundly ethical and philosophical religion. He arrived from India with a party of six other *bhikkhus* (monks) soon after Dēvānaṃpiya's second coronation. Two of Aśoka's grandsons, Sumana Samanara, a novice, and Bhanduka Upaska, a lay disciple, were included in the entourage. That Aśoka's son and two grandsons were part of the mission indicates its special prestige and also the esteem with which Tissa was regarded by the Indian monarch. Sri Lankan sources recount a popular notion that King Dēvānaṃpiya and Emperor Aśoka had been brothers in a former life. A Buddhist legend contends that Mahinda and his associates were magically transported through the air from Mount Vedisaka in India to Missaka-pabbata, a forested mountain some eight miles east of the Sri Lankan capital at Anuradhapura.

The Buddhist canons record that the first meeting between Mahinda and Tissa occurred while Tissa was engaged in a hunting expedition at Missaka-pabbata (also called Chettiya-pabbata), today known as Mihintale. On the day there happened to be a great festival known as Jettha-Mulanakkhatta, and the king was out with an entourage of forty thousand men. Following a deer, the group was led to the very spot where the missionaries were. Mahinda, on seeing the king, called out to him by name. Although startled at first, Tissa, having heard of Buddhism from Aśoka's ambassadors, received the Buddhist missionaries with great kindness. The visiting teacher began to pose a series of questions to Tissa, probing his capacity for understanding the complexities of Buddhism. Convinced of his goodness and intelligence,

Mahinda proceeded immediately to preach the *Cula-hatthipadopama Sutta* (*The Shorter Discourse on the Simile of the Elephant's Footprint*, 1912), a text that contains the principal teachings of the Buddha, including the Four Noble Truths. On completing the sermon, the king declared his allegiance to the new faith, and his entire entourage of expressed their willingness to embrace Buddhism as well.

The following morning, Mahinda and his companions entered the capital city, where they were received by the king and taken into the royal house. Tissa served his guests lunch and called on the five hundred women of the palace, including Anuladevi, a minor queen, to pay their respects to their Buddhist guests. After lunch, Mahinda addressed the royal household about various Buddhist canons for the spiritual development of all. Hearing him speak, all the ladies declared their desire to become Buddhists. Meanwhile, numerous other city dwellers, learning of the presence of the teachers, gathered at the palace gate, asking for an opportunity to hear Mahinda talk. Tissa ordered that the Elephant Hall be cleared and readied. There, Mahinda taught from the text called *Devaduta Suttanta*, and one thousand more from the assembly declared their intentions to follow the path laid down by the historical Buddha. Soon the Elephant Hall was overflowing with more and more seekers wanting Buddhist instruction, and the king ordered that sufficient seats be provided in Nandanavana Park on the south side of the city. It was there that Mahinda taught the *Asivisopama Sutta* and another thousand were converted. Thus, by the second day of his arrival, Mahinda had led twenty-five hundred Sri Lankans to the path of enlightenment.

Tissa urged the party of missionaries to take up residence in the royal pavilion in Mahameghavana Park, located a short distance outside the city. The location of the park was ideal; removed from the city, it afforded the monks quiet for their meditations, yet it was near enough that it was easily accessible to visitors. Once installed there, the king offered to give the park to the monks as a tangible evidence of his devotion and his firm dedication to support the faith. The transfer of the land was affirmed by the traditional gesture in which the king poured water over the hands of Mahinda. The chronicles relate that the act of transference was followed by many miraculous events. The gift of land not only assured the material well-being of the monks, but it also marked the establishment of the first official Buddhist complex in Tambapanni. The park came to be known as the famous Mahā-vīra or Great Monastery; it has continued throughout the

centuries to remain the primary center of Theravādin Buddhist culture and learning in Tambapanni. In 207 B.C.E., Dēvānaṃpiya and Mahinda laid out a vast planned complex on the site that thenceforth was known as the Holy City of Anuradhapura. In doing so, they established the sacred boundary (*sima*) so as to include the city in order that the king and his family could live within the Buddha's command. The gesture is important because it affirmed the inviolable position of a Buddhist king. From then until the nineteenth century, only a king who was Buddhist had the right to rule the country.

Mahinda continued to preach for several more days, converting the multitudes to the new faith. On the seventh day, he announced to Tissa that he was returning to Missaka-pabbata on the mountain; in accordance with the Buddhist tradition, the monks needed to spend the period of *vassa* (monsoon season) in remote isolation. Tissa then donated the mountain site to the teacher and the following; it became known as Cettiya-pabbata. On that very same day, the king's nephew Maha-Arittha joined the order with fifty-five of his elder and younger brothers. After the king ordered that sixty-eight caves be cleared for the monks' occupation, Mahinda and his fellow *bhikkus* spent the first *vassa* on the mountain. At the end of the season, the king ordered a *thupa* (*stupa* or burial monument) to be constructed to house relics of the body of the historical Buddha Śākyamuni.

Before the onset of the rainy season, Queen Anuladevi expressed her wish to take the Buddhist vows and become a full-fledged nun. Because only a ranking Buddhist nun was authorized to confer that station on the queen, Tissa sent an envoy to King Aśoka asking that he send his daughter Sanghamitta to Tambapanni so that she could establish an order of nuns (Bhikkhuni Sasana). While awaiting the arrival of Sanghamitta, Anuladevi and her companions observed the tenfold precepts of the faithful. Meanwhile, Tissa ordered construction of a building suitable for a nunnery so that all would be ready for the female community; it was called Hatthalhaka Vihara. Sanghamitta arrived, accompanied by several nuns. She initiated Anuladevi and her attendants and thus inaugurated the first female Buddhist establishment.

At the time he sent for Sanghamitta, Tissa also requested a branch of the Bodhi tree beneath which the Buddha had attained his enlightenment. The details of the manner in which Aśoka selected and cut the branch from the sacred tree and how it was sent to Tambapanni are recorded in the *Mahāvamsa* and the *Samantapāsādikā* (fifth century C.E.). Reception of the tree branch in Tambapanni was observed with a great ceremony in which

Tissa waded neck-deep in the ocean and carried the cutting on his head to the shore where he had a pavilion specially built for it. Soon the tree was permanently planted at the nunnery, Hatthalhaka Vihara, where Buddhists in Sri Lanka have paid it the utmost respect throughout the centuries. Eventually thirty-two saplings of the Bodhi tree were distributed throughout the island.

Along with the cutting from the Bodhi tree, Aśoka sent along more than fifty families among whom were learned ministers as well as representatives of various occupations and guilds. The gesture suggests that Aśoka wanted to introduce many forms of higher learning and skills to Tambapanni. Tradition relates that the begging bowl (*patra dhatu*) and various fragments from the body of the historical Buddha were sent to Tambapanni along with the tree limb. A fragment of the Buddha's right collarbone was housed in the Thumparama Dagaba (*stupa*) at Chettiya-pabbata, and the alms bowl was kept in the royal palace. Buddha's relics signified the presence of the Buddha himself and his residence on the island. During his forty years as king, Tissa continued to support the faith and to donate land and structures for the use of the *saṅgha* (Buddhist community). He built many other important structures including the Issarasamanaka Vihara, Vessagiri Vihara, the Mahapali refractory at Anuradhapura, and the Jambukolapattana in Nagadipa. Dēvānaṃpiya Tissa died in 207 B.C.E. His younger brother Uttiya, who actively continued to promote Buddhism, followed him on the throne. Mahinda died in 200 B.C.E. at Chettiya-prabbata, and his relics are enshrined in a *stupa* at the site.

SIGNIFICANCE

King Dēvānaṃpiya Tissa's influence was enormous. As a devout believer, he was instrumental in efforts to convert his family and subjects to Buddhism. It was he who made Buddhism the state religion and founded the indigenous monastic order for both men and women. In addition, he implemented many social programs for the welfare of the people. The course of the island's history was altered significantly by his conversion and included the introduction of foreign technologies, particularly large-scale, durable architecture. By donating lands and constructing monastic complexes he created an enduring stronghold for Theravāda (Hināyāna) Buddhism in Sri

Lanka. Not only was his patronage key for the establishment of Buddhism, but he also fostered a great age of higher learning in Sri Lanka. Under the wise stewardship of Tissa, a great influx of learning, both sacred and secular, occurred. These events mark Sri Lanka's transition from a provincial island culture to a complex civilization known for its erudition and its advanced material culture.

—*Katherine Anne Harper*

FURTHER READING

Adikaram, E. W. *Early History of Buddhism in Ceylon.* Migoda, Ceylon: D. S. Puswella, 1946. Provides an excellent and comprehensive history of early Sinhalese culture as revealed in Buddhist commentaries. Includes bibliography.

Sekhera, Kalalelle. *Early Buddhist Sanghas and Viharas in Sri Lanka (up to the Fourth Century A.D.).* Varanasi, India: Rishi, 1998. Review of early monastic life in Sri Lanka. Contains list and layout of important monasteries. Includes bibliography.

Smith, Bardwell L. *Religion and Legitimation of Power in Sri Lanka.* Chambersburg, Pa.: ANIMA Books, 1978. Considers Sri Lankan history and the role of Buddhism in state matters and politics. Includes bibliography.

Rahula, Walpola. *History of Buddhism in Ceylon: The Anuradhapura Period, Third Century B.C.-Tenth Century A.D.* 2d ed. Colombo, Ceylon: M. D. Gunasena, 1966. Addresses the pre-Buddhist social conditions of Sri Lanka and the establishment of Buddhism and its history for a period of one thousand years. Includes bibliography.

Trainor, Kevin. *Relics, Ritual, and Representation in Buddhism: Rematerializing the Sri Lankan Theravada Tradition.* New York: Cambridge University Press, 1997. A careful study of the cult of the relics of Siddhārtha Gautama, the historical Buddha, as manifested in Sri Lanka. Includes bibliography.

SEE ALSO: Aśoka; Buddha.
RELATED ARTICLES in *Great Events from History: The Ancient World*: 6th or 5th century B.C.E., Birth of Buddhism; 273/265-c. 238 B.C.E., Aśoka Reigns over India; c. 250 B.C.E., Third Buddhist Council Convenes; c. 247-207 B.C.E., Buddhism Established in Sri Lanka.

TIY
Egyptian queen

Wife of Pharaoh Amenhotep III and mother of Pharaoh Akhenaton (Amenhotep IV), Tiy was influential in political and religious affairs in the Eighteenth Dynasty.

BORN: c. 1410 B.C.E.; Thebes, Egypt
DIED: c. 1340 B.C.E.; Akhetaton (now Tell el-Amārna, Egypt)
ALSO KNOWN AS: Tiye; Tiyi
AREAS OF ACHIEVEMENT: Government and politics, religion

EARLY LIFE

Information on Tiy (tee) comes primarily from archaeological records. Tiy was the daughter of Yuya and Thuyu. Yuya, her father, was a chariot officer who bore the title "master of the horse," served as a priest of the god Min, and had the additional distinction of the title "god's father." Hailing from Akhmim in Upper Egypt, Yuya may have been a nonnative Egyptian. His name was uncommon in ancient Egypt, and he was of unusually tall stature. Some postulate that Yuya was of Asian origin, based on his name and expertise in horsemanship, a skill associated with Asiatics. Other scholars theorize that Tiy's family was of sub-Saharan African origin, basing this conclusion on depictions of Tiy from the reigns of her husband and her son and the features of the mummy commonly identified as the queen. Tiy's mother was also a woman of distinction who bore the title "chief lady of the harem of Amen," marking her as an important figure in the cult of Amen, the main god of Egypt. One of Tiy's brothers, Anen, was also an important religious figure; he held the title "second prophet of Amen."

Yuya and Thuyu were sufficiently important to the pharaoh that he allowed them a tomb in the royal necropolis at Thebes, an honor reserved for very few. Most likely, this honor was bestowed on Yuya and Thuyu as a result of Tiy's marriage to the pharaoh. The tomb of Tiy's parents was a significant find for archaeologists, as the burial was largely intact despite having been robbed in antiquity. Until the excavation of the tomb of Pharaoh Tutankhamen, the tomb of Yuya and Thuyu (KV46) held the most complete funerary equipment of all excavated Egyptian tombs. The tomb was excavated in 1905 by James Quibbell on behalf of Theodore Davis; the funerary equipment was placed on display at the Egyptian Museum in Cairo.

LIFE'S WORK

Although Tiy was the daughter of Egyptian officials, it is generally agreed that she was not related to the royal family. She is best known for her marriage to Pharaoh Amenhotep III (r. 1391-1349 B.C.E.) and as the mother of Akhenaton (1364-1334 B.C.E.) and at least five other children. As the wife of one pharaoh and the mother of another, Tiy was extremely influential; some argue she was one of Egypt's most powerful queens.

Tiy likely married Amenhotep III when she was a young girl, most probably in her early teens. While generally considered to have been a good ruler, Amenhotep III was not a pharaoh primarily engaged in expansion or warfare; by the time he was pharaoh, Egypt was strong and prosperous, and such shows of strength were rarely warranted. Tiy's husband maintained Egypt, going to war most notably to put down a revolt in Nubia in the fifth year of his reign. Egypt while Tiy was queen was a country with a strong economy and a wealth of trade; gold from Nubia; elephant tusks, giraffe hides, and ebony from Kush; lapis lazuli from Afghanistan; jars from Crete; and copper from Cyrus flowed into Egypt. Tiy traveled often with her husband, journeying north from Thebes to the administrative center of Memphis, likely visiting temples and shrines along the way. Because of Egypt's prosperity, Amenhotep III was better known for his sponsorship of art and architecture and for the opulent lifestyle of his family and court than for his military prowess. His chief architect, the famous Amenhotep, son of Hapu, built a new palace complex for the pharaoh at Malkata, near Thebes, which included a large artificial lake, Birket Habu, built for Queen Tiy to use for sailing on her barge.

The esteem in which Amenhotep III held his Great Royal Wife is evident in the frequency with which Tiy appears in the records of that period. Tiy is included in the commemorative scarabs issued by her husband. Images of the queen appear in reliefs and statues from Amenhotep III's reign. In many depictions, she is shown as equal in size to her husband, an uncommon portrayal in an era during which the wives of pharaohs were shown as considerably smaller. Amenhotep III further honored Tiy with the construction of a temple in Nubia at Sedeigna (present-day northern Sudan). Here, the queen was worshiped as a form of the goddess Hathor. More important, at this temple she was associated with the solar eye of the god Ra, and in this role, she ensured the maintenance of *ma'at* (divine order) throughout the region through her joining with the deity Nebmaatra.

Tiy's son, Amenhotep IV, most likely succeeded his father before Amenhotep III's death. Examination of the pharaoh's mummy indicates that he suffered from a variety of afflictions, including extensive dental abscesses. Some scholars theorize that Tiy urged her husband to make their son his coregent, thus assuring his eventual succession. In the first year of his reign, Amenhotep IV established a temple to the sun disk god Aton at Karnak; Aton had been the personal god of Amenhotep III. Yet Amenhotep IV took worship of Aton to a new level, changing his name in the fifth year of his reign to Akhenaton ("glory of the Aton") and beginning construction of a new capital city, to be called Akhetaton ("horizon of the Aton"). The new city, designed to replace Memphis and Thebes as both the religious and political capital of Egypt, was located in Middle Egypt on land that had not been dedicated to any other gods. Akhenaton, in promoting the worship of Aton above all other deities, engineered a religious revolution in Egypt. His new religion of Aton-worship has been called monotheistic by some and henotheistic by others. It is not clear to what extent Tiy participated in this new faith, but evidence indicates she visited the new capital and most likely died there.

Whether or not Tiy participated in her son's religious revolution, she most certainly exerted political influence over him after the death of his father. The Amarna Letters, a term given to diplomatic correspondence of the period between Egyptian and Asiatic rulers, demonstrate Tiy's political importance. Tushratta, the king of Mitanni, a state with which Amenhotep III's Egypt had friendly relations, urged Akhenaton to seek his mother's advice, as she was privy to all Amenhotep III's dealings with Mitanni and would provide the best counsel for the new pharaoh. In addition, Tushratta wrote directly to Tiy asking for her assistance in his transactions with her son. In one such letter, Tushratta urged Tiy to ensure that Egypt and Mitanni maintained their good relations and complained that Akhenaton was neglecting their alliance. Like her husband, her son also held Tiy in high esteem. The queen's image appears in reliefs and temples at Akhetaton, and evidence indicates Akhenaton built a palace at his new capital for his mother.

Although the queen most likely died at Akhetaton, recent work indicates that the mummy of Tiy, as well those of several other persons, was transported from the royal necropolis at Akhetaton and reburied in the Valley of the Kings at Thebes. The tomb associated with Tiy is KV 55, first discovered and excavated by Edward Ayrton for

Theodore Davis in 1907-1908. Although Ayrton located several burial items (including pots, furniture, boxes, and tools) belonging to Tiy, the excavation did not uncover Tiy's mummy. Before it was examined, the mummy found in KV55 was assumed to be Tiy; after it was unwrapped, it was discovered that the individual was a man. This male mummy is believed by some to be that of Smenkhare, a coregent of Akhenaton. Yet more recent work indicates that this mummy may in fact be that of Akhenaton himself.

The location of Tiy's mummy remains a subject for debate, but the prevailing theory holds that during the Twenty-first Dynasty, her mummy along with several others was moved from KV55 to KV35, the tomb of Amenhotep II. When this tomb was excavated in 1898 by Victor Loret on behalf of the Service des Antiquités, ten mummies (apparently cached there to prevent desecration by tomb robbers) in addition to the three for whom the tomb was built were found inside. The mummy nicknamed the "Elder Woman" is often said to be that of Tiy, a conclusion based in part on the similarity between the hair of the mummy and a lock of hair found in the tomb of Tutankhamen and identified as that of Tiy.

SIGNIFICANCE

Tiy is an interesting individual in Egyptian history. A commoner who rose to become the wife and mother of a pharaoh, she developed into a powerful religious and political figure who lived through some of the most turbulent times of the New Kingdom. While women in ancient Egypt had a broad range of rights that included the right to own property, conduct their own economic and legal affairs, work, trade, and divorce their husbands, women were not often involved in political affairs. The New Kingdom was an era that included many of Egypt's most memorable and noted women—Hatshepsut (c. 1525-c. 1482 B.C.E.), who reigned as pharaoh in her own name; Nefertari, beloved Great Wife of Ramses II (c. 1307-c. 1265 B.C.E.); and Nefertiti (c. 1364-c. 1334 B.C.E.), beautiful queen of Akhenaton. Tiy must certainly be listed with these women as among Egypt's most influential female figures.

As Amenhotep III's Great Wife, Tiy was a companion to her husband, played a crucial role in the maintenance of divine order at her temple in Nubia, was worshiped as an incarnation of Hathor, was mother to six children, including the next pharaoh, and was a trusted political confidante and adviser to Amenhotep III. On the death of her husband, Tiy did not fade from the scene; she had ensured the succession of her son and she continued to advise him on political and diplomatic affairs and to correspond in her own right with at least one foreign leader. Although her religious significance must have declined with the advent of the Aton cult, Tiy's importance to her son did not. Still revered as mother, adviser, and queen, Tiy continued to exert a powerful influence on Egyptian politics until her death.

—Amy J. Johnson

FURTHER READING

Brier, Bob. *The Murder of Tutankhamen.* New York: Berkeley Books, 1998. Details the history of the Eighteenth Dynasty, culminating in the death of Tutankhamen. Author makes a case for the pharaoh's murder by his officials.

Davis, Theodore. *The Tomb of Queen Tiyi.* London: Constable & Company, 1910. The report on the excavations of 1907, including the tomb and the body found within which is not that of the queen.

Hawass, Zahi A. *Silent Images: Women in Pharaonic Egypt.* New York: Harry N. Abrams, 2000. Uses images of women to discuss their roles in ancient Egyptian society. Contains images and discussions of Tiy.

Robins, Gay. *Women in Ancient Egypt.* Cambridge, Mass.: Harvard University Press, 1993. Discusses women's public and private lives in ancient Egypt.

Shaw, Ian, ed. *The Oxford History of Ancient Egypt.* New York: Oxford University Press, 2000. Good, detailed history of ancient Egypt, including two chapters on the Eighteenth Dynasty. Includes many photos and maps.

Silverman, David P., ed. *Ancient Egypt.* New York: Oxford University Press, 1997. Provides a general overview of ancient Egyptian history. While it does not discuss Tiy, it gives the reader a good background for the subject and includes many photos and maps.

Tyldesley, Joyce A. *Daughters of Isis: Women of Ancient Egypt.* New York: Penguin, 1995. Provides information about women's lives in ancient Egypt and includes not only royal women but lower class women as well.

SEE ALSO: Akhenaton; Amenhotep III; Hatshepsut; Nefertari; Nefertiti; Tutankhamen.

RELATED ARTICLES in *Great Events from History: The Ancient World*: c. 1600-c. 1300 B.C.E., Mitanni Kingdom Flourishes in Upper Mesopotamia; c. 1570 B.C.E., New Kingdom Period Begins in Egypt; From c. 1500 B.C.E., Dissemination of the Book of the Dead; c. 1450 B.C.E., International Age of Major Kingdoms Begins in the Near East; c. 1365 B.C.E., Failure of Akhenaton's Cultural Revival.

TRAJAN
Roman emperor (r. c. 98-117 C.E.)

The first of the adoptive emperors of Rome, Trajan became one of the most successful in both war and politics. During his reign, the Roman Empire reached its maximum territorial extent.

BORN: c. 53 C.E.; Italica, Baetica (now in Spain)
DIED: c. August 8, 117 C.E.; Selinus, Cilicia (now in Turkey)
ALSO KNOWN AS: Marcus Ulpius Trajanus (full name)
AREAS OF ACHIEVEMENT: Government and politics, war and conquest

EARLY LIFE

Marcus Ulpius Trajanus, known as Trajan (TRAY-juhn), was born in Baetica, in what is now southern Spain, an area of Roman conquests and Latin influences for more than a century. By the time of Trajan's birth, c. 53 C.E., much of the population spoke Latin rather than the native Iberian language. Trajan's father, also Marcus Ulpius

Trajanus, was a native of Baetica who came from an Italian family that had been long established in Spain. The senior Trajanus had a significant military and political career; he served as governor of Baetica and commanded a legion in the war Vespasian conducted against the Jews, then became a consul and a member of the patrician class before acting as governor of Syria and, ultimately, as Imperial proconsul in the East. His attainments showed that most positions in the Imperial hierarchy during the first century C.E. were open to non-Italians. His son, Trajan, would become the first provincial to become emperor.

Little is known of Trajan's early life. He served as a military tribune and accompanied his father to Syria during the latter's term as governor. Typically for one of his class, he held various judicial and political positions, but his primary experience was military. He held command in Spain, then in Germany, becoming governor of Upper Germany. Physically imposing, tall, and serious in manner, he was popular and successful in the military and also among the senators in Rome.

In 97, probably as a result of political pressure, Marcus Cocceius Nerva, emperor since the murder of Domitian the previous year, adopted Trajan as his successor. Nerva was a politician, not a warrior, who hoped to end the autocratic abuses of Domitian's reign. He was ill and had no children of his own, and his adoption of Trajan satisfied both military and civilian powers. Four months after Trajan's adoption Nerva died, in January, 98, and Trajan, despite his provincial birth, became emperor of Rome.

LIFE'S WORK

At the time of Nerva's death, Trajan was at Cologne, in Lower Germany. Before returning to Rome, he fought a series of engagements against nearby foes, both to impress on them the might of Roman power and to establish plans for subsequent military action. His belated arrival

in Rome, in the summer of 99, suggests the unchallenged position he had already achieved.

Like his predecessors, Trajan continued to wear the mantle woven by Augustus more than a century earlier. In reality he was an autocrat, but in theory he was merely the first citizen, the princeps. His power was nearly absolute, yet, unlike many of Augustus's successors, Trajan masked his powers so as to reassure rather than intimidate the former ruling body, the senate, and the aristocratic patricians who had governed during the era of the Republic. Republican sentiment still ran high, in spite of the many changes since the Republic's end, as reflected in the historical works of two of Trajan's contemporaries, Cornelius Tacitus and Suetonius. Trajan reconciled the reality of order with the appearance of freedom in a way that satisfied most people; the equilibrium sought by Nerva but established by Trajan ushered in an era that the English historian Edward Gibbon described as one of the golden ages of human history.

Trajan, shown seated. (Library of Congress)

Trajan stressed moderation and reinforced the values of an earlier Rome. His family's upright reputation, his public generosity and private frugality, his lack of interest in excessive ceremonies glorifying himself, and his accessibility all contributed to the general popularity of his rule. As an administrator, Trajan was conscientious and hardworking rather than radically innovative; he was willing merely to improve existing practices inherited from his predecessors. If the senate remained powerless collectively, Trajan made good use of the abilities of individual senators. He created new patricians and made greater use of the class known as the knights rather than the services of freedmen, who often had attained considerable responsibility during the first century of the Empire. His judicial decisions favored the rights of slave owners rather than those of the slaves, although there is considerable evidence that Trajan's own sympathies were generally humanitarian. In his actions and demeanor, he conveyed the ruling-class virtues of the Republic.

As the Empire reached its maximum extent and its most notable era, public works projects continued to be of great importance. Roads were built or improved, particularly in the eastern part of the Empire, and road milestones from Trajan's reign have been discovered far south in Egypt. Aqueducts constructed around Rome greatly increased water supply to the city's populace. Harbors were improved, including Ostia, the port for Rome. New public baths were developed, and temples, libraries, and business facilities enhanced the city. Plans for many of the projects existed before Trajan became emperor, but he fulfilled and often expanded them. The Empire continued to become more urbanized, particularly in the East, and local municipalities also experienced considerable construction.

Trajan oversaw the reorganization of the traditional importation of grain so important to the Romans and increased the number of people qualified to receive it free. Public shows and games, a major part of urban life during his reign, were especially notable after his military victories. Trajan's interests in the plight of the lower classes possibly reflected his humanitarian concerns, but those actions were also simply good politics. He was fortunate to be able to reduce taxes—partially because of administrative dedication, but also because of the economic benefits that resulted from his military victories. Personally popular with the legions, Trajan successfully controlled his armies. He created a new mounted bodyguard, primarily composed of non-Italians, thus moving toward parity between Italians and those from the provinces.

TRAJAN AND HIS SUCCESSORS	
Ruler	*Reign (C.E.)*
Trajan	98-117
Hadrian	117-138
Antoninus Pius	138-161
Lucius Verus	161-169
Marcus Aurelius	161-180
Commodus	180-192
Pertinax	193
Didius Julianus	193
Pescennius Niger	193-194
Septimius Severus	193-211

Concern for his personal security, given the record of violent deaths suffered by several of his predecessors, led to the development of a new secret service.

Trajan's religious beliefs, orthodox for members of his class and time, reflected his traditional and patriotic nature rather than a deep theological concern. He built and restored temples throughout the Empire, and like Augustus, he accepted the fact of emperor worship in the eastern part of the Empire but resisted its development in the West. Nevertheless, new religions, such as Christianity, were spreading throughout the Empire, and, although only a small minority of the population were Christians, questions arose about the new movement.

Pliny the Younger, a Roman aristocrat appointed by Trajan as governor of the province of Bithynia-Pontus, wrote often to ask for solutions to problems he faced, including how Christians were to be treated. Trajan seriously considered all such difficulties; he did not allow his subordinates to decide the many matters of governance. Given the intimate tie between the Roman gods and the Roman state, Trajan's instructions to Pliny were moderate and sensible. Fearing subversive threats that might affect the tranquillity of the Empire, Trajan ordered that Christians who would not recant should be punished according to the requirements of the laws, but Christians should not be sought out for special persecution, and anonymous accusations by others against them should not be accepted. Trajan's response was typical of his nature; he was not a religious fanatic, but he understood the necessity to uphold the laws that had traditionally been accepted by the society and that had been responsible for Roman well-being.

Predictably, war and military conquest, the enterprises that had led to his adoption by Nerva, became an important theme of Trajan's reign. In eastern Europe, the great rivers of the Rhine and the Danube had long served as the natural boundaries of the Empire. Yet, because of a great inward curve of the Danube, a portion of southeastern Europe, known as Dacia, had remained a dangerous enclave that threatened the security of the Empire. The Dacians had adopted at least part of the Greco-Roman culture, including certain military techniques; although the Romans considered them barbarians, they were not primitives, and periodically they aggressively raided Roman territory across the Danube.

Trajan waged two wars against the Dacians and their formidable king, Decebalus. The first war, lasting from 101 to 102, resulted in Trajan leading the legions to victory over the Dacians, but Decebalus refused to abide by the terms of peace, and a second Dacian war was fought in 105. Again, Trajan was victorious, and Decebalus committed suicide. Most of the population of Dacia was removed and the area was colonized by Roman soldiers and civilians. The province became an important part of the Empire, until it was abandoned in the late third century after the invasion of the Germanic Goths. Trajan's conquest was celebrated by coins and inscriptions throughout the Empire, but the most famous monument stood in Rome. A hundred-foot-high column was constructed that portrayed the course of the Dacian wars; running counterclockwise from bottom to top, twenty-five hundred carved figures decorated the column, which was crowned with a statue of Trajan. It was dedicated in 113 and remains one of the most impressive remains of the Roman Empire at the time of its greatest power.

After the victory against Decebalus, Trajan spent the next several years in Rome before responding to another threat to Rome's supremacy, this time in the East, from Parthia, whose ancient borders spread at times from the Euphrates River to India. Rome and Parthia had been adversaries as far back as the late Republic, when Pompey the Great had extended the boundaries of the Empire into the area south of the Black Sea. Trajan, in 113, decided to annex Armenia to Rome, claiming that the Parthians had upset the existing arrangements in that territory. Trajan's motives have been variously interpreted; he may have acted for economic reasons, to secure the overland trade routes from the Persian Gulf and beyond, or because of ambitions for personal fame (although even the wars against Dacia resulted more from Dacian incursions than Roman aggression). Trajan was sixty years old when the war against Parthia began, and in 114 his armies easily conquered Armenia, making it a Roman province, with client kingdoms extending even farther to the east.

The Roman advance continued south the following year into Mesopotamia. Behind the Roman lines, however, there was unrest; businessmen were upset by the uncertain changes brought by the new Roman regime, and many Jewish communities in the East again rose up against Roman authority. At the same time the Parthians, previously disunited, came together, forcing the Romans back. The military situation stabilized, but Trajan's health declined; there were matters at Rome that needed his presence, and he turned west toward home. Before reaching Rome, he died at Selinus in Cilicia, in southern Asia Minor, probably on August 8, 117. His ashes were deposited in a golden urn at the base of his famous column in Rome.

SIGNIFICANCE

Before he died, Trajan apparently adopted as his successor Publius Aelius Hadrianus (Hadrian), a distant relative who had been reared in Trajan's household. Trajan had no children of his own, and his wife, Pompeia Plotina, favored Hadrian's accession. One of the first acts of the new emperor was to reach an agreement with Parthia to have Rome withdraw from the advanced positions attained by Trajan. Hadrian's decision was both strategic and political. It is possible that under Trajan the Empire was overextended, that it lacked the resources necessary to hold the new territories. For his own success, Hadrian desired peace rather than a resumption of his predecessor's forward policy. Under Hadrian, and under his successors, the Roman Empire would never again reach the limits achieved by Trajan.

The adjustment made between the ruler as *princeps* and the ruler as tyrant distinguished Trajan's reign. Power resided solely in the emperor's hands, but he used that power responsibly. The practice of adopting one's successor, first established by Nerva, continued until 180, and during that period the Empire was governed by men of ability and much vision. It was not, however, a golden age; even under Trajan, increased centralization took place, Italy began to fall relatively behind other parts of the Empire, and the borders were never totally secure. The traditional governing classes of Rome turned more toward the literary life than toward politics and public service, while the Empire depended in large part on the labor of slaves for its prosperity.

Nevertheless, Trajan was one of the greatest of the emperors, both because of his military and territorial conquests and because of the standards he set as governor and statesman. Early in his reign he was hailed as *Optimus*, the best. Along with Augustus, Trajan was the standard by which later Romans measured the leadership of the Empire; their expressed hope, rarely attained, was that later emperors would be *felicior Augusto, melior Traiano*, or more fortunate than Augustus and better than Trajan.

—*Eugene S. Larson*

FURTHER READING

Bennett, Julian. *Trajan: Optimus Princeps*. 2d ed. Bloomington: Indiana University Press, 2001. The first full-length biography on Trajan in English. Comprehensive and detailed, although sometimes uninspired writing. Includes bibliographical references and indexes.

Garzetti, Albino. *From Tiberius to the Antonines: A History of the Roman Empire, A.D. 14-192*. Translated by J. F. Foster. London: Methuen, 1974. Trajan is one of the major figures and is the subject of a long chapter in the work. The author argues that Trajan was one of the best of all the emperors of Rome and that he successfully remained primarily princeps rather than dictator.

Gibbon, Edward. *History of the Decline and Fall of the Roman Empire*. 1787. Reprint. New York: Modern Library, 1995. In Gibbon's landmark work, the second century of the common era was one of humanity's golden ages. Trajan was one of the best of the emperors, whose only personal weakness was his military ambitions.

Grant, Michael. *The Army of the Caesars*. New York: Charles Scribner's Sons, 1974. The author, one of the most prolific historians of ancient Rome, has produced a well-written study of the armies of Rome from the late Republic through the fall of the Western Roman Empire in 476. Grant discusses the military conquests of Trajan in Dacia and against Parthia and argues that the latter was ultimately beyond the resources of the Empire.

_____. *The Roman Emperors: A Biographical Guide to the Rulers of Imperial Rome, 31 B.C.-A.D. 476*. London: Weidenfeld and Nicolson, 1996. The sketch on Trajan is brief but covers his accomplishments and characteristics.

Harris, B. F. *Bithynia Under Trajan: Roman and Greek Views of the Principate*. Auckland, New Zealand: University of Auckland, 1964. This brief monograph discusses the different but complementary views of the position and powers of the Roman emperor at the time of Trajan as expressed by the Roman governor in Bithynia, Pliny the Younger, and the Greek Dio Chrysostom.

Hoffer, Stanley E. *The Anxieties of Pliny the Younger*. London: Oxford University Press, 1999. Provides some useful biographical information on Trajan as well as criticism and interpretation of his times. Includes five pages of bibliographical references and an index.

Millar, Fergus. *The Emperor in the Roman World, 31 B.C.-A.D. 337*. Ithaca, N.Y.: Cornell University Press, 1977. This study of the emperors of Rome from Augustus to Constantine is one of the major works on the powers and responsibilities of the many rulers of the Empire. Long and not easily digested, it is still worth the effort because of its comprehensiveness and its insights. Although there is no single chapter on Trajan, he is frequently mentioned.

Rossi, Lino. *Trajan's Column and the Dacian Wars*. Translated by J. M. C. Toynbee. Ithaca, N.Y.: Cornell University Press, 1971. The author's historical interest is in warfare, Roman and modern. In this study, in the absence of written records, he uses one of the most famous monuments of the Roman Empire in order to dissect the course of Trajan's victorious wars against the Dacians, which represented one of the most important accomplishments of his reign.

Wilken, Robert L. *The Christians as the Romans Saw Them*. New Haven, Conn.: Yale University Press, 1984. Pliny the Younger's letters to the emperor have continued to be one of the major sources for the era. Among other topics, Pliny wrote to Trajan regarding Christians in Bithynia. The author places that correspondence in historical context from the Roman perspective.

SEE ALSO: Hadrian; Tacitus.

RELATED ARTICLES in *Great Events from History: The Ancient World*: 312-264 B.C.E., Building of the Appian Way; c. 110 C.E., Trajan Adopts Anti-Christian Religious Policy.

TUTANKHAMEN
Egyptian pharaoh (r. 1334-1325 B.C.E.)

Tutankhamen is one of the best-known and most studied of the Egyptian pharaohs because his tomb lay undisturbed and intact until its discovery in the early twentieth century. Although he was a relatively minor figure in the course of Egyptian history, the gold-laden contents of his tomb have captured the imagination of the world and contributed much to the knowledge of ancient Egyptian life, culture, and religion.

BORN: c. 1343 B.C.E.; probably Tell el-Amārna, Egypt
DIED: c. 1325 B.C.E.; place unknown
ALSO KNOWN AS: Tutankhaton
AREAS OF ACHIEVEMENT: Government and politics, art and art patronage

EARLY LIFE

The lineage of Tutankhamen (TEWT-ahn-KAH-muhn) is uncertain, and despite the vast assortment of riches discovered in his tomb, the exact dates and events of his rule remain shrouded in mystery. Presumably born in Tell el-Amārna during the reign of Akhenaton (1350-1334 B.C.E.), he was most likely the son of either Amenhotep III (1386-1349 B.C.E.) or Akhenaton. The identity of Tutankhamen's mother is less certain. She was most likely one of the secondary wives or concubines of the king. Kiya, a secondary wife of Akhenaton, is the most logical candidate, since she was referred to in numerous inscriptions as the "Greatly Beloved Wife." She was probably a relative of his father, as it was the practice of Egyptian nobility of the time to marry another member of the royal family and thus ensure the purity of royal blood.

The son-in-law of Akhenaton and Queen Nefertiti by marriage to their third daughter, Tutankhamen was only nine years old when he succeeded his brother Smenkhare. Tutankhamen's queen, Ankhesenpaaton, was also very young at the time of their marriage. The royal couple produced no known heirs. Two fetuses, however, were buried in the tomb of Tutankhamen and are assumed to be their offspring. He ascending the throne during the period of transition that followed the death of Akhenaton, who had promoted the cult of the solar disk, Aton; at such a time, the rule of Egypt would have been difficult for even the most adept of statesmen. Akhenaton had angered many by moving the capital from Thebes to Tell el-Amārna. Akhenaton's fervent monotheism, neglect of foreign affairs, and the decline of Egyptian power abroad, especially in Syria and Palestine, had created considerable unrest. During the final years of his reign, however, and during the brief reign of his coregent and successor, Smenkhare, the priesthood of Amen reemerged. When Tutankhamen succeeded his brother Smenkhare, he initially embraced the priesthood of Aton. It was the only cult he had ever known.

LIFE'S WORK

Although the new king originally took the name Tutankhaton, meaning "gracious of life is Aton," less than three years later he changed his name to Tutankhamen, meaning "gracious of life is Amen." It is likely that the achievements of Tutankhamen's reign were actually envisioned and carried out by the vizier Ay and the general Horemheb. Tutankhamen was probably no more than a puppet ruler who, because of his youth, was easily manipulated by others for much of his reign. Ay, possibly the father of Nefertiti, was the power behind the throne and was likely responsible for the return of polytheism. The transfer of the administrative capital of Egypt back to Memphis and the reestablishment of Thebes as the religious center should probably be credited to Ay as well. Meanwhile, Hasemhab, the commander of the Egyptian armies, reasserted Egyptian authority in Asia by halting Hittite advances. Tutankhamen was thus credited with successfully halting Hittite advances on the Egyptian empire in northern Syria.

Although several objects in his tomb depict the 5.5-foot (1.6-meter) Tutankhamen defeating enemies in battle, there is no evidence he ever actually participated in a campaign. It is not an impossibility, however, since some other pharaohs did engage the enemy at about the age of eighteen; most scholars, however, believe that the depictions represent the king's armies as an extension of his power. It is known that Tutankhamen was a trained archer. Inscriptions on the fans found in his tomb state that the ostrich plumes they contained were taken from trophies of the king's hunts. When Tutankhamen died at about the age of eighteen, he was succeeded by Ay, who married Tutankhamen's widow. The cause of his death is unknown. There is evidence from skull damage that he may have been killed in battle or assassinated.

Whatever the cause of his demise, he had not prepared for death. Tutankhamen was buried in the Valley of the Kings in a tomb that had been originally prepared for someone else. The tomb of Tutankhamen was not one typically prepared for persons of such status. It has been estimated that it took the artisans working on his tomb about ten weeks to complete the coffin and shrines that protected him. The mummification process took about the same amount of time. Before his burial, all of his internal organs, except the heart, were removed and placed in containers called Canopic jars. The body was then placed in a dry mineral, natron, for dehydration. Other substances known only to the ancients were also used to embalm the body before it was wrapped in linen bandages and placed in the solid-gold coffin. Although the entrance of the tomb was pillaged by grave robbers some years after his death, it was later resealed and buried under the debris of the Twentieth Dynasty tomb of Ramses VI, which was built literally on top of his tomb. Tutankhamen was all but forgotten, both by his successors and by historians, until the discovery of his tomb by Howard Carter more than three thousand years after his death.

In 1909, Theodore Davis, a noted archaeologist, uncovered what he believed to be the tomb of Tutankhamen. Howard Carter, a self-trained Egyptologist, disagreed with Davis and vowed to continue the search. He eventually convinced George Herbert, the fifth earl of Carnarvon, to purchase Davis's concession to work the Valley of the Kings. For the next eighteen years, the two men spent half of each year in the Egyptian desert searching for the tomb of Tutankhamen or some other rare antiquity. In 1922, Carter, whose work since 1909 had been financed by Carnarvon at a cost of more than $250,000, discovered the set of steps leading down to the entrance of Tutankhamen's tomb. Within days, news of the discovery of the massive golden treasures unearthed in the tomb captured the imagination of the world.

The tomb was stocked with everything the young king might need in the afterlife. Clothing, jewelry, musical instruments, chairs, lamps, weapons, chariots, jars, and baskets containing wine and food filled the rooms. The sepulchral chamber contained his throne, covered with gold, silver, and jewels. The sarcophagus contained three coffins placed one within the other. The innermost, made of solid gold and weighing 2,500 pounds (1,134 kilograms), was of human shape and bore the likeness of Tutankhamen.

Carter spent more than ten years extracting and documenting every artifact removed from the tomb. He maintained meticulous field notes on every aspect of the discovery and excavation. Carter's notes and drawings, and related photographs taken during the excavation by Harry Burton of New York's Metropolitan Museum of Art, were later donated to the University of Oxford. Carnarvon, on the other hand, died as the result of a mysterious infection soon after discovering the tomb. He was only one of a series of victims—including Carter's pet canary, which was eaten by a cobra—whose deaths were attributed to the "mummy's curse." The allegedly strange circumstances surrounding their deaths, however, only served to heighten the interest in the phenomenal discovery.

SIGNIFICANCE

Tutankhamen was a relatively minor Egyptian ruler. As a result of the discoveries of Carter and Carnarvon, however, the world became obsessed with Tutankhamen and all things Egyptian during the 1920's. Egypt greatly benefited from the publicity surrounding the discovery, as thousands of tourists flocked to the Valley of the Kings. Although the local economy was completely unprepared for the deluge, industrious entrepreneurs soon found ways to accommodate the visitors. The "Egyptian look" became the epitome of women's fashion, and when the

Death mask of Tutankhamen. (Library of Congress)

British Empire Exhibition of 1924 featured a replica of the tomb, it attracted more than 200,000 visitors on opening day.

The fascination with things Egyptian created by the discovery of Tutankhamen's tomb persists in popular culture. Many of the contents of the tomb remain on display in the Cairo Museum, but several exhibitions have been conducted abroad. In 1972, to commemorate the fiftieth anniversary of the tomb's discovery, an exhibit was held in the British Museum in London. A similar exhibit toured the United States in 1976. Thousands waited in line to catch a rare glimpse of the wealth and splendor of Egyptian antiquity. Tutankhamen's greatest legacy as ruler of Egypt was not political or military but rather the knowledge of the society in which he lived that has been gleaned from the contents of his tomb.

—*Donald C. Simmons, Jr.*

FURTHER READING

Brier, Bob. *The Murder of Tutankhamen*. New York: Putnam, 1997. A well-known paleopathologist and Egyptologist presents the case for Tutankhamen's murder, arguing that Ay, who replaced him on the throne, fomented the political intrigue. Although Brier's thesis is controversial, he is perhaps its most persuasive and knowledgeable proponent.

Carter, Howard. *The Tomb of Tutankhamen: Discovered by the Late Earl of Carnarvon and Howard Carter*. 3 vols. 1927. Reprint. London: Duckworth, 2000-2001. Carter describes the events of his discovery in detail. The photographs are of great interest.

Dersin, Denise, ed. *What Life Was Like on the Banks of the Nile: Egypt, 3050-3030 B.C.* Alexandria, Va.: Time-Life Books, 1997. Almost every aspect of Egyptian life, including the role of women in society, is addressed in this well-written volume. The timeline is extremely helpful for the novice Egyptologist, and the bibliography is excellent.

Descouches-Noblecourt, Christiane. *Tutankhamen: Life and Death of a Pharaoh*. 1984. Reprint. New York: Penguin Books, 1990. The text is complemented by more than seventy color photographs and numerous illustrations related to the life and death of Tutankhamen. The list of principal characters of his life is invaluable. The notes on the color photographs are an excellent resource.

El Mahdy, Christine. *Tutankhamen: The Life and Death of the Boy-King*. New York: St. Martin's Press, 2000. A thorough assessment of the evidence for Tutankhamen's life that can be gleaned from the contents of his tomb. El Mahdy argues that the pharaoh died of a tumor, and his death was covered up for a time in order to ensure a smooth transition of government.

James, T. G. H. *Tutankhamun: The Eternal Splendor of the Boy Pharaoh*. New York: Tauris Parke, 2000. One of the best-illustrated works on Tutankhamen's burial available. Provides detailed description of the discovery of the tomb and its contents. The photographs are of exceptionally high quality and include many lesser-known objects as well as the iconographical items such as the gold funerary mask.

Reeves, Nicholas. *The Complete Tutankhamen: The King, the Tomb, the Treasure*. 1990. Reprint. New York: Thames and Hudson, 2002. Outlines the events of the discovery of the now-famous tomb. Includes easy-to-read biographical information about the most important participants in the expedition, including often overlooked members of the excavation team. Also contains excellent photographs.

SEE ALSO: Akhenaton; Amenhotep III; Cleopatra VII; Hatshepsut; Imhotep; Menes; Menkaure; Montuhotep II; Piye; Psamtik; Ramses II; Sesostris III; Thutmose III; Zoser.

RELATED ARTICLES in *Great Events from History: The Ancient World*: c. 2575-c. 2566 B.C.E., Building of the Great Pyramid; c. 1570 B.C.E., New Kingdom Period Begins in Egypt; From c. 1500 B.C.E., Dissemination of the Book of the Dead; c. 1365 B.C.E., Failure of Akhenaton's Cultural Revival; 1069 B.C.E., Third Intermediate Period Begins in Egypt.

ULFILAS
Gothic Christian bishop

An apostle to the Goths, Ulfilas developed an alphabet for the Gothic language and made the first Gothic translation of the Bible. He was also instrumental in converting the Goths to Arianism, leading to conflicts once these peoples settled inside the predominantly Nicene Roman Empire.

BORN: 311 C.E.; the region of modern Romania
DIED: 383 C.E.; Constantinople (now Istanbul, Turkey)
ALSO KNOWN AS: Ulfila; Wulfila (Gothic)
AREA OF ACHIEVEMENT: Religion

EARLY LIFE

Not much is known about the early life of Ulfilas (UHL-fuh-las). Tradition has it that his grandparents were taken as slaves from Cappadocia into the Gothic settlements north of the Danube. This same tradition suggests that his father was a Goth. "Ulfilas" itself is a Gothic term meaning "little wolf."

Ulfilas was fluent in three languages: Greek, Latin, and Gothic. He must have learned something of all three in his youth, for in 332 he was sent to Constantinople, perhaps as an emissary of the Goths to the Romans, or perhaps as a hostage to the court of the emperor Constantine. While there, Ulfilas either acquired or further developed his mastery of Greek and Latin. By the time he was thirty, he had risen to the position of lector, which required that he be able to read and speak in all three languages to the Gothic Christians inside the Empire.

The adult Ulfilas was an Arian rather than a Nicene Christian. When he embraced this position has been debated since antiquity. Orthodox and Arian historians alike tended to advance dates more important for their partisan positions than for their historical accuracy; modern scholars are convinced that it was around 330, during his time at the court of Constantine, since Arianism was the predominant theological position there. Whatever the accurate date, in 341, during the reign of the Emperor Constantius II, Ulfilas was consecrated a bishop by the Arian bishop Eusebius. He would spend the remaining forty years of his life as an apostle to the Goths.

LIFE'S WORK

The Visigoths were a tribal people who, though nominally under a king, usually vested local control in the hands of "judges." In the region where Ulfilas began his preaching, the local judge, Athanaric, was a pagan. After Ulfilas had been preaching for seven years, Athanaric began to persecute both Arian and Nicene Christians. The danger became so great that Ulfilas sought refuge inside the Empire on the near side of the Danube. The emperor at the time, Constantius, also an Arian, granted his request for asylum. Ulfilas and his band of followers settled in Moetia, in modern Bulgaria.

A second, more severe persecution followed, lasting from 369 to 373. Many more Arians fled to Ulfilas's community. Apparently, Athanaric feared that Christianity was undermining the tribal nature of his society and threatening the old religion. If Ulfilas's community is any example, this would certainly have been the case. They remained steadfastly loyal to Rome and devoutly Arian Christian even in the following century, when they refused to join the whole remaining body of the Visigoths who, fleeing the Huns, entered and subsequently looted the falling Roman Empire. Indeed, the community Ulfilas had founded in Moetia was still there in the middle of the sixth century when Jordanes, a Gothic historian, distinguished them from the other, more warlike Goths.

In the midst of the persecution of 368, a civil war erupted between Athanaric and another chieftain, Fritigern. Fritigern, at first defeated, sought Imperial assistance. The emperor Valens, an Arian, was prepared to assist; Fritigern, in return, was prepared to convert to Arian Christianity along with all of his followers. With Valens's help, Athanaric was defeated. From his location on the Imperial side of the mountains, Ulfilas seems to have attempted to convert both peoples. In 376, when Fritigern's Visigoths entered the Empire fleeing the Huns, Ulfilas is said to have accompanied his embassy to the emperor in order to plead their case.

Ulfilas's specific activities in the remainder of his life are not well documented. That he was preaching and teaching the Goths and Romans in Moetia, and perhaps beyond, seems clear. Additionally, he must have devoted much of his time to developing the Gothic alphabet, which he used for his translation of the Greek Bible. He also must have instructed his followers in the use of the alphabet. Subsequently, his text was copied and disseminated among other Gothic groups. The only remaining copy of Ulfilas's translation, a fragment of some 118 pages of the New Testament preserved at the University of Uppsala in Sweden, was made in Ostrogothic Italy about a century after Ulfilas's death. It is known as the *Codex Argenteus* because its uncial letters are of silver on blue velum. A few additional manuscript fragments exist that bear a striking resemblance to the work of Ulfilas, but it is not possible to determine with certainty that they are his. Finally, there are later references to the text that include quotations from the Psalms as well as passages from Genesis. It was his intention to translate the entire Bible with the possible exception of the Book of Kings, which he said was too much about war for the Goths' own good. In all likelihood, he completed the major portion of his work.

He was also a tireless participant in the Trinitarian controversy of his day. His disciple Bishop Auxentius records that Ulfilas attended many councils and wrote much on the controversy. Independent sources mention him only at two councils, but Auxentius's own work speaks at length of Ulfilas's polemical writings.

Ulfilas occupied something of a moderate position in the controversy. He was Arian because he subordinated Jesus the Son to God the Father. On his deathbed, he repeated his creed in a form that would become synonymous with that of other Arians who subsequently converted to

Ulfilas. (F. R. Niglutsch)

this version of Christianity. He stated that he believed in one eternal God who existed alone from the beginning. It was this God who created the Son, "the only begotten God." The Son, in turn, was the creator of all things and regarded the Father as superior to himself. Finally, it was the Father through the Son who created the Holy Spirit before anything else was created. His creed was "Homoean" because it refers to Christ as being "like" the Father rather than being in any sense "of the same substance" with the Father, as the "Homousian" formula from the Nicene Council of 325 had decreed.

This debate was very important for subsequent Gothic history. Ulfilas, the apostle to the Goths, and his disciples doubtless worked tirelessly among them teaching an Arian gospel. Further, his Gothic Bible was influential in providing them with a written language and also with access to other writings, many of which would have been Arian in outlook. The Nicene community worked only in Latin and Greek. Some scholars, indeed, have suggested

that Ulfilas would have served the Goths better if he had taught his priests Greek or Latin instead of the language of the Goths. Others point out that, given the hostility between Roman and Goth in this period, Latin is not a language the Goths would have readily learned to read; their own language, though, was another matter.

It has been noted that Ulfilas's version of the Trinity was more compatible with the culture of the Goths than was the Nicene version. It was a society in which hierarchy of social rank was not only very significant but also very much threatened by the influence of Rome. A creed that made a clear subordination of Son to Father and Holy Spirit to both would have been more acceptable than the highly abstract notions of equality and co-eternity of the Nicene Creed. Finally, the centralizing tendencies of the Nicene tradition would have further weakened the traditional structures of Gothic society, making Christianity into a more threatening, less inviting religious creed.

There is a certain amount of conjecture in all these arguments. However, it is certain that in 376, when the remaining Goths crossed the Danube seeking the safety of the Empire, they embraced Arian Christianity, which they retained until their disappearance as independent successor states during the Gothic Wars of the Emperor Justinian in the sixth century.

Near the end of Ulfilas's life, the Nicene faction regained control of the Imperial court, and the Arians found their position under attack. In 380, the emperor Theodosius the Great convened a synod at Constantinople, ostensibly to deal with the matter. Ulfilas was among those summoned; that he was personally summoned by the emperor attests to his continuing importance among the Arian bishops of the era. In any event, he went and even testified; before the council completed its work, however, he died, in 383.

SIGNIFICANCE

Ulfilas's position was ultimately rejected at the Synod of Constantinople, which, following the Second Ecumenical Council, condemned Arianism. Yet the Goths did gain the recognition that, in their churches at least, the people would be governed in accordance with the manner of their forebears. In effect, Goths would be free to pursue their own beliefs. In this way, an opportunity was created for Arianism to spread. In the decades following 395, when large numbers of Huns crossed the Danube into the Empire, Ulfilas's Arian Gauls with their Gothic Bibles were prepared to convert the Gothic newcomers, who now included not only the few remaining Visigoths but the Ostrogoths, Vandals, and Gepids as well. Arianism would be a force to be reckoned with for centuries to come.

Finally, Ulfilas's translation of the Bible has been of inestimable value to scholars interested in the languages and practices of the Gothic peoples of the late Empire. By comparing the Gothic words Ulfilas used to translate the biblical text to the original Greek, it is possible to gain insights into the social, political, and theological ideas of the Goths. Scholars frequently refer to Gothic words gleaned from the *Codex Argenteus* when describing the cultural and social structure of the early Goths. Without Ulfilas's work, scholars would know far less about them.

Ulfilas was on the losing side of the Trinitarian argument, and almost all that he himself wrote was destroyed. Yet he helped to make possible the first step in the absorption of the Gothic peoples into the West; moreover, through his translation of the Bible, he provided modern scholars with invaluable insights into the lives of peoples who, though long vanished as political and ethnic communities, continue to survive in their descendants among the populations of southern France, Spain, and Italy.

—*Terry R. Morris*

FURTHER READING

Böhmer, H. "Ulfilas." In *The New Schaff-Herzog Encyclopedia of Religious Knowledge*, edited by Macauley Jackson. Vol. 12. Grand Rapids, Mich.: Baker, 1949-1950. A lengthy article on Ulfilas as well as a helpful bibliography. A source useful in organizing the major events of Ulfilas's life.

Bradley, Henry. *The Story of the Goths: From the Earliest Times to the End of the Gothic Dominion in Spain*. New York: G. P. Putnam's Sons, 1888. Although dated in some respects, still useful for its discussion of Ulfilas's Gothic alphabet and his biblical translation.

Schaff, Philip, ed. *A Select Library of the Nicene and Post-Nicene Fathers of the Christian Church*. 1890-1907. Reprint. 14 vols. Grand Rapids, Mich.: W. R. Eerdmans, 1983. An English source for the works of Greek Church historians of Ulfilas and the Trinitarian controversy; however, they are all partisans of the Nicene position. Available in most college libraries.

Scott, Charles A. Anderson. *Ulfilas, Apostle of the Goths: Together with an Account of the Gothic Churches and Their Decline*. Cambridge: Macmillan and Bowers, 1885. An older work that seeks to do justice to the Arian Goths at the hands of earlier partisan Nicene Christian writers. The author presents Ulfilas as a "monument to the Goths." Checked against more recent sources, it is still quite valuable.

Sumruld, William A. *Augustine and the Arians: The Bishop of Hippo's Encounters with Ulfilan Arianism*. Cranbury, N.J.: Associated University Presses, 1994. Although the focus is on Saint Augustine and his debates with Maximinus, there is much attention paid to the influence of Ulfilas. See in particular chapter 2, "The Rise of Ulfilan Arianism."

Thompson, E. A. *Romans and Barbarians: The Decline of the Western Empire*. Madison: University of Wisconsin Press, 1982. Presents the story of the end of the Western Roman Empire from the vantage point of the Goths. While the work contains little information on Ulfilas, it provides valuable insights into the culture of his people.

_____. *The Visigoths in the Time of Ulfila*. Oxford, England: Clarendon Press, 1966. As much about the Visigoths as Ulfilas, this work provides valuable insights into the working of Visigothic society. Helps explain Ulfilas's work and significance among the Visigoths.

Wolfram, Herwig. *History of the Goths*. Translated by Thomas J. Dunlap. Berkeley: University of California Press, 1988. A comparatively recent source on Ulfilas and his place in Gothic history; also the most complete work on the Goths as a whole. Covers all the Gothic peoples from their shadowy beginnings to their catastrophic end in the sixth century Gothic Wars.

SEE ALSO: Theodosius the Great.
RELATED ARTICLES in *Great Events from History: The Ancient World*: c. 3d-4th century C.E., Huns Begin Migration West from Central Asia; 325 C.E., Adoption of the Nicene Creed; 380-392 C.E., Theodosius's Edicts Promote Christian Orthodoxy.

UR-NAMMU
Sumerian king (r. c. 2112-2095 B.C.E.)

Ur-Nammu advanced agriculture with an irrigation canal, reclaimed land, constructed the best-preserved ziggurat of the ancient world, recorded the first known law code, and reestablished Sumerian Ur as the dominant force of Mesopotamia.

BORN: Late twenty-second century B.C.E.; Ur, Sumer (now Muqaiyir, Iraq)
DIED: 2095 B.C.E.; in war with Gutium (now in Iraq)
ALSO KNOWN AS: Ur-Namma; Ur-Engur; Zur-Nammu
AREAS OF ACHIEVEMENT: Architecture, government and politics, law, war and conquest

EARLY LIFE

Before Ur-Nammu (oor NAH-mu), Third Dynasty regent of Ur and 120th king, monarchs of legendary stature people the Sumerian king list. Eight preceded the great flood, the first of whom, Alulim of Eridu, ruled for 28,800 years. After the flood, Jucar of Kish ruled for 1,200 years. Etana of Kish (fl. c. 2800 B.C.E.) is reasonably credited with uniting the city-states of Sumer. Gilgamesh (fl. c. 2600 B.C.E.), the fifth king of Uruk, is said to have ruled for 126 years. He is credited, in the epic preserved by Mesopotamians who succeeded the Sumerians, with being the son of the goddess Ninsun and visiting Utnapishtim, the Sumerian Noah, who was granted eternal life. Mec-ane-padda, first regent from Ur, is said to have ruled for 80 years. These claims bear comparison to longevity in Genesis.

Excavations prove the historicity of Sargon of Akkad, the 82d king, who conquered Sumer in the twenty-fourth century B.C.E., creating the first known empire, a polity composed of different peoples. His existence is in no way challenged by the fact that Utu-hejal of Uruk, the 119th king, is said to have ruled after the flood for 427 years. Seven years, six months is another estimate. As for the historicity of Ur-Nammu, the ziggurat he built for the moon god, Nanna (the word means "Full Moon"), still stands. Fragmentary hymns for and about Ur-Nammu are extant, and his legislation and wise political innovations are celebrated in clay and stone.

Little is known of Ur-Nammu's personal origin. His hymn to Enlil (god of the air, "Lord Wind") credits the god with choosing Ur-Nammu to be king "from the multitude." According to the hymn "To Nanna for Ur-Nammu," his mother was Ninsun. The goddess Ninsun—literally "Lady Wild Cow"—is associated with cattle and healthy offspring. In the elegy on "The Death of Ur-Nammu," on her son's demise "holy Ninsun" is said to have wept and cried, "'Oh My heart!'"

One can reconcile the two claims of origin by arguing that Ur-Nammu's mother was a venerated woman named after the goddess who wept yearly at a ritual celebrating the death of her son, the wild bull Dumuzi (not to be confused at the outset with the god Tammuz, also called Dumuzi, though later conflated with him). Perhaps the elegy simply associates, through their names and the shared weeping, Ur-Nammu's human mother and the divinity. Perhaps it conflates the two. Lady Wild Cow herself may have been thought to be Ur-Nammu's mother. After all, the moon god Nanna, Ur's patron divinity, whose symbol, the crescent, was sometimes represented as the horns of a bull, was also associated with cattle, bestowing fertility and increase on both herds and vegetation. "Ur-Namma C" ("A Praise Poem of Ur-Nammu") credits the king with saying, "After my seed had been poured into the holy womb, Suen [Sumerian for "crescent moon," an alternative appellation for Nanna that led to the god's Babylonian name, Sin], loving its appearance [envisioning its possibilities?], made it partake of Nanna's attractiveness." The poem concludes, "I am the creature of Nanna! I am the older brother of Gilgamec [Gilgamesh, who preceded Ur-Nammu by centuries]! I am the son borne by Ninsun, a princely seed! For me, kingship came down from heaven! Sweet is the praise of me, the shepherd Ur-Nammu!"

Beyond the speculation such claims engender, the biography is short: Ur-Nammu, son of Ninsun, was a brother of Uruk's king Utu-hegal, under whom he served as governor of Ur before replacing him as king. In the course of cementing alliances, Ur-Nammu married a woman of Mari who was identified as Taram-Uram ("She loves Ur"). The approximate dates of his reign are known but not the date of his birth.

LIFE'S WORK

How exactly Ur-Nammu rose from king Utu-hegal's governor of Ur to king himself is not known. By defeating Lagash, he managed to direct trade through his city, enriching its life with foreign contacts and its coffers through commerce. He reestablished Ur as capital and declared himself king of a united Sumer and Akkad, the fertile and civilized area that the Akkadian Sargon first consolidated. It had passed from the Akkadians into the hands of Ur-nijin of Uruk, only to be lost four generations later to the Gutians, reputed barbarians. Some twenty rulers later, the Gutians were themselves defeated, and under Ur-Nammu, Sumer rose to its last glorious ascendancy, characterized by artistic, economic, social, legal, and technological heights of remarkable character.

As ruler, in addition to overseeing such advances, Ur-Nammu was responsible for the relationship between the people and the city's deity, Nanna (whose crescent currently graces flags and mosques of the region). In that capacity, Ur-Nammu constructed the god's temple, the best-preserved ziggurat of the ancient world. The structure employs what ancient Greeks would rediscover and call entasis, the sophisticated use of a slight convexity that effects a more aesthetically pleasing form than straight lines would produce. The weight of the upper stories seems to be more lightly sustained because of the convexity of the structures below them. The effect serves a religious purpose as well. It produces an upward movement, an ascent toward the top of the ziggurat, where the temple, Nanna's dwelling place, is located. Among other things, Ur-Nammu also erected the ziggurat at Uruk.

During his reign, the Sumerians used columns, arches, vaults, and domes in the service of architecture, a panoply of structural possibilities that exceeds what the ancient Greeks would develop.

For Sumerians, the religious commitments of Ur-Nammu were as practical as his contributions to commerce, architecture, and agriculture. His service to the gods fulfilled the divinely established purpose of humanity as Sumerians understood it, submission to the yoke of service for which the gods created humankind. Indeed, that concept still dominates the region. The name of the religion of present-day occupants, Islam, means "submission to the will of God." By honoring the gods, Ur-Nammu effected positive results, a comfortable and secure life for his people. Nanna, satisfied, preserved and benefited his devotees.

In addition to serving the gods, Sumerian kings performed ritually as the god Tammuz, who died and was reborn each year. His sacred marriage to Inanna (represented by and embodied in the highest ranking priestess), assured a fruitful year. The effect of the ritual union of king/Tammuz and priestess/Inanna, like the construction of temples, was thought to be as practical and efficacious as Ur-Nammu's construction of roads for commerce or the canal that helped farmers water their crops and the dyke with which he managed to dry marshland so that it could be used for agriculture. The gods dug out the beds of the rivers Tigress and Euphrates, and—almost as remarkable—Ur Nammu created the canal and expanded the area of arable land. In fact, Ur-Nammu is said to have dug the canal "for Nanna." His service to the Sumerian divinities may well have been thought most crucial, because without the blessing of the gods humanity was considered utterly helpless. Even today, "God is great," people of the region aver, implicitly acknowledging the justice of God's will, whether they are experiencing good or ill. The divinity trumps all.

Yet another of Ur-Nammu's reputed accomplishments having to do with justice was his publication, some three hundred years before Babylonian Hammurabi, of the first known law code—"written in stone," literally, though it was recovered, badly damaged, in a clay copy. Some attribute the code to Shulgi, Ur-Nammu's son, but Ur-Nammu was credited with its creation by his near contemporaries. What remains of it is not so much a code, a reasoned set of laws, as a document that begins praising Ur-Nammu's leadership; protection of widows, orphans, and the poor; and punishment of the wicked. Using legal precedents in specific examples of crimes and punishments, it specifies the cost of various misdeeds, including adultery, personal injury, the mistreatment and escape of slaves, false testimony, and issues of farming. Though the code is not without its primitive elements—the validity of a charge of witchcraft is tested in trial by water, for example—Ur-Nammu had moved beyond eye-for-eye justice. Different payments in silver are exacted for various forms of physical injury.

In the service of equity and universal economic understanding, Ur-Nammu created weights and measures and divided his empire into clearly demarcated provinces in a land register that declared him to be acting on behalf of the god of each province. Naram-Sin (fl. 2291 B.C.E.), a descendant of Sargon, is credited with providing standardized weights and measures earlier, but the attribution to Ur-Nammu indicates his awareness of their utility. In part as a result of such objectively fixed, and therefore apparently fair, measurements, procedures, and boundaries, Ur-Nammu ushered in a period of economic, political, and social peace and prosperity that was enjoyed most during the reign of his son. The Sumerians considered Ur-Nammu the great lawgiver.

The constructive quality of Ur-Nammu's reign is celebrated in the elegy on his death. Ur-Nammu, who shepherded his subjects, is gone, and they are terrified. Betrayed by the gods, Ur-Nammu has been slain in battle. The streets are full of sorrow. He and his loyal soldiers proceed to the underworld. There he presents offerings to the seven gatekeepers. Replacing the underworld's bitter food with a sumptuous feast, he sacrifices the cattle he has brought along and presents each god of the underworld with the proper offering. To the extent possible in such a place, he creates a better existence even for the dead, and he is rewarded, becoming a judge in the underworld of status equal to Gilgamesh.

SIGNIFICANCE

Credited with supporting the worthy and defeating the wicked in this world as well as in the next, Ur-Nammu saw the value of clarity and specificity, ordering polities no less than individual lives. The creation of clear boundary lines between provinces contributed to pacific relations among neighbors. The boundaries in his code delineate acceptable and unacceptable social action. Those who lusted after the virgin slaves of others could temper their desires in the light of the stated consequences. Slaves who were considering flight could weigh their risks and options. The physically injured could not demand unreasonable recompense, and those who injured

them were required to pay a penalty. The code set limits and established relationships among people. Ur-Nammu thus lent moral choices a sort of physical substance. The progeny of Hammurabi's near contemporary, the biblical Abraham, who came from Ur, as well as Hammurabi himself, may have been influenced by Ur-Nammu's code.

Ur-Nammu's canal was a service both to his people (who benefited from more plentiful crops and better-fed animals) and the gods (who enjoyed more sumptuous offerings from those riches). The significance of Sumer for biblical exegesis, sometimes clear but inexplicable, cannot be exaggerated. The statue from Ur of the Sumerian Ram god in the Thicket, contemporary with Gilgamesh and housed in Iraq's national museum, strikes one as crucially related to the ram caught in a thicket that Abraham sacrifices in place of his son in the biblical book of Genesis. Ur-Nammu's constructions for the gods were thought to benefit his subjects practically, evoking divine blessings that would ease their lives. He was a king who took his office as a moral responsibility rather than a tool of self-aggrandizement. Aesthetic effects were perhaps outside the realm of his intentions, but those who praised him honored the aesthetic value of both his person and works. They declared him comely and a magnificent creator, one who had crafted a beautiful, secure, and just world for both the living and the dead.

—*Albert Wachtel*

FURTHER READING

Fluckiger-Hawker, Esther. *Urnamma of Ur in Sumerian Literary Tradition*. Fribourg, Switzerland: University Press, 1999. Contains transliteration, composite text, translation, photographs, and commentary.

Kramer, Samuel Noah. *The Sumerians: Their History, Culture, and Character*. Chicago: University of Chicago Press, 1963. An informed overview, beginning with archaeological discoveries and the decipherment of Sumerian and concluding with mythology and literature. Photographs of recovered treasures are included as illustrations.

Postgate, J. N. *Early Mesopotamia: Society and Economy at the Dawn of History*. New York: Routledge, 1992. A careful history, grounded in details of language and a thorough assessment of extant texts, including remarkable photographs.

Potts, D. T. *Mesopotamian Civilization: The Material Foundations*. Ithaca, N.Y.: Cornell University Press, 1997. This study moves from climate, geography, and natural resources to the foundations' uses for physical, cultural, and religious purposes. Includes excellent illustrations.

Sasson, Jack M. *Civilization of the Ancient Near East, I-IV.* New York: Scribner, 1995. A wide-ranging, comprehensive survey of the entire region.

SEE ALSO: Abraham; Enheduanna; Gudea; Hammurabi.
RELATED ARTICLES in *Great Events from History: The Ancient World*: c. 4000 B.C.E., Sumerian Civilization Begins in Mesopotamia; c. 3800 B.C.E., Cities and Civic Institutions Are Invented in Mesopotamia; c. 3100 B.C.E., Sumerians Invent Writing; c. 2334-c. 2279 B.C.E., Sargon of Akkad Establishes the Akkadian Dynasty; c. 2112 B.C.E., Ur-Nammu Establishes a Code of Law; c. 2000 B.C.E., Composition of the Gilgamesh Epic; c. 1770 B.C.E., Promulgation of Hammurabi's Code.

VALENTINUS
Roman philosopher and Gnostic

A second century religious genius, Valentinus synthesized concepts drawn from such disparate sources as Christian theology, rabbinic mysticism, Neopythagoreanism, Neoplatonism, Hellenistic mystery religions, and theosophy into an elaborate system of Gnostic thought that attracted large numbers of converts in the patristic period. His influence was so great that the patristic heresiologists singled him out as one of the most formidable enemies of orthodox Christianity.

BORN: Probably early second century C.E.; Lower Egypt
DIED: c. 165 C.E.; Cyprus or Rome (now in Italy)
AREAS OF ACHIEVEMENT: Religion, philosophy

EARLY LIFE
Very little is known of the early life of Valentinus (val-uhn-TI-nuhs), except that he probably was born in Lower Egypt and obtained a Greek education in Alexandria. During his stay in Alexandria, he became a Christian; according to Irenaeus and others, he was taught by Theodas, one of Apostle Paul's students.

Some authors have suggested that Gnosticism influenced Valentinus even during these early days in Alexandria and that Theodas himself may have preached a Christian gnosis. The Gnostic stress on salvation through a secret gnosis, or transcendental knowledge, must have appealed to Valentinus, whose teachings, to the extent that they can be reconstructed from the scattered information found in writings of the church fathers who came to oppose him (and perhaps also from the Nag Hammadi papyruses), reflect an exceptionally creative mind with a strong aesthetic bent.

LIFE'S WORK
Valentinus apparently taught in Alexandria before going to Rome during the bishopric of Hyginus (c. 136-c. 140). Tertullian states that Valentinus himself almost became bishop of Rome but withdrew in favor of a man who was later martyred (probably Pius I). In fact, Valentinus also withdrew from the Christian community, for he had become a Gnostic; soon, the Church branded him a heretic. Subsequently, Valentinus gained a considerable following—he probably established his own school—and he remained in Rome for another twenty years, after which he may have gone to Cyprus; it is possible that he stayed in Rome until his death after 160.

Valentinus's move into Gnosticism may have been the result of a desire to go beyond the exclusivist teachings of Christianity and to integrate Jesus Christ's teachings with contemporary Hellenistic philosophies. Valentinus's teaching was done in the form of sermons, hymns, and psalms, as well as more formally through writing and lecturing.

Valentinian Gnosticism evolved so rapidly that it is difficult to disentangle the original Valentinian teachings from those of his disciples. Still, the Nag Hammadi works, combined with the heresiologies of the patristic writers, make it possible to describe the outlines of the Valentinian system.

As its core, it had a mythical cosmogony, offered as an explanation of the human predicament. This cosmogony was structured around "aeons": Everything that exists is an emanation of a perfect, primordially existent aeon, which is the origin and source of being for all subsequent aeons. The term "aeon" in the Valentinian system suggests eternal existence (*aei on*, "always being"). This means that in terms of temporal sequence there is no difference between the One and its progeny. The difference between them is, instead, ontological: All subsequent aeons are less perfect outpourings of the One's substance. The One is also called Proarche (First Principle), Propator (Forefather), and Buthos (Primeval Depth). The One is beyond conceptualization and is the storehouse of all perfections. In Buthos there is no difference of gender; it contains all the qualities of masculinity and femininity without distinction.

According to its inscrutable purpose, Buthos brings into being a sequence of secondary aeons. Unlike Buthos, this chain of beings is differentiated into gender pairs, or syzygies, arranged according to ontological perfection (relative perfection of being). Of these fifteen pairs, which together constitute the Pleroma (Fullness or Completion), only the first four and the last have significance in the Valentinian exposition of the ontological corruption of the universe.

The first syzygy is somewhat problematic, since Buthos transcends the qualities of masculinity and femininity yet is paired with Sige (Silence). From this first syzygy emanate Nous (Understanding) and Aletheia (Truth). From their union are produced Logos (Word) and Zoe (Life), and from the union of Logos and Zoe are produced Anthropos (Man) and Ekklesia (Church). Together, these four pairs (or two tetrads) form the Ogdoad (the Eight), from which issue the remaining eleven syzygies and, indeed, all the rest of reality.

According to the Valentinians, disharmony was introduced into reality in the following way. Of all the aeons, it was Nous who was best proportioned to understand the One and who took the greatest pleasure in this contemplation. Nous, in the abundance of his generosity, wished to share his knowledge with the other aeons, and the aeons themselves demonstrated a willingness to seek out and become more directly acquainted with the primacy and fullness of the One. Yet Nous was restrained from prematurely sharing this knowledge, for it was the desire of Buthos to lead the aeons to this awareness gradually, through steady application that might prove their worthiness. Buthos also was aware that the aeons had different capacities and therefore would have to be brought to this knowledge at different rates. The knowledge of Buthos's purpose was passed down through the successive aeons, and all except the malcontent Sophia (Wisdom) acceded to his will.

Sophia's desire could not be satisfied by either her station or her mate, Theletos (Will). She craved knowledge

Valentinus. (Library of Congress)

beyond her capacity: She wanted to comprehend the perfect wisdom of the Forefather. In her desire to grasp supernatural perfection, Sophia abandoned her station and stretched herself heavenward, nearly losing her distinctive character by being reabsorbed into the plentitude of the One, against its will. Alarmed by the hubris of Sophia, Buthos, in conjunction with Nous, generated Horos (the principle of limitation), who is also called Savior, One-Who-Imposes-Limitation, One-Who-Brings-Back-After-Conflict, and Cross. Horos was generated by Buthos for the purpose of restraining Sophia and stripping her of her presumptuousness. This was accomplished when Horos separated her from her passion and *enthumesis* (esteem, glory) and rejoined the purged Sophia to Theletos, while casting her passion in the abyss outside the Pleroma.

After the rebelliousness of Sophia was cast out, Buthos and Nous gave rise to another syzygy designed to perfect and strengthen the Pleroma. This syzygy is that of Christ and the Holy Spirit. Christ was sent to the aeons as a teacher to instruct them in the purpose of Buthos, leading them to be satisfied with the knowledge they possess by convincing them that only Nous can comprehend the One in its perfection. The aeon Christ thus was sent as a mediator of consoling knowledge concerning their stations and purpose. The Holy Spirit's function was to lead the aeons to give thanks for the knowledge revealed by Christ. Through contrition and thankfulness they were all brought into harmony.

The work of Christ, however, was not yet complete. The *enthumesis* and passion of Sophia had been banished from the Pleroma to smolder, a chaotic, self-consuming power without form and without purpose. The aeon Christ, seeing her state, did not forsake her but instead took pity on her. He extended himself beyond the limit of the Pleroma and imposed a substantial form on her, to give her a definite nature; he withdrew, however, before providing transcendental wisdom. The dim reflection of Sophia was thus given character and definition as Achamoth (Hebrew for "wisdom"). The form Christ provided resulted in a regretful awareness of Achamoth's severance from the Pleroma and made her aspire to immortality with her limited intelligence. From the confusion of passions that boiled in Achamoth, the matter of the world issued, and from the desire to return to unity with the One, all souls (including that of the Demiurge) sprang into being.

From her own psychic substance, Achamoth formed the Demiurge, but she concealed herself from him. The Demiurge, not recognizing another greater than himself, deluded himself into believing that he was the only creator god, and he immediately began to make corporeal substances and to populate the realm below Horos with all manner of things. It is he who is responsible for the creation of the seven heavens and everything in or under them. All the while he was creating, however, he was unaware that Achamoth was working through him and was adding spiritual substances to the psychic beings (animals) he created. Humans are therefore composites of matter, psyche, and spirit, although the Demiurge is ignorant of their spiritual dimension.

Achamoth, feeling pity and responsibility for the spiritual beings she had generated, decided to bring them to knowledge of the aeons. To give this knowledge to the Demiurge and his creation, she imitated the production of the Christ aeon and contributed a spiritual substance to a body prepared by the Demiurge in ignorance. The resulting composite being was Jesus the Savior. Jesus' mission thus was primarily a ministry of teaching; his mission was to teach the gnosis of the aeonic hierarchy. His mission will be accomplished when all worthy creations below the Pleroma are brought to perfection in knowledge. Then Achamoth and her perfected children will ascend to places above the Horos. The Demiurge will ascend to the eighth heaven along with those beings of a purely psychic nature, and the purely corporeal humans will be consumed in a final conflagration.

From complicated cosmological speculations such as these, the Valentinians wove a fabric of doctrines that resembled Christianity but that were, in every instance, of a much higher speculative order. Like the traditional Christians, the Valentinians had a distinctive Christology. Whereas the former emphasized the sacrificial death of Jesus as the means of remission of sins, the Valentinians thought that the spirit of Jesus ascended before he could suffer, a belief consistent with their understanding of his aeonic mission of teaching.

Anthropologically, traditional Christianity interpreted all humans as being equally capable of finding salvation in Jesus, since he had died for all. The Valentinians, however, worked out a doctrine of election that in some ways anticipated Calvinist teachings. They believed that the salvation of a given individual depended on whether Achamoth had implanted a bit of spiritual substance, a seed of light, in that individual. Those who are spiritual have the potential (if not certainty) of achieving gnosis and thus being raptured and carried aloft to the Pleroma. The best that other humans may hope for is either a place in the eighth heaven or to be burned as garbage at the end of time.

Ecclesiologically, Valentinians construed the body of Gnostics on earth as a dim reflection of the aeon Ekklesia. Basing their speculation on certain passages in Saint Paul and on obscure rabbinic doctrines, they saw the syzygy of Anthropos and Ekklesia as the Platonic archetype of the relationship that eventually will exist between Achamoth and the pneumatics. In the final rapture, Achamoth will be conjoined to her seeds of light in the nuptial chamber of the Pleroma. At that point, symmetry will be restored to the chain of aeons and the universe will exist in harmony, with the lower syzygies mirroring their higher paradigms and beings of all levels finding perfect satisfaction.

On the basis of this rich and intricate mythology and its resultant theology, the Valentinians taught a form of Christian theosophy that gained large numbers of converts in the second and third centuries. Of all the forms of Gnosticism it attracted the most followers. How such a complicated and seemingly arbitrary religious cosmology could have inspired droves to seek this brand of salvation is puzzling, but there are a few features that most likely made it attractive.

First, it offered a kind of salvation that placed a premium on knowledge and de-emphasized the moral rigor that was typical of the Christianity of the period. This, no doubt, appealed to the classes that Gnosticism attracted: the plebeians and the intellectual elite, who had no strong political or religious alliances but rather identified with their plebeian followers.

Second, although the Valentinians shunned the sacramentalism of many of the other Christian sects, they apparently practiced rituals of purification and made use of hymns and prayers, all of which were designed to culminate in a powerful ecstatic experience in which the individual would achieve spiritual intercourse with Achamoth in her nuptial chamber. In this way, Valentinian Gnosticism offered an experience that at least rivaled the charismatic experiences of the more traditional Christian groups.

Finally, a large part of the appeal of Valentinian theosophy was that it was continuous with other religious phenomena of the time. In that turbulent period when religious curiosity ran rampant and when contact with magicians, astrologers, and itinerant preachers of wisdom was the norm, Valentinian theosophy offered a model of the universe that allowed for the retention of a magical worldview. Unlike traditional Christianity, which was extremely strict in its rejection of alien gods and magic, the Valentinian system was syncretistic. It allowed its adepts to move freely between its sphere of concepts and other systems of theosophy and magic.

SIGNIFICANCE

Valentinus had a very large following and probably was the most influential of the Gnostics. There is no doubt that his teaching affected orthodox Christianity. Many Christian theologians were forced to sharpen their rhetorical and theological skills as they undertook to refute the Valentinians, and, as they engaged in this dialogue, they began to formulate explicit orthodox Christian doctrines and creeds. Valentinus, as a representative of Gnosticism, spurred Christians toward the establishment of a canon of inspired Scriptures so that they might be able to avoid syncretism and heresy.

Valentinus was very much a man of the second century in his tendency toward religious syncretism, evidenced by his application of Neoplatonic and Neopythagorean concepts to Christian theology. Thus, Valentinus's thought was a representative form of the prototheology that produced and encouraged reasoned dialogues and debates in the early years of Christianity.

—*Thomas Ryba and Ruth van der Maas*

FURTHER READING

Jonas, Hans. *The Gnostic Religion: The Message of the Alien God and the Beginnings of Christianity.* 3d ed. Boston: Beacon Press, 1991. A classic (although somewhat dated) and thorough introduction to the nature of Gnosticism. Useful because it describes the Gnostic categories and discusses various Gnostic systems. Shows how Gnosticism is both an interruption and a continuation of classic Greek thought. Chapter 5 constitutes a helpful treatment of Valentinus's system. Thorough, multilanguage bibliography.

Lacarrière, Jacques. *The Gnostics.* Translated from the French by Nina Rootes. New York: E. P. Dutton, 1977. Phenomenological treatment of Gnosticism, but only partly successful since the author regards Gnostics as Promethean heroes rebelling against established religion, and his bias is evident throughout. Valuable as a lively interpretation of the Gnostic mind-set. Chapter 6 deals with Valentinus in some detail. Contains a somewhat quirky bibliography.

Lampe, Peter. *From Paul to Valentinus: Christians at Rome in the First Two Centuries.* A pathbreaking examination of the earliest Christian churches in Rome from historical, theological, archaeological, and sociological perspectives.

Pagels, Elaine. *The Gnostic Gospels.* New York: Random House, 1989. Popular treatment, readable and interesting, but unsystematic. The feminist views of the author are evident. Tends to discuss the individualism of Gnostics in a manner inappropriate to the period and to impose twentieth century values on the second century. Valentinus is treated throughout rather than in a separate chapter. No bibliography.

Perkins, Pheme. *The Gnostic Dialogue: The Early Church and the Crisis of Gnosticism.* New York: Paulist Press, 1980. In part a response and corrective to some extremes in Pagels's work, this is a scholarly attempt to contextualize Gnosticism in setting of particular scriptural traditions, with research based on texts. Investigates Gnosticism in dialogue with Christianity and other religions. Valentinus is treated throughout. Good selected multilanguage bibliography; especially helpful are the references to the Nag Hammadi, the New Testament, and patristic sources.

Robinson, James M., ed. *The Coptic Gnostic Library: A Complete Edition of the Nag Hammadi Codices.* Boston: Brill Academic, 2000. A revealing collection of Gnostic scriptures available in English translation. Particularly useful because it contains fragments of second century treatises of probable or certain Gnostic origin such as the *Gospel of Truth*, the *Treatise on Resurrection*, the *Tripartite Tractate*, the *Apocalypse of Paul, A Valentinian Exposition, On the Anointing, On Baptism,* and *On the Eucharist.*

Rudolph, Kurt. *Gnosis: The Nature and History of Gnosticism.* Edited and translated by Robert McLachlan Wilson. San Francisco: Harper and Row, 1983. A comprehensive treatment by a specialist in Mandaean religion. Valentinus is cited frequently throughout, and the treatment of the Valentinian system is extensive. Extremely sensitive to all sources in all their complexity, though some Marxist bias is evident. Illustrations, photographs, maps, chronological table, and a multilanguage bibliography of original texts and secondary sources.

Williams, Jacqueline A. *Biblical Interpretation in the Gnostic Gospel of Truth from Nag Hammadi.* Atlanta: Scholars Press, 1988. Williams sheds light on Valentinus's impact on religious thought through a close examination of his use of allusion in the Gospel of Truth. A scholarly work based on Williams's doctoral dissertation.

SEE ALSO: Jesus; Plotinus; Pythagoras; Tertullian.

RELATED ARTICLES in *Great Events from History: The Ancient World*: c. 50-c. 150 C.E., Compilation of the New Testament; 200 C.E., Christian Apologists Develop Concept of Theology.

VĀLMĪKI
Indian sage poet

Vālmīki composed the first epic poem of India, a work describing the life of Prince Rāma.

FLOURISHED: c. 500 B.C.E.; Ayodhya?, India
AREA OF ACHIEVEMENT: Literature

EARLY LIFE

The historicity of Vālmīki (val-MEE-kee) is somewhat uncertain because the traditions referring to him are late and unsupported by anything other than still later texts repeating, modifying, or elaborating on the stories. Though the *Rāmāyaṇa* (c. 550 B.C.E.; English translation, 1870-1889) does not contain any information on Vālmīki's early life, we know from the Purāṇas, the *Mahābhārata* (400 B.C.E.-400 C.E., present form by c. 400 C.E.; *The Mahabharata of Krishna-Dwaipayana Vyasa*, 1887-1896), and the seventh book of the *Rāmāyaṇa* itself that he was born in the lineage of the Vedic savant Mahariśi Bhrigu. As Vālmīki is often mentioned with his patronymic Prachetasa, it is reasonable to speculate that his father's name was Prachetas.

In the first book of the *Rāmāyaṇa* (*Bāla-kāṇḍa*), which was a later interpolation, Vālmīki is introduced as a gifted saint who lived with his gifted pupils, such as the sage Bharadwaja, in a hermitage in the valley of the river Tamasa. The *Adhyātma Rāmāyaṇa* (esoteric *Rāmāyaṇa*), an anonymous work in Sanskrit, composed probably in the fifteenth century, describes him as a Brahman youth who associated with brigands and burglars and took to a violent life of an outlaw even as a married man with a family of his own. According to popular tradition, this wayward youth, named Ratnakara, was the tenth son of Varuṇa, one of the eight guardian deities of the quarters. When, in the course of one of his escapades, he overpowered seven sages, his victims reminded him that his sins incurred on account of his violent and lawless habits would not be shared by his family. He found this admonition to be right on the mark when in fact his wife and children refused to share his sins. Panicking, the hapless highwayman rushed to the hermits for spiritual help. They taught him the Vedas and counseled him to utter the name of Rāma even if it be in reverse order, Mara. Thereupon the penitent reprobate began chanting Rāma's name oblivious of time; gradually his body was covered under an anthill (*vālmīka*).

LIFE'S WORK

Years later, the sages rescued him from the anthill and the

reformed bandit came to be known as the sage Vālmīki. He built a hermitage on the bank of the River Tamasa (some miles south of Ayodhyā in north central India) and acquired disciples. The seventh book of the *Rāmāyaṇa* relates that one day, finishing his ritual bath in the Tamasa, Vālmīki saw a hunter shoot down a bird in the midst of its mating. Upset by the violent killing, the sage burst forth into a curse for the cruel archer expressed in a musical verse composed in the *anuṣṭubh* meter (a thirty-two-syllable stanza constructed in four quarters of eight syllables each).

> No fame be thine for endless time,
> Because, base outcast, of thy crime,
> When cruel hand was fain to slay
> One of this gentle pair at play.

Returning to his cottage, the saint brooded until he had a vision of the god Brahma appearing before him and advising him to write the lore of Rāma, the king of Ayodhyā.

The *Rāmāyaṇa*, consisting of some fifty thousand lines, is divided into seven books or parts (*kāṇḍas*): *Bāla-kāṇḍa* ("the book of childhood," describing the childhood and adolescence of Rāma), *Ayodhyākāṇḍa* ("the book of Ayodhyā," depicting the court of King Daśaratha and the scenes of Daśaratha's exchanges with his second queen Kaikeyī leading to the exile of Rāma in the forest of Daṇḍka), *Aranyakāṇḍa* ("the book of the forest," describing life in the forest and the abduction of Sītā by Rāvaṇa), *Kiśkindhākāṇḍa* ("the book of Kiśkindhā," describing Rāma's residence in Kiśkindhyā, his quest for Sītā, and his murder of Vālin, the monkey warrior), *Sundarakāṇḍa* ("the book of beauty," describing the beautiful terrains over which Rāma roamed in search of his abducted wife, the arrival of Rāma and his simian allies in Laṅkā, and Rāvaṇa's kingdom), *Yuddhakāṇḍa* (also known as *Laṅkākāṇḍa*, "the book of battle," describing Rāvaṇa's defeat, Sītā's release, and Rāma's return to Ayodhyā and his coronation), and the *Uttarakāṇḍa* ("the last book," detailing Rāma's life in Ayodhyā, Sītā's banishment, the birth of Lava and Kuśa, the reconciliation between Rāma and Sītā, Sītā's death or entry into the earth, and Rāma's suicide or ascent into heaven).

Rāma is the eldest son of King Daśaratha of Ayodhyā through his first wife, Kauśalyā. Though he is the legal heir to the throne, his father's other queen, Kaikeyī, contrives to have the heir apparent sent into exile for fourteen years and have her own son, Bharata, installed as king. Though Bharata is not a party to the plot—he in fact is a very loyal and respectful elder brother—Rama decides to defer to his stepmother's wishes and proceeds to the forest, accompanied by his wife Sītā and his brother Lakṣmaṇa, who is one of the two sons of Daśaratha's third queen, Sumitrā. In the forest, the royal youths encounter numerous adventures, but it is the abduction of Sītā by Rāvaṇa, the powerful demon-king of Laṅkā, which sets the stage for the titanic battle between Rāma and Rāvaṇa. In his enterprise to find Sītā's whereabouts, Rāma enlists the services of Hanumān, the powerful and resourceful monkey hero, who becomes the prince's factotum. Eventually Rāvaṇa is killed in battle, his traitorous brother Vibhīsana is installed on the throne of Laṅkā, and Rāma has Sītā undergo a fire ordeal to prove her chastity because she lived in another man's house; he returns to Ayodhyā triumphantly with his wife and brother.

The seventh book of the *Rāmāyaṇa* concerns the final years of Rāma and his family. After great adversity and adventure, Rāma begins his peaceful regime that has been celebrated in folklore as the righteous rule of Rāma, *Rāmarājya*. Yet Rāma's (actually Sītā's) tribulations are far from over. King Rāma is upset at ugly rumors of his wife's infidelity, her successful ordeal by fire notwithstanding. To maintain the honor of his kingship, Rāma banishes the pregnant queen even though he is personally convinced that the rumor is unfounded. After some years full of minor adventures, Rāma performs the horse sacrifice (*aśvamedha*), during which two young bards led by an old sage appear and recite the *Rāmāyaṇa*. The two boys are in fact Rāma's twin sons Lava and Kuśa, born during their mother's exile, and the sage turns out to be none other than the poet Vālmīki himself. Now Rāma realizes his hasty and unfair decision to succumb to canards and hastens to get Sītā back. However, Sītā finds her situation increasingly unbearable and invokes Earth, her mother, to receive her back into her folds. The ground opens and Sītā enters into the cavity, never to come out. Stung by remorse, Rāma abdicates his throne, divides the kingdom between his sons, and commits suicide by drowning in the waters of the Sarayu River (modern-day Ghāghara River) near the city of Kosala.

The original, or the *Vālmīki*, *Rāmāyaṇa* comprised only five books, from the *Ayodhyākāṇḍa* through the *Yuddhakāṇḍa*, according to Hermann Jacobi, one of the pioneers in critical *Rāmāyaṇa* scholarship. The first and last books were later interpolations or additions. This epic poem inspired generations of Sanskrit poets, some

of the most prominent of whom are Bhāsa, Bhavabhūti, and Kālidāsa. Even the Buddhist *Daśaratha Jātaka* and and the Jain poet Vimalasūri's *Paumacariyam* repeated the story of Rāma in their own ways, but following the basic structure of Vālmīki's narrative.

From the eleventh century C.E., the story of *Rāmāyaṇa* came to be written in various vernacular languages of India: in Kannada by Nāgacandra in the eleventh century C.E., in Tamil by Kampaṇ in the twelfth century, in Telegu by Ranganātha in the fourteenth century, in Bengali by Kṛttibasa Ojhā in the fifteenth century, in Hindi by Tulsīdās in the sixteenth century, and in Sikh or Gurmukhi by Guru Govind Singh in the seventeenth century. Additionally there are five proto-*Rāmāyaṇa*s: the *Ānanda Rāmāyaṇa*, the *Vashinstha Rāmāyaṇa*, the *Mula Rāmāyaṇa* (highlighting the glory of Hanumān), the *Adhyātma Rāmāyaṇa* mentioned earlier, and the *Adbhuta Rāmāyaṇa*, often dubbed the *Adbhutottarakāṇḍa*, an eighth *kāṇḍa* of the *Vālmīki Rāmāyaṇa*—a mixture of Vaishnava and Śakta religious perspectives, based in part on the great Śakta treatise the *Devi-Mahatmya*. The *Adbhuta Rāmāyaṇa* privileges Sītā as the incarnation of the ferocious Shakti, who annihilates Rāvaṇa. It has 1,353 verses in the form of a dialogue between Vālmīki and Bhāradwāja and is believed to have been composed sometime after the fifteenth century.

Historians and Sanskritists differ on the historicity of the *Rāmāyaṇa* story. Though a few experts believe that Rāma ruled about 1600 B.C.E., most scholars tend to push the date of the composition of the original epic (books 2 thru 6) somewhere between the eighth and the third century B.C.E. Some even maintain that the first part of the *Rāmāyaṇa*—extending up to Rāma's exile and his refusal to return and accept the crown of Ayodhyā at his brother Bharata's entreaties—has a historical basis, whereas the second part, consisting of Sītā's abduction by Rāvaṇa, Rāma's battle with the abductor, and his recovery of Sītā, may be an allegorical reading of a Vedic myth. Still others believe that Rāma's story as narrated by Vālmīki was intended to represent allegorically the first attempt of the Aryans of north India to conquer the south. Several scholars assume that Vālmīki drew his inspiration from some now-lost body of ballads or legends about heroism and self-sacrifice.

SIGNIFICANCE

The *Rāmāyaṇa* is arguably one of the finest works of Sanskrit poetry in respect of both contents and form. The beautiful and elegant descriptions of nature, flora, and fauna exhibit the artistry of the poet. His theme of the struggles among *annyaya* (injustice), *darpa* (arrogance), *moha* (infatuation), *dharma* (righteousness), and *nyaya* (justice) has formed the cornerstone of the Hindu world-view. In spite of references to numerous magical and ana-gogical episodes, Vālmīki remains one of the earliest authors of the Hindu morality tale. His significance was dramatically and eloquently expressed by the German poet Friedrich Ruckert (1788-1866), who, comparing the *Rāmayaṇa* with Homer's *Iliad* (c. 750 B.C.E.; English translation, 1611), wrote:

Such fantastic grimaces and such formless fermenting verbiage
As *Rāmāyaṇa* offers thee, that has Homer
Certainly taught thee to despise; but yet such lofty thoughts
And such deep feeling the *Iliad* does not show thee.

—*Narasingha P. Sil*

FURTHER READING

Blank, Jonah. *Arrow of the Blue-Skinned God: Tracing the Ramayana Through India*. New York: Grove, 2000. A journalist travels India, visiting places mentioned in the *Rāmāyaṇa* as a meditation on the state of modern India.

Brockington, J. L. *Epic Threads: John Brockington on the Sanskrit Epics*. New York: Oxford University Press, 2001. A collection of essays on specialized aspects of the *Rāmāyaṇa*, such as linguistic features and style, formulaic expression and proverbs, manuscript studies, and religion, by a renowned scholar.

Griffith, Ralph T. H., trans. *The Rāmāyaṇa of Vālmīki*.

1915. Reprint. Yucaipa, Calif.: Light Mission Publishing, 2003. An elegant translation in rhymed verse.

Richman, Paula, ed. *Questioning Rāmāyaṇas: A South Asian Tradition*. Berkeley: University of California Press, 2001. Scholarly discourse on the various proto-*Rāmāyaṇas*.

Sankalia, H. D. *The Rāmāyaṇa in Historical Perpective*. Delhi: Macmillan India Limited, 1982. A solid scholarly study by a noted expert.

Smith, H. Daniel, comp. *Select Bibliography of Rāmāyaṇa-Related Studies*. Bombay: Ananthacharya Indological Research Institute, 1989. Extremely helpful research tool for *Rāmāyaṇa* scholars.

Vālmīki. *The Rāmāyaṇa of Vālmīki*. Edited and translated by Robert P. Goldman et al. 5 vols. Princeton, N.J.: Princeton University Press, 1984-1996. A magisterial translation with superb scholarly glosses.

SEE ALSO: Aśvaghosa; Euripides; Hesiod; Homer; Kālidāsa; Sophocles; Vergil.

RELATED ARTICLES in *Great Events from History: The Ancient World*: 1500-1100 B.C.E., Compilation of the Vedas; c. 1000-c. 200 B.C.E., Compilation of the Upaniṣads; c. 550 B.C.E., Vālmīki Composes the *Rāmāyaṇa*; c. 400 B.C.E.-400 C.E., Composition of the *Mahābhārata*; c. 200 B.C.E., Birth of Hinduism; c. 200 B.C.E.-200 C.E., *Bhagavad Gita* Is Created; 5th or 6th century C.E., First Major Text on Hinduism's Great Goddess Is Compiled; c. 400 C.E., Kālidāsa Composes Sanskrit Poetry and Plays.

VARDHAMĀNA
Indian religious leader

By the example of his ascetic life and his charismatic leadership, Vardhamāna revived and systematized the religious tradition of Jainism.

BORN: c. 599 B.C.E.; Kundagrama, Bihar, Magadha (now in India)

DIED: 527 B.C.E.; Pavapuri, Bihar, Magadha (now in India)

ALSO KNOWN AS: Mahāvīra; Nigantha Nātaputra; Jina; Sanmati

AREA OF ACHIEVEMENT: Religion

EARLY LIFE

While the two sects of the Jains (Digambara and Svetambara) have differing traditions regarding the life of Var-

dhamāna (var-duh-MAN-uh) they are in agreement on the most essential features. Vardhamāna was born to Siddhārtha, chieftain of a warrior (Kṣatriya) clan, whose wife Trishalā was the sister of the king of Vaiśālī. Vardhamāna's conception was foretold to his mother in a series of dreams that are often described in Jain literature and represented artistically. About his youth virtually nothing is recorded, but probably he was trained in archery, horsemanship, and writing, as were other princes of his era. The two Jain sects disagree regarding one point concerning his adult life, the Svetambaras saying that Vardhamāna married and fathered one daughter, while the Digambaras say that he neither married nor had offspring.

By the age of thirty, Vardhamāna's parents had died. With the consent of his elder brother, he decided to abandon his royal position and become a wandering ascetic. He distributed his possessions, plucked out his hair, and renounced the life of the householder to pursue enlightenment. The most significant disagreement between the two sects of Jainism is highlighted by this incident in Vardhamāna's life, known as the Great Renunciation. Digambara ("sky-clad") Jains depict Vardhamāna as renouncing clothing as well as other possessions, choosing to remain nude and requiring this practice of his followers when they renounced the world. Svetambara ("white-clad") Jains depict Vardhamāna as wearing a single white cloth for thirteen months after the Great Renunciation, at which time he adopted nudity but did not require it of his followers after their renunciation. This difference in monastic practice has kept the two sects separate since about 300 B.C.E.

LIFE'S WORK

In the era in which Vardhamāna lived, dissatisfaction was growing with the then dominant religious tradition of Brahmanism, which was based on performance of sacrificial rituals and recitation of the sacred words of the Vedas. Asceticism—including endurance of hunger, thirst, pain, exposure to the elements, and celibacy—was an alternative way of being religious, by means of which individuals sought to accumulate power. It was widely believed that the actions (karma) of one's life would cause one to be reincarnated but that the power accumulated through asceticism could enable one to destroy one's karma and escape the otherwise endless cycle of rebirth.

Like a number of his contemporaries (such as the Buddha and ascetics of the Brahmanic Upaniṣads), Vardhamāna left his family to live as a homeless wanderer in the hope of escaping rebirth. For twelve years, subjecting himself to great hardship, including extended fasts, and engaging in deep meditation on the nature of the self, Vardhamāna single-mindedly persevered. Finally, after a fast of two and a half days during which he meditated continuously, he attained enlightenment accompanied by omniscience and was freed from the bondage of his karma. According to the scriptures, following his enlightenment Vardhamāna taught large assemblies of listeners and organized the community of monks, nuns, laymen, and laywomen. He was acclaimed as Mahāvīra (Great Hero), a title by which he is best known.

Vardhamāna Mahāvīra taught others the means of attaining what he had attained. The ultimate objective was

and is escape from the cycle of rebirth, with its suffering a result of the inevitability of disease, old age, and death. The infinite bliss of the cessation of such suffering was not to be attained by following the path of enjoyment of pleasures but by forsaking the finite pleasures and performing rigorous austerities. Restraint of body, speech, and mind and the performance of ascetic practices will destroy the effects of one's karma, thereby freeing one from rebirth.

In Vardhamāna's view, karma is a material substance that becomes attached to one's soul as a result of actions performed; Jainism is unique in its assertion of the material nature of karma. The souls of individuals who are subject to the passions (desire and hatred) will be further defiled by the adherence of karmic material, while the souls of those few individuals who are free from the passions will not be affected at all; karma will not adhere to such a soul.

Absolutely necessary to the successful escape from rebirth is the avoidance of causing injury to living beings, a practice known as *ahiṃsā*. As a consequence of this strongly held belief, Jains are strict vegetarians. For the same reason, they have traditionally avoided occupations involving injury to living beings, including farming, and have instead often engaged in commerce. Avoidance of injury to life in all of its forms is the first vow of the Jains, ascetics and lay followers alike.

The path of the devout layman or laywoman differs from that of the monk or nun only in the extent to which ascetic self-denial is practiced. For the lay follower, eleven stages of spiritual progress are prescribed by which one is purified and prepares oneself for the ascetic life of the monk or nun. By passing through all eleven stages, the lay follower demonstrates that he or she has overcome the passions and is ready to become a monk or nun. As a result of the severity of the rules of conduct for the Jain lay follower, relatively few individuals in reality are willing or able to adhere to this ideal. Most lay followers support the monks and nuns through donations.

All Jains regard Vardhamāna Mahāvīra as the twenty-fourth and last Jina (conqueror) or *tīrthaṅkara* (ford-maker) to have lived and taught in this world. His immediate predecessor, Parsva, apparently lived in Benares, India, in the ninth century B.C.E.; Western scholars, however, regard the other twenty-two saintly teachers in the Jain tradition as figures of myth rather than history. The parents of Vardhamāna are described as followers of Parsva's doctrine, and there are clear references in Buddhist scriptures to the existence of an established order of

Jain ascetics. This information suggests the existence of a Jain community composed of ascetics and lay followers, a community older than that of the Buddhists and predating Vardhamāna himself. Vardhamāna's teachings are presented as eternal truths and the same path as has been taught by all the Jinas. Thus, Vardhamāna's contribution was the reviving and reactualization of this ancient tradition. As one who has "crossed over" the ocean of suffering and reached the other side, Vardhamāna has demonstrated the efficacy of the spiritual discipline of the Jinas.

At the age of about seventy-two, Vardhamāna died. Although the Jain scriptures repeatedly state that he was a human being, lay followers often have regarded him as superhuman and endowed with marvelous attributes. The exemplary life of Vardhamāna Mahāvīra has greatly influenced the Jain community, which continues to revere his memory.

SIGNIFICANCE

Vardhamāna Mahāvīra was both a very able organizer and a thinker of striking originality. The social organization of Jain monks and nuns may well have been the world's first monastic orders. Thanks to the support of some Indian rulers and sympathetic lay followers, the monastic orders have been able to follow the example of Vardhamāna Mahāvīra for twenty-five centuries. Vardhamāna was one of the first to oppose the Brahmanic orthodoxy, a tradition of sacrificial ritual that was dominated by priests and aristocrats. In its place he offered a systematic explanation of the laws of the universe and humanity's place within it. Vardhamāna's teachings presented to everyone the possibility of attaining the ultimate state, whether female or male, regardless of social class.

The Jain insistence on *ahiṁsā*, refraining from injuring living beings, has influenced the whole of India and even some who are unfamiliar with Jainism. Vegetarianism, uncommon in India during Vardhamāna's lifetime, is now a way of life for many Hindus, and Jainism's uncompromising position is in part responsible for this change. The leader of India's independence movement in the first half of the twentieth century, Mahatma Gandhi, was profoundly influenced by a Jain layman named Raychandbhai Mehta, with whom he corresponded. He helped Gandhi realize the power of nonviolence, and Gandhi began to use nonviolent civil disobedience as a political weapon, agitating for India's independence from the British Empire. A generation later, Martin Luther King, Jr., with Gandhi as his inspiration, led similar nonviolent protests for civil rights in the United States. Vardhamāna's teachings, whether regarded as the ancient doctrine of all the Jinas or as his own unique contribution, are the core of a still-vital religious tradition.

—*Bruce M. Sullivan*

FURTHER READING

Dundas, Paul. *The Jains*. New York: Routledge, 2002. A scholarly introduction and overview from a Western perspective. Looks at Jainism in its social and doctrinal context; discusses its history, sects, scriptures, and ritual; and describes how the Jains have defined themselves as a unique religious community.

Jacobi, Hermann, trans. *Jaina Sutras*. 1884-1895. Reprint. New York: Taylor and Francis, 2001. A fine translation of selected scriptures of the Jain religious tradition, with an introduction by the translator that includes a brief treatment of the life of Vardhamāna. Volume 22 in the series contains Jain scriptures on the life of Vardhamāna, and volume 44 contains his teachings.

Jain, Kailash Chand. *Lord Mahavira and His Times*. 2d ed. New Delhi: Motilal Banarsidass, 1992. A biography of Vardhamāna and analysis of Jain religion.

Jaini, Padmanabh S. *The Jaina Path of Purification*. Berkeley: University of California Press, 1979. An excellent treatment of the Jain religious tradition, both ancient and modern, including the life of Vardhamāna. Includes an extensive bibliography, illustrations, and thirty-two photographs.

Schubring, Walther. *The Doctrine of the Jainas, Described After the Old Sources*. Translated by Wolfgang Beurlen. Rev. ed. 1962. Reprint. New Delhi: Motilal Banarsidass, 2000. A clear and concise presentation of Vardhamāna's teachings and the subsequent Jain scholastic traditions on cosmology, ethics, rebirth, and related topics.

SEE ALSO: Ānanda; Asaṅga; Aśoka; Aśvaghosa; Bodhidharma; Buddha; Chandragupta Maurya; Gośāla Maskarīputra; Kanishka; Vasubandhu; Vattagamani.
RELATED ARTICLES in *Great Events from History: The Ancient World*: 1500-1100 B.C.E., Compilation of the Vedas; c. 1000-c. 200 B.C.E., Compilation of the Upaniṣads; 6th or 5th century B.C.E., Birth of Buddhism; 527 B.C.E., Death of Vardhamāna, Founder of Jainism; c. 467 B.C.E., Gośāla Maskarīputra, Founder of Ājīvika Sect, Dies; c. 321 B.C.E., Mauryan Empire Rises in India; c. 200 B.C.E., Birth of Hinduism; c. 200 B.C.E.-200 C.E., *Bhagavad Gita* Is Created.

MARCUS TERENTIUS VARRO
Roman scholar

Varro contributed to every field of abstract and practical knowledge extant in his day, established the worthiness of intellectual pursuits such as linguistic study and encyclopedism, and left a body of knowledge that, directly or indirectly, has informed and influenced writers and scholars ever since.

BORN: 116 B.C.E.; Reate, near Rome (now Rieti, Italy)
DIED: 27 B.C.E.; Rome (now in Italy)
ALSO KNOWN AS: Marcus Terentius Varro Reatinus
AREA OF ACHIEVEMENT: Scholarship

EARLY LIFE

Marcus Terentius Varro (VAHR-oh) was sometimes called Marcus Terentius Varro Reatinus because he was born in Reate, in the Sabine region of modern Italy. His family, which owned vast estates there, was considered to be of equestrian, or knightly, rank, although certain ancestors had attained noble rank by holding office in the senate. Varro's parents had the means to obtain for him the best education available at the time. This included a long sojourn in the capital, where he studied under the Stoic Stilo Praeconinus (who taught Cicero ten years later) and afterward a period in Athens, during which he studied philosophy with Antiochus of Ascalon, the academic. Stilo Praeconinus, the first Roman grammarian and philologist, was also a learned historian of Roman antiquity, and under his tutelage Varro soon showed an extraordinary aptitude for these pursuits.

LIFE'S WORK

As a gifted scholar, Varro could have kept himself apart from public life had he so chosen. Until he was nearly seventy, however, he remained deeply involved in both politics and the military. To people of his own era, this was not contradictory, for few of Varro's contemporaries were inclined to draw a strict boundary between intellectual and public life. Julius Caesar, during his march through the Alps to Gaul, composed a treatise on Latin grammatical inflections that he dedicated to Cicero. Indeed, political leaders such as Cicero and Caesar spent many adult years studying philosophy and ancient history, trying to draw lessons that would help them govern justly and wisely.

Varro's political and military career was closely allied with that of Pompey the Great. In 76 B.C.E. he served under Pompey in a military campaign against the rebel Quintus Sertorius in Spain. Afterward, Varro entered public office, serving first as tribune (a magistrate of the people with veto power over senate actions), then as *curule aedile* (roughly, superintendent of public works), and finally as praetor, or judicial officer. In 67, he held a naval command under Pompey in the war against the Cilician pirates, who, for a time, had virtually controlled the Mediterranean Sea. From 66 to 63 Varro served, again under Pompey, in the third war against Mithradates the Great, king of Pontus. From 52 to 48, during the civil war between Pompey and Caesar, Varro commanded two legions for Pompey in Spain. On August 2, 48, two other Pompeian commanders in Spain capitulated to Caesar, and Varro, probably under pressure from his soldiers, was forced to follow suit. Afterward, like Cicero and Cato the Younger, he went to Dyrrachium, a sort of neutral corner, to await the outcome of the Battle of Pharsalus, which decided the entire conflict in Caesar's favor.

Varro and Caesar had remained on friendly terms during even the bitterest conflict between Caesar and Pompey. In 48 Pompey was murdered by agents of the Egyptian king, and the following year the victorious Caesar pardoned Varro and restored to him lands that had been seized by Marc Antony. Caesar also appointed Varro head of the great public library that was then being planned. Thus began the period of the works and accomplishments for which Varro is best remembered and which earned for him the title (bestowed by Quintilian in the first century C.E.) of "the most learned of Romans."

A profile of Varro, bearded and wearing a woolen, Greek-style cap, appears on an ancient coin now housed in the Museo Nazionale Romano. Most Roman men did not grow beards, although Greek men did, and Varro may have worn one along with the cap as a sign of his intellectual vocation, which was commonly associated with Greece rather than with Rome. Alternatively, regardless of Varro's actual appearance, the designer of the coin may have simply portrayed him in this fashion for symbolic purposes.

Varro is remembered, among many other reasons, for compiling in Rome what was to be the first library for public use. He concentrated on three types of prose works: the writings of the antiquarians, treatises by grammarians and philologists (by this time Stilo Praeconinus's new disciplines had come into their own), and works on practical subjects such as husbandry and domestic economy. His collection served as a kind of stylistic barometer for the times: The Ciceronian style dominated the prose of theoretical works, especially in philosophy, rhetoric, and history, while the sparser, more direct expression of Cato the Censor set the standard for practical treatises. In addition to Latin works in these genres, Varro acquired for his collection many volumes in Greek.

Although he seems generally to have ignored poetry (which was then in temporary eclipse), he is credited with establishing the canon of dramatic verse certifiably written by Plautus—some twenty-one plays, constituting what is called the *Fabulae Varronianae*—and, according to Aulus Gellius, Varro also wrote literary and dramatic criticism of Plautus.

Varro's unprecedented collection of books for public use proved of enormous benefit to contemporary scholars. As Rome passed from a republican to an Imperial form of government, interest in Roman antiquity grew rapidly, and there developed a new fraternity of researchers and historians who made whatever use they could of the early records and works by the pioneering annalists of Rome. Before the formation of Varro's public library—as in Great Britain and the United States at comparable periods of their development—a literary worker had to depend on the generosity of private library owners for a look at such rare works and records.

Though he now was devoted to the pursuits of scholarship and librarianship that were his forte, Varro had one remaining practical challenge to face. In 47, nearly seventy years old, he had retired altogether from political life when he accepted Caesar's appointment as librarian. Nevertheless, after Caesar was assassinated in 44 B.C.E. and Octavian, Marc Antony, and Marcus Aemilius Lepidus formed the Second Triumvirate, Antony declared Varro an enemy of the state and had him proscribed, that is, banished from the vicinity of Rome. Varro's home near the capital was destroyed, as was his private library, containing not only thousands of works by other writers but also many of the hundreds of volumes he himself had written up to his seventy-third year, when he was banished. If not for the proscription, with its destructive aftermath—an all-too-common occurrence in that period of Roman history—more might be known about the exact contents of the famous public library, for which Varro probably had earmarked many volumes in his private collection. Undoubtedly, too, many more of Varro's works would have survived down to the present day.

Indeed, Varro nearly lost his life during Antony's proscription—the same proscription that actually did lead to the death of Cicero in 43 B.C.E. Yet with the help of friends, led by Quintus Fufius Calenus, Varro received a pardon from Octavian and spent the rest of his days peacefully in Rome.

The vigorous, hardworking old man now turned most of his energies to his own writing. Varro claimed to have composed, over his entire career, seventy-four works comprising more than six hundred volumes. This assertion is supported by commentators such as Aulus Gellius, Macrobius, and Nonius Marcellus, who all lived and worked within a few centuries after Varro. His work spanned virtually all areas of learning and all genres of writing then known to Rome: poetry, philosophy, history, literary criticism, grammar, philology, science and mathematics, practical handbooks, and the like. Among his lost books are a work on geometry, one on mensuration, and a nine-volume encyclopedia that helped form the basis for what became the medieval program of education.

On the other hand, what Varro did for his contemporaries, in the way of preserving and concentrating sources for antiquarian research, many later scholars have done for certain of his works. For example, it is thanks in large part to quotations by Nonius Marcellus (fl. fourth century C.E.) that some six hundred lines and ninety titles of Varro's 150 books that form the *Saturae Menippiae* (c. 81-67 B.C.E.; *Menippean Satires*) are preserved for the twentieth century. (According to Cicero, Varro himself composed much verse, although Varro allowed little room for poetry in his library collection.)

Actually, the satires were an intermixture of prose and verse in the style of Menippus, a Greek Cynic of the third century B.C.E. The extant titles are greatly varied, some named after gods or persons, some quoting Latin or Greek proverbs—for example, *Nescis quid vesper serus vehat* (You know not what the evening may bring forth) and the famous Socratic dictum "Know thyself." The subject matter also varies: eating and drinking, literature, philosophy, politics, and the "good old days." The general themes are the absurdity of much Greek philosophy and the preoccupation among Romans of Varro's day with luxury and leisure. Varro expressed his disapproval for the First Triumvirate in a satire he called *Trikaranos* (the three-headed).

Modern opinion, based on the surviving fragments, varies as to the literary merit of the *Menippean Satires*. The ancients, however, quoted them so frequently as to make quite evident their popularity with Varro's contemporaries. In addition to his own poetic compositions, Varro wrote several treatises on literature and literary history, including *De poematis* (of poetry), *De compositione saturarum* (on the composition of satire), and *De poetis* (about poets).

He also made many lasting contributions to science and education, chief of which was to introduce the Greek concept of the encyclopedia, meaning "general education," into Roman thought. This he did by way of his now-lost *De forma philosophiae libri III* (on philosophical forms) and *Disciplinarum libri IX* (liberal arts). The latter set forth all the known liberal arts gathered from Greek sources. It was the Greeks who had originally divided the liberal arts into a trivium (grammar, logic, and rhetoric) and a quadrivium (geometry, arithmetic, astronomy, and music), and the *Disciplinarum libri IX* contained a chapter on each, as well as on architecture and medicine. Later scholars removed these last two from the scheme and made them professional studies, retaining the others as the basic program of education in the Middle Ages. Meanwhile, the encyclopedia, incorporating excerpts from and synopses of writings by earlier authors, became a respectable genre among the Romans, particularly in scientific circles. Other scientific contributions included two works on geography, *De ora maritima* (of the seashore) and *De aestuariis* (of estuaries), as well as numerous works on meteorology and almanacs for farmers and sailors.

Varro brought innovation in yet another area: His fifteen-volume *Imagines*, also known as *Hebdomades*, published about 39 B.C.E., introduced the illustrated biography to Romans. (Crateuas, the physician of Mithradates the Great, had earlier published an illustrated book on plants written in Greek.) Varro's *Imagines* contained brief life histories of seven hundred famous Greeks and Romans, accompanied by a likeness of each. Varro's choice of precisely seven hundred biographies is also interesting: He had a powerful attachment to the number seven, and Aulus Gellius quoted him as saying that the virtues of that number are many and various.

By ancient estimates, Varro's greatest work was one of which no trace now remains: the forty-one-volume *Antiquitates rerum humanarum et divinarum libri XLI* (of matters human and divine). Its importance lay in the complete account it gave of Roman political and religious life from the earliest times. Because the book displayed immense knowledge of the Roman past, the church fathers used it as a source of information about official Roman religion. Although this work is lost, much information from it is preserved in Gellius, Servius, Macrobius, and Saint Augustine.

Of those works by Varro that are preserved in the original, one, *De lingua Latina* (*On the Latin Language*), has come down in mutilated form. Only five of its twenty-five volumes survive, and even these are incomplete.

Varro composed the work between 47 and 45 and published it before the death of Cicero, to whom it is dedicated. It has value not only as an early study of linguistic origins and development but also as a source of quotations from early Roman poets. Although some of the etymologies are a bit fanciful, many more evince true wit and insight. Perhaps most important, this work is a pioneering systematic treatment—starting with word origins and the evolution of meanings, moving to a defense of etymology as a branch of learning, treating abstract concepts such as ideas of time and the rare and difficult words that poets often use, then introducing the debate over "anomaly" versus "analogy" (a controversy that survives to modern times). Varro's approach, the product of independent thought despite its heavy debt to his teacher Stilo Praeconinus, made the subject worthy of attention from other scholars.

His other surviving work, *De re rustica* (36 B.C.E.; *On Agriculture*), has come down almost completely intact. *On Agriculture* is a practical handbook rather than a theoretical treatise; Varro based it on his actual experience of running his family's three Sabine farms, as well as on lore and science drawn from ancient sources.

On Agriculture is important for several reasons: as an instance of the dialogue form, as a revelation of Roman agricultural ideas, as a source for Vergil's *Georgics* (c. 37-29 B.C.E.), and as a harbinger of at least one discovery of modern science. In this work, Varro cautioned farmers to choose a healthy site for their farmhouse and to avoid building near swamps because, as he wrote, "certain minute animals, invisible to the eye, breed there and, borne by the air, reach inside the body by way of the mouth and nose and cause diseases that are difficult to get rid of." Cicero and his circle, though friendly to Varro, apparently considered this theory of his absurd. Varro was possibly the only Roman who approached the germ theory of disease, which Louis Pasteur would fully develop more than eighteen hundred years later.

SIGNIFICANCE

Even the briefest survey of his work reveals how pervasive Marcus Terentius Varro's influence was—not only on his own age but also on posterity. Cicero praised Varro with the words, "When we were foreigners and wanderers—strangers, as it were, in our own land—your books led us home and made it possible for us at length to learn who we were as Romans and where we lived." Through the sheer range of his undertakings, he influenced later authors and scholars as diverse as Vergil, Petronius, Gellius, Augustine, and Boethius.

Despite the enormous scope of his abstract knowledge, Varro was primarily a shrewd, practical thinker, and, because the Roman mind looked for the practical significance of all things intellectual, he attempted to absorb and then pass on to his fellow citizens all that could be learned. So intent was he on transmitting what was knowable that he summarized some of his longer works so that less-educated Romans could comprehend them more easily. In this capacity, he became perhaps the world's first intellectual popularizer.

—*Thomas Rankin*

FURTHER READING

Duff, J. Wight. *A Literary History of Rome in the Silver Age from Tiberius to Hadrian.* New York: Charles Scribner's Sons, 1927. Reprint. Westport, Conn.: Greenwood Press, 1979. Contains a discussion of Varro's place in Roman literature.

_____. *Roman Satire: Its Outlook on Social Life.* 1936. Reprint. Hamden, Conn.: Archon Books, 1964. Includes a discussion specifically focusing on Varro's *Menippean Satires*, of which only fragments remain but which is thought by some scholars to have great literary merit.

Skydsgaard, Jens Erik. *Varro the Scholar: Studies in the First Book of Varro's "De re rustica."* Copenhagen, Denmark: Munksgaard, 1968. A lucid discussion of the first part of Varro's *On Agriculture.* Written by a respected scholar.

Stahl, William H. *Roman Science: Origins, Develop-* *ment, and Influence to the Later Middle Ages.* 1962. Reprint. Westport, Conn.: Greenwood Press, 1978. Includes a discussion of Varro's contributions to agriculture, mathematics, linguistic studies, geography, and encyclopedism.

Varro, Marcus Terentius. *De Lingua Latina X.* Translated by Daniel J. Taylor. Philadelphia: John Benjamins, 1996. Notes to this translation examine Book 10 of this work and Varro's work with linguistics.

_____. *On Agriculture.* Translated by William Davis Hooper and Harrison Boyd Ash. Rev. ed. Cambridge, Mass.: Harvard University Press, 1979. Varro's only complete surviving work. Written in dialogue form, with great descriptive and dramatic power. Cato's *De agri cultura* (c. 160 B.C.E.; *On Agriculture,* 1913) is printed in the same volume.

_____. *On the Latin Language.* Translated by Roland G. Kent. 2 vols. Rev. ed. 1951. Reprint. Cambridge, Mass.: Harvard University Press, 1993. Contains the surviving fragments of Varro's twenty-five-volume work on the derivation, grammar, and popular usage of the Latin language. Provides the Latin original opposite each page of translation.

SEE ALSO: Marc Antony; Julius Caesar; Cicero; Pompey the Great.

RELATED ARTICLES in *Great Events from History: The Ancient World*: 58-51 B.C.E., Caesar Conquers Gaul; 51 B.C.E., Cicero Writes *De republica*; 43-42 B.C.E., Second Triumvirate Enacts Proscriptions.

VASUBANDHU
Indian philosopher

Vasubandhu articulated and critiqued the Sarvāstivāda school of Buddhism and then developed the "consciousness-only" school, thus laying the metaphysical foundations of Yogācāra Buddhism.

BORN: c. 400 C.E.; Puruśapura, Gandhara (now Peshawar, Pakistan)
DIED: c. 480 C.E.; place unknown
AREA OF ACHIEVEMENT: Philosophy

EARLY LIFE

Access to the life and work of Vasubandhu (VAH-sew-BAHN-dew) begins with consideration of the activities of the Indian scholar and philosopher Paramārtha (c. 499-569 C.E.). Paramārtha was a Buddhist monk who traveled to China about 548 C.E., intending to spread the teachings of the *Abhidharmakośa* (fourth or fifth century C.E.; *The Abhidharmakosa of Vasubandhu*, 1983) and the *Mahāyānasaṁgraha* (fourth century C.E.; *The Summary of the Great Vehicle*, 1992). The former is a basic text of the Sarvāstivāda (or Vaibhāśika) school of Buddhism, written by Vasubandhu; the latter, a fundamental text of the Yogācāra school, written by Vasubandhu's brother Asanga and annotated by Vasubandhu. In addition to spreading these doctrines and composing many other works, Paramārtha wrote a biography of Vasubandhu.

This biography is the foundation of the opinion, held both traditionally and by most contemporary scholars, that Vasubandhu was a single individual, rather than two distinct persons separated in time by a century or so. Paramārtha's work of textual and doctrinal propagation supplies the grounds for the controversy. The Sarvās-tivāda ("all-things-exist") persuasion is a quite early (c. third century B.C.E.) deviation from the Theravāda school "Of the Elders," also (critically) termed Hīna-yāna, the "Lesser Vehicle." The Yogācāra or Vijñānavāda ("consciousness-only") position is a branch of Mahāyāna or "Greater Vehicle" Buddhism. The large designations Hīnayāna-Mahāyāna are usually understood as opposi-tional, as are the more detailed Sarvāstivāda-Vijñānavāda doctrines. This creates the "problem of Vasubandhu," that is, the need to consider whether he is a single person, which views he held when, and why. The core of the problem is the legitimate doubt that a single individual would have held what seem to be divergent, even op-posed positions.

Singularity is generally accepted. Vasubandhu is thought to have been born in the late fourth or early fifth century C.E. in the city of Puruśapura (modern Pesha-war), located in the territory of Gandhara. The elder Asanga was probably his half brother, born of the same mother but not the son of Vasubandhu's Brahman father. Vasubandhu was broadly educated in traditional Hindu texts but, like Asanga, chose to become a Buddhist monk. He was enrolled in the Sarvāstivāda school, then traveled to Kashmir for advanced instruction in *abhi-dharma*, that is, academic investigation into the nature of ultimate reality. Evidently, the young Vasubandhu's in-telligence was curious and searching, interested in the critical examination of arguments rather than adherence to any particular school or dogma.

LIFE'S WORK
Vasubandhu and his brother were both Buddhist monks of, broadly, the Mahāyāna persuasion. The purpose of Buddhism is to transcend *samsāra*—the distressing cy-cle of repeated births and deaths—through enlighten-ment. Mahāyāna Buddhism teaches that the bodhisattvas, "enlightenment-beings," seek transcendence or salvation not only for themselves but also for others. They help to provide the "greater vehicle" into which all may enter.

The philosophical Buddhist, then, seeks to gain en-lightenment and to end suffering through investigation into both what is ultimately real, and therefore worth seeking, and, on the other hand, what is merely apparent or passing, and therefore of little or no concern. The Vaibhāsika branch of the Sarvāstivāda school, of which Vasubandhu's *Abhidharmakośa* is the most important text, understands reality in terms of dharmas.

In this usage, a dharma is that which exists non-contingently or—what constitutes practically the same quality—is able to cause an event. It is, however, mislead-ing to attribute "thingness" of any sort (material or ideal, physical or mental) to dharmas. The comprehensive doc-trine is that dharmas, while they have existence, are im-permanent events or occurrences. Of course, "dharma-discourse" contains numerous details, most significantly the allocation of the seventy-five dharmas to five general categories. This categorization is in tension with the com-prehensive doctrine, since it amounts to a mind-matter du-alism; and it thus generates the question of how a physical occurrence is able to cause a mental event, and vice versa.

This categorical disjunction is secondary. Within the Buddhist frame, the "all-things-exist" position is deeply disturbing. It presents a world that is an endless sequence of momentary events, "the self" or "consciousness" in-cluded. Beyond this, it is unable to explain adequately ei-ther how, in the transmigratory cycle, the conscious self resumes following evident nonexistence, or how a self that is merely episodic and impermanent is able to achieve enlightenment and transcendence, that is, nir-vana. The former may be termed the continuity problem, the latter the enlightenment problem. In sum, what might be called categorical empiricism or analytical phenom-enology is hardly more than a starting point for mature Buddhist philosophical reflection.

In the tradition, a variety of homey and touching stories are told about how Asanga "converted" Vasubandhu from his Sarvāstivāda beliefs to the Yogācāra school of Mahā-yāna Buddhism. They amount to personal appeals from older to younger brother, in which Vasubandhu feels guilty about one or another fraternal misdeed. Be these as they may, attention to the *Abhidharmakośa* shows that Va-subandhu was presenting and examining Sarvāstivāda ar-guments, not subscribing to a creed. It is incomplete and ultimately misleading to argue that he was merely look-ing for solutions to philosophical problems. It is more ac-curate to say that Buddhist beliefs pose philosophical questions that must be thoughtfully resolved before the Buddhist soul may be in the greatest possible repose.

It is, then, the condition of consciousness (*vijñāna*), which must be considered carefully. To "consider care-fully" normally means to "think about"; thinking implies a thinker and a thing thought, and is inherently dualistic. Yogācāra thinking avoids this trap. Yogācāra means "the practice of *yogā*." *Yogā*, a Sanskirt word, is from the ver-bal root *yuj*, "to join"; *yogā* means "union." Two things are thus suggested: first, that consciousness is to be con-sidered and understood experientially, not abstractly or intellectually; second, that this understanding will be in the nature of a joining or a union.

It is not surprising, then, that Vasubandhu presents his mature reflections and conclusions in the *Triṃśikā* (fourth or fifth century C.E.; *Three Works of Vasubandhu in Sanskrit Manuscripts*, 1989) or "Thirty Verses." These verses are best considered as a report on the experience of consciousness, and not as a treatise on the philosophy of mind. Following Vasubandhu, and thus avoiding all technicalities, consciousness is experienced as threefold. The order of presentation intimates that the first consciousness experientially is the consciousness of self (*manas*). Vasubandhu repeatedly says of this consciousness that it is "always reflecting." It acts both to acquire and to look on its acquisitions. For example, it appropriates as "its own" the activities of the second sort of consciousness—perception—and thus has (knowledge of) events. The active self absorbs these experiences, and thus has thoughts and dispositions of its own. Furthermore, its relentless energy inevitably conjoins it with the "four afflictions"—view of self, confusion of self, pride of self, and love of self.

Consciousness of self, or "own-being," is prideful and (therefore) unenlightened. It is not aware of its own origins. Somehow, the practice of *yoga* reveals that there is a kind of consciousness more primitive than either perception or the reflective self. Vasubandhu calls this third consciousness *ālaya-vijñāna*, usually translated "store-consciousness." The store-consciousness is, as it were, the basket in which exist all the seeds (*bīja*), which subsequently develop into higher sorts of consciousness. It appears that the essence of store-consciousness is that it is nonintentional; that is, unfocused, all-accepting, and undirected by a purposeful, therefore partial, self.

The fundamental result of experiencing consciousness comprehensively is to place the self in a larger context, and thus to make evident the limitations of self-consciousness or "own-being." The self arises from a condition of undifferentiated consciousness, prior to and free from self-concern. Enlightenment is the experiential—that is, direct and unreflective—apprehension of this larger consciousness. This is, for a Yogācārin, the direct experience of reality; that is, of "no (particular) thing." One returns to that from which one has, as defined and limited self, arisen. This would seem to solve the continuity problem, since a ground in consciousness has been provided for each distinctive version of the self. In a formula, the self is diminished by expansion and transcends by returning; but it is of the essence of Yogācāra that such matters are experiential, not propositional.

SIGNIFICANCE

The influence of Vasubandhu may be suggested with an analogy. Imagine, counterfactually, that the ancient Greek philosopher Plato first articulated a theory of forms culminating in an all-generating Good, then on further consideration reversed himself, became in affect his dissenting pupil Aristotle, and argued for a pluralistic world. For the Buddhist tradition, Vasubandhu was Plato and Aristotle rolled into one, but with the idealism-pluralism pattern reversed. His work in the Vaibhāṣika division of the Sarvāstivāda school, classically expressed in the *Abhidharmakośa*, had a lasting effect on Indo-Tibetan Buddhist thought and remains a basic text in some curricula to this day. His Yogācāra works were a principal reason that this school of Mahāyāna Buddhism became dominant. Spreading into China, Korea, Japan, and later the West, Yogācāra became, among other things, the foundation of Zen Buddhism.

Above all, Vasubandhu realized the basic principle of Mahāyāna. If Buddhism was to have meaning for many people, it had to be other than either received religious dogma or learned philosophical disputation: It had to be a matter of experience and practice. In showing that consciousness could be understood and expanded through the practice of *yoga*, Vasubandhu was able to derive and therefore ground metaphysical categories in experience. This foundation was critical in making Buddhism a practical part of everyday life. In assisting many, Vasubandhu was a true bodhisattva.

—John F. Wilson

FURTHER READING

Conze, Edward. *Buddhist Thought in India: Three Phases of Buddhist Philosophy.* Ann Arbor: University of Michigan Press, 1967. A widely available paperback by the greatest English student of Buddhism. Although brief on Vasubandhu, Conze places Mahāyāna Yogācāra in developmental context, and illuminates characteristic differences between Eastern and Western thinking. Notes and index.

Griffiths, Paul J. *On Being Mindless: Buddhist Meditation and the Mind-Body Problem.* La Salle, Ill.: Open Court, 1986. In this excellent but demanding work, Griffiths examines the detailed philosophical argumentation of both of Vasubandhu's positions. The scholarly apparatus—glossary, appendices, notes, textual and interpretative bibliographies, and index—is extremely useful.

Kalupahana, David J. *Buddhist Philosophy: A Historical Analysis.* Honolulu: University of Hawaii Press,

1976. A brief but comprehensive scholarly treatment, available in paperback. Vasubandhu receives significant notice. Kalupahana pays particular attention to the meaning of Buddhist philosophical terms. Notes, bibliographies, and index.

Pandit, Moti Lal. *Sunyata: The Essence of Mahāyāna Spirituality.* New Delhi: Munshiram Manoharlal Publishers, 1998. A comprehensive contemporary treatment of the Mahāyāna persuasion. Vasubandhu is discussed largely in chapter 5, but his influence on Mahāyāna philosophizing is evident throughout. Reasonably accessible, especially the "Overview." Chapter notes and references, bibliography, and index.

Prebish, Charles S., ed. *Buddhism: A Modern Perspective.* University Park: Pennsylvania State University Press, 1975. An unusual cooperative effort by eight distinguished Buddhist scholars, resulting in short, topically specific chapters. Vasubandhu is discussed extensively. Chapter and comprehensive bibliographies, appendix, very full glossary, and index.

Raju, P. T. *Structural Depths of Indian Thought.* Albany: State University of New York Press, 1985. A masterwork by a veteran Indian scholar and philosopher. Raju places Vasubandhu, the Mahāyāna, and Buddhism generally in its larger Indian context and very usefully shows its influence on modern and contemporary Western thought. Notes, glossary, bibliography, and index.

Takakusu, Junjiro. *The Essentials of Buddhist Philosophy.* 3d ed. Delhi: Motilal Banarsidass, 1975. This useful book is worth seeking out. Takakusu, a leading Japanese Buddhist scholar, translated Paramārtha's "Life of Vasubandhu" and is persuaded of the "single Vasubandhu" view. He traces the influence of the various Buddhist schools in China and, especially, Japan. Contains helpful pullout tables of the dharmas, charts, and an index.

SEE ALSO: Ānanda; Asanga; Aśoka; Aśvaghosa; Bodhidharma; Buddha; Chandragupta Maurya; Gośāla Maskarīputra; Kanishka; Vardhamāna; Vattagamani.

RELATED ARTICLES in *Great Events from History: The Ancient World*: 6th or 5th century B.C.E., Birth of Buddhism; c. 5th-4th centuries B.C.E., Creation of the *Jātakas*; c. 321 B.C.E., Mauryan Empire Rises in India; 300 B.C.E.-600 C.E., Construction of the Māhabodhi Temple; c. 250 B.C.E., Third Buddhist Council Convenes; c. 250 B.C.E., *Tipiṭaka* Is Compiled; c. 247-207 B.C.E., Buddhism Established in Sri Lanka; c. 1st century B.C.E., Indian Buddhist Nuns Compile the *Therigatha*; 1st century B.C.E.-1st century C.E., Compilation of the *Lotus Sutra*; 1st century C.E., Fourth Buddhist Council Convenes; Late 4th-5th centuries C.E., Asanga Helps Spread Mahāyāna Buddhism; 460-477 C.E., Buddhist Temples Built at Ajanta Caves in India.

VATTAGAMANI
Sri Lankan religious leader and king (r. 103-102 and 89-77 B.C.E.)

Vattagamani was instrumental in supporting and defending the Buddhist religion that had been introduced to Sri Lanka in the third century B.C.E. Vattagamani called together the Fourth Buddhist Council, in which he ordered Buddhist writers and scribes to write down the Pāli Tipiṭaka*, or Pāli Canon, for the first time.*

BORN: Second century B.C.E.; place unknown
DIED: 77 B.C.E; place unknown
ALSO KNOWN AS: Vaṭṭagāmaṇi Abhaya; Valagam Ba
AREA OF ACHIEVEMENT: Religion

EARLY LIFE
Vattagamani (vat-ta-ga-MA-nih) was the son of King Saddhatissa and Queen Somadevi of Sri Lanka, a pearl-shaped island off the coast of southeastern India, for-

merly called Ceylon. Although little is known of his early life, he is inextricably linked with the history of Buddhism. Buddhism was founded by Siddhārtha Gautama (c. 566-c. 486 B.C.E.), a prince of the Śākya clan. After an early life of great luxury, at the age of twenty-nine, Siddhārtha renounced his life of ease and wealth and traveled in search of the answers to his questions about the causes of death and suffering. After several years of wandering, he achieved enlightenment while meditating under a tree (later known as the Bodhi tree) at Uruvelā, near Benares (modern-day Varanasi). Buddha spent the rest of his life teaching what he had learned. He also founded a group of monks to carry on his teachings.

The core of Buddha's teachings center on the Four Noble Truths that emerged from his meditation. One becomes awakened when focusing on these truths: (1) suffering exists; (2) desire or craving is the cause of suffering; (3) the end of suffering is brought about by cessation of desire; and (4) the path that leads to the end of suffering is the noble Eightfold Path. By learning to cease desire and thus end suffering, an individual creates a way to achieve nirvana, a state of freedom that is the ultimate goal of Buddha's teachings.

In the third century B.C.E., the emperor of India, King Aśoka (c. 302-c. 238 B.C.E.), adopted Buddhism and supported its spread throughout India and beyond. Around 251 B.C.E. Aśoka sent his son, Mahinda Thera (c. 279-c. 204 B.C.E.), to the island of Sri Lanka to introduce the religion there. During his nearly fifty years of missionary work, Mahinda translated the teachings of Buddhism into Sinhala, the language of the Sinhalese, the earliest colonizers of Sri Lanka, and established the monastery of Mahāvihāra (meaning "Great Monastery"), a center of Buddhist learning and culture where the doctrines of the Buddha were upheld. The monks living at Mahāvihāra became known as Theravādins. Major Buddhist shrines were established at Anuradhapura (founded in the fifth century B.C.E.), Kandy, and Dalada Maligawa.

The teachings of Buddha were transmitted orally by monks living within communities. By 250 B.C.E., the teachings had been arranged and organized into three basic divisions: one containing the rules and customs of the community of monks, another the sermon and words of the Buddha and his closest followers, and a third, an analysis of the doctrine and discipline or *dharma* of Buddhism. After Buddha's death, as his doctrines spread across India, several different approaches to Buddha's teachings arose. One of the sects was called Mahāyāna Buddhism (*Mahāyāna* meaning "great vehicle"); another was called Hīnayāna Buddhism (*Hīnayāna* meaning "lesser vehicle"). In time, they became the two main branches of Buddhism. Theravāda Buddhism is the surviving branch of the Hīnayāna school of Buddhism. It is inspired by the scriptures found in the *Tipiṭaka* (compiled c. 250 B.C.E.; English translation in *Buddhist Scriptures*, 1913). Today, it is the form of Buddhism found in southeast Asia and Sri Lanka.

LIFE'S WORK

This history formed the backdrop for the rise of Vattagamani, who ruled the island nation of Sri Lanka twice, from 103 to 102 B.C.E. and again from 89 to 77 B.C.E. The monks who followed Theravāda Buddhism suffered when Sri Lanka was invaded during Vattagamani's first reign by Hindu Tamils from southern India. King Vattagamani

went into hiding during this Tamil period. During the fourteen-year rule by the Tamils, Sri Lankans experienced widespread famine. Buddhist monks could not get enough food to sustain themselves in order to carry on the arduous practice of handing down Buddhist teachings from memory. In 80 B.C.E., they sought out the help of Vattagamani, who had sheltered them during his wanderings, in calling forth a council for the purpose of committing the teachings of Buddha to writing. A group of five hundred monks assembled to recite and copy the entire body of Buddhist teachings on *ola* (palm leaves). The name of the completed body of work is the *Pāli Tipiṭaka*. Thus, Theravāda Buddhism was rescued from extinction.

King Vattagamani eventually defeated the Tamil invaders and restored Theravāda Buddhist monks to their former place of authority. The king also built a monastery, the Abhayagiri, which he gave as a gift to a monk, Mahatissa, who had helped him during his times of difficulty. Mahatissa was expelled from the Mahāvihāra and went to live at the Abhayagiri, where he was joined by five hundred monks. As a result of Vattagamani's support of the Abhayagiri monks, there arose a schism in Theravāda Buddhism. The Mahāvihāra group represented a more conservative approach to the interpretation of the teachings of the Buddha, while the Abhayagiri represented a liberal, progressive outlook.

SIGNIFICANCE

The protection that Vattagamani gave to the monks and scribes who wrote down the *Pāli Tipiṭaka* enabled them to preserve a record of the teachings of Buddha. His defeat of the Tamil invaders of Sri Lanka reestablished Sri Lankan Buddhism, creating both the circumstances that maintained Theravāda Buddhism and the schism that created the Mahāvihāra and Abhayagiri schools.

—*Adriane Ruggiero*

FURTHER READING

Armstrong, Karen. *Buddha*. New York: Penguin, 2001. An overview of the life of the founder of Buddhism by a major, contemporary religion writer who is also a former Catholic nun.

Carter, John Ross. *On Understanding Buddhists: Essays on the Theravāda Tradition in Sri Lanka*. Albany: State University of New York Press, 1993. A series of essays focus on Sri Lanka's role in Theravāda Buddhism, illuminating notions of ethical living and faith, the religious life, the view of the world, the place of the monk, the role of music, and the origins and development of some of the core Buddhist concepts.

Robinson, R. H., and W. L. Johnson. *The Buddhist Religion: A Historical Introduction.* Belmont, Calif.: Wadsworth, 1997. A general overview of the history of Buddhism and its growth as a world religion; part of the Religious Life of Man series.

Smith, Huston, and Philip Novak. *Buddhism: A Concise Introduction.* San Francisco: HarperSanFrancisco, 2003. An erudite overview of Buddhism by a world-famous writer with a special emphasis on Theravāda Buddhism and a detailed description of the differences between the Buddhist traditions.

SEE ALSO: Ānanda; Asanga; Aśoka; Aśvaghosa; Bodhidharma; Buddha; Chandragupta Maurya; Gośāla Maskarīputra; Kanishka; Vardhamāna; Vasubandhu.

RELATED ARTICLES in *Great Events from History: The Ancient World*: 6th or 5th century B.C.E., Birth of Buddhism; c. 5th-4th centuries B.C.E., Creation of the *Jātakas*; c. 321 B.C.E., Mauryan Empire Rises in India; 300 B.C.E.-600 C.E., Construction of the Māhabodhi Temple; c. 250 B.C.E., Third Buddhist Council Convenes; c. 250 B.C.E., *Tipiṭaka* Is Compiled; c. 247-207 B.C.E., Buddhism Established in Sri Lanka; c. 1st century B.C.E., Indian Buddhist Nuns Compile the *Therigatha*; 1st century B.C.E.-1st century C.E., Compilation of the *Lotus Sutra*; 1st century C.E., Fourth Buddhist Council Convenes; Late 4th-5th centuries C.E., Asanga Helps Spread Mahāyāna Buddhism; 460-477 C.E., Buddhist Temples Built at Ajanta Caves in India.

VERCINGETORIX
Gallic leader

Vercingetorix fashioned a coalition of Gallic tribes to expel their Roman conquerors. Although he was captured at his capital of Alesia by Julius Caesar, Vercingetorix has long been identified as an early French national hero.

BORN: c. 75 B.C.E.; central Gaul (now in France)
DIED: c. 46 B.C.E.; Rome (now in Italy)
AREAS OF ACHIEVEMENT: Government and politics, war and conquest

EARLY LIFE

The Celts were a nonliterate society prior to the Roman era, so there are no written sources regarding the Roman conquest of Gaul from the Gallic point of view. From the Roman side, Julius Caesar's *Comentarii de bello Gallico* (52-51 B.C.E.; translated with *Comentarii de bello cinli*, 45 B.C.E., as *Commentaries*, 1609) is primarily a narration of his successes during his eight-year war against the tribes of Gaul. It is also one of the few surviving written accounts of Celtic political structures and culture. The Gallic Revolt of 52 B.C.E., which is described in book 7 of *Comentarii de bello Gallico*, provides the only source of information for the life of Vercingetorix (vuhr-sihn-JEHT-uhr-ihks). Caesar's work must be considered self-serving, for he was interested only in narrating his interpretation of his victories; moreover, his analysis and descriptions of the Gallic chief are limited to the revolt of 52 B.C.E.

According to Caesar, Vercingetorix was the son of Celtillus, chief of the Arverni, a Celtic tribe in central Gaul. The father had once claimed overlordship over the whole of Gaul but had been executed, probably by a conspiracy of his nobles and other Gallic tribal chiefs, for having sought to make himself king. Caesar, then about fifty years old, refers to Vercingetorix as a young man, which would mean that the Gaul was probably about thirty at the time of the revolt. Caesar credited Vercingetorix with numerous talents, including great strength of character, boundless energy, and the ability to lead a fractious society. It is clear from his writing that, of all of his Gallic opponents, Vercingetorix was the leader Caesar respected most.

Other aspects of the early life of Vercingetorix can only be inferred. He was a Gallic Celt of noble birth, and societal traditions would have demanded that he be schooled in the Druidical traditions. Celtic culture placed a premium on skill in warfare by adult males, and the youth would have been rigorously trained in Celtic battle tactics and weaponry. Celtic oral traditions of the period, which almost always focused on military virtues such as courage and bravery, were assuredly an integral part of his learning. Additionally, he was clearly an intelligent leader who learned quickly. He had watched and learned from the Roman conquests of Gallic tribes by the Romans, which had been accomplished over a six-year period (58-53 B.C.E.).

LIFE'S WORK

The Gaul into which Vercingetorix had been born was divided into dozens, perhaps hundreds, of tribal groupings of various Celtic peoples. Although Celts spoke similar dialects and shared many cultural traits, they were in no way a unified people. The Druids were especially significant in this society, and it was they who passed on Celtic traditions and beliefs. It was also they who resisted the spread of Roman hegemony in Celtic areas and who orchestrated resistance to Roman conquest. Celtic warriors were fiercely independent and high-spirited, according to Roman accounts. The Romans considered them to be brave but undisciplined warriors who could not, or would not, unite against a common danger.

When Caesar was appointed governor of the province of Cisalpine Gaul, in northwestern Italy, in 59 B.C.E., it had been at his own request. The Celts of Transalpine Gaul across the Alps had long been viewed as dangerous enemies, and Caesar viewed the position as an opportunity to enhance his military reputation. In 58 B.C.E., his legions conquered first the Suevi of southeastern Gaul and then the Helvetii, from the area of modern Switzerland, thereby extending Roman influence. He moved northward, down the Rhine River, against the Belgii of northwestern Gaul, then conquered the Veneti of western Gaul, and finally subdued the Aquitani in southwestern Gaul. Celtic Britain was attacked in 55-54 B.C.E., and his army raided the Germans in 55 and 53 B.C.E. Most of 54-53 B.C.E. was devoted to the brutal suppression of several Celtic uprisings in northern Gaul.

Roman success had been largely the result of the inability of the Celtic tribes to unite in the face of the Roman danger. Caesar had also avoided central Gaul, wherein lay the most formidable of his potential Gallic enemies. Militarily, central Gaul had been isolated and surrounded, a fact not unnoticed by the Gallic tribes there. When the whole of Gaul was treated as if it were a subservient province, it was clear that it was only a matter of time before central Gaul was attacked. During the winter of 53-52 B.C.E., when it was learned that Caesar had left his army in garrison in north Gaul while he returned to Rome, a coalition of tribes from central Gaul began plotting to expel the Romans. At Cenabum (modern Orleans), Roman officials and traders were slaughtered. The conspiracy turned quickly to the youthful Vercingetorix as commander in chief, showing that he was already held in high esteem by his peers. That they turned to the son of the chief who had been killed for having had the same pretensions is clear evidence that the Gallic tribes recognized the Roman threat for what it was.

Vercingetorix swiftly welded a confederacy of Celtic tribes on whom he could count in the coming war. As commander in chief, he demanded and received hostages as pledge of a willingness to fight with him. Allies were given quotas of troops to arm and prepare, and he himself set about extending the alliance to areas already conquered by the Romans. Vercingetorix hoped to smash the Roman presence in Gaul before Caesar could return, and he moved his forces against the Roman legions wintering in northern garrisons. Despite severe weather, and with his path blocked by mountains and deep snow, Caesar effected a crossing into Gaul. His first action was to harry the rebellious tribes of southeastern Gaul, forcing Vercingetorix to move southward to face the threat. Caesar then moved rapidly northward to rejoin his troops.

The war of the next few months was that of parry and thrust. Initially, each side attacked the *oppida*, or hillforts, loyal to the other. Each side also resorted to a scorched-earth policy to deprive the enemy of needed supplies. Vercingetorix besieged Gorgobina (modern St. Parize-le-Chatel), the capital for the pro-Roman Boii Celtic tribe; Caesar retaliated by first attacking Vallauno-

Vercingetorix. (Hulton|Archive by Getty Images)

dunum (modern Montargis) and then retaking Cenabum. One of the most brutal battles during this phase was the Roman siege of Avaricum (modern Bourges), during which Vercingetorix attempted and failed to relieve the siege. Caesar claimed to have killed all but eight hundred of the forty thousand inhabitants when he successfully stormed the city, although these numbers are surely inflated. Interestingly, his praise of Vercingetorix following this stunning defeat for the Gauls was high indeed, for he noted that it took a man of great ability to retain, let alone expand, his power after such a disaster.

In the spring of 52 B.C.E., Caesar moved to attack the *oppidum* of Gergovia (near modern Clermont), which Vercingetorix swiftly moved to protect. The two sides built camps facing each other, with neither willing to force an open battle. The Romans attempted to take the town by storm but failed, a disaster that prompted more Gallic tribes to join the rebellion. Caesar, though, stunned Vercingetorix by leaving the Gauls behind, marching northward towards Lutetia (modern Paris), all the while laying waste to the countryside. Vercingetorix was forced to leave his strong position and to advance against the Roman army. When Caesar moved against him, Vercingetorix attacked the Roman column with his cavalry. In this battle, the Gaulish cavalry, on which the rebellion had placed much hope, was defeated by the Roman cavalry.

Vercingetorix was forced to withdraw to Alesia, a strong *oppidum* located on a massif at the confluence of two streams. Although Alesia provided Vercingetorix with an excellent defensive position, he was swiftly besieged by Caesar. Within weeks, the Romans had completed their circumvallation of Alesia, with eight strong camps connected by redoubts and walls. An outer wall was also constructed to protect the Romans from the Gauls who would come to the aid of Vercingetorix. This relieving army, estimated at a hyperbolic 250,000 by Caesar, soon besieged the besiegers. Sadly for Vercingetorix and for Alesia, disunity among the Gallic forces sealed their fate, for attacks on the Roman lines were uncoordinated and failed at great cost. Even when Vercingetorix attacked from the inner side and Vercassivellaunus, a cousin of Vercingetorix, led a simultaneous attack from the outer side, the Roman lines remained unbroken. Realizing the futility of further fighting, the outer host departed; Vercingetorix submitted to Caesar, who took him to Rome and paraded him through the streets on display. According to Dion Cassius, the only extant Roman source to discuss the death of Vercingetorix, the Arverni leader was allowed to live for six more years and then publicly executed as part of a Roman spectacle.

SIGNIFICANCE

In life, Vercingetorix warranted little more than a footnote. His entire career spanned less than a year, and his success against the Romans was minimal. He won no major battles, and his capture meant the end of Gallic aspirations of expelling the Romans from Gaul. The greatness of Vercingetorix lay in his ability to form an alliance where one had never existed before. Through force of will and persuasiveness, he manipulated and cajoled many tribes into working together for the common good. Yet he never had the full support of all Gallic tribes, for many remained loyal to the Romans; nor did he have total commitment from his own confederates. Even had he succeeded in defeating the Romans, he would have quickly found his united Gaul to have been a chimera. It should not be considered his fault that other Gallic leaders were not as perceptive as he and that, ultimately, his efforts failed.

His legacy, however, is far greater than that of a failed military leader. Caesar ascribed to him the goal of "freedom of Gaul," an intent Vercingetorix surely promoted but which probably was a cover for his own personal goals. Still, in death, Vercingetorix became a symbol of resistance to foreign aggression and domination. Nineteenth century France rediscovered Vercingetorix and made him into a national hero. Statues were erected, with the portraits stamped on coins issued during his rebellion providing the image of his face. The lost cause of the Gaul had become the quest for national unity and the ideal state.

—*William S. Brockington, Jr.*

FURTHER READING

Caesar, Julius. *The Battle for Gaul*. Translated by Anne Wiseman and Peter Wiseman. Boston: D. R. Godine, 1980. The introduction includes perspectival information as well as interpretations based on recently discovered evidence.

_____. *The Conquest of Gaul*. Translated by S. Hartford. Baltimore: Penguin Books, 1951. The introduction serves to place the Gallic War within the dynamics of late republican Rome and of Roman Imperial expansion. It also outlines the nature of Gaul and of the Roman army of Caesar.

Cook, S. A., F. E. Adcock, and M. P. Charlesworth, eds. *The Roman Republic, 133-44 B.C.* Vol. 9 in *The Cambridge Ancient History*. Rev. ed. London: Cambridge University Press, 1966. Outlines the progress of the revolt in chapter 13, part 6. Caesar is used extensively as the source, but it provides details on geography and modern place names along with interpretations of events.

Holmes, Thomas Rice Edward. *Caesar's Conquest of Gaul.* 2d ed. New York: AMS Press, 1911. London: Oxford University Press, 1931. Holmes is still considered to be one of the finest interpreters of Caesar's military history of the war. Of particular value are his footnotes and references, which clarify and elucidate Caesar's narrative. Holmes also provides information about other Roman sources of the period.

Jiménez, Ramon L. *Caesar Against the Celts.* Edison, N.J.: Castle Books, 2001. Although Jiménez does not bring much new information to the topic, he does provide a very readable and accessible overview of the

Gallic Wars. Includes bibliographical references and an index.

King, Anthony. *Roman Gaul and Germany.* Berkeley: University of California Press, 1990. Although only a small portion of this work deals with Vercingetorix, it places the rebellion of 52 B.C.E. within the context of the times. The discussion of archaeological work done at Celtic sites in Gaul is most illuminating, for it demonstrates how historical insights can be inferred without written evidence.

SEE ALSO: Boudicca; Julius Caesar.

RELATED ARTICLES in *Great Events from History: The Ancient World*: 58-51 B.C.E., Caesar Conquers Gaul; 43-130 C.E., Roman Conquest of Britain; 60 C.E., Boudicca Leads Revolt Against Roman Rule.

VERGIL
Roman poet

Author of an epic poem celebrating the beginnings of the Roman race, pastoral poems, and a poem about the farmer's life, Vergil is among the greatest poets of all time.

BORN: October 15, 70 B.C.E.; Andes, near Mantua, Cisalpine Gaul (now in Italy)

DIED: September 21, 19 B.C.E.; Brundisium (now Brindisi, Italy)

ALSO KNOWN AS: Publius Vergilius Maro (full name); Virgil

AREA OF ACHIEVEMENT: Literature

EARLY LIFE

Publius Vergilius Maro, or simply Vergil (VUR-juhl), was born in Andes, a village near Mantua in Cisalpine Gaul, in 70 B.C.E., a generation before the death of the Roman Republic. His origins were humble; his father eked out a living by keeping bees on the family's small farm. Though no record of his father's name remains, it is known that his mother's name was Magia Polla. It also seems likely that Vergil received his early education at Cremona and Mediolanum (Milan) and that he received the *toga virilis* (the toga of manhood) in 55 B.C.E., on his fifteenth birthday. Wearing the *toga virilis* would signify full rights and privileges of citizenship.

Vergil is said to have learned Greek at Neapolis (Naples) from Parthenius, a Bithynian captive brought to Rome during the war with Mithradates the Great. Sup-

posedly, Vergil based one of his own poems, the *Moretum*, on a Greek model by Parthenius. The young poet also received instruction in Epicurean philosophy from Siron and training in rhetoric from Epidius. Most scholars believe that Vergil studied with Epidius at the same time as Octavian, the future emperor Augustus who would later become Vergil's champion and patron. In short, Vergil received a first-rate education in literature, philosophy, and rhetoric, and critics have discerned his broad learning in his *Georgics* (c. 37-29 B.C.E.), which deals with all elements relating to the farmer's work during the year. There is no indication that Vergil served in the military or engaged in politics. He was probably excused from these duties because of his fragile health and general bookishness.

About the year 45 B.C.E., on completing his education, Vergil returned to his family's property near Mantua, but in 42, after victory at Philippi, Octavian, in assigning grants of land to his veterans, allowed his aide, Octavius Musa, to determine boundaries of lands assigned in the Cremona district, and Vergil's paternal estate was deeded to a centurion named Arrius. Vergil's influential friends Asinius Pollio and Cornelius Gallus advised Vergil to appeal directly to Octavian; that he did, and the family farm was restored. Vergil would celebrate Octavian's understanding and kindness in this matter in eclogue 1 of the *Eclogues* (43-37 B.C.E.). Unfortunately, a second attempt to appropriate the family's estate, led by Milienus Toro, was successful several years later. (Vergil was almost killed by a ruffian named Clodius in the violence that ensued.)

Paradoxically, some good came from this sordid affair. Vergil took temporary refuge in a farmhouse owned by a neighbor named Siro but immediately thereafter moved to Rome, where he wrote the two collections of verse that attracted the notice of his first sponsor, Gaius Maecenas. The incident is referred to in section 10 of *Catalepton*, an ancient collection of poetry.

LIFE'S WORK

After Vergil's pastorals—the *Eclogues* (sometimes called the *Bucolics* and probably written with the countryside near Tarentum in mind)—appeared, Maecenas became interested in Vergil's work. Maecenas led a literary circle, was influential in matters of state, and had the ear of Octavian, soon to be known as Augustus. Although Vergil did not recover his family's farm, Augustus saw to it that he was compensated with another estate, probably the one located near Nola in Campania to which Aulus Gellius refers in *Noctes Atticae* (c. 143 C.E.; *Attic Nights*). Vergil also knew the poet Horace well by this time and was instrumental in admitting him to Maecenas's circle and securing a patron for him. Horace mentions his acquaintance with Vergil in the *Satires* (35, 30 B.C.E.; English translation, 1567), a description of a journey from Rome to Brundisium.

The *Georgics*, completed when its author had been fully accepted as a member of Maecenas's circle, is clearly the poem of which Vergil was most proud. It appears that he undertook its composition at Maecenas's suggestion and completed it at Naples sometime after the Battle of Actium (31 B.C.E.). Justifiably, the *Georgics* was compared with the idylls of Theocritus (c. 308-260 B.C.E.) and the *Erga kai Emerai* (c. 700 B.C.E.; *Works and Days*, 1618) of Hesiod, was found worthy of their Greek predecessors, and catapulted Vergil to prominence.

It is likely that for some time Vergil had considered writing the *Aeneid* (c. 29-19 B.C.E.), the epic poem for which he is best known. As early as 27, while Augustus was on military campaign in Spain, he wrote to Vergil suggesting composition of an epic that would celebrate Aeneas's founding of a so-called New Troy in Italy and set forth the ancient origins of the Roman people. It is likely that Vergil began the *Aeneid* soon thereafter. Dating composition of specific sections is difficult, but Vergil mentions the death of Marcellus, son of Octavia (the sister of Julius Caesar), in the *Aeneid*. Since it is known that Marcellus died in 23, one can assume that

Vergil. (Library of Congress)

Vergil had outlined the entire poem by this time, the reference appearing almost exactly at the epic's midpoint. Octavia, supposedly present at Vergil's reading of this passage, is said to have fainted on hearing the poet's allusion to her son as a young man of promise who died too young.

It is known that Vergil met Augustus in Athens late in the year 20. Possibly Vergil had intended to continue his tour of Greece, but his health, never strong, was rapidly declining, so he accompanied Augustus first to Megara, a district between the Corinthian and Saronic gulfs, then to Brundisium, on the tip of the Italian peninsula; he died there, at the age of fifty. His body was brought first to Naples, his summer residence, and supposedly interred in a tomb on a road between Naples and Puteoli (Pozzuoli), where, indeed, a tomb still stands. An epitaph, supposedly dating from Vergil's burial, reads: "Mantua me genuit, Calabri rapuere, tenet nunc Parthenope. Cecini pascua, rura, duces" ("Mantua bore me, Calabria ravished me, now Parthenope holds me. I have nourished flocks, fields, generals"; Parthenope is the ancient name of Naples after the Siren of that name). There is no evidence that Vergil himself composed this epitaph or even that it was on his tomb at the time of his death; nevertheless, the inscription is very old and has always been attributed to the poet.

One of the most dramatic events ensuing on Vergil's death concerns his will. He left half his property to his half brother Valerius Proculus and named Augustus, Maecenas, and his friends Lucius Varius and Plotius Tucca as other legatees. His final request, however, was that Varius and Tucca burn the *Aeneid*, which he did not consider in its finished state. Tradition has it that Augustus himself intervened to save the poem and that it was published with the revisions of Varius and Tucca.

Vergil died a wealthy man, thanks primarily to the generosity of Augustus and Maecenas. His residence on the Esquiline Hill included a garden located next to that of Maecenas. Generous grants from his patrons had enabled Vergil to find the security and leisure he needed for writing his verse and enjoying the friendship of amiable fellow artists, such as Horace. Vergil was also fortunate in finding acceptance for his works, which, even during his lifetime, became an essential part of the school curriculum.

One wonders what this most celebrated of Roman poets might have looked like. Though many ancient renderings of Vergil survive, none dates to his own time and all are idealized. Artists, focusing on the certain frailty of Vergil's health, inevitably portray him as a youthful, frail, and sensitive man with hair covering the ears, longer than the close-cropped Imperial style. In Renaissance paintings, he wears fillets or the poet's laurel crown and is often shown declaiming a passage from his works to an appreciative Augustus or Maecenas.

SIGNIFICANCE

During his lifetime and even more so after his death, the *Eclogues*, the *Georgics*, and the *Aeneid* became classics, known well by every patriotic Roman. They were memorized, recited, and used for rhetorical training. Soon after Vergil's death, the poet's works were credited with every variety of mystical allusion. The fourth eclogue, for example, was taken as prophecy of the birth of Jesus Christ, though the boy whose birth will signal a new golden age is more likely the emperor Augustus. Others regularly consulted the *Aeneid* and collected its "hidden meanings" as the so-called *Sortes Vergilianae* (Vergilian allotments). This practice began as early as the period immediately after Vergil's death, becoming an obsession in the Middle Ages. The unusual *praenomen* (first name) of Magia Polla, Vergil's mother, implied for many that the

poet was a gifted sorcerer as well. The alternate spelling of Vergil's name (Virgil) itself probably derives from the magician's *virga* (wand). That so many were able to see so much beyond the literal in Vergil's poems is testimony to their enduring value as masterpieces.

There is much information on Vergil's life, although much of it is embroidered with legend. Aelius Donatus's fourth century biography, appended to his commentary on Vergil's poems, is the most important ancient source, although it was derived in part from the rather random remarks in the *De viris illustribus* (second century C.E.; on famous men) of Suetonius. Suetonius is said to have derived his information from now-lost accounts by Varius (one of Vergil's literary executors) and from Melissus, a freedman of Maecenas. Other ancient biographies, less reliable, were written by Valerius Probus (first century C.E.) and Saint Jerome (c. 331-420 C.E.). An unattributed life of Vergil is also attached to the Vergil commentaries of Servius (late fourth century C.E.).

—*Robert J. Forman*

FURTHER READING

Commager, Steele, ed. *Virgil: A Collection of Critical Essays*. Englewood Cliffs, N.J.: Prentice-Hall, 1966. This book of essays discusses everything from the landscape that gave Vergil his inspiration to important imagery in his poetry. Includes a chronology of Vergil's life and a short bibliography.

Comparetti, Domenico. *Vergil in the Middle Ages*. Translated by E. F. M. Benecke. 1985. Reprint. Princeton, N.J.: Princeton University Press, 1997. This book remains the classic treatment of Vergil's literary legacy showing how it influenced both education and literature for centuries. It is still the best discussion of Vergilian bibliography available. A respected scholarly source.

Frank, Tenney. *Vergil: A Biography*. 1922. Reprint. New York: Russell and Russell, 1965. This standard biography discusses the poet's life through references to his works. Particularly interesting is Frank's use of the pseudo-Vergilian poems *Culex* and *Cirus*, the influence of Epicureanism, and his discussion of the circle of Maecenas.

Jenkyns, Richard. *Vergil's Experience, Nature, and History: Times, Names, and Places*. New York: Oxford University Press, 1998. This large-scale work concerns itself with examining Vergil's ideas of nature and historical experience as compared with similar ideas throughout the ancient world. Jenkyns also discusses the influence of Vergil's work on later thought.

Knight, W. F. Jackson. *Roman Vergil*. 1944. Reprint. New York: Barnes and Noble Books, 1968. How Vergil changed the literary world and how Augustus changed the political world are two important concerns in this biographical and literary study. There is also good discussion of Vergilian style, meter, and language, as well as appendices on how Vergil's poetry advanced Latin as a literary language and on the allegorical and symbolic applications of Vergil's poems.

Levi, Peter. *Virgil: His Life and Times*. New York: St. Martin's Press, 1999. This notable work by a leading classics scholar places Vergil in the context of his times.

Martindale, Charles, ed. *The Cambridge Companion to Virgil*. New York: Cambridge University Press, 1997. Twenty-one essays (including the editor's introduction) are divided into four sections covering the translation and reception of Vergil's works, his poetic career, historical contexts, and the content of his thought. Includes numerous bibliographies.

Otis, Brooks. *Virgil: A Study in Civilized Poetry*. Norman: University of Oklahoma Press, 1995. Excellent work that argues for Vergil as a sophisticated poet who presented mythic, well-known material in a new and meaningful style to his urban readers.

SEE ALSO: Augustus; Horace; Gaius Maecenas.

RELATED ARTICLES in *Great Events from History: The Ancient World*: 19 B.C.E., Roman Poet Vergil Dies; November 27, 8 B.C.E., Roman Lyric Poet Horace Dies.

MARCUS VERRIUS FLACCUS
Roman language and literature teacher

A onetime slave, Verrius established at Rome an innovative method for the teaching of Latin language and literature and, through his studies of Roman antiquities, contributed to modern understanding of Latin literature and Roman history.

BORN: c. 60 B.C.E.; place unknown
DIED: c. 22 C.E.; place unknown
AREA OF ACHIEVEMENT: Scholarship

EARLY LIFE

The biographer Suetonius supplies the basic biographical information about Marcus Verrius Flaccus (VEHR-ee-uhs FLAK-uhs) in his essay *De grammaticis et rhetoribus* (c. 120 C.E.; *Lives of the Grammarians*). This work by Suetonius, a discussion of teachers active in Rome during the last half of the first century B.C.E., includes the statement "Marcus Verrius Flaccus the freedman was especially renowned for his method of teaching." Nothing of Verrius's background is known except for his freedman's status and the probable name of his former master, Marcus Verrius. (Manumitted Roman slaves normally took the first and family names of their former owner.)

The name Verrius points to the region about Naples, where others with precisely the same nomenclature and many of the same family name are known. Scholarly work that Verrius did late in his life for the Roman town of Praeneste (modern Palestrina), however, has suggested to some that Verrius may have had an early connection with this town 23 miles (37 kilometers) southeast of Rome.

LIFE'S WORK

During Verrius's time, several men of letters with similar backgrounds established private schools in Rome for the instruction of Latin language and literature. These schools normally took children at the age of eleven for several years of training in the reading, recitation, and writing of Latin, while other schoolmasters might also have trained the same students in Greek language and literature. Verrius's school was notable because he forced his students to compete in writing and recitation, with prizes of rare literary editions for the victors. Verrius thus attracted the attention of the emperor Augustus, who invited Verrius to move his school to the Imperial palace and tutor—at a salary equal to that of a senior administrator—the emperor's young grandsons, Gaius and Lucius. The appointment of Verrius as Imperial tutor must have occurred between 8 and 11 B.C.E. and is no doubt the reason for Saint Jerome's assertion that Verrius "flourished" in 8 B.C.E.

Verrius wrote on a variety of subjects. *Rerum memoria dignarum* (things worth remembering), to judge from references to this work by Pliny the Elder and other ancient scholars, ranged from elephants to Roman religious lore and rituals. Other writings touched on the Etruscans and on Roman traditions. Several important works treated the Latin language: *De orthographia* (on correct spelling) apparently urged a return to old-fashioned ways of spelling (and pronouncing) Latin words; *De obscuris Catonis* (obscurities in Cato) explained unusual words in the orations and writings of Cato the Censor (who died in 149 B.C.E.). Verrius's most influential work was his dictionary, *De verborum significatu* (on the meaning of words). This work, the first Latin lexicon, was an alphabetical list of Latin words with definitions, etymologies, and frequent quotations of examples of usage drawn from archaic Latin texts (c. 250-100 B.C.E.) otherwise unknown. For example, the dictionary's entry under *quartarios* reads:

> Romans used to call muleskinners hired on contract "fourth-parters" [*quartarios*] because the muleskinners customarily charged for their services a fourth part of the profit. Thus Lucilius [a Roman satirist who wrote at the end of the second century B.C.E.]: "And then the unspeakable men, like a bad fourth-partner, crashed against all of the tombstones."

None of Verrius's works has survived intact.

Suetonius also reports that the town of Praeneste dedicated a statue of Verrius to honor his work on a great calendar inscribed on marble and set up prominently in a public area of the town. Enough fragments of this calendar have been discovered at Praeneste to indicate its size—6 feet (1.8 meters) high and more than 16 feet (4.8 meters) wide—and the scope of Verrius's work. The calendar listed the days of each month, with remarks on the religious and legal nature of each day and with notes on the pertinent religious festivals and historical and legendary events associated with each day. For example, he included this information for January 30:

> A day on which legal business may be transacted, a day for religious rites. Festival decreed by the senate, because on this date the Altar of the Augustan Peace was dedicated in Mars' Field [at Rome], when Drusus and Crispinus were consuls [9 B.C.E.].

The calendar has been dated to between 6 and 9 C.E. and therefore would have been the fruit of Verrius's later years.

Verrius died sometime during the reign of the emperor Tiberius (14-37 C.E.). His rise from slave to acclaimed teacher and scholar illustrates well the social mobility possible for talented freedmen in ancient Rome.

SIGNIFICANCE

Of Marcus Verrius Flaccus's teaching methods nothing more is known, although his practice of forcing his students to compete for literary prizes has clearly had a long (if unacknowledged) history.

Suetonius observed that Verrius's work on spelling was criticized by Scribonius Aphrodisius, a fellow freedman and contemporary rival in teaching, who attacked Verrius's morals as well as his scholarship. Yet Verrius's writings, especially his dictionary and his treatise on Cato's vocabulary, were widely consulted and discussed in the second century C.E., when Roman literary scholars took a particular interest in Cato and other early writers of Latin. About the year 200 C.E., an otherwise unknown Latin scholar, Sextus Pompeius Festus, made an abridged edition of Verrius's dictionary. The first half of Festus's edition is lost, but a further abridgment of all Festus's work was made by Paul the Deacon, a historian and teacher of Latin at the court of Charlemagne (c. 800 C.E.). Modern scholars, by studying what has survived of Festus's edition and Paul's condensed version of Festus, are thus able to judge the quality and content of Verrius's dictionary.

As Verrius's annotations to the Praenestine calendar have proved to be of significant value for those who study Roman history, so also Verrius's dictionary, even in the abridged editions in which it has survived, is a major source for students of the Latin language and early Roman literature.

—*Paul B. Harvey, Jr.*

FURTHER READING

Baldwin, Barry. *Studies in Aulus Gellius*. Lawrence, Kans.: Coronado Press, 1975. Chapter 4 ("Scholarly Interests") offers a lively discussion of Roman and Greek scholarship of the second century C.E. and of how students of Latin literature exploited previous studies, including the works of Verrius. Includes adequate notes citing the ancient and modern sources.

Bonner, Stanley Frederick. *Education in Ancient Rome: From the Elder Cato to the Younger Pliny*. Berkeley: University of California Press, 1977. The standard discussion of education in the ancient Roman world. Chapters 5 and 6 provide a general discussion of the schools of literature, language, and rhetoric in Rome. Includes sparse notes but a good bibliography.

Marrou, Henri Irénée. *A History of Education in Antiquity*. Translated by George Lamb. 1956. Madison: University of Wisconsin Press, 1982. A broader and more detailed study than Bonner's, this volume is arranged along chronological lines. In part 3, chapters 2 through 7 discuss the emergence and development of schools at Rome; chapter 5, in particular, covers what is known of schools of the type that Verrius established. Includes complete bibliographic notes.

Michels, Agnes Kirsopp. *The Calendar of the Roman Republic*. Princeton, N.J.: Princeton University Press, 1967. A technical discussion of calendars in ancient Rome, with particular attention to inscribed wall calendars such as that created by Verrius at Praeneste. Includes notes and fine schematic drawings of ancient wall calendars.

Rawson, Elizabeth. *Intellectual Life in the Late Roman Republic*. Baltimore: The Johns Hopkins University Press, 1985. Offers a concise discussion of the personalities associated with literary and language studies in ancient Italy in the time of Verrius and earlier generations. Contains detailed notes and a complete bibliography.

Suetonius Tranquillus, C. *De grammaticis et rhetoribus*. Edited and translated by Robert A. Kaster. New York: Oxford University Press, 1995. Kaster also provides an introduction and commentary. Suetonius's work is a primary source for information on Verrius Flaccus.

Treggiari, Susan. *Roman Freedmen During the Late Republic*. New York: Oxford University Press, 1969. The standard discussion in English of the social and legal circumstances of manumitted slaves in Roman history before c. 30 B.C.E. Discusses the prominence in Roman life of freedmen in education and other learned professions. Includes notes and a bibliography.

Wallace-Hadrill, Andrew. *Suetonius*. Reprint. London: Bristol Classical Press, 1995. The best study in English of the ancient biographer. Treats Suetonius's essay on ancient teachers of literature and rhetoric. The author discusses fully the history of the profession of teachers and literary men such as Verrius and Suetonius himself in Rome. Includes generous notes and a bibliography.

SEE ALSO: Artistotle; Augustus; Cato the Censor; Plato; Socrates.

RELATED ARTICLE in *Great Events from History: The Ancient World*: c. 440 B.C.E., Sophists Train the Greeks in Rhetoric and Politics.

VESPASIAN
Roman emperor (r. 69-79 C.E.)

After the chaos and civil war that followed the downfall of Nero, Vespasian restored peace and order to the Roman Empire and secured its survival as an enduring political and cultural institution.

BORN: November 17, 9 C.E.; Reate (now Rieti, Italy)

DIED: June 23, 79 C.E.; Aquae Cutilae (now Bagni di Paterno, Italy)

ALSO KNOWN AS: Titus Flavius Sabinus Vespasianus (full name)

AREA OF ACHIEVEMENT: Government and politics

EARLY LIFE

Titus Flavius Sabinus Vespasianus, better known as Vespasian (vehs-PAY-zhee-uhn), came from a family whose origins were probably humble and certainly obscure. The Flavians were of Sabine stock, and Vespasian's grandfather and father were both tax collectors and moneylenders. His father never advanced above the equestrian order (the rank below the senate) but was an associate of several influential members of the court of the emperor Claudius; through them, he obtained a military commission for his son.

Vespasian was appointed a tribune of soldiers in Thrace and demonstrated his considerable abilities within a short period of time. He advanced fairly rapidly for a man of his position and won the office of quaestor, which meant that provinces could be assigned to him; he was given Crete and Cyrene.

He married Flavia Domitilla, and they had three children. The two sons, Titus and Domitian, would succeed their father as emperors; the daughter died at a young age. After the death of his wife, Vespasian resumed a relationship with a woman named Caenis, a former slave who had been secretary to the mother of the emperor Claudius. Vespasian lived with Caenis as his wife in all but official ceremony until her death.

During 43 and 44, Vespasian was in command of Roman troops in Germany, and then in Britain, where he distinguished himself through vigorous military actions, including the defeat of several powerful tribes and the conquest of the Isle of Wight. For these accomplish-

Vespasian. (Library of Congress)

ments, he was awarded a consulship. He next served as governor of the Roman province of Africa (modern Tunisia) but was so honest that he left office without amassing the usual wealth. His career under Claudius's successor, Nero, took a disastrous turn in 66 when Vespasian fell asleep at one of the emperor's singing performances. For this heinous offense Vespasian narrowly escaped death and was instead banished from the court. Not until the outbreak of a serious revolt in Judaea, when an experienced general was required, was Vespasian rescued from oblivion.

Vespasian was strongly built, with a broad, sturdy frame. Throughout his life he enjoyed excellent health, partly because of his temperate habits and partly because of his active and energetic life. The coins and portrait busts of the period show a face that is humorous yet shrewd, with an expression that caused the ancient biographer Suetonius to compare it to a man straining to complete a bowel movement. Vespasian had a rough, often coarse humor, which was frequently directed at himself—in particular, at his well-known reputation for stinginess. His outstanding characteristics were hard work, administrative genius, and a profound wealth of common sense.

LIFE'S WORK

In 67, Vespasian was recalled from exile to lead Roman forces against the Jewish revolt, which was a serious threat to Rome's eastern borders and a danger to the vital grain supply from Egypt. By the summer of 68, Vespasian had regained most of Judaea, and the remnants of the rebel forces were detained in Jerusalem, which he put under siege. It was at this point that Vespasian learned of the uprising in Rome and the death of Nero.

"The year of the four emperors" followed, as Servius Sulpicius Galba, Marcus Salvius Otho, and Aulus Vitellius successively aspired to and gained the throne. While seeming to accept each in turn as the legitimate ruler, Vespasian was secretly establishing contacts and making plans with other influential governors and generals in the east; most notable were those of the two key provinces of Syria and Egypt. In 68, the troops of Vespasian's army declared him emperor; troops throughout the region quickly followed, and soon the forces pledged to him were advancing on Rome.

Vespasian himself reached Rome sometime in the fall of 70; his son, Titus, remained in Judaea to complete the reconquest of that territory. Later, the two would celebrate a splendid double triumph, which indicated that Titus was not only Vespasian's heir but also an important part of the government.

The disastrous end of Nero's reign and the fierce civil war and struggle over the Imperial power had left their harmful mark on Roman life and society, and it was Vespasian's first and most constant task to repair this damage. He reintroduced strict discipline and order into the military, hoping to remove the threat of another emperor being created far from Rome by a discontented army. He began an extensive series of construction and renovation projects throughout the Empire, especially in Rome, restoring years of neglect and destruction. At the rebuilding of the Forum in Rome, Vespasian himself carried away the first load of rubble.

A parallel effort was effected in the government and administration, as Vespasian assumed the title of censor and thoroughly revised the rolls of the senate and the equestrian orders. It was in his naming of new senators that Vespasian made one of his most innovative and lasting contributions to the Empire, for he included not only many Italians from outside Rome but also men from the provinces. Through this strategy, Vespasian enlarged not only the senate but also the entire concept of the Empire itself, making it less a collection of territories conquered by Rome and more a unified, organic whole. It is impossible to determine if Vespasian was working from a coherent, deliberate plan or merely responding to the situation in a sensible, practical fashion; either interpretation is possible. The result, however, was to create a broader and more lasting base for Roman power.

This reconstruction of Roman life demanded much effort from Vespasian, and he proved to be an outstandingly diligent administrator. The work also required vast amounts of money, and it was in search of these funds that Vespasian acquired the reputation for greed. He was quite open and shameless in obtaining funds, buying and selling on the commodity market and placing a tax on the public restrooms. When his son Titus found this last measure distasteful and protested to his father, Vespasian held up a coin and asked if the smell was offensive. When Titus said that it was not, Vespasian answered, "And yet it comes from urine." Even today, public restrooms in Italy are called *vespasianos*.

Although Vespasian was quick and crafty in gathering money, he was willing to spend it freely for worthwhile purposes. In addition to his extensive building projects, he was the first emperor to give grants and stipends to those who contributed to the liberal and practical arts: Teachers of rhetoric, poets, artists, and engineers received funds during his reign.

The years of Vespasian were marked by no major conquests or expansions of the Empire's boundaries. Even if he had aspired to such glories, the situation made the option highly dubious. Internally there was simply too much restoration to be done, as Rome was depleted from the recent succession of rival emperors and from the revolt in Judaea. Peace at home, rather than glory abroad, was the theme of Vespasian's reign.

This peace and the restoration it made possible were accomplished largely through Vespasian's abilities and

innate common sense. Unlike the rulers who preceded him, he had little fear of conspiracies or plots, launched no treason trials, and encouraged no informers. Historians have generally accorded him a high place, naming him one of Rome's best emperors.

From the time of Julius Caesar it had become a tradition that rulers of the Empire were deified on their deaths. When Vespasian was in his final hours, he took note of this practice and with rough good humor made his last remark: "Dear me, I seem to be turning into a god."

SIGNIFICANCE

Vespasian's great achievements were the restoration of peace and political sanity to the Roman Empire and the enlargement of its Imperial rather than strictly Roman foundations. After the disaster of Nero's final years and the almost fatal chaos of the struggle for power that followed, Vespasian was able to provide for domestic tranquillity, reassert military discipline, and establish a political framework that prevented, at least for a time, renewed outbreaks of self-destructive civil war.

At first glance, Vespasian might have seemed unlikely to be capable of such tremendous tasks: His origins were humble, his manner was common, even coarse, and his abilities, although genuine, seemed limited. Yet it is evident that these apparent defects, when allied with a solid basis of traditional Roman common sense and a broad view of the Empire, were in fact the very qualities needed to undo years of social uncertainty and internecine violence.

As an administrator Vespasian was diligent; his major concern was to ensure the proper functioning of those operations necessary to any state: tax collections, public works, defense, and commerce. Having achieved the Imperial position, he was more concerned to execute it conscientiously for the state than to defend it obsessively for himself. Ancient historians are unanimous in their view that he displayed none of the crippling suspicions and paranoid actions of earlier rulers. Cornelius Tacitus, that bleak and perceptive observer of Imperial Rome, gave Vespasian the rarest of praise when he wrote that he was the only ruler who became better, rather than worse, as time went on.

Vespasian's common origins were perhaps one reason that he could form a larger view of the Empire, including more of its population as citizens and senators. He was not trapped by the old views of patrician families seeking to retain their privileged status and their time-honored, yet ineffectual, control of the state. His wide-ranging experiences, from Britain to Judaea, also helped give him

VESPASIAN AND HIS SUCCESSORS	
Ruler	*Reign (C.E.)*
Vespasian	69-79
Titus	79-81
Domitian	81-96
Nerva	96-98
Trajan	98-117
Hadrian	117-138
Antoninus Pius	138-161
Lucius Verus	161-169
Marcus Aurelius	161-180
Commodus	180-192

this expanded perspective; there was not much doubt that this new direction enabled later emperors to maintain one of the world's most lasting political systems.

In this view, Vespasian certainly ranks as one of the best of the Roman emperors. This judgment is based on many factors, but focuses on Vespasian's renewal and expansion of the Empire, an expansion less in geographical territory than in political unity.

—Michael Witkoski

FURTHER READING

Grant, Michael. *The Roman Emperors: A Biographical Guide to the Rulers of Imperial Rome, 31 B.C.-A.D. 476*. London: Weidenfeld and Nicolson, 1996. Vespasian's rule is best judged not alone but as counterpoint to the disorder that preceded it. The brief selections in this volume provide an overview of the decline of the Empire during the last years of Nero and the near-fatal chaos that followed. Vespasian's accomplishments are viewed as the more outstanding in the comparison.

_____. *The Twelve Caesars*. New York: Charles Scribner's Sons, 1975. Grant continues where Suetonius's *Lives of the Twelve Caesars* (see below) leaves off in using anecdotes of character and personality to establish underlying psychological and political motives. By placing Vespasian within the tenor of his times, Grant not only makes the emperor more human but also shows the impressive nature of his achievements.

Greenhalgh, P. A. L. *The Year of the Four Emperors*. New York: Barnes and Noble Books, 1975. A large part of Vespasian's reputation is linked to the restoration of order to the Roman world after an intense period of chaos. This study concentrates on the events that brought him to power and reveals the extensive task of reconstruction he had to undertake.

Levick, Barbara. *Vespasian*. New York: Routledge, 1999. The first full-length biography of Vespasian in English. Although the writing is dry, the scholarship is sound and thorough. Addresses not only Vespasian's accomplishments in life but also his legacy. Includes indexes and eight pages of bibliographical references.

Marsh, Henry. *The Caesars: The Roman Empire and Its Rulers*. New York: St. Martin's Press, 1971. A brisk narrative in this popular collection of biographical portraits shows Vespasian in his roles as soldier, administrator, emperor, and rough-edged individual. The nonscholarly style is admirably suited to the character of Vespasian, with his practical common sense and coarse humor.

Suetonius. *Lives of the Twelve Caesars*. Translated by Michael Grant. New York: Welcome Rain, 2001. True to the standards of ancient biography, Suetonius shows the caesars less as actors on the grand political stage than as particular individuals with quirks and characteristics. This presentation, while missing much of importance, is still excellent for revealing the unmistakable individuality of a man such as Vespasian.

Wellesley, Kenneth. *The Year of the Four Emperors*. 3d ed. New York: Routledge, 2000. This edition includes an introduction by Barbara Levick. Places Vespasian in the context of the chaos and turmoil that preceded his reign. Addresses his childhood briefly but focuses on his rise to power. Includes bibliographical references, maps, and an index.

SEE ALSO: Claudius I; Nero.
RELATED ARTICLES in *Great Events from History: The Ancient World*: 43-130 C.E., Roman Conquest of Britain; 64-67 C.E., Nero Persecutes the Christians; 68-69 C.E., Year of the Four Emperors; September 8, 70 C.E., Roman Destruction of the Temple of Jerusalem.

SAINT VINCENT OF LÉRINS
Gallic theologian

Vincent was one of the leaders in the Gallic opposition to the concept of Augustinian predestination. After his death, Vincent came to be known primarily for his formula for distinguishing orthodoxy from heresy.

BORN: Late fourth century C.E.; probably in or near Toul, Belgica (now in France)
DIED: c. 450 C.E.; Lérins, Marseilles, or Troyes (now in France)
ALSO KNOWN AS: Vincentius Lerinensis (Latin); Peregrinus (pseudonym)
AREA OF ACHIEVEMENT: Religion

EARLY LIFE

Vincent of Lérins (lay-ra) was probably a native of Toul in northern Gaul and belonged to a well-to-do family. He and his brother, Lupus, would have received a classical education. Vincent also was learned in ecclesiastical literature: In the 490's, Gennadius of Marseilles described him as "a man learned in the holy scriptures and sufficiently instructed in the knowledge of ecclesiastical dogma." Sometime during his youth, Vincent held an unspecified civil or military secular office. Around 425-426, however, he and his brother, like many other young aristocrats, adopted the monastic life, going to the island of Lérins, near Nice. The abbot there, Honoratus, was another northerner; he perhaps came from near Dijon. Another monk who entered the monastery at about this same time was Honoratus's younger relative Hilary, whose sister Pimeniola married Lupus.

Unlike many of the monks, who remained laymen, Vincent was ordained a priest. He was active in the quasi-familial atmosphere of the monastery. Along with Honoratus, Hilary, and the priest Salvian, later of Marseilles, he assisted in the education of Salonius and Veranus, the young sons of the monk Eucherius. Many of these monks went on to become bishops in their own right, Honoratus and Hilary at Arles, Eucherius at Lyons, and Lupus at Troyes. Vincent, however, remained a monk and may have spent time also at Marseilles as well as with his brother in the north: "Avoiding the turmoil and crowds of cities, I inhabit a little dwelling on a remote farmstead and within it the retreat of a monastery."

LIFE'S WORK

Vincent is known primarily for his involvement in ecclesiastical debates, especially in the controversy in Gaul surrounding some of the teachings of Saint Augustine.

Augustine was much respected in Gaul, and every fifth century Gallic theologian cited him, at least on occasion, as an authority. Vincent compiled some *excerpta* from Augustine on the Trinity and the Incarnation. Augustine's opposition to Pelagianism, which denied original sin and the need for grace, was consistent with the prevalent Gallic orthodoxy. For example, according to a Gallic chronicler writing in 452, in 400 "the insane Pelagius attempts to befoul the churches with his execrable teaching."

The sticking point, however, was Augustine's concept of predestination, and according to that same source in the entry for the year 418, "the heresy of the predestinarians, which is said to have received its impetus from Augustine, once arisen creeps along." Predestination, which taught that only certain individuals were "predestined" for salvation, was seen as denying free will and as related to fatalism, Priscillianism, or Manichaean dualism.

The Gallic ambivalence toward Augustine ended in the mid-420's with the publication of his *De correptione et gratia* (426; *On Admonition and Grace*, 1873). In 426, John Cassian published an attack on both Pelagianism and unconditional predestination. At about that same time, two of Augustine's supporters, the laymen Prosper of Aquitane and Hilarius, wrote letters to him, still extant, decrying the situation in Gaul. According to Prosper,

> Many of the servants of Christ who live in Marseilles think that, in the writings which Your Sanctity composed against the Pelagian heretics, whatever you said in them about the choice of the elect according to the fixed purpose of God is contrary to the opinion of the fathers and to ecclesiastical feeling.

In order to strengthen his case against the Gallic antipredestinarians, Prosper went so far as to accuse them of being Pelagians, referring to their "spirit of Pelagianism" and describing some of their teachings as the "remnants of the Pelagian depravity." Prosper's accusation has gained sufficient credence that the antipredestinarian party in Gaul has been given the misleading designation "Semi-Pelagian," in spite of the fact that all known influential Gallic theologians, including the Semi-Pelagians, condemned Pelagianism as heartily as did Augustine himself.

A more accurate depiction of Gallic sentiments is given by Prosper in the same letter to Augustine, when he reported on the short-lived Bishop Helladius of Arles:

> Your Beatitude should know that he is an admirer and follower of your teaching in all other things, and with regard to that which he calls into question [predestination], he already wished to convey his own thoughts to Your Sanctity through correspondence. . . .

In 430, Augustine died. Shortly thereafter, Prosper, seeing himself as the defender of Augustine in the struggle against the Gallic antipredestinarians, returned to the attack in three tracts, including the *Pro Augustino responsiones ad capitula objectionum Vincentianarum* (c. 431-434; *The Defense of Saint Augustine*, 1963). As a result, the Gauls also entered the pamphlet war; one of their most important writers was Vincent of Lérins. Although none of these anti-Augustinian works survives, Prosper's responses to them give a good idea of Vincent's objections. Augustine was accused of fatalism, of denying that all share the chance for salvation, and even of asserting that predestination compelled some to sin. The Gauls denounced Augustine for teaching that those predestined to salvation had no need to lead a Christian life, to be baptized, or to have free will.

It soon appeared to Prosper, however, that he was unable to sway his Gallic opponents with his rhetoric. He and Hilarius then exercised the increasingly popular last resort of so many disgruntled Gallic ecclesiastics: They went to Rome and appealed to the pope. As a result, Pope Celestine I, probably in 431, addressed a letter to several Gallic bishops, rebuking them for allowing the teaching of improper beliefs. Celestine, however, had been led to believe that the Gauls were infected with Pelagianism and on this basis were questioning the Augustinian interpretation of free will. Scholars have searched Celestine's letter in vain for any reference to the real reason that the Gauls opposed Augustine.

The definitive Gallic response to Celestine and Prosper came in 434, when Vincent, under the pseudonym Peregrinus (the pilgrim), wrote *Commonitoria* (*The Commonitory of Vincent of Lérins*, 1554), also known as *Adversus haereticos*, a tract ostensibly issued as a general guide for discerning heresy from orthodoxy. Vincent, stating that "the fraudulence of new heretics demands great care and attention," issued what would become the standard definition of orthodoxy, the so-called Vincentian canon: Orthodox belief was "quod ubique, quod semper, quod ab omnibus creditum est"

(that which has been believed everywhere, always, and by all). Vincent therefore espoused a triple test—ecumenicity, antiquity, and universal consent.

Although Vincent taught that the true basis for orthodox belief lay in the Scriptures, he also placed great emphasis on church tradition, because the Scriptures were capable of many different interpretations. How was one to distinguish between legitimate doctrinal evolution, which came with greater maturity and understanding, and heretical innovation? In Vincent's view, the established Church and all the orthodox church fathers were collectively the holders of dogmatic truth and stood as the guarantors of the proper interpretation.

Vincent soon, however, narrowed his discussion down to a consideration of "novelty" and "recent heresies, when they first arise." Vincent's particular concerns were to respond to Celestine's letter and to defend the Gallic antipredestinarian position even though, as usual, Augustine was not mentioned by name. In his final argument against novelty, Vincent turned Celestine's own arguments against him: "Let [Celestine] speak himself, let him destroy the doubts of our readers himself. He said 'let novelty cease to assault tradition.'" The "inventors of novelty," whoever they might be, should be condemned.

Vincent concluded by arguing that because Pelagius, Coelestius (another Pelagian), and Nestorius, who had separated the human and divine natures of Christ, all had been condemned, it was necessary for Christians "to detest, pursue, and persecute the profane novelties of the profane." The doctrine of predestination also was novelty, and as such was to be condemned. By using Celestine's own arguments, Vincent rejected Celestine's and Prosper's claims that the Gallic antipredestinarians were guilty of wrongdoing. Vincent and the Gauls showed that, however much they might respect authorities such as Augustine and the bishop of Rome, they reserved final judgment for themselves. For the rest of the century, the Gallic theological establishment continued to reject predestination and to define ever more carefully its own conception of the interaction among grace, effort, and free will.

Vincent's treatise is the last extant evidence for the predestination controversy for nearly forty years. Prosper apparently gave up his efforts to influence the Gauls, admitted defeat, and permanently moved to Rome. His move did not mean, however, that there did not continue to be predestinarians in Gaul or that everyone agreed with the views expressed by Vincent. Gennadius of Marseilles reported that the reason the second book of *The*

Commonitory of Vincent of Lérins survived only in outline form was that the complete version had been stolen. Vincent himself is not heard from again, and Gennadius states that he was dead by the year 450.

SIGNIFICANCE

Vincent of Lérins wrote and taught at a time when the Western Church was in theological ferment. There was a growing concern with various kinds of heretical beliefs, their identification and suppression. One previously popular view, Pelagianism, had just been condemned. Another, more recent theory of Augustine, predestination, although accepted in other parts of the Roman Empire, in Gaul was considered heretical. This Gallic rejection of foreign influence was reflected in other spheres of the Church as well. Throughout the fifth century, for example, the Gauls, especially the monks of Lérins, refused to acknowledge any direct papal authority in Gaul.

Vincent was one of the primary figures in the Gallic theological discussions of the 420's and 430's. His articulate condemnation of predestination was accepted in Gaul for nearly a century. In the sixth century, however, after the fall of the Roman Empire in the West and the division of Gaul into barbarian kingdoms, the Gallic church no longer was able to maintain its independence. In 529, at the Second Council of Orange, the southern Gallic bishops, now under the influence of the pope and the Italian court, condemned the earlier rejection of strict predestination. Vincent's method for distinguishing orthodox from heretical beliefs, however, continued to be applied; it still provides the standard definition.

—*Ralph W. Mathisen*

FURTHER READING

Cooper-Marsdin, Arthur Cooper. *The History of the Islands of the Lérins: The Monastery, Saints, and Theologians of S. Honorat*. Cambridge, England: Cambridge University Press, 1913. An English-language account devoted to the monastery where Vincent lived and worked. Includes index.

Creswell, Dennis R. *Saint Augustine's Dilemma: Grace and Eternal Law in the Major Works of Augustine of Hippo*. New York: Peter Lang, 1997. A study that examines, among other topics, Saint Augustine's views on predestination.

Mathisen, Ralph W. *Ecclesiastical Factions and Religious Controversy in Fifth-Century Gaul*. Washington, D.C.: Catholic University of America Press, 1989. A detailed account of Vincent's ecclesiastical environment, including descriptions of the monastery at Lérins, Vincent's life and works, and the theological controversies in which Vincent became involved. Includes a detailed bibliography.

Vincentius Lerinensis, Saint. *The Commonitory of Vincent of Lérins*. Translated by C. A. Huertley. Vol. 11 in *A Select Library of Nicene and Post-Nicene Church Fathers*. Reprint. Grand Rapids, Mich.: Wm. B. Eerdmans, 1955. This English translation of Vincent's work includes a scholarly preface that discusses the background and context of Vincent's literary efforts in detail.

_____. *Vincent of Lérins: Commonitories*. Translated by Rudolph E. Morris. Vol. 7 in *Niceta of Remesiana*. New York: Fathers of the Church, 1949. An English translation of Vincent's most influential work. Includes critical commentary.

SEE ALSO: Saint Augustine.

RELATED ARTICLES in *Great Events from History: The Ancient World*: c. 6 B.C.E., Birth of Jesus Christ; c. 30 C.E., Condemnation and Crucifixion of Jesus Christ; 413-427 C.E., Saint Augustine Writes *The City of God*; 428-431 C.E., Nestorian Controversy; October 8-25, 451 C.E., Council of Chalcedon.

WANG BI
Chinese philosopher

Wang Bi was a major creative force behind the most important philosophical school of his day, and his commentaries on some of the most revered Chinese classics still help shape their interpretation.

BORN: 226 C.E.; China
DIED: 249 C.E.; China
ALSO KNOWN AS: Wang Pi (Wade-Giles)
AREA OF ACHIEVEMENT: Philosophy

EARLY LIFE

Wang Bi (wahng bee) died at the age of twenty-three. It is therefore difficult to separate the story of his early life from that of his mature period of productivity. A further handicap to the student of Wang Bi is the fact that very little is actually known about the details of his life. In an uncharacteristic omission, the Chinese dynastic histories do not even contain a biography for him.

Most of what is known about Wang Bi comes from a few short paragraphs appended as footnotes to the biography of another man and incorporated into a history called the *San guo zhi* (third century; *San Kuo: Or, Romance of the Three Kingdoms*, 1925). Wang Bi's thought, however, survives in the commentaries he wrote to three Chinese classics: the *Yijing* (eighth to third century B.C.E.; English translation, 1876; also known as *Book of Changes*, 1986), the *Dao De Jing* (possibly sixth century B.C.E., probably compiled late third century B.C.E.; *The Speculations on Metaphysics, Polity, and Morality of "the Old Philosopher, Lau-Tsze,"* 1868; better known as the *Dao De Jing*), and Confucius's *Lunyu* (late sixth or early fifth century B.C.E.; *The Analects*, 1861).

Wang Bi was a precocious child, and he soon proved himself remarkably adept at conversation—a skill that was much in vogue among the elite of third century China and that accounts for much of his contemporary reputation. He was a thorough master of the polite arts of the day, but, in keeping with his image as enfant terrible, he also was not quite sensitive enough to others' feelings and offended many of his acquaintances with his overly clever manner. He served in the relatively minor post of departmental secretary, which had also been his father's job, but failed to reach higher office because his patron, Ho Yen (He Yan; 190-249 C.E.), was outmaneuvered at court in his efforts to have Wang appointed. However, Wang was not really interested in administration anyway and preferred to devote his time and energy to philosophical speculation.

Wang flourished in the era of the Zhengshi reign (Cheng-shih; 240-249 C.E.), which is often cited as the high point of the so-called Neo-Daoist movement in China. This period came to an abrupt end in 249 C.E., when a *coup d'état* stripped real power away from the ruling family of the Wei state in northern China, where Wang lived, and placed it in the hands of a military dictator. Ho Yen perished in the wake of this coup, and Wang himself was dismissed from office; he died later that same year of unknown natural causes.

LIFE'S WORK

Wang Bi and his patron, Ho Yen, are traditionally credited with founding the movement known in the West as Neo-Daoism. This name is misleading, however, since the movement really grew as much out of Confucianism as it did out of Daoism. It began with studies of the Confucian classic the *Book of Changes*, was enthusiastically discussed with reference to the Daoist *Dao De Jing* and *Zhuangzi* (traditionally c. 300 B.C.E., probably compiled c. 285-160 B.C.E.; *The Divine Classic of Nan-hua*, 1881; also known as *The Complete Works of Chuang Tzu*, 1968; commonly known as *Zhuangzi*, 1991) in the later third century, and in the fourth century finally merged into a newly triumphant Mahāyāna Buddhism. The movement is probably most accurately known by its Chinese name: *xuanxue* (mysterious learning).

Wang himself stands accused of trying to interpret a Confucian classic, the *Book of Changes*, in Daoist terms, and, in the single most famous episode in Wang's life, of praising Confucius as the supreme Daoist because he knew better than to try and say anything about the ineffable Dao. The truth is that Wang was not much concerned with—indeed, he completely rejected—labels such as "Confucian" and "Daoist" and instead strove to unearth the ultimate truths concealed in each.

During the waning years of the Han Dynasty (206-220 C.E.), various thinkers, notably the great Wang Chong (Wang Ch'ung, 27-c. 100 C.E.), had become increasingly disillusioned with standard Confucian metaphysics, which in the mid-Han era had emphasized elaborate systems of correspondences between Heaven, Earth, and Man, cycles of the so-called Five Elements, and attempts to predict the future based on these. The desire to understand the basic principles of the universe was not lost, nor were the basic ideas entirely rejected, but the simplistic excesses—the teleology and the easy belief that Heaven was regular, purposeful, and concerned with humankind—were shaved away. At the same time, the so-called New Text versions of the Confucian classics that had supported the elaborate Han cosmological systems lost their standing and gradually were replaced by versions of the texts purporting to be older. These "Old Texts" did not fit neatly into vast cosmological systems and left a cosmological void in Confucian thought. By the end of the Han, the great pattern of the universe had seemingly dissolved into chaos.

In the third century, *xuanxue* emerged to fill this metaphysical vacuum. *Xuanxue* is predicated on the belief that the infinite phenomena of this universe are random, transitory, and without any meaningful pattern. Yet they all must, it was reasoned, be generated by one single, eternal verity. That was the "original nothingness" (*benwu*), or "nonbeing" (*wu*), the origin of all being.

Because of this emphasis on nonbeing as the root of all things, *xuanxue* thinkers have sometimes been dismissed as nihilistic. This casual dismissal is reinforced by the explanation that they were escapist Neo-Daoists, who turned from the traditional social concerns of Confucianism because of political repression, the collapse of the established Han world order, or aristocratic indifference. In fact, *xuanxue* was far more than mere escapism and represents an impassioned search for meaning in the universe by highly refined and critical intellects. The idea that nonbeing is the ontological foundation of the universe is similarly more than mere nihilism, since, in *xuanxue* thought, nonbeing becomes the positive principle that renders the universe intelligible.

Being and nonbeing coexist and are fundamentally indivisible. This great unity of being and nonbeing is "The Mystery" (*xuan*), also known as Dao, or the Way. It is the unifying principle of the universe, called a "mystery" because any name would be inadequate: It is absolute, and even to call it a mystery is to impose false and misleading limitations on it—better not to call it anything (but to call it "nothing" is not quite satisfactory either).

Wang's thought focused on this critical *xuanxue* relationship between being and nonbeing. His work took the form of exegesis, an attempt to achieve an understanding of the classics of China's formative age. Wang's scholarship was solidly in the tradition of the Jingzhou (Chingchou) school, a place in central China that had been a late Han center for Old Text scholarship and that was particularly famous for its study of the *Daixuan Jing* (c. 4 B.C.E.; *The T'ai Hsüan Ching: The Hidden Classic*, 1983). This book, in turn, was largely just an amplification of ideas to be found in the more venerable *Book of Changes*, and it

was to the *Book of Changes* that Wang turned his principal interest.

Working with an Old Text edition of the *Book of Changes*, Wang rejected the Han tradition of interpreting it in terms of astrological symbols and numerology and sought instead to return to what he thought was the original meaning of the text. The *Book of Changes* consists of the set of all sixty-four possible combinations of six broken and unbroken lines; the resulting hexagrams were then assigned oracular values and used in divination. Later, a set of "wings," or commentaries, was added that recast this fortune-teller's manual into a kind of cosmological blueprint of the universe. Although Wang rejected the neat teleology of Han Confucianism, he was still searching for some abstract principle that would reconcile the apparent diversity and disorder of the material universe, and he found in the *Book of Changes* exactly the kind of cosmic diagram for which he was looking.

The *Book of Changes* spoke of a Great Ultimate (*taiji*) that gives rise to the twin poles, yin and yang, which in turn generate the multitude of phenomena in the world. This schema is the primordial unity that in the third century was called The Mystery. Unlike the elaborate systems and cycles of earlier Han cosmology, this principle is spontaneous and unpremeditated. Heaven and Earth move without obvious purpose, yet naturally accord with the Dao. This system is a truth beyond words that must be looked at holistically; any attempt at analytical description violates its absolute quality. Consequently, in a typically Daoist paradox, the subject of Wang's intense investigations was beyond the power of his words to describe.

Wang belonged to the side of a raging third century debate that believed in the inadequacy of language. Characteristically, this idea harked back to a passage in the *Book of Changes* that said that "words cannot exhaustively [convey] meaning" (*yan bu jin yi*). Wang argued, therefore, that one should pay attention not to symbols or words but to their underlying, and more abstract, meanings. When one understands the meaning of a passage, one should forget the words.

Although the cosmic principle, or Dao, is unitary, it also has a binary extension—the dialectic between being and nonbeing. From these two, then, come the many. Wang liked to view the universe in terms of the interaction between a fundamental "substance" (*ti*), and its "applications" (*yong*) in the phenomenal world. This schema is reminiscent of the fourth century B.C.E. Greek philosopher Plato's famous duality between ideals and physical appearances, but, more important, it also resembles the later Neo-Confucian duality between "princi-ple" (*li*) and "matter" (*qi*). Wang, in fact, appears to have been one of the first Chinese thinkers to use *li* in essen-tially this sense, and, although he cannot be given credit for fully conceiving these ideas, he clearly contributed to the ongoing development of an important theme in later Chinese thought.

SIGNIFICANCE

In his short life, Wang Bi exerted a tremendous impact on philosophy. *Xuanxue* was the dominant mode of thought for some two centuries, and Wang's commentaries on the *Book of Changes* and the *Dao De Jing*, together with the commentary on the *Zhuangzi* by Guo Xiang (Kuo Hsiang; d. 312) and Xiang Xiu (Hsiang Hsiu; c. 230-c. 280), were the central texts of *xuanxue*. Later *xuanxue* thinkers and conversationalists measured themselves against Wang.

Wang's scholarship, if not *xuanxue* thought itself, also affects scholars even in modern times. It is well known that the *Dao De Jing* has been the most translated of all Chinese books, and, of the literally hundreds of Chinese commentaries on the *Dao De Jing*, that of Wang is con-sidered to be the very best that still remains. Most transla-tions of the *Dao De Jing* are therefore based on Wang's edition of the text and commentary. To be sure, Wang profoundly influenced his own time, but he also exerts an influence on modern scholarship, as the *Dao De Jing*, one of the most important books of all time, continues to be viewed partly through his eyes.

—*Charles W. Holcombe*

FURTHER READING

Fêng, Yu-lan. *The Period of Classical Learning*. Vol. 2 in *A History of Chinese Philosophy*. Translated by Derk Bodde. 1953. Reprint. Princeton, N.J.: Princeton Uni-versity Press, 1983. Although somewhat dated, and not without flaws, this work remains a classic. It is vir-tually the only English language study of some of the lesser known Chinese thinkers, such as Wang Bi.

Kohn, Livia, and Michael Lafargue, eds. *Lao-tzu and the Tao-Te-Ching*. Albany: State University of New York Press, 1998. This collection of essays on the wide range of approaches to the *Dao De Jing* includes one essay on Wang Bi in particular. As a whole, the collec-tion helps to illuminate Wang Bi's similarities with and differences from other Daoist interpretations.

Lin, Paul J. *A Translation of Lao Tzu's "Tao-te Ching" and Wang Bi's Commentary*. Ann Arbor: Center for Chinese Studies, University of Michigan, 1977. This book examines Wang's contribution to the study of the *Dao De Jing*. It includes a complete translation of a brief third century biography of Wang.

Wagner, Rudolf G. *The Craft of a Chinese Commenta-tor: Wang Bi on the "Laozi."* Albany: State Univer-sity of New York Press, 2000. This systematic study of Wang Bi's commentary on the *Laozi* both illumi-nates his scholarship and illustrates the differences between Chinese and Western interpretations of the classic.

_____. *Language, Ontology, and Political Philosophy in China: Wang Bi's Scholarly Exploration of the Dark (Xuanxue)*. Albany: State University of New York Press, 2003. An advanced philosophical explo-ration of Wang Bi's major contribution to Daoism.

SEE ALSO: Confucius; Hanfeizi; Laozi; Mencius; Wang Chong; Xie Lingyun; Xunzi; Zhuangzi.

RELATED ARTICLES in *Great Events from History: The Ancient World*: 500-400 B.C.E., Creation of the *Wujing*; 5th-1st century B.C.E., Composition of *The Great Learning*; 479 B.C.E., Confucius's Death Leads to the Creation of *The Analects*; Early 4th century B.C.E., Founding of Mohism; 3d century B.C.E. (tradi-tionally 6th century B.C.E.), Laozi Composes the *Dao De Jing*; 285-160 B.C.E. (traditionally, c. 300 B.C.E.), Composition of the *Zhuangzi*; 139-122 B.C.E., Com-position of the *Huainanzi*; 104 B.C.E., Dong Zhongshu Systematizes Confucianism; c. 60-68 C.E., Buddhism Enters China; c. 100-c. 127 C.E., Kushān Dynasty Ex-pands into India; 142 C.E., Zhang Daoling Founds the Celestial Masters Movement; c. 3d century C.E., Wang Bi and Guo Xiang Revive Daoism; 399 C.E., Chinese Monk Faxian Travels to India.

WANG CHONG
Chinese philosopher

During the Eastern Han Dynasty, apocryphal literature became popular, supplementing humanistic and rationalistic Confucianism and supporting the belief in portents and prophecies. Amid this change, Wang Chong was a rationalistic, naturalistic, and materialistic thinker whose philosophy contributed to clearing the atmosphere of superstition and occultism and to enhancing the spirit of skepticism, rationalism, and naturalism, which later bloomed in the form of Neo-Daoism during the Wei-Chin period.

BORN: 27 C.E.; Shangyu, Kuaiji (now Zhejiang Province), China
DIED: c. 100 C.E.; Shangyu, Kuaiji, China
ALSO KNOWN AS: Wang Ch'ung (Wade-Giles); Wang Zhongren (Pinyin), Wang Chung-jen (Wade-Giles)
AREA OF ACHIEVEMENT: Philosophy

EARLY LIFE

Wang Chong (wahng choong) was born in Shangyu, Kuaiji (now Zhejiang Province), China, in 27 C.E.; he lived during the period of transition from orthodox Confucianism to popular Neo-Daoism. During that time, China endured a series of crop failures that resulted in widespread famine and suffered from rebellions arising from the government's inability to find a solution to its people's problems. As a result, Confucianism, on whose training advancement in the civil service was based, declined in popularity; the country began to search for another ideology. Without a cohesive philosophy, the Chinese state and society would fragment and crumble.

While the country was going through this upheaval, Wang Chong suffered his own difficulties, having been born into a family whose fortunes were already on the decline. His rebellious grandfather and father had less-than-successful careers in government service. Eventually, both were forced into an erratic lifestyle, moving from one job to the next. To compound matters, Wang Chong was orphaned when he was very young.

Nevertheless, he always expressed an interest in learning. He continued to read, even in the most difficult of circumstances, in the local bookstores, going on to study at the national university in the capital city of Luoyang (Lo-yang). There he met Ban Biao (Pan Piao; 3-54 C.E.), an eminent scholar and the father of the noted historian Ban Gu (Pan Ku; 32-92 C.E.). Much of Wang Chong's education, however, was informal and irregular.

While teaching himself, he did not follow any of the traditional scholastic methods or values. Thus he has been classified as a member of the Miscellaneous school.

Like his grandfather and father before him, Wang Chong worked as a government official, coming into conflict with his superiors as a result of his uncompromising personality. During the course of his career, he held a few minor official positions on the local level, serving without distinction. In 88 C.E. he retired from circuit government, a job he had obtained as a favor from Dong Qin (Tung Ch'in), a provincial official. He returned to his hometown and devoted the remainder of his life to teaching and writing.

LIFE'S WORK

The intellectual situation in Wang Chong's lifetime was complex. Confucianism was supreme, yet it was being debased into a mysterious and superstitious doctrine. In addition, belief in the unity of humankind and nature was changing: Humankind and nature were seen as mutually influencing each other, and these influences were thought to be exerted through strange phenomena and calamities. Heaven, though not anthropomorphic, was purposeful, asserting its will through prodigies that it used to warn mortals; on a smaller scale, spiritual beings exercised a similar influence.

Wang Chong rejected these beliefs, declaring that Heaven takes no action; that natural events, including prodigies, occur spontaneously; that there is no such thing as teleology; that fortune and misfortune occur by chance; and that people do not become ghosts after death. In addition, he insisted that theories must be tested and supported by concrete evidence. He did not believe that the past is any sure guide with regard to the present, saying that there is no evidence that the past is better than the present, and vice versa. In short, he believed in human logic and nature's spontaneous manifestation.

Wang Chong also wrote three books: the *Jisu jieyi* (first century C.E.; ridiculing custom and decorum), in which he discussed the vagaries of politics and power. When he himself was out of power, he wrote the *Zhengwu* (first century C.E.; political affairs), in which he discusses the defects of the political system, and the *Lun heng* (85 C.E.; *On Balance*, 1907-1911), in which he calls for a logic based on tangible evidence and rejects superstition and speculation without foundation. Only *On Balance* has survived.

In *On Balance*, Wang Chong presented a variety of views on human nature. In it, he first quoted Confucius (551-479 B.C.E.): "By nature men are alike. Through practice they have become far apart." He then turned to Mencius (c. 372-c. 289 B.C.E.), one of Confucius's disciples, who saw humankind's nature as originally good, especially during childhood, and explained evil in terms of the circumstances of their lives. He also quoted Gaozi (Kao Tzu), Mencius's contemporary, who said that human nature is neither good nor evil: It is like the willow tree. Xunzi (Hsün-tzu), however, opposed Mencius, saying that "the nature of man is evil"; that is, just as a stone is hard as soon as it is produced, people are bad even in childhood. Dong Zhongshu (Tung Chung-shu) read the works of both Mencius and Xunzi and proposed eclectic theories of human nature and feelings: "Nature is born of yang and feelings are born of yin. The force of yin results in greed and that of yang results in humanity." He meant that human nature and feelings are both good and evil, for they are products of yin and yang. Liu Zizheng (Liu Tzu-cheng) concurred, saying that human nature is inborn and not expressed, but feelings are what come into contact with things; thus, human nature is yin (evil) and human feelings are yang (good).

Wang Chong dealt with these theories eclectically. He considered that Mencius's doctrine of the goodness of human nature referred only to people above the average, that Xunzi's doctrine of the evil of human nature applied to people below the average, and that the doctrine of Yang Xiong (Yang Hsiung)—human nature is a mixture of good and evil—referred to average people. Although his statements seemingly indicate that Wang Chong believed in three grades of human nature, he actually took this approach because he believed that human nature is neither good nor evil.

Nature and its spontaneity Wang Chong explained in terms of skepticism and rationalism. He did not believe that nature (or heaven and earth) produces anything purposely; instead, all things are spontaneously created when the material force (qi) of heaven and earth come together. Specifically, the calamities and changes produced unexpectedly by nature are not for the purpose of reprimanding or rewarding humanity. Their occurrence is nothing but a spontaneous, natural manifestation, known as nonaction (*wuwei*). Discussing this subject, he said, "What do we mean when we say that Heaven is spontaneous and takes no action? It is a matter of material force. It is tranquil, without desire, and is engaged in neither action nor business." Thus he rejected the teleological and anthropomorphic view of Heaven

then popular among his contemporary Confucianists.

He developed his view of fate similarly. He believed that human nature and fate have nothing to do with a good or bad life: A good-natured person can be unlucky, and an evil-natured person can be lucky. He concluded that nature dictates its own course in and of itself.

Death he explained again in terms of skepticism and rationalism. First, he did not believe in the existence of spirits or ghosts because after people die they are not conscious and thus are not capable of doing anything for themselves, asking, "How can the dead be spiritual beings if such is the case?" He then continued, "When other creatures die, they do not become spiritual beings. Why should man alone become a spiritual being when he dies?" He gave further reason in terms of naturalism and rationalism: "Man can live because of his vital forces. At death his vital forces are extinct. What makes the vital forces possible is the blood. When a person dies, his blood becomes exhausted. With this his vital forces are extinct, and his body decays and becomes ashes and dust." In short, he believed in nothing after death. Human death, according to Wang Chong, is like the extinction of fire: When fires are extinguished, their light shines no longer, and when people die, their consciousness has no more understanding. Here Wang Chong equated human (life) and matter (fire) in terms of material force (qi), which in turn is explained by nonaction (*wuwei*). Thus he can be identified as a materialist and naturalist.

Wang Chong also rejected the Confucian view that antiquity was a golden period in Chinese history. He believed in the equality of past and present, saying that the world was and is well governed because of sages and that it was and is ill governed because of unrighteous people; thus, good and bad governments, whether past or present, are not distinct. At times, however, he contradicted himself, saying that the present is better than the past. He came to this conclusion especially with the beginning of the later Han Dynasty (25-220 C.E.). The Han Dynasty's power and glory reached its pinnacle when it gained territorial expansion and political stability throughout the country; credit for these achievements was ascribed to the virtue of Han Dynasty rulers. Wang Chong was neither anti-Confucian nor pro-Confucian. Although he gave the impression that he was no follower of Confucianism, he actually buttressed Confucianism through his rational skepticism and criticism.

SIGNIFICANCE

Wang Chong believed in the power of nature and its spontaneity and stressed the importance of skepticism and rationalism. Yet he did not propose any new ideas. Instead, he attacked and accommodated the old ideas in an eclectic fashion. As a result, he is generally credited with ushering in the era of Neo-Daoism, which emphasized both the spontaneous power of nature (naturalism) and the critical ability of humans (rationalism) during the Wei-Jin period. Orthodox Confucianism was severely challenged by such emergent unorthodox ideologies as Neo-Daoism; Wang Chong, a typical Confucian scholar at heart, defended the basic Confucian tenets in his own unique way.

—*Key Ray Chong*

FURTHER READING

Chan, Wing-tsit. *A Source Book in Chinese Philosophy.* Princeton, N.J.: Princeton University Press, 1969. This book contains a chapter on Wang Chong's life, together with extensive excerpts of his philosophical writings taken from *On Balance.*

De Bary, William T., Wing-tsit Chan, and Burton Watson, eds. *Sources of Chinese Tradition.* 2d ed. New York: Columbia University Press, 2000. A brief introduction to Wang Chong's writings in relation to theories of the structure of the universe.

Fêng, Yu-lan. *The Period of Classical Learning.* Vol. 2 in *A History of Chinese Philosophy*, translated by Derk Bodde. 1953. Reprint. Princeton, N.J.: Princeton University Press, 1983. Interprets Wang Chong's philosophy.

Needham, Joseph. *Science and Civilization in China: History of Scientific Thought.* Vol. 2. 1956. Reprint. New York: Cambridge University Press, 1991. The scientific aspect of Wang Chong's philosophy is discussed.

Wang, Chong. *Lun-hêng.* 2 vols. Translated by Alfred Forke. 1907-1911. Reprint. New York: Paragon Books, 1962. An excellent, annotated translation of *On Balance*, the major result of Wang Chong's philosophy.

SEE ALSO: Confucius; Hanfeizi; Laozi; Mencius; Wang Bi; Xie Lingyun; Xunzi; Zhuangzi.

RELATED ARTICLES in *Great Events from History: The Ancient World*: 500-400 B.C.E., Creation of the *Wujing*; 5th-1st century B.C.E., Composition of *The Great Learning*; 479 B.C.E., Confucius's Death Leads to the Creation of *The Analects*; 3d century B.C.E. (traditionally 6th century B.C.E.), Laozi Composes the *Dao De Jing*; 285-160 B.C.E. (traditionally, c. 300 B.C.E.), Composition of the *Zhuangzi*; 139-122 B.C.E., Composition of the *Huainanzi*; 104 B.C.E., Dong Zhongshu Systematizes Confucianism; c. 60-68 C.E., Buddhism Enters China; 142 C.E., Zhang Daoling Founds the Celestial Masters Movement; c. 3d century C.E., Wang Bi and Guo Xiang Revive Daoism; 4th century C.E., Ge Chaofu Founds the Ling Bao Sect of Daoism; 399 C.E., Chinese Monk Faxian Travels to India.

WANG XIZHI
Chinese calligrapher

By refining the styles of earlier calligraphers and developing new ones, Wang Xizhi, through his innovative brushwork, set the aesthetic standards for all subsequent calligraphers in China, Korea, and Japan.

BORN: c. 307 C.E.; Linxi, Shandong Province, China
DIED: c. 379 C.E.; near Shanyin, Zhejiang Province, China
ALSO KNOWN AS: Wang Hsi-chih (Wade-Giles); Yishao (Pinyin), Yi-shao (Wade-Giles)
AREA OF ACHIEVEMENT: Art and art patronage

EARLY LIFE

In 317 C.E., because of military onslaughts by non-Chinese "barbarians," the Western Jin Dynasty (Chin; 265-316 C.E.) was forced to evacuate southward, reestablishing itself in refuge as the Eastern Jin (Chin; 317-420 C.E.). Wang Xizhi (wahng shur-dzur) was born some years before this move in what is today the province of Shandong, where the Wangs enjoyed the status of a leading aristocratic family. His father, Wang Kuang (Wang K'uang), was the cousin of Wang Dao (Wang Tao), a prominent minister of the Western Jin, who advocated moving to the south. Both Wang Kuang and Wang Dao were praised for helping save the Jin through this fortuitous move.

Many of Wang Xizhi's relatives, besides being active in politics, were literati well versed in philosophy, literature, and the arts, especially calligraphy, the technique of writing characters with brush and ink. Chinese characters, the oldest continuous form of writing in the world, evolved from primitive markings on Neolithic pottery, to first millennium B.C.E. graphs carved on tortoise shells and scapulae used in divination, and later to a complex script preserved on cast bronze ritual vessels and stone tablets. By the second century B.C.E., characters were being written on silk and bamboo slips using bamboo brushes with animal hair tips dipped in ink made from molded lampblack hardened with glue and dissolved in water on an ink slab.

As writing changed from carving, casting, and etching to a means of expressing, through a flexible brush, nuances of aesthetic feeling on a receptive surface such as silk or paper, the art of beautiful writing emerged. Writing had become not only a means of communication but indeed an expression of sentiment made manifest in ink. The ability to use the brush as both an artist's and a calligrapher's tool was a hallmark of the cultured gentleman. "A person's true character is revealed in one's calligraphy" according to a Chinese maxim; the facility to write Chinese characters in an elegant hand was judged to be a sign of talent and breeding.

Calligraphy is a discipline learned through practice and imitation. Wang was introduced to the "four treasures of the scholar's studio"—the brush, the ink stick, the ink stone, and paper or silk—in his youth by his father, who was adept in the *li* ("clerical") style of writing, and an uncle, Wang Yi, a master of the *xing* ("running") style. These styles of writing had evolved from earlier calligraphers' experiments with character forms and the movement of writing implements over the ages. Beginning with the Shang-period *jiaguwen* ("oracle bone") script, calligraphic styles progressed through the inscribed *guwen* ("ancient") script on bronze implements, the *dazhuan* ("large seal") script on Warring States-era ritual vessels, and the clerical style on Han Dynasty bamboo slips, to the *kaishu* ("block") script of the first century or so. By Wang's time, the running style, aptly named since the strokes run together, along with *zhang-cao* ("official grass"), were new styles emerging out of these historical predecessors.

As a teenager, Wang became a disciple of the noted calligrapher Lady Wei. She was impressed with his talent, reportedly saying, "This child is destined to surpass my fame as a calligrapher." Later, to broaden his knowledge of past masters' brushwork, Wang traveled the land examining inscriptions preserved on stone stelae. In the south, he encountered specimens of Li Si (Li Ssu; 280?-208 B.C.E.), the Legalist prime minister of the Qin Dynasty (221-206 B.C.E.), whose decrees unified the scripts of the rival feudal states into a single one based on Qin models. He was also impressed by the *zhenshu* ("regular") script works of Zhong Yao (Chung Yao), a Wei premier, and Liang Hu, noted for his large characters. The masterpieces of Cao Xi (Ts'ao Hsi), Cao Yong (Ts'ai Yung), and Zhang Chang (Chang Ch'ang) also had an effect on him. From their examples he learned the theoretical and technical essences of calligraphy to enable him to go beyond imitation to creativity.

Awakened to new inspirations, he reportedly lamented that he had wasted years in studying under Lady Wei. "I [then] changed my master," he wrote, "and have been taking lessons from the monuments." He absorbed all the styles that he encountered, adapting them to create new versions. Besides the running style, he was especially proficient in the *cao* ("grass") style, an abstract, cursive form of writing whereby individual strokes of a character are effortlessly blended together while the brush rapidly moves across the writing surface, producing characters as flowing as "grass undulating in the breeze."

LIFE'S WORK

Wang Xizhi held several government positions, including Censor of Kuaiji (K'uai-chi) and General of the Right Army (*Yujun*), a title frequently affixed to his surname. He held posts in the provinces of Hubei and Zhejiang, but he was far better known as a calligrapher than as a government official.

Many anecdotes, perhaps apocryphal, but repeated nevertheless in most Chinese biographies of Wang, attest his brilliance and dedication to his art. One such legend relates that he would practice writing from morning until dusk beside a pond at the Jiezhu (Chieh-chu) Temple in Shaoxing. Forgetting even to eat, he would copy characters repeatedly until he was satisfied. He washed out his brush and rinsed off the ink slab so frequently in the pond that its waters eventually turned black, and it became known as "Ink Pond."

Wang would practice even when he did not have paper, using his sleeve as a substitute. His writing was extremely forceful. Once, at Fenyang, he asked a craftsman to carve out the characters he had written on a board; the worker reported that the power of his brush strokes had been impressed through three-quarters of the wood, giving rise to the phrase "penetrating three-fourths of the wood" as a metaphor for profundity and keenness. His wife, a noted calligrapher in her own right, often could not get him to stop writing even to eat; once she found him absorbed in his work, munching on sticks of ink that he absentmindedly had mistaken for food.

On another occasion, a Daoist monk, taking advantage of Wang's love of geese, connived to induce him to write out a Daoist text for him by arranging for a particularly fine gaggle to swim near the artist's boat. Instead of selling the geese to Wang, who wanted them badly and was willing to pay a high price, the monk asked him to write out the *Huangting jing* (fourth century C.E.; *The Primordial Breath*, 1992) in exchange for the fowl. Wang promptly obliged and sailed off with his beloved geese in tow, leaving the clever monk with an invaluable treasure. Wang's fascination with geese was rooted in his admiration of their gliding movement in the water and their bearing, traits he studied to improve his use of the brush.

On another occasion, Wang supposedly encountered an old woman selling fans beside a bridge in Shaoxing. When she asked him to purchase one, he inquired as to how many she was able to sell each day. Admitting that her fans were out of fashion, the woman grumbled that she could barely make ends meet. Taking pity on her, Wang offered to write some poems on the fans and urged her to sell them at a high price. Though skeptical and thinking that her fans were spoiled by his writing, she followed his advice, and within a short period of time all the fans were sold. Now realizing the value of his calligraphy on her wares, she hounded Wang to decorate more, even pursuing him to his home. In desperation, he hid behind a stone grotto in the garden; later generations referred to this site as the "Old Woman Evading Stone." The bridge where the fans were reportedly inscribed is still popularly called the "Fan Writing Bridge."

The best-known event in Wang's life happened in 353 C.E. On the third day of the third lunar month, he joined a group of some forty men of letters, including Sun Tong (Sun T'ung) and Xie An (Hsieh An), to celebrate the spring festival at a scenic spot near Shaoxing, famous for the rare orchids supposedly planted there by a king of the fifth century B.C.E. There, at the Orchid Pavilion, they drank, challenged one another with word games, played chess, and composed poems. To commemorate the occasion, Wang wrote a preface to a collection of poetry created there by himself and his friends. This 324-character, twenty-eight-line masterpiece, the *Lanting xu* (after 353 C.E.; "preface to poems made at the Orchard Pavilion"), became treasured as one of Wang's greatest accomplishments.

This scroll's brushwork and composition were likened to "fairies flying among the clouds and dancing on the waves." Each character displayed his genius, and even where several characters, such as *zhi* (repeated twenty times) and *bu* (used in seven places), were duplicated in the composition, calligraphic variations were employed to prevent any single character from being exactly like another. Wang later tried to duplicate this success by making copies, but he was forced to admit that even he could not surpass his original in beauty.

Eventually, he became dissatisfied with court intrigue and corruption, preferring to retire to a reclusive life in order to devote himself exclusively to study and calligraphy. His last days were spent secluded in the picturesque hills of Zhejiang Province at the Jade Curtain Spring near Shanyin, where he died, probably around 379 (some sources say 361).

SIGNIFICANCE

Wang Xizhi is celebrated by connoisseurs of Chinese writing as the "Sage Calligrapher." His writing style was immortalized by the phrase "dragons leaping at the gate of heaven and tigers crouching before the phoenix hall," the words used by the sixth century Emperor Wu of the Liang Dynasty (502-557 C.E.) on being shown Wang's works. Several of his seven sons, particularly Wang Xianzhi (Wang Hsien-chih; nicknamed the "Little Sage") carried on their father's legacy, becoming important calligraphers in their own right and producing equally talented progeny.

Wang Xizhi's holographs were greatly coveted. The *Lanting xu*, for example, was passed on as a Wang family heirloom for seven generations, ending up in the possession of Zhi Yong (Chih Yung), a monk who was also well-known as a calligrapher. When Zhi Yong died, the scroll was entrusted to his disciple, Bien Cai (Pien Ts'ai). Emperor Tang Taizong (T'ang T'ai-tsung; r. 626-649) wanted this scroll in order to complete his collection of Wang originals. Thrice the monk refused to give it up. Wei Zheng (Wei Cheng), the prime minister, then devised a scheme whereby a confidant named Xiao Yi (Hsiao Yi), pretending to be a kind host, disarmed the monk's suspicion by plying him with wine; taking advantage of his drunken stupor, Xiao Yi was able to steal away the scroll, which had been hidden in a wooden temple beam. The emperor was overjoyed and ordered Zhao Mu (Chao Mu) and Feng Chengsu (Feng Ch'eng-su) to make copies for distribution to his ministers for their enjoyment and study.

On his death, Taizong ordered this scroll and all other original writings by Wang entombed with him so that he could enjoy them in the afterworld. The consensus of most experts is that none of Wang's originals exists today. Fortunately, many of his writings were carved in stone so that rubbings could be made for study, and other artists traced his originals to learn and to imitate his stroke style, thus preserving samples of Wang's genius for posterity.

—*William M. Zanella*

FURTHER READING
Froncek, Thomas, ed. *The Horizon Book of the Arts of China.* New York: Simon & Schuster, 1969. A concise biography of Wang is included under the heading "Wine, Weather, and Wang." Preceding page has a picture of Wang entitled "Wang Hsi-chi Writing on a Fan," painted by Liang Kai (Liang K'ai; c. 1140-c. 1210).
Long, Jean. *The Art of Chinese Calligraphy.* 1987. Reprint. New York: Dover, 2001. A general introduction, including chapters on history and the relationship of the characters to Chinese thought.
Moore, Oliver. *Reading the Past: Chinese.* Berkeley: University of California Press, 2001. This introduction to the Chinese writing system includes illustrations of many calligraphic styles and scripts. Wang Xizhi is covered in chapter 5.
Nakata, Yujiro. *Chinese Calligraphy.* Tokyo: Weather Hill/Tankosha, 1983. Historical overview of Chinese calligraphy originally published in Japanese. Chapter 6, "The Masterpieces of Wang Xizhi and Wang Xianzhi," gives a short biographical account. Numerous examples of Wang's work are illustrated and analyzed. Appendix contains a chronology of calligraphers and their works.
Willetts, William. *Chinese Calligraphy: Its History and Aesthetic Motivation.* New York: Oxford University Press, 1985. Contains a short account of the writing of the *Lanting xu* and reproduces a section of the scroll taken from a stone rubbing. Good bibliography on Chinese calligraphy in general.
Yee, Chiang. *Chinese Calligraphy: An Introduction to Its Aesthetic and Technique.* 3d ed. Cambridge, Mass.: Harvard University Press, 1973. Explains the history, philosophy, and aesthetics of Chinese calligraphy and its relationship to other genres of Chinese art.

SEE ALSO: Xie Lingyun.
RELATED ARTICLES in *Great Events from History: The Ancient World*: c. 3100 B.C.E., Sumerians Invent Writing; c. 1600 B.C.E., Shang Dynasty Develops Writing and Bronzework; 221-206 B.C.E., Legalist Movement in China.

WUDI
Chinese emperor (r. 140-87 B.C.E.)

The victorious campaigns led by Wudi's generals made Han China the paramount power throughout central Asia. Wudi's domestic and foreign policies exemplified the activist model, in contrast to the passive, laissez-faire policies of his predecessors.

BORN: 156 B.C.E.; place unknown
DIED: 87 B.C.E.; China
ALSO KNOWN AS: Wu-ti (Wade-Giles); Liu Che (Pinyin, birth name), Liu Ch'e (Wade-Giles, birth name)
AREA OF ACHIEVEMENT: Government and politics

EARLY LIFE
Wudi (wew-dee) became heir apparent at age nine and emperor at his father's death in his sixteenth year. His fifty-three-year reign was the longest in Chinese history until the eighteenth century. Foreign and domestic policy problems confronted the young emperor. Serious raids by the Xiongnu (Hsiung-nu) continued along the northern borders despite the peace treaty first signed by dynastic founder Liu Bang (Liu Pang; 256-195 B.C.E.), and renewed many times subsequently, generally to the advantage of the Xiongnu. Under Wudi, the Han were no longer willing to continue this unsatisfactory arrangement, but before they could declare war against the Xiongnu, domestic consolidation needed to take place and new foreign alliances had to be forged.

LIFE'S WORK
To centralize the government Wudi had to reduce the semi-autonomous feudal states that had been created by Liu Bang to reward relatives, in-laws, and meritorious officials. The system had been troublesome from the start, and had culminated in a major though unsuccessful revolt by the vassal kings in 154 B.C.E. Wudi's policies dramatically weakened these lords: He imposed heavy financial demands on them that bankrupted many (for instance, he demanded that they pay a tribute of white deer skin to him, and since the only herd of albino deer lived in his imperial park, the lords had to buy the skin from him at exorbitant prices); he also stripped many of their ranks for minor offenses and confiscated their do-

mains, which then became commanderies and counties. Most important, he made all noblemen divide their fiefs equally among all their sons on their death, thus fragmenting their domains.

Wudi inherited a prosperous country that had enjoyed seventy years of peace. It was reported that the coins in the state treasury storehouses could not be counted because the strings that tied them were rotten from long storage. However, the merchants had also profited enormously from the peace and low taxes. Some had engaged in speculation in grain and other essential items and in loaning money to peasants at high interest rates, and mortgage foreclosures had forced many farmers to tenancy and even slavery. To end the merchants' abuses, to add revenue to the treasury (to pay for the wars he was planning), and to prevent the sale of strategically important iron to the Xiongnu, Wudi introduced new taxes on merchant inventories, enacted laws that forbade merchants from owning farmland, introduced an "ever-normal granary" system to regulate the supply and price of grain, and made the production and wholesale distribution of iron, salt, and liquor state monopolies. He also enacted measures that forbade merchants to wear silk clothes or ride in carriages, among other bans, in order to humiliate them. Wudi's other measures that had economic consequences included flood control projects along the Yellow River, government-sponsored caravans to promote trade with western lands, and government-sponsored and supervised settlements in newly conquered lands.

These policies were intended to strengthen China for an eventual showdown with the Xiongnu, an enterprise for which it also needed allies. In 139 B.C.E. Wudi sent a courtier Zhang Qian (Chang Ch'ien; d. 114 B.C.E.) to find a nomadic people called the Yuezhi (Yüeh-chih) who had earlier been defeated by the Xiongnu and fled westward. Zhang's mission was to offer the Yuezhi an alliance against the Xiongnu. First, however, Zhang and his party of one hundred men had to cross Xiongnu territory, where they were captured. He settled among the Xiongnu, married one of their women, and waited for ten years before he could escape. Zhang eventually found the Yuezhi, who now called themselves Kushan and had settled in present-day northern Pakistan; they refused his offer of an alliance and Zhang began his return trip. He was again captured by the Xiongnu, again escaped, and finally returned to the Han capital Chang-an (modern-day Xian) in 126 B.C.E.

Although Zhang's mission was a failure, his report gave the court information about western regions hith-

EMPERORS OF THE WESTERN HAN DYNASTY	
Ruler	*Reign*
Gaozu (Liu Bang)	206-195 B.C.E.
Huidi	195-188
Shaoi Kong	188-180
Shaodi Hong	188-180
Wendi	180-157
Jingdi	157-141
Wudi	140-87
Zhaodi	87-74
Xuandi	74-49
Yuandi	49-33
Chengdi	33-7
Aidi	7-1
Pingdi	1 B.C.E.-6 C.E.
Ruzi	6-9 C.E.

erto unknown to the Chinese and about a breed of "heavenly horses" in Central Asia. He also reported rumors of trade routes between southwestern China and India. Both possible trade routes reinforced Wudi's intentions to expand Chinese conquests. In the meantime, Wudi had sent another emissary to another tribal people called the Wusun (Wu-sun), located in the northwest, whose land also produced fine horses; he offered the Wusun an alliance against the Xiongnu, a Han princess to marry the Wusun king, and rich gifts.

The massive campaigns against the Xiongnu began in 133 B.C.E. Wudi did not personally lead the expeditions; several of the leading generals were relatives of his wives and consorts. The Xiongnu were first cleared from the Ordos region, an area in the northern bend of the Yellow River, from which Xiongnu raids had threatened Changan; that region was settled by Chinese farmers. The armies then fanned out to the east and west, driving the Xiongnu from Inner Mongolia, Gansu (Kansu), and Chinese Turkestan. In 102 B.C.E., General Li Guangli (Li Kuang-li), brother of Wudi's favorite consort, reached Ferghana in Central Asia and induced its overawed king, as well as the rulers of numerous petty kingdoms in the region, to render submission to China.

A tributary relationship was established between the local states and China whereby Chinese protector-generals supervised local vassal rulers, who appeared periodically at the Chinese court with symbolic tribute and sometimes left sons in the Chinese capital as hostages, to be educated in Chinese ways. The tribute missions received in return lavish gifts from the Chinese court. Trade flourished as a result, with China exporting mainly silk and importing various local luxury products, most notably the noble Central Asian horses known in China as the "heavenly" or "blood-sweating" horses (a mite caused the capillaries under the horses' skin to rupture so that the horses' sweat was mixed with blood).

The Great Wall was extended to the Jade Gate in present-day Gansu Province and garrisons and military colonies were established beyond that point to defend China against raids and to protect trade. Other areas conquered by Wudi's generals included the southern coastal regions of present-day Chinese Yunnan and Guizhou (Kweichow) Provinces in the southwest, northern Vietnam, and Korea. These regions were organized into commanderies and counties and governed as regular parts of the Han Dynasty.

Other important accomplishments under Wudi include the establishment of an Imperial Academy that standardized the interpretation of the ancient classics and admitted an initial class of fifty students. On completion of their studies they were eligible for appointment to the civil service. This academy expanded to enroll thirty thousand students by the late Han Dynasty. All students studied Confucianism, the philosophies of Confucius and his disciples, which were defined during Wudi's reign by a famous scholar named Dong Zhongshu (Tung Chung-shu, c.179-104 B.C.E.). Confucianism had been growing in official stature since the beginning of the dynasty, but under Wudi it became the official doctrine of state and remained so until the beginning of the twentieth century.

China's most revered historians lived during Wudi's reign. They were a father-son duo, Sima Tan (Ssu-ma T'an, d. 110 B.C.E.) and his more famous son Sima Qian (Ssu-ma Ch'ien, 145-86 B.C.E.). They were jointly responsible for writing a monumental history of the world as known to China up to that time titled *Shiji* (first century B.C.E.; *Records of the Grand Historian of China*, 1960, rev. ed. 1993). It became the example for all subsequent histories because of its organization, comprehensiveness, and elegance of style. It also established a historiographic tradition that would be a hallmark of Chinese civilization.

The strain of Wudi's campaigns on manpower and finances, the undue severity of his rule to strengthen government control over the people, and the extravagance of his court led to severe crises during the last years of his reign. There were revolts by the exhausted people, but the most disruptive conflicts were between his wives and their relatives who vied for power. The first domestic cri-

sis of Wudi's household concerned his first wife, the Empress Chen (Ch'en) who had one daughter and no son. Her use of magic and witchcraft on the emperor so that she could bear a son led to her demotion from empress, the execution of their daughter, and the deaths of numerous other people.

In later years Wudi was unable to control the intense rivalry between the powerful family members of his second wife, the Empress Wei, and the family of one of his favorite consorts, the Lady Li. This rivalry culminated in an attempted coup by the Wei family in 91 B.C.E. In the intense fighting that ensued in Chang-an, thousands died and Wudi had to flee his capital city. In the end, both Empress Wei and her son, the crown prince, committed suicide. In 87 B.C.E., the gravely ill Wudi appointed an eight-year-old son crown prince mainly because his mother, the consort Zhao (Chao), had no powerful relatives. She died soon after her son's elevation—unproven rumor had it that she was murdered. Thus ended one of the most brilliant reigns in Chinese history.

SIGNIFICANCE

Wudi is one of the most celebrated grand monarchs in Chinese history. His long reign saw the reversal of Han domestic and foreign policy. His domestic reforms show a mixed record, but the reduction of the power of the semi-autonomous princes and nobles and the growing power of the central government promoted unity and uniformity in governance. His establishment of important state monopolies set a trend for later reigns and dynasties. His wars and foreign policy enlarged the empire to include southern and southwestern China, Inner Mongolia, and southern Manchuria, areas that would remain integral parts of China. Vietnam and Korea would eventually break away from direct Chinese rule but remain parts of the Chinese cultural area.

Wudi's campaigns against the Xiongnu swung the tide in Han-Xiongnu relations; under his successors, the wars would end in the break-up of Xiongnu power and their eventual expulsion from the Chinese frontier. In expanding Han power to central Asia, Wudi consolidated the Silk Roads that linked the Han and Roman Empires and expanded the Pax Sinica (Chinese peace) to prevail in much of the Asian continent. His espousal of Confucianism (despite his despotic ways) culminated in the establishment of Confucianism as China's state ideology, a trend that had begun under Liu Bang, the dynastic founder. Despite the family crises that marked the end of his reign, Wudi is regarded as a heroic figure in Chinese history.

—Jiu-Hwa Lo Upshur

FURTHER READING

Grousset, Rene. *The Empire of the Steppes: A History of Central Asia*. Translated by Naomi Walford. New Brunswick, N.J.: Rutgers University Press, 1994. Focuses on the nomadic neighbors of China from the Han Dynasty on. Index.

Jagchid, Sechin, and Van Jay Symons. *Peace, War, and Trade Along the Great Wall: Nomadic-Chinese Interactions Through Two Millenia*. Bloomington: Indiana University Press, 1989. An overview of Chinese-nomadic relations, with large sections devoted to the Han Dynasty. Glossary, bibliography, and index.

Kierman, Frank, and John K. Fairbank, eds. *Chinese Ways in Warfare*. Cambridge, Mass.: Harvard University Press, 1974. One long chapter is devoted to Wudi's campaigns. Glossary and index.

Loewe, Michael. *Crisis and Conflict in Han China, 104 B.C.-A.D. 9*. London: Allen and Unwin, 1974. An account of court intrigue and policy conflicts from Wudi's reign to the end of the Western Han. Glossary of Chinese and Japanese terms, and index.

Twitchett, Denis, and John K. Fairbank, eds. *The Ch'in and Han Empires, 221 B.C.-A.D. 220*. Vol. 1 in *The Cambridge History of China*. New York: Cambridge University Press, 1986. The definitive history of the Qin and Han Dynasties. Glossary, bibliography, and index.

Wang, Zhongshu. *Han Civilization*. Translated by K. C. Chang. New Haven, Conn.: Yale University Press, 1982. Richly illustrated account with recent archaeological information. Bibliography and index.

SEE ALSO: Confucius; Sima Qian.

RELATED ARTICLES in *Great Events from History: The Ancient World*: 221 B.C.E., Qin Dynasty Founded in China; 209-174 B.C.E., Maodun Creates a Large Confederation in Central Asia; 206 B.C.E., Liu Bang Captures Qin Capital, Founds Han Dynasty; 2d century B.C.E., Silk Road Opens; 140-87 B.C.E., Wudi Rules Han Dynasty China; 1st century B.C.E., Sima Qian Writes Chinese History; 9-23 C.E., Wang Mang's Rise to Power; 25 C.E., Guang Wudi Restores the Han Dynasty.

XANTHIPPE
Greek noblewoman

Through her aggressive behavior, Xanthippe forced men to reflect on and reconsider conventional assumptions about women's nature and social roles.

BORN: c. 445 B.C.E.; Athens, Greece
DIED: Early to mid-fourth century B.C.E.; probably Athens, Greece
AREA OF ACHIEVEMENT: Philosophy

EARLY LIFE

Xanthippe (zan-THIHP-ee) is known not as a mere name discovered through archaeological research but as a meaningful figure in ancient literature. Since almost no contemporary Athenian women thus are recognized, the implication is that Xanthippe was unusual. She was not a "normal" woman, of whom the Greek philosopher Aristotle (384-322 B.C.E.)—quoting the fifth century B.C.E. poet Sophocles—wrote, "Silence lends decorum to a woman." Xanthippe's concern was not male notions of decorum. She spoke, often shrilly, and her voice helped to create philosophical echoes across the centuries.

Nothing certain is known of Xanthippe's childhood and youth. Her date of birth can be estimated as 445 B.C.E., since she was the mother of one son in his late teens and two much younger sons when her husband, the Athenian political philosopher Socrates (469-399 B.C.E.), was executed. Several pieces of circumstantial evidence suggest that Xanthippe was born into a noble, or at least wealthy, Athenian family. Her name, meaning "Golden Horse," was of the sort traditionally favored by the aristocracy. The biographer Diogenes Laertius (late second-early third century C.E.) mentions that Xanthippe brought a dowry into her marriage. Athenian dowries were quite sizable and often included a large sum of money. At some point, Socrates virtually abandoned his early profession of stonecutting, perhaps living on the proceeds of invested money. Given that Socrates was not from a wealthy family, the money may have come from Xanthippe. Diogenes Laertius also mentions that Xanthippe felt ashamed of a dinner that Socrates gave for some rich men, suggesting her awareness of upper-class standards. The contemporary novelist John Gardner's *The Wreckage of Agathon* (1972), based loosely on the life of Socrates, supposes that Agathon's wife Tuka ("battle-ax") is of aristocratic background.

Xanthippe was an exception to the rule that Athenian daughters, especially those of aristocratic lineage, married very young, often in their mid-teens. Socrates' eldest son Lamprocles was born when the philosopher was in his early fifties, his youngest when Socrates was about sixty-five. If Xanthippe was twenty-four years younger than Socrates, she would have borne Lamprocles at twenty-eight and her youngest son at about forty-one. These figures suggest that Xanthippe married about ten years later than was customary.

There are two probable reasons why Xanthippe married late, perhaps below her social status, and to a notoriously ugly and unproductive man: She was difficult temperamentally, and she was physically unattractive. Her temper was infamous; her looks may be inferred from some Socratic advice reported by the historian Xenophon (c. 430-c. 354 B.C.E.). Socrates advises his companions to avoid sexual relations with beautiful people and to restrict their sexual activity to those who would be shunned unless there existed an overwhelming physical need. Whether or not he took his own advice in marrying Xanthippe, there is not the slightest hint that she was physically attractive.

LIFE'S WORK

The marriage of Xanthippe and Socrates would seem to be a match made in hell, between an overage, unattractive, difficult woman and an even older, ugly, underemployed frequenter of the Athenian streets. Many must have seen it this way: Socrates was put to death for his disturbing activities, and Xanthippe's name became synonymous with "shrew." This view, however, is superficial, ignoring the deep moral bond between the two.

That bond is suggested by the fact that the activities of Xanthippe and Socrates were both orthodox and unorthodox. In a number of important ways, each was a conventional Athenian of the time. Xanthippe married, reared children, managed a household, and stayed clear of political life; Socrates, in addition to establishing a family, served in military campaigns and took his turn in holding public office. Neither challenged practically the genderized Athenian division of functions.

This extraordinary couple's challenge to authority was verbal. This is thoroughly familiar in Socrates' case. He questioned and criticized powerful Athenians, comparing himself to a gadfly stinging that noble but complacent horse Athens. Antagonizing many, he was indicted for impiety, tried, convicted, and executed. In the process, Socrates became a hero of free speech and moral integrity. What is not so obvious is that Xanthippe's life may be understood in roughly the same terms, once the necessary revisions in perspective are made.

Athenian males ruled the city (and much of their known world), not only politically but with their public presence. Athenian women, especially those of the upper classes, were secluded and were segregated from men. Xanthippe appears to have had a complex response to these restrictions. On one hand, denied wider public access, she "stung" most frequently members of her own family. Xenophon tells the story of Socrates arguing Lamprocles out of his anger with his mother. Xanthippe has been abusing her son, not physically but verbally; Lamprocles protests that this is unjust, since he has done nothing wrong. Socrates induces his son to acknowledge that Xanthippe's scolding is not only not malicious but also motivated by special concern for Lamprocles. This implies that while Lamprocles may have done nothing wrong, he may also have done nothing right, and that his mother's words were needed to get him moving. There is a glimpse here of the power of women to shape men morally through daily "encouragement."

Xanthippe's activities, however, probably were not confined to the household. She appears to have known most of Socrates' friends and companions. There are a number of instances of Xanthippe appearing in public, as related by Diogenes Laertius and in Plato's *Phaedōn* (388-368 B.C.E.; *Phaedo*, 1675). In her house, in the streets, in the marketplace, in Socrates' jail cell, Xanthippe was a presence. She was not silent; she did not defer to or flatter men; she did not conceal her anger. In short, she frequently behaved like a man, being as visible, as outspoken, and as courageous—or at any rate as rash—as a man was expected to be. This presumption of equality amused but also unnerved Socrates' companions, to whom any outspoken, critical woman was abnormal and therefore a "shrew."

Xanthippe's attitude toward Socrates was straightforward. Anecdotes about her verbal and physical abuse of him have become legendary and form most of the traditional image of Xanthippe. No doubt, there is a basis in fact for these anecdotes; Socrates must have been a better philosopher than husband, father, and provider, and Xanthippe may well have been a frequent critic. Yet Xanthippe is also shown to have admired Socrates, especially for his justice, and to have been considerably more accepting of his friends than they were of her. Overall, she seems to have had few illusions about, but considerable affection for, Socrates. It is Plato, not Xanthippe, who portrays Socrates as "young and fair."

Socrates' experience with Xanthippe may have been of major importance for his political philosophy. Contemporary scholars have noted that Socrates was unusually well-disposed toward women. This seems paradoxical, given the horrific reputation of the woman to whom he was closest. Yet Xenophon makes it clear that Socrates very much appreciated Xanthippe. In part, this was because he believed her to be a very good mother, painstaking and selfless, if not especially patient, with her sons.

Beyond this, however, Socrates was clear-eyed about Xanthippe's nature, and he was unbiased by the prevailing antifemale prejudice. He understood that Xanthippe was high-spirited; perhaps punning on her name, he compared her to a horse. He was not interested in changing her nature by attempting to break her. Instead of forcing Xanthippe to conform to convention, Socrates conformed to her, believing that learning to live with Xanthippe would be excellent training for getting along with all others. Socrates' acknowledgment of Xanthippe's active, high-spirited nature is reflected in the imaginary "best city" of Plato's *Politeia* (388-368 B.C.E.; *Republic*, 1701). There, Socrates proposes that naturally gifted women as well as men be educated as the guardian-rulers of the city.

SIGNIFICANCE

Xanthippe disappeared from historical view following Socrates' execution in 399 B.C.E. It is easy to believe that her notoriety depended entirely on her relationship with a famous man—that she was a "mere appendage" to him, and an obnoxious one at that. Yet to believe this is to misunderstand the historical significance of both Socrates and Xanthippe.

It is clear that Xanthippe had an unusual degree of freedom in her relationship with Socrates. This is not because Socrates was an ideological "feminist," but because he was observant enough and honest enough to take each person as he or she was. He believed that persons were not merely "male" and "female" in a simple anatomical sense but also had "souls" significantly independent of gender. Xanthippe had a nobly rambunctious soul, and Socrates accorded it due respect.

Very likely, Xanthippe recognized this independence of mind and sense of justice in Socrates and chose him as fully as he chose her. Nevertheless, both Athenian conventions and Socrates' own freedom-loving nature made it impossible for Xanthippe to be simply his equal and companion. The philosopher's wife was, after all, a wife; Socrates and Xanthippe were not fellow guardians in his imagined city. It is easy to believe that Xanthippe, acutely attuned to justice by nature and circumstances, felt the injustice in both her situation and that of Athenian women generally. According to Socratic doctrine, the response of the high-spirited person to injustice is anger.

Xanthippe's "shrewishness," then, may be seen in two sympathetic ways. First, to view a woman as a shrew was the common male reaction to any female who was not sufficiently deferential. Second, shrewishness was the only form contextually available to Xanthippe to express her sense of injustice. Xanthippe was in a classic double-bind: She could not remain silent, but neither could she join her husband's circle of refined, sustained moral discourse. "Conversing daily about virtue" was not an option for Xanthippe; she was too busy rearing Socrates' children and keeping his house. Instead, she shouted occasionally about virtue, and she was misunderstood. Xanthippe's life thus serves as a reminder of both the demands of and constraints on perfect justice.

—*John F. Wilson*

FURTHER READING

Blundell, Sue. *Women in Ancient Greece*. Cambridge, Mass.: Harvard University Press, 1995. A well-illustrated survey of the topic, based on thorough scholarship and engagingly written. Part 2 covers the period of Xanthippe's life.

Cantarella, Eva. *Pandora's Daughters: The Role and Status of Women in Greek and Roman Antiquity*. Translated by Maureen B. Fant. Baltimore: The Johns Hopkins University Press, 1987. This influential interpretation of the position of women in antiquity stresses the breadth and depth of antifemale bias. Socrates is understood as an important dissenter, but his inspiration is seen as the courtesan Aspasia, not Xanthippe.

Caputi, Jane. *Gossips, Gorgons, and Crones: The Fates of the Earth*. Santa Fe, N.Mex.: Bear, 1993. An interesting, spirited interpretation of the role of "resistant women," written from an ecofeminist perspective. Xanthippe would be included under the category "Gorgon."

Diogenes Laertius. *Lives of Eminent Philosophers*. Vol. 1. Translated by R. D. Hicks. Cambridge, Mass.: Harvard University Press, 1991. Diogenes Laertius's biography of Socrates (in book 2, chapter 5) is the principal source of the colorful, "shrewish" anecdotes about Xanthippe.

Gardner, John. *The Wreckage of Agathon*. New York: Ballantine Books, 1972. This novel gives controversial historical life to Xanthippe ("Tuka") and Socrates ("Agathon"). The fictional pair are far more involved with one another (and with heterosexual relations generally) than historical scholarship would concede.

Plato. *Phaedo*. In *The Collected Dialogues of Plato*, edited by Edith Hamilton and Huntington Cairns. Princeton, N.J.: Princeton University Press, 1963. Provocative glimpses of Xanthippe begin and end Plato's treatment of Socrates' last day of life.

Scruton, Roger. *Xanthippic Dialogues*. South Bend, Ind.: St. Augustine's Press, 1998. An excellent, humorous, insightful parody of Plato's dialogues. Xanthippe is here portrayed as a brilliant observer and philosopher. This work serves as an excellent commentary on the original dialogues.

Xenophon. *Conversations of Socrates*. Translated by Hugh Tredennick and Robin Waterfield. London: Penguin Books, 1990. Xanthippe as a real-world example of woman, wife, and mother is present, explicitly and implicitly, throughout Xenophon's Socratic writings.

SEE ALSO: Plato; Socrates.

RELATED ARTICLES in *Great Events from History: The Ancient World*: 478-448 B.C.E., Athenian Empire Is Created; 399 B.C.E., Death of Socrates.

XENOPHANES
Greek philosopher

Xenophanes' critique of the Homeric gods marks the beginning of both systematic theology and the rational interpretation of myth in ancient Greek society.

BORN: c. 570 B.C.E.; Colophon, Ionia (now in Turkey)
DIED: c. 478 B.C.E.; Magna Graecia (now in Italy)
AREAS OF ACHIEVEMENT: Philosophy, literature, religion

EARLY LIFE

The childhood of Xenophanes (zeh-NOF-uh-neez), like that of most early Greek philosophers, is shrouded in mystery. By the time that Xenophanes himself appears in the literary record of ancient Greece, he is already a grown man, traveling from town to town as a professional poet. Scholars cannot even be certain of his father's name, since several ancient authorities have listed it as Dexius, others as Dexinus, and still others as Orthomenes. Scholars are certain, however, that Xenophanes was born in the city of Colophon (near the coast of Asia Minor) sometime during the middle of the sixth century B.C.E. Moreover, it is likely that he left this area in his youth, probably as the result of Persia's policy of imperial expansion. It was, then, during the very period of Xenophanes' youth that the Persian conquest of new territories began to lead, inevitably, to war between Persia and Greece.

Xenophanes himself would later allude to this stage of his life with these ambiguous words, taken from what is known as fragment 8:

> Already there have been seven and sixty years tossing my thoughts up and down the land of Greece. And from my birth there were another twenty-five in addition to these, if indeed I know how to speak truly of such things.

Since in another fragment Xenophanes had mentioned "the coming of the Mede," it seems probable that he left Colophon at about the time that this city fell to Harpagus the Mede in 546. For the rest of his life, Xenophanes would support himself through his poetry. He became a traveling rhapsodist, composing songs on various topics as he journeyed throughout the Greek world. Unlike many other archaic rhapsodists, however, Xenophanes used only his own compositions in his performances. It is probably from these works that the extant fragments are derived.

Diogenes Laertius states that Xenophanes spent much of his life in Sicily. Other authorities support this view, maintaining that Xenophanes had participated in founding the city of Elea, in what is modern Italy. Xenophanes, according to these scholars, is thus the spiritual forebear of the philosophers known as the Eleatics and one of the actual founders of Elea itself. The accuracy of this claim seems questionable, however, and the belief that Xenophanes was instrumental in founding Elea may have arisen solely because the philosopher had written a poem commemorating the event. In fact, Xenophanes seems unlikely to have had any permanent residence; he must have spent most of his life traveling extensively throughout Greece and Sicily, pausing in each community only for brief periods.

Xenophanes' lifelong travels had a profound influence on his thought. For example, after he had observed fossils in a quarry near Syracuse, Xenophanes developed the theory that life on earth is cyclic: Those creatures who had lived in earlier eras, he believed, were repeatedly "dissolved" by the encroaching seas, and life had to develop all over again. Yet even more important than what Xenophanes observed during these travels was his contact with the intellectual revolution in Greek philosophy, which, by this time, was well under way. For example, Thales of Miletus, whose views about the composition of matter are regarded as the origin of Greek philosophy, had by then been active for more than forty years. Anaximander, who was Thales' successor and who had originated the notion of the *apeiron* (the "unbounded" or "unlimited" as the source of all creation), died in about the same year that Colophon fell. Anaximenes of Miletus, who had believed that all matter was composed of rarefied or contracted air, is also likely to have lived in roughly the same period as Xenophanes.

The ideas of these philosophers were of great importance in the Greek world where Xenophanes traveled, lived, and wrote his poetry. The young philosopher seems to have listened to the theories of his predecessors, considered them, and then combined their views with his own thought to create the subjects of his songs. Unlike many other pre-Socratics, however, Xenophanes has left the modern world substantial portions of his poetry, written down either by himself or by those who studied with him. It is from these surviving words of Xenophanes— about 120 lines in all—that modern readers are able to form their clearest picture of the philosopher and of his life's work.

LIFE'S WORK

As was common among the pre-Socratic philosophers, Xenophanes devoted a substantial portion of his thought to considering the nature of the physical universe. Although it is uncertain whether he actually wrote the work titled *Peri physeōs* (on nature), which Stobaeus and Pollux attributed to him, a large number of Xenophanes' surviving fragments are concerned with matters of astronomy and the weather. In these passages, Xenophanes reveals that he was strongly influenced by Anaximenes, who had argued that clouds were merely condensed, or "thickened," masses of air. Xenophanes expressed a similar view, substituting only the notion of "sea" or "water" for that of air. In Xenophanes' theory, the sea gives rise to the clouds, winds, and rivers; the sun and heavenly bodies are created from thickened, or "ignited," bits of cloud. Rainbows, too, are said to be nothing more than colored fragments of cloud.

In two other passages, Xenophanes says that everything in the universe is made of earth and water. This theory is apparently an attempt to combine Thales' recognition that water is necessary to life and, as ice or steam, can change its shape with Anaximenes' belief that there must be some general process (condensation or rarefaction) that accounts for this change. That same general line of thought may also lie behind Xenophanes' belief that each day the sun is created anew, arising from fiery bits of dilated cloud.

Yet far more influential than these physical theories of Xenophanes were the philosopher's theological views and his statements about the nature of God. Xenophanes disagreed with earlier authors such as Homer and Hesiod who had presented the gods as immoral and had endowed them with the same physical traits and limitations as ordinary men. In two famous fragments, Xenophanes criticized the common assumption that the gods were merely immortal creatures similar in most ways to ordinary human beings:

> The Ethiopians claim that their gods are snub-nosed and black, the Thracians that theirs have blue eyes and blond hair.... But if cows and horses or lions had hands or could draw and do all the other things that men do, then horses would draw images of the gods which look like horses, and cows like cows, and they would depict the bodies of their gods in the same form as they had themselves.

The argument here is that all people wrongly assume the gods to be like themselves, in form and (it is suggested) in their vices and faults.

Xenophanes' own understanding of divinity was quite different. To begin with, Xenophanes was a monotheist, believing that there exists only a single god who is unlike humankind both in form and in character. Second, Xenophanes said that this deity perceives the universe differently from humankind, using all of its "body" simultaneously to think, to hear, and to see. Finally, in two important fragments, Xenophanes anticipated Aristotle's theory of the Prime Mover, asserting that this one god remains in a single place and guides the universe without movement, relying solely on the power of Mind.

Yet, by Xenophanes' own admission, even these statements about divinity are subject to debate. For "no man," he says, "either has known or will know the clear truth about the gods.... Belief [and not certain knowledge] is produced for all men." While not as general in focus as the skepticism of Plato's Academy, Xenophanes' remarks here do anticipate some of the views that would arise in later periods of Greek philosophy. His distinction between "believing" and "knowing," for example, was to have a crucial influence on the work of Plato himself. Moreover, Xenophanes' theory that human knowledge is necessarily limited would reappear in the works of many later Platonic scholars.

SIGNIFICANCE

If Xenophanes' statements about his life in fragment 8 are to be believed, he had already reached the age of ninety-two when those words were written. Xenophanes' lifetime would have encompassed a period of Greek history that witnessed the birth of both tragedy and philosophy in the Western world. At the time of his death, the Persian Wars were drawing to a close and the classical period of Greek history was about to begin.

The picture of Xenophanes that emerges from his writings is thus that of a man who was representative of his day: diverse in his interests, immensely curious, and unwilling to remain content with the dogma of the past. These are traits that characterize many of the other pre-Socratic philosophers as well.

Yet Xenophanes was also important for the impact that he would have on later scholars. His perception of divinity would influence Aristotle and, ultimately, Saint Thomas Aquinas. His belief that human knowledge was inherently limited was to reemerge in the skepticism of the Academy. Xenophanes was, in other words, a pivotal figure who helped to transform the empirical philosophy of antiquity into the more metaphysical philosophy of the classical age.

—Jeffrey L. Buller

FURTHER READING

Fraenkel, H. "Xenophanes' Empiricism and His Critique of Knowledge." In *The Pre-Socratics: A Collection of Critical Essays*, edited by Alexander P. D. Mourelatos. Garden City, N.Y.: Anchor Books, 1974. Fraenkel uses Xenophanes' theory of knowledge, and his rejection of early beliefs about the gods, as the basis for an exploration of the philosopher's worldview. Perhaps the best short summary available on the thought and contribution of Xenophanes to Greek philosophy.

Freeman, Kathleen. *Ancilla to the Pre-Socratic Philosophers: A Complete Translation of the Fragments in Diels, "Fragmente der Vorsokratiker."* Cambridge, Mass.: Harvard University Press, 1971. The most convenient source of information for anyone who is interested in examining the surviving texts of the pre-Socratics. Freeman translates, without commentary or interpretation, all the fragments included in Diels's exhaustive edition of the pre-Socratics.

_____. *The Pre-Socratic Philosophers*. Cambridge, Mass.: Harvard University Press, 1953. In this excellent survey, Freeman, taking each historical figure in turn, digests and summarizes all that is known about the philosophical views of the pre-Socratics. The fragments on which she has based her information are all listed in concise footnotes. A very thorough summary of the philosopher's life begins each entry. At the end of the work is an invaluable list that presents, in a sentence or two, an encapsulated view of what is known about the authors who are the sources for the fragments.

Jaeger, Werner Wilhelm. "Xenophanes' Doctrine of God." In *The Theology of the Early Greek Philosophers*. Translated by Edward S. Robinson. New York: Oxford University Press, 1968. The premise of Jaeger's book is that the pre-Socratics are important for their theological views as well as for their (more famous) doctrines on the physical universe. Xenophanes, as arguably the most theological of the pre-Socratics, naturally plays a central role in this work.

Kirk, Geoffrey S., and John E. Raven. *The Presocratic Philosophers: A Critical History with a Selection of Texts*. 1957. Rev. ed. New York: Cambridge University Press, 1983. A useful summary of pre-Socratic philosophers and their philosophy, containing both the major texts of the philosophers and reliable commentary on those texts. The extant fragments are grouped by topic rather than by number (as in many other editions). The 1983 edition contains more recent interpretations and a much-improved format: Translations follow Greek passages immediately, rather than in footnotes. Includes a short but important bibliography on each author.

Xenophanes. *Xenophanes of Colophon: Fragments, a Text and Translation with a Commentary*. Toronto: University of Toronto Press, 1992. Greek text with English translation and commentary by J. H. Lesher. A solid translation with helpful commentary. Includes bibliographical references and an index.

SEE ALSO: Anaximander; Anaximenes of Miletus; Parmenides; Plato; Thales of Miletus.

RELATED ARTICLES in *Great Events from History: The Ancient World*: c. 750 B.C.E., Homer Composes the *Iliad*; c. 700 B.C.E., Hesiod Composes *Theogony* and *Works and Days*; 600-500 B.C.E., Greek Philosophers Formulate Theories of the Cosmos; 480-479 B.C.E., Persian Invasion of Greece.

XENOPHON
Greek historian and philosopher

Through his writings on subjects ranging from the practical to the philosophical, Xenophon, a pupil of Socrates, sought in the fourth century B.C.E. to instruct and improve Greek society. His works provide the modern reader with a clearer picture of the ancient world.

BORN: c. 431 B.C.E.; Athens, Greece
DIED: c. 354 B.C.E.; Corinth, Greece
AREAS OF ACHIEVEMENT: Literature, philosophy

EARLY LIFE

Xenophon (ZEN-oh-fuhn) was born in Athens around 431 B.C.E. His father, Gryllus, was a wealthy Athenian aristocrat. Little is known of Xenophon's early life, but he would have come of age during the latter years of the Peloponnesian War (431-404 B.C.E.), the great conflict between Athens and Sparta. He probably served in one of the crack Athenian cavalry units.

As a youth, Xenophon became a pupil of Socrates, joining an intellectual circle that included at various times such diverse personalities as Alcibiades and Plato. Socrates' teaching was frequently conducted out of doors and in an informal manner. No citizen was barred from listening to him or taking part in the discussions, and in a sense his pupils taught themselves. Each student thus developed his own concepts of who Socrates was and what he was saying; therefore, Xenophon should not be faulted because his views of Socrates were not those of Plato, who was gifted with an entirely different quality of mind.

Socrates' belief in moral purposes and his emphasis on the essential goodness of humankind would have appealed to Xenophon's sense of conventional morality. He was not a clever or brilliant pupil but a solid, practical person; probably he took some notes during Socrates' conversations, which would become in later years part of his *Apomnēmoneumata* (c. 381-355 B.C.E.; *Memorabilia of Socrates*, 1712) and the *Apologia Sōcratous* (c. 384 B.C.E.; *Apology of Socrates*, 1762). The latter work was thought at one time to be by another author, but it is most likely genuine. Another brief work, the *Symposion* (*Symposium*, 1710), whose date, like much of Xenophon's writing, is unknown, places Socrates at an Athenian dinner party, where he discusses a variety of subjects, including the nature of love.

Athens was slipping beyond her golden age as the fifth century waned; Sparta's triumph and the political infighting between the parties of the right and left had tarnished the Athenian democracy. Socrates was increasingly viewed as a suspicious and even dangerous person, for he asked too many questions.

Xenophon was uncertain as to what career he should pursue. In 401, a friend and professional soldier, Proxenus, suggested that he join a band of mercenaries commanded by Prince Cyrus (Cyrus the Younger), son of King Darius II of Persia, on an expedition against his brother, Artaxerxes II. The lure of adventure, riches, and military glory was strong, but Xenophon hesitated and consulted Socrates, who advised him to seek counsel of the oracle at Delphi.

Xenophon went to Delphi but apparently had already made a decision before his arrival, since he asked Apollo not whether he should take service with the Persians, but how best the journey might be made. Returning home, he bade Socrates farewell, and the old man advised him to do the will of the god. They were never to meet again.

LIFE'S WORK

The high point of Xenophon's life was his military adventures in the Persian Empire, which he vividly describes in the *Kyrou anabasis* (between 394 and 371 B.C.E.; *Anabasis*, 1623). In March, 401, Prince Cyrus led his mixed force of Greeks, Persians, and other troops from the city of Sardis in western Asia Minor to the Euphrates River and on toward Babylon. At Cunaxa on September 3, 401, a battle was fought between his and Artaxerxes' forces, and Cyrus was killed. Leaderless and isolated in hostile country, the Greeks were further devastated by the murder of their officers, who had been negotiating after the conflict with the Persians, under a flag of truce. Among the slain was Xenophon's friend Proxenus.

There could be no time for mourning; the ten thousand Greeks who survived elected new commanders, Xenophon being one, and hastily retreated northward into the mountains of Kurdistan and Armenia and fought their way back to the Greek colony of Trapezus on the Black Sea. The March of the Ten Thousand took approximately five months, and Xenophon undoubtedly played a vital role in its success. He kept a journal, which he would use in writing the *Anabasis* decades later.

As Julius Caesar would later do, Xenophon told his story in the third person. Indeed, for reasons now unknown it was originally published under an assumed name. There is, however, no question of authorship; the writing style is Xenophon's, and several ancient authors, Plutarch being one, list the *Anabasis* among his works.

Lively and well written, the *Anabasis* is filled with details of army life, scenes of the countrysides through which the Greeks were passing, descriptions of strange animals and birds (such as ostriches, which ran too fast for the soldiers to catch), and the savage tribes that harassed the "Ten Thousand" on their long march to the sea. The *Anabasis* is Xenophon's most popular work.

The conclusion of these five months of danger and hardship was not as Xenophon had hoped. Denied the opportunity of enrichment and glory serving Prince Cyrus, Xenophon considered founding a colony on the Black Sea. Omens from the gods were unfavorable, however, and the Greeks were now divided in their aims. He and some of his friends were obliged to return to military life, first under the command of a petty Thracian king and then with a force of Spartans who had arrived in Asia Minor to defend the Ionian cities against a new Persian attack. During this latter campaign (399 B.C.E.), Xenophon captured a wealthy Persian family and managed at last to make his fortune with the large ransom paid for their release.

The year 399 also saw the trial, condemnation, and execution of Socrates. Xenophon's initial reaction to this injustice is not known, but the death of his old teacher

must have hastened his rejection of current Athenian democracy. To a professional military man, the order and discipline of the Spartans was more appealing.

During the campaign against the Persians and later in a war among the city-states, which pitted Sparta against Athens and Thebes (395-391 B.C.E.), Xenophon served on the staff of the Spartan king Agesilaus. In return, the Athenians banished him as a traitor. The Spartans then provided him with an estate at Scillus, near Olympia. Now married and with two sons, Xenophon had the leisure to pursue the life of a country gentleman, devoting his energies to hunting and entertaining his friends and guests, writing, and building a shrine to Artemis, the goddess of the hunt. It was probably during this period that his practical essays *Kynēgetikos* (394-371 B.C.E.; *On Hunting*, 1832), *Peri hippikēs* (c. 380 B.C.E.; *The Art of Riding*, 1584), and *Hipparchikos* (c. 357 B.C.E.; *On the Cavalry General*, 1832) were composed.

An altogether different sort of work is the *Kyrou paideia* (after 371? B.C.E.; *The Cyropaedia: Or, Education of Cyrus*, 1560-1567), a historical novel that treats not only the life and training of Cyrus the Great (not Prince Cyrus of the *Anabasis*) but also the history of the Persian Empire and Xenophon's views on what education and government should be. That *The Cyropaedia* is a complex work is evidenced by the fact that scholars still dispute what Xenophon hoped to accomplish. His contacts with Persians had given him a unique view of non-Greeks, whom many of his countrymen tended to dismiss as barbarians. Xenophon was both better informed and more appreciative of life outside Hellas than were most Greeks.

Local feeling against the Spartans and their allies after Sparta was defeated by Thebes at the Battle of Leuctra (371 B.C.E.) obliged Xenophon and his family to leave Scillus and reside in Corinth. There is some question as to whether Xenophon returned to Athens after his banishment was revoked (369-365 B.C.E.), but his sons were educated there, and the elder, Gryllus, enlisted in the cavalry as his father had done and died fighting for Athens at the Battle of Mantinea in 362.

In 361 or 360, King Agesilaus died, and Xenophon wrote the *Logos eis Agēsilaon Basilea* (*Agesilaus*, 1832) as a tribute to him. Another of his major works was probably completed in Corinth at about this time. *Ellēnika* (411-362 B.C.E.; *History of the Affairs of Greece*, 1685) was intended to complement and complete Thucydides' unfinished history of the Peloponnesian War and carry the narrative into contemporary times, ending with the Battle of Mantinea. *History of the Affairs of Greece* is

Xenophon. (Library of Congress)

generally considered to be inferior to its predecessor, however, because of Xenophon's open expressions of admiration for Sparta and dislike of Thebes.

The *Poroi* (c. 355-353 B.C.E.; *On Ways and Means*, 1832) is probably Xenophon's last work; most scholars believe that he died within five years of its completion. This essay addressing the financial difficulties of Athens in the mid-fourth century offers various remedies to aid in the city's recovery, including such practical suggestions as ownership by the state of a merchant fleet, more efficient working of the silver mines, and improvement in the status of resident aliens. Xenophon eloquently cites the benefits of peace, suggesting that a board of guardians be established to help maintain peace. In conclusion, he advises the Athenians to consult the gods, an echo of the counsel Socrates had given the young aristocratic cavalryman about to seek his fortune in Persia.

SIGNIFICANCE

Although Xenophon was a staff officer of considerable talent and wrote several essays relative to his profession, his most lasting achievements were in the field of historical writing. One of the pleasures of Xenophon, quite apart from the readability of his prose, is his variety; he was genuinely interested in many subjects and eager to impart to his audience as much information as possible.

Socrates had taught his students to seek out and learn the good, and this advice is reflected throughout Xenophon's works, whether he is discussing the management of horses or a household (*Oikonomikos*, c. 362-361 B.C.E.; *Xenophon's Treatise of Household*, 1532), describing constitutions, or exploring the nature of tyranny (*Hierōn ē tyrannikos*, date unknown; *Hiero*, 1832). At various times, it has been fashionable among scholars to dwell on Xenophon's limitations and to compare him unfavorably to Thucydides or Plato. Such comparisons are unwise, however, and further study impresses one with his versatility.

It is of interest that writers discussing Xenophon generally seem to fall naturally into one of two camps: those who concentrate on his military career and his more practical works and those who focus on his more philosophical writings. It is a measure of his complexity, coupled with the plethora of extant writings, that so many scholars have addressed his life and works.

—*Dorothy T. Potter*

FURTHER READING

Anderson, J. K. *Military Theory and Practice in the Age of Xenophon*. Berkeley: University of California Press, 1970. The title gives the focus of the work. This lengthy study (more than four hundred pages, including index and bibliography) is enhanced by diagrams of formations and battle plans, as well as nineteen black-and-white plates illustrating military costumes and weapons.

Dillery, John. *Xenophon and the History of His Times*. New York: Routledge, 1995. An extensive treatment of Xenophon's historical writing and the times they address. Includes discussions of the Battle of Mantinea, the March of Ten Thousand, and the Spartans in Asia as well as treatment of Xenophon's philosophies and political and social views. Includes bibliographical references and indexes.

Higgins, W. E. *Xenophon the Athenian: The Problem of the Individual and the Society of the Polis*. Albany: State University of New York Press, 1977. This study deals with Xenophon as a writer and a pupil of Socrates. The style is pleasant and clear. In addition to the index, the author's notes are extensive and impressive.

Nadon, Christopher. *Xenophon's Prince: Republic and Empire in the "Cyropaedia."* Berkeley: University of California Press, 2001. Focuses on Xenophon's political theory in *The Cyropaedia* and on the nature of politico-historical writing. Includes bibliographical references and indexes.

Prevas, John. *Xenophon's March: Into the Lair of the Persian Lion*. Cambridge, Mass.: Da Capo Press, 2002. An in-depth examination of Cyrus the Younger's failed expedition against his brother in Persia and the March of the Ten Thousand, as explored through Xenophon's writing. Includes illustrations, maps, bibliographical references, and an index.

Schmeling, Gareth L. *Xenophon of Ephesus*. Boston: Twayne Publishers, 1980. A solid, accessible, basic overview of Xenophon as a writer. Includes biographical information.

Strauss, Leo. *On Tyranny*. Rev. and expanded ed. Chicago: University of Chicago Press, 2000. Xenophon's *Hiero* is interpreted in detail, with an analysis of the text as well as a translation. Also included is an essay by another scholar, Alexandre Kojève, not only on Xenophon and his views on tyranny but also on Strauss's interpretations. This volume is for the serious student of Xenophon.

_____. *Xenophon's Socrates*. Ithaca, N.Y.: Cornell University Press, 1972. In this study, Strauss continues his interpretation of Xenophon as a man who wrote well and with wisdom, an important author who adds to the understanding of his teacher, Socrates. The book contains an appendix and an index and is intended for a scholarly audience.

_____. *Xenophon's Socratic Discourse: An Interpretation of the "Oeconomicus."* South Bend, Ind.: St. Augustine's Press, 1998. Xenophon's *Oikonomikos*, although in the form of a Socratic dialogue, is sometimes dismissed as an enjoyable essay on estate management, complete with a description of the character of the dutiful wife. Strauss writes that its purpose is misunderstood. As with previous references, this work is intended for the better understanding of Socrates as well as Xenophon. The later edition includes a new, literal translation of the *Oikonomikos* by Carnes Lord.

SEE ALSO: Agesilaus II of Sparta; Alcibiades of Athens; Cyrus the Great; Plato; Socrates.

RELATED ARTICLES in *Great Events from History: The Ancient World*: May, 431-September, 404 B.C.E., Peloponnesian War; 401-400 B.C.E., March of the Ten Thousand; 399 B.C.E., Death of Socrates; Between 394 and 371 B.C.E., Xenophon Writes the *Anabasis*; 386 B.C.E., King's Peace Ends Corinthian War.

XERXES I
Persian king (r. 486-465 B.C.E.)

Xerxes mobilized the largest army ever assembled in ancient times and marched against Greece; he crossed Thessaly and annexed Attica to the Persian Empire. Posterity remembers him for capturing Athens and burning the Acropolis and for building the magnificent Palace of Xerxes at Persepolis.

BORN: c. 519 B.C.E.; place unknown
DIED: 465 B.C.E.; Persepolis (now in Iran)
ALSO KNOWN AS: Ahasuerus (biblical); Iksersa; Khsayarsan (Persian); Khshayārshā; Xerxes the Great
AREAS OF ACHIEVEMENT: War and conquest, architecture

EARLY LIFE

Among Darius the Great's seven sons, Xerxes (ZURK-zees) was the youngest of two claimants to the throne of Persia. He was the eldest among the four children born to Atossa, the daughter of Cyrus the Great, whom Darius had married on accession to the throne. The other claimant, Artabazanes, was Darius's eldest son by the daughter of Gobryas, born when Darius was still a private individual. Of the two, Xerxes had a stronger claim for succession, not only because he had been born into the royal house and his line continued that of Cyrus the Great but also because he was an able individual. In his mid-twenties, he was assigned the governorship of Babylonia in preference to Artabazanes. By the time the question of succession arose, he had already governed this kingdom for twelve years.

A bas-relief in the Archaeological Museum in Tehran depicts Xerxes as the heir apparent: He stands behind his father's throne. The father and son occupy the pinnacle of a symbolic pyramid; below them are the nobles, priests, generals, and dignitaries. The bas-relief, two versions of which are in existence, is part of a larger picture in which the king gives audience to his subject nations on the occasion of the Now Ruz (Persian new year). The participation of Xerxes in the ceremony signifies Darius's attempt to create a mutual bond between the prince and the representatives of many nations bringing gifts to the court at Persepolis.

Xerxes was about thirty-seven years old when he became king on Darius's death in 486. His assumption of power did not represent an easy transition: His own brother, Aryamen the satrap of Bactria, rose against him and had to be brought within the fold. Following that revolt, Xerxes marched on Egypt, where a usurper had been ruling since 484—two years prior to the death of Darius. The Persian army defeated the pretender and devastated the Nile Delta. After destroying all Egyptian fortifications, Xerxes appointed one of his brothers, Achaemenes, satrap and then left Egypt. As a result of this revolt, Egypt lost its autonomy within the empire; Egyptian citizens, however, continued to enjoy their previous rights and privileges.

While still in Egypt, Xerxes was informed of a revolt in Babylonia; by then the revolt of a first leader had given way to that of a second, Shamash-eriba. Xerxes marched on Babylonia, defeated Shamash-eriba, and then treated the kingdom in the same way as he had Egypt. He went so far as to break with Achaemenian tradition—he removed the statue of Marduk, the god who had welcomed Cyrus to Babylon, and took it to Persia. Removal of the much-adored golden statue was tantamount to the demotion of Babylonia to the rank of a satrapy. Under Xerxes, therefore, both Egypt and Babylonia lost their status as autonomous kingdoms in the empire. After his return from Babylon, Xerxes no longer called himself "Lord of Nations." He was now "King of the Persians and the Medes."

LIFE'S WORK

After his conquests in Egypt and Babylonia, Xerxes intended to live a tranquil life and attend to matters of state. Exiled Greeks and other ambitious individuals holding prominent positions in Persia, Lydia, and Athens recognized a Persian victory in Europe as the avenue to their own success. Their efforts, therefore, were expended on convincing the king that Persia, ruled by a divine king, was superior and could easily defeat Greece. After giving the matter thought and keeping in mind his father's defeat at Marathon in 490 B.C.E., Xerxes assembled the notables of the empire and announced his intention to invade Greece. He proposed to build a bridge of boats across the Hellespont for the army to cross and further announced that he intended to set fire to the city of Athens in retaliation for the burning of the temple and sacred woods of Sardis by the Ionians.

The nobles, except for the king's uncle, Artabanus, agreed with the king and praised his foresight and might. Artabanus, speaking from experience, reminded the assembly of Darius's fruitless pursuit of the European Scythians in the steppes beyond the Danube. He reminded Xerxes of the enormous loss of life that had resulted from that futile endeavor. He further disagreed with those who claimed that the Persians could defeat the Athenians at sea. His advice to the king was to adjourn the meeting and continue with his plans to unify the empire.

Artabanus's words angered Xerxes. He shouted at the aged warrior that no Persian should sit idle while foreigners infringed on his domain and set fire to his cities. He recounted the great deeds of his ancestors and pledged to surpass them. The assembly agreed with the king's views that war with Greece was inevitable and compromise impossible. Either Persia had to rule Greece or Greece would rule Persia. Over the next few days, Xerxes won Artabanus's agreement and began preparations for a major invasion of Europe. The king's next four years were devoted to military preparations and to diplomatic negotiations before the invasion. These preparations included marshaling forces, digging a major canal at Athos to prevent the kind of disaster experienced by Darius, and dispatching envoys to certain Greek cities to demand "water and soil," that is, recognition of Persian suzerainty without recourse to war. Drawing on the satrap system, a system of government initially installed by Cyrus and later

expanded by Darius, Xerxes assembled an army the likes of which, according to Herodotus, no one had seen or remembered. This army gathered at Sardis in the spring of 480 B.C.E. and from there, led by the king himself, set out for Europe.

Among the obstacles that barred access to Europe, the most awesome was the formidable Hellespont. Ten years before, in his invasion of Europe, Darius had bypassed the Hellespont and built a bridge on the Bosporus. Xerxes, however, had decided to cross the Hellespont on a bridge made of warships. The first array of boats was easily washed away by stormy seas. For the lost ships and the wasted time, Xerxes had the two engineers responsible beheaded. He also ordered the sea to be whipped three hundred lashes to calm it. The second bridge, built with reinforced materials and heavy ropes, held for the seven days that it took the Persian army (estimated as anywhere from 360,000 to two million) to cross. The bridge was not disassembled so that, in the event of a Persian defeat, the king could return to Asia and not be stranded in Europe.

Xerxes I, seated on throne, commands the punishment of the sea. (F. R. Niglutsch)

From Thrace, Xerxes circled the Aegean Sea. He crossed Macedonia and Thessaly, where he stayed while the army deforested the land and built roads. He then headed for Attica, accompanied by his fleet, which remained a short distance offshore.

The Greek states, knowing of the enormity of the invading land army, set their internal squabbles aside so that they could present a united front against the Persians. The alliance, led by Sparta, chose the narrow pass at Thermopylae for the initial meeting with Xerxes. The Greek navy at nearby Artemisium was in constant contact with the land force.

Initially, the battle at Thermopylae did not go well for the Persians. Xerxes sent in a contingent of Medes for the first day and fielded his ten thousand Immortals the second day. Both failed to turn the tide. Worse yet, a significant part of the Persian fleet was destroyed in a storm. Undaunted, however, Xerxes continued to fight. After the third day, a large contingent of Persians, guided through a hidden path the previous night by a Greek defector, appeared on the mountain overlooking the pass. Its defenders found themselves trapped. Leonidas, the Spartan king in charge of the Greek contingent, marshaled the troops of Sparta, Thespiae, and Thebes to continue the defense of the pass. He sent the rest of his men to reinforce the allied army that would fight Xerxes beyond Thermopylae. Leonidas and his three hundred men fought bravely and died to the last man, allowing their compatriots time to withdraw to the narrow strait of Salamis. Attica, and consequently Athens, was left defenseless.

The Persian army, having lost four of Darius's sons at Thermopylae, entered Athens. Most of the inhabitants had already been evacuated. Those who remained took refuge in the Acropolis, the home of Athena, the patron goddess of the city. Xerxes, as he had vowed, burned the city and celebrated his conquest. He was now the only Persian ruler, indeed the only Asian ruler up until that time, to have set foot in Athens as a victor. He dispatched a messenger to Susa to apprise Artabanus, his vice-regent, of the victory.

Xerxes' celebration, however, was premature. He had won the battle at Thermopylae, but the war raged on. Artabanus had been right. The devastated Persian fleet was no match for the Athenian navy, especially when the latter was led by Themistocles, a general who had fought Darius at Marathon and who had spent his life building a formidable navy to match Persia's land army.

At Salamis, what had remained of the Persian fleet was dragged into narrow straits, outmaneuvered, and rammed by stout Greek ships. Witnessing the destruction of their fleet, the Persians fled the scene. Xerxes feared that he might become stranded in Europe. He immediately withdrew to Thessaly and from there to Asia. His hasty departure left the outcome of the war uncertain, especially when Mardonius, whom Xerxes had left in charge of the European campaign, was killed at Platae.

Henceforth, Xerxes became absolutely uninterested in the war and its outcome. Approaching forty, he returned to his palaces at Susa and Persepolis and watched from the sidelines as his appointees fought the war. The hostilities continued for another thirteen years.

At Persepolis, Xerxes devoted his time to the completion of Darius's Apadana and to the construction of his own palace, a magnificent complex erected southeast of Darius's palace. He also became involved in domestic politics and in the affairs of the court. A partial history of these involvements, especially in relation to the Jews of Persia, is found in the Book of Esther. Xerxes also became involved in harem intrigue. This latter involvement resulted in his death: Xerxes was murdered by his courtiers, among them Artabanus, his minister, in 465. He was fifty-four years old.

SIGNIFICANCE

Xerxes stayed in the wings for twelve years, administering the affairs of the kingdom of Babylonia. He watched his father's rise in power and prestige and his fall at Marathon. As king, he found himself on the horns of a dilemma. He had to choose between witnessing the demise of a disunited empire and attempting to rejuvenate it through war. In addition, he needed to show his people that he was the son of Darius and that he could surpass the deeds of kings of the past. Having already decided on a course of action, he revealed his plans and spent much time and energy preparing to bring them to fruition.

The goal of his European campaign was the capture of Athens and the destruction of that city in retaliation for the burning of Sardis. This goal, however, was in conflict with a larger goal nurtured by Greece—the replacement of the absolutism of the East with the free institutions of the West. Thus the victory in Athens had a bittersweet taste for Xerxes, who was compelled by circumstances to fight at Salamis against his wishes. His defeat at Salamis demoralized him to the point that he no longer recognized the potential of his enormous land army and the possibility of an eventual victory.

Against this background, it is doubtful whether Xerxes, on his own, could have prepared the army so that it could capture and burn Athens. Behind Xerxes was the formidable war machine of Darius, a machine created for the single purpose of reducing Europe to a Persian colony. Xerxes merely guided this instrument to its destined end and then into the ground.

Furthermore, Xerxes greatly underestimated the seriousness of the fragmentation that had occurred during the final year of Darius's reign. The defeat at Marathon was closely related to the unhappiness of the peoples of such well-established kingdoms as Egypt and Babylonia. Yet Xerxes took it on himself to further belittle these nations by reducing them to the rank of satrapies.

Rather than trying his hand at world conquest, Xerxes could have drawn on his forte, administration. Instead, he made the same mistake that his father had made: He took on Greece in Europe. Under Xerxes, therefore, the empire continued to disintegrate. Lack of leadership and squabbles among the future claimants further weakened the empire and caused its eventual demise.

Xerxes' view of himself was different. Like Darius, he attributed his success as king to Ahura Mazda, his god. He could do no wrong. Although he exercised great restraint in judgment, he allowed himself to be influenced and used by others. His inflexibility and self-confidence, both deriving from the incredible numbers he commanded rather than from the strength of his policies or that of his allies, played a major role in his demoralization and downfall. After Salamis, the man who had considered himself a good warrior, excelling in horsemanship, archery, and javelin throwing, became a womanizer and a manipulator of lowly lives at his own court.

—Iraj Bashiri

FURTHER READING

Burn, A. R. *Persia and the Greeks: The Defense of the West, 546-478 B.C.* New York: Minerva Press, 1968. This book contains detailed discussions of the various aspects of Xerxes' rule and an especially informative section on his campaign in Europe. Includes maps, charts illustrating battle formations, and genealogies for the major figures.

Cook, J. M. "The Rise of the Achaemenids and Establishment of Their Empire." *The Median and Achaemenian Period.* Vol. 2 in *The Cambridge History of Iran.* Cambridge, England: Cambridge University Press, 1985. This article examines the principal sources on ancient Iran and the extent and composition of the empire. Toward the end, Cook assesses the leadership that enabled the Persians to form a great empire.

Frye, Richard N. *The Heritage of Persia.* 1962. Reprint. New York: New American Library, 1966. Frye's account of ancient Iran is unique. It focuses on the eastern provinces of the ancient kingdom, but, unlike similar accounts, it is based on cultural, religious, and literary sources. The book is illustrated; it includes an index, maps, genealogies, and an informative bibliography.

Ghirshman, Roman. *Iran: From the Earliest Times to the Islamic Conquest.* 1954. Reprint. Baltimore: Penguin Books, 1965. In this account of Iran's prehistory to Islamic times, Ghirshman juxtaposes textual information and archaeological data to place ancient Iran in its proper perspective. The book is illustrated with text figures as well as with plates. It includes an index and a selected bibliography.

Green, Peter. *The Greco-Persian Wars.* Rev. ed. Berkeley: University of California Press, 1996. Originally published as *Xerxes at Salamis* (1970), this is a unique, though somewhat biased, account of the logistics of Xerxes' campaigns in Europe; it focuses on the leadership of Themistocles and on the divergent ideologies of the belligerents. The book has an index and a bibliography; it is sparsely illustrated.

Herodotus. *The Histories.* Translated by Aubrey de Sélincourt. 1954. 6th ed. New York: Penguin, 1996. This sixth edition of a standard translation is revised with introductory matter and notes by John Marincola. In this comprehensive classical account, Herodotus discusses Xerxes' planned invasion of Europe, his long march in Asia and Europe, his capture and burning of Athens, and his retreat to Asia. This book should be read alongside other authoritative sources. It includes poor maps but has a good index.

Hignett, Charles. *Xerxes' Invasion of Greece.* Oxford: Clarendon Press, 1963. This work deals exclusively with Xerxes and his campaigns against Greece. It critically examines previous research on Xerxes and discusses Xerxes' fleet, the number of infantry the king commanded, and the topography of Thermopylae and Salamis. The book includes a bibliography, a good index, and eight maps.

Olmstead, Arthur T. *History of the Persian Empire.* 1948. Chicago: University of Chicago Press, 1960. This detailed history of the Achaemenid period remains the chief secondary source for the study of ancient Iran. The book includes a topographical index, maps, and many carefully selected illustrations.

Szemler, G. J., W. J. Cherf, and J. C. Kraft. *Thermopylai: Myth and Reality in 480 B.C.* Chicago, Ill.: Ares Publishers, 1996. A close look at the devastating Battle of Thermopylae.

SEE ALSO: Atossa; Cyrus the Great; Darius the Great; Leonidas; Themistocles.
RELATED ARTICLES in *Great Events from History: The Ancient World*: 547 B.C.E., Cyrus the Great Founds the Persian Empire; 520-518 B.C.E., Darius the Great Conquers the Indus Valley; September 17, 490 B.C.E., Battle of Marathon; 483 B.C.E., Naval Law of Themistocles Is Instituted; 480-479 B.C.E., Persian Invasion of Greece; 478-448 B.C.E., Athenian Empire Is Created.

XIE LINGYUN
Chinese poet and philosopher

Xie Lingyun was the first and greatest of China's nature poets, the founder of a school of verse. A philosophical syncretist, he blended elements of Confucianism and Daoism with Buddhism to produce a uniquely Chinese synthesis.

BORN: 385 C.E.; Zhejiang Province, China
DIED: 433 C.E.; Canton, Nanhai, China
ALSO KNOWN AS: Hsieh Ling-yün (Wade-Giles); Xie Kanglo (Pinyin), Hsieh K'ang-lo (Wade-Giles)
AREAS OF ACHIEVEMENT: Literature, philosophy

EARLY LIFE

Xie Lingyun (shyee ling-yewn) was born into one of China's most powerful and illustrious aristocratic families of the Six Dynasties (420-589 C.E.). As secretary of the Imperial Library, his father was the least prepossessing member of the Xie clan, which had included a host of distinguished poets, calligraphers, and high-ranking imperial officials. The Liu, Xie Lingyun's mother's family, was distinguished by its calligraphers, notably Wang Xizhi (321-379 C.E.). In the light of his familial background, Lingyun surprised no one by his precocity. As a small child, he was placed under temporary adoption in Hangzhou with Du Mingshi (Tu Ming-shih), a devout Daoist. Calligraphy was an integral part of Du Mingshi's Daoism, and Lingyun proved an apt pupil. The boy remained with his foster family in the splendid aristocratic environs of Hangzhou until he was fifteen.

In 399 C.E., a rebel faction led by Sun En invaded Zhejiang and Jiangsu provinces, and in the ensuing struggle Lingyun's father was killed. His family decided to send Lingyun to the safety of their house in the capital, Jianye (Chienyeh; now Nanjing). There he came under the decisive influence of his uncle, Xie Hun (Hsieh Hun), a handsome, aristocratic figure who was recognized as one of China's foremost poets. Married to an imperial Jin princess and secure in worldly ways, Hun had drawn together a lively, exclusive literary salon, into which Lingyun was inducted. He was soon recognized as a stellar member. The precocious Lingyun cut a swath around Jianye even in an age notorious for social ostentation and eccentricity. He had inherited the title of duke of Kangluo (K'ang-lo); as such, he drew revenues from more than three thousand households. Xie Lingyun affected foppish dress, extravagant behavior, and a languor that challenged the efforts of scores of attendants. Dukedom also brought government appointments: He was made administrator to the grand marshal and, more important, administrator in the Redaction Office, a post that ensnared him in the political fortunes of Liu Yi (Liu I). It was thus that he was forced to endure a chain of misfortunes that dramatically altered the course of his life.

LIFE'S WORK

When Lingyun entered service with Liu Yi, Yi had emerged as the most distinguished leader of a revolt against another rebel, Huan Xuan (Huan Hsüan), who founded the abortive Chu (Ch'u) Dynasty in 404 C.E. Yi's victories against Huan brought him the dukedom of Nanping (Nan-p'ing) as well as a military governor generalship, these posts devolving on him from Liu Yu (Liu Yü), the titular restorer of the Jin Dynasty in 405 C.E. Lingyun's fortunes might have been assured if Liu Yi had accepted Liu Yu's political supremacy. He did not. Thus, between 405 and 411 C.E., a series of complex plots and inevitable military clashes between partisans of the two men resulted in Yi's defeat and disgrace. Through the course of these events, Lingyun served on his staff, ultimately suffering the consequences of his fall. Moved to the periphery of power, Yi, with Lingyun in tow, was obliged in 412 to establish his headquarters at Jiangling in Hubei Province. There, Lingyun's life changed decisively.

While posted to Jiangling, Lingyun visited the famed Buddhist center at the nearby Mount Lu. The Eastern Grove Monastery, which eventually became the most influential southern center of Chinese Buddhism, had been founded by Hui Yuan (Hui-yüan; 334-416 C.E.), himself the principal disciple of Dao An (Tao-an; 312-385 C.E.), who had been the first to emphasize the basic distinctions between Indian Buddhism—essentially an alien doctrine—and the casual versions of Buddhism that had been integrated with mainstream Chinese culture. Hui Yuan devoted himself to making the Chinese aware of the foreignness of Buddhist thought, hoping to make the purer form of its teachings and practices acceptable to well-educated Chinese aristocrats. Lingyun found that this transcendental, poeticized Buddhism, with its many concrete images, appealed to him far more than the intellectualized Buddhism common to the capital and his native region.

Moreover, Lingyun's poetic sensibilities were overwhelmed by the beauty of the Eastern Grove's setting—craggy, forested mountain peaks enshrouded in mists, lush gorges filled with tumbled boulders and riven by pure, roaring streams—and the austere way of life of its devotees. The contrast with the corruptions and hostilities of court life was compelling. In his poetic "Dirge for Hui Yuan," Lingyun revealed his yearning to immerse himself in Buddhist study and to accept a place even as the least of Hui Yuan's disciples.

As Lingyun was falling under the spell of Eastern Grove Buddhism, however, the fact that he and the Xie family had thrown in their lot with the wrong leader was becoming all too clear. Liu Yu, having consolidated his position, crushed Liu Yi, Lingyun's mentor, on December 31, 412 C.E.; Yi eventually was killed. Liu Yu spared Lingyun, however, and coopted him into his service in 413 C.E., first as administrator to the commander in chief, then as assistant director of the Imperial Library. During the time that Lingyun held these posts, the Chinese monk Faxian (Fa-hsien; c. 337-422 C.E.), after fourteen years in Afghanistan, returned to Jianye rich in Buddhist lore. He reported having seen a gigantic image of Buddha, in a cave, shining with brilliant light and casting mysterious shadows. Hoping to replicate this image, Hui Yuan arranged a similar shrine for the Eastern Grove. Painted shades of green on silk, the Buddha image was consecrated on May 27, 412 C.E. As a noted poet and calligrapher, Lingyun was invited to produce a poem that he entitled "Inscription on the Buddha-Shadow," one of his earliest surviving metaphysical verses.

As always, Lingyun's fortunes were linked to political events. In 415 C.E., he was dismissed from office, and the following year Hui Yuan died. Lingyun's fortunes improved, however, with new administrative posts. More important was Yu's liberation of Chang-an (Xian), the center of Northern Buddhism. Many of its monks there-

upon traveled southward, bringing about the mingling of the two schools of Buddhist thought from which a distinctive Chinese version was to emerge. Amid this intellectual and religious excitement, however, Lingyun was held responsible for eruption of a scandal and was again dismissed. Nothing is known of him for the next eighteen months. In 419 C.E., Liu Yu strangled the imbecilic Emperor An, ending the Jin Dynasty and allowing his assumption of power as Wudi (Wu-ti), first of the Song Dynasty (Sung; 420-479 C.E.).

In accordance with customary treatment of aristocrats after a coup, Lingyun was demoted to the rank of marquess over only one hundred households. Subsequently, the rise of his cousin Xie Huilian (Hsieh Hui-lien) as the chief of the emperor's henchmen and the courtly influence of a number of other relatives and friends drew him into succession politics. Unhappily, Lingyun's romanticism, imprudence, and willful personality led him to back the wrong forces. Shortly after the ascension of Yifu (I-fu) to the throne, the clique with which Lingyun associated was disgraced. Ill and impoverished, he was banished to the lowly post of grand warden to Yongjia, a backward town in Zhejiang Province.

The mournful poems written during Lingyun's exile from the capital reveal a distressed man confronting reality in full maturity. Middle-aged, bereft of significant income, beyond the pale of elusive political power, stricken by tuberculosis, and plagued by ulcerous legs, he had only his literary talents and religious beliefs to sustain him. Indeed, in accordance with esoteric Daoist and Buddhist teachings, he thereafter sought consolation in a search for truth in the wilderness into which he was exiled. The two months of hard travel that it took him to reach Yongjia evoked a series of fine nature poems, elegantly descriptive and brooding. On arrival, he also commenced his "Bienzong Lun" (c. 423-430; "On Distinguishing What Is Essential"), a major philosophical work.

Many earlier Chinese philosophers had wrestled with problems examined in Lingyun's "On Distinguishing What Is Essential," and in this sense it is a work of many authors. This fact, however, does not diminish the value of Lingyun's contribution to Chinese philosophical discourse. Two versions of truth preoccupied him: truth that was acquired gradually and truth that was revealed instantaneously. Many Buddhists believed that an arrival at truth (Nirvana) required several lengthy stages of spiritual and bodily preparation, involving faith, study, and good works. That, Lingyun acknowledged, was the gradualism that Siddhārtha Gautama, the Buddha, had taught. Yet Buddha, he argued, had used that explanation when teaching Indians, a people with a facility for learning but with scant predilection for intuitive understanding. Had Buddha preached to the Chinese, a people who had difficulty in acquiring learning but who were masters of intuitive comprehension, his message would have been different. Ultimate enlightenment—a state of nonbeing, or *wu*—although doubtless assisted by learning, would have been presented by Buddha to the Chinese as attainable in a flash, by a quantum leap in faith.

As his health improved and his literary reputation increased, Lingyun also became more intriguing because of his new character. He was neglectful of his official duties, despite some efforts to plant mulberry trees, improve local agriculture, and undertake hydraulic works. His change in priorities had to do less with an implicit criticism of the state than with an honest desire to withdraw from worldly vexations in a mystic pursuit of truth. The climbing boots with removable studs that he designed for expeditions into the mountains became fashionable at court, and a broad-brimmed peasant hat, knapsack, and staff came to be his personal hallmarks. Soon, he resigned from office. His Daoism, which promised immortality for the body as well as the soul, required a spartan regimen of yoga, breathing exercises, and preparations of drugs, herbs, and elixirs. His "*Fu* of the Homeward Road" and "On Leaving My District" signaled his return in 424 C.E. to the decayed family estate at Shining. There, moving toward a richer inner life, he labored assiduously in the mountainous wilderness. During the next several years, a number of monks joined him in his idyllic anchorite life. His continuous investigations into Buddhist meanings made him the most learned layman of his day.

The regard in which Lingyun's poetry was held, added to the renown of his family name, made him useful to Emperor Wen on his ascension to power. Lingyun's presence not only would grace the court with a leading poet and calligrapher but also would solidify support for the emperor among many who had wavered. Accordingly, Lingyun was offered the directorship of the Imperial Library. Because rejection would have constituted an affront to the emperor and meant peril for his friends, he accepted reluctantly. For several years, he collected and collated documents, including major Buddhist sutras; he wrote poems and painted for the emperor. Court life wearied him, however, and in spite of an impending promotion, he begged a sick leave, which in 428 allowed a return to Shining. He conceived of himself during this time as free from official obligations and lived healthily and actively as a result, but the emperor viewed his conduct as defiant. Eventually, Lingyun fell afoul of conflicts among the local gentry. In serious danger, he begged Wendi's forgiveness, and for a time the emperor protected him while he helped translate major sutras of Mahāyāna Buddhism into Chinese. Even his translations, however, were offensive to sectarians; the emperor found him a liability, and he was exiled to the wilds of Jiangxi Province. There Lingyun once again courted disaster by engaging in defiant conduct. Falsely implicated in a rebellious plot, he was called to Nanhai in 433 C.E. Philosophical, courageous, and aristocratic to the end, he was publicly executed the same year; he was buried in Guiji, among the mountains he loved.

SIGNIFICANCE

Of the thousands of Xie Lingyun's writings and poems, relatively few survive. Those extant clearly confirm his repute as China's greatest nature poet. Nature poetry—descriptive, mystical, impressionistic, and simultaneously reflective and mood-stimulating—in Lingyun's hands, was a disciplined, highly developed art form, particularly the five-word poem and the *yuefu*. Along with Ban Zhao (Pan Chao) and Tao Yunming (T'ao Yünming), he was in his own time—and has continued to be—recognized as one of the greatest poets in a uniquely Chinese genre.

As the most learned Buddhist layman of his day, Xie Lingyun exerted a major influence—through his poetry, calligraphy, essays, translations, associations, and later anchorite lifestyle—in the Sinicization of Buddhism. His profound understanding of Buddhism, always melded subtly with his Confucianism and Daoism, allowed him to translate and reinterpret main tenets of the religion for a distinctive Chinese context. Only a quintessential Chinese could have accomplished this task.

—*Clifton K. Yearley and Kerrie L. MacPherson*

FURTHER READING

Bingham, Woodbridge. *The Founding of the T'ang Dynasty.* New York: Octagon Press, 1970. Good background on the fall of the Sui Dynasty and early Tang, with observations on contributions of the Song. Lacks critical balance, but is accessible and gives the reader an accurate sense of the importance of the period. Limited bibliography; useful appendices.

Frodsham, J. D. *The Murmuring Stream: The Life and Works of the Chinese Nature Poet Hsieh Ling-yun (385-433), Duke of K'ang-Lo.* 2 vols. Kuala Lumpur: University of Malaya Press, 1967. Definitive scholarly study; eminently readable. Volume 1 is largely biographical; volume 2 translates and examines Lingyun's poetry extensively. Helpful footnotes throughout. Adequate appendices and index.

Fung Yu-Lan. *A History of Chinese Philosophy.* Translated by Derk Bodde. 2 vols. 1973. Reprint. Princeton, N.J.: Princeton University Press, 1983. Chapter 7 of the second volume of this excellent scholarly work carefully examines various aspects of Buddhism and Xie Lingyun's role and influence in its interpretations. Splendid comparative chronological tables of the period of classical learning; informative notes throughout; superb bibliography; fine index.

Xie, Lingyun. *The Mountain Poems of Hsieh Ling-Yün.* Translated by David Hinton. New York: New Directions, 2001. A translation that includes introduction, notes, a map, a list of key terms intended to outline the poet's worldview, and a bibliography. The poems are divided into three sections, from his first exile, his time in Shining, and his final exile.

SEE ALSO: Faxian; Wudi.

RELATED ARTICLES in *Great Events from History: The Ancient World*: 285-160 B.C.E. (traditionally, c. 300 B.C.E.), Composition of the *Zhuangzi*; 139-122 B.C.E., Composition of the *Huainanzi*; c. 60-68 C.E., Buddhism Enters China; 142 C.E., Zhang Daoling Founds the Celestial Masters Movement; 220 C.E., Three Kingdoms Period Begins in China; 4th century C.E., Ge Chaofu Founds the Ling Bao Sect of Daoism; 399 C.E., Chinese Monk Faxian Travels to India; 420 C.E., Southern Dynasties Period Begins in China; c. 470 C.E., Bodhidharma Brings Chan Buddhism to China.

XUNZI
Chinese philosopher

Through his development and modification of Confucian teachings, Xunzi built a synthesized and more realistic foundation for Confucian ideology that was influential throughout China during the Han Dynasty.

BORN: c. 307 B.C.E.; Zhao kingdom, China
DIED: c. 235 B.C.E.; Lanling, China
ALSO KNOWN AS: Hsün-tzu (Wade-Giles); Xun Qing (Pinyin), Hsün Ch'ing (Wade-Giles); Xun Guang (Pinyin), Hsün K'uang (Wade-Giles)
AREA OF ACHIEVEMENT: Philosophy

EARLY LIFE

Although Xunzi (shewn-dzur) is undoubtedly a great figure in Chinese philosophy, the basic facts of his life are still controversial among scholars. According to most Chinese scholars, he was born in the northern state of Zhao (Chao), and the period of his activities as a philosopher and politician covers sixty years, from 298 to 238 B.C.E. The most reliable sources about his life are his own writings, published posthumously, and Sima Qian's *Shiji* (first century B.C.E.; *Records of the Grand Historian of China*, 1960, rev. ed. 1993). Yet almost no information about his early life, his education, or even his family background can be found in these early sources, which provide an account of his life beginning at the age of fifty, when he first visited the state of Qi (Ch'i) and joined a distinguished group of scholars from various philosophical schools at the Jixia (Chi-hsia) Academy. This lack of information about his early life prompts some modern scholars to doubt the accuracy of the *Records of the Grand Historian* and suggest that Xunzi first visited the Jixia Academy at the age of fifteen, not fifty. These scholars contend that either Xunzi's age was erroneously recorded in the first place or the *Records of the Grand Historian* text was corrupted, and that his true date of birth is closer to 307 B.C.E. rather than the traditional c. 313.

LIFE'S WORK

Whether Xunzi first appeared on the stage of history at fifty or fifteen does not change much of his historical role, for he did not really affect his contemporaries or his immediate environment during his lifetime. Like his predecessors in the Confucian school, Confucius (Kong Qiu; 551-479 B.C.E.) and Mencius (Mengzi; c. 372-c. 289 B.C.E.) specifically, Xunzi traveled from state to state, trying to persuade the rulers of Qi, Qu (Ch'u), Zhao, and even the Legalist Qin to adopt his brand of Confucian statecraft. The dating of his various visits to these states is again an area of endless academic debate.

There are, however, two reliable historical dates in Xunzi's public career. In 255 B.C.E., he was invited by Lord Chunshen (Ch'un-shen) of Qu to serve as the magistrate of Lanling. He was soon forced to resign the post when Lord Chunshen gave credence to some slanderous rumors about the potential danger of the benevolent Confucian policy. Xunzi then left for his native Zhao. He stayed as an honored guest in the Zhao court until Lord Chunshen apologized for his suspicion and invited him to resume the magistrateship. Xunzi remained in the position until 238 B.C.E., the year Lord Chunshen was assassinated. Xunzi was immediately dismissed from office, and he died in Lanling, probably soon after the coup.

The most immediate impact of Xunzi on the political situation of the ancient Chinese world came, ironically, from his two best students, Hanfeizi (Han-fei; c. 280-233 B.C.E.) and Li Si (Li Ssu; 280?-208 B.C.E.). Both men deviated from his teachings of Confucian benevolence and turned his emphasis on pragmatic sociopolitical programming into realpolitik. Hanfeizi became a synthesizer of Legalist thought, and Li Si became a prime minister who helped Shu Huangdi (Shih Huang-ti; c. 259-210/209 B.C.E.) set up a totalitarian state after China was unified.

Xunzi's greatest contribution to Chinese civilization lies in the field of philosophy, or, more generally, in the intellectual formation of Chinese sociopolitical behavior. His writings were perhaps compiled by himself in his later years but were definitely supplemented with a few chapters from his disciples. The standard edition of Xunzi's works is the end product of a Han scholar, Liu Xiang (Liu Hsiang; c. 77-c. 6 B.C.E.), who collated and edited the available sources into thirty-two chapters. Since Xunzi lived through a period of fierce political strife, constant warfare, and tremendous social change on the eve of China's unification (also the golden age of Chinese philosophy known as the period of the Hundred Schools), his approach to the social and ethical issues of Confucian philosophy was markedly more realistic than those of Confucius and Mencius. In his defense of Confucian doctrine, he not only refuted the arguments and programs of other schools but also criticized the idealistic strain of thinking within his own camp, particularly in Mencius's philosophy. With an admirable command of scholarship and a powerful mind for critical analysis, Xunzi demonstrated the Confucian way of thinking in a most systematic and pragmatic manner.

In opposition to Mencius's contention that human nature is innately good and man need only go back to his original psychological urges to achieve goodness and righteousness, Xunzi states that human nature is evil and that only through education can man distinguish himself from animals. Despondent as it appears, Xunzi's conception of human nature is quite complex and far removed from pessimism. For him, human nature—though evil—does not determine human destiny, for people have a ca-

pacity for reasoning and learning and for attaining a higher and more civilized order. That humans created civilization and sloughed off their barbarism is clear testimony to the possibility of a brighter future for humankind, as long as the civilizing order is maintained and continued. The whole process of education and socialization thus becomes the focus of Xunzi's ethical concern.

It seems that when Xunzi addresses the question of human nature, he has no preconceived illusions and deals squarely with human psychology as such. The evil of which he speaks is simply a composite body of animal drives and has no likeness to the Judeo-Christian concept of Original Sin. With such a no-nonsense and down-to-earth approach, he is interested in human nature less as an ontological issue than as an epistemological one. His particular emphasis on "artificial endeavor" for humanity also attests this interest, which some scholars describe as a "moral epistemology."

Xunzi's interest in education and socialization centers on the Confucian concept of *li*, which has been translated in different contexts as propriety, decorum, rite, and etiquette. It is Xunzi's belief that proper social behavior is foundational for moral gentlemen and that institutionalized rites regulate human relations for a better society. Thus, education is not only a way of acquiring external knowledge for its own sake but also a process of internalizing all the knowledge for the molding of a good and moral person. On the other hand, society is not merely a background against which one develops his or her intellectual faculty or moral character: Society is the main source of personality development. Through interaction between the individual self and the social norm, a functioning structure takes shape and reveals a pattern of *li* that serves as the very basis of social order.

How did *li* first come into existence? Confucius did not talk about its origin. Mencius was not interested in it. For Xunzi, however, this question was of primary importance. In his treatise on *li*, Xunzi offers the following explanation:

> Man is born with desires. If his desires are not satisfied for him, he cannot but seek some means to satisfy them himself. If there are no limits and measures of regulation in his seeking, then he will inevitably fall to wrangling with other men. From wrangling comes disorder and from disorder comes exhaustion. The ancient kings hated such disorder, and therefore they institutionalized *li* and righteousness in order to define the relationship between men, to train men's desires and to provide for their satisfaction.

This explanation supports his argument that human nature is evil and also shows his concern for law and order.

For Confucius and Mencius, *li* is the internalized moral code that impels people to exhibit proper social behavior; it has nothing to do with the penal code, or law, imposed by government from outside to regulate social order. Xunzi's practical concern for institutionalized law and order greatly transformed this Confucian concept of *li*. Confucius and Mencius could not bear to see a society's peace and order being enforced by law, while Xunzi would acquiesce on this practical matter. Xunzi, however, was by no means a Legalist entrusting the programming of social order entirely to the institution of law; he always placed the benevolence of the ruling class, the moral behavior maintained by a gentlemanly social elite, and the education of the people ahead of the enforcement of law, a necessary evil.

Xunzi's concept of nature also complements his realistic approach to social and ethical issues. He believed that nature exists independent of human will. Heavenly matters have nothing to do with social and ethical issues, and, therefore, human beings are solely responsible for their behavior. This attitude underlies logically his idea that human nature is evil and that the good is the product of humanity's artificial endeavor. It also implies the unlimited potential of "evil-natured" humankind to do good and better the human world, because there is no supernatural force to hinder such a human endeavor. In this sense, Xunzi should be taken seriously as an ardent optimist with regard to human progress.

SIGNIFICANCE

During his lifetime, Xunzi did not have any major effect on historical events. War, suffering, and political intrigue continued in his country. It was during this time of chaos and disintegration that Xunzi developed his systematic reinterpretation of the Confucian tradition. If the unification of China and the institutionalization of the Legalist program toward the end of the third century B.C.E. can only be partly credited to his students Hanfeizi and Li Si, at least Xunzi can claim a lion's share in the formation of the Confucian system during the Han period, after the Legalist Qin Dynasty collapsed. This Han Confucian system, with its strong emphasis on the blending of practical sociopolitical institutions with moral concerns, has served as the foundation of Chinese social and political norms for two millennia.

—Pei-kai Cheng

FURTHER READING

Cua, A. S. *Ethical Argumentation: A Study in Hsün Tzu's Moral Epistemology.* Honolulu: University of Hawaii Press, 1985. Contains a detailed and stimulating analysis of Xunzi's ethical theory and the rationale and argumentative discourse in his philosophy. An in-depth study of an important but rarely touched area of Xunzi's thought. With a bibliography, notes, and an index.

Goldin, Paul Rakita. *Rituals of the Way: The Philosophy of Xunzi.* Chicago: Open Court, 1999. Analyzes Xunzi's thoughts on such typically Confucian topics as human nature, civilization, the relation of the individual to other people, Heaven, and the cosmos, the organization of the state, and the role of language.

Kline, T. C., III, and Philip J. Ivanhoe, eds. *Virtue, Morality, and Agency in the Xunzi.* Indianapolis, Ind.: Hackett, 2000. A collection of eleven essays on various aspects of Xunzi's Confucianism, both studying his own work and comparing it with that of other Confucian theorists.

Schwartz, Benjamin I. *The World of Thought in Ancient China.* Cambridge, Mass.: Harvard University Press, 1985. A remarkable study in the field of ancient Chinese thought, this book is scholarly but never dull. It presents all the major issues in clear language and compares them with Western philosophical concepts without losing their original meanings. The chapter on Mencius and Xunzi is informative. With a bibliography, notes, and an index.

Xunzi. *Xunzi: A Translation and Study of the Complete Works.* Translated by John Knoblock. 3 vols. Stanford, Calif.: Stanford University Press, 1988-1994. These three volumes contain annotated translations and full-scale studies of the complete works of Xunzi. With a glossary, notes, a bibliography, and an index.

SEE ALSO: Confucius; Hanfeizi; Laozi; Mencius; Mozi; Sima Qian.

RELATED ARTICLES in *Great Events from History: The Ancient World*: 500-400 B.C.E., Creation of the *Wujing*; 479 B.C.E., Confucius's Death Leads to the Creation of *The Analects*; c. 285-c. 255 B.C.E, Xunzi Develops Teachings That Lead to Legalism; 221 B.C.E., Qin Dynasty Founded in China; 221-206 B.C.E., Legalist Movement in China; 206 B.C.E., Liu Bang Captures Qin Capital, Founds Han Dynasty; 104 B.C.E., Dong Zhongshu Systematizes Confucianism.

ZENO OF CITIUM
Greek philosopher

Zeno founded Stoicism, the leading Hellenistic school of philosophy. Though not the school's greatest thinker, he created its unified, systematic teaching and guided it to prominence.

BORN: c. 335 B.C.E.; Citium (now Larnaca), Cyprus
DIED: c. 263 B.C.E.; Athens, Greece
ALSO KNOWN AS: Zeno the Stoic
AREA OF ACHIEVEMENT: Philosophy

EARLY LIFE

While a full biography of Zeno of Citium (ZEE-noh of SIHSH-ee-uhm) cannot be written from the anecdotes and sayings collected in late antiquity, principally available in the work of Diogenes Laertius, much can be learned from a critical reading of them. Diogenes quotes the honorific inscription that dates Zeno's death as well as the statement of Zeno's disciple Persaeus of Citium that the master lived to be seventy-two, which dates his birth.

Nevertheless, there is no information about his childhood; even the name of his mother no longer survives. Mnaseas, his father, has a name ambiguously meaningful both in Phoenician (equivalent to the Hebrew Manasseh, "one causing to forget") and in Greek ("mindful," a strong opposition). Mnaseas, contemporary with Citium's last Phoenician king, under whom the town was besieged and burned by Ptolemy Soter of Egypt in 312 B.C.E., may have initiated the family's break from Phoenician ways and turn to Greek and philosophical culture: The name he gave his son has no Semitic meaning but refers to the Greek god Zeus and was celebrated in a famous syncretic hymn by Zeno's disciple Cleanthes.

In one story, Mnaseas brought many books by Socratic writers back from Athens for Zeno. In another story, Zeno himself, shipwrecked on a commercial trip to Athens, consoled himself in a bookstore with Xenophon's *Apomnēmoneumata* (c. 381-355 B.C.E.; *Memorabilia of Socrates*) and rushed to follow the Cynic philosopher Crates of Thebes, when Crates was pointed out as a living Socratic teacher. Persaeus said that Zeno was twenty-two when he came to Athens; he never seems to have left. His arrival would have been in 311, the year after Citium fell to Ptolemy.

The failure of the records to mention close relationships with his parents or others may be significant: Stoicism was to teach, as Cynicism had, individual self-sufficiency and rational discipline of the emotions. Socrates exemplified this philosophy: Personally ugly but desirable, ethically committed but unwilling to be called a teacher or to write anything, sealing his commitment to philosophy with his death at the hands of democratic Athens, Socrates was publicized by his followers, including Plato and Xenophon, and became the personal inspiration of all the fourth century schools of philosophy. Plato's Academy was almost a formal alternative to the city-state that had killed its greatest thinker, and Aristotle's Lyceum was modeled on it. The Cynics, on the other hand, avoided institutional encumbrances, living and teaching in public to a scandalous degree: Their name means "doglike." In a symbolic story, Zeno, soon after he became Crates' follower, modestly covered his teacher and Crates' student-bride Hipparchia with a cloak as they consummated their "dog-wedding" in public in the Stoa Poecile. Cynics, including the young Zeno, maintained the ill-dressed, voluntarily poor, and combatively questioning, even anti-intellectual stance they claimed to derive from Socrates' teachings.

Zeno's Cynic period culminated before 300 in the publication of his most notorious book, *Politeia* (the Republic), a short work denouncing then current methods of education and calling for a city of wise men and women without temples, courts, or gymnasiums, with the god Eros to be honored by friendship and polymorphous, unrestricted sex. Zeno also studied and perhaps enrolled in the Academy (studying Plato's dialogues, dialectical method, and metaphysics—including incorporeal ideas as causes for physical events, which he rejected) and followed the dialectical teachers Diodorus Cronus and Stilpo, who arrived from Megara about 307. Their advanced modal logic, however, proved a form of determinism that Zeno found unacceptable. By about 300, Zeno, in his early thirties, was able to declare his independence from other teachers and begin his regular strolls up and down the Stoa Poecile with his own students.

LIFE'S WORK

The professional career of a philosopher is rich not so much in public as in internal events, and Zeno's development is hard to follow in the absence of extensive or datable writings. *Politeia* came early, and it was widely enough quoted that a dozen or more of the extant fragments of his writings can be identified as belonging to it; none of the other twenty-four titles of his canon allows for as definite a reconstruction. He was a powerful teacher, famous for an epistemological demonstration in which he closed one extended hand by stages and then steadied the fist with his other hand while he named the corresponding stages of knowledge: "An impression is like this; assent is like this; cognitive grasp is like this; and science is like this; and only the wise man has it."

He established, for all Stoics except his unorthodox pupil Aristo of Chios, the three-part division of philosophy into logic (philosophy of language and meaning), physics (philosophy of nature—including theology, since spirit as breath and *logos* as creative word are bodies and also divine), and ethics (the famous division of things into good, bad, and indifferent; the development of the Cynic's "life according to nature" as the only virtuous and happy way of life). To a degree not approached by Plato, by Aristotle, or by his contemporaries the Cynics, Megarians, Epicureans, and Skeptics, Zeno made of these subjects a single, unified whole, giving priority neither to metaphysics—as with Plato and Aristotle—nor to ethics—as with the Epicureans.

The system was seen as dogmatic, and debate with Stoicism played a large part in the Academy's move into skepticism from the 270's. The dogmatic system was not perfected by Zeno himself: He left his logic rudimentary, to be developed by his successor's successor, Chrysippus. Among other changes, later Stoics softened the antisocial side of his ethics toward a propriety more acceptable to dignified Roman adherents such as the Gracchi, Seneca the Younger, and Marcus Aurelius.

Zeno was remembered for his pithy comments about and to his students; these observations were perhaps made more pointed by his Phoenician accent and manners, which he never tried to overcome. During his thirty-nine years leading the school, his oval face hardened into the philosophic persona visible in surviving portraits. It is not a handsome face: The forehead recedes, the frown lines are pronounced, the expression seems severe or even morose; the neck bends forward, and Diogenes says that it crooked also to one side, adding that Zeno was rather tall, thin but flabby, and dark-complected. Self-control was the main attribute he projected. He lived on bread, water, and "a little wine of good bouquet"—coming from a commercial family, he seems never to have been really in want—avoiding dinners and drinking parties except when his pupil and patron, the Macedonian prince Antigonus Gonatas, the future king of Macedon, insisted. Zeno is said to have had a weak constitution—justifying his abstemiousness—but also to have been in good health until his death, which was voluntary and in response to a trivial fall that he took as a divine sign. As for his pleasures, they included green figs and sunbaths and boy slave-prostitutes, whom he "used sparingly." He did, to be sure, state in *Politeia* that Eros is a god of constructive political friendship, and he is recorded to have been in love with Chremonides, later the instigator of Athens's last, ill-starred war against the dominion of Macedon.

Zeno's school had a different sort of corporate existence from the more settled Academy, Lyceum, and Epicurean "Garden." The Academy and Lyceum were technically sodalities of the Muses and Apollo, meeting in public gymnasiums (religiously consecrated exercise grounds particularly used by Athenian *ephebes* in their compulsory military and civic-religious training). The Epicurean "Garden" was Epicurus's private house and garden, later inherited by the school's leaders. Zeno, barred as a foreigner from owning property and perhaps drawn to the Stoa Poecile from his studies with Crates, chose that public facility for his lessons. The Stoa Poecile was a sizable building (accommodating meetings of at least five hundred people) on the northwest corner of the Athenian civic center (Agora), with an open colonnade facing south across the Agora toward the Acropolis temple complex. The structure was roofed, with walls on three sides hung with paintings (hence the name Poikile, "decorated"), by Polygnotus and other masters, of great historical and mythic battles, which often suggested reason defeating emotion. It was fitting that this should be the scene for what amounted to a radical shift of the city from historical, civic excellence to philosophy. Because the building did not belong to them in any sense, the Stoics (as they came to be called in preference to "Zenoneans") must have done their administrative and library work elsewhere. In Zeno's time, given his Cynic background, administration must have been slight, though books were always important to this scholarly sect.

One sort of student was easy to find at the Stoa Poecile: The years after 307 marked the end of the compulsory *ephebeia*, and eighteen- to twenty-year-olds would have found themselves drawn to public lounging areas such as the Stoa Poecile. As a philosophical organization, however, the Stoa was formidably professional, and Zeno seems, according to remarks such as his threat to charge passersby for listening, to have discouraged random crowds. Most of his known disciples came from abroad—including non-Greek places such as Citium, Zeno's own home—drawn, as Zeno had been, by published books and Athens's educational reputation. The most illustrious of these people was Antigonus Gonatas, who was in Athens as overlord but who thought of himself as a Stoic and employed Zeno's fellow Citiote (housemate) and disciple Persaeus as a tutor for his son and even as a general. Of the more modest sort were Persaeus himself (sometimes rumored to have been Zeno's slave); Cleanthes of Assos, who made a living at the waterworks so as to be in Athens to hear Zeno lecture and who inherited Zeno's position as leader of the school; Aristo of Chios, who set up a rival school teaching ethics; and Sphaerus, the specialist in definition who advised Sparta's revolutionary, land-reforming king, Cleomenes III.

SIGNIFICANCE

Athens, during Zeno of Citium's fifty years there, passed through upheavals that largely left him untouched: Demetrius Eukairos, the philosopher-tyrant, was succeeded by a rivalry of democrats (who initially illegalized philosophy schools), oligarchs, and moderates, while the port of Piraeus was constantly garrisoned by Macedon. Historian William Scott Ferguson counts seven changes of government and four of constitution, three bloody uprisings, and four sieges during this period—with Zeno, though the teacher of a major warlord, never taking any prominent part. The turmoil may already have had for him the unreal quality it acquires in retrospect; the impassive Stoic (and stoic) remains.

Zeno did influence Hellenistic politics, however, contributing some enlightenment to what would in any case have been despotisms. He did not solve all the questions he addressed but left the school with room for future development over several generations: Forward-looking, even arrogant, thinkers liked the dynamic and the sense that human action is cosmically purposeful and significant, though Epicureans and Skeptics demurred. The detailed contributions of the Stoic thought that Zeno either began or left for great successors to begin are great. Finally, Athens honored him after his death with statues in the Academy and Lyceum, a public tomb, and a resolution praising him as a teacher of virtue and temperance who had lived the morality he taught.

—*Owen C. Cramer*

FURTHER READING

Arnold, E. Vernon. *Roman Stoicism: Being Lectures on the History of the Stoic Philosophy with Special Reference to Its Development Within the Roman Empire.* Reprint. New York: Humanities Press, 1958. Contains a fourteen page essay on Zeno in English, and the book—in spite of its title—is a classic treatment of Greek Stoicism in a religious context that was deemphasized in later English philosophical treatments. The chronology needs to be revised in the light of later works.

Camp, John M. *The Athenian Agora: Excavations in the Heart of Classical Athens.* 1986. Rev. ed. New York: Thames and Hudson, 1992. Photographs and discussion of the Stoa Poecile, where excavation began in 1981, in the context of extended archaeological presentation of the city center. A good background for the narratives of Ferguson, Tarn, and Walbank (see below).

Diogenes Laertius. *Lives of Eminent Philosophers.* Translated by R. D. Hicks. 2 vols. Cambridge, Mass.: Harvard University Press, 1991. The main source of information on Zeno. Includes symbolic anecdotes and apothegms in the same relation to Zeno as the Gospels are to Jesus. Hicks's terminology is not always philosophically sophisticated and should be compared to that of Long and Sedley (see below).

Dudley, Donald R. *A History of Cynicism from Diogenes to the Sixth Century A.D.* 1937. Reprint. London: Bristol Classical Press, 1998. The most vivid historical presentation in English of the philosophical environment in which Zeno studied. This edition includes a foreword and bibliography by Miriam Griffin.

Ferguson, William Scott. *Hellenistic Athens: An Historical Essay.* 1911. Reprint. Chicago: Ares, 1974. A classic narrative, hardly superseded though others have improved the chronology and updated the bibliography. Chapters 2 through 4 constitute the history of Athens in Zeno's time and pointedly end with his death. In the absence of a modern biography of Zeno, this work and Tarn's study (below) are the two most extensive substitutes.

Hunt, Harold Arthur Kinross. *A Physical Interpretation of the Universe: The Doctrines of Zeno the Stoic.* Melbourne, Australia: Melbourne University Press, 1976. Though philosophically and historically naïve, this is the only English monograph on Zeno. Not a biography, it presents 105 of the fragments of his teaching in acceptable translations, with commentary and a limited bibliography.

Long, A. A., and D. N. Sedley. *Translations of the Principal Sources, with Philosophical Commentary.* Vol. 1 in *The Hellenistic Philosophers.* New York: Cambridge University Press, 1987. The results of a generation's study of Stoicism are presented in the central 280 pages. Philosophically illuminating, not concentrating on the philosophers' personality or history. Contains a good glossary of technical terms, lists of philosophers and ancient sources, and a panorama of Athens showing the locations of the schools. Short bibliography.

Richter, Gisela M. A. *The Portraits of the Greeks*. 3 vols. London: Phaidon Press, 1965. Volume 2 presents the known ancient portraits of Zeno (except for a group of carved gems) and supports the author's detailed description of Zeno's physiognomy, which, absent further data, must stand for his character to some extent.

Sandbach, F. H. *The Stoics*. 2d ed. Indianapolis: Hackett, 1994. The short opening chapter mentions most of the data. The volume is competent, though not as vivid as that of Dudley (above; whose coverage it does not duplicate).

Sedley, David. "The School: From Zeno to Arius Didymus." In *The Cambridge Companion to the Stoics*, edited by Brad Inwood. New York: Cambridge University Press, 2003. A solid chapter on the beginnings of the Stoic school. Places Zeno in the context of his times and later chapters address his influence throughout time.

Tarn, William Woodthorpe. *Antigonos Gonatas*. 1913. Reprint. Oxford, England: Clarendon Press, 1969. A classic biography by an admirer of Alexander the Great and Hellenism, fitting Antigonus into the mold of adventurous, enlightened prince and featuring Zeno as one of his teachers and a member of his circle. Chronology and bibliography to be supplemented from Walbank (below).

Walbank, F. W., A. E. Astin, M. W. Frederiksen, and R. M. Ogilvie, eds. *The Hellenistic World*. Vol. 7 in *The Cambridge Ancient History*. 2d ed. Cambridge, England: Cambridge University Press, 1984. A useful, long chapter on the period of Antigonus places Zeno's adopted home in perspective with his princely student. Includes chronological improvements on Tarn's and Ferguson's works. Chronological chart, immense bibliography.

SEE ALSO: Aristotle; Plato; Socrates.

RELATED ARTICLE in *Great Events from History: The Ancient World*: c. 300 B.C.E., Stoics Conceptualize Natural Law.

ZENO OF ELEA
Greek philosopher

Although Zeno cannot be said to have succeeded in defending Paramenides' doctrine of the one, his paradoxes are still remembered, and his method of argument influenced all later philosophy.

BORN: c. 490 B.C.E.; Elea (now Velia, Italy)
DIED: c. 440 B.C.E.; Elea
AREA OF ACHIEVEMENT: Philosophy

EARLY LIFE

Little is known of the life of Zeno (ZEE-noh). In the early fifth century, when he was young, Greek philosophy was still in its cruder, experimental form, sometimes mythological, even borrowing from Oriental lore, sometimes resembling primitive science by trying to explain the physical world and basing its conclusions on observation if not on experiment. One tendency was to try to explain all material phenomena as variations on one particular element. Thus, Thales of Miletus taught that all material things were derived from water; Anaximenes of Miletus taught that all things were derived from air; and Heraclitus of Ephesus, though his philosophy was by no means as simple as those of his predecessors, thought that all things were derived from fire. Empedocles, on the other hand, rejected the idea of any single element as the source of all and saw the material world as the result of the mixture and separation of four elements: earth, air, fire, and water.

Zeno's master, Parmenides, rejected this notion of multiplicity in favor of a fundamental unity. His arguments, which were placed in a mythological setting and expressed in hexameter verse, have survived only in fragments; they are exceedingly involved and hard to follow but perhaps can best be summarized as saying that multiplicity is illogical, self-contradictory, or merely unthinkable. This leaves the one, which is not water or air or fire but simply is "being"—"individual, changeless, featureless, motionless, rock-solid being." Multiplicity, however, if contrary to logic, is nevertheless a fact of experience, and Parmenides apparently undertook to give a systematic account of it. A modern thinker might say that the world of reason and the world of experience were mutually exclusive and could never be reconciled.

LIFE'S WORK

Despite the paucity of biographical information about Zeno, Plato's dialogue *Parmenides* (c. 360 B.C.E.) reports the conversation of Socrates—then a young man—and the visiting Parmenides and Zeno. In that account, Zeno is described as "nearly forty years of age, tall and fair to look upon; in the days of his youth he was reported to have been beloved by Parmenides." In the dialogue, having finished reading aloud from his works, written in his youth, Zeno frankly explains their origin and his motive:

> The truth is, that these writings of mine were meant to protect the arguments of Parmenides against those who make fun of him and seek to show the many ridiculous and contradictory results which they suppose to follow from the affirmation of the one. My answer is addressed to partisans of the many, whose attack I return with interest by retorting on them that their hypothesis of the being of many, if carried out, appears to be still more ridiculous than the hypothesis of the being of one.

After Zeno confesses that his arguments were motivated not by "the ambition of an older man, but the pugnacity of a young one," Socrates endeavors to summarize Zeno's arguments:

> Do you maintain that if being is many, it must be both like and unlike, and that this is impossible, for neither can the like be unlike, nor the unlike like. . . . And if the unlike cannot be like, or the like unlike, then according to you, being could not be many, for this would involve an impossibility. In all that you say have you any other purpose except to disprove the being of the many? And is not each division of your treatise intended to furnish a separate proof of this, there being as many proofs of the not-being of the many, as you have composed arguments?

In the dialogue, Zeno acknowledges that Socrates has correctly understood him. Zeno's defense of Parmenides thus consists not of evidence supporting Parmenides' position nor even of positive arguments; rather, Zeno demonstrates that the opposite position is self-contradictory.

These proofs of the being of the one by proving the not-being of the many might not seem relevant in a scientific age, but some have survived and are known to those who are not otherwise learned in pre-Socratic philosophy. Aristotle summarized the most famous of Zeno's arguments, called the "Achilles": "In a race, the quickest runner can never overtake the slowest, since the pursuer must first reach the point where the pursued started, so that the slower must always hold a lead." Almost as famous is the paradox of the arrow, which can never reach its target. According to Zeno's argument, at each point of its flight, the arrow must be at that point and at rest at that point. Thus, all motion, and therefore all change, is illusory.

Zeno's famed pugnacity was not limited to philosophy. After a plot in which he was involved against the tyrant Nearchus of Elea was discovered, the philosopher died under torture, and his death became the subject of various anecdotes. Some claim that he revealed the names of the tyrant's own friends as conspirators. Another story states that Zeno bit off his tongue and spit it out at the tyrant; in another, he bit off the tyrant's ear or nose.

SIGNIFICANCE

Plato recognized in *Sophistēs* (365-361 B.C.E.; *Sophist*, 1804) that there is something futile about such arguments as those of Zeno and that those who make them may simply be showing off:

> Thus we provide a rich feast for tyros, whether young or old; for there is nothing easier than to argue that the one cannot be many, or the many one: and great is their delight in denying that a man is good; for man, they insist, is man and good is good. I dare say that you have met with persons who take an interest in such matters—they are often elderly men, whose meagre sense is thrown into amazement by these discoveries of theirs, which they believe to be the height of wisdom.

Zeno can be defended in a number of ways. One could argue that his motives were good—that he wanted only to defend Parmenides. In doing so, he simply showed that trait of loyalty that brought about his death. More seriously, one could argue that his position in the history of philosophy excuses his failures and could praise him for raising issues and developing methods of argument that Aristotle took seriously. In Zeno's arguments a recurring theme in philosophy can be seen: the conflict of reason and common sense. Periodically in philosophy, thinkers prove by logic things that ordinary people cannot accept. The British empiricists—John Locke, George Berkeley, and David Hume—did this by stripping away the qualities of objects until the real world had to be defended as an illusion. More recently, the poststructuralists have denounced the logocentric view of the world and have written *sous rature*—the world may be described rationally, but that analysis must be voided, since any logocentric analysis of the world by definition must be faulty. Periodically, it seems, logic and common sense must be at odds.

Nevertheless, in the twentieth century, Zeno found one eminent and eloquent defender, Bertrand Russell. Zeno, he said, for two thousand years had been pronounced an ingenious juggler, and his arguments had been considered sophisms, when "these sophisms were reinstated, and made the foundations of a mathematical renaissance, by a German professor," Karl Weierstrass. Russell concludes, "The only point where Zeno probably erred was in inferring (if he did infer) that, because there is no change, therefore the world must be in the same state at one time as at another." Thus, at the dawn of philosophy, when philosophers sometimes wrote in hexameters and were executed for their politics, Zeno expressed certain philosophical problems in a form that still amuses ordinary people and that still occasions profound debates among professional philosophers.

—*John C. Sherwood*

FURTHER READING

Aristotle. *The Physics*. Translated by Robin Waterfield. New York: Oxford University Press, 1999. Contains an analysis of Zeno's arguments. Important because Zeno's extant texts are so fragmentary. Introduction and notes by David Bostock. Includes bibliographical references.

Freeman, Kathleen. *The Pre-Socratic Philosophers: A Companion to Diels's "Fragmente der Vorsokratiker."* Cambridge, Mass.: Harvard University Press, 1959. Freeman's work contains translations of the extant fragments of Zeno's work, interspersed with analysis and commentary.

Hussey, Edward. *The Pre-Socratics*. 1972. Reprint. Indianapolis: Hackett, 1995. This volume contains a sympathetic analysis of Parmenides and Zeno. According to Hussey, "What is historically most important here is the logical analysis of such concepts as *time, change, diversity, separation, completeness*."

Plato. *Parmenides*. Translated with introduction and commentary by Samuel Scolnicov. Berkeley: University of California Press, 2003. Plato provides a glimpse of Zeno as a person as well as some idea of the thought of Parmenides. It is not certain that the dialogue form Plato favors was actually employed by Zeno. An "Eleatic stranger," said to be a disciple of Parmenides and Zeno, takes part in two of the dialogues, but it is not certain whether he expresses their thoughts.

Salmon, Wesley C., ed. *Zeno's Paradoxes*. Indianapolis: Bobbs-Merrill, 1970. Twelve essays by noted thinkers that take a modern look and interpretation of Zeno's puzzling concepts.

West, Martin. "Early Greek Philosophy." In *The Oxford History of the Classical World*, edited by John Boardman, Jasper Griffin, and Oswyn Murray. New York: Oxford University Press, 1986. Although this essay does not give much detail on Zeno, it is nevertheless useful in placing him in his historical and cultural context. The volume itself is illustrated and includes an index and bibliographies.

SEE ALSO: Parmenides; Plato; Socrates.
RELATED ARTICLES in *Great Events from History: The Ancient World*: 600-500 B.C.E., Greek Philosophers Formulate Theories of the Cosmos; c. 530 B.C.E., Founding of the Pythagorean Brotherhood.

ZENOBIA
Queen of the Roman East (r. 267-272 C.E.)

Zenobia conquered and unified Rome's eastern provinces during the late third century C.E. and formed a literary salon of Greek and Syrian intellectuals.

BORN: c. 240 C.E.; Palmyra (now Tadmor, Syria)
DIED: after 274 C.E.; near Tibur (now Tivoli, Italy)
ALSO KNOWN AS: Septimia Zenobia; Bat Zabbai
AREAS OF ACHIEVEMENT: War and conquest, government and politics, art and art patronage

EARLY LIFE

Little is known about Queen Zenobia (zee-NOH-bih-uh) other than she was the second wife of Septimius Odaenathus and mother of the young prince of Palmyra, Septimus Vaballathus (or Athenodorus, in Greek). Her beauty

must have been sublime if her name, in the Arabic form "al-Zabba," is taken to mean the one with beautiful long hair. She was the daughter of Julius Aurelius Zenobios, a military man of the city of Palmyra in the 240's C.E. Palmyra (modern Tadmor in Syria) had been a prosperous city in the Roman East, which had enjoyed the profits of the Silk Road as a nodal point in that long trade route spanning China and the Mediterranean region.

Zenobia's native tongue was Palmyrene, a dialect of Aramaic, and she most likely knew Greek. She attached her fortunes to a local Palmyrene senator (*vir consularis*) named Septimius Odaenathus, who eventually became the king of Palmyra. Their only child was a son named Vaballathus. The social and political backdrop to Zenobia's lifetime is that of the "crisis" period of Roman rule during the third century C.E. From 235 to 284, Roman government underwent a tremendous amount of political instability with no less that thirty different emperors claiming rule. The legitimacy of the emperorship was called into question as various generals, supported by their legions, vied for power. Serious incursions into Roman territory by the Germanic Herulian tribes in the north along the Danube River and by Sasanid Persians in the east had exacerbated the situation.

Severe financial difficulties plagued Rome as well. Over time, the silver content of Roman coins was debased, primarily to stretch the silver bullion supply. By the early third century, Roman currency was little more than a bronze coin with a thin wash of silver, and inflation was rampant. The security of the Roman provinces, particularly in the northern and eastern frontiers, was in jeopardy. A military disaster in 260 left the Roman emperor Valerian captured by the Persian king Shāpūr I and Rome's eastern provinces virtually defenseless. Odaenathus, as an ally of Rome, defeated Shāpūr's forces and helped secure Rome's eastern territories in 261.

LIFE'S WORK

On her husband's death in 267 (he may have been assassinated in a dynastic struggle), Zenobia had accepted Odaenathus's authority as king of Palmyra and de facto governor (*corrector*) of the Roman eastern provinces as a regent for her young son. Filling a power vacuum left by a weakened Roman military, Zenobia governed the provinces of Syria and secured Rome's eastern frontier from Sasanid Persian invasion. After the death of the emperor Claudius II in 270, however, the ambitious Zenobia expanded her authority and territory by swiftly overcoming the provinces of Arabia, heading west into Syria-Palestine, and then plunging south into Egypt.

Zenobia's campaign in Egypt, which is well documented, consisted of a direct assault on Alexandria with an army of seventy thousand. The army at its core comprised Palmyrene heavy calvary, supplemented by horse archers as well as light infantry made up of Syrians and other Near Easterners. It appears that the Palmyrene army depended on various mercenary troops made up of many different people. Sources mention that half of Zenobia's forces had Jewish, Nabataean, and perhaps Indian and Aksumitic elements. After Zenobia had taken

Zenobia, in white dress. (F. R. Niglutsch)

Egypt, she marched west into Asia Minor and reached the city of Ancyra. At its height, Zenobia's Palmyrene Empire extended over much of Syria, the Levantine coast, Arabia, Egypt, and a good deal of Asia Minor. The major metropolitan cities of Antioch, Bostra, and Alexandria were under Zenobia's control within a single year, a remarkable military achievement.

The major sources of the period that characterize the nature of Zenobia's regime are not wholly consistent. The *Historia Augusta* (a collection of biographies of the Roman emperors from Hadrian to Numerian, probably written in the late fourth century C.E. by unknown authors; no complete translation) portrays the Palmyrene queen as a Syrian Dido, a Queen Victoria, an Assyrian queen, and a self-styled Cleopatra VII. This contrasts with her own propaganda emphasizing her connection with the Hellenistic Seleucid line as well as legendary accounts that emphasize her "Jewishness." Early in her career in 267-268, Zenobia held, through her son, the formal Roman title of *corrector*, a governorship position that her husband had held. Early in 270 a series of coins was issued from the mints at Antioch and Alexandria featuring her son, Vaballathus, and the legitimate Roman emperor Aurelian, giving the appearance of joint rule.

Later that year, as the break from Rome grew more pronounced, she fully assumed the title of *augusta*, clearly revealing her aspirations to be equal with the emperors in Rome. Perhaps her assumption of such numerous and varied titles points to the diverse nature of the constituencies over whom she ruled. As a Ptolemaic queen, a daughter of Antiochus, or a Roman *augusta*, Zenobia wore many crowns, so to speak, for the many people that she ruled.

Despite Zenobia's wide-ranging constituency, there is evidence that her rule was far from stable. According to Tabari's *Tārīkh al-rusul wa-al-mulūk*; (ninth century C.E.; *The History of Al-Tabarī*, 1985-1999), an Arab tradition states that Zenobia had assassinated Jadhima, the ruling sheik of the Tanukh tribal confederation in northern Arabia. Jadhima's successor, 'Amir ibn 'Adi, avenged his uncle's death by leading the Tanukh against Palmyra, eventually destroying it. The accuracy of this legendary account is suspect, through it perhaps points to tension that existed between Zenobia and some Bedouin tribes. Zenobia and her Palmyrene forces had also earned the enmity of the Sasanid Persians, who had been defeated and driven from the Roman east back to Ctesiphon by Odaenathus. The disappearance of a Persian representative Aurelius Vorodes from the Palmyrene court is a sure indication that hostilities existed between the two powers after Zenobia's ascendancy.

One of the major achievements of Zenobia's rule is her establishment of a literary salon of writers, philosophers, and intellectuals. Cassius Longinus, the rhetorician and Platonic philosopher, is said to have been part of Zenobia's court and had written Odaenathus's funeral oration. The salon of Palmyra must have had an eastern flavor, with the historians Genathlius of Petra and Nicostratus of Trapezus, who penned histories of the Roman east. Rhetoricians and Sophists were also included, such as Callinicus. He, surpassing the realm of oral eloquence, wrote a history of Alexandria and presented it to his patron queen, Zenobia. Clearly the Palmyrene queen understood the importance of maintaining the trappings of queenly literary patronage, symbolizing

her status as a ruler. One can perhaps see some parallels with another Syrian empress, Julia Domna, who during the second century C.E. patronized a similar circle of literati.

Unfortunately, Zenobia's star fell as quickly as it had risen. In 272 the emperor Aurelian, bent on restoring the Roman Empire to its previous integrity, made war on the Palmyrenes. Aurelian's military victories in Asia Minor quickly caused support for the Palmyrene regime to evaporate. Zenobia and her general, Zabdas, fled before Aurelian's onslaught, first to Emesa and later to Palmyra, where she held her ground. It is not clear exactly what became of the Palmyrene queen. One tradition has Zenobia, not wishing to become part of Aurelian's triumph, fall in battle against the Romans. Others say that she was bound with gold fetters and did indeed become part of Aurelian's victory parade through Rome. This tradition also maintains that Zenobia, after being brought to Rome, was granted clemency by Aurelian and spent the remaining years of her life in a villa at Tivoli.

SIGNIFICANCE

Zenobia's Palmyrene Empire demonstrates the fragile nature of Roman Imperial government during the third century C.E. During this crisis of the third century, Rome's central government had been so weak as to have lost not only its eastern provinces to Zenobia but its northern provinces of Britannia and Gaul for a short number of years. It was truly an accomplishment that Zenobia took control of her city after her husband's death and then went on to conquer and rule the wealthiest and most populous of Rome's provinces. The diversity of peoples she ruled perhaps forced her to portray herself in ambiguous ways, adapting to the circumstances around her. During the early stages of her regime, Zenobia had ruled as a regent, but she then assumed full control, dispensing the guise of her rule along the lines of a patriarchy. It is unclear what plans she had for her son, Vaballathus, had he grown to maturity or how it would have affected her reign had it lasted.

—*Byron J. Nakamura*

FURTHER READING

Browning, Iain. *Palmyra*. Park Ridge, N.J.: Noyes Press, 1979. A richly illustrated work on the archaeological remains of Palmyra. Includes bibliography and index.

Colledge, M. A. R. *The Art of Palmyra*. Boulder, Colo.: Westview Press, 1976. A comprehensive study of the art and architecture of Palmyra. Includes bibliography and index.

Millar, Fergus. *The Roman Near East, 31 B.C.-A.D. 337.* Cambridge, Mass.: Harvard University Press, 1993. A thorough political survey of the Roman Near East that provides the larger political context for Palmyra and Zenobia. Includes bibliography and index.

Nakamura, Byron. "Palmyra and the Roman East." *Greek, Roman, and Byzantine Studies* 34 (1993): 133-172. Argues for the political pragmatism of Zenobia's propaganda and imperial images.

Stoneman, Richard. *Palmyra, Its Empire: Zenobia's Revolt Against Rome.* Ann Arbor: University of Michigan Press, 1992. An accessible introduction to the Palmyrene rebellion. Includes bibliography and index.

SEE ALSO: Arsinoe II Philadelphus; Boudicca; Cleopatra VII; Dido; Julia Domna; Sammu-ramat.

RELATED ARTICLE in *Great Events from History: The Ancient World*: 2d century B.C.E., Silk Road Opens.

ZHUANGZI
Chinese philosopher

Zhuangzi was the greatest thinker of the Chinese Daoist school of philosophy. He went much beyond its founder, Laozi, in constructing an apolitical, transcendental philosophy designed to promote an individual's spiritual freedom.

BORN: c. 365 B.C.E.; Meng, Kingdom of Song, China
DIED: c. 290 B.C.E.; Nanhua Hill, Caozhou, Kingdom of Chi, China
ALSO KNOWN AS: Chuang-tzu (Wade-Giles); Chuang Tzu; Chuang Chou
AREAS OF ACHIEVEMENT: Philosophy, religion, literature

EARLY LIFE

Zhuangzi (dzwahng-dzur) was born sometime around 365 B.C.E.; according to his biographer, Sima Qian (Ssuma Ch'ien; 145-86 B.C.E.), the philosopher was a native of the town of Meng in the Kingdom of Song. His personal name was Zhou. Beyond this, little is known regarding Zhuangzi's life and career. He was born into a time known as the Warring States period (475-221 B.C.E.), during which China had become divided into many small, fiercely competitive states as a result of the collapse of the Zhou (Chou) Dynasty. Thus, Zhuangzi was a contemporary of the famous Confucian philosopher Mencius (Mengzi; c. 372-c. 289 B.C.E.).

For a brief time, Zhuangzi served as a government official in Qiyuan (Ch'i-yuan), not far from his birthplace. He soon tired of public life, however, and resolved to pursue philosophical meditation and writing. Thereupon, he retired to the state of Qi (Ch'i), where he took up residence on Nanhua Hill, in the prefecture of Caozhou (Ts'ao-chou). Here he spent the remainder of his life.

Zhuangzi's disillusionment with law and politics is apparent in an anecdote recorded in chapter 17 of the *Zhuangzi* (traditionally c. 300 B.C.E.; probably compiled c. 285-160 B.C.E.; *The Divine Classic of Nan-hua*, 1881; also known as *The Complete Works of Chuang Tzu*, 1968; commonly known as *Zhuangzi*, 1991):

> Once, when Chuang Tzu [Zhuangzi] was fishing in the P'u River, the king of Ch'u [Chu] sent two officials to go and announce to him: "I would like to trouble you with the administration of my realm."
> Chuang Tzu held on to the fishing pole and, without turning his head, said, "I have heard that there is a sacred tortoise in Ch'u that has been dead for three thousand years. The king keeps it wrapped in cloth and boxed, and stores it in the ancestral temple. Now would this tortoise rather be dead and have its bones left behind and honored? Or would it rather be alive and dragging its tail in the mud?"
> "It would rather be alive and dragging its tail in the mud," said the two officials.
> Chuang Tzu said, "Go away! I'll drag my tail in the mud!"

A portrait of this stubbornly independent thinker has been preserved in Taipei's National Palace Museum. It shows a rather short, slightly built man with sparse hair and penetrating eyes. He stands with his hands clasped over his chest, a pose that conveys dignity and serenity.

LIFE'S WORK

The Daoism of Zhuangzi's time derived from the *Yijing* (eighth to third century B.C.E.; English translation, 1876; also known as *Book of Changes*, 1986), the ancient manual of divination based on the concept that the world and the laws of change are an ordered, interdependent unit, and from Laozi's *Dao De Jing* (possibly sixth century B.C.E., probably compiled late third century B.C.E.; *The Speculations on Metaphysics, Polity, and Morality of* "the Old Philosopher, Lau-Tsze," 1868; better known as the *Dao De Jing*), which described the workings of the Dao (the Way), the primordial generative principle that is the mother of all things. Dao was interpreted as "the Way of Heaven," or natural law, and the Daoists explained natural phenomena and the social order in reference to this principle. Proper human behavior consisted of not interfering with the Dao but living in harmony with it. Thus, the Daoists taught the doctrine of *wuwei* (not doing), or, more explicitly, *wei-wu-wei* (doing by not doing). This standard did not imply absolute quietism but rather acting intuitively, spontaneously, and effortlessly in imitation of the Dao, which manages to accomplish everything naturally. Although some Daoists retired entirely from the world and lived as hermits, Daoism was not designed for the hermit but for the sage king, who, though not withdrawing from the world, seeks to avoid interfering with it.

For the Daoists, then, the best government was the least government. Indeed, they reasoned, if all men acted in harmony with the Dao, government as an institution would be unnecessary. Government by law and even the notions of good and evil were regarded by the Daoists as deviations from the Dao and unwarranted interference with it. Such an attitude gave Daoists considerable independence in regard to politics and worldly affairs generally.

It is evident that Zhuangzi's decision to withdraw from political entanglements was amply supported by Daoist teachings. His interpretations of this and other doctrines have been passed down in the *Zhuangzi*, an imaginative compilation of anecdote and dialogue. In the words of a modern scholar, in the *Zhuangzi* "animals speak, natural forces are personified, and dialogues which begin in soberness unexpectedly veer into humor, fantasy, and absurdity."

Where the *Dao De Jing* of Laozi sets forth the universal Dao as a political and social ideal, the *Zhuangzi* is mostly concerned with the individual and his or her intellectual and spiritual freedom. Unlike Laozi's work, which is addressed to rulers, the *Zhuangzi* addresses anyone, ruler or private person, who wishes to become a member of the spiritual elite. To achieve this goal, the seeker must begin by achieving an awareness of the existence and workings of the universal Dao and of his or her own relation to the scheme of things.

The Dao is nameless; the name assigned to it is merely a convenient label. Though it is preexistent, formless, and imperceptible, it latently contains all forms, entities, and forces; it permeates all things. All Being issues from it and returns to it. The life and death of human beings take part in this transformation from Non-being into Being and back again to Non-being.

After accepting this metaphysical scheme, the seeker faces the second step on the ladder of knowledge: the realization of the importance of making full and free use of his natural ability. Whatever ability he possesses stems from his *tê*, the power within him that comes directly from the Dao. The individuated forms of things come from their *tê*, which confers on them their natural properties and abilities. Things differ both in their nature and in their natural abilities. One kind of bird can fly a thousand miles; another kind has difficulty flying from one tree to another. It is no use for a man to discuss the ocean with a frog that has lived its whole life in a well.

It is important for the seeker to distinguish between what is heavenly—that is, of nature—and what is entirely human. What is heavenly is internal; what is human is external. The human is all that is artificial: the artifacts of man; his institutions of government, education, and religion; his cultural codes of etiquette, law, and morals. All these artificialities involve restrictions on man's independence and freedom. To the extent that a person can exercise his natural abilities independently of or in spite of the restrictions imposed on him, he ought to do so. In so doing, he will achieve a measure of happiness, although it will be a relative, not an absolute, happiness. Interference with nature should be avoided, according to Zhuangzi's teachings. Government that seeks to rule people by strict laws and strong institutions is pictured as putting a halter around a horse's neck or a cord through an ox's nose. The use of violence by governments is like trying to lengthen the short legs of a duck or to shorten the long legs of a crane.

Relative happiness, then, can be attained by making good use of one's natural ability; yet, other factors such as avoiding injury and disease and overcoming fear of death are also necessary to happiness. If the seeker gains a proper understanding of the nature of things, he can greatly mitigate his anxiety regarding death as well as the grief he may feel when a loved one dies. Chapter 18 of the *Zhuangzi*, "Perfect Happiness," records an anecdote that illustrates this notion. Zhuangzi's wife had died, and Huizi (Hui-tzu) had gone to pay his condolences to the philosopher. On entering his house, Huizi was amazed to find the master "sitting with his legs sprawled, pounding on a tub and singing." Scandalized, Huizi hastened to remind Zhuangzi that he had lived with his wife a long time, that she had borne and reared his children, and that she had grown old along with him. Huizi reproached his friend: "It should be enough simply not to weep at her death. But pounding on a tub and singing—this is going too far, isn't it?" Zhuangzi replied:

> You're wrong. When she first died, do you think I didn't grieve like anyone else? But I looked back to her beginning and the time before she was born. Not only the time before she was born, but the time before she had a body. Not only the time before she had a body, but the time before she had a spirit. In the midst of the jumble of wonder and mystery a change took place and she had a spirit. Another change and she had a body. Another change and she was born. Now there's been another change and she's dead. It's just like the progression of the four seasons, spring, summer, fall, winter.
>
> Now she's going to lie down peacefully in a vast room. If I were to follow after her bawling and sobbing, it would show that I don't understand anything about fate. So I stopped.

Thus, death is simply a phase in the turning of the wheel of fortune that is the Dao. The turning of the wheel voids the identity and disintegrates the material body of the dead person. From the standpoint of the Dao, however, no state of being is more desirable than another. As a natural event in the cycle of human life, death is neither to be feared nor to be sorrowed over.

How does the seeker reach the third and last rung of his upward way? To answer this question, Zhuangzi proposed an epistemology, a theory of knowledge. Knowledge, he said, is of two kinds: lower and higher. The lower involves sense perception, reason, and language; it depends on relativity, finitude, and memory. Higher knowledge involves suprasensible perception, intuition, and silence; it depends on the unity of opposites, infinitude, and forgetfulness. Lower knowledge lacks understanding. Higher knowledge is filled with understanding, a condition in which everything is illuminated by "the light of Heaven."

To achieve higher knowledge, the seeker must forget the knowledge that he has acquired. He must transcend all relativity, finitude, and apparent contradictions implied in conventional opposites such as right and wrong, great and small, life and death. The seeker can transcend such distinctions when he realizes that the Dao makes them all one. Once he has attained this realization, he has no use for categories. Where "ordinary men discriminate and parade their discriminations before others," the enlightened man "embraces things." Thus, forgetfulness and "no-knowledge" constitute the highest wisdom.

The lower level of knowledge permits the use of speech. Good language is dispassionate and calm; bad language is "shrill and quarrelsome." At the higher level of knowledge, however, language is inadequate: "The Great Way is not named; Great Discriminations are not spoken. . . . If discriminations are put into words, they do not suffice." The holy man does not speak, for him silence reigns supreme. Content within himself because he has forgotten self and the world, he may be said to have entered Heaven. He has achieved absolute happiness.

SIGNIFICANCE

If the real Zhuangzi is a barely perceptible shadow cast by the dim light of history, he is brightly visible in the pages of the *Zhuangzi*. Here he emerges as a living, breathing, dynamic human being, radiant of mind, wideranging in imagination, full of wit and humor. The *Zhuangzi* is a monumental book and a great classic of Chinese literature. Its style is brilliant, full of clever rhetorical devices, satire, fantasy, metaphor, jokes, dreams, and parody. Although it is a work of philosophy, it may also be termed "protofictional." It not only uses historical characters, such as Confucius, fictionally, but also creates fictional characters as foils for its protagonist. In this way, the *Zhuangzi* contributed to the development of later Chinese fictional genres such as *xiaoshuo* and *zhiguai*.

Philosophically, Zhuangzi went beyond Laozi in offering a clear alternative to the philosophies of his age. He emphasized the personal ideal of the emancipation of the individual for his or her own sake in place of the social ideal of the harmonious society ruled by the Sage king. Although the *Zhuangzi* never gained the popularity and influence of the *Dao De Jing*, it continued to command the interest and admiration of Chinese rulers and philosophers. The Neo-Daoist philosophers Xiang Xiu (Hsiang Hsiu; c. 221-c. 300 C.E.) and Guo Xiang (Kuo Hsiang; d. c. 312 C.E.) both wrote commentaries on the *Zhuangzi*, seeking to reconcile the social ideal of Confucius with the private ideal of Zhuangzi. Despite their criticism of Zhuangzi, they performed the important service of transmitting his work and preserving it for posterity.

In the West, the *Zhuangzi* has made a decided impression on numerous prominent thinkers, beginning perhaps with the great German philosopher G. W. F. Hegel, who in 1816 lectured at the University of Heidelberg on Daoism and Confucianism, based on the *Book of Changes* and the *Zhuangzi*. His concept of the Absolute as a process rather than a source and his description of the dialectical process (thesis and antithesis merging into a synthesis) are reminiscent of Zhuangzi's concept of the Dao and the underlying unity of opposites. Later twentieth century thinkers such as Pierre Teilhard de Chardin, Carl Jung, Jacques Maritain, Jacques Lacan, and Thomas Merton all show evidence in their writing of an intimate acquaintance with Daoism and the thought of Zhuangzi.

—*Richard P. Benton*

FURTHER READING

Ames, Roger T., ed. *Wandering at Ease in the "Zhuangzi."* Albany: State University of New York Press, 1998. Eleven essays on the *Zhuangzi*, which collectively are intended to comprise a primer on how to read this Daoist classic.

Hochsmann, Hyun. *On Chuang Tzu*. Belmont, Calif.: Wadsworth/Thomson Learning, 2001. A brief introduction to Zhuangzi's life and thought, intended as a guide for students.

Kjellberg, Paul, and Philip J. Ivanhoe, eds. *Essays on Skepticism, Relativism, and Ethics in the "Zuangzi."* Albany: State University of New York Press, 1996. A collection of nine essays, whose main focus is the source and nature of Zhuangzi's cheerfulness.

Merton, Thomas. *The Way of Chuang Tzu*. 1965. Reprint. Boston: Shambhala, 1992. The author was a poet, prose writer, mystic, and Trappist monk. Knowing no

Chinese, he made an effort here to capture his intuitive sense of Zhuangzi's spirit on the basis of translations in Western languages. He succeeds as well as the translators.

Roth, Harold D. *A Companion to Angus C. Graham's "Chuang Tze: The Inner Chapters."* Honolulu: University of Hawaii Press, 2003. Collects the notes and commentary of one of the premier Zhuangzi scholars and translators.

Zhuangzi. *The Inner Chapters*. Translated by A. C. Graham. 1981. Reprint. Cambridge, Mass.: Hackett Publishing, 2001. A translation of the *Zhuangzi* as well as an extensive collection of ancient commentary. Also includes a thorough introduction, notes, a list of characters, and index.

SEE ALSO: Laozi; Mencius.

RELATED ARTICLES in *Great Events from History: The Ancient World*: 3d century B.C.E. (traditionally 6th century B.C.E.), Laozi Composes the *Dao De Jing*; 285-160 B.C.E. (traditionally, c. 300 B.C.E.), Composition of the *Zhuangzi*; 139-122 B.C.E., Composition of the *Huainanzi*; c. 60-68 C.E., Buddhism Enters China; 142 C.E., Zhang Daoling Founds the Celestial Masters Movement; 4th century C.E., Ge Chaofu Founds the Ling Bao Sect of Daoism.

ZOROASTER

Persian religious leader

The founder of one of the great ethical religions of the ancient world, Zoroaster exerted direct and indirect influence on the development of three other world religions: Judaism, Christianity, and Islam.

BORN: c. 628 B.C.E.; probably Rhages, Media (now Rey, Iran)

DIED: c. 551 B.C.E.; probably Media (now in northern Iran)

ALSO KNOWN AS: Zarathustra

AREA OF ACHIEVEMENT: Religion

EARLY LIFE

Zoroaster (ZOHR-uh-was-tur)—the corrupt Greek name of the Persian name Zarathustra (zah-rah-THEWS-trah)—was one of the most important religious reformers of the ancient world and the founder of a new religion that took his name: Zoroastrianism. Because very little is known about his life, the dates of his birth and death are

disputed. According to tradition, he "lived 258 years before Alexander" the Great. This has been interpreted as 258 years before Alexander's conquest of Persia in 330 B.C.E. The date has also been interpreted not as a birth date but as the date of one of three principal events in Zoroaster's life: his vision and revelation at the age of thirty, the beginning of his preaching at age forty, or the conversion of King Vishtaspa (or Hystapas) two years later. As, according to tradition, Zoroaster lived for seventy-seven years, he lived between 630 and 553, 628 and 551, or 618 and 541.

Although he was never deified, legends and pious embellishments began to grow about Zoroaster after his death. Such legends have both clarified and obscured modern knowledge about him. It was said that he was the product of a miraculous birth and that at birth he laughed aloud, thus driving away evil spirits. As an adult, he became a great lover of wisdom and righteousness, withdrawing to an isolated mountain wilderness, where he survived on cheese and wild fruit. There he was tempted by the devil but successfully resisted. He was then subjected to intense physical torture, which he endured by clinging to his faith in Ahura Mazda, the true god and the Lord of Light. He received a revelation from Ahura Mazda in the form of the *Avesta*, the holy book of his religion, and was commissioned to preach to humankind. After suffering ridicule and persecution for many years, he at last found a convert and patron in King Vishtaspa. Married and the father of a daughter and two sons, Zoroaster appears to have enjoyed a degree of local prominence at his patron's court. His daughter apparently married a leading minister of the king.

LIFE'S WORK

Like the other great ethical religions, Zoroastrianism had its origins in its founder's reaction to the religious beliefs and practices of his people. The religion of the pre-Zoroastrian Persians displays many features in common with Hinduism. This is understandable, because the ancient settlers of Persia and India came from the same Aryan tribes that had invaded Persia and India a millennium before Zoroaster's birth. Persian religion before Zoroaster was polytheistic, with specific deities attached to the three major classes of society: chiefs and priests, warriors, and farmers and cattle breeders. The deities known as *asuras* (lords), who alone were endowed with an ethical character, were attached exclusively to the first class. Two forms of sacrifice were practiced: animal sacrifice, apparently to propitiate the gods, and the drinking of the fermented juice of the sacred *haoma* plant, which, through the intoxication it induced, supplied a foretaste of immortality. To perform the sacrifices and the other rituals, a priestly class, the magi, rose to a position of great power in early Persian society.

Basing his teaching on the *Avesta*, a book of revelations from Ahura Mazda, Zoroaster conceived it as his mission to purify the traditional beliefs of his people by eradicating polytheism, animal sacrifice, and magic and to establish a new, more ethical and spiritual religion. Ultimately, Zoroastrianism succeeded because of its founder's and early followers' ability to accommodate their teachings with certain features of traditional Persian religion.

It is impossible to determine how many of the teachings of Zoroastrianism originated with its founder. The *Avesta*, as it has come down to the present, is composed of several divisions, including two liturgical texts, prayers, and two sets of hymns, only one of which, the *Gathas*, is definitely ascribed to Zoroaster. Much of the *Avesta* has been destroyed or lost. Zoroaster probably made additional contributions, as did his later followers. There is, however, general agreement that it was Zoroaster who provided the central teaching of his religion.

According to Zoroaster, the history of the world was the ongoing conflict between the forces of good and evil. God, Ahura Mazda, represented the former; the devil, Ahriman, the latter. Ahura Mazda, one of several of the *asuras* of traditional Persian religion, was elevated by Zoroaster to the place of the one high god; Zoroastrianism was originally a distinctly monotheistic religion, although later it absorbed polytheistic features. Zoroaster divided history into four three-thousand-year periods, during which Ahura Mazda and Ahriman competed for people's souls and the ultimate victory of their respective causes. At the end of the final stage, which some Zoroastrians interpreted as beginning with the birth of Zoroaster, Ahura Mazda would overpower Ahriman and his minions in a great conflagration and cast them into the

Zoroaster. (Hulton|Archive by Getty Images)

abyss. This would be followed by a resurrection of the dead, a last judgment, and the beginning of a new life for all good souls (believers in Ahura Mazda) in a world free of evil, darkness, pain, and death.

Zoroastrianism included concepts of a hell and purgatory as well as a paradise. At death, all souls would have to cross the narrow Sifting Bridge (also known as the Bridge of the Requiter), which was like a long sword. The good would be offered the broad (flat) side of the bridge and would be welcomed into paradise by a beautiful young maiden. There they would reside with Ahura Mazda throughout eternity. The evil souls—the followers of Ahriman—would be forced to walk along the razor's edge of the sword-bridge and would fall into a hell that would be their abode of darkness and terror forever. For the souls who had sinned but whose good works outweighed their bad, there would be a short period of temporary punishment to cleanse them in preparation for entrance into paradise. For sinners of greater degree, who had nevertheless performed some good works, suffering in hell would last until god's final victory and the last judgment, when they also would be welcomed into paradise. Those who subscribed to Zoroaster's teachings, therefore, could face death unafraid in anticipation of a blissful afterlife, if not immediately at least ultimately.

The religion of Zoraster was ethical. People's duties were threefold: to befriend their enemies, to lead the wicked to righteousness, and to educate the ignorant. The greatest virtue toward which the believer must strive was piety, followed by honor and honesty in both word and deed. The worst sin was unbelief, which was not only a denial of Ahura Mazda but also a rejection of his ethical code of conduct and an acceptance of evil. Because piety was the greatest virtue, the first obligation of the believer was to worship god through purification, sacrifice, and prayer.

Although Zoroaster rejected blood sacrifices, he retained the sacrifice of fire, which was a symbol of Ahura Mazda and thus of purity and truth. Although Zoroaster decried the drinking of the fermented juice of the *haoma* plant for its intoxicating qualities, it was retained as a medium of Holy Communion. Historically, the fire ritual became the central feature of Zoroastrian worship. Sacred fires are tended and preserved by priests in fire temples, where the king of fires, Bahram, is crowned and enthroned. Modern Zoroastrians (Parsees) have also retained the practices of wearing the *sadre*, the shirt that symbolizes their religion, and the daily untying and re-knotting of the *kushti*, the sacred thread whose seventy-two strands symbolize the chapters of the *Yasna*, one of

the sacred liturgical texts. The final act of piety is proper provision for the disposition of one's body after death. The corpse is neither cremated nor buried, because the first method would defile fire and the second method would defile the earth, both of which are regarded as good creations of god. Instead, the dead are exposed to the elements, where their flesh is consumed by vultures. This practice survives today in the famous Towers of Silence in Bombay among the Parsees (Persians), virtually the last significant surviving community of Zoroastrians.

Although Zoroaster was a monotheist, he nevertheless sought to accommodate his religious traditions. Surrounding Ahura Mazda are the six "Beneficent (or Holy) Immortal Ones" and the *yazads* (the worshiped ones), who probably had their origins in the deities worshiped by the lesser orders of ancient Persian society. These beings have been compared to the archangels and angels of Christianity. Because of the exalted nature of Ahura Mazda, it came to be believed that he should be approached indirectly through these servants, who came to personify certain facets of god's creation and qualities. The *yazad* Mithra, keeper of the sacred fire (the fire temples came to be called the courts of Mithra), who represented justice and friendship and who was Ahura Mazda's chief lieutenant in the struggle against evil, was himself to become the deity in a religious offshoot of Zoroastrianism, Mithraism, which was one of Christianity's chief competitors in the Roman Empire. Opposed to the servants of god were Ahriman and his hordes of demons, who were also associated with lesser ancient Persian demigods. They brought evil into the world in its various forms and worked to deny humans their blissful afterlife with Ahura Mazda and his servants. Zoroaster is thought to have died at the age of seventy-seven; legend states that he was murdered.

SIGNIFICANCE

The history of Zoroastrianism following the death of its founder was characterized by change, accommodation, decline, and revival. The most notable changes were the emergence of dualism, with the deification of Ahriman and the conception of history as the struggle between separate gods of good and evil, and the emergence of an increasingly powerful priestly class, the magi, who introduced elements of magic, astrology, and blood sacrifice in a perversion of Zoroaster's ideals. Following the Muslim conquest of Persia in the seventh century, Zoroastrians were alternately tolerated, persecuted, and forcibly converted to Islam. In the eleventh century, all but a small remnant left Persia and emigrated to India, where most of them settled in the area around Bombay. There they have remained, and, known as the Parsees, they have become among the wealthiest, best-educated, and most charitable members of Indian society, all the while holding fast to their religious beliefs and practices. In the nineteenth century, they reestablished contact with the remaining Zoroastrians in Iran, the Gabars.

There are significant parallels between Zoroastrianism and three of the world's great religions, Judaism, Christianity, and Islam, although the extent of Zoroastrianism's direct influence remains a subject of debate. Perhaps Zoroaster's greatest contribution, both to his own age and to later civilizations, was the elevation of religion from debasement, magic, blood sacrifice, and pessimism to a scheme that optimistically promises rewards to those who conform in word and deed to a high, but realizable, code of ethical conduct.

—J. Stewart Alverson

FURTHER READING

Duchesne-Guillemin, Jacques. *The Western Response to Zoroaster.* Reprint. Westport, Conn.: Greenwood Press, 1973. This is a valuable introduction to scholarship on Zoroaster and Zoroastrianism by one of the leading twentieth century scholars on the subject.

Durant, Will. *Our Oriental Heritage: Being a History of Civilization in Egypt and the Near East to the Death of Alexander, and in India, China, and Japan from the Beginning to Our Own Day, with an Introduction on the Nature and Foundations of Civilization.* Vol. 1 in *The Story of Civilization.* 1954. Reprint. New York: MJF Books, 1992. Contains an especially helpful and perceptive account of Zoroaster and Zoroastrianism. Durant considers the subject both in its ancient Persian context and as a powerful influence on later religions.

Kriwaczek, Paul. *In Search of Zarathustra: The First Prophet and the Ideas That Changed the World.* New York: Knopf, 2003. The publisher's note states: "Moving from present to past, Paul Kriwaczek examines the effects of the prophet's teachings on the spiritual and daily lives of diverse peoples." He covers the impact of Zoroastrianism and follows it back to the man himself.

Masani, Rustom. *The Religion of the Good Life: Zoroastrianism.* 1938. 2d ed. New York: Macmillan, 1968. This is a useful account by a Parsee of the teachings and practices of Zoroastrianism.

Olmstead, A. T. *History of the Persian Empire.* 1948. Reprint. Chicago: University of Chicago Press, 1960. This classic history of ancient Persia is useful in placing Zoroaster in his historical context.

Parrinder, Geoffrey, ed. *World Religions: From Ancient History to the Present.* Rev. ed. New York: Facts on File, 1983. In this revised and enlarged edition of a book first published in the United States in 1971 as *Religions of the World*, Zoroastrianism is traced from its origins to the present, including material on its most important offshoots, Mithraism and Manichaeanism.

Zoroaster. *The Hymns of Zarathustra: Being a Translation of the Gāthās Together with Introduction and Commentary.* Translated by Mrs. M. Henning. 1952. Reprint. Westport, Conn.: Hyperion Press, 1979. This translation of the *Gathas*, which contains the only teachings of Zoroastrianism that can definitely be attributed to its founder, is indispensable to serious study of the subject. Includes an introduction and commentary by Jacques Duchesne-Guillemin.

SEE ALSO: Akhenaton; Buddha; Jesus; Moses.

RELATED ARTICLES in *Great Events from History: The Ancient World*: c. 600 B.C.E., Appearance of Zoroastrian Ditheism; c. 500 B.C.E.-c. 600 C.E., Mithraism Emerges as Significant Religion.

ZOSER

Egyptian pharaoh (r. c. 2687-2650 B.C.E.)

Zoser was the first great king of the epoch known as the Old Kingdom, the Third through Eighth Dynasties. His outstanding achievement was the construction of the Step Pyramid at Saqqara near Memphis, the earliest of the great pyramids.

BORN: c. 2700 B.C.E.; probably Memphis, Egypt
DIED: c. 2650 B.C.E.; Memphis, Egypt
ALSO KNOWN AS: Djoser; Zosher; Netjerikhet
AREAS OF ACHIEVEMENT: Government and politics, architecture

EARLY LIFE

Zoser is usually regarded as either the first king of the Third Dynasty (c. 2687-c. 2613), although some historians include a predecessor, Nebka (Sanekht). Zoser's physical description is known from several reliefs found in the Step Pyramid complex and from a seated limestone statue, thought to be the oldest life-size statue found in Egypt. This portrayal of the king was discovered in a small, doorless room near his pyramid, positioned to look out two eyeholes in the wall so that the king could view food offerings brought to him by his funerary priests each day. Although the inlaid eyes have been gouged out and the nose has been damaged, the massive head, with its high cheekbones and prominent mouth, has lost none of its intimidating majesty. This is no idealized portrait, but the likeness of Zoser himself.

Apart from the members of his immediate family, only a few others can be linked to Zoser by name. Hesyra and Khabausokar have left impressive funerary monuments that testify to their importance in Zoser's court. Although his tomb remains to be discovered, there is one man, Imhotep, whose name must rank with that of the great king. In later antiquity he was credited with every kind of wisdom and was even accorded divine status as a god of healing. It is as Zoser's chief architect, however, that Imhotep has ensured his place in history, for the king entrusted to this innovative genius the construction of the Step Pyramid.

LIFE'S WORK

Ancient Egyptians believed that the king was the incarnation of the falcon god Horus, source of all goods and prosperity for the entire land. During his life on earth, the king displayed his effectiveness as a ruler by the wealth and beauty of his royal residence; after his death, he proclaimed his ability to continue to perform good services for his subjects by the magnificence of his tomb. When the king departed this life he became one with his father, Osiris, god of the land's fertility, and continued to bestow prosperity on his subjects through the new incarnation of the god Horus, that is, the king's son and successor.

From the very beginning, royal tombs were built on the analogy of the royal residence, for the king's tomb was his "house of eternity," in the common Egyptian expression. Thus, in very early times when the king lived in a circular hut, his tomb was circular; when the royal residence became rectangular in shape, the royal tomb became rectangular. The royal tomb, despite some changes, remained essentially the same until the time of Zoser. It consisted of a subterranean structure where the dead king was buried with his most valuable possessions, topped by a brick superstructure in the form of a rectangular platform, which Egyptologists refer to as a mastaba (Arabic for "bench").

When Zoser came to the throne, he had the same assumptions about his role as his predecessors. He was the god Horus, or rather a temporary incarnation of that god, whose special name for this particular incarnation was Netjerikhet ("divine of body"). It was by this name that the king identified himself everywhere in the Step Pyramid complex and not by the familiar name Zoser (found only in later writings together with the name Netjerikhet). Like his predecessors, Zoser assumed that one of his most important duties as king was to undertake the preparation of his "house of eternity." Fortunately, he had in his service the brilliant Imhotep.

Zoser's decision to construct a mastaba for his monument was dictated by tradition, but instead of employing the usual rectangular shape, he directed Imhotep to build it as a square, with each side facing the four cardinal points and measuring approximately 207 feet (63 meters). In addition, he ordered that the monument be constructed of limestone and not brick, the material used in all previous constructions of this sort. Rising to a height of 26 feet (8 meters), this square stone mastaba was enclosed in a rectangular area by a wall 33 feet (10 meters) high and more than 1 mile (1.6 kilometers) long.

Even as it stood, Zoser's monument displayed a number of bold innovations. Simply in point of size, it dwarfed anything in Egyptian experience because the area enclosed by the girdle wall was more than sixty times larger than any built so far. Almost immediately, however, Zoser began to rethink the plan of his monu-

MAJOR RULERS OF THE THIRD DYNASTY	
Ruler	Reign (B.C.E.)
Zoser	c. 2687–c. 2650
Sekhemkhet	c. 2648–c. 2640
Khaba	c. 2640–c. 2637
Huni	c. 2637–c. 2613

Note: Dynastic research is ongoing; data are approximate.

ment. In the end, the original mastaba underwent six major reconstructions and eventually emerged as a white stone pyramid rising in six unequal steps to a height of 204 feet (63 meters) and measuring at the base 411 by 358 feet (125 by 109 meters). Instead of viewing his tomb simply as his royal residence in death, Zoser had come to think of it also as a colossal staircase by which his transfigured body might climb up into the sky and join the sun god Ra in his solar barge as he passed through the sky each day (this according to information discovered in pyramids of the Fifth Dynasty).

Not until after the pyramid was finished did Zoser complete the numerous other temples and courts that he considered essential to the complex, for he envisioned it as a true necropolis, a city of the dead. Except for the Mortuary Temple and the smaller building in which Zoser's statue was found, none of the other buildings surrounding the Step Pyramid has any known precedent or parallel, and the purpose that many were intended to serve remains obscure. One group of buildings, partially restored, whose function is reasonably clear, relates to the celebration of the Sed or Jubilee Festival and requires special attention.

In earlier times, when the king's physical vigor was observed to weaken, he was put to death and replaced by a younger man because nature's bounty was thought to depend on the king's virility. In later times, this custom was supplanted by the Sed Festival, which enabled the aging king to renew his power through magic and thus ensure the welfare of his kingdom. Zoser most likely had celebrated this festival during his life and had intended that the complex of buildings south of his pyramid should provide him with the setting necessary for repeating this ceremony throughout eternity. One of the most important rites was the reenactment of the king's double coronation as king of Upper and Lower Egypt, during which he was presented with the white crown of the south and the red crown of the north. In another rite, which is depicted in a fine relief, the king is shown running a fixed course, ap-

parently to display his renewed strength to his subjects. An area was set aside for Zoser's eternal run.

Archaeologists have carefully examined the subterranean part of Zoser's tomb, where he was buried with his most valuable possessions. Despite having been plundered by tomb robbers over the course of four thousand years, the storage rooms have yielded to excavators some 90 tons (82 metric tons) of stone vessels made of such costly stones as alabaster, porphyry, and quartz. It is clear that Zoser was lavishly equipped for eternity, on a scale never attempted before.

SIGNIFICANCE

Menes, the semilegendary first king of the First Dynasty, unified Upper and Lower Egypt around 3050 B.C.E. An Egypt with a strong central government was able to undertake large hydraulic projects to control the annual inundations of the Nile. Under one king, the obedient army and conscripted peasants could increase the amount of arable land by draining swamps and irrigating the desert margins. During the first two dynasties, despite periods of civil strife, a unified Egypt was able to make enormous strides forward in every way. The invention of writing made it possible to conduct censuses of people and animals, make records of more complicated data, and communicate easily over long distances. Leisure provided the intelligentsia with an opportunity for speculative thought and for the fine arts as well as the practical.

Roughly five hundred years of progress culminated in Zoser's reign. Although written documents are generally lacking for this period, the Step Pyramid itself is very reliable testimony to the great prosperity and self-confidence that characterized Zoser's tenure. The size of his funerary monument alone implies much about the economic and political status of Egypt during this period. More important than mere size, however, are the architectural innovations, especially Zoser's decision to build his monument in the revolutionary shape of a pyramid and to use quarried stone for its material, the first large structure to be so raised. The Step Pyramid represents Zoser's vision of himself as king, able literally to ascend into the heavens by a stairway that would never perish. Zoser's vision was fully realized about one hundred years later in the Great Pyramid of Khufu, still a wonder to the world.

—*H. J. Shey*

FURTHER READING

Aldred, Cyril. *Egyptian Art in the Days of the Pharaohs, 3100-320 B.C.* Reprint. New York: Thames and Hudson, 1985. Primarily trained as an art historian,

Aldred has produced perhaps the most elegant and lucid descriptions of Egypt's art treasures available in any language. The chapter on the Third Dynasty is particularly informative on the precise nature and significance of the architectural innovations of Zoser's reign.

Firth, C. M., and J. E. Quibell. *Excavations at Saqqara, the Step Pyramid*. Architectural plans by J. Ph. Lauer. 2 vols. Cairo: L'Institut Français d'Archéologie Orientale, 1935-1936. Serious excavations around the Step Pyramid did not begin until after World War I, when Firth took charge of the work from 1920 until his death in 1931. Lauer joined Firth in 1927 as architect and is responsible for the extensive restoration work on the pyramid and surrounding buildings that is still in progress. This book is the fundamental work on the Step Pyramid complex.

Smith, W. S. "The Old Kingdom in Egypt." In *The Cambridge Ancient History*, vol. 1, edited by I. E. S. Edwards, C. J. Gadd, and N. G. L. Hammond. 3d ed. New York: Cambridge University Press, 1971. Smith's discussion of the Third Dynasty includes all the minutiae pertaining to Zoser's lineage and the chief monuments of officials of his court. In general, this admirable series of volumes is written by scholars for scholars, and Smith's account is no exception. Each chapter is furnished with an extensive bibliography, an indispensable guide to further study.

Verner, Miroslav. *The Pyramids: The Mystery, Culture, and Science of Egypt's Great Monuments*. Translated by Steven Rendall. New York: Grove, 2001. A very thorough study of the construction and cultural context of the pyramids. Traces the evolution of the form from the mastaba through the Great Pyramid, explaining the cult that produced Egyptian funerary rituals and the social conditions that supported them. Includes appendices of the basic dimensions of the pyramids, lists of Egyptologists and pyramid scholars, dynastic chronologies, and glossary.

SEE ALSO: Akhenaton; Amenhotep III; Cleopatra VII; Hatshepsut; Imhotep; Menes; Menkaure; Montuhotep II; Piye; Psamtik I; Ramses II; Sesostris III; Thutmose III; Tutankhamen.

RELATED ARTICLES in *Great Events from History: The Ancient World*: c. 3100-c. 1550 B.C.E., Building of Stonehenge; c. 3050 B.C.E., Unification of Lower and Upper Egypt; c. 2687 B.C.E., Old Kingdom Period Begins in Egypt; c. 2575-c. 2566 B.C.E., Building of the Great Pyramid; c. 1600-c. 1500 B.C.E., Flowering of Minoan Civilization; From c. 1500 B.C.E., Dissemination of the Book of the Dead.

Great Lives from History

The Ancient World

Prehistory - 476 C.E.

CHRONOLOGICAL LIST OF ENTRIES

The arrangement of personages in this list is chronological on the basis of birth years (where known; other vital years appear where birth year is unknown). All personages appearing in this list are the subjects of articles in *Great Lives from History: The Ancient World, Prehistory-476 C.E.*; Cleomenes I-III, the Gracchi, and the Tarquins are the subjects of multiple-person essays.

3100-1101 B.C.E.

Menes (c. 3100-c. 3000 B.C.E.)
Zoser (c. 2700-c. 2650 B.C.E.)
Imhotep (fl. 27th century B.C.E.)
Menkaure (2532-2503 B.C.E.)
Enheduanna (c. 2320-c. 2250 B.C.E.)
Ur-Nammu (late 22d century-2095 B.C.E.)
Gudea (c. 2120-c. 2070 B.C.E.)
Montuhotep II (2055-2004 B.C.E.)
Abraham (c. 2050-c. 1950 B.C.E.)
Sesostris III (d. 1843 B.C.E.)
Hammurabi (c. 1810-1750 B.C.E.)
Thutmose III (late 16th century-1450 B.C.E.)

Hatshepsut (c. 1525-c. 1482 B.C.E.)
Tiy (c. 1410-c. 1340 B.C.E.)
Amenhotep III (c. 1403-c. 1353 B.C.E.)
Aaron (c. 1395-c. 1272 B.C.E.)
Akhenaton (c. 1390-c. 1360 B.C.E.)
Nefertiti (c. 1390-c. 1360 B.C.E.)
Tutankhamen (c. 1370-c. 1352 B.C.E.)
Nefertari (c. 1307-c. 1265 B.C.E.)
Ramses II (c. 1300-1213 B.C.E.)
Moses (c. 1300-c. 1200 B.C.E.)
Deborah (fl. c. 1200-1125 B.C.E.)

1100-601 B.C.E.

Samuel (c. 1090-c. 1020 B.C.E.)
David (c. 1030-c. 962 B.C.E.)
Bathsheba (fl. 10th century B.C.E.)
Solomon (c. 991-930 B.C.E.)
Ashurnasirpal II (c. 915-859 B.C.E.)
Dido (mid-9th century-late 9th/early 8th century B.C.E.)
Sammu-ramat (c. 840-after 807 B.C.E.)
Homer (c. early 8th century-c. late 8th century B.C.E.)
Tiglath-pileser III (early 8th century-727 B.C.E.)
Piye (c. 769-716 B.C.E.)
Isaiah (c. 760-c. 701-680 B.C.E.)
Sargon II (second half of 8th century-705 B.C.E.)
Sennacherib (c. 735-Jan., 681 B.C.E.)
Hesiod (fl. c. 700 B.C.E.)
Draco (fl. perhaps 7th century B.C.E.)
Lucius Tarquinius Priscus (7th century-579 B.C.E.)

Ashurbanipal (c. 685-627 B.C.E.)
Psamtik I (c. 684-610 B.C.E.)
Tanaquil (fl. mid- to late 7th century B.C.E.)
Jeremiah (c. 645-after 587 B.C.E.)
Pittacus of Mytilene (c. 645-c. 570 B.C.E.)
Sappho (c. 630-c. 580 B.C.E.)
Nebuchadnezzar II (c. 630-562 B.C.E.)
Solon (c. 630-c. 560 B.C.E.)
Zoroaster (c. 628-c. 551 B.C.E.)
Ezekiel (c. 627-c. 570 B.C.E.)
Thales of Miletus (c. 624-c. 548 B.C.E.)
Aesop (c. 620-c. 560 B.C.E.)
Pisistratus (c. 612-527 B.C.E.)
Anaximander (c. 610-c. 547 B.C.E.)
Laozi (604-6th century B.C.E.)
Cyrus the Great (c. 601-590 to c. 530 B.C.E.)

600-501 B.C.E.

Ānanda (fl. 6th century B.C.E.)
Lucius Tarquinius Superbus (6th century-
    after 510 B.C.E.)
Lucretia (6th century-c. 509 B.C.E.)
Gośāla Maskarīputra (6th century-c. 467 B.C.E.)
Anaximenes of Miletus (early 6th century-second half
    of 6th century B.C.E.)
Vardhamāna (c. 599-527 B.C.E.)
Croesus (c. 595-546 B.C.E.)
Pythagoras (c. 580-c. 500 B.C.E.)
Eupalinus of Megara (c. 575-c. 500 B.C.E.)
Xenophanes (c. 570-c. 478 B.C.E.)
Cleisthenes of Athens (c. 570-after 507 B.C.E.)
Buddha (c. 566-c. 486 B.C.E.)
Simonides (c. 556-c. 467 B.C.E.)
Miltiades the Younger (c. 554-489 B.C.E.)
Confucius (551-479 B.C.E.)
Darius the Great (550-486 B.C.E.)

Atossa (c. 545-possibly c. 479 B.C.E.)
Heraclitus of Ephesus (c. 540-c. 480)
Thespis (before 535-after 501 B.C.E.)
Ezra (fl. late 6th/early 5th century B.C.E.)
Artemisia I (late 6th century-probably
    mid-5th century B.C.E.)
Pausanias of Sparta (late 6th century-c. 470 B.C.E.)
Aeschylus (525-524 to 456-455 B.C.E.)
Themistocles (c. 524-c. 460 B.C.E.)
Hanno (c. 520-510 B.C.E.)
Xerxes I (c. 519-465 B.C.E.)
Pindar (518 B.C.E.- 438 B.C.E.)
Pheidippides (probably c. 515-perhaps 490 B.C.E.)
Parmenides (c. 515-perhaps after 436 B.C.E.)
Leonidas (c. 510-Aug. 20, 480 B.C.E.)
Cimon (c. 510-c. 451 B.C.E.)
Alcmaeon (c. 510-c. 430 B.C.E.)

500-401 B.C.E.

Vālmīki (fl. c. 500 B.C.E.)
Polygnotus (c. 500-c. 440? B.C.E.)
Anaxagoras (c. 500-c. 428 B.C.E.)
Sophocles (c. 496-406 B.C.E.)
Pericles (c. 495-429 B.C.E.)
Cleomenes I (d. c. 490 B.C.E.)
Zeno of Elea (c. 490-c. 440 B.C.E.)
Phidias (c. 490-c. 430 B.C.E.)
Empedocles (c. 490-c. 430 B.C.E.)
Protagoras (c. 485-c. 410 B.C.E.)
Euripides (c. 485-406 B.C.E.)
Herodotus (c. 484-c. 425 B.C.E.)
Aspasia of Miletus (c. 475-after 428 B.C.E.)
Socrates (c. 470-399 B.C.E.)
Mozi (c. 470-c. 391 B.C.E.)
Polyclitus (c. 460-c. 410 B.C.E.)

Democritus (c. 460-c. 370 B.C.E.)
Hippocrates (c. 460-c. 370 B.C.E.)
Thucydides (c. 459-c. 402 B.C.E.)
Alcibiades of Athens (c. 450-404 B.C.E.)
Aristophanes (c. 450-c. 385 B.C.E.)
Xanthippe (c. 445-early to mid-4th century B.C.E.)
Antisthenes (c. 444-c. 365 B.C.E.)
Agesilaus II of Sparta (c. 444-c. 360 B.C.E.)
Isocrates (436-338 B.C.E.)
Aristippus (c. 435-365 B.C.E.)
Xenophon (c. 431-c. 354 B.C.E.)
Plato (c. 427-347 B.C.E.)
Scopas (possibly as early as 420-
    late 4th century B.C.E.)
Diogenes (c. 412-403 to c. 324-321 B.C.E.)
Epaminondas (c. 410-362 B.C.E.)

400-301 B.C.E.

Eudoxus of Cnidus (c. 390-c. 337 B.C.E.)
Lysippus (c. 390-c. 300 B.C.E.)
Aristotle (384-322 B.C.E.)

Demosthenes (384-322 B.C.E.)
Philip II of Macedonia (382-336 B.C.E.)
Antigonus I Monophthalmos (382-301 B.C.E.)

300-201 B.C.E.

200-101 B.C.E.

100-1 B.C.E.

Nabu-rimanni (early 1st century-late 1st century B.C.E.)
Julius Caesar (July 12/13, 100-March 15, 44 B.C.E.)
Lucretius (c. 98-Oct. 15, 55 B.C.E.)
Clodia (c. 95-after 45 B.C.E.)
Cato the Younger (95-46 B.C.E.)
Sosigenes (c. 90-1st century B.C.E.)
Sallust (86-35 B.C.E.)
Catullus (c. 85-c. 54 B.C.E.)
Marcus Junius Brutus (85-Oct. 23, 42 B.C.E.)
Marc Antony (c. 82-30 B.C.E.)
Vercingetorix (c. 75-c. 46 B.C.E.)
Herod the Great (73-spring, 4 B.C.E.)
Gaius Maecenas (c. 70-8 B.C.E.)
Vergil (Oct. 15, 70-Sept. 21, 19 B.C.E.)
Cleopatra VII (69-Aug. 3, 30 B.C.E.)
Horace (Dec. 8, 65-Nov. 27, 8 B.C.E.)
Strabo (64 or 63 B.C.E.-after 23 C.E.)
Marcus Vipsanius Agrippa (c. 63-March, 12 B.C.E.)
Augustus (Sept. 23, 63 B.C.E.-Aug. 19, 14 C.E.)

Marcus Verrius Flaccus (c. 60 B.C.E.-c. 22 C.E.)
Livy (59 B.C.E.-17 C.E.)
Livia Drusilla (Jan. 30, 58 B.C.E.-29 C.E.)
Sextus Propertius (c. 57-48 B.C.E.-d. c. 16 B.C.E.-2 C.E.)
Ovid (Mar. 20, 43 B.C.E.-17 C.E.)
Cassius (d. 42 B.C.E.)
Tiberius (Nov. 16, 42 B.C.E.-March 16, 37 C.E.)
Julia III (39 B.C.E.-14 C.E.)
Antonia Minor (Jan. 31, 36 B.C.E.-May 1, 37 C.E.)
Sulpicia (fl. late 1st century B.C.E.)
Aulus Cornelius Celsus (c. 25 B.C.E.-c. 50 C.E.)
Mary (b. 22 B.C.E.)
Philo of Alexandria (c. 20 B.C.E.-c. 45 C.E.)
Arminius (c. 17 B.C.E.-19 C.E.)
Phaedrus (c. 15 B.C.E.-c. 55 C.E.)
Claudius I (Aug. 1, 10 B.C.E.-Oct. 13, 54 C.E.)
Saint John the Baptist (c. 7 B.C.E.-c. 27 C.E.)
Jesus (c. 6 B.C.E.-30 C.E.)
Seneca the Younger (c. 4 B.C.E.-Apr., 65 C.E.)

I C.E. - 99 C.E.

Boudicca (1st century-60 C.E.)
Kanishka (1st or 2d century-c. 152 C.E.)
Saint Thomas (c. early 1st century-second half of
    1st century C.E.)
Arria the Elder (c. 1-42 C.E.)
Johanan ben Zakkai (c. 1 C.E.-c. 80 C.E.)
Saint Stephen (c. 5-c. 36 C.E.)
Vespasian (Nov. 17, 9-June 23, 79 C.E.)
Saint Paul (c. 10-c. 64 C.E.)
John the Apostle (c. 10-c. 100 C.E.)
Caligula (Aug. 31, 12-Jan. 24, 41 C.E.)
Agrippina the Younger (Nov. 6, c. 15-March 59 C.E.)
Valeria Messallina (c. 20-48 C.E.)
Arria the Younger (c. 21-28-c. 97-106 C.E.)
Pliny the Elder (probably 23-Aug. 25, 79 C.E.)
Wang Chong (27-c. 100 C.E.)
Ignatius of Antioch (c. 30-Dec. 20, 107 C.E.)
Poppaea Sabina (31-65 C.E.)

Ban Gu (32-92 C.E.)
Pontius Pilate (d. after 36 C.E.)
Flavius Josephus (c. 37-c. 100 C.E.)
Nero (Dec. 15, 37-Jun. 9, 68 C.E.)
Martial (March 1, 38-41-c. 103 C.E.)
Pedanius Dioscorides (c. 40-c. 90 C.E.)
Akiba ben Joseph (c. 40-c. 135 C.E.)
Gnaeus Julius Agricola (June 13, 40-Aug. 23, 93 C.E.)
Ban Zhao (c. 45-c. 120 C.E.)
Plutarch (c. 46-after 120 C.E.)
Trajan (c. 53-c. Aug. 8, 117 C.E.)
Tacitus (c. 56-c. 120 C.E.)
Juvenal (c. 60-c. 130 C.E.)
Hero of Alexandria (fl. 62-late 1st century C.E.)
Saint Peter (d. 64 C.E.)
Hadrian (Jan. 24, 76-July 10, 138 C.E.)
Aśvaghosa (c. 80-c. 150 C.E.)
Clement I (d. c. 99 C.E.)

100 C.E. - 199 C.E.

Aretaeus of Cappadocia (b. probably 2d century C.E.)
Valentinus (probably early 2d century-c. 165 C.E.)
Julia Mamaea (2d century-March 10, 235 C.E.)
Ptolemy, astronomer (c. 100-c. 178 C.E.)
Pausanias the Traveler (c. 110-115 to c. 180 C.E.)
Lucian (c. 120-c. 180 C.E.)
Saint Irenaeus (between 120 and 140-c. 202 C.E.)
Marcus Aurelius (April 26, 121-March 17, 180 C.E.)

Galen (129-c. 199 C.E.)
Dio Cassius (c. 150-c. 235 C.E.)
Cao Cao (155-220 C.E.)
Tertullian (c. 155-160-after 217 C.E.)
Julia Domna (c. 167-217 C.E.)
Hippolytus of Rome (c. 170-c. 235 C.E.)
Julia Soaemias (c. 180-222 C.E.)
Origen (c. 185-c. 254 C.E.)

200-299 C.E.

Saint Christopher (possibly 3d century-c. 250 C.E.)
Plotinus (205-270 C.E.)
Wang Bi (226-249 C.E.)
Porphyry (c. 234-c. 305 C.E.)
Zenobia (c. 240-after 274 C.E.)
Diocletian (c. 245-Dec. 3, 316 C.E.)
Saint Helena (c. 248-c. 328 C.E.)
Saint Denis (d. c. 250 C.E.)

Diophantus (fl. c. 250 C.E.)
Saint Anthony of Egypt (c. 251-probably Jan. 17, 356 C.E.)
Eusebius of Caesarea (c. 260-May 30, 339 C.E.)
Constantine the Great (Feb. 17/27, c. 272-285-May 22, 337 C.E.)
Saint Athanasius of Alexandria (c. 293-May 2, 373 C.E.)

300 C.E. - 500 C.E.

Jingū (early 4th century-late 4th century C.E.)
Pappus (c. 300-c. 350 C.E.)
Wang Xizhi (c. 303-c. 350 C.E.)
Ezana (c. 307-c. 379 C.E.)
Shāpūr II (309-379 C.E.)
Ulfilas (311-383 C.E.)
Gregory of Nazianzus (329/330-389/390 C.E.)
Saint Jerome (331-347 to probably 420 C.E.)
Gregory of Nyssa (c. 335-c. 394 C.E.)
Saint Siricius (c. 335/340-Nov. 26, 399 C.E.)
Faxian (c. 337-422 C.E.)
Saint Ambrose (339-Apr. 4, 397 C.E.)
Priscillian (c. 340-385 C.E.)
Kālidāsa (c. 340-c. 400 C.E.)
Theodosius the Great (Jan. 11, 346 or 347-Jan. 17, 395 C.E.)
Theodore of Mopsuestia (c. 350-428 C.E.)

Saint John Chrysostom (c. 354-Sept. 14, 407 C.E.)
Saint Augustine (Nov. 13, 354-Aug. 28, 430 C.E.)
Flavius Stilicho (c. 365-Aug. 22, 408 C.E.)
Tao Qian (365-427 C.E.)
Asanga (c. 365-c. 440 C.E.)
Hypatia (c. 370-March, 415 C.E.)
Ōjin Tennō (late 4th century-early 5th century C.E.)
Saint Vincent of Lérins (late 4th century-c. 450 C.E.)
Xie Lingyun (385-433 C.E.)
Saint Simeon Stylites (c. 390-459 C.E.)
Genseric (c. 390-477 C.E.)
Theodoret of Cyrrhus (c. 393-c. 458 C.E.)
Vasubandhu (c. 400-c. 480 C.E.)
Bodhidharma (5th century-6th century C.E.)
Attila (c. 406-453 C.E.)
Proclus (c. 410-485 C.E.)
Hengist (c. 420-c. 488 C.E.)

Category Index

List of Categories

GEOGRAPHICAL INDEX

PERSONAGES INDEX

SUBJECT INDEX